ISBN 978-0-260-63544-0
PIBN 10961006

SESSIONAL PAPERS

PUBLIC ACCOUNTS

VOL. LXV.—PART I.

FOURTH SESSION

OF THE

EIGHTEENTH LEGISLATURE

OF THE

PROVINCE OF ONTARIO

SESSION 1933

TORONTO
Printed and Published by Herbert H. Ball, Printer to the King's Most Excellent Majesty
1933

CONTENTS
FOR PART I.

PUBLIC ACCOUNTS

OF THE

PROVINCE OF ONTARIO

FOR THE

Year Ending 31st October

1932

PRINTED BY ORDER OF
THE LEGISLATIVE ASSEMBLY OF ONTARIO

SESSIONAL PAPER No. 1, 1933

ONTARIO

TORONTO
Printed by Herbert H. Ball, Printer to the King's Most Excellent Majesty
1933

TO THE HONOURABLE COLONEL HERBERT ALEXANDER BRUCE, M.D., R.A.M.C., F.R.C.S. (ENG.)

Lieutenant-Governor of the Province of Ontario.

MAY IT PLEASE YOUR HONOUR:

The undersigned has the honour to present to Your Honour the Public Accounts of the Province of Ontario for the year ended 31st October, 1932.

Respectfully submitted,

E. A. DUNLOP,
Treasurer.

Treasury Department, Ontario,
February 10th, 1933.

Audit Office,

February 10th, 1933.

THE HONOURABLE E. A. DUNLOP,
Provincial Treasurer.

SIR,—I have the honour to submit to you the Public Accounts for the year ended 31st October, 1932.

Respectfully submitted,

G. A. BROWN,
Provincial Auditor.

TABLE OF CONTENTS

Index to Details of Revenue and Expenditure

ALPHABETICAL INDEX AT BACK OF BOOK

INDEX TO STATEMENTS

THE GOVERNMENT OF THE

ASSETS AND LIABILITIES

Capital Assets

Page No.				
..	REALIZABLE OR INCOME-PRODUCING:			
	DOMINION OF CANADA			
	Capital Account—Capitalized at 5%—			
	Annual Subsidy, B.N.A. Act		$ 4,800,000 00	
	Annual Grant, B.N.A. Act		51,180,196 00	
	Annual (increased) Subsidy, 47 V, Cap. 4		2,848,289 60	
	Common School Fund—(Ontario and Quebec) Ontario's share of fund		1,454,481 06	
	Quebec Turnpike Trust—(Ontario and Quebec)		3,262 50	
			$60,286,229 16	
36	HYDRO-ELECTRIC POWER COMMISSION—			
	Advances	$204,488,631 44		
	Less—			
	Repayment from Sinking Fund	14,853,440 35		
			189,635,191 09	
..	TEMISKAMING AND NORTHERN ONTARIO RAILWAY— Advances		30,207,934 92	
36	LOANS TO MUNICIPALITIES, ETC		7,737,639 55	
				$287,866,994 72
36	BUILDINGS, ROADS, ETC			244,996,934 51
	ESTIMATED POTENTIAL REVENUE RESOURCES:			
	Log Timber, Pine, Spruce, Poplar, etc.	$ 241,050,000 00		
	Pulpwood Timber, Ties, Poles, etc.	337,200,000 00		
	Crown Lands	23,000,000 00		
	Water Powers	55,000,000 00		
	Fish, Game and Fur	15,000,000 00		
	Mines	20,000,000 00		
		$691,250,000 00		
	TOTAL CAPITAL ASSETS			$532,863,929 23

Current Assets

Page No.			
37	CASH IN BANKS	$15,709,648 01	
37	ACCOUNTS RECEIVABLE	5,153,301 42	
47	AGRICULTURAL DEVELOPMENT FINANCE ACT— INVESTMENTS AND CASH	45,721,554 49	
	BOWMANVILLE SCHOOL GYMNASIUM FUND—INVESTMENTS	10,000 00	
37	PLANT, LIVESTOCK, STORES AND EQUIPMENT	2,439,661 05	
	TOTAL CURRENT ASSETS		69,034,164 97
37	DEFERRED ASSETS	$ 146,816 13	
..	UNEMPLOYMENT RELIEF—DIRECT (LESS 1/5 WRITTEN OFF)	3,139,749 88	
			3,286,566 01
38	DISCOUNT ON LOANS	$ 8,396,847 64	
	TOTAL ASSETS		$605,184,660 21

PROVINCE OF ONTARIO

AS AT OCTOBER 31st, 1932

Capital Liabilities

Page No.			
40	Ontario Stock and Debentures	$499,986,011 19	
	Deduct—		
39	Sinking Funds	4,543,066 11	
			$495,442,945 08
42	Annuities and Certificates		1,261,299 84
43	Contingent Liabilities:		
	Bonds, etc., guaranteed by the Province $80,618,385 84		

Note:—The Hydro-Electric Power Commission has deposited with the Province, Ontario Bonds of par value of $2,101,000 on account of Sinking Fund for repayment of advances, in excess of cash payments called for under the Debt Retirement Plan.

	Total Capital Liabilities		$496,704,244 92

Current Liabilities

Page No.			
..	Temporary Loans—Treasury Bills	$37,505,000 00	
47	Province of Ontario Savings Office—Deposits	23,709,819 62	
47	Accounts Payable	385,944 71	
..	Accrued Interest on Public Debt	8,732,579 00	
47	Special Funds	7,381,804 76	
	Total Current Liabilities		77,715,148 09
	Total Liabilities		$574,419,393 01
	Debt Retirement Reserve:		
	Amount provided out of Ordinary Revenue to date in accordance with Debt Retirement Plan	$ 7,668,560 66	
	Balance—Excess of Total Assets over Total Liabilities		30,765,267 20
			$605,184,660 21

Statement
REVENUE AND
Fiscal Year ended

Page No.	Statement No.	Departments	Ordinary	Capital	Total
		Revenue	$ c.	$ c.	$ c.
10	2	Prime Minister	265,799 11	....	265,799 11
10	3	Legislation	26,484 38	....	26,484 38
11	4	Attorney-General	9,736,067 43	....	9,736,067 43
12	5	Insurance	174,541 05	....	174,541 05
12	6	Education	9,235 92	....	9,235 92
13	7	Lands and Forests	2,318,922 18	115,333 63	2,434,255 81
14	8	Northern Development	....	10,578 08	10,578 08
15	9	Mines	775,841 25	17,917 95	793,759 20
16	10	Game and Fisheries	613,784 70	....	613,784 70
16	11	Public Works	36,627 20	17,933 05	54,560 25
17	12	Highways	19,835,456 62	8,975 78	19,844,432 40
18	13	Health	35,556 83	....	35,556 83
18	14	Labour	350 25	....	350 25
19	15	Provincial Treasurer	19,665,423 89	....	19,665,423 89
24	16	Provincial Secretary	458,525 35	....	458,525 35
24	17	Agriculture	182 44	....	182 44
29	T10	Stationery Account (Excess of distribution over purchases during year)	17,817 94	....	17,817 94
			53,970,616 54	170,738 49	54,141,355 03
25	18	Interest	204,616 47	....	204,616 47
		TOTAL REVENUE	54,175,233 01	170,738 49	54,345,971 50

RECAPITULATION

ORDINARY REVENUE AND EXPENDITURE

Ordinary Revenue as above	$ 54,175,233 01
Ordinary Expenditure as per contra	52,173,086 91
Surplus before Special Expenditure	$ 2,002,146 10
Special Expenditure	4,062,944 41
Deficit after Special Expenditure	$ 2,060,798 31

CONSOLIDATED
Fiscal Year ended

Page No.	Statement No.	Receipts		
..	..	Balance in Banks—November 1st, 1931		$ 3,973,554 68
..	..	Revenue as above—		
		Ordinary	$ 54,175,233 01	
		Capital	170,738 49	
				54,345,971 50
26	19	Public Debt—		
		Proceeds of Bond and Treasury Bill Issues, etc.	$185,659,387 72	
28	20	Loan Repayments—Municipalities, Hydro-Electric Power Commission, etc.	6,504,777 83	
28	20	Special Funds—Deposits	1,495,774 94	
				193,659,940 49
				$251,979,466 67

No. 1

EXPENDITURE

October **31st, 1932**

Page No.	Departments	Ordinary	*Special	Capital	Total
	Expenditure	$ c.	$ c.	$ c.	$ c.
A2	Lieutenant-Governor	3,630 00			3,630 00
B2	Prime Minister	177,574 57		725,000 00	902,574 57
C2	Legislation	350,675 61			350,675 61
D2	Attorney-General	2,550,481 46	356,890 35		2,907,371 81
E2	Insurance	64,537 51			64,537 51
F2	Education	11,720,718 28		1,631,545 70	13,352,263 98
G2	Lands and Forests	1,835,078 01		572,714 05	2,407,792 06
H2	Northern Development	2,147,322 79		3,116,672 35	5,263,995 14
I 2	Mines	338,238 04		995 88	339,233 92
J2	Game and Fisheries	562,093 41		67,082 61	629,176 02
K2	Public Works	693,034 87		2,486,350 71	3,179,385 58
L2	Highways	3,865,847 02		6,712,739 10	10,578,586 12
M2	Health	5,870,270 53			5,870,270 53
N2	Labour	315,440 13	808,470 68	13,231,875 79	14,355,786 60
O2	Public Welfare	3,613,378 68	567,120 25		4,180,498 93
P2	Provincial Treasurer	973,979 29			973,979 29
Q2	Provincial Auditor	113,022 96			113,022 96
R2	Provincial Secretary	814,488 48		10,000 00	824,488 48
S2	Agriculture	2,017,618 50			2,017,618 50
T2	Miscellaneous	589,409 89		83,443 15	672,853 04
		38,616,840 03	1,732,481 28	28,638,419 34	68,987,740 65
P5	Public Debt—Charges	13,556,246 88	2,330,463 13		15,886,710 01
	TOTAL EXPENDITURE	52,173,086 91	4,062,944 41	28,638,419 34	84,874,450 66

*SPECIAL EXPENDITURE:

Attorney-General—Refund of Fines, City of Toronto	$ 356,890 35
Labour—Unemployment Relief—Direct (1/5 write off)	808,470 68
Public Welfare—Old Age Pensions—Adjustment—Dominion Government, 1931 contribution	567,120 25
Public Debt—Exchange on United States Funds	2,330,463 13
TOTAL SPECIAL EXPENDITURE	$4,062,944 41

REVENUE FUND

October **31st, 1932**

Page No.	Payments		
	Expenditure as above—		
	Ordinary	$ 52,173,086 91	
	Special	4,062,944 41	
	Capital	28,638,419 34	
			$ 84,874,450 66
UI	Public Debt—		
	Bonds and Treasury Bills, etc., matured and paid	$135,675,950 34	
UI	Loans Advanced—Municipalities:		
	Hydro-Electric Power Commission, etc	14,656,707 55	
U1	Special Funds—Repayments	678,073 05	
			151,010,730 94
	Balance—		
37	In Banks—October 31st, 1932	$ 16,093,100 41	
..	Returned Cheques held for collection, etc	1,184 66	
			16,094,285 07
			$251,979,466 67

Statement No. 2

DEPARTMENT OF THE PRIME MINISTER

Revenue for Fiscal Year 1932

ORDINARY—		
OFFICE OF EXECUTIVE COUNCIL—		
Sale of Orders-in-Conncil	$	2 00
OFFICE OF KING'S PRINTER—		
Ontario Gazette		31,373 57
PUBLICITY BUREAU—		
Miscellaneous		53 80
HYDRO-ELECTRIC POWER COMMISSION—		
Water Rentals—Queenston-Chippawa Plant		234,369 74
	$	265,799 11

Statement No. 3

LEGISLATION

Revenue for Fiscal Year 1932

ORDINARY—				
OFFICE OF LEGISLATIVE ACCOUNTANT—				
Sale of Legislative Papers—				
Statutes	$	4,947 26		
Publications		1,449 66		
Bills		1,755 20		
			$	8,152 12
Fees—				
Private Bills	$	18,313 26		
Certifying Bills		19 00		
				18,332 26
			$	26,484 38

Statement No. 4

DEPARTMENT OF THE ATTORNEY-GENERAL

Revenue for Fiscal Year 1932

ORDINARY—		
MAIN OFFICE—		
Refunds—Miscellaneous		$ 24 80
AUDITOR OF CRIMINAL JUSTICE ACCOUNTS—		
Perquisites	$ 5,414 55	
Refunds—Election Expenses, etc.	346 32	
		5,760 87
ONTARIO RAILWAY BOARD—Casual		4 40
INSPECTOR OF LEGAL OFFICES—		
Miscellaneous	$ 51 00	
Police Magistrates—		
Fines	23,083 05	
Fees	45,167 15	
Local Master of Titles—Fees	27,008 03	
Local and Surrogate Registrars—		
Fees	122,008 10	
Crown Attorneys—		
Fees	68,003 51	
Fines and Estreated Bail	2,887 96	
Sheriffs—Fees	20,493 34	
Division Court Clerks—		
Fees	57,821 85	
		366,523 99
ONTARIO SECURITIES COMMISSION—		
Fees		28,166 38
LAW ENFORCEMENT (Ontario Provincial Police)—		
Licenses—Detective Agencies	$ 3,000 00	
Less—Miscellaneous Refunds	363 65	
		2,636 35
FIRE MARSHAL—		
Fire Marshal's Tax—		
Licensed Companies	$ 70,101 27	
Unlicensed Companies	984 92	
Lightning Rod Act—License Fees, etc.	1,864 45	
		72,950 64
LIQUOR CONTROL BOARD—		
Profits, Fines, Licenses, etc.		9,260,000 00
		$ 9,736,067 43

Statement No. 5

DEPARTMENT OF INSURANCE

(Under the Attorney-General)

Revenue for Fiscal Year 1932

ORDINARY—		
ONTARIO INSURANCE ACT—		
Joint Stock Companies	$ 68,385 00	
Mutual and Cash Mutuals	15,025 00	
Fraternal and Mutual Benefit Societies	5,600 00	
Other Insurers	2,675 00	
Underwriters' Agency Licenses	1,900 00	
Agents, Brokers' and Adjusters' Licenses	61,058 00	
Special Brokers' Licenses	200 00	
Tax on Premiums—		
Unlicensed Companies	1,229 21	
Reciprocals	3,580 43	
Miscellaneous Fees	3,531 41	
		$ 163,184 05
LOAN AND TRUST CORPORATIONS ACT—		
Loan Corporations	$ 3,255 00	
Loaning Land Companies	285 00	
Trust Companies	6,875 00	
Miscellaneous Fees	617 00	
		11,032 00
MONEY LENDERS ACT—		
License Fees		325 00
		$ 174,541 05

Statement No. 6

DEPARTMENT OF EDUCATION

Revenue for Fiscal Year 1932

ORDINARY—	
MAIN OFFICE—	
Miscellaneous, School Acts, Manuals, etc.	$ 9,235 92

Statement No. 7

DEPARTMENT OF LANDS AND FORESTS

Revenue for Fiscal Year 1932

ORDINARY—			
MAIN OFFICE—			
Rentals—Crown Leases and Licenses of Occupation		$ 275,230 38	
Fees—Casual		319 88	
Refunds—Miscellaneous		62 50	
Lac Suel Dam		15,964 13	
			$ 291,576 89
BRANCHES—			
Lands—			
Sales—Crown Lands—			
Agricultural	$ 79,119 88		
Townsites	55,131 54		
		$ 134,251 42	
Clergy Lands		1,228 75	
Common School Lands		3,688 89	
University Lands		448 58	
Grammar School Lands		398 83	
		$ 140,016 47	
Less—Capital, 75 %		105,012 33	
			35,004 14
Land Tax—Provincial Land Tax			119,728 08
Woods and Forests—			
Bonus	$ 748,848 40		
Timber Dues	1,010,862 71		
		$ 1,759,711 11	
Rentals—Ground		73,801 07	
Fees—Transfer		980 15	
Mill Licenses		500 10	
			1,834,992 43
Forestry—Refunds—Fire Ranging, etc			993 56
Surveys—Refunds			1,710 13
Agents—Refunds			237 60
Parks and Beaches—			
Algonquin—			
Rentals		$ 4,348 89	
Perquisites, etc		1,719 63	
Licenses—Fishing, Guides and Boats		6,220 00	
Sales—Furs, Lumber, etc		479 88	
Miscellaneous		835 88	
			13,604 28
Rondeau—			
Rentals		$ 9,739 99	
Perquisites		390 00	
Sales—Lumber, Syrup, Venison, etc		1,116 79	
Miscellaneous		1,491 67	
			12,738 45
Quetico—			
Rentals		$ 15 00	
Perquisites		422 75	
Licenses—Fishing		2,569 07	
Sales—Furs		34 92	
Miscellaneous		5 76	
			3,047 50
Carried forward			$ 2,313,633 06

Statement No. 7—Continued

DEPARTMENT OF LANDS AND FORESTS

Brought Forward		$ 2,313,633 06
ORDINARY—		
Parks and Beaches—Continued		
Temagami—Rentals	$ 2,706 00	
Bruce Beach—Rentals	1,661 18	
Jordan Harbour—Rentals	921 94	
		5,289 12
TOTAL ORDINARY REVENUE		$ 2,318,922 18
CAPITAL—		
BRANCHES—		
Lands—		
Land Collections, 75 %	$ 105,012 33	
Forestry—		
Refunds	6,754 65	
Surveys—		
Lac Seul Dam—Dominion Government	3,566 65	
		115,333 63
		$ 2,434,255 81

Statement No. 8

DEPARTMENT OF NORTHERN DEVELOPMENT

(Under Minister of Lands and Forests)

Revenue for Fiscal Year 1932

	Capital	Ordinary
MAIN OFFICE—		
R.S.O. 1927, Chapter 36—		
Sec. 11 (D) Assistance of Settlers—Feed Shortage, Principal and Interest on Notes	$ 6 00	$ 2 86
(F) Seed Grain—Cash Sales and Principal and Interest on Notes	4,847 86	1,461 90
(F) Agricultural Implements—Principal and Interest on Notes	124 36	64 05
(H) Purchase of Cattle—Cash Sales and Principal and Interest on Notes	5,599 86	347 37
Bank Interest	....	2,357 31
	$ 10,578 08	$ 4,233 49
Interest (To Statement No. 18)	$ 4,233 49	
Capital Receipts	10,578 08	
	$ 14,811 57	

Statement No. 9

DEPARTMENT OF MINES

Revenue for Fiscal Year 1932

ORDINARY—			
MAIN OFFICE—			
Sand and Gravel—			
Royalties		$ 51,060 06	
Licenses		2,475 00	
Fees—Casual		663 76	
Sale of Record Books—Metal Sales Act		71 00	
Permits—Boring		100 00	
Leases—Gas		4,100 00	
			$ 58,469 82
BRANCHES—			
Inspection—Cable Testing			3,640 00
Assessment—Taxes—			
Acreage		$ 20,618 07	
Profit		515,153 59	
Gas		67,831 61	
			603,603 27
Chemical and Assay—Fees			976 23
Mining Recorders—			
Rentals—Mining Leases	$ 3,493 98		
Licenses of Occupation	1,858 23		
		$ 5,352 21	
Licenses—Miners		35,617 01	
Fees—Recording	$ 47,115 44		
Miscellaneous	2,112 01		
		49,227 45	
Sales—Maps		1,170 98	
			91,367 65
Natural Gas Commissioner—Permits			1,580 67
Sulphur Fumes Arbitrator—Damages			1,096 84
Temiskaming Laboratories—Fees			15,106 77
			$ 775,841 25
CAPITAL—			
Mining Recorders—Mining Land Sales			17,917 95
			$ 793,759 20

Statement No. 10

DEPARTMENT OF GAME AND FISHERIES
(Under Provincial Secretary)

Revenue for Fiscal Year 1932

ORDINARY—			
GAME—			
Royalty		$ 93,700 83	
Licenses—			
Trapping	$ 36,873 25		
Non-Resident—Hunting	46,420 00		
Deer	64,961 10		
Moose	6,242 50		
Gun	46,764 00		
Fur Dealers	29,318 00		
Fur Farmers	8,125 00		
Tanners	160 00		
Cold Storage	155 00		
Hotel and Restaurant	20 00		
		239,038 85	
			$ 332,739 68
FISHERIES—			
Royalty		$ 11,761 21	
Licenses—			
Fishing	$ 95,235 00		
Angling	136,077 35		
		231,312 35	
Sales—Spawn taking		1,114 16	
			244,187 72
GENERAL—			
Guides' Licenses		$ 5,142 00	
Fines		12,369 03	
Costs		1,068 14	
Sales—Confiscated Articles		8,222 62	
Rent		4,711 00	
Commission		2,218 50	
Miscellaneous		559 51	
			34,290 80
EXPERIMENTAL FUR FARM—			
Sale of Pelts			2,566 50
			$ 613,784 70

Statement No. 11

DEPARTMENT OF PUBLIC WORKS

Revenue for Fiscal Year 1932

ORDINARY—		
Perquisites	$ 1,396 00	
Sale of Material	1,283 50	
Commissions—Telegrams and Telephones	3,181 81	
Refunds—Miscellaneous	269 84	
Rentals	30,281 25	
Services of Building Equipment	214 80	
		$ 36,627 20
CAPITAL—		
Refunds—Miscellaneous	$ 672 37	
Sales—Property	17,360 48	
	$ 18,032 85	
Less—Deposit Guarantee of Contracts	99 80	
		17,933 05
		$ 54,560 25

Statement No. 12

DEPARTMENT OF HIGHWAYS

Revenue for Fiscal Year 1932

ORDINARY—				
MAIN OFFICE—				
Stationary—				
Maps			$ 490 37	
Sales—				
Sale of Supplies		$ 3,874 25		
Rental of Property		1,676 00		
Miscellaneous		1,433 19		
			6,983 44	
Interest—				
Repayments—				
County and Suburban			59,203 81	
Sale of Property—				
Lands and Buildings			363 52	
Permits—				
Garages		$ 17,757 50		
Signs		10,433 00		
Gas Pumps		19,396 86		
Franchises—				
Gas Lines		2,917 61		
			50,504 97	
Taxes—				
Gasoline			12,341,237 78	
				$12,458,783 89
MOTOR VEHICLES BRANCH—				
Licenses—				
Passenger		$4,289,695 40		
Commercial		1,843,390 85		
Convertibles		31,435 90		
Trailers		106,192 50		
Motor Cycles		11,412 50		
Dealers—				
Automobile	$ 25,522 00			
Commercial	5,562 00			
Motor Cycles	607 00			
		31,691 00		
Chauffeurs		165,232 30		
Operators		469,158 60		
Garages		15,685 00		
Public Vehicles		113,522 72		
Public Commercial Vehicles		88,325 53		
Incomplete Applications		13 50		
Miscellaneous		39 68		
			7,165,795 48	
Fees—				
In Transit		$ 5,305 00		
Duplicate Cards and Badges		7,521 00		
Transfers		110,804 80		
Certificates and Searches		116 01		
Lists		266 32		
Examinations		15,538 00		
Testing Headlights		225 00		
			139,776 13	
Fines—				
Breach of Highway Traffic Act			72,410 04	
			$ 7,377,981 65	
Less Charges paid by Agents			1,308 92	
				$ 7,376,672 73
TOTAL ORDINARY REVENUE CARRIED FORWARD				$19,835,456 62

Statement No. 12 (Continued)

DEPARTMENT OF HIGHWAYS

Revenue for Fiscal Year 1932

ORDINARY..Brought forward			$19,835,456 62
CAPITAL—			
MAIN OFFICE—			
Sales—			
Lands and Buildings................	$ 2,965 00		
Sand, Gravel, Scrap................	2,771 53		
		$ 5,736 53	
Branches—			
Garage—			
Sale of Equipment—Machines and Tools.....		3,239 25	
			8,975 78
			$19,844,432 40

Statement No. 13

DEPARTMENT OF HEALTH

Revenue for Fiscal Year 1932

ORDINARY—			
MAIN OFFICE—			
Miscellaneous....................................		$ 25	
BRANCHES—			
Preventable Diseases—			
Sale of Products—			
Wassermann Needles.........	$ 1,491 00		
Sale of Stock and Equipment.....	213 17		
		1,704 17	
Sanitary Engineering—			
Sale of Stock and Equipment..................		118 28	
Laboratory—			
Sales—Biological Products........	$ 406 26		
Fees—			
Pathology.................	2,182 55		
		2,588 81	
			$ 4,411 51
Public Health Education—			
Milk Bulletin Reprints....................................			37 65
INSPECTION OF TRAINING SCHOOLS FOR NURSES—			
Fees—			
Registration and Re-registration.................		$ 16,451 00	
Examinations................................		8,160 00	
Sales—Curriculum and Records.....................		63 75	
Miscellaneous..................................		21 05	
			24,695 80
HOSPITALS BRANCH—			
Patients' Maintenance............................		$ 1,132 25	
Private Hospitals................................		675 78	
Perquisites......................................		89 70	
Removal of Patients..............................		3,439 59	
Miscellaneous....................................		1,074 55	
			6,411 87
			$ 35,556 83

Statement No. 14

(Under Minister of Public Works and Labour)

Revenue for Fiscal Year 1932

ORDINARY—	
MAIN OFFICE—	
Fees—Private Employment Agencies..................................	$ 350 25

Statement No. 15

PROVINCIAL TREASURER'S DEPARTMENT

Revenue for Fiscal Year 1932

ORDINARY—			
MAIN OFFICE—			
Subsidies—Dominion Government—			
Annual Subsidy, B.N.A. Act, 1907		$ 240,000 00	
Annual Grant per Capita, B.N.A. Act, 1907		2,409,603 50	
Annual Subsidy (Increased), 47 Vic., Cap. 4		441,227 08	
		$ 3,090,830 58	
Permit Fees—Liquor Control Board		645,000 00	
Scholarships—Educational—			
Hon. J. R. Cooke		100 00	
Outstanding Cheques—Department of Highways		2,647 38	
Restitution—H. L. Austin		1,206 67	
Miscellaneous		10 29	
			$ 3,739,794 92
OFFICE OF CONTROLLER OF REVENUE—			
Taxes—			
Corporations (Statement 15 (a))	$7,910,562 25		
Succession Duty (Statement 15 (b))	6,136,624 02		
Amusements	1,016,793 44		
Wine	64,936 68		
		$15,128,916 39	
Licenses—			
Theatre and Cinematograph	$ 70,071 73		
Travelling Shows	9,924 18		
		79,995 91	
Fees—			
Land Transfer (Statement 15 (c))	$ 254,125 60		
Law Stamps (Statement 15 (d))	377,049 92		
		631,175 52	
Miscellaneous		69 28	
			15,840,157 10
BOARD OF CENSORS—Fees			85,471 87
			$19,665,423 89

Statement No. 15 (a)

PROVINCIAL TREASURER'S DEPARTMENT

THE CORPORATIONS TAX ACT

R.S.O. 1927, Cap. 29 with Amendments

Revenue for Fiscal Year 1932

From whom received:		
Life Insurance Companies		$ 1,289,480 18
Fire Insurance Companies		590,197 61
Miscellaneous Insurance Companies		106,731 93
Gas and Electric Companies		218,591 90
Trust Companies		88,545 81
Loan Companies		80,747 47
Banks		731,059 35
Finance Companies		23,967 08
Railways	$ 734,540 23	
Less—Amount to be set aside under Section 24 and deducted from municipalities in respect of indigent insane patients (transferred to Revenue of Public Institutions)	156,677 50	
		577,862 73
Street Railways		6,079 22
Telephones		183,276 44
Telegraphs		7,319 15
Express		55,229 94
Car Companies		15,027 05
Incorporated Companies		2,758,535 02
Race Tracks	$ 1,052,924 88	
Less—Rebates on account of races for Canadian-bred horses	23,604 00	
		1,029,320 88
Stock Transfer Tax		148,590 49
		$ 7,910,562 25

Statement No. 15 (b)

PROVINCIAL TREASURER'S DEPARTMENT

SUCCESSION DUTY

Revenue, by Counties, for Fiscal Year Ended October 31st, 1932

County	Amount
Algoma	$ 3,583 07
Brant	95,422 59
Bruce	15,662 73
Carleton	302,191 74
Cochrane	1,332 48
Dufferin	14,272 47
Elgin	20,854 77
Essex	126,803 72
Frontenac	83,195 25
Foreign	164,392 53
Grey	18,860 02
Great Britain	81,224 81
Haldimand	4,674 97
Halton	55,587 37
Hastings	26,299 22
Huron	22,848 98
Kenora	307 15
Kent	76,160 90
Lambton	60,019 45
Lanark	27,654 41
Leeds and Grenville	85,665 69
Lennox and Addington	6,918 46
Lincoln	656,686 63
Manitoulin	56 39
Middlesex	508,914 33
Muskoka	8,271 89
Nipissing	18,064 48
Norfolk	31,574 46
Northumberland and Durham	29,276 58
Ontario	45,569 07
Oxford	26,489 46
Parry Sound	3,459 96
Peel	29,960 01
Perth	48,695 04
Peterborough	67,660 18
Prescott and Russell	7,143 58
Prince Edward	3,165 78
Provinces outside of Ontario	92,976 28
Rainy River	5,453 41
Renfrew	46,556 99
Simcoe	20,593 87
Stormont, Dundas and Glengarry	18,704 47
Sudbury	37,429 47
Temiskaming	1,458 96
Thunder Bay	130,072 41
United States	62,540 85
Victoria	4,990 09
Waterloo	176,432 60
Welland	39,264 10
Wellington	62,702 69
Wentworth	393,092 26
York	2,265,434 95
Total	$ 6,136,624 02

Statement No. 15 (c)

PROVINCIAL TREASURER'S DEPARTMENT

LAND TRANSFER TAX

Revenue for Fiscal Year 1932

Algoma (Land Titles)	$ 269 99
Algoma	783 69
Brant	2,570 17
Bruce	1,866 20
Carleton	1,728 21
Cochrane	1,726 05
Dufferin	1,047 13
Dundas	629 21
Durham (East)	389 54
Durham (West)	736 74
Elgin	2,271 35
Essex	17,919 17
Fort William	1,030 65
Frontenac	2,173 04
Glengarry	501 67
Grenville	354 89
Grey (North)	1,630 00
Grey (South)	1,181 88
Haldimand	1,071 34
Haliburton	603 57
Halton	2,171 48
Hastings	2,044 19
Huron	1,947 49
Kenora	365 75
Kent	3,410 12
Lambton	2,734 85
Lanark (North)	305 59
Lanark (South)	452 49
Leeds	1,455 94
Lennox and Addington	712 44
Lincoln	4,101 73
London (City)	3,987 12
Manitoulin (R.O. & L.T.)	263 89
Middlesex (East)	2,972 29
Middlesex (West)	889 12
Muskoka	807 82
Nipissing	967 93
Norfolk	1,968 72
Northumberland (East)	810 59
Northumberland (West)	722 39
Ontario	$ 4,193 85
Ottawa (City)	7,195 70
Ottawa (Land Titles)	1,180 33
Oxford	3,160 32
Parry Sound (District)	328 77
Parry Sound (Land Titles)	283 28
Peel	2,504 20
Perth (North)	2,059 13
Perth (South)	743 36
Peterborough	1,799 43
Prescott	1,076 59
Prince Edward	617 85
Rainy River	530 81
Renfrew	1,254 92
Russell	874 07
Simcoe	3,605 65
Stormont	1,066 20
Sudbury	1,912 08
Temiskaming	1,714 68
Thunder Bay	785 92
Toronto (East and West)	60,867 91
Toronto and York (Land Titles)	22,153 70
Victoria	1,051 35
Waterloo	6,484 23
Welland	6,384 80
Wellington (North)	952 54
Wellington (South and Centre)	2,183 16
Wentworth	14,297 11
York (East and West)	28,099 53
York (North)	2,405 05
	$255,342 95
Deduct—	
Assurance Fund, E. and W. Toronto	1,217 35
	$254,125 60

Statement No. 15 (d)

PROVINCIAL TREASURER'S DEPARTMENT

LAW STAMPS

Revenue for Fiscal Year 1932

County or District	Distributor	Amount
Brant	F. G. Biscoe	$ 5,250 00
Bruce	J. W. Freeborn	3,665 00
Carleton	J. A. Ritchie	13,155 90
Dufferin	H. Endacott	1,701 52
Elgin	John D. Shaw	200 00
Elgin	E. Lindop	3,503 95
Essex	T. A. Mills	15,078 50
Frontenac	T. J. Rigney	4,711 00
Grey	M. M. Pringle	4,740 00
Haldimand	J. C. Eccles	1,515 00
Halton	W. I. Dick	2,660 70
Hastings	B. C. Donnan	3,708 25
Huron	Robert Johnston	4,918 00
Kent	D. E. Douglas	5,300 00
Lambton	W. S. Haney	4,323 00
Lanark	J. S. McNeely	3,010 00
Leeds and Grenville	A. E. Baker	5,295 00
Lennox and Addington	U. M. Wilson	1,553 00
Lincoln	E. H. Lancaster	5,550 00
Middlesex	Edmund Weld	13,000 00
Norfolk	Charles S. Buck	2,446 00
Northumberland and Durham	F. D. Boggs	4,545 00
Ontario	H. Bascom	5,540 00
Oxford	R. N. Ball	4,632 00
Peel	James R. Fallis	4,390 00
Perth	G. G. McPherson	5,820 00
Peterborough	Geo. I. Sherry	3,678 00
Prescott and Russell	J. Belanger	1,800 00
Prince Edward	M. R. Allison	1,450 50
Renfrew	J. McLaren Beatty	3,350 00
Simcoe	F. G. Evans	5,436 60
Stormont, Dundas and Glengarry	J. Harkness	3,867 00
Victoria	M. C. Sootheran	1,850 00
Waterloo	D. S. Bowlby	7,556 00
Welland	T. D. Cowper	5,952 00
Wellington	J. M. Kearns	6,170 00
Wentworth	G. W. Ballard	20,619 50
York	J. E. Thompson	63,343 00
Algoma District	T. J. Foster	1,905 00
Cochrane District	J. D. MacKay	1,150 00
Kenora District	E. Appleton	609 75
Manitoulin District	C. C. Platt	270 00
Muskoka District	Thos. Johnson	1,200 00
Nipissing District	T. E. McKee	1,391 00
Parry Sound District	F. Tasker	668 50
Rainy River District	Estate of W. A. Baker	573 00
Rainy River District	Alex. Thompson	119 00
Sudbury District	A. Irving	265 00
Sudbury District	A. H. Beath	1,432 50
Temiskaming District	F. L. Smiley	1,630 00
Thunder Bay District	N. Edmeston	2,275 00
Osgoode Hall	J. H. Carnegie	100,072 65
Ontario Railway and Municipal Board		8,202 00
Miscellaneous		2 10
		$ 377,049 92

Statement No. 16

PROVINCIAL SECRETARY'S DEPARTMENT

Revenue for Fiscal Year 1932

ORDINARY—		
MAIN OFFICE—		
Fees—		
Commissions, etc.	$ 1,990 00	
Marriage Licenses	80,086 00	
		$ 82,076 00
BRANCHES—		
COMPANIES AND BROKERS—		
Fees—		
Letters Patent	$ 96,105 40	
Supplementary Letters Patent	16,755 60	
Companies' Returns	160,729 50	
Extra-Provincial and Mortmain	20,206 50	
Prospectus, By-laws, Searches, etc.	12,144 01	
Real Estate Brokers	11,415 00	
Real Estate Salesmen	1,402 00	
		318,758 01
REGISTRAR-GENERAL—		
Fees—		
Searches and Certificates—		
Births, Marriages and Deaths	$ 25,318 03	
Miscellaneous	34 75	
		25,352 78
PUBLIC INSTITUTIONS—		
MAIN OFFICE—		
Counties, etc.—Removal of Prisoners and Insane	$ 21,751 89	
Miscellaneous	10,586 67	
		32,338 56
		$ 458,525 35

Statement No. 17

DEPARTMENT OF AGRICULTURE

Revenue for Fiscal Year 1932

ORDINARY—		
MAIN OFFICE—		
Licenses—Auctioneers	$ 50 00	
Miscellaneous	29 52	
		$ 79 52
BRANCHES—		
Statistics and Publications—		
Sales—Reports		102 92
		$ 182 44

Statement No. 18

INTEREST ACCOUNT

Interest Received for Fiscal Year 1932

NORTHERN DEVELOPMENT—		
Assistance to Settlers—Interest on Notes		$ 4,233 49
PROVINCIAL TREASURER—		
Dominion Government—		
Common School Fund—		
5% on Ontario's Share of Fund for Year ended July 1st, 1932	$ 73,304 06	
Municipal Debentures	242 71	
Various Municipalities—		
Municipal Drainage Debentures	13,197 54	
Tile Drainage Debentures	111,718 66	
Interest on Surplus Fees	135 60	
School of Medicine—		
Mortgage Interest	450 00	
Byron Telephone Company—Dividend	1 50	
Farm Loan Associations—Dividend	94 50	
		199,144 57
AGRICULTURE—		
J. Brillon, New Liskeard—Mortgage	$ 370 47	
Georgian Bay Fruit Growers—Loan	867 94	
		1,238 41
		$ 204,616 47

Statement No. **19**

PUBLIC DEBT

Proceeds of Loans for Fiscal Year 1932

Series	Description			
DEBENTURES: Series				
	R.S.O. 1927, Cap. 23 and 57—5%, 20 years, due November 1st, 1951, payable, Canada			$ 500,000 00
	R.S.O. 1927, Cap. 23 and 57—5%, 5 years, due November 1st, 1936, payable Canada			150,000 00
"AT"	21 Geo. V, Cap. 2 and R.S.O. 1927, Cap. 23—5½%—15 years, due February 1st, 1947, payable Canada.			
	Par value		$20,000,000 00	
	Less—Discount	$ 1,150,000 00		
	Commission and Expenses	40,019 29		
			1,190,019 29	
				18,809,980 71
"ZA-AT"	R.S.O. 1927, Cap. 23 and 57—5%, 15 years, due February 1st, 1947, payable Canada.			
	Par value		$ 2,000,000 00	
	Less—Discount		100,000 00	
				1,900,000 00
"AU"	R.S.O. 1927, Cap. 23 and 57—6%, 3 years, due February 1st, 1935, payable Canada.			
	Par value		$ 5,000,000 00	
	Less—Discount	$ 50,000 00		
	Commission and Expenses	10,476 48		
			60,476 48	
				4,939,523 52
"AV"	R.S.O. 1927, Cap. 23 and 57—4½%, 15-25 years, due June 1st, 1947/57, payable London, Eng., £250,000.			
	Par value		$ 1,216,666 65	
	Less—Discount		215,180 62	
				1,001,486 03
"AW"	21 Geo. V, Cap. 2 and R.S.O. 1927, Cap. 23—5½%, 14 years, due July 1st, 1946, payable Canada.			
	Par value		$ 20,000,000 00	
	Less—Discount	$ 800,000 00		
	Commission and Expenses	44,010 16		
			844,010 16	
				19,155,989 84
TREASURY BILLS: Series				
"CI"	R.S.O. 1927, Cap. 57—			
	5½% 1 month due February 5th, 1932. Payable Toronto			5,000,000 00
	R.S.O. 1927, Cap. 23 and 57 (Renewals)—			
	5½% 3 months due May 5th, 1932. Payable Toronto			5,000,000 00
	5½% 2 months due July 5th, 1932. Payable Toronto			5,000,000 00
"CJ"	R.S.O. 1927, Cap. 57—			
	6% 3 months due February 2nd, 1932. Payable New York			4,000,000 00
"CK"	R.S.O. 1927, Cap. 57—			
	6% 3 months due February 6th, 1932. Payable New York			5,000,000 00
"CL"	R.S.O. 1927, Cap. 57—			
	6% 3 months due February 16th, 1932. Payable New York			5,000,000 00
	R.S.O. 1927, Cap. 23 and 57 (Renewals)—			
	6% 3 months due May 16th, 1932. Payable New York			5,000,000 00
	6% 3 months due August 16th, 1932. Payable New York			2,500,000 00
	6% 3 months due November 16th, 1932. Payable New York			2,500,000 00
"CM"	21 Geo. V, Cap. 2—			
	5½% 3 months due February 13th, 1932. Payable Toronto			19,000,000 00
	Carried Forward			$104,456,980 10

Statement No. 19—Continued

PUBLIC DEBT

Proceeds of Loans for Fiscal Year 1932

TREASURY BILLS	Brought Forward		$104,456,980 10
"CN"	R.S.O. 1927, Cap. 57—		
	6% 3 months due February 29th, 1932. Payable New York		4,000,000 00
	R.S.O. 1927, Cap. 23 and 57 (Renewals)—		
	6% 3 months due May 29th, 1932. Payable New York		4,000,000 00
	6% 5 months due November 1st, 1932. Payable New York		2,000,000 00
"CO"	R.S.O. 1927, Cap. 57—		
	5½% due on demand. Payable Toronto		800,000 00
	21 Geo. V, Cap. 2—		
	5½% 1 month due February 15th, 1932. Payable Toronto		3,500,000 00
	R.S.O. 1927, Cap. 23 (Renewals)—		
	5½% 1 month due March 15th, 1932. Payable Toronto		3,500,000 00
	5½% 3 months due June 15th, 1932. Payable Toronto		3,500,000 00
	5½% 5 months due November 15th, 1932. Payable Toronto		3,500,000 00
"CP"	R.S.O. 1927, Cap. 57—		
	6% 3 months due May 6th, 1932. Payable New York		7,000,000 00
	R.S.O. 1927, Cap. 23 and 57 (Renewals)—		
	6% 3 months due August 6th, 1932. Payable New York		3,500,000 00
	6% 3 months due November 6th, 1932. Payable New York		3,500,000 00
"CQ"	R.S.O. 1927, Cap. 57—		
	5½% 3 months due June 30th, 1932. Payable Toronto.		
	Par value	5,000,000 00	
	Less—Discount	68,561 65	
			4,931,438 35
	R.S.O. 1927, Cap. 23 and 57—		
	5½% 2 months due June 30th, 1932. Payable Toronto.		
	Par value	$ 5,000,000 00	
	Less—Discount	45,959 00	
			4,954,041 00
"CR"	R.S.O. 1927, Cap. 23 and 57—		
	5% 5½ months due November 1st, 1932. Payable New York.		
	Par value	$ 3,000,000 00	
	Less—Discount	13,494 72	
			2,986,505 28
"CS"	R.S.O. 1927, Cap. 57—		
	5% 1 month due June 30th, 1932. Payable Toronto.		
	Par value	$ 5,000,000 00	
	Less—Discount	22,602 75	
			4,977,397 25
"CT"	20 Geo. V, Cap. 2—		
	5½% 4⅔ months due October 31st, 1932. Payable Toronto		100,000 00
	20 Geo. V, Cap. 2—		
	5½% 4 months due November 2nd, 1932. Payable Toronto		2,000,000 00
"CU"	20 Geo. V, Cap. 2—		
	5⅝% 4 months due November 1st, 1932. Payable Toronto		15,000,000 00
"CV"	R.S.O. 1927, Cap. 23 and 57—		
	6% 2 years due July 1st, 1934. Payable Toronto		5,000,000 00
"HY"	R.S.O. 1927, Cap. 57—		
	5½% payable on demand. Payable Toronto		1,950,000 00
SINKING FUNDS:	3½% Inscribed Stock—		
	Proceeds of sale of British 5% War Loan, 1929/1947		274,239 42
	Earnings on investments		49,650 56
	4% Inscribed Stock—		
	Proceeds of Sale of British 5% War Loan, 1929/1947		94,155 00
	Earnings on investments		45,649 85
	4½% Inscribed Stock—		
	Proceeds of Sale of British 5% War Loan, 1929/1947		15,057 98
	Earnings on investments		15,672 93
	Series "AM," Sinking Fund—		
	Sale of $8,000 "UU" and "XX," 6% due 1943		8,600 00
			$185,659,387 72

Statement No. 20

LOAN REPAYMENTS AND SPECIAL FUND DEPOSITS

Receipts for Fiscal Year 1932

Loan Repayments—			
Prime Minister's Department—			
Hydro-Electric Power Commission—			
Refund of advances not required		$ 902,314 82	
Sale of Properties—			
Bowmanville Distribution System		92,403 11	
Trenton Distribution System		204,646 99	
Repayment of advances from Sinking Fund—			
Advances prior to October 31st, 1925	$ 1,628,572 00		
Advances since October 31st, 1925	774,372 38		
		2,402,944 38	
Rural Loans—Repayment		6,431 07	
			$ 3,608,740 37
Attorney-General's Department—			
Housing Loans—Repayments			329,981 51
Northern Development Department—			
Settlers' Loans—Repayments			28,748 09
Public Welfare Department—			
Mothers' Allowances—Municipalities—Outstanding at October 31st, 1931		$ 107,345 50	
Old Age Pensions—Dominion, Municipalities and Other Provinces—Outstanding at October 31st, 1931		1,015,779 50	
			1,123,125 00
Provincial Treasurer's Department—			
Agricultural Development Board—Repayment of Debentures		$ 1,200,000 00	
Tile Drainage Loans—Repayments		163,451 74	
Municipal Drainage Loans—Repayments		36,048 78	
Farm Loans—Repayments		11,899 95	
Capital Stock		150 00	
Municipal Debentures—Repayments		2,305 38	
			1,413,855 85
Agriculture Department—			
J. Brillon—Repayment of Mortgage			327 01
			$ 6,504,777 83
Special Fund Deposits—			
Prime Minister's Department—			
Ontario Public Service Superannuation Fund—			
Contributions by Employees and Government		$ 847,749 12	
Interest earned on Fund		198,104 20	
			1,045,853 32
Education Department—			
Bequests			4,000 00
Lands and Forests Department—			
Back to Land Movement—Municipalities			20,765 39
Northern Development Department—			
Cochrane Co-operative Dairy Co., Ltd.—Proceeds, Sale of Creamery			4,000 00
Public Welfare Department—			
Bowmanville School—Rotary Club Gymnasium Fund			1,435 00
Provincial Treasurer's Department—			
Municipal Sinking Funds		$ 108,542 70	
Surplus Registry Office Fees deposited—R.S.O. 1927, Cap. 158		27,055 06	
Toronto Registry Office—Assurance Fund		1,217 35	
Discount on Bonds, etc		282,882 73	
Overpayment—Accountable Warrants, etc		23 39	
			419,721 23
			$ 1,495,774 94

Statement No. 21

KING'S PRINTER OFFICE

Government Stationery and Paper Account

Stock on hand, November 1st, 1931—				
Stationery				$ 37,719 54
Printing and binding				13,911 04
Contract Paper				7,168 39
				$ 58,798 97
Purchases during the year—				
Stationery			$ 159,579 74	
Printing and binding			347,588 89	
Contract paper			12,204 75	
				519,373 38
				$ 578,172 35
Deduct—				
Distribution to Departments—				
Stationery, printing and binding	$ 497,651 33			
Contract paper	13,386 37			
		$ 511,037 70		
Cash Sales—				
Stationery, printing and binding	$ 25,150 16			
Paper	1,003 46			
		26,153 62		
		$ 537,191 32		
Stock written off, 1931, and adjustments		367 86		
Stock on hand, October 31st, 1932—				
Stationery	$ 24,820 43			
Contract paper	4,864 84			
In course of distribution (on invoices)				
Stationery, printing and binding	10,685 51			
Paper	168 03			
		40,538 81		
				578 097 99
Loss in Distribution				$ 74 36
Distribution of stationery, printing and paper as above				$ 537,191 32
Purchases as above				519,373 38
Excess of distribution over purchases				$ 17,817 94

For details of Purchases, see pages T 7-10.

MISCELLANEOUS STATEMENTS

As at October 31st, 1932

(See Index, Page 5)

PROVINCIAL DEBT

Statement Showing Investment Thereof as at October 31st, 1932

FUNDED DEBT:			
Stock and Debentures outstanding			$499,986,011 19
Certificates and Annuities			1,261,299 84
			$501,247,311 03
Deduct—Sinking Fund Investments—			
Registered Stocks		$2,758,066 11	
"AM"—Sinking Fund		1,095,000 00	
"AN"— " "		690,000 00	
Hydro-Electric Power Commission—			
Ontario bonds deposited with Treasury		2,101,000 00	
			6,644,066 11
Total Funded Debt			$494,603,244 92
UNFUNDED DEBT:			
Treasury Bills		$37,505,000 00	
Savings Office Deposits		23,709,819 62	
Special Fuuds, Accounts Payable and Accrued Interest		16,500,328 47	
			77,715,148 09
Gross Debt			$572,318,393 01
INVESTMENT THEREOF:			
Revenue Producing and Realizable Assets—			
Hydro-Electric Power Commission—advances		$189,635,191 09	
Less—Sinking Fund Investments deposited		2,101,000 00	
		$187,534,191 09	
Temiskaming and Northern Ontario Railway—advances		30,207,934 92	
Farm, Housing and Settlers' Loans		53,459,194 04	
Cash and Accounts Receivable	$20,872,949 43		
King's Highways—Construction—Counties and Cities	2,570,302 99		
		23,443,252 42	
			294,644,572 47
Revenue Producing but not Realizable Assets—			
Roads and Highways	$181,663,253 50		
Less—Due by Cities and Counties	2,570,302 99		
		$179,092,950 51	
Niagara Parks		1,856,125 72	
Common School Fund—Trust Fund; Ontario and Quebec		1,457,743 56	
			182,406,819 79
Total Revenue Producing Assets			$477,051,392 26
Non-Revenue Producing Assets—			
Provincial buildings and public works		$61,477,555 29	
Plant, stores and equipment		2,439,661 05	
Deferred assets		146,816 13	
			64,064,032 47
Other Assets—			
Capitalized value of annual subsidy		$58,828,485 60	
Unemployment relief—Direct (less 1/5 written off)		3,139,749 88	
			61,968,235 48
Total Assets			$603,083,660 21
Excess of Assets over Liabilities			$ 30,765,267 20

GROSS PROVINCIAL DEBT

Statement Showing Increase

Fiscal Year ended October 31st, 1932

	1931	1932	Increase
FUNDED DEBT—	$ c.	$ c.	$ c.
Stocks, Debentures, Certificates and Annuities	453,151,596 04	496,704,244 92	43,552,648 88
Less: Hydro Sinking Fund—Ontario Bonds deposited	2,101,000 00	2,101,000 00	....
	451,050,596 04	494,603,244 92	43,552,648 88
UNFUNDED DEBT	67,515,904 67	77,715,148 09	10,199,243 42
Gross debt	518,566,500 71	572,318,393 01	53,751,892 30

INCREASE IN GROSS DEBT ACCOUNTED FOR THUS—

		$ c.
CASH IN BANKS—Increase		11,736,093 33
CAPITAL EXPENDITURE—		
Expenditure on Highways, Northern Development, Public Buildings and Works, etc	15,406,543 55	
Unemployment Relief—		
Municipal and Public Works	10,092,125 91	
Direct Relief (Less one-fifth written off)	3,139,749 88	
	28,638,419 34	
Less—Capital Revenue	170,738 49	
	28,467,680 85	
Less—Payable by Dominion Government	528,555 72	
		27,939,125 13
HYDRO-ELECTRIC POWER COMMISSION—advances	3,660,955 08	
Less: Repayments from Sinking Funds	2,402,944 38	
		1,258,010 70
AGRICULTURAL DEVELOPMENT FINANCE ACT— Increase in Investments		7,148,747 81
PENSIONS, MOTHERS' ALLOWANCES AND UNEMPLOYMENT RELIEF— Due to Province—Increase		213,998 89
DISCOUNT ON BONDS, ETC., ISSUED IN 1932		2,598,129 67
MISCELLANEOUS		10,328 43
DEFICIT IN ORDINARY REVENUE—1932		2,060,798 31
		52,965,232 27
Deduct:		
LOANS TO MUNICIPALITIES, ETC.—Decrease	113,264 20	
SINKING FUNDS—Earnings	110,973 34	
DISCOUNT WRITTEN OFF IN CURRENT YEAR	282,882 73	
		507,120 27
		52,458,112 00
BOOK ENTRIES—		
Increase in accrued liabilities at October 31st, 1932, included in Unfunded Debt—Accrued interest on Public Debt, Special Funds, etc		1,293,780 30
		53,751,892 30

NET PROVINCIAL DEBT

Statement Showing Increase

Fiscal Year Ended October 31st ,1932

	1931	1932	Increase
	$ c.	$ c.	$ c.
GROSS DEBT	518,566,500 71	572,318,393 01	53,751,892 30
REVENUE PRODUCING AND REALIZABLE ASSETS	274,539,371 85	294,644,572 47	20,105,200 62
Net Debt	244,027,128 86	277,673,820 54	33,646,691 68

INCREASE IN NET DEBT ACCOUNTED FOR THUS:

NET CAPITAL EXPENDITURE—		
Highways, Northern Development, Public Buildings and Works, Unemployment Relief, etc.	28,467,680 85	
Less—Payable by Dominion Government	528,555 72	
		27,939,125 13
DEBENTURE GUARANTEE ACT—		
Paid by Province—Repayment deferred		42,682 48
DISCOUNT ON BOND AND TREASURY BILLS—1932		
Less amount written off during year		2,315,246 94
MISCELLANEOUS		54 73
DEFICIT OF ORDINARY REVENUE—1932		2,060,798 31
		32,357,907 59
Deduct:		
SINKING FUND INVESTMENT ACCOUNTS—Earnings		110,973 34
		32,246,934 25
Add:		
BOOK ENTRIES—		
Accrued Liabilities—increase	1,293,780 30	
Accrued Accounts Receivable—decrease	105,977 13	
		1,399,757 43
		33,646,691 68

NOTE.—Net Debt represents indebtedness incurred in respect of expenditure on projects of a non-realizable nature, such as Highways, Buildings, Public Works, etc. It is further increased by items of the nature of discount on loans, deficits of ordinary revenue, etc.

STATEMENT SHOWING SOURCES OF ORDINARY REVENUE

Fiscal Year Ending October 31st, 1932

DOMINION GOVERNMENT—ANNUAL SUBSIDY		$3,090,830 58
REVENUE DERIVED FROM INDIVIDUALS AND CORPORATIONS RECEIVING THE BENEFIT OF PROVINCIAL SERVICES, SPECIAL PRIVILEGES OR THE USE OF NATURAL RESOURCES AND PROPERTIES AND PROFITS FROM TRADING, ETC.:		
Taxation Gasoline, Mines, Lands, Corporations, Race Tracks (betting), Amusements, Stock Transfers and Wine.	$21,967,906 97	
Licenses Motor Vehicles, Liquor Permits, Hunting and Fishing, Insurance, Loan and Trust Companies, Mines, Race Tracks, Theatres, etc.	8,682,892 72	
Fees Local Registrars, Police Magistrates, Crown Attorneys, etc.; Fire Marshal, Mine Recording, Companies and Brokers Registration, etc.; Land Transfers, Motor Vehicle Transfers, etc.	1,887,483 65	
Pines and Penalties	111,818 22	
Profits from Trading Activities Liquor Control Board—Profits, Fines, Sale of Confiscated Liquor, etc.	9,260,000 00	
Succession Duties	6,136,624 02	
Natural Resources	2,629,525 69	
Interest on Drainage and Sundry Loans	204,616 47	
Miscellaneous Ontario Gazette, sale of Government publications, and casual revenue.	203,534 69	
		51,084,402 43
		$54,175,233 01

NET PROVINCIAL [illegible]EBT

Statement Showing I[illegible]rease

Fiscal Year Ended Octob[illegible] 31st, 1932

	19[illegible]	1932	Increase
	$	$ c.	$ c.
Gross Debt	518,566,[illegible]	5[illegible]2,318,393 01	53,751,892 30
Revenue Producing and Realizable Assets	274,539,[illegible]	[illegible]4,644,572 47	20,105,200 62
Net Debt	244 02[illegible]	[illegible]77,673,820 54	33,646,691 68

Increase in Net Debt Accounted for thus:		
Net Capital Expenditure—		
Highways, Northern Development, Public B[illegible] and Works, Unemployment Relief, etc	[illegible]8,467,680 85	
Less—Payable by Dominion Government	528,555 72	27,939,125 13
Debenture Guarantee Act— Paid by Province—Repayment deferred	....	42,682 48
Discount on Bond and Treasury Bills 193[illegible] Less amount written off during year	....	2,315,246 94
Miscellaneous		54 73
Deficit of Ordinary Revenue—1932	....	2,060,798 31
		32,357,907 59
Deduct:		
Sinking Fund Investment Accounts- Earnings	....	110,973 34
		32,246,934 25
Add:		
Book Entries—		
Accrued Liabilities—increase	1,293,780 30	
Accrued Accounts Receivable—decrease	105,977 13	1,399,757 43
		33,646,691 68

Note.—Net Debt represents indebtedness incurr[illegible] in respect of expenditure on projects of a non-realizable nature, such as Highways, Build[illegible]s, Public Works, etc. It is furth[illegible] increased by items of the nature of discount on loans, [illegible]fi[illegible]ts of ordinary revenue, etc

STATEMENT SH WING SOURCES OF ORDINARY REVENUE

Fisc Year Ending October **31st, 1932**

DOMINION GOVERNMENT—ANN L SUBSIDY		$3,090,830 58
REVENUE DERIVED FROM I VIDUALS AND CORPORATIONS RECEIVING THE BEN FI OF PROVINCIAL SERVICES, SPECIAL PRIVILEGES OR T USE OF NATURAL RESOURCES AND PROPERTIES AND PR TS FROM TRADING, ETC.:		
Taxation	$21,967,906 97	
Gasoline, Mines, Lan , Corporations, Race Tracks (betting), Amusen its, Stock Transfers and Wine.		
Licenses	8,682,892 72	
Motor Vehicles, Li uo Permits, Hunting and Fishing, Insurance, Lo n d Trust Companies, Mines, Race Tracks, Ih res, etc.		
Fees	1,887,483 65	
Local Registrars, Polic Magistrates, Crown Attorneys, etc.; Fire Marsh Mine Recording, Companies and Brokers Reg ration, etc.; Land Transfers, Motor Vehicle T isfers, etc.		
Fines and Penalties	111,818 22	
Profits from Trading Ac ies	9,260,000 00	
Liquor Control Boa Profits, Fines, Sale of Confiscated Liquor, e		[illegible]84
Succession Duties	6,136,624 0[illegible]	[illegible]01 42
Natural Resources	2,629,525 [illegible]	
Interest on Drainage and ındry Loans	204,61[illegible]	
Miscellaneous		
Ontario Gazette, sale Government publications casual revenue.		

$ 40,538 81
12,231 55
1,150,000 00
49,884 31
528,903 52
40,000 00
10,635 75
532,697 11
74,770 00
$ 2,439,661 05

$ 52,153 49
16,168 02
20,830 25
2,183 14
1,579 00
$ 92,913 90
53,902 23
$ 146,816 13

HYDRO-ELECTRIC POWER COMMISSION OF ONTARIO

Advances by Province to October **31st, 1932**

Advanced on Capital Account to October 31st, 1931		$200,827,676 36
Advances during current year (see page B2)		4,860,320 00
		$205,687,996 36
Deduct:		
Refund of Capital Advances not required (see page 28)	$ 902,314 82	
Sale of Properties (see page 28)	297,050 10	
		1,199,364 92
Total Advances to date		$204,488,631 44
Repayments from Sinking Fund in accordance with Debt Retirement Plan—		
To October 31st, 1931	$12,450,495 97	
Current year	2,402,944 38	
		14,853,440 35
Net Advances to October 31st, 1932		$189,635,191 09

Note—Province of Ontario Bonds, $2,101,000, have been deposited with the Provincial Treasurer on account of Sinking Fund for the repayment of advances, in excess of cash payments called for and made under the Debt Retirement Plan.

LOANS TO MUNICIPALITIES, ETC.

As at October **31st, 1932**

Housing Loans		$ 4,216,057 33
Drainage Debentures—		
Tile Drainage Act	$ 2,182,643 09	
Municipal Drainage Aid Act	239,853 16	
		2,422,496 25
Settlers' Loans		712,003 61
Municipal Debentures—		
Town of Cochrane	$ 33,514 06	
Township of Whitney	17,147 85	
Village of Eganville	5,562 40	
		56,224 31
Rural Power Districts Loans Act		58,568 93
Soldiers' Aid Commission		22,191 62
J. Brillon—Mortgage		5,847 50
Co-operative Marketing Loan Act		244,250 00
		$ 7,737,639 55

BUILDINGS, ROADS, ETC.

As at October **31st, 1932**

Provincial Buildings and Lands	$ 48,735,763 01
Improvements to Highways, 1919-1932	136,556,183 07
Northern Development—Roads and Farms, 1919-1932	37,800,871 55
Colonization Roads—1919-1932	3,994,523 18
Trans-Canada Highway, 1930-1932	3,311,675 70
Niagara Parks Commission—Surplus of Assets	1,856,125 72
Hydro Power Plant—Monteith	27,061 10
Rural Power Transmission Lines—Bonus, 1927-1932	6,739,243 00
Unemployment Relief—Municipal Works, etc.	5,975,488 18
	$244,996,934 51

BANK BALANCES

As at October 31st, 1932

Balances Due by Banks—	
Commerce	$ 3,129,180 60
Dominion	387,546 27
Home (in liquidation)	250,000 00
Imperial	260,416 83
Montreal	5,432,554 98
Nova Scotia	4,918,113 96
Royal	1,140,244 17
Toronto	575,043 60
	$ 16,093,100 41
Deduct:	
Montreal, (London) Inscribed Stock Sinking Fund Accounts	383,452 40
	$15,709,648 01

ACCOUNTS RECEIVABLE

As at October 31st, 1932

Lands and Forests—Crown Land Sales and Interest, etc.	$ 378,154 87
" " Surveys Branch	14,747 10
Northern Development—Aid to Settlers—Notes Outstanding	349,655 53
Mines	53,433 09
Public Works—Rentals, etc.	2,475 00
Highways—Municipalities, Maintenance of Highways, etc	680,817 89
Treasury—Succession Duties, Corporation Tax, etc.	936,909 47
Hospitals and Institutions—Maintenance of Patients, etc	242,548 50
Provincial Secretary—Filing Fees, etc	85,000 00
Sale of Central Prison and Toronto Asylum—Balance	473,320 00
Unemployment Relief—Dominion Government	531,839 55
Old Age Pensions—Dominion Government, Municipalities and Other Provinces	1,254,523 42
Mothers' Allowances—Municipalities	121,165 00
Old School of Medicine—Sale	5,000 00
Returned Cheques held for collection	14,538 23
Byron Telephone Co.—Capital Stock	30 00
Back to the Land Movement—Dominion Government	2,933 93
Accountable Warrants—Administration of Justice in Districts	6,209 84
	$ 5,153,301 42

PLANT, LIVESTOCK, STORES AND EQUIPMENT

As at October 31st, 1932

King's Printer—Stationery Stock	$ 40,538 81
Education Department	12,231 55
Lands and Forests Department	1,150,000 00
Highways Department	49,884 31
Health—Ontario Hospitals	528,903 52
Public Health	40,000 00
Public Welfare	10,635 75
Provincial Secretary—Ontario Reformatories	532,697 11
Agriculture	74,770 00
	$ 2,439,661 05

DEFERRED ASSETS

As at October 31st, 1932

Debentures and Interest paid under Debenture Guarantee Act:	
Town of Matheson	$ 52,153 49
Town of Riverside	16,168 02
City of East Windsor	20,830 25
Town of Cobalt—High School	2,183 14
Robillard and Truax Union School Board	1,579 00
	$ 92,913 90
Promissory Notes Paid—	
Ottawa Separate Schools Commission	53,902 23
	$ 146,816 13

DISCOUNT ON LOANS, 1926-1932

	Balance October 31st, 1931	Charged off during 1932	Balance October 31st, 1932
	$ c.	$ c.	$ c.
Treasury Bills—			
Series "CI" 3 months—due January 5th, 1932.	42,009 13	42,009 13	....
" "CQ" 3 " " June 30th, 1932...	....	68,561 65	....
" "CQ" 2 " " June 30th, 1932...	....	45,959 00	....
" "CS" 1 " " June 30th, 1932...	....	22,602 75	....
" "CR" 5½ " " Nov. 1st, 1932....	....	13,494 72	....
	42,009 13	192,627 25	....
Debenture Issues refunding maturities issued prior to to October 31st, 1925:			
Series "A.J." 30 years—due 1928/56...........	553,300 00	22,132 00	531,168 00
" "A.K" 30 " " 1928/57...........	143,938 08	5,536 08	138,402 00
" "A.L." 38 " " 1928/66 (part).....	504,321 00	14,618 00	489,703 00
" "A.M" 30 " " 1959 "	74,410 33	2,705 83	71,704 50
" "A.P" 36 " " 1930/66 "	428,200 00	12,400 00	415,800 00
" "A.R" 3 " " 1932/34 "	19,508 00	9,754 00	9,754 00
	1,723,677 41	67,145 91	1,656,531 50
Premium received (on Debentures Issued):			
Series "A.N." 31 years—due 1960 (part)........	80,249 32	2,800 00	77,449 32
	1,643,428 09	64,345 91	1,579,082 18
Premiums paid on Debentures purchased for Debt Redemption and Sinking Funds................	221,039 90	25,909 57	232,955 33
Loan Floatation expenses:			
Series "A.T." 15 years—due 1947.............	....	....	40,019 29
" "A.U." 3 " " 1935.............	....	....	10,476 48
" "A.W." 14 " " 1946.............	....	....	44,010 16
	1,906,477 12	282,882 73	1,906,543 44
Debentures Issued—New Debt (since October 31st, 1925):			
Discount provided for by payment of annuity maturities and Sinking Fund instalments out of Ordinary Revenue:			
Series "A.L." 40 years—due 1968 (part).......	1,138,608 00	60,726 00	1,077,882 00
" "A.M." 30 " " 1959 "	198,297 92	7,210 83	191,087 09
" "A.P." 40 " " 1970 "	1,183,682 50	30,745 00	1,152,937 50
" "A.R." 40 " " 1971 "	360,523 80	9,244 20	351,279 60
" "A.S." 40 " " 1971.............	1,721,212 50	43,575 00	1,677,637 50
" "A.T." 15 " " 1947.............	....	58,500 08	1,091,499 92
" "AT-ZA" 15 " " 1947.............	....	5,000 00	95,000 00
" "A.U." 3 " " 1935.............	....	12,500 00	37,500 00
" "A.V." 25 " " 1957.............	....	4,303 67	210,876 95
" "A.W." 14 " " 1946.............	....	16,904 81	783,095 19
	4,602,324 72	248,709 59	6,668,795 75
Premiums received (on debentures issued):			
Series "A.N." 31 years—due 1960 (part).......	184,866 26	6,374 71	178,491 55
	4,417,458 46	242,334 88	6,490,304 20
	6,323,935 58	525,217 61	8,396,847 64

SINKING FUNDS—INVESTMENTS

As at October 31st, 1932

3½% Registered Stock, due January 1st, 1946—£422,549: 4:10:		
Ontario Registered 3½% Stock 1946. Par value..........$	618,710 48	
" " 4% " 1947 " "	194,556 96	
" " 4½% " 1965 " "	151,241 64	
Commonwealth of Australia, 5% Stock, 1945-75, £4,637: 6:10 at cost..............................	24,191 98	
Bank of Montreal, London, England—Cash uninvested....	274,239 42	
		$1,262,940 48
4% Registered Stock, due May 1st, 1947—£317,912:16: 4:		
Ontario Registered 3½% Stock, 1946. Par value..........$	251,113 37	
" " 4% " 1947 " "	454,360 51	
" " 4½% " 1965 " "	191,365 92	
Commonwealth of Australia, 5% Stock, 1945-75, £28,527:12: 8 at cost..............................	136,300 71	
Bank of Montreal, London, England—Cash uninvested....	94,155 00	
		1,127,295 51
4½% Registered Stock, due January 1st, 1946—£171,454:12: 8:		
Ontario Registered 3½% Stock, 1946. Par value..........$	61,810 59	
" " 4% " 1947. " "	109,438 98	
" " 4½% " 1965. " "	112,172 40	
Commonwealth of Australia, 5% Stock, 1945-75, £14,510:12: 6 at cost..............................	69,350 17	
Bank of Montreal, London, England—Cash uninvested....	15,057 98	
		367,830 12
Debenture Loan—Series "A.M." due May 1st, 1959—$35,000,000:		
Province of Ontario Debentures—		
Series "AD" 1942, 5% Par value..............$	10,000 00	
" "UU" & "XX" 1943, 6% " "	37,000 00	
" "WW" & "YY" 1943, 6% " "	79,000 00	
" "AW" 1946, 5% " "	25,000 00	
" "AT" 1947, 5% " "	30,000 00	
" "AF" 1948, 5% " "	307,000 00	
" "AB" 1952, 5% " "	20,000 00	
" "AM" 1959, 5% " "	587,000 00	
		1,095,000 00
Debenture Loan—Series "A.N." due December 2nd, 1960—$35,000,000:		
Province of Ontario Debentures—		
Series "AC" 1942, 5½% Par value............$	45,000 00	
" "UU" & "XX" 1943, 6% " "	60,000 00	
" "AN" 1960, 5% " "	585,000 00	
		690,000 00
		$4,543,066 11

DISCOUNT ON LOANS, 1926-1932

	Balance October 31st, 1931 $ c.	Charged off during 1932 $ c.	Balance October 31st, 1932 $ c.
Treasury Bills—			
Series "CI" 3 months—due January 5th, 1932	42,009 13	42,009 13	....
" "CO" 3 " " June 30th, 1932	.....	68,561 65	....
" "CQ" 2 " " June 30th, 1932	.....	45,959 00	....
" "CS" 1 " " June 30th, 1932	.....	22,602 75	....
" "CR" 5½ " " Nov. 1st, 1932	.....	13,494 72	....
	42,009 13	192,627 25	....
Debenture Issues refunding maturities issued prior to October 31st, 1925:			
Series "A.J." 30 years—due 1928/56	553,300 00	22,132 00	531,168 00
" "A.K" 30 " " 1928/57	143,938 08	5,536 08	138,402 00
" "A.L." 38 " " 1928/66 (part)	504,321 00	14,618 00	489,703 00
" "A.M" 30 " " 1959 "	74,410 33	2,705 83	71,704 50
" "A.P" 36 " " 1930/66 "	[illegible]28,200 00	12,400 00	415,800 00
" "A.R" 3 " " 1932/34 "	19,508 00	9,754 00	9,754 00
	[illegible]23,677 41	67,145 91	1,656,531 50
Premium received (on Debentures Issued): Series "A.N." 31 years—due 1960 (part)	80,249 32	2,800 00	77,449 32
	[illegible]43,428 09	64,345 91	1,579,082 18
Premiums paid on Debentures purchased for Debt Redemption and Sinking Funds	[illegible]1,039 90	25,909 57	232,955 33
Loan Floatation expenses:			
Series "A.T." 15 years—due 1947	....	....	**40,019 29**
" "A.U." 3 " " 1935	....	....	**10,476 48**
" "A.W." 14 " " 1946	....	....	**44,010 16**
	[illegible]06,477 12	282,882 73	1,906,543 44
Debentures Issued—New Debt (since October 31st, 1925):			
Discount provided for by payment of annual maturities and Sinking Fund instalments out of Ordinary Revenue:			
Series "A.L." 40 years—due 1968 (part)	[illegible]38,608 00	**60,726 00**	**1,077,882 00**
" "A.M." 30 " " 1959 "	[illegible]8,297 92	**7,210 83**	**191,087 09**
" "A.P." 40 " " 1970 "	1[illegible]3,682 50	**30,745 00**	**1,152,937 50**
" "A.R." 40 " " 1971 "	[illegible]0,523 80	**9,244 20**	**351,279 60**
" "A.S." 40 " " 1971	[illegible]21,212 50	**43,575 00**	**1,677,637 50**
" "A.T." 15 " " 1947	.....	**58,500 08**	**1,091,499 92**
" "AT-ZA" 15 " " 1947	.....	**5,000 00**	**95,000 00**
" "A.U." 3 " " 1935	.....	**12,500 00**	**37,500 00**
" "A.V." 25 " " 1957	.....	**4,303 67**	**210,876 95**
" "A.W." 14 " " 1946	.....	**16,904 81**	**783,095 19**
	4,602,324 72	248,709 59	6,668,795 75
Premiums received (on debentures issued): Series "A.N." 31 years—due 1960 (part)	184,866 26	6,374 71	178,491 55
	417,458 46	242,334 88	6,490,304 20
	[illegible],3[illegible]3,935 58	525,217 61	8,396,847 64

SINKIG FUNDS—INVESTMENTS

A at October 31st, 1932

3½% Registered Stock, due Janury 1st, 1946—£422,549: 4:10:		
Ontario Registered 3½% Stck 1946. Par value..........	$ 618,710 48	
" " 4% 1947 " "	194,556 95	
" " 4½% 1965 " "	151,241 64	
Commonwealth of Australia 5% Stock, 1945-75, £4,637: 6:10 at cost	24,191 98	
Bank of Montreal, London, ngland—Cash uninvested....	274,239 42	
		$1,262,940 48
4% Registered Stock, due May 1s 1947—£317,912:16: 4:		
Ontario Registered 3½% Sck, 1946. Par value..........	$ 251,113 37	
" " 4% 1947 " "	454,360 51	
" " 4½% 1965 " "	191,365 92	
Commonwealth of Australi 5% Stock, 1945-75, £28,527:12: 8 at co	136,300 71	
Bank of Montreal, London ngland—Cash uninvested....	94,155 00	
		1,127,295 51
4½% Registered Stock, due Janury 1st, 1946—£171,454:12: 8:		
Ontario Registered 3½% Sck, 1946. Par value..........	$ 61,810 59	
" " 4% 1947. " "	109,438 98	
" " 4½% 1965. " "	112,172 40	
Commonwealth of Australi 5% Stock, 1945-75, £14,510:12: 6 at co	69,350 17	
Bank of Montreal, London ngland—Cash uninvested....	15,057 98	
		367,830 12
Debenture Loan—Series "A.M." e May 1st, 1959—$35,000,000:		
Province of Ontario Debenture—		
Series "AD" 194 5% Par value..........	$ 10,000 00	
" "UU" & "XX" 194 6% " "	37,000 00	
" "WW" & "YY" 194 6% " "	79,000 00	
" "AW" 194 5% " "	25,000 00	
" "AT" 194 5% " "	30,000 00	
" "AF" 194 5% " "	307,000 00	
" "AB" 195 5% " "	20,000 00	
" "AM" 195 5% " "	587,000 00	
		1,095,000 00
Debenture Loan—Series "A.N." e December 2nd, 1960—$35,000,000:		
Province of Ontario Debentur —		
Series "AC" 194 5½% Par value..........	$ 45,000 00	
" "UU" & "XX" 194 6% " "	60,000 00	
" "AN" 19(5% " "	585,000 00	
		690,000 00
		$4,543,066 11

PROVINCE OF ONTARIO—STOCK AND DEBENTURES

Maturity	Nature	Date of Issue	Rate	Amount of Issue	Redeemed and Cancelled	Amount Outstanding
Instalment Issues			%	$	$	$
1932, Nov. 1......... (1928-1957).....	Serial	Nov. 1, 1927	4½	24,000,000	3,200,000	20,800,000
Dec. 1......... (1926-1955).....	Serial	Dec. 1, 1925	4½	21,000,000	4,200,000	16,800,000
1933, Jan. 15........ (1928-1957).....	Serial	Jan. 15, 1927	4½	24,000,000	4,000,000	20,000,000
1933, Jan. 15........ (1932-71).......	Annuity	Jan. 15, 1931	4½	30,000,000	961,000	29,039,000
May 15........ (1929-1968).....	Annuity	May 15, 1928	4	30,000,000	1,385,000	28,615,000
May 15........ (1931-1970).....	Annuity	May 15, 1930	4½	30,000,000	611,000	29,389,000
June 1......... (1932-71).......	Annuity	June 1, 1931	4	30,000,000	316,000	29,684,000
Straight Term Issues						
1935, Feb. 1..........	Bonds	Feb. 1, 1932	6	5,000,000	....	5,000,000
1935, April 1........	Bonds	April 1, 1920	6	2,000,000	19,000	1,981,000
Dec. 1........	Bonds	Dec. 1, 1920	6	16,000,000	767,000	15,233,000
1936, May 2........	Bonds	May 2, 1921	6	15,000,000	610,000	14,390,000
July 1........	B. & S.	July 1, 1906	3½	2,684,500	2,336,500	*348,000
Nov. 1........	Bonds	Nov. 1, 1931	5	150,000	....	150,000
1937, Jan. 3........	Bonds	Jan. 3, 1922	5½	15,000,000	....	15,000,000
1939, June 1........	B. & S.	June 1, 1909	4	1,150,000	....	1,150,000
June 1........	B. & S.	June 1, 1909	4	3,500,000	2,834,050	*665,950
1940, Oct. 31........	Bond	Oct. 31, 1930	4½	2,000,000	....	2,000,000
1941, Feb. 1........	Bonds	Feb. 1, 1921	6	10,000,000	496,500	9,503,500
May 1........	B. & S.	May 1, 1911	4	498,600	274,600	*224,000
Nov. 1........	B. & S.	Nov. 1, 1911	4	3,000,000	1,811,600	*1,188,400
1942, Oct. 1........	Bonds	Oct. 2, 1922	5	20,000,000	....	20,000,000
Dec. 1........	Bonds	Dec. 1, 1922	5½	20,000,000	1,360,500	18,639,500
1943, Sept. 15........	Bonds	Sept. 15, 1921	6	15,000,000	88,000	14,912,000
Sept. 15........	Bonds	Sept. 15, 1921	6	15,000,000	387,500	14,612,500
1944, Sept. 1........	Bonds	Sept. 1, 1924	4½	20,000,000	800,000	19,200,000
1946, July 1........	Bonds	July 1, 1932	5½	20,000,000	....	20,000,000
1947, Feb. 1........	Bonds	Feb. 1, 1932	5½	20,000,000	....	20,000,000
1947, Feb. 1........	Bonds	Feb. 1, 1932	5½	2,000,000	....	2,000,000
1948, Oct. 15........	Bonds	Oct. 15, 1923	5	40,000,000	1,693,500	38,306,500
1951, Nov. 1........	Bonds	Nov. 1, 1931	5	500,000	....	500,000
1952, April 1........	Bonds	April 1, 1922	5	15,000,000	....	15,000,000
1957, June 1........ £250,000/0/0...	Bonds	June 1, 1932	4½	1,216,666.65	....	a 1,216,666.65
1959, May 1........	Bonds	May 1, 1929	5	35,000,000	....	b 35,000,000
1960, Dec. 2........	Bonds	Dec. 2, 1929	5	35,000,000	....	c 35,000,000
1946, Jan. 1........ £422,549/4/10..	Stock	Jan. 1, 1906	3½	2,056,406.30	....	d 2,056,406.30
1947, May 1........ £317,912/16/4..	Stock	May 1, 1909	4	1,547,175.70	....	d *1,547,175.70
1965, Jan. 1........ £171,454/12/8..	Stock	Jan. 1, 1914	4½	834,412.54	....	d *834,412.54
				528,137,761.19	28,151,750	499,986,011.19

a Optional redemption by the Province on June 1st, 1947, or subsequent interest date on 3 months' notice. Sinking Fund provision ½ of 1% annually.
b Sinking Fund on 40-year retirement basis to provide 55 per cent. of issue at maturity in 1959.
c Sinking Fund to provide 68 per cent. of issue at maturity in 1960.
d Registered Stock—Bank of Montreal, London, England—Amount outstanding of which there has been purchased for Sinking Funds, $931,634.44, 3½ per cent. stock; $758,356.45, 4 per cent. stock, and $454,779.96, 4½ per cent. stock.
* Succession Duty Free.

OUTSTANDING AS AT OCTOBER 31st, 1932

Series	Authority	Interest Dates	Where Payable†	Denomination
AK	17 Geo. V, Cap. 2; R.S.O. 1914, Cap. 21	1 M & N	Prov. Treas. & Bk. Mtl., M., W., V., R., C., H., N.Y., L.	1,000
AH	15 Geo. V, Cap. 2; R.S.O. 1914, Cap. 21	1 J & D	Prov. Treas. & Bk. Mtl., M., W., V., R., C., H., St. J., N.Y., L.	1,000
AJ	16 Geo. V, Cap. 6; R.S.O. 1914, Cap. 21	15 J & J	Prov. Treas. & Bk. Mtl., M., W., V., R., C., H., St. J., N.Y., L.	1,000
AR	R.S.O. 1927, Cap. 23 & 57.....	15 J & J	Prov. Treas. & Bk. Mtl., M., W., V., R., C., H., St. J., N.Y., L.	1,000
AL	16 Geo. V, Cap. 6; 18 Geo. V, Cap. 6; R.S.O. 1927, Cap. 23	15 M & N	Prov. Treas. & Bk. Mtl., M., W., V., R., C., H., St. J., N.Y., L.	1,000
AP	R.S.O. 1927, Cap. 23 & 57.....	15 M & N	Prov. Treas. & Bk. Mtl., M., W., V., R., C., H., St. J., N.Y., L.	1,000
AS	20 Geo. V, Cap. 2, R.S.O. 1927, Cap. 23	1 J & D	Prov. Treas. & Bk. Mtl., M., W., V., R., C., H., St. J., N.Y., L.	1,000
AU	R.S.O. 1927, Cap. 57.........	1 F & A	Prov. Treas. & Bk. N.S. at M., W., V., H., St. J., O.	1,000
KK	R.S.O. 1914, Cap. 39.........	1 A & O	Prov. Treas. & Bk. Mtl., M.........	1,000
RR	R.S.O. 1914, Cap. 39.........	1 J & D	Prov. Treas. & Bk. Mtl., M., W.....	1,000 & 500
TT	R.S.O. 1914, Cap. 39.........	2 M & N	Prov. Treas. & Bk. Mtl., M.........	1,000 & 500
......	5 Ed. VII, Cap. 2; 6 Ed. VII, Cap. 4	1 J & J	Prov. Treas.	1,000 & 500
......	R.S.O. 1927, Cap. 23 & 57...	1 M & N	Prov. Treas........................	....
ZZ	11 Geo. V, Cap. 7...........	3 J & J	Prov. Treas. & Bk. Mtl., M., N.Y...	1,000
......	5 Ed. VII, Cap. 2 & 3.......	1 J & D	Prov. Treas. & Bk. Mtl., M.........	1,000 & 500
A	9 Ed. VII, Cap. 8...........	1 J & D	Prov. Treas. & Bk. Mtl., M., N.Y...	1,000 & 500
AQ	R.S.O. 1927, Cap. 331........	30 A & O	Prov. Treas........................	....
SS	R.S.O. 1914, Cap. 39.........	1 F & A	Prov. Treas. & Bk. Mtl., M.........	1,000 & 500
B	1 Geo. V, Cap. 9............	1 M & N	Prov. Treas. & Bk. Mtl., M., N.Y.....	1,000 & 500
C & D	1 Geo. V, Cap. 4............	1 M & N	Prov. Treas. & Bk. Mtl., M., N.Y.....	1,000
AC	12-13 Geo. V, Cap. 8..........	1 A & O	Prov. Treas. & Bk. Mtl., M., N.Y.....	1,000
AD	12-13 Geo. V, Cap. 8..........	1 J & D	Prov. Treas. & Bk. Mtl., M...........	1,000 & 500
UU & XX	R.S.O. 1914, Cap. 39.........	15 M & S	Prov. Treas. & Bk. Mtl., M., N.Y.....	1,000
WW & YY	R.S.O. 1914, Cap. 39.........	15 M & S	Prov. Treas. & Bk. Mtl., M., W.......	1,000 & 500
AG	14 Geo. V, Cap. 9............	1 M & S	Prov. Treas. & Bk. Mtl., M., N.Y., L..	1,000
AW	21 Geo. V, Cap. 2; R.S.O. 1927, Cap. 23	1 J & J	Prov. Treas. & Bk. Mtl., M., W., V., H., St. J., O.	1,000, 500, 100
AT	21 Geo. V, Cap. 2, R.S.O. 1927, Cap. 23	1 F & A	Prov. Treas. & Bk. Mtl., M., W., V., H., St. J., O.,	1,000 & 500
ZA — AT	R.S.O. 1927, Cap. 23 & 57...	1 F & A	Prov. Treas........................	....
AF	13-14 Geo. V, Cap. 2........	15 A & O	Prov. Treas. & Bk. Comm., M., W., V., H., St. J.	1,000 & 500
......	R.S.O. 1927, Cap. 23 & 57...	1 M & N	Prov. Treas........................	....
AB	R.S.O. 1914, Cap. 39.........	1 A & O	Prov. Treas. & Bk. Mtl., M., N.Y...	1,000
AV	R.S.O. 1927, Cap. 23 & 57...	1 J & D	Bk. Mtl., L. Eng.	....
AM	18 Geo. V, Cap. 6, R.S.O. 1927, Cap. 23	1 M & N	Prov. Treas. & Bk. Mtl., M., W., V., R., C., H., St. J., N.Y., L..	1,000
AN	19 Geo. V, Cap. 2; R.S.O. 1927, Cap. 23	2 J & D	Prov. Treas. & Bk. Mtl., M., W., V., R., C., H., St. J., N.Y., L.	1,000 & 500
......	5 Ed. VII, Cap. 2 & 3.......	1 J & J	Bk. Mtl., L........................	....
......	2 Geo. V, Cap. 2............	1 M & N	Bk. Mtl., L........................	....
......	4 Geo. V, Cap. 9............	1 J & J	Bk. Mtl., L........................	....

†M—Montreal; W—Winnipeg; V—Vancouver; R—Regina; C—Calgary; H—Halifax; St. J.—Saint John, N.B.; O—Ottawa; N.Y.—New York; L—London, England.

ANNUITIES

As at October 31st, 1932

Year	Annuities		
	Railway Aid Certificates	Annuities	University of Toronto
	$ c.	$ c.	$ c.
1932	....	14,350 00	....
1933	125,120 54	28,700 00	30,000 00
1934	123,021 74	28,700 00	30,000 00
1935	111,128 54	24,700 00	30,000 00
1936	105,090 01	16,700 00	....
1937	94,459 80	9,200 00	....
1938	90,961 80	2,850 00	....
1939	86,122 35	....	....
1940	82,239 02	....	....
1941	67,943 75	....	....
1942	31,818 40	....	....
1943	24,920 51	....	....
1944	22,695 08	....	....
1945	18,251 86	....	....
1946	18,251 86	....	....
1947	18,251 86	....	....
1948	18,251 86	....	....
1949	6,871 26	....	....
1950	699 60	....	....
	1,046,099 84	125,200 00	90,000 00

Maturities—
Railway Aid Certificates.............1st January and July.
Annuities...........................30th June, 31st December.
University of Toronto...............30th June.

Indirect Liabilities and Guarantees of the Province of Ontario
As at October 31st, 1932

(1) Temiskaming and Northern Ontario Railway Commission.		
Guaranteed by the Province of Ontario, under authority 17 Geo. V, cap. 16. Bonds of above Commission, due 1st February, 1939, to 1st February, 1968, 4 per cent........		$6,000,000 00
(2) Niagara Parks Commission.		
Guaranteed by the Province of Ontario, under authority 17 Geo. V, cap. 24. Bonds of above Commission, due 1st December, 1928, to 1st December, 1947, 4 per cent. Outstanding..	$1,714,000 00	
Guaranteed by the Province under authority Order-in-Council, July 26th, 1932. Bonds of the above Commission, due August 1st, 1947, 5½ per cent......................	300,000 00	
		2,014,000 00
(3) University of Toronto.		
Guaranteed by the Province of Ontario, under authority Order-in-Council, 15th July, 1908, and 16th June, 1909. Annuity Debentures of above University, payable 15th July, 1910, to 15th July, 1949, 40 years, $429,420.00 outstanding. Present value for 17 years at 4 per cent................	$307,304 82	
Guaranteed by the Province of Ontario, under authority Order-in-Council, 7th April, 1911. Annuity Debentures of above University, payable 1st January, 1912, to 1st January, 1951, 40 years, $124,792.00 outstanding. Present value for 19 years at 4 per cent................	86,263 72	
Guaranteed by the Province of Ontario, under authority Order-in-Council, 15th May, 1912. Annuity Debentures of above University, payable 1st January, 1912, to 1st January, 1951, 40 years, $287,983.00 outstanding. Present value for 19 years at 4 per cent...............	199,071 13	
Guaranteed by the Province of Ontario, under authority Order-in-Council, April 14th, 1915. Annuity Debentures of above University, payable April 15th, 1916, to April 15th, 1955, 40 years, $137,425.00 outstanding. Present value for 23 years at 4½ per cent.............	84,532 93	
Guaranteed by the Province of Ontario, under authority Order-in-Council, June 17th, 1924. Annuity Debentures of above University, payable July 15th, 1925, to July 15th, 1944, 20 years, $120,000.00 outstanding. Present value for 12 years at 5 per cent...............	88,632 50	
Guaranteed by the Province of Ontario, under authority Order-in-Council, November 15th, 1928. Annuity Debentures of above University, payable January 15th, 1930, to January 15th, 1949, 20 years, $1,091,281.00 outstanding. Present value for 17 years at 5 per cent................	723,716 38	
		1,489,521 48
(4) University of Western Ontario (London).		
Guaranteed by the Province of Ontario, under authority Order-in-Council, November 29th, 1928. Debentures of above University payable July 2nd, 1929, to July 2nd, 1958, 30 years, $440,000.00, 4½ per cent. Amount outstanding................................		410,000 00
(5) Town of Bruce Mines.		
R.S.O. 1914, cap. 266. January 1st, 1918, to January 1st, 1947, 6 per cent., outstanding......		17,639 62
Carried forward......$		9,931,161 10

Indirect Liabilities and Guarantees of the Province of Ontario—Continued

Brought forward...$		9,931,161 10
(6) Town of Matheson.		
7 Geo. V, cap. 9.		
June 1st, 1923, to June 1st, 1937, 6 per cent., outstanding..$	2,168 58	
9 Geo. V, cap. 4.		
April 1st, 1920, to April 1st, 1949, 6 per cent., outstanding..	23,977 28	
May 6th, 1924, to May 6th, 1948, 6 per cent., outstanding..	29,367 27	
		55,513 13
(7) Town of Capreol.		
10-11 Geo. V, cap. 7.		
December 1st, 1922, to December 1st, 1939, 6 per cent., outstanding.....		4,331 13
(8) Town of Cochrane.		
7 Geo. V, cap. 9.		
May 1st, 1918, to May 1st, 1947, 5 per cent., outstanding..	$ 27,008 46	
14 Geo. V, cap. 3.		
July 2nd, 1925, to July 2nd, 1944, 5½ per cent., outstanding	28,847 65	
July 2nd, 1924, to July 2nd, 1943, 5½ per cent., outstanding	74,489 59	
		130,345 70
(9) Town of Haileybury.		
14 Geo. V, cap. 3.		
April 1st, 1925, to April 1st, 1944, 6 per cent., outstanding	$ 14,618 83	
April 15th, 1925, to April 15th, 1944, 6 per cent., outstanding	1,260 33	
April 1st, 1925, to April 1st, 1934, 6 per cent., outstanding	923 08	
July 15th, 1924, to July 15th, 1943, 6 per cent., outstanding	10,314 22	
Feb. 12th, 1925, to Feb. 12th, 1934, 6 per cent., outstanding	1,245 50	
May 10th, 1925, to May 10th, 1934, 6 per cent., outstanding	4,039 80	
April 15th, 1925, to April 15th, 1944, 6 per cent., outstanding	1,719 63	
		34,121 39
(10) Board Trustees, R.C. Sep. School, Town of Timmins.		
7 Geo. V, cap. 27.		
Dec. 1st, 1918, to Dec. 1st, 1937, 5 per cent., outstanding	$ 12,218 61	
9 Geo. V, cap. 4.		
Nov. 1st, 1919, to Nov. 1st, 1938, 6 per cent., outstanding	7,300 39	
		19,519 00
(11) Town of Timmins.		
14 Geo. V, cap. 3 and 15 Geo. V, cap. 3.		
April 1st, 1926, to April 1st, 1940, 5½ per cent., outstanding	$ 80,778 88	
April 1st, 1926, to April 1st, 1940, 5½ per cent., outstanding	45,438 12	
		126,217 00
(12) Presqu'ile Park Commission.		
13-14 Geo. V, cap. 6.		
Payable May 1st, 1943, 6 per cent..................................		20,000 00
(13) Town of Kapuskasing.		
14 Geo. V, cap. 3.		
Aug. 1st, 1926, to Aug. 1st, 1945, 6 per cent., outstanding	$ 61,745 38	
Jan. 1st, 1928, to Jan. 1st, 1947, 6 per cent., outstanding	16,935 17	
		78,680 55
Carried forward......		$10,399,889 00

Indirect Liabilities and Guarantees of the Province of Ontario—Continued

Brought forward.....		$10,399,889 00
(14) Town of Englehart.		
15 Geo. V, cap. 4.		
Dec. 31st, 1924, to Dec. 31st, 1943, 6 per cent., outstanding	$ 4,500 00	
Dec. 31st, 1924, to Dec. 31st, 1943, 6 per cent., outstanding	9,000 00	
Dec. 31st, 1925, to Dec. 31st, 1944, 6 per cent., outstanding	2,470 00	
		15,970 00
(15) Guarantees under the authority of the Municipal Housing Act, 1920.		
Beaverton	$ 4,140 93	
Cochrane	48,126 46	
Fergus	547 00	
East Windsor	215,863 25	
Kitchener	73,088 75	
Listowel	34,691 09	
London	177,900 77	
Niagara Falls	47,722 04	
Oshawa	135,435 63	
Point Edward	29,625 27	
Riverside	132,424 13	
Sarnia	90,455 43	
Sioux Lookout	17,190 14	
Stamford Township	61,187 00	
Sudbury	83,788 50	
Tilbury	28,822 39	
Walkerville	25,667 48	
Windsor	575,547 32	
		$1,782,223 58
(16) Guarantees by the Province of Ontario, under authority of section 7 of the Department of Education Act and Amendments		3,182,228 29
(17) Hydro-Electric Power Commission of Ontario.		
Debentures issued by Commission:		
Re Dominion Power and Transmission Co., Ltd.		
40 years, 4¾ per cent. debentures due January 1st, 1970	$13,000,000 00	
5 years, 5 per cent. debentures due January 1st, 1935	8,000,000 00	
Issued in purchase of Undertakings and Companies.		
Re Ontario Power Company of Niagara Falls.		
40 years, 4 per cent. debentures due August 1st, 1957	8,000,000 00	
Issued in purchase of Capital Stock.		
20 years, 6% debentures due 1941	3,200,000 00	
Issued to retire debentures of Company due 1921.		
Re Toronto Power Company, Limited.		
20 years, 6 per cent. debentures due Dec. 1st, 1940 (part)	413,200 00	
Issued in purchase of Capital Stock.		
15 years, 5 per cent. debentures, due June 15th, 1939	4,000,000 00	
Issued to retire debentures of Company due 1924.		
Re Essex System.		
40 years, 4 per cent. debentures, due June 1st, 1958	200,000 00	
Issued in purchase of distribution lines.		
Re Thorold System.		
40 years, 4 per cent. debentures, due December 1st, 1958	100,000 00	
Issued in purchase of distribution lines.		
Re Sandwich, Windsor and Amherstburg Railway.		
40 years, 4½ per cent bonds due April 1st, 1960	2,100,000 00	
40 " 6 " " " July 1st, 1961	900,000 00	
20 " 5 " " " September 1st, 1943	966,205 00	
20 " 5 " " " July 1st, 1945	750,000 00	
20 " 5 " " " September 1st, 1945	100,000 00	
20 " 5 " " " July 15th, 1946	1,000,000 00	
Re Port Credit and St. Catharines Railway.		
50 years, 5 per cent bonds, due November 1st, 1969	500,000 00	
$1,200,000 pledged as security for Bank Loan of $500,000.		
Re Guelph Railway.		
39½ years, 5 per cent bonds, due November 1st, 1970	300,000 00	
Carried forward.....		$15,380,310 87

Indirect Liabilities and Guarantees of the Province of Ontario—Continued

Brought forward....		$15,380,310 87
(17) Hydro-Electric Power Commission of Ontario—(Continued).		
Re Toronto and York Radial Railway Company, and Schomberg and Aurora Railway Company.		
20 years, 6 per cent. bonds, due December 1st, 1940.......	$2,375,000 00	
Issued in purchase of Capital Stock.		
20 years, 6 per cent. bonds, due December 1st, 1940 (part).	205,800 00	
Issued in purchase of electrical power equipment of the Toronto and York Radial Railway.		
Bonds and Debenture Stock assumed by the Commission:		
Re Ontario Power Company of Niagara Falls.		
First mortgage 5 per cent. gold bonds, due Feb. 1st, 1943...	7,968,000 00	
Re Ontario Transmission Company, Limited.		
First mortgage 5 per cent. gold bonds, due May 1st, 1945...	1,304,000 00	
Re Toronto Power Company, Limited.		
Guaranteed 4½ per cent. debenture stock, due May 1st, 1941.	6,084,369 97	
Re Electrical Development Company of Ontario, Limited.		
First mortgage 5 per cent. gold bonds, due 1933...........	3,271,500 00	
		64,738,074 97
(18) Sandwich, Windsor and Amhurstburg Railway Co., Guarantee to Bank of Montreal of advances to Hydro-Electric Power Commission of Ontario as agent for the Railway Company		500,000 00
		$80,618,385 84

AGRICULTURAL DEVELOPMENT FINANCE ACT

R.S.O. 1927, Cap. 67

Statement Showing Deposits in Province of Ontario Savings Offices, and Agricultural Loans as at October 31st, 1932

Deposits in Savings Offices by Public at October 31st, 1932		$ 23,709,819 62
Agricultural Development Finance Act—Investments—		
Agricultural Development Board—Debentures	$ 51,538,000 00	
Less: Repayments to date	7,888,000 00	
	$ 43,650,000 00	
Accrued Interest	1,262,436 97	
		$44,912,436 97
Farm Loans Act—Farm Loan Associations		193,876 62
" " " —Capital Stock in Associations		2,445 00
		$ 45,108,758 59
Savings Offices—		
Cash on hand and in banks	$ 570,024 28	
Accounts receivable	1,000 00	
Fixtures (depreciated value)	41,771 62	
		612,795 90
		$ 45,721,554 49

ACCOUNTS PAYABLE

As at October 31st, 1932

Accounts due by Departments	$ 373,973 14
Bonds matured outstanding	10,000 00
Surplus Registry Office fees—re Land Titles Office	1,971 57
	$ 385,944 71

SPECIAL FUNDS

As at October 31st, 1932

Ontario Public Service Superannuation Fund—see page 48	$ 4,345,659 00
Municipal Sinking Funds—see page 49	1,641,093 33
Assurance Fund under Land Titles Act	299,234 85
Assurance Fund—Toronto Registry Office	23,398 56
Federal Subsidy for Agriculture—balance unexpended	457 11
Agricultural Development Finance Act—Reserves:	
Province of Ontario Savings Offices	260,691 14
For Farm Loans	488,260 92
Vimy Ridge Farm—Boys' Trust Fund	7 76
Sundry bequests	116,736 12
Brophy Estate—Estreated	162,966 94
Bowmanville School—Gymnasium Fund—Rotary Club—Contributions	18,525 00
Creamery Sold—Proceeds in suspense	4,000 00
Back-to-Land Movement—Deposits by Municipalities	20,765 39
Accountable Warrants—Overpayment	8 64
	$ 7,381,804 76

PUBLIC SERVICE SUPERANNUATION FUND

R.S.O. 1927, Cap. 16, Part III

As at October 31st, 1932

Balance at credit of Fund—November 1st, 1931				$3,802,798 96
Contributions to Fund—				
By Employees			$433,139 06	
By Government (Sec. 39)	$323,135 36			
" Various Commissions, etc.	110,003 70			
	433,139 06			
Less Refunds (Sec. 36)	37,973 21			
		$395,165 85		
By Government for Sheriffs (Sec. 60)		19,444 21		
			414,610 06	
Interest earned—				
On balance to credit of Fund at November 1st, 1931		$190,139 95		
On Employees' Contribution	$ 9,770 63			
On Government Contributions	9,770 63			
	$ 19,541 26			
Less interest allowed Government on payments	11,577 01			
		7,964 25		
			198,104 20	
				1,045,853 32
				$4,848,652 28
DEDUCT—				
Benefits Paid—				
Allowances to superannuates and beneficiaries			$449,521 03	
Lump sum payments, Secs. 34, 35 and 45			9,986 66	
Refunds under Sec. 36			37,973 21	
Interest on refunds and lump sum payments			5,512 38	
				502,993 28
Balance at Credit of Fund at October 31st, 1932				$4,345,659 00

STATEMENT OF RECEIPTS AND EXPENDITURES

November 1st, 1921, to October 31st, 1932

Year	Receipts	Expenditure	Surplus
	$ c.	$ c.	$ c.
1921	331,412 32	62,709 95	268,702 37
1922	406,744 96	111,728 78	295,016 18
1923	485,151 01	170,199 39	314,951 62
1924	467,864 22	199,815 11	268,049 11
1925	466,060 66	212,319 80	253,740 86
1926	491,070 84	227,197 06	263,873 78
1927	497,250 65	255,432 31	241,818 34
1928	696,402 12	297,711 92	398,690 20
1929	741,378 75	335,109 66	406,269 09
1930	812,817 26	336,993 11	475,824 15
1931	1,025,386 94	409,523 68	615,863 26
1932	1,045,853 32	502,993 28	542,860 04
Total	7,467,393 05	3,121,734 05	4,345,659 00

MUNICIPAL SINKING FUNDS

Municipal Sinking Funds on deposit with the Treasurer of Ontario to October 31st, 1932, with interest. (R.S.O. 1927, Cap. 233)

Municipality	By-law	Amount	Total
		$ c.	$ c.
Cities—			
Belleville	1,595	23,777 47	
"	1,637	26,015 34	
"	1,677	25,085 30	
"	1,871	32,211 03	
"	1,980	3,925 63	
"	2,408	27,573 12	
			138,587 89
St. Thomas	2,304	....	32,602 28
Towns—			
Gananoque	570	....	14,508 93
Gravenhurst	409	10,996 26	
"	410	14,573 03	
"	442	4,437 02	
"	479	2,059 89	
"	480	4,506 72	
			36,572 92
Ingersoll	731	....	74,877 31
Prescott	640	13,030 52	
"	641	3,475 15	
"	666	5,220 83	
"	673	2,459 42	
"	675	2,693 20	
"	687	3,670 92	
"	715	1,659 91	
"	717	2,251 01	
"	784	12,736 51	
"	854	1,724 23	
			48,921 70
St. Mary's	139	4,094 15	
"	239	17,143 39	
"	254	3,171 50	
"	259	1,500 47	
"	271	2,451 09	
"	293	16,906 69	
"	294	1,372 92	
"	295	6,865 85	
"	303	5,781 37	
"	332	1,141 08	
"	355	1,587 67	
			62,016 18
Thornbury	17 (1912)	14,128 62	
"	17 (1923)	3,177 02	
			17,305 64
Villages—			
Acton	500 B	501 43	
"	533 B	208 20	

MUNICIPAL SINKING FUNDS—Continued

Municipality	By-law	Amount	Total
Villages—Continued		$ c.	$ c.
Acton	547	188 74	
"	548	552 30	
"	564	383 11	
"	582	77 05	
			1,910 83
Beaverton	8	2,696 26	
"	114	8,493 52	
			11,189 78
Elora	688	....	1,696 87
Glencoe	348	....	3,246 88
Port Dalhousie	404	....	2,467 12
Counties—			
Lincoln	586	81,398 99	
"	604	66,637 94	
"	619	67,771 04	
"	637	122,775 07	
"	649	52,280 05	
"	672	37,004 20	
"	692	43,789 91	
"	708	85,459 72	
"	754	57,737 61	
"	755	14,154 95	
"	788	8,077 07	
"	837	10,056 65	
"	854	5,666 33	
"	855	16,776 85	
"	885	15,761 33	
"	886	2,148 96	
"	918	6,732 28	
			694,228 95
Welland	928	76,438 37	
"	959	44,250 09	
			120,688 46
Townships—			
Barton	875	22,672 41	
"	889	10,868 16	
"	904	364 44	
"	905	334 07	
"	909	9,341 49	
"	912	13,493 28	
"	918	28,062 84	
"	924	1,232 58	
"	946	19,095 03	
"	961	5,853 45	
"	967	458 49	
"	993	3,793 11	
"	994	12,377 05	
"	1,001	203 14	
"	1,003	4,773 48	
"	1,029	5,978 93	
"	1,065	20,357 71	
"	1,066	4,803 96	
"	1,089	1,598 74	
"	1,122	2,120 26	
"	1,129	16,376 40	

MUNICIPAL SINKING FUNDS—Continued

Municipality	By-law	Amount	Total
Townships—Continued		$ c.	$ c.
Barton	1,146	4,082 28	
"	1,154	9,825 76	
"	1,219	5,556 67	
"	1,257	3,402 29	
"	1,294	5,766 21	
"	1,327	27,629 83	
"	1,342	1,712 27	
"	1,365	15,863 30	
"	1,366	3,775 90	
"	1,369	2,492 87	
"	1,425	4,257 24	
"	1,426	10,375 42	
"	1,427	4,959 72	
"	1,448	14,322 93	
"	1,470	906 17	
"	1,471	7,770 18	
"	1,495	407 66	
"	1,496	4,341 79	
"	1,518	2,939 25	
"	1,520	3,321 41	
			317,868 17
Collingwood	2	9,541 75	
"	14	1,166 92	
"	8	1,319 35	
"	6	779 69	
"	8	1,507 60	
			14,315 31
Pelham	686	....	6,070 68
Saltfleet	683	....	1,065 42
School Boards—			
Pub. S. S. No. 1—Foleyet	3	....	1,494 33
" " " 2—Lorrain	1	....	452 14
" " " 1—McIrvine	160	....	10,967 37
" " " 1—Wicksteed	1	....	11,790 17
R.C. " " 4—Calvert	1	7,606 21	
" " " 4— "	8	3,648 46	
" " " 4— "	19	526 46	
			11,781 13
R.C. S. S. No. 10—Gloucester	1	1,751 51	
" " " 10— "	2	524 55	
			2,276 06
" " " 12—Nepean	4	....	2,190 81
Balance standing to credit of Municipal Sinking Fund Account at October 31st, 1932	......	....	1,641,093 33

ONTARIO HOUSING COMMISSION

Amounts Repaid Province on Account of Principal and Interest under The Ontario Housing Act, 1919, in Fiscal Year 1932

Municipality	Interest	Principal
	$ c.	$ c.
Barton Township	2,489 41	5,427 95
Beaverton	201 65	358 51
Belleville	172 25	800 21
Brampton	1,815 89	3,150 01
Brantford	5,738 96	12,174 52
Brantford Township	632 65	1,303 67
Bucke Township	800 00	....
Capreol	820 02	....
Charlton	293 66	359 38
Chippawa	417 41	770 81
Cochrane	1,711 05	3,458 07
East Windsor	2,824 52	6,564 49
Elmira	365 85	618 90
Englehart	25 15	....
Etobicoke Township	3,540 18	6,628 86
Fergus	570 30	1,559 16
Fort Frances	102 13	217 91
Fort William	856 20	1,799 88
Galt	667 63	2,864 32
Georgetown	1,633 82	3,098 86
Goderich	82 54	137 54
Guelph	6,641 05	12,926 27
Guelph Township	208 00	392 00
Haileybury	2,000 00	....
Hamilton	10,068 42	21,361 70
Hawkesbury	3,226 96	....
Humberstone	230 03	514 45
Ingersoll	622 48	1,405 76
Kapuskasing	9,018 44	12,443 80
Leamington	1,087 62	2,159 08
Leaside	2,677 59	5,278 41
Listowel	1,072 98	2,096 46
London	10,549 51	18,370 81
Merritton	519 50	2,229 89
Midland	1,333 01	3,151 63
Milton	288 77	527 35
Milverton	476 97	930 99
Mimico	292 18	536 56
New Toronto	4,462 99	6,780 41
Niagara Falls	5,513 57	12,899 75
Oshawa	11,058 30	21,680 27
Ottawa	21,394 10	39,038 26
Paris	1,685 96	3,916 39
Perth	484 45	1,056 35
Port Arthur	400 96	863 50
Port Colborne	3,657 08	3,711 64
Port Credit	544 31	1,135 69
Port Dalhousie	1,194 47	1,105 53
Point Edward	804 66	1,595 70
Port McNicoll	249 42	558 66
Renfrew	321 40	678 68
Richmond Hill	571 48	1,132 52
Sandwich	2,888 03	1,926 83
Sandwich East Township	504 04	....
Sarnia	1,923 85	4,052 51
Sault Ste. Marie	4,078 10	10,857 47

ONTARIO HOUSING COMMISSION—**Continued**

Amounts **Repaid** Province **on** Account **of Principal and** Interest **under The** Ontario **Housing** Act, **1919, in** Fiscal **Year 1932**

Municipality	Interest	Principal
	$ c.	$ c.
Scarborough Township	652 58	1,259 50
Sioux Lookout	470 73	729 27
Smith's Falls	606 61	1,185 59
Stamford Township	705 72	1,438 44
St. Catharines	3,359 81	7,499 95
Sturgeon Falls	306 59	493 41
Stratford	6,116 62	9,641 02
Sudbury	2,835 01	7,635 15
Tara	252 15	30 59
Thorold	1,089 59	2,442 73
Timmins	140 29	1,748 07
Trenton	211 66	476 54
Walkerville	6,305 77	5,787 94
Welland	4,213 48	2,595 56
Whitby	1,357 77	2,642 55
Windsor	19,406 98	13,402 09
Woodbridge	486 61	993 47
Woodstock	2,599 03	5,076 89
York Township	10,993 32	16,294 38
Total	199,922 77	329,981 51

MOTHERS' ALLOWANCES COMMISSION

Amount received from Municipalities during the Fiscal Year 1932

Counties—		Cities—	
Brant	$ 6,137 50	Belleville	9,975 00
Bruce	7,002 50	Brantford	18,392 50
Carleton	13,175 00	Chatham	6,825 00
Dufferin	3,687 50	East Windsor	11,595 00
Elgin	4,765 50	Fort William	11,145 00
Essex	12,037 50	Galt	5,355 00
Frontenac	4,040 00	Guelph	9,415 00
Grey	13,312 50	Hamilton	80,482 50
Haldimand	5,497 50	Kingston	13,102 50
Haliburton	1,630 00	Kitchener	12,480 00
Halton	8,090 00	London	38,060 00
Hastings	13,467 50	Niagara Falls	7,705 00
Huron	11,212 50	North Bay	10,352 50
Kent	11,310 00	Oshawa	10,127 50
Lambton	4,937 50	Ottawa	74,742 50
Lanark	10,117 50	Owen Sound	6,340 00
Leeds and Grenville	10,102 50	Peterborough	10,651 00
Lennox and Addington	4,695 00	Port Arthur	11,770 00
Lincoln	8,610 00	St. Catharines	16,093 50
Middlesex	15,725 00	St. Thomas	6,097 50
Norfolk	6,875 00	Sarnia	6,815 00
Northumberland and Durham	14,725 00	Sault Ste. Marie	8,955 00
Ontario	9,537 50	Stratford	10,162 50
Oxford	5.655 00	Sudbury	3,835 00
Peel	5,267 50	Toronto	295,005 37
Perth	3,395 00	Welland	6,044 75
Peterborough	8,787 50	Windsor	22,302 50
Prescott and Russell	18,342 50	Woodstock	3,215 00
Prince Edward	5,112 50	Towns—	
Renfrew	47,920 25	Brockville	3,765 00
Simcoe	31,915 00	Gananoque	1,455 00
Stormont, Dundas and Glengarry	34,405 00	Ingersoll	1,705 00
Victoria	9,750 00	Prescott	2,640 00
Waterloo	10,615 00	Smith's Falls	1,585 00
Welland	17,327 50	St. Mary's	1,295 00
Wellington	6,285 00	Trenton	2,460 00
Wentworth	7,580 00	Walkerville	1,540 00
York	61,807 50	Indian Reserves	2,462 50
			$1,220,805 37

On account, 1930-1931 (See page 28)	$ 107,345 50
On Account of Current Year:	
Deducted from expenditure (See page O14)	1,113,459 87
	$1,220,805 37

OLD AGE PENSIONS COMMISSION

Amount Received from Dominion Government, Provinces and Municipalities for Fiscal Year 1932

Dominion Government	$6,420,517 78
Interprovincial	22,413 84
Municipalities	965,124 10

Counties—	
Brant	$6,240 41
Bruce	9,198 01
Carleton	13,924 67
Dufferin	3,428 81
Elgin	13,359 83
Essex	10,972 31
Frontenac	7,774 22
Grey	13,064 47
Haldimand	5,164 44
Halton	7,956 33
Hastings	20,848 33
Huron	15,760 58
Kent	10,409 04
Lambton	9,108 86
Lanark	9,780 71
Leeds and Grenville	14,853 36
Lennox and Addington	7,183 96
Lincoln	6,934 67
Middlesex	15,275 82
Norfolk	12,171 98
Northumberland and Durham	19,389 69
Ontario	13,763 42
Oxford	7,987 55
Peel	7,349 42
Perth	7,502 13
Peterborough	6,499 16
Prescott and Russell	10,171 10
Prince Edward	9,004 98
Renfrew	26,176 65
Simcoe	30,154 01
Stormont, Dundas and Glengarry	20,966 98
Victoria	7,377 95
Waterloo	11,813 90
Welland	9,376 77
Wellington	15,474 79
Wentworth	7,578 61
York	34,414 64
	$458,362 56

Cities—	
Belleville	$4,486 09
Brantford	12,915 03
Chatham	4,297 77
East Windsor	1,892 90
Fort William	2,765 83
Galt	4,846 39
Guelph	6,015 12
Hamilton	41,925 13
Kingston	11,906 58
Kitchener	4,145 11
London	30,518 71
Niagara Falls	2,487 94
North Bay	3,764 32
Oshawa	3,849 43
Ottawa	43,952 32
Owen Sound	4,566 29
Peterborough	8,354 13
Port Arthur	3,294 45
St. Catharines	6,851 80
St. Thomas	6,413 97
Sarnia	4,681 61
Sault Ste. Marie	5,255 72
Stratford	5,558 17
Sudbury	1,978 52
Toronto	244,865 02
Welland	1,772 51
Windsor	10,758 74
Woodstock	3,291 70
	$487,411 30

Towns—	
Brockville	4,884 07
Gananoque	2,171 59
Ingersoll	1,720 74
Prescott	965 14
St. Mary's	1,795 30
Smith's Falls	2,916 55
Timmins	858 59
Trenton	2,902 60
Walkerville	1,135 66
	$ 19,350 24

$7,408,055 72

On Account, 1930-31 (See page 28)	$1,015,779 50
On account of Current Year: Deducted from Expenditure (See page O16)	6,392,276 22
	$7,408,055 72

EXPENDITURE STATEMENT

Statement of Expenditure for the Twelve Months Ended October 31st, 1932

Department	Details	Ordinary	Capital	Total
		$ c.	$ c.	$ c.
Lieutenant-Governor's Office	Part A	3,630 00	....	3,630 00
Prime Minister	" B	177,574 57	725,000 00	902,574 57
Legislation	" C	350,675 61	....	350,675 61
Attorney-General	" D	2,907,371 81	....	2,907,371 81
Insurance	" E	64,537 51	....	64,537 51
Education	" F	11,720,718 28	1,631,545 70	13,352,263 98
Lands and Forests	" G	1,835,078 01	572,714 05	2,407,792 06
Northern Development	" H	2,147,322 79	3,116,672 35	5,263,995 14
Mines	" I	338,238 04	995 88	339,233 92
Game and Fisheries	" J	562,093 41	67,082 61	629,176 02
Public Works	" K	693,034 87	2,486,350 71	3,179,385 58
Highways	" L	3,865,847 02	6,712,739 10	10,578,586 12
Health	" M	5,870,270 53	....	5,870,270 53
Labour	" N	1,123,910 81	13,231,875 79	14,355,786 60
Public Welfare	" O	4,180,498 93	....	4,180,498 93
Provincial Treasurer	" P	16,860,689 30	....	16,860,689 30
Provincial Auditor's Office	" Q	113,022 96	....	113,022 96
Provincial Secretary	" R	814,488 48	10,000 00	824,488 48
Agriculture	" S	2,017,618 50	....	2,017,618 50
Miscellaneous	" T	589,409 89	83,443 15	672,853 04
Total		56,236,031 32	28,638,419 34	84,874,450 66
Public Debt, Loans Advanced, Special Fund Repayments, etc.	" U	....	151,010,730 94	151,010,730 94
Grand Total		56,236,031 32	179,649,150 28	235,885,181 60

Comparative Statement of Expenditure by Departments for the Years 1931 and 1932

Departments	Ordinary 1931	Ordinary 1932	Capital 1931	Capital 1932
	$ c.	$ c.	$ c.	$ c.
Lieutenant-Governor's Office..	6,116 62	3,630 00	....	....
Prime Minister's Department:				
Main Office and Branches..	149,437 91	144,756 23	....	....
Hydro-Electric Power Commission..........	....	....	13,430,698 00	4,846,320 00
Statutory..........	15,299 17	14,508 32	409,523 68	502,993 28
Bonuses to Rural Primary and Secondary Transmission Lines........	....	....	1,414,299 00	725,000 00
Rural Power District Loan Act, 1930..........	....	....	....	65,000 00
Special Warrants..........	8,649 63	21,612 00	....	....
Hydro-Electric, Purchase of Power Interests.....	....	....	481,005 00	....
Construction Rural Primary and Secondary Transmission Lines on Island of Manitoulin...	....	....	....	14,000 00
	173,386 71	180,876 55	15,735,525 68	6,153,313 28
Less Salary Assessment....		3,301 98		
Deduct:—Advances to Hydro-Electric Power Commission and Public Service Superannuation Fund Payments........	....	....	14,321,226 68	5,428,313 28
Total..........	173,386 71	177,574 57	1,414,299 00	725,000 00
Legislation..........	379,906 15	351,435 56	....	....
Less Salary Assessment....	....	759 95	....	....
Total..........	379,906 15	350,675 61	....	....
Attorney-General's Dept.:				
Main Office..........	52,879 82	48,455 86	....	....
General..........	173,468 74	183,563 09	....	....
Commutation of Fees......	771 13	1,600 00	....	....
Supreme Court..........	113,595 09	108,847 57	....	....
Law Enforcement Fund....	1,004,104 08	918,241 77	....	....
Toronto and York Crown Attorney's Office........	27,115 38	27,659 89	....	....
Administration of Justice...	1,036,733 70	837,453 85	....	6,209 84
Inspection of Legal Offices..	33,249 93	33,714 00	....	....
Land Titles Office..........	36,156 57	33,301 81	....	....
Local Masters of Titles.....	29,427 52	29,395 64	....	....
Miscellaneous..........	129,346 31	104,512 03	....	....
Statutory..........	147,837 20	607,221 21	....	....
Special Warrants..........	....	6,000 00	....	....
	2,784,685 47	2,939,966 72	....	6,209 84
Less Salary Assessment....	....	32,594 91	....	....
Deduct, Outstanding Accountable Warrants...	....	....	....	6,209 84
Total..........	2,784,685 47	2,907,371 81	....	....
Insurance Department.......	72,021 88	65,552 86	....	....
Less Salary Assessment....	....	1,015 35	....	....
Total..........	72,021 88	64,537 51	....	....

EXPENDITURE STATMENT

Statement of Expenditure for the Twelve Mo hs Ended October 31st, 1932

Department	Details	Ordi[illegible]		Capital		Total	
		$	c.	$	c.	$	c.
Lieutenant-Governor's Office	Part A	3,[illegible]	[illegible]	....		3,630	00
Prime Minister	" B	177,[illegible]	[illegible]	725,000	00	902,574	57
Legislation	" C	350,[illegible]	[illegible]	....		350,675	61
Attorney-General	" D	2,907,[illegible]	[illegible]	....		2,907,371	81
Insurance	" E	64,[illegible]	[illegible]	....		64,537	51
Education	" F	11,720,[illegible]	[illegible]	1,631,545	70	13,352,263	98
Lands and Forests	" G	1,835,[illegible]	[illegible]	572,714	05	2,407,792	06
Northern Development	" H	2,147,2[illegible]	[illegible]	3,116,672	35	5,263,995	14
Mines	" I	338,[illegible]	[illegible]	995	88	339,233	92
Game and Fisheries	" J	562,[illegible]	[illegible]	67,082	61	629,176	02
Public Works	" K	693,[illegible]	[illegible]	2,486,350	71	3,179,385	58
Highways	" L	3,865,[illegible]	[illegible]	6,712,739	10	10,578,586	12
Health	" M	5,870,[illegible]	[illegible]	....		5,870,270	53
Labour	" N	1,123,[illegible]	[illegible]	13,231,875	79	14,355,786	60
Public Welfare	" O	4,180,[illegible]	[illegible]	....		4,180,498	93
Provincial Treasurer	" P	16,860,[illegible]	[illegible]	....		16,860,689	30
Provincial Auditor's Office	" Q	113,[illegible]	[illegible]	....		113,022	96
Provincial Secretary	" R	814,[illegible]	[illegible]	10,000	00	824,488	48
Agriculture	" S	2,017,[illegible]	[illegible]	....		2,017,618	50
Miscellaneous	" T	589,[illegible]	[illegible]	83,443	15	672,853	04
Total		56,236,[illegible]	32	28,638,419	34	84,874,450	66
Public Debt, Loans Advanced, Special Fund Repayments, etc.	" U			151,010,730	94	151,010,730	94
Grand Total		56,236,[illegible]	32	179,649,150	28	235,885,181	60

Comparative Statement of Expiditure by Departments for the Years 1931 and 1932

Departments	Ordinary		Capital	
	931	1932	1931	1932
	$ c.	$ c.	$ c.	$ c.
Lieutenant-Governor's Office	6,116 62	3,630 00	....	....
Prime Minister's Department				
Main Office and Branches	49,437 91	144,756 23	....	....
Hydro-Electric Power Commission		....	13,430,698 00	4,846,320 00
Statutory	15,299 17	14,508 32	409,523 68	502,993 28
Bonuses to Rural Primary and Secondary Transmission Lines		....	1,414,299 00	725,000 00
Rural Power District Loan Act, 1930		....	....	65,000 00
Special Warrants	8,649 63	21,612 00	....	....
Hydro-Electric, Purchase of Power Interests		....	481,005 00	....
Construction Rural Primary and Secondary Transmission Lines on Island of Manitoulin			....	14,000 00
	73,386 71	180,876 55	15,735,525 68	6,153,313 28
Less Salary Assessment		3,301 98		
Deduct:—Advances to Hydro-Electric Power Commission and Public Service Superannuation Fund Payments			14,321,226 68	5,428,313 28
Total	73,386 71	177,574 57	1,414,299 00	725,000 00
Legislation	79,906 15	351,435 56	....	....
Less Salary Assessment		759 95	....	....
Total	79,906 15	350,675 61	....	....
Attorney-General's Dept.:				
Main Office	52,879 82	48,455 86	....	....
General	73,468 74	183,563 09	....	....
Commutation of Fees	771 13	1,600 00	....	....
Supreme Court	13,595 09	108 847 57	....	....
Law Enforcement Fund	04,104 08	918,241 77	....	....
Toronto and York Crown Attorney's Office	27,115 38	27,659 89	....	....
Administration of Justice	36,733 70	837,453 85	....	6,209 84
Inspection of Legal Offices	33,249 93	33,714 00	....	....
Land Titles Office	36,156 57	33,301 81	....	....
Local Masters of Titles	29,427 52	29,395 64	....	....
Miscellaneous	129,346 31	104,512 03	....	....
Statutory	147,837 20	607,221 21	....	....
Special Warrants	....	6,000 00	....	....
	784,685 47	2,939,966 72	....	6,209 84
Less Salary Assessment		32,594 91	....	....
Deduct, Outstanding Accountable Warrants	....	....	....	6,209 84
Total	784,685 47	2,907,371 81	....	....
Insurance Department	72,021 88	65,552 86	....	
Less Salary Assessment	....	1,015 35	....	...
	[illegible]	[illegible]		

Comparative Statement of Expenditure by Departments for the Years 1931 and 1932—Continued

Departments	Ordinary 1931	Ordinary 1932	Capital 1931	Capital 1932
	$ c.	$ c.	$ c.	$ c.
Education Department:				
Main Office	92,303 74	84,649 61		
Public and Separate Schools	4,687,605 00	4,380,227 35		
Inspection of Schools	692,327 46	634,281 36		
Departmental Examinations	275,953 65	145,729 31		
Text Books	69,628 45	66,921 32		
General	1,200 00	1,200 00	130 78	130 78
Training Schools	117,964 13	121,875 53		
Normal and Model Schools	564,024 92	625,069 57		
High Schools and Collegiate Institutes	499,398 46	468,902 46		
Departmental Museum	7,754 81	4,998 10		
Public Libraries	106,939 34	94,633 78		
Technical Education	1,584,508 01	1,509,786 32		
Ontario Training College for Technical Teachers	29,901 39	27,141 92		
Superannuated Teachers	19,328 00	15,873 00		
Provincial and other Universities	2,172,136 85	1,938,513 34	223,025 15	140,661 66
Belleville School for the Deaf	130,048 46	135,046 67		
Brantford School for the Blind	68,495 20	62,078 81		
Northern Academy, Monteith	28,668 66	25,362 55		
Miscellaneous	44,881 02	21,708 55		
Statutory	567,195 84	1,289,671 38	65,638 43	65,638 43
Special Warrants	69,158 90	93,930 40	744,086 42	1,427,428 75
	11,829,422 29	11,747,601 33	1,032,880 78	1,633,859 62
Less Salary Assessment		26,883 05		
Deduct, Redemption of Debentures guaranteed by the Province			130 78	2,313 92
Total	11,829,422 29	11,720,718 28	1,032,750 00	1,631,545 70
Lands and Forests Dept.:				
Main Office and Branches	158,762 07	147,076 31		
Miscellaneous	333,718 96	306,734 49	219,814 15	76,073 69
Forestry Branch	1,579,408 23	1,329,090 50	761,697 78	396,448 30
Surveys Branch	44,714 34	47,792 65	125,000 00	99,984 05
Statutory	11,990 41	10,368 99	381 53	208 01
Special Warrants	1,831 82	7,741 83		2,933 93
	2,130,425 83	1,848,804 77	1,106,893 46	575,647 98
Less Salary Assessment		13,726 76		
Deduct:—Back to the Land Movement				2,933 93
Total	2,130,425 83	1,835,078 01	1,106,893 46	572,714 05
Northern Development Dept.:				
Colonization Roads Branch	10,121 47	9,686 48		
Miscellaneous	195,004 88	173,842 57	292,139 58	260,094 71
Statutory	1,858,332 71	1,964,797 96	4,691,060 96	2,556,869 33
Special Warrants	2,597 05	1,300 03	382,520 31	406,303 31
	2,066,056 11	2,149,627 04	5,365,720 85	3,223,267 35
Less Salary Assessment		2,304 25		
Deduct, Loans advanced to Settlers' Loan Commission			118,835 00	106,595 00
Total	2,066,056 11	2,147,322 79	5,246,885 85	3,116,672 35

Comparative Statement of Expenditure by Departments for the Years 1931 and 1932—Continued

Departments	Ordinary 1931	Ordinary 1932	Capital 1931	Capital 1932
	$ c.	$ c.	$ c.	$ c.
Mines Department:				
Main Office and Branches..	201,680 53	182,983 10	....	....
Miscellaneous............	170,951 07	150,176 37	307,520 96	995 88
Statutory................	10,000 00	10,433 33	....	....
	382,631 60	343,592 80	307,520 96	995 88
Less Salary Assessment....	....	5,354 76	....	....
Total...............	382,631 60	338,238 04	307,520 96	995 88
Game and Fisheries Dept.:				
Main Office..............	55,899 27	53,270 42	....	....
Biological and Fish Culture Branch................	201,299 29	188,758 20	....	....
Miscellaneous............	368,499 07	326,030 08	118,372 33	67,082 61
	625,697 63	568,058 70	118,372 33	67,082 61
Less Salary Assessment....	....	5,965 29	....	....
Total...............	625,697 63	562,093 41	118,372 33	67,082 61
Public Works Department:				
Main Office	82,748 31	77,760 33	....	....
Maintenance and Repairs...	706,770 83	583,066 18	....	....
Public Works and Bridges..	36,373 42	24,896 37	176,414 20	144,179 62
Public Buildings..........	....	....	2,857,462 82	2,224,103 39
Statutory................	11,956 25	10,000 00	115,225 00	98,143 00
Special Warrants..........	166 40	5,278 97	24,459 00	19,924 70
	838,015 21	701,001 85	3,173,561 02	2,486,350 71
Less Salary Assessment....	....	7,966 98	....	....
Total...............	838,015 21	693,034 87	3,173,561 02	2,486,350 71
Highways Department:				
Main Office..............	336,749 54	350,127 27	32,659 27	32,334 59
Motor Vehicles Branch.....	171,731 72	157,775 02	5,687 98	....
Miscellaneous............	157,723 49	106,733 85	....	....
Statutory................	3,568,638 70	3,266,354 92	12,606,130 27	6,680,404 51
	4,234,843 45	3,880,991 06	12,644,477 52	6,712,739 10
Less Salary Assessment....	....	15,144 04	....	....
Total...............	4,234,843 45	3,865,847 02	12,644,477 52	6,712,739 10
Health Department:				
Main Office and Branches..	834,502 18	795,492 72	....	....
Hospitals Branch..........	153,588 35	168,591 69	29,000 00	....
General Hospitals and Charities..................	1,771,744 70	1,916,596 09	....	....
Mental Hospitals..........	3,298,590 53	2,923,423 32	....	....
Statutory................	20,104 40	10,925 00	....	....
Special Warrants..........	9,500 11	103,798 74	....	....
	6,088,030 27	5,918,827 56	29,000 00	....
Less Salary Assessment....	....	48,557 03	....	....
Total...............	6,088,030 27	5,870,270 53	29,000 00	....

Comparative Statement of Expenditure by Departments for the Years 1931 and 1932—Continued

Departments	Ordinary		Capital	
	1931	1932	1931	1932
	$ c.	$ c.	$ c.	$ c.
Labour Department:				
Main Office and Branches..	336,399 36	319,915 57	....	....
Statutory..................	787,963 62	517,817 27	3,891,420 11	11,815,630 77
Special Warrants..........	8,541 46	292,453 41	....	1,416,245 02
	1,132,904 44	1,130,186 25	3,891,420 11	13,231,875 79
Less Salary Assessment....	....	6,275 44	....	....
Total................	1,132,904 44	1,123,910 81	3,891,420 11	13,231,875 79
Public Welfare Department:				
Main Office and Branches..	255,796 03	294,949 24	....	....
Grants....................	244,168 29	209,186 65	....	....
Boys' Training School, Bowmanville................	99,989 04	38,879 87	....	....
Mothers' Allowances Commission.................	1,479,174 54	1,538,187 44	107,345 50	121,165 00
Old Age Pensions Commission....................	2,248,978 56	2,080,713 32	753,134 33	687,403 17
Statutory................	12,625 00	10,000 00	....	....
Special Warrants..........	22,180 68	14,204 05	....	....
	4,362,912 14	4,186,120 57	860,479 83	808,568 17
Less Salary Assessment....	....	5,621 64	....	....
Deduct, Mothers' Allowances and Old Age Pensions..................	....	....	860,479 83	808,568 17
Total................	4,362,912 14	4,180,498 93	....	....
Treasury Department:				
Main Office and Branches..	544,686 99	525,448 56	....	....
Statutory................	1,559,262 72	458,521 55	8,274,554 06	8,784,337 84
	2,103,949 71	983,970 11	8,274,554 06	8,784,337 84
Public Debt Charges.......	11,461,861 84	15,886,710 01	125,541,624 99	135,675,950 34
	13,565,811 55	16,870,680 12	133,816,179 05	144,460,288 18
Less Salary Assessment....	....	9,990 82	....	....
Deduct, Public Debt Maturities, Loans advanced and repayments on Account of Special Funds...	....	....	133,816,179 05	144,460,288 18
Total................	13,565,811 55	16,860,689 30	....	....

Comparative Statement of Expenditure by Departments for the Years 1931 and 1932—Continued

Departments	Ordinary		Capital	
	1931	1932	1931	1932
	$ c.	$ c.	$ c.	$ c.
Provincial Auditor's Office:				
Salaries and Contingencies..	110,096 06	108,717 09	....	....
Statutory (Auditor's salary)	6,500 00	6,500 00	....	....
	116,596 06	115,217 09	....	....
Less Salary Assessment....	....	2,194 13	....	....
Total...............	116,596 06	113,022 96	....	....
Provincial Secretary's Dept.:				
Main Office and Branches..	172,239 26	114,009 92	....	....
Public Institutions Branch..	73,339 81	91,274 56	....	....
Reformatories and Industrial Farms................	718,231 25	606,375 57	19,000 00	10,000 00
Statutory................	10,225 06	10,000 00	....	....
Special Warrants..........	250 00	3,600 00	630 00	....
	974,285 38	825,260 05	19,630 00	10,000 00
Less Salary Assessment....	....	10,771 57	....	....
Total...............	974,285 38	814,488 48	19,630 00	10,000 00
Agriculture Department:				
Main Office and Statistical Branch...............	32,749 44	29,227 71	....	....
Agricultural and Horticultural Societies Branch....	212,085 70	165,011 82	....	....
Live Stock Branch.........	218,432 91	198,061 57	....	....
Institutes Branch..........	96,477 27	78,958 16	....	....
Dairy Branch.............	168,786 05	145,635 75	....	....
Fruit Branch.............	127,335 04	99,524 82	....	....
Agricultural Representatives Branch...............	415,936 35	363,934 38	....	....
Crops, Co-operation and Markets Branch.........	69,794 79	77,069 49	....	4,800 00
Agricultural Development Board..................	42,294 06	4,798 77	....	....
Colonization and Immigration Branch............	127,266 21	80,990 24	....	....
Kemptville Agricultural School................	66,005 45	58,270 87	....	....
Ontario Veterinary College.	40,217 45	38,378 23	....	....
Western Ontario Experimental Farm............	18,406 02	15,947 13	....	....
Demonstration Farms, Northern Ontario...........	33,996 06	20,881 97	....	....
Ontario Agricultural College	638,866 27	558,829 34	....	....
Miscellaneous............	68,977 32	63,109 73	....	....
Statutory................	10,075 40	10,000 00	....	....
Special Warrants..........	136,010 07	33,815 68	....	126,000 00
	2,523,711 86	2,042,445 66	....	130,800 00
Less Salary Assessment....	....	24,827 16	....	....
Deduct, Loans Advanced Cold Storage Plants, etc..	....	....	....	130,800 00
Total...............	2,523,711 86	2,017,618 50	....	....

Comparative Statement of Expenditure by Departments for the Years 1931 and 1932—Continued

Departments	Ordinary		Capital	
	1931	1932	1931	1932
	$ c.	$ c.	$ c.	$ c.
General Miscellaneous:				
Miscellaneous.............	199,848 90	245,549 22	142,500 76	111,191 34
Statutory.................	5,110 77	11,929 67	....	....
Special Warrants..........	354,573 96	331,931 00	....	36,960 43
	559,533 63	589,409 89	142,500 76	148,151 77
Deduct, Repayments on account of Special Funds...	....	....	42,678 34	64,708 62
Total...............	559,533 63	589,409 89	99,822 42	83,443 15
Grand Total excluding Part U............	54,846,994 28	56,236,031 32	29,084,632 67	28,638,419 34
Public Debt, Loans Advanced, Special Fund, Repayments, etc..................	....	....	149,159,529 68	151,010,730 94
Grand Total..........	54,846,994 28	56,236,031 32	178,244,162 35	179,649,150 28

EXPENDITURE

IN DETAIL BY

DEPARTMENTS

PART A

LIEUTENANT-GOVERNOR'S OFFICE

FISCAL YEAR, 1931-32

GENERAL INDEX AT BACK OF BOOK

PART A—LIEUTENANT-GOVERNOR'S OFFICE

Statement of Expenditure Showing Amounts Expended, Unexpended and Overexpended for the Twelve Months Ended October 31st, 1932

Lieutenant-Governor's Office	Estimates	Expended			Un-expended	Over-expended	Treas. Bd. Minute
		Ordinary	Capital	Total Ordinary and Capital			
	$ c.	$ c.	$ c.	$ c.	$ c.	$ c.	$ c.
Salaries	4,400 00	3,600 00	....	3,600 00	800 00	....	....
Allowances for contingencies	2,050 00	30 00	....	30 00	2,020 00	....	....
Lieutenant-Governor's Office	6,450 00	3,630 00	....	3,630 00	2,820 00	....	....

LIEUTENANT-GOVERNOR'S OFFICE

Salaries ($3,600.00)

Col. Alexander Fraser	Official Secretary	(T) 12 months	1,400 00
Capt. Eric Haldenby	First Assistant Secretary	12 "	600 00
Marjorie P. Johnson	Secretarial Stenographer	12 "	1,600 00

Contingencies ($30.00)

His Honour the Lieutenant-Governor, allowance 30 00

Total Expenditure, Lieutenant-Governor's Office **$3,630 00**

DEPARTMENT

OF THE

PRIME MINISTER

FISCAL YEAR 1931-32

TABLE OF CONTENTS

GENERAL INDEX AT BACK OF BOOK

PART B—DEPARTMENT OF THE PRIME MINISTER

Statement of Expenditure Showing Amounts Expended, Unexpended and Overexpended for the Twelve Months Ended October 31st, 1932

Department of the Prime Minister	Page	Estimates	Expended			Unexpended	Over-expended	Treas. Bd. Minute
			Ordinary	Capital	Total Ordinary and Capital			
		$ c.	$ c.	$ c.	$ c.	$ c.	$ c.	$ c.
Main Office:								
Salaries	6	15,250 00	13,014 40	....	13,014 40	2,235 60	....	....
Executive Council Office:								
Salaries	6	10,900 00	10,577 00	....	10,577 00	323 00	....	....
Contingencies	6	4,000 00	9,714 17	....	9,714 17	....	5,714 17	6,000 00
Publicity and Information Bureau:								
Salaries	6	3,800 00	3,800 00	....	3,800 00	....	....	....
Advertising, publications, etc.	6	30,000 00	52,948 02	....	52,948 02	....	22,948 02	30,000 00
Sundry investigations	7	5,000 00	330 40	....	330 40	4,669 60	....	....
Entertainment of Distinguished Visitors	7	5,000 00	455 20	....	455 20	4,544 80	....	....
Civil Service Commissioner's Office:								
Salaries	7	15,000 00	15,000 00	....	15,000 00	....	....	....
Contingencies	7	2,500 00	753 80	....	753 80	1,746 20	....	....
King's Printer's Office:								
Salaries	8	29,175 00	29,175 00	....	29,175 00	....	....	....
Contingencies	8	4,500 00	3,061 82	....	3,061 82	1,438 18	....	....
Cartage of departmental stationery	8	900 00	188 25	....	188 25	711 75	....	....
Cost of Ontario Gazette	8	8,000 00	5,738 17	....	5,738 17	2,261 83	....	....
Total, Main Office and Branches	..	134,025 00	144,756 23	....	144,756 23	17,930 96	28,662 19	....
Hydro-Electric Power Commission:								
Niagara System:								
Developments,								
Chats Falls	8	2,200,000 00	....	1,048,731 00	1,048,731 00	1,151,269 00	....	....
Niagara River Plants	8	100,000 00	....	50,000 00	50,000 00	50,000 00	....	....
St. Lawrence and Ottawa River	8	100,000 00	....	....	....	100,000 00	....	....
Transformer Stations,								
220-K.V. Stations	8	850,000 00	....	780,116 00	780,116 00	69,884 00	....	....
110-K.V. Stations	8	800,000 00	....	166,675 00	166,675 00	633,325 00	....	....
Distributing Stations	8	300,000 00	....	118,000 00	118,000 00	182,000 00	....	....

[illegible] 220-KV. Lines	8	1,500,000 00	....	1,362,138 00	1,362,138 00	137,862 00	....	....
Miscellaneous extensions a[illegible]d [illegible]ments for all voltages	8	200,000 00	....	120,000 00	120,000 00	80,000 00	....	....
R[illegible]l [illegible]n	8	1,000,000 00	....	513,090 00	513,090 00	486,910 00	....	....
[illegible] Bay System:								
Developments,								
[illegible]	8	300,000 00	....	....	....	300,000 00	....	....
[illegible]us [illegible]ts to g[illegible]ting plants	8	50,000 00	....	9,000 00	9,000 00	41,000 00	....	....
T[illegible] [illegible]d distributing s[illegible]ns	8	90,000 00	....	37,908 00	37,908 00	52,092 00	....	....
[illegible]								
[illegible]us [illegible]	8	150,000 00	....	18,283 00	18,283 00	131,717 00	....	....
Rural [illegible]	8	200,000 00	....	106,017 00	106,017 00	93,983 00	....	....
Eastern [illegible] System:								
Developments,								
Miscellaneous [illegible]ts to generating, i[illegible]ding [illegible] station, [illegible]	8	60,000 00	....	....	....	60,000 00	....	....
Miscellaneous [illegible]ts to generating stations	8	50,000 00	....	13,000 00	13,000 00	37,000 00	....	....
[illegible] and Distributing S[illegible]s:								
[illegible]us extensions and [illegible]ts 110,000 K.V.-A s[illegible]s	8	60,000 00	....	25,000 00	25,000 00	35,000 00	....	....
Miscellaneous [illegible] [illegible]d betterments	8	50,000 00	....	34,000 00	34,000 00	16,000 00	....	....
Transmission [illegible]:								
[illegible]	8	50,000 00	....	19,400 00	19,400 00	30,600 00	....	....
R[illegible]	8	400,000 00	....	177,000 00	177,000 00	223,000 00	....	....
Thunder Bay System:								
Developments:								
Miscellaneous extensions and betterments	8	50,000 00	....	50,000 00	50,000 00	....	....	....
Transformer Stations:								
Miscellaneous extensions and betterments	8	25,000 00	....	4,036 00	4,036 00	20,964 00	....	....
Transmission Lines:								
Miscellaneous betterments	8	25,000 00	....	3,014 00	3,014 00	21,986 00	....	....
Rural distribution	8	10,000 00	....	27,229 00	27,229 00	....	17,229 00	17,229 00
Northern System:								
Developments:								
Dam reconstruction, Wahnapitae	8	25,000 00	....	....	....	25,000 00	....	....
Miscellaneous extensions and betterments	8	20,000 00	....	1,209 00	1,209 00	18,791 00	....	....
Transformer and Distributing Stations:								
Miscellaneous extensions and betterments	8	30,000 00	....	2,000 00	2,000 00	28,000 00	....	....
Transmission Lines:								
110,000 K.V.-A. Line, Hunta to Copper Cliff	8	350,000 00	....	58,000 00	58,000 00	292,000 00	....	....
Miscellaneous extensions and betterments	8	50,000 00	....	5,948 00	5,948 00	44,052 00	....	....

PART B—DEPARTMENT OF THE PRIME MINISTER—Continued

Statement of Expenditure Showing Amounts Expended, Unexpended and Overexpended for the Twelve Months Ended October 31st, 1932

Department of the Prime Minister	Page	Estimates	Expended			Unexpended	Over-expended	Treas. Bd. Minute
			Ordinary	Capital	Total Ordinary and Capital			
		$ c.	$ c.	$ c.	$ c.	$ c.	$ c.	$ c.
Miscellaneous:								
Administration Building	8	1,500,000 00	....	94,328 00	94,328 00	1,405,672 00	....	....
Miscellaneous extensions and betterments	8	10,000 00	....	2,198 00	2,198 00	7,802 00	....	....
*Hydro-Electric Power Commission	..	10,605,000 00	....	4,846,320 00	4,846,320 00	5,775,909 00	17,229 00	....
Supply Bill	..	10,739,025 00	144,756 23	4,846,320 00	4,991,076 23	5,793,839 96	45,891 19	....
Statutory:								
Minister's salary	8	....	14,000 00	....	14,000 00	....	....	....
Salaries unprovided for	8	....	225 00	....	225 00	....	....	....
Public Service Superannuation Act:								
Administration	8	....	283 32	....	283 32	....	....	....
*Allowances	8	....	....	502,993 28	502,993 28	....	....	....
Bonuses re costs, Rural, Primary and Secondary Transmission Lines	9	....	....	725,000 00	725,000 00	....	....	....
*Rural Power District Loan Act, 1930	9	....	....	65,000 00	65,000 00	....	....	....
Statutory	..	....	14,508 32	1,292,993 28	1,307,501 60	....	....	....
Special Warrants:								
Advertising, general	9	....	2,579 40	....	2,579 40	....	....	....
Grant to Canadian Olympic Committee	9	....	5,000 00	....	5,000 00	....	....	....
Grant to Navy League of Canada	9	....	500 00	....	500 00	....	....	....
Balance of salary, Hon. E. C. Drury	9	....	8,825 00	....	8,825 00	....	....	....
Accounts re Royal Commission of Investigation re Hydro-Electric Power Commission	9	....	4,707 60	....	4,707 60	....	....	....

Hydro-Elec. Power Commission, *Construction of Rural, Primary and Secondary Transmission Lines on Manitoulin Island	9	....	....	14,000 00	14,000 00	....	....	....
Special Warrants	..	....	21,612 00	14,000 00	35,612 00	....	....	....
Total	..	....	180,876 55	6,153,313 28	6,334,189 83	....	....	....
Less Salary Assessment	..	....	3,301 98	....	3,301 98	....	....	....
Department of Prime Minister	....	....	177,574 57	6,153,313 28	6,330,887 85	....	....	....

SUMMARY

Department of the Prime Minister	Page	Ordinary	Capital	Total
		$ c.	$ c.	$ c.
Main Office and Branches	6-8	144,756 23	....	144,756 23
Hydro-Electric Power Commission	8	....	4,846,320 00	4,846,320 00
Statutory	8-9	14,508 32	1,292,993 28	1,307,501 60
Special Warrants	9	21,612 00	14,000 00	35,612 00
		180,876 55	6,153,313 28	6,334,189 83
*Deduct—Transferred to:				
Loans and Special Funds (see Part U),				
Advances to Hydro-Electric Power Commission	8	....	4,925,320 00	4,925,320 00
Superannuation Fund Payments	8	....	502,993 28	502,993 28
	..	....	5,428,313 28	5,428,313 28
Total	..	180,876 55	725,000 00	905,876 55
Less Salary Assessment	..	3,301 98	....	3,301 98
Department of the Prime Minister	..	177,574 57	725,000 00	902,574 57

DEPARTMENT OF THE PRIME MINISTER

Hon. George S. Henry, Premier and President of the Council (statutory), $14,000.00

PRIME MINISTER'S OFFICE

Salaries ($13,014.40)

Name	Position	Period		Amount
Horace Wallis	Deputy Minister	9 months	3,836 97	
" "	" " (T)	3 "	837 43	
				4,674 40
Charles J. Foster	Secretary	12 months		3,000 00
Charles Chase	Confidential Messenger to Prime Minister (T)	12 "		740 00
R. P. Ferguson	Assistant Secretary	12 "		2,000 00
A. Langstaff	Senior Clerk Stenographer	12 "		1,400 00
M. E. Robertson	" " "	12 "		1,200 00

EXECUTIVE COUNCIL OFFICE

Salaries ($10,577.00)

Name	Position	Period	Amount
C. F. Bulmer	Clerk of the Executive Council	12 months	4,500 00
A. Stewart	Senior Clerk	12 "	1,800 00
I. Leaman	Senior Clerk Stenographer	12 "	1,400 00
K. A. Murray	Clerk Stenographer, Group 1	½ "	52 00
John Young	" " " 2 (T)	12 "	825 00
L. G. Dewsbury	Secretary to Minister without Portfolio	12 "	2,000 00

Contingencies ($9,714.17)

Temporary Services, $7,738.22.

Name	Position	Period	Amount
C. C. Hele	General Secretary	12 months	4,000 00
Fred R. Batchelor	Junior Clerk Messenger	12 "	525 00
P. F. Cronin	Assistant	12 "	2,400 00
Edward W. Dodds	Junior Clerk Messenger	7 "	311 30
Bessie Long	Clerk Typist, Group 1	6½ "	501 92

Travelling Expenses, $205.64.

C. J. Foster, 7.15; C. C. Hele, 198.49 .... 205 64

Miscellaneous, $1,770.31.

Canadian Gazette Publishing Co., directory, 25.00; King's Printer, 1,021.81; McCann & Alexander, platen, etc., 11.00; Might Directories, Ltd., maps, 17.00; United Typewriter Co., Ltd., repairs, etc., 164.08. Sundries—car tickets, 15.00; express, 1.55; newspapers and periodicals, 252.49; telegrams, 252.19; petty disbursements, 10.19 .... 1,770 31

PUBLICITY AND INFORMATION BUREAU

Salaries ($3,800.00)

Name	Position	Period	Amount
L. B. Jackes	Photographer	12 months	2,400 00
R. E. Houston	Senior Clerk Stenographer	12 "	1,400 00

Printing and Distributing Booklets, Advertising Tourist Attractions and General Expenses ($52,948.02)

Temporary Services, $2,625.00.

Name	Position	Period	Amount
L. R. Arnett	Representative (Peace Bridge)	6 months	1,800 00
Sherman Galvin	" (Ambassador Bridge)	6 "	825 00

Travelling Expenses, $370.84.

L. R. Arnett, 71.87; L. B. Jackes, 298.97 .... 370 84

Advertising, $17,254.31.

Canadian Traveller, 246.96; Gossip, Ltd., 950.00; Norris-Patterson, Ltd., 15,566.17; Summer Guests, 100.00; Toronto Convention & Tourist Association, 87.18; Toronto Hotel Association, Inc., 304.00 .... 17,254 31

Publicity and Information Bureau—Continued

Miscellaneous, $32,697.87.

G. E. Atkinson, camera repairs and supplies, 50.50; Canadian Association of Tourist and Publicity Bureaus, subscription, 100.00; Copp, Clark Co., Ltd., road map, 100.00; Dept. of Highways, garage account, 32.40; Eastman's Kodak Stores, Ltd., photo supplies, 284.28; General Advertising Service, lettering window, 29.80; King's Printer, 27,037.76; Kodascope Libraries of Canada, rental of reels, 14.41; Latimer, Ltd., photo supplies, 34.28; Light & Sound Engineering Co., Ltd., sign rental, 100.00; Lockhart's Camera Exchange, rental, photo supplies, 426.81; Proctor & Proctor, postage on Vacation Books, addressing and mailing, 3,040.00; E. L. Ruddy Co., Ltd., metal sign, 16.00; Toronto Convention & Tourist Association, subscription, 1,000.00; H. C. Tugwell & Co., Ltd., films, etc., 170.77. Sundries—car tickets, 6.00; customs, 1.42; express, 146.20; newspapers and periodicals, 40.00; telegrams, 4.08; petty disbursements, 63.16.................. 32,697 87

Sundry Investigations

Advisory Committee on Unemployment ($330.40)

Temporary Services, $36.45.

Gladys S. Snyder...........Stenographer.................................. 36 45

Travelling Expenses, $293.95.

H. S. Higman, 157.55; A. C. McFarlane, 49.40; A. G. Stone, 42.90; S. K. Watt, 44.10.. 293 95

Entertainment of Distinguished Visitors ($455.20)

Canadian Association of Tourist and Publicity Bureaus:	
Royal York Hotel, dinner	166 75
Deputy Ministers:	
E. Longstaff, dinner	58 85
Royal Commission on Transportation:	
E. Longstaff, luncheon	36 50
British Business Men's Visit to Canada:	
Thompson, J. B., travelling expenses	57 85
Advisory Committee on Unemployment:	
E. Longstaff, luncheon	13 75
Order of Sons of Temperance:	
Muskoka Lakes Navigation & Hotels Co., Ltd., transportation	121 50

CIVIL SERVICE COMMISSIONER'S OFFICE

Salaries ($15,000.00)

J. M. McCutcheon	Commissioner	12 months	6,000 00
F. V. Glenny	Principal Clerk	12 "	2,000 00
Reta Woltz	Senior Clerk Stenographer	12 "	1,400 00
R. M. Shier	Clerk, Group 1	12 "	1,400 00
Colena M. Harper	Clerk Typist, Group 1	12 "	1,200 00
Gladys I. Murray	Clerk Stenographer, Group 1	12 "	1,125 00
Constance A. Lawrie	" " " 2	12 "	975 00
Asta Larsen	" " " 2	3 "	225 00
Isobel I. Downey	" " " 2	9 "	675 00

Salaries not Otherwise Provided for (Statutory), ($225.00)

Isobel I. Downey	Clerk Stenographer, Group 2	3 months	225 00

Contingencies ($753.80)

Temporary Services, $125.00.

Jean Waters	Clerk Typist, Group 2	2 months	125 00

Travelling Expenses, $227.91.

J. M. McCutcheon.. 227 91

Miscellaneous, $400.89.

King's Printer, 349.64; United Typewriter Co., Ltd., inspections, 50.00. Sundries, telegrams, 1.25.. 400 89

KING'S PRINTER'S OFFICE

Salaries ($29,175.00)

H. H. Ball	King's Printer	12 months	3,600 00
R. B. Magill	Assistant King's Printer	12 "	2,700 00
T. W. Heron	Principal Clerk	12 "	2,400 00
T. E. Bowman	" "	12 "	2,400 00
A. Whelan	Accountant, Group 4	12 "	1,900 00
Chas. J. F. Price	Senior Clerk	12 "	2,000 00
F. Petley	" "	12 "	1,800 00
W. F. Caldwell	" "	12 "	1,900 00
P. D. Shea	Clerk, Group 1	12 "	1,500 00
P. L. Chandler	" " 1	12 "	1,500 00
F. W. Sprague	" " 2	12 "	1,200 00
F. F. Fogg	3	12 "	975 00
R. Edwards	" " 3	12 "	975 00
H. Knowles	Clerk Typist, " 2	12 "	825 00
J. N. Lea	Stock Clerk, " 1	12 "	1,400 00
Dorothy McWatters	Clerk Typist, " 1	12 "	1,050 00
Lillian E. Church	" " " 1	12 "	1,050 00

Contingencies ($3,061.82)

Temporary Services, $750.00.

S. Fallis....................Clerk, Group 3....................12 months 750 00

Miscellaneous, $2,311.82.

T. E. Bowman, allowance re use of auto, 200.00; Burroughs Adding Machine Co., Ltd., inspections, 27.30; W. H. Forgie Typewriter Co., repairs, 15.00; King's Printer, 1,257.89; McCann & Alexander, typewriter inspections, 27.75; A. P. Reed, services taking stock, 600.00; Remington Typewriters, Ltd., inspections, 37.00; Thomas & Corney Typewriters, Ltd., typewriter inspections, 12.00; United Typewriter Co., Ltd., inspections, 70.00. Sundries—express, 58.58; freight, .30; newspapers, 6.00.................... 2,311 82

Cartage of Departmental Stationery ($188.25)

John Hill.................... 188 25

Cost of Official Gazette ($5,738.17)

King's Printer.................... 5,738 17

Main Office and Branches....................$144,756.23

HYDRO-ELECTRIC POWER COMMISSION OF ONTARIO

Advances under various appropriations (see statement, pages B 2-4)....................4,846,320 00

STATUTORY

Prime Minister's salary (see page B 6).................... 14,000 00
Salaries not otherwise provided for (see page B 7).................... 225 00

ONTARIO PUBLIC SERVICE SUPERANNUATION ACT

R.S.O. 1927, Chap. 16, Part III

Administration Expenses of the Board ($283.32)

Members of Board Attending Meetings, $90.00.

F. H. Greenlaw, 30.00; M. MacVicar, 30.00; S. L. Squire, 30.00.................... 90 00

Miscellaneous, $193.32.

King's Printer, 193.02; telegrams, .30.................... 193 32

Allowances, Lump Sum Payments and Refunds ($502,993.28)

Allowances, $449,521.03.

Sundry persons	449,842 04	
Less refund, M. A. Sinclair 1931 allowance	321 01	
		449,521 03

Lump Sum Payments, $10,533.74.

Sundry Persons under Sec. No. 34	2,806 34	
" " " Sec. No. 35, 6,771.30, interest, 547.08	7,318 38	
" " " Sec. No. 45	409 02	
		10,533 74

Ontario Public Service Superannuation Act—Continued

Refunds, $42,938.51.

Sundry Persons under Sec. No. 36, 37,973.21; interest, 4,965.30	42,938 51

Bonuses to Rural, Primary and Secondary Transmission Lines

R.S.O. 1927, Chap. 59, Sec. 2

Hydro-Electric Power Commission	725,000 00

Rural Power District Loans Act 1930 ($65,000.00)

20 Geo. V, chap. 14

Hydro-Electric Power Commission, advance	65,000 00

Statutory $1,307,501.60

SPECIAL WARRANTS

General Advertising ($2,579.40)

Border Cities Star, 180.00; Canadian Labour Press, 250.00; Evening Telegram, 457.60; Globe Printing Co., 404.80; Hamilton Spectator, 180.00; Kingston Whig Standard, 90.00; London Free Press, 225.00; Mail and Empire, 440.00; Ottawa Journal Dailies, 124.00; Toronto Daily Star, 168.00; Tribune, Nassau, Bahamas, 60.00	2,579 40

Grant to the Canadian Olympic Committee ($5,000.00)

Canadian Olympic Committee	5,000 00

Grant to the Navy League of Canada ($500.00)

Navy League of Canada	500 00

Royal Commission of Investigation re the Purchase of certain Properties by the Hydro-Electric Power Commission of Ontario ($4,707.60)

W. J. Angus, travelling expenses, 40.65; L. C. Christie, travelling expenses, 46.05; Estate of late Mr. Justice Orde, part honorarium, 2,500.00; Globe Printing Co., advertising, 25.20; Greene, Hill & Co., legal services, 12.00; H. B. Griffiths, travelling expenses, 37.42; McLaren, Fletcher & Co., travelling expenses of Mr. Young, 97.10; C. A. Magrath, travelling expenses, 138.70; Mail and Empire, advertising, 24.00; A. J. Nesbitt, travelling expenses, 43.40; R. O. Sweezey, travelling expenses, 37.43; Thorne, Mulholland, Howson & McPherson, audit services, 1,185.00; Tilley, Johnston & Co., sundry persons as witnesses, 10.00; D. J. Walker, services and expenses as secretary, 460.19; J. B. Woodyatt, travelling expenses, 42.70; petty disbursements, 7.76	4,707 60

To pay balance of salary to Hon. E. C. Drury, Premier and President of Council for the years 1919 to 1922 for said office as provided by the Executive Council Act ($8,825.00)

Hon. E. C. Drury	8,825 00

Construction of Rural, Primary and Secondary Transmission Lines on the Island of Manitoulin ($14,000.00)

Hydro-Electric Power Commission, advance	14,000 00

Special Warrants $35,612.00

Total	6,334,189 93
Less Salary Assessment	3,301 98
Total Expenditure, Department of the Prime Minister	**$6,330,887 85**

LEGISLATION

FISCAL YEAR, 1931-32

TABLE OF CONTENTS

GENERAL INDEX AT BACK OF BOOK

PART C—LEGISLATION

Statement of Expenditure Showing Amounts Expended, Unexpended and Overexpended for the Twelve Months Ended October 31st, 1932

Legislation	Page	Estimates	Expended: Ordinary	Expended: Capital	Expended: Total Ordinary and Capital	Un-expended	Over-expended	Treasury Bd. Minute
		$ c.	$ c.	$ c.	$ c.	$ c.	$ c.	$ c.
Legislation:								
Salaries	4	14,925 00	13,847 64	....	13,847 64	1,077 36	....	....
Clerks of Committees	4	1,600 00	700 00	....	700 00	900 00	....	....
Sessional Writers, Messengers, Pages, etc.	4	25,000 00	24,582 65	....	24,582 65	417 35	....	....
Contingencies	5	5,000 00	7,166 85	....	7,166 85	....	2,166 85	2,500 00
Indemnity to Members, including mileage	6	230,500 00	217,128 00	....	217,128 00	13,372 00	....	....
Stationery, Distributing Statutes, Printing, etc.	6	30,000 00	34,991 73	....	34,991 73	....	4,991 73	5,000 00
Allowance to Mr. Speaker in lieu of contingencies	6	1,000 00	1,000 00	....	1,000 00	....	....	....
Legislative Committee for Art Purposes	6	1,500 00	687 00	....	687 00	813 00	....	....
Legislation		309,525 00	300,103 87	....	300,103 87	16,579 71	7,158 58	....
Law Clerk's Office:								
Salaries	6	16,000 00	14,500 00	....	14,500 00	1,500 00	....	....
Clerk of the Crown in Chancery:								
Salaries	6	3,200 00	3,200 00	....	3,200 00	....	....	....
Contingencies	6	500 00	102 07	....	102 07	397 93	....	....
Clerk of the Crown in Chancery		3,700 00	3,302 07	....	3,302 07	397 93	....	....
Legislative Library:								
Salaries	6	16,225 00	12,675 00	....	12,675 00	3,550 00	....	....
Purchase of books, contingencies, etc.	6	11,000 00	9,668 33	....	9,668 33	1,331 67	....	....
Purchase of Legal Publications	7	550 00	490 35	....	490 35	59 65	....	....
Legislative Library	..	27,775 00	22,833 68	....	22,833 68	4,941 32	....	....
Supply Bill	..	357,000 00	340,739 62	....	340,739 62	23,418 96	7,158 58	....

Special Warrants:								
Services and Expenses re Security Frauds Prevention Act	7	....	10,695 94	....	10,695 94	....	....	....
Special Warrants	..	....	10,695 94	....	10,695 94	....	....	....
Total	..	....	351,435 56	....	351,435 56	....	....	....
Less Salary Assessment	..	....	759 95	....	759 95	....	....	....
Legislation	..	....	350,675 61	....	350,675 61	....	....	....

SUMMARY

Legislation	Page	Ordinary	Capital	Total
		$ c.	$ c.	$ c.
Legislation	4-6	300,103 87	....	300,103 87
Law Clerk's Office	6	14,500 00	....	14,500 00
Clerk of the Crown in Chancery	6	3,302 07	....	3,302 07
Legislative Library	6-7	22,833 68	....	22,833 68
Special Warrants	7	10,695 94	....	10,695 94
Total	..	351,435 56	....	351,435 56
Less Salary Assessment	..	759 95	....	759 95
Legislation	..	350,675 61	....	350,675 61

LEGISLATION

Salaries ($13,847.64)

Hon. Thomas A. Kidd	Speaker		2,500 00
A. C. Lewis	Clerk of the House	12 months	5,000 00
G. Hunter Ogilvie	Sergeant-at-Arms	(T) 12 "	1,999 92
Robert Brown	Clerk, Group 1	(T) 12 "	676 92
Roy Dies	" " 1	12 "	1,700 00
Grace Jones	Clerk Stenographer, Group 1	12 "	1,125 00
May E. Lindner	Secretary to Mr. Speaker	(T) 5⅔ "	845 80

Clerks of Committees ($700.00)

W. G. W. Harvey	Chief Clerk of Committees	400 00
J. J. Dingman	Clerk of Game and Fisheries	75 00
Douglas Oliver	" " Agriculture	75 00
Ralph Hyman	" " Printing	75 00
R. Regan	" " Public Accounts	50 00
J. O. Hambleton	" " Colonization	25 00

Sessional Writers, Messengers, Pages, etc. ($24,582.65)

Sessional Writers, $15,075.15.

Geo. Creighton (special), 274.99 F. S. Ebbs (special), 1,000.00; Ethel M. Ferguson (Supervisor), 325.00; S. R. Payne (special), 228.00; Charles Reed (special), 312.49; W. J. Reynolds (special), 256.67; Ethel Anderson, 102.00; Olive Armstrong, 84.00; Betty Barchard, 84.00; Lorraine Barchard, 102.00; Ann Berry, 102.00; Ida Bland, 102.00; Joey Bond, 102.00; Margaret Bowen, 102.00; Margaret Burley, 102.00; Sayde L. Carter, 102.00; Marjorie Chatterton, 102.00; Lora Colquhoun, 102.00; Helen A. Cooper, 144.00; Helen Cosens, 114.00; Mrs. Catherine Cote, 75.00; Lillian Cox, 102.00; Hilda Cryer, 162.00; Elsie Currie, 102.00; Nancy Davis, 102.00; Mary Denholm, 126.00; Marie Devlin, 102.00; Jean Donald, 114.00; Grace Donaldson, 102.00; Aileen Doyle, 102.00; Zelma Drinkill, 102.00; Pearl Dunbar, 84.00; Ferne Eagen, 102.00; Vivian G. Eaton, 102.00; Margaret E. D. Ecks, 126.00; Florence E. Elson, 102.00; Berneice English, 102.00; Kathleen Eplett, 102.00; Edith Fell, 48.00; Annie Fox, 102.00; Inga Fraser, 102.00; J. H. Fraser, 102.00; Marie Fraser, 102.00; Anne Freedman, 114.00; Helen Galloway, 102.00; Phyllis Gault, 102.00; Lillian Glassier, 102.00; Gertrude Goldhar, 84.00; Marjorie Golding, 102.00; Alice Gordon, 102.00; Jean Gordon, 162.00; Helen J. Greive, 102.00; Helen Groves, 114.00; Dora Hale, 102.00; A. V. Harrison, 144.00; May Harrison, 102.00; Edna Heagle, 114.00; Rita Henderson, 102.00; Dorothy Holliday, 114.00; Rhea Hooper, 102.00; Marion Houston, 114.00; Wilma Hunter, 102.00; Vera A. Ireton, 102.00; Doris Jackson, 102.00; Kathleen G. Killing, 102.00; Laura C. Knight, 78.00; Mae Lake, 189.00; Muriel Lane, 93.00; Thelma Lee, 102.00; Nina A. Lewis, 342.00; Christina Leitch, 78.00; Louise Livingstone, 102.00; Bessie Long, 144.00; Jean MacKenzie, 102.00; Velma C. MacKenzie, 102.00; Madeline MacMorine, 114.00; Edythe Marsh, 114.00; Ruby Marshall, 102.00; Nora Manion, 102.00; Isabel McAlpine, 102.00; Molly McAvoy, 114.00; Annie B. McCorkell, 102.00; Hilda McKechnie, 126.00; T. McLellan, 102.00; Elsie McVeity, 102.00; Marjory L. Morrison, 102.00; Elizabeth Myers, 57.00; G. Nicholas, 102.00; Audrey Noecker, 114.00; Mildred Price, 114.00; Floretta Pritchard, 162.00; Eileen Redfearne, 138.00; Edith M. Richards, 102.00; Lucy B. Richardson, 114.00; Margaret K. Roberts, 102.00; Dorothy Robertson, 114.00; Lorraine Roder, 171.00; Alma Rowden, 30.00; Katherine Rutherford, 102.00; Marion Scott, 102.00; Marion Shaver, 102.00; Hallie Shearer, 96.00; Helen Shepard, 114.00; Jessie Smith, 102.00; Maude Smith, 102.00; Maud D. Smith, 114.00; Marjory Spalding, 135.00; Florence E. Speck, 102.00; Eleanor P. Strong, 114.00; Gertrude E. Taylor, 102.00; Muriel E. Tester, 105.00; Eleanor K. Thomson, 102.00; Dorothy Trimble, 102.00; Mona Tyler, 102.00; Gertrude E. Webb, 99.00; Miriam Whaley, 114.00; Alice Williams, 210.00; P. C. Williams, 102.00; Muriel Willoughby, 102.00; Eleanor Winterfield, 102.00; Eileen P. Wooton, 102.00; Genvea Wright, 114.00 .... 15,075 15

Messengers, $8,082.00.

R. A. Allen, 114.00; Wm. Baillie, 114.00; H. P. Barnes, 102.00; T. A. Blakely, 84.00; Wm. Boag, 114.00; John Body, 102.00; Adam Boyd, 114.00; George Brooks, 114.00; Jack E. Brown, 102.00; George Brunton, 114.00; Wm. Burnett, 114.00; Chase Burrows, 102.00; W. A. Caldwell, 114.00; George Carpenter, 102.00; Walter Carter, 102.00; J. Carey, 66.00; Joseph Champagne, 102.00; John Chisholm, 114.00; Lionel Choquette, 66.00; Doug. Christie, 102.00; R. H.

Sessional Writers, Messengers, Pages, etc.—Continued

Messengers—Continued

Coleman, 114.00; R. H. Craddock, 102.00; W. H. Creighton, 114.00; E. J. Crottie, 114.00; J. G. Dearing, 114.00; Earl Dignan, 114.00; E. Dodds, 120.00; Art. T. Eagen, 66.00; Henry Floyd, 114.00; J. Gibson, 102.00; Jack S. Gibson, 102.00; George Glackin, 102.00; James Graham, 102.00; J. J. Hagerty, 102.00; C. F. Hahn, 114.00; William Hanna, 114.00; Fred Hartt, 102.00; Eddie Jackson, 102.00; Jack Jarvis, 102.00; Carl J. Kane, 96.00; Robert Kearns, 102.00; Edison Kent, 102.00; William Kiel, 102.00; J. J. King, 114.00; Daniel Kinsman, 114.00; P. J. Loughrin, 102.00; J. D. Mann, 102.00; J. J. McCarthy, 114.00; George McCausland, 114.00; Douglas McColl, 102.00; Archie McCraw, 102.00; G. H. McKenzie, 102.00; F. McCumber, 48.00; John McNamara, 114.00; Robert McWhinney, 114.00; Albert Moore, 114.00; J. P. Morgan, 102.00; Joseph Murphy, 102.00; Allen Newman, 102.00; W. Nuttall, 102.00; W. J. O'Grady, 15.00; Douglas Park, 96.00; Walter Pate, 102.00; Thomas Pettit, 114.00; L. J. Pitt, 129.00; Edward Randall, 114.00; Bernard Saunders, 93.00; F. Seeger, 123.00; David Sinclair, 102.00; Donald Sivitz, 102.00; Charles J. Smith, 114.00; Charles H. Standish, 114.00; E. Stone, 102.00; George Sydenham, 102.00; Maxwell Wigle, 18.00; Wm. Wilkins, 102.00; F. C. Williams, 84.00; Alfred Wilson, 102.00; William Younger, 114.00 .... 8,082 00

Pages, $977.50.

Frank Boon, 92.50; Beverley Burley, 95.00; J. R. Burns, 92.50; Arthur Carr, 92.50; George Hawkins, 92.50; Archie Parker, 92.50; Allan C. Peck, 92.50; Alex. Stewart, 50.00; Robert W. Stiff, 92.50; Charles Watkins, 92.50; Gordon Young, 92.50 .... 977 50

Cleaners, $448.00.

Mona Hart, 86.00; Marie A. McGillivray, 68.00; Ellen M. Smith, 76.00; Elizabeth Veal, 114.00; L. Wales, 104.00 .... 448 00

Contingencies, including Stationery and Equipment for Reporters ($7,166.85)

Temporary Services, $2,080.00.

D. K. Black .... Assistant to the Law Clerks .... 12 months 2,080 00

Advertising Private Bills, $823.12.

Algoma Advocate, 11.00; Belleville Ontario Intelligencer, 18.75; Border Cities Star, 38.55; Brockville Recorder and Times, 12.00; Bruce Mines Spectator, 13.00; Chatham Daily News, 18.75; Clinton Publishing Co., 15.00; Cochrane Northland Post, 15.00; Evening Telegram, 69.30; Fort William Daily Times Journal, 10.00; Galt Daily Reporter, 15.00; Globe Printing Co., 61.80; Guelph Daily Mercury, 18.75; The Haileyburian, 15.00; Hamilton Spectator, 26.25; Kenora Mirror & News, 15.00; Kingston Whig Standard, 48.75; London Free Press, 35.00; Mail and Empire, 68.10; Municipal World, 36.00; North Bay Nugget, 20.00; Oshawa Daily Times, 18.75; Ottawa Journal Dailies, 35.00; Pembroke Standard Observer, 12.00; Peterborough Examiner, 15.12; Porcupine Advocate, 13.00; Port Arthur News Chronicle, 10.00; Powassan News, 8.75; St. Catharines Standard, 18.75; Sarnia Canadian Observer, 11.25; Sault Daily Star, 18.00; Service Press, 7.00; Stratford Beacon Herald, 14.00; Sudbury Star, 25.00; Toronto Daily Star, 18.00; Woodstock Sentinel Review, 17.50 .... 823 12

Travelling Expenses, $294.65.

D. K. Black, 36.70; H. L. Cummings, 257.95 .... 294 65

Extra Services, $675.00.

J. Bennett, 75.00; R. Brown, 75.00; W. Campbell, 50.00; T. Cordell, 75.00; S. Lowe, 50.00; S. McKenzie, 50.00; H. Petley, 200.00; E. M. Sexsmith, 50.00; W. Thompson, 50.00 .... 675 00

Public Accounts Committee, $116.65.

N. R. Butcher & Co., reporting, 90.60; F. D. Hogg, expenses, 26.05 .... 116 65

Municipal Committee, $450.00.

A. Ellis, 60.00; F. W. Elliott, 105.00; T. W. Jutten, 90.00; F. G. McBrien, 30.00; Hon. P. Poisson, 60.00; T. K. Slack, 105.00 .... 450 00

Contingencies—Continued

Miscellaneous, $2,727.43.

George Coles Ltd., maid service, 25.00; Gray Coach Lines, rental of busses, 24.00; Mrs. H. Kilbride, repairs to uniforms, 30.00; King's Printer, 436.83; E. Longstaff, meals for members, re late sessions, 371.40; National Publishing Syndicate, pictures for members, 300.00; W. E. Phillips Co., Ltd., framing pictures for members, 427.40; Remington Typewriters, Ltd., rental of machines, 100.00; Rose Cleaners & Dyers, cleaning and pressing suits, 14.00; A. E. Semple, reporting Budget Speech, 45.00; United Typewriter Co., Ltd., inspection, rentals, etc., 369.60. Sundries—car tickets, 15.00; cartage, 9.00; express, 174.36; newspapers and periodicals, 283.65; telegrams, 75.46; petty disbursements, 26.73 — 2,727 43

Indemnity to Members, including Mileage ($217,128.00)

Indemnity to Members, including mileage	228,228 00	
Less Indemnity Assessment	11,100 00	
		217,128 00

Stationery, including Printing Paper, Printing Bills, Distributing Statutes, Printing and Binding ($34,991.73)

King's Printer, stationery, 6,848.68; printing, 25,033.59; paper, 3,108.11; express charges, 1.35 — 34,991 73

Allowance to Mr. Speaker in Lieu of Contingencies ($1,000.00)

Hon. T. A. Kidd — 1,000 00

Legislative Committee for Art Purposes ($687.00)

Leatherdale Studios, photos of members — 687 00

LAW CLERK'S OFFICE

Salaries ($14,500.00)

Name	Position	Period	Amount
A. M. Dymond	Law Clerk of Public Bills	10 months	4,500 00
Herbert L. Cummings	Law Clerk of Private and Municipal Bills	12 "	4,600 00
A. E. Baker	Principal Clerk	12 "	2,400 00
C. S. Berthon	Senior Clerk Stenographer	12 "	1,500 00
D. H. McCleary	" " "	12 "	1,500 00

CLERK OF THE CROWN IN CHANCERY

Salaries ($3,200.00)

Name	Position	Period	Amount
W. G. W. Harvey	Clerk, Group 1	12 months	1,700 00
M. B. Rice	Senior Clerk Stenographer	12 "	1,500 00

Contingencies ($102.07)

King's Printer, 64.95; United Typewriter Co., Ltd., inspections, etc., 25.12. Sundries—newspapers, 12.00 — 102 07

LEGISLATIVE LIBRARY

Salaries ($12,675.00)

Name	Position	Period	Amount
A. T. Wilgress	Librarian	12 months	3,600 00
Geo. E. Barnes	Senior Library Assistant	12 "	2,050 00
E. King	" " "	12 "	2,000 00
Hugh Ray	" " " (T)	12 "	900 00
O. M. Bright	" " "	12 "	1,800 00
E. J. Leckie	Library Assistant, Group 2	12 "	1,200 00
Wm. A. Powell	" " Group 2	12 "	1,125 00

Contingencies ($9,668.33)

Temporary Services, $2,245.38.

Name	Position	Period	Amount
Lillian Bligh	Library Clerk	12 months	936 00
Mildred Fraser	Library Assistant, Group 2	6 "	484 38
Bessie E. Hunter	Clerk Stenographer, Group 2	12 "	825 00

Purchase of Books, $4,312.05.

Acadia University, 1.07; E. G. Allen & Sons, Ltd., 701.63; American Antiquarian Society, 4.00; American Geographical Society, .50; American Ornithologists' Union, 3.40; J. R. Angus, 1.00; Army Historical Research Society, 5.11; C. G. Bailey, 4.80; Baker & Taylor Co., 45.69; Bibliographical Society of America, 33.01; G. Bouchard, .25; R. R. Bowker Co., 18.24; H. W. Bragg, 1.00; A. Britnell Book Shop, 164.85; Canadian Bankers' Association, .30; Canadian Citizens' Institute Research, 12.00; Canadian Comment, 2.00; Canadian Facts

Contingencies—Continued

Purchase of Books—Continued.

Publishing Co., 1.50; Canadian Gazeteer Publishing Co., Ltd., 20.00; Canadian Geographic Society, .35; Canadian Historical Association, 6.00; Canadian Magazine, .30; Canadian Pacific Railway Co., 1.00; Canadian Review Co., 8.00; C. D. Cazenove & Son, 2,015.36; Clark Irwin & Co., Ltd., 3.60; Colonial Society of Massachussets, 5.00; Copp-Clark Co., Ltd., 8.77; J. M. Dent & Sons, Ltd., 24.99; Department of Public Printing and Stationery, Ottawa, 2.50; The Dickens' Fellowship, 87.72; Dominion Publishing Co., Ltd., 42.50; G. Ducharme, 1.50; Empire Club of Canada, 3.00; Europa Publications, Ltd., 10.22; W. S. Evans Statistical Service, 2.25; Evans Bros., Ltd., .48; F. W. Faxon Co., 2.11; Federation of Ontario Naturalists, 1.00; Fishery Research Commission, .50; W. J. Gage Co., Ltd., .76; Gazette Printing Co., Ltd., 4.00; General Board of Religious Education, .90; Golden Vesta Press, 3.40; Graphic Publishers, Ltd., 4.34; J. Hardwick Co., 41.15; Harvard University Press, 4.05; Heaton Publishing Co., 7.50; Henry George & Barron, 15.33; J. Hill, 5.00; The Johns Hopkins Press, 3.39; Houston's Standard Publications, 15.00; Hudson's Bay Co., 2.50; Imperial War Graves Commission, 39.42; International Press, 10.00; International Railway Publishing Co., 2.00; The Jackson Press, 1.50; Jamaica Government Printing Office, 2.15; R. Jocelyn, 10.75; Kelly Publishing Co., 20.00; H. A. Kennedy, 3.00; P. S. King & Son, Ltd., 203.73; League of Nations Society in Canada, 3.05; A. Legree, 2.00; H. T. Lennon, 14.00; Libraire Beauchemin, Ltd., .82; Libraire d'Action Canadienne Francaise, .35; The Library Association, 17.03; Lions Gate Publishing Co., 2.12; Longmans Green & Co., 1.75; H. McIntosh, 57.95; A. McKim, Ltd., 3.00; McMullen Publishers, 4.00; Macmillan Co. of Canada, Ltd., 49.40; N. L. Martin, 19.80; Michigan Historical Society, 2.00; Might Directors, Ltd., 37.00; Minnesota Historical Society, 2.80; Mississippi Valley Historical Association, 5.00; Museum Book Store, Ltd., 9.73; Musson Book Co., Ltd., 4.75; National Alumni, Ltd., 35.60; National Educational Association, 5.00; T. Nelson & Sons, Ltd., 20.17; Newspaper Press Directory, 1.58; New York Times Index, 12.00; Ogilvie & Boyd, Ltd., 9.11; Oregon Historical Association, 2.00; Oxford University Press, 13.39; D. H. Peffers, 1 83; M. E. Perry, 1.00; Pine Tree Publishing Co., 5.00; Sir Isaac Pitman & Sons, Ltd., 2.50; Planet Book Service, 6.00; G. R. F. Prowse, 1.00; Bernard Quaritch, Ltd., 13.71; Royal Geographical Society, 7.96; Royal Society of Canada, 2.00; Ryerson Press, Ltd., 26.78; Saskatchewan Government, .30; Scolefield's Who's Who in New Zealand, 3.73; C. Scribner's Sons, 3.75; R. Simpson Co., Ltd., 5.39; T. Skinner & Co., 1.80; W. H. Smith & Sons, Ltd., 20.50; Smithsonian Institution Service, 49.50; H. M. Stationery Office, 17.03; Elliott Stock, 8.20; Times Book Club, 5.67; Torontonian Society Blue Book, 15.00; A. V. Turner, 17.36; Unemployment Research Committee of Ontario, 2.10; University of Chicago Press, 2.89; University of North Carolina 8.02; University of Toronto Press, 6.00; Verlag der intern Zeitschrift, 14.50; O. K. Watson, 1.00; L. Wharton, .50; H. W. Wilson Co., 69.45; Windsor Public Library, 1.50; Women's Institute, .25; Wrigley Hotel Directory, 5.00; Wrigley Printing Co., Ltd., 2.06 .... 4,312 05

Miscellaneous, $3,110.90.

R. Jackson, maps, etc., 16.50; King's Printer, 1,954.44; H. McIntosh, binding books, 21.00; C. Tarling Co., mounting maps, 32.65; United Typewriter Co., Ltd., inspections, etc., 22.00. Sundries—express, 9.40; newspapers and periodicals, 1,037.16; telegrams, 1.44; petty disbursements, 16.31 .... 3,110 90

Purchase of Legal Publications ($490.35)

Burroughs & Co., Ltd., weekly reports, etc., 26.50; Butterworth & Co., Ltd., law books, etc., 51.50; Canada Law Book Co., Ltd., law reports, 122.50; Canada Law List Publishing Co., law lists, 5.00; Carswell Co., Ltd., English law reports, etc., 278.85; Wilson & Lefleur Limitee, Raports de Pratique, 6.00 .... 490 35

Legislation **$340,739.62**

SPECIAL WARRANTS

Services and Expenses re Security Frauds Prevention Act ($10,695.94)

Clarkson, Gordon, Dilworth, Guilfoyle & Nash, 7,695.94; Edwards Morgan & Co., 3,000.00 .... 10,695 94

Special Warrants **$10,695.94**

Total	$351,435 56
Less Salary Assessment	759 95
Total Expenditure, Legislation	**$350,675.61**

DEPARTMENT

OF THE

ATTORNEY-GENERAL

FISCAL YEAR, 1931-32

TABLE OF CONTENTS

GENERAL INDEX AT BACK OF BOOK

PART D—DEPARTMENT OF ATTORNEY-GENERAL

Statement of Expenditure Showing Amounts Expended, Unexpended and Overexpended for the Twelve Months Ended October 31st, 1932

Department of Attorney-General	Page	Estimates	Expended			Un-expended	Over-expended	Treasury Board Minute
			Ordinary	Capital	Total Ordinary and Capital			
		$ c.	$ c.	$ c.	$ c.	$ c.	$ c.	$ c.
Main Office:								
Salaries	8	47,650 00	43,464 94	....	43,464 94	4,185 06	....	....
Contingencies	8	5,000 00	4,494 72	....	4,494 72	505 28	....	....
Law Library	8	500 00	496 20	....	496 20	3 80	....	....
Main Office	..	53,150 00	48,455 86	....	48,455 86	4,694 14	....	....
General:								
Deputy Clerks of Crown, etc	8	25,075 00	25,075 00	....	25,075 00	....	....	....
Shorthand Reporters:								
Salaries	9	24,000 00	23,922 60	....	23,922 60	77 40	....	....
Contingencies	9	7,000 00	8,991 31	....	8,991 31		1,991 31	2,000 00
Crown Counsel Prosecutions	9	35,000 00	42,943 68	....	42,943 68	....	7,943 68	8,000 00
Civil Litigation	10	10,000 00	26,460 74	....	26,460 74	....	16,460 74	21,000 00
Commissions and Sundry Investigations	11	5,000 00	1,553 87	....	1,553 87	3,446 13	....	....
Services not provided for	11	1,000 00	500 00	....	500 00	500 00	....	....
Grant to conference on improving Laws in the Provinces, etc	11	800 00	600 00	....	600 00	200 00	....	....
County Law Libraries	11	4,000 00	4,000 00	....	4,000 00	....	....	....
Compassionate Allowances	11	5,000 00	1,900 00	....	1,900 00	3,100 00	....	....
Ontario Securities Commission:								
Services and Expenses	11	35,525 00	47,615 89	....	47,615 89	....	12,090 89	13,500 00
General	..	152,400 00	183,563 09	....	183,563 09	7,323 53	38,486 62	....
Supreme Court:								
Salaries	12	92,125 00	78,246 93	....	78,246 93	13,878 07	....	....
Contingencies	12	6,000 00	9,401 10	....	9,401 10	....	3,401 10	3,500 00
Commutation of Fees, Judges of Surrogate	13	1,600 00	1,600 00	....	1,600 00	....	....	....
Allowances to Judges	13	19,000 00	18,899 54	....	18,899 54	100 46	....	....
Grant to Judges' Library	13	700 00	700 00	....	700 00	....	....	....

Grant to Judges' Library (Chancery)	13	600 00	600 00	....	600 00	....	....	....
Judges' Petty Expenses Fund	13	1,000 00	1,000 00	....	1,000 00	....	....	....
Supreme Court	..	121,025 00	110,447 57	....	110,447 57	13,978 53	3,401 10	....
Law Enforcement Fund	14	900,000 00	918,241 77	....	918,241 77	....	18,241 77	25,000 00
Toronto and York Crown Attorney's Office:								
Salaries	20	22,725 00	22,725 00	....	22,725 00	....	....	....
Contingencies	20	5,000 00	4,934 89	....	4,934 89	65 11	....	....
Toronto and York Crown Attorney's Office	..	27,725 00	27,659 89	....	27,659 89	65 11	....	....
Administration of Justice:								
Audit of Criminal Justice Accounts,								
Salaries	21	10,875 00	10,875 00	....	10,875 00	....	....	....
Contingencies	21	1,000 00	742 42	....	742 42	257 58	....	....
General Administration of Justice,								
Fees	21	475,000 00	386,818 43	....	386,818 43	88,181 57	....	....
Districts	21	130,000 00	138,516 56	6,209 84	144,726 40	....	14,726 40	15,000 00
Police Magistrates,								
Salaries, Contingencies, etc.	22	120,000 00	127,987 03	....	127,987 03	....	7,987 03	8,000 00
Revision of Voters' Lists	24	2,500 00	2,496 17	....	2,496 17	3 83	....	....
Algoma District,								
Salaries	24	2,400 00	2,400 00	....	2,400 00	....	....	....
Engineers, gaolers, turnkeys, etc.	24	8,500 00	8,486 72	....	8,486 72	13 28	....	....
Fuel, light and water	24	10,100 00	7,321 54	....	7,321 54	2,778 46	....	....
District of Cochrane,								
Salaries	24	1,400 00	1,400 00	....	1,400 00	....	....	....
Fuel, light and water	24	5,500 00	3,914 62	....	3,914 62	1,585 38	....	....
District of Kenora,								
Salaries	24	2,100 00	2,100 00	....	2,100 00	....	....	....
Gaolers, lock-up keepers, etc.	24	7,000 00	9,305 93	....	9,305 93	....	2,305 93	2,500 00
Fuel, light and water	24	7,000 00	5,972 35	....	5,972 35	1,027 65	....	....
District of Manitoulin,								
Salaries	25	2,950 00	2,950 00	....	2,950 00	....	....	....
Allowance for office rent	25	175 00	175 00	....	175 00	....	....	....
Gaolers, lock-up keepers, etc.	25	1,810 00	1,771 66	....	1,771 66	38 34	....	....
Fuel, light and water	25	2,675 00	2,547 65	....	2,547 65	127.35	....	....
District of Muskoka,								
Salaries	25	1,850 00	1,850 00	....	1,850 00	....	....	....
Gaolers, lock-up keepers, etc.	25	1,950 00	1,850 00	....	1,850 00	100 00	....	....
Fuel, light and water	25	2,000 00	985 89	....	985 89	1,014 11	....	....

PART D—DEPARTMENT OF ATTORNEY-GENERAL—Continued

Statement of Expenditure Showing Amounts Expended, Unexpended and Overexpended for the Twelve Months Ended October 31st, 1932

Department of Attorney-General	Page	Estimates	Expended			Un-expended	Over-expended	Treasury Board Minute
			Ordinary	Capital	Total Ordinary and Capital			
		$ c.	$ c.	$ c.	$ c.	$ c.	$ c.	$ c.
District of Nipissing,								
Salaries	25	1,900 00	1,900 00	....	1,900 00	....	....	....
Clerks of the Peace, office rent	25	200 00	200 00	....	200 00	....	....	....
Gaolers, lock-up keepers, etc.	25	9,100 00	8,958 38	....	8,958 38	141 62	....	....
Fuel, light and water	25	6,500 00	6,959 18	....	6,959 18	....	459 18	1,200 00
District of Parry Sound,								
Salaries	25	1,600 00	1,600 00	....	1,600 00	....	....	....
Gaolers, lock-up keepers, etc.	25	4,600 00	4,125 50	....	4,125 50	474 50	....	....
Fuel, light and water	25	3,800 00	3,799 85	....	3,799 85	15	....	....
District of Rainy River,								
Salaries	26	2,000 00	2,000 00	....	2,000 00	....	....	....
Gaolers, lock-up keepers, etc.	26	4,780 00	5,065 33	....	5,065 33	....	285 33	350 00
Fuel, light and water	26	3,500 00	2,244 89	....	2,244 89	1,255 11	....	....
District of Sudbury,								
Salaries	26	1,850 00	1,600 00	....	1,600 00	250 00	....	....
Gaolers, lock-up keepers, etc.	26	13,200 00	14,603 19	....	14,603 19	....	1,403 19	1,500 00
Fuel, light and water	26	12,500 00	14,984 64	....	14,984 64	....	2,484 64	4,000 00
District of Temiskaming,								
Salaries	26	2,000 00	2,000 00	....	2,000 00	....	....	....
Gaolers, lock-up keepers, etc.	26	9,500 00	10,653 00	....	10,653 00	....	1,153 00	2,000 00
Fuel, light and water	26	11,500 00	11,307 13	....	11,307 13	192 87	....	....
District of Thunder Bay,								
Salaries	26	2,100 00	2,100 00	....	2,100 00	....	....	....
Gaolers, lock-up keepers, etc.	26	10,500 00	12,543 66	....	12,543 66	....	2,043 66	2,100 00
Fuel, light and water	27	13,050 00	10,142 13	....	10,142 13	2,907 87	....	....
Provisional County of Haliburton Registrar of Deeds	27	200 00	200 00	....	200 00	....	....	....
Administration of Justice	..	911,165 00	837,453 85	6,209 84	843,663 69	100,349 67	32,848 36	....

Inspection of Legal Offices:								
Salaries	27	22,000 00	22,000 00		22,000 00			
Printing, stationery and contingencies	27	8,000 00	7,926 82		7,926 82	73 18		
Fidelity Bonds, Division Court officers	27	3,000 00	1,808 90		1,808 90	1,191 10		
Typewriters, contingencies for Judicial Officers, etc.	27	2,000 00	1,978 28		1,978 28	21 72		
Inspection of Legal Offices	..	35,000 00	33,714 00		33,714 00	1,286 00		
Land Titles Office:								
Salaries	27	39,100 00	30,676 33		30,676 33	8,423 67		
Contingencies	28	3,000 00	2,625 48		2,625 48	374 52		
Land Titles Office	..	42,100 00	33,301 81		33,301 81	8,798 19		
Local Masters of Titles:								
Sault Ste. Marie,								
Salaries and expenses	28	3,600 00	3,511 00		3,511 00	89 00		
Haileybury,								
Salaries and expenses	28	8,700 00	7,257 35		7,257 35	1,442 65		
North Bay,								
Salaries and expenses	28	7,100 00	5,978 94		5,978 94	1,121 06		
[illegible],								
Salaries and expenses	28	9,800 00	7,457 54		7,457 54	2,342 46		
Registrars and Local Masters in Districts,								
Forms, copying and contingencies	28	3,000 00	2,395 81		2,395 81	604 19		
Registrations of [illegible]	28	5,000 00	2,795 00		2,795 00	2,205 00		
Local Masters of Titles	..	37,200 00	29,395 64		29,395 64	7,804 36		
Miscellaneous:								
Ontario Municipal Board,								
Salaries	29	44,275 00	21,136 86		21,136 86	23,138 14		
Contingencies	29	13,500 00	3,324 18		3,324 18	10,175 82		
Drainage Trials Act,								
Salaries	29	4,000 00	4,000 00		4,000 00			
Contingencies	29	900 00	548 55		548 55	351 45		
Public Trustees' Office,								
Salaries	29	49,150 00				49,150 00		
[illegible] Fee	30	3,000 00				3,000 00		
Contingencies	30	5,000 00				5,000 00		
Fire Marshal's Office,								
Salaries	30	44,350 00	41,152 53		41,152 53	3,197 47		
Division of Fire Investigation	31	21,150 00	25,436 76		25,436 76		4,286 76	6,000 00

PART D—DEPARTMENT OF ATTORNEY-GENERAL—Continued

Statement of Expenditure Showing Amounts Expended, Unexpended and Overexpended for the Twelve Months Ended October 31st, 1932

Department of Attorney-General	Page	Estimates	Expended			Un-expended	Over-expended	Treasury Board Minute
			Ordinary	Capital	Total Ordinary and Capital			
		$ c.	$ c.	$ c.	$ c.	$ c.	$ c.	$ c.
Miscellaneous—Continued								
Fire Marshal's Office—Continued								
Division of Fire Prevention	32	10,000 00	5,185 56	....	5,185 56	4,814 44	....	....
Division of Lightning Rod Act	32	7,500 00	3,727 59	....	3,727 59	3,772 41	....	....
Miscellaneous	..	202,825 00	104,512 03	....	104,512 03	102,599 73	4,286 76	....
Supply Bill	..	2,482,590 00	2,326,745 51	6,209 84	2,332,955 35	246,899 26	97,264 61	....
Statutory:								
Minister's salary	32	....	10,000 00	....	10,000 00	....	....	....
Salaries [illegible] provided for	32	....	1,125 00	....	1,125 00	....	....	....
County Judges	32	....	71,849 77	....	71,849 77	....	....	....
Sheriffs, to make up incomes to $1,800.00	33	....	1,250 45	....	1,250 45	....	....	....
Registrars of Deeds, to make up incomes to $1,800.00	33	....	8,911 08	....	8,911 08	....	....	....
Special investigations	33	....	8,529 30	....	8,529 30	....	....	....
Probation Officers	33	....	30,329 73	....	30,329 73	....	....	....
Expenses of elections	33	....	16,425 01	....	16,425 01	....	....	....
Administration of Justice Expenses Act	33	....	56,541 89	....	56,541 89	....	....	....
Ontario Municipal Board, 22 Geo. V., Chap. 27 Sec. 38	34	....	24,865 99	....	24,865 99	....	....	....
Refund of Fines imposed on Aemilius Jarvis et al and interest	34	....	356,890 35	....	356,890 35	....	....	....
R.S.O. 1927 Chap. 25, Sec. 17	34	....	4,500 00	....	4,500 00	....	....	....
21 Geo. V., Chap. 48, Sec. 10, Securities Act, 1931	34	....	13,074 83	....	13,074 83	....	....	....
R.S.O. 1927, Chap. 22, Sec. 5	35	....	2,927 81	....	2,927 81	....	....	....
Statutory	..	....	607,221 21	....	607,221 21	....	....	....
Special Warrant:								
Grant to Ontario Provincial Command Canadian Legion B.E.S.L.	35	....	6,000 00	....	6,000 00	....	....	....

Total	....	..	....	2,939,966 72	6,209 84	2,946,176 56	....	....	....
Less Salary Assessment	....	..	....	32,594 91	....	32,594 91	....	....	....
Department of Attorney-General		..	....	2,907,371 81	6,209 84	2,913,581 65	....	....	....

SUMMARY

Department of Attorney-General	Page	Ordinary	Capital	[illegible]
		$ c.	$ c.	$ c.
[illegible]	8	48,455 86	....	[illegible]8,455 86
[illegible]	8-12	183,563 09	....	[illegible]3,563 09
[illegible] of Fees	13	1,600 00	....	[illegible] 00
[illegible]	12-13	108,847 57	....	[illegible]8,847 57
[illegible]	14-20	918,241 77	....	[illegible]8,241 77
[illegible] York Crown Attorney	20	27,659 89	....	27,659 89
[illegible]	21-27	837,453 85	6,209 84	843,663 69
[illegible] of Legal Offices	27	33,714 00	....	33,714 00
Land Titles [illegible]	27-28	33,301 81	....	33,[illegible] 81
Local Masters of Titles	28	29,395 64	....	29,[illegible] 64
[illegible]	29-32	104,512 03	....	104,[illegible] 03
Statutory	32-25	607,221 21	....	607,[illegible] 21
Special [illegible]	35	6,000 00	....	6,[illegible] 00
Total	....	2,939,966 72	6,209 84	2,946,176 56
Deduct—Transfered to Loans and Special Funds (see Part U);	....	....	6,209 84	6,209 84
	....	2,939,996 72	....	2,939,966 72
Less Salary Assessment	....	32,594 91	....	32,594 91
Department of Attorney-General	....	2,907,371 81	....	2,907,371 [illegible]

ATTORNEY-GENERAL'S DEPARTMENT

Hon. W. H. Price, Attorney-General (Statutory) $10,000.00

ATTORNEY-GENERAL'S OFFICE

Salaries ($43,464.94)

Edward Bayly	Deputy Attorney-General	12 months	7,200 00
I. A. Humphries	Solicitor	12 "	5,200 00
Joseph Sedgwick	"	12 "	4,400 00
W. B. Common	"	12 "	3,450 00
Henry C. Draper	"	12 "	3,000 00
P. S. Golding	"	12 "	2,850 00
M. Currey	Secretary to Minister	(T) 12 "	1,332 61
C. Magone	Chief Clerk	12 "	3,000 00
A. W. Nicol	Clerk	12 "	1,700 00
M. Mooney	Secretarial Stenographer	12 "	1,600 00
Mona S. Jones	Clerk Stenographer, Group 1	(T) 12 "	1,200 00
M. L. McGillivray	Senior Clerk Stenographer	12 "	1,500 00
Marie C. Hurst	Clerk Stenographer, Group 2	(T) 12 "	825 00
M. Bamford	" " " 1	8 "	866 46
H. I. Lobb	" " " 1	12 "	1,200 00
Margaret Browning	" " " 2	(T) 4¼ "	290 87
Clara M. Marron	" " " 1	12 "	1,300 00
Edith M. Jack	" " " 1	12 "	1,050 00
M. C. Trotter	" " " 2	12 "	975 00
Gordon F. Beddis	Office Boy	(T) 12 "	525 00

Salaries not Otherwise Provided for (Statutory), ($1,125.00)

Dr. E. R. Frankish..........Pathologist.................. 4½ months 1,125 00

Contingencies ($4,494.72)

Temporary Services, $525.00.

William C. Bowman......Office Boy..............................12 months 525 00

Travelling Expenses, $729.85.

E. Bayly, 123.15; I. A. Humphries, 53.00; J. Sedgwick, 145.45; Hon. W. H. Price, 500.00 .... 821 60

Less repayment, I. A. Humphries, accountable, 1931 .... 91 75

729 85

Miscellaneous, $3,239.87.

King's Printer, 2,228.33; Newsom & Gilbert, forms, 20.70; H. C. Tugwell, photo supplies, 68.39; United Typewriter Co., Ltd., inspections, etc., 172.03. Sundries—car tickets, 30.00; customs, .29; express, 2.28; newspapers and periodicals, 75.03; postage, 5.00; telegrams, 594.33; petty disbursements, 43.49.................. 3,239 87

Law Library ($496.20)

Burroughs & Co., Ltd., books, 24.60; Butterworth & Co., Ltd., books, 93.25; Canada Law Book Co., Ltd., binding, etc., 52.50; Carswell Co., Ltd., books, 78.00; Ontario Citator, index, 16.00. Sundries, subscriptions to law reports, etc., 231.85......... 496 20

Main Office..$48,455.86

GENERAL

Deputy Clerks of the Crown and Local Registrars

Salaries ($25,075.00)

H. J. Wallace	Brant	675 00
R. E. Clapp	Bruce	675 00
J. A. V. Preston	Dufferin	675 00
I. D. Cameron	Elgin	675 00
Angus McKinnon	Essex	675 00
Chester H. Wood	Frontenac	675 00
T. J. Rutherford	Grey	750 00
J. C. Eccles	Haldimand	600 00
W. J. McClenahan	Halton	600 00
John A. Kerr	Hastings	750 00
Robt. Johnston	Huron	750 00
D. E. Douglas	Kent	675 00

General—Continued

Deputy Clerks of the Crown and Local Registrars, Salaries—Continued

Alex Saunders	Lambton	675 00
J. S. McNeely	Lanark	675 00
A. E. Baker	Leeds and Grenville	750 00
W. P. Deroche	Lennox and Addington	600 00
E. J. Lovelace	Lincoln	675 00
E. Weld	Middlesex	500 00
C. S. Buck	Norfolk	675 00
J. T. Field	Northumberland	750 00
Horace Bascom	Ontario	675 00
Peter McDonald	Oxford	750 00
J. R. Fallis	Peel	600 00
R. A. Norman	Prince Edward	600 00
F. H. Thompson	Perth	675 00
Geo. J. Sherry	Peterborough	675 00
J. Bellanger	Prescott and Russell	675 00
J. M. Beatty	Renfrew	600 00
John McKay	Simcoe	750 00
A. I. Macdonell	Stormont, Dundas and Glengarry	750 00
J. E. Anderson (acting)	Victoria	675 00
Chas. C. Hahn	Waterloo	675 00
J. E. Cohoe	Welland	800 00
L. W. Goetz	Wellington	300 00
G. T. Inch	Wentworth	750 00
T. J. Foster	Algoma	150 00
W. L. Worrell	Cochrane	600 00
C. S. Salmon	Muskoka	150 00
J. T. Bourke	Nipissing	150 00
Fred Tasker	Parry Sound	150 00
A. H. Beath	Sudbury	150 00
T. J. Meagher	Temiskaming	150 00
Keith Munro	Thunder Bay	150 00

SHORTHAND REPORTERS

Salaries ($23,922.60)

Ernest Nield	Court Reporter Supreme Court of Ontario	12 months	3,000 00
F. Clitheroe	" " " " "	4⅔ "	1,750 00
J. E. Henderson	" " " " "	7 "	1,172 60
J. Buskard	" " " " "	12 "	3,000 00
R. N. Dickson	" " " " "	12 "	3,000 00
A. E. Cabeldu	" " " " "	12 "	3,000 00
S. W. Brown	" " " " "	12 "	3,000 00
H. O. Taylor	" " " " "	12 "	3,000 00
E. C. Foot	" " " " "	12 "	3,000 00

Contingencies ($8,991.31)

Services Reporting, $941.50.

W. W. Buskard, 35.10; N. R. Butcher & Co., 156.00; F. Clitheroe, 216.00; A. M. Good, 8.00; B. Lake, 16.00; A. G. Newell & Co., 192.00; W. W. Perry, 148.00; T. Pyburn, 162.40; L. M. Sagar, 8.00 ... 941 50

Travelling Expenses, $8,049.81.

S. W. Brown, 797.45; J. Buskard, 348.00; W. W. Buskard, 283.55; A. E. Cabeldu, 1,062.90; F. Clitheroe, 307.65; R. N. Dickson, 588.85; C. L. Empringham, 112.60; E. C. Foot, 1,154.35; J. E. Henderson, 431.60; B. Lake, 68.75; E. Nield, 941.10; W. W. Perry, 510.80; G. H. Playle, 31.55; H. O. Taylor, 1,410.66 ... 8,049 81

Crown Counsel Prosecutions ($42,943.68)

Fall, Winter and Spring Assizes.

M. R. Allison, Prince Edward, 20.00; J. E. Anderson, Victoria, 20.00; H. Arrell, Haldimand, 40.00; W. G. Atkins, Algoma, 20.00; H. Atkinson, Leeds and Grenville, 40.00; R. N. Ball, Oxford, 40.00; T. F. Battle, Essex, Wellington, 802.75; A. W. Beament, Ontario, 206.80; D. S. Bowlby, Waterloo, 20.00; W. S. Brewster, Kent, 228.38; G. L. T. Bull, Huron, 570.30; S. A. Caldbeck, Cochrane, 34.95; H. P. Cooke, Kenora, 60.00; D. J. Cowan, Thunder Bay, 634.65; N. L. Croome, Rainy River, 300.75; A. B. Cunningham, Ontario, 302.70; W. I. Dick, Halton,

General—Continued

Crown Counsel Prosecutions—Continued

26.00; J. M. Donahue, Welland, 260.37; A. R. Douglas, Kent, 183.80; J. A. B. Dulmage, Lanark, 20.00; R. D. Evans, Dufferin, 40.00; J. W. Freeborn, Bruce, 40.13; L. M. Frost, Halton, 411.90; C. M. Garvey, Northumberland and Durham, 453.75; N. B. Gash, Lennox and Addington, 248.90; W. M. Gordon, Brant, 273.10; R. H. Greer, York, 860.00; W. L. Haight, Parry Sound, 40.00; W. R. Hall, Lanark, 200.29; W. S. Haney, Lambton, 20.00; J. G. Harkness, Stormont, Dundas and Glengarry, 20.00; W. D. Henry, Gray, 40.00; D. E. Holmes, Huron, 20.00; J. J. A. Hope, Carleton, Prince Edward, 502.35; W. B. Horkins, Welland, Cochrane, Sudbury, 1,488.66; W. C. Inch, Temiskaming, 415.88; Thos. Johnson, Muskoka, 20.00; H. B. Johnston, Renfrew, 20.00; J. M. Kearns, Wellington, 20.00; W. E. Kelly, Norfolk, 20.00; P. Kerwin, Leeds, Middlesex, Wentworth (Hamilton), 1,639.74; A. C. Kingstone, Toronto and York, Wentworth, 4,806.50; E. H. Lancaster, Lincoln, 40.00; J. E. Lawson, Muskoka, 383.65; R. W. Lent, Peel, 20.00; R. P. Locke, Elgin, Hastings, 1,024.00; J. D. Lucas, York, 1,340.00; V. S. McClenaghan, Peel, 531.20; V. J. McElderry, Peterborough, 20.00; G. F. McFarlane, Middlesex, 359.40; T. E. McKee, Nipissing, 40.00; W. F. McRae, Manitoulin, 20.00; H. J. Macdonald, Temiskaming, Sandwich, 572.95; N. S. Macdonnell, Wentworth, 542.70; J. K. MacKay, Thunder Bay, Carleton, 2,441.25; J. C. Makins, York, Perth, 1,455.00; C. W. A. Marion, Prescott and Russell, 20.00; Sir A. Morine, Simcoe, 398.45; J. Murray, Perth, 147.85; J. L. O'Flynn, Algoma, 322.68; C. A. Payne, Northumberland and Durham, 270.34; D. F. Pepler, Elgin, 225.25; N. Phillips, Victoria, 336.80; R. D. Ponton, Grey, 514.50; F. C. Richardson, Stormont, Dundas and Glengarry, 233.05; T. J. Rigney, Frontenac, 20.00; H. Saint Jacques, Prescott and Russell, 618.75; G. N. Shaver, Wentworth, Essex, 1,435.37; J. L. Sheard, Kenora, Middlesex, 756.35; N. Sommerville, York, 1,900.39; H. A. Tibbetts, Norfolk, Kenora, 1,186.30; F. L. Ward, Renfrew, 330.05; Peter White, Simcoe, Carleton, Brant, 8,521.55; W. H. Williams, Sudbury, Frontenac, Waterloo, 1,463.20; N. M. Wilson, Lennox and Addington, 20.00........ 42,943 68

General Litigation ($26,460.74)

Aeronautics Reference:		
Blake & Redden, legal services	190 15	
Arrow River Appeal:		
Edward Bayly, travelling expenses, 53.55; Hogg & Hogg, legal services, 150.60	204 15	
Bell Telephone Enquiry:		
R. A. Reid, on account, legal services	2,200 00	
Divorce Case, Kerr & Kerr:		
R. W. Ralfe, copies of evidence	12 60	
Distribution of Criminal Fines, City of Toronto vs. The King:		
Blake & Redden, legal services, 656.58; W. N. Tilley, legal services, 3,500.00	4,156 58	
Insurance Reference, Attorney-General of Ontario vs. Attorney-General of Canada:		
Edward Bayly, travelling expenses, 60.60; Blake & Redden, legal services, 833.57; Hogg & Hogg, legal services, 12.00; W. N. Tilley, legal services, 7,509.32	8,415 49	
Litigation re Ownership of Ship Island, Attorney-General of Canada vs. Attorney-General of Ontario:		
A. H. Neeb, copy of Abstract	1 50	
Ownership of Property re W. L. Forrest, et al, Attorney-General of Canada vs. Attorney-General of Ontario.		
Hogg & Hogg, legal services	32 22	
Proprietary Articles Trade Association:		
W. N. Tilley, legal services	5,000 00	
Radio Reference:		
Blake & Redden, legal services	587 27	
Securities Frauds Legislation, Attorney-General of Ontario, half cost, Lymburn vs. Mayland:		
Blake & Redden, legal services, 634.78; Province of Alberta, half expenses of Appeal to Privy Council, 5,000.00	5,634 78	
Walker, Hiram, vs. Town of Walkerville:		
Hunter Rose Co., copies of factums	26 00	26,460 74

General—Continued

Commissions and Sundry Investigations ($1,553.87)

Juvenile Court, London:	
I. A. Humphries, travelling expenses	34 90
Renfrew Investigation:	
E. L. Featherston, services reporting, travelling expenses, and copies of evidence, 1,271.32; I. A. Humphries, travelling expenses, 123.95; D. J. Ritza, services as constable, 46.30	1,441 57
Workmen's Compensation Enquiry:	
Globe Printing Co., advertising, 27.00; Mail and Empire, advertising, 26.40; Evening Telegram, advertising, 24.00	77 40

Services not Otherwise Provided for ($500.00)

H. L. Cummings, special services as supervisor for Municipalities	500 00

Grant to Conference on Improving Laws in the Province, and to pay Allowances in lieu of Travelling and other Expenses ($600.00)

John D. Falconbridge, grant, 400.00; E. Rene Richard, grant, 200.00	600 00

County Law Libraries ($4,000.00)

Sundry County Law Libraries, grants	4,000 00

Compassionate Allowances for Incapacitated Officers ($1,900.00)

H. R. Bedford, 500.00; M. Brennan, 1,200.00; T. Dougherty, 200.00	1,900 00

ONTARIO SECURITIES COMMISSION ($47,615.89)

Salaries, $28,809.48.

Geo. A. Drew	Commissioner	12 months	10,000 00
Arthur W. Rogers	Solicitor and Deputy Commissioner	1 "	500 00
Helen B. Palen	Deputy Registrar	12 "	3,000 00
Wm. A. Brant	Solicitor	12 "	3,000 00
Norman Harris	Financial Assistant	12 "	3,000 00
W. B. Livett	Clerk, Group 1	12 "	1,600 00
Elsie Teasdall	Secretarial Stenographer	12 "	1,600 00
Muriel Browne	Clerk Stenographer, " 1	12 "	1,300 00
Edna M. Browne	" " " 1	12 "	1,125 00
L. N. Lester	" Stenographer, " 1	½ "	46 88
G. Hagar	Filing Clerk, " 1	12 "	1,050 00
M. A. Murphy	" " " " 1 (T)	12 "	900 00
A. A. Pringle	Clerk Stenographer " 3	10 "	937 60
A. M. McBain	Clerk, " 3 (T)	12 "	750 00

Temporary Services, $8,512.53.

C. M. Anderson	Assistant Filing Clerk	12 months	900 00
J. Bond	Clerk Stenographer, Group 2	3½ "	239 00
James Clare	Office Boy	12 "	522 93
James McBride	Accountant	12½ "	2,870 00
M. E. Smith	Clerk Typist, Group 2	3½ "	216 99
W. Stuart Banks	Accountant	12 "	3,010 00
Jean C. Thompson	Clerk Stenographer, Group 2	11 "	753 61

Travelling Expenses, $685.56.

W. S. Banks, 51.40; W. A. Brant, 396.11; J. C. Clare, 2.87; G. A. Drew, 47.80; W. Harris, 46.39; J. McBride, 132.00; Ontario Provincial Police, 8.99	685 56

Miscellaneous, $9,608.32.

C. G. Bailey, book, 12.50; Bain, Bicknell, White & Bristol, legal services, 804.05; Bourne & Ironsides, map, 12.35; Bradstreet Co., reports, 276.10; W. W. Buskard, services reporting, 19.50; N. R. Butcher & Co., services reporting, 16.45; W. J. Clark, court costs, Rex vs. Conroy & Hazzard, 35.76; Coo & Thompson, services reporting, 520.65; Cronyn & Betts, legal services, 35.22; Dictaphone Sales Co., Ltd., machines, inspections, etc., 2,541.38; R. G. Dun & Co., subscription, 125.00; Ediphone Co., Ltd., rental and inspections, 52.55; W. Henry, legal fees, 50.00; Imperial Bank, services re Rex vs. G. W. Miles, 20.00; King's Printer, 1,583.92; MacLean Publishing Co., Ltd., corporation services, 27.50; P. S. Ross & Sons, services investigating Ingoldsby Fur Farm Co., 1,012.20; C. W. Sime, audit services, 756.18; Sundry clerks, meals re overtime, 67.50; Thorne, Mulholland, Howson & McPherson, audit services, 1,205.00; United Typewriter Co., Ltd., inspections, 187.02; C. Wells, services reporting, 11.00; R. P. Wilson,

Crown Counsel Prosecutions—Co. nued

General—Continued

Ontario Securities Commission—Continued

Miscellaneous—Continued.

engineering service, 50.00. Sundries—car tickets, 51.75; excise stamps, .50; newspapers, etc., 66.50; telegrams, 92.25; petty disbursements, 66.30 .... 9,699 13
Less repayment: A. W. Rogers, accountable .... 90 81 | 9,608 32

General **$183,563.09**

SUPREME COURT

Salaries ($78,246.93)

Name	Position	Period	Amount
Jessie C. Wylie	Librarian	12 months	1,125 00
R. N. Davies	Stenographer and Reporter	12 “	2,000 00
E. M. Coles	“ to Judges	12 “	1,600 00
Laura E. Farrow	“ “ “	12 “	1,600 00
H. Loveys	“ “	12 “	1,600 00

Master's Office

Name	Position	Period	Amount
I. Hilliard	Master	12 months	6,600 00
W. J. Reilly	Assistant Master	11 “	4,216 62
F. Gordon Cook	“ “	1 “	291 66
E. W. Boyd	“ “	6 “	2,032 17
“		(T) 6 “	983 93
O. E. Lennox	“	12 “	3,450 00
A. S. Marriott	Clerk	12 “	2,400 00

Registrar's Office

Name	Position	Period	Amount
E. Harley	Senior Registrar	12 months	5,000 00
D'Arcy Hinds	Assistant Registrar	12 “	3,300 00
Clarence Bell	“ “	12 “	3,300 00
A. E. Trow	“ “	(T) 12 “	1,380 80
Frank J. Turville	Solicitor	10½ “	1,293 26
Cyril E. Rudge	“ Registrar	12 “	2,550 00
W. S. Anderson	Surrogate Clerk	12 “	2,500 00
Fred W. Scott	Principal Clerk	12 “	2,400 00
R. W. Ralfe	“ “	12 “	2,400 00
W. J. Davies	“ “	12 “	2,400 00
Lewis C. Ling	Senior Clerk	12 “	2,000 00
D. Bristol	Clerk, Group 1	(T) 12 “	1,200 00
Geo. K. McBride	Clerk, “ 1	12 “	1,600 00
Albert G. Stubbert	Junior Messenger	12 “	750 00
M. L. Garvey	“ “	12 “	900 00
Belle J. Currie	Clerk Stenographer, “ 1	12 “	1,200 00
Mary M. Staples	“ “ “ 1	12 “	1,125 00
Marjory Colloton	“ “ “ 2	12 “	975 00
C. G. Spanner	Stenographer and Reporter	12 “	2,000 00
E. Boys	Clerk Stenographer, Group 1	(T) 2 “	162 49
A. P. Gorman	Stenographer and Reporter	12 “	2,000 00
W. Denne	Usher and Messenger	(T) 12 “	700 00
T. S. Chambers	“ “	12 “	1,300 00
Wm. F. Irvine	“ “	(T) 12 “	1,200 00
N. J. Harrison	Allowance to Housekeeper as Chief Messenger	11 1/6 “	186 00
Norman M. Carrie	Messenger	12 “	600 00
Clare E. Grant	Office Boy	(T) 12 “	525 00

Taxing Office

Name	Position	Period	Amount
J. F. McGillivray	Taxing Officer	12 months	5,400 00

Contingencies ($9,401.10)

Temporary Services ($3,761.48)

Name	Position	Period	Amount
Chas. Bradley	Office Boy	1 month	48 72
Vera E. Cameron	Clerk Typist, Group 2	10½ “	605 77
Hilda Fisher	“ “ “ 2	10½ “	610 58

Supreme Court—Continued

Contingencies—Continued

Temporary Services—Continued

Chas. J. McCabe	Surrogate Clerk		1 month (1931)	100 26
Dorothy Smith	Clerk Typist,	Group 2	9 months	564 90
Elizabeth L. Spiers	Assistant Librarian,	" 3	12½ "	781 25
Eugenie Stead	Clerk Typist,	" 1	12 "	900 00
E. Williams	" "	" 1	2 "	150 00

Miscellaneous, $5,639.62.

Bell Telephone Co., tolls, 46.85; Canada Law Book Co., Ltd., reports, 26.00; Carswell Co., Ltd., books, 44.50; Coo & Thompson, services reporting, 350.00; General Office Equipment Co., Ltd., machine parts, maintenance charges, 44.00; C. H. Gundy, services reporting, 126.00; Harcourt & Son, Ltd., gown, 50.00; King's Printer, 4,302.62; B. Lake, services reporting, 44.00; A. G. Newall & Co., Ltd., services reporting, 60.00; W. W. Perry, services reporting, 16.00; United Typewriter Co., Ltd., inspections, 146.51. Sundries—car tickets, 55.00; express, 3.25; postage, 200.00; telegrams, 111.39; petty disbursements, 13.50.... 5,639 62

Commutation of Fees—Judges of Surrogate ($1,600.00)

His Honour F. M. Morson........ 1,600 00

Allowances to Judges under R.S.O. 1927, Chap. 89 ($18,899.54)

Court of Appeal for Ontario

Right Hon. Sir William Mulock, K.C.M.G., P.C., C.J.O.	1,000 00
Hon. F. R. Latchford, C.J.A.	1,000 00
Hon. James Magee, J.A.	1,000 00
Hon. Frank Hodgins, J.A.	884 25
Hon. W. R. Riddell, J.A.	1,000 00
Hon. W. E. Middleton, J.A.	1,000 00
Hon. C. A. Masten, J.A.	1,000 00
Hon. D. I. Grant, J.A.	1,000 00

High Court of Ontario

Hon. H. E. Rose, C.J., President	1,000 00
Hon. H. T. Kelly, J.	1,000 00
Hon. W. J. Logie, J.	1,000 00
Hon. J. F. Orde, J.	750 00
Hon. R. G. Fisher, J.	1,000 00
Hon. W. H. Wright, J.	1,000 00
Hon. J. M. McEvoy, J.	1,000 00
Hon. W. E. Raney, J.	1,000 00
Hon. Nicol Jeffrey, J.	1,000 00
Hon. Chas. Garrow, J.	1,000 00
Hon. Geo. H. Sedgewick, J.	1,000 00
Hon. A. C. Kingstone, J.	166 66
Hon. P. Kerwin, J.	98 63

Grant to Judges' Library for Upkeep ($700.00)

Hon. F. E. Hodgins, Treasurer........ 700 00

Grant to Judges' Library (Chancery) S.C.O. ($600.00)

L. Boyd, Treasurer........ 600 00

Allowance to Treasurer of Judges' Petty Expense Fund for Petty Expenses of Judges ($1,000.00)

Hon. W. E. Middleton........ 1,000 00

Supreme Court........$110,447.57

LAW ENFORCEMENT ($918,241.77)

Payments made Pursuant to The Constables' Act, R.S.O. 1927, Chap. 125, Sec. 35

Ontario Provincial Police

Salaries ($719,083.63)

Headquarters, $64,450.00.

Name	Position	Period	Amount
V. A. S. Williams	Commissioner	12 months	6,000 00
Alfred Cuddy	Assistant Commissioner	12 "	4,200 00
John Miller	Senior Inspector, C.I.B.	12 "	3,200 00
A. B. Boyd	Inspector, "	12 "	3,200 00
W. H. Stringer	" "	12 "	3,200 00
E. C. Gurnett	" "	12 "	3,000 00
E. D. L. Hammond	" "	12 "	3,000 00
A. H. Ward	" "	12 "	3,000 00
W. G. Dobson	Senior Clerk	12 "	2,000 00
F. E. Elliott	Chief Inspector, L.C.A.I.B.	12 "	3,300 00
Ephraim Zinkann	Inspector, "	12 "	2,100 00
W. C. Killing	Staff Inspector	12 "	3,000 00
Arthur Moss	" "	12 "	3,000 00
E. T. Doyle	" "	12 "	2,550 00
J. J. Monkman	Accountant	12 "	2,850 00
G. T. Kernick	Senior Clerk	12 "	1,800 00
E. H. Jackson	Clerk	12 "	1,400 00
B. M. Gregg	"	12 "	1,200 00
Harold McCullough	"	12 "	1,200 00
Norman Phelps	"	12 "	825 00
Alex Swan	Office Boy	12 "	600 00
R. A. Bullick	" "	12 "	600 00
E. C. Hoag	Secretarial Stenographer	12 "	1,750 00
B. I. Pidgeon	Clerk	12 "	1,400 00
Polly McKessock	Clerk Stenographer, Group 1	12 "	1,200 00
C. F. Moore	" " " 1	12 "	1,200 00
A. M. Bell	" " " 2	12 "	975 00
O. E. Edwards	" " " 2	12 "	975 00
M. L. Handforth	" " " 2	12 "	975 00
D. B. Chew	Junior Clerk	12 "	750 00

District Inspectors, $32,100.00.

C. F. Airey, 2,700.00; F. B. Creasy, 2,200.00; A. R. Elliott, 2,550.00; Hamor Gardner, 2,550.00; W. G. Ingram, 2,550.00; C. A. Jordon, 2,700.00; W. H. Lougheed, 2,700.00; W. T. Moore, 2,700.00; Sidney Oliver, 2,200.00; A. H. Palmer, 2,550.00; J. H. Putman, 2,700.00; A. E. Storie, 1,600.00; Philip Walter, 2,400.00 ..... 32,100 00

Sergeants, $29,408.38.

S. H. Bush, 2,100.00; T. W. Cousans, 2,100.00; Richard Cox, 2,100.00; G. W. Delves, 1,400.00; W. B. Elliott, 2,000.00; Francis Gardner, 2,100.00; P. T. Hake, 2,100.00; Eric Hand, 2,100.00; A. R. Knight, 2,100.00; R. P. Labelle, 1,108.38; W. C. Oliver, 2,000.00; W. A. Page, 2,100.00; W. A. Scott, 2,000.00; Hayston Storey, 2,100.00; H. E. Thompson, 2,000.00 ..... 29,408 38

Constables, $360,344.27.

Joseph Allen, 1,900.00; H. V. Allsopp, 1,900.00; F. W. Barrett, 1,700.00; James Bartlett, 1,800.00; W. A. Bayes, 1,800.00; R. G. Beatty, 1,900.00; R. J. Beatty, 1,900.00; Stanislaus Berard, 1,800.00; John Berry, 1,900.00; Wilfred Bertrand, 1,900.00; H. E. Blair, 1,700.00; A. L. Bonnycastle, 1,600.00; W. H. Boyd, 1,900.00; F. R. Bromfield, 1,700.00; J. R. Brown, 1,900.00; Finlay Buchanan, 1,900.00; S. G. Burgess, 1,700.00; Harry Butler, 1,900.00; W. R. Byrne, 1,900.00; D. G. Campbell, 1,700.00; Dorema Campeau, 1,900.00; W. J. Carey, 1,800.00; G. B. Carmichael, 1,900.00; L. C. Carr, 1,900.00; R. E. Carter, 1,800.00; W. R. Caverly, 1,800.00; B. L. Cayen, 1,900.00; W. V. C. Chisholm, 29.59; A. R. Clark, 1,700.00; John Clark, 1,900.00; W. H. Clark, 1,700.00; E. J. Cleland, 1,800.00; G. V. Clubbe, 1,900.00; Harold Cole, 237.48; J. V. Considine, 1,900.00; S. H. Cooke, 1,900.00; G. E. Cookman, 1,900.00; T. G. Corsie, 1,900.00; Alex Craik, 1,900.00; T. S. Crawford, 1,700.00; Ralph Crozier, 1,700.00; H. H. Dent, 1,600.00; L. A. Denton, 1,001.86; W. A. Diamond, 1,274.94; J. R. Dickson, 1,800.00; F. R. Dobson, 1,564.62; J. M. Douglas, 1,600.00; B. L. Drennan, 1,800.00; W. D. Duncan, 1,900.00; W. M. Durnford, 1,900.00; Arnold Eady, 1,600.00; R. G. Elliott, 1,900.00; W. A. Embleton, 1,900.00; A. S. Ericksen, 1,700.00; M. W. Ericksen, 1,800.00; L. S. Evans, 1,900.00; C. W. Farrow, 1,900.00; W. G. Ferguson, 1,700.00;

Law Enforcement—Continued

Ontario Provincial Police, Salaries—Continued

Constables—Continued

H. O. Finger, 1,800.00; Frank Fox, 1,564.62; W. J. Franks, 1,900.00; H. S. Gall, 1,564.62; Hugh Gibson, 1,900.00; A. F. Grant, 1,700.00; G. O. Grassick, 1,900.00; W. F. Gray, 1,900.00; David Hamilton, 1,700.00; H. T. Hammer, 1,900.00; L. S. Hardwick, 1,900.00; E. L. Harris, 1,900.00; E. F. Hartleib, 1,900.00; C. G. Hayes, 1,800.00; James Higgins, 1,800.00; T. W. Higgins, 1,800.00; E. A. Hoath, 1,700.00; W. H. Hocken, 1,564.62; T. A. Houldcroft, 1,900.00; B. C. Jakeman, 79.16; L. E. James, 1,800.00; F. R. Jarvis, 1,600.00; H. S. Johns, 1,600.00; J. E. Johnson, 1,600.00; W. J. Johnston, 1,800.00; J. W. Joslin, 1,600.00; L. T. Keeler, 1,564.62; E. W. Keen, 1,900.00; F. C. Kelly, 1,800.00; J. F. Kelly, 1,564.62; John Kelly, 1,804.17; T. J. Kennedy, 1,800.00; W. H. Kennedy, 1,564.62; J. A. Kenny, 1,900.00; Alex, Kidd, 1,700.00; G. W. Kierman, 1,155.00; C. H. Knight, 791.62; R. P. Labelle, 791.62; H. C. N. Langton, 1,800.00; G. J. Maguire, 1,800.00; W. A. Markle, 1,700.00; J. H. Marsland, 1,800.00; A. L. Mennie, 1,800.00; W. H. Metcalfe, 1,900.00; J. E. Miller, 1,600.00; Benjamin Milligan, 1,900.00; T. W. Mitchell, 1,900.00; D. P. Morris, 1,900.00; Benjamin Mulholland, 1,800.00; G. T. Murdock, 150.00; George MacKay, 1,900.00; J. F. MacLean, 925.43; Alex Macleod, 1,900.00; A. R. MacLeod, 1,800.00; E. J. MacMillan, 1,800.00; J. S. McBain, 1,900.00; W. J. McBride, 1,700.00; W. H. McBrien, 1,800.00; S. V. McClelland, 1,900.00; Otto McClevis, 1,900.00; J. W. McCord, 1,700.00; P. E. McCoy, 1,800.00; R. A. McCuaig, 1,800.00; David McCulloch, 300.00; T. M. McDonough, 1,800.00; Albert McDougall, 1,900.00; John McGetrick, 1,900.00; John McKee, 1,900.00; William McNab, 1,700.00; E. V. McNeill, 1,900.00; J. A. McQueen, 1,600.00; F. J. Naphan, 1,900.00; Joseph Nelson, 1,900.00; John Nixon, 1,800.00; Harry Noakes, 1,600.00; Harry Noble, 1,900.00; R. E. Noble, 1,800.00; Wm. Noyes, 1,700.00; T. W. Oldfield, 1,800.00; A. J. Oliver, 1,800.00; H. C. Ostrander, 283.32; T. H. Owens, 1,900.00; J. N. Page, 1,900.00; K. A. Patterson, 1,900.00; R. S. Patterson, 1,700.00; T. E. Pearson, 1,800.00; H. H. Peel, 1,800.00; R. E. Penner, 1,600.00; A. R. Peters, 1,900.00; W. N. Peters, 1,700.00; John Pike, 1,900.00; P. J. Poland, 1,700.00; D. H. Porter, 1,900.00; J. W. F. Pretorius, 1,800.00; E. L. Priest, 1,900.00; W. R. Pringle, 1,900.00; R. E. Purvis, 1,900.00; Harry Ramsbottom, 1,800.00; J. W. Reavley, 1,900.00; V. T. Reed, 1,900.00; Reginald Reynolds, 1,800.00; Thomas Richardson, 1,800.00; Thomas Riding, 1,700.00; Isaac Robbie, 1,900.00; T. P. K. Robinson, 1,900.00; W. A. T. Robinson, 1,900.00; J. F. Rose, 1,900.00; J. A. Rowe, 1,900.00; Frank Scott, 1,800.00; P. P. Seibert, 1,700.00; A. M. Shaughnessy, 1,800.00; J. B. Sheff, 1,700.00; E. A. Shepard, 1,700.00; D. C. Shervill, 1,800.00; J. A. Shields, 1,900.00; L. L. Shipley, 1,800.00; David Silvester, 1,900.00; Frederick Simpson, 1,900.00; C. N. C. Smaill, 1,900.00; C. E. Smith, 654.10; W. E. Smith, 1,900.00; Mason Spearman, 1,800.00; A. W. Stewart, 1,800.00; D. R. Stewart, 1,900.00; J. A. Stringer, 1,900.00; R. O. Stromberg, 1,700.00; J. D. Sutherland, 1,600.00; R. A. Taggart, 702.34; R. J. Taggart, 1,700.00; Cecil Taylor, 1,800.00; G. E. Taylor, 1,800.00; V. A. Taylor, 829.92; S. McD. Thomson, 1,564.62; F. C. Thurston, 1,800.00; W. G. Tomlinson, 1,800.00; Francis Tompkins, 1,700.00; L. A. Treganza, 1,800.00; N. R. Vyse, 1,600.00; L. G. A. Walker, 1,600:00; R. H. Wannell, 1,564.62; A. F. Whiteside, 1,900.00; R. J. Whiting, 1,900.00; E. F. Widmeyer, 1,900.00; Thomas Wilkinson, 1,900.00; A. S. Wilson, 1,604.16; D. E. Wilson, 1,800.00; C. W. Wood, 1,900.00; Wm. Wood, 1,900.00; G. G. Woodward, 1,600.00; T. R. Wright, 1,900.00; R. B. Young, 431.30; Stewart Young, 1,900.00; R. H. Hawkshaw, 1,416.68.......... 360,344 27

Motor Cycle Patrol, $154,942.84.

Inspectors—J. A. Grant, 2,550.00; Sydney Hunter, 2,200.00; F. G. Jerome, 2,200.00; T. G. P. Lucas, 2,200.00. Constables—D. F. Bell, 1,700.00; F. R. T. Blucher, 1,700.00; A. E. Bond, 1,800.00; A. E. Bosworth, 1,600.00; D. H. Brown, 1,700.00; G. E. Buck, 1,800.00; L. B. Byles, 1,900.00; J. W. Callander, 1,700.00; R. J. Clark, 1,600.00; W. H. Coles, 1,700.00; J. S. Culp, 1,800.00; D. H. Darby, 1,900.00; A. J. Davies, 1,900.00; W. H. Delaney, 1,600.00; V. H. Dentenbeck, 1,800.00; Percy Dowsley, 1,900.00; R. S. Dukes, 1,700.00; Samuel Ervine, 1,700.00; A. J. Ferguson, 1,900.00; J. H. Foxton, 1,700.00; W. O. Frink, 1,900.00; N. R. Gardner, 1,800.00; Gordon Hallick, 1,900.00; P. E. Harkness, 1,800.00; R. H. Hawkshaw, 283.32; Chas. Hefferon, 910.34; S. A. Hilliard, 1,900.00; J. M. Hinchliffe, 1,800.00; Clifford Hood, 1,800.00; A. E. Hornick, 1,700.00; H. W. Howell, 1,900.00; T. L. G. Howell, 1,900.00; D. H. Huffman, 1,800.00; Clarence Hunter, 1,900.00; C. R. Imrie, 1,600.00; H. F. Jackman, 1,700.00; Allie Jackson, 1,900.00; E. L. Jess, 1,800.00; Henry Jillings, 1,800.00; Carl Johns, 1,700.00; John Kay, 1,900.00; F. W. Kirk, 1,700.00; E. D. Kyle, 1,274.94; George Law, 1,800.00; Allister Lawrence, 1,600.00; Bertram LeGrand, 900.00; H. F. Lemon, 1,800.00; R. L. W.

Law Enforcement—Continued

Ontario Provincial Police, Salaries—Continued

Inspectors—Continued

Lemon, 1,900.00; Jack Lewis, 1,600.00; T. E. Logan, 1,700.00; A. E. Martin, 1,800.00; J. C. Massingham, 1,700.00; W. A. Melbourne, 1,700.00; J. I. Mitchell, 283.32; E. C. Mitchener, 1,700.00; L. A. Montgomery, 1,900.00; B. C. Moore, 1,800.00; N. F. Morris, 1,700.00; L. A. McClure, 1,700.00; J. H. Palmer, 849.96; J. J. Palmer, 1,800.00; C. E. Parmenter, 1,700.00; E. G. Purves, 1,700.00; H. R. Ransom, 1,900.00; L. O. Rawlins, 1,700.00; R. E. Raymer, 1,600.00; A. W. Reilly, 1,900.00; G. H. Richardson, 266.64; W. G. Robinson, 1,600.00; D. H. Rogers, 1,800.00; Eugene Rose, 1,600.00; J. W. Rowcliffe, 1,900.00; A. F. Runciman, 1,600.00; C. F. Russell, 1,800.00; A. R. Smith, 1,900.00; E. S. Spence, 124.32; I. R. Spencer, 1,900.00; O. E. Storey, 1,700.00; V. W. Summerfield, 1,700.00; H. W. Swain, 1,800.00; Clarence Thompson, 1,600.00; W. F. S. Thompson, 1,800.00; L. E. Throop, 1,600.00; G. R. Waud, 1,700.00; J. L. Whitty, 1,700.00; D. W. Wilson, 1,900.00; Albert Witts, 1,700.00; Wm. Wood, 1,600.00 .... 154,942 84

Special Constables, $25,063.74.

Arthur DeHaitre, 1,800.00; Richard Edmonds, 1,353.90; R. K. Fraser, 1,700.00; John Gagne, 1,900.00; Percy Gray, 1,700.00; Fred Hill, 1,700.00; J. J. McGregor, 909.84; M. H. Moore, 1,800.00; R. R. Moore, 1,600.00; Robert Reevely, 1,800.00; Matthew Side, 1,800.00; W. J. Thomlison, 1,700.00; D. B. Wagar, 1,700.00; William Warren, 1,800.00; Harry Wright, 1,800.00 .... 25,063 74

Drivers and Mechanics, $37,904.17.

M. S. Amey, 1,600.00; C. R. Armstrong, 1,300.00; W. W. Bibby, 1,200.00; H. C. Black, 1,300.00; E. G. Blood, 1,300.00; D. M. Bond, 1,800.00; Herbert Braney, 1,404.17; J. E. Cantwell, 1,600.00; A. E. Cook, 1,300.00; A. K. Cumming, 1,400.00; C. E. Dearborn, 1,400.00; A. V. Dymond, 1,300.00; Edward Hales, 1,600.00; B. F. Harper, 1,800.00; M. R. Hodgson, 1,200.00; W. C. Jones, 1,500.00; W. J. D. Kennedy, 1,500.00; J. H. Lindop, 1,400.00; H. B. Lindsay, 1,400.00; Lloyd Lonsdale, 1,600.00; L. E. Nix, 1,200.00; Ambrose Pearson, 1,500.00; D. H. Sarvis, 1,600.00; George Segar, 1,600.00; Clifford Sharp, 1,600.00; J. M. Thomas, 1,500.00 37,904 17

District Headquarters, Clerk Stenographers, $10,275.00.

Maretta Campbell, 975.00; Mary Gray, 975.00; Myrtle Hodgkins, 975.00; Alice Jones, 975.00; Isabelle Keehn, 825.00; Doris Kidney, 900.00; M. I. McCulloch, 975.00; Marjorie Miller, 825.00; Mary Pollock, 900.00; Aileen Thomas, 975.00; Bernice Tremeer, 975.00 .... 10,275 00

Temporary Salaries, Travelling Expenses and Disbursements ($4,595.23)

Sundry persons 4,595 23

District Disbursements ($152,658.29)

District No. 1—Headquarters, Windsor.—Comprising the border cities of Windsor, Walkerville, East Windsor, Sandwich, Riverside and the remainder of the County of Essex:		
Criminal disbursements	1,214 09	
L.C.A. disbursements	6,932 92	
	8,147 01	
Less costs recovered	2,036 73	
		6,110 28
District No. 2—Headquarters, London.—Comprising the Counties of Kent, Lambton, Middlesex, Elgin, Oxford, Brant, Norfolk and the Town of Tilbury:		
Criminal disbursements	13,086 44	
L.C.A. disbursements	2,557 71	
	15,644 15	
Less costs recovered	6,847 05	
		8,797 10
District No. 3—Headquarters, Hamilton.—Comprising the City of Hamilton, the remainder of the County of Wentworth and the County of Halton:		
Criminal disbursements	1,423 21	
L.C.A. disbursements	4,179 00	
	5,602 21	
Less costs recovered	634 35	
		4,967 86

Law Enforcement—Continued

Ontario Provincial Police, District Disbursements—Continued

District No. 4—Headquarters, Niagara Falls.—Comprising the Counties of Haldimand, Lincoln and Welland:		
Criminal disbursements	6,508 44	
L.C.A. disbursements	2,266 30	
	8,774 74	
Less costs recovered	3,076 66	
		5,698 08
District No. 5—Headquarters, Toronto.—Comprising the City of Toronto the remainder of the County of York, Peel County and the Townships of Scott, Uxbridge, Pickering, Beach, East Whitby, Brock, Thora and Whitby in the County of Ontario:		
Criminal disbursements	2,439 88	
L.C.A. disbursements	594 15	
	3,034 03	
Less costs recovered	1,437 97	
		1,596 06
District No. 6—Headquarters, Kitchener.—Comprising the Counties of Bruce, Perth, Grey, Wellington, Waterloo and Huron:		
Criminal disbursements	10,616 63	
L.C.A. disbursements	5,041 48	
	15,658 11	
Less costs recovered	7,099 73	
		8,558 38
District No. 7—Headquarters, Barrie.—Comprising the Counties of Simcoe, Dufferin, the Townships of Mara and Rama in the County of Ontario and the Districts of Muskoka and Parry Sound:		
Criminal disbursements	12,005 31	
L.C.A. disbursements	3,621 34	
	15,626 65	
Less costs recovered	5,010 76	
		10,615 89
District No. 8—Headquarters, Belleville.—Comprising the Counties of Victoria, Haliburton, Peterborough, Northumberland and Durham, Hastings, Lennox and Addington, Prince Edward and Frontenac:		
Criminal disbursements	12,072 78	
L.C.A. disbursements	3,205 63	
	15,278 41	
Less costs recovered	10,333 60	
		4,944 81
District No. 9—Headquarters, Ottawa.—Comrpsing the Counties of Renfrew, Lanark, Carleton, Grenville, Russell, Prescott, Glengarry, Leeds, Dundas and Stormont:		
Criminal disbursements	15,768 43	
L.C.A. disbursements	4,579 00	
	20,347 43	
Less costs recovered	8,810 13	
		11,537 30
District No. 10—Headquarters, Haileybury.—Comprising the Districts of Temiskaming, Cochrane and Nipissing and the northern portion of the District of Algoma extending from an imaginary line running parallel to the Canadian National Railway and twenty miles south of it and to include that portion of the Canadian National Railway in the District of Thunder Bay up to and including Grant:		
Criminal disbursements	18,035 96	
L.C.A. disbursements	3,396 75	
	21,432 71	
Less costs recovered	2,424 47	
		19,008 24

Law Enforcement—Continued

Ontario Provincial Police, District Disbursements—Continued

District No. 11—Headquarters, Sudbury.—Comprising the Districts of Sudbury, Manitoulin Island and the southern portion of the District of Algoma extending from an imaginary line running parallel to the Canadian National Railway and twenty miles south of it:

Criminal disbursements		15,047 75	
L.C.A. disbursements		3,333 87	
		18,381 62	
Less costs recovered		2,652 48	
			15,729 14

District No. 12—Headquarters, Port Arthur.—Comprising the Districts Kenora, Rainy River, Thunder Bay and Patricia:

Criminal disbursements		17,396 82	
L.C.A. disbursements		4,319 53	
		21,716 35	
Less costs recovered	1,869 58		
Refund, Department of Northern Development re Trans-Canada expenses	1,742 91		
		3,612 49	
			18,103 86

Motorcycle Patrol—Headquarters, Toronto:

Criminal disbursements		27,507 13	
Depreciation allowances on motorcycles		20,959 38	
		48,466 51	
Less costs recovered		11,475 22	
			36,991 29

Trans-Canada Highway Patrol:

Expenses paid by Headquarters		893 65	
Less: Refund by Department of Northern Development		893 65	
			Nil
			152,658 29

Travelling Expenses—Headquarters, $1,782.49.

V. A. S. Williams, 94.71; Alfred Cuddy, 84.25; W. C. Killing, 75.53; Arthur Moss, 242.35; E. T. Doyle, 1,007.93; F. E. Elliott, 154.62; Ephraim Zinkann, 40.42; W. H. Boyd, Acting Inspector of Automobiles re district cars, 82.68 .... 1,782 49

Insurance, $10,358.14.

Employers' Liability Assurance Corporation, Limited, accident insurance, Motorcycle Patrol		4,401 40	
Flaxton, Hueston & Company, accident insurance, Main Force		2,482 51	
James E. Dimock & Company:			
Automobile fleet insurance		1,638 15	
Motorcycle fleet insurance		2,128 31	
		10,650 37	
Less Refund Unearned Premium:			
Employers' Liability Corporation, Ltd.	129 65		
Flaxton, Hueston & Company	51 97		
James E. Dimock & Company	110 61		
		292 23	
			10,358 14

Medical expenses paid by Department in excess of insurance adjustments....... 1,874 78

Law Enforcement—Continued

Ontario Provincial Police, District Disbursements—Continued

Criminal Investigation Branch, $3,175.83.

Travelling expenses and disbursements of officers, C.I.B.	4,853 92	
Extradition expenses	680 66	
	5,534 58	
Less: Costs recovered	2,358 75	
		3,175 83

Automobiles, Supplies and Repairs, $14,433.98.

Acme Caretakers' Supply Co., garage accessories, 198.20; J. C. Adams & Co., Ltd., auto accessories, 12.25; Allatt Machine & Tool Co., auto parts, 9.32; Walter Andrews, Ltd., motorcycle accessories, 993.47; Auto Electric Service Co., Ltd., repairs and parts, 402.10; Automobile & Supply, Ltd., auto parts, 80.12; Barter's, Ltd., repairs, 5.55; Bear Equipment Co., repairs, 115.25; Bennet & Elliott, Ltd., auto accessories, 195.75; B. C. Berry & Co., repairs and parts, 40.20; The Big "A" Co., Ltd., garage accessories, 10.00; S. F. Bowser Co., Ltd., accessories, 11.70; British-American Oil Co., Ltd., gasoline and oil, 1,629.57; Bernard Cairns, Ltd., garage accessories, 19.45; Canadian Fairbanks-Morse Co., Ltd., auto accessories, 38.35; Canadian General Electric Co., Ltd., garage accessories, 5.35; Consolidated Plate Glass Company of Canada, Ltd., glass, 42.47; Cozens' Spring Service Co., Ltd., auto accessories, 36.56; Crystal Gasoline Co., oil, 32.30; Cutten & Foster, Ltd., accessories, 144.99; Domestic Brake Service, brake service, 214.07; Dunlop Tire & Rubber Goods Co., Ltd., tires and tubes, 105.98; Flexo Piston Ring Agency (C. J. Brasier), accessories, 6.60; Garage Supply Co., Ltd., auto accessories, 238.25; Goodyear Tire & Rubber Co. of Canada, Ltd., tires and tubes, 276.04; A. D. Gorrie & Co., Ltd., accessories, 38.36; George Green Welding Co., repairs, 239.50; Gutta Percha & Rubber, Ltd., tires and tubes, 392.52; Hart Battery Co., Ltd., accessories, 48.00; J. F. Hartz Co., Ltd., garage accessories, 7.50; Imperial Oil, Limited, gasoline and oil, 1,606.48; Kennedy & Menton, motorcycle accessories, 49.95; McColl-Frontenac Oil Co., Ltd., gasoline and oil, 2,365.26; McGee & Scully, repairs and parts, 841.50; J. C. McLaren Belting Co., Ltd., accessories and brake service, 17.42; McVey's Garage Supply Co., repairs and parts, 42.85; J. W. Madigin, repairs, 24.75; Motor Tool Specialty Co., garage accessories, 15.97; National Automotive Parts, Ltd., repairs and parts, 392.64; National Motors, Ltd., auto parts, 27.50; Ontario Automobile Co., Ltd., accessories, 27.26; Ontario Gasoline and Oils, Ltd., gasoline and oil, 916.90; Fred Powell Motors, Ltd., parts, 28.66; Provincial Tire Corporation, Ltd., tires, tubes, etc., 525.38; Pryal & Nye, accessories and repairs, 104.05; Reo Motor Sales Company of Toronto, Ltd., parts, 8.29; Rice Lewis & Son, Ltd., garage supplies, 52.29; F. E. Rosser, accessories and repairs, 10.00; See & Duggan Motors, Ltd., repairs and parts, 173.68; Simplex Piston Ring Sales Company of Ontario, accessories, 114.28; Snap-On Tools of Canada, Ltd., accessories, 15.75; Solar Products Co., garage accessories, 12.00; Spring Service, Ltd., repairs, 5.00; Supertest Petroleum Corporation, Ltd., gasoline, 117.24; Sutherland Plating, parts, 8.50; Swayze's (Artcraft Top & Trimming Co.), repairs, 24.10; Tiverton Tire Repair, tires and tubes, 47.80; Toronto Battery & Electric Co., Ltd., battery service and repairs, 254.15; Trelco, Ltd., garage accessories, 20.09; United Motors Service, Inc., accessories, 36.25; Wagner Electric Mfg. Company of Canada, Ltd., repairs and parts, 14.86; C. C. Wakefield & Co., Ltd., motor oil, 221.67; Wentworth Radio & Auto Supply Co., Ltd., accessories, 8.27; Wheel and Rim Company of Canada, Ltd., repairs, 29.43; Willys-Overland Sales Co., Ltd., automobiles and accessories, 1,630.80; Yellow Cab Company of Essex County, Ltd., Windsor, repairs, 11.82; W. H. Boyd, Acting Inspector of Automobiles, Headquarters' garage, disbursements, 1,009.74 .... 16,402 35

Less Repayments: Soldiers' Aid Commission, 545.08; London Guarantee & Accident Co., Ltd., 28.50; Trans-Canada Insurance Co., 465.00; Pilot Insurance Co., 13.82; Bunnell, Hitchon, Hendry, Ltd., 9.58; Dept. of Public Welfare, 113.25; Liquor Control Board of Ontario, 84.14; British American Assurance Co., 6.00; sale of used Headquarters' cars, 703.00 .... 1,968 37

14,433 98

Uniforms and Equipment, $17,457.09.

A. A. Allen & Co., Ltd., police caps, 201.44; J. & A. Aziz, sweaters, 100.00; Bernard Cairns, Ltd., badges, etc., 182.50; A. R. Clarke & Co., Ltd., caps, gauntlets, etc., 131.19; Classic Leather Wear, repairs, 32.65; Crown Tailoring Co., Ltd., police uniforms, 2,785.50; C. B. Dayfoot & Co., police boots, 333.30;

Law Enforcement—Continued

Ontario Provincial Police, District Disbursements—Continued

Uniforms and Equipment—Continued

J. Fowlie, mitts, holsters, leggings, etc., 149.60; J. R. Gaunt & Son (Can. Co., Ltd.), uniform buttons, etc., 297.50; Gutta Percha & Rubber, Ltd., police boots, 260.55; Hamilton Uniform Cap Co., uniform caps, 156.00; Lufkin Rule Company of Canada, Ltd., steel tapes and repairs, 74.54; Kahn Optical Co., Ltd., motorcycle goggles, 97.20; Muir Cap & Regalia, Ltd., uniform caps, 151.50; Rex Tailoring Co., Ltd., police uniforms, 9,261.53; Rice Lewis & Son, Ltd., ammunition and revolver repairs, 129.90; St. John Ambulance Association, First Aid lectures, etc., 72.10; Scythes & Co., Ltd., police slickers, 471.78; Robert Simpson Co., Ltd., uniform gloves, shirts, etc., 349.25; Spittal Bros., police coats, gauntlets, mitts and leggings, 823.00; Tower Canadian, Ltd., special police slickers, 103.68; Williams Shoe, Ltd., police boots, 1,339.03 .... 17,503 74

Less Repayments: Provincial Constable T. P. K. Robinson........ 46 65 — 17,457 09

Office Supplies and Equipment, $7,059.54.

Bank of Montreal (Grosvenor-Yonge), excise stamps, 1.00; Border Cities Star, subscription, 16.00; Burroughs Adding Machine of Canada, Ltd., maintenance service, 13.50; Canadian National Express Co., express charges, 293.91; Canadian National Telegraphs, telegrams, 100.07; Canadian Pacific Express Co., express charges, 219.55; Canadian Pacific Railway Co., freight charges, 2.84; Canadian Pacific Railway Telegraphs, telegrams, 99.15; Detective Publishing Co., subscription, 2.35; Globe Printing Co., subscriptions, 24.00; King's Printer, stationery and printing, 5,918.42; Mail and Empire, subscriptions, 18.00; Might Directories, Ltd., map, 8.50; K. & L. Motor Express, cartage, .75; Saturday Night, subscription, 5.00; Edward Tobin, newspaper subscriptions, 24.00; Toronto Railway & Steamboat Guide Co., Railway Guide subscription, 7.50; United Typewriter Co., Ltd., inspection service, 305.00........ 7,059 54

Miscellaneous Payments, $342.00.

T. H. Lennox, K.C., counsel fees........ 342 00

Total........	928,225 77
Less Refund: Dept. of Northern Development re salaries, Trans-Canada Highway patrol........	9,984 00
Law Enforcement........	**$918,241.77**

TORONTO AND YORK CROWN ATTORNEY'S OFFICE

Salaries ($22,725.00)

Name	Position	Period	Amount
Eric N. Armour	Crown Attorney	12 months	8,500 00
J. W. McFadden	Assistant Crown Attorney	12 "	4,600 00
W. Osmond Gibson	" " "	12 "	3,600 00
F. I. Malone	" " "	12 "	2,850 00
Loretta Walsh	Clerk	12 "	1,600 00
V. M. Foster	Clerk Stenographer, Group 1 ....(T)	12 "	975 00
Aubrey A. Wice	Office Boy	12 "	600 00

Contingencies ($4,934.89)

Temporary Services, $4,500.00.

Name	Position	Period	Amount
C. F. Moore	Assistant Crown Attorney	12 months	1,800 00
C. T. Snyder	" " "	12 "	2,700 00

Miscellaneous, $434.89.

G. Bellanger, copies of evidence, 12.00; Bell Telephone Co., tolls, 29.63; Burroughs & Co. (Eastern), Ltd., books, 16.00; Canada Law Book Co., Ltd., books, 31.00; J. G. Collinson, services reporting, 25.00; R. W. H. Hooper, services in library, 10.00; Kelly's Law Book Co., law books, 29.67; Sundries—car tickets, 1.96; express, 1.22; newspapers and periodicals, 22.75; postage, 198.05; telegrams, 24.08; petty disbursements, 33.53........ 434 89

Toronto and York Crown Attorney........ $27,659.89

ADMINISTRATION OF JUSTICE

Audit of Criminal Justice Accounts

Salaries ($10,875.00)

C. A. Fitch	Auditor	12 months	3,300 00
E. A. Mockler	Senior Clerk	12 "	2,000 00
Frank LeBrock	" "	12 "	1,900 00
A. Grace Haig	Clerk	12 "	1,125 00
M. Parkhill	Senior Clerk Stenographer	12 "	1,500 00
Dora J. Knight	Clerk Stenographer	12 "	1,050 00

Contingencies ($742.42)

Travelling Expenses, $247.60.

C. A. Fitch 247 60

Miscellaneous, $494.82.

Burroughs Adding Machine of Canada, Ltd., inspections, etc., 15.50; King's Printer, 413.17; United Typewriter Co., Ltd., inspections, 26.50. Sundries—newspapers and periodicals, 6.00; telegrams, 28.90; petty disbursements, 4.75 494 82

General Administration of Justice in Counties ($386,818.43)

Counties, $334,023.22.

Brant, 6,664.64; Bruce, 4,119.31; Carleton, 12,798.59; Dufferin, 1,766.40; Elgin 7,742.45; Essex, 19,122.93; Frontenac, 4,859.16; Grey, 7,170.08; Haldimand, 1,975.26; Halton, 4,764.29; Hamilton (Wentworth), 8,764.48; Hastings, 7,035.85; Huron, 4,383.45; Kent, 10,243.54; Lambton, 88.00; Lanark, 3,423.57; Leeds & Grenville, 6,286.13; Lennox and Addington, 3,452.53; Lincoln, 5,847.89; Middlesex, 12,957.00; Norfolk, 2,950.77; Northumberland and Durham, 8,815.09; Ontario, 6,062.52; Oxford, 4,805.62; Peel, 3,654.16; Perth, 3,282.28; Peterborough, 4,441.86; Prescott and Russell, 5,026.70; Prince Edward, 1,926.27; Renfrew, 3,856.28; Simcoe, 9,243.38; Stormont, Dundas and Glengarry, 44.20; Victoria, 7,002.00; Waterloo, 11,116.49; Welland, 9,859.93; Wellington, 3,796.60; Wentworth, 10,938.33; Toronto and York, 97,801.42; York, 5,933.77 .... 334,023 22

Crown Attorneys, Salaries in Lieu of Fees, $36,861.66.

J. S. Allan (Essex), 6,000.00; G. W. Ballard (Wentworth), 5,600.00; R. D. Evans (Dufferin), 1,400.00; J. G. Harkness (Stormont, Dundas and Glengarry), 3,230.00; A. M. Judd (Middlesex), 6,000.00; J. M. Kearns (Wellington), 4,200.00; W. E. Kelly (Norfolk), 4,050.00; J. C. Makins (Perth), 756.66; H. B. Morphy (Perth), 3,625.00; L. J. St. Pierre (Essex), 2,000.00 .... 36,861 66

Expenses re Prosecutions, $20,410.29.

M. Chertkoff, 128.72; F. Clitheroe, 89.15; Hands Studios, Ltd., 60.00; Dr. A. J. Kilgour, 3.00; Dr. J. R. McGeoch, 11.70; Dr. B. J. McGhie, 16.22; J. A. Mc-Gibbon, 100.00; Dr. R. C. Montgomery, 1.50; W. N. Tilley, 20,000.00 ...... 20,410 29

Total	391,295 17
Less Refund from Superannuation Fund re Sheriffs	4,476 74
	386,818 43

General Administration of Justice in Districts ($144,726.40)

Algoma:

T. J. Foster, D.C.C., attending court, 74.15; W. Grainger, crier, attending court, 30.00; King's Printer, 142.36; C. M. Macreath, treasurer, 18,236.27; accountable, 2,000.00; C. M. Macreath, sheriff, attending court, 365.00. Less outstanding Accountable Warrant, 1930-31, 452.22 .... 20,395 56

Cochrane:

King's Printer, 306.87; J. D. MacKay, treasurer, 17,963.75; accountable, 745.66; K. MacNab, court reporter, 1,409.90; W. L. Worrell, D.C.C., attending court, 32.00. Less outstanding Accountable Warrant, 1930-31, 200.00 .... 0,258 18

Kenora:

C. Appleton, D.C.C., attending court, 32.00; L. Campbell, court reporter, attending court, 150.00; H. P. Cooke, Crown Attorney, services, 2,120.00; King's Printer, 51.50; Robt. Nairn, treasurer, 9,238.62; accountable, 1,050.10. Less outstanding Accountable Warrant, 1930-31, 2,000.00 .... 10,642 22

Administration of Justice—Continued

Administration of Justice in the Districts—Continued

Manitoulin: King's Printer, 13.68; W. F. McRae, treasurer, 5,534.80; accountable, 500.00; C. C. Platt, D.C.C., attending court, 4.00	6,052 48
Muskoka: King's Printer, 38.91; C. E. Lount, treasurer, 6,060.29; accountable, 500.00; C. S. Salmon, D.C.C., attending, court 20.15	6,619 35
Nipissing: T. J. Bourke, D.C.C., attending court, 12.42; T. J. Bourke, treasurer, 10,245.25; J. Frizell, court reporter, attending court, 1,200.00; King's Printer, 113.11	11,570 78
Parry Sound: J. E. Armstrong, sheriff, attending court, 10.00; A. Greer, crier, attending court, 6.00; W. L. Haight, treasurer, 4,724.57; accountable, 200.00; W. L. Haight, Crown Attorney, services, 2,000.00; T. W. Keating, constable, attending court, 5.00; King's Printer, 51.90; F. Tasker, D.C.C., attending court, 8.35. Less outstanding Accountable Warrant, 1930-31, 315.00	6,690 82
Rainy River: W. A. Baker, treasurer, 10,465.20; accountable, 580.59; King's Printer, 4.73; W. P. Pilkey, D.C.C., attending court, 45.83. Less outstanding Accountable Warrant, 1930-31, 4,000.00	7,096 35
Sudbury: A. H. Beath, D.C.C., attending court, 32.00; A. Irving, treasurer, 16,026.75; accountable, 133.49; King's Printer, 109.18; A. Pomeroy, court reporter, 1,642.06; E. D. Wilkins, Crown Attorney, services, 5,000.00. Less outstanding Accountable Warrant, 1930-31, 2,364.62	20,578 86
Temiskaming: J. Gould, court reporter, services and expenses, 1,271.95; J. Gould, treasurer, 15,303.62; accountable, 500.00; King's Printer, 346.81; T. J. Meagher, D.C.C., attending court, 64.75; W. Shane, constable, attending court, 2.50	17,489 63
Thunder Bay: G. Cottingham, services, fireman, 618.34; N. Edmeston, treasurer, 17,840.70; N. Edmeston, sheriff, attending court, 90.00; King's Printer, 48.71; K. Munroe, D.C.C., attending court, 40.00. Less Judge McKay, refund, 32.00	18,605 75

Total	145,999 98
Less Refund from Superannuation Fund re Sheriffs	1,273 58
	144,726 40

POLICE MAGISTRATES

Salaries, Travelling and Office Expenses ($127,987.03)

Salaries, $114,392.75.

Name	Place	Period		Amount
J. A. Connell	Algonquin	1	month	125 00
J. T. Kirkland	Almonte	12	"	500 00
Walter E. Wiggins	Bancroft	12	"	1,200 00
Compton Jeffs	Barrie	12	"	1,000 00
W. C. Mikel	Belleville	12	"	1,700 00
N. H. Peterson	Bruce Mines	12	"	1,800 00
Jos. G. Myers	Bracebridge	12	"	600 00
W. T. Malkin	Bridgeburg	12	"	800 00
Geo. A. Wright	Brockville	12	"	100 00
John J. Wilson	Burk's Falls	12	"	1,700 00
G. R. Boucher	Carp	12	"	2,000 00
Thos. H. Wolfe	Chapleau	12	"	2,500 00
S. B. Arnold	Chatham	12	"	1,000 00
W. H. Floyd	Cobourg	12	"	1,600 00
E. R. Tucker	Cochrane	12	"	3,250 00
Howard Gover	Coldwater	12	"	1,000 00
W. A. Hogg	Collingwood	12	"	600 00
Thos. Stoddard	Copper Cliff	12	"	3,000 00
John C. Milligan	Cornwall	12	"	1,500 00
R. H. Pronger	Dryden	12	"	1,200 00
J. C. Massie	Dunnville	12	"	3,500 00
Wm. Blyth	Dunvegan	12	"	1,500 00

Administration of Justice—Continued

Police Magistrates—Salaries, Travelling and Office Expenses—Continued

Salaries—Continued

Name	Place	Period		Amount
Ed. Arthurs	Espanola	12	months	1,900 00
Henry L. Cruso	Fort Frances	12	"	2,000 00
Wm. Palling	Fort Willaim	12	"	800 00
Samuel C. Young	Fort William	12	"	2,000 00
J. R. Blake	Galt	12	"	1,600 00
C. A. Reid	Goderich	12	"	2,500 00
F. W. Major	Gore Bay	12	"	1,800 00
F. Watt	Guelph	12	"	1,000 00
S. Atkinson	Haileybury	12	"	3,600 00
J. F. Vance	Hamilton	12	"	1,800 00
H. W. Lawlor	Hawkesbury	12	"	1,600 00
J. L. Patterson	Ingersoll	12	"	1,600 00
A. Hellyer	Kenilworth	12	"	1,000 00
J. A. Kinney	Kenora	12	"	1,200 00
J. W. Bradshaw	Kingston	12	"	1,400 00
J. J. A. Weir	Kitchener	12	"	1,400 00
Burton L. MacLean	Lindsay	1	"	150 00
C. W. Hawkshaw	Lucan	12	"	2,500 00
Robt. R. Casement	Madoc	12	"	1,200 00
D. Davidson	Mimico Beach	12	"	1,500 00
H. D. Payne	Mimico Beach	12	"	1,300 00
G. A. Jordan	Minden	12	"	1,800 00
Frank Cook	Midland	12	"	400 00
Mark P. Graham	Napanee	12	"	1,200 00
John L. Loyd	Northbrook	12	"	600 00
C. S. McGaughey	North Bay	12	"	2,000 00
W. E. McIlveen	Oakville	12	"	1,800 00
Hugh Falconer	Orangeville	12	"	1,200 00
Dan McCaughrin	Orillia	12	"	1,300 00
John F. McKinley	Ottawa	1	"	172 60
E. C. Spereman	Owen Sound	12	"	1,500 00
Fred T. Zapfe	Parkhill	12	"	1,500 00
J. D. Broughton	Parry Sound	12	"	1,920 00
Wm. Stewart	Pelee Island	12	"	300 00
A. E. Calnan	Picton	12	"	1,500 00
W. W. O'Brien	Port Arthur	12	"	1,200 00
G. E. Copeland	Penetanguishene	12	"	500 00
O. A. Langley	Peterborough	12	"	1,300 00
H. E. Holland	Pineridge	12	"	600 00
S. T. Chown	Renfrew	12	"	2,500 00
W. A. Smith	Sandwich	12	"	2,500 00
C. S. Woodrow	Sarnia	12	"	1,500 00
Andrew Elliott	Sault Ste. Marie	12	"	600 00
R. E. Gunton	Simcoe	12	"	2,300 00
Jos. A. Cousineau	Sturgeon Falls	5	"	412 00
J. A. Makins	Stratford	12	"	1,000 00
J. H. Campbell	St. Catharines	12	"	1,000 00
C. F. Maxwell	St. Thomas	12	"	1,250 00
J. S. McKessock	Sudbury	12	"	2,100 00
Jas. E. Finlay	Tory Hill { 6 mos. 1931. $ 613.15; 12 " 1932, 1,200.00 }			1,813 15
A. B. Carscallen	Wallaceburg	12	"	1,000 00
F. W. Walker	Walkerton	12	"	2,000 00
John McCartney	Wiarton	12	"	1,000 00
John McCormick	Winchester	12	"	1,500 00
Sundry Magistrates, office assistance				5,100 00

Travelling and Office Expenses, $13,302.06.

C. A. Adams, 45.68; S. B. Arnold, 32.41; Ed. Arthurs, 128.63; S. Atkinson, 1,331.70; G. R. Boucher, 151.40; J. W. Bradshaw, 9.00; J. D. Broughton, 61.52; A. B. Carscallen, 5.00; R. R. Casement, 168.03; S. T. Chown, 190.27; J. A. Cousineau, 58.40; H. L. Cruso, 161.40; D. Davidson, 785.56; J. H. Davidson, 31.22; R. T. Dynes, 26.40; H. Falconer, 25.56; J. E. Finlay, 180.56; W. H. Floyd, 639.85; W. L. Fortier, 133.50; R. E. Gunton, 18.00; A. Hellyer, 163.98; W. A. Hogg, 75.67; H. E. Holland, 54.50; C. Jeffs, 97.25; G. A. Jordan, 20.45; J. T. Kirkland, 84.11; O. A. Langley, 100.21; J. L. Lloyd, 104.55; D. McCaughrin, 232.00; J. McCormick, 140.77; C. S. McGaughey, 488.70; J. S.

Administration of Justice—Continued

Police Magistrates—Salaries, Travelling and Office Expenses—Continued

Travelling and Office Expenses—Continued

McKessock, 13.30; F. W. Major, 1,082.66; J. A. Makins, 9.00; J. C. Massie, 1,147.62; C. F. Maxwell, 90.03; J. G. Myers, 85.60; W. Falling, 5.20; J. L. Paterson, 666.14; N. H. Peterson, 727.89; C. A. Reid, 141.70; J. H. Sampson, 22.30; E. C. Sanders, 15.44; W. J. Smith, 29.50; E. C. Spereman, 251.80; T. Stoddart, 286.65; E. R. Tucker, 906.11; F. W. Walker, 544.10; J. J. A. Weir, 79.00; W. E. Wiggins, 51.11; J. J. Wilson, 277.15; L. H. Wilson, 76.22; T. H. Wolfe, 410.21; C. S. Woodrow, 45.17; S. C. Young, 585.88; F. T. Zapfe, 6.00.... 13,302 06

Miscellaneous, $292.22.

Bain & Cubit, Ltd., reports, 35.60; S. R. Hart Co., Ltd., books, etc., 25.33; King's Printer, 231.29.... 292 22

Revision of Voters' List ($2,496.17)

Algoma, 65.35; Brant, 42.94; Bruce, 182.03; Carleton, 19.30; Cochrane, 40.65; Dufferin, 14.40; Elgin, 9.40; Essex, 118.60; Frontenac, 35.00; Grey, 34.40; Hastings, 279.30; Huron, 123.75; Kent, 61.78; Lambton, 60.90; Lanark, 80.16; Leeds and Grenville, 41.90; Lennox and Addington, 158.20; Lincoln, 31.20; Manitoulin, 17.92; Middlesex, 53.60; Muskoka, 28.20; Nipissing, 5.65; Northumberland and Durham, 29.00; Ontario, 39.68; Oxford, 35.00; Parry Sound, 12.10; Peel, 37.00; Perth, 157.47; Peterborough, 50.00; Prince Edward, 21.93; Renfrew, 59.70; Simcoe, 151.60; Stormont, Dundas and Glengarry, 59.10; Temiskaming, 17.20; Thunder Bay, 14.42; Victoria and Haliburton, 48.93; Welland, 117.20; Wellington, 35.00; Wentworth, 19.90; York, 86.31.... 2,496 17

ADMINISTRATION OF JUSTICE IN DISTRICTS

Algoma ($18,208.26)

Salaries, $10,886.72.

Name	Office	Period	Amount
C. M. Macreath	Sheriff	12 months	1,000 00
C. M. Macreath	Treasurer	12 "	400 00
W. G. Atkin	Clerk of the Peace and District Attorney	12 "	400 00
T. G. Foster	Clerk of the District Court	12 "	600 00
Robt. Milton Hearst	Gaoler	12 "	1,800 00
Mrs. M. A. Hearst	Matron	12 "	300 00
Dr. S. E. Fleming	Gaol Surgeon	12 "	300 00
James Thompson	Turnkey	12 "	1,200 00
Wm. Johnson	"	8 "	834 52
Sundry Engineers, Caretakers, etc.			4,052 20

Fuel, Light, Water and Contingencies, $7,321.54.

C. M. Macreath, Treasurer, 7,315.14; King's Printer, 6.40.... 7,321 54

Cochrane ($5,314.62)

Salaries, $1,400.00.

Name	Office	Period	Amount
J. D. Mackay	Sheriff	12 months	750 00
S. A. Caldbick	Clerk of the Peace	12 "	250 00
J. D. Mackay	District Treasurer	12 "	400 00

Fuel, Light and Water, $3,914.62.

J. D. Mackay, Treasurer.... 3,914 62

Kenora ($17,378.28)

Salaries, $11,405.93.

Name	Office	Period	Amount
L. D. MacCallum	Sheriff	12 months	1,000 00
E. Appleton	Registrar and Clerk of the District Court	12 "	700 00
R. Nairn	District Treasurer	12 "	400 00
Edwin Walter Cox	Gaoler	12 "	1,500 00
Maud Frances Cox	Matron	12 "	300 00
Dr. W. J. Gunne	Gaol Surgeon	12 "	200 00
Harry R. Warner	Turnkey	12 "	1,400 00
Sundry Engineers, Caretakers, etc.			5,905 93

Fuel, Light and Water, $5,972.35.

R. Nairn, Treasurer.... 5,972 35

Administration of Justice—Continued

Administration of Justice in the Districts—Continued

Manitoulin ($7,444.31)

Salaries, $4,721.66.

Name	Position	Period		Amount
J. H. Fell	Sheriff	12	months	950 00
W. F. McRae	Clerk of the Peace and District Attorney	12	"	250 00
C. C. Platt	Registrar of Deeds and Master of Titles	12	"	600 00
C. C. Platt	Clerk of the District Court and Surrogate Court	12	"	850 00
W. F. McRae	Treasurer	12	"	300 00
John W. Griffith	Gaoler	12	"	1,200 00
Mrs. Hilda E. E. Griffith	Matron	12	"	300 00
Dr. F. A. Strain	Gaol Surgeon	10	"	166 66
Sundry Engineers, Caretakers, etc.				105 00

Fuel, Light and Water, $2,547.65.

W. F. McRae, Treasurer	2,547 65

Allowance for Rent ($175.00)

W. F. McRae, Treasurer	175 00

Muskoka ($4,685.89)

Salaries, $3,700.00.

Name	Position	Period		Amount
Joseph C. Myers	Sheriff	12	months	750 00
Thomas Johnson	Clerk of the Peace and District Attorney	12	"	250 00
Charles S. Salmon	Clerk of the District Court	12	"	450 00
Chas. E. Lount	Treasurer	12	"	400 00
Duncan McDonald	Gaoler	12	"	1,400 00
Alice McDonald	Matron	12	"	300 00
Dr. P. B. McGibbon	Gaol Surgeon	12	"	150 00

Fuel, Light and Water, $985.89.

Chas. E. Lount, Treasurer	985 89

Nipissing ($18,017.56)

Salaries, $10,858.38.

Name	Position	Period		Amount
W. S. Wagar	Sheriff	3	months	200 00
Robert Y. Angus	"	5⅔	"	382 79
T. E. McKee	Acting Sheriff	3⅓	"	217 21
"	Clerk of the Peace and District Attorney	12	"	250 00
T. J. Bourke	Clerk of the District Court	12	"	450 00
"	Treasurer	12	"	400 00
E. Turner	Gaoler	12	"	1,800 00
A. E. Ranney	Gaol Surgeon	12	"	300 00
W. Rayner	Turnkey and Caretaker	12	"	1,460 00
Sundry Engineers, Caretakers, etc.				5,398 38

Fuel, Light, Water, etc., $6,959.18.

T. J. Bourke, Treasurer, 6,954.77; King's Printer, 4.41	6,959 18

Allowance for Rent ($200.00)

T. E. McKee, Treasurer	200 00

Parry Sound ($9,525.35)

Salaries, $5,725.50.

Name	Position	Period		Amount
J. E. Armstrong	Sheriff	12	months	750 00
F. Tasker	Clerk of the District Court	12	"	450 00
W. L. Haight	Treasurer	12	"	400 00
Thos. Keating	Gaoler	12	"	1,400 00
Mrs. Thos. Keating	Matron	12	"	300 00
M. H. Limbert	Gaol Surgeon	12	"	150 00
Wm. J. Tait	Turnkey	12	"	1,200 00
Sundry Engineers, Caretakers, etc.				1,075 50

Fuel, Light and Water, $3,799.85.

W. L. Haight, Treasurer	3,799 85

Administration of Justice—Continued

Administration of Justice in the Districts—Continued

Rainy River ($9,310.22)

Salaries, $7,065.33.

Name	Position	Period		Amount
W. A. Baker	Sheriff	9	months	562 50
Alex. Thompson	"	1	"	62 50
N. L. Croome	Acting Sheriff	2	"	125 00
"	Clerk of the Peace and District Attorney	12	"	250 00
"	Acting Treasurer	3	"	100 00
W. H. Pilkey	Clerk of the District Court	12	"	600 00
W. A. Baker	Treasurer	9	"	300 00
John E. King	Gaoler	12	"	1,600 00
Mrs. Margaret King	Matron	12	"	300 00
John Miller	Turnkey	12	"	1,300 00
Robt. Moore	Gaol Surgeon	10	"	83 33
Sundry Engineers, Caretakers, etc.				1,782 00

Fuel, Light and Water, $2,244.89.

W. A. Baker, Treasurer	2,244 89

Sudbury ($31,187.83)

Salaries, $16,203.19.

Name	Position	Period		Amount
Alexander Irving	Sheriff	11	months	687 50
A. H. Beath	Clerk of the District Court	12	"	450 00
Alexander Irving	District Treasurer	11	"	366 67
Arthur J. Manley	Sheriff	1	"	62 50
"	Treasurer	1	"	33 33
W. O'Leary	Gaoler	12	"	1,900 00
Mrs. W. O'Leary	Matron	12	"	300 00
Dr. W. C. Morrison	Gaol Surgeon	12	"	500 00
Chas. Shelswell		12	"	1,400 00
Richard Cornthwaithe	Turnkey	12	"	1,400 00
Leonard Marchant	"	12	"	1,400 00
John R. Warlow	"	$6^1/_6$	"	723 34
Sundry Engineers, Caretakers, etc.				6,979 85

Fuel, Light and Water, $14,984.64.

Arthur J. Manley, Treasurer	14,984 64

Temiskaming ($23,960.13)

Salaries, $12,653.00.

Name	Position	Period		Amount
Geo. Caldbick	Sheriff	12	months	1,000 00
F. L. Smiley	Clerk of the Peace	12	"	250 00
T. J. Meagher	Clerk of the District Court	12	"	450 00
Jay Gould	Treasurer	12	"	300 00
John L. Maltby	Gaoler	12	"	1,800 00
James Anderson	Turnkey	12	"	1,400 00
Charles W. Austin	"	12	"	1,400 00
Mrs. Cora L. Terrill	Matron	12	"	300 00
Dr. Walter C. Arnold	Gaol Surgeon	12	"	300 00
W. T. Joy	Caretaker	12	"	1,400 00
H. S. Burton	Turnkey	12	"	1,300 00
Sundry Engineers, Caretakers, etc.				2,753 00

Fuel, Light and Water, $11,307.13.

Jay Gould, Treasurer	11,307 13

Thunder Bay ($24,785.79)

Salaries, $14,643.66.

Name	Position	Period		Amount
Newton Edmeston	Sheriff	12	months	1,000 00
Keith Munro	Clerk of the District Court	12	"	450 00
W. F. Langworthy	Clerk of the Peace and District Attorney	12	"	250 00
Newton Edmeston	Treasurer	12	"	400 00
G. F. Lasseter	Gaoler	12	"	2,000 00
Mrs. Violet Lasseter	Matron	12	"	350 00
Dr. J. A. Crozier	Gaol Surgeon	12	"	250 00
C. M. York	Turnkey	12	"	1,460 00
Colin M. Smith	"	12	"	1,300 00
Sundry Engineers, Caretakers, etc.				7,183 66

Administration of Justice—Continued

Administration of Justice in the Districts—Continued

Fuel, Light and Water, $10,142.13.

Newton Edmeston, Treasurer 10,142 13

Provisional County of Haliburton ($200.00)

Delbert C. Brown	Registrar of Deeds		200 00

Administration of Justice $843,663.69

INSPECTION OF LEGAL OFFICES

(Including Registry Offices and Division Courts)

Salaries ($22,000.00)

W. W. Denison	Inspector	12 months	5,000 00
W. W. Ellis	Assistant Inspector	12 "	3,300 00
H. A. Locke	" "	12 "	2,700 00
W. A. James	Head Audit Clerk	12 "	2,850 00
H. R. Polson	Assistant Inspector	12 "	2,300 00
M. Irish	Senior Clerk	12 "	1,800 00
M. E. Tracey	Senior Clerk Stenographer	12 "	1,500 00
R. B. Bailey	Clerk Stenographer	12 "	1,050 00
M. Kearney	Secretarial Stenographer	12 "	1,500 00

Printing, Stationery and Contingencies ($7,926.82)

Travelling Expenses, $6,190.99.

W. W. Denison, 1,669.40; car allowance, 500.00; W. W. Ellis, 896.65; W. A. James, 1,744.09; H. A. Locke, 892.45; H. R. Polson, 488.40 .... 6,190 99

Miscellaneous, $1,735.83.

King's Printer, 1,206.55; United Typewriter Co., Ltd., inspections, 45.27. Sundries—car tickets, 10.00; cartage, .50; express, 17.80; newspapers and periodicals, 27.80; postage, 400.00; telegrams, 27.91 .... 1,735 83

Fidelity Bonds for Division Court Officers ($1,808.90)

Armstrong, DeWitt & Crossin, Ltd., 346.00; The Canada Surety Co., 303.15; Jas. E. Dimock & Co., 164.50; London Guarantee & Accident Co., Ltd., 319.00; Medland & Son, 317.00; Moore & Tew, 359.25 .... 1,808 90

Typewriters, Office Equipment and Contingencies for Judicial Officers etc. ($1,978.28)

Circuit Guide, copies of guide, 24.00; Fort Frances Publishing Co., printing, 17.50; Gore Bay Recorder, stationery supplies, 19.50; King's Printer, 1,842.98; Miner Publishing Co., index cases, 8.50; Sundries—express, 21.80; postage, 44.00 .... 1,978 28

Inspection of Legal Offices $33,714.00

LAND TITLES OFFICE

Salaries ($30,676.33)

C. R. Deacon	Master of Titles	12 months	4,600 00
W. J. Lander	Deputy Master of Titles	12 "	3,000 00
W. F. Young	Senior Clerk	12 "	2,000 00
S. Mercer	" "	12 "	1,900 00
G. G. Y. Willis	" "	12 "	1,700 00
J. M. Martin	Clerk	12 "	1,800 00
B. C. Durrant	"	12 "	1,600 00
E. Pollard	"	12 "	1,600 00
A. A. Crawford	"	12 "	1,600 00
M. M. Kell	"	1⅓ "	176 33
R. G. Cowling	"	12 "	1,600 00
S. A. Mason	"	12 "	1,600 00
A. W. Knapp	"	12 "	1,600 00
C. B. McCool	"	12 "	1,500 00
J. W. Harper	"	12 "	1,500 00
C. E. Clarke	Senior Clerk Stenographer	12 "	1,600 00
J. C. Perrins	" " "	12 "	1,300 00

Land Titles Office—Continued

Contingencies ($2,625.48)

Temporary Services, $1,599.96.

T. N. Poole	Senior Clerk	12 months	1,599 96

Miscellaneous, $1,025.52.

Burroughs & Co., Ltd., binding, 12.50; King's Printer, 949.95; Might Directories, Ltd., maps, 12.50; United Typewriter Co., Ltd., inspections, 25.57. Sundries—postage, 25.00 .... 1,025 52

Land Titles Office.... $33,301.81

LOCAL MASTERS OF TITLES

Salaries and Office Expenses

Sault Ste. Marie ($3,511.00)

Salaries, $3,511.00.

V. MacNamara	Local Master of Titles	12 months	2,500 00
Muriel Patterson	Clerk Stenographer, Group 2	12 "	975 00
Jewell Foster	Clerk Stenographer	(T) ½ "	36 00

Haileybury ($7,257.35)

Salaries, $7,050.00.

L. H. Ferguson	Local Master of Titles	(T) 12 months	4,200 00
Laura McKay	Deputy Local Master	12 "	1,200 00
Alice Beaton	Clerk	12 "	900 00
Margaret Ferguson	Stenographer	(T) 12 "	750 00

Office Expenses, $207.35.

United Typewriter Co., Ltd., repairs, etc., 9.75. Sundries—express, .60; postage, 197.00 .... 207 35

North Bay ($5,978.94)

Salaries, $5,850.00.

Gordon R. Brady	Master of Titles and Registrar	12 months	3,000 00
Edith Robertson	Clerk, Group 2	12 "	1,200 00
Mary Thackney	Clerk	12 "	900 00
Mary C. Stewart	Clerk Stenographer	12 "	750 00

Office Expenses, $128.94.

Bell Telephone Co., rental, 45.00; tolls, .22; Cochrane-Dunlop Hardware Co., Ltd., supplies, 2.35; Commercial Press, printing, 5.72; F. S. Fosdick, stationery, 1.45; J. A. Newsom, Ltd., stationery, 3.10; J. W. Richardson, bulbs, 1.95. Sundries—express, 3.90; postage, 65.25 .... 128 94

Cochrane ($7,457.54)

Salaries, $7,125.00.

J. A. Clermont	Local Master of Titles	12 months	4,500 00
Ada Caswell	Clerk Stenographer, Group 2	12 "	975 00
Nellie Le Barron	Clerk Typist, " 2	12 "	900 00
Blanche A. Levesque	Clerk, " 3	12 "	750 00

Office Expenses, $332.54.

J. E. Bester, repairs to typewriter, 10.00; Sundries—express, 5.25; postage, 317.29 .... 332 54

Forms, Copying and Contingencies ($2,395.81)

City Typewriter Co., inspections, etc., 21.00; Cliffe Printing Co., books, 26.75; Copeland-Chatterson, Ltd., books, 25.34; Department of Lands and Forests, mining forms, 12.50; General Office Equipment Co., Ltd., repairs, 19.95; C. W. Jarvis, services, copying abstracts, 136.20; King's Printer, 1,982.67; J. H. Tutty, services, copying abstracts, 86.25; Underwood Elliott Fisher Co., ribbons, 11.70; Sundries—express, 28.45; freight, 4.45; postage, 11.00; petty disbursements, 29.55 .... 2,395 81

Registration of Patents under R.S.O., Cap. 158, Section 158, including Allowance for Postage and Stationery ($2,795.00)

G. R. Brady, 163.25; M. Brunette, 385.75; J. A. Clermont, 629.50; E. A. Cunningham, 337.00; W. G. Dunn, 122.50; L. H. Ferguson, 593.75; W. L. Haight, 83.50; C. W. Jarvis, 139.00; W. J. Keating, 125.75; C. E. Lount, 38.00; V. McNamara, 155.00; C. C. Platt, 12.50; B. Wilson, 9.50 .... 2,795.00

Local Masters of Titles.... $29,395.64

Miscellaneous Services

ONTARIO RAILWAY AND MUNICIPAL BOARD

Salaries ($21,136.86)

Name	Position		Period		Amount
C. R. McKeown	Chairman		6	months	3,499 92
A. B. Ingram	Vice-Chairman	(T)	6	"	1,249 92
J. A. Ellis	Member of the Board and Director of Municipal Affairs		6	"	2,999 88
F. Dagger	Supervisor of Telephone Service		6	"	1,999 92
H. C. Small	Secretary		6	"	1,800 00
J. A. McDonald	Inspector of Telephone Service		6	"	1,275 00
A. C. McKee	Clerk, Group 1		6	"	799 92
E. Crossland	Inspector of Street Railway Operations		6	"	799 92
M. Sanderson	Senior Clerk Stenographer		6	"	750 00
B. Skelton	" " "		6	"	750 00
F. K. Balshaw	Clerk Stenographer		6	"	600 00
A. Campbell	" "		6	"	600 00
George A. Brown	Traffic Expert		6	"	450 00
W. J. Crawford	Municipal Auditor		6	"	1,200 00
J. J. Hoolihan	Senior Clerk		6	"	999 96
G. D. Kennedy	Clerk	(T)	6	"	799 98
A. Becker	Clerk Stenographer, Group 1		6	"	562 44

Contingencies ($3,324.18)

Temporary Services, $24.00.

Gertrude Taylor......Stenographer.............................. 8 days 24 00

Travelling Expenses, $1,091.87.

E. Crossland, 61.20; F. Dagger, 243.85; J. A. Ellis, 231.12; A. B. Ingram, 190.70; J. A. McDonald, 58.65; C. R. McKeown, 224.85; G. A. Thompson, 81.50....... 1,091 87

Miscellaneous, $2,208.31.

Burroughs Adding Machine of Canada, Ltd., repairs, 1.82; Canadian Electric Railway Association, membership fee, 10.00; Canadian Independent Telephone Association, annual dues, 15.00; Canada Law Book Co., Ltd., reports, 28.00; Carswell Co., Ltd., law reports, 50.50; Coo & Thompson, services reporting, 160.00; E. V. Deverall, services and expenses as consulting engineer, 15.00; King's Printer, 1,854.21; United Typewriter Co., Ltd., inspections, etc., 46.00. Sundries—newspapers and periodicals, 25.10; telegrams, 2.68.......................... 2,208 31

DRAINAGE TRIALS ACT

Salaries ($4,000.00)

Name	Position	Period		Amount
Geo. F. Henderson	Referee	12	months	3,500 00
L. M. Sager	Stenographer	12	"	500 00

Contingencies ($548.55)

G. F. Henderson, travelling expenses, 492.30; L. M. Sager, travelling expenses, 16.25; Helen Ely, services reporting, 40.00.. 548 55

PUBLIC TRUSTEE'S OFFICE

Salaries ($46,500.00)

Name	Position	Period		Amount
A. N. Middleton	Public Trustee	12	months	5,700 00
H. S. Jones	Trust Officer	12	"	3,450 00
R. G. Mainer	Accountant	12	"	3,300 00
G. F. Adams	Assistant Trust Officer	12	"	1,800 00
I. N. Draper	Investigator of Estates	12	"	2,200 00
P. Maginnis	" "	12	"	1,900 00
Bertram G. Williams	" "	12	"	1,800 00
P. M. Puley	Principal Clerk	12	"	2,300 00
J. S. Jordan	Senior Clerk	12	"	1,900 00
C. G. Hindle	Clerk	12	"	1,600 00
J. R. Thomas	Clerk Stenographer	12	"	825 00
M. G. Butler	" "	12	"	1,200 00
E. A. Gelinas	" "	12	"	975 00
H. Wixon	Senior Clerk Stenographer	12	"	1,500 00
M. E. Thurgerland	" " "	12	"	1,500 00
Mary H. Carr	" " "	12	"	1,500 00

Public Trustee's Office—Continued

Salaries—Continued

M. A. Moore	Clerk Stenographer	12 months	1,200 00
E. G. Trewick	" "	12 "	1,200 00
M. J. Williamson	" "	12 "	975 00
E. M. Dawson	" "	12 "	1,050 00
G. G. Thompson	" "	12 "	975 00
D. Wright	Filing Clerk	12 "	1,050 00
E. Simpson	" "	12 "	975 00
David Koznets	Office Boy	12 "	600 00
G. Tower Fergusson	Advisory Committee	7 "	966 35
W. C. McBrien	" "	12 "	1,500 00
G. R. Sweeny	" "	12 "	1,500 00
Baptist L. Johnston	"	4⅓ "	533 65
Sidney F. Cook	Office Boy	12 "	525 00

Auditor's Fees ($3,000.00)

Clarkson, Gordon, Dilworth, Guilfoyle & Nash, audit services.......... 3,000 00

Contingencies ($15,892.60)

Temporary Services, $5,632.87.

H. S. Clark	Assistant Trust Officer, Group 2	12 months	1,699 92
D. G. Cunningham	Clerk, " 3	1 "	43 33
E. T. Godwin	Assistant Trust Officer, " 2	12 "	1,599 96
Beatrice M. Hitchcock	Clerk Stenographer	½ "	39 66
R. McCrea	Investigator of Estates, " 2	12 "	1,500 00
H. F. White	Clerk, " 3	12 "	750 00

Travelling Expenses, $5,320.47.

G. F. Adams, 2.00; H. S. Clark, 61.44; I. N. Draper, 2,250.39; E. T. Godwin, 24.14; P. Maginnis, 505.80; A. N. Middleton, 49.85; H. F. White, 21.15; B. G. Williams, 2,405.70.......... 5,320 47

Miscellaneous, $4,939.26.

Bell Telephone Co., tolls, 99.12; Burroughs Adding Machine of Canada, Ltd., repairs, etc., 17.30; J. H. Carnegie, law stamps, 75.00; Denison, Foster & Williams, legal fees re Poole Estate, 155.40; Dominion Bank, rental safety deposit box, etc., 260.00; I. N. Draper, allowance re insurance on auto, 50.00; C. M. Garvey & Co., legal services, 16.66; General Indemnity Corporation of America, premiums, 15.00; J. M. Greer, legal services re M. and W. Wells, 10.00; King's Printer, 2,267.05; St. Paul Fire & Marine Insurance Co., premiums, 11.20; Todd Sales Co., repairs to check writing machine, 32.00; Turner & Fraser, legal fees re Poole Estate, 97.00; United Typewriter Co., Ltd., inspections, etc., 190.90; B. G. Williams, allowance re insurance on auto, 50.00; Willis, Faber & Co., insurance premiums, 90.00; Wilson, Pike & Stewart, legal fees, re Tyhurst Estate, 137.19. Sundries—car tickets, 90.00; express, 13.20; postage, 1,200.00; telegrams, 38.81; petty disbursements, 23.43.......... 4,939 26

Total Expenditure, Public Trustee's Office	65,392 60
Less refunded by Public Trustee	65,392 60

FIRE MARSHAL'S OFFICE

Salaries ($41,152.53)

E. P. Heaton	Fire Marshal (T)	12 months	2,500 00
Geo. F. Lewis	Deputy Fire Marshal	12 "	3,600 00
E. E. Starr	Secretarial Stenographer	12 "	1,600 00
Ruby Welbourne	Clerk Stenographer	12 "	1,500 00
E. D. Jordan	Fire Investigator	12 "	2,000 00
D. H. Saville	" "	12 "	2,000 00
J. W. Pointon	" "	12 "	2,000 00
F. G. Baker	" "	12 "	1,900 00
C. H. Cowan	" "	12 "	1,800 00
A. Burnett	" "	12 "	1,800 00
Arthur R. Stell	" "	12 "	1,800 00
Edward Desjardins	" "	12 "	1,800 00
Chas. E. Foley-Bennett	" "	12 "	1,683 87

Fire Marshal's Office—Continued

Salaries—Continued

Ina Smith	Clerk	12 months	1,600 00
F. McDonald	"	12 "	1,300 00
A. McDonald	"	9 "	843 66
Edith Pym	Junior Clerk	12 "	900 00
J. E. Ritchie	Fire Prevention Engineer	12 "	3,000 00
W. H. Halstead	" " Inspector	12 "	1,500 00
L. J. Bishop	Lightning Rod Inspector	12 "	2,000 00
W. L. Clairmont	" " "	12 "	2,000 00
M. J. Billinghurst	Clerk	12 "	1,200 00
Jessie M. Lacey	"	12 "	825 00

Division of Fire Investigation ($25,436.76)

Temporary Services, $2,017.00.

Audrey Deyell	Clerk Typist,	Group 2	3 months	201 92
J. Paton	Clerk Stenographer,	" 2	12 "	825 00
Helen Perkins	Filing Clerk,	" 1	12 "	900 00
Arthur F. Skelley	Office Boy		2⅛ "	90 08

Travelling Expenses, $12,663.50.

W. Atkin, 35.00; F. G. Baker, 1,046.03; C. F. Bennett, 61.05; A. B. Boyd, 12.85; A. Burnett, 746.78; F. Clitheroe, 723.17; C. H. Cowan, 1,304.15; E. Desjardins, 1,845.38; C. E. Foley-Bennett, 881.02; W. H. Halsted, 243.38; E. P. Heaton, 1,211.82; I. A. Humphries, 226.00; E. D. Jordan, 1,292.61; R. J. Marsh, 24.80; Expenses of Operators, Ontario Commissioner of Police, 571.79; S. E. Parker, 84.15; J. W. Pointon, 703.15; E. B. Reid, 73.80; D. H. Saville, 1,011.06; A. R. Stell, 564.91 .... 12,663 50

Services re Investigations, $5,381.82.

J. W. Aikens, 32.10; D. Armstrong, 24.60; N. R. Butcher, 117.60; F. Clitheroe, 2,865.39; F. W. Farncomb, 227.00; Fire Underwriters Investigation and Information Bureau, 166.66; J. A. Gunton, 50.00; R. J. Marsh, 202.50; H. Oliver, 114.00; A. Pomeroy, 401.00; E. B. Reid, 1,180.97 .... 5,381 82

Legal Fees and Expenses, $828.43.

M. R. Allison, 15.15; W. M. Charlton, 15.00; B. C. Donnan, 31.68; W. S. Haney, 48.60; I. A. Humphries, 500.00; J. M. Kearns, 20.00; G. L. Mitchell, 52.00; C. F. Moore, 25.00; A. Seguin, 60.00; E. D. Wilkins, 61.00 .... 828 43

Miscellaneous, $4,546.01.

J. W. Bald, photos, 28.50; J. Bell, fees, 10.00; Bell Telephone Co., tolls, 10.25; R. Browne, court officer fees, 10.00; Burroughs Adding Machine of Canada, Ltd., inspections, etc., 22.60; Campbell's Studio, Ltd., photos, 14.00; Can. Credit Men's Association, services, 21.55; Canada Law Book Co., Ltd., books, 18.00; A. Carty News Service, photos, 15.00; A. Caver, services, 17.75; B. Chadwick, stenographic services, 16.57; J. Clark, constable fees, 43.00; Joan Clark, stenographic services, 10.00; K. Coates, stenographic services, 13.00; Department of Highways, garage account, 420.07; Department of Public Works, rental of office, 500.00; E. Desjardins, photo supplies, rental of office, 76.05; A. Donoghue, copies of evidence, 10.70; Doreen Downs, stenographic services, 24.15; Employers Liability Association, insurance premium, 78.75; B. Evans-Jackson, copies of evidence, 13.03; W. H. Halsted, rental of garage, 52.50; H. Kaufman, services as watchman, 10.00; C. Kelso, stenographic services, 23.80; A. Kent & Sons, Ltd., badges, 10.00; King's Printer, 1,239.36; Lyons Letter Service, stenographic service, 11.00; Mackay & Mackay, plans, 70.00; M. D. Macphail, services as valuator, 25.00; C. W. Martin, stenographic services, 10.00; P. Maxwell, constable fees, 17.68; W. J. Michels, stenographic services, 16.25; Might Directories, Ltd., map, 15.00; Miller's Furniture Exchange, cabinet, 12.75; C. A. Mott, plans, 10.00; B. Mullins, copies of evidence, 51.83; T. B. Murray, services watchman, 20.00; T. O'Brien, stenographic services, 52.26; Ontario Motion Picture Bureau, photos, 51.00; Pringle & Booth, photos, 62.83; E. Reaume, services, 13.30; J. P. Reid, services as watchman, 20.00; L. J. Rogers, analyses, 140.00; M. Sauve, serving summons, 12.50; E. Skelton, copies of evidence, 19.70; W. H. Spray, photos, 32.50; Cora Stack, stenographic services, 25.10; Sundry persons, interpreters' fees, 104.00; Sundry persons, witness fees, 503.78; M. Tichborne, stenographic services, 35.47; J. S. Watkinson, stenographic services, 36.30; E. Welsh, copies of evidence, 21.90; A. S. Whyte, photos, 76.25. Sundries—car tickets, 90.00; customs, 21.28; express, 50.20; newspapers and periodicals, 31.00; telegrams, 57.93; petty disbursements, 120.57 .... 4,546 01

Fire Marshal's Office—Continued

Division of Fire Prevention ($5,185.56)

Temporary Services, $480.00.

A. E. Caldwell..........Fire Prevention Officer.................. 4 months 480 00

Travelling Expenses, $1,134.88.

L. J. Bishop, 192.21; W. L. Clairmont, 138.02; G. F. Lewis, 316.65; J. E. Ritchie, 488.00.............. 1,134 88

Advertising, $509.00.

Animal Life, 84.00; Dominion Association of Fire Chiefs, 100.00; Fire Fighters' Federation, 100.00; Firemen's Association, Province of Ontario, 50.00; Labour News, 50.00; Niagara District Firemen's Association, 25.00; Temiskaming Firemen's Association, 100.00.............. 509 00

Miscellaneous, $3,061.68.

Addressograph-Multigraph, Ltd., inspections, etc., 18.19; Association of Can. Fire Marshals, assessment of fire insurance premiums, 176.39; B. Cairns, Ltd., dies, 13.50; Dept. of Public Works, rental of office, 1,000.00; Dominion Association of Fire Chiefs, subscription, 10.00; R. G. Dun & Co., Ltd., subscription to Mercantile Agency, 125.00; Farm Fire Prevention, copies, 45.00; Field, Love & House, Ltd., inspections, etc., 44.00; Fire Prevention Hand Book Co., copies, 50.00; W. S. Haney, legal fees, 20.00; King's Printer, 907.05; National Fire Protection Co., subscription, copies of circular, 30.00; Sundry persons, witness fees, 36.50; Sundry Fire Chiefs, fees for reporting fires, 466.00; Typewriter Sales & Service, Ltd., inspections, etc., 13.50. Sundries—car tickets, 45.00; customs, .53; newspapers and periodicals, 25.50; petty disbursements, 35.52.... 3,061 68

Division of Lightning Rod Act ($3,727.59)

Travelling Expenses, $1,076.83.

F. G. Baker, 54.35; L. J. Bishop, 511.66; W. L. Clairmont, 483.57; J. E. Ritchie, 27.25.............. 1,076 83

Auto Repairs and Supplies, $1,078.42.

L. J. Bishop, 52.50; W. L. Clairmont, 60.00; Dept. of Highways, 833.72; G. C. Edwards, 132.20.............. 1,078 42

Miscellaneous, $1,572.34.

Bishop Electric Co., flash light, 2.15; Dept. of Public Works, office rent, 1,250.00; T. Eaton Co., Ltd., flash lights, etc., 15.25; Field, Love & House, inspections, etc., 14.00; D. Gestetner Co., Ltd., stencils, etc., 24.30; King's Printer, 266.64 1,572 34

Miscellaneous..........$104,512.03

STATUTORY

Minister's Salary (see page D8).............. 10,000 00
Salaries not otherwise provided for (see page D 8).............. 1,125 00

Allowances to County Judges ($71,849.77)

R.S.O. 1927, Cap. 90, Sec. 9

His Honour Judge—Boles, 1,000.00; Campbell, 1,000.00; Carpenter, 1,000.00; Caron, 1,000.00; Clement, 1,000.00; Constantineau, 1,000.00; Costello (Dundas), 1,000.00; Costello (Huron), 1,000.00; Coughlin, 1,000.00; Currey, 750.00; Daly, 1,000.00; Denton, 1,600.00; Deroche, 1,000.00; Dowler, 1,000.00; Field, 1,600.00; Grout, 500.00; Justin, 719.45; Hall, 1,000.00; Hardy, 1,000.00; Hartman, 1,000.00; Hayward, 1,000.00; Hewson, 249.00; Hopkins, 332.00; Holmes, 1,000.00; Huycke, 1,000.00; Ingram, 1,000.00; Jackson, 1,600.00; Kenny, 1,000.00; Killoran, 1,000.00; Lavell, 1,000.00; Leask, 1,000.00; Lee, 1,600.00; Livingstone, 1,000.00; Madden, 1,000.00; Mahaffy, 1,000.00; Mahon, 1,000.00; Morley, 750.00; Moon, 1,000.00; Mulcahy, 1,000.00; Munro, 1,000.00; McFadden, 1,000.00; McKay, 1,000.00; McKinnon, 1,000.00; McLean, 1,000.00; McLennan, 1,000.00; Owens, 1,083.33; O'Brien, 1,000.00; O'Connor, 1,000.00; O'Connell, 1,600.00; Parker, 1,600.00; Proulx, 1,000.00; Robb, 833.33; Ross, 1,000.00; Ruddy, 1,000.00; Scott, 1,000.00; Stone, 1,000.00; Sutherland, 166.00; Swayze, 1,000.00; Taylor, 1,000.00; Thompson (Hamilton), 1,000.00; Thompson (Whitby), 1,000.00; Tudhope, 1,000.00; Tytler, 1,600.00; Valin, 1,000.00; Wallace, 1,000.00; Wearing, 1,000.00; West, 666.66; Widdifield, 1,600.00; Wills, 1,000.00; Willson, 1,000.00; Wismer, 1,000.00.............. 71,849 77

Statutory—Continued

Sheriffs, to make up Incomes to $1,800.00 per annum ($1,250.45)

J. H. Ebbs, 126.64; H. Endacott, 487.69; Wm. McGhee, 301.12; R. J. Patterson, 310.00; S. W. Wright, 25.00 .... 1,250 45

Registrars, to make up Incomes to $1,800.00 per annum ($8,911.08)

Jas. Armour, 631.15; H. C. Bowland, 542.15; F. S. Broder, 821.59; D. C. Brown, 1,282.23; Mrs. E. A. Cunningham, 68.58; J. A. Gamble, 204.70; R. H. Hodgson, 717.30; W. S. Johnston, 766.40; H. McCullough, 736.85; J. A. McRae, 335.56; W. P. Pilkey, 1930—481.45; 1931—221.99; G. D. Rice, 846.05; Jas. Tucker, 275.25; J. H. Tully, 638.73; Geo. Weeks, 341.10 .... 8,911 08

Special Investigations, R.S.O. 1927, Chap. 25, Sec. 17 ($8,529.30)

Sundry Persons: Services and disbursements in connection with the Administration of Justice 8,529 30

PROBATION OFFICERS ($30,329.73)

Salaries ($29,114.38)

Name	Position	Period		Amount
Judge Mott	Chief Probation Officer	12	months	1,200 00
O. St. G. Freer	Chief Assistant Probation Officer	12	"	2,700 00
J. A. Netterfield	Deputy Probation Officer	12	"	2,100 00
J. B. Grimshaw	Assistant Probation Officer	12	"	2,000 00
A. Browne	" " "	12	"	1,900 00
J. A. Hyland	" " "	12	"	1,900 00
Miss M. Macdonald	" " "	12	"	1,800 00
A. V. Reddick	" " "	12	"	1,700 00
Jno. Young	" " "	12	"	1,700 00
John R. McKnight	" " "	12	"	1,500 00
J. F. McKinley	" " "	12	"	1,200 00
Geo. F. Jelfs	" " "	12	"	1,000 00
Ernest J. Leith	" " "	12	"	1,064 38
Dr. George Anderson	Psychiatrist	12	"	400 00
H. Bowen	Intelligence Officer	12	"	1,500 00
B. Howell	Investigator	12	"	1,400 00
Isabel Hetherington	Office Assistant	12	"	1,050 00
G. Smith	" "	12	"	1,050 00
H. Robinson	Clerk Stenographer	12	"	975 00
Violet Richardson	" "	12	"	975 00

Travelling Expenses, $926.46.

Judge H. S. Mott, 379.87; G. S. Postlethwaite, 6.35; A. V. Reddick, 500.00 (car allowance); J. Young, 40.24 .... 926 46

Miscellaneous, $288.89.

Grand & Toy, Ltd., stationery supplies, 8.00; King's Printer, 280.89 .... 288 89

ELECTIONS ($16,425.01)

By-Elections, 1931-32, $15,432.64.

Wellington South, 6,435.44; York West, 8,997.20 .... 15,432 64

Miscellaneous, $160.82.

King's Printer, 156.07; Sundries—express, 3.17; telegrams, 1.58 .... 160 82

R.S.O. 1927, Chap. 8, Section 6, $831.55.

Dept. of Highways, rental of car, 31.55; A. M. Dymond, services as chief election officer, 800.00 .... 831 55

ADMINISTRATION OF JUSTICE EXPENSE ACT, R.S.O., CHAP. 126, SECTION 13 ($56,541.89)

W. G. Atkin, 50.00; W. L. Breckell, 28.05; Carswell Co., Ltd., 166.34; E. R. C. Clarkson & Son, 437.31; Clarkson, Gordon, Dilworth, Guilfoyle & Nash, 250.00; F. Clitheroe, 14.90; Commercial Reproducing Co., Ltd., 618.59; Dr. C. M. Crawford, 28.75; Disbursing Clerk, Secretary of State of Washington, D.C., 322.89; F. Donnelly, 150.00; J. M. Donohue, 14.60; W. C. Eddis & Co., 3,397.50; Edwards, Morgan & Co., 9,163.01; Dr. J. H. Erb, 30.00; W. B. Fenwick, 19.25; Dr. E. R. Frankish, 692.20; A. M. Goode, 53.10; R. H. Greer, 9,000.00; Dr. J. T. Grieve, 28.45; W. L. Haight, 194.75; Fred Page, Higgins & Co., 10,080.00; Hogg & Hogg, 70.30; W. C. Inch, 150.00; C. Kelso, 32.75; A. C. Kingstone, 292.50; F. J. Kinzinger,

Statutory—Continued

Administration of Justice Expense Act—Continued

80.00; J. P. Langley & Co., 800.00; T. H. Lennox, 5,474.40; D. L. McCarthy, 1,500.00; Dr. B. T. McGhie, 74.78; J. A. McKay, 41.80; J. C. McRuer, 988.73; N. A. MacColl, 225.00; J. K. MacKay, 1,628.05; C. R. Magone, 293.47; J. Megan, 22.69; C. F. Moore, 1,670.00; Murray, Hollman & Lockwood, 101.89; E. Nield, 736.30; A. G. Newall & Co., 255.50; R. E. Park, 15.00; L. J. Rogers, 65.00; R. W. Ralfe, 566.13; Royal Canadian Mounted Police, 110.00; K. F. Sadleir, 18.50; J. Sedgwick, 130.51; Silverblatt Organization, Shorthand Reporters, 63.88; N. Sommerville & Co., 350.00; E. C. Spearman, 13.00; O. B. Stanton, 210.00; R. N. Stockhall, 11.10; V. C. Thomas, 50.00; W. N. Tilley, 5,000.00; W. H. Williams, 442.85; M. Yewchuck, 10.00; M. P. Zall, 250.00; petty disbursements, 58.07 .... 56,541 89

ONTARIO MUNICIPAL BOARD, 22 GEORGE V, CHAPTER 27, SECTION 38 ($24,865.99)

Salaries, $22,012.98.

Name	Position	Period	Amount
C. R. McKeown, K.C.	Chairman	6 months	4,000 08
J. A. Ellis	Vice-Chairman	6 "	3,500 12
H. L. Cummings	Member	6 "	500 00
A. B. Ingram	Expert Advisor on Railway Matters (T)	6 "	624 96
F. Dagger	Supervisor, Telephone Systems	6 "	2,000 08
H. C. Small	Secretary	6 "	1,800 00
J. A. McDonald	Inspector, Telephone Systems	6 "	1,275 00
A. C. McKee	Clerk	6 "	800 08
E. Crossland	Street Railway Inspector	6 "	800 08
M. Sanderson	Senior Clerk Stenographer	6 "	750 00
B. Skelton	" " "	6 "	750 00
A. Campbell	Clerk Stenographer	6 "	600 00
W. M. K. Balshaw	" "	6 "	600 00
George A. Brown	Traffic Expert	6 "	450 00
W. J. Crawford	Provincial Municipal Auditor	6 "	1,200 00
J. J. Hoolihan	Senior Clerk	6 "	1,000 04
G. D. Kennedy	Clerk (T)	6 "	799 98
A. Becker	Clerk Stenographer	6 "	562 56

Contingencies ($2,853.01)

Travelling Expenses, $1,444.10.

M. E. Coo, 20.60; E. A. Crossland, 86.45; F. Dagger, 483.10; J. A. Ellis, 357.40; A. B. Ingram, 9.30; J. A. McDonald, 127.95; C. R. McKeown, 282.85; G. A. Thompson, 76.45 .... 1,444 10

Miscellaneous, $1,408.91.

Canadian Independent Telephone Association, fees, 15.00; Carswell Co., Ltd., reports, 60.50; Coo & Thompson, services, 234.60; E. V. Deverall, services, 46.90; King's Printer, 936.70; United Tupewriter Co., Ltd., repairs, etc., 74.98. Sundries—freight, .30; newspapers and periodicals, 25.00; telegrams, 5.73; petty disbursements, 9.20 .... 1,408 91

R.S.O. 1927, CHAP. 22, SECTION 5 ($356,890.35)

City of Toronto—Refund of fines with interest:

Fine imposed re Æmelius Jarvis	60,000 00		
Interest	19,882 19		
Costs of Trial and Appeal	4,473 92		
		84,356 11	
Fine imposed re Solloway Mills & Co	250,000 00		
Interest	22,534 24		
		272,534 24	
			356,890 35

R.S.O. 1927, CHAP. 25, SEC. 17 ($4,500.00)

Trusts & Guarantee Co., Ltd., Hubbs & Hubbs & Rex vs. J. C. Hamilton 4,500 00

THE SECURITIES ACT, 1931, CHAP. 48, SECTION 10 ($13,074.83)

Better Business Bureau, services, re F. B. Robins & Co., 1,000.00; Clarkson, Gordon, Dilworth, Guilfoyle, and Nash, fee re Can. Terminal Systems, Ltd., Willison, Neely Corp., Ltd., et al, 12,074.83 .... 13,074 83

Statutory—Continued

R.S.O. 1927, CHAP. 22, SECTION 5 ($2,927.81)

Receiver General of Canada, Rex vs. Irwin, 2,246.25; interest, 681.56............. 2,927 81

Statutory...$607,221.21

SPECIAL WARRANTS

GRANT TO ONTARIO PROVINCIAL COMMAND, CANADIAN LEGION, B.E.S.L. TO ASSIST EX-SERVICE MEN RE UNEMPLOYMENT ($6,000.00)

Ontario Provincial Command, Canadian Legion, B.E.S.L........................ 6,000 00

Special Warrants...................................$6,000.00

Total..$2,946,176 56
Less Salary Assessment... 32,594 91

Total Expenditure, Department of Attorney-General..............$2,913,581 65

PART E

DEPARTMENT OF INSURANCE

FISCAL YEAR, 1931-32

GENERAL INDEX AT BACK OF BOOK

PART E—INSURANCE DEPARTMENT

Statement of Expenditure Showing Amounts Expended, Unexpended and Overexpended for the Twelve Months Ended October 31st, 1932

Department of Insurance	Page	Estimates	Expended			Un-expended	Over-expended	Treasury Board Minute
			Ordinary	Capital	Total Ordinary and Capital			
		$ c.	$ c.	$ c.	$ c.	$ c.	$ c.	$ c.
Salaries	3	49,525 00	46,625 00		46,625 00	2,900 00		
Contingencies	3	12,000 00	11,714 52		11,714 52	285 48		
Printing Annual Reports, etc	3	6,500 00	7,113 34		7,113 34		613 34	800 00
Grant to Association of Superintendents of Insurance	3	100 00	100 00		100 00			
Supply Bill	..	68,125 00	65,552 86		65,552 86	3,185 48	613 34	
Total	..		65,552 86		65,552 86			
Less Salary Assessment	..		1,015 35		1,015 35			
Insurance Department	..		64,537 51		64,537 51			

DEPARTMENT OF INSURANCE

Salaries ($46,625.00)

Name	Position	Period		Amount
R. Leighton Foster	Superintendent of Insurance and Registrar of Loan Corporations	12	months	6,000 00
H. B. Armstrong	Deputy Superintendent of Insurance	12	"	3,150 00
Frank Sanderson	Consulting Actuary (T)	12	"	3,600 00
W. K. Colin Campbell	Chief Inspector	12	"	4,000 00
Oscar B. Henry	Inspector	12	"	2,700 00
William A. Cork	"	12	"	2,700 00
H. C. Ness	"	12	"	2,300 00
Jno. Edwards	Assistant Inspector	12	"	2,000 00
Joel G. Gibbons	" "	12	"	2,000 00
Geo. N. Sheppard	" "	12	"	1,900 00
C. C. Johnson	Agency Officer	12	"	2,400 00
W. J. Smelt	Secretary	12	"	2,000 00
Edith N. Beswick	Secretarial Stenographer	12	"	1,500 00
Jessie W. McGlashan	Senior Clerk Stenographer	12	"	1,500 00
Jean A. Elliott	" " "	12	"	1,300 00
J. S. Laird	Clerk Stenographer, Group 1	12	"	1,050 00
M. Thomson	" " " 1	12	"	1,050 00
Edna Hinch	Clerk, Group 1	12	"	1,500 00
William Rhodes	" " 3	12	"	900 00
Elsie F. Thomson	Filing Clerk, Group 1	12	"	1,200 00
Z. Cliffe	" " " 1	12	"	1,200 00
Joseph A. Gill	Office Boy	12	"	675 00

Contingencies ($11,714.52)

Temporary Services, $2,923.35.

Name	Position	Period		Amount
M. B. Babcock	Filing Clerk, Group 2	2¼	months	134 65
Elsie M. Gates	Clerk Typist, Group 2	1	"	57 69
Alice E. Gazey	" " " 2	1	"	57 69
Irene M. Hall	" " " 2	2	"	187 50
Percy L. Marshment	Office Boy	11¼	"	493 03
Margaret D. Peace	Clerk Stenographer, Group 1	3	"	237 50
Margaret Reeder	Clerk Typist, Group 2	12	"	750 00
J. Scholes	" " " 2	2	"	122 60
A. P. Smith	Clerk Stenographer, Group 2	12	"	825 00
Verna M. Williams	Clerk Typist, Group 2	1	"	57 69

Travelling Expenses, $4,107.38.

H. B. Armstrong, 28.20; W. K. C. Campbell, 270.95; W. A. Cork, 258.45; J. Edwards, 326.99; R. L. Foster, 1,276.50; J. G. Gibbons, 214.35; O. B. Henry, 440.35; C. C. Johnson, 561.79; H. C. Ness, 287.50; F. Sanderson, 50.50; G. N. Sheppard, 389.80; W. J. Smelt, 2.00 .... 4,107 38

Miscellaneous, $4,683.79.

Addressograph-Multigraph of Canada, Ltd., inspections, etc., 19.39; D. S. Bowlby, legal services, 67.00; Burroughs Adding Machine of Canada, Ltd., 132.27; Can. Law Book Co. Ltd., books and reports, 46.00; F. W. Cowper, legal fees, 18.50; Dept. of Pub. Printing and Stationery, Ottawa, reports, etc., 41.05; Ediphone Co. Ltd., inspections, etc., 67.14; T. G. Evans, legal services, 21.80; Grand & Toy, Ltd., chairs, 12.90; B. L. Johnson, fees, etc., re Current Market Values, 200.00; King's Printer, 1,339.57; G. M. Orr, attending board meetings, 440.00; K. M. Pringle, services valuating and appraising securities, 600.00; Recording & Statistical Corporation, Ltd., consolidation of statement re fire insurance premiums and losses, 750.00; Stone & Cox, Ltd., books, 155.00; United Typewriter Co. Ltd., inspections, etc., 210.55; J. E. Whitmeyer, witness fees, 13.25; Sundries—car tickets, 50.00; express, 1.85; newspapers and periodicals, 125.94; telegrams, 308.26; petty disbursements, 63.32 .... 4,683 79

Grant to Association of Superintendents of Insurance of the Provinces of Canada, Toward Expense of Annual Conference ($100.00)

Association of Superintendents of Insurance 100 00

Printing Annual Reports, etc., ($7,113.34)

King's Printer 7,113 34

Total	65,552 86
Less Salary Assessment	1,015 35
Total Expenditure, Department of Insurance	**$64,537 51**

DEPARTMENT

OF

EDUCATION

FISCAL YEAR, 1931-32

TABLE OF CONTENTS

GENERAL INDEX AT BACK OF BOOK

PART F—DEPARTMENT OF EDUCATION

Statement of Expenditure Showing Amounts Expended, Unexpended and Overexpended for the Twelve Months Ended October 31st, 1932

Department of Education	Page	Estimates	Expended			Un-expended	Over-expended	Treasury Board Minute
			Ordinary	Capital	Total Ordinary and Capital			
		$ c.	$ c.	$ c.	$ c.	$ c.	$ c.	$ c.
Main Office:								
Salaries	16	89,625 00	75,621 37	....	75,621 37	14,003 63	....	....
Contingencies	16	10,000 00	9,028 24	....	9,028 24	971 76	....	....
Extra Services	..	3,000 00	....	....	....	3,000 00	....	....
Main Office	..	102,625 00	84,649 61	....	84,649 61	17,975 39	....	....
Public and Separate School Education:								
Grants [illegible] [illegible]s,								
[illegible] and Separate Schools	17	2,757,000 00	3,486,322 74	....	3,486,322 74	....	729,322 74	750,000 00
Assisted Public and Separate Schools	19	110,000 00	108,647 68	....	108,647 68	1,352 32	....	....
Special Grants,								
Ragged Rapids and Swift Rapids Schools	..	500 00	....	....	....	500 00	....	....
School at Cameron Falls	..	1,000 00	....	....	....	1,000 00	....	....
Special Grant to School at [illegible]te Fish Falls	19	500 00	500 00	....	500 00	....	....	....
Tarentorus [illegible]ip School Board	20	500 00	319 82	....	319 82	180 18	....	....
Rural and Urban Schools [illegible] by [illegible] Crown Property	..	2,500 00	....	....	....	2,500 00	....	....
Rural School [illegible]s	20	25,000 00	24,997 01	....	24,997 01	2 99	....	....
Public, Separate and Continuation Schools, Cadet Corps	20	12,500 00	8,563 00	....	8,563 00	3,937 00	....	....
Kindergarten Schools	20	13,000 00	13,277 22	....	13,277 22	....	277 22	500 00
Night Schools	21	6,500 00	5,853 37	....	5,853 37	646 63	....	....
[illegible] [illegible] Schools	21	65,000 00	42,708 82	....	42,708 82	22,291 18	....	....
Agricultural and [illegible] [illegible] Grants to School Boards, [illegible]s and [illegible]s	21	110,000 00	193,132 86	....	193,132 86	....	83,132 86	84,000 00
Industrial Arts, Manual Training and [illegible] Science Boards and [illegible]s	22	45,000 00	87,107 60	....	87,107 60	....	42,107 60	42,550 00
Correspondence [illegible], etc.	22	25,000 00	22,285 09	....	22,285 09	2,714 91	....	....
Continuation Schools	22	192,000 00	210,836 17	....	210,836 17	....	18,836 17	20,000 00
Fifth [illegible]s	24	50,000 00	58,288 15	....	58,288 15	....	8,288 15	8,625 00

Associations:								
Teachers	24	12,000 00	8,175 56	....	8,175 56	3,824 44	....	....
Ontario Educati[illegible]al	25	5,000 00	3,500 00	....	3,500 00	1,500 00	....	....
Ontario Educational Trustees' Section	25	8,000 00	4,000 00	....	4,000 00	4,000 00	....	....
[illegible]n Trustees	25	500 00	250 00	....	250 00	250 00	....	....
Canadian Educational	..	200 00	....	....	....	200 00	....	....
[illegible] Council of Education	25	2,400 00	2,400 00	....	2,400 00	....	....	....
Ontario [illegible] of [illegible] and School	25	2,000 00	2,000 00	....	2,000 00	....	....	....
Grant to Frontier College	25	7,500 00	7,500 00	....	7,500 00	....	....	....
Grant to Canadian Bureau for the Advancement of Music	25	1,000 00	1,000 00	....	1,000 00	....	....	....
Spring [illegible] Summer Schools	25	55,000 00	37,756 66	....	37,756 66	17,243 34	....	....
League of the Empire Expenses	25	500 00	230 67	....	230 67	269 33	....	....
Art Department [illegible] Expenses	25	7,300 00	8,372 43	....	8,372 43	....	1,072 43	1,175 00
To encourage courses in Music	26	20,000 00	27,372 50	....	27,372 50	....	7,372 50	7,485 00
Medical and Dental [illegible]	26	15,000 00	14,830 00	....	14,830 00	170 00	....	....
[illegible] in Schools	..	1,000 00	....	....	....	1,000 00	....	....
Public and Separate School Education	..	3,553,400 00	4,380,227 35	....	4,380,227 35	63,582 32	890,409 67	....
Inspection of Schools:								
Salaries (Inside Staff)	26	75,175 00	72,427 28	....	72,427 28	2,747 72	....	....
Public School Inspection	27	295,000 00	283,358 00	....	283,358 00	11,642 00	....	....
District Public Schools, Salaries	28	56,200 00	53,341 34	....	53,341 34	2,858 66	....	....
Separate Schools, Salaries	28	72,600 00	71,600 00	....	71,600 00	1,000 00	....	....
Travelling and Moving Expenses, Contingencies, etc.	29	100,000 00	98,633 50	....	98,633 50	1,366 50	....	....
Inspection of Indian Schools	29	3,500 00	2,525 78	....	2,525 78	974 22	....	....
Aux[illegible]iary Classes	29	21,000 00	52,395 46	....	52,395 46	....	31,395 46	32,075 00
Inspection of Schools	..	623,475 00	634,281 36	....	634,281 36	20,589 10	31,395 46	....
Departmental Examinations:								
Salaries	30	45,575 00	42,679 16	....	42,679 16	2,895 84	....	....
Services and Travelling Expenses	30	222,000 00	212,736 03	....	212,736 03	9,263 97	....	....
Assistants	30	40,000 00	40,785 00	....	40,785 00	....	785 00	1,000 00
Contingencies, etc	31	18,500 00	17,043 48	....	17,043 48	1,456 52	....	....
Extra Services	..	1,000 00	....	....	....	1,000 00	....	....
Extra Services Professional and Supervising Boards	31	7,750 00	7,650 00	....	7,650 00	100 00	....	....
Departmental Examinations	..	334,825 00	320,893 67	....	320,893 67	14,716 33	785 00	....
Less Fees and Appeals	..	....	175,164 36	....	175,164 36	175,164 36	....	....
Departmental Examinations	..	334,825 00	145,729 31	....	145,729 31	189,880 69	785 00	....

PART F—DEPARTMENT OF EDUCATION—Continued

Statement of Expenditure Showing Amounts Expended, Unexpended and Overexpended for the Twelve Months Ended October 31st, 1932

Department of Education	Page	Estimates	Expended			Un-expended	Over-expended	Treasury Board Minute
			Ordinary	Capital	Total Ordinary and Capital			
		$ c.	$ c.	$ c.	$ c.	$ c.	$ c.	$ c.
Text Books:								
Salaries	31	6,400 00	6,400 00	....	6,400 00	....	....	....
Preparation of Text Books	31	15,000 00	14,992 49	....	14,992 49	7 51	....	....
Subventions to Publishers	31	55,000 00	45,528 83	....	45,528 83	9,471 17	....	....
Text Books	..	76,400 00	66,921 32	....	66,921 32	9,478 68	....	....
General:								
Redemption of Debentures	32	2,000 00	....	130 78	130 78	1,869 22	....	....
Grant to Soldiers' Hostel, Bon Air	32	1,500 00	1,200 00	....	1,200 00	300 00	....	....
General	..	3,500 00	1,200 00	130 78	1,330 78	2,169 22	....	....
Training Schools:								
Salaries	32	6,200 00	6,200 00	....	6,200 00	....	....	....
Travelling, Moving Expenses and Contingencies	32	1,000 00	391 45	....	391 45	608 55	....	....
Grants to Teachers engaged in Model School Training at Hamilton, etc	32	60,000 00	73,850 00	....	73,850 00	....	13,850 00	15,000 00
Caretakers in Model Schools used for Training Teachers	32	1,700 00	1,680 00	....	1,680 00	20 00	....	....
Lecturers, courses for training first class Teachers	32	800 00	60 00	....	60 00	740 00	....	....
Temporary Teachers, Normal and Model Schools	32	7,000 00	4,053 98	....	4,053 98	2,946 02	....	....
Moving Expenses, Normal and Model School Teachers transferred	32	4,000 00	286 89	....	286 89	3,713 11	....	....
Grants to School Boards, etc., for use of Schools	32	5,000 00	4,875 00	....	4,875 00	125 00	....	....
Teachers in Public and Separate Schools used for observation purposes	32	13,000 00	13,809 45	....	13,809 45	....	809 45	1,000 00
Travelling Expenses, Normal School Students for Nature Study	33	6,700 00	6,212 30	....	6,212 30	487 70	....	....
Grants to Public and Separate School Inspectors re Visits of Normal School Students	33	600 00	260 00	....	260 00	340 00	....	....
Travelling Expenses, Normal School Masters	..	500 00	....	....	....	500 00	....	....

Classes in Manual Training and Household Science, etc.	33	6,500 00	5,806 26	....	5,806 26	693 74	....	....
Special Lectures at Normal Schools	..	500 00	....	....	....	500 00	....	....
Attendance of County Inspectors at Training Schools, etc.	..	3,000 00	....	....	....	3,000 00	....	....
Fees of returned soldiers attending course	33	1,000 00	148 00	....	148 00	852 00	....	....
Per diem allowances and travelling expenses of returned soldiers	33	8,000 00	4,242 20	....	4,242 20	3,757 80	....	....
Training Schools	..	125,500 00	121,875 53	....	121,875 53	18,283 92	14,659 45	....
Normal and Model Schools:								
Toronto Normal and Model:								
Salaries	33	112,600 00	102,666 66	....	102,666 66	9,933 34	....	....
Extra Services and Additional Teachers	..	500 00	....	....	....	500 00	....	....
Reference Books, Contingencies, etc.	34	6,600 00	4,648 47	....	4,648 47	1,951 53	....	....
Apparatus, Chemicals, Domestic Science and Manual Training Supplies	35	1,500 00	1,846 38	....	1,846 38	....	346 38	350 00
Kindergarten Supplies	35	1,000 00	529 72	....	529 72	470 28	....	....
Physical Culture Apparatus, etc.	35	375 00	388 05	....	388 05	....	13 05	100 00
Grant in aid of Games	35	100 00	100 00	....	100 00	....	....	....
Grant for Rink	35	100 00	50 00	....	50 00	50 00	....	....
Payment to Toronto Board of Education	35	2,000 00	1,600 00	....	1,600 00	400 00	....	....
Fuel, Light and Power	35	6,000 00	4,478 22	....	4,478 22	1,521 78	....	....
Water	35	1,450 00	980 59	....	980 59	469 41	....	....
Furniture and Furnishings	35	1,500 00	215 49	....	215 49	1,284 51	....	....
Expenses of Grounds, Trees, etc.	35	1,250 00	590 74	....	590 74	659 26	....	....
Wages, Porter, Fireman, etc.	35	6,000 00	3,349 17	....	3,349 17	2,650 83	....	....
Scrubbing, Cleaning, etc.	36	5,500 00	5,737 07	....	5,737 07	....	237 07	400 00
Repairs, Services, Materials	36	2,000 00	545 88	....	545 88	1,454 12	....	....
	..	148,475 00	127,726 44	....	127,726 44	21,345 06	596 50	....
Less Fees, etc.	..	....	9,452 00	....	9,452 00	9,452 00	....	....
Toronto Normal and Model	..	148,475 00	118,274 44	....	118,274 44	30,797 06	596 50	....
Ottawa Normal and Model:								
Salaries	36	75,175 00	68,758 33	....	68,758 33	6,416 67	....	....
Extra Services and Additional Teachers	..	500 00	....	....	....	500 00	....	....
Reference Books, Contingencies, etc.	36	5,600 00	2,674 81	....	2,674 81	2,925 19	....	....
Apparatus, Chemicals, Domestic Science and Manual Training Supplies	37	1,500 00	543 78	....	543 78	956 22	....	....
Physical Culture Apparatus, etc.	37	100 00	6 00	....	6 00	94 00	....	....
Kindergarten Supplies	37	800 00	779 89	....	779 89	20 11	....	....
Grant in aid of Games	37	100 00	100 00	....	100 00	....	....	....

PART F—DEPARTMENT OF EDUCATION—Continued

Statement of Expenditure Showing Amounts Expended, Unexpended and Overexpended for the Twelve Months Ended October 31st, 1932

Department of Education	Page	Estimates	Expended			Un-expended	Over-expended	Treasury Board Minute
			Ordinary	Capital	Total Ordinary and Capital			
		$ c.	$ c.	$ c.	$ c.	$ c.	$ c.	$ c.
Ottawa Normal and Model —Continued								
Grant for Rink	37	100 00	100 00	....	100 00	....	....	....
Payment to the Ottawa Public School Board	37	1,000 00	750 00	....	750 00	250 00	....	....
Fuel, Light and Power	37	5,000 00	4,093 22	....	4,093 22	906 78	....	....
Water	38	800 00	658 91	....	658 91	141 09	....	....
Furniture, Repairs and Incidentals	38	1,500 00	594 65	....	594 65	905 35	....	....
Expenses of Grounds	38	900 00	284 41	....	284 41	615 59	....	....
Scrubbing, Cleaning, etc	38	2,500 00	2,064 05	....	2,064 05	435 95	....	....
Snow Cleaning, Cartage, etc	38	900 00	124 10	....	124 10	775 90	....	....
	..	96,475 00	81,532 15	....	81,532 15	14 942 85	....	....
Less Fees, etc	..	....	8,008 00	....	8,008 00	8,008 00	....	....
Ottawa Normal and Model	..	96,475 00	73,524 15	....	73,524 15	22,950 85	....	....
London Normal:								
Salaries	38	35,450 00	33,578 37	....	33,578 37	1,871 63	....	....
Extra Services and Additional Teachers	..	500 00	....	....	....	500 00	....	....
Office Books, Contingencies, etc	38	2,800 00	1,283 88	....	1,283 88	1,516 12	....	....
Apparatus, Models, Domestic Science and Manual Training Supplies	39	800 00	259 71	....	259 71	540 29	....	....
Physical Culture Apparatus, etc	39	100 00	40 50	....	40 50	59 50	....	....
Grant to London Board of Education	39	1,900 00	1,600 00	....	1,600 00	300 00	....	....
Fuel, Light and Power	39	2,000 00	1,628 57	....	1,628 57	371 43	....	....
Water	39	300 00	90 62	....	90 62	209 38	....	....
Furniture, Repairs and Incidentals, etc	39	1,000 00	585 50	....	585 50	414 50	....	....
Expenses of Grounds, Trees, etc	39	1,500 00	1,091 61	....	1,091 61	408 39	....	....
Scrubbing, Cleaning, Cartage, etc	39	2,000 00	1,706 70	....	1,706 70	293 30	....	....
London Normal	..	48,350 00	41,865 46	....	41,865 46	6,484 54	....	....

Hamilton Normal:								
Salaries	40	33,250 00	32,144 33	....	32,144 33	1,105 67	....	....
Extra Services and Additional Teachers	..	500 00	....	....	....	500 00	....	....
Reference Books, Contingencies, etc	40	2,100 00	1,516 04	....	1,516 04	583 96	....	....
Apparatus, Chemicals, Domestic Science and Manual Training Supplies	40	1,000 00	615 99	....	615 99	384 01	....	....
Physical Culture Apparatus, etc	40	200 00	195 90	....	195 90	4 10	....	....
Payment to Hamilton Board of Education	40	1,900 00	1,750 00	....	1,750 00	150 00	....	....
Fuel, Light and Power	41	2,000 00	791 30	....	791 30	1,208 70	....	....
Water	41	200 00	136 05	....	136 05	63 95	....	....
Furniture, Repairs and Incidentals, etc	41	1,000 00	518 76	....	518 76	481 24	....	....
Expenses of Grounds, Trees, etc	41	500 00	325 03	....	325 03	174 97	....	....
Scrubbing, Cleaning, Cartage, etc	41	1,500 00	1,236 33	....	1,236 33	263 67	....	....
Hamilton Normal	..	44,150 00	39,229 73	....	39,229 73	4,920 27	....	....
Peterborough Normal:								
Salaries	41	36,700 00	35,350 00	....	35,350 00	1,350 00	....	....
Extra Services and Additional Teachers	..	500 00	....	....	....	500 00	....	....
Reference Books, Contingencies, etc	41	2,000 00	1,396 55	....	1,396 55	603 45	....	....
Apparatus, Chemicals, Domestic Science and Manual Training Supplies	42	800 00	532 81	....	532 81	267 19	....	....
Physical Culture Apparatus, etc	42	100 00	8 00	....	8 00	92 00	....	....
Payment to Peterborough Board of Education	42	1,100 00	1,100 00	....	1,100 00	....	....	....
Fuel, Light and Power	42	2,000 00	1,285 63	....	– 1,285 63	714 37	....	....
Water	42	350 00	203 01	....	203 01	146 99	....	....
Furniture, Repairs and Incidentals, etc	42	500 00	121 94	....	121 94	378 06	....	....
Expenses of Grounds, Trees, etc	42	600 00	197 15	....	197 15	402 85	....	....
Scrubbing, Cleaning, Cartage, etc	42	1,200 00	1,003 71	....	1,003 71	196 29	....	....
Peterborough Normal	..	45,850 00	41,198 80	....	41,198 80	4,651 20	....	....
Stratford Normal:								
Salaries	42	36,050 00	36,050 00	....	36,050 00	....	....	....
Extra Services and Additional Teachers	..	500 00	....	....	....	500 00	....	....
Reference Books, Contingencies, etc	43	2,000 00	1,848 11	....	1,848 11	151 89	....	....
Apparatus, Chemicals, Domestic Science and Manual Training Supplies	43	1,200 00	464 94	....	464 94	735 06	....	....
Physical Culture Apparatus, etc	43	375 00	331 89	....	331 89	43 11	....	....
Annual Grant for Rink	43	50 00	45 00	....	45 00	5 00	....	....
Payment to Stratford Board of Education	43	1,200 00	1,500 00	....	1,500 00	....	300 00	300 00
Fuel, Light and Power	43	2,000 00	979 91	....	979 91	1,020 09	....	....
Water	44	300 00	115 20	....	115 20	184 80	....	....
Furniture, Repairs and Incidentals	44	800 00	504 92	....	504 92	295 08	....	....

PART F—DEPARTMENT OF EDUCATION—Continued

Statement of Expenditure Showing Amounts Expended, Unexpended and Overexpended for the Twelve Months Ended October 31st, 1932

Department of Education	Page	Estimates	Expended			Un-expended	Over-expended	Treasury Board Minute
			Ordinary	Capital	Total Ordinary and Capital			
		$ c.	$ c.	$ c.	$ c.	$ c.	$ c.	$ c.
Stratford Normal—Continued								
Expenses of Grounds, Trees, etc.	44	800 00	382 89	....	382 89	417 11	....	....
Scrubbing, Cleaning, Cartage, etc.	44	1,200 00	1,120 07	....	1,120 07	79 93	....	....
Stratford Normal	..	46,475 00	43,342 93	....	43,342 93	3,432 07	300 00	....
North Bay Normal:								
Salaries	44	32,600 00	31,207 65	....	31,207 65	1,392 35	....	....
Extra Services and Visiting Lecturers	..	500 00	....	....	....	500 00	....	....
Reference Books, Contingencies, etc.	44	2,000 00	1,249 18	....	1,249 18	750 82	....	....
Art, Music, Domestic Science and Manual Training Supplies	45	800 00	301 96	....	301 96	498 04	....	....
Physical Culture Appliances, etc.	..	100 00	....	....	....	100 00	....	....
Students' Board and Travelling Expenses	45	45,000 00	42,665 50	....	42,665 50	2,334 50	....	....
Fuel, Light and Power	45	2,000 00	1,355 77	....	1,355 77	644 23	....	....
Water	45	300 00	162 14	....	162 14	137 86	....	....
Furniture, Repairs and Incidentals	45	1,000 00	241 30	....	241 30	758 70	....	....
Expenses of Grounds, Trees, etc.	45	900 00	210 88	....	210 88	689 12	....	....
Scrubbing, Cleaning, Cartage, etc.	45	1,200 00	1,166 84	....	1,166 84	33 16	....	....
North Bay Normal	..	86,400 00	78,561 22	....	78,561 22	7,838 78	....	....
University of Ottawa, Normal:								
Salaries	45	15,875 00	15,874 90	....	15,874 90	10	....	....
Reference Books, Contingencies, etc.	45	5,000 00	4,512 05	....	4,512 05	487 95	....	....
University of Ottawa, use of Building, Equipment, etc.	46	14,000 00	14,000 00	....	14,000 00	....	....	....
R. C. Separate School Board, Ottawa, for use of Schools for Training Teachers	46	620 00	750 00	....	750 00	....	130 00	130 00
Students' Board and Travelling Expenses	46	50,000 00	47,728 27	....	47,728 27	2,271 73	....	....
University of Ottawa, Normal	..	85,495 00	82,865 22	....	82,865 22	2,759 78	130 00	....

Model Schools:								
Sturgeon Falls,								
Salaries	46	14,200 00	11,900 00	....	11,900 00	2,300 00	....	....
Free Books, Contingencies, etc.	46	1,850 00	459 47	....	459 47	1,390 53	....	....
[illegible] Apparatus, etc.	..	100 00	....	....	....	100 00	....	....
R.C. Separate School Board for use of Schools for Training Pupils	46	1,000 00	800 00	....	800 00	200 00	....	....
Students' Board and Travelling Expenses	46	43,000 00	34,213 35	....	34,213 35	8,786 65	....	....
Fuel, Light and Power	46	1,500 00	458 74	....	458 74	1,041 26	....	....
Water	46	150 00	117 80	....	117 80	32 20	....	....
[illegible], Repairs and Incidentals	47	600 00	6 63	....	6 63	593 37	....	....
Expenses of [illegible]	..	300 00	....	....	....	300 00	....	....
Scrubbing, Cleaning, etc.	47	200 00	41 95	....	41 95	158 05	....	....
Sturgeon Falls	..	62,900 00	47,997 94	....	47,997 94	14,902 06	....	....
Sandwich,								
Salaries	47	6,475 00	6,475 00	....	6,475 00	....	....	....
Free [illegible], Contingencies, etc.	47	350 00	215 80	....	215 80	134 20	....	....
Physical [illegible] Apparatus, etc.	47	100 00	2 75	....	2 75	97 25	....	....
R.C. Separate School Board for use of Schools for Training Pupils	..	600 00	....	....	....	600 00	....	....
Students' Board and Travelling Expenses	47	8,000 00	5,024 37	....	5,024 37	2,975 63	....	....
Fuel, Light and Power	47	700 00	213 55	....	213 55	486 45	....	....
Water	47	100 00	19 81	....	19 81	80 19	....	....
[illegible], Repairs and Incidentals	47	400 00	53 24	....	53 24	346 76	....	....
Expenses of [illegible]	..	100 00	....	....	....	100 00	....	....
Scrubbing, Cleaning, etc.	47	100 00	46 81	....	46 81	53 19	....	....
Sandwich	..	16,925 00	12,051 33	....	12,051 33	4,873 67	....	....
[illegible],								
Salaries	47	11,550 00	11,201 71	....	11,201 71	348 29	....	....
Free Books, Contingencies, etc.	48	500 00	1,281 89	....	1,281 89	....	781 89	800 00
[illegible] Supplies	48	100 00	26 43	....	26 43	73 57	....	....
Grant for Rink	..	100 00	....	....	....	100 00	....	....
Grant to Separate School Board for use of School for Training Pupils	48	300 00	300 00	....	300 00	....	....	....
Students' Board and Travelling Expenses	48	37,000 00	32,852 90	....	32,852 90	4,147 10	....	....
Fuel, Light and Power	48	1,000 00	386 90	....	386 90	613 10	....	....
Water	..	200 00	....	....	....	200 00	....	....
[illegible], Repairs and Incidentals	48	500 00	6 03	....	6 03	493 97	....	....

PART F—DEPARTMENT OF EDUCATION—Continued

Statement of Expenditure Showing Amounts Expended, Unexpended and Overexpended for the Twelve Months Ended October 31st, 1932

Department of Education	Page	Estimates	Expended			Un-expended	Over-expended	Treasury Board Minute
			Ordinary	Capital	Total Ordinary and Capital			
		$ c.	$ c.	$ c.	$ c.	$ c.	$ c.	$ c.
Embrun—Continued								
Expenses of Grounds	..	200 00	....	....	....	200 00	....	....
Scrubbing, Cleaning, etc.	48	200 00	102 49	....	102 49	97 51	....	....
Embrun	..	51,650 00	46,158 35	....	46,158 35	6,273 54	781 89	....
High Schools [illegible] Collegiate Institutes:								
Salaries (Inspection)	48	25,450 00	23,450 00	....	23,450 00	2,000 00	....	....
[illegible], G[illegible]s	48	420,000 00	418,677 02	....	418,677 02	1,322 98	....	....
[illegible] [illegible] o[illegible]s	49	14,000 00	10,093 29	....	10,093 29	3,906 71	....	....
High School [illegible] G[illegible]s	49	4,500 00	3,750 00	....	3,750 00	750 00	....	....
Travelling [illegible] Moving Expenses	50	5,000 00	5,673 07	....	5,673 07	....	673 07	1,300 00
G[illegible]s [illegible] School Boards, etc., to [illegible] [illegible]s of Music in High Schools	50	1,000 00	1,052 16	....	1,052 16	....	52 16	100 00
G[illegible]s to [illegible] Schools [illegible] Collegiate [illegible]s to [illegible]t [illegible]s [illegible]d by [illegible] G[illegible] [illegible]y	50	1,200 00	1,255 39	....	1,255 39	....	55 39	200 00
Stati[illegible], [illegible], Contingencies	50	5,000 00	4,951 53	....	4,951 53	48 47	....	....
High Schools and Collegiate Institutes	..	476,150 00	468,902 46	....	468,902 46	8,028 16	780 62	....
Departmental Museum:								
Salaries	50	4,900 00	3,850 00	....	3,850 00	1,050 00	....	....
Contingencies	50	3,000 00	241 10	....	241 10	2,758 90	....	....
Archaeological Researches, etc.	50	2,000 00	782 00	....	782 00	1,218 00	....	....
Natural History Collections, etc.	50	500 00	125 00	....	125 00	375 00	....	....
Departmental Museum	..	10,400 00	4,998 10	....	4,998 10	5,401 90	....	....
Public Libraries:								
Salaries	50	14,200 00	8,866 66	....	8,866 66	5,333 34	....	....
Grants, Contingencies, etc.	51	60,000 00	52,134 65	....	52,134 65	7,865 35	....	....

Travelling Expenses	52	1,000 00	903 24	....	903 24	96 76	....	300 00
Library Institutes	52	2,200 00	191 98	....	191 98	2,008 02	....	....
Travelling Libraries, Books, Services and Contingencies	52	5,000 00	2,637 25	....	2,637 25	2,362 75	....	....
Grants to Ottawa Association for the Blind	53	1,000 00	1,000 00	....	1,000 00	....	....	....
Ont. College of Art and other Art Societies	53	25,500 00	25,500 00	....	25,500 00	....	....	....
Royal Canadian Institute, Toronto	53	2,500 00	2,500 00	....	2,500 00	....	....	....
Astronomical Society	53	600 00	600 00	....	600 00	....	....	....
Institut Canadien, Ottawa	53	300 00	300 00	....	300 00	....	....	....
Public Libraries	..	112,300 00	94,633 78	....	94,633 78	17,666 22	....	....
Vocational Education:								
Salaries	53	28,100 00	24,741 66	....	24,741 66	3,358 34	....	....
Grants and Contingencies, Manual Training and Household Science Departments	53	64,000 00	62,914 21	....	62,914 21	1,085 79	....	....
Sudbury High School for Mining Education	53	7,000 00	7,000 00	....	7,000 00	....	....	....
Haileybury High School for Mining Department	53	10,000 00	10,000 00	....	10,000 00	....	....	....
Agricultural Training in High Schools, etc.	53	40,000 00	39,995 49	....	39,995 49	4 51	....	....
Vocational Education, Day and Evening Classes	54	1,100,000 00	1,360,813 40	....	1,360,813 40	....	260,813 40	267,453 89
Travelling Expenses	54	5,000 00	4,321 56	....	4,321 56	678 44	....	....
Vocational Education	..	1,254,100 00	1,509,786 32	....	1,509,786 32	5,127 08	260,813 40	....
[illegible] College for [illegible]hical [illegible]s:								
Salaries	54	29,400 00	24,114 00	....	24,114 00	5,286 00	....	750 00
[illegible], etc.	55	2,500 00	984 57	....	984 57	1,515 43	....	....
[illegible] Shop Supplies	55	1,500 00	363 12	....	363 12	1,136 88	....	....
[illegible] to [illegible] Board of [illegible]ation	..	1,550 00	....	....	....	1,550 00	....	....
[illegible]	55	2,000 00	1,120 68	....	1,120 68	879 32	....	....
[illegible]	55	100 00	21 52	....	21 52	78 48	....	....
[illegible]s of [illegible]s, Trees, etc.	55	800 00	318 67	....	318 67	481 33	....	....
[illegible]	55	500 00	92 05	....	92 05	407 95	....	....
Scrubbing, [illegible], Cartage, etc.	55	1,500 00	127 31	....	127 31	1,372 69	....	....
Ontario Training College for Technical Teachers	..	39,850 00	27,141 92	....	27,141 92	12,708 08	....	....
Superannuated Teachers:								
Annual Retiring Allowances	55	20,000 00	15,873 00	....	15,873 00	4,127 00	....	....
Medical Examination, Fees, Contingencies, etc.	..	150 00	....	....	....	150 00	....	....
Superannuated Teachers	..	20,150 00	15,873 00	....	15,873 00	4,277 00	....	....

PART F—DEPARTMENT OF EDUCATION—Continued

Statement of Expenditure Showing Amounts Expended, Unexpended and Overexpended for the Twelve Months ended October 31st, 1932

Department of Education	Page	Estimates	Expended			Un-expended	Over-expended	Treasury Board Minute
			Ordinary	Capital	Total Ordinary and Capital			
		$ c.	$ c.	$ c.	$ c.	$ c.	$ c.	$ c.
Provincial and Other Universities, Grants:								
Toronto University Training School	56	234,175 00	234,175 00	....	234,175 00	....	....	....
Toronto University, Special Grant	56	1,200,000 00	1,059,338 34	140,661 66	1,200,000 00	....	....	....
Queen's University	56	300,000 00	300,000 00	....	300,000 00	....	....	....
Western Ontario University	56	300,000 00	300,000 00	....	300,000 00	....	....	....
Royal Ontario Museum	56	50,000 00	40,000 00	....	40,000 00	10,000 00	....	....
Royal Ontario Museum for Cataloguing	56	5,000 00	5,000 00	....	5,000 00	....	....	....
Connaught Laboratories	56	3,750 00	....	....	....	3,750 00	....	....
Provincial and Other Universities	..	2,092,925 00	1,938,513 34	140,661 66	2,079,175 00	13,750 00	....	....
Belleville School for the Deaf:								
Salaries	56	96,700 00	91,747 79	....	91,747 79	4,952 21	....	....
Expenses	57	50,000 00	59,775 88	....	59,775 88	....	9,775 88	10,000 00
To provide for Refunds to Teachers in Training	59	1,150 00	1,150 00	....	1,150 00	....	....	....
	..	147,850 00	152,673 67	....	152,673 67	4,952 21	9,775 88	....
Less Fees, etc.	..	....	17,627 00	....	17,627 00	17,627 00	....	....
Belleville School for the Deaf	..	147,850 00	135,046 67	....	135,046 67	22,579 21	9,775 88	....
Brantford School for the Blind:								
Salaries	59	61,159 00	56,159 79	....	56,159 79	4,999 21	....	....
Expenses	60	30,000 00	29,664 23	....	29,664 23	335 77	....	....
	..	91,159 00	85,824 02	....	85,824 02	5,334 98	....	....
Less Fees, etc.	..	....	23,745 21	....	23,745 21	23,745 21	....	....
Brantford School for the Blind	..	91,159 00	62,078 81	....	62,078 81	29,080 19	....	....

Northern Academy, Monteith:								
Salaries	61	29,665 00	26,925 98	....	26,925 98	2,729 02	....	....
Expenses	61	10,000 00	13,902 18	....	13,902 18	....	3,902 18	9,000 00
Farm and Power Plant	63	5,000 00	4,986 24	....	4,986 24	13 76	....	....
	..	44,655 00	45,814 40	....	45,814 40	2,742 78	3,902 18	....
Less Fees, etc	..	....	20,451 85	....	20,451 85	20,451 85	....	....
N ... Monteith	..	44,655 00	25,362 55	....	25,362 55	23,194 63	3,902 18	....
Mi... :								
...of ...of Mini... Report	63	2,500 00	1,447 72	....	1,447 72	1,052 28	....	....
... ...c School ...	..	3,500 00	....	....	....	3,500 00	....	....
...e of ...t Books by Schools, Grants and Contingencies	..	1,000 00	....	....	....	1,000 00	....	....
Cost of Litigation	63	1,000 00	150 00	....	150 00	850 00	....	....
... of ...e Acts of the Department of ...	63	3,000 00	231 71	....	231 71	2,768 29	....	....
Advertising in ... and ot...r Papers	63	5,000 00	8,985 42	....	8,985 42	....	3,985 42	4,000 00
Fees of ...	63	300 00	24 83	....	24 83	275 17	....	....
...ng ...	63	2,000 00	72 95	....	72 95	1,927 05	....	....
Historical ...	63	3,000 00	2,000 00	....	2,000 00	1,000 00	....	....
Grant to ...' ...' Superannuation ... of ...	..	4,000 00	....	....	....	4,000 00	....	....
Grant to ... Bank of ...	63	1,000 00	1,000 00	....	1,000 00	....	....	....
Compassionate ... to ...	63	5,000 00	6,795 92	....	6,795 92	....	1,795 92	2,000 00
...ng ... of ... to France	..	1,000 00	....	....	....	1,000 00	....	....
Grant to Students' ...	64	1,000 00	1,000 00	....	1,000 00	....	....	....
School ...ciati..., Contingencies	..	500 00	....	....	....	500 00	....	....
Miscellaneous	..	33,800 00	21,708 55	....	21,708 55	17,872 79	5,781 34	....
Supply Bill	..	9,876,209 00	10,363,999 55	140,792 44	10,504,791 99	591,528 40	1,220,111 39	....
Statut...y:								
Sal...s ...erwise ...	64	....	235 44	....	235 44	....	....	....
Succession ...	64	....	500,000 00	....	500,000 00	....	....	....
... of ... ...r 60 Vic. Chap. 59	64	....	7,000 00	....	7,000 00	....	....	....
... Aid ..., 1928	64	....	....	13,480 75	13,480 75	....	....	....
... ..., 1928	64	....	....	52,157 68	52,157 68	....	....	....
...n Scholarships	64	....	5,137 08	....	5,137 08	....	....	....
...r Scholarships	64	....	4,860 00	....	4,860 00	....	....	....
... ...	64	....	53,197 20	....	53,197 20	....	....	....
...o Government, ...ri...tion to Teachers' and I...' Superannuation ...	..	....	719,241 66	....	719,241 66	....	....	....
Statutory	..	....	1,289,671 38	65,638 43	1,355,309 81	....	....	....

PART F—DEPARTMENT OF EDUCATION—Continued

Statement of Expenditures Showing Amounts Expended, Unexpended and Overexpended for the Twelve Months Ended October 31st, 1932

Department of Education	Page	Estimates	Expended			Un-expended	Over-expended	Treasury Board Minute
			Ordinary	Capital	Total Ordinary and Capital			
		$ c.	$ c.	$ c.	$ c.	$ c.	$ c.	$ c.
Special [illegible]:								
[illegible] Mn, [illegible] of [illegible]	64	....	....	873,000 00	873,000 00	....	....	....
[illegible] ad Distributi on of Books for El[illegible] Schools	64	....	11,930 40	....	11,930 40	....	....	....
[illegible]'s U[illegible], Kingston [illegible]	64	....	50,000 00	....	50,000 00	....	....	....
To [illegible] of the Ontario [illegible] of [illegible]	64	....	....	35,245 61	35,245 61	....	....	....
[illegible], T[illegible] re [illegible] of [illegible] of Botanical Building	64	....	....	517,000 00	517,000 00	....	....	....
[illegible] of [illegible] of Grant to F[illegible]	64	....	22,500 00	....	22,500 00	....	....	....
[illegible] of [illegible] Col[illegible] of Paintings	64	....	5,000 00	....	5,000 00	....	....	....
[illegible] to [illegible] to aid the Developing of [illegible]	64	....	500 00	....	500 00	....	....	....
[illegible] to [illegible] Bank [illegible]	65	....	4,000 00	....	4,000 00	....	....	....
[illegible] Town of [illegible], to [illegible] High School Debentures and Interest	65	....	....	2,183 14	2,183 14	....	....	....
Special Warrants	..	....	93,930 40	1,427,428 75	1,521,359 15	....	....	....
Total	..	....	11,747,601 33	1,633,859 62	13,381,460 95	....	....	....
Less Salary Assessment	..	....	26,883 05	....	26,883 05	....	....	....
Department of Education	..	....	11,720,718 28	1,633,859 62	13,354,577 90	....	....	....

SUMMARY

Department of Education	Page	Ordinary	Capital	Total
		$ c.	$ c.	$ c.
[illegible]	16-17	84,649 61	....	84,649 61
[illegible] Separate Schools	17-26	4,380,227 35	....	4,380,[illegible]27 35
[illegible] of Schools	26-30	634,281 36	....	[illegible] 36
Departmental [illegible]	30-31	145,729 31	....	[illegible] 31
Text Books	31	66,921 32	....	66,[illegible]21 32
[illegible]	32	1,200 00	130 78	[illegible]30 78
[illegible] Schools	32-33	121,875 53	....	[illegible] 53
[illegible] Schools	33-48	625,069 57	....	[illegible] 57
High Schools [illegible] Collegiate Institutes	48-50	468,902 46	....	[illegible] 46
Departmental [illegible]	50	4,998 10	....	4,998 10
[illegible]	50-53	94,633 78	....	94,[illegible]63[illegible] 78
[illegible]	53-54	1,509,786 32	....	[illegible] 32
[illegible] College for Technical Teachers	54-55	27,141 92	....	27,[illegible] 92
Superannuated [illegible]	55-56	15,873 00	....	15,[illegible] 00
[illegible] Universiti[illegible]	56	1,938,513 34	140,661 66	[illegible] 00
Belleville School [illegible] Deaf	56-59	135,046 67	....	[illegible]5,046 67
[illegible]	59-61	62,078 81	....	62,[illegible] 81
[illegible]	61-63	25,362 55	....	25,[illegible] 55
[illegible]	63-64	21,708 55	....	21,[illegible] 55
Statutory	64	1,289,671 38	65,638 43	1,[illegible] 81
Special [illegible]	64-65	93,930 40	1,427,428 75	1[illegible] 15
	..	11,747,601 33	1,633,859 62	13,381,460 95
Deduct:—				
Transferred to Loans and Special Funds (See Part U)				
Redemption of debentures guaranteed by the Province	..	....	2,313 92	2,313 92
Total	..	11,747,601 33	1,631,545 70	13,379,147 03
Less Salary Assessment	..	26,883 05	....	26,883 05
Department of Education	......	11,720,718 28	1,631,545 70	13,352,263 98

DEPARTMENT OF EDUCATION

Hon. G. S. Henry, Minister

MAIN OFFICE

Salaries ($75,621.37)

A. H. U. Colquhoun	Deputy Minister	1 month	516 44	
" "	" " (T)	11 "	3,662 09	4,178 53
F. W. Merchant	Chief Advisor to the Minister of Education (T)	12 "		5,000 00
Geo. F. Rogers	Chief Director of Education	12 "		5,400 00
R. A. Croskery	Assistant to the Deputy Minister of Education	12 "		5,000 00
M. E. Saunderson	Secretary to Minister and Departmental Secretary	12 "		2,700 00
Gladys Dix	Secretary to Chief Director of Education	12 "		2,000 00
Frank L. Woodley	Chief Clerk	12 "		3,600 00
George Whitelaw	Principal Clerk	12 "		2,400 00
A. M. Campbell	" "	12 "		2,200 00
T. J. Greene	Senior Clerk	12 "		2,000 00
C. D. Creighton	" "	12 "		2,000 00
Thomas W. Aikens	" "	12 "		2,000 00
R. W. Joyce	" "	12 "		1,800 00
S. W. Jackson	" "	12 "		1,800 00
Lillian E. Brown	" "	12 "		1,800 00
Hugh M. Craig	" "	12 "		1,600 00
Geo. Walton	Clerk, Group 1	12 "		2,000 00
J. P. Clougher	" " 1	12 "		1,600 00
M. C. Higginson	" " 1	12 "		1,600 00
Alfred P. Frohns	" " 1	12 "		1,600 00
James A. Waring	" " 1	12 "		1,600 00
J. S. Ward	" " 1	12 "		1,600 00
G. Moran	" " 1	12 "		1,400 00
T. Edward P. Ellis	" " 1	12 "		1,300 00
E. I. Brown	" " 2	12 "		1,200 00
A. Watchorn	" " 2	12 "		1,200 00
D. E. Keough	" " 2—Full salary	4½ "	411 96	
" "	" " 2—Half "	7½ "	355 88	767 84
Ralph C. Bullock	" " 3	12 "		825 00
Carl H. Tapscott	" " 3	12 "		825 00
A. MacPherson	Senior Clerk Stenographer	12 "		1,500 00
Gladys M. Black	" " "	12 "		1,500 00
A. Haughland	" " "	12 "		1,500 00
Eula A. Humphrey	Clerk Stenographer, Group 1	12 "		1,125 00
Muriel L. Soanes	" " " 2	12 "		825 00
Jean G. Chidley	Filing Clerk, " 1	12 "		1,200 00
D. Creighton	" " " 1	12 "		1,200 00
Mabelle E. Young	" " " 1	12 "		975 00
W. A. Humphries	Senior Clerk Messenger	12 "		1,400 00
R. Marter	Vault Caretaker	12 "		1,400 00

Contingencies ($9,028.24)

Temporary Services, $3,129.81.

A. N. Burns	Clerk,	Group 1	1 month	100 CO
Alyce Daly	Clerk Typist,	" 2	12 "	750 00
Margaret E. Donson	Clerk Stenographer,	" 2	12 "	825 00
Cecil W. McNally	Clerk,	" 2	12 "	1,200 00
Robert Thomas	"	" 2	2 "	162 50
George Trumbell	"	" 1	1 "	92 31

Travelling Expenses, $774.23.

F. W. Merchant, 274.30; G. F. Rogers, 499.93	774 23

Advertising, $29.00.

Globe Printing Co., 12.00; London Free Press, 5.00; Mail & Empire, 12.00	29 00

Main Office—Continued

Contingencies—Continued

Miscellaneous, $5,095.20.

Angus Mack Co., maps, etc., 15.70; Burroughs Adding Machine of Canada, Ltd., inspections, 67.90; Bourne & Towse, maps, 12.50; Canadian Review Co., Ltd., books, 16.00; B. M. Dick, typing, 40.00; Evans Bros. Ltd., books, 17.60; Field, Love & House, inspection, etc., 104.00; King's Printer, 3,418.55; Might Directories Ltd., maps, etc., 17.00; Remington Typewriters, Ltd., inspections, 31.00; Thomas & Corney Typewriters Ltd., inspections, etc., 91.35; United Typewriter Co., Ltd., inspections, 316.50; George Walton, care of clocks, 70.72. Sundries—car tickets, 25.00; cartage, 59.55; express, 58.72; newspapers and periodicals, 319.89; telegrams, 344.90; petty disbursements, 68.32.................................. 5,095 20

Main Office.. $84,649.61

PUBLIC AND SEPARATE SCHOOLS

Grants and Contingencies ($3,486,322.74)

Public Schools, Counties, $1,710,657.33.

Brant, 15,514.44; Bruce, 42,696.15; Carleton, 42,154.23; Dufferin, 20,053.55; Elgin, 23,382.67; Essex, 36,833.99; Frontenac, 65,688.71; Grey, 49,450.97; Haldimand, 21,176.12; Haliburton, 32,603.65; Halton, 10,903.12; Hastings, 82,794.82; Huron, 36,687.87; Kent, 28,942.31; Lambton, 30,456.19; Lanark, 33,943.06; Leeds and Grenville, 66,357.79; Lennox and Addington, 35,991.81; Lincoln, 25,862.65; Middlesex, 37,319.25; Norfolk, 21,265.27; Northumberland and Durham, 50,751.26; Ontario, 36,232.25; Oxford, 25,240.22; Peel, 27,643.31; Perth, 19,174.00; Peterborough, 42,244.36; Prescott and Russell, 25,228.85; Prince Edward, 17,334.82; Renfrew, 58,045.13; Simcoe, 59,219.24; Stormont, Dundas and Glengarry, 64,222.15; Victoria, 26,376.01; Waterloo, 24,570.50; Welland, 46,335.17; Wellington, 29,140.75; Wentworth, 19,138.92; York, 379,681.77...1,710,657 33

Separate Schools, Counties, $145,736.74.

Bruce, 4,639.27; Carleton, 11,129.88; Essex, 10,717.62; Frontenac, 3,013.17; Grey, 2,153.81; Hastings, 1,822.02; Huron, 1,838.65; Kent, 2,668.59; Lambton, 538.27; Lanark, 1,057.89; Leeds and Grenville, 823.00; Lennox and Addington, 857.91; Middlesex, 803.61; Norfolk, 432.90; Northumberland and Durham, 1,382.09; Ontario, 559.35; Peel, 209.37; Perth, 4,090.27; Peterborough, 1,163.81; Prescott and Russell, 35,745.17; Renfrew, 13,679.71; Simcoe, 2,499.91; Stormont, Dundas and Glengarry, 16,684.66; Victoria, 718.22; Waterloo, 3,417.33; Wellington, 1,559.14; Wentworth, 717.20; York, 20,813.92........................... 145,736 74

Public Schools, Districts, $548,341.98.

Algoma, 49,331.32; Cochrane, 52,275.50; Kenora, 21,653.75; Manitoulin, 27,004.55; Muskoka, 53,092.65; Nipissing, 43,865.67; Parry Sound, 87,143.63; Rainy River, 41,547.46; Sudbury, 78,289.46; Temiskaming, 46,715.30; Thunder Bay, 47,422.69... 548,341 98

Separate Schools, Districts, $153,315.57.

Algoma, 2,719.80; Cochrane, 44,698.93; Kenora, 912.29; Muskoka, 1,304.55; Nipissing, 29,650.50; Rainy River, 1,804.69; Sudbury, 52,136.43; Temiskaming, 19,588.87; Thunder Bay, 499.51.. 153,315 57

Public Schools, Cities, $287,737.86.

Belleville, 3,998.19; Brantford, 11,758.09; Chatham, 9,173.36; Fort William, 11,029.75; Galt, 4,994.55; Guelph, 5,785.23; Hamilton, 27,002.39; Kingston, 6,433.25; Kitchener, 9,747.06; London, 11,677.30; Niagara Falls, 6,972.57; North Bay, 5,494.07; Oshawa, 10,361.61; Ottawa, 13,885.20; Owen Sound, 5,841.54; Peterborough, 8,226.38; Port Arthur, 4,941.09; St. Catharines, 9,343.54; St. Thomas, 4,038.71; Sarnia, 7,413.07; Sault Ste. Marie, 10,433.03; Stratford, 6,229.13; Sudbury, 4,812.13; Toronto, 64,555.20; Welland, 4,665.71 Windsor, 10,141.62; Windsor East, 5,674.56; Woodstock, 3,109.53.................... 287,737 86

Separate Schools, Cities, $74,230.69.

Belleville, 619.65; Brantford, 1,592.27; Chatham, 796.50; Fort William, 2,511.90; Galt, 570.60; Guelph, 1,634.54; Hamilton, 4,619.13; Kingston, 1,251.59; Kitchener, 2,800.58; London, 1,243.00; Niagara Falls, 805.46; North Bay, 3,356.90; Oshawa, 1,039.29; Ottawa, 19,511.48; Owen Sound, 247.05; Peterborough, 1,725.75; Port Arthur, 1,234.41; St. Catharines, 1,541.93; St. Thomas, 329.40; Sault Ste. Marie, 4,465.84; Stratford, 585.54; Toronto, 13,616.39; Windsor, 2,941.11; Windsor East, 4,982.03; Woodstock, 208.35.............. 74,230 69

Public and Separate Schools—Continued

Grants and Contingencies—Continued

Public Schools, Towns, $249,500.12.

Alexandria, 162.00; Alliston, 816.61; Almonte, 694.80; Amherstburg, 718.64; Arnprior, 1,224.28; Aurora, 1,479.83; Aylmer, 1,864.65; Bala, 361.80; Barrie, 3,321.68; Blenheim, 1,932.56; Blind River, 1,109.20; Bothwell, 677.57; Bowmanville, 930.44; Bracebridge, 1,393.20; Brampton, 2,276.05; Brockville, 3,314.16; Bruce Mines, 1,350.54; Burlington, 1,215.27; Cache Bay, 1,261.71; Campbellford, 1,517.85; Capreol, 4,740.12; Carleton Place, 1,579.41; Chesley, 1,705.95; Clinton, 1,832.40; Cobalt, 4,513.31; Cobourg, 1,117.26; Cochrane, 2,823.08; Collingwood, 3,303.12; Copper Cliff, 1,591.11; Cornwall, 1,315.22; Deseronto, 1,838.34; Dresden, 1,104.31; Dryden, 2,381.40; Dundas, 1,611.59; Dunnville, 2,447.16; Durham, 2,092.54; Eastview, 1,957.50; Elmira, 702.14; Englehart, 3,427.88; Essex, 2,783.82; Forest, 957.20; Fort Frances, 4,422.02; Frood Mines, 76.50; Gananoque, 816.98; Georgetown, 800.33; Goderich, 1,887.91; Gore Bay, 1,194.21; Gravenhurst, 2,778.48; Grimsby, 2,189.72; Haileybury, 1,274.41; Hanover, 1,442.97; Harriston, 739.68; Harrow, 1,285.17; Hawkesbury, 332.36; Hearst, 730.62; Hespeler, 1,912.26; Huntsville, 1,366.20; Ingersoll, 1,627.11; Iroquois Falls, 821.21; Kearney, 1,205.34; Keewatin, 1,186.43; Kenora, 3,014.28; Kincardine, 1,719.95; Kingsville, 1,009.43; La Salle, 69.95; Latchford, 1,232.61; Leamington, 2,288.97; Leaside, 698.87; Lindsay, 2,727.40; Listowel, 716.40; Little Current, 1,390.41; Massey, 1,411.38; Matheson, 1,563.32; Mattawa, 139.23; Meaford, 1,995.57; Merritton, 1,423.77; Midland, 2,978.64; Milton, 1,317.26; Mimico, 4,654.96; Mitchell, 1,163.52; Mount Forest, 811.91; Napanee, 1,519.56; Nesterville, 396.08; New Liskeard, 1,908.05; Newmarket, 2,056.59; New Toronto, 4,608.00; Niagara-on-the-Lake, 813.98; Oakville, 1,222.43; Orangeville, 1,334.70; Orillia, 3,499.38; Palmerston, 1,086.93; Paris, 1,323.00; Parkhill, 459.30; Parry Sound, 2,493.00; Pembroke, 2,769.62; Penetanguishene, 2,762.10; Perth, 1,733.40; Petrolia, 1,596.15; Picton, 708.84; Port Colborne, 5,018.61; Port Hope, 1,058.77; Powassan, 1,368.90; Prescott, 952.20; Preston, 2,336.44; Rainy River, 3,369.96; Renfrew, 1,043.10; Ridgetown, 1,871.28; Riverside, 4,939.04; Rockland, 56.69; Sandwich, 4,096.64; Seaforth, 1,576.80; Simcoe, 1,755.51; Sioux Lookout, 3,631.14; Smith's Falls, 2,914.20; Smooth Rock Falls, 738.27; Southampton, 1,814.04; St. Marys, 1,152.00; Stayner, 567.00; Strathroy, 844.42; Sturgeon Falls, 556.29; Tecumseth, 119.25; Thessalon, 2,138.94; Thornbury, 669.78; Thorold, 2,346.33; Tilbury, 635.76; Tillsonburg, 1,401.51; Timmins, 8,381.59; Trenton, 2,259.65; Trout Creek, 857.49; Uxbridge, 1,467.36; Vankleek Hill, 806.54; Walkerton, 776.34; Walkerville, 3,429.03; Wallaceburg, 3,011.08; Waterloo, 2,576.70; Webbwood, 2,236.95; Weston, 2,390.37; Whitby, 999.90; Wiarton, 3,222.00; Wingham, 1,955.70 .... 249,500 12

Separate Schools, Towns, $140,086.17.

Alexandria, 1,417.22; Almonte, 703.11; Amherstburg, 484.37; Arnprior, 897.44; Barrie, 187.20; Blind River, 2,174.00; Bonfield, 4,009.32; Cache Bay, 2,244.24; Campbellford, 127.80; Charlton, 559.48; Chelmsford, 3,397.90; Cobalt, 6,449.54; Cobourg, 286.20; Cochrane, 2,103.75; Collingwood, 388.80; Cornwall, 4,566.79; Dundas, 133.21; Eastview, 12,287.34; Essex, 1,137.73; Forest Hill, 36.90; Fort Frances, 435.52; Gananoque, 346.95; Goderich, 156.60; Haileybury, 4,591.80; Hanover, 269.73; Hawkesbury, 5,782.50; Hearst, 1,398.23; Hespeler, 113.36; Ingersoll, 299.70; Iroquois Falls, 2,250.90; Kearney, 630.90; Keewatin, 314.67; Kenora, 1,316.27; La Salle, 678.60; Lindsay, 1,162.71; Little Current, 1,401.47; Massey, 978.97; Mattawa, 4,426.38; Merritton, 320.89; Midland, 3,188.42; Mimico, 1,191.60; Mount Forest, 337.68; New Liskeard, 866.62; Newmarket, 290.79; Oakville, 93.15; Orillia, 563.85; Paris, 309.29; Parkhill, 190.80; Pembroke, 11,281.57; Penetanguishene, 715.50; Perth, 403.79; Picton, 69.48; Prescott, 217.44; Preston, 908.10; Rainy River, 1,099.16; Renfrew, 797.40; Riverside, 1,360.49; Rockland, 3,742.70; Sandwich, 3,351.31; Seaforth, 423.00; Sioux Lookout, 1,610.68; Smith's Falls, 303.73; Smooth Rock Falls, 4,072.60; St. Marys, 126.90; Sturgeon Falls, 6,772.34; Tecumseth, 7,283.15; Thorold, 925.72; Tilbury, 1,866.60; Timmins, 7,874.37; Trenton, 1,087.65; Vankleek Hill, 1,491.95; Walkerton, 1,110.60; Walkerville, 205.08; Wallaceburg, 1,167.30; Waterloo, 890.01; Weston, 1,229.13; Whitby, 197.73 .... 140,086 17

Public Schools, Villages, $157,812.42.

Acton, 1,226.51; Ailsa Craig, 365.31; Alvinston, 567.63; Arkona, 296.55; Arthur, 604.35; Athens, 848.70; Ayr, 925.20; Bancroft, 4,919.40; Bath, 585.90; Beamsville, 1,348.62; Beaverton, 589.05; Beeton, 340.97; Belle River, 74.27; Bloomfield, 448.65; Blyth, 671.40; Bobcaygeon, 935.82; Bolton, 658.89; Bradford, 688.86; Braeside, 793.35; Brighton, 1,374.30; Brussels, 774.18; Burks Falls, 1,990.08; Caledonia, 2,150.55; Cannington, 429.30; Cardinal, 2,100.60; Cayuga, 1,426.14;

Public and Separate Schools—Continued

Grants and Contingencies—Continued

Public Schools, Villages—Continued

Chatsworth, 431.10; Chesterville, 1,017.90; Chippawa, 1,489.05; Clifford, 269.55; Cobden, 897.98; Colborne, 944.10; Coldwater, 1,158.30; Courtright, 368.10; Creemore, 523.53; Delhi, 1,141.70; Deloro, 1,663.20; Drayton, 251.42; Dundalk, 1,190.70; Dutton, 550.96; Eganville, 526.86; Elora, 964.41; Embro, 364.37; Erieau, 556.28; Erin, 275.05; Exeter, 1,442.34; Fenelon Falls, 588.20; Flesherton, 404.64; Fergus, 744.86; Finch, 292.05; Fonthill, 1,231.65; Forest Hill, 415.80; Fort Erie, 7,257.36; Frankford, 1,191.87; Glencoe, 601.87; Grand Valley, 603.63; Hagersville, 2,255.40; Hastings, 390.60; Havelock, 5,778.99; Hensall, 492.30; Hepworth, 734.49; Hilton Beach, 1,013.22; Holland Landing, 768.24; Humberstone, 4,433.04; Iroquois, 857.45; Jarvis, 632.12; Kemptville, 1,724.40; Killaloe Station, 1,000.62; Lakefield, 2,145.20; Lanark, 880.56; Lancaster, 391.77; Lions Head, 639.72; Long Branch, 8,451.36; L'Orignal, 2,038.14; Lucan, 317.47; Lucknow, 1,115.73; Madoc, 1,848.96; Markdale, 1,254.11; Markham, 461.70; Marmora, 2,520.50; Maxville, 818.51; Merrickville, 1,049.40; Mildmay, 646.08; Millbrook, 458.91; Milverton, 828.90; Morrisburg, 1,162.44; Neustadt, 560.79; Newboro, 633.03; Newburgh, 601.20; Newbury, 333.18; Newcastle, 569.79; New Hamburg, 817.20; Norwich, 958.23; Norwood, 1,322.49; Oil Springs, 426.60; Omemee, 307.83; Paisley, 1,268.83; Point Edward, 2,232.00; Port Carling, 445.86; Port Credit, 1,839.47; Port Dalhousie, 1,443.58; Port Dover, 834.64; Port Elgin, 1,438.38; Port McNicoll, 2,127.60; Port Perry, 919.26; Port Rowan, 460.86; Portsmouth, 576.90; Port Stanley, 644.09; Richmond, 367.20; Richmond Hill, 2,285.87; Ripley, 608.99; Rockcliffe Park, 269.55; Rodney, 456.53; Rosseau, 769.32; St. Clair Beach, 93.68; Shallow Lake, 536.62; Shelburne, 1,175.85; South River, 1,281.78; Springfield, 386.17; Stirling, 618.66; Stoney Creek, 816.93; Stouffville, 1,110.60; Streetsville, 640.26; Sutton West, 633.49; Swansea, 4,898.40; Tara, 611.73; Tavistock, 756.81; Teeswater, 969.12; Thamesville, 696.62; Thedford, 489.78; Thornloe, 638.65; Tiverton, 266.40; Tottenham, 664.47; Victoria Harbour, 3,015.00; Vienna, 511.89; Wardsville, 124.65; Waterdown, 616.32; Waterford, 554.00; Watford, 1,096.02; West Lorne, 565.43; Westport, 592.61; Wheatley, 1,070.10; Winchester, 946.80; Windermere, 253.80; Woodbridge, 1,355.94; Woodville, 286.02; Wyoming, 414.81...................... 157,812 42

Separate Schools, Villages, $16,128.38.

Arthur, 490.86; Belle River, 801.00; Casselman, 2,207.34; Chesterville, 625.38; Eganville, 498.42; Elora, 204.21; Fergus, 59.76; Hastings, 522.14; Killaloe Station, 2,655.76; Lancaster, 2,912.41; L'Orignal, 329.24; Marmora, 757.80; Mildmay, 1,032.11; Port Dalhousie, 528.37; Portsmouth, 272.71; Swansea, 450.87; Teeswater, 200.70; Thornloe, 610.38; Tweed, 727.56; Westport, 241.36.. 16,128 38

Contingencies, $2,775.48.

King's Printer,.. 2,775 48

Assisted Public and Separate Schools, Grants and Contingencies ($108,647.68)

Public School Boards, Counties, $14,097.16.

Bruce, 280.00; Carleton, 1,000.00; Frontenac, 1,880.00; Haliburton, 3,178.50; Hastings, 1,343.33; Lanark, 42.13; Lennox and Addington, 200.01; Leeds and Grenville, 294.75; Lincoln, 350.00; Middlesex, 250.00; Ontario, 704.73; Oxford, 50.00; Peterborough, 292.50; Renfrew, 2,881.00; Simcoe, 100.00; Victoria, 103.80; Wellington, 927.41; Wentworth, 219.00 .... 14,097 16

Separate School Boards, Counties, $16,922.75.

Carleton, 10,075.00; Hastings, 300.00; Northumberland and Durham, 40.00; Prescott and Russell, 5,375.00; Renfrew, 275.00; Simcoe, 807.75; Stormont, Dundas and Glengarry, 50.00.. 16,922 75

Public School Boards, Districts, $56,352.60.

Algoma, 4,879.00; Cochrane, 5,721.95; Kenora, 9,195.72; Manitoulin, 1,550.00; Muskoka, 3,261.12; Nipissing, 2,800.00; Parry Sound, 1,924.70; Rainy River, 7,749.10; Sudbury, 8,413.00; Temiskaming, 4,635.25; Thunder Bay, 6,222.76... 56,352 60

Separate School Boards, Districts, $21,275.17.

Algoma, 1,550.00; Cochrane, 4,984.39; Kenora, 800.00; Muskoka, 325.00; Nipissing, 1,400.00; Sudbury, 10,805.78; Temiskaming, 1,410.00;............. 21,275 17

Special Grant to School at Whitefish Falls, District of Algoma ($500.00)

The Lord Bishop of Algoma.. 500 00

Public and Separate Schools—Continued

Grants and Contingencies—Continued

Special Grant to Tarentorus Township School Board in Aid of Education of Children at Children's Shelter ($319.82)

Treasurer, Tarentorus Township School Board 319 82

Rural School Libraries, Grants and Contingencies ($24,997.01)

Public School Grants, Counties, $20,332.08.

Brant, 177.95; Bruce, 1,177.98; Carleton, 318.44; Dufferin, 433.07; Dundas, Stormont and Glengarry, 1,020.57; Elgin, 579.63; Essex, 432.15; Frontenac, 570.39; Grey, 769.75; Haldimand, 322.29; Haliburton, 172.54; Halton, 198.24; Hastings, 990.97; Huron, 783.67; Kent, 899.84; Lambton, 280.70; Lanark, 638.88; Leeds and Grenville, 823.74; Lennox and Addington, 273.12; Lincoln, 454.39; Middlesex, 505.44; Norfolk, 207.80; Northumberland and Durham, 952.48; Ontario, 385.21; Oxford, 426.45; Peel, 337.47; Perth, 834.92; Peterborough, 341.55; Prescott and Russell, 179.38; Prince Edward, 289.87; Renfrew, 433.83; Simcoe, 717.99; Victoria, 239.60; Waterloo, 634.78; Welland, 368.46; Wellington, 745.92; Wentworth, 353.22; York, 1,059.40 .... 20,332 08

Separate School Grants, Counties, $1,199.59.

Bruce, 82.96; Carleton, 64.62; Dundas, Stormont and Glengarry, 97.77; Essex, 150.30; Frontenac, 65.57; Grey, 29.62; Hastings, 28.27; Huron, 37.17; Kent, 57.43; Lambton, 7.05; Lanark, 21.00; Middlesex, 30.87; Norfolk, 8.04; Northumberland and Durham, 20.62; Ontario, 8.84; Peel, 6.70; Perth, 53.48; Peterborough, 21.34; Prescott and Russell, 207.99; Renfrew, 88.59; Simcoe, 10.00; Victoria, 15.87; Waterloo, 50.00; Wellington, 17.85; York, 17.64 .... 1,199 59

Public School Grants, Districts, $2,936.79.

Algoma, 304.50; Cochrane, 221.75; Kenora, 107.79; Manitoulin, 183.24; Muskoka, 347.17; Nipissing, 225.31; Parry Sound, 381.26; Rainy River, 296.78; Sudbury, 264.19; Temiskaming, 248.52; Thunder Bay, 356.28 .... 2,936 79

Separate School Grants, Districts, $435.70.

Cochrane, 124.40; Nipissing, 185.94; Rainy River, 6.70; Sudbury, 46.70; Temiskaming, 65.26; Thunder Bay, 6.70 .... 435 70

Contingencies, $92.85.

King's Printer 92 85

Public, Separate and Continuation Schools, Cadet Corps, Grants and Contingencies ($8,563.00)

Public School Boards, $6,500.00.

Belleville, 100.00; Bowmanville, 50.00; Dundas, 50.00; Eganville, 50.00; Hamilton, 1,350.00; Havelock, 50.00; Iroquois Falls, 50.00; London, 50.00; Niagara Falls, 200.00; Ottawa, 250.00; Peterborough, 50.00; Port Hope, 50.00; St. Catharines, 50.00; Schumacher, 50.00; Stratford, 300.00; Toronto, 3,500.00; Trenton, 100.00; Walkerville, 50.00; Welland, 50.00; Weston, 50.00; York East, 50.00 .... 6,500 00

Separate School Boards, $2,000.00.

Hamilton, 650.00; Toronto, 1,350.00 .... 2,000 00

Continuation School Boards, $50.00.

North Mountain Consolidated, Hallville 50 00

Contingencies, $13.00.

King's Printer 13 00

Kindergarten Schools, Grants and Contingencies ($13,277.22)

Public School Boards, Cities, $8,399.04.

Brantford, 292.20; Chatham, 232.20; Fort William, 199.80; Galt, 140.40; Guelph, 72.90; Hamilton, 925.56; Kingston, 124.20; Kitchener, 448.20; London, 605.88; Niagara Falls, 81.00; North Bay, 21.60; Oshawa, 151.20; Ottawa, 580.50; Owen Sound, 129.60; Peterborough, 156.60; Port Arthur, 124.20; St. Catharines, 216.00; Sarnia, 75.60; Sault Ste. Marie, 189.00; St. Thomas, 129.60; Stratford, 148.50; Toronto, 2,817.00; Welland, 108.00; Windsor, 345.60; Windsor East, 83.70 .... 8,399 04

Public and Separate Schools—Continued

Kindergarten Schools, Grants and Contingencies—Continued

Public School Boards, Towns, $2,877.84.

Aurora, 36.00; Aylmer, 46.80; Barrie, 108.00; Campbellford, 28.80; Cóbourg, 36.00; Cochrane, 72.00; Collingwood, 50.40; Eastview, 36.00; Elmira, 36.00; Englehart, 28.80; Essex, 36.00; Fort Erie, 172.08; Goderich, 36.00; Grimsby, 36.00; Hanover, 72.00; Harrow, 36.00; Hawkesbury, 28.80; Hespeler, 46.80; Ingersoll, 72.00; Iroquois Falls, 28.80; Kincardine, 36.00; Kingsville, 64.80; Leamington, 172.80; Leaside, 36.00; Matheson, 36.00; Merritton, 14.40; New Liskeard, 72.00; Newmarket, 18.00; Niagara-on-the-Lake, 36.00; Pembroke, 93.60; Picton, 28.80; Port Colborne, 213.12; Preston, 97.20; Renfrew, 36.00; Riverside, 28.80; Sandwich, 72.00; Seaforth, 36.00; Simcoe, 72.00; Smooth Rock Falls, 36.00; Southampton, 36.00; Tillsonburg, 36.00; Timmins, 162.00; Trenton, 28.80; Vankleek Hill, 36.00; Walkerville, 93.60; Waterloo, 141.84; Whitby, 100.80 — 2,877 84

Public School Boards, Villages, $517.80.

Brighton, 54.00; Chesterville, 27.00; Cobden, 21.60; Delhi, 54.00; Eganville, 54.00; Lucknow, 43.20; Merrickville, 48.00; Stouffville, 54.00; Swansea, 162.00.. — 517 80

Public School Sections, $1,169.64.

No. 11, Bertie, 21.60; No. 3, Brantford, 54.00; No. 3, Buchanan, 27.00; No. 8, Grantham, 43.20; No. U2, Grantham, 54.00; No. 1, Grimsby North, 43.20; No. U2, North Algoma, 21.60; No. 1, O'Brien, 105.84; No. 12, Scarborough, 108.00; No. 14, Scarborough, 43.20; No. 1, Stamford, 54.00; No. 4, Stamford, 43.20; No. 6, Stamford, 25.92; No. U2, Teck and Lebel, 54.00; No. U1, Tisdale, 47.52; No. 16, Wellesley, 17.28; No. 6, Woolwich, 17.28; No. 13, York, 54.00; No. 15, York, 43.20; No. 25, York, 97.20; No. 32, York, 151.20; No; 35, York, 43.20......... — 1,169 64

Separate Schools, $269.70.

Kitchener, 27.00; Niagara Falls, 43.20; Port Arthur, 18.00; Preston, 36.00; Sault St. Marie, 32.94; Sudbury, 22.56; Toronto, 18.00; Waterloo, 72.00............. — 269 70

Consolidated School Sections, $43.20.

Falls View.. — 43 20

Night Schools, Grants and Contingencies ($5,853.37)

Grants, Public Schools, $5,654.37.

No. 1, Atikokan, 250.00; Burriss, 650.00; No. 4, Clinton, 66.66; No. 3, Eilber, 75.00; Port Colborne, 425.00; No. 2, Thorold, 246.66; Toronto, 3,904.39; No. 8, Tudor, 36.66.. — 5,654 37

Grants, Separate Schools, $160.00.

No. 4, Glackmeyer.. — 160 00

Contingencies, $39.00.

King's Printer.. — 39 00

Consolidated Schools ($42,708.82)

Grants, $42,708.82.

Barwick, 924.00; Burriss, 1,990.58; Byng Inlet, 807.60; Charlton, 1,345.74; Dorion, 1,881.10; Falls View, 1,553.50; Gooderham, 1,044.90; Grant, 558.60; Grantham, 1,343.11; Hudson, 1,255.94; Humber Heights, 1,268.00; Jaffray and Mellick, 326.70; Katrine, 983.35; MacDonald, 625.64; Mallorytown, 1,281.25; Mindemoya, 1,419.39; Morley, 2,093.76; Nipigon, 1,836.50; Nobel, 2,000.00; North Mountain, 2,046.82; Pointe au Baril, 2,520.18; Quibell, 1,626.77; Savard, 2,255.60; Sundridge, 950.00; Tamworth, 2,245.12; Tweed, 2,213.32; Wellington, 2,285.00; West Guilford, 1,380.00; Wilberforce, 627.60; York North, 18.75................... — 42,708 82

Agricultural and Horticultural Grants to School Boards, Teachers, Inspectors, and Contingencies ($193,132.86)

Ungraded Public Schools, $99,774.53.

School Boards, 12,394.09; teachers, 87,380.44................................ — 99,774 53

Ungraded Separate Schools, $2,478.90.

School Boards, 269.62; teachers, 2,209.28.................................. — 2,478 90

Graded Public Schools, $49,921.69.

School Boards, 10,161.46; teachers, 39,760.23.............................. — 49,921 69

Public and Separate Schools—Continued

Agricultural and Horticultural Grants to School Boards, Teachers, Inspectors and Contingencies—Continued

Graded Separate Schools, $11,155.73.

School Boards, 3,440.04; teachers, 7,715.69	11,155 73

Inspectors, $29,624.10.

Public Schools, 28,246.20; Separate Schools, 1,377.90	29,624 10

Contingencies, $177.91.

King's Printer	177 91

Industrial Arts, Manual Training and Household Science, Grants to Boards, Teachers, and Contingencies ($87,107.60)

Public Schools, $80,890.35.

Boards, 30,346.42; teachers, 50,543.93	80,890 35

Separate Schools, $6,206.25.

Boards, 2,056.75; teachers, 4,149.50	6,206 25

Contingencies, $11.00.

King's Printer	11 00

Correspondence Courses and Courses by Itinerant Teachers for Pupils in Isolated Districts, including Services and Equipment ($22,285.09)

Salaries, $12,500.00.

Name	Position	Period	Amount
F. G. Sloman	Teacher	12 months	1,800 00
W. H. McNally	"	12 "	1,800 00
Wm. Wright	"	12 "	1,700 00
Wm. J. Fleming	"	12 "	1,700 00
Lillian McBride	"	12 "	1,600 00
Andrew D. Clement	"	12 "	1,500 00
Gladys Dale	"	12 "	1,200 00
M. Frances Hinchcliffe	"	12 "	1,200 00

Temporary Services $3,161.53.

Name	Position	Period	Amount
Margaret K. Mungovan	Teacher	6½ months	650 00
Rhea Scott	"	2½ "	250 00
F. M. Stevens	"	8¾ "	888 46
Lucy A. Williams	"	4⅔ "	473 07
Norman A. Vale	Clerk Typist, Group 1	12 "	900 00

Extra Services, $675.75.

Andrew D. Clement, 111.00; Wm. J. Fleming, 273.00; W. H. McNally, 105.00; F. G. Sloman, 165.75; Wm. Wright, 21.00	675 75

Text Books and Supplies, $1,163.48.

Canadian Watchman Press, 44.99; Copp, Clark Co., Ltd., 87.20; J. M. Dent & Sons, Ltd., 23.68; T. Eaton Co., Ltd., 88.07; W. J. Gage & Co., Ltd., 216.63; G. M. Hendry Co., Ltd., 19.60; Hobbies, Ltd., 12.15; Longmans, Green & Co., 19.72; Macmillan Co., Ltd., 20.30; Marshall Wells Co., 17.43; Thomas Nelson & Sons, Ltd., 250.62; Nicholson's Tire Surgery, 12.75; Oxford University Press, 50.15; Rapid Grip & Batten, Ltd., 147.15; Ryerson Press, 36.11; Smith & Chapple, Ltd., 18.84; Thomas & Corney Typewriters, Ltd., 17.70; petty disbursements, 80.39	1,163 48

Miscellaneous, $4,864.72.

Canadian National Railways School Car, rent, repairs and supplies, 1,738.72; Canadian Pacific Railway Co. School Car, rent, repairs and supplies, 1,358.28; King's Printer, 1,446.63. Sundries—newspapers and periodicals, 80.01; express, 93.13; freight, 7.94; postage, 20.75; petty disbursements, 38.87	4,784 33

Continuation Schools, Grants and Contingencies ($210,836.17)

Continuation School Boards, $25,712.39.

Ayr, 819.98; Bancroft, 810.86; Blackstock, 817.18; Coniston, 1,611.88; Dorchester, 817.37; Espanola, 1,653.73; Freelton, 371.66; Holstein, 804.96; Ilderton, 822.88; Lefroy, 595.07; Lobo, 831.10; Lyndhurst, 793.32; Marmora, 801.95; Mount Brydges, 812.69; Mount Pleasant, 795.10; Onondaga, 399.63; Pelee Island, 1,297.84; Richard's Landing, 1,206.12; St. George, 833.47; Smooth Rock Falls, 1,599.44; Sparta, 813.65; Stella, 782.97; Sundridge, 1,556.75; Tamworth, 821.14; Thorndale, 801.27; Thornton, 799.98; Wales, 791.78; Wilberforce, special, 848.62	25,712 39

Public and Separate Schools—Continued

Continuation Schools, Grants and Contingencies—Continued

Public School Boards, Towns, $36,112.97.

Blind River, 1,662.19; Bothwell, 805.49; Bruce Mines, 1,649.46; Capreol, 1,646.66; Dresden, 807.54; Dryden, 2,136.38; Englehart, 1,628.19; Gore Bay, 1,643.15; Iroquois Falls, 5,227.49; Keewatin, 1,620.83; Little Current, 1,628.21; Massey, 1,696.17; Mattawa, 1,403.55; Palmerston, 809.29; Powassan, 2,588.39; Rainy River, 1,613.11; Sioux Lookout, 2,642.00; Southampton, 814.81; Stayner, 816.37; Sturgeon Falls, 1,633.25; Tilbury, 813.77; Thornbury, 826.67.................. 36,112 97

Public School Boards, Villages, $52,258.33.

Acton, 826.99; Ailsa Craig, 818.69; Alvinston, 821.26; Arkona, 319.31; No. 2, Assignack, 239.53; Bancroft, 2,000.00; Bath, 810.14; Beaverton, 819.97; Beeton, 818.46; Blyth, 812.93; Bobcaygeon, 813.40; Bolton, 812.00; Brussells, 811.84; Burk's Falls, 1,633.54; Cannington, 807.46; Cardinal, 824.78; Chatsworth, 820.09; Clifford, 830.86; Cobden, 400.64; Coldwater, 821.19; Creemore, 817.88; Delhi, 818.39; Drayton, 810.33; Eganville, 825.29; Embro, 826.10; Erin, 818.32; Frankford, 826.56; Grand Valley, 805.41; Havelock, 817.46; Hensall, 809.36; Hepworth, 832.00; Highgate, 816.25; Jarvis, 807.37; Lanark, 804.63; Lion's Head, 812.97; Lucknow, 825.43; Merrickville, 813.79; Millbrook, 825.46; Milverton, 829.28; New Hamburg, 813.14; Oil Springs, 805.93; Paisley, 823.75; Port Carling, 1,186.38; Richmond, 812.15; Rodney, 818.24; South River, 1,578.60; Springfield, 829.57; Stouffville, 821.01; Sutton, 830.16; Tara, 815.57; Tavistock, 817.95; Teeswater, 819.96; Thamesville, 819.56; Thedford, 805.12; Tiverton, 791.47; Tottenham, 796.03; Wellington, 831.54; West Lorne, 810.09; Westport, 808.42; Wheatley, 798.80; Woodville, 826.86; Wroxeter, 792.67................ 52,258 33

Separate School Boards, Villages, $1,604.93.

Eganville, 819.91; Westport, 785.02.. 1,604 93

Consolidated Schools, $4,482.64.

Mallorytown, 818.99; Mindemoya, 1,648.55; Nipigon, 1,184.35; North Mountain and Hallville, 830.75.. 4,482 64

Public School Boards, Townships, $90,339.56.

No. 14, Albion, 808.38; U 3 Amabel and Arran, 783.18; 3 Amaranth, 325.14; U 17 and 19 Ameliasburg and Hillier, 583.97; 1 Anson, 1,397.37; 2 Assignack, 1,196.23; 17 Augusta, 803.68; 11 Bastard, 785.55; 2 Bayham, 824.40; 9 Bertie, 818.97; U 4 Beverley, 807.35; 11 Blenheim, 812.70; U 21 Blenheim, 805.30; U 24 Blenheim, 817.60; 13 Brock, 792.63; 7 Bromley, 375.74; 3 Buchanan, 404.13; U 18 Burford and Oakland, 824.23; 4 Caledon, 603.32; 15 Caledon, 800.25; U 16 Caradoc, 821.64; 12 Clarke, 824.09; 9 Colchester S., 829.31; 22 Cramahe, 807.05; 5 Crosby, 819.29; 3 Cumberland, 814.17; 5 Cumberland, 561.52; 16 Darlington, 383.06; 2 Delaware, 800.60; 5 Denbigh, 386.75; 12 Dereham, 824.54; 5 Dereham, 832.31; 11 Dorchester S., 821.16; 3 Dysart, 2,437.27; 15 Edwardsburg, 801.90; 4 Ennismore, 787.31; 9 Eramosa, 802.03; 13 Ernestown, 806.10; 5 Essa, 809.53; 12 Etobicoke, 822.63; 5 Euphemia, 794.71; 8 Fitzroy, 782.69; 11 Fitzroy, 816.03; 5 Flos, 1,711.34; 1 Freeman, 1,180.96; 5 Gloucester, 330.22; 13 Gwillimbury E., 825.78; 7 Hay, 388.67; 17 Howick, 816.45; 3 Huntley, 805.19; 10 Huron, 805.39; 2 Kaladar, 564.62; 14 King, 819.39; 5 Lash, 1,756.47; 9 Leeds and Landsdowne, 801.96; 8 Leeds and Lansdowne, 794.84; 7 Manvers, 354.49; 15 Manvers, 393.14; 3 Marlborough, 577.87; U 1 McMurrich and Ryerson, 1,488.36; 8 Mariposa, 799.61; 8 Monk, 1,585.26; 1 Mountain, 820.31; 5 Mulmur, 798.39; U 16 and 18 Murray and Brighton, 800.85; 10 Nepean, 398.24; U 5 Nissouri East and 1 Oxford North, 790.18; U 3 North Gower, 812.84; U 6 North Gower, 803.66; U 3 Norwich North and Oxford East, 813.48; 6 Norwich South, 822.24; U 5 Nottawasaga and Osprey, 571.26; 2 Orillia, 1,198.81; 12 Orillia, 808.90; 4 Osnabruck, 555.92; 11 Osgoode, 800.41; 15 Osgoode, 802.04; 18 Osgoode, 820.20; 7 Osprey, 806.48; 4 Pakenham, 808.52; 9 Pelham, 829.13; 2 Percy, 815.16; 15 Pickering, 814.15; 4 Pickering W., 813.88; U 5 Raleigh, 797.05; 6 Ross, 564.76; 2 Russell, 774.20; 14 Scarborough, 820.28; 1 Schrieber, 1,639.48; 3 Somerville, 596.17; 12 Southwold, 821.09; 4 Tilbury West, 816.07; U 1A Tisdale, 6,499.43; 2 Toronto, 780.22; 9 Vespra, 597.78; 3 Walpole, 805.52; 16 Wellesley, 582.43; 2 Westmeath, 785.04; 7 Westmeath, 812.20; 17 Westminister, 829.65; 3 Whitby, 812.30; 1 Wickstead, 1,171.55; 1 and 3 Wilmot and Blenheim, 802.79; 4 Wolf Island, 370.68......... 90,339 56

Contingencies, $325.35.

Irwin & Gordon, Ltd., books, 89.20; King's Printer, 236.15................... 325 35

Public and Separate Schools—Continued

Fifth Classes, Grants and Contingencies ($58,288.15)

Public School Boards, Counties and Districts, $43,237.63.

Algoma, 1,758.09; Bruce, 533.06; Cochrane, 826.51; Dufferin, 1,143.57; Dundas, 199.69; Elgin, 614.48; Frontenac, 650.73; Grey, 1,023.41; Haldimand, 410.72; Haliburton, 2,192.17; Halton, 72.71; Hastings, 765.00; Huron, 1,439.35; Kenora, 778.68; Kent, 528.61; Lambton, 807.86; Lanark, 582.39; Lennox and Addington, 78.44; Lincoln, 60.98; Manitoulin, 1,552.16; Middlesex, 1,006.54; Muskoka, 2,866.50; Nipissing, 150.98; Norfolk, 327.66; Northumberland and Durham, 1,321.74; Ontario, 697.90; Oxford, 765.59; Parry Sound, 2,459.24; Peel, 72.63; Perth, 624.34; Peterborough, 872.72; Prescott and Russell, 650.28; Prince Edward, 484.09; Rainy River, 2,388.70; Renfrew, 597.40; Simcoe, 2,639.53; Sudbury, 3,012.36; Temiskaming, 2,700.56; Thunder Bay, 1,414.19; Victoria, 748.74; Waterloo, 337.72; Welland, 80.51; Wellington, 274.96; Wentworth, 275.42; York, 448.72 ..... 43,237 63

Public School Boards, Towns, $2,140.92.

Bala, 249.71; Hearst, 195.03; Kearney, 270.00; Latchford, 289.53; Mathieson, 306.32; Trout Creek, 227.88; Webbwood, 313.92; Windsor East, 288.53 ..... 2,140 92

Public School Boards, Villages, $1,780.29.

Erieau, 97.51; Hilton Beach, 226.15; Holland Landing, 102.42; Killaloe Station, 171.82; Mildmay, 124.49; Newboro, 189.36; Port McNicoll, 189.38; Rosseau, 358.38; Victoria Harbour, 185.78; Woodbridge, 135.00 ..... 1,780 29

Separate School Boards, Counties and Districts, $7,496.67.

Algoma, 145.28; Bruce, 306.59; Carleton, 112.35; Cochrane, 212.24; Essex, 643.70; Frontenac, 56.98; Grey, 147.06; Hastings, 142.46; Huron, 344.82; Kent, 115.87; Lennox and Addington, 193.66; Nipissing, 290.57; Norfolk, 69.66; Ontario, 88.29; Perth, 526.52; Prescott and Russell, 893.33; Rainy River, 154.92; Renfrew, 1,059.90; Simcoe, 118.11; Stormont, Dundas and Glengarry, 650.30; Sudbury, 350.61; Victoria, 136.35; Waterloo, 426.60; Wellington, 144.00; Wentworth, 166.50 ..... 7,496 67

Separate School Boards, Towns, $2,541.44.

Blind River, 342.00; Bonfield, 274.01; Charlton, 200.07; Chelmsford, 342.00; Hearst, 196.68; Kearney, 109.85; La Salle, 133.20; Preston, 138.55; Riverside, 94.37; Sandwich, 171.00; Tecumseh, 187.65; Tilbury, 181.06; Windsor East, 171.00 ..... 2,541 44

Separate School Boards, Villages, $1,030.60.

Belle River, 193.50; Casselman, 166.41; Hastings, 131.04; Killaloe Station, 193.50; Lancaster, 171.00; L'Orignal, 175.15 ..... 1,030 60

Contingencies, $60.60.

King's Printer 60 60

Teachers' Associations, Grants and Contingencies ($8,175.56)

Teachers' Institutes, Cities, $1,775.00.

Brantford, 50.00; Chatham, 25.00; Fort William and Port Arthur, 100.00; Guelph, 25.00; Hamilton, 200.00; Kingston, 50.00; Kitchener, 50.00; London, 100.00; Oshawa, 50.00; Ottawa, 175.00; Peterborough, 50.00; Sarnia, 50.00; St. Catharines, 50.00; Toronto, 675.00; Windsor, 125.00 ..... 1,775 00

Teachers' Institutes, Counties and Districts, $4,300.00.

5 Algoma East, 50.00; 8 Algoma, 50.00; Brant and Norfolk North, 50.00; Brockville and Leeds, 50.00; Bruce West, 50.00; Bruce East, 50.00; Carleton East, 50.00; Carleton West, 50.00; Cochrane North, 50.00; Dufferin, 50.00; Dundas, 50.00; Elgin East, 50.00; Elgin West, 50.00; Essex North, 75.00; Essex South, 50.00; Frontenac North and Addington, 25.00; Frontenac South, 50.00; Grey East, 50.00; Grey South, 50.00; Grey North and Bruce North, 50.00; Glengarry, 50.00; Haliburton, 25.00; Haldimand and Wentworth South, 50.00; Halton, 50.00; Hastings Centre, 50.00; Hastings North, 25.00; Hastings South, 50.00; Huron East, 50.00; Huron West, 50.00; Kenora, 50.00; 1 Kent, 50.00; 2 Kent, 50.00; Lambton East, 50.00; Lambton West, 50.00; Lanark East, 50.00; Lanark West and Smith's Falls, 50.00; 1 Leeds and Grenville, 50.00; Lennox, 50.00; Lincoln, 50.00; Manitoulin, 50.00; Middlesex East, 50.00; Middlesex West, 50.00; Muskoka 50.00; Nipissing, 50.00; Norfolk, 50.00; 1 Northumberland and Durham, 50.00; 2 Northumberland and Durham, 50.00; 3 Northumberland and Durham, 50.00;

Public and Separate Schools—Continued

Teachers' Associations, Grants and Contingencies—Continued

Teachers' Institutes, Counties and Districts—Continued

Ontario North and York, 50.00; Ontario South, 50.00; Oxford, 75.00; Parry Sound East, 50.00; Parry Sound West, 50.00 Peel (part) and York (part), 50.00; Perth, 75.00; Peterborough, 50.00; Prescott and Russell, 75.00; Prince Edward, 50.00; Rainy River, 50.00; Renfrew North, 50.00; Renfrew South, 50.00; Simcoe East, 50.00; Simcoe Centre, 50.00; Simcoe South (part), York (part) and Peel (part), 50.00; Simcoe West, Grey (part) and Dufferin (part), 50.00; Stormont, 50.00; 6 Sudbury, 50.00; 7 Sudbury, 50.00; Temiskaming South, 50.00; Temiskaming North and Cochrane (part), 50.00; Thunder Bay, 50.00; Victoria East and West, 50.00; Waterloo North, 50.00; Waterloo South, 50.00; Welland North, 75.00; Welland South, 50.00; Wellington South and City of Guelph, 50.00; Wellington North, 50.00; Wentworth, 50.00; 1 York, 50.00; 2 York, 50.00; 3 York, 50.00; 4 York, 50.00; 5 York, 50.00; 6 York, 50.00.................................. 4,300 00

Travelling Expenses, $43.30.

H. L. Banford, 13.60; C. H. Edwards, 11.50; D. Emory, 7.95; A. Marsh, 10.25.. 43 30

Contingencies, $2,057.26.

King's Printer.. 2,057 26

Grants ($20,650.00)

Ontario Educational Association, 3,500.00; Trustees' Section, Ontario Educational Association, 4,000.00; Urban Trustees' Association, 250.00; National Council of Education for Secretarial Work, 2,400.00; Ontario Federation of Home and School Association, 2,000.00; Frontier College, 7,500.00; Canadian Bureau for the Advancement of Music, 1,000.00....................................... 20,650 00

Spring and Summer Schools ($37,756.66)

Lectures, $35,166.13.

Services, 34,689.31; expenses, 476.82....................................... 35,166 13

Rent of Class Rooms and Caretakers' Services, $1,338.24.

Rentals, 240.00; services, 1,098.24.. 1,338 24

School Supplies, etc., $1,252.29.

Anderson Langstaff Co., seeds, 10.43; Bell Telephone Co., rentals, 12.88; tolls, 4.83; Chair Man Mills, rental of tables, 15.00; C. Chapman & Co., stationery, 17.50; Dale Estate, labels, 20.10; Douglas Seed Co., seed, 28.75; W. Fitzgerald, gymnasium supplies, 46.20; E. Grainger & Co., Ltd., flowers, 19.94; Gummer Press, Ltd., printing, 93.50; Hamilton Technical Institute, machine shop supplies, 35.81; J. Hope & Sons, Ltd., books, 10.00; Kemptville Agricultural School, stationery, etc., 14.25; King's Printer, 262.29; K. McDonald & Sons, Ltd., seeds, 54.10; New Method Laundry Co., Ltd., towelling, 27.74; Ontario Hughes, Owens Co., Ltd., instruments, 13.86; Ruddy Manufacturing Co., bee veils, 11.00; Soclean, Ltd., cleaning supplies, 31.30; United Typewriter Co., Ltd., rentals, 256.25; University of Toronto, registration cards, 40.85; Wilson Scientific Co., Ltd., beakers, 150.25. Sundries—express, 2.25; postage, 6.78; telegrams, .45; petty disbursements, 65.98... 1,252 29

League of the Empire ($230.67)

Gilchrist-Wright, Ltd., paper, 45.55; W. M. Morrow, services, 47.92; F. M. Standish, services, 100.00; postage, 37.20.................................. 230 67

Grants to Art Department and Teachers in Art ($8,372.43)

Public Schools, $7,200.68.

Boards, 1,797.08; teachers, 5,403.60....................................... 7,200 68

Separate Schools, $1,161.00.

Boards, 837.00; teachers, 324.00.. 1,161 00

Miscellaneous, $10.75.

King's Printer.. 10 75

Public and Separate Schools—Con ued

Fifth Classes, Grants and Contingencies 8,?88.15)

Public School Boards, Counties and Districts, $43,237.63.

Algoma, 1,758.09; Bruce, 533.06; Cochrane, 826.51; Duffer 1,143.57; Dundas, 199.69; Elgin, 614.48; Frontenac, 650.73; Grey, 1,023.41; Haldimand, 410.72; Haliburton, 2,192.17; Halton, 72.71; Hastings, 765.00; Hur , 1,439.35; Kenora, 778.68; Kent, 528.61; Lambton, 807.86; Lanark, 582.39; Le ıox and Addington, 78.44; Lincoln, 60.98; Manitoulin, 1,552.16; Middlesex, ,006.54; Muskoka, 2,866.50; Nipissing, 150.98; Norfolk, 327.66; Northumb and and Durham, 1,321.74; Ontario, 697.90; Oxford, 765.59; Parry Sound, 59.24; Peel, 72.63; Perth, 624.34; Peterborough, 872.72; Prescott and Russell, 6 .28; Prince Edward, 484.09; Rainy River, 2,388.70; Renfrew, 597.40; Simcoe 2,639.53; Sudbury, 3,012.36; Temiskaming, 2,700.56; Thunder Bay, 1,414. ; Victoria, 748.74; Waterloo, 337.72; Welland, 80.51; Wellington, 274.96; Wentworth, 275.42; York, 448.72 .... 43,237 63

Public School Boards, Towns, $2,140.92.

Bala, 249.71; Hearst, 195.03; Kearney, 270.00; Latchfor 289.53; Mathieson, 306.32; Trout Creek, 227.88; Webbwood, 313.92; Windsor . st, 288.53 .... 2,140 92

Public School Boards, Villages, $1,780.29.

Erieau, 97.51; Hilton Beach, 226.15; Holland Landing, 10 2; Killaloe Station, 171.82; Mildmay, 124.49; Newboro, 189.36; Port McNi l, 189.38; Rosseau, 358.38; Victoria Harbour, 185.78; Woodbridge, 135.00 .... 1,780 29

Separate School Boards, Counties and Districts, $7,496.67.

Algoma, 145.28; Bruce, 306.59; Carleton, 112.35; Coc ne, 212.24; Essex, 643.70; Frontenac, 56.98; Grey, 147.06; Hastings, 142.46; uron, 344.82; Kent, 115.87; Lennox and Addington, 193.66; Nipissing, 29 7; Norfolk, 69.66; Ontario, 88.29; Perth, 526.52; Prescott and Russell, 893.33 Rainy River, 154.92; Renfrew, 1,059.90; Simcoe, 118.11; Stormont, Dundas a Glengarry, 650.30; Sudbury, 350.61; Victoria, 136.35; Waterloo, 426.60; Wel gton, 144.00; Wentworth, 166.50 .... 7,496 67

Separate School Boards, Towns, $2,541.44.

Blind River, 342.00; Bonfield, 274.01; Charlton, 200.07 Chelmsford, 342.00; Hearst, 196.68; Kearney, 109.85; La Salle, 133.20; Pres ı, 138.55; Riverside, 94.37; Sandwich, 171.00; Tecumseh, 187.65; Tilbury, 1 .06; Windsor East, 171.00 .... 2,541 44

Separate School Boards, Villages, $1,030.60.

Belle River, 193.50; Casselman, 166.41; Hastings, 131 ·; Killaloe Station, 193.50; Lancaster, 171.00; L'Orignal, 175.15 .... 1,030 60

Contingencies, $60.60.

King's Printer 60 60

Teachers' Associations, Grants and Continge ies ($8,175.56)

Teachers' Institutes, Cities, $1,775.00.

Brantford, 50.00; Chatham, 25.00; Fort William and Port A hur, 100.00; Guelph, 25.00; Hamilton, 200.00; Kingston, 50.00; Kitchener, 5)0; London, 100.00; Oshawa, 50.00; Ottawa, 175.00; Peterborough, 50.00; Sarnia 0.00; St. Catharines, 50.00; Toronto, 675.00; Windsor, 125.00 .... 1,775 00

Teachers' Institutes, Counties and Districts, $4,300.00.

5 Algoma East, 50.00; 8 Algoma, 50.00; Brant and Norfoll North, 50.00; Brockville and Leeds, 50.00; Bruce West, 50.00; Bruce East,).00; Carleton East, 50.00; Carleton West, 50.00; Cochrane North, 50.00; Du ·rin, 50.00; Dundas, 50.00; Elgin East, 50.00; Elgin West, 50.00; Essex Nortl 75.00; Essex South, 50.00; Frontenac North and Addington, 25.00; Frontenac S th, 50.00; Grey East, 50.00; Grey South, 50.00; Grey North and Bruce North, 5(0; Glengarry, 50.00; Haliburton, 25.00; Haldimand and Wentworth South, .00; Halton, 50.00; Hastings Centre, 50.00; Hastings North, 25.00; Hastings South, 50.00; Huron East, 50.00; Huron West, 50.00; Kenora, 50.00; 1 Kent, 0.00; 2 Kent, 50.00; Lambton East, 50.00; Lambton West, 50.00; Lanark Eas 50.00; Lanark West and Smith's Falls, 50.00; 1 Leeds and Grenville, 50.00; L nox, 50.00; Lincoln, 50.00; Manitoulin, 50.00; Middlesex East, 50.00; Middlesex West, 50.00; Muskoka 50.00; Nipissing, 50.00; Norfolk, 50.00; 1 Northumberlan and Durham, 50.00; 2 Northumberland and Durham, 50.00; 3 Northumberlan and Durham, 50.00;

Pub.'c ıd Separate Schools—Continued

Teachers' Asᵹɔc ions, Grants and Contingencies—Continued

Teachers' Institutes, Counties ɾnc)istricts—Continued

Ontario North and York, 50.0 0 ntario South, 50.00; Oxford, 75.00; Parry Sound East, 50.00; Parry Sound V. st :0.00 Peel (part) and York (part), 50.00; Perth, 75.00; Peterborough, 50.00: Pı :ott and Russell, 75.00; Prince Edward, 50.00; Rainy River, 50.00; Renfre :th, 50.00; Renfrew South, 50.00; Simcoe East, 50.00; Simcoe Centre, 50.0: S coe South (part), York (part) and Peel (part), 50.00; Simcoe West, Grey ;a) and Dufferin (part), 50.00; Stormont, 50.00; 6 Sudbury, 50.00; 7 Sudbur ,).00; Temiskaming South, 50.00; Temiskaming North and Cochrane (part), 50); Thunder Bay, 50.00; Victoria East and West, 50.00; Waterloo North, 50 0 Vaterloo South, 50.00; Welland North, 75.00; Welland South, 50.00; Well g ı South and City of Guelph, 50.00; Wellington North, 50.00; Wentworth, 5).(1 York, 50.00; 2 York, 50.00; 3 York, 50.00; 4 York, 50.00; 5 York, 50.0 6 ork, 50.00 ..... 4,300 00

Travelling Expenses, $43.30.

H. L. Banford, 13.60; C. H. E(ards, 11.50; D. Emory, 7.95; A. Marsh, 10.25.. 43 30

Contingencies, $2,057.26.

King's Printer 2,057 26

Grants ($20,650.00)

Ontario Educational Associat 500.00; Trustees' Section, Ontario Educational Association, 4,000.00; Url 1 stees' Association, 250.00; National Council of Education for Secretarial c , 2,400.00; Ontario Federation of Home and School Association, 2,00 mtier College, 7,500.00; Canadian Bureau for the Advancement of Music, 1,(.00 ..... 20,650 00

Sprin nd Summer Schools ($37,756.66)

Lectures, $35,166.13.

Services, 34,689.31; expense .82 ..... 35,166 13

Rent of Class Rooms and Caretak r Services, $1,338.24.

Rentals, 240.00; services, 1 8 4 ..... 1,338 24

School Supplies, etc., $1,252.29.

Anderson Langstaff C s 0.43; Bell Telephone Co., rentals, 12.88; tolls, 4.83; Chair Man Mills, r 1 tables, 15.00; C. Chapman & Co., stationery, 17.50; Dale Estate, label , 1 Douglas Seed Co., seed, 28.75; W. Fitzgerald, gymnasium supplies, 46.) rainger & Co., Ltd., flowers, 19.94; Gummer Press, Ltd., printing, 93.50, lton Technical Institute, machine shop supplies, 35.81; J. Hope & Sons, l. ooks, 10.00; Kemptville Agricultural School, stationery, etc., 14.25; Kii l ıter, 262.29; K. McDonald & Sons, Ltd., seeds, 54.10; New Method Laundr C Ltd., towelling, 27.74; Ontario Hughes, Owens Co., Ltd., instruments, 13. R dy Manufacturing Co., bee veils, 11.00; Soclean, Ltd., cleaning supplies, 3) nited Typewriter Co., Ltd., rentals, 256.25; University of Toronto, r on cards, 40.85; Wilson Scientific Co., Ltd., beakers, 150.25. Sundries ex ess, 2.25; postage, 6.78; telegrams, .45; petty disbursements, 65.98 ..... 1,252 29

l gue of the Empire ($230.67)

Gilchrist-Wright, Ltd., pa . 55; W. M. Morrow, services, 47.92; F. M. Standish, services, 100.00 t e, 37.20 ..... 230 67

Grants to Art partment and Teachers in Art ($8,372.43)

Public Schools, $7,200.68.

Boards, 1,797.08; teachers, 5,4 .60 7,200

Separate Schools, $1,161.00.

Boards, 837.00; teachers, 324 .....

Miscellaneous, $10.75.

King's Printer .....

Public and Separate Schools—Continued

Grants to School Boards and Teachers for Music ($27,372.50)

Public School Boards, $25,993.00.
Boards, 16,896.60; teachers, 9,096.40 .... 25,993 00

Separate School Boards, $1,367.00.
Boards, 387.00; teachers, 980.00 .... 1,367 00

Miscellaneous, $12.50.
King's Printer 12 50

Medical and Dental Inspection Grants ($14,830.00)

Public Schools, Cities and Towns, $8,194.80.
Barrie, 165.00; Belleville, 138.00; Brockville, 165.00; Chatham, 159.00; Dundas, 85.00; Fort Frances, 135.00; Fort William, 297.00; Galt, 156.00; Hamilton, 1,710.00; Kingston, 195.00; London, 702.00; Midland, 135.00; Mimico, 130.00; Niagara Falls, 198.00; Ottawa, 810.00; Owen Sound, 150.00; Pembroke, 135.00; Peterborough, 222.00; Sandwich, 245.00; Sarnia, 201.00; St. Catharines, 270.00; Sault Ste. Marie, 249.00; Sudbury, 120.00; Walkerville, 350.00; Waterloo, 150.00; Welland, 153.00; Windsor, 610.80; Windsor East, 159.00 .... 8,194 80

Public Schools, Townships, $6,218.00.
No. U 2 Beamsville, Grimsby and Clinton, 400.00; Brampton, Port Credit and Toronto, 400.00; U 2A and 2B Bridgeburg, Fort Erie and Bertie, 720.00; U 2 Barton East and West Flamboro, 280.00; Dunnville, Cayuga and Caledonia, 400.00; 11A and 11B Etobicoke, 74.00; Glanford and Beverley, 330.00; 1 and 2 Nepean, 360.00; U 1 Port Dalhousie, Merritton and Grantham, 400.00; 15 Scarboro, 80.00; 12 Scarboro, 200.00; 10 Scarboro, 200.00; U 1 Stamford, Chippawa, Stamford and Willoughby, 400.00; U 3 Stoney Creek and Saltfleet, 270.00; U 3 Thorold and Thorold, 340.00; Wiarton, Chesley, Tara, etc., 250.00; S.S. 29, 32, 33 York, 400.00; 28 York, 98.00; 13 York, 215.00; 15 York, 400.00 .... 6,218 00

Separate Schools, $417.20.
Barrie, 15.00; Galt, 15.00; Niagara Falls, 30.00; Riverside, 30.00; St. Catharines, 63.00; Sudbury, 67.20; Waterloo, 50.00; Windsor East, 147.00 .... 417 20

Public and Separate School Education $4,380,227.35

INSPECTION OF SCHOOLS

Salaries (Inside Staff) $72,427.28)

V. K. Greer	Chief Inspector of Public and Separate Schools	12 months			5,400 00
J. D. Campbell	Assistant Chief Inspector	12	"		4,200 00
John Hartley	Assistant to the Chief Inspector	12	"		3,600 00
Neil McDougall	Director of School Correspondence Branch and Summer Courses	12	"		4,200 00
James B. MacDougall	Director of School Attendance	12	"		4,200 00
Constance R. Boulton	Provincial School Attendance and Field Work Officer	12			1,900 00
Norman Davies	Inspector, Group 1	4	"		1,266 66
J. B. Dandeno	Inspector of Agricultural Classes	1½	"	234 62	
" "	" " " (T)	3	"	1,001 00	1,235 62
G. K. Mills	Inspector of Continuation Schools	12	"		4,600 00
J. P. Hoag	" " "	12	"		4,600 00
Stanley D. Rendall	" " "	12	"		4,000 00
A. H. Leake	Inspector of Manual Training and Household Science	12	"		3,800 00
Harold E. Amoss	Inspector of Auxiliary Classes	12	"		4,400 00
Helen De Laporte	Assistant Inspector of Auxiliary Classes	12	"		2,550 00
W. J. Karr	Director of English Instruction	12	"		5,000 00
A. J. Beneteau	Director of French Instruction	12	"		5,000 00
W. J. McCoy	Clerk, Group 1	12			1,600 00
E. Francis	" Group 2	12	"		1,125 00
R. A. Patterson	Senior Clerk Stenographer	12			1,500 00
M. K. Drew	" " "	12	"		1,400 00
Laura Kirkland	" " "	12	"		1,400 00
Helen A. Boyd	" " "	12	"		1,300 00

Inspection of Public Schools—Continued

Salaries—Continued

E. H. Ross	Clerk Stenographer, Group 1	5½ months	550 00
J. M. Smyth	Clerk Typist, Group 1	12 "	1,200 00
Kathleen Burns	" " "	12 "	1,200 00
V. O. Kerr	" " "	12	1,200 00

Inspection of Public Schools ($283,358.00)

Walter Joyce	Inspector,	Brant	10 months	2,500 00
T. W. Standing	"	"	2 "	600 00
J. M. Game	"	Bruce E	10 "	2,500 00
John McCool	"	"	2 "	600 00
W. F. Bald	"	Bruce W	12 "	3,600 00
T. P. Maxwell	"	Carleton E	12 "	3,600 00
R. C. Rose	"	Carleton W	12 "	3,600 00
W. T. Liddy	"	Dufferin	12 "	3,600 00
W. J. Stewart	"	Dundas	12 "	3,150 00
J. C. Smith	"	Elgin E	12 "	3,600 00
J. A. Taylor	"	Elgin W	12 "	3,600 00
W. L. Bowden	"	Essex S	12 "	3,600 00
Thos. Preston	"	Essex N	12 "	3,600 00
M. R. Reid	"	Frontenac N	12 "	3,600 00
S. A. Truscott	"	Frontenac S	12 "	3,600 00
G. N. Edwards	"	Glengarry	12 "	3,000 00
S. A. Morrison	"	Grey E	12 "	3,400 00
J. J. Wilson	"	Grey W	12 "	3,150 00
Robt. Wright	"	Grey S	12 "	3,600 00
J. L. Mitchener	"	Haldimand	12 "	3,600 00
J. M. Denyes	"	Halton	12 "	3,600 00
A. W. McGuire	"	Hastings Centre	12 "	3,600 00
James Colling	"	Hastings N	12 "	3,600 00
H. J. Clarke	"	Hastings S	12 "	3,600 00
J. M. Field	"	Huron E	12 "	3,600 00
E. C. Beacom	"	Huron W	12 "	3,400 00
G. A. Pearson	"	Kent E	12 "	3,400 00
A. B. Lucas	"	Kent W	12 "	3,000 00
H. B. Galpin	"	Lambton W	12 "	3,400 00
J. J. Edwards	"	Lambton E	12 "	3,600 00
J. C. Spence	"	Lanark E	12 "	3,600 00
Thos. C. Smith	"	Lanark W	12 "	3,600 00
J. F. McGuire	"	Leeds, No. 1	12 "	3,600 00
W. C. Dowsley	"	Leeds, No. 2	12 "	3,600 00
T. A. Craig	"	Leeds, No. 3	10 "	3,000 00
Gordon Young	"	Leeds and Grenville	2 "	500 00
E. J. Corkill	"	Lennox	10 "	3,000 00
G. A. Carefoot	"	Lincoln	12 "	3,600 00
Albert Brown	"	Lennox and Addington	2 "	500 00
P. J. Thompson	"	Middlesex E	12 "	3,600 00
J. H. Sexton	"	Middlesex W	12 "	3,600 00
H. Frank Cook	"	Norfolk	12 "	3,600 00
E. E. Snider	"	Northumberland and Durham No. 1	12 "	3,600 00
J. W. Odell	"	Northumberland and Durham No. 2	12 "	3,600 00
Allan A. Martin	"	Northumberland and Durham No. 3	12 "	3,150 00
T. R. Ferguson	"	Ontario N	12 "	3,600 00
R. A. Hutchison	"	Ontario S	12 "	3,600 00
George M. Mather	"	Oxford N	12 "	3,200 00
R. A. Paterson	"	Oxford S	4 "	1,200 00
J. W. Hagen	"	Oxford S	8 "	2,400 00
M. R. Fydell	"	Peel	12 "	3,400 00
A. E. Nelson	"	Perth N	12 "	3,600 00
Jas. H. Smith	"	Perth S	12 "	3,600 00
L. W. Copp	"	Peterborough E	12 "	3,600 00
R. F. Downey	"	Peterborough W	12 "	3,600 00
Archibald McVicar	"	Prescott	12 "	3,600 00
C. E. Stothers	"	Prince Edward	12 "	3,600 00
Norman Campbell	"	Renfrew N	12 "	3,400 00

Inspection of Public Schools—Continued

Salaries—Continued

Colin W. Lees	Inspector,	Renfrew S.	12 months	3,000 00
J. L. Garvin	"	Simcoe	12 "	3,600 00
W. H. Carlton	"	Simcoe S.	12 "	3,150 00
Wm. A. Marshall	"	Simcoe W.	12 "	3,000 00
James Froats	"	Stormont	12 "	3,600 00
E. W. Jennings	"	Victoria W.	12 "	3,600 00
R. H. Roberts	"	Waterloo, No. 1	12 "	3,400 00
Lambert Norman	"	Waterloo, No. 2	12 "	3,600 00
J. A. Marlin	"	Welland	12 "	3,600 00
J. W. Marshall	"	Welland N.	12 "	3,600 00
Jas. McNiece	"	Welland S.	12 "	3,600 00
G. G. McNab	"	Wellington	12 "	3,600 00
J. A. Gibson	"	Wellington N.	12 "	3,150 00
L. P. Menzies	"	Wellington S.	12 "	3,150 00
J. B. Robinson	"	Wentworth	12 "	3,600 00
Robt. Gillies	"	York	12 "	3,600 00
A. L. Campbell	"	York S.	12 "	3,600 00
A. A. Jordan	"	York E.	12 "	3,600 00
W. A. Fydell	"	York N.	12 "	3,200 00
W. W. A. Trench	"	York, Division 3	12 "	3,600 00
J. E. Wilkinson	"	York	12 "	3,600 00

Grants to School Boards, Cities, $25,458.00.

Brantford, 678.00; Chatham, 300.00; Fort William, 600.00; Hamilton, 3,342.00; Kingston, 390.00; Kitchener, 588.00; London, 1,332.00; Oshawa, 522.00; Ottawa, 1,608.00; Peterborough, 444.00; Port Arthur, 426.00; Sandwich, 240.00; Sarnia, 396.00; Sault Ste. Marie, 498.00; St. Catharines, 558.00; Toronto, 11,874.00; Walkerville, 246.00; Welland, 306.00; Windsor, 1,110.00 — 25,458 00

District Public Schools ($53,341.34)

J. L. Moore	Inspector	12 months	3,600 00
J. W. Hagan	"	4 "	1,200 00
W. Roy McVittie	"	12 "	3,000 00
C. F. Ewers	"	12 "	3,600 00
Donald G. Smith	"	12 "	3,600 00
W. A. Wilson	"	12 "	2,307 00
George E. Pentland	"	12 "	3,600 00
P. W. Brown	"	12 "	3,600 00
D. T. Walkom	"	12 "	3,034 34
Samuel Shannon	"	12 "	3,600 00
L. J. Williams	"	12 "	3,600 00
Geo. S. Johnston	"	12 "	3,600 00
Oliver M. McKillop	"	12 "	3,600 00
R. A. A. McConnell	"	12 "	3,400 00
Lorne Skuce	"	12 "	3,000 00
Harold G. Elborn	"	12 "	3,000 00
Norman R. Wightman	"	8 "	2,000 00

Separate Schools ($71,600.00)

Joseph T. Anderson	Inspector	12 months	3,000 00
W. J. Lee	"	12 "	3,600 00
J. F. Sullivan	"	12 "	3,600 00
J. M. Bennett	"	12 "	3,600 00
Vincent C. Quarry	"	12 "	3,600 00
Thomas S. Melady	"	12 "	3,600 00
Henry J. Payette	"	12 "	3,600 00
J. S. Gratton	"	12 "	3,600 00
J. C. Walsh	"	12 "	3,600 00
James Scanlon	"	12 "	3,600 00
Charles A. Latour	"	12 "	3,600 00
Rosario Masse	"	12 "	3,000 00
Louis Charbonneau	"	11½ "	3,452 06
F. J. McDonald	"	12 "	3,600 00
Robert Gauthier	"	12 "	3,600 00
F. Choquette	"	12 "	3,600 00
Charlemagne Charron	"	12 "	3,200 00
Charles P. Matthews	"	12 "	3,000 00
William J. Greening	"	12 "	3,000 00

Inspection of Separate Schools—Continued

Salaries—Continued

Adelard J. Gascon	Inspector	12 months	3,000 00
Joseph Lapensee	"	½ "	147 94
Raymond B. Maurice	"	12 "	3,000 00

Travelling, Moving and Other Expenses ($98,633.50)

Temporary Services, $1,223.00.

Velma Caven	Clerk, Group 3	2 months	125 00
Pearl Lainson	Clerk Stenographer, Group 2	12 "	825 00
Willa McNally	Clerk, Group 2	3 "	273 00

Travelling and Office Expenses, $83,725.46.

H. E. Amoss, 806.61; J. T. Anderson, 637.52; W. F. Bald, 535.89; E. C. Beacom, 526.74; A. J. Beneteau, 1,231.52; J. M. Bennet, 334.85; C. N. Boulton, 498.45; W. L. Bowden, 387.85; F. W. Brown, 639.68; A. L. Campbell, 341.80; J. D. Campbell, 237.28; N. Campbell, 926.56; Geo. A. Carefoot, 648.00; W. H. Carlton, 585.53; L. Charbonneau, 1,025.28; L. Charron, 1,543.72; F. Choquette, 961.62; H. J. Clark, 357.26; J. Colling, 467.91; H. F. Cook, 622.72; L. W. Copp, 608.89; E. J. Corkhill, 236.08; T. A. Craig, 470.21; J. B. Dandeno, 20.95; N. Davies, 397.62; C. H. De Laporte, 593.27; J. M. Denyes, 427.86; F. F. Downey, 384.96; W. C. Dowsley, 449.37; J. J. Edwards, 486.35; G. N. Edwards, 744.56; H. C. Elborn, 704.56; C. F. Ewers, 786.45; T. R. Ferguson, 514.13; J. M. Field, 622.34; J. Froates, 657.09; W. A. Fydell, 188.77; M. R. Fydell, 642.81; H. B. Galpin, 582.95; J. M. Game, 687.47; J. L. Garvin, 276.58; A. Gascon, 1,137.40; R. Gauthier, 588.99; J. A. Gibson, 513.64; R. Gillies, 734.20; J. S. Gratton, 637.06; W. J. Greening, 536.65; V. K. Greer, 718.33; J. Hartley, 15.25; D. C. Hetherington, 4.40; J. W. Hagan, 1,017.13; J. P. Hoag, 1,300.77; R. A. Hutchinson, 567.90; E. W. Jennings, 674.88; G. S. Johnson, 1,289.95; A. A. Jordan, 194.61; W. Joyce, 422.71; W. J. Karr, 1,159.26; J. Lapensee, 25.50; C. A. Latour, 381.71; A. H. Leake, 866.76; C. W. Lees, 971.72; W. J. Lee, 108.46; W. R. Liddy, 601.34; A. B. Lucas, 677.71; O. M. Mackillop, 1,005.95; R. A. A. McConnell, 553.85; J. McCool, 197.45; F. J. McDonald, 214.39; J. B. McDougall, 762.92; A. W. McGuire, 496.47; J. F. McGuire, 497.90; G. G. McNab, 849.26; J. McNiece, 500.47; A. McVicar, 415.38; W. R. McVittie, 906.05; L. A. Marlin, 886.45; J. W. Marshall, 218.99; W. A. Marshall, 745.15; A. A. Martin, 692.48; R. Masse, 2,214.45; G. M. Mather, 646.87; C. P. Matthews, 836.05; T. P. Maxwell, 322.68; R. R. Maurice, 840.66; T. S. Melady, 406.05; L. P. Menzies, 519.01; G. K. Mills, 1,479.54; J. L. Mitchener, 446.31; J. L. Moore, 879.29; S. A. Morrison, 560.44; A. C. Nelson, 1,124.85; L. Norman, 495.78; J. W. O'Dell, 496.58; R. A. Patterson, 162.93; H. J. Payette, 1,074.99; G. A. Pearson, 713.68; G. E. Pentland, 1,131.32; Thos. Preston, 422.31; U. C. Quarry, 1,013.25; M. R. Reid, 451.22; R. H. Roberts, 441.41; J. P, Robinson, 826.31; R. C. Rose, 455.29; S. L. Rendall, 1,398.50; J. V. Scanlon, 867.76; J. H. Sexton, 479.71; S. Shannon, 728.29; L. Skuce, 829.20; D. G. Smith, 800.64; J. H. Smith, 259.12; J. C. Smith, 1,184.02; J. H. Smith, 234.12; T. C. Smith, 537.16; E. E. Snider, 531.05; J. C. Spence, 706.19; T. W. Standing, 148.88; W. J. Stewart, 463.62; C. E. Stothers, 658.01; J. F. Sullivan, 164.55; J. A. Taylor, 772.49; F. J. Thompson, 436.49; W. A. Trench, 517.78; S. A. Truscott, 604.18; D. T. Walkom, 661.20; J. C. Walsh, 682.76; N. F. Wightman, 806.87; J. E. Wilkinson, 438.86; L. J. Williams, 1,044.43; J. J. Wilson, 752.59; W. A. Wilson, 378.11; R. H. Wright, 739.19; G. Young, 48.87 .... 83,725 46

Miscellaneous, $13,685.04.

King's Printer, 13,440.05; Ryerson Press, Ltd., books, 225.00. Sundries—express, 8.75; petty disbursements, 11.24 .... 13,685 04

Inspection of Indian Schools ($2,525.78).

Sundry Inspectors, services, 1,768.00; expenses, 757.78 .... 2,525 78

Auxiliary Classes, Grants and Contingencies ($52,395.46)

Public School Boards, Grants, $45,070.14.

Barrie, 237.01; Belleville, 256.29; Blandford, No. 1, 45.00; Brantford, 775.40; Chatham, 558.66; Cobourg, 199.84; Collingwood, 208.73; East Zorra, 5.79; Fort Francis, 213.92; Fort William, 845.78; Galt, 201.92; Guelph, 542.23; Hamilton, 2,252.75; Ingersoll, 246.60; Kitchener, 1,189.13; Leamington, 197.48;

Auxiliary Classes, Grants and Contingencies—Continued

Public School Boards, Grants—Continued

London, 2,909.21; Midland, 166.50; Mimico, 138.94; Nepean, 16.30; New Toronto, 516.31; Niagara Falls, 793.87; Nassagaweya, 6.14; North Bay, 977.37; Orillia, 263.04; Oshawa, 183.37; Ottawa, 4,417.82; Owen Sound, 316.57; Parry Sound, 241.40; Pembroke, 242.81; Peterborough, 190.40; Port Arthur, 359.46; Renfrew, 199.59; St. Catharines, 759.27; St. Thomas, 275.49; Sarnia, 902.14; Sault Ste. Marie, 237.87; 15 Scarboro, 255.75; 12 Scarboro, 262.02; Smith's Falls, 251.53; Stratford, 180.92; Sudbury, 230.56; Swansea, 185.21; Tavistock, 45.00; Toronto, 15,504.10; Walkerville, 208.17; Waterloo, 211.50; Welland, 136.26; Weston, 206.11; Windsor East, 221.94; Windsor, 1,527.51; 15 Etobicoke, 292.50; 8 Etobicoke, 242.01; York North, 252.70; 26 East York, 477.70; 7 York, 494.17; 27 York, 237.95; 15 York, 372.25; 32 York, 221.56; 25 York, 285.23; 28 York, 532.91; 13 York, 144.18 .... 45,070 14

Separate School Boards, Grants, $3,747.63.

Hamilton, 1,004.55; Kitchener, 226.89; London, 258.55; Port Arthur, 263.68; Toronto, 1,465.10; Windsor East, 528.86 .... 3,747 63

Services and Expenses, $2,864.50.

H. E. Amoss, 1,512.00; L. H. De Laporte, 618.00; F. B. Palen, 306.00; F. Rothman, 84.40; H. A. Stirk, 139.15; E. Teasdall, 114.15; R. Patterson, 90.80 .... 2,864 50

Contingencies, $713.19.

King's Printer, 624.41; National Stationers, Ltd., rental of duplicator, 60.00; Sundries—express, 2.90; petty disbursements, 25.88 .... 713 19

Inspection of Schools $634,281.36

DEPARTMENTAL EXAMINATIONS

Salaries ($42,679.16)

J. P. Cowles	Registrar	12 months	4,600 00
Geo. Lyons	Chief Clerk	12 "	3,300 00
W. A. Beecroft	Head Clerk	12 "	3,000 00
A. M. Burnham	Principal Clerk	12 "	2,500 00
B. Riddell	" "	12 "	2,300 00
B. Leadbetter	Confidential Printer	12 "	2,400 00
Wm. Parr	Assistant Confidential Printer	12 "	1,600 00
Ida N. Spence	Senior Clerk	12 "	2,000 00
Irene Hynes	" "	12 "	1,800 00
Gordon J. Westwood	" "	12 "	1,600 00
M. Sutton	Clerk, Group 1	12 "	1,600 00
E. Trowell	" Group 1	12 "	1,600 00
W. R. Thornton	" Group 1	12 "	1,500 00
Una Truax	" Group 1	12 "	1,300 00
D. Ferguson	" Group 2	12 "	1,200 00
A. B. Wrenn	" Group 2	½ "	50 00
Ruth M. Duff	" Group 2	12 "	1,200 00
F. J. Blake	" Group 2	11 "	962 50
G. Arnoldi	" Group 2	1 "	91 66
Martha E. Coleman	" Group 2	12 "	1,050 00
M. Nesbitt	Senior Clerk Stenographer	12 "	1,500 00
M. E. Dilks	" " "	12 "	1,400 00
H. M. Simpson	Clerk Stenographer, Group 1	12 "	1,125 00
Nora Foy	" " Group 2	12 "	1,050 00
Thelma J. Standeaven	" " Group 2	12 "	1,050 00
Marjorie Johnston	" " Group 2	12 "	900 00

Salaries not Provided for (Statutory) $87.50)

Fred J. Blake .... Clerk, Group 2 .... 1 month 87 50

Examiners ($212,736.03)

Sundry examiners, services, 190,163.55; expenses, 22,572.48 .... 212,736 03

Clerical Assistance ($40,785.00)

Sundry clerks 40,785 00

Departmental Examinations—Continued

Contingencies ($17,043.48)

Addressograph-Multigraph Co., Ltd., inspections, 32.42; Ault & Wiborg Co., Ltd., printing, 46.75; Brigdens, Ltd., maps, drawings, etc., 323.74; Burroughs Adding Machine of Canada, Ltd., rental of machine, etc., 161.00; Commissioner of Police for Ontario, investigating impersonations, 57.39; King's Printer, 14,325.07; Manton Bros., repairing trees, etc., 67.25; Mitchell & McGill, rent of tables, 60.00; Porter Safety Seal Co., seals, 35.25; Remington Typewriters, Ltd., inspection and overhauling machines, 170.65; W. H. Steele, repairs to bags, 174.75; Thomas & Corney Typewriters, Ltd., inspection, rental, etc., 96.50; Thompson, Ahern & Co., customs, 13.32; United Typewriter Co., Ltd., overhauling machines, rental, etc., 75.83; University of Toronto, rent of classrooms, etc., 1,005.98. Sundries—cartage, 5.00; express, 110.19; freight, 2.05; postage, 240.00; petty disbursements, 40.34	17,043 48

Extra Services of Professional and Supervising Boards of Examiners ($7,650.00)

W. A. Beecroft, 150.00; A. J. Beneteau, 300.00; J. P. Cowles, 500.00; J. P. Hoag, 300.00; A. G. Hooper, 500.00; W. J. Karr, 300.00; J. A. Lajeunesse, 500.00; A. E. Lang, 500.00; I. M. Levan, 500.00; J. F. Macdonald, 500.00; Norman Miller, 500.00; K. P. R. Neville, 500.00; W. Pakenham, 500.00; G. F. Rogers, 800.00; R. W. Smith, 500.00; D. Walker, 800.00		7,650 00
Total	$320,893 67	
Less fees and appeals	175,164 36	
Departmental Examinations	$145,729.31	

TEXT BOOKS

Salaries ($6,400.00)

Horace W. Kerfoot	General Editor of Text Books	12 months	4,400 00
E. G. Denison	Assistant	12 "	2,000 00

Preparation of Text Books, etc. ($14,992.49)

Temporary Services ($825.00)

Helen R. Anderson	Clerk Stenographer, Group 2	12 months	825 00

Services Revising, $9,286.95.

W. J. Alexander, 907.50; H. E. Amoss, 45.00; J. J. Bailey, 225.00; A. J. Beneteau, 400.00; H. W. Brown, 99.05; N. W. De Witt, 1,000.00; Ambia Going, 428.70; V. K. Greer, 30.00; D. E. Hamilton, 303.00; Maud M. Hawkins, 82.50; E. S. Hogarth, 121.50; A. J. Husband, 52.50; F. C. A. Jeanneret, 72.00; W. J. Karr, 30.00; R. Lamoureux, 400.00; A. E. Lang, 1,200.00; I. M. Levan, 52.50; Arthur Lismer, 362.50; J. F. MacDonald, 75.00; G. W. McGill, 210.00; Miss A. M. McIntyre, 150.00; Annette Marsh, 433.00; G. H. Needler, 1,200.00; T. W. Oates, 225.00; S. W. Perry, 432.20; Ethel Sealey, 88.50; A. E. Sherin, 150.00; B. Tarte, 58.80; H. J. Vallentyne, 234.00; R. H. Wallace, 68.70; M. M. Watterworth, 150.00	9,286 95

Travelling Expenses, $521.70.

W. C. Dowsley, 36.60; Ambia Going, 38.75; Geo. L. Gray, 5.20; E. S. Hogarth, 14.20; Annie M. McIntyre, 204.65; T. W. Oates, 4.45; A. E. Sherin, 216.15; R. H. Wallace, 1.70	521 70

Advertising, $72.00.

Globe Printing Co., 36.00; Mail and Empire, 36.00	72 00

Miscellaneous, $4,286.84.

T. H. Best Printing Co., Ltd., printing pamphlets, etc., 1,269.00; T. L. Crossley, testing paper, 50.00; T. Eaton Co., Ltd., books, printing, 101.10; W. J. Gage & Co., Ltd., books, 1,875.10; King's Printer, 480.56; Macmillan Co., Ltd., books, 13.88; Ontario Publishing Co., Ltd., books, 10.58; Ryerson Press, 19.73; Sundry persons, use of poems, 425.02; United Typewriter Co., Ltd., inspections, 15.00. Sundries—express, 1.05; petty disbursements, 25.82	4,286 84

Subventions to Publishers ($45,528.83)

Canadian Watchman Press, 7,717.87; T. Eaton Co., Ltd., 37,810.96		45,528 83
Text Books	$66,921.32	

GENERAL

Redemption of Debentures Guaranteed by the Province of Ontario ($130.78)

Union P.S. 4 Robillard and Truax 130 78

Grant to Soldiers' Aid Hostel, Bon Air ($1,200.00)

Soldiers' Aid Commission 1,200 00

General $1,330.78

TRAINING SCHOOLS

Salaries ($6,200.00)

Duncan Walker	Director of Professional Training Schools	12 months	5,000 00
E. V. Crawford	Clerk Typist, Group 1	12 "	1,200 00

Travelling and Moving Expenses and Contingencies ($391.45)

Travelling Expenses, $363.05.
D. Walker 363 05

Contingencies, $28.40.
King's Printer, 18.65; Ryerson Press, 9.75 ..... 28 40

Grants to Teachers engaged in Model School Training ($73,850.00)

Sundry Teachers:
Embrun, 1,500.00; Hamilton, 12,428.00; London, 11,832.00; North Bay, 5,170.00; Ottawa, 5,060.00; Peterborough, 7,315.00; Stratford, 10,475.00; Sturgeon Falls, 2,250.00; Toronto, 12,760.00; University of Toronto, 5,060.00 ..... 73,850 00

Grants to Caretakers for Services in Model Schools ($1,680.00)

Embrun, 60.00; Hamilton, 260.00; London, 280.00; Ottawa, 180.00; Peterborough, 200.00; Stratford, 280.00; Sturgeon Falls, 60.00; Toronto, 200.00; University of Toronto, 160.00 ..... 1,680 00

Services and Expenses of Lecturers in connection with Normal and Other Training Schools ($60.00)

F. H. Nelson 60 00

Temporary Teachers in Normal and Model Schools in Case of Illness or on Leave ($4,053.98)

Sundry teachers 4,053 98

Travelling and Moving Expenses of Normal and Model School Teachers Transferred ($286.89)

Janet M. Bowden, 6.50; W. J. McCulloch, 135.00; C. E. Mark, 20.39; Chas. E. Percy, 125.00 ..... 286 89

Grants to Public, Separate, High and Continuation School Boards for Use of Schools for Observation Purposes ($4,875.00)

No. 7 Barton, 150.00; Burlington Beach, 150.00; 11 Douro and Otonabee, 150.00; 3 Downie, 150.00; 9 Easthope N. and S., 150.00; 1 Ellice, 75.00; 2 Ellice, 150.00; 7 Etobicoke, 150.00; 10 Etobicoke, 150.00; 12 Etobicoke, 150.00; 1 B Ferris, 300.00; 2 Gloucester, 150.00; 3 Gloucester, 150.00; 10 Gloucester, 150.00; 4 Himsworth North and Ferris, 150.00; 1 King and Whitchurch, 150.00; Lambeth Continuation, 150.00; 22 London, 150.00; 4 and 21 Markham and Vaughan, 150.00; Millbrook Continuation, 150.00; Nepean H.S., 150.00; 20 North York, 150.00; Omemee H.S. Board, 150.00; 16 Otonabee, 150.00; 3 Smith, 150.00; Tavistock Continuation School, 150.00; 2 Toronto, 150.00; 3 U W. Flamboro and Ancaster, 150.00; 4 Westminster, Brick, 150.00; 8 Westminister, Glendale, 150.00; 8 Westminster, Cove Rd., 150.00; 5 Widdifield, 150.00 ..... 4,875 00

Grants to Teachers in Public, Separate, High and Continuation Schools for Observation Purposes ($13,809.45)

D. O. Arnold, 300.00; C. I. Baldwin, 330.00; Gladys Barber, 330.00; E. J. Barnby, 330.00; V. E. Barnby, 330.00; L. M. Barton, 28.00; R. E. Boucher, 330.00; I. Brownlee, 330.00; J. S. Bell, 272.00; M. Bell, 106.45; H. H. Carlyle, 440.00;

Training Schools—Continued

Grants to Teachers in Public, Separate, High and Continuation Schools for Observation Purposes—Continued

S. A. Cawker, 330.00; J. D. Coombs, 440.00; H. M. Coveney, 330.00; J. De Long, 330.00; R. J. Dodds, 330.00; D. Evans, 330.00; E. Gale, 168.00; H. Harris, 330.00; Beryl Hart, 330.00; Evelyn Hartley, 209.00; R. A. Hocking, 66.00; C. B. Hope, 330.00; F. M. Johnson, 36.00; L. Jones, 440.00; W. H. Jordan, 330.00; E. Kalbfleisch, 165.00; Lily Kay, 330.00; M. I. Kerr, 330.00; Laura Laventure, 330.00; Ruth Lawton, 330.00; I. Leppington, 330.00; J. D. Lindsey, 330.00; E. M. MacKay, 440.00; L. L. MacNeil, 166.00; R. J. Moon, 330.00; A. Ney, 330.00; E. Owens, 121.00; Catherine Perry, 330.00; Gordon Pool, 50.00; E. M. Pringle, 36.00; Victor E. Pyke, 330.00; D. Quipp, 165.00; J. Rennie, 165.00; W. G. Rigney, 330.00; Elsie M. Soule, 330.00; E. L. Turpin, 28.00; R. W. Warnica, 330.00; Marion Wells, 24.00; M. J. Wilker, 44.00; B. R. Wilson, 330.00; P. D. Windrim, 330.00 .... 13,809 45

Travelling Expenses of Normal School Students to Rural Public and Separate Schools for Nature Study ($6,212.30)

Transport of Students, $6,212.30.

Canadian National Railways, 183.70; Canadian Pacific Railway Co., 47.70; Doyle's Taxi & Garage, 588.60; A. T. Fontaine, 655.00; Hamilton Bus Lines, 117.50; Highway King Bus, 45.80; H. Howell, 43.50; Thos. A. Johns, 474.85; M. Landreville, 460.25; Mahon & Hayball, 291.15; O'Meara Taxi, 204.00; A. D. Ormerod, 528.10; Ottawa Electric Railway, 67.00; H. M. Risk & Sons, 87.50; Smitty's Taxi, 33.90; G. H. Switzer, 19.50; Temiskaming and Northern Ontario Railway, 42.50; Toronto Cab, Ltd., 1,713.50; Toronto Transportation Commission, 412.00; Union Taxi, 185.75; E. B. Wilson, 10.50 .... 6,212 30

Grants to Public and Separate School Inspectors for Services re Visits to Public and Separate Schools by Normal School Students and Masters ($260.00)

W. H. Ballard, 20.00; A. L. Campbell, 20.00; W. H. Carlton, 20.00; L. W. Copp, 20.00; R. F. Downey, 20.00; Robt. Gillies, 20.00; A. Mowat, 20.00; A. E. Nelson, 20.00; J. B. Robinson, 20.00; J. H. Smith, 20.00; P. J. Thompson, 20.00; G. A. Wheable, 20.00; J. E. Wilkinson, 20.00 .... 260 00

Classes in Manual Training and Household Science for Rural School Teachers ($5,806.26)

Services, $5,001.00.

G. F. Apperley, 400.00; T. T. Carpenter, 400.00; Jas. Chrysler, 300.00; C. M. Degroat, 400.00; David Duncan, 62.50; Clara Elliott, 400.00; Stephen Emery, 47.50; Rita Lindsay, 276.00; J. D. Medcof, 400.00; Frances Newton, 300.00; A. J. Painter, 400.00; R. H. Pomeroy, 400.00; A. E. Shorey, 400.00; L. Slaughter, 15.00; T. C. Talbot, 400.00; Rita E. Williams, 400.00 .... 5,001 00

Miscellaneous, $805.26.

Geo. M. Hendry Co., Ltd., spheres, 3.65; J. H. Simmens, groceries, 36.51; J. M. Stanley, groceries, 100.25; Treasurer, Board of Education, Toronto, stationery, 664.85 .... 805 26

Payment of Fees of Returned Soldiers Attending Academic Courses ($148.00)

Bursar, University of Toronto 148 00

Per Diem Allowances and Travelling Expenses incurred by Returned Soldiers Attending Courses ($4,242.20)

Sundry Persons, allowances 4,242 20

Training Schools $121,875.53

NORMAL AND MODEL SCHOOLS

TORONTO

Salaries ($102,666.66)

Normal School Staff.

David Whyte	Principal	12 months	4,600 00
J. W. Firth	Master	12 "	3,800 00
T. Mustard	"	12 "	3,800 00
E. E. Ingall	"	12 "	3,800 00
A. M. Patterson	"	12 "	3,800 00

Normal and Model Schools, Toronto—Continued

Salaries—Continued

F. F. Halliday	Master	12 months	3,800 00
W. Mooney	"	12 "	3,800 00
W. K. F. Kendrick	"	12 "	3,300 00
M. C. Young	"	12 "	3,000 00
M. E. Hay	Instructor, Group 1	12 "	2,550 00
C. S. Apperly	" " 1	12 "	2,550 00
A. A. Powell	" " 1	10 "	2,250 00
N. A. Ewing	" " 1	10 "	2,250 00
L. B. Harding	" " 1	12 "	2,100 00
E. H. Price	" " 1	12 "	1,900 00
C. E. Percy	" " 1	12 "	1,800 00
Eleanor Sheppard	" " 1	2 "	300 00
Olga Johnston	" " 1	2 "	300 00
M. G. DeLestard	" " 3	12 "	800 00
A. F. Hare	" " 3	12 "	675 00
M. W. Brown	" " 3	12 "	600 00
J. L. Merchant	Librarian	12 "	2,400 00
D. I. Kerr	Assistant Librarian	12 "	1,300 00

Normal Model School Staff.

Frank McCordic	Head Master	12 months	3,800 00
C. D. Bouck	Assistant Master	12 "	2,700 00
Charters T. Sharp	" "	12 "	2,700 00
Adam McLeod	" "	12 "	2,700 00
Alice A. Harding	" "	12 "	2,100 00
Jessie I. Cross	" "	12 "	2,100 00
M. Maud Watterworth	" "	12 "	2,100 00
R. Kendall	" "	12 "	1,900 00
Norma M. Lindsay	" "	12 "	1,900 00
Cecil E. McMullen	" "	12 "	1,800 00
Jean D. Currie	" "	12 "	1,600 00
Doris R. Soden	" "	12 "	1,500 00
Vera S. Fuller	" "	12 "	1,500 00
Bessie C. Bunker	Instructor, Group 3	12 "	525 00
M. E. McIntyre	Kindergarten Directress	10 "	2,250 00
M. E. Hodgins	" "	2 "	300 00
" "	Assistant Kindergarten Directress	10 "	1,500 00
Rhea S. Mossop	" " "	2 "	216 66
Jean Greig	Pianist	12	300 00
E. B. Rennie	Secretary	12 "	1,200 00
Edith A. Dallimore	Clerk Stenographer	12 "	975 00
Charles Soady	Superintendent of Buildings and Grounds	12 "	2,000 00
George F. Chandler	Stationary Engineer, Group 3	12 "	1,600 00
T. R. Turner	Fireman	12 "	1,400 00
John Sloan	"	12 "	1,400 00
Fred L. Travis	"	12 "	1,200 00
J. Cormack	Cleaner and Helper	12 "	1,400 00
Stephen A. Coombs	" "	12 "	1,400 00
Wilbert G. Worley	" "	12 "	1,125 00

Reference Books, Periodicals, Stationery, Services and Contingencies ($4,648.47)

Reference Books, $713.97.

T. Allen, 1.60; Blackie & Sons, Ltd., .80; Canadian Facts Publishing Co., 5.85; Canadian Review Co., Ltd., 8.00; Canadian Watchman Press, 35.84; Clark, Irwin & Co., 2.64; Copp, Clark Co., Ltd., 64.00; J. M. Dent & Sons, Ltd., 92.82; T. Eaton Co., Ltd., 33.19; W. J. Gage & Co., Ltd., 87.46; J. Hardwicke, 1.50; Hunter Rose Co., Ltd., 11.52; Irwin & Gordon, .36; James Texts, 12.28; Longmans, Green & Co., 112.56; McClelland & Stewart, Ltd., 7.45; MacLean Publishing Co., Ltd., 1.87; Macmillan Co., of Canada, Ltd., 50.36; T. Nelson & Sons, Ltd., 16.18; W. F. Quarrie & Co., 1.00; Ryerson Press, 161.12; R. Simpson Co., Ltd., 4.97; United Church Publishing Co., .60 .... 713 97

Periodicals, $208.80.

Animal Life, 1.00; Wm. Dawson Subscription Service, Ltd., 161.03; Globe Printing Co., 6.00; Mail & Empire, 6.00; University of Toronto Press, 2.00; H. W. Wilson Co., 32.77 .... 208 80

Normal and Model Schools, Toronto—Continued

Reference Books, Periodicals, Stationery, Services and Contingencies—Continued

Stationery, $3,197.46.

King's Printer, 3,189.38; petty disbursements, 8.08 .... 3,197 46

Advertising, $15.00.

Mail and Empire 15 00

Miscellaneous, $513.24.

Bell Telephone Co., rental, 293.80; tolls, 7.21; Bookshelf Bindery, binding, 75.68; Remington Typewriters, Ltd., cylinder, feed rolls, etc., 20.85; Robt. Simpson Co., Ltd., oilcloth, etc., 16.40; United Typewriter Co., Ltd., inspections, etc., 14.21. Sundries—cartage, 4.31; freight, 1.41; postage, 63.80; telegrams, .63; petty disbursements, 14.94 .... 513 24

Apparatus, Chemicals, Musical Instruments, Domestic Science and Manual Training Supplies ($1,846.38)

Belle Ewart Ice Co., Ltd., ice, 15.40; Brown Bros., Ltd., paper, millboard, 38.83; T. Eaton Co., Ltd., scrub brushes, etc., 15.27; Geo. M. Hendry Co., Ltd., paste, etc., 29.60; Ingram & Bell, Ltd., powder, tape, etc., 52.09; King's Printer, 156.30; Rice Lewis & Son, Ltd., hardware, etc., 214.65; A. W. Neal, acid, 15.08; Robt. Simpson Co., Ltd., ice cream freezer, cake tester, etc., 50.82; H. Slater Co., Ltd., benches, 658.56; J. B. Smith & Sons, Ltd., lumber, 355.79; J. M. Stanley, groceries, 157.86; Sturgeon's, Ltd., paint, 29.47; petty disbursements, 56.66 .... 1,846 38

Supplies for Kindergarten ($529.72)

Andrewes Mountain Seed Co., Ltd., Christmas trees, etc., 20.50; King's Printer, 435.78; E. N. Moyer Co., Ltd., posters, etc., 18.70; Simmons & Son, Ltd., rental of plants, etc., 46.00; petty disbursements, 8.74 .... 529 72

Physical Training including Apparatus and Athletic Supplies ($388.05)

Toronto Board of Education, use of gymnasium and pool, 333.00; H. A. Wilson Co., Ltd., basketballs, bats, etc., 51.95; petty disbursements, 3.10 .... 388 05

Annual Grant in aid of Boys' and Girls' Model School Games ($100.00)

D. Whyte 100 00

Annual Grant for Rink ($50.00)

D. Whyte 50 00

Payment to Toronto Board of Education ($1,600.00)

Treasurer, Toronto Board of Education 1,600 00

Fuel, Light and Power ($4,478.22)

Canada Coal Co., Ltd., 1,460.35; Consumers Gas Co., 87.50; Doan Coal Co., Ltd., 40.50; Milnes Coal Co., Ltd., 1,681.54; Toronto Hydro Electric System, 1,208.33 4,478 22

Water ($980.59)

Treasurer, Corporation of City of Toronto 980 59

Furniture and Furnishings ($215.49)

Canadian General Electric Co., Ltd., electric supplies, 176.54; Robt. Simpson Co., Ltd., window shade, matting, etc., 38.75; petty disbursements, .20 .... 215 49

Expenses of Grounds, Trees, Supplies, etc. ($590.74)

Aikenhead Hardware, Ltd., garden border mower, 29.98; Andrewes Mountain Seed Co., Ltd., seeds, flowers, etc., 305.53; R. H. Ellarby, sod, 49.00; Jas. W. Harris, manure, cartage, etc., 46.50; Marchment Co., Ltd., manure, 45.00; S. B. McCready, bulbs, 79.52; G. Rathbone Lumber Co., Ltd., lumber, 21.71; petty disbursements, 13.50 .... 590 74

Wages of Porters, Extra Firemen and Labourers on Grounds ($3,349.17)

Pay list, wages of men 3,349 17

Normal and Model Schools, Toronto—Continued

Scrubbing, Cleaning and Supplies ($5,737.07)

Associated Chemical Co. of Canada, Ltd., soap, etc., 39.49; Atlas Chemical Co., floor dressing, 30.00; Canadian Germicide Co., Ltd., liquid soap, 31.53; Diamond Cleansers, Ltd., sweeping compound, 22.35; Excelsior Brushes, Ltd., cleaner, etc., 149.87; Harron's Dye Works, Ltd., cleaning curtains, 20.62; Huntington Laboratories of Canada, Ltd., cleaning crystals, 24.14; King's Printer, 97.43; The Levi's, furniture polish, etc., 40.00; Pay list, wages of charwomen, 4,929.50; E. Pullan Wipers and Waste Co., Ltd., mops, etc., 29.68; Robt. Simpson Co., Ltd., baskets, etc., 93.40; Whirlwind Carpet Cleaners, Ltd., cleaning carpets, 25.50; Yorkville Laundry, Ltd., laundry, 190.10; petty disbursements, 13.46.......... 5,737 07

Repairs, including Materials, Services, Incidentals, etc. ($545.88)

Aikenhead Hardware, Ltd., nails, etc., 74.13; Bird Archer Co., Ltd., chemicals, 25.50; Canadian Germicide Co., Ltd., chemicals, 23.27; J. W. Cormack, care of clocks, 166.40; Henry Disston & Sons, Ltd., tools, etc., 59.44; Heintzman & Co., Ltd., repairing pianos, 27.00; Rice Lewis & Son, Ltd., hardware, 16.75; Geo. Pearsall & Son, Ltd., hardware, 15.11; Geo. Rathbone Lumber Co., Ltd., lumber, 62.20; W. Richmond & Co., locks, keys, 20.95; Robt. Simpson Co., Ltd., sash cord, screws, etc., 24.85; petty disbursements, 30.28.......... 545 88

Total	$127,726 44
Less fees, etc	9,452 00
Toronto Normal School	$118,274.44

OTTAWA

Salaries ($68,758.33)

Normal School Staff.

Name	Position	Period		Amount
Frank A. Jones	Principal	12	months	4,200 00
G. A. Miller	Master	12	"	3,800 00
M. K. Clifford	"	12	"	3,800 00
Henry Bowers	"	12	"	3,300 00
O. E. Ault	"	12	"	3,000 00
G. R. Smith	"	2	"	633 33
J. S. Harterre	Instructor, Group 1	12	"	2,700 00
Roy Fleming	" " 1	12	"	2,700 00
C. E. Green	" " 1	12	"	2,700 00
L. E. Monaghan	" " 1	12	"	2,700 00
Edna P. Dunning	" " 1	12	"	2,100 00
F. Luella Barriger	" " 2	12	"	1,400 00
J. C. Logan	" " 3	12	"	675 00
Cherry Grant	Librarian	12	"	2,200 00

Normal Model School Staff.

Name	Position	Period		Amount
Elwood Oakes	Head Master	12	months	3,000 00
K. O. Birkin	Assistant Master	12	"	2,400 00
Rose Lynch	" "	12	"	2,100 00
Elsie A. Sherrin	" "	12	"	2,100 00
E. M. Cluff	" "	12	"	2,100 00
A. M. Delaney	" "	12	"	2,100 00
M. R. Elliott	" "	12	"	2,100 00
C. E. Timanus	" "	12	"	1,800 00
H. G. Redfern	" "	12	*	1,800 00
L. M. Lorriman	" "	2	"	250 00
Gaston Louvray	Instructor, Group 3	12	"	800 00
A. H. Baker	Kindergarten Directress	12	"	2,200 00
E. Mitchell	Kindergarten Primary	12	"	1,900 00
D. Graham	Asst. Kindergarten Directress	12	"	1,600 00
E. M. Marshall	Secretary	12	"	1,300 00
A. Heeney	Stationary Engineer	12	"	1,600 00
B. Pearce	Carpenter's Helper	12	"	1,400 00
Arthur Hardy	Caretaker, Group 1	10	"	1,000 00
James McCorkill	Watchman	12	"	1,300 00

Reference Books, Periodicals, Stationery, Services and Contingencies ($2,674.81)

Reference Books, $525.17.

Blackie & Sons, Ltd., 30.24; Canadian Facts Publishing Co., Ltd., 5.85; Canadian Review Co., Ltd., 8.00; Canadian Watchman Press, 14.11; Clarke Irwin & Co.,

Normal and Model Schools, Ottawa—Continued

Reference Books, Periodicals, Stationery, Services and Contingencies—Continued

Reference Books—Continued.

2.05; Copp, Clark Co., Ltd., 22.00; J. M. Dent & Sons, Ltd., 16.69; Doubleday, Doran & Gundy, Ltd., 4.51; T. Eaton Co., Ltd., 28.31; W. J. Gage & Co., Ltd., 84.35; General Board of Religious Education, 3.70; Grolier Society, Ltd., 138.50; Jas. Hope & Son, Ltd., 10.80; A. H. Jarvis, 24.60; Longmans, Green & Co., 2.88; McClelland & Stewart, Ltd., 5.05; MacLean Publishing Co., Ltd., 2.04; Macmillan Co., Ltd., 17.71; E. N. Moyer Co., Ltd., .80; Musson Book Co., Ltd., .10; National Gallery of Canada, 6.00; Thos. Nelson & Sons, Ltd., .65; Oxford University Press, 3.55; Palmer Co., 1.13; Plymouth Press, 2.23; Public School Publishing Co., 3.82; Ryerson Press, 79.60; T. Skinner & Co., 2.00; Superintendent of Documents, Government Printer, Washington, 3.90 .... 525 17

Periodicals, $162.10.

Animal Life, 1.00; Wm. Dawson Subscription Service, Ltd., 152.10; University of Toronto Press, 2.00; H. W. Wilson Co., 7.00 .... 162 10

Stationery, $1,328.23.

Federal Typewriter Co., Ltd., 14.18; King's Printer, 1,195.98; A. A. Laflamme, 53.55; Progressive Printers, 25.00; Roneo Co. of Canada, Ltd., 16.20; Runge Press, Ltd., 10.50; petty disbursements, 12.82 .... 1,328 23

Advertising, $19.20.

Journal Dailies, 9.60; Ottawa Evening Citizen, 9.60 .... 19 20

Miscellaneous, $640.11.

Bell Telephone Co., rental, 186.00; tolls, 4.31; C. H. Horton, services as caretaker, 233.33; F. A. Jones, travelling expenses, 28.10; United Typewriter Co., Ltd., repairs, 17.50; J. Wesson, services as watchman, 44.00. Sundries—customs, .10; express, 47.15; freight, 6.77; postage, 39.60; telegrams, 1.16; petty disbursements, 32.09 .... 640 11

Apparatus, Chemicals, Musical Instruments, Domestic Science and Manual Training Supplies ($543.78)

Barrett Bros., lumber, 73.00; Central Scientific Co. of Canada, Ltd., bottles, 23.22; J. M. Garland Son & Co., Ltd., flannel, 21.43; Geo. M. Hendry Co., Ltd., paper, 91.60; McKechnie Music Co., Ltd., stands, etc., 21.25; W. J. Moreland & Son, provisions, etc., 18.29; C. Ogilvy Co., Ltd., flannel and cotton, 47.66; R. E. Powell, provisions, 59.22; Producers' Dairy, Ltd., milk and butter, 34.75; Thorburn & Abbott, Ltd., pictures, stationery, etc., 35.35; Thornton & Truman, Ltd., sharpening tools, 19.20; petty disbursements, 98.81 .... 543 78

Physical Training, including Apparatus and Athletic Supplies ($6.00)

Chas. Ogilvy, Ltd., baseballs 6 00

Supplies for Kindergarten ($779.89)

King's Printer, 713.97; E. N. Moyer Co., Ltd., books, 17.50; Chas. Ogilvy, Ltd., toys, 22.99; F. W. Woolworth Co., Ltd., crepe paper, etc., 12.25; petty disbursements, 13.18 .... 779 89

Annual Grant in Aid of Boys' and Girls' Model School Games ($100.00)

F. A. Jones 100 00

Annual Grant for Rink ($100.00)

F. A. Jones 100 00

Payment to the Ottawa Public School Board ($750.00)

Treasurer, Public School Board 750 00

Fuel, Light and Power ($4,093.22)

Canadian Pacific Rly. Co., 36.54; Independent Coal Co., Ltd., 3,189.84; Ottawa Gas Co., 27.16; Ottawa Hydro Electric Commission, 722.23; Stinson-Reeb Builders Supply Co., Ltd., 117.45 .... 4,093 22

Normal and Model Schools, Ottawa—Continued

Water ($658.91)

Corporation of the City of Ottawa.. 658 91

Furniture, Repairs and Incidentals ($594.65)

Bryson-Graham, Ltd., mop handles, etc., 27.75; W. J. Carson, repairs, 22.23; Grand & Toy, Ltd., chairs, 185.40; J. Jones, services, 45.50; McKinley & Northwood, Ltd., washers, 87.00; Ottawa Hydro-Electric System, lamps, 19.20; W. A. Rankin, Ltd., locks, cement, etc., 102.62; Trudel & McAdam, Ltd., chair plates, 16.45; United Hardware & Supply of Ottawa, Ltd., saw blades, etc., 27.18; E. E. Wildman, shelving, 25.00; petty disbursements, 36.32........................... 594 65

Expenses of Grounds ($284.41)

Oliver Birtch, fertilizer, etc., 25.50; Graham Bros., seeds, 59.21; J. Jones, clearing garden, 10.00; Mahoney & Rich, Ltd., fertilizer, 12.00; A. V. Main, planting flowers, bulbs, 142.10; J. Wesson, work on grounds, 31.60; petty disbursements, 4.00.. 284 41

Scrubbing, Cleaning, etc. ($2,064.05)

Bryson-Graham, Ltd., wax, etc., 30.62; E. B. Eddy Co., Ltd., towels, etc., 49.10; J. H. Jones, washing windows, 50.02; Pay list, wages of charwomen, 1,859.04; A. Thompson, brooms, 25.30; J. Wesson, services, whitewashing, 30.02; petty disbursements, 19.95.. 2,064 05

Snow Cleaning, Cartage, etc. ($124.10)

McKinley & Northwood, shovelling snow, etc., 93.60; Mahoney & Rich, cartage, 10.00; J. Wesson, shovelling snow, 20.50.................................. 124 10

Total..	$81,532 15
Less fees, etc..	8,008 00
Ottawa Normal School..............................	$73,524.15

LONDON NORMAL

Salaries ($33,578.37)

Clarence E. Mark	Principal	12 months		4,000 00
G. W. Hoffard	Master	12 "		3,800 00
T. E. Clarke	"	12 "		3,800 00
J. G. McEachern	"	12 "		3,800 00
E. H. McKone	"	12 "		3,800 00
S. Pickles	Instructor, Group 1	12 "		2,700 00
A. B. Neville	" " 1	12 "		2,400 00
Dorothy Emery	" " 2	12 "		1,400 00
Albert D. Jordan	" " 2	10¼ "		895 13
Wm. F. Marshall	" " 3	12 "		675 00
A. Slatter	" " 3	12 "		675 00
L. Gahan	Librarian	12 "		2,400 00
N. Heffernan	Secretary	12 "		1,300 00
W. Casey	Stationary Engineer, Group 3	7½ "		995 45
G. Fitchett	Watchman	6½ "	360 10	
" "	"	(T) 5½ "	577 69	937 79

Reference Books, Periodicals, Stationery, Services and Contingencies ($1,283.88)

Reference Books, $249.51.

Blackie & Sons, Ltd., .60; Bruce Publishing Co., 3.16; Canadian Facts Publishing Co., Ltd., 5.85; Canadian Review Co., Ltd., 8.00; Clarke, Irwin & Co., 1.40; J. M. Dent & Sons, Ltd., 7.50; Wendell Holmes, Ltd., 2.25; McClelland & Stewart, Ltd., 5.05; Maclean Publishing Co., Ltd., 2.04; Macmillan Co., Ltd., 3.68; T. Nelson & Sons, Ltd., 8.63; Mrs. E. I. Paterson, 164.00; Ryerson Press, 37.35.. 249 51

Periodicals, $28.30.

Animal Life, 1.00; Globe Printing Co., 7.80; Hay Stationery Co., Ltd., 2.50; School Arts Magazine, 8.00; University of Toronto, 2.00; H. W. Wilson Co., 7.00 28 30

Normal School, London—Continued

Reference Books, Periodicals, Stationery, Services and Contingencies—Continued

Stationery, $621.61.

Hay Stationery Co., Ltd., 35.44; King's Printer, 549.35; C. R. Smith Stationery Co., 27.38; petty disbursements, 9.44 ..... 621 61

Miscellaneous, $384.46.

Anglo-Canadian Music Co., music sheets, 22.00; Bell Telephone Co., rental, 77.40; tolls, 8.97; British Empire Art Co., prints, 17.25; Miss M. Davis, secretarial work, 34.05; London Printing and Litho Co., Ltd., class lists, 63.75 ; Treasurer, London Board of Education, use of school, 60.75. Sundries—cartage, 4.25; excise stamps, 2.00; express, 22.34; postage, 52.00; telegrams, .65; petty disbursements, 19.05 ..... 384 46

Apparatus, Chemicals, Musical Instruments, Domestic Science and Manual Training Supplies ($259.71)

Book and Novelty Shop, bristol board, etc., 24.84; W. S. Caldwell, nails, etc., 18.92; L. Caswell, groceries, 34.55; W. Gerry & Sons, lumber, 13.85; Learie's Pure Food Grocery, provisions, 22.65; London Floral Exchange, flowers, 12.00; Smallman & Ingram, Ltd., dry goods, 77.34; T. N. Sumner, drugs, 11.03; R. J. Young & Co., Ltd., dimity, etc., 17.48; petty disbursements, 27.05 ..... 259 71

Physical Training including Apparatus and Athletic Supplies ($40.50)

T. Munro, basket balls 40 50

Payment to the London Board of Education ($1,600.00)

Treasurer, London Board of Education 1,600 00

Fuel, Light and Power ($1,628.57)

City Gas Co., 19.38; Hunt Coal Co., Ltd., 1,273.31; Public Utilities Commission, 335.88 ..... 1,628 57

Water ($90.62)

Public Utilities Commission 90 62

Furniture, Repairs and Incidentals ($585.50)

W. S. Caldwell, hardware, 79.26; City Chimney Sweep & Cartage, cleaning, etc., 14.50; Gutta Percha & Rubber, Ltd., mats, 37.87; Johnson Temperature Regulating Co., valves, etc., 15.00; Kingsmills, Ltd., rug, 31.00; London Window Cleaning Co., removing storm windows, 165.00; W. McPhillips, Ltd., wire, 12.50; Alex. Milne, plumbing, 68.10; W. J. Mortimer, repairs to map racks, 10.56; W. A. Reid, weatherstripping, 10.00; E. H. Russell, installing range boiler, 25.80; Superior Barn Equipment Co., stools, 15.36; F. H. Thompson, purchase and installation of door stops, etc., 45.70; W. J. White, gasolene, etc., 15.80; petty disbursements, 39.05 ..... 585 50

Expenses of Grounds, Trees, etc. ($1,091.61)

Alf. Cotterill, manure, 25.00; Morgan's Supply House, Ltd., seed, etc., 19.01; J. Pawlitzki, flowers, 68.15; Pay list, wages of men, 939.60; F. H. Thompson, sharpening mower, 12.00; petty disbursements, 27.85 ..... 1,091 61

Scrubbing, Cleaning, Cartage, etc. ($1,706.70)

City Chimney Sweep & Cartage, removing ashes, etc., 32.00; London Cleansers Supply House, soap, soda, etc., 95.05; Pay list, wages of charwoman, 1,568.55; petty disbursements, 11.10 ..... 1,706 70

London Normal School $41,865.46

HAMILTON NORMAL

Salaries ($32,144.33)

Name	Position	Period		Amount
G. O. McMillan	Principal	12	months	4,200 00
H. G. Lockett	Master	12	"	3,800 00
J. H. Davidson	"	12	"	3,800 00
M. G. N. Irving	"	12	"	3,800 00
J. A. Partridge	"	12	"	3,300 00
C. E. Elliott	Instructor, Group 1	12	"	2,700 00
H. A. Stares	" " 2	12	"	1,400 00
A. J. Painter	" " 2	12	"	1,400 00
Marjorie G. Seavey	" " 2	12	"	1,050 00
A. J. Park	" " 3	12	"	675 00
J. M. Grindlay	" " 3	2½	"	138 37
Mary L. McCready	Librarian	12	"	1,900 00
G. I. Carruthers	Secretary	12	"	1,300 00
David Duncan	Stationary Engineer, Group 3	12	"	1,600 00
Stephen Emery	Caretaker, Group 1	11	"	1,080 96

Reference Books, Periodicals, Stationery, Services and Contingencies ($1,516.04)

Reference Books, $206.79.

Canadian Facts Publishing Co., Ltd., 5.85; Canadian Review Co., Ltd., 8.00; Clarke, Irwin & Co., Ltd., 5.67; J. M. Dent & Sons, Ltd., 7.50; R. Duncan & Co., Ltd., 51.20; J. H. French & Co., Ltd., 8.08; W. J. Gage & Co., Ltd., 2.90; H. M. Stationery Office, 1.18; McAinsh & Co., Ltd., 9.60; McClelland & Stewart, 5.05; Maclean Publishing Co., Ltd., 2.04; Morris Book Shop, 1.43; T. Nelson & Sons, Ltd., 5.00; Ryerson Press, 18.79; F. G. Smith, 70.00; University of Toronto, Students' Book Department, 4.50 .... 206 79

Periodicals, $177.76.

Animal Life, 1.00; Wm. Dawson Subscription Service, Ltd., 168.60; University of Toronto Press, 2.00; H. W. Wilson Co., 6.16 .... 177 76

Stationery, $594.90.

R. Duncan & Co., Ltd., 44.05; King's Printer, 536.01; J. E. Poole Co., ink powder, 11.55; petty disbursements, 3.29 .... 594 90

Miscellaneous, $536.59.

Bell Telephone Co., rental, 83.40; tolls, 17.35; R. Duncan & Co., Ltd., chalk, etc., 22.35; Florence Dyment, services as stenographer, 15.00; W. R. Filken, removing ashes, 10.50; Heintzman & Co., Ltd., rental and cartage of piano, 35.00; J. C. Lougheed, music books, 10.80; National Child Welfare Association, hygiene charts, 10.00; National Stationers, Ltd., stencils, 22.50; L. Slaughter, services as caretaker, 179.76; R. G. Smith, typing, 30.00; Stephens Sales, Ltd., paper, 11.25. Sundries—cartage, 2.60; express, 20.00; postage, 48.00; telegrams, .50; petty disbursements, 17.58. .... 536 59

Apparatus, Chemicals, Musical Instruments, Domestic Science and Manual Training Supplies ($615.99)

D. Aitchison Lumber Co., Ltd., lumber, 15.74; J. R. Brown, biology supplies, 33.75; Buntin, Gillies & Co., Ltd., paper, etc., 147.46; Canadian Laboratory Supplies, Ltd., tubing, etc., 90.55; T. Eaton Co., Ltd., dishes, etc., 29.07; Geo. M. Hendry Co., Ltd., reed, plasticine, etc., 93.25; J. C. Lougheed, books and albums, 11.45; Mills Hardware Co., Ltd., saw blades, hardware, 21.23; Jos. Mossip, lumber, 17.05; Parke & Parke, Ltd., chemicals, etc., 18.27; G. H. Robinson, film, etc., 16.80; G. W. Robinson & Co., Ltd., flannelette, etc., 17.67; J. Semmens, groceries, 49.03; petty disbursements, 54.67 .... 615 99

Physical Training, Apparatus and Athletic Supplies ($195.90)

Sam Manson, Ltd., basket ball, etc., 39.50; G. W. Robinson Co., Ltd., matting, etc., 6.40; Zion Gymnasium Committee, rent of gymnasium floor, 150.00 .... 195 90

Payment to Hamilton Board of Education ($1,750.00)

Treasurer, Hamilton Board of Education, use of rooms 1,750 00

Normal School, Hamilton—Continued

Fuel, Light and Power ($791.30)

Burton Coal Co. of Hamilton, Ltd., coal, 159.90; Hamilton Hydro-Electric System, light and power, 304.19; Sherring Coal Co., coal, 318.21; United Gas & Fuel Co. of Hamilton, Ltd., gas, 9.00 .... 791 30

Water ($136.05)

Corporation City of Hamilton 136 05

Furniture, Repairs and Incidentals ($518.76)

D. Aitchison Lumber Co., Ltd., lumber, etc., 73.09; Grand & Toy, Ltd., lockers, 77.00; Hamilton Paper Box Co., fibre boxes, 10.50; R. Haygarth, plumbing repairs, etc., 34.65; Johnson Temperature Regulating Co., repairs, 10.40; Mills Hardware Co., Ltd., hardware, 68.55; J. Mossip, repairing lockers, etc., 51.30; Ed. Reid, carpenter work, etc., 38.30; A. M. Souter & Co., Ltd., chairs, 47.28; Wood, Alexander & James, Ltd., hardware, 45.15; petty disbursements, 62.54.. 518 76

Expenses of Grounds, etc. ($325.03)

Ed. Bollen, work on grounds, 10.00; J. Brown, work on grounds, 10.00; M. Davidson, shrubs, 16.25; W. R. Filkin, manure, 31.00; Geo. T. Sones & Son, preparing flower beds, etc., 66.00; Steele, Briggs Seed Co., Ltd., sprayer, seeds, 165.37; petty disbursements, 26.41 .... 325 03

Scrubbing, Cleaning, Cartage, etc. ($1,236.33)

Balfour's, Ltd., soap, 17.35; W. Banks, cleaning windows, 12.00; Finch Bros., cheese cloth, etc., 26.06; Pay list, wages of charwomen, 1,028.00; Sunlight Laundry Co., Ltd., laundry, 43.52; Superior Oil & Supply Co., Ltd., sweeping compound, 10.00; West Disinfecting Co., towels, etc., 57.75; petty disbursements, 41.65 .... 1,236 33

Hamilton Normal School $39,229.73

PETERBOROUGH NORMAL

Salaries ($35,350.00)

Name	Position	Period		Amount
J. A. Bannister	Principal	12	months	4,200 00
A. J. Madill	Master	12	"	3,800 00
A. Macdonald	"	12	"	3,800 00
C. H. Edwards	"	10	"	3,000 00
John V. McIntyre	"	12	"	3,150 00
Maurice H. Parke	"	10	"	2,750 00
E. MacVannel	Instructor, Group 1	12	"	2,700 00
M. R. Rannie	" " 2	12	"	2,075 00
A. F. Hagerman	" " 2	12	"	1,400 00
Ambia L. Going	" " 2	12	"	1,300 00
J. A. McKone	" " 3	12	"	675 00
E. M. Munro	Librarian	12	"	2,400 00
B. Latimer	Secretary	12	"	1,300 00
H. A. Bonney	Stationary Engineer, Group 3	12	"	1,600 00
Elias A. Stinson	Caretaker, Group 1	12	"	1,200 00

Reference Books, Periodicals, Stationery, Services and Contingencies ($1,396.55)

Reference Books, $109.63.

Canadian Facts Publishing Co., 5.85; Canadian Review Co., Ltd., 8.00; Clarke, Irwin & Co., Ltd., .41; J. M. Dent & Sons, Ltd., 12.83; W. J. Gage & Co., Ltd., 1.99; The James Texts, .50; McClelland & Stewart, Ltd., 5.05; Maclean Publishing Co., Ltd., 2.04; Macmillan Co. of Canada, Ltd., 4.57; Madrigal Singers, 7.50; E. N. Moyer Co., Ltd., 4.05; Thos. Nelson & Sons, Ltd., 1.29; Sir Isaac Pitman & Sons, Ltd., .78; Renauf Publishing Co., 6.21; Ryerson Press, 45.06; Stanford University Press, 2.70; Trebilcock Bros., .80 .... 109 63

Periodicals, $147.33.

American Library Association, 1.00; Animal Life, 1.00; Wm. Dawson Subscription Service, Ltd., 137.55; Pictorial Education, 4.50; University of Toronto Press, 2.00; Woodward Press, 1.05; petty disbursements, .23 .... 147 33

Normal School, Peterborough—Continued

Reference Books, Periodicals, Stationery, Services and Contingencies—Continued

Stationery, $645.12.

King's Printer, 644.42; petty disbursements .70 ... 645 12

Services and Travelling Expenses, $8.00.

J. A. Bannister, travelling expenses ... 8 00

Miscellaneous, $486.47.

Bell Telephone Co., rental, 57.00; tolls, 8.32; Canadian Pacific Railway Co., peat, 85.40; Wm. Gibbs, services as janitor, 58.33; A. F. Hagerman, bird-house pole, etc., 10.00; Library of Congress, catalogue cards, 28.59; Peterborough Review Co., paper, 24.50; Sundries—cartage, 21.95; express, 25.69; freight, 61.03; postage, 42.75; telegrams, .35; petty disbursements, 62.56 ... 486 47

Apparatus, Chemicals, Musical Instruments, Domestic Science and Manual Training Supplies ($532.81)

Artists Supply Co., Ltd., crayons, etc., 17.37; Art Metropole, stand, etc., 30.50; Miss I. Elcome, mounting birds, 15.00; R. Fair & Co., Ltd., canvas, flannels, etc., 130.84; General Biological Supply House, Inc., aquarium, etc., 15.86; D. M. Goheen, mounting birds, 27.00; A. F. Hagerman, lantern tables, 15.00; R. Hall, Ltd., cloth, etc., 20.20; Higgins Hardware Co., glue, 36.30; J. Juby, provisions, 43.93; A. MacDonald Lumber Co., cuttings, lumber, 13.06; H. S. Routley, saucers, 11.38; E. Wand, lumber, 49.25; petty disbursements, 107.12 ... 532 81

Physical Training including Apparatus and Athletic Supplies ($8.00)

Peterborough Hardware Co., balls and bats ... 8 00

Payment to Peterborough Board of Education ($1,100.00)

Treasurer, Peterborough Board of Education ... 1,100 00

Fuel, Light and Power ($1,285.63)

Peterborough Utilities Commission, light and power, 216.09; Stinson-Reeb Builders' Supply Co., peat fuel, 233.33; H. B. Taylor & Son, coal, 835.71; petty disbursements, .50 ... 1,285 63

Water ($203.01)

Peterborough Utilities Commission ... 203 01

Furniture, Repairs and Incidentals ($121.94)

S. Ephgrave, repairs to floor and door, 13.75; Higgins Hardware Co., picture wire, soap, etc., 36.44; Johnson Temperature Regulating Co., Ltd., repairs, 19.45; McIntosh Service Station, oil, 12.65; E. Wand, tables, 18.00; petty disbursements, 21.65 ... 121 94

Expenses of Grounds, Trees, etc. ($197.15)

K. G. Brown, soil, 15.00; A. B. Davis, fertilizer, 12.00; R. F. Ivey, work on grounds, 19.60; D. Jordan, seed, 29.70; J. D. McIntosh, fertilizer, 10.00; Peterborough Floral Co., seed, 26.10; H. Wilson, work on grounds, 50.20; petty disbursements, 34.55 ... 197 15

Scrubbing, Cleaning, Cartage, etc. ($1,003.71)

Fanning's Steam Laundry, laundry, 50.83; Higgins Hardware Co., brooms, soda, etc., 52.09; G. S. Kingdon, removing ashes, 11.25; Pay list, wages of charwomen, 877.63; petty disbursements, 11.91 ... 1,003 71

Peterborough Normal School ... $41,198.80

STRATFORD NORMAL

Salaries ($36,050.00)

S. Silcox	Principal	12 months	4,600 00
H. G. Martyn	Master	12 "	3,800 00
H. G. Manning	"	12 "	3,800 00
L. R. Halnan	"	12 "	3,800 00
Wm. E. M. Aitken	"	12 "	3,300 00
E. A. Miller		12 "	3,150 00

Normal School, Stratford—Continued

Salaries—Continued

E. M. Everson	Instructor, Group 1	12 months	2,700 00
H. Mayberry	" " 2	12 "	1,400 00
E. M. Cottle	" " 2	12 "	1,400 00
W. B. Rothwell	" " 2	12 "	1,400 00
A. J. Johnston	Librarian	12 "	2,400 00
M. M. Sebben	Secretary	12 "	1,300 00
Wm. Ellis	Stationary Engineer, Group 3	12 "	1,600 00
C. Bell	Caretaker, Group 1	12 "	1,400 00

Reference Books, Periodicals, Stationery, Services and Contingencies ($1,848.11)

Reference Books, $506.84.

Alexander Book Shop, 24.70; Blackie & Son, Ltd., 1.85; Canadian Facts Publishing Co., 5.85; Canadian Review Co., Ltd., 8.00; Clarke, Irwin & Co., Ltd., 2.40; J. Cooper, 4.50; J. M. Dent & Sons, Ltd., 76.44; General Publishing Co., Ltd., 3.65; Ginn & Co., 1.64; J. H. Kenner, 11.49; Longmans, Green & Co., 127.60; McClelland & Stewart, Ltd., 9.27; Maclean Publishing Co., Ltd., 2.04; Macmillan Company of Canada, Ltd., 17.95; H. G. Manning, .65; Manual Arts Press, 2.00; Manufacturers' Press, Ltd., 42.00; National Geographic Society, .50; Thos. Nelson & Sons, Ltd., 1.42; Superintendent of Documents, Ottawa, 1.32; Oxford University Press, 5.53; Ryerson Press, 154.36; University of Chicago Press, 1.68.. 506 84

Periodicals, $140.40.

Animal Life, 1.00; Wm. Dawson Subscription Service, Ltd., 113.20; Globe Printing Co., 3.75; Mail and Empire, 3.75; T. Nelson & Sons, Ltd., 5.00; Stratford Beacon-Herald, 11.70; University of Toronto Press, 2.00 140 40

Stationery, $667.96.

Alexander Book Shop, 128.15; Commercial Printers, 32.50; King's Printer, 426.79; Murdock Stationery, 23.50; National Stationers, Ltd., 11.00; A. E. Taylor, 27.00; petty disbursements, 19.02 667 96

Travelling Expenses, $292.95.

S. Pickles, travelling expenses, 285.95; S. Silcox, travelling expenses, 7.00...... 292 95

Miscellaneous, $239.96.

Bell Telephone Co., rental, 59.40; tolls, 16.29; Copp, Clark Co., Ltd., maps, 16.67; Heintzman & Co., Ltd., music, 31.54. Sundries—cartage, 5.50; express, 24.42; freight, .50; postage, 60.00; petty disbursements, 25.64 239 96

Apparatus, Chemicals, Musical Instruments, Domestic Science and Manual Training Supplies ($464.94)

Alexander Book Shop, wax paper, etc., 58.75; W. R. Bradshaw, lumber, etc., 17.10; Central Scientific Company of Canada, Ltd., apparatus, 64.41; D. D. Fraser, needles, etc., 25.44; Gordan & Orr, towels, thread, etc., 47.20; Kalbfleisch Bros., Ltd., lumber, 12.90; W. J. McCully, fruit, coffee, etc., 130.50; J. R. Meyers & Sons, Ltd., tadpoles, etc., 19.30; J. W. Rogers, photos, 10.50; Silverwood's Stratford Dairy, Ltd., milk, cream, etc., 14.40; petty disbursements, 64.44...... 464 94

Physical Training including Apparatus and Athletic Supplies ($331.89)

His Master's Voice, Ltd., records, 12.82; Ryerson Leather Goods Co., hockey sticks, 11.57; Y.M.C.A., use of swimming tank and gymnasium, 176.00; Y.W.C.A., rent of gymnasium, 120.00; petty disbursements, 11.50 331 89

Annual Grant for Rink ($45.00)

S. Silcox 45 00

Payment to Stratford Board of Education ($1,500.00)

Treasurer, Stratford Board of Education 1,500 00

Fuel, Light and Power ($979.91)

E. Burdett & Sons, 728.44; Stratford Public Utilities Commission, 251.47......... 979 91

Normal School, Stratford—Continued

Water ($115.20)

Stratford Public Utilities Commission.. 115 20

Furniture, Repairs and Incidentals ($504.92)

Bennington Electric Co., Ltd., light bulbs, etc., 12.05; Dawn & Fleming, shades, 15.34; Kalbfleisch Bros., Ltd., lumber, 95.85; E. N. Moyer Co., Ltd., maps, 16.65; Peter & Sylvester, waste baskets, 12.75; Preston-Noelting, Ltd., desk tops, etc., 47.08; Stratford Hardware, tools, nails, etc., 277.65; petty disbursements, 27.55.. 504 92

Expenses of Grounds, Trees, etc. ($382.89)

E. G. Budd, flowers, 11.80; E. Burnham, bulbs, 110.25; A. Keane, manure, 18.75; H. Thorne, removing storm windows, and work on grounds, 60.40; Treasurer, Board of Park Management, care of lawns, 176.00; petty disbursements, 5.69.... 382 89

Scrubbing, Cleaning, Cartage, etc. ($1,120.07)

J. Lloyd & Son, towels, 34.22; Pay list, wages of charwoman, 994.82; E. Pullan Wipers & Waste Co., Ltd., klenser kloths, 20.00; E. Ramsden, services, 52.00; petty disbursements, 19.03.. 1,120 07

Stratford Normal School...............................$43,342.93

NORTH BAY NORMAL

Salaries ($31,207.65)

Name	Position	Period		
J. C. Norris	Principal	8½ months	2,809 03	
"	"	(T) 1½ "	265 29	3,074 32
H. E. Ricker	"	2 months		666 73
"	Master	10 "		3,166 60
G. Morgan	"	12 "		3,800 00
W. J. Neale	"	12 "		3,800 00
Floyd S. Rivers	"	12 "		3,300 00
C. Ramsay	Instructor, Group 1	12 "		2,700 00
J. E. Chambers	" " 1	12 "		2,700 00
H. L. Bamford	" " 1	12 "		1,900 00
E. Preston	" " 1	12 "		1,900 00
K. McCubbin	Secretary	12 "		1,300 00
F. Wharram	Stationary Engineer, Group 3	12 "		1,600 00
H. E. Jackson	Caretaker, Group 1	12 "		1,300 00

Reference Books, Periodicals, Stationery, Services and Contingencies ($1,249.18)

Reference Books, $147.54.

Canadian Facts Publishing Co., 5.85; Canadian Review Co., Ltd., 8.00; J. M. Dent & Sons, Ltd., 37.80; W. J. Gage & Co., Ltd., .66; Canadian Geographic Society, 3.00; Grolier Society, Ltd., 69.50; McClelland & Stewart, Ltd., 5.05; Maclean Publishing Co., Ltd., 2.04; Macmillan Company of Canada, Ltd., 5.08; E. N. Moyer Co., Ltd., 3.05; Thos. Nelson & Sons, Ltd., .30; Ryerson Press, 7.93 147 54

Periodicals, $128.20.

Animal Life, 1.00; Wm. Dawson Subscription Service, Ltd., 117.70; Nuggett Publishing Co., 4.00; Thomas Co., 3.50; University of Toronto Press, 2.00...... 128 20

Stationery, $511.37.

F. S. Fosdick, 26.29; King's Printer, 484.72; petty disbursements, .36.......... 511 37

Services and Travelling Expenses, $121.88.

Wm. Andrews.. 121 88

Miscellaneous, $340.19.

Bell Telephone Co., rental, 47.40; tolls, 1.95; E. N. Moyer Co., Ltd., maps, 14.60; J. C. Norris, travelling expenses, 14.90; The Nuggett, copies of registrations, 63.70. Sundries—express, 30.88; freight, 114.35; postage, 38.00; telegrams, 1.36; petty disbursements, 13.05.. 340 19

Normal School, North Bay—Continued

Apparatus, Chemicals, Musical Instruments, Domestic Science and Manual Training Supplies ($301.96)

Canadian Department Stores, Ltd., thread, cloth, 24.69; Central Scientific Company of Canada, Ltd., clamps, etc., 35.46; T. Eaton Co., Ltd., canvas, etc., 21.05; King's Printer, 94.65; Rankin's Grocery, tea, sugar, etc., 13.50; J. W. Richardson, hack saw blades, etc., 12.05; A. C. Rorabeck, acid, films, etc., 21.48; R. B. Tennant & Co., lumber, 41.50; petty disbursements, 37.58 .... 301 96

Students' Board and Travelling Expenses ($42,665.50)

Sundry students 42,665 50

Fuel, Light and Power ($1,355.77)

Hydro-Electric Power Commission, power and light, 339.21; Lindsay & McCluskey, coal, 20.89; S. Rigby, cartage on fuel, 20.75; Stinson-Reeb Builders Supply Co., peat fuel, 116.73; Valley Camp Coal Co., coal, 846.69; petty disbursements, 11.50 1,355 77

Water ($162.14)

Corporation of the City of North Bay 162 14

Furniture, Repairs and Incidentals ($241.30)

Cochrane-Dunlop Hardware, Ltd., drills, hardware, etc., 100.24; Electric Supply Co., flush switches, etc., 11.30; Hume Paint & Wall Paper Store, glass, 35.43; S. Montgomery, unloading coal, 40.33; Office Specialty Manufacturing Co., Ltd., lockers, 31.95; petty disbursements, 22.05 .... 241 30

Expenses of Grounds, Trees, etc. ($210.88)

W. Andrews, work on grounds, 102.42; W. M. Oliver, work on grounds, 18.55; W. D. Parks, manure, 24.50; Rankin's Grocery, seeds, 21.11; D. Wharron, work on grounds, 31.85; petty disbursements, 12.45 .... 210 88

Scrubbing, Cleaning, Cartage, etc. ($1,166.84)

Cochrane-Dunlop Hardware, Ltd., hardware, 52.54; Dustbane Products, Ltd., brooms, etc., 27.42; S. Montgomery, cartage, 94.37; Pay list, wages of charwomen, 963.20; E. Pullan Wipers & Waste Co., Ltd., mops, etc., 13.50; petty disbursements, 15.81 .... 1,166 84

North Bay Normal School $78,561.22

UNIVERSITY OF OTTAWA NORMAL SCHOOL

Salaries ($15,874.90)

Name	Position	Period	Amount
Rene Lamoureux	Principal	12 months	4,400 00
Roger St. Denis	Master	12 "	3,450 00
Edward J. Watson	"	12 "	3,450 00
Joseph Bechard	Assistant Master	12 "	3,600 00
M. Bernadette Tarte	Secretary and Librarian	10 "	812 40
A. M. Isabelle Parent	" "	2 "	162 50

Salaries not Provided for (Statutory) ($147.94)

Louis Charbonneau .... Master .... ½ months 147 94

Reference Books, Periodicals, Stationery, Equipment and Contingencies ($4,512.05)

Reference Books, $41.89.

Canadian Facts Publishing Co., 5.85; Canadian Review Co., Ltd., 8.00; J. M. Dent & Sons, Ltd., 7.50; J. Hope & Sons, 5.75; Lafontaine Librairie, 2.40; Longmans, Green & Co., 5.28; McClelland & Stewart, Ltd., 5.04; Maclean Publishing Co., Ltd., 2.07 .... 41 89

Stationery, $387.12.

Beaugerard Press, 44.00; James Hope & Son, Ltd., 19.00; King's Printer, 267.78; University of Ottawa, 36.45; petty disbursements, 19.89 .... 387 12

Periodicals, $17.00.

Animal Life, 1.00; Evans Bros., Ltd., 9.00; National Geographic Society, 3.50; The School, 1.50; University of Toronto Press, 2.00 .... 17 00

University of Ottawa Normal School—Continued

Reference Books, Periodicals, Stationery, Equipment and Contingencies—Continued

Services and Travelling Expenses, $1,247.80.

J. A. Lajeunesse, services as instructor in Art and Music, 720.00; L. Lamoureux, travelling expenses, 52.80; J. C. Logan, services as writing instructor, 475.00.... 1,247 80

Miscellaneous, $2,818.24.

Bell Telephone Co., tolls, 2.45; Grand & Toy, Ltd., counter, etc., 125.00; McFarlane, Son & Hodgson, Ltd., paper towels, 45.50; Office Specialty Mfg. Co., Ltd., furniture, etc., 2,569.39; Sundries—cartage, 1.56; express, 13.23; postage, 20.00; revenue stamps, 3.00; telegrams, 9.17; petty disbursements, 28.94....... 2,818 24

University of Ottawa for Use of Building and Equipment ($14,000.00)

Bursar, University of Ottawa, rental.......... 14,000 00

Roman Catholic Separate School Board for Use of Schools ($750.00)

Treasurer, Roman Catholic Separate School Board.......... 750 00

Students' Board and Travelling Expenses ($47,728.27)

Sundry students.......... 47,728 27

University of Ottawa Normal School..........$82,865.22

STURGEON FALLS MODEL SCHOOL

Salaries ($11,900.00)

Name	Position		Period	Amount
J. M. Kaine	Principal		12 months	3,600 00
Henri Lemieux	Associate Principal		12 "	3,300 00
Margaret O. Cleland	Teacher Group 2		12 "	2,300 00
Gabrielle Gourand	" " 4		12 "	1,500 00
Arthur Dumont	Caretaker, Group 1	(T)	12 "	1,200 00

Reference Books, Periodicals, Stationery, Equipment, Musical Instruments, Services and Contingencies ($459.47)

Reference Books, $42.90.

Canadian Facts Publishing Co., 3.25; Jno. Cooper, .93; Copp Clarke Co., Ltd., 19.82; Doubleday, Doran & Gundy, Ltd., 1.59; Geographical Survey, Dept. of Mines, 4.15; L'Action Catholique, 4.00; J. M. Kaine, .44; Ryerson Press, 8.72.... 42 90

Periodicals, $13.00.

Mail and Empire, 5.00; National Geographic Society, 3.50; Ottawa Newspapers Subscription Bureau, 4.50.......... 13 00

Stationery, $216.18.

King's Printer, 196.44; Pharmacie Maranda, 19.74.......... 216 18

Miscellaneous, $187.39.

Bell Telephone Co., rental, 32.40; tolls, 6.77; Dr. Cornell, rent of piano, 24.00; E. R. Kaine, typing, 16.96; Michaud Bros., provisions, etc., 24.08; Sundries—express, 34.03; postage, 30.95; petty disbursements, 18.20.......... 187 39

Payment to Roman Catholic Separate School Board for Use of Schools ($800.00)

Treasurer, Roman Catholic School Board.......... 800 00

Students' Board and Travelling Expenses ($34,213.35)

Sundry students.......... 34,213 35

Fuel, Light and Power ($458.74)

J. B. Moore, coal, 382.31; Town of Sturgeon Falls, electric service, 76.43.......... 458 74

Water ($117.80)

Town of Sturgeon Falls.......... 117 80

Model School, Sturgeon Falls—Continued

Furniture, Repairs and Incidentals ($6.63)

Mageau Lumber Co., Ltd., lumber, 1.85; Michaud & Levesque, Ltd., oil, gas, etc., 4.78 .... 6 63

Scrubbing, Cleaning and Supplies ($41.95)

Michaud Bros., Ltd., dustbane, etc., 21.75; Michaud & Levesque, Ltd., floor oil, 20.20 41 95

Sturgeon Falls Model School........ $47,997.94

SANDWICH MODEL SCHOOL

Salaries ($6,475.00)

D. M. Eagle	Principal	12 months	3,600 00
Albina Sabourin	Teacher, Group 2	12 "	1,900 00
John V. Rudge	Caretaker, Group 2	12 "	975 00

Reference Books, Periodicals, Stationery, Equipment, Musical Instruments, Services and Contingencies ($215.80)

Reference Books, $60.61.

Canadian Facts Publishing Co., 3.25; J. M. Dent & Sons, Ltd., 15.36; Manufacturers' Press, Ltd., encyclopoedia, 42.00........ 60 61

Stationery, $95.75.

King's Printer, 39.43; V. E. Marentette & Son, 52.07; petty disbursements, 4.25.. 95 75

Miscellaneous, $59.44.

Bell Telephone Co., rental, 50.40; Sundries—cartage, .90; postage, 7.69; petty disbursements, .45........ 59 44

Physical Training including Apparatus and Athletic Supplies ($2.75)

Marentette Hardware, coat hooks........ 2 75

Students' Board and Travelling Expenses ($5,024.37)

Sundry students........ 5,024 37

Fuel, Light and Power ($213.55)

Sandwich Hydro-Electric System, light, 20.44; Wm. Woollatt Sons, Ltd., wood and coal, 193.11........ 213 55

Water ($19.81)

Sandwich Water Board........ 19 81

Furniture, Repairs and Incidentals ($53.24)

J. L. Sieber, plumbing, etc., 23.70; Geo. Thornton, repairing doors, etc., 19.20; petty disbursements, 10.34........ 53 24

Scrubbing, Cleaning and Supplies ($46.81)

Geo. J. Dupuis, cleaning supplies, 21.12; J. Rudge, laundry, 16.05; petty disbursements, 9.64........ 46 81

Sandwich Model School........ $12,051.33

EMBRUN MODEL SCHOOL

Salaries ($11,201.71)

Joseph Lapensee	Principal	11½ months	3,452 06
Harvey H. Andrews	Acting Principal	½ "	123 28
Harvey H. Andrews	Teacher	11½ "	2,301 37
Maurice Brunet	"	12 "	2,000 00
Camille M. Blanchard	"	12 "	2,200 00
Gloriana Martineau	" Group 2	1 "	75 00
Antoine Bourdeau	Caretaker, Group 2	12 "	1,050 00

Model School, Embrun—Continued

Reference Books, Periodicals, Stationery, Equipment, Musical Instruments, Services and Contingencies ($1,281.89)

Reference Books, $226.66.

Canadian Facts Publishing Co., 3.25; Copp, Clarke Co., Ltd., 102.05; T. Eaton Co., Ltd., 16.00; LaPatrie, 4.00; Omer Mahen et Fils Ltee, 67.20; Manufacturers' Press, Ltd., encyclopoedia, 23.52; Ryerson Press, 10.64	226 66

Periodicals, $7.50.

Canadian Geographic Society, 3.00; La Patrie, 3.00; The School, 1.50	7 50

Stationery, $210.11.

King's Printer	210 11

Miscellaneous, $837.62.

Bell Telephone Co., rental, 32.40; tolls, .50; Dominion Loose Leaf Co., Ltd., cards, 15.00; Embrun Convent, rent of rooms, 682.50; C. W. Lindsay, Ltd., rent of piano, 24.50; Sundries—cartage, 25.38; express, 21.86; postage, 30.35; telegrams, .88; petty disbursements, 4.25	837 62

Physical Training including Apparatus and Athletic Supplies ($26.43)

Ketchum, Ltd., soccer ball, 7.40; Omer Mahen & Fils, Ltee, hockey outfit, etc., 7.40; Sport Shop, baseballs, 11.63	26 43

Payment to Roman Catholic School Board, Embrun, for Use of Schools for Training of Teachers ($300.00)

Trustees Roman Catholic School Section No. 6, Russell	300 00

Students' Board and Travelling Expenses ($32,852.90)

Sundry students	32,852 90

Fuel, Light and Power ($386.90)

A. T. Emard, coal, 304.84; Hydro-Electric Power Commission, electric light, 59.81; Independent Coal Co., Ltd., wood, 22.25	386 90

Furniture, Repairs and Incidentals ($6.03)

Omer Mahen et Fils, Ltee., repairs to furniture	6 03

Scrubbing, Cleaning and Supplies ($102.49)

Omer Mahen et Fils, Ltee, paint, cleansers, etc.	102 49

Embrun Model School.....$46,158.35

Normal and Model Schools.....$625,069.57

HIGH SCHOOLS AND COLLEGIATE INSTITUTES

Salaries ($23,450.00)

Name	Position	Period	Amount
R. W. Anglin	Inspector	12 months	4,600 00
A. J. Husband	"	12 "	4,600 00
Wm. A. Jennings	"	12 "	4,600 00
A. G. Hooper	"	12 "	4,600 00
I. M. Levan	"	(T) 12 "	2,600 00
M. Manion	Senior Clerk Stenographer	12 "	1,400 00
Winnifred Beech	Clerk Stenographer, Group 1	12 "	1,050 00

Grants, High Schools and Collegiate Institutes ($418,677.02)

Alexandria, 1,620.57; Alliston, 1,558.48; Almonte, 1,801.22; Amherstburg, 1,870.24; Arnprior, 1,778.82; Arthur, 1,517.62; Athens, 1,784.42; Aurora, 1,879.83; Avonmore, 1,379.38; Aylmer, 1,638.79; Barrie, 1,897.50; Beamsville, 1,853.00; Belleville, 1,869.50; Blenheim, 1,713.16; Bowmanville, 1,850.80; Bracebridge, 7,294.66; Bradford, 1,556.47; Brampton, 1,914.50; Brantford, 1,981.50; Brighton, 1,541.91; Brockville, 1,954.50; Burford, 1,651.41; Burlington, 1,864.50; Caledonia, 1,836.32; Campbellford, 1,824.50; Carleton Place, 1,796.69; Cayuga, 1,710.60; Chapleau, 3,426.68; Chatham, 1,715.50; Chesley, 1,592.88; Chesterville, 1,320.70; Clinton, 1,869.50; Cobalt, 6,185.92; Cobourg, 1,709.50; Cochrane, 5,776.41; Colborne,

High Schools and Collegiate Institutes—Continued

Grants—Continued

1,542.94; Collingwood, 1,929.50; Cornwall, 1,946.72; Deseronto, 1,330.34; Dundalk, 1,216.28; Dundas, 1,903.10; Dunnville, 1,742.50; Durham, 1,716.45; Dutton, 1,811.09; Elmira, 1,639.52; Elora, 1,165.70; Essex, 1,886.28; Etobicoke, 1,909.04; Exeter, 1,496.93; Fergus, 1,903.21; Finch, 1,366.39; Flesherton, 1,567.30; Forest, 1,598.66; Fort Erie, 1,888.57; Fort Frances, 3,777.00; Fort William, 8,323.17; Galt, 1,941.50; Gananoque, 1,635.00; Georgetown, 1,600.10; Glencoe, 1,517.61; Goderich, 1,920.50; Gravenhurst, 2,999.78; Grimsby, 1,910.81; Guelph, 1,673.18; Hagerville, 1,825.59; Haileybury, 4,796.17; Hamilton, 5,667.70; Hanover, 1,670.50; Harriston, 1,429.90; Hawkesbury, 2,375.07; Huntsville, 4,286.00; Ingersoll, 1,557.90; Iroquois, 1,668.31; Kapuskasing, 3,114.36; Kemptville, 1,479.02; Kenora, 3,744.34; Kincardine, 1,661.04; Kingston, 1,808.50; Kingsville, 1,603.05; Kirkland Lake, 3,743.24; Kitchener, 1,819.50; Lakefield, 1,215.07; Leamington, 1,889.32; Lindsay, 1,867.50; Listowel, 1,604.00; London, 5,763.42; Lucan, 1,337.89; Madoc, 1,451.23; Markdale, 1,184.80; Markham, 1,607.56; Maxville, 1,442.00; Meaford, 1,857.41; Midland, 1,914.50; Milton, 1,717.04; Mimico, 1,864.50; Mitchell, 1,807.69; Morewood, 1,034.02; Morrisburg, 1,870.39; Mount Forest, 1,545.00; Napanee, 1,843.50; Nepean, 3,684.96; Newburgh, 1,239.64; Newcastle, 958.89; New Liskeard, 7,759.29; Newmarket, 1,907.14; Niagara Falls, 1,915.50; Niagara-on-the-Lake, 1,541.12; North Bay, 5,514.85; Norwich, 1,620.00; Norwood, 1,360.21; Oakville, 1,682.50; Omemee, 852.72; Orangeville, 1,690.13; Orillia, 1,865.75; Oshawa, 1,915.76; Ottawa, 3,765.00; Owen Sound, 1,951.50; Paris, 1,824.91; Parkhill, 1,381.61; Parry Sound, 3,129.00; Pembroke, 1,863.50; Penetanguishene, 1,673.61; Perth, 1,965.50; Peterborough, 1,847.50; Petrolia, 1,889.69; Picton, 1,961.50; Plantaganet, 1,346.17; Port Arthur, 3,669.00; Port Colborne, 1,823.86; Port Credit, 1,813.04; Port Dover, 1,282.98; Port Elgin, 1,335.76; Port Hope, 1,818.06; Port Perry, 1,758.89; Port Rowan, 926.16; Prescott, 1,803.29; Renfrew, 1,981.50; Richmond Hill, 1,856.72; Ridgetown, 1,626.10; Ridgeway, 1,903.52; Rockland, 1,316.52; Saltfleet, 1,677.31; Sandwich, 1,694.19; Sarnia, 1,974.91; Sault Ste. Marie, 3,905.40; Scarborough, 1,981.50; Seaforth, 1,584.50; Shelburne, 1,780.23; Simcoe, 1,642.23; Smith's Falls, 1,816.50; Smithville, 1,490.06; St. Catharines, 1,951.50; St. Mary's, 1,903.50; St. Thomas, 1,755.23; Stamford, 1,969.50; Stirling, 1,701.30; Stratford, 1,887.28; Strathroy, 1,905.50; Streetsville, 1,192.21; Sudbury, 3,330.82; Sydenham, 1,599.64, Thessalon, 3,581.03; Thorold, 1,880.34; Tillsonburg, 1,878.48; Timmins, 9,190.30; Toronto, 17,166.50; Trenton, 1,892.39; Tweed, 1,682.82; Uxbridge, 1,894.50; Vankleek Hill, 1,777.50; Vienna, 899.16; Walkerton, 1,525.00; Walkerville, 1,981.50; Wallaceburg, 1,648.50; Wardsville, 877.10; Waterdown, 1,867.12; Watford, 1,879.50; Waterford, 1,606.82; Welland, 1,885.50; Weston, 1,765.00; Whitby, 1,880.50; Wiarton, 1,592.21; Williamstown, 1,451.45; Winchester, 1,590.74; Windsor, 3,910.43; Wingham, 1,519.42; Woodstock, 1,790.50; York, 5,940.50; York East, 1,981.50; York North, 1,909.87........................ 418,677 02

Night High Schools ($10,093.29)

Belleville, 172.33; Brantford, 127.50; Cornwall, 125.00; Fort William, 86.66; Galt, 56.33; Guelph, 40.00; Hamilton, 865.50; Kitchener, 370.00; Niagara Falls, 181.33; Niagara Falls South, 156.00; Ottawa, 430.00; Pembroke, 92.50; Peterborough, 110.00; Petrolia, 101.00; Picton, 87.50; Port Arthur, 18.33; Runnymede Road, Toronto, 996.76; St. Thomas, 216.66; Stratford, 146.66; Sudbury, 303.58; Tillsonburg, 100.00; Toronto, 2,608.76; Vaughan Road, Toronto, 881.15; Walkerville, 729.00; Welland, 80.00; York East, 371.33; York Memorial, 639.41............ 10,093 29

High School Cadet Corps ($3,750.00)

Athens, 50.00; Aurora, 50.00; Barrie, 50.00; Belleville, 50.00; Birchcliff, 50.00; Bowmanville, 50.00; Brampton, 50.00; Brockville, 50.00; Caledonia, 50.00; Campbellford, 50.00; Carleton Place, 50.00; Chapleau, 50.00; Chatham, 100.00; Cobourg, 50.00 ; Cornwall, 50.00; Dundas, 50.00; Dunnville, 50.00; Fort Frances, 50.00; Galt, 50.00; Goderich, 50.00; Hamilton, 200.00; Kenora, 50.00; Leamington, 50.00; Lindsay, 50.00; Meaford, 50.00; Midland, 50.00; Morrisburg, 50.00; Napanee, 50.00; Niagara Falls, 50.00; North Bay, 50.00; Orillia, 50.00; Oshawa, 50.00; Ottawa, 150.00; Pembroke, 100.00; Perth, 50.00; Peterborough, 50.00; Picton, 50.00; Port Arthur, 50.00; Port Perry, 50.00; Renfrew, 50.00; Ridgetown, 50.00; Sarnia, 50.00; St. Catharines, 50.00; St. Thomas, 50.00; Smith's Falls, 50.00; Stratford, 50.00; Strathroy, 50.00; Sudbury, 50.00 Thorold, 50.00 Tillsonburg, 50.00; Toronto, 550.00; Trenton, 50.00; Vankleek Hill, 50.00; Welland, 50.00; Weston, 50.00; Whitby, 50.00; Windsor, 50.00; Woodstock, 50.00. 3,750 00

High Schools and Collegiate Institutes—Continued

Travelling and Moving Expenses ($5,673.07)

R. W. Anglin, 930.00; A. G. Hooper, 1,266.15; A. J. Husband, 1,323.63; W. A. Jennings, 1,463.09; I. M. Levan, 690.20 .... 5,673 07

Grants to School Boards, Supervisors and Teachers to Encourage Courses of Music in High Schools and Collegiate Institutes ($1,052.16)

Teachers and Supervisors, $955.00.

W. H. Bishop, 100.00; Leila Carroll, 100.00; Harry Duxbury, 80.00; W. A. Fisher, 50.00; Harry Hill, 100.00; Flossie Kinnaird, 100.00; P. G. Marshall, 200.00; Dorothy Myers, 25.00; J. T. Priest, 100.00; H. C. Renaud, 100.00 .... 955 00

School Boards, $97.16.

Fort Frances High School, 30.00; Glencoe High School, 30.00; Norwood Board of Education, 30.00; Port Dover Board of Education, 7.16 .... 97 16

Grants to High Schools and Collegiate Institutes to offset Losses Occasioned by Unassessed Crown Property ($1,255.39)

Penetanguishene High School Board, 748.07; Whitby Board of Education, 317.17; Woodstock Board of Education, 190.15 .... 1,255 39

Stationery, Postage, Printing, Services and Contingencies ($4,951.53)

Committee Preparing Catalogue and British History—Services, $2,745.00; Expenses, $104.05.

Winnifred Barnstead, services, 511.00; F. E. Clarke, services, 100.00; A. M. Hamill, services, 130.00; A. G. Hooper, services, 45.00; A. J. Husband, services, 45.00; Alfred Johnson, services, 45.00; expenses, 10.80; H. W. Kerfoot, services, 565.00; I. M. Levan, services, 256.00; James McQueen, services, 45.00; expenses, 30.40; A. I. Ogilvie, services, 958.00; expenses 62.85; Blanche Snell, services, 45.00 .... 2,849 05

Miscellaneous, $2,102.48.

Irwin & Gordon, Ltd., books, 89.20; King's Printer, 1,984.26; Ryerson Press, 27.44; petty disbursements, 1.58 .... 2,102 48

High Schools and Collegiate Institutes $468,902.46

DEPARTMENTAL MUSEUM

Salaries ($3,850.00)

Rowland B. Orr	Director of Ontario Provincial Museum .... (T)	12 months	1,050 00
Robert Virtue	Museum Assistant	12 "	1,600 00
H. Borthwick	Clerk Stenographer, Group 1	12 "	1,200 00

Contingencies ($241.10)

Miscellaneous, $241.10.

G. H. Hamilton, soap chips, etc., 20.87; King's Printer, 27.52; Geo. Pearsall & Son, paint and hardware, 11.48; Robt. Simpson Co., Ltd., coats, etc., 22.01; United Typewriter Co., Ltd., inspections, 12.00; R. E. Virtue, travelling expenses, 11.50. Sundries—express, 4.10; newspapers and periodicals, 35.72; postage, 63.00; petty disbursements, 32.90 .... 241 10

Expenses of Archaeological Researches, etc. ($782.00)

Muriel Edwards, painting casts, 172.00; M. Foster, repairs to plaster busts, 10.00; Arthur Heming, painting, 600.00 .... 782 00

Natural History Collections ($125.00)

Thos. Emack, mounting birds, 120.00; Wm. J. Robertson, snake, 5.00 .... 125 00

Departmental Museum $4,998.10

PUBLIC LIBRARIES

Salaries ($8,866.66)

Frederick C. Jennings	Inspector of Public Libraries	4 months	1,266 66
S. B. Herbert	Principal Clerk	12 "	2,400 00
William E. Smith	Senior Clerk	12 "	2,000 00
P. Spereman	Senior Library Assistant	12 "	1,700 00
Jessie Craig	Senior Clerk Stenographer	12 "	1,500 00

Public Libraries—Continued

Grants, Organization, Services, Books and Expenses ($52,134.65)

Grants, etc., $40,891.19.

Acton, 62.98; Agincourt, 131.05; Ailsa Craig, 118.15; Allenford, 16.99; Alliston, 39.96; Alma, 10.00; Almonte, 148.68; Alvinston, 58.57; Alton, 13.57; Amherstburg, 122.94; Ancaster, 26.80; Apple Hill, 15.32; Arkona, 13.10; Arnprior, 101.50; Arthur, 91.34; Athens, 41.11; Atwood, 34.39; Auburn, 18.91; Aurora, 95.04; Aylmer, 155.00; Ayr, 140.47; Badgeros, 19.28; Bala, 81.03; Bancroft, 80.32; Barrie, 160.00; Bayfield, 43.49; Bayville, 23.95; Beachville, 29.86; Beamsville, 126.10; Beaverton, 89.35; Beechwood, 60.59; Beeton, 24.76; Belleville, 160.00; Belwood, 38.23; Belmont, 77.90; Belmore, 21.10; Birchcliffe, 101.72; Blenheim, 116.74; Blind River, 85.81; Bloomfield, 67.33; Blyth, 15.14; Bobcaygeon, 99.43; Bolton, 19.67; Bond Head, 45.22; Bothwell, 65.45; Bowmanville, 153.16; Bracebridge, 119.25; Brampton, 160.00; Brantford, 160.00; Brighton, 64.08; Brockville, 160.00; Brooklin, 27.88; Bronte, 24.47; Brougham, 29.39; Brown's Corners, 37.03; Brownsville, 21.50; Brucefield, 14.71; Bruce Mines, 78.95; Brussels, 87.44; Burgessville, 15.00; Burk's Falls, 117.90; Burlington, 146.87; Caledon, 10.00; Callander, 30.59; Cambray, 36.91; Camden East, 38.10; Campbellford, 148.55; Camlachie, 22.37; Canfield, 47.61; Cannington, 25.37; Cardinal, 54.00; Cargill, 10.00; Carleton Place, 118.04; Carlisle, 65.72; Castleton, 10.00; Cayuga, 23.12; Chalk River, 20.99; Chapleau, 101.31; Chatham, 160.00; Chatsworth, 22.26; Cheapside, 10.00; Chesley, 134.70; Chesterville, 20.00; Claremont, 60.91; Clarksburg, 83.86; Clarkson, 31.46; Claude, 5.45; Clifford, 60.31; Clinton, 155.00; Cobalt, 10.00; Cobourg, 119.50; Cochrane, 107.31; Colborne, 92.35; Coldstream, 44.51; Coldwater, 10.49; Collingwood, 160.00; Collins Bay, 20.25; Comber, 71.68; Cookstown, 14.17; Copper Cliff, 100.00; Cornwall, 160.00; Cottam, 31.09; Creemore, 30.80; Delaware, 50.64; Delhi, 114.90; Delta, 18.51; Depot Harbour, 25.55; Deseronto, 26.25; Don, 21.92; Dorchester, 84.88; Drayton, 96.26; Dresden, 137.00; Drumbo, 19.56; Dryden, 94.42; Dundalk, 64.60; Dundas, 160.00; Dungannon, 52.39; Dunnville, 100.00; Durham, 115.49; Dutton, 121.68; Elmira, 151.00; Elmvale, 23.15; Elmwood, 49.37; Elora, 147.35; Embro, 60.49; Emo, 22.47; Englehart, 15.00; Ennotville, 71.61; Erin, 23.38; Espanola, 59.72; Essex, 146.85; Ethel, 52.49; Exeter, 84.25; Fenelon Falls, 61.87; Fenwick, 19.80; Fergus, 154.55; Flesherton, 28.91; Fonthill, 81.77; Fordwich, 16.56; Forest, 129.50; Foresters Falls, 10.00; Fort Erie, 117.63; Fort Erie North, 105.75; Fort Frances, 149.35; Fort William, 320.00; Frankford, 107.86; Fulton, 15.80; Galt, 160.00; Gananoque, 160.00; Garden Island, 18.52; Georgetown, 139.02; Glamis, 10.00; Glanworth, 74.08; Glencoe, 96.37; Glen Allen, 17.88; Glen Morris, 33.71; Goderich, 160.00; Gore Bay, 89.04; Gore's Landing, 31.01; Gorrie, 18.08; Grafton, 34.13; Grand Valley, 72.19; Granton, 49.38; Gravenhurst, 101.50; Grimsby, 150.77; Guelph, 160.00; Hagersville, 126.25; Haileybury, 100.00; Haliburton, 35.04; Hamilton, 803.68; Hanover, 84.52; Harrietville, 61.25; Harrington West, 27.87; Harriston, 111.51; Harrow, 42.52; Harrowsmith, 21.17; Havelock, 40.10; Hensall, 71.51; Hepworth, 11.52; Hespeler, 389.69; Hickson, 120.00; Highgate, 105.49; Highland Creek, 21.85; Hillsburg, 58.18; Hillsdale, 25.35; Hilton Beach, 20.00; Holstein, 22.68; Honeywood, 26.02; Humber Bay, 54.16; Huntsville, 96.11; Ignace, 10.00; Ilderton, 71.78; Ingersoll, 160.00; Inglewood, 27.47; Inwood, 43.15; Iroquois, 29.60; Iroquois Falls, 100.00; Islington, 83.06; Ivanhoe, 31.72; Jarvis, 28.43; Kearney, 20.06; Kemble, 42.78; Kemptville, 84.08; Kenora, 160.00; Kimberley, 15.27; Kincardine, 257.11; Kingston, 160.00; Kingsville, 154.45; Kinsale, 34.43; Kintore, 35.06; Kirkfield, 77.24; Kirkland Lake, 100.00; Kirkton, 28.15; Kitchener, 160.00; Komoka, 38.45; Lake Charles, 5.00; Lakefield, 99.54; Lakeside, 38.07; Lambeth, 59.10; Lambton, 35.00; Lanark, 81.16; Lancaster, 40.07; Leamington, 160.00; Lefroy, 12.46; Lindsay, 160.00; Linwood, 31.96; Listowel, 149.12; Little Britain, 83.28; Little Current, 100.00; London, 550.00; Long Branch, 43.49; Lorne Park, 62.32; Lucan, 50.14; Lucknow, 122.85; Lyn, 5.00; Madoc, 94.92; Mandamin, 33.62; Manilla, 116.80; Manotick, 12.61; Markdale, 101.80; Markham, 57.24; Marmora, 103.50; Martintown, 15.00; Maxwell, 29.21; Maxville, 38.06; Meaford, 151.20; Melbourne, 10.00; Merrickville, 34.27; Merritton, 81.74; Midland, 160.00; Mildmay, 20.52; Millbank, 15.00; Millbrook, 115.96; Millgrove, 18.50; Milton, 64.13; Milverton, 109.30; Mimico, 160.00; Minden, 10.00; Mitchell, 132.82; Moorefield, 18.87; Monkton, 15.00; Mono Road, 11.34; Morrisburg, 72.04; Morriston, 18.93; Mount Albert, 86.64; Mount Brydges, 31.75; Mount Dennis, 124.65; Mount Elgin, 38.87; Mount Forest, 146.22; Mount Hope, 15.00; Nanticoke, 11.77; Napanee, 152.07; Napier, 16.17; Newburgh, 28.12; Newbury, 18.55; Newcastle, 148.97; New Dundee, 68.64; New Hamburg, 143.00; Newington, 19.09; New Liskeard, 147.51; New Lowell, 27.67; Newmarket, 143.13; New Toronto, 388.00; Niagara Falls, 294.50; Niagara-on-the-Lake, 112.54; Norland, 10.00; North Bay, 160.00; North Gower, 20.80; Norwich, 144.05; Norwood, 80.38; Oakville, 155.00; Oakwood, 50.42; Odessa, 45.12; Oil

Public Libraries—Continued

Grants, Organization, Services, Books and Expenses—Continued

Grants, etc.—Continued

Springs, 16.92; Omemee, 47.65; Orangeville, 160.00; Orillia, 160.00; Orono, 18.80; Osgoode, 33.19; Oshawa, 160.00; Ottawa, 767.30; Otterville, 58.17; Owen Sound, 160.00; Oxford Mills, 10.00; Paisley, 106.79; Palermo, 31.46; Palmerston, 118.18; Paris, 160.00; Park Head, 18.30; Parkhill, 74.97; Parry Sound, 100.00; Pembroke, 160.00; Penetanguishene, 142.80; Perth, 160.00; Peterborough, 160.00; Pickering, 49.71; Picton, 160.00; Pinkerton, 21.23; Plattsville, 33.63; Point Edward, 56.47; Port Arthur, 160.00; Port Carling, 83.13; Port Colborne, 115.75; Port Credit, 93.73; Port Dover, 137.02; Port Elgin, 109.73; Port Hope, 160.00; Port Lambton, 30.28; Port Perry, 96.38; Port Rowan, 51.63; Port Stanley, 61.43; Powassan, 41.22; Prescott, 152.07; Preston, 160.00; Princeton, 66.29; Queensville, 20.13; Rebecca, 50.94; Renfrew, 160.00; Richard's Landing, 10.00; Richmond Hill, 120.68; Ridgetown, 143.15; Ridgeway, 105.48; Ripley, 20.95; Rittenhouse, 110.68; Rodney, 54.25; Romney, 47.87; Rosedale, 22.11; Runnymede, 38.23; St. George, 58.64; St. Helen's, 31.82; St. Marys, 160.00; St. Thomas, 320.00; Saltfleet, 100.00; Sandwich, 141.42; Sarnia, 160.00; Sault Ste. Marie, 296.22; Scarborough, 119.97; Scarborough Bluffs, 12.97; Schomberg, 77.67; Schrieber, 104.45; Scotland, 32.98; Seaforth, 150.32; Shedden, 25.77; Shelburne, 155.00; Shetland, 16.54; Simcoe, 160.00; Smith's Falls, 381.92; Solina, 24.39; Sombra, 36.17; Southampton, 91.25 South Porcupine, 133.07; South Mountain, 5.00; South River, 19.69; South Woodslee, 51.83; Sparta, 46.54; Springfield, 20.12; Sprucedale, 23.18; Stayner, 26.52; Stevensville, 60.60; Stirling, 135.98; Stouffville, 140.46; Stratford, 160.00; Strathroy, 160.00; Strathcona, 10.00; Stratton, 18.42; Streetsville, 79.25; Sudbury, 160.00; Sunderland, 20.43; Sundridge, 49.14; Sutton West, 87.68; Swansea, 86.24; Sydenham, 68.40; Tara, 73.72; Tavistock, 139.18; Teeswater, 108.05; Thamesford, 64.76; Thamesville, 86.32; Thedford, 62.15; Thessalon, 36.70; Thornbury, 49.57; Thorndale, 37.96; Thornhill, 37.80; Thorold, 195.04; Tillsonburg, 154.40; Timmins 160.00; Tiverton, 10.00; Tobermory, 39.04; Toronto, 2,646.37; Tottenham, 24.89; Trenton, 155.00; Trout Creek, 10.00; Tweed, 84.67; Underwood, 48.88; Unionville, 50.89; Uxbridge, 151.77; Varna, 64.97; Vars, 10.00; Victoria, 10.00; Victoria Mines, 25.20; Vineland, 46.37; Walkerton, 417.00; Walkerville, 315.00; Wallaceburg, 160.00; Walton, 10.00; Wardsville, 38.71; Warkworth, 15.00; Warren Park, Toronto, 10.00; Waterdown, 44.03; Waterford, 35.58; Waterloo, 160.00; Watford, 94.69; Welland, 406.20; Wellburn, 18.27; Wellesley, 53.60; Wellington, 46.22; West Lorne, 24.76; Weston, 151.22; Whitby, 365.72; Whitevale, 33.02; Wiarton, 80.92; Williamstown, 10.00; Winchester, 27.68; Windsor, 361.43; Wingham, 160.00; Woodbridge, 40.37; Woodville, 33.25; Woodstock, 160.00; Wroxeter, 24.58; Wyoming, 95.41; Zepher, 20.93; Zurich, 25.86........................ 40,891 19

Books, $406.75.

American Library Association, 31.41; Blackie & Son, Ltd., 3.20; R. R. Bowker Co., 19.89; Canadian Forum, 2.00; Wm. Dawson Subscription Service, Ltd., 18.25; Library Review, 2.00; Royal Astronomical Society of Canada, 300.00; Ryerson Press, 5.60; F. I. Weaver, Publisher, 2.00; H. W. Wilson Co., 19.90; Windsor Public Library, 2.50.. 406 75

Miscellaneous, $10,836.71.

Addressograph Co., Ltd., inspections, 28.56; F. B. Dixon Co., cartage, 76.00; King's Printer, 10,663.63; Remington Typewriters, Ltd., inspections, 12.64; Ryerson Press, cards, 16.36; United Typewriter Co., Ltd., inspections, 34.20; Sundries—customs, .22; petty disbursements, 5.10..... .... 10,836 71

Travelling Expenses ($903.24)

S. B. Herbert, 163.20; F. C. Jennings, 496.74; Miss P. Spereman, 243.30........... 903 24

Library Institutes ($191.98)

Sundry persons, travelling expenses... 191 98

Travelling Libraries, Cost of Books, Services and Contingencies ($2,637.25)

Books, $2,109.65.

T. Allen, 28.69; Blackie & Son, Ltd., 44.40; A. Britnell, 71.66; Canadian Facts Publishing Co., Ltd., 26.00; Canadian Review Co., Ltd., 400.00; Copp Clark Co., Ltd., 55.89; J. M. Dent & Sons, Ltd., 23.00; Doubleday, Doran & Gundy Co., Ltd., 68.41; Longmans, Green & Co., 322.17; McClelland & Stewart, Ltd., 69.51; Geo. J. McLeod, Ltd., 54.67; Macmillan Company of Canada, Ltd., 64.48; Musson Book Co., Ltd., 96.39; Thos. Nelson & Sons, Ltd., 173.70; Geolcgical Survey of Canada, 12.50; Ryerson Press, 523.57; S. J. R. Saunders, 40.00; Wm. Tyrrell & Co., Ltd., 25.20; petty disbursements, 9.41.................... 2,109 65

Public Libraries—Continued

Travelling Libraries, Cost of Books, Services and Contingencies—Continued

Miscellaneous, $527.60.

King's Printer, 82.50; express, 315.78; freight, 124.32; petty disbursements, 5.00.. 527 60

Grants ($29,900.00)

Ottawa Association for the Blind	1,000 00
Ontario College of Art	25,000 00
Ontario Society of Artists	500 00
Royal Canadian Institute (Toronto)	2,500 00
Royal Astronomical Society of Canada	600 00
Institut Canadien Francais	300 00

Public Libraries....$94,633.78

VOCATIONAL EDUCATION

Salaries ($24,741.66)

Frank S. Rutherford	Director of Vocational Education	12 months	4,600 00
A. M. Moon	Inspector, Group 1	10 "	3,166 66
Louis S. Beattie	" " 1	12 "	4,000 00
Alice M. Hamill	" " 2	12 "	3,600 00
J. E. Uffen	Head Clerk	12 "	2,850 00
E. M. Strange	Clerk, Group 1	12 "	1,500 00
Wm. Paterson	" " 2	12 "	1,500 00
Violet G. English	" " 2	12 "	1,200 00
M. Foy	Clerk Stenographer, Group 1	12 "	1,200 00
W. E. Lattimore	" " " 1	12 "	1,125 00

Manual Training and Household Science Departments including Grants ($62,914.21)

Public School Boards, Grants, $62,914.21.

Brantford, 930.73; Bridgeburg, 718.10; Brockville, 762.50; Chatham, 471.71; Cobourg, 167.12; Fairbank, 435.43; Guelph, 444.80; Hamilton, 6,834.74; Ingersoll, 422.95; Kingston, 451.43; Kitchener, 991.97; London, 2,959.51; Ottawa, 5,980.84; Owen Sound, 550.17; Pembroke, 319.41; Peterborough, 547.95; St. Catharines, 481.26; Sarnia, 1,348.44; Stirling, 173.75; Stratford, 977.73; Swansea, 572.32; Toronto, 31,009.86; Walkerville, 910.43; Waterloo, 461.95; Windsor, 2,686.51; Woodstock, 519.48; York, 783.12.... 62,914 21

Grants to High Schools for Mining Education ($17,000.00)

Treasurer, Haileybury High School	10,000 00
Treasurer, Sudbury High School	7,000 00

Agricultural Training in High Schools and Collegiate Institutes Grants ($39,995.49)

Grants to High Schools and Teachers, $23,367.79.

Amherstburg, 34.66; Beamsville, 222.50; Bowmanville, 89.00; Bracebridge, 91.35; Bradford, 89.00; Brighton, 169.10; Burlington, 222.50; Caledonia, 216.27; Cayuga, 215.91; Cobalt, 111.25; Dundas, 139.93; Dunnville, 219.83; Elmira, 976.88; Essex, 56.28; Fergus, 213.60; Fort Francis, 81.35; Haileybury, 17.75; Iroquois, 26.34; Kincardine, 202.74; Kingsville, 222.50; Leamington, 63.55; Listowel, 1,335.44; Madoc, 94.75; Midland, 178.00; Mitchell, 190.49; Nepean, 46.76; New Liskeard, 222.50; Norwich, 222.50; Oakville, 166.62; Petrolia, 106.10; Port Elgin, 89.00; Port Perry, 2,540.67; Ridgetown, 222.50; Ridgeway, 222.50; Saltfleet, 204.25; Shelburne, 86.45; Smithville, 81.76; Stamford, 222.50; Thessalon, 44.50; Uxbridge, 64.97; Waterdown, 135.66; Watford, 195.64; Welland, 86.52; Whitby, 1,343.85; Williamstown, 89.00; Winchester, 207.37. Sundry teachers, 11,285.20.... 23,367 79

Grants to Collegiate Institutes and Teachers, $8,149.53.

Barrie, 178.00; Belleville, 178.00; Brockville, 222.50; Cobourg, 92.74; Cornwall, 66.98; East York, 89.00; Fort William, 98.43; Goderich, 87.80; Ingersoll, 60.67; Kitchener, 33.94; Lindsay, 222.50; Napanee, 222.50; Orillia, 79.39; Perth, 89.00; Picton, 123.36; Port Arthur, 51.67; Renfrew, 222.50; Runnymede, 89.00; Scarborough, 222.12; Smiths Falls, 143.58; Strathroy, 222.50; Walkerville, 89.00; York, 89.00. Sundry teachers, 5,175.35.... 8,149 53

Vocational Education—Continued

Agricultural Training in High Schools and Collegiate Institutes,
Grants—Continued

Grants to Continuation Schools and Teachers, $8,150.10.

Agincourt, 125.10; Belmont, 67.24; Brownsville, 69.85; Coldwater, 18.33; Comber, 198.38; Drayton, 1,029.93; Drumbo, 222.02; Embro, 87.08; Fordwich, 65.35; Ilderton, 34.98; Kinmount, 8.72; Lobo, 100.15; Lynden, 133.12; Lyndhurst, 46.01; Mindemoya, 80.10; Minden, 37.88; Mount Bridges, 69.26; Mount Elgin, 219.91; Mount Pleasant, 195.30; Pakenham, 56.44; Pelham, 175.86; Princeton, 220.01; Seeley's Bay, 32.17; Sparta, 79.66; Stouffville, 29.28; Thamesford, 160.18; Thornbury, 178.00; Thorndale, 168.13; Wheatley, 541.74. Woodville, 221.78. Sundry teachers, 3,478.14 .... 8,150 10

Grants to Fifth Classes, $328.07.

Port McNicholl, 6.20; No. 7, Biddulph, 92.65; No. 4, Wellesley, 24.52. Sundry teachers, 204.70 .... 328 07

Day and Evening Classes ($1,360,813.40)

Special Committee on Nurses Examinations, $637.50.

W. J. Dunlop, 87.50; Jean I. Gunn, 87.50; A. M. Hamill, 162.50; A. M. Munn, 87.50; W. J. Salter, 137.50; W. R. Saunders, 75.00 .... 637 50

Boards of Education, Grants, $1,030,477.54.

Barrie, 6,062.24; Beamsville, 6,715.52; Belleville, 18,134.11; Brantford, 12,787.14; Brockville, 6,862.52; Chatham, 16,899.57; Collingwood, 1,824.71; Dryden, 120.00; Dundas, 931.65; Dunnville, 636.00; Fort Erie, 813.75; Fort Frances, 3,108.93; Fort William, 14,704.09; Galt, 21,857.90; Guelph, 18,157.36; Hamilton, 153,176.91, Hespeler, 452.10; Ingersoll, 1,291.05; Kapuskasing, 1,219.80; Kenora, 161.40; London, 60,887.62; Midland, 204.00; Napanee, 5,747.94; Niagara Falls, 10,625.16; New Toronto, 799.88; Oshawa, 20,624.49; Owen Sound, 24,391.08; Perth, 5,878.26; Peterborough, 8,834.32; Petrolia, 396.00; Port Arthur, 33,465.69; Preston, 1,039.31; Renfrew, 7,552.31; Sarnia, 9,467.07; St. Catharines, 10,923.91; St. Thomas, 21,604.93; Stratford, 7,753.28; Toronto, 474,992.29; Welland, 15,602.59; Weston, 17,076.71; Windsor East, 941.93; Woodstock, 5,752.02 .... 1,030,477 54

High School Boards, Grants, $133,017.90.

Amherstburg, 316.65; Burlington, 333.00; Essex, 353.36; Fort Erie, 5,809.82; Fort Frances, 2,985.18; Haileybury, 4,508.86; Hanover, 1,385.02; Kirkland Lake, 274.22; Midland, 1,158.30; Ridgetown, 3,556.01; Scarborough, 7,112.26; Stamford, 7,029.91; Sudbury, 15,336.41; Timmins, 75,358.74; York East, 7,198.78; York North, 301.38 .... 133,017 90

Vocational School Boards, Grants, $66,927.65.

Apprenticeship Branch, Department of Labour, proportion of various amounts paid to Vocational Schools, 1,389.44; Windsor-Walkerville, 65,538.21 .... 66,927 65

Collegiate Institute Boards, Grants, $128,667.13.

Cornwall, 7,447.84; Goderich, 170.33; Kitchener-Waterloo, 23,009.07; North Bay, 30,679.03; Ottawa, 26,371.79; Picton, 4,667.60; Sault Ste. Marie, 17,469.20; York, 14,844.64; York East, 4,007.63 .... 128,667 13

Miscellaneous, $1,085.68.

King's Printer, 998.20; W. J. Salter, travelling expenses, 77.35; Sundries—customs, .50; petty disbursements, 9.63 .... 1,085 68

Travelling Expenses of Instructors ($4,321.56)

L. S. Beattie, 1,242.90; A. M. Hamill, 991.77; A. M. Moon, 930.48; W. Paterson, 93.93; F. S. Rutherford, 606.43; M. A. Sorsoleil, 116.70; J. F. Uffen, 339.35 .... 4,321 56

Vocational Education $1,509,786.32

ONTARIO TRAINING COLLEGE FOR TECHNICAL TEACHERS

Salaries ($24,114.00)

Name	Position	Period	Amount
F. P. Gavin	Principal	12 months	5,000 00
Cyril G. Ashcroft	Master	12 "	4,000 00
Elsie J. McKim	"	12 "	4,000 00
Arthur Styles	"	12 "	4,000 00
Edith Gardener	Librarian and Secretary	12 "	1,300 00
T. W. Nicholls	Caretaker, Group 1	12 "	1,400 00
Sundry critic and other teachers			4,414 00

Ontario Training College for Technical Teachers—Continued

Reference Books, Periodicals, Stationery, Furniture, Services and Expenses ($984.57)

Reference Books, $113.93.

Canadian Fine Art Guild, 43.75; Grolier Society, Ltd., 69.00; Macmillan Company of Canada, Ltd., 1.18 .... 113 93

Periodicals, $56.95.

R. Duncan & Co., 52.95; petty disbursements, 4.00 .... 56 95

Stationery, $407.89.

Brown Bros., Ltd., 18.55; Buntin, Gillies & Co., Ltd., 13.86; Hamilton Vocational Institute, 11.10; King's Printer, 308.72; Smith Bros., 29.60; petty disbursements, 26.06 .... 407 89

Services, $100.50.

A. Henderson, 2.50; F. H. Kirkpatrick, 10.00; A. McLeish, 60.00; E. Milroy, 18.00; Wm. Rambo, 10.00 .... 100 50

Travelling Expenses, $105.45.

F. P. Gavin 105 45

Miscellaneous, $199.85.

Bell Telephone Co., rental, 83.40; tolls, 20.21. Sundries—cartage, .50; express, 8.05; postage, 76.34; telegrams, 1.50; petty disbursements, 9.85 .... 199 85

Apparatus, Chemicals and Shop Supplies ($363.12)

Buntin-Gillies & Co., Ltd., paper, 25.16; Chadwick-Carroll Brass Co., Ltd., copper, 28.44; Cody Hardware Co., hardware, 22.48; Consumers' Lumber Co., lumber, 180.48; Gordon MacKay & Co., Ltd., cotton, 16.56; Hamilton Engineering Service, Ltd., ivory, 13.50; Hamilton Vocational Institute, cast iron, etc., 23.85; Phillips, Toronto, Ltd., packing, etc., 17.82; petty disbursements, 34.83 .... 363 12

Heat, Light and Power ($1,120.68)

Treasurer, Hamilton Board of Education, heating, 890.66; Hamilton Hydro-Electric System, 230.02 .... 1,120 68

Water ($21.52)

Corporation of the City of Hamilton 21 52

Expenses of Grounds, etc. ($318.67)

W. Charlesworth, rolling lawn, 1.25; Corporation, City of Hamilton, 50% cost of services re roadway, 317.42 .... 318 67

Repairs and Incidentals ($92.05)

Adam Clark, Ltd., repairs, 6.00; Cody Hardware Co., hardware, 85.35; Mills Hardware Co., .70 .... 92 05

Scrubbing, Cleaning, Cartage, etc. ($127.31)

Buntin, Gillies & Co., Ltd., towels, 75.95; Hamilton Window Cleaning Co., cleaning windows, 25.00; Walter Wood, Ltd., paper, 12.00; petty disbursements, 14.36 .... 127 31

Ontario Training College for Technical Teachers $27,141.92

SUPERANNUATED TEACHERS

Retiring Allowances ($15,873.00)

C. F. Adair, 293.00; Wm. Chas. Allin, 433.00; Isaac J. Birchard, 506.00; Robert W. Bright, 494.00; Edward Byfield, 402.00; Thos. B. Caswell, 445.00; Jno. G. Cochrane, 416.00; Robt. Cowling, 323.00; Peter Crawford, 358.00; F. A. Cull, 347.50; Rebecca De Cou, 572.00; Benj. Forster, 485.00; A. A. Gould, 361.00; Henry Gray, 518.00; Robt. F. Greenlees, 455.00; R. E. Hamilton, 143.00; Hy. Horton, 299.50; Jno. Houston, 260.00; Jas. S. Jameson, 374.00; Wm. D. Johnston, 272.00; Wm. L. Judge, 392.00; Jane Kessack, 332.00; Richard H. Knowles, 350.00; Frederick Lees, 172.00; Mrs. Margaret Levergood, 227.00; Donald MacDonald, 308.00; A. J. McKinnon, 243.50; Jas. McLean, 157.00; Jno. Matthews, 177.50; Jas. W. Morgan, 404.00; Jas. P. Pegg, 134.00; Thos. Rankin,

Superannuated Teachers—Continued

Retiring Allowances—Continued

436.00; Albert W. Reavley, 302.00; M. Y. Richardson, 326.00; D. J. Ritchie, 398.50; Robert P. Shanks, 366.00; Jessie A. Simpson, 512.00; Estate of D. Smith, 295.00; Wm. H. Smith, 562.50; Thos. F. Spafford, 347.00; Edward A. Stevens, 485.50; Jno. Telfer, 111.50; John S. Thomas, 531.50; H. Vanderburgh, 275.00; A. W. Wright, 270.50 .... 15,873.00

PROVINCIAL AND OTHER UNIVERSITIES ($2,079,175.00)

Grants.

University of Toronto, Ontario College of Education, training High School Assistants	234,175 00
University of Toronto, Special Grant	1,200,000 00
Queen's University	300,000 00
University of Western Ontario	300,000 00
University of Toronto, Royal Ontario Museum	40,000 00
University of Toronto, Royal Ontario Museum for Cataloguing	5,000 00

BELLEVILLE SCHOOL FOR THE DEAF

Salaries ($91,747.79)

Name	Position	Time			Amount
H. B. Fetterly, M.A.	Superintendent and Principal	12	months		4,800 00
Robert McTennant, M.D.	Physician	1	"		75 00
W. W. Boyce, M.D.	"	11	"		825 00
C. B. McGuire	Bursar	12	"		2,100 00
H. McCluggage	Matron and Dietitian	12	"		1,600 00
C. Ford	Directress of Professional Training	12	"		2,500 00
W. J. Campbell	Supervising Teacher	4	"	745 35	
	(T)	6	"	337 35	1,082 70
Clifford L. Ellis	" "	12	"		1,500 00
E. B. Lally	" "	12	"		2,200 00
E. Dennard	" "	12	"		2,000 00
M. Blanchard	" "	12	"		2,000 00
V. G. Handley	Teacher, Group 1	12	"		1,700 00
E. Nurse	" " 1	12	"		1,700 00
L. Carrol	" " 1	12	"		1,700 00
B. Rierden	" " 1	12	"		1,600 00
C. A. Holmes	" " 1	2	"		250 00
E. Panter	" Group 2	12	"		1,500 00
Mabel Cass	" " 2	12	"		1,500 00
A. C. Stratton	" " 2	6	"		750 00
Alec Gordon	" " 2	12	"		1,400 00
F. M. Bell	" " 2	12	"		1,400 00
M. E. Benedict	" " 2	12	"		1,400 00
Alice W. Sweetman	" " 2	12	"		1,125 00
A. Wannamaker	" " 2	12	"		1,300 00
K. B. Daly	" " 2	12	"		1,300 00
C. O'Connell	" " 2	12	"		1,300 00
G. Burt	" " 2	12	"		1,400 00
Phylis Blanchard	" " 2	12	"		1,200 00
F. P. Cunningham	" " 2	12	"		1,100 00
G. E. Rathbun	" " 2	12	"		1,100 00
Doris C. Matthews	" " 2	11	"		1,055 44
M. B. Code	" " 2	12	"		1,200 00
M. Totton	" " 2	12	"		1,200 00
Marjorie W. Ketcheson	" " 2	10	"		937 50
Nora M. Tett	" " 2	12	"		1,200 00
Helen M. Keeler	" " 2	12	"		1,125 00
Vera L. Sheffield	" " 2	10	"		937 50
M. Lally	" " 2	12	"		1,125 00
M. Heagle	" " 2	12	"		1,125 00
R. Van Allen	" " 2	12	"		1,125 00
A. J. Clare	" " 2	12	"		950 00
Gladys S. Parry	" " 2	12	"		1,050 00
K. Bawden	Clerk Stenographer, Group 1	12	"		1,200 00
M. Allison	Nurse	12	"		1,300 00
J. J. O'Gorman	Supervisor of Boys	12	"		1,200 00
Frank H. Chesher	Stationary Engineer, Group 2	8½	"		1,133 33
C. J. Peppin	" " " 2	3½	"		547 86

Belleville School for the Deaf—Continued

Salaries—Continued

E. Doran	Assistant Engineer and Fireman	7¼ months	786 79
Simon Kerr	Fireman and Watchman	12 "	1,200 00
Percy Mott	Farmer	12 "	1,500 00
James Sweet	Farm Hand	12 "	1,050 00
J. N. Boyd	Baker	2½ "	258 59
G. A. Gibson	" (T)	7 "	700 00
T. W. O'Hara	Instructor in Carpentry	12 "	1,700 00
Thomas Truman	Shoemaker	12 "	1,300 00
L. E. Morrison	Instructor in Printing	12 "	1,600 00
Robert Coles	Caretaker, Group 1	12 "	1,400 00
M. Glenn	Seamstress	12 "	850 00
Russell Flagler	Porter and Messenger	12 "	1,200 00
Joseph Chant, M.D	Occulist and Aurist (part time)	12 "	150 00
Supervisors			2,924 00
Engineering Staff			1,256 63
Farmhands			907 50
Cooks, Laundresses, Housemaids, etc			6,161 61
Temporary Assistance			2,983 34

Expenses ($59,775.88)

Medicine and Medical Comforts, $682.20.

Colgate-Palmolive-Peet Co., Ltd., 24.60; Hygiene Products, Ltd., 25.90; Dr. O. A. Marshall, 30.00; J. S. McKeown, 185.61; Ostrom's Drug Store, 371.67; G. Rogers, 30.00; petty disbursements, 14.42 ... 682 20

Groceries and Provisions, $18,522.29.

R. H. Ashton, 41.40; Associated Quality Canners, Ltd., 70.00; Avonhurst Fruit Farm, 15.00; R. J. Bird, 26.60; Braeside Orchards, 75.00; Citizens Dairy, Ltd., 2,841.44; G. Dafoe, 25.50; Dickens & Son, 25.75; A. F. Downey, 14.00; Evans' Fish Store, 150.88; Farm Dept. School, 4,043.35; F. W. Fearman Co., Ltd., 15.40; H. Fiddick, 40.00; W. Gray, 40.00; H. G. Green, 4,415.95; Harris Bread Co., 78.00; R. B. Hayhoe & Co., 299.24; H. Horne Co., Ltd., 47.75; E. A. Kellaway, 304.78; H. Kennedy, 61.46; B. Ketcheson, 31.50; J. A. Ketcheson, 11.63; Mackenzie & Co., 1,219.10; MacLaren-Wright, Ltd., 308.89; S. M. Maybee, 81.00; H. McCoy, 10.50; G. W. Metzler, 77.48; C. B. Meyers, 62.50; E. Morris, 12.00; R. Z. Morrow, 45.00; National Grocers Co., Ltd., 347.87; Ontario Reformatory Industries, 30.13; G. F. Ostrom, 411.60; J. W. Parks, 13.95; Mrs. R. Perry, 24.00; A. Reid, 20.00; Mrs. W. M. Reid, 24.00; H. A. Seeley, 14.75; W. Shaw, 16.70; Smithfield Milling Co., 16.00; Standard Brands, Ltd., 111.86; Swift Canadian Co., Ltd., 23.00; W. Thompson, 50.00; P. G. Van Allan, 12.75; Wallbridge & Clarke, 233.33; J. E. Walmsley Co., Ltd., 2,501.63; Zion Cheese Factory, 130.47; petty disbursements, 49.15 ... 18,522 29

Bedding, Clothing and Shoes, $3,719.62.

Beardmore Leathers, Ltd., 229.46; B. W. Brown, 18.40; Caldwell Linen Mills, Ltd., 337.92; Canadian Department Stores, Ltd., 246.40; J. W. Cook, 387.32; Dominion Linens, Ltd., 94.25; T. Eaton Co., Ltd., 107.19; Gordon MacKay & Co., Ltd., 499.48; Haines Shoe House, 18.13; G. H. Hees Son & Co., Ltd., 46.45; J. King, 106.08; Leslie Shoe Store, 13.45; McIntosh Bros., 57.27; Ontario Reformatory Industries, 774.00; T. C. Thompson, 165.50; Toronto Feather & Down Co., Ltd., 197.40; Walker Stores, Ltd., 126.78; J. E. Walmsley Co., Ltd., 14.40; Warren Bros., Ltd., 265.17; petty disbursements, 14.57 ... 3,719 62

Fuel, Light, Power and Water, $15,044.57.

Beardmore Leathers, Ltd., 52.22; Canadian Westinghouse Co., Ltd., 21.24; Conger Lehigh Coal Co., Ltd., 11,277.99; Garlock Packing Co. of Canada, Ltd., 13.65; Hibbard Electric Co., 85.82; Hydro-Electric Power Commission, 2,288.42; W. H. Oliphant, 110.34; Riley Engineering & Supply Co., Ltd., 17.70; J. E. Walmsley Co., Ltd., 2.23; Waterworks Dept., City of Belleville, 1,174.96 ... 15,044 57

Laundry, Soap and Cleaning, $1,960.89.

Alexander Hardware Co., Ltd., 16.50; Beaver Laundry Machinery Co., Ltd., 17.28; Colgate-Palmolive-Peet Co., Ltd., 330.07; Diamond Cleanser, Ltd., 55.40; Dustbane Products, Ltd., 109.50; Electric Boiler Compound Co., Ltd., 325.00; Excelsior Brushes, Ltd., 262.88; S. C. Johnson & Son, Ltd., 148.60; Lavoline Cleanser Co., Ltd., 86.98; S. F. Lawrason & Co., Ltd., 21.32; National Grocers Co., Ltd., 61.18; Sunelo Products, 16.50; J. Taylor & Co., Ltd., 79.50; J. E. Walmsley Co., Ltd., 96.91; G. H. Wood & Co., Ltd., 294.50; petty disbursements, 38.77 ... 1,960 89

Belleville School for the Deaf—Continued

Expenses—Continued

Furniture and Furnishings, $2,599.80.

Belleville Electric and Stampings, Ltd., 27.94; Canadian Department Stores, Ltd., 431.72; Canadian Industries, Ltd., 95.25; Cassidy's, Ltd., 477.06; J. W. Cook, 37.70; F etcher Manufacturing Co., Ltd., 10.00; General Steel Wares, Ltd., 107.00; J. F. Hartz Co., Ltd., 90.00; G. H. Hees Son & Co., Ltd., 105.87; C. L. Hyde, 15.45; Jones Bros. of Canada, Ltd., 47.25; Kilgours, Ltd., 29.70; Ontario Reformatory Industries, 324.00; Radio & Refrigeration Shop, 235.00; Singer Sewing Machine Co., 148.80; D. Stroud, 116.22; Tickell & Sons Co., 227.85; G. H. Wood & Co., Ltd., 37.50; petty disbursements, 35.49............ 2,599 80

Farm Expenses, $2,499.81.

D. F. Ashley, 12.00; T. W. Bamford, 14.20; C. E. Bishop & Son, 442.51; British-American Oil Co., Ltd., 78.90; H. Brown, 28.90; H. M. Brown, 71.20; Chalmers & Hubbs, 13.95; Dolan the Druggist, 11.00; D. A. Hall, 65.76; J. V. Hanley, 123.50; H. Hill, 81.50; C. E. Hogle, 14.00; Hygiene Products, Ltd., 16.50; International Stock Food Consumers Co., Ltd., 54.50; G. F. Kellar, 25.00; MacKenzie & Co., 624.80; B. L. Redner, 36.97; R. Roblin, 27.50; F. M. Rutherford, 130.00; E. D. Smith & Sons, Ltd., 48.50; G. Stokes, 80.57; Supertest Corporation, Ltd., 51.25; Tweed Milling Co., Ltd., 35.62; J. E. Walmsley Co., Ltd., 10.00; H. Welbanks, 22.25; White Hardware Co., 12.75; H. Wood, 300.00; petty disbursements, 66.18.. 2,499 81

Repairs and Alterations, $3,937.08.

American Hardware Corporation of Canada, Ltd., 29.88; Beardmore Leathers, Ltd., 19.83; Beaver Laundry Machinery Co., Ltd., 11.00; Belleville-Sargent & Co., Ltd., 25.37; R. M. Brown, 11.55; Canadian Department Stores, Ltd., 27.51; Canadian General Electric Co., Ltd., 30.46; Canadian Johns-Manville Co., Ltd., 12.56; Canadian Powers Regulator Co., Ltd., 16.45; J. M. Christie, 42.90; Coulter Copper & Brass Co., Ltd., 48.05; M. E. Crosby, 27.00; H. Disston & Sons, Ltd., 20.13; C. A. Dunham Co., Ltd., 19.35; Everlasting Valve Co., Ltd., 49.72; Fruit Machinery Co., Ltd., 130.85; Garlock Packing Co., Ltd., 19.21; General Steel Wares, Ltd., 24.70; Good Specialties, Ltd., 82.56; Hibbard Bros., 126.18; D. Houston, 10.00; Houston Co., Ltd., 449.53; Howard Welding Co., 17.75; C. L. Hyde, 597.02; Hydro-Electric Power Commission, 15.94; Jenkins Bros., Ltd., 15.44; Kilgours, Ltd., 16.20; Lamont & Co., Ltd., 23.00; A. F. Lazier, 126.24; J. Lewis Co., 89.10; G. A. Matthews Co., Ltd., 41.18; W. J. McCullough, 10.50; J. Morrison Brass Mfg. Co., Ltd., 29.88; Riley Engineering & Supply Co., Ltd., 10.80; St. Charles Motor Co., 12.60; Singer Sewing Machine Co., 18.79; Smart-Turner Machine Co., Ltd., 21.00; R. E. Smith, 17.25; Waterworks Dept., City of Belleville, 29.40; R. L. Webster, 14.00; R. P. White, 667.16; White Hardware Co., 857.01; petty disbursements, 72.03.................................... 3,937 08

School Supplies and Equipment, $6,310.92.

American Annals of the Deaf, 46.00; Angus Mack Co., 14.70; British Empire Art Co., 21.66; Bunton-Reid Co., Ltd., 372.44; Canada Printing Ink Co., Ltd., 16.40; T. R. Cuykendell, 30.00; Doyle's Drug Store, 12.20; A. L. Green, 2,472.27; D. Gestetner, Canada, Ltd., 118.35; G. M. Hendry Co., Ltd., 1,350.51; Moore Type Foundry, 41.76; Office Specialty Mfg. Co., Ltd., 17.30; W. E. Rowsome, 258.30; Sill's Stationery Store, 18.75; Singer Sewing Machine Co., 86.06; N. Slater Co., Ltd., 162.00; Tickell & Sons Co., 83.50; Toronto Type Foundry Co., Ltd., 66.74; United Church Publishing House, 87.11; United Paper Mills, Ltd., 162.26; United Shoe Machinery Co. of Canada, Ltd., 115.87; United Typewriter Co., Ltd., 370.00; University Publishing Co., 47.64; White Hardware Co., 268.00; F. W. Woolworth Co., Ltd., 10.75. Sundries—newspapers and periodicals, 4.00; petty disbursements, 56.35.. 6,310 92

Purchase and Maintenance of Motor Conveyances, $1,344.06.

B. Boland, 20.50; J. B. Boyce, 43.78; City Battery Service, 19.29; Rigg's Motor Sales, 967.55; Supertest Corporation, Ltd., 237.21; petty disbursements, 55.73.. 1,344 06

Travelling Expenses, $932.55.

F. M. Bell, .75; M. S. Blanchard, 5.30; W. J. Campbell, 3.70; M. J. Cass, 6.25; E. Deannard, 4.00; C. L. Ellis, 3.95; H. B. Fetterly, 200.73; C. Ford, 70.24; V. G. Handley, 5.65; E. B. Lally, 11.95; C. B. McGuire, 22.27; L. E. Morrison, 2.75; E. M. Nurse, 35.35; J. K. O'Gorman, 11.01; E. N. Panter, 16.55; B. Rierdon, 1.20; Sundry pupils and attendants, 525.80; A. Wannamaker, 5.10............. 932 55

Belleville School for the Deaf—Continued

Expenses—Continued

Contingencies, $2,222.09.

Bell Telephone Co. of Canada, rentals, 216.96; tolls, 47.97; Brigden's, Ltd., halftones, 17.55; Canadian Bank of Commerce, cheque books, 61.08; D. Christie, literary services, 200.25; H. J. Clarke, literary services, 200.00; Dept. of Trade and Commerce, Ottawa, testing scales, 12.00; E. B. Eddy Co., Ltd., toilet tissue, 56.25; Graham Cold Storage, ice, 45.00; Kilgours, Ltd., toilet tissue, 127.00; S. Licence, sporting goods, 99.07; Ontario Intelligencer, advertising, 54.08; Ostrom's Drug Store, prizes, 22.40; Pay list, wages of men, 43.16; Province of Ontario Pictures, film rentals, 43.25; Ratcliff Paper Co., Ltd., toilet tissue, 70.50; Trophy Craft, Ltd., medals, 56.94; Yateman's Garage & Taxi Service, trucking, 25.50; Y.M.C.A., membership fees for pupils, 20.00. Sundries—cartage, 133.20; express, 142.50; freight, 59.05; newspapers and periodicals, 16.40; postage, 390.00; telegrams, 13.79; petty disbursements, 48.39 .... 2,222 09

Refunds to Teachers-in-Training ($1,150.00)

F. M. Bell, 115.00; M. E. Benedict, 115.00; G. E. I. Burt, 115.00; M. B. Code, 115.00; K. B. Daly, 115.00; M. I. Heagle, 115.00; C. O'Connell, 115.00; A. C. Stratton, 115.00; R. Van Allan, 115.00; A. Wannamaker, 115.00 .... 1,150 00

Total		$152,673 67
Less Perquisites	$7,228 62	
Fees	4,389 50	
Sale of Produce	5,164 83	
Miscellaneous	844 05	
		17,627 00
Belleville School for the Deaf		$135,046.67

BRANTFORD SCHOOL FOR THE BLIND

Salaries ($56,159.79)

Name	Position	Time		Amount
W. B. Race	Superintendent and Principal	12 months		5,000 00
G. A. Cole	Assistant Principal	12 "		2,400 00
J. A. Marquis, M.D.	Physician	12 "		750 00
G. H. Ryerson	Bursar	12 "		2,488 00
E. L. Scace	Matron	4⅓ "	415 24	
" "	" (T)	5⅔ "	276 61	
L. J. Langan	Supervising Teacher	12 "		1,900 00
I. Draper	Teacher, Group 1	12 "		1,700 00
J. Babb	" " 2	12 "		1,500 00
A. O'Donohue	" " 2	12 "		1,500 00
J. McClure	" " 2	12 "		1,125 00
R. Taylor	" 2	10 "		875 00
Esther A. C. Murray	" " 2	2 "		162 50
Z. Perry	Teacher of Music	12 "		1,200 00
S. Miller	" "	12 "		1,125 00
D. Lord	Teacher of Violin	12 "		400 00
L. Behrns	Teacher of Domestic Science	12 "		1,200 00
K. Strowger	Teacher of Knitting (Full salary)	3 "	225 00	
" "	" " (Half salary)	9 "	337 50	562 50
F. Lord	Musical Director	12 "		1,200 00
J. D. Ansell	Teacher of Piano Tuning	12 "		1,600 00
W. B. Donkin	Trades Instructor	12 "		1,800 00
P. King	Physical Instructor	12 "		1,500 00
Grace H. Turnbull	Nurse	10 "		875 00
E. Wright	"	1⅓ "		143 95
M. Milne	Girls' Nurse Supervisor	12 "		1,050 00
B. Cameron	Boys' Nurse Supervisor	12 "		975 00
R. Troughton	Supervisor of Boys, Group 2	12 "		975 00
V. Kellett	Clerk Stenographer	12 "		1,125 00
A. MacGillivray	Attendant	12 "		825 00
H. Bond	Caretaker	12 "		1,486 00
D. Doyle	Stationary Engineer, Group 3	12 "		1,600 00
D. Saunders	Fireman, Group 2	12 "		1,300 00
W. Crawshaw	" " 2	12 "		1,300 00

Brantford School for the Blind—Continued

Salaries—Continued

D. Scott	Farmer	12 months	1,300 00
W. Rockett	Porter and Messenger	12 "	1,200 00
Domestic Help, Cooks, Maids and Laundresses			6,572 99
Temporary Assistance			4,752 00

Expenses ($29,664.23)

Medicine and Medical Comforts, $336.97.

Brantford General Hospital, 12.50; N. M. Lee, 252.19; M. H. Robertson, Ltd., 72.28 ..... 336 97

Groceries and Provisions, $11,070.63.

Associated Quality Canners, Ltd., 108.84; A. H. Baker & Co., 16.68; Brantford Produce Co., Ltd., 934.40; I. Brazil, 89.94; Canada Bread Co., Ltd., 223.24; R. M. Copeland, 79.02; A. Coulbeck, 101.38; Dominion Bakeries, Ltd., 250.07; Eddy's, 172.48; Farm Dept. School, 2,581.60; W. C. Good, 34.75; Gordon, Grierson & Co., 32.05; H. Horne Co., Ltd., 66.50; Johnston's Bakery, 545.82; J. Kew, 80.59; Klinkhammer's Grocery, 116.30; F. McGregor, 79.62; J. McHutcheon, Ltd., 664.69; Messecar Fish Store, 339.65; F. A. Mitchell, 621.72; Nicholson & Stetler, Ltd., 11.70; Ontario Reformatory Industries, 1,956.49; W. A. Ratcliffe, 301.00; T. E. Ryerson, 1,066.02; R. W. Simons & Co., 135.00; Suddaby's, Ltd., 79.37; Terrace Hill Dairy, Ltd., 142.59; R. & J. Welsh, 176.48; White Bakery, 34.32; petty disbursements, 28.32 ..... 11,070 63

Bedding, Clothing and Shoes, $105.27.

J. M. A. Lefebre, 40.50; Textile Products Co., 12.00; J. M. Young & Co., Ltd., 41.72; petty disbursements, 11.05 ..... 105 27

Fuel, Light, Power and Water, $9,549.41.

A. Ballantyne, 9.60; Brantford Hydro-Electric System, 1,520.53; Canadian General Electric Co., Ltd., 22.07; Lyon's Electric Co., Ltd., 40.70; Waterworks Dept., City of Brantford, 947.93; Welsh Fuel Co., 7,008.58 ..... 9,549 41

Laundry Soap and Cleaning, $572.88.

A. Ballantyne, 34.20; Brantford Laundry. Ltd., 12.67; J. Burns, 34.88; Canadian National Institute for the Blind, 18.00; F. Haynes, 10.00; E. Jones, 10.00; Lavoline Cleanser Co., Ltd., 10.00; London Cleansers Supply House, 22.28; M. Packowski, 10.00; T. E. Ryerson, 17.91; C. C. Snowdon, 11.00; Stedman's Book Store, 297.20; Mrs. P. Stevens, 15.00; Sunclo Products, 19.25; Swift Canadian Co., Ltd., 15.44; petty disbursements, 65.05 ..... 602 88

Furniture and Furnishings, $382.06.

Canadian Department Stores, Ltd., 93.96; O. Dickert, 21.00; R. Feely, 40.82; Turnbull & Cutcliffe, Ltd., 16.45; Vanstone's China Hall, 67.05; R. G. Venn, 11.40; J. M. Young & Co., Ltd., 80.88; petty disbursements, 50.50 ..... 382 06

Farm and Garden, $1,466.82.

C. R. Bier, 11.35; J. Bishop & Son, Ltd., 15.20; W. E. Buck, 12.00; Campbell Bros., 15.92; Douglas Seed Co., 591.29; F. C. Ginn, 41.60; A. Kerr, 24.25; Lake of the Woods Milling Co., Ltd., 192.55; B. Lowe, 72.00; F. McIntyre, 12.98; National Canned Goods, 14.36; J. H. Norris, 11.95; H. Taws, 225.00; N. Welsh, 58.00; G. E. Wood, 64.59. Sundries—customs, .30; petty disbursements, 103.48 ..... 1,466 82

Repairs and Alterations, $864.21.

C. K. Addison, 44.18; Anguish & Whitfield, 35.78; A. Ballantyne, 22.80; R. H. Ballantyne, 11.10; J. Bishop & Son, Ltd., 47.40; Brantford Novelties and Builders' Supplies, Ltd., 211.80; W. Elliott, 16.00; R. Feely, 129.63; Hobbs Glass Mfg. Co., Ltd., 30.17; S. C. Johnson & Son, Ltd., 10.50; Lyons Electric Co., Ltd., 23.27; Minnes Bros., 11.36; Scarfe & Co., 11.85; W. S. Sterne, 92.60; W. Tipper & Son, 69.87; Waterous, Ltd., 23.25; petty disbursements, 72.65 ..... 864 21

School Supplies and Equipment, $1,618.55.

T. Anderson, 19.36; J. Bishop & Son, Ltd., 26.50; Bradley Machine Co., 20.40; Brantford Novelties and Builders' Supplies, Ltd., 102.86; Brantford Pattern Works, 52.48; Brantford Willow Works, 59.80; Canadian Bank of Commerce, 39.24; Canadian National Institute for the Blind, 216.88; Cummings Button Co., 17.38; F. Goldspink, 48.80; G. M. Hendry Co., Ltd., 34.14; E. Miltenberg, Inc., 103.53; National Institute for the Blind, 54.51; Needlecraft Shop, 84.05;

Brantford School for the Blind—Continued

Expenses—Continued

School Supplies and Equipment—Continued

E. H. Newman & Sons, 18.00; P. Ryan, 11.00; J. M. Shaw, 27.60; Stedman's Book Store, Ltd., 397.11; Sun Oil Co., 27.82; United Typewriter Co., Ltd., 18.00; J. M. Young & Co., Ltd., 92.04. Sundries—newspapers and periodicals, 55.70; petty disbursements, 91.35 .... 1,618 55

Inspection of Literary and Musical Classes, $262.50.

Mrs. P. Greenwood, 12.50; Dr. A. Ham, 150.00; W. Morrison, 100.00 .... 262 50

Dental and Oculist Services, $388.25.

Dr. N. M. Bragg, 150.00; Dr. J. R. Will, 238.25 .... 388 25

Purchase and Maintenance of Motor Conveyances, $724.63.

Bradley's Garage, 13.85; Bradley's Machine Co., 12.35; Dell's Rubber Stores, 300.38; R. F. Foster, 10.00; McGraw's Service Station, 369.23; petty disbursements, 18.82 .... 724 63

Travelling Expenses, $103.89.

G. A. Cole, 37.09; L. J. Langan, 8.55; S. Miller, 4.60; W. B. Race, 43.75; G. H. Ryerson, 7.20; R. Troughton, 2.70 .... 103 89

Contingencies, $2,218.16.

American Foundation for the Blind, reports, 10.00; Bell Telephone Co. of Canada, rentals, 258.65; tolls, 114.86; Brant Ave. United Church, pew rental, 50.00; Brantford General Hospital, charges, 213.85; Brantford Municipal Railway, bus service, 22.00; R. M. Campbell, nursing services, 88.50; Farm Dept. School, labour, 358.75; Graham Bros., wreath, 10.00; J. McKay, haircutting, 60.00; M. Milne, haircutting, 94.00; E. L. Quillie, nursing services, 24.00; Pay list, wages of men, 127.00; St. Andrew's United Church, pew rental, 50.00; St. Basil's R.C. Church, pew rental, 50.00; St. James Anglican Church, pew rental, 50.00; A. Troughton, nursing services, 67.50; G. H. Turnbull, nursing services, 100.00; United Typewriter Co., Ltd., inspections, 57.00; Vernon Directories, Ltd., directory, 12.00; Y.M.C.A., fees for pupils, 100.00. Sundries—cartage, 46.18; express, 8.33; freight, 3.56; newspapers and periodicals, 5.71; postage, 134.50; telegrams, 5.95; petty disbursements, 65.82 .... 2,218 16

Total		$85,824 02	
Less Perquisites	$5,873 70		
Fees	14,533 33		
Sale of Produce	3,338 18		
		23,745 21	
Brantford School for the Blind		$62,078.81	

MONTEITH NORTHERN ACADEMY

Salaries ($26,925.98)

Name	Position	Months	Amount
Wm. F. Hiscocks	Principal	12 months	4,200 00
Allan G. Ward	Teacher, Group 1	12 "	2,700 00
Constance Connell	" " 2	10 "	1,846 66
F. A. Moreau	" " 2	12 "	2,000 00
Francis Tanton	" " 2	12 "	2,000 00
C. H. Smylie, M.D	Medical Officer (T)	12 "	1,200 00
Lydie E. Moore	Dietitian, Group 2	12 "	1,600 00
Margaret Payne	Nurse	12 "	1,125 00
P. E. Armstrong	Secretary and Stenographer (T)	12 "	950 00
E. W. Critchley	Stationary Engineer, Group 3	12 "	1,600 00
H. Johnson	Caretaker	12 "	1,400 00
Nightwatchman, Fireman and Janitor			3,630 00
Domestic Help			2,100 00
Temporary Assistance			574 32

Expenses ($13,902.18)

Medicine and Medical Comforts, $122.96.

Gordon, MacKay & Co., Ltd., 63.04; Ingram & Bell, Ltd., 37.26. Sundries—express, 16.75; freight, 3.34; petty disbursements, 2.57 .... 122 96

Brantford School for the Blind—Continued

Salaries—Continued

D. Scott	Farmer	12 months	1,300 00
W. Rockett	Porter and Messenger	12 "	1,200 00
Domestic Help, Cooks, Maids and Laundresses			6,572 99
Temporary Assistance			4,752 00

Expenses ($29,664.23)

Medicine and Medical Comforts, $336.97.

Brantford General Hospital, 12.50; N. M. Lee, 252.19; . H. Robertson, Ltd., 72.28 ... 336 97

Groceries and Provisions, $11,070.63.

Associated Quality Canners, Ltd., 108.84; A. H. Baker C .. 16.68; Brantford Produce Co., Ltd., 934.40; I. Brazil, 89.94; Canada I Co., Ltd., 223.24; R. M. Copeland, 79.02; A. Coulbeck, 101.38; Dominion s Ltd., 250.07; Eddy's, 172.48; Farm Dept. School, 2,581.60; W. C 34 75; Gordon, Grierson & Co., 32.05; H. Horne Co., Ltd., 66.50; J. 's Bakery, 545.82; J. Kew, 80.59; Klinkhammer's Grocery, 116.30; F. M r, 79.62; J. McHutcheon, Ltd., 664.69; Messecar Fish Store, 339.65; A. Mitchell, 621.72; Nicholson & Stetler, Ltd., 11.70; Ontario Reformat Industries, 1,956.49; W. A. Ratcliffe, 301.00; T. E. Ryerson, 1,066.02; R. W rs & Co., 135.00; Suddaby's, Ltd., 79.37; Terrace Hill Dairy, Ltd., 112.5 . & J. Welsh, 176.48; White Bakery, 34.32; petty disbursements, 28.32 ... 11,070 63

Bedding, Clothing and Shoes, $105.27.

J. M. A. Lefebre, 40.50; Textile Products Co., 12.00; J I Y ung & Co., Ltd., 41.72; petty disbursements, 11.05 ... 105 27

Fuel, Light, Power and Water, $9,549.41.

A. Ballantyne, 9.60; Brantford Hydro-Electric Sys , 1,520.53; Canadian General Electric Co., Ltd., 22.07; Lyon's Electric Co. d 40.70; Waterworks Dept., City of Brantford, 947.93; Welsh Fuel Co., 7,00 ... 9,549 41

Laundry Soap and Cleaning, $572.88.

A. Ballantyne, 34.20; Brantford Laundry, Ltd., 12.67; Burns, 34.88; Canadian National Institute for the Blind, 18.00; F. Haynes, 10.00 . J es, 10.00; Lavoline Cleanser Co., Ltd., 10.00; London Cleansers Supply Ho , 22.28; M. Packowski, 10.00; T. E. Ryerson, 17.91; C. C. Snowdon, 11.00 Stedman's Book Store, 297.20; Mrs. P. Stevens, 15.00; Sunelo Products, 19.25; in Canadian Co., Ltd., 15.44; petty disbursements, 65.05 ... 602 88

Furniture and Furnishings, $382.06.

Canadian Department Stores, Ltd., 93.96; O. Dickert 21.00; R. Feely, 40.82; Turnbull & Cutcliffe, Ltd., 16.45; Vanstone's China ll, 67.05; R. G. Venn, 11.40; J. M. Young & Co., Ltd., 80.88; petty disbursements, 50.50 ... 382 06

Farm and Garden, $1,466.82.

C. R. Bier, 11.35; J. Bishop & Son, Ltd., 15.20; W. I Buck, 12.00; Campbell Bros., 15.92; Douglas Seed Co., 591.29; F. C. Ginn, 41); A. Kerr, 24.25; Lake of the Woods Milling Co., Ltd., 192.55; B. Lowe, 72); F. McIntyre, 12.98; National Canned Goods, 14.36; J. H. Norris, 11.95; H. aws, 225.00; N. Welsh, 58.00; G. E. Wood, 64.59. Sundries—customs, .30; petty disbursements, 103.48 ... 1,466 82

Repairs and Alterations, $864.21.

C. K. Addison, 44.18; Anguish & Whitfield, 35.78; A. Ballantyne, 22.80; R. H. Ballantyne, 11.10; J. Bishop & Son, Ltd., 47.40; Brantford Novelties and Builders' Supplies, Ltd., 211.80; W. Elliott, 16.00; R. Feely, 1 63; Hobbs Glass Mfg. Co., Ltd., 30.17; S. C. Johnson & Son, Ltd., 10.50; . ons Electric Co., Ltd., 23.27; Minnes Bros., 11.36; Scarfe & Co., 11.85; W. S. err.e, 92.60; W. Tipper & Son, 69.87; Waterous, Ltd., 23.25; petty disbursements, 72.65 ... 864 21

School Supplies and Equipment, $1,618.55.

T. Anderson, 19.36; J. Bishop & Son, Ltd., 26.50; Bra ey Machine Co., 20.40; Brantford Novelties and Builders' Supplies, Ltd., 10.86; Brantford Pattern Works, 52.48; Brantford Willow Works, 59.80; Canadian Bank of Commerce, 39.24; Canadian National Institute for the Blind, 2 .88; Cummings Button C ., 17.38; F. Goldspink, 48.80; G. M. Hendry Co., L ., 34.14; E. Miltenberg, Inc., 103.53; National Institute for the Blind, 54.51; Needlecraft Shop, 84.05;

Brantfcl School for the Blind—Continued

Expenses—Continued

School Supplies and Equipment—›ntinued

E. H. Newman & Sons, 18.00 P. Ryan, 11.00; J. M. Shaw, 27.60; Stedman's Book Store, Ltd., 397.11; Sun (Co., 27.82; United Typewriter Co., Ltd., 18.00; J. M. Young & Co., Ltd., 92.(Sundries—newspapers and periodicals, 55.70; petty disbursements, 91.35.... 1,618 55

Inspection of Literary and Musical ›sses, $262.50.

Mrs. P. Greenwood, 12.50; Dr. . Ham, 150.00; W. Morrison, 100.00.......... 262 50

Dental and Oculist Services, $388.25.

Dr. N. M. Bragg, 150.00; Dr. R. Will, 238.25.......... 388 25

Purchase and Maintenance of Motor :onveyances, $724.63.

Bradley's Garage, 13.85; Bradv's Machine Co., 12.35; Dell's Rubber Stores, 300.38; R. F. Foster, 10.00; M:raw's Service Station, 369.23; petty disbursements, 18.82.......... 724 63

Travelling Expenses, $103.89.

G. A. Cole, 37.09; L. J. Lan 'ai 8.55; S. Miller, 4.60; W. B. Race, 43.75; G. H. Ryerson, 7.20; R. Troughtoı , 2).......... 103 89

Contingencies, $2,218.16.

American Foundation for the Bl l, reports, 10.00; Bell Telephone Co. of Canada, rentals, 258.65; tolls, 114.8 ; ant Ave. United Church, pew rental, 50.00; Brantford General Hospital, c ·ges, 213.85; Brantford Municipal Railway, bus service, 22.00; R. M. Camp ll, nursing services, 88.50; Farm Dept. School, labour, 358.75; Graham Br s. wreath, 10.00; J. McKay, haircutting, 60.00; M. Milne, haircutting, 94.0); L. Quillie, nursing services, 24.00; Pay list, wages of men, 127.00; St. A ı rc's United Church, pew rental, 50.00; St. Basil's R.C. Church, pew rental, 50 00 St. James Anglican Church, pew rental, 50.00; A. Troughton, nursing ser i s 7.50; G. H. Turnbull, nursing services, 100.00; United Typewriter Co., Lt l., ıspections, 57.00; Vernon Directories, Ltd., directory, 12.00; Y.M.C.A., c for pupils, 100.00. Sundries—cartage, 46.18; express, 8.33; freight, 3.56; ı e ›apers and periodicals, 5.71; postage, 134.50; telegrams, 5.95; petty disburs n ıts, 65.82.......... 2,218 16

Total..........		$85,824 02
Less Perquisites..........	$5,873 70	
Fees..........	14,533 33	
Sale of Produce..........	3,338 18	
		23,745 21
Brantford School f r th Blind..........		$62,078.81

MON :ITH NORTHERN ACADEMY

Salaries ($26,925.98)

Wm. F. Hiscocks..........	[illegible]al..........	12 months	4,200 00
Allan G. Ward..........	[illegible]r, Group 1..........	12 "	2,700 00
Constance Connell..........	" 2..........	10 "	1,846 66
F. A. Moreau..........	" 2..........	12 "	2,000 00
Francis Tanton..........	" 2..........	12 "	2,000 00
C. H. Smylie, M.D..........	Medl ıl Officer.......... (T)	12 "	1,200 00
Lydie E. Moore..........	Diet ın, Group 2..........	12 "	[illegible]
Margaret Payne..........	Nur..........	12 "	[illegible]
P. E. Armstrong..........	Secrtary and Stenographer.......... (T)	12 "	[illegible]
E. W. Critchley..........	Stat ıary Engineer, Group 3..........	12 "	[illegible]
H. Johnson..........	Care ker..........	12 "	[illegible]
Nightwatchman, Fireman and Janit..........			[illegible]
Domestic Help..........			[illegible]
Temporary Assistance..........			[illegible] 32

Expenses ($13,902.18)

Medicine and Medical Comforts, $122.$

Gordon, MacKay & Co., Ltd., 604; Ingram & Bell, Ltd., 37.26. Sundries—express, 16.75; freight, 3.34; pett disbursements, 2.57.......... 1.

Monteith Northern Academy—Continued

Expenses—Continued

Groceries and Provisions, $7,262.85.

Canadian Canners, Ltd., 423.68; H. & G. Critchley, 58.92; J. H. Dick, 102.02; Gamble, Robinson, Ltd., 56.00; A. Gerard, 154.72; D. D. Gibbon, 35.50; Gorman, Eckert & Co., Ltd., 106.30; R. B. Hayhoe & Co., 39.60; J. Johnston, 449.28; Lake of the Woods Milling Co., Ltd., 26.75; J. Lupien, 38.27; National Grocers Co., Ltd., 841.83; Northern Academy Farm, 3,003.96; C. L. Rawson, 90.93; E. D. Smith & Sons, Ltd., 28.36; Swift Canadian Co., Ltd., 428.61; Teeswater Creamery, 426.60; Val Gagne Creamery, 60.75; J. H. Wethey, Ltd., 292.29; White's Fish Co., Ltd., 51.60; Whyte Packing Co., Ltd., 356.55; Young-Winfield, Ltd., 21.68. Sundries—express, 38.38; freight, 104.97; petty disbursements, 25.30 .... 7,262 85

Bedding, Clothing and Shoes, $233.19.

Bird Woollen Mill Co., Ltd., 168.60; T. Eaton Co., Ltd., 20.93; Gordon, MacKay & Co., Ltd., 39.32. Sundries—express, 1.35; freight, 2.99 .... 233 19

Fuel, Light, Power and Water, $2,906.99.

Brandram-Henderson, Ltd., 13.85; Canadian Fairbanks-Morse Co., Ltd., 17.16; Canadian General Electric Co., Ltd., 56.97; F. Demrah, 66.25; Empire Brass Mfg. Co., Ltd., 37.71; S. D. Eplett & Sons, Ltd., 109.08; Hawk Lake Lumber Co., Ltd., 24.13; Jack Frost Service, 16.50; C. James, 70.50; J. Kruiswerta, 94.00; J. Larabee, 206.00; Rice Lewis & Son, Ltd., 28.27; G. Lawrence, 133.20; J. Lupien, 199.00; J. Malley, 51.00; McColl-Frontenac Oil Co., Ltd., 18.00; Northern Academy Farm, 843.26; J. C. O'Brien, 30.00; Pay list, wages of men, 783.70; G. Taylor Hardware, Ltd., 32.28. Sundries—express, 8.88; freight, 37.15; petty disbursements, 30.10 .... 2,906 99

Furniture and Furnishings, $224.51.

Canadian General Electric Co., Ltd., 14.42; Cassidy's, Ltd., 54.49; Hill, Clarke, Francis, Ltd., 91.00; G. Sparrow & Co., 22.78; M. Sunders Fabrics, Ltd., 11.40; Sundries—express, 11.62; freight, 8.31; petty disbursements, 10.49 .... 224 51

Laundry, Soap and Cleaning, $377.17.

Canada Colors & Chemicals, Ltd., 35.53; Ingram & Bell, Ltd., 10.81 Rice Lewis & Son, Ltd., 28.74; McColl-Frontenac Oil Co., Ltd., 75.03; National Grocers Co., Ltd., 139.63; Pugsley-Dingman & Co., Ltd., 58.50. Sundries—express, 6.05; freight, 13.00; petty disbursements, 9.88 .... 377 17

Grounds and Garden, $605.19.

Canadian Fairbanks-Morse Co., Ltd., 35.89; D. McPhail, 10.20; Pay list, wages of men, 449.15; Wm. Rennie Co., Ltd., 53.70; Winona Nursery Co., 35.25. Sundries—freight, 8.50; petty disbursements, 12.50 .... 605 19

Repairs and Alterations, $408.95.

Abitibi Power & Paper Co., Ltd., 16.00; Hawk Lake Lumber Co., Ltd., 111.95; Hill, Clark, Francis, Ltd., 73.48; Provincial Glass Co., Ltd., 35.09; Sturgeon's, Ltd., 30.94; G. Taylor Hardware, Ltd., 90.25. Sundries—express, 17.74; freight, 25.96; petty disbursements, 7.54 .... 408 95

Books, Apparatus, Chemicals, Manual Training Supplies, $836.50.

A. Britnell Book Shop, 43.05; Central Scientific Co. of Canada, Ltd., 35.48; Copp, Clark Co., Ltd., 136.85; J. M. Dent & Sons, Ltd., 21.60; T. Eaton Co., Ltd., 42.47; W. J. Gage & Co., Ltd., 37.94; E. N. Moyer Co., Ltd., 421.75; Murdock Stationery, 21.65; Spencer Lens Co., 18.90; James Texts, 11.16. Sundries—express, 21.20; freight, 14.02; petty disbursements, 10.43 .... 836 50

Physical Culture Supplies, $45.99.

A. G. Spalding & Bros., Ltd., 39.67. Sundries—express, 1.60; freight, 4.72 .... 45 99

Travelling Expenses, $269.10.

E. Haughland, 39.00; F. Tanton, 230.10 .... 269 10

Contingencies, $608.78.

Beare & Son, supplies, 16.94; Bell Telephone Co. of Canada, rentals, 33.00; tolls, 32.24; T. Eaton Co., Ltd., frames, 12.43; C. Kelly, tuning piano, 10.00; King's Printer, 57.87; H. L. Lugsdin, toilet tissue, 120.50; National Stationers, Ltd., stencil, 22.50; Chas. G. D. Roberts, lecturer, 10.00; United Typewriter Co., Ltd., inspections, 10.75. Sundries—express, 24.10; freight, 13.72; newspapers and periodicals, 48.30; postage, 135.00; telegrams, 15.11; petty disbursements, 46.32 .... 608 78

Monteith Northern Academy—Continued

Farm and Power Plant ($4,986.24)

Canadian General Electric Co., Ltd., 52.88; Canadian Industries, Ltd., 14.36; H. & G. Critchley, 24.70; Holstein-Friesian Association, 15.50; Lake of the Woods Milling Co., Ltd., 245.77; J. Lupien, 684.04; D. McPhail, 146.75; Northern Academy Farm, 82.50; Pay list, wages of men, 3,548.35; Wm. Rennie Co., Ltd., 99.88. Sundries—freight, 49.23; petty disbursements, 22.28 ..... 4,986 24

Total		$45,814 40
Less Perquisites	$1,931 45	
Fees	13,487 85	
Farm	3,417 22	
Light and Power	1,615 33	
		20,451 85
Monteith Northern Academy		$25,362.55

MISCELLANEOUS

Proportion of Cost of Minister's Report ($1,447.72)

King's Printer 1,447 72

Cost of Litigation ($150.00)

Tilley, Johnston, Thomson & Parmenter, fees re MacKell, injunctions 150 00

Consolidation and Revision of the Acts of the Department of Education ($231.71)

King's Printer 231 71

Advertising ($8,985.42)

Animal Life, 49.00; British American Publishing Co., 124.80; Canadian Baptist, 182.28; Canadian Brotherhood of Railway Employees, 350.00; Canadian Churchman, 576.00; Canadian Congress Journal Publishing Co., 152.00; Canadian Countryman Publishing Co., Ltd., 929.50; Canadian Jewish Review, 129.00; Canadian Labour Press, Ltd., 336.00; Canadian Labour World, 41.66; Canadian Magazine Publishing Co., Ltd., 315.00; Canadian Review Co., Ltd., 50.00; Canadian Trade Unionist, 49.98; Canadian Unionist, 200.00; Catholic Record, 428.40; Catholic Register, 61.60; Echoes, 105.00; Educational Publishing Co., 91.00; Farm & Dairy, 232.80; Farmer's Sun, 179.20; J. J. Gibbons, Ltd., 180.00; Jewish Standard, 77.00; Labour Leader Publishing Co., 340.00; Labour News, 87.50; The Legionary, 204.00; National Council of Women, 100.00; New Outlook, 182.00; Ontario Farmer, 364.00; Ontario Milk Producers Association, 144.00; Ontario School Trustee and Ratepayers Association, 180.00; Ottawa Farm Journal, 134.40; Postal Journal of Canada, 150.00; Presbyterian Record 120.00; Queen's Quarterly, 8.00; Rural Publishing Co., 294.00; The Sailor,, 64.80; The School, 228.00; Standard Weekly Publications, Ltd., 55.00; Toronto Daily Hebrew Journal, 140.40; Toronto Humane Society, 21.00; University of Toronto Monthly, 61.10; University of Toronto Press, 100.00; Wm. Weld Co., Ltd., 626.40; Wilson Publishing Company, 540.00 ..... 8,985 42

Fees of Officials to Archaeological and Other Associations ($24.83)

American Anthropological Association, 6.00; American Library Association, 5.00; Champlain Society, 10.00; The Library Association, 1.83; National League of Compulsory Education, 2.00 ..... 24 83

Travelling Expenses ($72.95)

E. C. Guillet 72 95

Historical Research Work ($2,000.00)

Treasurer, Ontario Historical Society 2,000 00

Grant to the Penny Bank of Ontario ($1,000.00)

Penny Bank of Ontario 1,000 00

Compassionate Allowances to Ex-Teachers ($6,795.92)

Sundry ex-teachers 6,795 92

Miscellaneous—Continued

Grant to Students' Hostel in Paris ($1,000.00)

Treasurer, Students' Hostel........ 1,000 00

Miscellaneous $21,708.55

STATUTORY

Salaries not otherwise provided for (see pages 30-45)........ 235 44

Grants

University of Toronto, Succession Duty, 6. Edw. VII, Chap. 55........	500,000 00
" " Grant, 60 Victoria, Chap. 59........	7,000 00
" " University Aid Act, 1928, Twenty years annuity re new buildings, seventh instalment........	13,480 75
" University Lands Act, 1928, Chap. 55........	52,157 68

French Scholarships, 16 Geo. V, Chap. 103 ($5,137.08)

Helen S. C. Armstrong, 600.00; Miss H. E. Black, 684.27; Miss M. B. Ferguson, 600.00; Mollie Harper, 600.00; Miss M. Jones, 684.27; Miss K. Pless, 684.27; Helen B. St. John, 600.00; Miss M. M. Wilson, 684.27........ 5,137 08

Carter Scholarships, R.S.O. 1927, Chap. 22, Sec. 6 ($4,860.00)

Sundry pupils........ 4,860 00

Grant to Royal Ontario Museum, R.S.O., Chap. 343, Sec. 16 ($53,197.20)

Bursar, University of Toronto........ 53,197 20

Ontario Government's Contribution to Teachers' and Inspectors' Superannuation Fund ($719,241.66)

Teachers' and Inspectors' Superannuation Fund........ 719,241 66

Statutory........ $1,355,309.81

SPECIAL WARRANTS

Board of Trustees of the Royal Ontario Museum in Payment on account of cost of New Building and other Incidental Works ($873,000.00)

Royal Ontario Museum........ 873,000 00

Purchase and Distribution of Books for the Elementary and Secondary Schools and Public Libraries and Contingencies ($11,930.40)

Oxford University Press........ 11,930 40

Grant to Queen's University re the Extension of the Kingston General Hospital ($50,000.00)

Treasurer, Queen's University........ 50,000 00

University of Toronto, to Provide for the Extension of the Ontario College of Education and for Equipment and Furnishings ($35,245.61)

Bursar, University of Toronto........ 35,245 61

Grant to the Board of Governors, University of Toronto, Cost of Erection of the Botanical Building ($517,000.00)

Bursar, University of Toronto........ 517,000 00

Payment of Arrears of Grants to the Frontier College ($22,500.00)

Treasurer, Frontier College........ 22,500 00

Payment towards Purchase of the Robert Holmes Collection of Wild Flower Paintings ($5,000.00)

The Art Gallery of Toronto........ 5,000 00

Grant to the Ontario Temperance Association to Aid in the Developing of Temperance Education ($500.00)

Treasurer, Ontario Temperance Association........ 500 00

Special Warrants—Continued

Grant to the Penny Bank of Ontario ($4,000.00)

Penny Bank of Ontario		4,000 00

Corporation Town of Cobalt, to meet the Payment of High School Debentures and Interest due on October 1st, 1932 ($2,183.14)

Canadian Bank of Commerce—Account Independent Order of Foresters	1,681 66	
" Pension Fund	501 48	2,183 14
Special Warrants	$1,521,359.15	
Total		$13,381,460 95
Less Salary Assessment		26,883 05
Total Expenditure, Department of Education		**$13,354,577 90**

DEPARTMENT

OF

LANDS AND FORESTS

FISCAL YEAR, 1931-32

TABLE OF CONTENTS

GENERAL INDEX AT THE BACK OF BOOK

PART G—DEPARTMENT OF LANDS AND FORESTS

Statement of Expenditure Showing Amounts Expended, Unexpended and Overexpended for the Twelve months Ended October 31st, 1932

Department of Lands and Forests	Page	Estimates	Expended			Un-expended	Over-expended	Treasury Board Minute
			Ordinary	Capital	Total Ordinary and Capital			
		$ c.	$ c.	$ c.	$ c.	$ c.	$ c.	$ c.
Main Office and Branches:								
Salaries	5	147,440 00	121,619 99	....	121,619 99	25,820 01	....	....
Contingencies	6	25,000 00	25,101 44	....	25,101 44	....	101 44	3,000 00
Advertising	6	3,000 00	354 88	....	354 88	2,645 12	....	....
Extra Services	..	1,000 00	....	....	....	1,000 00	....	....
Main Office and Branches	..	176,440 00	147,076 31	....	147,076 31	29,465 13	101 44	....
General:								
Legal Fees and Expenses	6	2,000 00	192 00	....	192 00	1,808 00	....	....
Insurance	6	7,500 00	6,957 82	....	6,957 82	542 18	....	....
Display at Toronto Exhibition	6	1,500 00	463 16	....	463 16	1,036 84	....	....
Moving Expenses of Officials	7	250 00	32 10	....	32 10	217 90	....	....
Ontario Volunteer Veterans' Land Grants	7	500 00	150 00	....	150 00	350 00	....	....
Agents' Salaries and Disbursements	7	100,000 00	103,099 33	....	103,099 33	....	3,099 33	5,000 00
Ottawa Agency	..	2,700 00	....	....	....	2,700 00	....	....
Forest Ranging	8	360,000 00	98,496 32	50,934 62	149,430 94	210,569 06	....	....
Forest Reserves	10	8,000 00	7,802 95	....	7,802 95	197 05	....	....
[illegible]rs' Act	..	500 00	....	....	....	500 00	....	....
Expenditure under Forestry Act	10	45,000 00	....	23,666 00	23,666 00	21,334 00	....	....
Algonquin Provincial Park, Services and Expenses	10	55,000 00	48,607 84	1,473 07	50,080 91	4,919 09	....	....
Cleaning up right-of-way	..	1,000 00	....	....	....	1,000 00	....	....
Rondeau Provincial Park, services and expenses	12	20,000 00	19,925 42	....	19,925 42	74 58	....	....
Quetico Provincial Park, services and expenses	13	20,000 00	20,982 39	....	20,982 39	....	982 39	2,500 00
Creation, Extension and Maintenance of Parks	13	1,000 00	25 16	....	25 16	974 84	....	....
General	..	624,950 00	306,734 49	76,073 69	382,808 18	246,223 54	4,081 72	....
Forestry Branch:								
Salaries	13	45,625 00	45,543 75	....	45,543 75	81 25	....	....
Contingencies	14	10,000 00	6,152 83	....	6,152 83	3,847 17	....	....

Reforestation	14	375,000 00	....	235,109 92	235,109 92	139,890 08	....	....
Fire Ranging	17	1,250,000 00	1,265,103 26	139,673 81	1,404,777 07	....	154,777 07	300,000 00
Clearing Townsites, etc.	32	55,000 00	....	21,664 57	21,664 57	33,335 43	....	....
Grant, Canadian Forestry Association	32	1,000 00	1,000 00	....	1,000 00	....	....	....
Forest Research	32	15,000 00	5,297 46	....	5,297 46	9,702 54	....	....
Grants to Township School Sections,								
South Walsingham	32	150 00	150 00	....	150 00	....	....	....
Vespra	32	250 00	250 00	....	250 00	....	....	....
Charlotteville, Norfolk County	32	150 00	150 00	....	150 00	....	....	....
Clarke, Durham County	32	150 00	150 00	....	150 00	....	....	....
Insect Control	32	6,000 00	4,647 78	....	4,647 78	1,352 22	....	....
Displays at Exhibitions and Fall Fairs	32	1,000 00	645 42	....	645 42	354 58	....	....
Forestry Branch	..	1,759,325 00	1,329,090 50	396,448 30	1,725,538 80	188,563 27	154,777 07	....
Surveys Branch:								
Salaries	33	39,525 00	34,675 00	....	34,675 00	4,850 00	....	....
Contingencies	33	20,000 00	12,204 04	....	12,204 04	7,795 96	....	....
Board of Surveyors	33	200 00	200 00	....	200 00	....	....	....
Surveys	33	100,000 00	....	99,984 05	99,984 05	15 95	....	....
Inspection of Drains and other Engineering Works, etc.	34	1,000 00	115 00	....	115 00	885 00	....	....
Lac Seul Storage Dam, maintenance, etc	34	50,000 00	598 61	....	598 61	49,401 39	....	....
Surveys Branch	..	210,725 00	47,792 65	99,984 05	147,776 70	62,948 30	....	....
Supply Bill	..	2,771,440 00	1,830,693 95	572,506 04	2,403,199 99	527,200 24	158,960 23	....
Statutory:								
Minister's Salary	35	....	10,000 00	....	10,000 00	....	....	....
Refund, University of Toronto re wild lands	35	....	69 34	208 01	277 35	....	....	....
" 2 per cent. on Crown Dues	35	....	299 65	....	299 65	....	....	....
Statutory	..	....	10,368 99	208 01	10,577 00	....	....	....
Special Warrants:								
Grant, Canadian Lumbermen's Association	35	....	2,000 00	....	2,000 00	....	....	....
Back to the Land Movement	35	....	5,741 83	2,933 93	8,675 76	....	....	....
Special Warrants	..	....	7,741 83	2,933 93	10,675 76	....	....	....
Total	..	....	1,848,804 77	575,647 98	2,424,452 75	....	....	....
Less Salary Assessment	..	....	13,726 76	....	13,726 76	....	....	....
Department of Lands and Forests	..	....	1,835,078 01	575,647 98	2,410,725 99	....	....	....

SUMMARY

Department of Lands and Forests	Page	Ordinary	Capital	Total
		$ c.	$ c.	$ c.
Main Office and Branches	5-6	147,076 31	....	147,076 31
Miscellaneous	6-13	306,734 49	76,073 69	382,808 18
Forestry Branch	13-32	1,329,090 50	396,448 30	1,725,538 [illegible]
Surveys Branch	33-34	47,792 65	99,984 05	147,776 [illegible]
Statutory	34	10,368 99	208 01	10,577 00
Special Warrants	34-35	7,741 83	2,933 93	10,675 [illegible]
Total	....	1,848,804 77	575,647 98	2,424 [illegible] 75
Deduct—Transfered to Loans and Special Funds (see Part U)	....	....	2,933 93	[illegible] 93
	....	1,848,804 77	572,714 05	2, [illegible]
Less Salary Assessment	....	13,726 76	....	13,726 76
Department of Lands and Forests	....	1,835,078 01	572,714 05	2,407,792 06

DEPARTMENT OF LANDS AND FORESTS

Hon. Wm. Finlayson..........Minister (Statutory)........10,000 00

MAIN OFFICE AND BRANCHES

Salaries ($121,619.99)

Name	Position	Term		Amount
W. C. Cain	Deputy Minister	12	months	6,000 00
A. Ferguson	Assistant to Deputy Minister	12	"	3,450 00
John B. Thompson	Secretary to Minister and Departmental Secretary	12	"	3,000 00
E. Harrison	Secretarial Stenographer	12	"	1,600 00
V. M. Molesworth	Senior Clerk Stenographer	12	"	1,400 00
Dorothy Smedley	Clerk Stenographer, Group 1	12	"	1,200 00
A. M. Stephens	" " " 1	12	"	1,125 00
F. Budd	Office Boy	12	"	675 00

LANDS BRANCH

Name	Position	Term		Amount
S. Draper	Chief Clerk	12	months	3,450 00
W. R. Ledger	Head Clerk, Group 2	12	"	2,700 00
C. E. Burns	" " " 2	12	"	2,700 00
J. W. Millar	Principal Clerk (T)	12	"	1,095 00
J. Hutcheon	Senior Clerk	12	"	1,700 00
A. E. Robillard	" "	12	"	2,000 00
M. E. Bliss	" "	12	"	1,700 00
E. E. Halliday		12	"	1,700 00
E. F. O'Neil	"	12	"	1,700 00
S. Ross	" "	12	"	1,700 00
B. M. Benson	Clerk, Group 1	12	"	1,600 00
A. R. Carey	" " 1	12	"	1,200 00
E. F. Eaton	" " 2	12	"	1,125 00
F. Griffith	Senior Clerk Stenographer	12	"	1,300 00
A. V. Pepler	" " "	12	"	1,300 00
M. I. Sutherland	" " "	12	"	1,300 00
L. McLeod	Clerk Stenographer, Group 1	12	"	1,200 00
M. G. Burke	" " " 1	12	"	1,200 00
R. M. Feehley	" " " 1	12	"	1,200 00
Audrey Mason	" " 2	12	"	975 00
J. P. Kelly	Vault Caretaker	12	"	1,400 00
Geo. W. McGuire	Clerk, Group 2	12	"	1,050 00
Audrey M. Anderson	Clerk Typist, Group 1	12	"	975 00

WOODS AND FORESTS BRANCH

Name	Position	Term		Amount
J. Houser	Chief Clerk	12	months	3,450 00
H. D. Gillard	Head Clerk, Group 2	12	"	2,700 00
A. H. O'Neil	Principal Clerk	12	"	2,300 00
S. D. Meeking	" "	12	"	2,200 00
E. H. Telfer	Senior "	12	"	2,000 00
J. T. Lee	" "	12	"	2,000 00
G. Potter	Clerk, Group 1	3	"	399 99
W. A. McCord	" " 1	12	"	1,600 00
S. Mulholland	" " 1	12	"	1,600 00
E. F. Quigley	" 1	12	"	1,500 00
Wm. Judd	" " 2	12	"	1,125 00
E. C. Armour	Senior Clerk Stenographer	12	"	1,500 00
J. Ferguson	" " "	12	"	1,500 00
J. Bryce	" " "	12	"	1,500 00
F. E. Stewart	" " "	12	"	1,300 00

ACCOUNTS BRANCH

Name	Position	Term		Amount
H. M. Lount	Accountant, Group 2	12	months	3,000 00
C. J. Clarke	Head Clerk, Group 2	12	"	2,550 00
W. A. Burritt	Senior Clerk	12	"	2,000 00
Alexander MacLean	" "	12	"	2,000 00
J. F. Warren	Clerk, Group 1	12	"	1,600 00
C. Bowland	" " 1	12	"	1,600 00
L. G. Donald	" " 1	12	"	1,600 00
J. Bryson	1	12	"	1,600 00
M. A. Whyte	" " 1	12	"	1,500 00
Dorothy E. Stuart	Office Appliance Operator, Group 2	12	"	1,125 00
M. J. Langevin	Cheque Writer, Group 2	12	"	1,050 00
M. Armitage	Clerk Stenographer, Group 2	12	"	975 00

Main Office and Branches—Continued

Salaries—Continued

FILES BRANCH

Name	Position	Period	Amount
F. Samuels	Senior Clerk	12 months	2,000
E. Hills	Clerk, Group 1	12 "	1,
R. N. Black	" " 1	12 "	1,
H. Harris	" " 1	12 "	1,600 00
Thomas A. Meredith	Senior Clerk Messenger	12 "	1,600 00

PROVINCIAL LAND TAX BRANCH

Name	Position	Period	Amount
L. M. Ryan	Land Tax Collector	12 months	2,5
G. J. Hinton	Senior Clerk	12 "	1,7
Maud M. Craddock	Clerk, Group 2	12 "	1,1
C. H. Deacon	" " 2	12 "	1,0
F. E. Stephens	" " 2	12 "	1,0
E. P. Riches	Clerk Stenographer, Group 1	12 "	1,1
H. M. Lyons	" " " 1	12 "	1,100
S. Madill	" " " 1	12 "	1,000 00
May E. Lomas	Clerk Typist, Group 2	12	900 00

Contingencies ($25,101.44)

Temporary Services, $8,480.44.

Name	Position	Period	Amount
M. N. Adams	Clerk Stenographer, Group 2	12 months	825 00
Beverly B. Burley	Office Boy	1½ "	62 27
A. M. Doyle	Clerk Typist, Group 2	7 "	451 92
David Evans	Cleaning Vault	¼ "	16 25
B. P. Foster	Filing Clerk, Group 1	12 "	900 00
A. H. G. Gray	Clerk, Group 2	12 "	975 00
G. E. Gray	" " 2	12	975 00
H. Hayes	Clerk Stenographer, Group 1	12	975 00
N. B. McMahan	Filing Clerk, Group 1	12	900 00
G. L. Nicol	Clerk Stenographer, Group 1	12	975 00
K. M. Pack	Clerk, Group 3	12	750 00
M. E. Rawlinson	Office Boy	12	525 00
F. E. Ross	Clerk Typist, Group 2	2	150 00

Travelling Expenses, $1,592.97.

J. A. Alexander, 27.20; W. C. Cain, 177.05; H. C. Draper, 139.00; S. Draper, 166.00; A. Ferguson, 259.22; Hon. Wm. Finlayson, 300.00; Charles G. Knight, 288.20; J. W. Millar, 29.60; L. M. Ryan, 142.60; J. B. Thompson, 64.10........ 1,592 97

Miscellaneous, $15,028.03.

Burroughs Adding Machine of Canada, Ltd., inspections, etc., 23.85; General Office Equipment Corp., inspection of machines, 18.00; King's Printer, 12,642.27; W. H. Price, sign, 13.50; Remington Typewriters, Ltd., inspections, 195.00; Thomas and Corney Typewriters, Ltd., inspections, 12.00; United Typewriter Co., Ltd., inspections and repairs, 435.36; Robert F. Vair, notice of hearing, 15.00. Sundries—car tickets, 49.00; excise stamps, 44.00; express, 179.95; freight, 7.11; newspapers and periodicals, 201.16; telegrams, 1,132.65; petty disbursements, 59.18........ 15,028 03

Advertising ($354.88)

Canada Lumberman, 8.75; Cochrane Northland Post, Ltd., 14.52; Fort William Times-Journal, 16.90; Miner Publishing Co., 3.36; Municipal Intelligence Bureau, 50.00; New Liskeard Speaker, 18.25; Porcupine Advance, 19.80; Port Arthur News-Chronicle, 21.50; C. Prouty, 14.40; Sault Daily Star, 5.40; Sudbury Star, 11.00; Toronto Daily Star, 27.00; Toronto Globe, 58.50; Toronto Mail and Empire, 58.50; Toronto Telegram, 27.00........ 354 88

Main Office and Branches........ $147,076.31

Legal Fees and Expenses ($192.00)

Cowan and Seaman, 40.00; H. J. Donley, 50.00; A. D. George, 50.00; Hugill and Hesson, 40.00; H. B. Johnson, 12.00........ 192 00

Insurance ($6,957.82).

Sundry Insurance Companies, insurance premiums........ 6,957 82

Display at Toronto Exhibition ($463.16)

Travelling Expenses, $263.06

P. J. Gervais, 87.25; J. W. Millar, 87.41; J. Shields, 88.40........ 263 06

Main Office and Branches—Continued

Miscellaneous, $200.10.

C. A. Fraser, cartage, 52.25; W. F. Petry, repairs, 25.00; Province of Ontario Pictures, pictures, 38.25. Sundries—express, 62.95; petty disbursements, 21.65 ... 200 10

Moving Expenses of Officers and Officials ($32.10)

S. G. Noble, from Clarkson to Hearst ... 32 10

Commutation Volunteer Veterans' Land Grants ($150.00)

Miss Minnie Bacon, 50.00; Estate J. B. Bartram, 50.00; A. W. Moodie, 50.00 ... 150 00

Agents' Salaries and Disbursements ($103,099.33)

Salaries, $74,787.29.

J. I. Hartt	Inspector of Crown Timber Agencies (T)		12 months	4,600 00
S. J. Hawkins	Principal Clerk		12 "	2,500 00
J. A. Alexander	Crown Timber Agent,	Fort Frances	12 "	2,500 00
C. A. Duval	" " "	Timmins	12 "	2,500 00
N. B. Fletcher	" " "	Parry Sound	12 "	2,000 00
A. H. Huckson	" " "	Sault Ste. Marie	12 "	2,500 00
J. T. McDougall	" " "	North Bay	12 "	2,500 00
S. C. MacDonald	" " "	New Liskeard	12 "	2,500 00
Jos. H. Milway	" " "	Port Arthur	9⅓ "	1,936 70
J. G. McCaw	" " "	Sudbury	12 "	2,500 00
J. D. C. Smith	" " "	Kenora	12 "	2,500 00
A. Stevenson	" " "	Peterborough	12 "	2,000 00
H. T. Vincent	" " "	Cochrane	12 "	2,200 00
P. J. Whelan	" " "	Renfrew	12 "	2,500 00
C. B. Bell	Clerk Stenographer,	Sault Ste. Marie	12 "	975 00
P. O. Shubring	" "	Fort Frances	12 "	975 00
E. Arthurs	Crown Lands Agent,	Espanola Mills	12 "	600 00
F. Blank	" " "	Wilno	12 "	600 00
C. Both	" " "	Denbigh	12 "	300 00
John Bresnahan	" " "	Hearst	5⅓ "	532 88
Wm. Cameron	" " "	Stratton	12 "	500 00
I. M. Campbell	" " "	Parry Sound	12 "	650 00
John Clark	" " "	Englehart	12 "	900 00
J. A. Fink	" " "	Mattawa	12 "	500 00
J. S. Freeborn	" " "	Magnetawan	12 "	500 00
D. Fuller	" " "	Bancroft	12	500 00
J. E. Gibson	" " "	Dryden	12 "	1,400 00
Albert Grigg	" " "	Bruce Mines	12 "	1,000 00
J. A. Hough	" " "	Matheson	12 "	1,400 00
John S. Lowe	" " "	Massey	8⅔ "	432 88
J. R. McCrea	" " "	New Liskeard	12 "	1,400 00
J. K. MacLennan	" " "	Sudbury	12 "	700 00
W. F. MacPhie	" " "	North Bay	12 "	1,125 00
T. Millichamp	" " "	Markstay	12 "	700 00
W. J. Trainor	" " "	Hilton Beach	12 "	300 00
F. Watt	" " "	Pembroke	12 "	300 00
A. N. Wilson	" " "	Kinmount	12 "	175 00
S. H. Wilson	" " "	Port Arthur	12 "	1,400 00
W. R. Smyth	Supervisor of Settlement (T)		10 1/5	3,154 26
E. H. Barnes	Homestead Inspector,	Sault Ste. Marie	3½ "	330 57
J. C. Barr	" "	Fort Frances	12 "	1,900 00
J. A. Bastien	" "	Chelmsford	12 "	1,400 00
W. V. Cragg	" "	New Liskeard	12 "	1,900 00
Wm. G. Gerhart	" "	Bracebridge	12 "	1,400 00
Wm. Hough	" "	Englehart	12 "	1,400 00
H. B. Owens	" "	Cache Bay	12 "	1,400 00
H. E. Sheppard	" "	Kapuskasing	12 "	1,900 00
D. Smith	" "	Cochrane	12 "	1,900 00
Lauchlan Torrie	" "	Kakabeka Falls	12 "	1,200 00
L. E. Van Horn	" "	Monteith	12 "	1,900 00
R. G. Wigle	" "	Dryden	12 "	1,900 00

Temporary Services, $5,126.77.

Name	Position	Period	Amount
John Dent	Caretaker	12 months	50 00
G. E. Godkin	"	12 "	50 00
W. H. Jamieson	"	12 "	50 00
Helmi Lassi	Clerk Stenographer	12 "	840 00

Agents' Salaries and Disbursements—Continued

Salaries—Continued

J. P. Marchildon	Acting Crown Lands Agent	12 months	487 75
J. L. Regan	" " Timber Agent	12 "	1,963 00
Mary C. Rumsey	Clerk Stenographer	½ "	45 00
Margaret Rumsey	" "	12 "	1,020 00
Joseph Tilson	Homestead Inspector	5½ "	584 10
Katherine Tyndall	Clerk Stenographer	½ "	36 92

Travelling Expenses, $12,420.56.

J. A. Alexander, 22.40; E. H. Barnes, 4.00; J. C. Barr, 736.50; J. A. Bastien, 1,410.15; J. Bresnahan, 8.80; W. V. Cragg, 398.50; W. Crebo, 71.70; C. A. Duval, 217.71; N. B. Fletcher, 18.00; W. G. Gerhart, 153.00; A. Grigg, 180.15; H. G. Guin, 6.80; J. I. Hartt, 1,035.70; S. J. Hawkins, 421.70; W. Hough, 360.95; A. H. Huckson, 224.36; S. C. MacDonald, 165.23; J. G. McCaw, 27.75; J. T. McDougall, 62.04; J. P. Marchildon, 11.00; J. H. Milway, 335.12; H. B. Owens, 1,214.95; J. L. Regan, 314.00; H. E. Sheppard, 523.95; J. D. C. Smith, 139.10; D. Smith, 559.28; W. R. Smyth, 1,323.42; D. Stringer, 1.60; A. Stevenson, 212.78; J. Tilson, 334.70; L. Torrie, 637.90; Thomas Thorpe, 2.30; L. E. Vanhorn, 450.95; H. T. Vincent, 204.33; P. J. Whelan, 336.88; R. G. Wigle, 292.86 .... 12,420 56

Office Rent, Light, Telephone and Telegraph Service, $7,504.60.

E. L. Banner Insurance Agency, 360.00; F. Blank, 90.00; Bradburns, Ltd., 180.00; V. Brisson, 180.00; I. M. Campbell, 110.00; Mrs. E. Chenette, 15.00; J. Clark, 120.00; Department of Agriculture, 177.22; Department of Northern Development, 101.65; Empire Cafe, 207.00; J. A. Fink, 102.00; Leo. Geroux, 240.00; I. E. Gibson, 120.00; A. Grigg, 130.00; Charles Howe, 69.00; Hydro-Electric Power Commission, 21.06; Town of Kapuskasing, 65.66; Kenora Public Utilities Commission, 10.77; Lindsay and McCluskey, 780.00; J. S. Lowe, 76.50; J. P. Marchildon, 60.00; T. A. Millichamp, 120.00; Northern Ontario Power Co., Ltd., 14.36; Peterborough Public Utilities Commission, 8.13; G. M. Rioch, 540.00; Rothschilds & Co., Ltd., 720.00; H. E. Sheppard, 165.00; Mrs. F. Soucie, 35.00; Spruce Falls Power and Paper Co., Ltd., 204.00; Timmins Theatres, Ltd., 420.00; Mrs. W. Trombley, 145.10; Mrs. I. F. Waller, 330.00; P. J. Whelan, 180.00. Sundries—telegrams, 76.84; telephone, rental, 809.81; tolls, 520.50 .... 7,504 60

Miscellaneous, $3,260.11.

Canadian Fairbanks-Morse Co., Ltd., parts, 23.32; Cochrane-Dunlop Hardware, Ltd., hardware, 11.48; Mrs. A. Denomme, cleaning office, 16.00; Dingwall Motors, gas, 21.65; J. C. Dix, livery, 54.50; M. Fingland, moving garage, 14.50; S. Goodwin, provisions, 47.86; Mrs. A. Hadwin, cleaning, 22.00; Thomas Hughes, services as Homestead Inspector, 52.83; Kapuskasing Supply Co., Ltd., coal oil, etc., 111.38; King's Printer, 336.00; G. Lemaire, wood, 27.00; J. S. Lowe, services as Inspector, 50.40; J. Lupien, hay, oats, etc., 24.35; Lynch Auto Sales Co., repairs, 16.19; Mrs. R. J. Miller, cleaning, 40.00; Peterborough Fuel & Transfer Co., Ltd., coal, 39.50; Remington Typewriters, Ltd., inspections, 10.75; Sault Stationers, Ltd., repairs, 24.50; E. Sheremeto, cleaning office, 78.50; J. Stewart, livery, 32.00; G. Taylor Hardware, Ltd., hardware, etc., 16.49; Tyne Motor Co., gas, 20.13; United Typewriter Co., Ltd., inspections, 95.31; A. R. Wood, repairs to car, 51.32. Sundries—cartage, 53.62; express, 71.80; freight, 32.60; postage, 1,593.47; petty disbursements, 270.66 .... 3,260 11

Forest Ranging ($149,430.94)

Salaries ($124,325.23)

H. H. Parsons	Assistant Forester	12 months	2,300 00
H. L. McCausland	" "	12 "	2,100 00
A. P. Leslie	" "	2 "	316 66
J. A. Brodie	" "	2 "	400 00
J. P. Legris	Fire Inspector	2 "	450 00
Thos. J. Kennedy	Check Scaler	12 "	2,200 00
J. M. Horn	" "	12 "	2,200 00
E. A. Ferguson	" "	12 "	2,200 00
C. R. Richardson	" "	12 "	2,200 00
J. R. McDonell	" "	12 "	2,200 00
J. P. L'Abbe	" "	12 "	2,200 00
Thos. Thorpe	" "	12 "	2,200 00
Wm. Elliott	" "	12 "	2,200 00
J. R. Dillon	" "	12 "	2,200 00
J. A. Brown	" "	12 "	2,200 00

Forest Ranging—Continued

Salaries—Continued

D. C. McInnis	Check Scaler	12 months		2,200 00
Andrew Moran	" "	12 "		2,200 00
P. O'Gorman	" "	12 "		2,200 00
A. Hurd	" "	12 "		2,200 00
J. P. McKee	" "	12 "		2,200 00
John Durrell	" "	6½ "		1,208 47
Geo. Fisher	" "	12 "		2,200 00
P. A. Stein	" "	12 "		2,200 00
E. G. Hagan	" "	12 "		2,200 00
Wm. Crebo	" "	12 "		2,200 00
J. J. Fink	" "	12 "		2,000 00
J. H. Caldwell	" "	12 "		2,000 00
Sundry Rangers			95,945 18	
Less repayment by sundry lumber companies of scalers' wages			24,195 08	
				71,750 10

Travelling Expenses, $19,206.70.

R. Alcock, 56.20; R. A. Allen, 116.65; T. J. Anderson, 343.40; M. Ardenne, 60.09; E. Beaumont, 60.55; B. Blastorah, 58.60; A. Blair, 200.65; E. A. Boice, 167.75; W. G. Boland, 59.45; W. H. Brennan, 41.55; E. H. Bromley, 115.80; J. L. Bromley, 61.60; W. H. Bromley, 528.05; T. A. Bromley, 155.80; W. J. Brooks, 67.70; J. A. Brown, 204.90; C. P. Cain, 27.10; J. H. Caldwell, 494.15; J. W. Colley, 674.60; J. A. Costello, 230.00; P. H. Coyne, 7.00; W. Crebo, 322.60; W. H. Croteau, 22.10; J. T. Cuddihey, 311.56; F. J. Dennie, 174.35; J. Dickson, 10.60; J. R. Dillon, 138.70; J. E. Doxsee, 151.30; D. Duncan, 10.50; W. A. Duncan, 16.50; J. R. Durrell, 20.60; W. J. Durrell, 55.30; R. Duval, 88.05; W. Elliott, 465.75; A. Fenson, 78.85; E. A. Ferguson, 184.35; J. J. Fink, 196.45; G. Fisher, 36.40; A. L. Galbraith, 4.15; B. Gorman, 563.30; J. Grant, 197.37; E. G. Hagan, 257.82; T. C. Haley, 235.75; J. J. Harkins, 60.55; I. C. Hartt, 254.32; F. R. Hayward, 22.20; J. M. Horn, 219.75; J. F. Horne, 14.40; E. Huckson, 812.81; A. D. Hunt, 3.85; A. Hurd, 149.10; C. Hurd, 107.25; E. Irving, 35.70; R. A. Johnston, 83.20; T. J. Kennedy, 509.22; J. Kerby, 36.45; D. King, 5.70; P. L'Abbe, 255.68; P. D. Lacasse, 39.10; J. Mackay, 16.30; R. Mantle, 8.60; J. Marconi, 266.65; E. D. Meeking, 122.20; R. Millar, 381.30; O. A. Mockler, 4.80; A. Moran, 595.85; H. Morel, 23.10; J. B. Morrison, 16.00; W. A. Morgan, 620.45; W. D. McAuley, 33.75; S. C. MacDonald, 46.85; N. McDonald, 123.83; J. R. McDonell, 281.91; A. McDougall, 25.33; J. M. McDougall, 561.10; J. M. McGonigal, 10.00; T. N. McGown, 130.35; D. C. McInnis, 164.15; J. A. McIntyre, 44.40; J. P. McKee, 43.35; A. McLay, 8.45; J. D. McManus, 174.70; J. S. McPherson, 71.00; N. C. McVittie, 43.70; P. O'Gorman, 368.25; I. S. Palmer, 41.92; J. A. Park, 620.85; J. D. Pennock, 116.35; C. Prouty, 241.89; A. C. Rattew, 495.70; C. R. Richardson, 120.27; R. Ridley, 48.00; T. G. Robinson, 18.80; F. E. Rowe, 424.80; W. J. Rudd, 6.40; W. J. Saunders, 100.15; A. Shaw, 365.70; G. Sheffield, 3.00; J. D. C. Smith, 75.43; J. D. Spence, 44.20; F. A. Sprague, 118.00; P. A. Stein, 117.90; J. L. Stewart, 331.00; J. A. Thompson, 201.05; L. Thomson, 7.10; T. Thorpe, 48.65; M. Vanderburgh, 572.65; G. O. Wallingford, 205.35; T. F. Waller, 24.15; R. M. Warren, 18.85; F. Widdifield, 298.00; F. G. Young, 444.25; W. D. Young, 26.70 ..... 19,206 70

Camp Supplies, Equipment and Repairs, $4,528.44.

Aikenhead Hardware, Ltd., 11.53; W. R. H. Bauer, 63.98; Nick Blakey, 66.90; E. Bliss, 41.62; Bowman's General Store, 17.90; H. Burrows, 577.14; Canadian Johnson Motor Co., Ltd., 32.58; Christoff & Co., 21.82; Cochrane-Dunlop Hardware, Ltd., 19.59; H. Coolican, 10.50; S. Goodwin, 109.55; H. H. Green, 17.11; Hinsperger's Outfitters, 99.65; Hobson-Gauthier, Ltd., 96.57; Kapuskasking Supply Co., Ltd., 46.29; Kert and Co., 451.65; Keyes Hardware, Ltd., 20.06; J. H. Leng, 30.80; McGill Hardware Co., Ltd., 365.37; Marshall-Wells Co., Ltd., 94.00; Neale and Heath, 412.02; North Bay Garage, 38.81; S. Onerheim, 30.85; Quality Meat and Gocery Co., Ltd., 202.75; J. A. Richards and Sons, 50.00; St. Marys Marine Supply Co., 1,173.62; Service Inn, 30.75; M. Silverstone, 17.60; Stewarts, Ltd., 27.43; C. O. Thacker, 20.05; Tweed Hardware, 11.25; Watson and Lloyd, 71.06; Williams Hardware Co., 72.91; Winds Supply Station, 16.95; A. R. Wood, 110.38; petty disbursements, 47.40 ..... 4,528 44

Miscellaneous, $1,370.57.

G. E. Atkinson, camera repairs, 83.90; D. Bell Insurance Agency, rent, 180.00; E. Brown, pasture, 42.50; Canadian Photo Copy Co., photostats, 20.54; F. J. Dampier, boat hire, 33.00; J. Duclois, meals, 28.40; Eastman Kodak Stores, Ltd., films, etc., 59.15; J. Fitzgerald, meals, 31.00; Instruments, Ltd., stereoscope

Forest Ranging—Continued

Miscellaneous—Continued.

repairs, 30.00; Journal Printing Co., cards, 30.00; B. Leacy & Co., Ltd., provisions, 24.04; Lynch Auto Sales Co., Ltd., auto repairs, 74.30; Neale and Heath, hay, etc., 33.06; New Method Dyers and Cleaners, cleaning, 20.26; S. Onerheim, repairs, 21.10; T. Pocklington Co., repairs, 24.75; J. F. Raw Co., Ltd., repairs, etc., 10.31; Service Inn Station, gasoline, 28.25; Shevlin-Clarke Co., Ltd., meals, 78.20; Shell Co. of Canada, Ltd., gasoline, 20.65; A. H. Skene, rent, 84.00; F. M. Wallingford, rent, 21.00; Williams Hardware Co., rent, oil, etc., 89.65. Sundries—express, .60; telephone, tolls, 2.15; postage, .79; cartage and livery, 259.48; petty disbursements, 44.49 .... $1,375 57
Less repayments from previous year 5 00
1,370 57

FOREST RESERVES ($7,802.95)

Salaries ($7,527.85)

C. E. Hindson	Superintendent, Temagami	12 months	1,
J. P. Legris	Forest Supervisor	10 "	2,[illegible]00 00
Sundry Rangers, wages			3,[illegible] [illegible]

Travelling Expenses, $126.85

H. Elkington, 25.30; V. H. Prewer, 82.60; R. E. Watson, 18.95 .... 126 85

Miscellaneous, $148.25.

Eastman Kodak Stores, Ltd., films, etc., 144.20; petty disbursements, 7.65 .... 151 85
Less repayment from previous year, sale of blueprints 3 60
148 25

Expenditure under The Forestry Act ($23,666.00)

I. C. Marritt	Forester	12 months	3,000 00
Wages of men			16,962 37

Travelling Expenses, $2,196.56.

M. Ardenne, 60.92; J. M. Bishop, 9.00; J. A. Brodie, 98.35; A. F. Catto, 45.60; F. T. Garnham, 11.95; E. E. Grainger, 27.60; D. W. Gray, 50.15; R. N. Johnston, 63.43; N. M. Kensit, 46.13; A. P. Leslie, 45.45; A. P. MacBean, 101.70; I. C. Marritt, 1,365.49; J. F. Sharpe, 95.15; W. D. Start, 175.64 .... 2,196 56

Miscellaneous, $1,507.07.

H. Burrows, oats, 17.13; A. P. Campbell, log building, 25.00; Canada Canoe Co., Ltd., canvas, 38.47; Canadian Photo Copy Co., photostats, 18.10; Cochrane-Dunlop Hardware, Ltd., hardware, etc., 13.32; Connelly & Mewett, hardware, 17.90; Eastman Kodak Stores, Ltd., film, etc., 32.67; W. Gardner, boat hire, 25.00; Gregory, Greek & Co., provisions, 170.78; Hinsperger Harness Co., Ltd., repairing tents, 34.28; International Stock Food Co., Ltd., feed, 10.77; Keuffel and Esser Co., prints, etc., 35.86; A. Legree, provisions, 16.81; McIntosh Grain & Feed Co., Ltd., feed, 240.16; A. J. Maynes, provisions, 73.89; C. R. Parker, provisions, 88.57; Percy the Optician, lenses, 12.50; Pratt and Shanacy, provisions, 14.03; Province of Ontario Pictures, slides, 19.35; J. F. Raw Co., Ltd., prints, etc., 10.08; Remington Typewriters, Ltd., rentals, 51.50; J. W. Richardson, seeds, etc., 35.82; A. L. Rooks, veterinary services, 20.00; Star Grocery, provisions, 141.40; Superior Chain Stores, provisions, 42.44; R. Wallace & Sons, bricks, 10.50; H. Weeks, moving expenses, 59.40; Woods Manufacturing Co., cleaning robes, 83.59; T. C. Young, veterinary services, 25.50. Sundries—express, 2.15; freight, 13.37; telegrams, .30; petty disbursements, 106.43 .... 1,507 07

PROVINCIAL PARKS

Algonquin ($50,080.91)

Salaries ($40,058.68)

F. A. MacDougall	Superintendent	12 months	3,600 00
M. Robinson	Chief Ranger	12 "	1,600 00
J. Shields	" "	12 "	1,600 00
J. R. Boyle	" "	12 "	1,300 00
Z. A. Nadon	Ranger	12 "	1,200 00
P. Ranger	"	12 "	1,200 00
D. Valentine	"	12 "	1,200 00

Provincial Parks—Continued

Algonquin Park—Continued

Salaries—Continued

Name	Position	Period		Amount
J. Christie	Ranger	8¼	months	826 30
W. A. Mooney	"	12	"	1,200 00
G. Holmberg	"	12	"	1,200 00
Ed. Godin	"	8¼	"	829 59
C. E. Brewer	"	5	"	500 00
M. McNamara	"	12	"	1,200 00
M. J. Newell	"	12	"	1,200 00
P. J. Gervais	"	12	"	1,200 00
Andrew M. Grant	"	12	"	1,200 00
J. McIntyre	"	12	"	1,200 00
F. X. Robichaud	"	12	"	1,200 00
N. J. Bowers	"	12	"	1,200 00
Daniel Stringer	"	12	"	1,200 00
John E. Stringer	"	12	"	1,200 00
Albert Patterson	"	12	"	1,200 00
Ross Edwards	"	12	"	1,125 00
D. McMeekin	"	12	"	1,130 25
J. Kennedy	Deputy Chief (Temporary)	7	"	943 30
John McIntyre	" " "	7	"	943 30
J. S. Foulds	Utility Ranger, "	7	"	775 50
H. J. Boehme	Ranger "	6	"	533 90
John Burchat	" "	7	"	623 80
M. P. Coulas	" "	7	"	568 75
R. Curley	" "	7	"	623 80
Stewart Eady	" "	7	"	623 80
B. McClelland	" "	7	"	623 80
S. Sunstrum	" "	6	"	533 90
I. Turcotte	" "	7	"	623 80
L. Turcotte	" "	7	"	623 80
Mrs. P. J. Gervais	Housekeeper "	6	"	272 96
Thos. Cannon	Cook "	6	"	494 10
Sundry Rangers (part time)				739 03

Travelling Expenses, $1,504.43.

H. J. Boehme, 16.65; N. J. Bowers, 12.20; J. R. Boyle, 89.32; J. Burchat, 11.20; John Christie, 3.50; M. P. Coulas, 15.40; C. S. Eady, 16.90; R. Edwards, 16.55; P. J. Gervais, 34.55; A. M. Grant, 17.65; I. R. Humble, 13.00; J. Kennedy, 235.70; S. W. Knight, 15.00; F. A. MacDougall, 285.84; Blake McClelland, 9.90; J. McIntyre, 162.63; D. McMeekin, 8.75; W. A. Mooney, 25.05; T. Mulcahy, 22.37; Z. A. Nadon, 36.25; M. J. Newell, 11.65; P. Ranger, 22.35; F. X. Robichaud, 20.25; M. Robinson, 41.42; J. Shields, 234.80; D. Stringer, 86.06; I. Turcotte, 39.49 .... 1,504 43

Miscellaneous, $8,517.80.

Aikenhead Hardware, Ltd., hardware, screen head, etc., 19.89; J. W. Anderson, & Co., oilcloth, etc., 28.50; G. Andrews, harness, etc., 44.00; Barrys Bay Lumber Co., Ltd., lumber, 117.74; Bigwin Laundry, washing, 11.40; Canadian Industries, Ltd., stain and paint, 192.49; Canadian Liquid Air Co., rods, torch, etc., 134.32; Canadian National Railways, rental car house, 60.00; Canadian Wright, Ltd., spark plugs, etc., 64.88; Chestnut Canoe Co., Ltd., parts, 16.00; N. T. Clarke, boat rental, etc., 36.39; Cochrane-Dunlop Hardware, Ltd., hardware, 12.44; Cockburn & Archer, shingles, heater, etc., 1,112.25; J. Cousineau, soap, etc., 21.13; Delco Appliance Corporation, piston, springs, etc., 107.44; Dominion Wire & Rope Co., Ltd., cable, 11.76; P. A. Duff, Ltd., lumber, 80.00; T. Eaton Co., Ltd., cotton, sheeting, etc., 457.29; Exide Batteries of Canada, Ltd., batteries, etc., 248.00; Fairchild Aircraft, Ltd., tubing, parts, etc., 59.53; Fassett Lumber Corporation, Ltd., flooring and lumber, 84.11; Findlay's, Ltd., stove, repairs, etc., 113.22; F. W. Fischer, doors, etc., 67.99; Grand & Toy, Ltd., cases, stationery, etc., 44.60; Grimm Manufacturing Co., Ltd., strainers, 12.89; Hinsperger's Outfitters, snowshoes, sleeping bag, etc., 287.98; Huntsville Planing Mills, shingles, etc., 28.89; Imperial Oil, Ltd., oil and aeroplane spirits, 1,390.55; Instruments, Ltd., section paper, 14.00; Johnson Water Gardens, plants, 17.25; Keuffel & Esser Co., rule, compass, etc., 103.94; J. Leckie, Ltd., duck, 32.95; Felix Lynch, shingles, 84.28; McCall & Co., lumber, 23.50; K. McDonald & Sons, Ltd., seeds, 46.05; C. McFarland, cement mixer, 30.00; J. S. L. McRae, lumber, etc., 118.32; A. A. Mask, sash and frames, 59.25; H. H. Middleton, provisions, etc., 19.50; H. Morris Crane & Hoist Co., Ltd., chain block, etc., 102.38; C. & D.

Provincial Parks—Continued

Algonquin Park—Continued

Miscellaneous—Continued.

Murray, Ltd., cement, 81.75; Muskoka & Parry Sound Telephone, Ltd., tolls, 91.55; National Grocers Co., Ltd., provisions, 22.10; Northern Electric Co., Ltd., cable, wire, etc., 555.38; Wm. Okum, lumber, 26.40; Ontario Hughes Owens Co., Ltd., platter, chronometer, etc., 83.91; Peterborough Canoe Co., canoe filler, etc., 71.28; Phenotos Chemical Co., Inc., oil, etc., 77.00; O. E. Post, roofing paper, hardware, etc., 355.04; Province of Ontario Pictures, framing, etc., 29.20; Estate late Father Reynolds, contents of cabin, 25.00; Richards-Wilcox Canadian Co., Ltd., hardware, 345.00; J. D. Shier Lumber Co., Ltd., lumber, 22.50; Stewart's Drug Store, drugs, 12.85; United Typewriter Co., Ltd., repairs, 21.21; White Drug Stores, drugs, 17.35; Woods Manufacturing Co., Ltd., overalls, etc., 10.13. Sundries—customs, 11.58; express, 191.41; freight, 596.86; postage, 170.03; telegrams, 32.65; telephone, 155.46; petty disbursements, 178.76.... 8,701 50

Less refund, oil drums	168 70		
Sale of stove	15 00		
		183 70	
			8,517 80

Rondeau ($19,925.42)

Salaries ($14,032.47)

R. S. Carman	Superintendent	12 months	2,700 00
A. Hitchcock	Ranger	12 "	1,125 00
A. Townsend	Gamekeeper	12 "	1,050 00
H. Atkinson	Ranger	12 "	1,050 00
Herbert Hitchcock	" (Temporary)	12 "	952 05
Vester Russell	" "	12 "	928 85
Fred Walters	" "	12 "	999 02
A. Whitfield	" "	12 "	927 40
O. Stirling	" "	12 "	1,000 62
W. Reeves	" "	12 "	908 44
N. Cumming	" "	9 "	546 67
R. Thompson	" "	5½ "	428 60
E. A. Grant	Traffic Officer (Temporary)	4 "	477 72
Sundry Rangers (part time)			938 10

Travelling Expenses, $135.03.

R. S. Carman	135 03

Miscellaneous, $5,757.92.

A. E. Baker, repairing tires, etc., 35.45; W. J. Bannister, professional services, 16.00; F. Coll, hay, 35.00; H. Coll, sale of furs, etc., 279.83; Department of Highways, calcium chloride, 290.28; H. Disston & Sons, Ltd., hammer, etc., 10.23; E. B. Eddy Co., Ltd., paper, 52.06; Electric Shop, wiring, etc., 165.72; G. T. Garson, plumbing, etc., 40.70; Gilson Manufacturing Co., Ltd., saw, 10.00; W. H. Goodhue, hardware, etc., 172.56; Goodyear Tire & Rubber Co., Ltd., tire, 12.87; T. G. Griffith, chemicals, 78.00; Hydro-Electric Power Commission, light, services, etc., 649.13; Imperial Oil, Ltd., oil and gas, 903.61; F. Kennedy, lumber, 269.59; MacDonald Manufacturing Co., Ltd., syrup cans, 16.15; J. MacGregor, harness repairs, etc., 41.55; C. W. MacPherson, oil, 11.25; McIrvine's Garage, repairs, etc., 18.57; G. T. Mickle & Sons, feed, 421.39; Municipal Spraying & Oiling Co., Ltd., spraying, 502.39; W. N. Parker, chain, etc., 10.25; Ridgetown Fire Chief, services at fire, 25.00; Ridgetown Green House, shrubs, 10.40; Ridgetown Hydro-Electric Power Commission, light, 202.53; Ridgetown Public Utilities, repairs, 105.07; S. Scott, horseshoes, etc., 52.55; Shanks Garage, repairs, etc., 517.99; Shillington Hardware, cement, etc., 11.54; A. J. Silcox, hardware, rope, etc., 443.08; C. Stirling, straw, etc., 27.00; Universal Machine & Tool Works, pulleys, etc., 44.97; Warwick & Son, shingles, etc., 66.75; Watson & Taylor, lumber, etc., 31.75; G. Wedge, fertilizer, etc., 18.90; Willson Press, cards, etc., 11.50. Sundries—express, 6.22; freight, 10.03; postage, 63.00; telegrams, 5.03; telephone, 131.93; petty disbursements, 171.00.... 5,998 82

Less Refund, Gasolene tax	222 50		
" T. Eaton Co., Ltd	18 40		
		240 90	
			5,757 92

Provincial Parks—Continued

Quetico ($20,982.39)

Salaries ($18,812.30)

John Jamieson	Superintendent, Group 2	12 months	1,900 00
T. Dettbarn	Ranger	12 "	1,200 00
Thos. Quinn	"	10⅔ "	1,011 47
Thos. Brady	"	9½ "	924 93
Mrs. V. Jameson	Housekeeper	12 "	300 00
R. Wells	Ranger (Temporary)	12 "	991 25
E. Elliott	" "	12 "	918 35
J. C. Valley	" "	12 "	991 25
A. Dumas	" "	12 "	991 25
A. Lemay	" "	10 "	818 45
A. Matchett	" "	10 "	818 45
J. R. Ferguson	" "	10 "	823 85
J. W. Hendrickson	" "	10 "	823 85
G. Stewart	" "	10 "	818 45
E. Kelly	" "	10 "	818 45
E. E. Godin	" "	9 1/6	756 35
J. V. Bannister	" "	9 1/6	756 35
Robert Halliday	" "	7 "	577 80
Thomas Callaghan	" "	6⅔ "	558 00
A. Brewer	" "	5½ "	426 95
F. Sly	" "	5 "	402 65
John Bullied	" "	5 "	402 30
M. Ritchie	" "	4⅓ "	356 75
Sundry Rangers (part time)			425 15

Travelling Expenses, $426.46.

A. Brewer, 28.25; T. Callaghan, 16.70; E. Elliott, 16.25; E. E. Godin, 8.35; J. Jamieson, 295.56; M. MacDonald, 8.90; A. Matchett, 20.55; G. Stewart, 31.90.. 426 46

Miscellaneous, $1,743.63.

G. G. Barker, drugs, 16.00; Black Bros., hay, etc., 126.80; Canadian Johnson Motor Co., Ltd., parts, etc., 45.68; T. Eaton Co., Ltd., pillows, etc., 145.80; Ely Gas & Oil Co., gas, 58.63; Fort Frances Wholesalers, Ltd., provisions, 94.33; Gillmor & Noden, hardware, snowshoes, etc., 608.40; Imperial Oil, Ltd., oil, 29.05; J. Leckie, Ltd., paddles, etc., 175.34; J. A. Mathieu, Ltd., lumber, 53.18; Monarch Oil Co., Ltd., gas, 117.60; Northern Electric Co., Ltd., test set, 39.37; Shevlin-Clarke Co., Ltd., lumber, etc., 120.63. Sundries—customs, 11.59; express, 4.40; freight, 89.34; postage, 16.81; telegrams, 12.20; petty disbursements, 15.68 .... 1,780 83

Less Refund of gasolene tax 37 20

1,743 63

Creation, Extension and Maintenance of Parks ($25.16)

Hydro-Electric Power Commission of Ontario, light 25 16

Miscellaneous $382,808.18

FORESTRY BRANCH

Salaries ($45,543.75)

E. J. Zavitz	Deputy Minister	12 months	5,700 00
C. R. Mills	Assistant Provincial Forester	12 "	4,000 00
A. H. Richardson	Forester	12 "	3,300 00
R. N. Johnson	"	12 "	3,300 00
J. F. Sharpe	"	12 "	3,300 00
Wm. R. Haddow	Forest Pathologist	12 "	2,700 00
C. E. Westland	Assistant Forester, Group 1	12 "	2,400 00
G. Bayly	" " " 1	12 "	2,400 00
J. F. L. Simmons	" " " 2	12 "	2,100 00
J. M. Bishop	Draughtsman, Group 1	12 "	2,000 00
N. L. Rogers	Principal Clerk	12 "	2,100 00
G. W. Harris	Senior Clerk	12 "	2,000 00
E. W. Cooper	" "	12 "	1,800 00
M. C. Rowland	Senior Clerk Stenographer	12 "	1,500 00
J. Bald	" " "	12 "	1,500 00
A. S. McKyes	" " "	12 "	1,400 00
F. A. Cuthbertson	Clerk Stenographer, Group 1	12 "	1,125 00
M. E. Overend	" " " 1	12 "	1,050 00
K. H. DeNure	" " " 2	12 "	975 00
G. H. Evans	Clerk Typist, Group 1	11 "	893 75

Forestry Branch—Continued

Contingencies ($6,152.83)

Dorothy Stewart	Clerk Stenographer, Group 2 ... 12 months	825 00
C. R. Mills, Travelling Expenses		63 43

Miscellaneous, $5,264.40.

Canadian Forestry Association, advertising, 45.00; Department of Public Works, blue print paper, 180.12; Eastman Kodak Stores, Ltd., film, etc., 56.91; Forest & Outdoors, advertising, 180.00; King's Printer, 3,316.35; L. A. Philip & Co., rental of machine, 45.00; Thos. Pocklington Co., land level, etc., 78.25; Province of Ontario Pictures, slides, etc., 42.75; J. F. Raw, Ltd., blue prints, etc., 25.51; Remington Typewriters, Ltd., inspections, 48.75; University of Toronto, books, etc., 64.29; United Typewriter Co., Ltd., inspections, etc., 129.46; Wisely Bragg Publishing Co., advertising, 100.00. Sundries—freight, .50; newspapers and periodicals, 13.00; telegrams, 915.25; petty disbursements, 23.26 ... 5,264 40

REFORESTATION ($235,109.92)

Main Office.

Name	Position	Period	Amount
J. F. Cowan	Clerk, Group 1, Forestry Branch	12 months	1,500 00
R. J. Crossley	" " 1, " "	12 "	1,400 00

Norfolk Forest Station:

Name	Position	Period	Amount
F. S. Newman	Superintendent, Group 1	12 months	4,000 00
J. A. Watts	Foreman, Group 1	12 "	1,500 00
E. Telford	Deputy Foreman	12 "	1,400 00
R. Addison	Deputy Foreman	12 "	1,300 00
Theo. Balcombe	Assistant "	12 "	1,050 00
Fred A. Cline	" "	12 "	1,039 93
Archie W. Colwell	" "	12 "	1,050 00
Stanley Day	" "	12 "	1,050 00
J. M. Drinkwater	" "	12 "	1,050 00
Wm. Proper	" "	12 "	1,044 25
Clarence Starling	" "	12 "	1,050 00
Frank Will	" "	12 "	1,047 12
Ernest Smith	Teamster	12 "	1,100 00
John McKim	"	12 "	1,100 00
Frank Pratt	Gardener	12 "	1,125 00
Chas. Smith	Mechanic	12 "	1,050 00
Alfred Walter	Clerk, Group 2	12 "	1,050 00
R. A. MacInnes	" " 2	12 "	1,050 00
J. C. M. Kirk	Forestry Helper	12 "	1,050 00

Midhurst Forest Station:

Name	Position	Period	Amount
M. A. Adamson	Superintendent, Group 3	12 months	2,300 00
Wm. Kennedy	Clerk, Group 2	12 "	1,125 00
A. H. Spence	Foreman, Group 1	12 "	1,600 00
S. A. McLean	Assistant Foreman	12 "	1,200 00
John Marton	" "	12 "	1,200 00
John Pain	" "	12 "	1,200 00
L. R. Brown	" "	12 "	1,200 00
A. D. Patterson	"	12 *	1,050 00
R. H. Poole	Teamster	12 "	1,200 00
J. J. Kissock	"	12 "	1,050 00
A. H. Bishop	"	12 "	1,050 00
S. J. Cox	Caretaker, Group 2	12 "	975 00

Orono Forest Station:

Name	Position	Period	Amount
G. M. Linton	Superintendent, Group 3	12 months	2,700 00
W. J. Hall	Foreman, Group 2	12 "	1,400 00
G. R. L. Sutton	Assistant Foreman	12 "	1,200 00
D. Harness	" "	12 "	1,050 00
W. C. Mitchell	Caretaker, Group 2	12 "	1,050 00
J. Middleton	Forestry Helper	12 "	975 00
A. W. Clough	" "	12 "	975 00

Pay List, wages of men ... 134,522 24

Reforestation—Continued

Travelling Expenses, $4,174.67.

M. A. Adamson, 96.35; Arlington Hotel, 52.50; A. S. L. Barnes, 253.54; Geo. Bayly, 1,012.00; Richard Boultbee, 10.10; R. J. Crossley, 376.82; Gordon Crutcher, 12.10; E. J. Dearlove, 37.00; Charles Drinkwater, 62.19; C. W. Duckworth, 51.30; Thos. H. Honey, 6.15; F. Latimer, 38.66; Jas. Lapalm, 96.20; G. M. Linton, 79.89; Charles McGhie, 17.00; Robt. F. Nelson, 4.00; F. S. Newman, 116.19; W. J. Noden, 16.50; Clifford Plaxton, 33.65; Miller Plaxton, 5.60; A. H. Richardson, 399.84; J. F. L. Simmons, 572.29; Frank Stanley, 34.55; Geo. Telford, 144.50; C. M. Wattie, 93.73; A. B. Wheatley, 524.02; Howard Willoughby, 28.00 .... 4,174 67

Maintenance-General, $22,631.08.

Wm. H. Abbey, 74.70; M. A. Adamson, 50.72; The Adams Vandusen Co., 21.13; Aikenhead Hardware Co., 6.45; D. R. Aldread, 14.00; Alliston Milling Co., 5.00; American Tent and Awning Co., Ltd., 96.45; B. W. Anderson, 3.70; J. R. Anderson, 3.50; Andrewes Mountain Seed Co., Ltd., 5.30; Lorne Anger, 14.00; Armstrong and Rainford, 22.07; Alex. Armstrong, 20.00; C. G. Armstrong, 61.28; Harry Armstrong, 2.90; Asagh and Davey, 24.00; John Ashdown, 21.60; Ball Planing Mill, 580.71; Barrie Fuel and Supply Co., 448.34; Barrie Planing Mill, 44.63; H. Barringer, 41.95; Geo. Bayly, 207.60; J. Beleskey, 2.35; W. C. Bell, 18.40; Eugene Bennett, 5.00; J. Bigelow, 23.50; Wm. Binney, 19.25; H. S. Blakeley, 4.00; H. C. Bonathon, 5.75; N. H. Bowers, 11.36; W. L. Brennan, 28.33; Bridge Bros., 3.15; F. Bronson, 10.85; Brown & Co., 124.74; Chas. Brown, 100.00; A. A. Burk & Co., 7.45; E. A. Button, 6.15; Andrew Byerlay, 10.00; Geo. Caldwell, 3.75; David Campbell, 3.00; Can. Builders' Materials, Ltd., 9.03; Canadian Credit Men's Association, 25.44; Can. Elec. Co., Ltd., 133.33; Can. Fairbanks-Morse Co., Ltd., 2.30; Can. Gen. Elec. Co., Ltd., 27.92; Can. Metal Co., Ltd., 5.00; Can. Oil Co., Ltd., 525.74; Geo. Cane, 13.50; E. Carson, 10.00; T. Carson, 5.00; J. P. Cassidy, 12.95; Cassidy's, Ltd., 1.26; Ed. Cavanagh, 95.25; Central Scientific Co., 1.80; Frank Chappell, 28.00; J. W. Church, 7.45; Oscar A. Clark, 1.25; C. F. Cole, 20.00; W. J. Cook, 61.73; Cooper and Glanville, 34.86; Copeland Milling Co., 258.75; Harry Couch, 7.80; Coulter's Garage, 28.35; Jas. Coutts, 95.00; A. E. Cousins, 13.50; S. J. Cox, 4.00; Crane, Ltd., 15.13; Roy Cridland, 62.50; R. J. Crossley, 74.57; O. Davis, 97.50; Thos. Dawes & Sons, 20.45; W. H. Dayton, 96.55; A. S. Deadrick, 100.00; E. J. Dearlove, 29.50; Ernest Dent, 4.75; Henry Disston & Sons, 5.60; Dominion Glass Co., 15.88; Walter Downey, 10.00; M. Drenan, 4.80; C. W. Duckworth, 4.35; T. Eaton Co., Ltd., 10.55; E. B. Eddy Co., 12.78; Electric Shop, 11.93; A. F. Emphe, 22.53; F. R. Evans, 31.00; S. A. Foy, 270.39; H. Feagan, 188.91; Fibre Box, Ltd., 135.12; Film & Slide Co., Ltd., 32.44; Firstbrooks, Ltd. (boxes), 182.15; Bruce Fiske, 23.00; Fleming Hardware, 14.15; Flexible Shaft Co., Ltd., 4.13; Foster Pottery Co., 11.59; Frost Steel & Wire Co., 141.80; D. M. Gallaughan, 7.00; J. C. Gallaughan, 8.00; R. J. Gamble, 4.50; General Steel Wares, Ltd., 32.89; G. Gilbert, Estate, 10.61; Garfield Gilbert, 17.35; John J. Gilfellen, 41.37; Henry Gilner, 5.00; The Gilson Mfg. Co., 166.33; Golf, Ltd., 26.25; Gould, Shapley & Muir, Ltd., 85.00; Graham Nail & Wire Co., Ltd., 68.54; John Graves, 20.50; Robt. Greening, 9.75; B. Greening Wire Co., Ltd., 21.42; Gurney Foundry Co., Ltd., 19.89; Haddads, 58.54; C. E. Haddon, 54.16; Halliday & Co., Ltd., 66.35; E. Hammon, 423.06; W. A. Hannah, 13.88; Geo. Patterson, 13.60; Hartwell Bros., 8.41; Herbert Hawkins, 11.57; James Henry & Sons, 371.37; Hepburn & Cohoun Motors, 25.26; Fred. O. Heskett, 25.30; Hesson Lumber Co., Ltd., 76.45; F. T. Hill & Co., 14.10; Harold Hill, 25.25; John E. Hill, 11.25; Hinde & Dauch Paper Co., 149.10; Edmund Hind Lumber Co., Ltd., 102.28; Hogg & Lytle Co., Ltd., 23.40; Fred Hollidge, 20.75; John Holmberg, 24.00; Thos. H. Honey, 3.52; H. Marshall Howell, 100.00; W. Howey, 115.47; H. S. Howland & Son, Ltd., 40.01; Hubbard's Hardware, 522.59; Chas. Hutchinson, 46.00; Imperial Oil, Ltd., 1,150.71; Instruments, Ltd., 20.10; Dave Jackson, 6.80; E. H. Jackson Co., Ltd., 55.77; W. R. Jackson & Co., 14.50; Jamieson's Garage, 7.50; Geo. Jamieson, 11.00; Robt. Jennings, 2.50; W. H. Jewel & Son, 811.62; F. E. Johnson & Co., 102.08; Irvin Johnson, 316.25; J. H. Johnson, 3.50; W. H. Johnson & Son, 18.76; H. A. Kane, 6.00; Smith Kane, 63.40; N. M. Kensit, 11.80; A. Knapp, 144.75, A. W. Laidman, 51.35; Charles Lees, 3.00; A. T. Leedham, 121.98; Jas. Lapalm, 81.79; G. M. Linton, 270.68; Jas. S. Livingstone, 6.30; E. Long, Ltd., 17.76; Lord & Burnham Co., Ltd., 17.30; M. J. Lovelace, 66.38; Lundy Fence Co., Ltd., 2.92; R. Lytton, 76.00; McColl & Co., 2,440.87; The R. McDougall Co., 28.05; W. J. McGuire, 27.30; McKenzie & McNabb, 58.19; Robt. McKinney, 70.00; Wm. McKracken, 4.50; W. A. McLean, 55.00; A. McMahon, 21.14; A. D. McNabb, 33.00; Thos. McQuade, 1.75; Massey-Harris Co., Ltd., 15.00; A. S. Maw, 30.00; Meredith-Simmond Co., Ltd., 3.07; The Metallic Roofing Co., of Canada Ltd., 25.14; A. Middlebrook, 8.43; The

Reforestation—Continued

Maintenance—General—Continued.

Midland Steam Laundry Co., Ltd., 122.75; Millbrook Coal Co., 328.13; A. Moffat, 30.56; John Moffatt, 36.00; T. Moran, 8.00; P. J. Moran, 1.70; F. F. Morris, 6.00; The Jas. Morrison Brass Mfg. Co., Ltd., 35.66; Geo. E. Mottashead, 1.89; J. H. Mouncey, 11.84; W. P. Muir, 1.80; National Electric Heating Co., 5.64; F. S. Newman, .75; J. E. Nicholson, 106.00; Noble Bros., 13.35; W. J. Noden, 29.65; Norfolk Co-operative, Ltd., 57.69; Northern Electric Co., 71.20; T. J. O'Flynn, 223.29; N. L. Oliver, 28.40; Ontario Cheese Box Co., 20.70; Ontario Fertilizer, Ltd., 66.32; Ontario Wind Engine & Pump Co., 1.28; Milton Orchard, 44.00; Orono Coal & Lumber Co., 614.94; Orono Telephone Co., 49.50; Harold Orser, 24.00; Oshawa Electric Supply Co., 20.81; P. Patton, 56.25; Pease Foundry Co., Ltd., 115.09; The Pedlar People, Ltd., 77.49; Peterboro Canoe Co., 4.00; W. F. Petry, 380.50; R. H. Poaps, 295.87; Port Rowan Brick & Tile Co., 15.00; H. S. Prelipp, 49.78; Province of Ontario Pictures, 8.10; Queen City Glass Co., 3.68; Remington Typewriters, Ltd., 6.25; Wm. Rennie Seeds, Ltd., 45.33; A. H. Richardson, 73.78; Richardson Bros., 30.53; Jas. Robertson Co., Ltd., 14.71; John Robinson, 15.00; Robertson Hardware, 18.73; Rolph Hardware, 591.44; S. Rowe, 20.00; H. D. Russell, 40.00; J. C. Rutherford, 2.00; The Sargeant Co., Ltd., 202.70; Norman Schanellen, 85.25; J. M. Schneider & Sons, Ltd., 14.00; John Schwartz, 11.00; Geo. Scott & Son, 8.85; L. L. Scott, 12.12; J. C. Shanahan, 43.00; Alfred Shaw, 130.08; Sheppard & Gill, 1,407.19; J. A. Simmers, 13.87; W. Simms, 10.00; W. G. Slorach, 5.15; Harry Smith, 152.73; S. G. Smith & Co., 5.00; Smythe Bros., 3.11; Spencer C. Smith, 12.25; J. J. Spilker, 12.92; Standard Underground Cable Co. of Canada, Ltd., 3.54; Frank Stanley, 8.17; H. S. Stark, 17.00; Steel Co. of Canada, Ltd., 5.00; Steele, Briggs Seed Co., 17.50; A. Stephoff, 27.00; David Stevens, 31.25; Oscar Stevens, 100.00; John Stewart, 24.00; Sturgeons, Ltd., 205.38; Taylor-Forbes Co., Ltd., 41.14; Edward Taylor, 12.00; The Thomas-Laker Sign Co., 18.00; Peter Thompson & Sons, 386.61; T. Thornton, 12.80; Toronto Asphalt Roofing Co., 187.51; Jas. Torpey, 222.75; J. W. Towne & Co., 197.28; Matti Tuomi, 66.50; J. J. Turner & Sons, Ltd., 20.00; Universal Lightning Rod Co., 34.60; Urry Bros., 2.55; Uxbridge Hardware Co., 4.50; Vacu-Draft, Ltd., 98.50; Vego-Humus, Ltd., 25.00; Victoria Paper & Twine Co., 4.56; T. M. Ward, 5.00; R. Ward, 13.70; Watson & Rorabeck, 4.93; Watson, Jack, Ltd., 58.94; C. M. Wattie, 6.00; C. Wattie, 24.00; West Toronto Iron & Building Co., 19.35; West, Peachy & Sons, 2.43; A. B. Wheatley, 34.78; Wheeler & Bain, Ltd., 16.41; A. H. Wilson, 39.14; Howard Willoughby, 7.50; Wood, Alexander & James, Ltd., 4.82; Woods Manufacturing Co., 126.76; A. E. Wrigglesworth, 77.10; C. E. Wright, 50.00; G. O. Wright, 13.25; W. H. Young, 4.90 .... 22,631 08

Maintenance—Automobiles, $5,376.74.

Gordon Armstrong, 2.61; A. E. Atkin & Sons, 29.38; A. S. L. Barnes, 20.63; Geo. Bayly, 50.90; Bay View Garage, 57.64; Bloomfield Garage, 152.18; W. L. Brennan, 10.82; Canadian Oil Cos., Ltd., 1,103.72; Chittick Motor Sales, 170.17; W. L. Christmas & Son, 2.38; Roger L. Corbett, 4.10; Coulter's Garage, 363.59; L. C. Cratt, 23.20; Gordon Crutcher, 6.95; Dept. of Highways, 807.01; H. Feagan, 6.90; Goodyear Tire & Rubber Co., 11.57; Harpham Bros., 33.52; Hepburn & Cohoun Motors, 31.87; Harold Hill, 33.58; E. L. Hoover, 17.84; Imperial Oil, Ltd., 746.05; W. H. Jewel & Son, 113.98; Herman Kleinsteuber, 113.57; Jas. Lapalm, 90.07; Joseph A. Lobraico, 87.17; F. E. MacCartney, 48.00; Mansfield Garage, 149.46; Mills Garage, 10.80; Geo. E. Mottashead, 40.25; F. S. Newman, 4.35; Noble Bros., 9.78; North Bay Garage, 41.65; Ontario Motor Sales Co., 77.94; Orono Garage, 56.06; A. L. Phillips, 19.28; Wm. Phillips, 63.21; H. F. Prelipp, 9.38; I. A. Procunier, 105.03; A. H. Richardson, 58.71; Richardson Bros., 132.70; Service Garage, 5.75; Shelburne Garage, 3.95; J. F. Simmons, 30.38; R. E. Smith, 105.92; Spencer C. Smith, 33.82; Turton's Garage, 6.00; R. Ward, 88.64; Watson's Garage, 4.25; Willys-Overland Sales Co., Ltd., 90.98; Woodman & Ross, 9.00; Geo. O. Wright, 80.05 .... 5,376 74

Express, Freight, etc., $9,890.07.

M. A. Adamson, 145.06; Atkey Transport Co., 80.16; A. S. L. Barnes, 3.68; Bell Telephone Co., 230.53; Geo. Bayly, 298.73; Canadian National Railways, 7,570.81; Canadian Pacific Railway Co., 56.98; Oscar A. Clarke, 53.56; S. J. Cox, 22.40; R. J. Crossley, .50; E. J. Dearlove, 80.93; C. W. Duckworth, 1.19; H. Elkington, 7.12; Galt Transport, .50; W. H. Golden & Son, 49.01; Haldimand Ruel Telephone Co., Ltd., 6.30; G. J. Hass, 6.16; Hendry & Co., .40; Jno. D. Hill, 20.50; Hoar's Transport, 173.29; Fred Hollidge, 19.75; Thos. H. Honey, 12.66; Herbert Jennings, 12.00; H. M. Legris, 2.85; Jas. Lapalm, 48.15; G. M. Linton, 100.08; P. McEwen, 25.36; R. H. McKee, 8.10; Maguire's Transport, 104.44;

Reforestation—Continued

Express, Freight, etc.—Continued.

F. S. Newman, 171.15; Chas. G. Petherick, 165.00; Postage, 113.75; A. H. Richardson, 14.95; J. F. Simmons, 67.50; Southern Ontario Phone Co., 107.48; Chas. Strong, 84.00; C. M. Wattie, 5.59; A. B. Wheatley, 19.45 .... 9,890 07

Seed Collecting, $14,116.43.

Sundry persons for cone collecting 14,116 43

Light and Power, $4,701.57.

Hydro-Electric Power Commission 4,701 57

Miscellaneous, $1,659.51.

M. A. Adamson, 201.83; Andrewes Mountain Seed Co., Ltd., 34.55; Armstrong & Rainford, 6.50; Harry Armstrong, 7.10; Art Sign Co., 7.50; A. S. L. Barnes, 14.15; Geo. Bayly, 116.55; Chas. A. Brown, 4.90; David Campbell, 1.80; Canadian National Railways, 3.00; Canadian Photo Co., 3.60; Canadian Press Clipping Co., 108.40; Oscar A. Clarke, 22.00; Cox & Andrews, 10.00; R. H. Creech, 8.10; R. J. Crossley, 2.37; Dominion Glass Co., 9.85; E. B. Eddy Co., 2.25; W. A. Edye-de-Hearst, 19.86; Electric Shop, .65; Endean Nurseries, 2.75; F. F. Fallis, 82.10; Film & Slide Co., Ltd., 15.85; Garfield Gilbert, 3.18; Jno. J. Gilfillen, 16.89; His Master's Voice, Ltd., 5.10; Jas. Holden, 3.10; Holland Bulb Gardens, 9.90; Fred Hollidge, 1.00; Thos. H. Honey, 2.00; Dave Jackson, 2.00; Dr. E. G. Kerslik, 3.00; King's Printer, 330.65; Laboratory of Bacteriology, O.A.C., 10.00; Jas. Lapalm, 163.05; G. M. Linton, 12.55; S. B. McCready, 35.00; P. McEwen, 1.00; Thos. C. Martin, 12.50; The James Morrison Brass Mfg. Co., Ltd., .95; F. S. Newman, 12.00; Northern Electric Co., 2.02; Office Specialty Mfg. Co., 7.60; Orono News, 4.10; Powell & Hook, 8.00; Province of Ontario Pictures, 102.65; J. Frank Raw Co., Ltd., 2.25; Wm. Rennie Seeds, Ltd., 5.00; A. H. Richardson, 39.47; The Sault Daily Star, 14.40; Scarboro Gardens Co., Ltd., 5.90; J. A. Simmers, 16.35; J. F. Simmons, 11.15; Harry Smith, 2.03; T. Smith, 5.00; Frank Stanley, 5.80; C. Tarling Co., 2.75; Taylor Instrument Co. of Canada, Ltd., 3.96; Wagner Electric Mfg. Co., Ltd., 2.55; C. M. Wattie, 17.27; Edward Webb & Sons, 16.55; Howard Willoughby, 72.88; George York, 2.30 .... 1,659 51

Total, Reforestation		248,578 61	
Less Repayments, Sale of Seeds	13,450 00		
Refund on freight overcharge	5 92		
" T. Eaton Company	2 77		
" Customs charges	10 00		
		13,468 69	
Reforestation			$235,109.92

FIRE RANGING ($1,404,777.07)

Ground Work ($1,276,645.17)

Salaries, $698,869.59.

P. McEwen	District Forester, Georgian Bay Inspectorate	12	months	3,300 00
A. B. Connell	" " Hudson "	12	"	3,300 00
K. A. Stewart	" " Sudbury "	12	"	3,300 00
W. D. Cram	" " Kenora "	12	"	3,000 00
H. W. Crosbie	" " Trent "	12	"	2,850 00
C. E. Foote	" " Port Arthur "	12	"	2,850 00
N. M. Kensit	" " Sault Ste. Marie "	12	"	2,550 00
T. E. Mackey	" " Oba "	12	"	2,400 00
W. B. Greenwood	" " North Bay "	12	"	2,700 00
E. S. Davidson	" " Rainy River "	12	"	2,300 00
J. R. B. Coleman	Assistant "	12	"	2,100 00
R. D. L. Snow	" "	12	"	2,000 00
R. Boultbee	" "	12	"	1,900 00
Wm. A. Hooper	" "	12	"	2,100 00
E. L. Ward	" "	12	"	2,100 00
R. F. Goodall	" "	12	"	2,000 00
M. Ardenne	" "	12	"	2,100 00
W. D. Pigott	Fire Inspector, Sudbury Inspectorate	12	"	2,500 00
F. Hamilton	" " Cochrane, "	12	"	2,500 00
J. Kirkpatrick	Stock Clerk, Group 1	12	"	1,560 00
Rangers Pay Lists				649,459 59

Fire Ranging—Continued

Ground Work—Continued

Travelling Expenses, $25,650.13.

Lloyd Acheson, 92.65; K. Acheson, 79.00; R. Alcock, 3.15; J. C. Alt, 96.65; C. Amm, 52.70; J. B. Amm, 420.85; H. S. Anderson, 26.90; J. Anderson, 8.40; H. Autayo, 3.15; Geo. Ash, 39.15; Geo. Austin, 44.95; M. H. Baker, 317.00; M. Bamford, 6.75; W. I. Barber, 49.60; E. Beaumont, 32.00; Wm. Belisle, 19.00; J. W. Bell, 109.85; F. Belmore, 54.45; Louis Berlinquette, 231.22; H. E. Bickmore, 14.50; J. A. Bissonnette, 11.55; R. H. Bliss, 392.50; A. C. Bouchey, 92.90; E. Bouchey, 175.33; R. Boultbee, 12.60; J. J. Bowland, 297.50; Alex. Brown, 20.95; John Brown, 30.00; G. C. Buckingham, 9.10; Don Burns, 99.80; J. B. Burns, 296.25; R. C. Burns, 141.60; Thos. Campbell, 257.15; T. E. Cassidy, 50.15; H. A. Canning, 213.30; H. M. Carnahan, 4.40; J. Charron, 58.25; J. H. Clavelle, 28.75; A. Cleavely, 79.45; S. J. Clement, 96.30; J. R. B. Coleman, 84.45; A. B. Connell, 81.10; G. A. Coutanche, 13.45; S. J. Cowan, 83.45; W. D. Cram, 440.10; S. Crockett, 27.35; H. W. Crosbie, 244.20; N. A. Cross, 80.85; G. L. Crouch, 171.15; A. E. Crump, 46.45; J. H. Cunning, 140.79; W. Darby, 100.60; H. S. Davis, 11.80; E. S. Davison, 124.70; W. D. Dixon, 18.35; J. C. Dillon, 236.80; J. Dodd, 148.90; P. M. Dolan, 14.00; Tom Dolan, 11.75; W. A. Draper, 150.05; Chas. R. Dunn, 22.70; A. L. Dunne, 22.00; A. J. Dusang, 85.95; W. L. Eckersley, 7.50; H. Elkington, 83.60; John Eno, 129.55; A. S. Ericson, 8.80; W. E. Fenn, 104.30; A. Fenton, 85.34; H. Ferguson, 3.55; C. E. Foote, 181.55; W. A. Forsythe, 59.95; J. A. Foster, 37.70; W. H. Foyle, 41.57; H. R. Fuller, 7.85; A. I. Furlong, 190.70; A. E. Gardiner, 82.15; W. R. Gardner, 89.00; F. T. Garnham, 40.35; E. C. Gatien, 33.50; W. J. Gibson, 53.65; J. A. Gillespie, 301.27; E. J. Gilligan, 56.65; F. S. Godfrey, 27.90; R. F. Goodall, 18.25; F. Gordon, 242.75; W. H. Graham, 110.35; A. Grasser, 125.55; H. Green, 106.05; J. H. Green, 64.05; W. B. Greenwood, 127.60; T. Guerard, 9.50; Oscar Gulin, 18.85; T. C. Haley, 22.50; F. Hamilton, 196.40; E. C. Hart, 223.55; G. J. Hass, 341.65; S. Hawken, 4.13; Wm. H. Hawkins, 137.90; L. Henderson, 15.70; R. J. Henderson, 78.55; W. M. Henry, 9.90; Ben Hey, 763.90; C. E. Hindson, 11.50; P. Hoffman, 80.65; A. Holinshead, 139.35; W. A. Hooper, 60.10; M. R. Horn, 37.45; H. E. Hutchinson, 23.00; Edwin Jarman, 84.25; H. S. Johns, 46.65; C. Johnson, 37.50; Jno. H. Johnson, 5.60; R. N. Johnston, 90.40; W. H. Kearns, 56.20; H. E. Kedey, 244.90; E. W. Keen, 8.50; D. J. Kennedy, 83.05; Jerry Kennedy, 12.60; N. M. Kensit, 336.29; A. C. Kilby, 23.20; J. Lalonde, 57.90; F. S. Landry, 8.50; R. Languerand, 47.65; G. V. Lawrence, 41.35; G. B. Lawrence, 194.00; H. M. Legris, 106.20; J. P. Legris, 141.00; Lorne LeSieur, 22.85; C. E. Lloyd, 138.44; Hugh Logan, 44.75; J. R. Loucks, 34.50; Ben Love, 7.80; F. A. MacDougall, 167.28; Thos. McCoshen, 27.90; H. L. McCausland, 201.10; C. McChesney, 68.15; Thos. McCormick, 170.25; C. W. McDonald, 56.95; Colin McDougall, 26.10; A. H. McEwen, 305.25; P. McEwen, 135.16; J. W. McGloan, 37.85; Colin McInnis, 232.65; Jno. McIntyre, 10.30; C. McKinnon, 48.95; W. McLaren, 9.00; J. J. McLellan, 49.15; Jno. McNamara, 55.10; K. W. McNeill, 256.35; M. E. McNulty, 161.25; Roy McPhail, 12.95; T. E. Mackey, 479.10; E. W. Maher, 7.00; V. Mawn, 140.45; J. B. Matthews, 140.94; E. D. Meeking, 125.70; C. R. Mills, 142.41; S. Miles, 39.40; W. W. Milne, 15.33; A. C. Mitchell, 109.75; Frank B. Moran, 7.55; H. Morel, Jr., 147.85; J. W. Murdock, 56.20; J. E. Morin, 105.71; G. J. M. Munro, 38.45; T. J. Murphy, 15.50; Jno. Nelson, 76.85; H. Nicholas, 130.05; Jno. Nixon, 12.85; H. V. Orr, 83.80; C. A. Osborne, 30.15; Jas. O'Shea, 145.10; L. J. Oulette, 253.05; F. R. Parmeter, 32.50; C. C. Parr, 138.50; H. H. Parsons, 120.85; M. Patterson, 55.00; L. W. Peddie, 177.45; D. Pender, 111.35; B. Perrigo, 19.50; W. D. Pigott, 170.44; E. E. Potter, 87.30; V. H. Prewer, 429.90; F. Pritchard, 42.15; J. C. R. Punchard, 101.20; Max Rabbitts, 36.65; Jno. Raeburn, 47.20; J. L. Rannie, 11.50; G. O. Reesor, 6.50; M. Roadhouse, 5.95; C. H. Robinson, 62.90; H. Robinson, 47.30; W. J. Robinson, 619.50; Jas. Ruxton, 80.45; S. V. Ryan, 50.60; A. E. Sach, 53.55; Ole Sand, 332.15; W. Sangster, 60.10; F. G. Saunders, 944.75; Jno. S. M. Sewell, 50.60; L. E. Simpson, 129.60; R. Simpson, 106.85; R. J. Smith, 28.70; V. H. Smith, 30.35; J. R. G. Smyth, 44.80; R. L. Snow, 336.84; F. Snyder, 18.10; D. Y. Solandt, 183.65; S. D. Spence, 68.35; K. A. Stewart, 150.70; Otto Stein, 2.35; J. H. Stirrett, 27.60; J. H. Strain, 91.85; Wm. Stringer, 170.50; Alf. Tait, 94.05; Angus G. Taylor, 553.34; D. W. Taylor, 69.25; Jas. S. Taylor, 62.15; D. T. Thaw, 23.00; Lloyd Thomson, 22.05; S. B. Trainer, 96.00; Eric A. Turl, 43.25; W. E. Van Clieaf, 129.60; J. S. Walker, 138.25; R. B. Walker, 53.75; Jas. I. Walsh, 125.60; C. Ward, 198.55; E. L. Ward, 245.30; G. Watson, 47.50; R. E. Watson, 93.10; N. F. Welsh, 89.60; W. J. Werry, 15.45; H. Whitefield, 59.50; Bogert Wilson, 67.70; E. Wilson, 152.25; R. K. Wilson, 330.70; C. Wither, 60.85; Geo. Wither, 44.30; Chas. E. Wolgar, 84.35; Alex. Wylie, 20.20; Murray Young, 92.30; H. Zufelt, 116.85 .... 25,650.13

Fire Ranging—Continued

Transportation of Extra Fire Fighters, $3,970.13.

J. Boivin, 162.00; S. Buckburrough, 156.50; Wm. Bull, 157.50; Canadian Pacific Railway Co., 4.10; Chas. Carr, 151.50; Thos. Clark, 178.50; Donald Connelly, 27.05; E. S. Davison, 8.04; R. F. Goodall, 68.76; O. Harris, 160.50; Hudson's Bay Co., 13.85; J. U. Lauzon, 148.50; J. H. Leng, 5.48; Lesage Motor Sales, 3.00; Lynch Auto Sales, 157.29; A. Maisonneuve, 151.50; E. Morley, 42.00; W. L. Morissey, 9.35; Neale & Heath, 12.48; J. Porco & Co., Garage 50.00; V. H. Prewer, 280.98; W. J. Robinson, 57.50; Geo. Sheridan, 162.00; Sioux Motor Sales, 25.00; Star Grocery, 34.32; J. W. Stone Boat Manufacturing Co., 2.00; J. H. Strain, 6.00; W. S. Tennant, 15.50; J. Z. Vinet, 9.31; Watson & Lloyd, 42.73; Wesley Taxi & Transfer Co., 42.95; Alf. Wilkie, 133.50; H. Wilkins, 160.50; Frank Wright, 160.50; Thos. Yarrow, 151.50. **Miscellaneous disbursements by Forestry Branch Officers**—Lloyd Acheson, 24.55; M. Ardenne, 5.30; Ed. Bliss, 2.00; R. H. Bliss, 19.40; A. C. Bouchey, 33.40; E. Bouchey, 13.75; A. B. Connell, 11.50; W. D. Cram, 12.60; H. W. Crosbie, 2.00; Wm. Darby, 8.90; E. S. Davison, 26.85; W. D. Dixon, 6.30; J. A. Gillespie, 22.85; W. B. Greenwood, 9.15; G. J. Hass, 2.75; W. H. Hawkins, 24.30; P. Hoffman, 24.90; M. R. Horn, 11.85; D. J. Kennedy, 14.30; N. M. Kensit, 79.60; T. E. Mackey, 64.17; J. B. Matthews, 5.40; A. C. Mitchell, 18.00; Gerald Munroe, 2.90; John McIntyre, 16.64; H. V. Orr, 11.35; David Pender, .50; W. D. Pigott, 2.50; V. H. Prewer, 4.50; Max Rabbitts, 15.45; Jas. Ruxton, 2.30; S. D. Spence, 3.80; K. A. Stewart, 223.10; J. H. Strain, 157.05; E. L. Ward, 126.08; Bogert Wilson, .95; Murray Young, 7.00 .... 3,970 13

Equipment, $88,017.22.

Abitibi Power & Paper Co., 11.50; Acme Drug Co., 8.35; C. T. Adams, 27.00; Aikenhead Hardware, Ltd., 12.94; Jas. Algie, 7.28; Aluminium (VI), Ltd., 4.53; Geo. Andrews, 15.00; John Arthur, 12.00; G. E. Atkinson, 135.60; Austin & Nicholson, 5.40; C. A. Bailey, 8.45; F. A. Barhouse, 40.00; Wm. Barton, 20.00; Barton Devices Co., 75.00; A. E. Beamish, 9.00; Walter Beatty Estate, 2.25; Wm. Beatty Co., 20.02; Beauchesne Bros., 1.80; A. Beauparlant, 4.07; Bertrand Bros., 75.05; A. C. Blakeley, 3.50; Blind River Garage, .25; E. Bliss, 1.25; J. R. Booth, Ltd., 16.00; Bowman's General Store, 8.15; F. Y. W. Braithwaite, 64.40; V. Brisson, 15.00; British Xylonite Co. of Canada, Ltd., 141.00; Brown Bros., 2.43; Burk & Avery, 10.00; A. A. Burke Co., .25; W. T. Bush, 43.20; Canadian Department Stores, 19.30; Canadian Fairbanks-Morse Co., Ltd., 118.21; Canadian Fire Hose Co., 22.00; Canadian General Electric Co., 39.70; Canadian Industries, Ltd., 13.38; Canadian Johnson Motors, 44.64; Canadian National Railways, 321.71; Canadian Pacific Railway Co., 134.71; Canadian Photo Co., 77.20; Canadian Telephone & Supplies, 51.45; Central Drug Store, 2.30; Central Motors, 12.57; Channell, Ltd., 24.01; Chapleau Drug Co., 6.00; H. B. Christilaw, 9.74; Christoff & Co., 8.32; D. W. Clayton, .50; Cliffe Printing Co., 5.25; Cockburn & Archer, 965.45; Cochrane-Dunlop Hardware Co., 2,202.38; Commercial Reproducing Co., 4.35; Connelly-Mewett, .50; Donald Connelly, 198.69; Consumers' Trading Co., 9.20; Coulter's Pharmacy, 16.35; W. J. Craig, 1.45; Craig Bros., 5.00; Crawley & McCracken, 27.40; A. Dalgleish, 30.00; De Forest Crosley, Ltd., 45.00; Department of Health, .60; Dingwall Motors, 7.68; Dominion Rubber Co., 759.50; Dougall Motor Car Co., 200.00; Dunlop Tire & Rubber Co., 808.45; Dunn Hardware Co., Ltd., 2,405.82; Durance Bros., 25.63; John East Co., 15.87; Eastman Kodak Stores, 1,599.62; T. Eaton Co., 31.71; Edwards Hardware, .94; Englehart Hardware, 2.86; Evans Co., Ltd., 83.90; Fairchild Aerial Camera Corporation, 2,900.00; Fairway Stores, 186.10; A. N. Fenn, 155.35; Findlay's, Ltd., 18.92; Harry Fisher, 54.30; P. Flynn, 17.70; Fort Frances Times, 10.75; F. S. Fosdick, 4.00; Fowler Hardware Co., 247.55; Fraser, Grieve & Co., 14.25; Fyr-Fyter Co. of Canada, 24.50; Galt Stove & Furnace Co., 20.43; Paul Gamache, 1.00; Garage Supply Co., Ltd., 13.58; A. E. Gardiner, 1.75; F. S. Gardiner, 7.00; Gem Electric Shop, 5.25; Gillmor & Noden, 37.29; H. Goodman & Son, 24.29; W. Gordon Steel Works, 6.00; Gordon E. Graham, 10.00; Grand & Toy, Ltd., 33.05; Grant-Holden-Graham, 552.78; John T. Gravelle, 15.00; Greenwood Electric & Hardware, 16.90; Chas. A. Guenette, 8.75; R. Gustafson, 28.30; Gutta Percha & Rubber Co., 817.98; Hartwell Bros., Ltd., 28.14; J. F. Hartz Co., 3.41; Hill-Clark-Francis, Ltd., 34.86; Hinsperger Harness Co., 175.75; Hose Hardware Co., 48.70; H. S. Howland Sons & Co., Ltd., 7.19; Hudson's Bay Co., 145.26; D. S. Humphrey, 44.45; Hutchings Transport Co., 40.50; Ideal Drug Co., 16.50; Instruments, Ltd., 22.78; International Paints (Canada), Ltd., 53.75; Jack & Co., 8.30; H. H. Joanisse, .85; D. Johnston & Son, 1.25; Kapusasking Supply Co., 77.22; Harry B. Kennedy, 7.50; Kert & Co., 10.01; Keuffel & Esser Co., 160.27; Keys Hardware, 143.39; Keyes Supply Co., 40.15; Cecil J. Kidd, 2.55; King's Printer, 9,325.13; S. N. Knight, 11.00; Arthur

Fire Ranging—Continued

Equipment—Continued.

Labbe, 2.50; J. B. Lacroix, .88; Lang & Ross, Ltd., 16.17; J. A. Lapalme, 6.90; John Leckie, Ltd., 431.76; Geo. H. Lees & Co., 11.65; Legree Hardware, 14.90; Lesage Motor Sales, 5.66; Lindstrom & Nilson, 10.80; H. T. Lloyd, 7.97; Lovelady Studio, 6.22; Marshall-Ecclestone, 17.90; Marshall Motor Car Co., Ltd., 719.61; Marshall-Wells Co., Ltd., 227.61; L. McCloskey, 59.87; Alex. McDonald, .50; Allan A. J. MacDonald, 43.25; McDowell Motors, 7.88; McGill Hardware, 247.08; B. R. McKenzie, 11.90; Mrs. M. F. McKey, 6.31; McLeod Garage, 5.85; McNaught Lumber Co., 4.60; Merrill, Rhind & Walmsley, 2.10; S. Miles, 6.64; Monarch Motors, 12.00; Monarch Oil Co., 421.00; Moore Bros., 6.00; W. L. Morrissey, 8.80; A. A. Moses, .88; Motor Trade Supply Co., 16.00; F. C. Muirhead, 2.00; C. W. Mullet, 20.55; Harry L. Mundell, 27.60; Chas. Murphy, 16.71; C. & D. Murray, Ltd., 14.73; James Murray, 54.20; Frank G. Myers, 3.25; Myles & Son Hardware, 10.45; National Grocers, Ltd., 23.86; Nichols Corporation, 199.06; Nicholson's Tire Surgery, 23.98; Norris Shoe Co., 15.00; Northern Canada Supply Co., Ltd., 120.49; Northern Drug Co., 3.95; Northern Electric Co., 953.23; Northern Garage, .34; Northern Ontario Power Co., 4.10; The Nugget, 2.40; Sam Onarheim, 2.50; Ontario Hughes-Owens Co., 14.84; Gilbert Ostler, 1.15; M. Pardy, 11.05; C. R. Parker, 8.30; Peerless Hardware, 1.20; E. Pellow, 1.50; Pembroke Service Garage, 25.60; A. L. Perkins & Co., 2.15; Peter Perlin, 226.90; Mrs. A. Peterson, 3.45; H. W. Petrie, Ltd., 4.55; W. F. Petry, 156.63; Pierce & Radke, 19.15; Thos. Pocklington Co., 164.10; Corporation of the City of Port Arthur, 8.61; Port Arthur Shipbuilding Co., Ltd., 228.75; Porter & Co., 9.90; O. E. Post, 22.99; Poupore Lumber Co., 230.15; Powassan Garage, 1.50; Pratt & Shanacy, 23.87; B. H. Rands, 1,003.80; J. Frank Raw Co., 294.95; G. H. Reid, 58.25; Arthur Reynart, 2.00; J. W. Richardson, 1.50; Wm. Richmond & Co., 26.40; J. Robert, 18.85; F. R. Robertson, 12.60; C. S. Rollins, 6.60; Rossport Trading Co., 1.20; N. Salo, 2.00; F. Sanderson, 194.80; Sault Stationers, Ltd., 8.85; Reg. Seller, 4.00; Robert Simpson Co., 1,136.85; Singer Sewing Machine, 25.00; Howard Smith Paper Mills, 6.00; Smith & Chapple, Ltd., 32.72; Soo Lumber & Mill Co., 21.50; Spanish River Lumber Co., 3.41; Spruce Falls Power & Paper Co., 19.04; Sudbury Boat & Canoe Co., 80.00; Superior Chain Stores, 3.25; Tapp & Hobbs, 29.00; C. Tarling Co., 110.50; L. S. Tarshis & Sons, 15.00; Thunder Bay Lumber Co., 49.17; A. W. Tingey, 5.00; Triangle Fish Co., 37.72; Tweed Hardware, 10.50; Twin City Grain, 8.00; Vernon Directories, Ltd., 12.00; Watson, Jack & Co., 49,190.31; Watson & Lloyd, 1.80; Wells Hardware Co., Ltd., 24.30; Western Grocers, Ltd., 14.90; White Drug Store, 22.85; Williams Hardware, 982.35; The A. R. Williams Machinery Co., Ltd., 1.92; Wolfe & Collins, Ltd., 3.45; Woods Manufacturing Co., 1,785.26; Wright Furniture Co., Ltd., 5.05. **Miscellaneous disbursements by Forestry Branch Officers.**—Lloyd Acheson, 2.00; R. H. Bliss, 1.40; A. C. Bouchey, 33.67; E. Bouchey, .30; Alex. Brown, .25; J. B. Burns, .80; A. B. Connell, 98.38; W. D. Cram, 345.26; H. W. Crosbie, 9.60; E. S. Davison, 8.86; J. C. Dillon, 1.80; Chas. R. Dunn, .75; H. Elkington, 5.61; C. E. Foote, .60; W. A. Forsythe, 2.46; W. J. Gibson, 2.13; H. Green, .75; W. B. Greenwood, 14.43; T. C. Haley, .35; F. Hamilton, 4.22; G. J. Hass, 31.48; W. H. Hawkins, 23.02; C. E. Hindson, 1.25; P. Hoffman, 13.48; M. R. Horn, 19.87; D. J. Kennedy, 4.98; N. M. Kensit, 44.24; H. M. Legris, 10.54; J. R. Loucks, 34.26; T. E. Mackey, 3.50; Thos. McCormick, 26.42; C. W. McDonald, 1.56; P. McEwen, 25.30; M. E. McNulty, .20; H. V. Orr, 3.81; W. D. Pigott, 14.71; Jas. Ruxton, 3.75; R. Simpson, 1.50; R. L. Snow, 1.10; S. D. Spence, 4.24; K. A. Stewart, 96.24; J. H. Strain, 2.25; Wm. Stringer, 7.50; E. L. Ward, 12.23; R. E. Watson, 4.05; Bogert Wilson, 7.80; Geo. Wombwell, 4.05 .... 88,017 22

Improvements, $26,781.47.

Aikenhead Hardware, Ltd., 14.50; Algoma Central & H.B. Ry., 5.35; Allcock, Laight & Westwood Co., 3.00; Barton & Fisher, 40.54; Beatty & Beatty, 25.00; Wm. Beatty Co., 5.40; Geo. Blanchard, 87.40; F. Bosley, 48.00; Gordon R. Brady, 2.38; F. Y. W. Braithwaite, 2.10; V. Brisson, 7.70; Daniel Bronson, 49.60; Campbell Heating Co., .75; Canadian General Electric Co., Ltd., 2.42; Canadian Industries, Ltd., 10.25; Canadian National Railways, 316.41; Canadian Pacific Railway Co., 4.70; Cardiff Township of Highland Grove, 20.00; Cockburn & Archer, 28.76; Cochrane-Dunlop Hardware, 20.14; R. L. Collins, 3.13; Donald Connelly, 1.51; H. F. Corbett, 832.00; Crane, Ltd., 712.22; Cross Machine Shop, 4.87; A. Dalgleish, 73.20; Day Lumber Co., 4.00; R. W. DeMorest, 1.00; Diamond State Fibre Co. of Canada, Ltd., 4.50; Dingwall Motors, Ltd., 57.75; Dunn Hardware Co., Ltd., 435.45; Fairway Stores, 131.14; G. E. Farlinger, 73.73; Jno. Fee, 14.46; A. N. Fenn, 32.83; Fisher Dray Line, 8.85; Fowler Hardware Co., 3.00; General Radio Co., 19.16; H. Goodman & Son, 5.00; Goold, Shapley & Muir Co., 1.20; L. G. Greene Co., 4.00; Greenwood Electric & Hardware, 5.32; Gregory, Greek Co., 148.86; R. Gustafson, 272.19; A. N. Haddad, 43.07;

Fire Ranging—Continued

Improvements—Continued.

Halliday Co., Ltd., 80.59; Jno. Harju, 72.00; Hawkins Bros., 1.50; Pete Hawryluk, 82.80; Hydro-Electric Power Commission, 76.73; International Resistance Co., Ltd., 4.41; W. R. Jackson & Co., 6.76; D. Johnston & Son, 4.35; Keys Hardware, 55.62; Laberge Lumber Co., 8.95; J. A. Laflamme, 135.88; W. F. Langworthy, 18.10; J. A. Lablanc, 11.70; Mahon Electric Co., Ltd., .82; Marshall-Wells Co., Ltd., 10.51; E. J. Maxwell, 78.00; Allan A. J. MacDonald, 220.45; McGill Hardware, 13.00; D. McLellan, 12.57; C. W. Mullet, 9.60; Northern Canada Supply Co., Ltd., .30; Northern Electric Co., 4,610.13; Penage Property Owners' Association, 4.04; A. L. Perkins & Co., 61.41; Peter Perlin, 55.53; Eugene F. Phillip Electric Works, 609.46; Thos. Pocklington Co., 6.00; City of Port Arthur Building Inspection Department, 1.50; Corporation of the City of Port Arthur, 2.24; Poupore Lumber Co., 2.24; Jos. Puurula, 99.00; B. H. Rands, 244.45; J. W. Robertson, 627.00; L. F. Robertson, 2.50; Rossport Trading Co., 12.45; Rowland & Atkins, 50.00; Jno. Russell, 42.90; T. S. Ryan, 10.25; Sim-Mac Lines, Ltd., 1.60; W. J. Snellgrove, 238.20; Standard Chemical Co., Ltd., 29.25; Star Grocery, 13.70; Stirling's Plumbing Service, 2.14; Elijah Switzer, 22.10; Tapp & Hobbs, 68.53; Thunder Bay Lumber Co., 447.69; Toronto Radio & Sports, Ltd., 3.15; Tucker Bros., 350.00; Scott Vader, 34.00; Watson & Lloyd, 9.90; Williams Hardware, 31.97; Woodside Bros., 16.40. **Miscellaneous disbursements by** Forestry **Branch Officers.**—M. H. Baker, 44.30; Alex. Brown, 1.00; A. B. Connell, 56.92; H. W. Crosbie, 3.40; E. S. Davison, 41.25; T. A. Fenton, 14.00; G. J. Hass, 6.81; W. H. Hawkins, 3.75; N. M. Kensit, 281.09; H. M. Legris, 13.09; Thos. McCormick, 45.85; P. McEwen, 116.96; Chas. McGie, 8.60; Colin McInnis, 24.00; Jno. McNamara, 19.00; W. D. Pigott, 7.72; R. L. Snow, 22.50; S. D. Spence, .90; K. A. Stewart, 1.25; Wm. Stringer, 2.00; E. L. Ward, 10.00; Carl Wither, 7.00; Geo. Wither, 10.00 .... 12,942 60

Fire Fighting, Provisions, etc., $313,201.53.

Abitibi Power & Paper Co., 58.71; Algoma Central & H. B. Ry., 78.30; B. Ames, 12.00; G. Ames, 159.99; J. Antoine, 2.50; F. C. Armstrong Estate, 12.32; Geo. Armstrong, 25.00; Mrs. J. Armstrong, 102.22; Ashley Gold Mining Corporation, 37.75; Austin & Nicholson, 59.49; Rev. Father Bate, 10.00; Barnes & Oliver, 11.78; Paul Bateman, 18.00; N. Bazinette, 13.50; Bear Lake Camps, 5.00; Beauchesne Bros., 68.20; R. H. Beaulieu, 22.00; W. Beaulieu, 29.25; I. Bedard, 12.00; Joe Belanger, 107.84; S. Beltson, 1.25; Geo. Benger, 858.67; J. O. Bernier, 76.50; A. C. Bernier, 5.00; Bertrand Bros., 243.74; Alf. Berube, 6.09; Fabien Bissonette, 12.50; J. R. Booth, 152.21; D. Bowers, 25.63; Bowman's General Store, 237.63; T. B. Bradley, 40.67; F. Y. W. Braithwaite, 2.95; H. S. Brennan, 8.32; J. Brohm, 6.60; W. S. Bruce, 134.55; Bryce's Bakery, 19.26; Geo. Bucciarelli, 79.04; J. E. Buchanan, 12.35; G. A. Bullied & Son, 11.75; Chas. Burlanyett, 10.01; Burns & Co., Ltd., 430.93; Burns Transfer, 164.25; G. Burstrom, 9.00; A. Caccame, 170.16; C. Campbell, 12.00; Campbell & Gibbon, 201.70; F. C. Campbell, 15.05; M. C. Campbell & Co., 207.49; Canada Airways, Ltd., 13,459.28; Canadian Department Stores, 4.00; Canadian National Railways, 2,238.56; Canadian Oil Cos., Ltd., 571.41; Canadian Pacific Railway Co., 2,112.14; Cardinal Company, 3.00; Geo. Carlton, 16.85; Chalykoff & Co., 16.03; E. J. Chandonet, 78.71; Chapleau Drug Co., 3.25; A. Chauvin, 90.84; H. B. Christilaw, 156.17; Christoff & Co., 180.15; City Service Transfer, 52.63; D. A. Clark, 19.20; Elsie Closs, 88.08; Cockburn & Archer, 1.45; Cochrane-Dunlop Hardware Co., 4.00; J. H. Collins, 9.50; Donald Connelly, 945.02; Consumers Trading Co., 1,667.08; C. W. Cook, 10.00; Richard Cooper, 6.00; I. Corbett, 19.18; Frank Cosco, 23.01; A. A. Cotman, 5.75; Mrs. E. Cousineau, 12.50; S. D. Coveney, 89.87; Craig Lumber Co., 24.00; Crawley & McCracken, 6.25; C. Christonen, 1.60; H. F. Crowder, 2.00; F. G. Cybulskie, 1.87; N. Dainio, 2.00; J. A. Daoust, 30.15; E. Daoust, 273.17; Dolphis Daoust, 5.00; N. Daneff, 185.29; H. S. Davis, 125.24; Joe Deguire, 3.00; A. M. Delamere, 5.95; Geo. Delaney, 2.00; Mrs. A. Dellaire, 38.00; O. Demhemont, 63.65; Department of Indian Affairs, 186.75; Department of Northern Development, 104.99; L. Deshaies, 1.19; Joe Dessureault, 62.14; J. Dimoff, 18.00; Mike Dominick, 25.00; Dominion Stores, 154.37; Estate of David Dover, 4.65; L. Dubeau, 7.66; Duggan Bros., 9.46; Dunn Hardware Co., Ltd., 151.20; Mrs. C. R. Dunne, 5.05; T. Eaton Co., Ltd., 725.10; J. R. Ellet, 108.33; H. England, 14.51; A. S. Ericksen, 8.80; C. Ethier, 203.50; A. E. Fader, 80.00; Fairway Stores, 1,881.46; Falardeau & Forget, 42.53; G. E. Farlinger, 25.00; H. Feagan, 31.38; Frank Fera, 631.48; Ph. Filion, 18.58; Fisher Dray Line, 2,938.00; M. J. E. Fitzgerald, 40.94; Fitzergald Drug Store, Ltd., 39.00; Fitzsimmons Fruit Co., 49.50; H. H. Flesher & Co., 107.79; R. Foster, 43.93; Fowler Hardware Co., 26.38; Francey's Drug Store, 217.75; J. Fraser, 17.16; W. Fraser, 70.00; G. Freeberg, 37.50; Township of Freeman, 18.58; Jos.

Fire Ranging—Continued

Fire Fighting, Provisions, etc.—Continued.

Gagne, 24.00; W. R. Gardner, 13.90; Wm. Gavin, 31.50; General Airways, Ltd., 2,903.26; J. E. Gervais, 10.91; W. J. Gibson, 48.10; Gillies Bros., 6.50; Albert Giroux, 12.35; Mrs. Z. Giroulx, 8.00; Sam Godard, 1.00; H. Goodman & Son, 290.43; A. Gove, 1.25; H. H. Grace, 28.88; R. L. Graham, 2,639.03; S. A. Graham, 12.00; Green's Camp, 64.02; Grieve & Powell, 211.55; G. Guerin, 2.75; E. Guertin, 2.00; Judson A. Gunter, 17.40; John Hall, 25.50; R. Hagard, 7.50; J. A. Hamilton, 5.46; J. Harju, 379.48; Harris Abattoir, 3,383.19; Haverluck & Koval, 55.45; John A. Hawkins, 98.13; B. Hayes, 7.73; John W. Heald, 614.74; J. Herbert, 18.00; Geo. Hickerson, 5.00; W. Hickson, 10.50; Hoag Bros., 140.85; Mrs. R. Hobin, 3.50; Hobson, Gauthier, Ltd., 183.86; Hornepayne Baking Co., 9.58; Veikko Horppu, 2.00; Jos. Houle, 1.00; Hudson's Bay Co., 5,834.35; T. C. Huffman, 40.50; Humphrey Township, 11.08; Wm. Hunter, 4.10; Hydro-Electric Power Commission, 34.79; Ideal Grocery, 63.89; Industrial Farm, Burwash, 230.92; International Store, 66.52; International Transit, Ltd., 20.00; J. E. Jacques, 29.87; Jaffrey & Mellick Municipality, 231.72; Emile Janveau, 5.00; Leo Jean, 3.00; V. J. Jewell, 26.17; Johnson's Pharmacy, .60; C. Johnson, 12.00; A. E. Johnstone, 4.29; G. N. Johnston & Son, 59.85; S. R. Johnston, 21.00; Mrs. T. Keeting, 56.00; Kena Store, 247.26; J. D. Kenneally, 25.00; Kert & Co., 41.11; Cecil J. Kidd, 3.73; K. Kobal, 12.00; Wm. Kruschenski, 53.57; Lacey's Taxi, 2.50; J. B. LaCroix, 151.91; Fred LaFreniere, 13.50; D. Laframboise, 49.00; J. H. Lahie, 27.00; Lake Travers Camp, 32.09; Lang Lake Camps, 5.50; Lang & Ross, Ltd., 100.00; Robert Lang, 10.00; M. Lanin, 302.45; J. A. Lapalme, 908.66; Frank Lapointe, 40.00; R. Lemieux, 45.00; J. H. Leng, 2.80; Leonard's Transfer, 9.00; J. H. Lessard, 8.05; H. T. Lloyd, 290.25; E. T. Lozien, 110.70; Lynch Auto Sales, 39.47; Township of Machar, 5.75; L. A. Maki, 938.51; R. M. Mantyla, 1.50; Marine Laundry, 5.25; Marshall-Wells Co., Ltd., 1,332.74; F. Mathieson, 3.50; Mattawa Bakery, 25.67; Wm. McAuley, 10.00; Jas. McCann, 24.00; Larry McCann, 24.00; H. McDermid, 24.00; J. A. MacDonald, 68.00; Murray C. MacDonald, 87.87; L. MacDougall, 20.70; Wm. McGaughey, 76.54; A. M. McKechnie, 68.02; Township of McKellar, 10.00; E. J. McKinnon, 28.20; H. L. McKinnon & Co., 390.65; P. McMuldrock, 445.00; Township of Medora and Wood, 290.33; C. Merrill, 190.43; Merrill, Rhind & Walmsley, 406.05; Fred Michaud, 25.00; H. H. Middleton, 42.80; S. Miles, 10.50; Mining Corporation of Canada, Ltd., 19.50; Missinaibi Timber Co., 11.85; Monarch Oil Co., 3,034.84; Moore Bros., 1,549.24; Mrs. M. Morin, 12.00; E. Morley, 12.76; D. P. Morris, 15.83; W. L. Morrissey, 217.39; R. J. Mousseau, 16.00; Jas. Muir, 95.00; Wm. Muncaster, 45.00; H. L. Mundell, 267.97; J. H. Murphy, 20.00; C. & D. Murray, Ltd., 59.41; H. Naananen, 32.47; Nakina Bakery, 44.98; Nakina Fur & Supply Co., 288.19; Wm. G. Napier, 106.00; National Air Transport, 5,210.13; National Grocers, Ltd., 189.16; R. G. Nault, 3.50; Neale & Heath, 683.60; H. Nesbitt, 12.00; Nicholson Tire Surgery, 9.93; Nipigon Service Garage, 18.00; John Nixon, 12.85; Noelville Trading Co., 45.62; North Shore Transport Co., 15.20; Oak Airways, Ltd., 19,143.06; M. O'Connor, 35.75; Gilbert Ostler, 11.47; Mrs. Moise Paquette, 4.00; M. Pardy, 296.76; Alex. Parent, 2.10; Leslie Park, 50.00; C. R. Parker, 354.37; J. Parviainen, 5.00; Mrs. E. Patterson, 17.50; Mrs. J. A. Pelletier, 27.45; Wm. Pelletier, 1.20; A. L. Perkins & Co., 2.78; Mrs. A. Peterson, 171.78; S. Petrooch, 20.00; G. L. Pidgen, 79.21; B. Pigeon, 35.48; Pigeon Timber Co., Ltd., 5,138.56; J. C. Pinch, 128.96; Alf. Pitt, Ltd., 99.99; F. Ploufe, 6.00; A. Poitras, 5.00; H. H. Porlier, 379.68; Corporation of the City of Port Arthur, 8.40; Port Arthur Public Utilities, 85.78; Porter & Co., 235.33; O. E. Post, 356.33; H. Pow, 96.00; Pratt & Shanacy, 116.24; J. Prieur, 5.00; O. H. Pronger, 17.60; Provencher Bros., 238.25; Quality Meat & Grocery Co., Ltd., 1,838.91; R. L. Racicot, 94.15; V. Ragala, 15.75; A. Rahal, 3.50; A. Ramond, 1.60; Jos. Rancourt, 234.75; J. Randle, 25.00; Reamsbottom & Edwards, 25.47; E. L. Reid, 42.29; G. H. Reid, 4.40; Revillon Trading Co., 24.78; P. Richer, 6.00; Alphonse Rioux, 15.75; Emile Ritchie, 6.00; W. D. Ritchie & Son, 29.02; J. Robert, 71.45; Robinhood Mills, 69.81; J. Robinson, 8.00; C. S. Rollins, 9.11; Rossport Trading Co., 1,251.32; Harry Rouse, 5.00; H. H. Roy, 4.23; N. T. Roy, 7.00; D. V. Rumsey, 21.90; Sadowski & Co., 31.15; N. Salo, 173.83; Paul B. Sammons, 11.66; Zim Schell, 4.50; Tom Schell, 29.50; D. W. Scott, 30.67; Scott Motor Sales, 41.50; A. V. J. Selkirk, 594.62; Jos. Seymour, 10.50; Alf. Shaw, 6.80; Sioux Lookout Cash Store, 64.88; Colin Smith, 1.76; D. R. Smith, 27.55; Mrs. R. J. Smith, 5.50; Otto Somes, 10.00; Spadoni Bros., 630.36; Spanish River Lumber Co., 121.27; J. Spillett, 50.00; Standard Laundries, 253.50; Star Grocery, 1,073.41; Ed. Steep, 20.25; H. Stenlund, 150.00; Stevenson & Co., Ltd., 2.10; Wm. Stinson, 2.50; J. W. Stone Boat Manufacturing Co., 2.00; J. H. Strain, 3.00; Mrs. O. Strasein, 51.50; P. Strycholski, 9.50; D. M. Stuart, 34.63; Sudbury Boat & Canoe Co., 40.00; Sudbury Steam Laundry, 31.00; Sullivan's Grocery, 4.31; P. Sundstrom, 14.68 ;

Fire Ranging—Continued

Fire Fighting, Provisions, etc.—Continued.

Superior Chain Stores, 29.06; Frank Suszek, 24.50; Swift Canadian Co., Ltd., 2,722.52; Tapp & Hobbs, 8,259.44; B. Taracani, 12.00; Thos. Tario, 3.00; Timagami Timber Co., 131.95; N. Tessier, 4.00; J. A. Thompson, 7.30; Thomson's Restaurant, 68.25; Fred Tiplady, 435.93; Triangle Fish Co., 8.50; Alex. Tulloch & Sons, 38.60; Twin City Grain, 101.22; John Tyson, 24.95; Dean Udy, 60.67; J. A. Vaillancourt, 27.85; Louis Vaillancourt, 187.11; W. F. VanKoughnett, 40.00; F. A. Van Norman, 4.00; J. Z. Vinet, 329.00; John Vitkuske, 11.85; Jim Volpini, 5.00; D. B. Wagar, 10.30; Waldhof Farmers' Co-operative Club, 2.85; Wm. Wardrop, 46.75; Watson & Lloyd, 554.35; C. Webbs, 7.00; Wesley Taxi & Transfer Co., 57.00; Western Grocers, Ltd., 9,924.99; Western Oil Co., 320.06; William Wheeler, 18.50; White Drug Store, 6.20; Stan. White, 8.80; M. J. White, 733.79; Ida Wideman, 2.40; T. Wideman, 18.20; Mrs. W. Wilcox, 1.10; J. Williams, 5.00; J. S. Wilson, 36.50; A. Winer, 3.15; Wolfe & Collins, Ltd., 97.54; Joe Wood, 67.42; C. J. Wright, 95.38; L. Wutanaki, 5.00; Chas. Young, 9.00; A. Ziebell, 178.11. **Miscellaneous disbursements by Forestry Branch Officers**—Lloyd Acheson, 103.95; J. C. Alt, 120.18; Geo. Austin, 1.05; J. A. Bissonnette, 1.75; R. H. Bliss, 114.22; A. C. Bouchey, 54.60; E. Bouchey, .30; Alex. Brown, 5.00; J. B. Burns, 62.52; A. B. Connell, 988.85; W. D. Cram, 563.02; Wm. Darby, 6.60; E. S. Davison, .20; W. D. Dixon, 10.05; J. C. Dillon, 9.45; Thos. Dolen, 9.70; H. Elkington, 89.07; T. A. Fenton, 43.49; C. E. Foote, 949.24; Oscar Gulin, 12.00; W. J. Gibson, 22.48; J. A. Gillespie,733.45; E. J. Gilligan, 29.50; W. B. Greenwood, 96.05; G. J. Hass, 88.73; W. H. Hawkins, 260.26; P. Hoffman, 156.32; A. Holinshead, .40; W. A. Hooper, 10.00; M. R. Horn, 55.85; D. J. Kennedy, 438.38; N. M. Kensit, 44.24; H. M. Legris, 12.30; J. P. Legris, 4.25; J. R. Loucks, 1.20; T. E. Mackey, 7.50; J. B. Matthews, 5.35; A. C. Mitchell, 2.50; Gerald Munro, 7.60; Thos. McCormick, 162.10; P. McEwen, 31.20; Chas. McGhie, 10.91; J. McGloan, 3.15; Colin McInnis, 5.60; John McNamara, 5.98; M. E. McNulty, 2.68; H. V. Orr, 8.40; F. Parmeter, 3.40; C. C. Parr, 70.52; David Pender, 16.70; E. E. Potter, 37.25; V. H. Prewer, 3.50; Max Rabbitts, 113.87; Jas. Ruxton, .40; S. V. Ryan, 2.00; W. Sangster, .48; R. Simpson, 13.15; R. L. Snow, 7.50; S. D. Spence, 12.65; K. A. Stewart, 3,850.69; J. H. Strain, 241.81; Wm. Stringer, 26.28; Alfred Tait, 13.25; W. E. Van Clieaf, 8.55; E. L. Ward, 9.93; R. E. Watson, 121.20; Bogert Wilson, 21.03; Alex. Wylie, 2.00; W. Yeomans, 16.00; Murray Young, 3.50. Wages for extra fire fighters, 172,047.70 .... 313,201 53

Express, Freight, Telephone, Telegrams, etc. $19,858.38.

Algoma Central & H. B. Ry., 86.47; I. Bedard, 10.00; Bell Telephone Co., 75.40; Brougham & Gratton Telephone Co., 154.50; R. M. Brunton, 27.00; Calabogie & Renfrew Phone Co., 15.00; Canadian National Railways, 1,365.99; Canadian Pacific Railway, 198.51; Mrs. Carmichael, 40.00; J. A. Cassidy, 1.50; Chapleau Telephone System, 35.00; Chappe Municipal Telephone System, 59.90; Joseph Charron, 12.00; Cockburn & Archer, 1.76; Donald Connelly, 3.21; N. S. Coughlin, 114.00; J. A. Daoust, 5.00; De Luxe Transport, 145.00; Department of Highways, .50; Department of Marine and Fisheries, 25.45; Joe Donnelly, 6.00; Dungannon Municipal Telephone System, 21.00; Frank Edwards, .75; Mrs. H. Elkington, 100.00; Exide Batteries of Canada, Ltd., 28.66; Fairway Stores, 4.87; Fisher Dray Line, 64.25; Forest Fraser, 7.00; A. E. Gardiner, 34.51; Glamorgan Municipal Telephone System, 15.75; Mrs. Stanley Gregg, 100.00; Hagarty Municipal Telephone System, 43.15; J. A. Hamilton, 1.50; W. Harju, 4.00; Hopetown Phone Co., 10.00; Hutchings Trans. Co., 15.99; Hydro-Electric Power Commission, 100.00; Kapuskasing Garage, 7.20; Town of Kapuskasing, 46.16; Kert & Co., 5.00; S. Koruna, 8.50; J. B. LaCroix, 1.50; Lake of Bays & Haliburton Phone Co., 6.00; John Leckie, Ltd., 1.20; Lynch Auto Sales, 158.06; Frank Lyon, 30.00; Thos. McCormick, 25.25; Mrs. J. McLaren, 100.00; C. Merrill, 41.37; S. Miles, 3.75; Monarch Oil Co., 2.06; Monteagle & Herschel Telephone Co., 46.00; J. B. Moore, 10.00; Muskoka-Parry Sound Telephone Co., 24.03; J. W. Nicholson, 30.00; Nipissing Municipal Telephone Co., 10.00; Northern Telephone Co., 38.45; C. B. Oakes, 42.00; O'Connor Telephone System, 2.10; Opeongo Lumber Co., 4.00; C. Oullette, 25.00; E. Pellow, 14.38; People's Telegraph & Telephone Co., 141.42; Mrs. P. Plotz, 100.00; Port Arthur Public Utilities, 1,069.73; O. E. Post, 6.83; Y. Rajala, 6.75; L. F. Robertson, 2.50; Sherwood Municipal Telephone System, 70.90; Shevlin-Clarke Co., Ltd., 610.00; Town of Sioux Lookout, 21.35; Otto Somes, 10.00; Spence & Monteith Telephone Co., 11.50; James Sprackett, 20.00; Temiskaming and Northern Ontario Railway Commission, 34.28; F. Upland, 23.50; A. Vick, 9.90; Jas. Vogan, 40.00; Wesley Taxi & Transfer Co., 62.00; Municipality of Widdifield, 20.00; Widdifield Telephone System, 9.00. **Miscellaneous disbursements by Forestry Branch Officers**—K. Acheson, 3.34; Lloyd Acheson, 300.56; J. C. Ault, 1.50; Geo. Ash,

Fire Ranging—Continued

Express, Freight, Telephone, Telegrams, etc.—Continued.

5.00; Geo. Austin, 2.00; Ed. Bliss, 2.00; R. H. Bliss, 317.01; A. C. Bouchey, 116.07; E. Bouchey, 72.06; Alex. Brown, 3.20; J. B. Burns, 44.67; A. C. Cleaveley, 17.00; A. B. Connell, 801.88; W. D. Cram, 1,011.92; H. W. Crosbie, 717.06; Wm. Darby, 4.10; E. S. Davison, 339.63; W. D. Dickson, 6.02; J. C. Dillon, 67.06; C. R. Dunn, 5.08; H. Elkington, 99.38; John Eno, 1.25; T. A. Fenton, 19.73; C. E. Foote, 298.66; W. A. Forsythe, .50; W. R. Gardner, 182.42; W. J. Gibson, 45.65; J. A. Gillespie, 271.01; E. J. Gilligan, 252.21; W. H. Graham, 4.00; H. Green, 7.99; W. B. Greenwood, 444.34; T. C. Haley, 11.32; F. Hamilton, 269.19; G. J. Hass, 216.75; W. H. Hawkins, 340.96; C. E. Hindson, 39.65; P. Hoffman, 150.33; W. A. Hooper, 37.43; M. R. Horn, 135.39; D. J. Kennedy, 412.54; N. M. Kensit, 1,150.19; F. Landry, 5.25; H. M. Legris, 86.45; J. P. Legris, 85.55; J. R. Loucks, 62.36; T. E. Mackey, 266.20; J. B. Matthews, 11.74; A. C. Mitchell, 9.17; Gerald Munro, 12.69; H. L. McCausland, 157.38; Thos. McCormick, 163.03; C. W. McDonald, 13.34; P. McEwen, 626.54; Chas. McGhie, 2.50; Colin McInnis, 13.32; John McIntyre, 1.90; John McNamara, 6.15; K. W. McNeill, 18.76; M. E. McNulty, 13.00; H. V. Orr, 399.33; F. Parmeter, 18.09; H. H. Parsons, 23.79; C. C. Parr, 114.15; David Pender, 1.97; Ben Perrigo, 11.50; W. D. Pigott, 95.25; E. E. Potter, 274.98; V. H. Prewer, 15.86; Max Rabbitts, 105.25; Geo. Reesor, 9.00; M. Roadhouse, 3.00; C. H. Robinson, 5.50; Jas. Ruxton, 83.10; F. G. Saunders, 21.30; R. Simpson, 38.46; R. L. Snow, 3.82; S. D. Spence, 280.29; K. A. Stewart, 1,973.21; J. H. Strain, 141.23; Wm. Stringer, 11.60; Alfred Tait, 21.80; A. Taylor, 1.00; W. E. Van Clieaf, 9.50; E. L. Ward, 402.28; R. E. Watson, 26.34; N. F. Welch, 2.00; Bogert Wilson, 14.90; R. K. Wilson, 52.67; Geo. Wombwell, 28.54.......................... 19,858 38

Gas and Oil, $42,465.03.

Algoma Central & Hudson's Bay Ry., 4.53; Austin & Nicholson, 24.98; John Bartholomew, 25.50; A. Beauparlant, 6.03; Berini Motor Sales, 3.70; A. M. Blemkie, 1.75; Blind River Garage, 316.19; J. R. Booth, 58.75; W. N. Boyes, 13.95; F. Y. W. Braithwaite, 47.74; V. Brisson, 2.25; Geo. Bucciarelli, 183.66; Burk & Avery, .99; Canadian Johnson Motors, 13.61; Canadian National Railways, 13.58; Canadian Oil Cos., 7,826.98; Canadian Pacific Railway, 3.77; Carpenter-Hixon Co., 4.55; Chalykoff & Co., 338.15; D. W. Clayton, 223.50; Cockburn & Archer, 23.45; Cochrane-Dunlop Hardware, 32.85; Donald Connelly, 5.16; J. A. Daoust, 1.75; E. Daoust, 16.20; Department of Highways, 69.32; Dunn Hardware Co., Ltd., 10.80; Herb Edwards, 5.94; Elk Lake Garage & Machine, 104.34; Englehart Hardware, 1.15; Fairway Stores, 1,314.40; A. N. Fenn, .20; Get Gas, Ltd., 1,459.24; Gibson Garage, 129.39; Goddard's Garage, 32.80; H. Goodman & Son, 8.40; Gordon E. Graham, 7.86; Grieve & Powell, 1.05; Chas. A. Guenette, .80; N. Heita, 7.50; Hudson's Bay Co., 27.30; Imperial Oil Co., 15,089.81; Industrial Farm, Burwash, 3.45; E. W. Jones, 238.93; Kapuskasing Supply Co., 93.78; Keyes Hardware, 4.40; Cecil J. Kidd, 171.38; J. B. Lacroix, 2.00; Lesage Motor Sales, 81.08; H. T. Lloyd, 2.80; Marshall Motor Car Co., 2.75; Maxwell Bros., 13.17; L. McCloskey, 368.25; McColl-Frontenac Oil Co., 2,388.63; H. McDermott, 25.42; Allan A. J. MacDonald, 3.91; R. McGarvey, 7.83; Mrs. M. F. McKey, 15.50; McNaught Lumber Co., 5.85; Monarch Oil Co., 2,538.92; J. B. Moore, 57.00; W. L. Morrissey, 44.73; C. W. Mullet, 1.60; Myles & Son Hardware, .05; National Auto Sales, 3.00; Northern Garage, 5.10; Northern Oil Co., 848.92; Northern Telephone Co., 3.20; Opeongo Lumber Co., 15.30; Gilbert Ostler, 33.85; Patricia Transportation Co., Ltd., 636.55; Pembroke Service Garage, 9.13, A. L. Perkins & Co., 14.40; Bill Phillips, 25.00; Pierce & Radke, 1.75; J. Porco & Co., garage, 7.72; H. H. Porlier, 15.30; O. E. Post, 278.74; Powassan Garage, 7.08; Pratt & Shanacy, 3.55; F. R. Robertson, .50; E. A. Rogers, 14.85; Scott's Boat Livery, 1,007.39; Scott Motor Sales, 1,094.80; Shiel's Garage, 6.25; Smith & Chapple, Ltd., 137.91; Soo Gasoline & Oil Co., Ltd., 358.40; Spanish River Lumber Co., 54.50; Geo. Stephens, 202.67; Triangle Fish Co., 2.80; J. A. Vaillancourt, 2.45; Louis Vaillancourt, 16.23; W. A. Warlick, 6.40; Wesley Taxi & Transfer Co., 30.00; Western Oil Co., 508.23; R. H. Wilson, 27.00; A. R. Wood, 2,663.09. **Miscellaneous disbursements by Forestry Branch Officers**—Lloyd Acheson, 19.40; M. Ardenne, 3.30; Geo. Austin, 7.28; A. C. Bouchey, 1.94; E. Bouchey, 4.88; Alex. Brown, 1.63; J. B. Burns, 4.45; A. B. Connell, 4.90; W. D. Cram, 1.68; H. W. Crosbie, 34.75; J. C. Dillon, 105.63; H. Elkington, 52.66; W. J. Gibson, 2.05; J. A. Gillespie, 32.59; R. F. Goodall, 2.80; W. B. Greenwood, 20.47; G. J. Hass, 100.21; W. H. Hawkins, 10.80; C. E. Hindson, 3.49; P. Hoffman, 15.53; M. R. Horn, 1.51; D. J. Kennedy, 66.76; H. M. Legris, 49.09; T. E. Mackey, 7.21; Thos. McCormick, 28.02; C. W. McDonald, 5.69; Colin McInnis, 4.07; John McNamara, 1.75; M. E. McNulty, 28.16; H. V. Orr, 2.00; David Pender, .76;

Fire Ranging—Continued

Gas and Oil—Continued.

W. D. Pigott, 3.97; V. H. Prewer, 5.25; R. Simpson, 6.39; S. D. Spence, 3.15; K. A. Stewart, 93.80; J. H. Strain, 15.94; Wm. Stringer, 73.78; Alfred Tait, 3.72; E. L. Ward, 13.05; R. E. Watson, 43.16............................ 42,465 03

Repairs, $59,635.75.

Abitibi Power & Paper Co., 2.00; Acme Laundry, 269.35; Acme Timber Co., 31.49; Aikenhead Hardware, Ltd., 15.36; H. Alcock, 7.50; Algoma Central & H. B. Ry., 736.62; Algoma Steel Corporation, 1.00; Mrs. Alex. Alves, 20.00; Carl Anderson, 7.00; Anderson Boat Co., 19.00; Arco Co., Ltd., 5.75; M. Armstrong, 15.84; Arrow Garage & Service, 2.60; Art Metropole, 4.93; G. E. Atkinson, 7.50; Atlas Radio Corporation, Ltd., 8.00; Austin & Nicholson, 6.30; Auto Electric Service Co., 19.28; Auto Glass Supplies, 12.85; Bakelite Corporation, 15.00; H. J. Baldwin, 27.53; Bannon Bros., 10.34; Bartlett Auto Service, 8.00; Barton & Fisher, 24.00; Battery Service Station, 31.97; K. N. Baturensky, 7.70; Bay City Machine Works, 224.52; Walter Beatty Estate, 111.28; Wm. Beatty Co., 80.99; Beauchesne Bros., .30; Jos. Beaulieu, 5.25; A. Beauparlant, 2.01; A. Beauvais, 18.00; M. Beauvais, 2.00; T. Beauvais, 4.00; I. Bedard, 23.25; Estate of J. H. Bell, 6.65; Bell Fuel Service, 178.97; Bell Telephone Co., 12.16; Berini Motor Sales, 2.00; J. O. Bernier, 35.00; Bertrand Bros., 15.00; Bert's Battery, 8.50; Black & Decker, 27.97; Oliver Blais Co., 105.81; A. M. Blemkie, 24.05; Blind River Garage, 344.52; Boden & Bassingthwaite, 27.55; D. Bohm, 30.45; Jos. Bois, 18.23; J. R. Booth, 16.50; Bottan, Beebe & Grainger, 1.50; F. Y. W. Braithwaite, 88.96; Green Motor Co., 1.00; J. T. Brett, 44.61; V. Brisson, 67.39; F. L. Buchanan, Ltd., 59.00; Burgess Battery Co., 69.95; A. A. Burke, 14.77; Burns Transfer, 6.00; Burton's Garage, Ltd., 5.25; Chas. Bush, Ltd., .50; Lorne Callahan, 30.25; D. A. Campbell, 960.00; Campbell Heating Co., 49.35; Canada Creosoting Co., 5.00; Canada Paint Co., 89.23; Canada Power & Paper Corporation (Consolidated Paper Corporation, Ltd.), 8.00; Canada Wire & Cable Co., 16.27; Canadian Canoe Co., 137.76; Canadian Fairbanks-Morse Co., Ltd., 4,177.50; Canadian General Electric Co., Ltd., 72.36; Canadian Industries, Ltd., 839.21; Canadian Johnson Motor Co., 1,339.53; Canadian Marconi, 3.25; Canadian National Railways, 2,192.83; Canadian Pacific Railway Co., 200.18; Canadian S.K.F. Co., Ltd., 1.48; Joe Capute, 6.25; J. F. Card, 8.95; H. Carlbonn, 17.35; Ed. Caron, 9.50; Carpenter-Hixon Co., 103.97; Cascade Laundry, 60.00; Central Garage, 4.00; Central Motors, 226.16; Central Tent & Awning, 40.45; Charland's Battery Service, 32.25; Joe Charron, 10.00; S. J. Cherry, 95.07; H. Cheyne, 86.25; H. P. Christilaw, 2.24; Christoff & Co., 1.50; Clare Bros. & Co., 2.25; D. W. Clayton, 6.42; Cockburn & Archer, 554.52; Cochrane-Dunlop Hardware, 1,560.96; Cochrane Machine Works, 148.17; Collins Tire & Battery, 4.00; Connelly-Mewett, 36.60; Donald Connelly, 69.45; Consolidated Plate Glass Co., 1.39; Consumers Trading Co., 1.00; Coulas Garage, 8.40; A. M. Cowey, 185.75; Chas. W. Cox, 77.36; Crane, Ltd., 18.99; A. Cross & Co., 19.12; Cross Machine Co., 169.13; Crosswell Bros., 21.70; A. W. Daball, 51.20; J. A. Daoust, 12.00; A. Dalgleish, 15.25; K. Daniels, 9.75; J. J. Darlington, 4.50; Davey Bros., 26.25; E. S. Davison, 10.52; Davison's Garage, 17.55; Day Lumber Co., 9.90; Department of Health, 5.40; Department of Highways, 264.86; Department of Northern Development, 12.10; S. Deslauriers, 39.35; Dingwall Motors, Ltd., 355.47; Domic Tie & Lumber Co., Ltd., 153.16; Dominion Motors, Ltd., 61.73; Dominion Oxygen Co., 9.50; Dougall Motor Car Co., 112.39; Doyle's Garage, 13.30; Town of Dryden, 9.52; Dryden Motors, .75; Duncan Bros., 191.99; Dunn Hardware Co., Ltd., 736.46; Mrs. C. R. Dunne, 19.20; Gus Dupont, 20.00; Durance Bros., 110.64; John East Co., 81.27; Eastern Lumber Co., 2.50; Eastman Kodak Stores, .78; T. Eaton Co., Ltd., 42.44; Edward's Hardware, 9.40; Electric Specialty Co., 4.48; Elk Lake Garage & Machine, 289.77; A. E. Elliott, .75; C. Ellis, 2.05; Empire Coal & Lumber Co., 37.00; Endress & Auld, Ltd., 95.67, Englehart Hardware, .70; Espanola Garage, 1.00; Evans Co., Ltd., 317.74; Exide Batteries of Canada, Ltd., 423.85; Fairyway Stores, 353.97; A. Falkoski, 5.00; G. E. Farlinger, 48.12; Fassett Lumber Co., 35.96; John Fee, 58.46; Feldman Timber Co., 3.62; A. N. Fenn, 409.42; Ferguson Electric, 9.13; Frank Findlay, 2.70; Findlay's, Ltd., 42.22; F. W. Fischer, 23.10; Fisher Dray Line, 54.00; Flockhart Bros., 4.80; Corporation of City of Fort William, 50.00; E. Fortin, 9.00; Fowler Hardware Co., 68.17; Francey's Drug Store, 7.85; D. M. Fraser, Ltd., 76.25; Forest Fraser, 5.00; Fyr-Fyter Company of Canada, 22.05; M. Gagnon, 9.50; Paul Gamache, 1.50; Garage Supply Co., Ltd., 129.40; A. E. Gardiner, .70; F. S. Gardiner, 3.50; Gardner's Garage, 7.46; Gastmeier & Co., .10; Gem Electric Shop, 22.39; J. D. Gemmell, 12.00; Get Gas, Ltd., 299.90; Gibson Garage, 315.51; Gillies Bros., 6.00; Gillmor & Noden, 1.72; H. Goodman & Son, 112.95; Goold, Shapley & Muir Co., 25.60; Gordon E. Graham, 215.04; Grain Port Motors, Ltd., 305.42;

Fire Ranging—Continued

Repairs—Continued.

Grant-Holden-Graham, 6.43; H. L. Graton, 10.00; Greenwood Electric & Hardware, 119.62; Gregory, Greek Co., 27.13; Grieve & Powell, 10.25; Grove Motors, 16.85; Chas. H. Guenette, 35.46; R. Gustafson, 104.45; Adam Hall, 12.41; Halliday Superior, Ltd., 82.70; Halliday Co., Ltd., 95.23; John Harju, 2.00; Hawkins Bros., 29.80; N. Heita, 55.00; Henry Motor Co., 12.50; Hesson Lumber Co., 4.85; Higgins & Burke, Ltd., 3.85; Hill, Clark, Francis, Ltd., 32.62; Hinsperger Harness Co., 60.65; Hose Hardware Co., 457.90; H. S. Howland Sons & Co., 7.12; Hudson's Bay Co., 153.18; D. S. Humphrey, 82.90; J. P. Hunt, 7.90; Wm. Hunter, 20.00; Hydro-Electric Power Commission, 21.66; Industrial Farm, Burwash, 2.40; Instruments, Ltd., 30.40; International Nickel Co., 6.00; International Paint (Canada), Ltd., 119.36; International Resistance Co., Ltd., 7.20; C. H. Jackson, 4.97; W. R. Jackson & Co., 8.43; F. C. James, 3.80; H. H. Joanisse, 1.90; Johnson Bros., 6.00; Johnson & Co., 143.94; E. W. Jones, 315.26; M. Kanokko, 10.00; Kapuskasing Garage, 60.02 ; Kapuskasing Supply Co., 275.05; Town of Kapuskasing, 2.38; Kay Supply Co., 1.21; Keewatin Lumber Co., 464.93; Kelly & Kimberley, 223.65; Town of Kenora, 22.00; Kermath Manufacturing Company of Canada, Ltd., 337.07; Kert & Co., 13.81; Keuffel & Esser Co., 6.92; Keyes Hardware, 176.89; Keys Supply Co., 354.85; Cecil J. Kidd, 11.08; S. Koruna, 16.00; John Kron & Son, 26.50; Arthur Labbe, 3.28; W. Ladouceur, 2.00; L. L. Lafleur, 9.00; Lakehead Motor Co. 176.60; P. Lantheir, 18.00; J. A. Lapalme, 65.90; J. A. Leblanc, 17.19; John Leckie, Ltd., 199.47; Lee Bros., 29.75; Legree Hardware, 2.25; Lesage Motor Sales, 233.43; Lindstrom & Nilson, 584.72; Link-Belt, Ltd., 9.54; Thos. Linklater, 3.00; H. T. Lloyd, 2.20; Lundy Fence Co., 24.48; Lynch Auto Sales, 112.63; MacKay-Morton, Ltd., 36.50; Oscar Macklin, 8.25; J. W. Magnus Co., 41.00; Mahon Electric Co., Ltd., 14.57; Marshall-Ecclestone, 60.53; Marshall Motor Car, Ltd., 107.12; Marshall-Wells Co., Ltd., 129.69; Massey-Harris Co., Ltd., 1.50; Matheson Garage, 4.25; A. Matthews, Ltd., 2.95; Maxwell Bros., 598.52; L. McCloskey, 38.15; H. McDermott, 42.63; Alex. McDonald, 15.00; Allan A. J. McDonald, 177.88; K. McDonald & Sons, 2.40; McDowell Motors, 32.99; R. McGarvey, 212.01; McGill Hardware, 1,101.87; Mrs. M. F. McKey, 77.29; J. W. McKinley, 5.95; McKinley Hardware Co., 33.17; D. K. McLaren, 16.62; D. McLellan, 19.78; McLeod Garage, 450.53; McNaught Lumber Co., 12.05; J. S. L. McRae, 90.28; J. McVey, 229.14; C. Merrill, 11.20; Merrill, Rhind & Walmsley, 3.25; C. Michelson, 15.00; Mickle, Dyment & Son, 8.65; Milne's Garage, 47.45; Minaki Boathouse, 3.00; Missinaibi Timber Co., 53.60; Mitchell's Service Station, 61.40; Monarch Motors, 62.37; Monarch Oil Co., 51.28; Moore's Hotel, 15.00; J. R. Morris, 11.60; Fred Morrison, 2.75; W. L. Morrissey, 75.02; C. W. Mullett, 13.52; Harry L. Mundell, 41.07; C. & D. Murray, Ltd., 77.90; Jas. Murray, 10.01; Muskoka-Parry Sound Telephone Co., 7.20; Frank G. Myers, 4.10; Myles & Son Hardware, 21.43; Nash & Chrysler Motors, 18.07; National Auto Sales, 248.16; National Co., Inc., 9.61; National Grocers, Ltd., 2.75; Neale & Heath, 14.85; Nicholson's Tire Surgery, 409.78; Nipissing Electric Supply Co., Ltd., 12.20; Nipissing Laundry Co., Ltd., 67.95; North Bay Garage, 776.14; North Star Garage, 6.50; Northern Canada Supply Co., Ltd., 256.78; Northern Coal & Wood Co., 113.75; Northern Electric Co., 2,503.69; Northern Garage, 32.53; Northern Oil Co., 4.25; Northern Telephone Co., 1.15; The Nugget, 1.85; Oba Public School Board, 132.00; J. C. O'Brien, 23.50; Sam Onarheim, 118.80; Ontario Hughes-Owens Co., 6.86; Opeongo Lumber Co., 8.18; Osborne & Macklain, 45.05; Gilbert Ostler, 2.01; C. Oullette, 16.00 ; Packard-Ontario Motor Co., 35.00; Geo. Page, 10.50; Pakesley Lumber Co., 20.00; Palangio Motor Sales, 10.75; M. Pardy, 10.50; Town of Parry Sound, 6.51; C. R. Parker, 33.00; Patterson Bros., Ltd., 2.00; Patterson Machine Works, 9.05; H. J. Paul, 4.00; Geo. Pearsall & Son, 3.60; Pearson Batteries, Ltd., 1.00; Peckover's, 3.59; Peerless Hardware, 2.05; E. Pellow, 104.80; Pembroke Laundry, Cleaning Dyeing Co., 115.56; Pembroke Motors, 40.84; Pembroke Service Garage, 157.80; A. L. Perkins & Co., 69.87; Peter Perlin, 99.10; Perron & Marsh, 17.75; Peterborough Canoe Co., 497.35; Mrs. A. Peterson, 18.85; W. F. Petry, 25.25; E. Phillips, 2.00; Pierce & Radke, 130.63; D. Pike Co., 2.00; Thos. Pocklington Co., 160.98; J. Porco & Co. Garage, 64.02; Port Arthur Garage, 1.20 ; Corporation of the City of Port Arthur, 118.95; Port Arthur Ship Building Co., 9.90; Porter & Co., .70; O. E. Post, 48.05; Poupore Lumber Co., 5.38; Powassan Garage, 160.88; Powassan Planing Mill, 5.00; Pratt Engineering Co., 59.85; Pratt & Shanacy, 66.17; Preston Machine Co., 10.00; Provincial Tire Corporation, 76.98; Quality Meat & Grocery Co., Ltd., 5.74; B. H. Rands, 363.24; Rashotte Bros., 140.26; Red Wing Motor Co., 31.88; Remington Typewriters, Ltd., 16.00; Renfrew Wood Products, 7.95; J. W. Richardson, 1.20; Amedie Ritchie, 20.00; J. Robert, 64.83; C. Robertson Transfer, 36.00; F. R. Robertson, 35.20; Rothschild's Garage, 42.55; Alex. Russell, 138.00; Russell Bros., Port Arthur, 1.50; Russell Bros., Fort Frances, 73.04; Sagamo Co., Ltd., 5.70; Scott's Boat Livery, 30.53; Scott

Fire Ranging—Continued

Repairs—Continued.

Motor Sales, 239.98; Searchmont Lumber Co., 38.82; Louis, Seguin & Fils, 4.80; A. V. J. Selkirk, 66.00; Reg. Seller, 32.20; Service Station Equipment, 1.32; Len Shaw, 52.40; Sherwin-Williams Co., 117.60; Shevlin-Clarke Co., Ltd., 206.07; Shur-Line Automatic, 7.50; Sid's Service Station, 12.54; Signal Electric Mfg., 9.74; Chas. Sims, 12.00; J. A. Simmers, Ltd., 37.36; Sim-Mack Lines, Ltd., 1.60; Town of Sioux Lookout, 288.00; Smith Agricultural Chemical Co., 7.00: W. E. Smith, 3.89; Smith & Chapple, Ltd., 70.72; Smith & Travers Co., 187.78; Smyth Bros. Garage, 9.52; Soo Garage, Ltd., 21.14; Soo Lumber & Mill Co., Ltd., 22.80; Spadoni Bros., 66.00; Spruce Falls Power & Paper Co., 33.55; St. Lawrence Engine Co., 23.40; Standard Chemical Co., Ltd., 53.50; Standard Laundries, Ltd., 676.21; Standard Planing Mills and Lumber Co., Ltd., 12.66; Star Grocery, 17.18; J. W. Stone Boat Mfg. Co., 73.54; Mrs. G. H. Stubbins, 30.40; Sudbury Boat & Canoe Co., 230.27; City of Sudbury, 81.05; Sudbury Steam Laundry, 36.40; Superior Chain Stores, 7.20; Superior Welding Co., 5.15; Frank Suszek, 103.19; Swayze's, 1.25; Elijah Switzer, 10.00; Tallack Bros., 74.25; Tapp & Hobbs, 24.75; J. M. Taylor, 4.10; Teck Motor Sales, 42.47; T. & N. O. Railway Commission, 531.98; Jos. Thibeault, 3.00; Thunder Bay Lumber Co., 813.71; J. B. Tiefenbacker, 8.35; Timmins Garage Co., 12.00; Toronto Battery & Electric Co., 21.05; Toronto Bearing & Parts, 11.85; Toronto Simonizing Co., 8.00; Trout Creek Lumber Co., 28.11; Trudeau Motor Sales, 25.94; Municipal Corporation of Tweed, 470.06; Twin City Grain, .80; Twinport Auto Sales, 18.38; United Motor Service, 1.96; United Typewriter Co., 89.99; Valspar Corporation, Ltd., 13.13; Frank Virkus, 15.00; Wabi Iron Works, Ltd., 36.44; W. C. Warburton & Co., 7.62; W. A. Warlick, 42.90; Watson, Jack & Co., 8,468.65; Wells Hardware Co., Ltd., 25.98; Wesley Taxi & Transfer Co., 1.00; Western Grocers, Ltd., 44.25; White & McDowell, 36.90; H. Wilkins, 171.40; Williams Hardware, 467.49; A. R. Williams Machinery Co., Ltd., 60.57; Williams & Wilson, 7.20; Willys-Overland Sales, Ltd., 112.86; J. Winterbottom, .55; Wolfe & Collins, Ltd., 5.35; A. R. Wood, 83.05; Woods Mfg. Co., 9.50; Yull's Auto Electric Service, 1.25; A. Ziebell, 38.50;—**Miscellaneous Disbursements by Forestry Branch Officers**—Lloyd Acheson, 95.41; Geo. Austin, 4.25; R. H. Bliss, 59.24; A. C. Bouchey, 24.10; E. Bouchey, 23.21; Alex. Brown, 1.00; J. B. Burns, 5.65; A. C. Cleaveley, 5.00; A. B. Connell, 295.23; W. D. Cram, 154.97; H. W. Crosbie, 19.10; Wm. Darby, 9.05; H. S. Davis, .85; E. S. Davison, 22.13; W. D. Dickson, 1.30; J. C. Dillon, .95; A. L. Dunne, 8.40; H. Elkington, 95.62; John Eno, .70; T. A. Fenton, 11.35; C. E. Foote, 8.08; W. A. Forsythe, 2.50; W. J. Gibson, 19.31; J. A. Gillespie, 128.83; E. J. Gilligan, 11.01; H. Green, 4.25; W. B. Greenwood, 65.88; T. C. Haley, 6.80; Fred Hamilton, 167.56; G. J. Hass, 93.32; W. H. Hawkins, 29.06; C. E. Hindson, 20.74; P. Hoffman, 64.39; M. R. Horn, 39.19; Percy Ianson, 1.50; D. J. Kennedy, 126.96; N. M. Kensit, 7.42; H. M. Legris, 87.26; J. R. Loucks, 14.86; C. E. Lucas, 1.50; T. E. Mackey, 143.92; J. V. Matthews, .70; C. R. Mills, 14.78; A. C. Mitchell, 3.50; H. L. McCausland, 1.33; Thos. McCormick, 106.05; C. W. McDonald, 7.40; P. McEwen, 325.29; Colin McInnis, 24.20; John McIntyre, 2.60; John McNamara, 31.57; M. E. McNulty, 21.13; H. V. Orr, 20.67; F. Parmeter, 3.00; C. C. Parr, 23.39; W. D. Pigott, 24.55; E. E. Potter, 2.69; V. H. Prewer, 42.90; Max Rabbitts, 70.00; Jas. Ruxton, 11.01; R. Simpson, 93.07; R. L. Snow, 3.30; S. D. Spence, 18.30; K. A. Stewart, 247.36; J. H. Strain, 36.94; Wm. Stringer, 56.55; E. L. Ward, 345.68; Gordon Watson, 44.00; R. E. Watson, 26.54; Bogert Wilson, 11.87; Geo. Wombwell, 71.95;—Wages for extra labour—412.93 .... 59,635 75

Rent, $7,683.86.

Acme Timber Co., 200.00; Algoma Central & H. B. Ry., 5.00; Mrs. E. Appleton, 175.00; I. Bedard, 3.00; J. O. Bernier, 63.67; Mrs. J. Burke, 87.50; Canada Power & Paper Corporation (Consolidated Paper Corporation, Ltd.), 163.03; Canadian National Railways, 110.00; Mrs. E. Cousineau, 36.00; Mrs. Thos. Cousineau, 22.45; Dept. of Public Works, 438.63; W. D. Dickson, 60.00; Mrs. W. Edwards, 93.50; Hubert Elkington, 80.00; Empire Cafe, 360.00; B. Forbes, 60.00; Fort Frances Masonic Building Association, 315.00; E. Gardiner, 50.00; F. D. Henderson, 12.00; Geo. M. Ingram, 50.00; Kerr & Co., 308.00; Frank Knapp, 20.00; Mrs. D. T. Kovalckink, 50.00; Alphonse Labrecque, 550.00; Mrs. T. Lafrance, 62.50; H. M. Legris, 180.00; Calvin Lewis, 30.00; Luke Manzuk, 80.00; Jno. C. A. Martin, 750.00; Mrs. C. A. Martin, 150.00; Matheson Garage, 5.00; Mrs. Mary T. McEachern, 1,020.00; McLeod's Garage, 56.50; Moore's Hotel, 37.58; Fred Morrison, 155.00; Rothschild & Co., 1,440.00; Spanish River Lumber Co., 35.00; G. Vincent, 50.00; R. O. Whyte, 138.00;—**Miscellaneous disbursements by Forestry Branch Officers**—C. E. Foote, 35.00; W. B. Greenwood, 65.50; Thos. McCormick, 25.00; E. L. Ward, 56.00 .... 7,683 86

Fire Ranging—Continued

Miscellaneous, $4,350.95.

Acme Drug Co., 10.43; C. T. Adams Co., 2.89; H. J. Baldwin, 4.00; Canadian National Railways, 386.68; Chapleau Drug Co., 2.94; City Typewriter Co., 50.00; Commercial Reproducing Co., 2.20; H. P. Cook, K.C., 24.15; T. D. Corcoran, 8.50; E. A. Cunningham, 13.40; Dept. of Highways, 2,924.98; Hudson's Bay Co., 1.40; Ideal Drug Co., 1.60; Johnson's Pharmacy, 3.75; King's Printer, 116.19; E. Kotanen, 2.00; Legros Bros., 11.50; Lesage Motor Sales, 2.50; T. E. McKee, 35.00; Myles & Son Hardware, 4.30; Pakseley Lumber Co., 6.76; C. R. Parker, 302.80; Thos. Pocklington Co., 20.56; Corporation of the City of Port Arthur, 1.05; Porter & Co., 2.45; Pratt & Shanacy, .70; Province of Ontario Pictures, 1.00; J. Robert, .50; Sault Stationers, Ltd., 53.00; R. M. Smith, 100.00; Sault Business College, 25.00; Sudbury High & Technical School, 30.00; Sudbury Star, 16.80; Superintendent of Documents, Ottawa, 1.50; C. Tarling Co., 1.50; Mrs. A. B. Watson, 19.50; Mrs. F. Wilkinson, 4.00; A. R. Wood, 7.50—**Miscellaneous Disbursements by Forestry Branch Officers**—Lloyd Acheson, 3.75; A. C. Bouchey, .60; A. B. Connell, 25.50; S. J. Cowan, 1.75; W. D. Cram, 12.85; H. W. Crosbie, 5.67; W. B. Greenwood, 7.55; G. J. Hass, 16.50; W. H. Hawkins, 5.72; D. J. Kennedy, 4.10; N. M. Kensit, .75; H. M. Legris, 13.35; Gerald J. Munro, .45; P. McEwen, 5.95; H. V. Orr, 1.67; W. D. Pigott, .35; Max Rabbitts, 4.65; R. L. Snow, .55; S. D. Spence, 3.30; K. A. Stewart, 14.10; J. H. Strain, 9.46; Wm. Stringer, .30; E. L. Ward, 5.95; R. E. Watson, 3.10 .... 4,350 95

Air Service ($407,074.51)

Salaries, $227,204.89.

Wm. R. Maxwell	Director of Air Service	12 months		5,500 00
G. H. R. Phillips	District Superintendent	12 "		3,600 00
Wm. H. Ptolemy	" "	12 "		3,600 00
J. F. Hyde	Plant Superintendent	12 "		3,600 00
Wm. J. Hill	Assistant Plant Superintendent	12 "		2,700 00
D. A. McIntyre	Senior Pilot	12 "		3,150 00
A. L. Harvey	" "	12 "		3,000 00
F. J. Dawson	" "	12 "		3,000 00
C. C. Crossley	" "	12 "		3,000 00
Wm. H. Lyons		12 "		3,000 00
Gifford Swartman	" "	12 "		3,000 00
H. W. Westaway	" "	12 "		3,000 00
E. Billington	Junior Pilot	12 "		2,400 00
G. Delahaye	" "	12 "	2,400 00	
	Less Leave of Absence		200 00	
				2,200 00
A. M. D. Delamere	" "	12 "		2,400 00
M. V. Gillard	" "	12 "		2,400 00
E. A. Hodgson	" "	12 "		2,400 00
R. M. Smith	" "	12 "	2,400 00	
	Less Leave of Absence		200 00	
				2,200 00
Thos. Woodside	" "	12 "		2,400 00
G. R. Hutt	Foreman, Engine Shop	12 "		2,700 00
E. C. Thompson	Engineer	12 "		2,700 00
S. Macauley	"	12 "		2,700 00
Geo. E. Miles	"	12 "		2,400 00
J. H. Tyrrel	"	12 "		2,400 00
H. J. Phillips	"	12 "		2,400 00
G. A. Gill	"	12 "		2,400 00
A. H. Simard	"	12 "		2,400 00
J. Sherborne	"	12 "		2,400 00
F. P. Batchelor	"	12 "		2,200 00
Wm. I. Hughes	"	12 "		2,200 00
F. J. Allen	"	12 "		2,100 00
C. E. Wright	"	12 "		2,000 00
W. N. McDevitt	"	12 "		1,800 00
G. M. Clucas	Superintendent of Stores	12 "		2,700 00
J. C. Noble	Senior Clerk	12 "		2,000 00
D. H. Murray	" "	12 "		1,900 00
W. H. Wilcox	Carpenter	12 "		2,100 00
J. Hendry	"	12 "		2,100 00

Fire Ranging—Continued

Air Service—Continued

Salaries—Continued.

P. T. Hancox	Tailor and Sailmaker	12 months	1,800 00
T. H. Lake	Blacksmith	12 "	1,800 00
J. Terry	Caretaker	12 "	1,300 00
Pay list, wages of men			122,154 89

Travelling Expenses of Air Service Officers, $4,223.49.

John Aitken, 2.25; W. J. Atkins, 27.50; D. S. Atkinson, 35.25; G. L. Beveridge, 27.50; W. B. Buckworth, 33.90; J. T. Cairns, 109.95; H. Christensen, 59.40; C. M. Clucas, 109.95; accountable, 6.95; G. A. R. Cowan, 41.75; J. P. Culliton, 21.55; H. W. Day, 55.35; G. Delahaye, 121.25; A. M. Delamere, 35.60; A. E. Denning, 5.35; K. H. DeNure, 64.40; O. G. Dewell, 30.20; Francis Duguay, 8.65; G. A. Doan, 7.25; G. Edmunds, 4.80; R. P. Edwards, 48.55; R. H. Fraser, 32.05; W. W. Fuller, 20.05; P. Gascoigne, 6.00; Emery Gee, 29.65; M. V. Gillard, 140.35; A. R. Grundy, 11.20; E. C. Hart, 50.95; A. L. Harvey, 111.70; G. Hastings, 27.35; A. C. Heaven, 33.00; J. Hendry, 59.40; G. R. Hicks, 5.50; W. J. Hill, 46.85; E. Hodgson, 46.20; J. G. Horn, 1.50; F. T. Hughes, 54.70; W. I. Hughes, 20.90; J. R. Humble, 34.50; J. Hyde, 121.10; S. N. Knight, 33.25; J. Lamontagne, 7.05; D. Logan, 35.20; W. H. Lyons, 48.90; Sam Macauley, 73.05; E. S. MacKay, 16.50; J. Madden, 29.35; T. L. Mahon, 33.25; W. R. Maxwell, 995.37; J. H. McCoy, 30.90; J. M. McDevitt, 42.40; W. N. McDevitt, 40.30; D. A. McIntyre, 140.25; D. McPhail, 30.60; H. R. Mericle, 11.00; A. K. Murray, 78.30; M. D. Nelan, 9.45; W. L. Nesbitt, 50.25; J. C. Noble, 67.10; G. O'Reilly, 61.60; R. F. Overbury, 5.50; G. H. R. Phillips, 105.25; H. J. Phillips, 38.75; O. Radford, 5.80; R. G. Reid, 54.45; C. R. Ruse, 109.42; Robt. M. Smith, 21.60; W. G. Thompson, .75; G. E. Trussler, 45.45; W. W. Tweed, 5.50; J. G. Twist, 42.60; E. B. Waller, 20.65; R. J. Watson, 15.15; H. W. Westaway, 108.85; S. G. Williams, 30.55; Thos. Woodside, 5.25; E. Wright, 63.60 .... 4,223 49

Equipment, $36,113.19.

C. T. Adams & Co., 7.00; Aikenhead Hardware, Ltd., 26.35; American News Co., Ltd., 37.62; Barnes Drug Co., 69.50; Barton Devices Co., 180.55; E. L. Bedard, 125.44; Bennett & Elliott, 82.03; Bert's Electric Battery, 6.00; Black & Decker, 161.34; Canadian General Electric Co., 52.88; Can. Hanson & Van Winkle Co., 43.20; Can. Pratt & Whitney Co., Ltd., 148.43; Can. Vickers, Ltd., 28.70; Wilfrid Caron, 17.58; Cochrane-Dunlop Hardware, 509.71; C. J. Collins, 13.60; W. H. Cooper & Co., 36.15; Coulter's Pharmacy, 86.18; De Havilland Aircraft of Canada, 14,236.27; De Vilbiss Mfg. Co., 100.90; Dominion Rubber Co., 29.72; Dominion Wire Rope Co., Ltd., 1.15; Dunn Hardware Co., 13.45; John East Co., 35.45; Edwards Hardware Co., 30.85; Fairchild Aircraft, Ltd., 15,130.04; Fairway Stores, 147.65; R. Foster, 8.30; Fowler Hardware Co., Ltd., 15.46; Fyr Fyter Company of Canada, 50.06; Grand & Toy, 24.50; Greenfield Tap & Die Corp., 16.17; Greenwood Electric & Hardware Co., 77.35; Hesson Lumber Co., Ltd., 80.94; Wm. Hill Hardware, 23.13; Hinsperger Harness Co., 539.51; Hudson's Bay Co., 2.70; Imperial News, Ltd., 7.28; International Paints (Canada), Ltd., 53.75; Instruments, Ltd., 89.00; Kapuskasing Supply Co., 3.00; Keuffel & Esser, 7.21; Keyes Hardware, Ltd., 351.47; King's Printer, 689.51; Wm. S. Leask, 13.35; John Leckie, Ltd., 33.15; Mahon Electric Co., Ltd., 1.00; Marshall-Wells Co., 28.36; J. A. Mathieu, Ltd., 3.20; Allan A. J. MacDonald, 139.95; Norman MacDonald, 87.29; Herbert Morris Crane & Hoist Co., 69.98; Motor Meter Gauge & Equipment Corporation, 168.56; Munderloh & Co.,Ltd., 4.17; Nakina Fur & Supply Co., 12.29; National Grocers, Ltd., 2.38; Northern Feed & Seed Co., Ltd., 9.00; Northern Foundry & Machine Co., Ltd., 27.01; Ontario Hughes-Owens Co., 3.18; Peckover's, Ltd., 32.81; Peterborough Canoe Co., 58.32; H. W. Petrie, Ltd., 77.20; J. C. Pinch, 82.64; Pratt & Shanacy, 58.52; Pratt & Whitney Company of Canada, 5.06; Preston Woodworking Machinery Co., Ltd., 300.00; Province of Ontario Pictures, 18.95; Scythes & Co., Ltd., 445.13; Seno Sign Co., 108.00; N. Slater Co., Ltd., 4.56; Sudbury Boat & Canoe Co., 7.00; C. Tarling Co., 115.50; W. I. Thayer, 139.56; C. L. Turnbull Co., Ltd., 28.60; Vernon Directories, 12.00; Watson, Jack & Co., Ltd., 31.30; White Drug Store, 13.85; Williams Hardware Co., 57.10; Williams & Wilson, Ltd., 199.62; A. R. Williams Co., Ltd., 74.59; Wood, Alexander & James, Ltd., 12.72. **Miscellaneous Disbursements by Air Service Officers**—F. J. Dawson, 4.84; G. Delahaye, 4.47; M. V. Gillard, 4.80; J. G. Horne, 1.85; D. A. McIntyre, 13.55; R. F. Overbury, 1.00; C. M. Clucas, 199.70 .... 36,113 19

Improvements, $3,831.23.

Cochrane-Dunlop Hardware, 66.31; Flockhart Bros., 7.80; Greenwood Electric & Hardware Co., 3.80; Halliday Co., 86.37; Hesson Lumber Co., Ltd., 86.75;

Fire Ranging—Continued

Air Service—Continued

Improvements—Continued.

Jamieson Electric Co., Ltd., 115.54; Keyes Hardware, Ltd., 81.67; Lindstrom & Nilson, 135.25; Allan A. J. MacDonald, 105.90; Lloyd Acheson, 1.59; McLartys, Harten & Webber, 2,708.19; Northern Aerial Minerals Exploration and Jno. E. Hammell, 13,838.87; Pratt & Shanacy, 48.15; Soo Lumber & Mill Co., 383.91.... 17,670 10

Express, Freight, Telephone, Telegrams, etc., $6,764.07.

Bell Telephone Co., 409.78; R. M. Brunton, 401.00; Canada Steamship Lines, 306.24; Canadian National Railways, 689.79; Canadian Pacific Railway Co., 510.01; City Water and Light Department (Soo), 2,017.13; Cossey's Repair Shop, 3.50; Fisher Dray Line, 10.78; Town of Fort Frances, 3.00; Great Northern Gas, 256.26; Ireland Cartage & Storage, 24.00; Kenora Public Utilities, 116.05; John Kron & Son, 19.50; J. A. Mathieu, Ltd., 19.60; Isidore Ouellette 66.00; M. Pardy, 16.00; Patricia Transport Co., Ltd., 114.00; Postmaster, 374.00; M. Rawlinson, Ltd., 227.00; Sioux Lookout Public Utilities, 485.80; Sudbury Boat & Canoe Co., 1.00; Wesley Taxi & Transfer, 315.75. **Miscellaneous disbursements by Air Service Officers**—E. Billington, 17.35; C. M. Clucas, 42.20; C. C. Crossley, 18.90; F. J. Dawson, 74.58; G. Delahaye, 23.13; A. M. Delamere, 23.21; M. V. Gillard, 17.62; J. H. Horne, 16.92; W. R. Maxwell, 2.77; A. K. Murray, 10.00; D. A. McIntyre, 35.96; R. F. Overbury, 43.00; W. H. Ptolemy, 24.99; G. E. Trussler, 14.00; H. W. Westaway, 13.25................ 6,764 07

Gas and Oil, $39,019.81.

Algoma Central & H. B. Ry., 15.00; E. L. Bedard, 1.40; Canada Steamship Lines, 325.45; Cochrane-Dunlop Hardware, 3.15; Endress & Auld, 5.25; Fairway Stores, 12.40; John Harju, 12.50; M. Heita, 144.75; Hudson's Bay Co., 147.38; Imperial Oil, Ltd., 37,762.40; Keyes Hardware, Ltd., 1.62; John Kron & Son, 118.03; McKinnon's Store, 24.00; C. Merrill, 17.67; Nakina Fur & Supply Co., .20; Isidore Ouellette, 32.75; Patricia Transport Co., Ltd., 161.00; Pratt & Shanacy, 7.20; Revillion Freres Trading Co., Ltd., 36.40; C. Robertson's Transfer, 39.14; W. Sangster, 15.50; Soo Garage, Ltd., 20.80; Superior Chain Stores, 3.50; William's Hardware Co., 2.40. **Miscellaneous disbursements by Air Service Officers**—D. S. Atkinson, 5.68; C. C. Crossley, 65.25; A. M. Delamere, 6.00; J. H. Horn, 1.20; D. A. McIntyre, 21.42; W. H. Ptolemy, 10.37............... 39,019 81

Repairs, $75,433.61.

Abitibi Power & Paper Co., 11.28; Acme Laundry, 14.38; Aeronautical Corp. of Canada, 218.77; Aircraft Accessories Co., 573.52; Algoma Central & H. B. Railway, 1,213.01; Algoma Steel Corp., 54.33; Aluminum, Ltd., 37.98; American Chemical Paint Co., 6.57; D. L. Auld, 521.93; Auto Starter Co., Ltd., 70.00; F. Bacon & Co., 61.73; Barton Devices Co., 150.00; E. L. Bedford, 268.53; Bendix Stromberg Carlson, 157.87; Bennett & Elliott, 56.65; Black & Decker, 3.84; Boeing Aeroplane Co., 899.09; Nelson Boyes, 15.00; V. Brisson, 17.60; British-American Express Co., 246.75; Buhl Stamping Co., 250.00; Burroughs Adding Machine of Canada, Ltd., 43.26; Canadian Department Stores, 4.75; Canadian Fairbanks-Morse Co., 18.08; Canadian General Electric Co., 61.08; Canadian Hanson & Van Winkle Co., 8.80; Canadian Industries, Ltd., 129.83; Canadian Johnson Motors, 156.13; Canadian Liquid Air, 4.80; Canadian National Railways, 280.88; Canadian Oil Companies, Ltd., 9.50; Canadian Pacific Railway Co., 1,239.01; Canadian Pratt & Whitney Co., Ltd., 9,386.38; Canadian Vickers, Ltd., 118.25; Canadian Wright, Ltd., 2,792.00; Wilfrid Caron, 40.06; Carpenter-Hixon Co., Ltd., 701,87; Wm. G. Carson, 189.60; Chantler & Chantler, 28.00; H. Cheyne, 1.50; Chicago Screw Co., 54.28; Chicago Tubing & Grading Co., 3.80; Cleveland Pneumatic Tool Co., 45.52; Cochrane-Dunlop Hardware, 1,533.30; C. J. Collins, 2,125.48; Cossey's Repair Shop, 15.45; Coulter Copper & Brass Co., 162.37; Coulter's Pharmacy, 10.70; Cross Machine Shop, 4.00; Day Lumber Co., 428.65; B. W. Deane & Co., 28.24; De Havilland Aircraft of Canada, 16,295.12; Delco Aviation Corporation, 40.96; Dominion Oxygen Co., 193.52; Dominion Wire Rope Co., Ltd., 54.15; I. J. Downey & Sons, 300.76; Drummond, McCall & Co., 21.46; Dunn Hardware Co., 18.15; Dunseath & McClary, 54.27; John East Co., 41.55; Eastern Steel Products, 5.20; Eclipse Machine Co., 826.53; Edwards Hardware, 82.73; Ellis Bros., Ltd., 5.00; Exide Batteries of Canada, 136.15; Fairchild Aircraft, Ltd., 126.87; Fairway Stores, 412.77; G. E. Farlinger, 58.40; Thos. Firth & John Brown, Ltd., 21.08; Flockhart Bros., 8.81; Fowler

Fire Ranging—Continued

Air Service—Continued

Repairs—Continued.

Hardware Co., Ltd.; 10.85; Fyr Fyter of Canada, 216.78; Bilmond Gagnon, 18.00; B. B. Glove Mfg. Co., 27.29; Greenfield Tap & Die Corporation, 1.23; Greenwood Electric & Hardware Co., 556.01; Gutta Percha & Rubber Co., Ltd., 80.17; Hesson Lumber Co., 167.66; Wm. Hill Hardware, 26.15; Hinsperger Harness Co., 76.46; International Paints (Canada), Ltd., 2,378.50; International Varnish Co., 418.26; Johnson & Carlbon, 53.50; Kapuskasing Supply Co., 12.70; Keewatin Lumber Co., 2.70; Keyes Hardware, Ltd., 399.38; John Kron & Son, 19.60; Laberge Lumber Co., Ltd., 60.49; R. Laidlaw Lumber Co., Ltd., 1,928.58; Wm. S. Leask, 188.68; John Leckie, Ltd., 61.95; Wm. Lightfoot, 5.43; J. A. Link, 73.00; The Lowe Bros. Co., 93.92; Lyman Tube & Supply Co., Ltd., 97.35; J. W. Magnus Co., 59.98; M. J. Mahon, 16.46; Mahon Electric Co., Ltd., 43.70; Marine Laundry, Ltd., 126.58; Marshall-Wells Co., 34.37; A. Mascotte, 228.00; J. A. Mathieu, Ltd., 39.85; MacDonald Bros. Aircraft, Ltd., 13,049.69; Allan A. J. MacDonald, 426.68; J. H. McDonald, 2,295.20; J. Roy MacDonald, 102.59; Norman MacDonald, 1.14; Wm. McKirdy & Sons, 17.50; McLartys, Harten & Webber, 128.85; McNaught Lumber Co., 11.52; John McVey, 8.50; MacWhyte Co., 20.97; Menzies Bros., Ltd., 16.70; Herbert Morris, Crane & Hoist Co., 22.07; Nakina Fur & Supply, 7.20; Nicholson's Tire Surgery, 73.67; Northern Electric Co., 6.43; Northern Feed & Seed Co., 40.00; Northern Foundry & Machine Co., Ltd., 69.23; Northwest Airways, Inc., 336.00; Ontario Hughes-Owens Co., 278.03; Ontario Plate Glass, 2.05; Mrs. Antoine Ouellet, 25.50; Peckover's, Ltd., 426.65; The Peterborough Canoe Co., 11.30; H. W. Petrie, Ltd., 203.34; W. E. Phillips, Ltd., 72.59; J. C. Pinch, 3.31; Port Arthur Shipbuilding Co., Ltd., 46.09; Power Light Devices, 23.18; Pratt & Shanacy, 132.62; Pyrene Mfg. Company of Canada, Ltd., 88.07; Railway & Power Engineering Corporation, 6.88; Red Wing Motor Co., 18.00; Remington Typewriters, Ltd., 7.50; C. Robertson's Transfer, 40.00; G. B. Rousseau, 36.55; P. T. Rowland, 150.00; Rugby Transfer, 200.00; Russel Bros., Ltd., 1.80; City of Sault Ste. Marie, 160.50; Saulte Ste. Marie Coal & Wood Co., 36.10; Scintilla of Canada, 181.11; Scythes & Co., Ltd., 49.56; T. E. Simpson, Ltd., 128.40; Town of Sioux Lookout, 275.00; Sky Specialties Corp., 3.00; Soo Garage, 2.25; Soo Lumber & Mill Co., 222.85; Standard Chemical Co., Ltd., 173.14; J. W. Stone Boat Mfg. Co., Ltd., 102.50; Sturgeon's, Ltd., 182.03; Sudbury Boat & Canoe Co., 7.00; Sudbury Steam Laundry, 6.85; Superior Ice Co., 42.00; Tapp & Hobbs, 6.01; W. I. Thayer, 46.00; Thunder Bay Lumber Co., 187.59; United Carr Fastener Company of Canada, 16.75; United Typewriter Co., Ltd., 49.51; Utilities Accessories, Inc., 8.20; Neil Weibe, 152.50; Wells & Emerson, 4.50; Willard Storage Battery Co., 107.64; Williams Hardware Co., 79.83; Williams & Wilson, Ltd., 14.19; The A. R. Williams Machinery Co., Ltd., 60.76; Rutherford Williamson, F.C.A.R., 10.35; Wood, Alexander & James, Ltd., 13.18; T. C. Young, 7.50. **Miscellaneous disbursements by Air Service Officers.** —D. S. Atkinson, 9.35; E. Billington, 31.47; J. T. Cairns, 23.97; C. M. Clucas, 521.67; C. C. Crossley, 49.87; F. J. Dawson, 61.63; H. W. Day, 15.27; G. Dalahaye, 20.68; A. M. Delamere, 4.65; A. E. Denning, 13.00; R. P. Edwards, 4.12; D. Fleming, 10.53; R. H. Fraser, 4.00; W. W. Fuller, 6.70; E. Gee, 17.53; M. V. Gillard, 48.37; A. L. Harvey, 1.46; G. Hastings, 5.56; A. C. Heaven, 2.25; G. R. Hicks, 3.73; J. G. Horne, 19.59; F. T. Hughes, 8.56; W. I. Hughes, 2.98; J. R. Humble, 9.43; S. N. Knight, 12.53; W. H. Lyons, 11.28; A. K. Murray, 14.50; J. M. McDevitt, 9.53; D. A. McIntyre, 80.85; M. D. Nelan, 2.98; W. L. Nesbitt, 13.38; G. O'Reilly, 7.96; R. F. Overbury, 46.69; H. J. Phillips, 3.13; W. H. Ptolmey, 334.95; R. G. Reid, 19.59; C. R. Ruse, 8.50; R. Simard, 16.74; R. M. Smith, 15.56; G. E. Trussler, 59.50; W. W. Tweed, 15.93; J. W. Twist, 6.80; J. H. Tyrrel, 5.15; P. M. Vooges, 5.86; S. Williams, 3.28; T. Woodside, 3.58; E. Wright, 19.81; Canada Customs, duty, 2,373.50............ 75,433 61

Rent.

Geo. H. Fanning.. 240 00

Miscellaneous, $405.35.

Coulter's Pharmacy, 3.10; Fort Frances Times, 30.00; L. J. Jodouin, 98.00; United Typewriter Co., Ltd., 2.00; C. M. Clucas, 230.25; F. J. Dawson, 20.00; M. V. Gillard, 20.00; D. A. McIntyre, 2.00................................ 405 35

Fire Ranging—Continued

Total		1,683,719 68
Less repayments:		
Sundry persons re fire fighting	1,970 08	
Radio and telephone messages	2,400 00	
Sale of equipment	110 17	
Refund on films, Department of Mines	296 53	
Refund on rent	1 00	
Unused railway tickets	29 15	
Revenue from telephone rentals	1,406 18	
Repayment of wages, fire protection	1,514 05	
Refund on material, Crane, Limited	68 75	
Refund on freight overcharge	57 60	
Refund on telephone charges	7 01	
Overpayment, J. R. Ellet	8 98	
Fire Protection Act	270,515 42	
Miscellaneous refunds	557 69	
		278,942 61
Total, Fire Ranging		1,404,777.07

Clearing Townsites and Removing Fire Hazards ($21,664.57)

Travelling Expenses, $1,596.36.

L. Acheson, 14.21; J. B. Burns, 47.55; N. A. Cross, 6.00; A. J. Dusang, 75.80; A. E. Gardiner, 13.40; W. R. Gardner, 93.95; T. Garrard, 18.75; E. J. Gilligan, 28.00; L. Henderson, 18.65; B. Hey, 131.55; A. Holinshead, 104.50; L. Languerand, 31.70; J. R. Loucks, 17.50; C. McKinnon, 19.35; V. Mawn, 75.55; J. E. Morin, 34.20; H. Nicholas, 18.20; J. O'Shea, 4.10; C. C. Parr, 50.45; B. Perrigo, 12.00; E. E. Potter, 24.85; F. Pritchard, 19.45; H. Pritchard, 21.60; J. Reeston, 15.10; M. Roadhouse, 3.00; S. V. Ryan, 9.50; W. Sangster, 147.45; M. Sauerbrie, 14.10; W. Stringer, 40.60; L. Swardfager, 66.65; D. T. Thaw, 7.90; W. E. Van Clieaf, 166.60; M. E. Walker, 47.40; N. F. Welch, 86.05; M. Young, 110.70 .... 1,596 36

Miscellaneous, $20,068.21.

Hudson's Bay Co., toboggans, 27.00; McIntosh Grain & Feed Co., Ltd., oats, 16.68; Monarch Oil Co., Ltd., gas, etc., 179.81; Northern Telephone Co., rental, 4.80; tolls, 2.55; Pay list, wages of men, 19,647.77; Watson, Jack & Co., Ltd., pumps, 159.25. Sundries—express, .95; postage, 3.00; petty disbursements, 26.40 .... 20,068 21

Grant to Canadian Forestry Association ($1,000.00)

Canadian Forestry Association 1,000 00

Forest Research, $5,297.46.

Salaries ($3,583.34)

J. A. Brodie	Assistant Forester, Goup 1	10 months	2,000 00
A. P. Leslie	" " " 2	10 "	1,583 34

Temporary Services, $1,183.35.

D. W. Gray	Assistant Forester, Group 2	8 months	1,183 35

Travelling Expenses, $80.58.

A. Crealock, 12.30; D. W. Gray, 35.23; J. F. Sharpe, 33.05 .... 80 58

Miscellaneous, $450.19.

Canadian Canoe Co., Ltd., canvas, etc., 19.45; Canadian Photo Copy Co., photostats, 49.01; Cochrane-Dunlop Hardware, Ltd., hardware supplies, 10.01; Le Sage Motor Sales, brake lining 66.64; Pay list, wages of men, 274.75; Sundries—cartage, 3.95; freight, 5.34; petty disbursements, 21.04 .... 450 19

Allowances to Township School Sections ($700.00)

Treasurer—Township of Charlotteville, 150.00; Township of Clarke, 150.00; Township of Vespra, 250.00; Township of South Walsingham, 150.00 .... 700 00

Insect Control ($4,647.78)

Travelling Expenses, $447.12.

C. W. Duckworth, 35.28; E. E. Grainger, 112.65; W. R. Haddow, 114.09; G. K. Marshall, 68.18; W. W. Milne, 17.01; C. H. Plaxton, 34.76; K. A. Stewart, 65.15.. 447 12

Miscellaneous, $4,200.66.

Austin & Nicholson, Ltd., provisions, 10.48; G. Bucciarelli, provisions, 20.22; Evans Co., Ltd., lumber, etc., 42.41; Pay list, wages of men, 3,999.66; T. Pocklingtou Co., tape, etc., 32.60; Pratt & Shanacy, Ltd., provisions, 10.73; Steele, Briggs Seed Co., Ltd., spramotor, 32.00; Sundries—express, 6.80; freight, 9.52; postage, .50; telegrams, .34; petty disbursements, 35.40........................ 4,200 66

Displays at Exhibitions and Fall Fairs ($645.42)

Travelling Expenses, $95.96.

G. A. Crutcher, 37.75; C. H. Plaxton, 38.16; F. W. Stanley, 20.05............. 95 96

Miscellaneous, $549.46.

M. Armstrong, repairs, 56.40; Ball Planing Mill Co., Ltd., lumber, 31.55; Canadian General Electric Co., Ltd., bulbs, 14.61; Cox & Andrew, cards, 18.50; O. J. Evans & Son, sign, 156.25; Film & Slide Company of Canada, Ltd., transparencies, 22.05; Hamilton Exhibition, electric supplies, etc., 20.00; Hutchins & Sillicks, tubes, etc., 103.87; John Leckie, Ltd., flags, etc., 22.23; Province of Ontario Pictures, transparencies, 78.00; R. Simpson Co., Ltd., rental of chairs, etc., 26.00.............. 549 46

Forestry Branch....................................$1,725,538.80

SURVEYS BRANCH

Salaries ($34,675.00)

Name	Position	Period		Amount
L. V. Rorke	Surveyor General	12	months	5,400 00
J. L. Morris	Inspector of Surveys	12	"	3,650 00
Wm. F. Weaver	Surveyor and Senior Draughtsman	12	"	2,400 00
N. A. Burwash	Assistant Inspector	12	"	2,550 00
W. H. Heath	Geographer	12	"	2,850 00
Wm. A. C. Barnard	Senior Map Draughtsman, Group 1	12	"	2,400 00
F. L. Barr	Senior Draughtsman, Group 2	12	"	2,100 00
E. M. Jarvis	Senior Clerk	12	"	2,000 00
H. Treeby	Map Draughtsman	12	"	2,000 00
F. E. Blanchett	" "	12	"	2,000 00
Archie Wilson	Draughtsman, Group 3	12	"	1,050 00
Victor Vance	Clerk, Group 2	12	"	1,050 00
S. O. Dennis	Senior Clerk Stenographer	12	"	1,400 00
M. B. Pugh	Filing Clerk, Group 1	12	"	975 00
G. E. M. Stork	Clerk Stenographer, Group 1	12	"	1,200 00
M. C. Haskett	" " " 2	12	"	900 00
P. Aylesworth	" " " 2	10	"	750 00

Contingencies ($12,204.04)

Temporary Services, $2,085.82.

Name	Position	Period		Amount
William E. Carroll	Draughtsman, Group 2	12	months	1,200 00
N. L. Chard	Clerk Stenographer, Group 2	12	"	825 00
Isabel M. Hatley	" " " 2	1	"	60 82

Travelling Expenses, $928.52.

N. A. Burwash, 78.55; H. C. Draper, 24.65; J. L. Morris, 296.90; L. V. Rorke, 528.42.. 928 52

Advertising, $32.40.

Simcoe Reformer.. 32 40

Miscellaneous, $9,157.30.

Association of Ontario Land Surveyors, fees, 14.00; Architectural Bronze & Iron Works, castings, 187.00; Canadian Photo Copy Co., Ltd., photostats, 249.63; Dept. of Public Works, blueprint paper, 509.17; Dept. of Interior, Ottawa, maps, 15.00; D. Evans, services, 19.80; W. L. Haight, registrations, 10.94; Harris Litho Co., Ltd., maps, 1,072.00; King's Printer, 3,007.87; Rolph-Clark-Stone, Ltd., maps, 3,534.10; Sutcliffe Co., Ltd., engineering services, 250.00; United Typewriter Co., Ltd., inspections, etc., 62.50. Sundries—cartage, 5.00; express, 158.60; telegrams, 38.33; newspapers and periodicals, 6.00; petty disbursements, 17.36... 9,157 30

Surveys Branch—Continued

Board of Surveyors ($200.00)

Ontario Land Surveyors' Association, grant	200 00

Surveys ($99,984.05)

Algoma District.—C. R. Kenny, 2,994.61, less accountable, 1931, 2,500.00=494.61; T. J. Patten, accountable, 2,000.00	2,494 61
Algoma and Thunder Bay Boundary.—Elihu Stewart, accountable	1,500 00
Cochrane District.—J. T. Ransom, 9,464.00, less accountable, 1931, 7,491.25= 1,972.75; Speight & Van Nostrand, 8,100.00, less accountable, 1931, 6,075.00= 2,025.00; H. W. Sutcliffe, 9,720.00, less accountable, 1931, 7,290.00=2,430.00	6,427 75
Cochrane District, Township Lines.—Speight & Van Nostrand, accountable, 4,335.00; H. W. Sutcliffe, accountable, 5,500.00	9,835 00
Cochrane District Roads.—C. E. Bush, accountable, 6,368.00; J. Lanning, accountable, 3,400.00	9,768 00
Cochrane District, Meridian Line.—Beatty & Beatty, accountable	5,100 00
Cochrane District, Seventh Base Line.—Beatty & Beatty, 8,575.45, less accountable, 1931, 6,430.00=2,145.45; E. L. Moore, 8,921.19, less accountable, 1931, 6,600.00= 2,321.19	4,466 64
Inverhuron Town Plot Corrections.—E. D. Bolton	45 90
Kenora District.—A. McMeekin, accountable, 100.00; Phillips & Benner, accountable, 3,800.00	3,900 00
Lake St. Clair.—R. W. Code, 3,133.15, less accountable, 1931, 1,800.00	1,333 15
Lake Superior Traverse and Islands.—J. S. Dobie, 8,553.64, less accountable, 6,500.00=2,053.64; accountable, 1932, 4,586.00	6,639 64
Moose and Harricanaw Rivers and Shores of James Bay.—C. R. Kenny, accountable	3,300 00
Nipissing District.—E. L. Cavana, 8,453.78, less accountable, 1931, 2,200.00	6,253 78
Nipissing-Parry Sound Districts.—J. T. Coltham, 8,215.60, less accountable, 1931, 3,657.22	4,558 38
Ontario-Manitoba Boundary Line (retracement of part).—J. W. Pierce, accountable	2,000 00
Ontario-Quebec Boundary Line.—N. A. Burwash, 184.05; J. A. Shirley King, 8,662.37, less accountable, 1931, 6,900.00=1,762.37; accountable, 1932, 4,000.00	5,946 42
Parry Sound District Roads.—E. L. Cavana, accountable	1,534 53
Temiskaming and Nipissing Districts.—C. E. Bush, 10,288.78, less accountable, 1931, 8,085.00	2,203 78
Thunder Bay District.—R. S. Kirkup, 7,433.28, less accountable, 1931, 4,363.20	3,070 08
Thunder Bay District Roads.—R. S. Kirkup, accountable	4,070 00
Thunder Bay Township Outlines.—Phillips & Benner, 9,516.92, less accountable, 1931, 7,200.00	2,316 92
Thunder Bay District, re Survey of McTavish Township—Phillips & Benner	2,575 69
Township of Bigwood Roads.—L. Mooney	122 84
Townships of Caron and Moose.—G. P. Angus, accountable	1,500 00
Township of Cleland.—L. Mooney	450 63
Township of Dryden.—R. W. de Morest, accountable	500 00
Township of Horden.—E. L. Moore, accountable	3,500 00
Townships of Laird and Tarbutt.—C. R. Kenny	52 00
Township of McKay.—J. T. Coltham, accountable	2,500 00
Township of Wicklow.—T. F. Webster, 555.10, less accountable, 1927, 300.00	255 10
Miscellaneous Surveys.—E. Stewart, re inspection, 4,263.21, less accountable, 1931, 2,500.00	1,763 21

Salaries, Expenses and Equipment in Connection with Inspection of Dams, and other Engineering Works and Valuations ($115.00)

E. L. Hughes, travelling expenses, 13.00; W. F. MacPhie, services, regulating water levels and travelling expenses, 102.00	115 00

Lac Seul Storage Dam, Maintenance and Damage Accruing from Flooding or Other Causes by Reason of Dam ($598.61)

E. A. Cunningham, registration fees, 2.93; Dr. T. H. Hogg, 12 months remuneration, 1,000.00; Hydro-Electric Power Commission, power, etc., 581.38; L. V. Rorke, 12 months remuneration, 1,000.00		2,584 31	
Less—Repayment by Dominion Government	1,584 31		
Refunded by Workmen's Compensation Board	401 39		
		1,985 70	
			598 61

Surveys Branch $147,776.70

STATUTORY

Minister's salary (see page G 5) 10,000 00

Refunds to University re Wild Lands ($277.35)

Bursar, University of Toronto 277 35

Refund of 2 per cent., Crown Dues ($299.65)

Sundry municipalities, R.S.O. 1927, Chap. 38, Sec. 15 .... 299 65

Statutory $10,577.00

SPECIAL WARRANTS

Canadian Lumbermen's Association re Information in Connection with Forest Products Industries at Imperial Economic Conference ($2,000.00)

Canadian Lumbermen's Association, grant 2,000 00

Back to the Land Movement ($8,675.76)

Temporary Services, $995.67.

Wm. J. Magladery	Secretary, Advisory Committee	3½	months	427 88
John W. Russell	Superintendent, Fort William District	2⅛	"	227 40
T. Brown	Clerk Stenographer, Group 2	2⅛	"	234 62
G. N. Johnston	Clerk Typist, Group 2	1⅝	"	105 77

Travelling Expenses, $852.70.

W. G. Armstrong, 58.25; J. Clark, 63.22; G. A. Elliott, 9.95; A. Ferguson, 101.90; G. E. Gray, 59.95; T. E. Heron, 50.90; W. Magladery, 99.30; J. W. Russell, 181.92; H. E. Sheppard, 24.55; J. B. Thompson, 123.13; H. T. Vincent, 28.53; F. Widdifield, 51.10 .... 852 70

Miscellaneous, $6,827.39.

H. G. Armstrong, services, 125.00; B. Angi, team horses, 300.00; Beauchesne Bros., provisions, 252.58; A. Bernard, lumber, 112.50; M. Breland & Co., Ltd., clothing, etc., 181.99; V. Brisson, lumber, etc., 609.42; Canadian Pacific Railway Co., fares, 230.75; G. Chartrand, stoves, 79.50; H. Chevrier, meals, 34.00; City of St. Catharines, transportation men, etc., 179.70; Cochrane-Dunlop Hardware, Ltd., hardware, 56.43; J. Cole, clothing, 58.55; J. A. Coles, hardware, 75.38; Commercial Hotel, meals, etc., 77.60; M. C. Dupuis, meals, 55.65; Economy Store, rubbers, 11.20; P. H. Filion, hardware, etc., 18.31; J. J. Fink, hardware, 46.96; Grand River Railway Co., freight, 96.00; C. A. Guerenette, hardware, 428.97; L. Guillemette, lumber, 60.00; Haileybury Lumber Co., Ltd., lumber, 344.91; Hawk Lake Lumber Co., lumber, 328.34; J. A. Hough, accountable, 300.00; J. E. Jacques, hardware and provisions, 36.63; Kapuskasing Supply Co., Ltd., blankets, etc., 106.59; King's Printer, 705.21; J. A. Lacombe, provisions, 10.68; J. Lupien, hardware, 30.80; P. McLeod, provisions, etc., 15.03; A. Mercer, lumber, 30.00; Mercier & Shirley, Ltd., provisions, 110.06; E. Morton, lumber, 27.82; H. G. Murdock, blankets, etc., 29.20; National Grocers Co., Ltd., provisions, 49.64; Peerless Hardware, hardware, 32.13; Pellow Lumber & Hardware Co., hardware, 396.08; M. Purcell, lumber, 70.00; O. D. Stevens, lumber, 20.00; G. Taylor Hardware, Ltd., hardware, 459.66; L. Vaillancourt, provisions, 44.98; L. Walker, lumber, 276.77; Waverley Hotel, room rent, 32.50; E. J. Weeks, lumber, 20.00; West & Co., provisions, 360.47; Williams & Scott, hardware, 205.46. Sundries—cartage, 128.95; freight, 2,216.50; telegrams, 150.05; petty disbursements, 58.05 .... 9,687 00

Less assessment paid by municipalities 2,859 61

6,827 39

Special Warrants $10,675.76

Total $2,424,452 75

Less Salary Assessment 13,726 76

Total Expenditure, Department of Lands and Forests **$2,410,725 99**

PART H

DEPARTMENT

OF

NORTHERN DEVELOPMENT

FISCAL YEAR, 1931-1932

TABLE OF CONTENTS

GENERAL INDEX AT BACK OF BOOK

PART H—DEPARTMENT OF NORTHERN DEVELOPMENT

Statement of Expenditures Showing Amounts Expended, Unexpended, and Overexpended for the Twelve Months Ended October 31st, 1932

Department of Northern Development	Page	Estimates	Expended			Un-expended	Over-expended	Treasury Board Minute
			Ordinary	Capital	Total Ordinary and Capital			
		$ c.	$ c.	$ c.	$ c.	$ c.	$ c.	$ c.
Colonization Roads Branch:								
Salaries	4	15,350 00	8,800 00	....	8,800 00	6,550 00	....	....
Contingencies	4	2,500 00	886 48	....	886 48	1,613 52	....	....
Colonization Roads Branch	..	17,850 00	9,686 48	....	9,686 48	8,163 52	....	....
Miscellaneous:								
Colonization Roads By-laws	5	250,000 00	95,928 35	143,892 46	239,820 81	10,179 19	....	....
Construction, maintenance and repairs of roads, bridges, etc.	5	350,000 00	68,490 99	102,736 35	171,227 34	178,772 66	....	....
Inspection of roads and bridges	11	20,000 00	8,512 26	12,768 43	21,280 69	....	1,280 69	2,000 00
Storage and insurance of road-making machinery, etc.	11	600 00	446 00	....	446 00	154 00	....	....
Engineering, surveying and locating roads	11	2,500 00	406 97	610 47	1,017 44	1,482 56	....	....
Salaries and expenses not otherwise provided for	11	1,000 00	58 00	87 00	145 00	855 00	....	....
Miscellaneous	..	624,100 00	173,842 57	260,094 71	433,937 28	191,443 41	1,280 69	....
Supply Bill	..	641,950 00	183,529 05	260,094 71	443,623 76	199,606 93	1,280 69	....
Statutory:								
Northern Development Department,								
Salaries and contingencies	11	....	143,575 52	....	143,575 52	....	....	....
Making roads	13	....	1,809,083 95	2,431,237 18	4,240,321 13	....	....	....
Purchase and care of cattle, etc.	40	....	484 22	5,586 65	6,070 87	....	....	....
Purchase and distribution of seed grain	40	....	617 76	13,450 50	14,068 26	....	....	....
Assistance of agriculture (creameries)	41	....	500 00	....	500 00	....	....	....
Loans to settlers, administration expenses	41	....	10,536 51	....	10,536 51	....	....	....
Loans to settlers	41	....	....	106,595 00	106,595 00	....	....	....
Statutory	..	....	1,964,797 96	2,556,869 33	4,521,667 29	....	....	....

Special Warrants:								
Unemployment Relief, Board Camps	41	....	....	399,209 33	399,209 33	....	....	....
Northern Development Exhibit, C.N.E.	43	....	1,300 03	....	1,300 03	....	....	....
Unemployment Relief, Improvement and Construction of Roads in Township of Swayze	44	....	....	7,093 98	7,093 98	....	....	....
Special Warrants	..	....	1,300 03	406,303 31	407,603 34	....	....	....
Total	..	....	2,149,627 04	3,223,267 35	5,372,894 39	....	....	....
Less Salary Assessment	..	....	2,304 25	....	2,304 25	....	....	....
Department of Northern Development	..	....	2,147,322 79	3,223,267 35	5,370,590 14	....	....	....

SUMMARY

Department of Northern Development	Page	Ordinary	Capital	Total
Colonization Roads Branch	4-5	9,686 48	....	9,686 48
Miscellaneous	5-11	173,842 57	260,094 71	433,937 28
Statutory	11-41	1,964,797 96	2,556,869 33	4,521,667 29
Special Warrants	41-44	1,300 03	406,303 31	407,603 34
	..	2,149,627 04	3,223,267 35	5,372,894 39
Deduct—Loans Advanced:				
Settlers' Loan Commission (see Part "U")	..	....	106,595 00	106,595 00
Total	..	2,149,627 04	3,116,672 35	5,266,299 39
Less Salary Assessment	..	2,304 25	....	2,304 25
Department of Northern Development	..	2,147,322 79	3,116,672 35	5,370,590 14

DEPARTMENT OF NORTHERN DEVELOPMENT

Hon. Wm. Finlayson, Minister

Salaries (Statutory)

C. H. Fullerton	Deputy Minister	12 months		5,700 00
Jas. Sinton	Chief Engineer	12 "		4,200 00
C. H. Meader	Assistant Chief Engineer	12 "		3,600 00
W. L. Lawer	Accountant, Group 1	12 "		3,150 00
C. L. Dicker	Principal Clerk	12 "		2,200 00
Jas. Smith	Principal Audit Clerk	12 "		2,000 00
L. D. N. Stewart	Surveyor	12 "		2,850 00
Alex Reid	Engineering Draughtsman	12 "		2,850 00
Jno. Gourlay	Senior Draughtsman, Group 2	12 "		2,300 00
J. Boyd	" " " 2	12 "		2,200 00
P. S. Van Raalte	Draughtsman, Group 1	12 "		2,000 00
J. E. D. Tonks	" " 1	12 "		1,800 00
A. S. Williamson	" " 2	12 "		1,500 00
S. Adams	Senior Clerk	12 "		1,700 00
Ethel Fleming	Clerk, Group 1	12 "		1,600 00
Margaret Harper	Senior Clerk Stenographer	12 "		1,500 00
Florence Talbot	Clerk, Group 1	12 "		1,500 00
Florence Embleton	" " 1	12 "		1,500 00
Mary I. McGregor	Senior Clerk Stenographer	12 "		1,300 00
Gwendoline Didsbury	" " "	12 "		1,300 00
Irene Chadwick	Clerk Typist, Group 1	12 "		1,200 00
Margaret Lyons	" " " 1	12 "		1,200 00
Helen Hozack	Filing Clerk, " 1	12 "		1,200 00
Vera Asher	Clerk Typist, Group 1	8 "		800 00
Annabel Downey	" " " 1	5½ "		550 00
F. Flegg	Clerk, Group 2	12 "		1,125 00
Sybil Murray	Clerk Stenographer, Group 1	12 "		1,050 00
Mollie Sturmey	Clerk Typist, Group 1	12 "		1,050 00
Lillian Kirton	" " " 1	11½ "		1,006 25
M. Merle Tisdall	Clerk Stenographer, Group 1	12 "		1,050 00
Enid L. Roberts	" " " 2	6 "		487 44
Frances I. McPhail	Clerk Typist, Group 1	12 "	975 00	
	Less leave of absence		40 63	934 37
Lillian Elliott	Clerk Stenographer, Group 2	12 "		900 00
G. J. Lamb	District Road Engineer	12 "		3,300 00
E. J. Hosking	" " "	12 "		3,300 00
K. Rose	" " "	12 "		3,300 00
D. J. Miller	" " "	12 "		3,300 00
G. A. White	" " "	12 "		3,300 00
C. Tackaberry	" " "	12 "		3,150 00
A. M. Mills	" " "	12 "		3,150 00
R. T. Lyons	" " "	12 "		3,150 00
A. J. Isbester	" " "	12 "		3,150 00
W. E. Buchan	Senior Clerk	12 "		1,900 00
R. V. Shave	" "	12 "		1,900 00
E. W. Geddes	" "	12 "		1,900 00
M. B. Mather	" "	1 "		158 34
J. A. Paul	" "	12 "		1,800 00
D. V. Reid	" "	1 "		141 66
Jos. Anderson	Office Boy	12 "		675 00
Chas. Tompsett	"	12 "		600 00
				97,478 06

COLONIZATION ROADS BRANCH ($443,623.76)

Salaries ($8,800.00)

Main Office.

R. G. Sneath	Road Engineer	12 months	3,300 00
T. C. Swartman	Assistant Engineer	12 "	1,900 00
A. Gamey	Senior Clerk	12 "	1,800 00
V. Jacques	Clerk Stenographer, Group 2	12 "	900 00
J. W. Perry	" " " 2	12 "	900 00

Contingencies ($886.48)

Association of Professional Engineers, fees, 1929-1932, 20.00; Bank of Toronto, blank cheques, 10.35; Canadian Bank of Commerce, blank cheques, 20.75; Department

Colonization Roads Branch—Continued

Contingencies—Continued

of Public Works, blue printing and paper, 67.21; King's Printer, 574.10; Remington Typewriters, Ltd., Dalton machine, 136.00; Royal Bank of Canada, blank cheques, 15.52; United Typewriter Co., Ltd., inspections, 36.00. Sundries—telegrams, 6.55 .... 886 48

Colonization Roads, Main Office $9,686.48

By-laws ($239,820.81)

Admaston, 2,366.68; Alice and Frazer, 1,452.00; Anson and Hindon, 100.00; Armour, 2,700.00; Bagot and Blythfield, 1,300.00; Bala (Town of), 750.00; Bangor, Wicklow and McClure, 763.93; Bedford, 934.08; Bexley, 2,896.61; Bonfield, 208.04; Bromley, 2,507.18; Brougham, 250.00; Brunel, 5,484.98; Burleigh and Anstruther, 1,019.69; Carden, 3,416.28; Cardiff, 775.00; Cardwell, 1,784.54; Carling, 3,168.27; Carlow, 995.16; Chaffey, 2,767.77; Chandos, 1,821.47; Chapman, 2,257.50; Chisholm, 2,910.21; Christie, 364.98; Clarendon and Miller, 1,604.59; Dalton, 5,876.42; Denbigh, Abinger and Ashby, 1,600.50; Draper, 3,039.79; Dungannon, 1,156.65; Dysart, 3,480.85; Eldon, 2,159.94; Elzevir and Grimsthorpe, 325.00; Faraday, 700.00; Foley, 3,813.13; Franklin, 3,716.92; Freeman, 56.25; Galway and Cavendish, 100.00; Glamorgan, 646.59; Grattan, 867.92; Griffith and Matawatchan, 962.50; Hagarty and Richards, 795.50; Hagerman, 946.74; Harvey, 1,736.78; Himsworth North, 1,357.42; Himsworth South, 3,021.05; Hinchinbrooke, 3,012.64; Humphrey, 2,273.64; Hungerford, 5,772.15; Huntingdon, 315.90; Kaladar, Anglesea and Effingham, 1,249.53; Kennebec, 1,857.90; Laxton, Digby and Longford, 1,113.85; Limerick, 583.34; Lutterworth, 100.00; Macaulay, 1,543.01; Machar, 1,848.44; Madoc, 1,059.88; Marmora and Lake, 1,871.64; Matchedash, 443.99; Mayo, 875.00; McDougal, 3,700.00; McKellar, 1,373.24; McLean, 967.77; McMurrich, 2,777.10; Medora and Wood, 17,117.49; Minden, 615.99; Monck, 10,082.60; Monmouth, 1,869.02; Monteagle and Herschel, 1,298.34; Morrison, 3,128.59; Muskoka, 3,149.25; Nipissing, 1,569.07; North Algona, 200.00; North Crosby, 2,500.00; Oakley, 1,085.08; Olden, 1,862.53; Orillia, 9,292.26; Oro, 4,892.74; Oso, 2,435.00; Pakenham, 1,467.12; Palmerston and Canonto, 1,575.00; Pembroke, 300.00; Perry, 3,351.46; Port Carling, 1,867.50; Raglan, 600.00; Rama, 2,004.65; Ridout, 1,000.00; Ross, 2,000.00; Rosseau Village, 225.00; Ryde, 2,884.63; Ryerson, 1,997.51; Sheffield, 4,056.18; Sherborne, 397.24; Sherwood, Jones and Burns, 300.00; Snowdon, 904.71; Somerville, 3,058.35; South Crosby, 770.37; Stafford, 650.00; Stanhope, 174.87; Stephenson, 2,968.59; Stisted, 1,700.00; Strong, 1,850.00; Sunnidale, 2,875.00; Tay, 5,702.95; Tiny, 8,750.00; Vespra, 2,230.42; Watt, 2,913.37; Westmeath, 3,250.00; Wilberforce, 1,250.00; Wollaston, 1,950.00 .... 239,820 81

Construction, Maintenance and Repair of Roads and Bridges ($171,227.34)

Addington.—Wages, 4,193.80; H. Bishop, gravel, 29.50; E. Bosley, gravel, 5.20; C. Both, blacksmithing, 10.55; W. Both, grease, wire, etc., 3.35; J. F. Davidson, blacksmithing, 4.00; T. Ervin, cedar, 50.00; P. Lloyd, gravel, 111.00; E. Morley, gasoline, etc., 26.60; The Pedlar People, Ltd., culverts, 34.32; P. Peterson, gravel, 4.70; J. A. Pringle, explosives, tools, etc., 268.94; T. Rodberg, gravel, 10.00; W. H. Simonette, grease and oil, 43.75; C. C. Thompson, gasoline, tools, etc., 92.00; I. Wickware, gravel, 29.00; V. Wieneckie, lumber, 3.50; S. E. Wise & Son, gasoline, oil, etc., 151.26 .... 5,071 47

Admaston.—Wages, 986.80; Devine & Legree, explosives, 8.86; R. G. Reinke, Ltd., explosives, 6.50 .... 1,002 16

Airy and Sproule.—Wages, 51.20; Canadian National Express, charges, .90 .... 52 10

Algona North.—Wages 200 00

Algona North and Hagarty.—Wages, 168.50; M. Paplenski, gravel, 9.15; G. Wagner, gravel, 21.75 .... 199 40

Algona South.—Wages 602 40

Alice and Fraser.—Wages, 1,480.30; H. Biesenthal, gravel, 9.80; W. Carson, gravel, 12.30; Cochrane Dunlop Hardware, Ltd., explosives, 36.75; G. Hamel, gravel, 14.40 .... 1,553 55

Alice and Wilberforce.—Wages 100 60

Anson and Hindon.—Wages 199 60

Apsley-Bancroft.—Wages, 1,237.70; W. Kidd, gravel, 11.60 .... 1,249 30

Bagot and Blythfield.—Wages, 3,206.05; Devine & Legree, explosives, 77.82; D. Kipper, gravel, 36.00; J. S. Legris, lumber, 6.50; J. J. McCann, gravel, 31.50; P. Quilty, gravel and cedarwood, 15.20; The Scott Hardware, fencing, etc., 18.15; N. Stoughton, gravel, 10.80 .... 3,402 02

Bangor-Wicklow and McClure.—Wages, 1,755.60; B. Parisien, gravel, 25.00; A. Pesheau, gravel, 18.50 .... 1,799 10

Colonization Roads Branch—Continued

Construction, Maintenance and Repair of Roads and Bridges—Continued

Barrie.—Wages, 801.10; H. Bishop, gravel, 45.00; J. R. Gray, gravel, 29.40; E. Morley, gasoline, 55.65; W. Perry, gravel, 14.10; T. M. Thompson, gravel, 10.70; S. E. Wise & Son, gasoline, 5.08	961 03
Barry's Bay-Madawaska Trunk Roads.—Wages	200 00
Barry's Bay Road, east through Wilno and Killaloe.—Wages, 4,351.60; F. B. Chapeski, gravel, 44.70; R. Chapeski, gravel, 25.50; C. & D. Murray, Ltd., explosives, 26.97; Sherwood Municipal Telephone, work on telephone lines, 26.00; A. Sheshack, gravel, 9.50	4,484 27
Baxter.—Wages, 326.07; Coldwater Crushed Stone, Ltd., stone, 7.37; A. Dupuis, gravel, 34.35; Manning Hardware & Furniture Supply Co., explosives, 5.00	372 79
Bedford.—Wages, 1,465.62; S. Barr, gravel, 19.80; A. Bridges, gravel, 9.50; W. B. Dalton & Sons, Ltd., tools, 1.50; F. W. Harris, cedar, 9.87; T. McEwen, blacksmithing, 3.10; R. McGinnis, gravel, 12.60; F. O'Reilly, gravel, 2.30; T. H. Swerbrick, explosives, gasoline, etc., 24.77; J. A. Wilson, gravel, 8.40	1,557 46
Bethune.—Wages, 246.00; R. A. Flavelle, tools, etc., 14.69; C. Holland, cedar and gravel, 11.68; W. Millar, lumber, etc., 18.08; H. White, cedar, 10.08	300 53
Bexley.—Wages	349 07
Bonfield.—Wages, 2,236.10; J. Duchesne, gravel, 7.70; I. Foisy, gravel, 5.80; C. Genven, gravel, 2.90; S. Levesque, gravel, 14.60; E. Perron, gravel, 16.00; M. Vaillancourt, gravel, 25.50	2,308 60
Boulter.—Wages	201 10
Bromley.—Wages, 867.15; A. Sheedy, gravel, 12.30; W. Sherrill, gravel, 6.90; J. Shirley, gravel, 18.00;	904 35
Brougham.—Wages, 3,279.50; P. Barrett, grader repairs, 16.83; M. Foley, gravel, 55.00; W. L. Hunt, screen, etc., 15.19; Legree Hardware, explosives, 130.50	3,497 02
Brudenell and Algona South.—Wages	100 40
Brudenell and Lyndoch.—Wages, 298.00; T. Finnerty, gravel, 5.70	303 70
Brudenell and Radcliffe.—Wages	100 00
Brunel.—Wages, 457.60; G. W. Ecclestone, Ltd., explosives, etc., 23.37; Hern Hardware, Ltd., explosives, 20.70	501 67
Buckhorn.—Wages, 558.20; D. Bernt, gravel, 1.90; G. Irwin, gravel, 2.00; J. Jones, gravel, 27.90; E. R. Windover, gravel, 6.10; T. S. Wood, blacksmithing, 1.30	597 40
Burleigh Trunk Road.—Wages, 2,908.20; D. Brown, cartage, 1.75; W. E. Boulton, gravel, 4.70; J. Downing, planks, .64; I. Dunford, gravel, 48.40; Imperial Oil, Ltd., grease, 3.38; Kingan Hardware, Co. explosives, 26.00; R. Knox, gravel, 1.60; W. W. Leonard, fuse, 1.00; J. McColl, sign board, 2.50; C. McFadden, gravel, 1.60; G. Stevens, coal oil, etc., 20.70; W. Thompson, tools, etc., 22.45; C. A. Wilson, crowbars, 1.50; M. Wilson, gravel, 1.50; S. Windsor, gravel, 5.40	3,051 32
Burleigh and Anstruther.—Wages, 630.50; C. McFadden, gravel, 2.00; J. Tucker, gravel, 3.20; F. Wilson, gravel, 2.30; V. Windsor, grader repairs, 2.00	640 00
Burton-McKenzie.—Wages, 429.90; J. Ainsley, spikes, 1.20; W. Beatty Co., Ltd., spikes, 1.65; E. C. Bennett, cedar, 16.64; J. Bottrell, cedar and gravel, 27.86; L. Crossman, blacksmithing, 6.75; J. Ervin, gravel, 9.40; F. Harrison, blacksmithing, 4.00; Tudhope & Ludgate, explosives, 12.00; S. R. Wainwright, lumber, etc., 10.34	519 74
Calabogie-Black Donald.—Wages, 1,067.70; Black Donald Graphite Co., Ltd., explosives, etc., 28.76; Legree Hardware, explosives, 4.00	1,100 46
Calabogie-Burnstown.—Wages, 458.40; F. Arno, gravel, 45.15; Hydro-Electric Power Commission of Ontario, gravel, 189.75	693 30
Calvin.—Wages, 1,862.30; F. Beckett, cedar, 5.07; W. Beckett, gravel, 15.48; J. H. Bell (estate of), explosives, 18.30; A. Chapman, gravel, 33.10; R. Cross, gravel, 9.00; R. Larrett, gravel, 9.70; W. Sullivan, gravel, 9.90; F. E. Whaley, gravel, 5.00	1,967 85
Cameron.—Wages	802 00
Carden.—Wages	350 35
Cardiff.—Wages, 909.90; U. A. Hubbell, hardwood, 20.00; C. W. Mullett, explosives, etc., 62.89; A. Vance, cartage, .50; H. Welch, blacksmithing, 1.50; G. White, plank, 4.80	999 59
Carlow.—Wages, 558.50; P. Foran, gravel, 13.80; H. Haryett, explosives, 6.25; W. Mackey, lumber, 4.00; A. McDiarmid, gravel, 17.40	599 95
Chandos.—Wages, 1,742.90; J. Brien, gravel, 5.00; G. Couch, gravel, 4.40; J. Mace, gravel, 1.10; J. O'Brien, gravel, 1.00; F. Pomeroy, gravel, 1.50; G. Stevens, grease, etc., 4.90; G. Wease, gravel, 29.50; L. Young, gravel, etc., 7.00	1,797 30
Chisholm.—Wages, 2,605.75; R. W. Butler, explosives, 73.36; P. Chayer, cedar, 3.84; G. W. Hall, blacksmithing, 7.25; G. Periad, cedar, 7.80	2,698 00

Colonization Roads Branch—Continued

Construction, Maintenance and Repair of Roads and Bridges—Continued

Christie and Foley.—Wages, 1,529.00; S. G. Avery, lumber, etc., 16.44; Beagan Motors, cartage, 6.25; A. J. Campbell, blacksmithing, 9.90; Canadian Industries, Ltd., explosives, 99.98; A. N. Fenn, explosives, tools, etc., 129.70; M. Lawson, gravel, 2.10; J. Ricco, gravel, 2.40; A. R. Thompson, gravel, .75; W. Thompson, explosives, 2.91 .... 1,799 43

Clarendon-Miller.—Wages, 1,571.60; J. Derne, caps, .30; E. J. Lemke, blacksmithing, 3.00; The Pedlar People, Ltd., culvert, 30.14; R. Watkins, explosives, 2.24 ...... 1,607 28

Coboconk-Minden-Dorset.—Wages, 9,333.70; F. Angiers, gravel, 5.70; Central Garage, gasoline, oil, etc., 83.74; W. Cooper, gasoline, etc., 63.26; J. Cox, gravel, 81.50; Department of Northern Development, purchase of rights-of-way, 1,988.76; M. Ellis, gravel, 6.80; J. E. Emmerson, gasoline, etc., 42.79; R. Fry, grader repairs, 8.70; D. Gibbs, gravel, 32.00; W. Harrison, gravel, 4.80; D. J. Hartle, tools, etc., 12.43; W. H. Hewitt, gravel, 2.50; A. Jewell, cartage, 8.00; C. Kay, cordwood, 12.00; LeCrow Bros., gasoline, 57.82; W. A. Lindop, gasoline, grader parts, etc., 108.27; E. E. McElwain, roofing, etc., 13.21; L. A. Pritchard, freight charges, 2.64; Reliable Garage, gasoline, etc., 6.40; T. H. Rogers & Son, gasoline, oil, etc., 38.85; W. E. Rogers, gasoline, oil, etc., 41.59; J. E. Shier, express charges, 3.44; O. Sisson, gravel, 3.00; E. E. Valentine, gasoline, etc., 37.54; J. Welch, blacksmithing, 9.10; S. S. Wessell, fencing, etc., 20.16; A. Wilson, gravel, 3.92 ... 12,032 62

Cormac-Eganville Road in Sebastopol Township.—Wages, 2,309.00; R. J. Reinke, Ltd., explosives, 160.76; J. Walsh, gravel, 45.50 .... 2,515 26

Croft.—Wages, 360.65; Burk's Falls Hardware, Ltd., explosives, 9.15; W. J. Fraser, cedar, 17.00; J. Jeffery, blacksmithing, .90; A. H. McLachlan, blacksmithing, 1.30; H. Wager, explosives, 9.20 .... 398 20

Crosby North.—Wages, 1,064.00; A. Egan, gravel, 14.50; W. A. Hutchings, gravel, 24.00; H. Martin, gravel, 22.35; E. McGlad, gravel, 1.95; G. A. Myers, gravel, 18.60; J. S. Myers, gravel, 11.10; J. F. Perkins, gravel, 18.75; J. A. Pringle, explosives, 10.50; G. Speagle, gravel, 1.05; G. Wright, gravel, 12.25 .... 1,199 05

Crosby South.—Wages, 265.45; W. Kerr, gravel, 34.20 .... 299 65

Cross Lake.—Wages, 548.60; Caverhill Learmount & Co., wire, 43.20; H. S. Davis, tools, 2.25; P. Flynn, explosives, etc., 24.30; C. & D. Murray, explosives, 28.25; G. Reynolds, gravel, 4.00; G. A. Tiva, blacksmithing, 1.30 .... 651 90

D'Acre-Caldwell.—Wages, 774.00; J. Donohue, plow repairs, 5.00; J. P. Hunt, blacksmithing, 41.87; B. J. Hunter, gravel, 50.50; Legree Hardware, explosives, 32.38; H. Richards, gravel, tools, etc., 97.37 .... 1,001 12

Dalton.—Wages 300 60

Darling.—Wages, 1,244.00; J. James, gravel, 8.80 .... 1,252 80

Denbigh.—Wages 699 80

Draper.—Wages 100 00

Dungannon.—Wages, 556.80 ; P. Hawley, gravel, 25.00; C. W. Mullett, explosives, 7.30; W. E. Smith, gravel, 11.50 .... 600 60

Dysart.—Wages, 396.05; J. Roberts, gravel, 7.00 .... 403 05

Eldon.—Wages 299 70

Elzevir-Grimsthorpe.—Wages 401 31

Faraday.—Wages, 563.90; W. McEatheron, gravel, 17.90; C. W. Mullett, explosives, 18.15 .... 599 95

Ferguson.—Wages, 270.50; E. Kirkham, gravel, 13.70; W. Kirkham, gravel, 9.80; A. Lockse, gravel, 4.20; W. Vowels, spikes, 1.80 .... 300 00

Ferris East.—Wages, 4,688.00; J. Beaulieu, gravel, 1.50; E. Belecque, gravel, 13.00; J. H. Bell (estate of), explosives, 75.26; R. W. Butler, explosives, 9.10; Canadian Timber Co., Ltd., lumber, 10.80; E. Cantin, gravel, 12.80; H. Champayne, gravel, 8.00; Cochrane Dunlop Hardware, Ltd., explosives, etc., 15.67; B. Crosgery, gravel, 11.60; A. Demers, gravel, 6.95; R. Demers, blacksmithing, 3.20; O. Desjardines, cedar, 24.40; O. Dionne, gravel, 4.20; A. Ethier, gravel, 1.80; A. R. Gauthier, tools, 2.60; J. Gauthier, gravel, 11.25; O. Gauthier, gravel, etc., 43.50; J. Gravelle, gravel, 32.20; H. Grenier, gravel, 6.20; J. Guillemette, gravel, 4.50; A. Houle, gravel, 3.15; J. Lanouette, gravel, 8.25; H. Lascelles, cedar, 3.36; J. Lazura, gravel, 11.25; Lindsay & McCluskey, Ltd., coal, .80; G. K. Morrison, tools, 3.30; A. Marrossa, gravel, 21.20; A. Perron, gravel, 45.40; H. Perron, coal, .80; P. Racicot, gravel, 14.20; J. Voyer, gravel, 12.80 .... 5,111 04

Foley.—Wages, 270.00; A. N. Fenn, explosives, 6.20; Treasurer, Foley Township, explosives, 23.44 .... 299 64

Franklin.—Wages, 431.40; G. W. Ecclestone, Ltd., explosives, etc., 68.16 .... 499 56

Franklin and Brunel T. L. Road.—Wages 148 80

Freeman.—Wages, 340.00; J. Reva, gravel, 10.00 .... 350 00

Colonization Roads Branch—Continued

Construction, Maintenance and Repair of Roads and Bridges—Continued

Frontenac Trunk Road.—Wages, 4,299.05; L. P. Bateman, gasoline, etc., 20.65; J. Derne, explosives, 5.68; B. Greening Wire Co., Ltd., cable, etc., 35.26; J. Gray, tile, 29.25; B. Hannah, gasoline, etc., 52.50; F. Hardwick, earth fill, 9.00; G. Hermer, gravel, 9.75; H. Johnston, cedar posts, 7.00; E. Martin, gravel, 35.25; M. Mills, blacksmithing, 1.60; E. Morley, gasoline, oil, etc., 41.79; The Pedlar People, Ltd., culverts, 62.40; R. Price, gravel, 1.50; J. A. Pringle, explosives, 343.64; W. H. Simonette, tools, etc., 4.30; B. J. Snider, gasoline, etc., 21.41; A. Weiss, explosives, 6.60; C. D. York, gravel, 54.80	5,041 43
Galway-Cavendish.—Wages, 1,128.50; J. Allen, gravel, 7.00; H. Bolt, gravel, 10.20; T. Davis, gravel, 4.10; G. Henderson, gravel, 6.20; Hopkins Mark Co., fuse, .75; J. McGann, gravel, 1.50; C. Molyneaux, cedar and gravel, 37.95; J. R. Umphrey, blacksmithing, 1.00; F. Wright, gravel, 1.60	1,198 80
Gibson.—Wages	717 65
Glamorgan.—Wages	399 30
Golden Lake-Lake Dore.—(1931 accounts), wages	980 63
Grattan.—Wages, 721.20; Legree Hardware, explosives, etc., 10.00; A. St. Louis, gravel, 6.40; A. Tiegs, gravel, 16.00	753 60
Griffith-D'Acre.—Wages, 470.40; Legree Hardware, explosives, 31.00	501 40
Griffith-Matawatchan.—Wages, 981.60; Legree Hardware, explosives, 4.75; R. G. Reinke, Ltd., explosives, 13.20; J. B. Wilson, caps, 2.25	1,001 80
Gurd.—Wages, 110.40; E. Evers, gravel, 14.56	124 96
Hagarty-North Algona.—Wages	99 50
Hagarty-Richards.—Wages, 1,685.40; J. McCarthy, gravel, 17.20	1,702 60
Hardy-Mills.—Wages, 264.80; Department of Northern Development, Huntsville, explosives, 14.00; L. McCloskey, explosives, 9.50; C. Moore, coal, 4.80; C. Simms, cedar and gravel, 12.60	305 70
Harvey.—Wages, 924.80; J. Carew Lumber Co., Ltd., gravel, 4.20; J. J. Coones, gravel, 2.10; P. Graham, gravel, 1.00; J. Jones, gravel, .50; W. Moore, gravel, 1.40; O. Thompson, gravel, 11.60; H. Windover, gravel, 3.90	949 50
Henvey.—Wages, 1,163.90; O. Ambeau, crushed rock, 24.90; A. C. Beaner, crushed rock, 23.30; A. N. Fenn, wire fence, explosives, etc., 103.50; D. Fletcher, cedar, 7.04; J. Garon, cedar, 22.00; B. Greening Wire Co., Ltd., rail cable, 30.95; G. Urchuck, cedar, 22.00	1,397 59
Himsworth North.—Wages, 435.70; S. Dufresne, blacksmithing, etc., 8.20; B. Greening Wire Co., Ltd., cable, etc., 19.49; W. Jamieson, cedar, 15.00; L. McCloskey, explosives, 15.00; H. Ricker, timber, 5.00	498 39
Hinchinbrooke.—Wages, 1,084.97; J. N. Ackerman, gravel, 25.50; M. Cronk & Son, gasoline, etc., 48.17; G. M. Goodberry, cedar posts, 13.20; G. H. Goodfellow, gasoline, oil, etc., 9.80; R. A. Hamilton, gravel, 52.00; R. McGinnis, posts, etc., 21.50; J. A. Pringle, explosives, 9.50; T. H. Swerbrick, gasoline, oil, etc., 104.12; C. D. York, gravel, 33.10	1,401 86
Humphrey (Peninsular Road).—Wages, 192.10; C. K. Beley, cedar, 16.50; Brown & Co., nails, 1.38; G. C. Clubbe, explosives, 12.78; L. Houle, bolts, 4.00; C. F. Jacklin, planks, 29.79	256 55
Hungerford.—Wages, 256.50; W. Martin, gravel, 5.50	262 00
Huntingdon.—Wages, 15.00; Treasurer, Hastings County, crushed rock, 252.00	267 00
Kaladar.—Wages, 1,137.05; J. N. Baker, culverts, 32.00; P. Bay, gravel, 15.90; O. Cole, gravel, 5.60; F. Lessard, gravel, etc., 32.30; Myles & Son, explosives, 1.00; H. O'Donnell, gravel, 18.80; J. S. Slater, gravel, 14.70; D. Trepanier, cartage, 2.00; Tweed Hardware, explosives, 4.00; S. A. Wheeler, gasoline, oil, etc., 10.84; S. E. Wise & Son, gasoline, etc., 9.93; B. Yanch, gasoline, 54.59; S. Yanch, cartage, 3.00	1,341 71
Kennebec.—Wages, 1,270.30; B. Arney, gravel, 6.30; H. Black, gravel, 8.70; M. Detlor, gravel, 14.00; B. Hannah, gravel, 3.30; B. Hayes, gravel, 4.00; G. Hayes, gravel, 1.80; E. Morley, gasoline, etc., 32.03; J. A. Pringle, explosives, gasoline, etc., 57.34; G. Shorts, blacksmithing, .40; E. Wilkes, gravel, 5.00	1,403 17
Kearney to Sand Lake Road.—Wages, 444.12; R. A. Flavelle, explosives, 28.90; M. Holland, gravel, 9.00; W. Miller, draw bars, 8.28	490 30
Lake Dore to Killaloe Trunk Road.—Wages, 6,625.40; A. A. Biederman, gravel, 136.35; A. G. Biederman, explosives, 3.49; T. A. Boland, tools, 4.00; G. Brox, gravel, 35.85; T. Carty, blacksmithing, 5.05; F. Felske, cedar posts, 15.75; W. J. Hughli, explosives, etc., 136.73; H. Kutochke, cedar posts, 56.25; W. Levair, cedar posts, 8.55; E. Luloff, gravel, 11.00; W. Mundt, gravel, 50.60; P. Passaw, gravel, 58.60; W. A. Pilatzke, blacksmithing, 3.80; R. G. Reinke, 316.35; J. M. Roche, cement, 48.30; P. S. Ryan, lumber, 27.20; H. Shaw, gravel and lumber, 57.98; F. W. Springer, gravel, 26.10	7,627 35

Colonization Roads Branch—Continued

Construction, Maintenance and Repair of Roads and Bridges—Continued

L'Amable to Maynooth.—Wages, 6,190.75; J. Beaudrie, gravel, 58.00; H. F. Conlin, explosives, 27.21; D. Goodwin, plank, etc., 2.52; A. Hall, gravel, 65.00; H. Haryett, gasoline, etc., 46.43; P. A. Kellar, gasoline, etc., 74.10; C. W. Mullett, explosives, 188.07; W. Newman, gravel, 12.80; W. Olmstead, gravel, 29.50; F. White, gravel, 17.95; E. Whyte, gravel, 5.60	6,717 93
Lauder.—Wages	100 00
Lavant.—Wages	899 70
Laxton, Digby and Longford.—Wages	350 60
Limerick.—Wages	600 30
Lount.—Wages, 180.80; A. Sohm, gravel, 18.80	199 60
Lutterworth.—Wages	399 80
Macaulay-Draper.—Wages, 885.50; G. W. Ecclestone, Ltd., explosives, 40.25; T. Grau, explosives, 73.90	999 65
Madawaska to Barry's Bay Road.—Wages, 678.00; H. S. Davis, tools, 21.20	699 20
Madoc.—Wages	401 85
Marmora and Lake.—Wages, 380.20; A. McCoy, gravel, 19.80	400 00
Matchedash.—Wages, 448.57; Coldwater Crushed Stone, Ltd., crushed stone, 154.60	603 17
Maynooth-Whitney (North Hastings end).—Wages, 931.20; P. Flynn, explosives, etc., 81.75	1,012 95
Maynooth-Whitney (Nipissing end).—Wages, 2,581.15; P. Flynn, explosives, etc., 10.00; J. A. Gunter, bolts, .92; E. Laundry, bolts, .48; J. Pigeon, cedar, 9.40	2,601 95
Mayo.—Wages, 529.60; W. Bruce, gravel, 5.00; G. Caldwell, gasoline, etc., 9.35; P. A. Kellar, gasoline, etc., 22.61; C. W. Mullett, explosives, 36.59	603 15
Medonte.—Wages, 950.10; Coldwater Crushed Stone, Ltd., stone screenings, 118.93; H. Gibson, gravel, 25.12; W. Johnston, gravel, 15.20; J. Mercer, gravel, 20.00; W. J. Reynolds, gravel, 14.00; A. Snelgrove, tile, 51.00	1,194 35
Medora-Wood.—Wages	200 00
Minden.—Wages	400 30
Monmouth.—Wages	602 35
Monteagle-Herschell.—Wages, 673.85; P. Flynn, explosives, 13.12; L. Jenkins, gravel, 5.85; A. Waddell, gravel, 15.50	708 32
Monteith.—Wages, 541.97; S. Anderson, gravel, 5.00; W. H. Dixon & Son, explosives, 6.05; J. Nelson, gravel, 11.00; A. H. Vigras, explosives and lumber 36.49	600 51
Morrison.—Wages, 2,314.75; W. Brunson, gravel, 11.70; J. S. Clipsham & Sons, Ltd., explosives, 2.25; H. R. Cook, coal, etc., 2.50; N. W. Cook, coal, etc., 1.50; W. E. Cooper, explosives, 16.25; Gravenhurst Hardware Co., Ltd., explosives, 97.45; J. McPhee, earth fill, 8.00; Mickle, Dyment & Son, hemlock, 9.60; C. E. Robinson, blower repairs, 1.00; E. Struthers, earth fill, 10.00; G. Whitelaw, cedar posts, etc., 12.40	2,487 40
Mowat.—Wages, 324.60; Burk's Falls Hardware Co., tools, 2.40; A. N. Fenn, nails, etc., 12.90	339 90
McMurrich.—Wages, 84.00; H. Watson, tile, 16.00	100 00
Nipissing.—Wages, 170.50; T. Byers, gravel, 11.00; W. Hinchberger, timber, 16.36; L. McCloskey, explosives, 2.12	199 98
Oakley.—Wages, 1,051.70; W. N. Boyes, explosives, 36.92; G. W. Ecclestone, Ltd., explosives, 10.89	1,099 51
Olden.—Wages, 956.40; T. Ayers, explosives, 16.70; J. Drew, gravel, 8.00; M. Donnelly, blacksmithing, 3.57; R. McGinnis, cedar and gravel, 65.20; J. A. Pringle, explosives, 15.50; H. Smith, blacksmithing, 1.40; W. Smith, gravel, 12.00; T. H. Swerbrick, gasoline, oil, etc., 20.25	1,099 02
Orillia.—Wages, 1,142.60; T. Gammon, gravel, 14.25; Limestone Products, Ltd., stone, 29.72; W. O'Connor, gravel, 20.20; Stinson Bros., explosives, 9.38	1,216 15
Oro.—Wages, 722.30; W. Anderson, gravel, 5.00; A. Cameron, gravel, 8.40; W. Locking, gravel, 15.60; C. O'Brien, gravel, 15.60; G. Rugman, gravel, 13.20; A. Snelgrove, tile, 16.00	796 10
Oso.—Wages, 697.90; E. Clements, gravel, 4.80; W. R. Hawley, cedar posts, 6.00; H. E. Norris, cedar, 5.00; J. A. Pringle, explosives, 46.63; H. Smith, blacksmithing, 14.75; H. J. Thomson, gasoline and gravel, 25.45	800 53
Pakenham.—Wages	100 10
Palmerston-Canonto.—Wages, 1,261.15; G. Gemmell, cartage, 8.00; James Bros., explosives, 58.46; P. McIntyre, blacksmithing, 17.24; J. McKinnon, gravel, 14.10; A. E. Park, explosives, 8.75; E. Riddell, gravel, 9.00; J. Riddell, blacksmithing, 1.42; R. Sargeant, cartage, 32.00; R. J. Sergeant, tiling, 19.04; R. White, gravel, 18.40; A. M. Wood, rent of steel, 2.19	1,449 75

Colonization Roads Branch—Continued

Construction, Maintenance and Repair of Roads and Bridges—Continued

Papineau.—Wages, 2,223.00; B. Charette, gravel, 57.00; A. Chenier, hemlock, 12.75; P. Delaire, gravel, 7.00; J. Gilligan, explosives, 8.70; Mattawa Hardware, explosives, etc., 8.63; J. Minor, gravel, 34.00; O. Minor, gravel, 4.00; J. Morin, cedar, 10.50; J. B. Porrier, gravel, 1.50; A. Seguin, gravel, 16.60; M. T. Seguin, gravel, 2.80; J. Smiley, gravel, 14.00; S. Soucie, gravel, 2.40	2,402 88
Pembroke.—Wages, 211.20; E. Sullivan, gravel, 38.85	250 05
Perry.—Wages	499 95
Petawawa.—Wages	450 00
Port Severn Road in Tay Township.—Wages, 217.25; Coldwater Crushed Stone, Ltd., stone, screenings 32.18; The Pedlar People. Ltd., culvert, 27.40	276 83
Pringle.—Wages, 87.20; Department of Northern Development, Huntsville, explosives, 8.00; J. Knight, coal, 1.35; L. McCloskey, fuse, 1.50; O. Moore, cartage, 2.00	100 05
Radcliffe.—Wages, 487.30; A. E. Lidkie, explosives, 13.00	500 30
Raglan.—Wages	500 10
Rolph, Buchanan and Wylie.—Wages	600 00
Ross.—Wages, 876.40; W. E. Burns, gravel, 21.30; W. Gibson, gravel, 8.00; S. Gilman, gravel, 10.50; T. Guest, gravel, 12.30; J. J. Jeffrey, gravel, 11.70; A. Johnson, gravel, 14.40; C. Kolschmidt, gravel, 13.50; H. Kolschmidt, gravel, 17.40; W. J. Moore, explosives, 12.68	998 18
Ryde.—Wages, 622.90; J. E. Clipsham & Sons, Ltd., explosives, 28.50; N. W. Cook, coal, etc., 1.35; W. E. Cooper, explosives, etc., 14.75; H. H. Hill, nails, .52; The Whitten Co., Ltd., explosives, etc., 31.90	699 92
Sabine.—Wages, 488.60; J. S. L. McRae, hemlock, 12.63	501 23
Sebastopol.—Wages, 642.40; J. Rose, gravel, 8.80	651 20
Sebastopol-Lyndoch.—Wages	100 00
Severn Falls Road, in Matchedash Township.—Wages, 2,631.85; W. Borland, lumber, 109.47; Canadian National Railways, freight charges, 12.28; C. H. Jermey, hemlock, 30.29; J. Kingsborough, explosives, tools, etc., 111.23; C. Lovering, lumber, 14.00; D. & L. Lovering, washing blankets, etc., 22.75; Manning Hardware & Furniture Supply Co., tools, 4.00; McNab & Sons, crumper, 1.25; Meaford Steel Products, Ltd., scrapers, 77.22; A. C. Robinson, blacksmithing, 28.09; W. W. Templeman, provisions, tools, etc., 371.07; G. Tyrrell, plow repairs, 3.75	3,417 25
Sheffield.—Wages, 444.00; D. W. Detlor, gravel, 46.10; M. Detlor, gravel, 9.90	500 00
Sherborne.—Wages	250 60
Sherwood, Jones and Burns.—Wages	502 50
Sinclair.—Wages, 473.20; G. W. Ecclestone, Ltd., explosives, etc., 25.27	498 47
Snowdon.—Wages	400 70
Somerville.—Wages, 395.35; G. Truax, pick points, 3.50	398 85
Stafford.—Wages, 391.00; O. Dament, gravel, 6.60	397 60
Stanhope.—Wages	399 00
Stephenson.—Wages, 590.20; J. Pascall, blacksmithing, 8.70	598 90
Stisted.—Wages, 475.35; Hern Hardware, Ltd., explosives, etc., 23.50; H. Joiner, cartage, .40	499 25
Tay.—Wages, 1,041.70; J. Caughey, gravel, 24.80; Coldwater Crushed Stone, Ltd., stone screenings 55.65; W. J. Edwards, gravel, 4.00; H. Gratrix, gravel, 6.80; W. Heasman, gravel, 8.00; F. J. Lockhart, gravel, 4.00; W. J. H. Montgomery, gravel, 14.20; H. Revard, gravel, 15.20; H. Robinson, gravel, 18.00; W. R. Wallace, gravel, 6.80	1,199 15
Tiny.—Wages	350 50
Tudor and Cashel.—Wages, 365.00; M. W. Connor & Sons, explosives, etc., 32.58; W. A. McMurray, explosives, 3.55	401 13
Vespra.—Wages	100 00
Wallbridge and Henvey.—Wages, 50.00; A. N. Fenn, explosives, 50.00	100 00
Watt-Bracebridge-Port Carling.—Wages, 412.90; J. A. Edington, purchase of right-of-way, 90.00; A. Fowler, gravel, 62.40; W. A. Pooler, putting in culvert and fill, 73.00	638 30
Westmeath.—Wages, 509.20; P. Hickey, gravel, 12.50; J. Valliant, gravel, 30.00	551 70
Whitney-Madawaska.—Wages, 4,211.35; S. Bush, tools, 1.00; Canadian National Express, charges, 1.80; H. S. Davis, tools, etc., 26.10; H. Fuller, blacksmithing, 19.70; S. Heggart, cartage, etc., 7.95; J. P. Kubesensky, cartage, 6.00; W. O'Malley, tools, etc., 11.00; J. S. L. McRae, gravel and lumber, 17.02; C. & D. Murray, Ltd., explosives, 107.50; O. E. Post, tools, 49.45; G. Reynolds, gravel, 3.90	4,462 77
Wilberforce.—Wages, 1,290.10; R. G. Reinke, Ltd., explosives, 26.69; C. Timm, gravel, 32.85	1,349 64

Colonization Roads Branch—Continued

Construction, Maintenance and Repair of Roads and Bridges—Continued

Wilson and McConkey.—Wages, 134.80; Department of Northern Development, Huntsville, explosives, 10.00; O. Moore, coal, 4.80 .... 149 60

Wollaston.—Wages, 661.00; F. Dafoe, explosives, etc., 30.00; W. N. Gilroy, explosives, etc., 8.64 .... 699 64

Purchase and Maintenance of Equipment.—D. A. Barker, compressor repairs, 12.31; Cockburn & Archer, scrapers, 22.70; Compressed Air Equipment, Ltd., rotator and parts, 203.80; Davie's Garage, 1 sedan car, 506.94; Dominion Road Machinery Co., Ltd., grader repairs, 9.58; General Supply Company of Canada, Ltd., blacksmith's forge, 35.20; B. Good, truck repairs, 20.00; J. McCrae Machine & Foundry, Ltd., tractor repairs, 22.37; L. A. Pritchard, cartage and freight charges, 65.29; W. E. Rogers, tractor repairs, 30.00; Sawyer-Massey, Ltd., 1 grader, 2,400.00; grader parts and repairs, 1,088.59; W. H. Simonette, truck repairs, 6.50; B. J. Snider, 1 sedan car, 562.00; truck repairs, 786.37; Sullivan Machinery Co., compressor repairs, 82.11; Trudeau Motor Sales, truck repairs, 7.67; W. E. Wiggins, express charges, .45 .... 5,861 88

Inspection of Roads and Bridges ($21,280.69)

Inspectors: Services, $12,852.71; Expenses, $8,427.98.

W. Anderson, services, 1,370.50; expenses, 613.35; C. H. Jermey, services, 1,538.75; expenses, 793.18; W. C. Millar, services, 1,168.85; expenses, 502.40; D. Mitchell, services, 1,455.05; expenses, 752.37; W. W. Pringle, services, 1,442.36; expenses, 784.35; L. A. Pritchard, services, 1,499.90; expenses, 27.57; J. A. Rochefort, services, 1,654.85; expenses, 985.57; R. G. Sneath, expenses, 754.64; W. A. Suffern, services, 1,745.55; expenses, 646.21; T. C. Swartman, expenses, 2,043.90; W. E. Wiggins, services, 976.90; expenses, 524.44 .... 21,280 69

Storage and Insurance of Roadmaking Machinery ($446.00)

C. S. Ball, storage of compressor, 8.00; Bark and Mortimer, premiums on cars, 93.60; M. J. Billings, storage of supplies, etc., 60.00; E. Casey, storage of equipment, 30.00; W. J. Cooper, storage of tractor, 12.00; L. Godson, premiums on cars, 40.30; D. A. Goodfellow, storage of trucks, 11.00; L. A. Pritchard, moving equipment, etc., 127.40; Smith and Walsh, Ltd., premiums on cars, 63.70 .... 446 00

Engineering, Surveying and Locating Roads ($1,017.44)

R. M. Best, search for titles, 11.13; S. Blaney, purchase of land, 11.32; J. Bloedow, purchase of land, 40.00; G. M. Busch (estate of), purchase of land, 125.00; R. A. Campbell, registration of deeds, 7.66; M. Dombroski, purchase of right-of-way, 160.00; E. Evers, purchase of right-of-way, 175.00; B. Giffen, purchase of right-of-way, 168.60; P. Passaw, purchase of land, 40.00; Pirie & Stone, registration fees, etc., 41.56; N. Ricker, purchase of right-of-way, 150.00; R. J. Sanderson, registration fees, 9.67; T. C. Swartman, wages of men, 75.50; purchase of options, 2.00 .... 1,017 44

Salaries, Travelling and Other Expenses Not Otherwise Provided for ($145.00)

E. Casey, services taking charge of equipment, 105.00; W. Prince, claim for loss of horse, 40.00 .... 145 00

Miscellaneous $433,937.28

Colonization Roads $443,623.76

Statutory

EXPENDITURES UNDER NORTHERN DEVELOPMENT ACT ($4,521,667.29)

Summary

Administration ($143,575.52)

(R.S.O. 1927, Chapter 36, Section 9)

Permanent salaries (see page 4)	97,478 06		
Temporary salaries (see page 12)	16,214 87		
		113,692 93	
Contingencies (see page 12)		29,882 59	
		143,575 52	
Salaries of Deputy Minister and Officials (see page 4)			97,478 06

Statutory—Continued

Administration—Continued

Temporary Services, $16,214.87.

Harold Benson, clerk typist at 73.50 per mo., 441.00; I. Bishop, clerk typist at 61.25 per mo., 367.50; Harry Burch, messenger boy at 42.87 per mo., 516.20; C. Chesterfield, clerk at 73.50 per mo., 378.80; M. Dickin, stenographer at 67.37 per mo., 404.22; E. J. Dodds, draughtsman at 97.92 per mo., 1,179.20; W. Draper, draughtsman at 130.42 per mo., 1,570.86; F. Elson, clerk typist at 61.25 per mo., 367.50; K. Eplett, typist at 61.25 per mo., 61.25; A. S. Falconer, assistant storekeeper at 73.50 per mo., 441.00; M. Gould, stenographer at 67.37 per mo., 404.22; M. Higgins, stenographer at 67.37 per mo., 811.20; Anne Hunt, stenographer at 85.38 per mo., 1,028.80; Thos. Magladery, clerk stenographer at 79.62 per mo., 477.72; Wm. Marks, clerk at 61.25 per mo., 367.50; D. Moore, clerk typist at 61.25 per mo., 367.50; Ernest Potter, clerk at 61.25 per mo., 367.50; Margaret Potts, clerk stenographer at 61.25 per mo., 737.50; L. Robe, stenographer at 67.37 per mo., 811.20; I. Shankland, stenographer at 67.37 per mo., 811.20; Jessie Smith, clerk at 61.25 per mo., 367.50; Marian Sparling, stenographer clerk at 67.37 per mo., 233.20; Dorothy Trimble, clerk at 61.25 per mo., 367.50; Geo. Trumbell, clerk at 79.62 per mo., 477.72; Fane Waterbury, clerk at 79.62 per mo., 477.72; Jean Waters, clerk at 61.25 per mo., 367.50; W. Wilkinson, draughtsman at 130.42 per mo., 1,570.86; D. Wilson, clerk typist at 73.50 per mo., 441.00...... 16,214 87

Travelling Expenses, $4,518.17.

C. H. Fullerton, 268.43; J. Gourlay, 135.92; C. H. Meader, 1,189.08; A. Reid, 55.48; J. Sinton, 975.68; Jas. Smith, 1,767.58; R. G. Sneath, 59.50; L. D. N. Stewart, 66.50.. 4,518 17

Contingencies, $25,364.42.

American Road Builders Association, annual dues, 3.00; The Art Metropole, draughting and engineering supplies, 330.22; Bailey & May, gas, oil, 13.63; Bark & Mortimer, auto insurance, 29.92; Burroughs Adding Machine of Canada, Ltd., inspections, repairs, 47.73; The Canadian Engineer, advertising and subscription, 303.85; The Canadian Facts Publishing Co., copies, 7.50; Canadian Geographical Society, subscription, 3.00; Canadian Good Roads Association, subscription, 4.00; Canadian Grocer, subscription, 2.00; Canadian National Express, express, 497.11; Canadian National Railways, freight, 1.56; Canadian National Telegraph, telegrams, 316.65; Canadian Pacific Express Co., 1,122.25; Canadian Pacific Railway Co., freight, .30; Canadian Pacific Railway Co.'s Telegraph, telegrams, 751.17; E. O. Casselman Garage, car parts, gas, oil, 135.44; Commercial Reproducing Co., Ltd., blueprinting, photostat, 18.85; Contract Record & Engineering Review, advertising, 123.00; H. S. Crabtree, Ltd., blueprint, draughting supplies, 191.04; A. G. Cumming, Ltd., draughting instruments and supplies, 18.70; Engineering Institute, fee and subscription, 10.00; Engineering News-Record, subscription, 7.50; Felt & Tarrant, Ltd., inspections, 8.00; Film & Slide Co. of Canada, Ltd., slides, 16.50; Lionel Godson, auto insurance, 44.20; E. Gruenig, bridge building book, 2.25; Instruments, Ltd., draughting supplies, 69.82; King Edward Hotel, meals, 26.25; King's Printer, 14,816.78; C. G. Knight, gas, oil, 504.11; W. L. Lawer, disbursements, 236.05; Hugh C. MacLean Publications, Ltd., subscription, 3.00; Miller Lithographic Co., Ltd., copies of road map, 1,670.00; Milne's Garage, repairs, 138.61; Murdock Stationery, carbon paper, 232.75; Association of Ontario Land Surveyors, annual dues, 14.00; Province of Ontario Pictures, lantern slides, prints, 16.80; Thos. Pocklington Co., Ltd., repairs to instruments, 143.48; Postmaster, stamps, 61.63; Association of Professional Engineers, annual fees, 15.00; Dept. of Highways, gas, oil, repairs, 2,124.40; Dept. of Public Printing and Stationery, advertising, subscription, 24.60; Dept. of Public Works, blueprints, supplies, 599.39; The J. Frank Raw Co., Ltd., draughting supplies, 53.01; Remington Typewriters, Ltd., inspections, etc., 33.00; Smith & Walsh, auto insurance, 27.30; E. B. Smyth, tire and tube, 8.40; Thomas & Corney Typewriters, Ltd., inspections, ribbons, 128.50; The Todd Sales Co., Ltd., inspections, 5.50; Toronto Railway & Steamboat Guide, annual subscriptions, 15.00; Toronto Transportation Commission, car tickets, 18.00; Toronto United Garage, Ltd., air seal, 10.63; United Typewriter Co., Ltd., inspections, repairs, 356.24; Willys-Overland Sales Co., Ltd., car parts, 2.80.... 25,364 42

Total Administration................................ 143,575 52

Statutory—Continued

ROADS AND BRIDGES ($4,240,321.13)

District No. 1, Huntsville	557,289 76	
District No. 2, North Bay	434,552 04	
District No. 3, Sudbury	523,067 49	
District No. 4, Sault Ste. Marie	406,038 17	
District No. 5, New Liskeard	533,256 69	
District No. 6, Matheson	447,417 87	
District No. 7, Cochrane	309,241 54	
District No. 8, Fort William	638,499 86	
District No. 9, Kenora	266,483 26	
District No. 10, Fort Frances	131,565 92	
	4,247,412 60	
Less Repayments Transferred from Refund Account	7,091 47	
		4,240,321 13

DISTRICT No. 1 ($557,289.76)

Engineer, K. Rose, Huntsville

Ferguson Highway	278,584 14	
Bracebridge-Baysville-Dorset Road	39,444 49	
Rosseau Road	23,454 82	
Burk's Falls-Parry Sound Road	19,019 36	
Trout Creek-Loring Road	17,228 95	
Powassan-Restoule Road	13,718 30	
Gravenhurst-Bala-Parry Sound Road	13,596 70	
Huntsville-Dwight-Dorset Road	7,651 18	
Sundridge-Magnetawan Road	6,003 20	
Parry Sound-Nobel Road	3,544 28	
Emsdale-Sprucedale Road	2,704 63	
Equipment and tools	74,673 89	
General maintenance, settlers' and other roads, sundry expenditure	57,665 82	
		557,289 76

Travelling Expenses, $2,149.83.

D. H. Campbell, 937.33; A. A. Cooper, 117.47; G. H. Cooper, 76.36; E. W. Geddes, 41.30; Geo. McKenzie, 92.52; Ross Miller, 131.01; P. Mulveney, 210.60; John Paris, 15.88; R. E. Richardson, 221.21; K. Rose, 306.15 .... 2,149 83

Advertising, Newspapers, Printing and Stationery, $152.82.

Harry Booth, 57.35; Gilchrist's Drug Store, 10.10; Huntsville Forrester, 16.80; National Stationers, Ltd., 18.00; Royal Bank of Canada, 50.57 .... 152 82

Autos, Trucks, Accessories, Parts and Repairs, $18,597.77.

Bailey & May, 229.98; Burk's Falls Garage, 368.81; Canadian Fairbanks-Morse Co., Ltd., 90.53; Canadian Ingersoll-Rand Co., Ltd., 15.39; Central Garage, Huntsville, 40.65; Central Garage, Minden, 36.79; Dominion Road Machinery Co., Ltd., 976.45; Emsdale Garage, 37.05; General Supply Co. of Canada, Ltd., 4,271.65; Gravenhurst Auto Repairs, 1,022.54; Gravenhurst Service Station, 790.82; H. S. Howland Sons & Co., Ltd., 164.05; International Harvester Co. of Canada, Ltd., 652.53; W. J. Jessup, 534.06; David Johnston & Son, 14.70; Don T. Johnston, 387.00; Kaiser's Auto Service, 296.23; Henry Langford, 73.65; Massey-Harris Co., Ltd., 187.56; Milne's Garage, 15.50; R. J. Mitchell, 2,160.94; Mitchell's Service Station, 1,283.11; Muskoka Garage, 14.55; Muskoka Foundry, Ltd., 50.18; North Star Garage, 100.39; Osbourne & Macklain, 65.09; Powassan Garage, 91.28; Dept. of Highways, 259.28; Sawyer-Massey, Ltd., 1,335.81; Reg. Scott, 56.75; E. T. Shortland, 406.56; Sullivan Machinery Co., Ltd., 19.07; Sundridge Garage, 729.48; K. Thomson, 101.61; Trout Creek Garage, 423.63; Truck & Tractor Equipment Co., Ltd., 80.36; Union Garage, 344.53; Frank Virkus, 94.50; Wettlaufer Machinery Co., 54.25; G. S. Yearley, 720.46 .... 18,597 77

Camp and Road Supplies and Equipment, $123,912.52.

I. H. Alexander, 155.49; Ed. Barber, 69.00; Barrett Co., Ltd., 3,368.87; Bethune Pulp & Lumber Co., Ltd., 156.73; Bituminous Spraying & Contracting Co., Ltd., 8,227.47; Mrs. Louisa Bower, 27.34; British American Oil Co., Ltd., 47.20; C. Burns, 40.40; A. Busch, 321.00; Sam Butti, 71.19; Walker Camick, 38.40; Canada Paint Co., Ltd., 194.46; Canadian Timber Co., Ltd., 12.95; E. O. Casselman, 1,052.72; Frank Cassie, 586.50; Clarke & Shea, 110.00; D. W. Clayton, 10.05;

Statutory—Continued

Roads and Bridges—Continued

District No. 1—Continued

Camp and Road Supplies and Equipment—Continued

J. E. Clipsham & Sons, Ltd., 854.15; Cochrane Dunlop Hardware, Ltd., 99.71; Cockshutt Plow Co., Ltd., 1,009.56; Colas Roads, Ltd., 14,441.98; Coldwater Crushed Stone, 11,058.64; Frank Cook, 10.52; J. P. Cook, 62.60; A. G. Cumming, 57.40; Alf. Davis, 15.18; M. & M. A. Deans, Ltd., 23.90; W. Dillane, 25.55; F. Dobbs, 25.50; Dominion Bridge Co., Ltd., 40.00; Bert Doolittle, 10.66; Dow Chemical Co., 4,383.51; W. Driver, 13.89; A. N. Fenn, 209.10; Sylvester Gaido, 75.00; General Steel Wares, Ltd., 11,955.42; M. S. Godfrey, 10.90; Gold Medal Furniture Manufacturing Co., Ltd., 928.27; Grand & Toy, Ltd., 48.50; Grant-Holden-Graham, Ltd., 6,323.61; B. Greening Wire Co., Ltd., 380.81; Adam Hall, Ltd., 4,030.88; Horace G. Harper, 30.13; Hern Hardware, Ltd., 1,230.03; E. Hillman. 75.00; Francis W. Holt, 327.75; Leonard Hummel, 14.00; Huntsville Planing Mills, 369.67; Huntsville Trading Co., 8,414.47; Imperial Oil, Ltd., 267.65; Instruments, Ltd., 40.75; A. B. Jardine & Co., Ltd., 3,766.00; Jestin & Blanchard, 67.50; J. P. Johnstone, 20.60; N. A. Kelly, 14.40; Cecil T. Kidd, 150.00; D. R. Kidd, 32.40; King's Printer, 169.29 ; J. Knowles, 25.89; John Leckie, Ltd., 911.22; W. G. Leigh, 114.00; L. McCloskey, 208.65; Jos. McEwen, 49.20; McKinley Hardware Co., 646.85; McKinnon Industries, Ltd., 66.24; Metallic Roofing Co. of Canada, Ltd., 316.08; Mickle, Dyment & Son, 133.41; H. S. Miller, 64.17; Miller's Service Station, 36.65; Geo. K. Morrison, 23.36; Alex. Murray & Co., Ltd., 4,033.72; Muskoka Wood Manufacturing Co., Ltd., 69.14; Lloyd Nicholl's Garage, 77.19; Non-Skid Pavement Ltd., 2,155.56; Geo. F. Olan, 15.00; Ontario Reformatory Industries, 2,261.51; John Paris, 200.00; Ernest Patterson, 590.90; Pedlar People, Ltd., 372.90; A. L. Perkins, 25.11; Thos. Pocklington Co., 77.48; Postmasters, 1,193.63; J. Frank Raw Co., Ltd., 413.17; Wm. J. Rice Co., 968.49; R. Roberts, 32.40; Roebuck & Sharp, 1,817.01; Sawyer-Massey, Ltd., 5,090.01; A. E. Shaw, 241.08; R. Shay, 28.47; Shell Co. of Canada, Ltd., 34.10; J. D. Shier Lumber Co., Ltd., 136.29; Jos. Shoemaker, 28.92; R. Shoemaker, 71.00; Slingsby Manufacturing Co., Ltd., 1,485.00; Wm. Sloan, 29.60; John B. Smith & Sons, Ltd., 172.47; Smith's Hardware & Grocery, 83.60; Solvay Sales Corporation, 4,273.50; South River Trading Co., 12.00; Sturgeons, Ltd., 949.18; K. E. Thomson, 46.58; Trout Creek Lumber Co., 1,032.15; J. W. Troyer, 25.35; Tudhope-Anderson, Ltd., 1,290.94; Watson, Jack & Co., Ltd., 702.81; John Welch, 26.00; S. W. Welch, 33.95; The Whitten Co., Ltd., 19.45; Wood, Alexander & James, Ltd., 1,191.80; Wm. Woodruff, 97.40

Woods Manufacturing Co., Ltd., 10,429.67; Geo. Wye, 11.90.......		130,016 80	
Less transferred to Fort William Stores Account.....	3,494 82		
Less transferred to Temiskaming Stores Account....	2,609 46		
		6,104 28	
			123,912 52

Contracts $63,857.74.

Bituminous Spraying & Contracting Co., Ltd., reshaping and rolling of sub-grade and laying 3-inch consolidated bituminous retread surface, between Novar and Powassan, between Powassan and Callendar on the Ferguson Highway, 42,936.02; Muskoka Construction Co., cutting, burning, stumping and grubbing right-of-way, Ferguson Highway, Township Armour, 16,007.21; Wm. Dillane, Bridges, Trout Creek-Powassan Section, Ferguson Highway, Township Himsworth, 3,502.20; Wm. Dillane, bridges and culverts, Burk's Falls-South River Section, Ferguson Highway, Townships Armour and Strong, 1,412.31.................. 63,857 74

Gravel, Rock and Stone, $15,609.54.

Mrs. Wm Acton, 23.80; Thos. Allan, 33.37; Mrs. T. N. Armstrong, 84.60; Ed. Barber, 13.10; John Barrager, 31.20; A. E. Bastedo, 223.00; T. G. Boothby, 73.20; W. Bottrell, 65.70; Mrs. Louisa Bower, 651.60; Thos. Boyce, 20.50; Arthur Boyes, 20.08; Cecil Bradfield, 19.85; David Bradford, 235.35; P. Brock, 140.05; Henry Brook, 59.25; Adam Brownlee, 21.20; Angus Buchanan, 78.00; Chas. Burke, 62.00; Muriel S. Burnes, 38.40; Bert Campbell, 96.25; E. Casselman, 742.40; J. Ciglen, 331.40; Geo. Clubbe, 10.35; Abraham Code, 283.90; Henry Creasor, 128.90; D. Crossthwaite, 764.70; B. Dashney, 11.86; Mrs. Mary Doley, 402.25; John Draper, 48.44; Mrs. Jane Dunbar, 18.75; Jas. Duncan, 39.75; Geo. Dunker, 11.70; Edward Durnin, 67.80; Harvey Ego, 44.30; F. E Emberson, 31.00; L. Emlaw, 24.70; Henry Etler, 106.10; R. Fry, 48.75; John Gougeon, 30.40; Jas. Graham, 47.20; Wm. Grant, 11.70; Mrs. Sarah Green, 23.10; Arthur Harrow, 22.25; T. B. Hearn, 66.80; E. Hillman, 224.40; Philip Holt, 12.00; O. Hubener, 45.52; A. Hubner, 21.15; Ignatius Hummel, 11.30; John Hunter, 68.50; Jos. E. Hunter, 135.10; R. J. Hutchison, 20.40; Charlie Jacklin, 48.15; Wm. Jackson, 35.00; Herb H. Jamieson, 82.60; Arthur Jeffrey, 171.60; N. A. Kelly, 187.20; Geo. Keown, 25.60; Ernest Kirk, 27.00; V. Kundel, 17.47; Albert Lamb,

Statutory—Continued

Roads and Bridges—Continued

District No. 1—Continued

Gravel, Rock and Stone—Continued

36.70; Wm. Lang, 13.95; Samuel Langmaid, 314.10; Geo. Law, 39.75; F. and Mrs. Lawson, 97.65; Chas. Lick, 96.47; Limestone Products, Ltd., 58.42; Longford Crushed Stone, Ltd., 2,413.63 ; Geo. Loxton, 589.05 ; W. T. Lundy, 100.00; Roy McCoubrey, 60.80; N. McDonald, 15.00; Jas. Mathewson, 80.25; Townships of Medora and Wood, 196.10; Clifford Miller, 150.17; Stanley Mills, 157.92; Mrs. Robt. Moore, 94.70; T. J. Moore, 61.45; J. Morgan, 78.50; Stan. Morris, 25.90; J. Neely, 339.30; Geo. O'Brien, 14.80; Thos. Paget, 357.15; W. Parolin, 73.30; Alfred Parton, 171.67; R. Patterson, 96.55; Roland Peacock, 58.00; G. Perry, 41.13; Percy Price, 599.60; Alex. Proudfoot, 176.40; W. Restoule, 15.62; J. B. Rich, 27.99; Martin Rich, 15.06; Jos. Riva, 42.20; Mrs. E. J. Roberts, 18.75; Mrs. Geo. Roberts, 55.20; Lee Roberts, 169.65; G. L. Robertson, 15.00; Henry Robins, 20.00; Ian Robins, 247.38; A. Rochefort, 25.20; R. Rowlandson, 148.60; Jas. Shelley, 43.60; E. Shortland, 120.60; W. Simpson, 339.40; Daniel Sinclair, 20.00; Nelson Sinclair, 17.25; Wm. Sloan, 15.30; John Smith, 92.60; Soldiers' Settlement Board of Canada, 21.50; L. Sommacal, 66 70; M. G. Stevenson, 69.25; Thos. Stewart, 15.45; Jos. Tapley, 11.40; W. Thorne, 71.50; Mrs. Geo. Tibbell, 80.40; Frank Welsh, 14.10; John Willoughby, 20.25; J. Wurm, 47.90; Geo. Wye, 67.49; R. Zimmerman, 623.80 .... 15,609 54

Pay Lists, $239,585.64.

Wages of men 239,585 64

Board and Lodging, $1,232.65.

Bayview Lodge, 230.02; Mrs. Louisa Bower, 71.40; Hugo Evers, 25.00; Mrs. M. Fawcett, 140.50; Mrs. H. G. Hurtibise, 146.00; Kent House, 18.22; Mrs. A. McKechnie, 22.35; New Windsor Hotel, 89.00; Mrs. B. Richardson, 356.06; Mrs. Geo. Tibbell, 19.50; Valley View Inn, 39.80; Mrs. Fred Vanclieaf, 74.80 .... 1,232 65

Proportionate Cost of Roads, $612.50.

Township of Macauley 612 50

Purchase of Property, Right-of-Way, $25,69 .07.

Agricultural Development Board, 556.00; Misses Sarah and Susan Beaumont, 1,199.50; Mrs. Alice Bouskill, 15.00; Mrs. Louisa Bower, 482.85; Arthur Boyes, 89.38; David Bradford, 689.03; Angus Buchanan, 729.50; Clem Bunn, 420.70; Geo. Butson, 697.50; A. B. Caldwell, 356.00; Edward Candelore, 813.63; Mrs. Annie Grace Carr, 21.00; Pauline Esther Christian, 250.00; A. M. Church, 175.00; Abraham Code, 721.70; Miss Mary Corkery, 950.00; Henry Creasor, 325.00; Colin H. Cudmore, 140.00; Mrs. Margaret V. Doeg, 50.00; Mrs. Jane Dunbar, 423.25; Jas. Duncan, 292.50; Edward Durnin, 225.00; Hugo Evers, 375.00; John Gibbs, 501.25; B. E. Green, 100.00; T. B. Hearn, 450.00; Alvin Hogg, 50.00; Ignatius Hummel, 1,500.00; Wm. Hummel, 553.00; Mrs. Eleanor Jackson, 175.00; Mrs. A. E. Johnstone, 125.00; Geo. W. Kidd, 85.00; Wm. Lang, 320.00; Mrs. Mary Logan, 125.00; Jas. McClocklin, 25.00; John and Martha Minorgan, 50.75; T. J. Moore, 1,543.00; Alex. Norrie, 543.00; Levi Nutt, 100.00; Thos. Nutt, 100.00; Geo. O'Brien, 467.50; Wm. O'Shaughnessy, 715.00; Wilbert Parker, 730.80; Ernest Parker, 327.35; Roland Peacock, 1,218.00; Frank W. Prince, 25.00; Henry Rawson, 25.00; B. B. Rick, 343.50; Henry Robins, 758.73; Ian Robins, 765.33; John W. Sedore, 400.00; H. M. Shaw, 800.00; Mrs. Jennie Shields, 97.22; Strong Agricultural Society, 127.00; Mrs. Geo. Tibbell, 343.40; Mrs. Hugh Tibbell, 341.70; N. Tugendhaft, 550.00; John Verasco, 30.00; Mrs. Kate Wall, 1,250.00; Ace Willard, 35.00 .... 25,694 07

Miscellaneous, $65,884.68.

Mrs. I. Armstrong, cleaning office, 182.00; Bark & Mortimer, auto insurance, 11.70; Bell Telephone Co., telephone services, etc., 949.01; R. M. Best, professional services, 398.49; Bigwin Laundry, washing blankets, 1,225.99; John Billingsley, damages to property, 23.00; Bituminous Spraying & Contracting Co., Ltd., demurrage, 57.00; Christie Boe, car rental, 12.00; Alf. Bower, car rental, 202.00; H. R. Brock, damage to property, 150.00; D. H. Campbell, car rental, 658.00; Canadian Inspection & Testing Co., Ltd., testing paint, 36.44; Canadian National Express, express, 72.61; Canadian National Railways, freight, etc., 20,419.99; Canadian National Telegraphs, telegrams, 62.34; Canadian Pacific Railway Co., freight, 12.76; Gordon S. Cook, blacksmithing, 19.85; N. W. Cook, blacksmithing, 19.35; G. H. Cooper, car rental, 344.00; B. Cottrill & Son, rent of rooms, light, 469.75; A. Cowden, car rental, 42.00; Stephen Dougan, plumbing, etc., 208.40; F. E. Emberson, fencing, 15.00; Fred Fisher, rent of stables, etc.,

Statutory—Continued

Roads and Bridges—Continued

District No. 1—Continued

Miscellaneous—Continued

15.00; Galbraith & Burgess, surveying land, 34.00; G. Gavin, car rental, 18.00; E. W. Geddes, car rental, 49.00; B. E. Green, fencing, 15.00; building, 700.00; W. L. Haight, searching titles, 16.50; Horace G. Harper, fencing, 21.50; Geo. Hayes, cartage, 130.00; The Huntsville Club, office rent, 20.00; Town of Huntsville, surface treading road, 2,181.72; Town of Huntsville, light, water, 16.42; Hutchins Service Station & Transport, cartage, 146.62; Wm. Hutchins, cartage, 662.75; Hydro-Electric Power Commission of Ontario, repairs to line, 42.75; E. Jacklin, car rental, 30.00; A. Kellock & Sons, rent of building, storage, 45.50; Kirkfield Garage, hauling timber, 135.00; Jas. Knight, blacksmithing, 126.12; H. Lalonde, rental of barn, 12.33; C. E. Lount (Registrar), professional services, 15.20; J. McCabe, cartage, 19.00; R. H. McFarland, car rental, 14.00; Herb McKelvie, rent of office, cleaning, 15.00; Geo. McKenzie, car rental, 666.00; Magnetawan Municipal Telephone System, moving poles, etc., 40.00; E. W. Meloy, damage to property, $70.00; Ross Miller, car rental, $604.00; Minden Municipal Telephone System, telephone services, 44.92; Mrs. Newlove, cartage, 70.49; John Paris, car rental, 78.00; Ernest Patterson, hauling, 183.50; H. A. Peacock, car rental, 68.00; Pirie & Stone, legal services, 2,088.21; Dept. of Highways, 50 per cent. of construction of bridge, 29,861.95; E. W. Richards, cartage, 710.25; R. E. Richardson, car rental, 400.00; Cecil A. Roberts, trucking, 187.50; Wm. Shier, car rental, 20.00; Val Thompson, replacing fence, 15.00; Watt Municipal Telephone System, moving poles, 31.50; A. E. Wilson & Co., Ltd., auto insurance, 52.00; petty disbursements, unenumerated, $720.27 .... 65,984 68

Less Expenditure Refund .... 100 00 | 65,884 68

DISTRICT No. 2 ($434,552.04)

Engineer, G. A. White, North Bay

Trans-Canada Highway	156,064 06	
North Bay-Sault Road	66,894 93	
Sturgeon Falls-Field Road	47,105 48	
Warren-Rutter Road	17,523 67	
Ferguson Highway	17,036 58	
Pembroke-Callander Road	16,368 24	
Warren-River Valley Road	6,099 10	
Trout Lake Road	2,881 75	
Field-River Valley Road	2,522 41	
Equipment and tools	10,288 22	
General maintenance, settlers' and other roads, sundry expenditure	91,767 60	
		434,552 04

Travelling Expenses, $1,864.70.

E. G. Adams, 183.97; G. A. Crane, 240.80; J. A. Levis, 34.57; R. M. McCaffrey, 62.99; K. C. McDonald, 30.35; J. MacKenzie, 373.62; Thos. Nicholls, 23.50; Jno. Pichette, 40.23; W. E. Roberts, 23.95; P. Rochefort, 220.85; Fred Saynor, 137.25; G. A. White, 492.62 .... 1,864 70

Advertising, Newspapers, Printing, Stationery, $148.58.

F. S. Fosdick, 86.09; Bank of Nova Scotia, 42.00; The Nugget, 20.49 .... 148 58

Autos, Trucks, Accessories, Parts and Repairs, $15,382.86.

J. D. Adams (Canada), Ltd., 204.84; Allis-Chalmers Mfg. Co. (Milwaukee), 26.97; Allis-Chalmers Mfg Co. (Toronto), 1,036.55; Bay City Machine Works, 1,301.29; E. Berriault, 13.60; N. Boufford, 25.23; V. Boufford, 13.49; A. Bourgault, 95.70; Central Garage, 169.38; Charland's Battery Service, 16.60; S. J. Cherry, 103.20; Dominion Road Machinery Co., Ltd., 225.66; Doyle's Garage, 17.75; General Supply Co. of Canada, Ltd., 229.98; E. Giesebrecht, 96.78; Omer Gignac, 43.35; International Harvester Co. of Canada, Ltd., 466.37; Keyes Supply Co., Ltd., 98.18; Wilfred Laforge, 11.00; Wm. Laforge, 437.02; Mattawa Garage, 86.82; John Morrow Screw & Nut Co., Ltd., 928.07; Murdock & Smith, 16.00; North Bay Garage, 785.02; Northern Foundry & Machine Co., Ltd., 207.27; Northern Supplies, Ltd., 546.62; A. C. O'Connor, 213.97; O'Connor's Garage, 106.50; Patterson Machine Works, 15.19; J. A. Prieur, 2,488.78; Sawyer-Massey, Ltd., 1,528.25; P. Sherwin, 2,770.81; Smyth Bros. Garage, 36.90; H. Stockdale, 30.00;

Statutory—Continued

Roads and Bridges—Continued

District No. 2—Continued

Autos, Trucks, Accessories, Parts and Repairs—Continued

John R. Taylor, 14.00; Truck & Tractor Equipment Co., Ltd., 193.67; Albert Trudel, 123.39; W. C. Warburton Co., Ltd., 249.81; White & McDowell, 422.20; less Baines & David, Ltd., 13.35 credit.................................... 15,382 86

Camp and Road Supplies and Equipment, $44,049.44.

Adanac Service, Ltd., 77.49; W. D. Advitt, 68.42; J. G. Armstrong, 46.91; Art Metropole, 77.50; Omer Asslin, 51.01; Jos. Baechler, 280.00; Fred T. Baker, 41.20; Barrett Co., Ltd., 30.36; Estate of Walter Beatty, 59.02; Estate of J. H. Bell, 291.92; A. D. Bellefeuille, 20.52; Eug. Bertrand, 33.85; Bituminous Spraying & Contracting Co., Ltd., 48.00; A. Branconnier, 123.16; A. Breault, 16.80; Victor Brisson, 38.71; Burlington Steel Co., Ltd., 121.03; Canada Cement Co., Ltd., 537.50; Canada Bitumuls Co., Ltd., 11,333.21; Canadian Ingersoll-Rand Co., Ltd., 1,036.04; Canadian Oil Companies, Ltd.. 8,533.28; Canadian Timber Co., Ltd., 47.33; J. Carey, 63.50; Municipalities of Casimir, Jennings and Appelby, 59.25; R. Chevrefels, 28.48; Phillippe Chretien, 27.60; Clarke & Lounsbury, 70.55; Cochrane Dunlop Hardware Co., Ltd. (North Bay), 953.52; Cochrane Dunlop Hardware Co., Ltd. (Pembroke), 71.92; Jos. Contu, 64.32; Andrew Cotnam, 79.73; A. O. Cotnam, 104.39; C. Cousineau, 44.70; E. Daoust, 61.82; D. Dashnay, 10.92; A. Desrosiers, 45.72; W. Dixon, 139.56; Aug. Doust, 20.68; Estate of David Dover, 600.40; F. England, 15.75; Foisy Garage, 52.81; Jas. Foisy, 42.00; Goodyear Tire & Rubber Co. of Canada, Ltd., 20.63; Geo. Gordon & Co., Ltd., 30.80; Hector Goulard, 17.85; Clo Guenette, 1,126.65; E. Guenette, 11.80; Jos. Guenette, 13.10; J. Herman, 546.77; Jas. Kilby, 45.00; King's Printer 214.29; W. E. Kinsey, 80.75; Art Lafrenniere, 48.58 ; C. H. Lafrenniere, 83.68; T. Lalonde, 58.50; Emile Langlois, 37.75; O. Larocque & Sons, 457.60; Mrs. E. Lee, 81.48; Jos. Levigny, 21.96; Lindsay & McCluskey, Ltd., 83.03; McColl-Frontenac Oil Co., Ltd., 11.96; D. McDonald, 60.00; F. McDonald, 347.45; A. A. McIntosh, Ltd., 391.48; Mrs. A. McKechnie, 124.66; Hugh McPharland, 14.00; Mageau Lumber Co., Ltd., 319.09; Mattawa Hardware, 65.02; Lou Mersineau, 142.40; Metallic Roofing Co. of Canada, Ltd., 132.00; Michaud Bros., Ltd., 82.10; Michaud & Levesque, 24.61; J. H. Mulligan, 348.25; Alex. Murray & Co., Ltd., 2,793.91; National Grocers Co., Ltd., 1,389.08; Noelville Trading Co., 2,965.72; Northern Oil Co., Ltd., 1,447.06; Ontario Reformatory Industries, 308.83; Peerless Baking Co., 57.60; Jos. Perreault, 33.93; N. L. Piper Railway Supplies, Ltd., 153.60; W. Poitras, 12.60; Postmasters, 171.50; G. Price, 18.00; Rapid Service Station, 31.46; Zenon Riberdy, 13.00; J. W. Richardson, 13.97; J. O. Roberge, 58.80; J. O. Robert, 347.65; Alfred Rogers, Ltd., 537.50; H. Roy, 1,582.94; Adelard St. Aubin, 31.00; Henri Savage, 25.78; J. Sevigny, 199.23; Standard Planing Mills & Lumber Co., Ltd., 93.20; Steel Equipment Co., Ltd., 24.25; Stratford Chair Co., 185.00; Sturgeons, Ltd., 88.42; R. B. Tennant & Co., 32.64; F. Trottier, 19.44; G. Z. Trudeau, 10.30; Jack Turner, 10.20; Louis Vaillancourt, 383.81; J. Z. Vinet, 76.79; A. J. Walker, 222.80; Chas. Warnock & Co., Ltd., 30.00; West.Arm Inn, 147.31; H. P. Whyte, 18.00........ 44,049 44

Contracts, $24,370.34.

The Edgar Irvine Co., Ltd., scarifying, reshaping and rolling of sub-grade on the Trans-Canada Highway and laying thereon of 3-inch consolidated bituminous retread, from the Town of Pembroke ten miles northwesterly, 19,557.00; Leitch Construction Co., removal and erecting bridges, widening culvert, Trans-Canada Highway, Township of Buchanan, 3,861.49; Standard Steel Construction Co., fabrication and erection of steel bridge over Chalk River on the Trans-Canada Highway, Township of Buchanan, 951.85.................................. 24,370 34

Gravel, Rock and Stone, $67,310.00.

Mrs. A. Audet, 18.90; E. A. Bartlett, 15.50; Jos. Beaulieu, 25.00; J. E. Bedard, 22.65; J. S. Bedard, 44.50; H. Benette, 13.20; J. Bertrand, 20.80; Paul Binette, 24.00; S. Binnette, 27.30; J. Boudreau, 28.40; D. Bouffard, 16.00; Nap. Bouffard, 66.20; S. Bouffard, 22.05; Jos. Brassard, 81.40; Mrs. Jos. Brause, 23.40; A. Breault, 38.44; E. Breault, 12.70; M. Brisson, 10.90; D. Buffard, 14.90; S. Buffard, 19.40; Albert E. Burton, 196.10; J. Carey, 24.90; H. Champagne, 15.90; E. Chartrand, 10.80; C. Chenier, 75.55; T. Chenier, 112.35; R. Chevrefels, 64.20; L. S. Clarke, 114.90; E. Contou, 13.95; E. Contu, 61.00; N. T. Cooper, 33.60; G. Cretien, 15.60; C. T. R. Crompton, 233.75; F. Dagg, 770.25; Victor Dalcourt, 41.40; A. Deforge, 18.40; A. Dignard, 47.50; A. Ducharme, 83.50; E. Dufour, 428.40; O. Dufrense, 20.45; Justine Dupois, 14.25; A. Durant, 53.60; C. Duval, 32.50; Mrs. N. P. Eden, 32.50; H. Filliatreau, 10.20; V. Fink, 12.45; Mrs. Albertine Forget, 17.35; Mrs. Albertine Fortin, 15.40; Mrs. Arthur Fortin, 68.60; D. Fraser, 21.90; R. Fraser,

Statutory—Continued

Roads and Bridges—Continued

District No. 2—Continued

Gravel, Rock and Stone—Continued

60.00; Thos. Gallagher, 342.75; D. Gascon, 15.60; L. Gaudette, 324.85; O. Gauthier, 63.30; P. Gauthier, 51.40; O. Gervais, 13.90; C. E. Gorman, 50.20; G. Gorman, 27.05; O. Hansen, 29.60; Harry Horner, 115.70; E. Hurtibese, 23.50; E. A. Hurtibese, 129.45; Edgar Irvine Co., Ltd., 2,869.00; O. Lachance, 16.00; Z. Lachappel, 121.50; A. Lafortune, 31.00; Art Lafrenniere, 56.90; L. Lafrenniere, 129.70; F. Lance, 13.60; Alex. Lang, 46.90; E. Lapance, 35.90; A. Lapierre, 25.20; V. Larochelle, 39.40; Art Larocque, 289.70; E. Laurin, 77.80; A. Lavasseur, 63.45; Eug. Lavasseur, 46.55; O. Lavoie, 29.40; J. E. Leblanc, 65.50; Joe Leclair, 21.10; Raoul Lecompte, 60.80; A. Legault, 37.50; Jos. Legault, 119.70; Jos. Legrandeau, 29.40; D. Legris, 24.00; N. Lemieux, 33.20; R. Lemieux, 87.00; A. Levasseur, 112.80; Eug. Lavasseur, 208.85; M. McNulty, 32.90; O. Martin, 13.20; Wm. Matthews, 43.00; G. Meilleur, 16.20; M. Menard, 12.90; Henry Mielkie, 19.40; L. Montroy, 113.05; W. Nadon, 54.35; L. Neault, 15.40; A. Norena, 22.55; G. E. Norena, 50.00; J. Norenda, 68.55; E. Norman, 46.75; A. Parks, 63.50; F. Pedneault, 70.10; Town of Pembroke, 54,541.21; A. Perry, 309.00; J. Piette, 16.40; Mrs. Point, 19.00; J. B. Porrier, 17.80; A. Poitras, 20.20; E. Potvin, 28.70; J. Powers, 33.60; Henry Quesnel, 15.70; Jos. Quesnel, 24.30; A. Rainville, 22.20; J. B. Rochon, 73.30; M. Rochon, 58.70; Louis Romillard, 11.25; G. Ronario, 24.15; D. Roy, 46.20; J. B. Roy, 19.60; S. Sanfrene, 36.20; E. Sarazen, 20.00; S. Saufrene, 266.60; J. Schill, 43.70; A. Seguin, 153.80; Mr. and Mrs. F. Seguin, 11.35; Jos. Seguin, 44.20; Estate of J. Shane, 88.50; Soldiers' Settlement Board of Canada, 75.00; C. Souter, 190.00; Frank Stevens, 21.75; H. Sullivan, 36.45; W. Sullivan, 95.30; H. Therien, 23.20; O. Turpin, 167.35; A. Vachon, 474.60; M. Viancourt, 34.20; I. Viau, 38.20; Mrs. A. Walsh, 29.20; A. Wegner, 43.70; J. White, 349.50 .... 67,310 00

Pay Lists, $222,960.94.

Wages of men 222,960 94

Board and Lodging, $1,671.10.

Omer Asslin, 19.50; Fred T. Baker, 57.25; Mrs. J. Campbell, 53.00; F. Champagne, 84.60; J. A. Clement, 94.80; J. Corbeil, 251.85; Paul Cote, 39.70; Crawley & McCracken Co., Ltd., 16.40; Field Hotel, 35.60; Thos. Hill, 124.50; Mrs. H. Leach, 19.80; Mrs. McDonald, 10.85; Mrs. A. McKechnie, 687.75; Mrs. O'Connor, 26.00; Mrs. G. O'Connor, 56.00; A. Poitras, 15.00; West Arm Inn, 78.50 .... 1,671 10

Proportionate Cost of Roads, $15,833.04.

Townships of—Caldwell, 2,890.75; Casimir, Jennings and Appelby, 2,317.70; Cosby and Mason, 799.88; West Ferris, 1,360.00; Field, 972.50; Martland, 1,000.00; Ratter and Dunnett, 1,675.00; Springer, 1,067.21; Widdifield, 3,750.00 15,833 04

Purchase of Property, Right-of-Way, $2,290.00.

Mrs. Norah Crompton, 2,250.00; J. A. Roy, 40.00 .... 2,290 00

Miscellaneous, $38,671.04.

E. G. Adams, car rental, 40.00; T. H. Armitage, blacksmithing, 20.75; J. G. Armstrong, car rental, 75.50; C. Auger, blacksmithing, 1,069.67; Bark & Mortimer, auto insurance, 19.72; G. R. Bartlett, car rental, 259.00; H. A. Batsford, car rental, 94.50; Bell Telephone Co., telephone services and moving poles, 1,747.48; J. Bennett, cartage, 14.00; R. Bole, car livery, 54.25; Misses G. and I. Burritt, fencing, 225.00; John Burritt, fencing, 360.00; Canada Power & Paper Corporation, rent of building, 12.00; Canadian Inspection & Testing Co., Ltd. (Toronto), testing cement, 20.00; Canadian Inspection & Testing Co., Ltd. (Montreal), testing paint, 36.44; Canadian National Express, express, 10.65; Canadian National Telegraphs, protecting wires, telegrams, 141.88; Canadian Pacific Express Co., express, 21.39; Canadian Pacific Railway Co., protecting lines, freight, 912.60; Canadian Pacific Railway Co., constructing subway, 20,601.39; Canadian Pacific Railway Co.'s Telegraph, telegrams, 73.26; T. Chapman, car rental, 604.50; Ed. Chauvin, rent of shed, 30.00; car rental, 262.00; E. Chenier, car rental, 43.60; W. Chenier, car rental, 57.65; O. Cregerson, damages to property by fire, 11.50; Paul Dechene, fencing, 150.00; De Luxe Taxi & Transfer, trucking, 50.25; A. Leo Devost, fencing, 156.00; Ed. Dupuis, rent of blacksmith shop, etc., 11.42; John Ferguson, rent of office, 45.00; Napoleon Galipeau, Jr., car rental, 511.35; Paul Galipeau, car rental, 69.00; R. Gauthier, blacksmithing, 13.90; Lionel Godson, auto insurance, 23.40; Mary Huhta, fencing, 120.00; Hydro-Electric Power Commission of Ontario, lighting, 147.34; Hydro-Electric Power Commission of Ontario, repairs to cable, 28.70; Mrs. Oscar

Statutory—Continued

Roads and Bridges—Continued

District No. 2—Continued

Miscellaneous—Continued

Ilamaki, fencing, 60.00; Edgar Irvine Co., Ltd., work on roads, 2,117.72; John Jacques, cartage, 40.50; C. R. James, fencing, 240.00; K. Kataja, fencing, 31.50; Carlo Koivistu, fencing, 120.00; Wm. Laforge, car rental, 35.00; Wm. F. Lamon, cartage, 40.00; D. Laporte, rent of warehouse, 60.00; Joe Leclair, car rental, 132.00; Leitch Construction Co., work on bridge, 1,479.75; K. C. McDonald, car rental, 268.00; J. MacKenzie, car rental, 771.05; R. McLeod, fencing, 300.00; S. J. McMeekin, fencing, 120.00; H. Malmloff, cartage, 14.15; J. A. Martin, car rental, 242.00; Tom Mattson, fencing, 112.50; Alex. A. Montgomery, clearing land, 139.70; D. C. Moore, car rental, 302.00; W. Nadon, fencing, 120.00; John Narrena, fencing, 90.00; Nipissing Laundry Co., Ltd., cleaning blankets, 14.40; The Nugget, rent of office, 975.00; alterations to office, 1,097.35; J. A. Paiment, estimating jobs, 62.50; John Paris, car rental, 20.00; Ced. Price Signs, lettering doors, etc., 18.00; Theo Rabishaw, fencing, 67.50; Z. Ranger, fencing, 45.00; Remington Typewriters, Ltd., rental of machines, 37.50; P. Reordow, damages to property by fire, 30.00; D. Rousseau, car rental, 108.00; Emil Saari, fencing, 120.00; J. R. Savard, blacksmithing, 11.50; Smith & Walsh, auto insurance, 46.80; Star Taxi & Transfer, cartage, 11.50; C. F. Szammers, car rental, 160.00; W. J. Tobin, blacksmithing, 110.53; United Typewriter Co., Ltd., rental and inspections of machines, 132.50; R. H. Wilson, blacksmithing, 31.15; petty disbursements, unenumerated, 590.85 .... 38,671 04

DISTRICT No. 3 ($523,067.49)

Engineer, E. J. Hosking, Sudbury

North Bay-Sault Road	184,234 03	
Espanola-Little Current Road	27,143 17	
Sudbury-Levack Road	19,401 41	
Little Current-Gore Bay Road	13,999 09	
Sudbury-Massey Bay Road	11,898 48	
Sudbury-Milnet Road	11,020 78	
Chapleau-Devon Road	9,757 33	
Chelmsford-Blezard-Capreol Road	9,515 76	
Gore Bay-Meldrum Bay Road	7,836 28	
Little Current-Manitowaning Road	6,247 13	
Gore Bay-Providence Bay Road	6,223 81	
Providence Bay-Manitowaning Road	4,664 75	
Sudbury-Burwash Road	4,212 92	
Bidwell-Green Bay Road	3,038 64	
Sandfield-Mindemoya Road	2,431 13	
Sudbury-Long Lake Road	2,383 09	
Long Bay-Perivale-Spring Bay Road	1,944 85	
Copper Cliff-Creighton Road	1,714 88	
Equipment and tools	19,606 34	
General maintenance, settlers' and other roads, sundry expenditure	175,793 62	
		523,067 49

Travelling Expenses, $5,194.90.

Robt. T. Crawford, 168.70; W. J. Fillion, 167.08; Harold French, 11.10; Geo. Gingras, 40.07; Louis Gratton, 40.50; Geo. Holmes, 1,186.07; E. J. Hosking, 1,021.82; John McAnsh, 1,002.20; A. L. McDonald, 14.41; A. R. McDonald, 232.30; Duncan J. McEachren, 633.51; N. N. McLean, 228.11; M. W. Moore, 37.05; F. Papineau, 54.60; D. D. Snaith, 267.24; Thos. Travers, 90.14 .... 5,194 90

Advertising, Newspapers, Printing, Stationery, $251.25.

F. C. Muirhead, 111.30; Sudbury Star, 37.55; Bank of Toronto, 102.40 .... 251 25

Autos, Trucks, Accessories, Parts and Repairs, $16,697.09.

J. D. Adams (Canada), Ltd., $66.05; Austin & Nicholson, Ltd., $793.80; O. Bourgeois, 11.75; Wm. Bracken, 12.96; Burton's Garage, Ltd., 297.80; Campbell's Garage, 194.17; Canada Ingot Iron Co., Ltd., 1,001.73; Canadian Ingersoll-Rand Co., Ltd., 783.16; Davison's Garage, 246.37; Delongchamp Truck Sales & Service, 628.60; Dominion Road Machinery Co., Ltd., 894.96; Duncan Bros., 1,038.46; Espanola Garage, 491.80; Gardiner's Garage, 1,910.17; General Welding Co., 136.50; Gore Bay Garage, 73.16; Holman Machine Co., 328.16; Hudson-Essex

Statutory—Continued

Roads and Bridges—Continued

District No. 3—Continued

Autos, Trucks, Accessories, Parts and Repairs—Continued

Garage, 75.01; Kay Supply Co., 81.86; Geo. A. Lockerby, 30.65; N. J. McColeman, 21.17; L. McDougall, 27.30; McLaughlin-Buick & Marquette Sales & Service, 143.89; McLeod Garage, 4,445.84; Northern Foundry & Machine Co., Ltd., 202.94; A. M. Rumley, 18.35; Sawyer-Massey, Ltd., 117.70; Scott Motor Sales, 46.00; Smith & Travers Co., 20.56; Sudbury Construction & Machinery Co., Ltd., 814.56; Sudbury Motors, 36.95; Wm. Terry, 15.00; N. Trotter, 870.79; Tudhope-Anderson, Ltd., 450.24; Ed. Valiquette, 35.00; Waterous, Ltd., 13.46; R. O. Watson, 14.85; Willys-Overland Sales Co., Ltd., 293.37; F. H. Wood, 12.00 ...... 16,697 09

Camp and Road Supplies and Equipment, $68,311.77.

John Ajola, 140.00; Azilda Carage, 579.40; Bannon Bros., 91.30; Oscar T. Bennett, 198.76; F. Berichon, 77.50; Bituminous Spraying & Contracting Co., Ltd., 3,004.58; T. Blais, 280.80; W. G. Blanchette, 41.80; Jos. Bois, 36.00; Louis Bois, 33.60; Teles Bonin, 98.08; Octave Boucher, 28.95; Brandow Bros., 44.75; E. Brown, 24.50; Geo. Bucciarelli, 39.84; Norman Buchanan, 66.75; L. A. Buck, 140.95; H. Buis, 74.13; James Byrnes, 12.80; Wm. Campbell, 15.00; Canada Creosoting Co., 777.17; Canada Paint Co., Ltd., 21.36; Canadian Industries, Ltd., 2,328.70; Canadian Oil Companies, Ltd., 566.46; Frank Cassie, 362.99; Chapleau Meat Market, 36.59; Stewart Clarke, 24.00; Cochrane Dunlop Hardware, Ltd., 1,671.26; Cockshutt Plow Co., Ltd., 134.65; Colas Roads, Ltd., 426.33; Coldwater Crushed Stone, Ltd., 729.22; Martin Connell, 26.80; August Daoust, 472.10; M. K. Dickinson, 96.10; Dominion Oxygen Co., Ltd., 272.82; Delphis Drolet, 12.50; Clifford Duboy, 49.00; Evans Co., Ltd., 1,359.22; P. Falzetta, 269.39; Fowler Hardware Co., Ltd., 376.35; Frost Steel & Wire Co., Ltd., 512.64; J. D. Gemmell, 533.70; George & Riching, 95.76; Get Gas, Ltd., 1,981.34; Albert Gibson, 10.05; H. W. Golden, 96.00; Goodman & Co., 152.60; H. Goodman & Son, 15.11; J. Gordon, 22.00; Grand & Toy, Ltd., 291.10; B. Greening Wire Co., Ltd., 48.36; Harpham Bros., 383.73; A. Harvey, 23,73; P. W. Herron, 1,262.64; Hocken Lumber Co., Ltd., 26.28; Albert Houle, 144.15; D. S. Humphrey, 37.20; Imperial Oil, Ltd., 1,442.40; J. C. Irving & Co., 17.45; R. J. Jaffray & Co., 884.95; Mr. and Mrs. R. Jalbert, 115.70; E. Jones, 21.00; Joe Kelly, 12.75; King George Hotel, 45.92; Kingsboro & Baxter, 57.90; A. C. Kitchen, 28.79; J. Korli, 21.40; Laberge Lumber Co., Ltd., 933.11; R. Lacoste, 21.15; P. S. Lane, 23.94; Jos. Larocque, 228.32; K. Lehto, 10.08; A. Lepage, 32.90; N. Lepage, 360.00; Z. R. Lepage, 11.85; Town of Little Current, 16.88; J. Luopa, 27.80; N. J. McColeman, 81.02; McColl-Frontenac Oil Co., Ltd., 1,471.78; H. McConnell, 22.50; Mr. and Mrs. J. McDonald, 633.73; Herbert McKnight, 783.20; Wm. Madaby, 10.50; J. T. May, 12.50; Metallic Roofing Co. of Canada, Ltd., 18,516.16; Moore Bros., 25.14; P. Morrison, 154.94; Alex. Murray Co., Ltd., 1,120.48; National Grocers Co., Ltd., 70.55; Nickel City Service, 1,047.63; North Country Supply Co., Ltd., 497.85; Northern Coal & Wood Co., 13.50; Northern Drug Co., Ltd., 10.05; Northern Paint & Varnish Co., Ltd., 124.35; J. T. Paquette, 22.11; Paramount Petroleum Co., Ltd., 12,470.01; E. Pellow, 10.03; Pellow's Garage & Taxi Service, 586.68; Nick. Perkovitch, 111.72; Jno. Polychuck, 34.51; Postmasters, 593.80; Jno. E. Powell, 39.10; E. Pullan Wipers & Waste Co., Ltd., 98.50; James Purvis & Sons, 381.35; E. Ranger, 13.44; J. Frank Raw Co., Ltd., 15.25; Theo Rochon, 17.50; Omer Rodrigue, 96.00; F. Romana, 131.90; E. Roy, 61.38; H. H. Roy, 135.12; Nap. Roy, 179.12; Joe Rumley, 13.20; S. Russell, 53.76; Jno. Salminen, 15.00; L. B. Scannell, 27.30; Philip W. Shaw, 314.25; Sherwin-Williams Co. of Canada, Ltd., 106.82; A. Shewchuk Co., 34.03; J. Sicord, 28.00; K. Sillanpaa, 13.20; J. Sloss, 17.50; Smith & Chapple, Ltd., 160.70; Spanish River Lumber Co., Ltd. (Skead), 47.78; Spanish River Lumber Co., Ltd. (Sudbury), 804.56; Sturgeon's, Ltd., 570.88; Byron H. Turner Co., Ltd., 12.89; A. B. Vaillancourt, 1,158.91; A. J. Wagg, 22.65; G. L. White, 29.71; H. Wilson, 13.40; Geo. H. Winsor, 121.46; Wolfe & Collins, 159.19 .... 68,311 77

Contracts, $33,347.12.

The Bituminous Spraying & Contracting Co., Ltd., supplying stone and chips, reshaping where necessary and rolling sub-grade, North Bay-Sault Ste. Marie Highway—from Copper Cliff to Vermillion River Bridge—11.5 miles and laying thereon 2½-inch consolidated bituminous retread top, 30,059.26; The Law Construction Co., the scarifying, reshaping and rolling of North Bay-Sault Ste. Marie Trunk Road, from Sudbury to Copper Cliff, approximately 1.3 miles and laying thereon 4-inch colasmix macadam pavement, Township of McKim, 3,287.86 .... 33,347 12

Statutory—Continued

Roads and Bridges—Continued

District No. 3—Continued

Gravel, Rock and Stone, $11,770.35.

Davis Aho, 38.10; Ed. Ahonen, 35.30; Donald Ainslie, 42.70; P. Albert, 45.50; Hugh Bailey, 13.80; Julian Batman, 125.30; Alex. Beaudry, 34.80; D. Beaudry, 44.75; J. Blackburn, 16.50; G. Bonin, 24.60; Allan Bowerman, 83.50; Peter Boyuck, 37.00; Ed. Brocklebank, 26.70; Bill Bukowski, 57.60; Herb. Caddell, 23.40; Stan Cadieux, 30.00; D. Calford, 36.20; Geo. Campbell, 54.95; Wm. Campbell, 18.00; Canadian Pacific Railway Co., 1,347.20; John Cannard, 36.60; James Carter, 11.75; Charrette Estate, 92.00; Stewart Clarke, 12.45; Wm. Clarke, 57.80; W. H. Clarke, 16.80; Isaac Collins, 68.60; Harry Cooper, 13.35; Jos. Wm. Coutu, 51.30; Geo. Croft, 13.95; Lillie Cryderman, 75.00; Annie Debossige, 26.50; L. Debossige, 25.90; Harry Debossige, 12.10; Mrs. Peter Debossige, 15.00; Julien Denis, 83.60; J. Dever, 24.00; Wm. K. Dinsmore, 30.30; G. Duhamel, 60.00; A. Duxbury, 33.40; W. Duxbury, 10.20; Robt. Eade, 70.00; Chas. Eadie, 10.80; Wm. Eadie, 29.80; W. F. Edmonds, 40.00; Earle Edson, 195.05; A. Ethier, 14.10; J. Ethier, 25.30; Archie Ferguson, 44.70; Percy Ferguson, 72.60; Bert Finch, 11.90; Bert Fisher, 32.20; Mrs. Elizabeth Forsythe, 117.40; G. L. Fraser, 48.60; L. Fraser, 14.40; Paul Gamache, 19.80; N. Gareau, 21.00; Roy Graham, 22.80; R. L. Graham, 106.50; Wm. Graham, 27.10; Wm. Granger, 49.30; Geo. Hall, 10.65; Wm. Haner, 61.30; Wm. Head, 35.70; J. E. Huard, 23.40; Elias Hutchinson, 11.70; Ish. Johnson, 142.60; David Johnston, 15.00; I. Johnston, 48.15; Charlie Joyce, 15.40; M. Kannakko, 42.90; Mrs. John Kemp, 18.00; Mrs. Wm. Kemp, 30.00; A. Koivula, 27.50; A. Kolari, 49.60; J. Lahti, 42.30; Phil. Lavignew, 135.60; Law Construction Co., Ltd., 3,253.75; Thos. Leclair, 317.50; R. J. Lewis, 56.40; N. Luotos, 16.80; Clifford Luscombe, 16.40; Mrs. J. McArthur, 31.45; J. G. McColeman, 13.30; Wesley McColeman, 13.20; John McCormick, 35.80; W. McCormick, 31.70; Clifford McCutcheon, 18.60; Wm. McDonald, 26.80; Angus McDougall, 25.60; J. J. McFadden, Ltd., 166.00; Wm. McGibbon, 44.70; Geo. McIvor, 50.80; Jas. McKinley, 31.70; D. McLean, 25.50; W. A. McMitchell, 145.10; W. F. McRae, 24.75; M. Maensivu, 20.40; Jacob Maki, 21.30; Otto Maki, 24.50; Wm. Marshall, 20.20; Tom Merrylees, 50.80; Wallace Moore, 24.00; A. Morrell, 36.60; Jos. Newburn, 47.40; Mrs. Lillian Noakes, 56.80; Johnston Noble, 69.00; J. T. Paquette, 198.00; T. Peura, 21.60; William Peura, 42.90; Geo. Pharand, 556.70; John Pitle, 31.30; David Poulin, 112.50; James Purvis & Son, 28.80; Mrs. M. Regal, 37.00; W. Robb, 77.00; A. A. Robertson, 19.30; Edward Robson, 42.00; Alf. Rochon, 13.20; Harvey Rogers, 10.10; Cliff. Roszel, 22.00; W. Rowe, 57.75; J. B. Rumley, 26.40; Leslie Rumley, 36.10; J. T. Rutledge, 32.60; J. Saikkonen, 40.40; David Sloss, 55.45; Tom Smeltzer, 55.70; Soldiers' Settlement of Canada, 14.70; E. Stubbington, 149.70; J. Takala, 95.40; John Turpeinen, 51.10; Raoul Vaillancourt, 378.00; A. Warren, 45.00; Alfred Williams, 58.45; Tom Williams, 11.10; Peter Williamson, 43.10; Oscar Wirtenen, 37.80; Sandy Wright, 11.50; H. Yade, 51.20 .... 11,770 35

Pay Lists, $305,222.91.

Wages of men 305,222 91

Board and Lodging, $674.40.

Mrs. I. Ballantyne, 391.25; Espanola Hotel, 134.00; Mrs. D. T. Labelle, 13.50; Alex. McLean, 20.90; Mansion House, Little Current, 114.75 .... 674 40

Proportionate Cost of Roads, $24,199.63.

Townships of—Assiginack, 1,492.92; Balfour, 1,205.89; Billings, 600.00; Blezard, 846.37; Carnarvon, 1,500.00; Cockburn Island, 600.00; Dowling, 124.17; Drury, Dennison and Graham, 1,631.32; Gordon and Allan, 1,200.00; Hagar, 1,145.00; Hanmer, 1,567.61 ; Howland, 1,400.00; McKim, 3,765.00; Neelon and Garson, 4,500.00; Nairn, 150.00; Rayside, 1,271.35; Sandfield, 500.00; Tehkummah, 700.00 .... 24,199 63

Purchase of Property, Right-of-Way, $1,383.40.

D. H. Haight, 800.00; James McCreary, 400.00; James Mathie, 183.40 .... 1,383 40

Miscellaneous, $56,014.67.

Abitibi Power & Paper Co., blacksmithing, 20.78; re-locating poles, 12.13; H. Alie, blacksmithing, 16.45; Bark & Mortimer, auto insurance, 98.15; Bell Telephone Co., telephone services and moving poles, etc., 1,392.32; J. H. Bisaillon, car rental, 26.00; C. R. Bradley, cartage, 73.64; S. J. Bradley, blacksmithing, 55.34; M. Brunnett, searching titles, 26.70; Norman Buchanan, blacksmithing, 14.65; Burn's Transfer, cartage, 523.35; Canadian Inspection & Testing Co., Ltd.,

Statutory—Continued

Roads and Bridges—Continued

District No. 3—Continued

Miscellaneous—Continued

Ltd., inspection paint, 34.10; Canadian National Express Co., express, 34.84; Canadian National Railways, freight, 47.03; Canadian Pacific Express Co., express, 36.98; Canadian Pacific Railway Co., constructing subway, 17,781.84; Canadian Pacific Railway Co., protecting lines, freight, etc., 3,878.04; Canadian Pacific Railway Company's Telegraph, telegrams, 75.98; Town of Capreol, work on road, 488.49; Wm. Connaughton, car rental, 60.00; Town of Copper Cliff, paving Sudbury-Copper Cliff Road, 17,466.19; Robt. T. Crawford, car rental, 96.00; John Cyr, ground rent, 18.00; Delongschamp Cartage Co., Ltd., cartage, 699.37; Arthur Elliott, cartage, 15.00; W. J. Fillion, car rental, 106.00; Mrs. Eli Fraser, cleaning office, 27.50; A. H. Fraser, cartage, 12.50; Paul Gamache, blacksmithing, 62.05; Lionel Godson, auto insurance, 75.40; J. Gourlay, damages to car, 50.00; D. L. Hennessy, rent of farm house, 105.00; F. Henry, blacksmithing, 11.25; Geo. Holmes, car rental, 632.00; J. Hunt, installing buzzers, 16.40; Hydro-Electric Power Commission of Ontario, protecting lines, 141.80; Geo. Johnson, blacksmithing, 88.51; Tobias Liscomb, blacksmithing, 39.14; Town of Little Current, lighting, 18.83; Geo. A. Lockerby, rent of boiler, 75.00; A. L. McDonald, car rental, 136.00; Duncan J. McEachren, car rental, 488.00; J. A. McGill, blacksmithing, 47.00; M. McKechnie, janitor service, 180.00; P. McLachlan, car and truck rental, 93.00; N. N. McLean, car rental, 168.00; Manitoulin and North Shore Telephone & Telegraph Co., Ltd., telephone services, etc., 131.17; Wm. Moore, blacksmithing, 20.45; James Purvis & Son, blacksmithing, 23.10; Henry Quennville, blacksmithing, 10.55; Mrs. S. Petty, washing blankets, 59.15; P. Rouleau, blacksmithing, 37.25; D. St. Denis, clearing lands, 100.00; J. Sicord, clearing land, 81.60; A. Silverman & Sons, rental of office, 1,504.44; Smith & Walsh, auto insurance, 70.20; A. Steed, blacksmithing, 22.45; R. Stringer, blacksmithing, 11.75; Sudbury Steam Laundry, washing blankets, 93.60; City of Sudbury, paving of road, 6,307.24; City of Sudbury, lighting, water, 291.82; John Swanson, rental of canoe, 13.00; Lary Talevi, livery, 82.00; Henry Thibbault, car rental, 87.00; Thos. Travers, car rental, 474.00; Norman Trotter, office rent, 130.00; A. E. Wilson & Co., Ltd., auto insurance, 104.00; D. Wyman, blacksmithing, 14.55; petty disbursements, unenumerated, 780.60.............. 56,014 67

DISTRICT No. 4 ($406,038.17)

Engineer, G. J. Lamb, Sault Ste. Marie

North Bay-Sault Road	174,066 27		
Sault-Searchmont Road	28,854 64		
Sault-Batchewana Road	23,336 69		
St. Joseph Island Roads	9,581 56		
Second Line Road	7,908 93		
Iron Bridge-Parkinson Road	3,909 10		
People's Road	3,550 03		
Dunn Valley and Bruce Mines Road	3,116 59		
Lake Matinenda Road	2,945 86		
Wa-Wa-Minto Mine Road	2,615 32		
Gordon Lake Road	1,751 11		
Wharncliffe Road	1,371 80		
Blind River-Iron Bridge Road	1,102 69		
Equipment and tools	56,220 33		
General maintenance, settlers' and other roads, sundry expenditure	85,707 25		
		406,038 17	

Travelling Expenses, $3,578.20.

Robt. Agnew, 30.71; L. O. Armstrong, 23.50; Jas. Barkley, 345.68; Chas. R. Brown, 176.25; W. W. Christopherson, 42.10; G. A. Crane, 160.69; O. L. Flanagan, 61.47; W. W. Hare, 134.25; W. J. Harris, 63.71; A. Hill, 37.85; W. G. Hopper, 60.10; W. Huber, 88.95; Thos. Humphries, 150.30; Alonzo Hurley, 11.75; G. S. Ireland, 34.75; G. J. Lamb, 568.67; W. W. Lethbridge, 10.25; Earl Lyons, 52.00; Archie McHardy, 11.75; D. Mitchell, 357.69; E. W. Neelands, 815.04; Geo. Reid, 48.29; Joe Shewfelt, 18.15; C. F. Thornton, 198.55; E. L. White, 10.15; W. S. Wilson, 65.60.............. 3,578 20

Advertising, Newspapers, Printing and Stationery, $194.02.

Wm. E. Fountain, 56.77; Bank of Montreal, 125.25; Vernon Directories, Ltd., 12.00.............. 194 02

Statutory—Continued

Roads and Bridges—Continued

District No. 4—Continued

Autos, Trucks, Accessories, Parts and Repairs, $31,016.49.

J. D. Adams (Canada), Ltd., 143.31; Advance-Rumley Thresher Co., Inc., 52.78; Allis-Chalmers-Rumley, Ltd., 554.03; G. E. Andrews, 138.45; Arrow Garage & Service, Ltd., 25.64; Auto Starter Co., Ltd., 45.69; Battery Service Station, 319.97; J. S. Boville, 38.75; Bruce Mines Garage, 1,326.86; A. A. Burk & Co., 859.78; Canadian Fairbanks-Morse Co., Ltd., 29.25; Canadian Ingersoll-Rand Co., Ltd., 1,148.47; Collin's Tire & Battery Service, 216.15; Desbarats Garage, 1,050.40; Dominion Road Machinery Co., Ltd., 3,745.19; Dunseath & McClary, 1,725.64; C. N. Eddy, 34.40; Espanola Garage, 211.22; Garage Supply Co., Ltd., 348.30; General Supply Co. of Canada, Ltd., 5,130.00; Gibson's Service Station, 380.68; T. A. Heye, 2,088.81; Thos. Humphries, 529.75; J. S. Innes, Ltd., 6,445.16; International Harvester Co. of Canada, Ltd., 303.46; Joliette Steel, Ltd., 27.50; Keetch Motor Sales, 708.50; A. Leclair, 19.00; Lynch Auto Sales Co., Ltd., 59.40; Marshall Motor Car Co., 405.38; R. J. Mitchell, 234.53; Mussens, Ltd., 35.50; J. C. Neyrinck, 12.76; Parr Motor Sales, 308.54; W. G. Plewes, 161.63; Thos. Pocklington Co., 42.81; Pratt Engineering Co., 408.61; Republic Trucks, Ltd., 683.68; Soo Garage, Ltd., 161.30; Spanish Garage, 421.15; Sullivan Machinery Co., Ltd., 284.99; Tallack Bros., 48.85; F. H. Teskey, 15.43; Willys-Overland Sales Co., Ltd., 84.79 .... 31,016 49

Camp and Road Supplies and Equipment, $69,219.12.

Algoma Produce Co., Ltd., 552.94; Edwin Ansley, 55.00; The Art Metropole, 334.90; E. Ault, 28.50; Baines & David, Ltd., 86.29; Barnes & Oliver, 14.55; Mirton Bean & Son, 136.10; E. L. Bedford, 5,610.78; Reuben Beilhartz, 57.22; A. C. Bernier, 10.35; Blind River Garage, 1,704.75; Chas. Bolls, 39.95; N. H. Bower, 278.93; W. J. Bradshaw, 160.18; J. C. Braniff, 12.20; F. Y. W. Brathwaite, 1,195.54; Bridge Bros., 59.22; J. E. Buchanan, 167.56; Emo Burnside, 16.00; Jas. Burnside, 25.00; E. Cameron, 37.50; Canada Creosoting Co., 92.09; Canadian Industries, Ltd., 825.01; Canadian Oil Companies, Ltd., 1,847.54; Carpenter-Hixon Co., Ltd., 1,037.20; Melvin Carter, 234.89; Frank Cassie, 1,368.00; J. A. Cheer, 27.14; Cochrane Dunlop Hardware, Ltd., 1,217.85; Cockshutt Plow Co., Ltd., 235.34; Geo. Cornelius, 19.00; Corrugated Pipe Co., Ltd., 694.03; Crane Lumber Co., Ltd., 40.00; A. G. Cumming, 239.35; W. J. Detweiler, 91.95; H. P. Dolson, 32.12; Dominion Oxygen Co., Ltd., 332.33; Dominion Tar & Chemical Co., Ltd., 14.00; H. A. Drury Co., Ltd., 16.74; Edwards Hardware, 2,668.80; Ernie's Gas Station, 52.87; V. and Mrs. Fillion, 149.95; Friar-Rath Lumber Co., Ltd., 15.04; Gasaccumulator Co. (Canada), Ltd., 88.23; Wm. Graham, 113.36; Grand & Toy, Ltd., 160.05; S. Gratton, 26.03; The B. Greening Wire Co., Ltd., 325.84; Greenwood Electric & Hardware, 157.55; Aide. Hamelin, 48.00; Eldy Hamlin, 39.00; John Harman, 73.15; T. Harman, 10.60; Harpham Bros., 510.36; Harris Abattoir Co., Ltd., 781.38; Hinsperger Harness Co., Ltd., 619.15; John Holmes, 30.18; E. F. Houghton & Co., 61.74; Mrs. R. A. Hunt, 15.00; S. Hunt, 39.35; Imperial Oil, Ltd., 2,967.58; G. S. Ireland, 12.00; Instruments, Ltd., 34.00; D. A. Jones & Son, 13.81; N. Joseph, 94.90; J. Junor, 128.18; Wm. Karlash, 20.00; Kentvale General Merchants, 18.70; Keyes Hardware, Ltd., 105.04; H. Kirby, 131.20; N. W. Kirby, 69.52; A. J. Kirstin Co., 33.96; L. H. Knoll, 26.00; Lang & Ross, 45.08; E. Leishman, 78.00; Line & Cable Accessories, 43.93; T. J. McCauley, 26.88; McColl-Frontenac Oil Co., Ltd., 385.69; N. R. McDonald, 19.20; Russell McDonald, 33.06; Stewart McElrea, 12.80; J. J. McFadden, Ltd., 249.48; John McIntyre, 19.30; Wm. McLean, 14.00; D. W. McMillan, 12.73; Hugh B. McMullin, 28.00; B. Maaho, 27.36; T. H. Magill & Co., 24.00; Geo. Maguire, 24.40; R. Maitland, 13.48; Andrew Marshall, 84.50; J. R. Marshall, 453.56; Meaford Steel Products, Ltd., 181.68; Jas. Meeks, 15.84; Kurt Meincke, 23.50; Menzies Bros., Ltd., 23.15; Metallic Roofing Co. of Canada, Ltd., 160.00; Mills Bros., 122.29; Harry Mills, 42.00; Jas. Mills, 13.00; Geo. Montgomery, 42.00; Peter R. Moore, 64.11; Alex. Murray & Co., Ltd., 6,342.65; J. B. Myers & Son, 144.60; L. Nanne, 22.00; National Grocers Co., Ltd., 501.83; Northern Foundry & Machine Co., Ltd., 11,381.49; Norman Pace, 22.95; Archie Patterson, 40.80; Mrs. E. G. Paul, 63.50; Pen-Link Construction Co., 1,255.50; People's Meat Market, 20.05; Mrs. Peter Peterbaugh, 17.90; Bill Phillips, 85.48; Ben Pittman, 12.00; Geo. Powley, 66.26; E. Pullan Wipers & Waste Co., Ltd., 110.00; Ransome's General Store, 51.08; J. Frank Raw Co., Ltd., 70.10; Redman's Garage, 113.81; Richard's Landing Garage, 19.76; H. Rogerson, 82.50; N. Rosenburg, 139.49; Rydal Bank Garage, 53.43; Sadowski & Co., 397.46; Sault Fuel & Oil, Ltd., 417.07; Sault Ste. Marie Coal & Wood Co., Ltd., 428.57; Sawyer-Massey, Ltd., 3,291.56; Lloyd Schoales, 423.81; B. Schwartz, 16.18; Searchmont Lumber Co., Ltd., 547.30; Sherwin-Williams Co. of Canada, Ltd., 82.57; Shiels Garage, 1,509.62; W. Shipman, 161.00; Henry Sims, 17.28; Geo. Singleton,

Statutory—Continued

Roads and Bridges—Continued

District No. 4—Continued

Camp and Road Supplies and Equipment—Continued

23.50; Wm. Smith, 99.74; Soo Gasoline & Oil Co., Ltd., 2,079.73; Soo Jobbing Co., Ltd., 12.90; Soo Lumber & Mill Co., 1,593.14; Soo Tinsmiths & Roofers, 29.10; Paul Spooner, 91.40; Chas. Stewart, 13.60; Sturgeon's, Ltd., 327.54; Peter Sunstrom, 13.20; Superior Iron & Steel Co. of Canada, Ltd., 676.00; Ernest B. Symes, 31.45; Taylor Bros., 133.01; Norah Tessier, 73.05; W. I. Thayer, 14.40; Chris Thompson, 23.10; Thompson, Ltd., 12.00; Frank Thornton, 213.73; Trap Rock, Ltd., 1,100.27; Matt Trivers, 10.04; A. W. Trotter, 15.84; Alex. Tulloch & Sons, 670.49; R. Tulloch, 51.00; Peter Tuovi, 17.40; Webbwood Garage, 50.51; C. E. Weeks, 27.00; E. A. White, 338.75; Wm. Wilkins, 21.92; Bruce Wilkinson, 10.20; Albert R. Wood, 2,601.78; Clifford Yates, 20.00; Geo. Young, 42.15...... 69,219 12

Contracts, $22,503.38.

The Municipal Road Spraying & Oiling Co., Ltd., supplying stone and chips, reshaping and rolling sub-grade, North Bay-Sault Trunk Road, from Sault Ste. Marie easterly, a distance of 3¼ miles and laying thereon 3-inch bituminous consolidated retread top, Township of St. Mary's,........................... 22,503 38

Gravel, Rock and Stone, $14,237.84.

Dr. Allen, 33.40; Wesley Archibald, 30.00; Roy Beemer, 17.70; Robt. Beharriel, 37.93; Chas. Belisle, 118.40; Albert Booth, 59.60; Robt. Boyle, 25.10; W. J. Bradshaw, 97.40; Wm. Brayley, 21.10; Robt. Brown, 81.90; Thos. Budge, 13.90; P. Burns, 87.30; Duncan Campbell, 57.80; Chas. Catling, 12.00; J. B. Chenier, 1,376.60; Ben Cohen, 10.60; Fred Coulson, 33.00; F. Daigle, 18.50; R. Davis, 111.10; H. Delhinty, 14.00; Geo. Doucette, 97.65; I. J. Downey & Sons, 49.65; Chas. Draper, 20.00; Paul Dufour, 196.60; Lorne Eaket, 27.90; Henry Edgar, 216.40; David Euler, 57.50; John Finlayson, 42.30; Paul Fremont, 141.19; R. A. Gamble, 30.00; Edwin Gay, 14.10; W. Goodchild, 73.00; Wm. Graham, 13.20; Albert Grigg, 59.60; Wm. Guild 82.20; Geo. Hainsworth, 23.40; Wallace Hall, 73.58; A. A. Hallett, 112.65; Mrs. H. I. Hamilton, 20.00; J. Hanrahan, 97.50; Ed. Harris, 18.00; A. Hartman, 349.65; P. C. Hawdon, 47.10; P. Helferty, 61.80; Robt. Hill, 23.20; Albert Houle, 43.25; Bert Houle, 42.00; Fred Humes, 48.40; Dept. of Indian Affairs (Ottawa), 210.90; Dept. of Indian Affairs (Sault), 30.40; T. H. and A. D. Jackson, 175.00; P. J. Jeffrey, 155.21; Hans Jensen, 20.00; Peter Jensen, 27.50; Jno. Kennedy, 61.00; N. Krmpotich, 17.90; J. Lautain, 190.00; Arthur Lees, 359.18; F. Lees, 68.40; A. Littleton, 43.70; D. McCauley, 17.70; Mrs. Margaret McCluskie, 37.00; Hugh McCrea, 12.00; P. D. McDonald, 38.00; Roderick McDonald, 42.40; John McKinnon, 17.00; J. D. McLennan, 57.00; Mrs. M. McLeod, 18.80; Town of Massey, 341.00; Donald Matheson, 77.60; Mrs. S. O'Neil, 71.50; G. Pearson, 12.60; T. C. Penno, 17.20; Wm. Pickering 75.70; Nelson Reemer, 11.00; Medie Ritchie, Sr., 49.00; Chas. Rosbeck, 86.60; D. Roy, 34.45; E. L. Russell, 60.80; Geo. Rutledge, 13.00; City of Sault Ste. Marie, 24.90; F. H. Schoales, 271.80; Archie Seabrooke, 14.70; Dan See, 26.80; Mrs. M. Sharp, 18.60; J. Shields, 19.80; Geo. Smith, 56.60; Soldiers' Settlement Board of Canada, 24.00; Geo. Steinberg, 31.50; Herb Steinberg, 42.80; E. F. E. Steinke, 25.60; Jas. Stewart, 69.30; Wray Stewart, 22.50; Wm. Suon, 66.20; Jas. Tallon, 26.50; Emerson Taylor, 15.20; W. C. Tomlinson, 85.00; Trap Rock, Ltd., 5,897.55; Geo. Tweedle, 39.25; Richard Williton, 10.50; Geo. Wilson, 86.60; John Wood, 38.60; R. F. Wyman, 15.60; Yens Yensen, 113.00; F. Young, 52.90; Geo. Young, 29.25; Young Men's Christian Association, 261.85; R. Young, 37.55; Jos. Zettler, 24.70.. 14,237 84

Pay Lists, $225,316.76.

Wages of men.. 225,316 76

Board and Lodging, $2,706.89.

Algoma Hotel, 96.00; H. Buchanan, 14.00; J. B. Chenier, 102.00; Desbarats Hotel, 66.65; Phillip Halferty, 360.00; A. T. Hartwick, 46.14; Alex. J. M. Hayes, 66.50; The Hefferman Hotel, 818.50; Mrs. Holmes, 17.00; John Holmes, 29.60; J. C. Hunter, 58.00; Huron Hotel, 387.50; Mrs. E. Maki, 33.25; J. Newton, 22.00; Robt. Nicholson, 66.75; Herb. Rodehouse, 472.75; Mrs. Ed. Smith, 16.00; Geo. Stringer, 34.25.. 2,706 89

Proportionate Cost of Roads, $14,477.24.

Townships of—Day and Bright, Additional, 300.00; Hilton, 500.00; Johnson, 1,650.00; Korah, 3,700.00; Laird, 1,850.00; McDonald, Meredith and Aberdeen, Additional, 865.24; Plummer Additional, 1,412.50; Prince, 300.00; St. Joseph, 1,624.51; Tarbutt and Tarbutt, Additional, 1,000.00; Tarentorus, 1,107.02; Thompson, 167.97.. 14,477 24

Statutory—Continued

Roads and Bridges—Continued

District No. 4—Continued

Purchase of Property, Right-of-Way, $3,309.66.

L. O. Armstrong, 1,022.50; Andrew Drysdale and Mrs. E. Houle, 360.00; Jas. Hamilton, 522.50; Jno. Haney, 297.50; Wm. Ed. Hinchley and Jas. Van Egmond, 192.00; Hugh Irwin, 133.00; Angus McIvor, 195.00; J. D. McLennan, 75.00; Mrs. Anne W. Rowland, 25.00; John Shaughnessy, 50.00; Chas. G. Willoughby, 66.16; Jos. Zettler, 371.00 .... 3,309 66

Miscellaneous, $19,478.57.

Abitibi Power & Paper Co., Ltd., clearing for road, 40.00; C. T. Adams & Co., developing and printing films, 48.36; Robt. Agnew, car rental, 177.00; Fred Albert, blacksmithing, 43.90; Algoma Central & Hudson Bay Railway, freight, telephone calls, fares, 530.71; Jas. Anderson, blacksmithing, 201.19; L. O. Armstrong, hauling stone, 16.00; Mrs. W. Armstrong, making flags, 25.00; Lloyd Barber, cartage, 20.00; Fred Barill, repairing damage to property caused by blasting, 300.00; Bark & Mortimer, auto insurance, 46.80; Jas. Barkley, car rental, telephone calls, etc., 818.36; Beckett & Smith, blacksmithing, 57.25; Bell Telephone Co., moving poles, telephone services, 1,625.48; Jas. Blight, blacksmithing, 73.70; Mrs. A. Booth, washing blankets, 160.87; W. J. Bradshaw, car hire, 12.00; Chas. R. Brown, car rental, etc., 95.09; Henry Bruijninck, washing blankets, 102.78; M. Brunette, searching titles, etc., 10.13; Albert Cameron, blacksmithing, 19.70; Canada Steamship Lines, Ltd., freight, 28.81; Canadian Inspection & Testing Co., Ltd., inspection of paint, 34.09; Canadian National Railways, freight, fares, 43.00; Canadian National Telegraphs, telegrams, 88.42; Canadian Pacific Express Co., express, 191.16; Canadian Pacific Railway Co., freight, fares, protecting lines, 3,032.66; Canadian Pacific Railway Co.'s Telegraphs, telegrams, 76.96; T. Carlyle, truck hire, 235.00; J. B. Chenier, garage rent, 60.00; W. W. Christopherson, rent of transit, 70.00; W. W. Climie, rent of transit, 50.00; Canada Customs, duty, 15.62; Ed. Deagle, moving poles, 68.10; Frank Germain, clearing land, 150.00; Mrs. Wm. Gillespie, clearing land, 150.00; Fred Gjos, blacksmithing, 132.10; Lionel Godson, auto insurance, 65.00; Steve Golec, blacksmithing, 44.15; Graham & Graham, developing films, 12.65; Great Lakes Power Co., Ltd., lighting, 62.06; Helen Hamilton, cleaning up land, 85.00; Mrs. H. I. Hamilton, wood cut in trespass, 25.00; Jas. Hamilton, clearing land, 50.00; W. W. Hare, car rental, 208.00; W. J. Harris, car rental, 249.00; W. J. Harris, searching titles, etc., 11.50; John Harrison & Sons, crown dues on cedar posts, 27.00; J. Harten, blacksmithing, 31.40; The Hefferman Hotel, rent of office, 30.00; Alex. Heye, truck rental, 36.00; John Holmes, rent of house and camp equipment, 100.00; Thos. Humphries, car rental, 352.00; G. S. Ireland, car rental, 362.00; Hugh Irwin, clearing land, 42.00; Johnson Municipal Telephone System, rental of telephone, 16.15; G. J. Lamb, garage rental, 55.00; W. W. Lethbridge, car rental, 44.00; Livingstone Rural Telephone Co., Ltd., labour, moving poles, 29.00; J. L. Luxton, car rental, 102.00; Earl Lyons, car rental, 95.00; J. H. McAuley, car rental, 26.00; Mrs. Ed. McColeman, car rental, 21.60; MacInnis & Brien, barristers, professional services, 30.00; Alex. MacIntyre, car rental, 86.00; Mrs. Emily McKie, clearing land, 37.20; E. V. McMillan, barrister, professional services, 11.70; T. H. Magill & Co., truck rental, cartage, 66.50; Alf. Maitland, blacksmithing, 69.74; R. Maitland, car and truck rental, 162.00; Chas. Marcelles, cartage, 148.60; Marine Laundry, Ltd., washing blankets, 61.15; Neil Merritt, tent destroyed by fire, 12.50; D. Mitchell, car rental, 614.00; D. Mitchell, telephone calls, stamps, etc., 99.67; J. L. Moxam, rent of car, 11.00; Municipal Road Spraying & Oiling Co., Ltd., scarifying road, 1,314.11; Pen-Link Construction Co., rental of crusher, 460.00; Postmasters, stamps, 853.00; V. Rains, car rental, 30.00; Geo. Reid, car and truck rental, 227.00; Stanley Robinson, car rental, 101.75; Lorne Rothwell, blacksmithing, 18.00; S. Rowe, compensation for damage to property, 60.00; Rowland & Atkin, Barristers, professional services, 340.85; J. St. Laurent, car rental, 90.00; City of Sault Ste. Marie, lighting, water, etc., 182.79; Henry Selin, sawing lumber, 100.18; J. F. Sidock, blacksmithing, 67.30; C. O. Somes, rent of buildings, 70.87; Soo Business College, rent of typewriters, 22.74; Mrs. Delima Tassey, cleaning and fencing land, 91.67; Jas. A. Templeton, cartage, etc., 497.00; Jas. Terry, cleaning offices, 120.00; C. F. Thornton, car rental, 102.15; Frank Thornton, car rental, 22.00; F. C. Thornton, car rental, 16.00; Mrs. J. Uhlman, washing blankets, 31.63; Walker & Horne, Blacksmithing, 62.90; Lloyd T. Wesley, car rental, 898.50; Wesley-Rent-A-Car Co., car rental, 206.00; J. H. Whalen, blacksmithing, 35.45; W. A. White, cartage, 41.50; A. E. Wilson & Co., Ltd., auto insurance, 52.00; Mrs. Jno. S. Wilson, rent of building, 35.00; W. S. Wilson, searching titles, 18.85; A. S. Wishart, professional services, 12.00; Jos. Zettler, clearing land, 112.00; petty disbursements, unenumerated, 743.52 .... 19,478 57

Statutory—Continued

Roads and Bridges—Continued

DISTRICT No. 5 ($533,256.69)

Engineer, D. J. Miller, New Liskeard

Ferguson Highway	235,341 97	
Elk Lake-Ashley Mine Road	53,210 58	
Haileybury West Road	33,081 07	
New Liskeard-Elk Lake Road	17,798 86	
Krugerdorf Road	10,295 01	
Matabichawan Road	9,104 47	
North Road	5,489 77	
South Lorrain Road	4,414 00	
Casey-Brethour Road	4,264 84	
New Liskeard-North Temiskaming Road	3,676 17	
Gowganda Road	3,109 29	
Elk Lake-Charlton Road	3,001 14	
Milberta Road	1,965 74	
McCool-Thornloe Road	1,551 21	
Bartlett's Point Road	1,515 13	
Equipment and tools	20,612 41	
General maintenance, settlers' and other roads, sundry expenditure	124,825 03	
		533,256 69

Travelling Expenses, $1,480.83.

A. C. Blair, 18.90; G. H. Bryson, 110.85; G. A. Crane, 31.68; W. A. Dalgleish, 297.80; K. Irvine, 12.60; J. S. Leitch, 135.90; V. H. Longstaffe, 119.60; J. Lott, 20.85; W. E. McCready, 34.90; D. J. Miller, 173.50; J. T. Morrow, 22.95; J. W. Neelands, 18.90; Geo. A. Powles, 124.05; W. H. Rice, 55.10; W. E. Roberts, 11.60; R. V. Shave, 35.40; J. Sheedy, 37.75; W. R. Thompson, 89.15; J. Ward, 14.20; H. Weeks, 12.60; H. P. Williams, 102.55 .... 1,480 83

Advertising, Newspapers, Printing and Stationery, $77.19.

Anderson's Stationery, 14.55; Contract Record and Engineering Review, 26.00; The Haileyburian, 36.64 .... 77 19

Autos, Trucks, Accessories, Parts and Repairs, $13,310.70.

Baines & David, Ltd., 960.85; Bartlett's Auto Electric Service, 13.02; Canada Carriage & Body Co., 16.43; Canadian Fairbanks-Morse Co., Ltd., 100.00; J. Christo, 374.00; The Cobalt Foundry, 90.07; Darling's Garage, 57.70; Dominion Road Machinery Co., Ltd., 112.02; Thos. Drinkill, 166.50; Earlton Garage, 1,383.54; Elk Lake Garage & Machine Works, 395.16; P. M. Fleming, 133.99; Garage Supply Co., Ltd., 682.91; General Supply Co. of Canada, Ltd., 1,495.22; E. F. Goddard, 78.23; Grant's Garage, 24.31; H. Hartley, 17.00; Holman Machines Ltd., 510.33; J. S. Innes, Ltd., 73.75; International Harvester Co. of Canada, Ltd. (Hamilton), 12.12; International Harvester Co. of Canada, Ltd. (Montreal), 35.91; Keyes Supply Co., Ltd., 194.09; Kirkland Machine Works, 19.50; Liskeard Motors, 39.98; J. W. McKinley, 873.02; National Auto Sales, 86.74; Northern Canada Supply Co., Ltd., 3,092.25; Henry O'Grady & Son, 155.05; Sullivan Machinery Co., 49.44; Tire Chain & Accessories, 127.37; Truck & Tractor Equipment Co., Ltd., 72.91; Tudhope-Anderson, Ltd., 176.49; Wabi Iron Works, Ltd., 1,556.34; W. C. Warburton & Co., Ltd., 122.70; Wettlaufer Machinery Co., 11.76 .... 13,310 70

Camp and Road Supplies and Equipment, $86,113.72.

John Alberta, 36.00; Anglo Traders, Ltd., 30.00; Austin's Meat Market, 567.21; Simon Bean, 45.00; Geo. Beaven, 84.25; The Oliver Blais Co., Ltd., 991.99; J. R. Booth, Ltd., 1,383.98; D. B. Bowen, 122.70; D. Bowers, 109.85; O. E. Bowman & Sons, 133.73; I. B. Bradley, 678.04; H. S. Brennan, 35.20; Wm. J. Briggs, 198.00; J. G. Brisco, 267.51; British American Oil Co., Ltd., 397.52; T. Burk, 76.56; Burlington Steel Co., Ltd., 1,278.63; Canada Cement Co., Ltd., 4,515.00; Canada Creosoting Co., 12,845.20; Canadian Industries, Ltd., 1,510.95; Canadian Liquid Air Co., Ltd., 89.60; Canadian Oil Companies, Ltd., 490.70; P. R. Carter, 36.25; Frank Cassie, 686.91; J. Christie, 151.90; John Clark, 41.49; Arthur Cloutier & Co., Ltd., 29.24; Colas Roads, Ltd., 344.52; Jas. A. Coles, 545.71; Conlin Bros., 276.53; Conlin & Hogan, 94.64; Donald Connelly, 691.45; H. S. Crabtree, Ltd., 94.10; Thos. Cragg, 501.00; Craig Bros., 873.28; Daily Commercial News, 22.50; Wm. Davis, 49.00; H. E. Didier, 27.90; Dominion Oxygen Co., Ltd., 17.62; U. Ducharme, 25.75; J. S. Duff, 27.60; The Englehart Hardware, 28.55; John W. Fogg, Ltd., 192.35; Alf. Gehrig, 667.01; A. Gignac,

Statutory—Continued

Roads and Bridges—Continued

District No. 5—Continued

Camp and Road Supplies and Equipment—Continued

46.30; Graham Bros., 21.74; Grant-Holden-Graham, Ltd., 412.52; P. J. Grant, 171.60; S. Greenwood & Son, 1,813.51; Gutta Percha & Rubber, Ltd., 396.73; Hall Foundry Co., Ltd., 108.78; Harpham Bros., 418.09; H. Heroux, 51.75; Hill-Clark-Francis, Ltd., 256.71; Alex Holmes, 36.20; C. Holmes, 36.72; O. Holmes, 26.15; A. Hurst, 171.91; Imperial Oil, Ltd., 5,691.72; R. Imrie Lumber Co., Ltd., 41.89; Milton Irvine, 1,142.10; Ives Bedding Co., Ltd., 586.56; Henry Jackson, 39.20; T. F. Johnston, 251.00; J. H. Keeler, 17.28; O. Labonte, 26.40; U. LaChapelle, 24.68; Lake Shore Mines, Ltd., 61.78; Jos. Larabee, 10.50; J. H. Leng, 84.57; H. T. Lloyd, 60.95; C. Lorimer, 32.30; McColl-Frontenac Oil Co., Ltd., 4,779.04; McCurdy-Simard, Ltd., 3,451.97; C. McFayden, 179.25; D. McLellan, 128.00; Peter McLeod, 1,471.90; McNamara Construction Co., Ltd., 622.41; Louis Marguerat, 26.20; John Mason, 27.65; Maxwells, Ltd., 40.70; E. Melitzer, 286.65; Art. Messenger, 12.00; Metallic Roofing Co. of Canada, Ltd., 132.00; L. Middleton, 17.60; Mitchell Hardware & Supply Co., Ltd., 24.01; J. A. Mitchell, 249.00; Modern Supply House, 55.49; J. B. Moyneur, 570.58; A. J. Murphy, 36.77; National Grocers Co., Ltd., 5,077.33; T. G. Neelands, 15.00; Olaf Nelson, 226.60; New Liskeard Brick Works, 21.60; Norfolk & Rochester Hardware Co., Ltd., 71.21; Northern Auto Company, 25.10; Northern Farmers' Co-Operative Co., Ltd., 337.21; Northern Paving & Materials, Ltd., 862.20; Pedlar People, Ltd., 5,520.16; R. Peever, 60.40; P. J. Perry, 25.64; W. H. Phillips, 132.97; Thos. Pocklington Co., 49.45; Wm. Pollock & Son, Ltd., 15.75; C. H. Powell & Son, 266.46; Quality Meat Market, 336.42; J. Quast, 44.95; J. Frank Raw Co., Ltd., 21.60; C. L. Rawson, 299.47; Chas. Reckin & Sons, 1,044.11; Wm. J. Rice Co., 490.90; J. A. Robitaille, 143.09; Alfred Rogers, Ltd., 3,855.00; P. Rolands, 16.65; H. W. Rowdon, 2,285.89; Sackrider's Garage, 29.39; Chas. Saunders, 48.30; Sawyer-Massey, Ltd., 3,748.02; Arthur Seed, 29.04; H. A. Semple, 43.80; Sherwin-Williams Co. of Canada, Ltd., 21.85; J. Shortt, 187.00; E. Simon, 265.50; W. Simon, 17.40; A. P. Simpkins, 42.80; N. Slater Co., Ltd., 52.84; J. E. Smith, 544.50; Steel Company of Canada, Ltd., 1,738.36; Sturgeons, Ltd., 507.17; Jas. B. Tarzwell, 312.09; Geo. Taylor Hardware, 12.63; Thorpe Bros., 22.25; Tomstown Lumber Co., Ltd., 229.34; E. Vahey, 64.80; S. E. Wallis, 31.16; Geo. Welsh, 280.00; John White, 12.75; Williams & Scott, 3,483.87; Willow Grove Market Gardens, 22.02; Woods Manufacturing Co., Ltd., 440.28; R. R. Woods, 1,092.37; T. S. Woolling, 137.95 .... 90,126 42

Less Expenditure Refund 6,000 00

84,126 42

Less transferred to South Cochrane District Stores Account 622 16

83,504 26

Add transferred from Muskoka District Stores Account 2,609 46

86,113 72

Contracts, $120,669.71.

The Chatham Dredging & General Contracting Co., construction steel and concrete bridge over Blanche River at Englehart on the Ferguson Highway, 41,619.67; The Hamilton Bridge Co., Ltd., fabrication of steel super-structure bridge over Blanche River at Englehart on the Ferguson Highway, 46,720.26; Messrs. Angus & Taylor, cutting, burning, stumping, grubbing, grading and gravelling right-of-way, 13 miles, Sheley Mine Road from Montreal River East, Townships Cairo, Bannockburn, Powell, 29,674.87; Chatham Dredging & General Contracting Co., grading, gravelling approaches to Englehart bridge, Ferguson Highway, 2,654.91 .... 120,669 71

Gravel, Rock and Stone, $6,170.82.

H. Anderson, 84.20; Ed. Atthill, 107.63; J. R. Bailey, 537.38; R. Batty, 119.65; C. Beatty, 137.40; Chas. Berard, 62.60; T. Blackburn, 613.80; Herman Boileau, 70.00; Mrs. F. Bowland, 13.70; R. Church, 127.60; Tom Cowan, 23.90; J. Davie, 57.45; N. Dennis, 77.85; W. Dickinson, 99.08; J. Dubois, 16.50; G. Dudgeon, 47.20; T. G. Eaton, 16.80; Leo. Eckensviller, 128.93; Estate of John A. Fernholm, 172.13; Chas. Grey, 47.70; Omer Hamelin, 13.65; H. Hammond, 303.30; E. Heaslip, 252.00; W. Hooper, 81.45; E. James, 25.60; W. C. Johnston, 31.95; John Jones, 41.20; C. Knight, 46.50; Felix LaCarte, 67.00; R. Laframboise, 63.00; J. Libby, 35.78; D. McDonald, 303.00; G. A. McLean, 44.05; C. Marshall, 32.90; H. Mersey, 71.10; Wellington Middleton, 141.76; F. Newell, 14.10; New Liskeard Brick Works, 81.50; John O'Hara, 73.60; Thos. Poole, 432.05; L.

Statutory—Continued

Roads and Bridges—Continued

District No. 5—Continued

Gravel, Rock and Stone—Continued

Porteous, 73.43; W. Powell, 165.40; Alfred Ribble, 11.00; A. Sariol, 42.60; Henry Schaffner, Sr., 74.30; Joe Schaffner, 47.00; W. M. Shore, 68.40; E. Simon, 189.50; D. Smylie, 21.50; Sure Run Mining Co., 322.65; J. Therriault, 14.40; D. Vahey, 63.60; S. J. Vosburgh, 86.85; G. Waldrif, 16.50; Sid. Wallis, 34.90; John Waters, 10.10; Wm. Waters, 53.80; Steve West, 30.70; Ed. Wood, 15.00; V. Woolings, 66.70; T. S. Woollings, 20.00; Tom Wright, 25.50 .... 6,170 82

Pay Lists, $238,985.11.

Wages of men 238,985 11

Board and Lodging, $1,317.50.

Angus & Taylor, 630.80; Albert Beaudin, 22.40; H. Blackburn, 16.50; Jos. Boisbert, 16.00; Commercial House, 215.50; Grand Union Hotel, 32.50; Mrs. Geo. Harman, 14.35; Nipissing Central Railway Co., 300.00; Mrs. E. Simms, 41.60; Mrs. G. Stephenson, 10.85; Windsor Hotel, 17.00 .... 1,317 50

Proportionate Cost of Roads, $26,029.26.

Townships of — Armstrong, 829.15; Brethour, 360.72; Bucke, 1,507.09; Casey, 1,034.08; Chamberlain, 943.69; Dack, 1,500.00; Dymond, 3,991.76; Evanturel, 3,128.31; Harley, 1,851.09; Harris, 267.25; Hilliard, 1,459.71; Hudson, 514.57; Kerns, 5,000.00; Teck, 3,493.34; Thornloe, 148.50 .... 26,029 26

Purchase of Property, Right-of-Way, $3,855.55.

Jos. N. Collins, 69.55; Evan Davies, 42.00; LaRose-Rouyn Mines, Ltd., 3,500.00; J. C. Maurer, 144.00; Alexander Player, 100.00 .... 3,855 55

Miscellaneous, $35,246.30.

Ontario Department of Agriculture, cost of Government office building, 88.61; Angus & Taylor, repairs to bridge, etc., 95.61; Angus & Taylor, teaming, hauling, 51.28; Ed. Arbuckle, taxi service, 21.00; Cecil Armour, checking bridge plans, 320.00; P. H. Armstrong, taxi service, car rental, 244.15; Bark & Mortimer, auto insurance, 11.70; Benson-Bastien Transportation Co., car hire, trucking, etc., 248.57; Benson Transportation Co., transportation livery, etc., 1,513.72; J. R. Booth, Ltd., rental of camps and office, 105.00; Claude Bowen, car rental, 37.50; Geo. L. Brewer, cartage and trucking, 15.00; Municipal Corporation of the Township of Bucke, rental of lots, 50.00; McCarthy Burns, boat hire, etc., 30.00; Canadian Inspection & Testing Co., Ltd. (Toronto), testing cement, etc., 213.50; Canadian Inspection & Testing Co., Ltd. (Montreal), testing cement, 34.11; Canadian National Express, express, 124.30; Canadian Pacific Express Co., express, 19.94; Canadian Pacific Railway Co., fares, freight, etc., 729.63; Chatham Dredging & Contracting Co., Ltd., driving and loading test piles, fitting steel, etc., 14,601.02; E. Copner, erecting chimney in warehouse, 20.25; W. A. Dalgleish, car rental, 457.50; Wm. Daw, trucking, 87.45; Miles Doherty, blacksmithing, 13.34; Town of Englehart, water, 15.45; Gordon Ferguson, snowmobile hire, etc., 226.00; Lorne H. Ferguson, searching titles, etc., 57.30; Lionel Godson, auto insurance, 78.00; L. Gordon, blacksmithing, 32.62; Gowganda Road Committee, keeping road open during winter, 284.07; R. Grant, transportation, 51.75; Edgar Hack, clearing and grubbing, 30.00; W. D. Harris, taxi service, 55.00; Bruce Kerr, car rental, 371.25; H. J. Leggott, blacksmithing, 26.41; J. H. Lever, locating and towing scow, 10.50; Liskeard Laundry, washing blankets, 117.23; W. E. Lobb, car rental, 415.00; O. A. McCracken, rent of house and table, 102.00; McLean's, developing and printing films, 25.50; McLellan Transportation Co., car hire, etc., 14.00; Mrs. R. T. McPherson, damages to farm, 52.50; B. I. Merkley, trucking, 85.50; Mining Corporation of Canada, Ltd., sharpening steel, 19.80; Ambrose Murphy, blacksmithing, etc., 19.65; Corporation of the Town of New Liskeard, 50 per cent. cost of paving through town of New Liskeard, water rates, etc., 6,927.58; Nipissing Central Railway Co., freight, 15.04; Northern Ontario Power Co., Ltd., lighting, 204.33; Northern Telephone Co., Ltd., telephone services, 1,214.41; Jas. Paddon, cartage, 15.00; John Paris, car rental, 28.50; Ed. Pelissier, blacksmithing, etc., 120.84; Postmaster (Englehart), stamps, etc., 63.00; Postmaster (New Liskeard), stamps, etc., 152.30; W. H. Rice, car rental, 732.50; John W. Rodie, trucking, etc., 119.94; E. Shaw, cartage, hauling and trucking, etc., 689.60; J. E. Smith, livery, 45.00; Smith & Walsh, auto insurance, 111.86; Sutcliffe Co., Ltd., surveying, etc., 100.00; Temiskaming & Northern Ontario Railway, lease on ground, 75.00; Temiskaming & Northern Ontario Railway, work

Statutory—Continued

Roads and Bridges—Continued

District No. 5—Continued

Miscellaneous—Continued

on crossing, 894.89; Temiskaming & Northern Ontario Railway, freight, 1,024.69; Temiskaming & Northern Ontario Railway Telegraph, telegrams, 61.22; W. R. Thompson, car rental, 362.50; Triangle Truck & Taxi Service, livery, 50.00; United Typewriter Co., Ltd., inspections, etc., 29.25; Chas. Warnock & Co., Ltd., inspecting steel, 108.43; H. Weeks, car rental, 477.50; Geo. Walsh, trucking, 15.00; petty disbursements, unenumerated, 385.21........................... 35,246 30

DISTRICT No. 6 ($447,417.87)

Engineer, D. Lough, Matheson

Kirkland Lake-Cheminis Road	100,513 22	
Ferguson Highway	93,256 43	
Porquis Junction-Timmins Road	53,870 00	
Goldthorpe-Kirkland Lake Road	26,080 71	
Porquis Junction-Iroquois Falls Road	16,803 20	
Shillington-Monteith-Iroquois Falls Road	6,697 57	
Matheson-Shillington-Connaught Road	4,712 36	
Iroquois Falls-Nellie Lake Road	2,192 67	
Equipment and tools	30,635 06	
General maintenance, settlers' and other roads, sundry expenditure	112,656 65	
		447,417 87

Travelling Expenses, $2,663.83.

E. K. Beam, 25.70; E. A. Cash, 262.08; W. W. Christopherson, 18.85; M. G. Clark, 179.15; E. B. Corbould, 27.20; Wm. Darcy, 14.45; Reg. Doal, 246.10; Wm. J. Yorke Hardy, 21.75; A. J. Hough, 45.20; F. A. Knapp, 40.10; R. Leavoy, 35.20; O. E. Loney, 28.95; D. Lough, 488.27; F. McCallum, 58.55; C. O. McLean, 85.45; R. Pollock, 71.85; G. L. Roberts, 37.33; G. Smith, 90.10; S. Smith, 427.05; Alex. Stirling, 136.70; T. L. Watts, 323.80.................................. 2,663 83

Advertising, Newspapers, Printing and Stationery, $67.79.

Contract Record & Engineering Review, 20.40; Daily Commercial News, 18.00; Northern News, Pearce Northern, Ltd., 26.29; J. B. Smith, 3.10............... 67 79

Autos, Trucks, Accessories, Parts and Repairs, $15,061.15.

Abitibi Power & Paper Co., Ltd., 21.01; J. D. Adams (Canada), Ltd., 120.95; Auto Electric Service Co., 290.05; Autoveyers, 14.60; Berini Motor Sales, 16.90; The Oliver Blais Co., Ltd., 184.25; Canada Ingot Iron Co., 121.84; Canadian Fairbanks-Morse Co., Ltd., 492.52; Canadian Ingersoll Rand Co., Ltd., 332.48; Dominion Road Machinery Co., 735.72; Dominion Rubber Co., Ltd., 42.14; Garage Supply Co., Ltd., 30.00; General Supply Co. of Canada, Ltd., 2,386.40; Goodyear Tire & Rubber Co. of Canada, Ltd., 162.03; J. S. Innes, Ltd., 2,420.25; International Harvester Co. of Canada, Ltd., 74.35; Keyes Supply Co., Ltd., 2,122.24; McDonald's Garage, 1,018.42; Marshall-Ecclestone, Ltd., 129.20; Matheson Garage, 83.30; R. J. Mitchell, 501.75; Motor Tool Specialty Co., 22.85; New Ontario Machine Works, 31.03; Northern Canada Supply Co., Ltd., 43.55; Porquis Junction Garage, 13.00; Sawyer-Massey, Ltd., 666.80; South End Garage, 2.00; Truck & Tractor Equipment Co., Ltd., 2,740.31; United Typewriter Co., Ltd., 1.40; W. C. Warburton & Co., Ltd., 100.67; Willys-Overland Sales Co., Ltd., 139.14.. 15,061 15

Camp and Road Supplies and Equipment, $79,213.86.

Abitibi Power & Paper Co., Ltd., 107.07; Hans Anderson, 114.40; F. Ashton, 140.00; W. A. Bannerman, 1,836.30; J. D. Bastien & Sons, 13.15; S. Bird, 1,256.70; Heber Briden, 30.00; Brown & Averell, 143.97; Canada Packers, Ltd., 912.53; Canadian Industries, Ltd., 2,914.05; Canadian Oil Companies, Ltd., 7,948.80; Frank Cassie, 475.41; J. H. Cole, 115.20; Corrugated Pipe Co., Ltd., 5,361.32; H. S. Crabtree, Ltd., 68.00; R. H. Craig, 14.00; Francis Desjardin, 88.00; Dunlop Tire & Rubber Goods Co., Ltd., 125.66; N. Evoy, 412.00; Feldman Bros., 18.03; Fred Findlay, 650.36; Felix Florrent, 109.20; John W. Fogg, Ltd., (Kirkland Lake), 1,041.92; John W. Fogg, Ltd. (Timmins), 938.97; General Supply Co. of Canada, Ltd., 1,045.00; J. T. Goldthorpe, 362.81; John H. Grainger, 922.48; A. Gullberg, 1,350.34; N. Hagar, 33.30; Hawk Lake Lumber Co., Ltd.,

Statutory—Continued

Roads and Bridges—Continued

District No. 6—Continued

Camp and Road Supplies and Equipment—Continued

1,832.18; J. Herron, 70.00; F. Hetu, 57.72; V. Hill, 76.74; Hill-Clark-Francis, Ltd., 123.73; Hy-Way Service Station, 2,452.16; Imperial Oil, Ltd., 4,856.10; Instruments, Ltd., 303.80; F. C. James, 12.40; Mrs. A. Kari, 37.75; John Leckie, Ltd., 151.14; John Ledingham, 360.89; John Lupine, 801.03; McColl-Frontenac Oil Co., Ltd., 1,515.13; Jas. W. McLeod, 87.19; McLeod's Service Station, 549.29; Donald McRae, 127.85; Marshall-Ecclestone, Ltd., 6,055.58; Metallic Roofing Co. of Canada, Ltd., 167.40; Geo. Mitchell, 12.50; Mitchell's Hardware & Supply Co., Ltd., 674.06; D. Moffatt, 17.00; R. Murphy, 24.96; National Grocers Co., Ltd., 2,090.96; Northern Canada Supply Co., Ltd., 2,452.28; Northern Lumber Sales, Regd., 240.00; M. O'Connor, 109.47; Ontario Reformatory Industries, 843.10; Pedlar People, Ltd., 17,506.84; Peerless Hardware, 496.66; Perkus, Ltd., 21.30; Chas. Pierce & Sons, Ltd., 351.87; Postmasters, 274.13; Purity Oxygen Sales, 27.93; John Ranger, 50.00; The J. Frank Raw Co., Ltd., 127.90; F. C. Richardson, 10.15; Shillington General Store, 311.43; South End Garage, 1,306.59; Teck Fuel & Ice Co., 395.25; Teck Motor Sales Co., 31.25; Jas. Thompson, 12.00; S. O. Tickner, 495.00; R. J. Vigrass, 2,522.02— 78,591 70
Add Transferred New Liskeard Stores Account.................. 622 16
79,213 86

Contracts, $99,820.80.

The McNamara Construction Co., Ltd., repairing Timmins-South Porcupine road from South Porcupine to Timmins, distance approximately 6 miles and applying seal coat to the whole surface of the existing pavement, Township of Tisdale, 12,607.65; The McNamara Construction Co., Ltd., supplying and gravelling Timmins-Porquis Junction Trunk Road, 18,900.00; Northern Paving & Materials, Ltd., cutting, burning, stumping and grubbing right-of-way and grading of approximately 10.4 miles, Kirkland Lake-Cheminis Road from Larder City to Cheminis, Townships Hearst, McVittie and McGarry, 68,313.15........ 99,820 80

Gravel, Rock and Stone, $21,707.70.

J. Carlson, 82.20; A. Champagne, 30.40; J. Champagne, 50.20; J. A. Craig, 60.00; Christy Crites, 163.40; J. Dambrovitz, 79.30; A. D'Amour, 362.30; Mrs. J. Deering, 42.40; Public Trustee of Jos. Fontaine Estate, 101.00; N. Gadoury, Sr., 11.80; Jack Gale, 401.00; John Gauthier, 335.80; R. Gauthier, 202.10; H. Gelinas, 41.40; Carl Hanson, 11.40; A. E. Heavens, 187.40; F. Hetu, 144.90; D. L. Jemmett, 149.20; B. Johnson, 60.20; Edward Journeau, 40.60; Alphonse Lambert, 363.70; Alfred Levacque, 74.00; J. J. McDonald, 677.40; Robt. Martin, 200.00; M. Miller, 429.25; Oswald Miller, 138.20; W. Mills, 33.40; Geo. Morgan, 206.80; F. Newlove, 96.20; Northern Paving & Materials, Ltd., 13,832.65; O. Olsen, 142.00; H. B. Peart, 107.20; T. Plouffe, 121.10; E. Potter, 169.60; G. Renwick, 58.10; Thos. G. Renwick, 118.30; Geo. Scace, 20.80; J. B. Smith, 120.20; Corporation of the Township of Teck, 2,050.00; Chesley Tomlinson, 16.50; W. Vanclief, 175.30........ 21,707 70

Pay Lists, $210,317.90.

Wages of men........ 210,317 90

Board and Lodging, $796.05.

Abitibi Power & Paper Co., Ltd., 38.50; Charlies Hotel, 233.55; P. E. Doal, 65.00; S. Latvala, 39.50; J. McCosh, 419.50........ 796 05

Proportionate Cost of Roads, $5,730.11.

Townships of—Playfair, 484.88; Tisdale, 5,245.23........ 5,730 11

Purchase of Property, $433.60.

Albert Boucher, 212.00; Narcisse Boucher, 93.00; Anton Laine, 105.60; Jos. Tremblay, 23.00........ 433 60

Miscellaneous, $11,605.08.

O. Ackles, rent of camps, 20.00; Percy Armstrong, car rental, 40.00; Bark & Mortimer, auto insurance, 105.30; E. K. Beam, transportation, 15.00; Canada Creosoting Co., loading lumber, 29.93; Canadian Liquid Air Co., Ltd., rental of cylinders, 233.94; Canadian National Express, express, 313.57; Canadian Pacific Express, express, 145.68; Canadian Pacific Railway Co., freight, 78.75; E. A. Cash, car rental, 172.50; D. Charlebois, transportation, 12.10; J. Leo Charpentier, clearing and grubbing land, 204.00; Consolidated Fire & Casualty Insurance Co., damages to car, 100.00; J. Deforge, transportation, 72.00; Geo. Dodds, car rental

Statutory—Continued

Roads and Bridges—Continued

District No. 6—Continued

Miscellaneous—Continued

and livery, 156.00; Hugh Dysart, clearing and grubbing land, 114.00; Donald Frood, boat hire, 14.00; Gordon H. Gauthier, clearing and grubbing land, 12.60; Lionel Godson, auto insurance, 52.00; J. T. Goldthorpe, rent of buildings, 90.00;W. Green, cleaning office, 78.00; A. Gullberg, rent of ground, 50.00; L. Hart, clearing and grubbing land, 138.10; R. Hembruff, car rental, 589.00; Herman's Dry Cleaning & Dyeing, washing blankets and mattresses, 25.60; T. Hylands, motor boat hire, 17.50; N. Jakower, cleaning blankets and mattresses, 80.05; F. C. James, blacksmithing, 180.95; J. Kempi, rent of building, 25.00; Mrs. A. Levacque, livery, 11.50; Walter Little, Ltd., Truck hire, 260.00; F. McCallum, car rental, 257.50; J. McInnes, car rental, 45.00; C. O. McLean, car rental, 341.00; E. C. McLean, car rental, 44.00; McLelland Transportation Co. (Kirkland Lake), car rental and storage, 36.95; McLelland Transportation Co. (Swastika), car rental, 278.65; McNamara Construction Co., Ltd., patching road, 250.00; Town of Matheson, water, 66.00; Walter Monahan, rent of powder house and horse, 87.60; H. Mould, removing truck from creek, 36.50; F. Newlove, rent of cutter and labour packing equipment, 5.30; Nipissing Central Railway Co., freight, and moving pole, 45.97; Northern Ontario Power Co., Ltd., lighting, repairs to line, 251.82; Northern Telephone Co., telephone services, 1,802.89; T. Nylands, motor boat hire, 97.50; R. Pollock, car rental, 550.00; E. Potter, rent of tractor, 27.75; John Rawlinson, Sr., clearing and grubbing land, 49.00; C. Scarffe, car rental, 29.37; A. Shorwen, blacksmithing, 14.50; W. E. Simpson, office rent, 60.00; Alex. Stirling, car rental, 585.00; Kenneth Stirling, car rental, 134.00; Corporation of the Township of Teck, water, 5.00; Temiskaming and Northern Ontario Railway, freight, fares, moving poles and flagging protection, 1,984.62; Temiskaming and Northern Ontario Telegraph, telegrams, 244.40; Temiskaming and Northern Ontario Telephone, telephone services, 101.30; Wm. C. Thompson, light, 17.50; Timmins Laundry Co., washing blankets, 12.60; Town of Timmins, taxes, 13.50; J. F. Tremblay, rent of building, 15.00; T. L. Watts, car rental, 325.00; I. P. Wilson, clearing and grubbing land, 125.13; petty disbursements, unenumerated, 227.66 .... 11,605 08

DISTRICT No. 7 ($309,241.54)

Engineer C. Tackaberry, Cochrane

Cochrane-Hearst Road	57,136 61	
Ferguson Highway	17,050 49	
Hearst-Coppell Road	10,793 17	
Cochrane-Norembega Road	7,708 52	
Genier Road	3,493 94	
Gardner Road	3,452 92	
Lake Road	1,968 20	
Clute Road	1,874 33	
Equipment and tools	41,342 26	
General maintenance, settlers' and other roads, sundry expenditure	164,421 10	
		309,241 54

Travelling Expenses, $3,168.47.

F. Bogie, 141.75; A. Corbeil, 67.00; W. Corbeil, 282.45; F. Draves, 494.95; Chas. R. Ellis, 17.50; R. Grasser, 144.55; W. B. Hutcheson, 439.74; T. J. Kennedy, 47.05; C. Landreville, 41.70; H. H. R. D. McDonald, 41.00; R. D. McGregor, 17.15; G. A. McMeekin, 106.10; A. Proulx, 41.90; D. V. Reid, 198.25; T. L. Ripley, 338.65; S. Smith, 46.00; W. B. Smith, 29.05; C. Tackaberry, 663.63; R. Williams, 10.05 .... 3,168 47

Advertising, Newspapers, Printing and Stationery, $130.66.

Chalykoff & Co., Ltd., 12.88; Cochrane Photo Studio, 60.30; C. Ellis, 41.73; The Northern Tribune, 15.75 .... 130 66

Autos, Trucks, Accessories, Parts and Repairs, $18,541.06.

Leger Brunelle, 39.20; Lorne Callahan, 118.57; Canada Ingot Iron Co., Ltd., 18.90; Canadian Fairbanks-Morse Co., Ltd., 151.98; Cochrane Machine Works, 1,294.72; Dominion Road Machinery Co., 659.32; General Supply Co. of Canada, Ltd., 743.56; Hearst Garage, 39.01; J. S. Innes, Ltd., 454.99; International Harvester

Statutory—Continued

Roads and Bridges—Continued

District No. 7—Continued

Autos, Trucks, Accessories, Parts and Repairs—Continued

Co. of Canada, Ltd., 403.52; Kapuskasing Garage, 66.25; Kapuskasing Supply Co., Ltd., 68.61; Keyes Supply Co., Ltd., 398.87; McGill Hardware, Ltd., 1,023.06; A. Marquis, 14.25; Meaford Steel Products, Ltd., 96.95; Motor Tool Specialty Co., 35.55; Nash & Chrysler Motors, 328.70; Northern Garage, 340.00; Palangio Motor Sales, 4,157.43; Thos. Pocklington Co., 73.55; Sawyer-Massey, Ltd., 1,434.04; Spruce Falls Power & Paper Co., Ltd., 239.09; Toronto Tractor & Equipment Co, 148.38; Truck & Tractor Equipment Co., Ltd., 5,951.10; Wabi Iron Works, Ltd., 112.20; W. C. Warburton Co., Ltd., 98.66; Willys-Overland Sales Co., Ltd., 30.60 .... 18,541 06

Camp and Road Supplies and Equipment, $84,431.90.

Adanac Service, Ltd., 18.00; Wm. Allen, 34.80; D. Andrewonick, 15.00; The Art Metropole, 38.00; J. B. Barrette, 40.50; J. A. Bentley, 595.08; F. Bondy, 264.40; Bondy & Johnson, 208.80; Leon Bouchard, 77.25; Jos. Brassard, 28.00; Vital Brisson, 1,071.18; Wm. Brush, 48.30; Canadian Industries, Ltd., 3,531.05; Canadian Oil Companies, Ltd., 12,490.01; J. Carson, 99.15; Carter Bros., 125.09; Chalykoff & Co., Ltd., 302.82; John Christianson, 795.00; R. J. Clifford, 47.25; A. P. Collins, 37.25; R. B. Croysdale, 60.42; J. H. Dallaire, 36.31; S. Deslauriers, 73.19; A. Dexter, 261.00; Andy Doyle, 41.08; M. Doyle, 132.33; Paul H. Dubois, 234.57; Leo Dumoulin, 24.30; H. C. Dunbar, 21.86; L. Flood, 90.32; Z. Fontaine, 112.79; R. Foster, 55.78; Alodar Gagnon, 12.00; Gasaccumulator Co. (Canada), Ltd., 21.20; A. Gauthier, 47.25; John Gibson, 150.00; E. Girard, 11.25; Gold Medal Furniture Manufacturing Co., Ltd., 283.99; L. Gregoire, 50.25; A. Chas. Guenette, 54.05; Jos. Guillemette, 55.17; Lorenzo Guillemette, 14.15; Geo. Hackett, 40.50; A. Hakala, 54.00; A. Hamon, 48.20; Hawk Lake Lumber Co., Ltd., 2,596.51; Hobson-Gauthier, Ltd., 135.69; Geo. Holledge, 103.00; Jean Houle, 16.68; Hudson's Bay Co., 45.18; Imperial Oil, Ltd., 10,463.31; Fred C. Ivy Co., 51.40; J. C. Jacques, 12.00; H. H. Joanisse, 305.85; P. Johnson, 50.60; Richard Peterson Kanne, 17.50; Kapuskasing Supply Co., Ltd., 1,441.93; M. B. Kellar, 14.25; Wm. Knight, 41.10; W. Kurtsweg, 87.30; A. Laflame, 34.80; J. A. Laflame, 44.75; Lang & Ross, 10.15; J. Lanthier, 38.40; L. Lapointe, 18.00; J. A. Leblanc, 177.17; John Leckie, Ltd., 1,700.09; Line & Cable Accessories, 246.49; W. Lloyd, 14.60; A. Loucks, 69.55; McColl-Frontenac Oil Co., Ltd., 535.76; McGill Hardware, Ltd., 4,815.48; R. D. McKay, 35.25; Honore Mallais, 42.00; Marshall-Ecclestone, Ltd., 2,862.00; T. Mercier, 453.60; Metallic Roofing Co. of Canada, Ltd., 6,045.76; Monarch Drug Co., Ltd., 33.57; National Grocers Co., Ltd., 291.91; Northern Canada Supply Co., Ltd., 65.44; Northland Grocers, Ltd., 26.95; Ontario Reformatory Industries, 1,058.06; Pedlar People, Ltd., 18,981.12; Pellow Lumber & Hardware Co., 1,166.06; M. Perkus, Ltd., 28.00; Onesime Perron, 13.47; D. Plamendon, 50.00; Thos. Pocklington Co., 16.55; Postmasters, 809.70; The J. Frank Raw Co., Ltd., 8.85; H. Reid, 24.73; Louis Seguin & Fils, 1,028.80; Sherwin-Williams Co. of Canada, Ltd., 16.02; M. Silverstone, 14.40; Jos. Simard, 281.43; C. Smith, 12.80; John B. Smith & Sons, Ltd., 315.75; R. M. Smith, 10.98; Sturgeons, Ltd., 94.03; The Geo. Taylor Hardware, Ltd., (Cochrane), 774.43; The Geo. Taylor Hardware, Ltd., (New Liskeard) 76.75; S. O. Tickner, 2,793.06; H. Toal, 21.00; Lucien Trottier, 136.70; Tudhope-Anderson, Ltd., 28.06; Union Lumber Co., Ltd., 153.51; Narcisse Veilleux, 12.00; Phillipe Veilleux, 422.99; Raoul Villeneuve, 170.04; H. T. Vincent, 57.57; Mrs. A. J. Wilkie, 54.60; C. Wilkie, 57.48; Wilson Bros., 12.06; Woods Manufacturing Co., Ltd., 701.49; A. J. Yelle, 19.00; Yelle Co., Ltd., 104.50; P. Zebruk, 109.00 .... 84,431 90

Contracts, $10,181.64.

J. Valliere, chopping and clearing right-of-way, Township of Devitt, 25.00; Isaac Walli, ditching, Township of Lamarche, 32.75; Nick Solovey, ditching, Township of Calder, 100.00; Steve Kulich, ditching, boundary Townships of Calder and Ottaway, 32.00; Lauritz Bakke, grubbing, burning, ditching, Township Eilber, 68.05; Ulysse Tremblay, grubbing, burning, ditching, Township of Idington, 25.00; H. Flood, grubbing, burning, ditching, Township of McCrea, 25.00; J. B. Levesque, cutting, burning, Township of Devitt, 300.00; J. B. Levesque, ditching, Township of Devitt, 632.64; K. Frobergh, stumping, burning, boundary Townships, of Hanlan and Way, 10.00; J. B. Levesque, stumping, burning, Township of Devitt, 397.73; K. Frobergh, ditching, boundary of Townships of Hanlan and Way, 117.14; H. Hurium, cutting, clearing, Township of Eilber, 45.76; H. Hurium, grubbing, burning, ditching, Township of Eilber, 723.82; Jos. Lacasse, grubbing, burning, ditching, Township of McCrea, 52.96; T.

Statutory—Continued

Roads and Bridges—Continued

District No. 7—Continued

Contracts—Continued

Bobov, cutting, burning, Township of Way, 46.20; J. Savalienen, ditching, Township of Devitt, 701.20; J. Savalienen, grubbing, stumping, burning, Township of Devitt, 216.30; H. Frisk, ditching, boundary of Townships of Hanlan and Way, 351.20; Steve Hornadek, grubbing, burning, ditching, spreading, Township of Williamson, 646.87; A. Laroche, ditching, spreading, boundary of Townships of Kendall and Casgrain, 102.86; A. Laroche, cutting, burning, boundary of Townships of Kendall and Casgrain, 50.60; A. Laroche, grubbing, stumping, burning, boundary of Townships of Kendall and Casgrain, 81.00; Peter Berg, cutting, burning boundary of Townships of McCrea and Barker, 44.49; Peter Berg, grubbing, burning, ditching, spreading, boundary of Townships of McCrea and Barker, 373.77; Peter Berg, grubbing, burning, ditching and spreading, boundary of Townships of McCrea and Barker, 116.24; Peter Berg, grubbing, burning, ditching, boundary of Townships of McGowan and Eilber, 1,594.35; H. Rask, ditching, spreading, Township of Hanlan, 159.12; R. P. Kanne, ditching, Township of Kendall, 470.20; F. B. Anderson, ditching, Township of Hanlan, 120.06; F. B. Anderson, cutting, burning, Township of Hanlan, 25.50; F. B. Anderson, grubbing, burning, stumping, Township of Hanlan, 17.80; A. Lapointe, grubbing, stumping, burning, Township of Way, 185.75; A. Lapointe, ditching, Township of Way, 314.60; K. Norhi, ditching, Township of Way, 605.25; J. Martin, ditching, Township of Way, 141.80; E. Luivo, ditching, Township of Hanlan, 292.50; S. Urkovitch, cutting, burning, Township of Hanlan, 50.60; S. Urkovitch, grubbing, stumping, burning, Township of Hanlan, 82.80; A. Lacasse, grubbing, burning, stumping, Township of Devitt, 452.34; L. Lapointe, grubbing, burning, stumping, Township of Hanlan, 113.45; L. Lafontaine, ditching, Township of Hanlan, 152.28; A. Drysdale, grubbing, stumping, burning, Township of Hanlan, 55.85; A. Drysdale, cutting, burning, Township of Hanlan, 28.80.................... 10,181 64

Gravel, Rock and Stone, $3,119.31.

A. Brunet, 10.35; John Christianson, 297.36; Dominique Gilbert, 172.20; L. Gregoire, 88.10; O. J. Haigh, 73.10; Richard Peterson Kanne, 300.00; Jos. Lawless, 1,202.55; J. Levis, 67.00; Carl Palangio, 93.10; A. Pinion, 196.40; A. Sirois, 387.70; Wm. Streahorn, 125.05; S. Zagrebalney, 106.40................. 3,119 31

Pay Lists, $171,963.61.

Wages of men.. 171,963 61

Board and Lodging, $3.70.

Lang & Ross.. 3 70

Proportionate Cost of Roads, $5,092.12.

Townships of—Fauquier, 118.88; Glackmeyer, 4,973.24...................... 5,092 12

Purchase of Property Right-of-Way, $306.00.

J. C. Maure.. 306 00

Miscellaneous, $12,303.07.

Mrs. J. J. Arseneault, washing blankets, 12.75; E. and Mrs. Audet, rent of office, 150.00; Bark & Mortimer, auto insurance, 46.80; Canadian Inspection & Testing Co., Ltd., inspection of paint, 34.10; Canadian National Express, express, 188.39; Canadian National Railways, lease of siding, rent of motor car house, freight, threading steel rods, 1,430.07; Canadian National Telegraphs, 108.15; Canadian Pacific Express Co., express, 7.27; John Christianson, blacksmithing, 21.85; Cochrane Steam Laundry, washing blankets, 30.98; Town of Cochrane, telephone, light, water, 879.41; Mrs. Geo. Comfort, washing blankets, 12.75; A. Corbeil, car rental, 361.00; W. Corbeil, car rental, 652.50; H. Cuillerier, livery, 45.00; A. Daze, cutting and grubbing land, 22.00; Chas. J. Dix, livery, 226.50; Dominion Oxygen Co., Ltd., cylinder rental, 173.70; J. Dufour, clearing and grubbing land, 57.20; Mrs. L. Duguay, clearing and grubbing land, 95.97; Experimental Farm (Kapuskasing), hauling gravel, 354.00; Murray Fingland, cartage, 15.00; J. Gagnon, grubbing and burning land, 35.25; Nap Gagnon, grubbing and burning land, 179.30; Estate of Jos. Gauthier, cutting and grubbing land, 54.80; Lionel Godson, auto insurance, 72.80; Grant Brothers Construction, Ltd., rent of cement mixer, 60.00; G. H. Greeley, clearing and grubbing land, 39.15; John M. Greer, drawing transfer, 20.30; J. Grenier, grubbing and burning land, 35.25; Jules Guindon, clearing and grubbing land, 42.05; Hearst Feed & Sale Stable, livery, 84.00; Hearst Garage, car rental, 15.00; Imperial Bank of Canada, interest on overdraft, 14.85; Cecil James, taxi service, 20.00; August Johnson, damage

Statutory—Continued

Roads and Bridges—Continued

District No. 7—Continued

Miscellaneous—Continued

to car and personal injuries, 250.00; Kapuskasing Garage, car rental, 47.65; Town of Kapuskasing, lighting, 23.79; Peter Kluke, taxi service and blacksmithing, 91.30; Mrs. Marie Kovachuk, rent of typewriter, 15.00; Adelard Lacasse, clearing, grubbing and burning land, 68.55; Jos. Lacasse, grubbing and ditching, 352.74; Mrs. H. Lafort, washing blankets, 11.08; W. Lamontagne, blacksmithing, 34.55; Hong Lee, washing blankets, 40.20; John Lepage, blacksmithing, 15.25; Mrs. L. Levesque, washing blankets and cleaning, 56.20; W. McEachern, cartage, 43.33; G. A. McMeekin, car rental, 790.00; Ol. Morel, clearing, grubbing and burning land, 57.20; R. M. Myers, legal services, 11.00; Northern Telephone Co., telephone services, 935.88; Owens Cartage Co., cartage, unloading timber, 126.50; Palangio Motor Sales, car rental, 145.50; Wm. Piette, rent of road, 50.00; E. Provost, clearing and grubbing land, 112.31; G. Rassel, stumping and brushing land, 290.41; C. Ringborg, cutting, burning and grubbing land, 22.00; P. Rousson, compensation for cows killed at crossing, 50.00; A. St. John, cutting and grubbing land, 158.95; Alex. M. Smith & Sons, cartage, 22.00; W. B. Smith, car rental, 490.00; N. Solovey, stumping land, 75.00; Mrs. J. Steenson, washing blankets, 12.75; The Temiskaming & Northern Ontario Railway, freight, lease of warehouse, 1,292.24; Temiskaming & Northern Ontario Railway Telegraph, telegrams, 2.16; S. O. Tickner, car rental, 148.00; E. Topaloff, rent of building, 75.00; Mrs. E. Tremblay, washing blankets, 15.60; United Typewriter Co., Ltd., inspection of typewriter, 20.50; Arthur Valley, taxi service, 147.75; I. Vandette, taxi service, 44.50; Wabi Iron Works, Ltd., blacksmithing, 27.70; Mrs. and W. Willmer, washing blankets, 133.61; Wilson Bros., blacksmithing, 19.05; petty disbursements, unenumerated, 379.68 .... 12,303 07

DISTRICT No. 8 ($638,499.86)

Engineer, A. J. Isbester, Fort William

International Highway	205,031 31	
Trans-Canada Highway	138,608 42	
Dawson Road	19,881 20	
Oliver Road	10,228 43	
Moss Mine Road	9,233 41	
Silver Creek Road	6,047 62	
Silver Mountain and Gunflint Road	5,456 09	
Finmark-Goldie Road	4,505 85	
Sibley West Road	4,331 10	
Scoble Road	3,923 33	
Forbes West Road	3,562 53	
Devon Road	3,163 10	
Kakabeka Falls-Hymers Road	2,895 14	
Forbes Centre Road	2,853 12	
Dog Lake Road	2,434 60	
Pass Lake Road	1,975 89	
Armstrong-Caribou Lake Road	1,858 12	
Nakina West Road	1,731 37	
Shebandowan Lake Road	1,576 31	
Sibley East Road	1,548 75	
Marks Road	1,455 68	
Scoble-Hymers Road	1,334 40	
Equipment and tools	38,395 72	
General maintenance, settlers' and other roads, sundry expenditure	166,468 37	
		638,499 86

Travelling Expenses, $828.73.

A. J. Isbester, 128.30; W. R. Maher, 145.13; D. C. Rea, 158.65; H. P. Sisson, 109.60; B. Sutherland, 69.80; John Welsh, 44.20; Jas. Wilson, 173.05 .... 828 73

Advertising, Newspapers, Printing and Stationery, $236.44.

Daily Times Journal, 39.24; D. Gestetner (Canada), Ltd., 19.92; Lowery's, Ltd., 19.95; News-Chronicle Publishing Co., Ltd., 24.00; Bank of Nova Scotia, 35.00; Remington Typewriters, Ltd., 13.35; J. Edgar Rutledge, 84.98 .... 236 44

Statutory—Continued

Roads and Bridges—Continued

District No. 8—Continued

Autos, Trucks, Accessories, Parts and Repairs, $27,981.59.

Barton & Fisher, 24.75; D. Bohm, Ltd., 92.10; J. Brown, 113.35; Canada Ingot Iron Co., Ltd., 287.39; Canadian Ingersoll-Rand Co., Ltd., 884.80; City Typewriter Co., 31.40; Coslett Hardware Co., 2,073.59; Coslett Machinery & Equipment Co., 2,184,83; A. Dalgleish, 23.50; Dominion Motors, 177.85; Dominion Road Machinery Co., Ltd., 1,153.88; Endress & Auld, Ltd., 980.62; Grain Port Motors, Ltd., 1,330.03; S. J. Hill & Co., 103.80; Kam Motors, Ltd., 4,313.15; Massey-Harris Co., Ltd. (Toronto), 80.40; Massey-Harris Co., Ltd. (Winnipeg), 334.80; Nicholson's Tire Surgery, 291.03; Northern Engineering & Supply Co., Ltd., 1,127.90; Northland Tractor & Equipment Co., Ltd., 736.79; N. M. Patterson & Co., Ltd., 70.00; Thos. Pocklington Co., 17.10; Ross Service Station, 8,843.36; Sawyer-Massey, Ltd., 1,184.42; Twinport Auto Sales, 485.14; Western Engineering Service, Ltd., 1,035.61 .... 27,981 59

Camp and Road Supplies and Equipment, $136,007.55.

A. Allard, 50.00; J. Arrow, 46.44; The Art Metropole, 104.70; Ball Bros., 230.00; E. E. Barrie, 161.58; E. A. Bell, 460.00; Bell Lumber Co., Ltd., 55.66; Romeo Bracci, 13.86; J. Broome, 86.25; Percy Broughton, 420.15; J. Brown, 36.40; Burns & Co., Ltd., 3,376.62; Campbell & Muir, 8,863.79; Canada Culvert Co., Ltd., 3,074.70; Canadian Liquid Air Co., Ltd., 43.49; Canadian Oil Companies, Ltd. (Port Arthur), 3,779.53; Canadian Oil Companies, Ltd. (Winnipeg), 94.36; Canadian Packing Co., Ltd., 1,136.89; Frank Cassie, 1,155.00; Central Tent & Awning Co., 495.95; Corrugated Pipe Co., Ltd., 4,561.54; Jas. Davidson & Co., Ltd., 350.35; Dominion Tar & Chemical Co., Ltd., 213.11; Dunn Hardware Co., Ltd., 3,327.17; Geo. J. Ellett, 363.05; Edward C. Ellis, 100.44; Ellis-Watts Co., 72.19; M. Engstrom, 11.28; Uno Erickson, 24.00; Fairway Stores, 136.26; Fallis Foote Co., 337.76; Fife Hardware Co., 159.28; Fitzgerald's Drug Store, Ltd., 22.30; Fitzsimmons Fruit Co., Ltd., 384.55; The Milton Francis Lumber Co., Ltd., 41.69; Gasaccumulator Co. (Canada), Ltd., 19.50; General Supply Co. of Canada, Ltd., 1,567.50; Gerry Hardware Electric, 75.80; Mrs. S. Goodfellow, 16.06; Grand & Toy, Ltd., 113.60; H. T. Gray, 296.70; M. Guyan, 115.00; J. A. Hamilton, 44.89; Harpham Bros., Ltd., 159.21; J. Hastings, 191.53; Hewitson Construction Co., Ltd., 11,998.34; S. J. Hill & Co., 404.45; Hans Hogan, 126.62; B. Hoglaf, 15.00; Hudson's Bay Co., 104.26; Hunt's Service Store, 87.43; Imperial Oil, Ltd., 1,419.84; A. Kaki, 605.80; Mark Leiterman & Sons, 15.85; Lovelady Studio, 23.10; Lowe Bros. Co., Ltd., 370.95; McColl-Frontenac Co., Ltd., 569.44; MacDonald's Consolidated, Ltd., 1,435.34; MacKenzie Inn, 163.15; H. L. McKinnon Co., Ltd., 454.43; Marshall-Wells Co., Ltd., 3,824.07; Matthews Sash & Door Co., 75.64; Metallic Roofing Co. of Canada, Ltd., 79.20; Thos. Miller, 94.45; Monarch Oil Co., Ltd., 2,783.42; Moss Gold Mines, Ltd., 72.58; Mount McKay Feed Co., Ltd., 1,326.97; Alex. Murray & Co., Ltd., 107.93; A. H. Nash, 280.88; Geo. Neve, 195.59; J. Nicholson, 88.83; Eddie Nielson, 11.25; Ontario Reformatory Industries, 4,042.15; W. Oskanen, 40.00; Paramount Petroleum Co., Ltd., 38,685.78; Hugh Parslow & Co., Ltd., 93.85; Pedlar People, Ltd., 12,385.91; Pigeon River Hotel, 31.60; Piper Hardware Co., 8,370.76; Port Arthur Hardware, Ltd., 90.90; City of Port Arthur 38.31; Postmasters, 260.00; John Rajakivisti, 16.00; J. Frank Raw Co., Ltd., 14.57; A. Rossignal, 19.20; D. V. Rumsey, 146.81; Mrs. R. Sedore, 102.18; Sherwin-Williams Co. of Canada, Ltd., 267.05; N. Slater Co., Ltd., 188.51; Spadoni Bros., 38.59; B. Strom, 37.44; S. Stroud, 11.70; Sturgeons, Ltd., 550.97; Superior Brick & Tile Co., 349.14; Sutton's Tourist Resort, 13.50; Jas. Swallow, 44.15; Thunder Bay Lumber Co. (Fort William), 155.94; Thunder Bay Lumber Co. (Port Arthur), 1,019.35; J. W. Tripp, 24.00; O. B. Turk, 35.20; Twin City Grain, Ltd., 70.70; Louis Walsh Coal Co., Ltd., 115.45; Wells & Emerson, 18.00; Western Grocers, Ltd., 1,909.02; J. Winters, 201.06 .... 132,512 73

Add—Transferred Huntsville Store Account 3,494 82

136,007 55

Contracts, $59,255.91.

J. F. Hewitson, the supplying of stone chips, reshaping and rolling of sub-grade, International Highway from Fort William approximately 15 miles southerly and laying thereon 2½" consolidated bituminous retread top, 36,611.60; J. F. Hewitson, the supplying of stone chips, reshaping and rolling of sub-grade, Trans-Canada Highway from Loon Lake, a distance of approximately 11 miles and laying thereon 2½" consolidated bituminous retread top, 16,223.00; The Standard Steel Construction Co., fabrication and erection of steel bridge over McKenzie River, Trans-Canada Highway, 6,421.31 .... 59,255 91

Statutory—Continued

Roads and Bridges—Continued

District No. 8—Continued

Gravel, Rock and Stone, $65,727.82.

Animikie Mines, Ltd., 70.00; Mrs. E. Breillie, 50.20; F. Brown, 58.72; F. Bruner, 18.55; Mrs. Ida Burman, 10.65; Theo. Fournier, 20.20; Mr. Galloway, 16.55; J. A. Hamilton, 107.57; Hewitson Construction Co., Ltd., 61,252.50; S. Kallio, 42.57; E. Killino, 78.30; J. Lethorn, 149.92; T. McCranor, 3,453.00; Chas. Manty, 10.37; J. H. Parsons, 28.70; Jos. Purella, 52.93; O. Rvynonen, 48.65; W. Saarnio, 19.90; T. Salnie, 50.00; J. Seed, 13.30; A. Tenkula, 67.20; Fred Wallberg, 82.55; Alec Wamsley, 25.49 .... 65,727 82

Pay Lists, $287,771.62.

Wages of men 287,771 62

Board and Lodging, $1,745.90.

Mrs. S. Goodfellow, 58.70; Hewitson Construction Co., Ltd., 494.25; A. E. McDonald, 40.50; Mrs. G. McKinley, 241.20; Moss Gold Mines, Ltd., 18.00; D. Olsen, 26.25; Pigeon River Hotel, 764.30; Queen's Hotel, 25.60; Young Men's Christian Association, 77.10 .... 1,745 90

Proportionate Cost of Roads, $36,784.23.

Townships of—Gillies, 937.86; Neebing, 6,927.58; Nipigon, 2,423.21; Oliver, 3,181.86; O'Connor, 2,361.75; Paipoonge, 4,159.03; Schreiber, 474.16; Shuniah, 16,318.78 .... 36,784 23

Purchase of Property Right-of-Way, $100.00.

Morris & Babe, 50.00; Harry Wood, 50.00 .... 100 00

Miscellaneous, $22,060.07.

Algoma Laundry, washing blankets, 628.75; A. Allard, rent of buildings, 100.00; E. Baker, car rental, 148.00; Bark & Mortimer, auto insurance, 89.68; Angus Bell, cartage, 71.20; R. Biesenthal, car rental, 628.00; Canada Steamship Lines, Ltd., freight, 20.42; Canadian Inspection & Testing Co., Ltd., testing paint, 47.86; Canadian National Express, express, 13.19; Canadian National Railways, freight, 576.78; Canadian National Telegraph, telegrams, 29.49; Canadian Northern Railway, freight, 11.17; Canadian Pacific Express Co., express, 35.56; Canadian Pacific Railway Co., freight, 558.70; Canadian Pacific Railway Co.'s Telegraph, telegrams, 69.53; Roy Cooke, car rental, 256.00; J. W. Crooks & Co., developing films, etc., 14.60; R. Falshaw, clearing land, 45.00; D. C. Fellowes, car rental, 636.00; City of Fort William, telephone services, water, etc., 263.00; Lionel Godson, auto insurance, 90.24; M. C. Greer, car rental, 324.00; Higginbottom & Co., installing heating plant, 509.39; Geo. Hymers, rent of ground, 40.00; Hydro-Electric Power Commission, lighting, 95.78; Kaministiquia Power Co., Ltd., lighting, 126.67; John Lysnes, blacksmithing, 33.35; McLeod Motor Transfer, cartage, 22.44; Morris & Babe, professional services, 75.10; Moss Gold Mines, Ltd., transportation, 35.00; N. M. Patterson & Co., Ltd., rent of machine shop, 190.00; Port Arthur Garage, storage, 40.00; City of Port Arthur, phone services, 64.50; City of Port Arthur, constructing road, 15,292.82; Jas. Wilson, car rental, 496.00; Chas. Wood, clearing and grubbing land, 100.00; Woodside Bros., blacksmithing, 71.80; petty disbursements, unenumerated, 210.05 .... 22,060 07

DISTRICT No. 9 ($266,483.26)

Engineer, R. T. Lyons, Kenora

Trans-Canada Highway	74,596 97	
Kenora-Fort Frances Highway	13,659 79	
Richan Road	7,044 67	
Sioux Lookout-Dinorwic Road	6,271 99	
Ostersund Road	4,812 65	
Vermillion Bay-Quibell Road	3,896 74	
Pellatt Road	2,863 56	
Muriel Lake Road	2,543 67	
Kenora-Redditt Road	2,093 79	
Lac Lu Road	1,919 25	
Rice Lake Road	1,322 19	
Equipment and tools	61,228 67	
General maintenance, settlers' and other roads, sundry expenditure	84,229 32	
		266,483 26

Statutory—Continued

Roads and Bridges—Continued

District No. 9—Continued

Travelling Expenses, $3,311.59.

J. A. D. Aaron, 138.63; John D. Baby, 284.03; A. J. Cairns, 32.85; H. F. Cairns, 158.56; G. A. Crane, 168.54; R. A. Emerson, 623.20; A. W. Fisher, 25.25; C. Holland, 115.10; R. T. Lyons, 1,034.69; Geo. Noble, 366.45; F. Petursson, 129.09; Bruce Sarvis, 29.80; W. B. Scott, 19.25; H. Smith, 127.85; R. O. Smith, 21.85; L. C. Wright, 36.45 .... 3,311 59

Advertising, Printing and Stationery, $428.77.

The Miner Publishing Co., 136.90; The Bank of Nova Scotia, 105.00; G. W. Smith, 186.87 .... 428 77

Autos, Trucks, Accessories, Parts and Repairs, $21,377.19.

J. D. Adams, Ltd. (Canada), 165.29; Advance-Rumley Thresher Co., Inc., 201.75; Allis-Chalmers-Rumley, Ltd., 105.87; Austin Manufacturing Co., 231.62; Automotive Rewinding Co., 125.85; Breen Motor Co., Ltd., 37.62; Canada Ingot Iron Co., Ltd., 269.31; Canada Tractor & Equipment Co., 78.25; Canadian Automobile Equipment, Ltd., 420.77; Canadian Fairbanks-Morse Co., Ltd., 327.59; Canadian Ingersoll Rand Co., Ltd., 1,108.77; Canadian Johnson Motor Co., 26.02; Canadian Pacific Railway Co., 34.21; Nicholas Chomic, 18.00; J. S. Corner, 72.10; Coslett Machinery & Equipment Co., 212.93; Alex Cowey, 313.56; Dingwall Motors, Ltd., 3,743.44; Dominion Motor Co., Ltd., 16.47; Dominion Road Machinery Co., 108.31; Dryden Motors, 553.37; The Dryden Paper Co., Ltd., 220.55; Durance Bros. & Co., 69.58; D. M. Griffith, 57.00; Hall Gear & Machine Co., Ltd., 102.00; J. S. Innes, Ltd., 2,048.31; International Harvester Co., Ltd., 33.00; A. Olaf Isakson, 20.42; Jeffrey Manufacturing Co., Ltd., 127.00; J. A. Link, 115.89; Meaford Steel Products, Ltd., 1,401 62; The Peterborough Canoe Co., 37.23; Plewes, Ltd., 17.53; Thos. Pocklington Co., 111.10; Sawyer-Massey, Ltd., 4,234.34; J. W. Stone Boat Manufacturing Co., Ltd., 511.62; Sullivan Machinery Co., Ltd., 36.19; Truck & Tractor Equipment Co., Ltd., 3,889.15; Vulcan Iron Works, Ltd., 159.57; Willys-Overland Sales Co., Ltd., 13.99 .... 21,377 19

Camp and Road Supplies and Equipment, $61,714.53.

Acme Waste Manufacturing Co., Ltd., 37.06; Mrs. J. Armstrong, 35.70; The Art Metropole, 5,094.56; Russell Barker, 189.01; Geo. Beatty & Son, Ltd., 271.75; J. B. Bellair, 1,072.75; F. Blackley, 55.00; C. Bohn, 15.00; Brandram-Henderson, Ltd., 96.70; Cain Bros., 21.36; The Campbell Heating Co., 106.32; Canada Culvert Co., Ltd., 3,147.00; Canada Paint Co., Ltd., 53.41; Canadian Oil Companies, Ltd. (Dryden), 58.76; Canadian Oil Companies, Ltd. (Winnipeg), 5,355.66; H. Cheyne, 12.40; Frank Cosco, 518.47; Alex Cowey, 239.55; W. Dingey, 12.00; Dryden Lumber Co., Ltd., 3,512.42; Dryden Pharmacy, Ltd., 18.00; Alan Durance, 21.30; Durance Bros. & Co., 3,925.23; Eastman Kodak Stores, Ltd., 35.55; The T. Eaton Co., Ltd., 1,595.12; Ellis-Watts Co., 73.11; Fairway Stores, 445.55; Falcon Oils, Ltd., 258.76; A. T. Fife & Co., 15.20; Fort Frances Wholesalers, Ltd., 545.68; A. J. Gardiner, 153.15; Gasaccumulator Co. (Canada), Ltd., 16.01; General Supply Co of Canada, Ltd., 2,917.00; Goodyear Tire & Rubber Co. of Canada, Ltd., 341.57; Grand & Toy, Ltd., 24.25; P. Guernsey, 487.66; H. Holmstrom, 12.50; The Hose Hardware Co., 499.48; Hughes-Owens Co., Ltd., 71.11; J. S. Hunter, 39.40; Imperial Oil, Ltd., 2,564.40; Jack & Connor, 56.50; Johnson's Pharmacy, 18.90; The Keewatin Lumber Co. (Kenora), 1,318.74; Kelly & Kimberley, 18.75; E. A. Klose, 200.78; John Kron & Son, 188.32; Laing Bros., Ltd., 152.48; John Leckie, Ltd., 487.62; C. G. Linde, 67.25; Lindstrom & Nilsen, 1,175.84; Lowery's Limited, 134.78; H. S. McIlwraith, 40.00; Alex McKenzie, 18.12; MacKay-Morton, Ltd., 54.75; Manitoba Stencil & Stamp Works, 15.50; Maple Leaf Milling Co., Ltd. (Kenora), 71.50; Maple Leaf Milling Co., Ltd. (Toronto), 58.05; Merril, Rhind & Walmsley, 126.30; Metallic Roofing Co. of Canada, Ltd., 130.00; T. A. Miles, 84.00; Birjer Mortenson, 180.00; A. L. Murray, 649.88; Neale & Heath, 164.21; Office Specialty Manufacturing Co., Ltd., 45.70; Ontario Reformatory Industries, 2,822.80; Peter Perlin, 1,264.52; J. Peterson, 409.47; Alfred Pitt, Ltd., 344.67; Thos. Pocklington Co., 487.35; Postmasters, 262.62; W. Powell, 213.87; Pronger & Armstrong, 30.50; O. H. Pronger, 11.05; R. J. Pronger, 40.15; Pullan Wipers & Waste Co., Ltd., 28.00; The J. Frank Raw Co., Ltd., 4,679.05; John Reid, 700.92; Scythes & Co., Ltd., 1,541.01; Shield Development Co., Ltd. (Montreal), 450.00; The Star Office Specialty Co., 15.81; The Steel Equipment Co., Ltd. (Ottawa), 24.25; The Steel Equipment Co., Ltd. (Pembroke), 24.25; M. Steiner, 444.40; Sturgeons, Limited, 160.72; Taylor & Tackaberry, 52.55; Tilley's Palace

Statutory—Continued

Roads and Bridges—Continued

District No. 9—Continued

Camp and Road Supplies and Equipment—Continued

Photo Studio, 19.70; M. Wager, 42.05; Waldhof Farmers' Co-Operative Club, Ltd., 35.62; H. B. Wellenbotter, 35.00; Wells Hardware Co., Ltd., 38.26; Western Grocers, Ltd., 583.54; Western Oil Co., Ltd., 154.18; W. Wilder, 16.08; Williams Hardware Co., 6,114.86; Winnipeg Map & Blue Print Co., Ltd., 379.12; Woods Manufacturing Co., Ltd., 966.28; Less Credit, McColl-Frontenac Oil Co., Ltd., 101.00........ 61,714 53

Gravel, Rock and Stone, $839.89.

E. Anderson, 62.16; J. T. Breet, 19.70; E. Fanden, 24.15; Albert Francis, 21.56; Robert Fuller, 23.82; John Gould, 62.16; E. Griffiths, 85.73; F. Hendrickson, 10.92; Andrew Jones, 115.78; Claire Lillie, 22.12; C. McLeod, 11.20; J. W. McMaster, 153.56; A. McPhail, 15.19; L. O. Mounk, 57.05; W. D. Neely, 85.47; J. W. Norris, 69.32........ 839 89

Pay Lists, $163,289.98.

Wages of men........ 163,289 98

Board and Lodging, $377.57.

Crawley & McCracken, Ltd., 345.40; Mrs. B. Rochon, 32.17........ 377 57

Proportionate Cost of Roads, $2,124.07.

Townships of—Jaffray & Melick, 1,069.97; Van Horne, 1,054.10........ 2,124 07

Purchase of Property, Right-of-Way, $162.50.

Canadian Pacific Railway Co.,........ 162 50

Miscellaneous, $12,857.17..

P. O. Baker, rent of lot, 60.00; Bark & Mortimer, auto insurance, 54.51; Tom Beggs, compensation for loss of horse, 50.00; Bernard's, washing blankets, 39.75; A. Blomquist, taxi service, 220.25; Canadian Inspection & Testing Co., Ltd., inspection of paint, 36.44; Canadian National Railways, installing crossing, freight, 29.28; Canadian Pacific Express Co., express, 266.42; Canadian Pacific Railway Co., freight, fares, ditching, loading, protecting crossings, 2,297.13; Canadian Pacific Railway Company's Telegraphs, telegrams, 559.89; Lloyd A. Clark & Co., overhauling adding machines, 13.05; Cossey's Repair Shop, blacksmithing, 136.27; E. A. Cunningham, searching titles, 20.05; Canada Customs, duty, 95.39; Geo. Drewry, rent of ground, 240.00; Town of Dryden, water, light and telephone, 592.65; Robert Duncan, compensation for loss of horse, 200.00; P. A. Ferguson, veterinary services, 69.80; James Fox, livery, car rental, 21.00; Lionel Godson, auto insurance, 37.70; D. M. Griffith, blacksmithing, 899.82; Mrs. W. Hanley, cleaning office, 156.00; A. W. Hoffstrom, sawing lumber, 403.06; C. Holland, rental of outboard motor, 100.00; Jeffries Taxi, taxi service, 25.50; J. A. Johnson, sawing timber, 150.14; Jones, lettering signs, 42.00; The Keewatin Lumber Co. (Keewatin), compensation for loss of horse, 75.00; The Keewatin Lumber Co. (Kenora), launching boat, 88.20; Kenora Paper Mills, Ltd., blacksmithing, 34.14; Town of Kenora, water, light, telephone, 1,152.55; Hartley King, washing blankets, 228.00; J. A. Link, car rental, 39.60; Mrs. O. Lundmark, compensation for loss of horse, 150.00; M. J. Lupton, car rental, 260.00; J. W. McRae, compensation for loss of horse, 200.00; Machin & Donley, legal services, 45.45; Department of Mines and Natural Resources, application for timber permit, 12.20; Monroe Calculating Machines, rental of machine, 95.00; Sam Onarheim, blacksmithing, 2,206.40; H. Park, car rental, 18.00; W. Powell, taxi service, 15.00; Shield Development Co., Ltd. (Kashabowie), freight and loading charges, 150.00; V. Sothe, taxi hire, 12.00; J. W. Stone Boat Manufacturing Co., Ltd., launch hire, 38.25; J. A. Strutt, blacksmithing, 422.17; C. Swanson, compensation for loss of horse, 100.00; Robert Sweeney, blacksmithing, 141.55; United Typewriter Co. of Manitoba, Ltd., rental of machines, 203.50; A. Vick, hauling lumber, gravel, etc., 22.00; Vulcan Iron Works, Ltd., blacksmithing, 66.30; W. A. Wilson, livery, 18.00; petty disbursements, unenumerated, 247.76........ 12,857 17

Statutory—Continued

Roads and Bridges—Continued

DISTRICT No. 10 ($131,565.92)

Engineer, A. M. Mills, Fort Frances

Fort Frances-Rainy River Road	25,162 42		
Sleeman-Bergland-Minahico Road	7,386 48		
Indian Mission Road	5,581 32		
Stratton-Sifton-Dewart Road	3,956 96		
Spohn River Road	3,838 52		
Barwick-Black Hawk Road	3,318 40		
Kenora-Fort Frances Road	3,176 04		
Arbor Vitae Road	2,342 74		
Dredge	2,169 46		
Barnhart-Off Lake Road	2,035 70		
River Road	1,581 32		
Bergland-Budreau-Tovell Road	1,116 46		
Devlin Road	1,045 80		
Crozier Road	1,031 85		
Equipment and tools	3,398 40		
General maintenance, settlers' and other roads, sundry expenditure	64,424 05		
		131,565 92	

Travelling Expenses, $1,152.89.

Frank Clement, 22.00; Harry Engebretsen, 120.79; A. M. Mills, 1,010.10........ 1,152 89

Advertising, Printing and Stationery, $104.63.

G. G. Baker, 27.38; Fort Frances Publishing Co., Ltd., 27.50; Fort Frances Times, 49.75........ 104 63

Autos, Trucks, Accessories, Parts and Repairs, $5,252.70.

Coslett Machinery & Equipment Co., Ltd., 131.81; Dominion Road Machinery Co., Ltd., 133.05; Graham's Garage, 422.05; Henry Motor Co., 38.68; J. S. Innes, Ltd., 58.69; International Harvester Co., Ltd., 93.08; John McVey, 2,395.83; Preston's Machine Shop, 94.56; Remi Roelens, 38.00; Russell Brothers, Ltd., 111.56; Sawyer-Massey, Ltd., 1,634.39; P. J. Tyne, 22.00; Vulcan Iron Works, Ltd., 79.00........ 5,252 70

Camp and Road Supplies and Equipment, $21,504.88.

Alex. Anderson, 2,556.52; Black Bros., 16.40; M. Bragg, 62.19; Burns & Co., Ltd., 31.62; Andrew Bynkoski, 106.83; Canada Ingot Iron Co., Ltd., 7,269.00; Canada Paint Co., Ltd., 106.82; Canadian Oil Companies, Ltd. (Fort Frances), 1,024.69; Canadian Oil Companies, Ltd. (Winnipeg), 1,879.57; The Cloverleaf Creamery, 13.44; Economy Meat Market, 62.67; Fort Frances Creamery Co., Ltd., 11.00; Fort Frances Service Station, 178.27; Fort Frances Wholesalers, Ltd., 281.65; Pierre Gariepy, 70.92; Gillmor & Noden, 204.79; Grant-Holden-Graham, Ltd., 1,727.55; T. Gunderson, 14.80; J. S. Hunter, 12.00; Imperial Oil, Ltd., 951.57; Theo. Jodoin, 75.75; L. Judson, 23.75; Langstaff, Schurg & Co., Ltd., 528.00; Langstaff Mercantile Co., 12.00; Line & Cable Accessories, 23.67; Loughead Bros., 22.91; W. B. Lowe, 17.65; D. A. McQuarrie, 36.33; Manitoba Bridge & Iron Works, Ltd., 146.05; J. A. Mathieu, Ltd., 254.62; Metallic Roofing Company of Canada, Ltd., 388.80; Alexander Murray & Co., Ltd., 492.56; Tom Nolan, 77.60; North Star Oil, Ltd., 266.25; Northern Wholesalers, Ltd., 67.57; W. M. Oglestean, 49.00; Ontario Reformatory Industries, 368.90; E. Overholser, 75.67; Postmasters, 178.00; The Red & White Store, 123.31; Ben Roen, 356.66; Service Sign Studios, 13.30; Sturgeons, Ltd., 402.94; W. F. Sullivan, 40.89; Tompkin's Hardware, 225.62; Van's Fruit Store, 10.60; Wells Hardware Co., Ltd., 446.41; Western Grocers Co., Ltd., 129.05; Winnipeg Map & Blue Print Co., Ltd., 11.60; Geo. Woods, 57.12........ 21,504 88

Gravel, Rock and Stone, $4,833.71.

L. W. Berg, 25.12; W. J. Bolton, 38.10; S. O. Braaton, 33.60; Pat Campbell, 602.40; W. Canfield, 169.20; Wm. Cooke, 122.10; E. T. Cornell, 24.00; A. H. Davis, 12.00; J. W. Davis, 313.30; Geo. Dawson, 226.40; Arvid Edberg, 15.00; J. Erickson, 42.00; Axel Fisk, 44.40; Nells Fosso, 72.00; Thos. Ganton, 117.66; Mrs. Henry Herron, 284.30; H. J. Hodges, 44.25; O. Holmberg, 24.20; Isaac Hyatt, 32.50; Department of Indian Affairs, 133.80; Ida Jane Jelly, 37.20; August Johnson, 25.80; C. Johnson, 116.40; Fred Kruger, 37.60; Nap. LaPointe, 56.05; Mrs. A. H. Larson, 13.05; Carl Leif, 13.35; H. Lennox, 99.55; G. Littlefield, 206.40; Wm. Lockhart, 980.18; W. B. Lowe, 15.25; Ernest McKelvie, 177.95; T. McLeod, 12.00; Chester Mosbeck, 154.40; Geo. Munroe, 55.50; A. Patterson, 22.80; J. Patterson, 42.90; Wm. Smith, 61.15; Ethel Stern, 33.60; Ed. Tompkins, 21.50; A. Topham, 31.50; Joe Trenchard, 14.20; W. J. Weir, 60.95; Mrs. Minnie Wolfe, 69.50; Geo. Wright, 98.60........ 4,833 71

Statutory—Continued

Roads and Bridges—Continued

District No. 10—Continued

Pay Lists, $81,396.77.

Wages of men........ 81,396 77

Board and Lodging, $115.60.

Emo Hotel, 92.60; Wm. Tribe, 23.00........ 115 60

Proportionate Cost of Roads, $13,414.61.

Townships of—Alberton, 1,410.22; Blue, 530.52; Chapple, 5,201.80; Dilke, 523.75; Emo, 1,311.99; Lavalle, 1,461.87; McCrossom and Tovell, 1,087.55; McIrvine, 496.40; Morley, 911.64; Morson, 478.87........ 13,414 61

Purchase of Property, Right-of-Way, $362.65.

The Baptist Church, 20.00; John Craigen, 266.65; Edward Jerry, 76.00........ 362 65

Miscellaneous, $3,427.48.

Canadian Inspection & Testing Co., Ltd., inspection of paint, 36.43; Canadian National Express, express, 41.08; Canadian National Railways, freight, 202.62; Canadian National Telegraphs, telegrams, 81.03; Canadian Pacific Railway Company's Telegraphs, telegrams, 64.43; Frank Clement, car rental, 907.55; Canada Customs, duty, 18.54; Municipal Corporation of Emo, telephone service, 117.05; Harry Engebretsen, car rental, 259.38; Town of Fort Frances, light and telephone, 280.10; Angus Galbraith, taxi service, 87.50; Lionel Godson, auto insurance, 11.70; Fred Holmes, car rental, 13.50; Thomas Jackson, rental of lot, 35.00; Chas. Langstaff, car rental, 19.50; E. A. Lockhart & Son, blacksmithing, 11.95; C. Robertson's Transfer, blacksmithing, 29.05; S. Rowland, blacksmithing, 34.60; Russell Brothers, Ltd., boat trips, 30.00; Smith & Walsh, auto insurance, 23.40; A. L. Steele, blacksmithing, 35.09; G. A. Stethem, rental of office, 700.00; Ellen M. Young, cleaning office, 91.00; petty disbursements, unenumerated, 296.98........ 3,427 48

Sec. 11 (B) Roads total........4,247,412 60
Less repayments transferred from refund account...... 7,091 47
——4,240,321 13

Purchase of Cattle and Other Live Stock for Settlers and Farmers ($6,070.87)

Section 11 (H)

Purchase of Cattle, $4,903.00.

J. A. Belisle, 55.00; Herbert E. Bolton, 230.00; C. Campbell, 50.00; Wm. Cashian, 150.00; Hugh Christie, 50.00; Linden Clark, 185.00; H. Cleave, 60.00; James Cross, 60.00; W. A. Edwards, 115.00; Experiemental Farm, Kapuskasing, 545.00; A. Farlinger, 100.00; G. E. File, 360.00; Lee Foster, 75.00; Lorne Fraser, 50.00; Wm. Gareau, 55.00; Morden Gilbert, 160.00; Joseph Girouard, 60.00; Wm. H. Gough, 215.00; Clifford McDermid, 90.00; A. B. McLennan, 50.00; John J. May, 90.00; M. A. Munro, 80.00; Wesley Murray, 540.00; A. H. Robertson, 300.00; Stewart Robertson, 605.00; Guy Spink, 45.00; D. M. Stewart, 225.00; Ralph Stone, 88.00; Salem Thomson, 105.00; G. Urquhart, 110.00........ 4,903 00

Miscellaneous, $1,167.87.

J. Broderick & Co., hay, oats, straw, 51.42; W. F. Bruce, travelling expenses, 63.95; John Cairns, freight on cows, 54.45; Canadian National Railways, freight, 384.65; Carter Bros., rope, pail, fork, 7.76; L. R. Clarke, services re cows, 15.00; Colliver & Huff, hay, oats, 20.60; W. H. Dayton, lumber, nails, 21.95; Hodgins Lumber Co., lumber, hardware, 44.49; Fred H. Hubbs, driver services, 30.00; Ives Bedding Co., Ltd., empty barrels, 1.50; C. Joubut, freighting, 24.00; King's Printer, 34.28; Cyprien Proulx, travelling expenses, 71.85; N. Ludwin Proulx, travelling expenses, 58.10; Smith Hardware, hardware, 23.87; Temiskaming & Northern Ontario Railway, freight, 260.00........ 1,167 87

Purchase and Distribution of Seed Grain ($14,068.26)

Section 11 (F)

Seed Grain, $11,988.04.

F. W. Hendry, 30.80; Hudson's Bay Co., 499.37; Mount McKay Feed Co., Ltd., 544.00; Steele, Briggs Seed Co., Ltd., 9,653.87; United Farmers Store, Manotick, 1,260.00........ 11,988 04

Statutory—Continued

Purchase and Distribution of Seed Grain—Continued

Miscellaneous, $2,053.82.

Gordon R. Brady, K.C., searching titles, etc., 26.85; M. Brunette, searching titles, 164.41; Canadian National Railways, freight, 517.35; Canadian Pacific Railway Co., freight, 289.07; J. A. Clermont, searching titles, 9.29; Cochrane Dunlop Hardware, Ltd., hooks, .65; Geo. Dunn, searching titles, etc., 7.75; W. L. Haight, searching titles, 47.60; F. W. Hendry, unloading, storing, 160.30; C. W. Jarvis, searching titles, 12.00; W. J. Keating, searching titles, 8.50; King's Printer, 96.87; C. E. Lount, searching titles, 7.78; V. McNamara, searching titles, 9.00; H. J. Moorhouse, searching titles, 9.45; Mount McKay Feed Co., Ltd., freight, cartage, 37.21; Owens Cartage, trucking, 33.50; Royal Bank of Canada, excise stamps, 3.00; Steele, Briggs Seed Co., Ltd., freight, 104.03; Temiskaming and Northern Ontario Railway, freight, 229.75; R. M. Tipper, searching titles, 2.21; J. H. Tully, searching titles, 16.26; United Farmers Store, Manotick, freight, 249.89; J. M. York, travelling expenses, 11.10........................ 2,053 82

Pay Lists, $26.40.

Wages of men.. 26 40

The Encouragement and Assistance of Agriculture, Hearst ($500.00)

Pay Lists, $500.00.

Wages of men.. 500 00

LOANS TO SETTLERS ($117,131.51)

Administration ($10,536.51)

F. Dane	Commissioner	(T) 12 months	3,000 00		
A. E. MacLean	Senior Clerk	12 "	2,500 00		
F. M. Jack	Clerk Stenographer	12 "	1,200 00		
F. L. Wilson	" "	12 "	1,050 00		
				7,750 00	

Contingencies, $2,786.51.

Edw. Arthurs, inspections, 50.50; E. H. Barnes, inspections, 5.00; J. C. Barr, inspections, 86.74; J. A. Bastien, inspections, 149.75; R. M. Best, legal expenses, 4.74; G. R. Brady, legal expenses, 8.85; M. Brunette, cost of certificates of search, 3.40; Canadian National Telegraphs, telegrams, 1.89; Canadian Pacific Railway Co.'s Telegraph, telegrams, 2.92; W. V. Cragg, inspections, 68.50; W. Crebo, inspections, 60.50; A. Grigg, inspections, 113.80; Wm. Hough, inspections, 53.65; King's Printer, 910.25; J. S. Lowe, inspections, 5.00; J. P. Marchildon, inspections, 8.00; H. B. Owens, inspections, 357.50; Postmaster, stamps, 10.00; H. J. Reynolds, legal expenses, 10.00; D. Smith, inspections, 192.20; L. Torrie, inspections, 401.90; W. J. Trainor, inspections, 25.00; United Typewriter Co., Ltd., typewriter rental and repairs, 39.50; L. E. Van Horn, inspections, 121.40; P. H. Whelan, inspections, 10.40; R. G. Wigle, inspections, 60.95; S. H. Wilson, inspections, 24.17.......... 2,786 51

Loans to Settlers ($106,595.00)

Sundry persons, loans.. 106,595 00

Statutory..$4,521,667.29

SPECIAL WARRANTS

Board Camps, Unemployment Relief ($399,209.33)

Trans-Canada Highway—Unemployment Relief.

Ottawa Valley Section:

From Pembroke through Mattawa to North Bay................. 121,287 94

Thunder Bay Section:

From Schreiber to Nipigon through Port Arthur and Fort William to English River.. 107,492 71

Western Section:

From English River through Dyment, Dinorwic, Dryden, Kenora to Manitoba Boundary.................................... 143,378 05

General Expense.. 55 44

372,214 14

Special Warrants—Continued

Board Camps, Unemployment Relief—Continued

General Work—Unemployment Relief.

DISTRICT No. 3

E. J. Hosking, Engineer, Sudbury

Sudbury Electoral District.

Chapleau-Iron Bridge Road	2,400 61		
Levack-Cartier Road	2,715 84		
		5,116 45	

DISTRICT No. 9

R. T. Lyons, Engineer, Kenora

Kenora Electoral District.

Kenora-Fort Frances Road	14,637 02		
Sioux Lookout-Dinorwic Road	7,226 72		
		21,863 74	
General Expense		15 00	
			26,995 19
Total			399,209 33

Albert Allin, hay, 19.20; Albert Anderson, provisions, 12.50; Bainbridge Stores, provisions, 22.60; Leo Baker, meat, 24.71; Estate of J. H. Bell, gas, oil, hardware, 810.67; C. Bohm, provisions, 23.40; S. H. Bolton, gas, parts, 2.60; S. Bowers, trucking, 64.00; J. T. Brett, hay, 232.78; British American Oil Co., Ltd., gas, 54.40; Percy Broughton, hay, 88.40; D. Brunette, trucking, 152.00; Burns & Co., Ltd., provisions, 149.87; John Burritt, wood, 17.50; Albert E. Burton, gravel, 3.70; D. Campbell, hay, 24.90; Campbell Heating Co., iron, hardware, etc., 52.41; R. Campbell, oats, 30.76; Canada Cement Co., Ltd., cement, 552.50; Canadian Industries, Ltd. (Montreal), explosives, 72.30; Canadian Industries, Ltd. (Winnipeg), explosives, 3,697.50; Canadian Ingersoll-Rand Co., machine parts, 22.30; Canadian Inspection & Testing Co., Ltd., testing cement, 4.00; Canadian National Express, express, .30; Canadian National Railways, freight, 142.80; Canadian National Telegraphs, telegrams, .88; Canadian Oil Companies, Ltd., North Bay, gas, oil, etc., 1,409.67; Canadian Oil Companies, Ltd., Port Arthur, gas. oil, 299.54; Canadian Oil Companies, Ltd., Winnipeg, gas, oil, 2,031.42; Canadian Pacific Express Co., express, 1.95; Canadian Pacific Railway Co., freight, 2,175.91; L. Carey, trucking, 37.00; Central Motors, car parts, 2.00; B. Charette, gravel, wood, rent of blacksmith shop, storage, 171.10; Ed. Clark, meat, 12.74; Cochrane Dunlop Hardware, Ltd. (North Bay), hardware, etc., 38.39; Cochrane Dunlop Hardware, Ltd. (Pembroke), hardware, etc., 96.63; Cochrane Dunlop Hardware, Ltd. (Sudbury), hardware, etc., 324.65; Cockburn & Archer, grease, coal, 58.71; C. Condie, fencing, 41.40; Corrugated Pipe Co., Ltd., pipe, 2,561.56; Frank Cosco, provisions, 2,357.93; Crawley & McCracken, Ltd., board, 161.80; C. Danielson, hay, 28.01; J. Danielson, hay, 111.43; James Davidson & Co., Ltd., hay, oats, 1,274.91; Thos. Draycott, meat, 14.21; Dryden Lumber Co., Ltd., tar paper, etc., 2.75; Dryden Pharmacy, Ltd., veterinary supplies, 1.40; Ben Dufoe, gravel, 148.70; Robert Duncan, hay, 65.48; Durance Brothers & Co., hardware, 31.35; Chesley P. Elliott, meat, 23.73; Evans Co., Ltd., lumber, cement, 428.25; Falcon Oils, Ltd., gas, oil, 788.54; Fallis-Foote Co., Ltd., hardware, cement, 1,218.57; G. E. Farlinger, provisions, hay, repairs, 191.39; Isaac Fearron, oats, 32.70; P. A. Ferguson, veterinary services, 67.15; H. Fisher, wood, 75.00; Fitzgerald's Drug Store, Ltd., veterinary supplies, 12.35; Fort Frances Creamery Co., Ltd., butter, 19.00; Fort Frances Publishing Co., Ltd., stationery, 5.50; Fort Frances Wholesalers, Ltd., provisions, 1,860.15; Foster's Meat Market, provisions, 77.98; Fowler Hardware Co., Ltd., hardware, 22.00; William Fraser, chain, 8.10; General Supply Co. of Canada, Ltd., machine parts, 24.70; Gerry Hardware Electric, hardware, tools, 9.20; Gillmor & Noden, hardware, 3.71; Glengarry Dray, cartage, 168.75; C. Gorman, travelling expenses, 3.10; S. Grenier, provisions, 22.68; D. M. Griffith, blacksmithing, 195.60; Harris Abattoir (Western), Ltd., provisions, 480.19; Wm. Hayes, oats, 23.55; Jos. Herty, hay, 551.70; W. Hicklin, travelling expenses, 19.81; Herman Hill, wood, 36.00; F. Hoksell, hay, 327.72; H. Holstrom, fly fluid, 123.45; Hose Hardware Co., Ltd., hardware, etc., 143.43; A. Huhta, wood, 34.68; D. S. Humphrey, sink, 6.28; J. S. Hunter, provisions, 64.29; J. M. Hutcheson, hay, 252.87; Imperial Oil, Ltd., Winnipeg, gas, oil, grease, 11,176.70; B. Jardine, wood, 64.00; Theo. Jodoin, provisions, 113.08; Howard Johnson, livery, 5.00; M. P. Johnson, hay, 27.67; Johnson's Pharmacy, veterinary supplies, 90.15; G. Keatley, hay, 72.46; Keewatin Lumber Co., Ltd., repairs, 311.55; Hans Kellberg, hay, 21.49; Otto Kellberg, hay, 19.76; Kelly & Kimberley, coal, 372.62; Town of Kenora, use of scales, 8.25; Wm. Kent, cartage, 1.72; King's Printer, 70.44; E. A. Klose, tools, 40.00;

Special Warrants—Continued

Board Camps, Unemployment Relief—Continued

L. Kohli, rental of blacksmith shop, 30.00; John Kron & Son, coal, 221.94; I. Kendry, hay, 58.76; Laberge Lumber Co., Ltd., lumber, 1.50; Laing Bros., hay, 1,167.23; Lake of the Woods Milling Co., Ltd., flour, oats, 1,842.40; F. Lance, gravel, 367.60; Langstaff Mercantile Co., eggs, 5.10; Thos. H. Lewis, hay, 67.67; Lindstrom & Nilson, lumber, hardware, 1,458.05; C. Linquist, potatoes, 6.25; H. Lutry, meat, 20.09; McColl-Frontenac Oil Co., Ltd., gas, oil, 321.30; Allan A. J. MacDonald, hardware, explosives, etc., 488.97; MacDonald's Consolidated, Ltd., provisions, 10.75; K. C. MacDonald, travelling expenses, 175.35; D. A. MacIver, travelling expenses, 63.27; Mrs. Allen McKechnie, grease, etc., 5.30; S. J. McMeekin, gas, repairs, 23.15; D. McMillan, hay, 57.09; Wm. McMillan, hay, 46.77; Maple Leaf Milling Co., Ltd., oats, bran, 1,732.95; Marshall-Wells Co., Ltd., hardware, oil, etc., 256.46; Mattawa Garage, gas, oil, repairs, 7.35; Mattawa Hardware, hardware, 8.08; Tom Mattson, damage to building, 26.25; John Meilleur, clay, 114.57; H. H. Middleton, hay, 206.43; Miller's Departmental Store, towelling, etc., 30.58; Miller's Store, towelling, 7.50; Peter Moline, hay, 18.10; Mrs. Annie Moore, wood, 71.50; Geo. Moore, drawing wood, 3.75; I. A. Moore, hay, 587.46; James Moran, timber, 14.00; Mount McKay Feed Co., oats, hay, coal, 1,735.19; National Grocers Co., Ltd., provisions, 71.80; Neale & Heath, bran, oats, 5.40; W. D. Neely, hay, 16.09; Geo. Noble, travelling expenses, 6.35; J. Norena, wood, 120.00; Northern Engineering & Supply Co., steel, 24.32; Northern Wholesalers, Ltd., provisions, 778.16; C. E. O'Gorman, gravel, 16.20; A. Oroskovics, meat, 11.97; Arvo J. Paju, hay, 414.75; Patterson Machine Works, machine parts, 26.40; Dick Payne, cartage, 20.00; A. Pearson, hay, 28.05; E. Pellow, lumber, oats, hay, 188.40; Pellow's Garage & Taxi Service, gas, oil, 211.01; Peter Perlin, explosives, 257.06; O. B. Peters, oats, 18.00; S. Peterson, hay, 139.09; Piper Hardware Co., hardware, oil, etc., 1,320.98; Alfred Pitt, Ltd., oats, etc., 14.00; J. Porco & Co., repairs, 2.40; Port Arthur Hardware Co., roofing, 26.00; Postmaster, stamps, 10.00; Producers Co-operative Creamery Co., provisions, 487.00; R. H. Pronger, hay, 50.92; E. Prouse, harness parts, 379.15; Victor Rajala, wood, 160.00; B. H. Rands, hardware, grease, 30.63; A. Rask, hay, 23.89; G. Reid, hay, 19.20; C. W. Roark, car rental, 218.00; Oli Roberts, hay, 82.23; E. Robitaille, cartage, 6.40; Rorabeck's Drug Store, oil, 24.00; Alex Ross & Son, Ltd., hay, 4.20; John Rowat, Jr., hay, 67.61; Stanley Sawickie, meat, 49.91; M. L. Schoales, repairs, 26.00; E. Shrumm, meat, 9.45; J. F. Shrumm, meat, 10.22; L. Shrumm, meat, 11.69; Sibley Township, wood, 198.00; Sioux Lookout Bakery & Grocery, provisions, 80.90; H. Sjostrom, hay, 292.21; C. Skene, oats, hay, 48.79; H. A. Skene, oats, 145.00; Wm. Smart, meat, 29.75; Smith & Chapple, Ltd., gas, hardware, 77.35; G. W. Smith, mucilage, .10; E. Stearns, hay, 67.95; J. Steiner, hay, 994.44; W. F. Sullivan, provisions, 209.67; Robert Sweeney, blacksmithing, 12.00; Swift-Canadian Co., Ltd., provisions, 263.86; Taylor's, Ltd., flannel, 2.30; Mrs. A. Thompson, meat, 26.32; Thunder Bay Lumber Co., Ltd., Fort William, lumber, 4.32; Thunder Bay Lumber Co., Ltd., Port Arthur, lumber, 30.65; Tompkins Hardware, hardware, 58.87; Donald Tucker, hay, 86.25; Twin City Grain, Ltd., hay, oats, bran, 2,964.56; A. B. Vaillancourt, lumber, oats, 210.70; Raoul Vaillancourt, hay, oats, bran, 133.81; C. Vandrunen, provisions, 13.00; Van's Fruit Store, vegetables, 5.00; Waldhof Farmers Co-operative Club, hay, 119.81; Alfred Weiske, hay, 94.65; John Welch & Co., gravel, 100.00; Wells Hardware Co., Ltd., hardware, etc., 518.36; Western Grocers Co., Ltd., Fort Frances, provisions, 1,013,77; Western Grocers Co., Ltd., Kenora, provisions, 81.88; F. Willard, harness parts, 6.53; Williams Hardware Co., hardware, 4,171.03; F. Willes, provisions, 7.50; Geo. H. Winsor, hardware, etc., 17.84; Winnipeg Map & Blueprints Co., Ltd., blueprints, 2.16; W. Winters, hay, 79.84; Wolfe & Collins, hardware, 6.80; D. Woodgate, fly fluid, 28.50; S. Zimring, fly fluid, 11.25........ 68,317 99

Pay Lists, $330,891.34.

Wages of men........ 330,891 34

399,209 33

Northern Development Exhibit, C.N.E. ($1,300.03)

Canadian National Exhibition, installing drain at Department's Exhibit in Ontario Government Buildings, 5.00; Roy Davenport, supplying material and erecting rail at Department's Exhibit, Ontario Government Building, 65.00; Ernest J. Dodd, meals, etc., 16.75; O. J. Evans & Sons, building models at C.N.E., furnishing office space and dismantling and covering models, etc., 1,135.00; Dept. of Highways, trucking, etc., 8.93; The Map Specialty Co., remounting maps, etc., 30.00; Toronto Transportation Commission, street car fares, 7.00; W. S. Wilkinson, meals, etc., 16.25; A. S. Williamson, meals, etc., 16.10.............. 1,300 03

Special Warrants—Continued

Sultan-Swayze Township Road ($7,093.98)

Pay Lists, $7,093.98

Wages of men		7,093 98
Special Warrants	**$407,603.34**	
Total		5,372,894 39
Less Salary Assessment		2,304 25
Total **Expenditure, Department** of Northern **Development**		**$5,370,590 14**

STATUTORY

R.S.O. 22, Geo V, Chapter 4
For Accounting, see Department of Labour, page N 19

Trans-Canada Highway, Unemployment Relief ($6,070,193.61)

Ottawa Valley Section:	
From Pembroke through Mattawa to North Bay	1,403,127 23
Thunder Bay Section:	
From Schreiber to Nipigon through Port Arthur and Fort Willaim to English River	2,068,895 49
Western Section:	
From English River through Dyment, Dinorwic, Dryden, Kenora to Manitoba Boundary	2,552,051 52
General Expenses	194,119 37
Northern Development Department, Cash Accountable	2,000 00
	6,220,193 61
Less Cash Accountable, 1931	150,000 00
	6,070,193.61

E. Abrahamson, travelling expenses, 19.45; Acme Waste Manufacturing Co., Ltd., wipers, 23.22; C. Adams, cases, 15.00; E. G. Adams, travelling expenses, 34.55; W. Adams, wood, 75.00; Adanac Hotel, board, 49.80; R. Affleck, fare, 3.05; Aikenhead Hardware, Ltd., hardware, 1.93; Hedley Alcock, provisions, 48.60; J. J. Aldred, travelling expenses, 82.44; Algoma Laundry, washing blankets, 824.25; R. J. Allan, board, 7.00; A. Allard, slabs, 40.00; E. R. Allen, travelling expenses, 3.00; Dave Allen, travelling expenses, 10.75; Dr. H. Allen, services, examining men, 44.00; Norman Allen, travelling expenses, 4.75; Allis-Chalmers Manufacturing Co., machinery parts, 29.87; B. Almos, rental of motor boat, fish, 69.70; John Alto, freight, 28.38; R. B. Amos, blacksmithing, 8.25; A. Amoyet, wood, 169.25; E. Amyotte, lumber, 77.11; C. E. Anderson, travelling expenses, 148.40; F. O. Anderson, hay, 172.55; Angus & Taylor, blacksmithing, dump carts, harness, 1,081.43; C. Annis, travelling expenses, 3.50; Tony Antoniuk, beets, 3.23; C. L. Archibald, travelling expenses, 147.15; Dr. John F. Argue, services, examining men, 11.00; E. F. Armstrong, travelling expenses, 13.00; Geo. Armstrong, cartage, 16.00; Jas. Armstrong, fare, 3.30; Mrs. J. and J. Armstrong, board, hire of horse and equipment, 311.25; T. S. Armstrong, transit, level, travelling expenses, 305.15; Dr. W. J. M. Armstrong, services, examining men, 6.00; The Art Metropole, draughting supplies, levels, transits, 7,278.77; Avenue Hotel, board, 59.75; Jno. D. Baby, travelling expenses, rent of horse and equipment, 567.75; W. C. Bain, railroad fare, 3.60; Baines & David, Ltd., steel, cartage, 204.97; E. Baker, travelling expenses, 148.00; Fred T. Baker, board, gas, oil, rental of camp site, 116.75; Ball Bros., wood, 22.31; J. Ball, wood, 43.56; Dr. J. C. Ball, services, examining men, 10.00; G. R. Balloch, travelling expenses, 259.85; R. M. Bannerman, travelling expenses, 4.10; Russell Barker, board, hardware, gas, livery, 1,223.70; Dr. J. W. Barnett, services, examining men, 83.00; Alex. Barr, hardwood, 157.50; R. Barr, lumber, 58.86; L. D. Barrett, travelling expenses, 49.65; Geo. Barriball, railroad fares, .85; Les. Barrow, travelling expenses, 3.65; Barton & Fisher, hardware, oilcloth, tar felt, 160.18; G. T. Bastedo, travelling expenses, 435.42; Bateman-Wilkinson Co., plows, barrows, 5,586.67; Bates Valve Bag Co., Ltd., barrels, 5.00; R. Baxendale, wagon repairs, 9.10; E. J. Baxter,

Statutory—Continued

Trans-Canada Highway, Unemployment Relief—Continued

travelling expenses, 2.00; J. H. Beamish, lumber, 465.00; F. Beattie, oats, 76.39; Beatty Bros., Ltd., pump, pipe, etc., 286.14; Geo. Beatty & Son, Ltd., rubber boots, 1,360.50; H. Beatty, oats, 31.73; Estate of Walter Beatty, lumber, sash, 750.58; F. Beaulieu, wood, 45.00; Dr. J. R. Beaven, services, examining men, 33.00; Chas. Beckett, cartage, 6.00; Tony Beda, railroad fare, 2.50; T. A. Beebee, timber, rental of camp site, 507.30; T. J. Beggs, provisions, hardware, snowshoes, 559.36; A. G. Bell, travelling expenses, 8.50; Angus Bell, trucking explosives, 305.30; Frank V. Bell, travelling expenses, 147.05; Estate of J. H. Bell, hardware, tools, explosives, gas, paint, iron, etc. 7,568.55; Bell Telephone Co., telephone services, 262.08; E. X. Bellaire, wood, 6.00; A. A. Bennett, cedar, 78.75; A. W. Bennett, Ltd., stationery, .50; L. G. Bennett, travelling expenses, 19.75; W. Bennett, fares, 7.65; D. Benzie, express, .65; Bergman & Nelson, lumber, sash, 2.355.53; Bernard's (Kenora), washing blankets, 207.50; J. Bertrand, wood, 21.75; Dr. F. L. Bickford, services, examining men, 25.00; Mrs. D. Bicknell, board, 679.60; R. Biesenthal, travelling expenses, 11.95; Jno. W. Billington, explosives, tool boxes, 21.76; W. Bilodeau, wood, 5.00; H. A. Bird, travelling expenses, 168.95; H. H. Bird, travelling expenses, 17.05; Dr. Homer Black, services, examining men, 17.00; Dr. H. Black, services, examining men, 33.00; Dr. A. M. Blackely, services, examining men, 76.00; A. Blaikie, railroad fare, travelling expenses, 13.95; Blanchard Auto Service, gas, oil, trucking, car parts and and repairs, car rental, 185.24; N. Blay, wood, 108.12; C. L. Bliss, half cost of horse hurt on train, 25.00; A. Blomquist, taxi service, 345.00; E. Bloudin, wood, rental of magazine site, 535.80; W. J. Boddy, travelling expenses, 56.29; W. Boissoneault, wood, 30.94; A. Boivin, car rental, 48.00; J. A. Boivin, travelling expenses, 47.80; Matt Boivin, lumber, wood, 255.22; F. A. Bolch, travelling expenses, 5.55; C. H. Boom, fish, 18.07; Mrs. F. Boomhower, hay, washing blankets, 224.85; Dr. Gordon E. Booth, services, examining men, 99.00; Geo. Boucher, rental of camp site, 80.00; Wm. Boucher, Sr., wood, poles, 1,113.00; J. Boudreau, re cow mired in ditch, 25.00; B. W. Boulton, travelling expenses, 4.45; J. M. Bourke, travelling expenses, 13.20; R. Bowers, travelling expenses, 5.55; Dr. J. H. Box, services, examining men, 22.00; The Brantford Clinic, services, examining men, 43.00 The Brantford Roofing Co., Ltd., roofing, sheathing, 1,256.60; J. Brazeau, wood, 19.50; Jas. A. Brennan, travelling expenses, 16.55; Breslaurer & Warren, stationery, 5.35; F. H. Brodigan, travelling expenses, 3.00; Fred Broome, railroad fare, 1.70; J. Broome, railroad fare, 1.70; Leslie Broomfield, railroad fare, .60; Dr. Wm. J. Brough, services, examining men, 139.00; Percy Broughton, wood, gas, oil, hardware, 1,167.37; F. Brown, gravel, wood, 137.60; Fred Brown, lumber, 114.50; Geo. Brown, railroad fare, 7.00; L. M. Brown, travelling expenses, 23.20; L. O. Brown, travelling expenses, 3.65; G. Brunello, railroad fares, 1.70; F. Bruner, gravel, 68.40; Thos. Brunner, wood, 27.50; Bryce's Bakery, provisions, towelling, oil, matches, 1,471.91; A. Bryer, travelling expenses, 12.55; Geo. Bucher, lumber, 116.76; Burgess Battery Co., batteries, 45.50; A. G. Burbidge, travelling expenses, 7.80; The Burlington Steel Co., Ltd., steel, 580.21; Burney's Taxi, taxi service, 1.00; Burns & Co., Ltd. (Fort William), provisions, 980.09; Burns & Co., Ltd. (Kenora), provisions, 7,469.12; Geo. Burns, travelling expenses, 7.35; Misses G. and I. Burritt, rental of land, 80.00; Jno. Burritt, wood, 185.00; J. A. Burritt, lumber, wood, 117.00; Burroughs Adding Machine of Canada, Ltd., rental charge and inspection of adding machines, 384.60; Dr. F. J. Burrows, services, examining men, 15.00; Albert E. Burton, rent of camp site, gas, 45.52; Dr. G. B. Burwell, services, examining men, 23.00; W. F. Busch, provisions, 11.65; M. Bussineault, wood, 22.50; S. W. Butt, travelling expenses, 9.25; C. W. Caddo, railroad fare, 1.30; Estate of John Cahill, hardware, grease, stationery, 35.49; H. T. Cairns, travelling expenses, 61.60; J. Cameron, wood, 451.56; Cameron Saw Mill Co., repairs to sawmill building, 72.44; D. M. Campbell, travelling expenses, 1.75; Mrs. E. J. Campbell, board, 35.00; Mrs. J. E. Campbell, car rental, gas, oil, 48.50; The Campbell Heating Co., pipe, hardware, iron, 2,924.51; R. A. Campbell, Registrar, fees, 39.60; Mrs. V. Campbell, board, 358.80; The Canada Cement Co., Ltd., cement, 402.50; Canada Culvert Co., Ltd., culverts, 6,223.36; Canada Ingot Iron Co., pipe, 2,929.40; Canada Power & Paper Corporation, lumber, gyproc, 442.04; Canadian Bank of Commerce, printing cheques, 45.00; Canadian Fairbanks-Morse Co., Ltd., machinery parts, 14.20; Canadian General Electric Co., Ltd., machinery parts, 8.19; Canadian Industries, Ltd. (Montreal), explosives, 97,011.85; Canadian Industries, Ltd. (Toronto), explosives, 53.00; Canadian Industries, Ltd. (Winnipeg), explosives, repairs to blasting machine, blasting machines, batteries, 254,704.61; Canadian Ingersoll-Rand Co., Ltd., compressors, jack hammers, machinery parts, 42,571.55; Canadian Inspection & Testing Co., Ltd., testing cement, 8.00; Canadian National Express, express, 73.54; Canadian National Railways, freight,

Statutory—Continued

Trans-Canada Highway, Unemployment Relief—Continued

fares, 2,033.91; Canadian National Telegraphs, telegrams, 329.70; Canadian Northern Railway, freight, 27.00; Canadian Oil Companies, Ltd. (Dryden), gas, 131.82; Canadian Oil Companies, Ltd. (Fort William), gas, oil, 195.43; Canadian Oil Companies, Ltd. (North Bay), gas, grease, oil, 7,575.60; Canadian Oil Companies, Ltd., (Port Arthur), gas, oil, grease, 4,369.62; Canadian Oil Companies, Ltd. (Winnipeg), gas, oil, grease, 3,628.21; Canadian Pacific Express Co., express, 605.56; Canadian Pacific Railway Co., fares, freight, protecting lines, temporary railroad crossing, unloading materials, constructing subway, 125,713.52; Canadian Pacific Railway Co.'s Telegraphs, telegrams, 613.01; Canadian Packing Co., Ltd., provisions, 5,596.96; Canadian Timber Co., Ltd., lumber, 9,412.34; J. Carey, gas, oil, wood, car rental, car repairs, 289.16; R. Carey, travelling expenses, 18.90; H. M. Carnahan, travelling expenses, 11.65; M. T. Caron, fare, 5.40; W. Caron, hire of dump wagon, 24.00; Ewart G. Carr, travelling expenses, 26.35; Hector Carriere, wood, 24.75; A. M. Casselman, travelling expenses, 3.00; Frank Cassie, cable, 1,691.25; J. A. Cassidy, trucking, 30.00; T. Cedarwall, potatoes, hay, 133.00; The Central Hotel, board, 213.20; Central Tent & Awning Co., mail bags, cover, 102.75; R. A. Chambers, dump carts, 875.00; A. Champagne, wood, 30.25; O. Champagne, timber, 1.60; A. Chapman, wood, 17.50; H. Chapute, wood, 12.00; Frank Charbonneau, wood, 50.00; Charland's Battery Service, car repairs, 44.00; J. Charron, car rental, 194.00; Geo. Chenery, railroad fare, 1.75; C. Chenier, wood, gravel, 40.80; E. Chenier, wood, 22.00; P. Chenier, lumber, wood, 174.55; W. Chenier, car rental, 302.00; H. Cheyne, tube and globe, 5.90; Jules Chouniard, wood, 32.00; Dan Cicinski, railroad fare, 1.30; City Typewriter Co., rent of machines and inspection, 61.00; Dr. R. W. Clark, services, examining men, 14.00; Thos. Clark, travelling expenses, 3.50; Dr. S. R. Clemes, services, examining men, 71.00; Thos. Clouthier, wood, 1,010.00; Cochrane Dunlop Hardware, Ltd. (North Bay), hardware, explosives, tools, iron, oil, etc., 14,453.96; Cochrane Dunlop Hardware, Ltd. (Pembroke), hardware, tools, roofing, explosives, oil, 9,589.08; Cockburn & Archer, hardware, tools, iron, coal, cartage, 3,421.42; Cockshutt Plow Co., Ltd., dump wagons, plows, machinery parts, 15,191.69; W. W. Code, travelling expenses, 47.50; C. Collen, oats, 40.13; The Commercial Hotel, board, 25.25; Commercial Reproducing Co., Ltd., negative photostats, 4.50; Compressed Air Equipment, steel, machinery parts, 9,553.87; A. Condie, wood, 219.50; B. Connoly, travelling expenses, 1.25; Consumers' Co-operative Store Co., Ltd., provisions, wood, hardware, lumber, 81.49; Dr. J. W. Cook, services, examining men, 1,137.00; Roy Cooke, car rental, 314.00; Gordon A. Cooper, shale, 5,017.00; G. Cooper, railroad fare, 2.50; N. T. Cooper, gas, oil, hardware, 4.66; Dr. Edwin S. Copeman, services, examining men, 11.00; J. Corbeil, wood, 1,045.00; Hoe Corbeil, board, 38.50; N. Corbeil, board, 470.00; Wilfred Corbeil, wood, 113.60; R. A. Corbett, travelling expenses, 11.35; J. Cornelius, hay, 16.71; Corrugated Pipe Co., Ltd., culvert pipe, 14,770.87; Thos. Cosgrove, wood, 13.50; The Coslett Hardware Co., hardware, paint, tools, oil, 1,090.80; Coslett Machinery & Equipment Co., machinery parts and repairs, 820.23; Cossey's Repair Shop, car repairs, gas, 35.18; Sam Cote, wood, 5.50; Ernest Cotie, wood, 45.00; Andrew Cotnam, wood, oil, 367.00; A. O. Cotnam, board, gas, oil, wood, 747.09; Miss J. A. Cotnam, gravel, 38.20; Dr. J. D. Cotnam, services, examining men, 24.00; D. E. Coveney, provisions, wood, 57.00; Alex. Cowey, mail bags and repairs, 281.23; H. S. Crabtree, Ltd., blueprints, draughting supplies, 32.55; G. A. Crane, travelling expenses, 37.90; Dr. J. G. Cranston, services, examining men, 22.00; A. W. Crawford, travelling expenses, 3,715.24; Crawley & McCracken Co, Ltd., board, unloading cars, matches, soap, stamps, etc., 17,480.00; J. B. Craymer, hay, 2,332.86; A. T. Crosbie, rent of transit and level, 16.00; H. T. Crosbie, rent of transit and level, 32.00; M. J. Crosier, oats, 77.47; J. Cross, cable, 7.00; Reuben Cross, wood, 18.00; Dr. J. A. Crozier, services, examining men, 1,024.00; Dr. W. W. Cruise, services, examining men, 92.00; Albert E. Crump, travelling expenses, board, 370.25; Dr. Jas. H. Cully, services, examining men, 43.00; Dr. Jos. H. Cully, services, examining men, 310.00; A. G. Cumming, draughting supplies, levelling rods, 1,001.18; A. Cummings, travelling expenses, 55.55; Canada Customs, duty, 6.91; Thos. Curran, wood, 25.50; J. H. Curzon, travelling expenses, 28.30; Ira D. Cuthbert, lumber, 22.80; Wm. Cuthbert, board, scantling, 243.40; Isaac Cyr, car rental, transportation, 100.50; Peter S. Dahl, travelling expenses, 7.60; Daily Times Journal, stationery, advertising, 45.50; Dalamore Hotel, board, 332.65; D. Davidson, wood, 103.24; G. Davidson, hay, oats, 200.55; Jas. Davidson & Co., Ltd., oats, hay, bran, 6,732.25; R. Davidson, wood, 8.12; Thos. Davidson, travelling expenses, freight, 16.43; C. L. Davis. railroad fares, 8.25; Dr. D. Davis, services, examining men, 82.00; W. Davis, hay, 295.67; C. B. Dawson, telephone box, 5.75; J. A. Dean, travelling expenses, railroad fares,

Statutory—Continued

Trans-Canada Highway, Unemployment Relief—Continued

15.85; A. Debratz, wood, 15.75; W. M. Deeley, candles, 1.50; W. Defoe, hay, 189.67; A. Delaforge, potatoes, 5.40; Drs. F. C. Delahey and J. H. Joyner, services, examining men, 2.00; A. Deloughery, travelling expenses, 63.60; Deluxe Taxi & Transfer, trucking, livery, 1,933.60; J. R. Denley, travelling expenses, 296.20; E. Deoosh, board, 21.00; Dr. Wilfred Derbyshire, services, examining men, 11.00; Peter Desmoulin, rent of tent, 10.00; Desrochers Bros., repairs, 15.55; E. Devost, timber, poles, 176.80; Henri Devost, timber, 24.72; W. D. Dickson, straw, hay, steel, 96.16; Dr. R. W. Digby, services, examining men, 43.00; Dingwall Motors, Ltd., car parts, repairs, glycerine, 131.41; Leo Dionne, gas, 5.48; Alex. Dobratz, wood, 26.25; Arthur Dobratz, wood, 41.44; Geo. Dobratz, wood, 11.87; E. Dobratz, wood, 24.16; Dominion Motor Co., Ltd., car repairs, 22.10; Dominion Road Machinery Co., Ltd., plows and parts, 3,414.77; Dominion Rubber Co., Ltd. (Toronto), rubber boots, 233.16; Dominion Rubber Co., Ltd. (Winnipeg), rubber boots, 167.23; Dominion Steel & Coal Corporation, drill steel, 679.54; W. Doubleday, cartage, travelling expenses, 58.83; Alf. Doudiet, vegetables, 144.46; W. A. Douglas, travelling expenses, 3.45; Estate of David Dover, gas, oil, 33.07; H. L. Dowd, taxi service, 6.00; Beverley Downer, travelling expenses, 9.65; H. C. Draper, travelling expenses, 304.45; Wm. Drazeclsey, wood, 5.00; Dryden Lumber Co., Ltd., lumber, hardware, coal, 8,757.20; Dryden Motors, car parts and repairs, gas, 34.48; Dryden Paper Co., Ltd., hay, oats, hardware, welding, 372.99; Dryden Pharmacy, Ltd., stationery, veterinary supplies, 340.67; Town of Dryden, light, telephone services and supplies, water, 192.06; E. Duchene, timber, 12.00; Jos. P. Dufaure, livery, 4.00; Sam Dufresne, blacksmithing, 11.00; W. N. Dufresne, wood, 22.00; Robt. Duncan, hay, oats, 255.98; Dunn Hardware Co., Ltd., explosives, hardware, blasting machine, tools, cement, 64,127.25; Edward Dupras, timber, 3.00; Mrs. E. Duquette, gravel, timber, rental of camp site, board, 258.14; Alan Durance, explosives, car rental, 1,418.35; Durance Brothers & Co., car rental, oil, truck rental, hardware, car parts, and repairs, explosives, tools, kitchenware, 24,840.89; Jos. Durand, wood, 109.37; Dr. U. J. Durocher, services, examining men, 36.00; Edward Dutton, travelling expenses, 3.55; Eastman Kodak Stores, Ltd., photograph supplies, 56.13; Geo. C. P. Eaton, travelling expenses, 3.85; Geo. F. Eaton, wood, 20.00; The T. Eaton Co., Ltd. (Toronto), tents, radios, 3,684.40; The T. Eaton Co., Ltd. (Winnipeg), pump and fittings, 35.39; Frank Edwards, wood, 100.00; Dr. L. Edwin, services, examining men, 49.00; W. K. Edye, sacks, 1.40; T. Ehn, travelling expenses, 9.80; J. R. Ellett, provisions, hardware, explosives, tools, 5,330.83; Ellis-Watts Co., steel, 70.10; R. A. Emerson, travelling expenses, 59.10; Alex. Emond, board, 456.00; Empire Taxi, taxi service and car rental, 90.50; N. Enders, wood, 9.56; H. England, wood, gas, hardware, provisions, snowshoes, 197.96; Dr. J. A. C. Evans, services, examining men, 28.00; Exide Batteries of Canada, Ltd., batteries, 17.50; John Fahlgren, travelling expenses, 10.40; Fairway Stores (Hurkett), wood, hay, hardware, wheelbarrows, oil, oats, 4,565.97; Fairway Stores (Ignace), hardware, provisions, oilcoth, tools, oats, 2,739.77; The Fallis Foote Co., wheelbarrows, explosives, hardware, tools, coal, cement, 11,991.64; G. R. Fanset, travelling expenses, 37.80; Dr. C. D. Farquharson, services, examining men, 42.00; J. W. Fenton, travelling expenses, 13.35; N. O. C. Fenton, railroad fare, 1.00; Dr. John Ferguson, services, examining men, 11.00; P. A. Ferguson, meal, veterinary services and supplies, fare, 154.00; H. J. Field, hay, 156.68; Dr. E. M. V. Fielding, services, examining men, 78.00; A. T. Fife & Co., explosives, hardware, tools, coal, 373.76; Fife Hardware Co., tools, hardware, grease, chains, 4,564.92; A. J. Fink, barrels, borax, etc., 7.90; V. Fink, wood, 67.50; A. W. Fisher, travelling expenses, 11.90; John Fisher, water tank, 15.00; M. R. Fisher, hay, 108.50; Fitzgerald's Drug Store, Ltd., films, veterinary supplies, 624.06; Fitzsimmons Fruit Co., Ltd., provisions, 883.57; Dr. H. G. Fletcher, services, examining men, 12.00; C. Flint, travelling expenses, 318.85; M. B. Flood, railroad fare, 1.15; R. J. Flowers, travelling expenses, 1.30; A. G. Foisy, wood, 175.00; Davis Foisy, wood, 44.00; Foisy Garage, repairs, gas, 10.60; Jas. Foisy, gas, oil, repairs, 7.75; John Foisy, wood, 68.25; Paul Foisy, taxi service, 6.00; S. Foisy, wood, 81.00; F. J. Follis, travelling expenses, 89.95; Fort Garry Tire & Service, Ltd., tire repairs, 9.00; F. S. Fosdick, stationery, 102.30; Dr. J. G. Foster, services, examining men, 94.00; Foster's Meat Market, provisions, 7,352.80; Jas. Fox, auto livery, transportation, 205.00; Thos. A. Frair, travelling expenses, 27.90; The Milton Francis Lumber Co., Ltd., lumber, 5,874.75; D. M. Fraser, Ltd., machinery part, 1.00; J. D. Fraser, travelling expenses, 32.50; Mrs. W. Fraser, board, 43.50; Walter L. Fraser, travelling expenses, 47.70; H. Frost, travelling expenses, 5.05; Fyr-Fyter Co. of Canada, Ltd., Fyr-Fyter fluid, extinguishers, 163.20; refills for fire extinguishers, 5.70; Dr. C. L. Fuller, services, examining men, 3.00; H. C. Gaboury, travelling expenses, 1.15;

Statutory—Continued

Trans-Canada Highway, Unemployment Relief—Continued

Mrs. E. Gabrieson, board, 26.00; Aug. Gagne, wood, timber, 48.00; Henry Gagne, wood, 28.75; Nap. Gagne, cedar, 7.50; Fred Gagnon, transportation, 11.90; R. J. Gagnon, railroad fare, 1.60; P. Gallagher, car rental, 108.00; R. J. Gallagher, travelling expenses, 168.30; Gamble-Robinson, Ltd., provisions, 56.02; A. J. Gardiner, tools, hardware, explosives, steel, gas, rubber boots, 10,567.63; D. Gardiner, oats, 49.35; A. Gavin, tarpaulin for compressor, 18.00; General Supply Co. of Canada, Ltd., compressors, anvils, wheelbarrows, bunks, ticks, machinery parts, 19,492.76; A. German, wood, 52.00; Fred Gerow, wood, 405.25; Gerry Hardware Electric, hardware, tools, coal, explosives, 3,624.46; J. Gibson, hay, 181.68; E. Giesebrecht, gas, oil, 43.52; Dr. Jas. C. Gillie, services, examining men, 683.00; R. O. Gilson, travelling expenses, 48.08; M. Glavotka, cutting, hauling wood, 168.00; Dr. H. Glendinning, services, examining men, 39.00; R. S. Godfrey, travelling expenses, 5.25; Goodyear Tire & Rubber Co. of Canada, Ltd., drill hose, 42.98; Geo. Gordon & Co., Ltd., lumber 16,341.61; Geo. Gordon, tool steel, 49.50; Frank Gork, use of car, 5.00; G. Gorman, gravel, 19.80; G. Goselin, wood, 6.00; Geo. Gough, hay, oats, 9.04; C. Gracie, travelling expenses, 2.50; J. M. Graham, chain, blocks, 36.63; W. Graham, wood, 266.87; Grain Port Motors, Ltd., car parts and repairs, 370.57; Grant-Holden-Graham, Ltd., tents, blankets, flags, tarpaulins, 6,028 22; Dr. F. T. Green, services, examining men, 11.00; W. T. Green, travelling expenses, .65; Jas. V. Greer, railroad fare, 6.65; A. Grevelle, trucking, 18.75; D. M. Griffith, blacksmithing, 2,777.59; W. Grossberndt, hay, 229.07; Albert Guay, meal, .50; J. W. Guest, travelling expenses, 27.85; A. Guilbault, car rental, 57.50; Hy. Guillemette, wood, 105.00; R. Gustafson, repairs, 6.60; Dr. J. Guthrie, services, examining men, 3.00; J. Hackenbrock, timber, gravel, 223.20; Hadash Bros., hay, 157.68; L. Hadley, car hire, 2.50; C. D. Hall, travelling expenses, 3.40; Halliday-Superior, Ltd., lumber, hardware, 1,465.24; A. T. Hamer, travelling expenses, 8.95; J. Geo. Hamilton, travelling expenses, 25.60; T. Hamilton, railroad fare, 7.75; J. Hammer-Schow, travelling expenses, 3.55; S. G. Hancock, travelling expenses, 9.75; F. R. Hanright, travelling expenses, 43.75; Jno. Hansen, fish, 2.40; J. Hardie, railroad fare, .30; A. Hargrave, railroad fare, 2.50; Dr. J. Graham Harkness, services, examining men, 27.00; W. M. Harman, sacks, 5.00; Harris Abattoir (Western), Ltd., provisions, 333.06; W. Harrison, travelling expenses, 4.15; A. W. Harvey, travelling expenses, 19.30; J. Hastings, provisions, 2,080.63; J. Hatch, sacks, 4.05; A. Hayward, travelling expenses, 7.85; G. Hayward, travelling expenses, 34.34; A. Heinmetz, rent of house, 60.00; Dr. Fred H. Heming, services, examining men, 10.00; D. Henderson, railroad fare, 2.90; J. J. Heney, postage on equipment, .65; Robt. Hennessey, travelling expenses, 28.05; J. Herman, tools, hardware, gas, oil, provisions, wood, 2,652.29; W. Herranen, wood, 87.50; P. W. Herron, board, 7.50; Jos. Herts, board, provisions, 1,083.00; W. Heslop, travelling expenses, 17.85; W. Hicklin, travelling expenses, 52.50; J. Higbee, travelling expenses, 6.45; J. Herb Hill, wood, 160.50; J. M. Hill, travelling expenses, 25.00; Milton Hill, board, 23.70; S. J. Hill & Co., lumber, wagon repairs, 594.18; Wm. Hill, Jr., timber, 32.22; C. E. Hogarth, travelling expenses, 5.10; C. Holland, travelling expenses, stamps, telegrams, 314.37; L. R. Holland, travelling expenses, 116.50; Wm. Holland, wood, 1,671.25; J. Hollmer, wood, 117.50; H. Holmstrom, fly fluid, etc., 59.30; Dr. Herbet E. Hopkins, services, examining men, 53.00; The Hose Hardware Co., hardware, oil, iron, tools, 2,762.16; Geo. Huckell, wagon axle, 4.50; Hudson's Bay Co. (Mobert), provisions, hardware, snowshoes, 744.64; Hudson's Bay Co. (Nipigon), hardware, stationery, 8.59; Hudson's Bay Co. (Winnipeg), provisions, hardware, 1,789.65; A. E. Huether, travelling expenses, 42.74; T. C. Huffman, trucking, 62.00; F. W. Huggins, travelling expenses, 16.95; Hughes-Owens Co., Ltd., draughting supplies, 1,362.37; A. Huhta, wood, 163.50; H. A. Humphries, travelling expenses, 5.05; L. Hunt, railroad fare, 3.85; R. Hunt, lumber, 76.49; Hunt's Service Store, provisions, 89.06; A. G. Hunter, travelling expenses, 7.90; G. W. Hunter, travelling expenses, 3.70; H. W. Hurrell, railroad fare, 6.25; Robt. F. Hurst, instrument repairs, 1.00; Sydney A. Hustwitt, travelling expenses, 15.20; J. Hutcheon, level with tripod, 100.00; A. Hutchinson, hay, 290.80; H. C. Hutchison, travelling expenses, 7.60; Jas. Hutchinson, oats, 35.35; H. N. Hutchison, travelling expenses, 7.30; John Hutchison, oats, hay, 350.52; Dr. W. G. Hutchison, services, examining men, 13.00; Dr. R. L. Hutton, services, examining men, 45.00; Hydro-Electric Power Commission (Fort William), lighting, 6.95; Hydro-Electric Power Commission of Ontario, re-locating lines, level, transit, cost of lineman during blasting, 2,836.22; Oscar Ilomaki, repairs, 5.00; Imperial Oil, Ltd., gas, oil, grease, 18,919.35; Imperial Order Daughters of the Empire, express, freight, 3.77; Independent Order of Foresters, room, 8.70; Indian Lake Lumber Co., Ltd., lumber, anvil, tongs, oats, hay, 4,270.38; E. L. Ingo, travelling expenses, 130.45; J. W. Ingram, travelling expenses, 2.25; J. S. Innes, Ltd., machinery parts, 998.04; Instruments, Ltd., rods,

Statutory—Continued

Trans-Canada Highway, Unemployment Relief—Continued

draughting supplies, 1,042.55; International Transit, Ltd., fares, transportation, freight, 799.30; F. Irmscher, wood, 14.75; J. Irmscher, oats, hay, 387.87; J. S. Irven, hay, oats, 934.10; R. J. Isaacs, travelling expenses, 42.30; Jack & Co., hardware, 670.38; Jackson Bros., provisions, 21.00; F. C. Jackson, travelling expenses, 10.35; V. Jackson, oats, 79.68; Walter Jackson, fill, 19.08; Wm. Jackson, rental of camp site, 40.00; A. W. Jacobson cedar, 55.68; F. Jahnert, hay, oats, 7.13; Dr. A. Jamieson, services, examining men, 32.00; B. Jardine, wood, lumber, 1,188.00; S. Jarvinen, oats, 70.94; L. R. Jarvis, travelling expenses, 7.55; R. C. Jary, travelling expenses, 4.90; Jeffrey & Taylor, repairing harness, 12.28; Jeffries Taxi, transportation, taxi service, 24.75; S. D. Jenner, travelling expenses, 11.35; S. W. Jenner, travelling expenses, 1.50; Dr. G. H. Jennings, services, examining men, 24.00; Geo. Johnson, travelling expenses, 70.50; J. Johnson, board, 49.40; Mrs. L. R. Johnson, room and board, 13.00; Johnson's Pharmacy, veterinary supplies, 401.20; R. Johnson, car rental, 88.00; B. P. Johnston, cleaners, .10; Dr. W. J. Johnston, services, examining men, 16.00; A. Jones, wood, 40.62; E. Jones, car rental, 92.00; Dr. H. G. Joyce, services, examining men, 15.00; Dr. J. H. Joyner, services, examining men, 36.00; Kaministiquia Lumber Co., Ltd., lumber, 4,166.38; Keewatin Lumber Co., Ltd., rental of Short's property, lumber, stove, oil, hay, veterinary supplies, 63,892.14; Town of Keewatin, use of scales, .50; Dr. E. P. Kelly, services, examining men, 45.00; F. Kelly, travelling expenses, 2.25; Kelly & Kimberley, coal, cement, sand, 1,888.11; R. Kelly, railroad fare, 1.60; Donald I. M. Kennard, travelling expenses, 1,008.21; Town of Kenora, light, water, telephone services, use of scales, 393.62; A. C. Kerr, travelling expenses, 3.70; N. J. Kerr, railroad fare and travelling expenses, 13.90; Thos. Kerr, wood, 6.00; M. Keswick, board, 514.80; O. Ketonen, gas drums, 40.00; Keyes Supply Co., Ltd., thermostat, 1.92; W. R. Keyes, travelling expenses, 20.60; Jas. Kilby, forges, battery, 50.00; Alex. King, freight, 2.42; H. King, washing blankets, 41.60; Shirley King, travelling expenses, 47.15; The King's Printer, 4,672.25; Jas. A. Kinney, legal services, .50; E. P. Kirsht, travelling expenses, 11.35; C. Kloepfer, Ltd., hardware, 2,162.53; E. A. Klose, hardware, roofing, tools, 84.67; Ivan Klose, hay, 141.63; Frank Knott, rent of house, 15.00; J. A. Knox, railroad fare, 36.25; A. Kohli, rent of blacksmith shop, 8.00; L. Kohli, rental of blacksmith shop, coal, 18.85; U. Kokko, travelling expenses, 7.75; Karl Kovisto, timber, 22.50; T. H. Kribs, travelling expenses, 18.25; John Kron & Son, coal, lumber, teaming, hire of team, wood, 2,413.04; Paavo Kujansuu, hay, 62.65; I. Kurz, hay, 172.23; Dept. of Labour, Ottawa, railway fares of men to road camps, 65,337.32; Lacey's Car Co., taxi service, 1.50; Geo. Lafleur, wood, 1,502.00; Laing Bros., Ltd., hay, 10,553.25; Dr. Geo. F. Laing, services, examining men, 220.00; Lake of the Woods Milling Co., Ltd., flour, oats, bran, 8,815.53; E. Lamothe, wood, 143.88; Dept. of Lands and Forests, timber dues, 12.50; Dr. Jurben Lannin, services, examining men, 143.00; Mrs. E. Larochelle, rent of blacksmith shop, 12.00; V. Larochelle, gravel, 11.00; O. Larocque & Sons, provisions, hay, 298.67; Ronald Lassman, travelling expenses, 3.95; Dr. R. H. Latimer, services, examining men, 5.00; F. Launder, oats, 54.25; C. Laundry, plow repairs, 5.85; R. Laurette, wood, 18.00; Robt. Law, freight, 3.03; G. V. Lawrence, travelling expenses, 168.60; L. Leach, travelling expenses, 2.25; Dr. F. A. Leacy, services, examining men, 31.00; Geo. B. Leblanc & Co., blacksmithing, 167.85; L. B. Leblanc, rods, 4.30; O. Leblond, birch, 25.00; Mrs. Catherine Lebrache, rental of camp site, 40.00; John Leckie, Ltd., tents, tarpaulins, tent parts, 944.43; C. Leclaire, wood, 176.00; Joe Leclair, wood, 26.00; Mrs. E. Lee, gas, oil, board, rent of camp site, timber, 939.51; R. Lee, meals, 2.70; L. J. Lehto, travelling expenses, 55.95; Mark Leiterman & Sons, lath, 46.00; Wm. Leith, gravel, 83.30; R. Leivtas, hay, 194.32; Dr. J. Albert LeMay, services, examining men, 98.00; P. Lemieux, wood, 15.00; C. C. Lemmon, travelling expenses, 23.85; Mrs. J. W. Lemmon, board, 32.80; Ed. Lever, hay, 31.15; Thos. H. Lewis, oats, hay, lumber, 127.11; C. G. Linde, photographs, negatives, 838.24; H. Lindsay, travelling expenses, 5.15; Lindsay & McCluskey, Ltd., coal, tile, 877.67; Lindstrom & Nilson, lumber, roofing, hardware, iron, creosote, 27,804.10; J. A. Link, gas, car rental, coal, 315.86; Dr. E. D. Linton, services, examining men, 21.00; C. B. Little, travelling expenses, 20.85; Dr. J. M. Lloyd, services, examining men, 215.00; H. Lomas, travelling expenses, 2.90; Dr. H. O. Lough, services, examining men, 9.00; Alex. Loumi, wood, 7.00; G. Loundsbury, hay, oats, 118.60; H. G. Lovell, rental of adding machine, 15.00; Chas. A. Low, travelling expenses, 7.85; F. H. Lowe, travelling expenses, 31.10; Lowery's, Ltd., office supplies, 415.25; D. J. Ludgate, travelling expenses, 53.90; J. P. Ludgate, travelling expenses, 11.20; K. Ludvigsin, posts, 15.00; M. J. Lupton, car rental, travelling expenses, 271.10; S.S. No. 1, Lyon Township, wood, 55.00; H. McAuley, lumber, 89.83; J. McBridge, travelling expenses, 2.65; R.

Statutory—Continued

Trans-Canada Highway, Unemployment Relief—Continued

McCammon, provisions, 23.88; W. J. McCann, travelling expenses, 104.70; W. N. McCann, travelling expenses, 1.30; M. McCarthy, hay, oats, 18.67; Dr. G. E. McCartney, services, examining men, 1.00; Mr. McCauley (Upsala), hay, 179.18; McColl-Frontenac Oil Co., Ltd. (Toronto), gas, oil, grease, 279.44; McColl-Frontenac Oil Co., Ltd. (Winnipeg), gas, oil, 703.64; Dr. J. M. McCormack, services, examining men, 177.00; Dr. W. McCormack, services, examining men, 22.00; T. McCranor, rock, 7,427.00; Dr. S. R. McCreary, services, examining men, 16.00; A. McDonald, axle, irons, 12.00; MacDonalds Consolidated Ltd., provisions, soap, matches, 77.34; H. R. MacDonald, travelling expenses, 11.95; Dr. J. O. McDonald, services, examining men, 222.00; K. C. MacDonald, travelling expenses, car rental, 1,201.53; Mrs. M. McDonald, board, 27.05; A. R. McDougall, travelling expenses, 4.45; C. R. McDougall, travelling expenses, 10.35; K. McDougall, travelling expenses, provisions, 8.03; P. J. McDevitt, railroad fare, 3.95; W. McDowell, travelling expenses, 15.90; McGaughey & Little, hay, 445.16; D. D. McGibbon, travelling expenses, 8.54; Dr. C. F. McGillivray, services, examining men, 12.00; Arthur McGravey, travelling expenses, 5.55; McIntosh Grain & Feed Co., Ltd., oats, 409.00; Dr. Thos. J. McInnis, services, examining men, 5.00; G. J. McIntyre, travelling expenses, 50.30; D. A. MacIver, travelling expenses, 349.69; Dr. Chas. R. Mackay, services, examining men, 20.00; Mrs. A. McKechnie, board, gas, oil, office rent, 2,098.76; Dr. A. E. MacKenzie, services, examining men, 29.00; Dr. D. W. MacKenzie, services, examining men, 21.00; MacKenzie Inn, gas, 17.87; H. L. McKinnon Co., Ltd., provisions, 2,114.28; McKinnon & Ronan, provisions, 309.17; C. O. McLean, travelling expenses, 5.65; E. J. McLean, travelling expenses, 11.35; E. H. McLean, travelling expenses, 5.10; G. O. McLean, travelling expenses, 8.25; John McLean, wood, 45.79; The J. H. McLennan Lumber Co., lumber, hardware, 4,351.07; W. E. McLennan, travelling expenses, 19.55; G. McLeod, poles, posts, 19.50; J. G. McLeod, travelling expenses, 10.10; D. C. McMillan, travelling expenses, 8.15; N. McMillan hay, oats, 367.01; Stanley McMinn, plank, 36.00; Drs. McMurchy, McMurchy & Campbell, services, examining men, 472.00; Peter McNabb, fares, 2.90; W. E. McNeely, rent of camp site, 80.00; Dr. D. Marshall MacPherson, services, examining men, 11.00; Municipality of Machin, lumber, 75.00; Victor Macki, timber, 3.00; Dr. K. L. Mackinnon, services, examining men, 23.00; W. R. Maher, travelling expenses, freight, towelling, 535.27; Mahon Electric Co., Ltd., electrical supplies, 40.00; T. Mahon, gravel, 181.25; A. W. R. Maisonville, travelling expenses, 7.75; E. Maki, hay, 266.70; R. Malette, wood, 15.00; B. Malpas, provisions, 1.50; Manitoba Stencil & Stamp Works, rubber stamp 2.90; L. Mann, railroad fare, 5.55; E. Mannisto, wagon repairs, 11.00; E. Manuel, lumber, poles, 247.76; Maple Leaf Milling Co., Ltd. (Kenora), flour, oats, bran, 4,317.40; Maple Leaf Milling Co., Ltd. (Toronto), bran, oats, flour, etc., 9,177.62; A. Marcell, travelling expenses, 9.65; Mariaggi Hotel, board, 319.70; Dr. M. Markson, services, examining men, 12.00; D. Marosse, timber, 9.00; Dr. Del. Marr, services, examining men, 13.00; Frank Marr, gas, trucking, 47.50; Marshall-Wells Co., Ltd., provisions, kitchenware, scrapers, rubber boots, tools, hardware, wheelbarrows, snowshoes, steel, tents, 47,105.19; J. A. Martin, car rental, 106.00; O. Martin, lumber, trucking, hardware, gas, oil, 227.95; O. G. Martin, travelling expenses, 43.45; Percy Martin, gas, oil, 69.51; R. Martin, travelling expenses, 2.25; Mrs. W. Martin, hay, 86.45; Massey-Harris Co., Ltd., machinery parts, 41.10; Carl J. Matson, travelling expenses, 13.35; Matthews Sash & Door Co., lumber, 916.72; Mattawa Garage, gas, oil, car storage, repairs, 396.70; Mattawa Hardware, tools, hardware, lumber, explosives, oats, gas, oil, trucking, hay, 10,191.49; A. Maxwell, wood, 128.12; H. Maxwell, wood, 269.86; Herb Maxwell, wood, 297.94; Maxwell's, Ltd., wheelbarrows, scrapers, 4,580.14; Meaford Steel Products, Ltd., scrapers, machinery parts, wharfage charges, 8,727.12; John Meilleur, lumber, car rental, 46.03; Mellor Timber Co., Ltd., camp, 500.00; E. Menard, wood, lumber, rental of camp site, 505.69; Dr. J. R. Mencke, services, examining men, 13.00; D. Menzie, travelling expenses, 2.35; J. M. Merchant, vegetables, 12.31; Merrill, Rhind & Walmsley, hardware, gas, provisions, 72.68; Metallic Roofing Co. of Canada, Ltd., culverts, 30,911.16; Dr. W. A. Metcalfe, services, examining men, 10.00; Phil Miault, taxi service, 5.00; H. H. Middleton, hay, oats, 938.64; E. Mikkela, drums, 40.00; F. Milanese, hay, 120.25; Wm. Milne & Sons, lumber, 1,064.34; The Miner Publishing Co., stationery, 307.10; F. Mitchell, railroad fares, 2.90; J. H. Moeser, hay, 14.00; Victor Moir, wood, posts, 106.20; Peter Moline, hay, 163.93; Molinski Bros., wood, lumber, 105.17; The Monarch Oil Co., Ltd., gas, oil, 829.95; Moncrieff & Endress, Ltd., compressor parts, 16.80; Monroe Calculating Machines, rental of machines, 95.00; H. F. Monty, travelling expenses, 1.10; A. Moore, fares, 3.35; Mrs. Annie Moore, wood, 12.50; D. C. Moore, car rental,

Statutory—Continued

Trans-Canada Highway, Unemployment Relief—Continued

349.00; J. A. Moore, trucking, hay, oats, 1,366.76; Dr. Jas. Moore, services, examining men, 59.00; W. H. Moore, gas, 4.50; Jas. Moran, wood, 18.00; O. Morancy, railroad fare, 4.60; Geo. Moreau, travelling expenses, 1.25; Mrs. Eliza Morel, board, 175.20; Leo Morel, car rental, 78.00; Milton Morgan, horse killed on work, 90.00; Joe Morin, wood, 101.25; O. and Mrs. Morley, wood, 63.37; Guiseppi Moroni, beef, 24.00; Dr. D. A. Morrison, services, examining men, 38.00; C. Morrow, lumber, cement, hardware, 5,302.69; John Morrow Screw & Nut Co., Ltd., puljacks, pulleys, 1,871.21; Birjer Mortenson, potatoes, 6.75; C. A. Morton, hay, 135.85; Harold A. Morton, hay, 262.92; W. Morton, travelling expenses, 14.75; W. Morton, hay, 146.84; Mount McKay Feed Co., Ltd., oats, hay, bran, coal, lumber, 24,787.38; J. McK. Mugan, travelling expenses, 46.30; J. H. Mulligan, hardware, gas, oil, transportation, 39.60; Dr. F. Munroe, services, examining men, 10.00; Alex. Murray & Co., Ltd., sheathing, 187.50; A. L. Murray, provisions, 17,565.54; A. Murray, railroad fare, 3.35; F. Murphy, railroad fare, 1.70; T. W. Murphy, hay, 12.60; Wm. Murphy, lumber, 70.59; H. J. Murtagh, travelling expenses, 6.00; Carl J. Mutson, travelling expenses, 2.50; A. Napper, railroad fare, 2.90; H. D. Nash, gas, 28.71; John Neal, railroad fare, 3.95; Neale & Heath, straw, hay, provisions, 2,004.04; R. E. Neely, oats, 104.83; W. E. Neely, hay, 127.72; P. Neidecken, hay, 148.43; Neilson's, towelling, oilcloth, flannel, 188.44; Dr. F. H. Nelson, services, examining men, 9.00; H. E. Nelson, travelling expenses, 8.10; Dr. Jas. S. Nelson, services, examining men, 17.00; Dr. W. H. Nelson, services, examining men, 42.00; Dr. Jas. H. Nesbitt, services, examining men, 44.00; Geo. Neve, gas, oil, 18.96; Neville Drug Co., Ltd., veterinary supplies, 59.10; W. Newberry, wagon parts, 2.00; New Dryden Jobbing Co., sacks, 24.00; New Empire Hotel, board, 38.50; S. G. Newland, car rental, travelling expenses, 54.51; E. Newton-White, travelling expenses, photographic supplies, office supplies, 580.70; Ed. Nichol, flour, oil, gas, 7.45; Thos. Nicholls, travelling expenses, 33.97; J. Nicholson, travelling expenses, 300.35; Nicholson's Tire Surgery, battery service, .80; Eddie Nielson, wood, 933.57; Nester Nieppola, cedar, 162.96; Axel Nilson, travelling expenses, 10.10; Nipigon Hydro-Electric Commission, repairing line to Bungalow camp, 3.00; Nipigon Inn, board, 659.25; Nipigon Service Garage, charging batteries, 5.50; N. C. Nixon, travelling expenses, 111.75; S. G. Noble, travelling expenses, 578.05; Geo. Noble, travelling expenses, 1,213.75; Geo. Nord, travelling expenses, 1.70; Fred Nordstrom, wood, 62.65; J. Norenda, timber, 162.75; North Shore Transportation Co., Ltd., transportation, 739.45; Northern Engineering & Supply Co., Ltd., blacksmithing, hardware, tools, iron, 394.25; Northern Development, cash accountable, 2,000.00; Northern Supplies, Ltd., machinery parts, 6.19; Northland Tractor & Equipment Co., Ltd., machinery parts, 69.54; Dr. A. E. Northwood, services, examining men, 20.00; Bank of Nova Scotia, Kenora, interest on overdraft, 11.13 ; Bank of Nova Scotia (North Bay), interest on overdraft, 10.35; Bank of Nova Scotia (Toronto), printing cheques, 126.00; J. Novosad, provisions, trees used for culverts, 64.90; The Nugget, ink, 3.60; S. J. O'Brien, sand, 1.50; A. C. O'Connor, gas, oil, hardware, repairs, trucking, 331.23; Office Specialty Manufacturing Co., Ltd. (Newmarket), pressboards, stationery, 78.46; Office Specialty Manufacturing Co., Ltd. (Winnipeg), stationery, 62.55; W. R. Ogden, travelling expenses, 4.00; O. O'Grady, wood, 23.25; A. Oikanen, wood, 63.00; J. Olafson, travelling expenses, 5.05; G. Olsen, wood, posts, 378.78; E. Olsen, travelling expenses, 9.60; Olympia Cafe, board, 183.85; Sam Onarheim, blacksmithing, 933.67; Ontario Provincial Police, patrolling highway, 12,620.56; Ontario Reformatory Industries, blankets, 1,941.84; N. O'Neil, wood, 11.25; U. Ordersen, railroad fare, 3.05; J. Pacaud, car rental, 150.00; B. Parden, potatoes, 2.70; Dr. J. P. Parent, services, examining men, 26.00; Hugh Parslow & Co., Ltd., oats, hay, bran, straw, 4,163.11; W. F. Parslow, lumber, 90.50; M. Parsons, wood, 97.75; Mrs. Mary Partington, board, 30.00; Albert Pasternak, travelling expenses, 4.15; A. Paterson, provisions, 3,725.64; Patterson Machine Works, machinery repairs, 2.60; Dr. W. S. Paul, services, examining men, 100.00; W. Ralph Pearce, travelling expenses, 147.75; A. Pearson, hay, 171.81; M. Pearson, tamarac, 4.25; Mrs. A. Pechette, board, 48.05; Angus Pecore, lumber, 140.29; Pedlar People, Ltd., culverts, 17,696.86; Wm. J. Peever, rental of camp site, 80.00; Fred Pelland, timber, 51.20; Pembroke Lumber Co., Ltd., lumber, 944.54; The Pembroke Milling Co., Ltd., oats, hay, 3,269.33; A. R. Perkins, travelling expenses, 4.55; G. W. Perram, travelling expenses, 14.50; A. Perrault, travelling expenses, 5.95; J. Peterson, lumber, 84.00; S. Peterson, hay, 147.65; Wm. Petrie, railroad fares, 2.50; F. Peturisson, travelling expenses, 223.08; H. J. Peturisson, travelling expenses, 59.72; J. Phillips, travelling expenses, 5.81; A. Pichette, wood, car rental, 23.50; Mrs. A. Pichette, board, 174.55; Jno. Pichette, wood, 87.50; G. L. Pidgeon, gas, 22.95; R. Pifer, building logs, 10.00; Piper Hardware Co., hardware, tools, heaters, kitchenware, explosives,

Statutory—Continued

Trans-Canada Highway, Unemployment Relief—Continued

tarpaulins, towelling, coal, 38,296.01; Alfred Pitt, Ltd., provisions, tools, kitchenware, towelling, oats, oilcloth, 4,066.45; W. Platford, board, 1,772.40; Thos. Pocklington Co., draughting supplies, repairs to instruments, 338.57; J. Poimo, boards, scantling, 75.18; J. B. Poirrier, gravel, 4.05; Paul Poitras, wood, 50.59; S. Poitras, wood, 113.76; Dr. S. S. Polack, services, examining men, 186.00; R. Pollard, hay, 152.00; W. Pollard, oats, 91.58; Howard C. Poole, railroad fares, 7.50; J. B. Porrier, trucking, gravel, transportation, 24.00; Port Arthur Hardware, Ltd., hardware, tools, coal, iron, explosives, 835.99; City of Port Arthur, blueprints, phone services, 349.52; Postmaster (Dryden), stamps, 87.00; Postmaster (Fort William), stamps, 405.00; Postmaster (Hawk Lake), stamps, stationery, 3.90; Postmaster (Ignace), stamps, 9.26; Postmaster (Kenora), stamps, 119.00; Postmaster (Mattawa), stamps, 1.45; Postmaster (North Bay), stamps, 407.00; Postmaster (Vermilion Bay), stamps, stationery, 1.00; Wm. Potts, railroad fare, 2.85; Dr. C. Powell, services, examining men, 569.00; R. Powell, travelling expenses, 4.90; W. Powell, taxi service, 48.00; Drs. Pratt, Ballantyne, Harold and Duff, services, examining men, 2.00; Dr. W. C. Pratt, services, examining men, 12.00; L. Priebe, snowshoes, 84.00; A. Primeau, travelling expenses, 2.45; Jos. Primo, Sr., lumber, 14.96; J. Prokah, railroad fare, 1.60; Pronger & Armstrong, stationery, 21.95; O. H. Pronger, provisions, towelling, matches, 1,255.06; Public Library of Toronto, books, 624.80; E. Pullan Wipers & Waste Co., Ltd., klenser kloths, 85.00; Dr. G. A. Publow, services, examining men, 41.00; R. Purcell, car rental, 114.00; Queen's Hotel, board, 253.67; Jos. Quimette, wood, 82.50; J. B. Quinlan, travelling expenses, 12.20; Bernard Quinland, travelling expenses, 2.85; E. M. Quirt, trucking, 480.38; Robt Rabishaw, board, 16.00; Theophile Rabishaw, blacksmithing, 15.90; Radio Corporation, Ltd., radio parts, 86.88; Railway & Power Engineering Corporation, Ltd., steel, 1,893.68; Victor Rajala, wood, fill, 1,065.40; W. Rand, oats, 15.44; E. Ranto, wood, 6.50; J. Ranto, wood, 40.00; The J. Frank Raw Co., Ltd., transits, levels, transit repairs, draughting supplies, 4,174.50; D. C. Rea, travelling expenses, 403.09; J. Ready, oats, 38.32; Geo. Recourd, wood, 25.00; R. H. Redding, testing radio tubes, 1.50; Red Indian Service Station, gas, 1.65; Dr. R. C. Redmond, services, examining men, 10.00; E. Rea, railroad fare, 6.60; A. Reid, oats, 110.25; Chas. Reid, lumber, 5.00; G. H. Reid, kitchenware, hardware, explosives, oil, snowshoes, anvil, gas, 7,249.79; H. Reid, railroad fare, 1.60; John Reid, oats, skid blocks, 72.55; Remington Typewriters, Ltd., typewriter, 189.00; Geo. Rencourd, wood, 20.00; B. A. Rennick, travelling expenses, 19.25; Dr. E. F. Richardson, services, examining men, 179.00; Geo. R. Richardson, wood, 33.75; S. Richardson, hay, 111.86; S. Rigby, trucking, transportation, 1,191.50; G. M. Rioch, stationery, .75; F. Roberts, travelling expenses, 4.00; Dr. Clyde H. Robertson, services, examining men, 40.00; Dr. H. E. Robertson, services, examining men, 12.00; Dr. W. A. Robertson, services, examining men, 115.00; Dr. W. N. Robertson, services, examining men, 31.00; Theophile Robinshaw, blacksmithing, 8.40; B. E. Robinson, wood, 26.25; S. Robinson, hay, 92.48; Ed. Robitaille, lumber, wood, 27.75; Dr. R. B. Robson, services, examining men, 32.00; Mrs. B. Rochon, board, 2.00; Delphis Rochon, blacksmithing, 26.82; Roebuck & Sharp, tents, 4,578.67; Alfred Rogers, Ltd., cement, 393.75; Rogers Fruit, distilled water, 7.75; Dr. Norman W. Rogers, services, examining men, 11.00; P. Roisboluex, railroad fare, 1.15; J. Ronson, wood, 21.25; Alex. Ross & Son, Ltd., oats, hay, 219.01; Dr. J. C. Ross, services, examining men, 10.00; Ross Service Station, charging battery, car parts, repairs, gas, oil, 538.28; Rossport Trading Co., hardware, provisions, roofing, tools, 272.89; Chas. Rotmark, cedar, 6.52; J. Routhier, lumber, 256.20; Royal Edward Hotel, board, 26.25; Geo. Ruete, oats, hay, 346.63; D. V. Rumsey, hardware, 24.20; Alex. Ryan, horse killed by rock, 200.00; Edward Ryan, travelling expenses, 23.50; J. E. R. Ryan, rent of camp site, 40.00; Dr. A. F. Rykert, services, examining men, 13.00; J. St. Jean, rent of canoes, 15.00; St. Louis Hotel, board, 257.95; Edward St. Pierre, wood, rental of camp site, repairs, 248.60; F. St. Pierre, timber, 15.00; O. L. Sadler, hay, oats, 115.88; M. Salo, hardware, 6.10; C. Sandrelli & Co., tool boxes, transportation, 579.00; Sawyer-Massey, Ltd., plows, machinery parts, 1,121.77; M. L. Schoales, tire repairs, 66.50; A. W. Schorse, travelling expenses, 63.90; J. H. Schou, travelling expenses, 41.62; W. C. Schwitzer, travelling expenses, 3.45; D. W. Scott, provisions, hardware, oil, soap, 685.54; Dr. P. J. Scott, services, examining men, 16.00; W. B. Scott, travelling expenses, 180.98; W. J. Scott, bran, oats, hay, bread, barrels, salt, 1,702.59; Scythes & Co., Ltd., tents, 3,076.34; W. Seargeant, travelling expenses, 6.25; Mack Sequin, taxi service, 31.00; C. O. Self, board, 224.50; Service Garage, repairs, 14.50; Jack Shable, railroad fare, 2.50; A. Shail, oats, 50.23; H. J. Shanacy, railroad fare and taxi, 6.85; L. Shank, wood, 247.23; F. Shapland, lumber, 312.75; A. P.

Statutory—Continued

Trans-Canada Highway, Unemployment Relief—Continued

Sharpe, travelling expenses, 41.50; L. C. Sharpe, travelling expenses, 18.70; W. Shastal, cedar logs, 40.00; Geo. M. Shaw, travelling expenses, 4.05; R. Shaw, railroad fares, 14.85; J. F. Shea, travelling expenses, 46.15; Ed. Sheedy, transportation, 15.00; P. Shiel, oats, 38.32; Shield Development Co., Ltd. (Kashabowie), freight, loading charges, rails, 1,750.00; Shield Development Co., Ltd., (Montreal), rails, loading, 2,200.00; Alex. W. Shorse, travelling expenses, 16.80; Dr. J. R. Simmons, services, examining men, 18.00; The Robt. Simpson Co., Ltd., radios, 900.00; Geo. Simpson, wood, 440.62; A. R. Sinclair, travelling expenses, 2.55; Dr. A. Sinclair, services, examining men, 213.00; J. Sinclair, railroad fare, 2.90; C. Skeats, travelling expenses, 6.60; C. Skene, oats, 40.08; J. Skene, oats, 86.80; D. R. Small, travelling expenses, 2.25; Campbell Smith, travelling expenses, 15.40; Con Smith, cedar, 357.00; E. Smith, travelling expenses, 184.43; F. C. Smith, travelling expenses, 6.15; G. Smith, railroad fare, 1.60; G. W. Smith, stationery, 263.05; H. Smith, travelling expenses, 585.55; Jas. Smith, hay, 335.79; Smyth Bros. Garages, repairs, 2.75; R. G. Sneath, travelling expenses, 197.45; Snelgrove-Evans Fuel & Supply Co., Ltd., lumber, nuts, 696.53; Dr. W. G. Snyder, services, examining men, 135.00; Robt. Sopher, Ltd., tents, 984.72; Mike Soroske, provisions, 6.00; Simon Soucie, hay, 6.00; A. E. Souliere, travelling expenses, 7.25; J. M. Souter, wood, 1,158.00; Wm. Sovereign, cedar, 95.04; Spadoni Bros. (Schreiber), canvas, twine, 8.06; Spadoni Bros. (White River), snowshoes, provisions, rubber boots, canvas, 115.27; J. Spalding, oats, 37.10; Dr. A. J. Sparling, services, examining men, 144.00; Dr. E. Spence, services, examining men, 1.00; Mrs. Albert Sperberg, gas, 1.60; J. Spillett, transportation, express, travelling expenses, 13.30; J. Spinks, wood, 97.49; C. Holmes Stalker, travelling expenses, 12.21; Standard Planing Mills & Lumber Co., Ltd., lumber, sash, 1,562.77; Star Taxi & Transfer, trucking, 225.00; O. Stanley, travelling expenses, 96.20; Star Cafe, meals, 8.40; Dr. John H. Stead, services, examining men, 10.00; J. Steiner, hay, 2,626.67; F. Stephens, travelling expenses, 67.70; Dr. R. W. Stephens, services, examining men, 10.00; Dr. Geo. R. Stewart, services examining men, 15.00; Jake E. Stewart, wood, 45.00; J. A. Stewart, travelling expenses, 9.60; E. Stiller, railroad fares, 5.30; Stirrett Lumber Co., lumber, 1,860.91; H. Stockdale, lumber, slabs, carts, teaming, 2,714.53; J. W. Stone Boat Manufacturing Co., Ltd., hire of launch, gas, bulbs, oil, 549.40; J. B. Stowski, travelling expenses, 3.65; O. A. Strey, cedar, 10.16; J. B. Striowski, travelling expenses, 25.85; Mrs. S. C. Stroud, hay, 177.96; J. A. Strutt, blacksmithing, 2,656.21; Geo. Stunden, travelling expenses, 10.35; Wm. Sundberg, railroad fares, 3.15; B. Sutherland, travelling expenses, 145.87; M. Sutherland, charging batteries, 14.00; Dr. H. C. Sutton, services, examining men, 10.00; Richard Sutton, railroad fare, 1.85; Conrad Swanson, windows, sashes, 149.30; S. O. Swanson, hay, 202.62; Robt. Sweeney, blacksmithing, 278.30; Fred H. Sykes, travelling expenses, 10.35; C. F. Szammers, travelling expenses, 75.90; Alfred Tait, steel, rails, switch, 144.41; L. Tanney, travelling expenses, 2.25; Tapp & Hobbs, provisions, 10.00; W. J. Tarrant, travelling expenses, 6.75; Drs. Taugher and McPherson, services, examining men, 5.00; Taylor & Co., provisions, matches, 7.02; Dr. H. A. Taylor, services, examining men, 24.00; John Taylor, cedar, 38.00; John R. Taylor, wheelbarrows, compressor, tools, hose, 3,663.36; Temiskaming & Northern Ontario Railway, freight, 87.78; J. Temple, travelling expenses, 1.60; R. B. Tennant & Co., lumber, 11.20; Dr. Robt. W. Tennent, services, examining men, 16.00; Dr. F. G. Thompson, services, examining men, 12.00; Geo. Thompson, hay, 187.20; W. R. Thomson, travelling expenses, car rental, 329.67; H. H. Thornton, travelling expenses, 49.60; H. W. Thorpe, travelling expenses, 4.75; Dr. C. A. M. Thrush, services. examining men, 18.00; Thunder Bay Lumber Co., Ltd. (Fort William), lumber, felt, 28,299.07; Thunder Bay Lumber Co., Ltd. (Port Arthur), lumber, sash, felt, 41,853.83; Geo.Thur, wood, 477.75; Tilley's Palace Photo Studio, photographs, 48.10; W. Tooley, rental of camp site, 80.00; The Tourtellot Hardware Co., Ltd., hardware, wheelbarrows, levels, heaters, windows, coal, etc., 1,693.15; Wilfred Traham, wood, 68.25; McWilliams Transport Co., cartage on books, 1.25; R. M. Treloar, travelling expenses, 34.45; J. Trelver, travelling expenses, 4.00; Richard Trist, board, hay, 632.01; G. Trottier, gravel, wood, block, 11.88; Abe Truax, travelling expenses, 4.60; Tudhope-Anderson, Ltd., stone boats, wheelbarrows, heaters, 11,748.66; T. Turcotte, wood, blocks, lumber, 830.16; Jas. S. Turner, railroad fares, board, 13.60; J. J. Turner & Sons, Ltd., tents, dunnage bags, 5,955.28; Twin City Grain, Ltd., hay, oats, bran, 27,624.33; Twin City Sash & Door Co., Ltd., lumber, 2,555.20; United Typewriter Co., Ltd., rental of typewriters, 47.50; United Typewriter Co. of Manitoba, Ltd., rental of typewriters and inspections, 133.10; M. Vaillincourt, wood, 191.87; A. Valois, car rental, 4.00; P. A. Valois, board, trans-

Statutory—Continued

Trans-Canada Highway, Unemployment Relief—Continued

portation, 8.25; Leonard L. Venney, travelling expenses, 16.55; J. A. Vetter, travelling expenses, 4.20; A. Vick, hauling lumber, 9.00; Victoria Hotel, board, 341.25; Jos. Voyer, wood, lumber, trucking, hardware, gas, oil, 1,183.64; Chas. Wadson, wood, 497.25; F. A. Walberg, gas, 6.23; Waldhof Farmers' Co-operative Club, Ltd., gas, hardware, provisions, oil, stationery, 364.33; W. K. Walker, travelling expenses, 74.60; F. Walkma, lumber, 51.31; P. Wall, oats, 116.38; E. E. Wallace, sleigh shoes, 8.25; W. Walters, stove, 7.00; P. Wanson Lumber Co., Ltd., lumber, scantling, 3,516.78; Roy H. Warne, travelling expenses, 4.00; Mrs. Warren filling, 93.19; R. S. Warwick, travelling expenses, 9.40; R. A. Watchorn, blacksmithing, 190.71; A. G. Waters, travelling expenses, 11.75; Fred Watts, travelling expensès, 10.60; H. D. Watts, travelling expenses, 5.20; W. A. Weare, oats, 114.92; Dr. W. A. Weaver, services, examining men, 14.00; S. Webb, railroad fare, 3.05; J. Weir, oats, 170.22; Alfred Weiske, hay, timber, 1,028.70; H. Weiss, hay, 25.08; Wells & Emerson, hardware, coal, tools, snowshoes, 743.04; John Welsh, travelling expenses, 161.09; G. R. West, travelling expenses, 2.60; Western Engineering Service, Ltd., machinery repairs, 9.02; Western Grocers, Ltd. (Fort William), provisions, brooms, 1,851.04; Western Grocers, Ltd. (Kenora), provisions, matches, veterinary supplies, 19,086.78; Dr. R. E. Weston, services, examining men, 13.00; W. D. C. Whalley, wood, 156.87; H. Wheeler, travelling expenses, 21.20; White & McDowell, battery repairs, 1.75; W. White, travelling expenses, hay, 363.49; Drs. Whitely and Graham, services, examining men, 7.00; A. W. Whitney, travelling expenses, 60.35; F. Willard, harness, parts, 1,019.36; Williams Hardware Co., hardware, tools, roofing, heaters, lath, office supplies, paint, steel, 176,652.06; Dr. Ralph Williams, services, examining men, 17.00; Wm. Williams, railroad fare, 4.15; Fred Willows, travelling expenses, 4.10; Jas. Wilson, travelling expenses, 174.76; L. Wilson, car parts, rails, 30.00; W. A. Wilson, horse feed, 34.00; Winnipeg Map & Blue Print Co., Ltd., blue prints, negatives, 1,598.42; R. Winter, wood, hauling, 144.00; W. Winters, hay, 641.24; J. Winterbottom, lumber, hardware, cartage, 756.09; Witherspoon's Drug Store, lime, veterinary supplies, 25.65; E. A. Wood, travelling expenses, 7.25; Woods Manufacturing Co., Ltd., tent flys, tents, 2,304.39; W. H. Woolley, railroad fare, 3.05; C. J. Wright, provisions, oil, soap, 658.91; H. Wright, oats, 49.88; Young Men's Christian Association (Ignace), board, 943.30; Young Men's Christian Association (Kenora), board, 1.90; Young Men's Christian Association Railway (Schreiber), board, 237.10; Young Men's Christian Association (White River), board, 238.05; R. M. Young, travelling expenses, 34.30; W. Young, travelling expenses, 137.20; E. L. Zealand, travelling expenses, 3.30; Guido Zentel, railroad fare, .85; S. Znameroski, car rental, 30.00; Mrs. Zolern, hay, 172.51; Dr. Frank F. Zwick, services, examining men, 17.00...... 1,933,880 43

Pay lists, wages of men	4,198,368 18
Workmen's Compensation Board, compensation to injured workmen	87,945 00
Total	6,220,193 61
Less Cash Accountable, 1931	150,000 00
	6,070,193 61

General Work—Unemployment Relief ($4,733,748.90)

District No. 1, Huntsville	1,027,695 51
District No. 1, County of Haliburton	372,478 16
District No. 2, North Bay	500,055 48
District No. 3, Sudbury	553,423 17
District No. 4, Sault Ste. Marie	864,836 93
District No. 5, New Liskeard	234,438 59
District No. 6, Matheson	302,025 68
District No. 7, Cochrane	236,140 74
District No. 8, Fort William	326,288 17
District No. 9, Kenora	220,500 01
District No. 10, Fort Frances	131,068 50
General Expense Account	63,797 96
	4,832,748 90
Northern Development Dept.—Cash Accountable	1,000 00
	4,833,748 90
Less Cash Accountable, 1931	100,000 00
	4,733,748 90

Statutory—Continued

General Work, Unemployment Relief—Continued

DISTRICT No. 1 ($1,027,695.51)

Engineer, K. Rose, Huntsville

Bracebridge-Baysville-Dorset Road	217,560 34	
Burks Falls-Parry Sound Road	186,220 63	
Trout Creek-Loring Road	107,449 18	
Gravenhurst-Bala-Parry Sound Road	93,723 79	
Huntsville-Dwight-Dorset Road	93,690 71	
Rosseau Road	84,268 98	
Powassan-R'estoule Road	74,891 97	
Sundridge-Magnetewan Road	74,022 95	
Ferguson Highway	56,587 61	
Bracebridge-Port Carling Road	4,991 40	
Emsdale-Sprucedale Road	3,456 93	
Settlers' and other Roads, Sundry Expenditure	30,831 02	
		1,027,695 51

County of Haliburton, $372,478.16.

Coboconk-Minden-Dorset Road		372,478 16

DISTRICT No. 2 ($500,055.48)

Engineer, G. A. White, North Bay

Sturgeon Falls-Field Road	90,923 64	
North Bay-Sault Road	54,847 94	
Field-Marten River Road	53,342 06	
Warren-Rutter Road	36,191 42	
Sturgeon Falls-Crystal Falls Road	13,874 86	
North Bay-Ferris Road	13,301 01	
River Road	11,337 87	
Phelps Road	10,635 85	
Trans-Canada Highway	8,257 45	
Pembroke-Callander Road	5,765 00	
North Bay-Trout Lake Road	5,246 84	
Verner-Field Road	4,791 04	
Verner-Lavigne Road	4,667 43	
Field-River Valley Road	3,578 11	
Ferguson Highway	1,938 35	
Warren-River Valley Road	1,513 56	
Noelville-Monetville Road	1,120 45	
Settlers' and other roads, sundry expenditure	178,722 60	
		500,055 48

DISTRICT No. 3 ($553,423.17)

Engineer, E. J. Hosking, Sudbury

Chapleau-Devon Road	80,490 26	
North Bay-Sault Road	65,027 35	
Espanola-Little Current Road	46,791 13	
Sudbury-Milnet Road	39,803 86	
Sudbury-Levack Road	32,694 66	
Little Current-Manitowaning Road	18,548 50	
Cartier-Levack Road	18,249 40	
Little Current-Gore Bay Road	15,689 82	
Capreol-Ella Lake Road	8,212 46	
Shining Tree Road	6,568 46	
Sudbury-Massey Bay Road	3,803 47	
Gore Bay-Providence Bay Road	2,550 90	
Gore Bay-Meldrum Bay Road	2,094 75	
Bidwill-Green Bay Road	1,938 80	
Providence Bay-Manitowaning Road	1,771 00	
Sandfield-Mindemoya Road	1,734 50	
Sudbury-Burwash Road	1,294 73	
Settlers' and other Roads, sundry expenditure	206,159 12	
		553,423 17

DISTRICT No. 4 ($864,836.93)

Engineer, G. J. Lamb, Sault Ste. Marie

North Bay-Sault Road	279,357 68	
Sault-Batchewana Road	86,486 89	

Statutory—Continued

General Work, Unemployment Relief—Continued

Wa-Wa-Minto Mine Road	64,614 78	
Iron Bridge-Parkinson Road	50,549 18	
Sault-Searchmont Road	39,949 81	
North Korah Road, Korah	32,951 21	
Second Line Road	28,912 82	
Blind River-Lake Duborn Road	22,717 69	
Lee Valley Road	15,653 10	
Creek Road, Prince	13,510 24	
Northland Road	11,761 35	
St. Joseph Island Roads	11,168 78	
Blind River-Iron Bridge Road	8,375 57	
Bellevue Valley Road	5,902 03	
Dunn Valley Road	5,242 03	
Shakespeare Road	3,635 10	
Old Goulais Bay Road	3,560 27	
Hornepayne Road	1,152 06	
Michipicoten River Wharf Road	1,142 32	
People's Road	1,012 89	
Settlers' and other roads, sundry expenditure	177,181 13	
		864,836 93

DISTRICT No. 5 ($234,438.59)

Engineer, D. J. Miller, New Liskeard

Ferguson Highway	91,523 45	
Elk Lake-Ashley Mine Road	43,243 72	
Gowganda-Shiningtree Road	27,344 20	
New Liskeard-Elk Lake Road	7,469 32	
Savard and Robillard Twp. Boundary Road	5,940 00	
Bartlett's Point Road	4,839 95	
Wendigo Road	3,649 11	
Casey-Brethour Road	3,352 29	
North Road	3,215 00	
Uno Park Road	2,855 08	
Greenwood's Bridge Road	2,290 95	
Earlton-Hilliardton Road	1,238 35	
Settlers' and other roads, sundry expenditure	37,477 17	
		234,438 59

DISTRICT No. 6 ($302,025.68)

Engineer, D. Lough, Matheson

Ferguson Highway	110,290 46	
Porquis Junction-Timmins Road	47,268 07	
Porquis Junction-Iroquois Falls Road	24,271 17	
Kirkland Lake-Cheminis Road	12,400 58	
Matheson-Shillington-Connaught Road	5,521 29	
Timmins West Road	2,374 00	
Settlers' and other roads, sundry expenditure	99,900 11	
		302,025 68

DISTRICT No. 7 ($236,140.74)

Engineer, C. Tackaberry, Cochrane

Cochrane-Hearst Road	77,488 37	
Ferguson Highway	38,375 94	
Hearst-Coppell Road	10,328 20	
Gardner Road	1,980 72	
Settlers' and other roads, sundry expenditure	107,967 51	
		236,140 74

DISTRICT No. 8 ($326,288.17)

Engineer, A. J. Ishester, Fort William

International Highway	133,328 37	
Dawson Road	80,486 17	
Silver Mountain and Gunflint Road	23,487 99	
John St. Road	13,730 55	

Statutory—Continued

General Work, Unemployment Relief—Continued

District No. 8—Continued

Dog Lake Road	12,144 45	
Shebandowan Lake Road	8,975 92	
Armstrong-Caribou Lake Road	7,945 51	
Twin Lake-Nakina Road	7,301 60	
Oliver Road	6,414 95	
Current River—Kam Road	3,663 88	
Devon Road	3,073 81	
Cloud Lake Road	3,064 59	
Kakabeka-Hymers Road	2,705 09	
Trans-Canada Highway	2,183 59	
Onion Lake Road	2,155 75	
Hymers-Scoble Road	1,449 80	
Settlers' and other roads, sundry expenditure	14,176 15	
		326,288 17

DISTRICT No. 9 ($220,500.01)

Engineer, R. T. Lyons, Kenora

Kenora-Fort Frances Highway	76,405 45	
Sioux Lookout-Dinorwic Road	56,246 47	
Kenora-Redditt Road	25,318 69	
Lac Lu Road	23,267 96	
Round Lake Road	17,482 15	
Rice Lake Road	16,886 13	
Alcona-Superior Junction Road	1,718 60	
Settlers' and other roads, sundry expenditure	3,174 56	
		220,500 01

DISTRICT No. 10 ($131,068.50)

Engineer, A. M. Mills, Fort Frances

Fort Frances-Rainy River Road	18,580 13	
Wildland Reserve Road	14,117 60	
Kenora-Fort Frances Highway	11,998 68	
Devlin Road	11,617 75	
Emo-Off Lake Road	6,643 76	
Stratton-Sifton Road	4,426 45	
Arbor Vitae Road	3,792 60	
LaVallee Road North	3,043 85	
Bergland-Budreau-Tovell Road	2,485 40	
Barwick-Black Hawk Road	2,090 60	
Black Hawk-Deerlock Road	1,979 13	
Indian Mission Road	1,951 41	
Crozier Road	1,762 84	
Spohn Road	1,529 40	
Sleeman-Minahico Road	1,375 60	
Black Hawk-Off Lake Road	1,216 40	
Settlers' and other roads, sundry expenditure	42,456 90	
		131,068 50
General Expense Account		63,797 96
Dept. of Northern Development, Cash Accountable		1,000 00
		4,833,748 90
Less Cash Accountable, 1931		100,000 00
Total		4,733,748 90

Jennie Abbleson, sand, 40.62; Abitibi Power & Paper Co., Ltd. (Espanola), bolts, rods, 7.06; Abitibi Power & Paper Co., Ltd. (Iroquois Falls), hardware, welding, kitchenware, laundry, 397.73; Abitibi Power & Paper Co., Ltd. (Sudbury), cutting timber, 246.51; O. Ackles, rent of camps, 80.00; Jas. Adams, timber, 93.88; Robt. Agnew, travelling expenses and car rental, 263.11; H. Aherns, provisions, gas, 50.34; Amil Aho, wood, 91.00; Aho's Service Garage, wood, 12.00; Jos. Aiken, lumber, 8.00; Thos. Aikins, explosives 12.50; Fred Albert, blacksmithing, 11.90; Albion Hotel, board, 5.00; Chas. Alexander, gravel, 86.65; Ernie Alexander,

Statutory—Continued

General Work, Unemployment Relief—Continued

wood, 41.63; Tom Alexander, wood, 65.00; Chas. Alexandria, hardwood, 50.00; Algoma Central & Hudson Bay Railway, fares, freight, phone calls, protecting tracks, 4,319.47; Algoma Central & Hudson Bay Express, express, 7.35; Algoma Hotel, cartage, transportation, 370.70; Algoma Produce Co., Ltd., provisions, 2,647.47; Robt. Allan, travelling expenses, 4.85; Thos. Allan, provisions, 16.96; Wm. Allard, hardware, 70.71; Geo. Alldred, livery, 5.00; C. Allen, gas, repairs, 2.00; Dr. H. Allen, services, examining men, 46.00; L. Allen, hay, oats, 15.40; Norman Allen, travelling expenses, 45.20; N. Allie, meat, 10.44; U. Allie, provisions, 19.84; Dr. Duncan Allison, services, examining men, 18.00; W. Alphonse, coal, 8.00; Frank Ames, lumber, 16.00; Alex. Anderson, lumber, oats, 732.13; Frank Anderson, provisions, oats, 706.90; H. A. Anderson, hay, 949.66; H. N. Anderson, hay, provisions, 3,152.48; L. Anderson, gravel, 12.60; Norman Anderson, gravel, 117.00; R. Anderson, transportation, 55.19; Roy Anderson, oats, 84.64; Stanley Anderson, provisions, 11.28; Clarence Andrews, provisions, 21.60; Roger Andrews, posts, 97.40; Angst Bros., gas, hardware, provisions, 424.24; F. Angus, provisions, 19.74; Angus & Taylor, blacksmithing, 263.00; Animikie Mines, Ltd., shale, 317.70; Ivan Anness, hay, 72.07; Fred Ansley, potatoes, 17.50; Nelson Ansley, provisions, 24.08; Ansonville Transfer, transportation, 216.00; E. Antalfy, rock, 15.00; Applebe & Co., Ltd., sulphuric acid, etc., 2.00; A. Arbour, gravel, 12.50; Mrs. Harold Archer, board, 182.00; Robt. Archer, wood and board, 247.20; Russell Archer, wood, cleaning camp site, rental and compensation for fence repairs, 93.00; T. Archer, gas, oil, rent of boat, 32.90; Mrs. Thos. Archer, board, 263.90; Mrs. Violet Archer, board, 16.20; Archibald Bros., repairs, 4.30; Dr. A. E. Ardagh, services examining men, 21.00; T. Ariss, gravel, 20.00; J. H. Armitage, blacksmithing, 7.75; C. Armstrong, blacksmithing, hardware, 25.40; Ed. Armstrong, tool box, 4.50; F. C. Armstrong Estate, hardware, 10.25; J. Armstrong, pork, 16.00; J. G. Armstrong, gas, oil, livery, hardware, 71.20; Lester Armstrong, cedar, 47.80; L. O. Armstrong, lumber and gravel 172.75; P. H. Armstrong, transportation, 175.50; R. T. Armstrong, provisions, hardware, oil, etc., 2,494.45; Mrs. T. N. Armstrong, gravel, 4.60; W. J. Armstrong (Richards Landing), provisions, 10.90; W. J. Armstrong (Powassan), lumber, 4.89; Armstrong's Meat Market, provisions, 226.93; Harve Arnold, blacksmithing, 17.25; Oliver Arnold, potatoes, 5.60; Roy G. Arnold, blacksmithing, 6.95; Arrow Publishing House, signs, 4.20; The Art Metropole, draughting supplies and repairs, 54.30; Sam Arthurs, blacksmithing, 11.50; S. N. Asbury, travelling expenses, 9.85; Jas. W. Asbury, hardware, provisions, 3,972.42 ; N. Asslin, cedar and gravel, 13.64; Omer Asslin, car rental, 193.25; Ben Atkinson, gravel, 15.80 ; W. J. Atkinson, milk and hay, 67.36; Mrs. W. J. Atkinson, board, 5.50; Jos. Aubertin, provisions, 42.00; A. Aubin, gravel, 68.30; C. M. Auer, gravel, 41.00; C. Auger, blacksmithing, hardware, 1,548.02; E. Ault, provisions, 122.00; Geo. A. Aultman, cedar, 151.45; Edwin Ausley, gravel, 43.20; C. R. Austin, meat, 16.00; J. Austin, slabs, 85.00; J. Austin & Sons, lumber, slabs, 2,624.00; Willard Austin, meat, 14.90; Austin & Nicholson, Ltd., lumber, hardware, provisions, blankets, repairs, 4,048.53; L. D. Averell, cedar, 8.50; Jas. Avery, wood, 8.00; Russell Avery, hay, 361.56; S. G. Avery, provisions, 346.36; Azilda Garage, gas, 84.60; J. D. Baby, travelling expenses, 7.85; J. H. Badger, provisions, barrels, 327.45; J. Cecil Badour Hotel, meals, 6.50; F. A. Baschler, rent of camping ground, 1.00; G. G. Baeker, stationery and liniment, 10.45; Bill Bailey, hauling equipment, 1.92; Hugh Bailey, gravel, 14.10; John Bailey, hay, 217.40; Bailey & May, gas, oil, repairs, 131.98; Alex. J. Bain, meat, 37.71; Geo. Bain, travelling expenses, 15.65; J. H. Bain, Sr., provisions, 16.02; Bainbridge Stores, provisions, fly spray, 76.69; A. Baker, gravel, 21.20; Alfred Baker, provisions, 3.75; Ed. Baker, cedar, 21.60; Nels Baker, pork, 40.40; Dr. J. C. Ball, services, examining men, 19.00; J. H. Ball, timber, 10.00; Mrs. I. Ballantyne, board, 67.50; W. A. Bannerman, gravel, 928.20; Cliff Barber, cutting wood, 4.00; Ed. Barber, gravel, 24.00; Geo. Barber, teaming, 7.50; Jno. Barber, gravel, 4.60; Lloyd Barber, hog, cartage, transportation, 25.06; Ted Barber, cedar, 277.15; J. Barchard, lumber, 25.00; Mrs. Clarsie Barker, gravel, 55.20; Robt. Barker, gravel, 68.90; Norman Barn, wood, 62.50; Dr. J. W. Barnett, services, examining men, 34.00; Miss Mary Barr, butter, 22.32; Ern. Barricks, gravel, 86.40; Bazil Barry, board, 11.20; Hiram Barry, gas, oil, repairs, livery, 122.40; Oscar Barry, taxi service, 2.00; E. A. Bartlett, board, gravel, rent of blacksmith tools and forge, 228.25; Chas. Barton, lumber, 251.62; Barton & Fisher, hardware, 124.10; Ted Barton, cedar, 3.80; Wm. Barton, hemlock, potatoes, 24.00; Calixte Bastien, cartage, transportation, 90.06; J. D. Bastien & Sons, provisions, hardware, gas, 496.20; Milburn Bates, cedar, 17.20; H. A. Batsford, car rental, timber, 219.63; battery Service Station, car parts, 4.28; R. Batty, gravel, 31.50; Karly N. Baturensky, repairs to tripod, stone, 5.00; Wm. Bayley, provisions, 50.90; Baysville Hotel

Statutory—Continued

General Work, Unemployment Relief—Continued

(Baysville), board, .50; Baysville Hotel (Huntsville), board, 9.00; Bayview Lodge, board, 363.18; Beagan Motor Sales, gas, repairs, cartage, car rental, 711.84; J. H. Beamish, lumber, 170.80; R. Beattie, milk, rent of camp site, 52.80; Geo. Beatty & Son, Ltd., rubber boots, 7.50; Jas. Beatty, cedar, 57.75; Robt. Beatty, rent of camp site, 4.00; Mrs. Robt. Beatty, milk, 11.00; Estate of Walter Beatty, lumber, signs, 36.18; The Wm. Beatty Co., Ltd., oilcloth, fishing line, 34.30; W. C. Beatty, provisions, 22.50; Albert Beaudin, provisions, soap, 16.00; Alex. Beaudry, gravel, 4.00; A. Beaudry, cedar, 24.00; Nap Beaudry, gravel, 3.00; Albert Beaulieu, gravel, 19.95; Emil Beaulieu, lumber, repairs, 13.55; A. Beauparlant, hardware, 56.99; G. Beauparlant, cartage, 18.00; Beckett & Smith, blacksmithing, 1.30; J. E. Bedard, gravel, fill, 189.35; J. S. Bedard, gravel, 80.10; E. L. Bedford, hardware, tile, iron, etc., 2,859.81; Ernest Begin, wood, 6.00; Geo. B. Begy, travelling expenses, 1.42; V. Beharriell, gravel, 60.00; W. J. Beharriell, hardware, 16.84; Harry Beiers, timber, 1.50; Carl Beilhartz, hay, 3.69; Reuben Beilhartz, lumber, 174.03; J. A. Belair, hardware, repairs, 3.50; Emile Belanger, wood, 10.05; J. Belanger, wood, 12.75; J. A. Belanger, shovels, 6.00; Jos. Belanger, provisions, soap, barrels, 759.44; Garnet Bell, gravel, 12.80; Bell Telephone Co., telephone services, moving and repairing lines, 595.84; E. Bellaire, gravel, 1.90; D. Bellamy, wood, 19.12; A. Bennett, provisions, 60.52; J. Bennett, trucking, transportation, 185.45; Oscar T. Bennett, tools, hardware, coal, 93.68; Stan Benniger, oats, 62.10; Leo Benoil, gravel, 1.40; Benson-Bastien Transportation Co., livery, cartage, 14.69; Benson Transportation Co., freighting, transportation, 499.68; Dr. O. L. Berdan, services, examining men, 20.00; Chas. Berdux, transportation, 149.75; L. W. Berg, gravel, 165.38; Eugene Bergeron, wood, 6.00; Bergman & Nelson, lumber, 21.42; E. Beriault, blacksmithing, 15.90; A. Berlinghoff, straw, 13.00; Bernard hotel, board, 117.00; T. Bernardo, cedar, 332.50; A. C. Bernier, board, 7.70; C. Bernstein, provisions, 300.38; David Berry, provisions, 9.75; Sam Bertolo, car rental, board, 43.00; Eug. Bertrand, coal, repairs, 109.10; F. Bertrand, blankets, 75.00; Alex. Besaw, wood, 3.00; Wm. Best, gravel, 212.80; Jos. Bibeau, repairs, 4.50; Bigwin Laundry, washing blankets, 660.90; Wm. Bird, gravel, 95.60; Henry Birmingham, wood, 24.75; Jas. Birmingham, wood, 23.25; Ernest Bisaillon, stone boat runners, 12.50; Frank Bishop, board, provisions, 145.45; J. F. Bishop, provisions, hardware, office supplies, 751.05; Black Bros., hardware, lumber, 90.44; Dr. Homer Black, services, examining men, 14.00; H. G. Black, rent of camp site, 18.45; J. Black, hay, 15.00; J. Blackburn, gravel, 4.20; Dr. A. M. Blakely, services, examining men, 23.00; Wm. Blackstock, gravel, 12.00; Jos. Blair, car rental and travelling expenses, 282.95; Jas. Blight, blacksmithing, coal, 21.15 ; Blind River Garage, gas, tires, tubes, hardware, 16.69; J. Bobyk, wood, provisions, 151.50; Christie Boe, car rental, travelling expenses, 205.65; F. Bogie, travelling expenses, 14.50; C. Bohm, eggs, 117.60; Jos. Bois, lumber, 72.00; Louis Bois, cedar, 54.60; T. Boisenue, gravel, 17.50; O. Boisvert, provisions, 65.04; A. Bolduc, lumber, 130.55; Jos. Bolduc, lumber, 6.50; R. Bole, car livery, 57.00; F. Bondy, gravel, 46.20; Teles Bonin, gas, 65.10; J. Bonner, provisions, 48.62; Miss Eva Booker, provisions, 23.21; John Booker, provisions, 48.20; Sanford Boomhower, cedar, 7.00; Mrs. A. Booth, washing blankets, 20.75; Alex. Booth, provisions, lumber, 99.25; Harry Booth, ink, .90; J. R. Booth, Ltd., rental of camp, provisions, hardware, hay, etc., 680.80; Sam Booth, blacksmithing, 2.25; Thos. Booth, provisions, 37.68; Wm. Booth, travelling expenses, 2.70; E. P. Boothby, provisions, 72.99; John Boothby, provisions, 28.35; Norman C. Boothby, provisions, oil, oats, transportation, cartage, 2,714.21; T. G. Boothby, lumber, 4.73; Peter Borachoff, cartage, taxi service, 7.00; Dick Born, wood, 30.00; W. Bottrell, rent of camp site, gravel, 56.88; Arthur Bouchard, provisions, 7.95; L. A. Boucher, travelling expenses, 79.57; Octave Boucher, provisions, 2,089.48; D. Bouffard, car parts, repairs, gravel, 73.05; S. Bouffard, gravel, 43.50; V. Bouffard, blacksmithing, 28.07; Alphonse Boulet, gravel, 13.72; Arthur Bourassa, cartage, 10.00; F. Bourdon, repairs, 3.00; A. Bourgault, car repairs, gas, oil, grease, 213.88; O. Bourgeois, blacksmithing, 7.60; J. V. Bourke, travelling expenses, 1.40; J. S. Boville, blacksmithing, 19.50; Sam Boville, blacksmithing, 16.90; Walter Bowen, hay, wood, 44.10; Alf Bower, car rental, travelling expenses, 69.25; Mrs. Louisa Bower, provisions, 9.50; N. H. Bowers, hardware, explosives, oil, 109.76; J. Bowman, oats, 21.00: Thos. Bowman, wood, 10.00; Boxall & Matthie, Ltd., iron, hardware, 66.84; S. J. Boyce, telegram, .60; Perrie Boyd, hay, oats, 24.52; John R. Boyd & Son, provisions, hay, soap, 853.09; J. M. Boyes, gravel, 20.00; John Boyes, milk, 50.00; Thos. Boyes, borrow, gravel, provisions, 212.40; Robin Boyle, rent of camp site, 40.00; W. A. Boyt, hardware, towelling, provisions, tools, 1,828.84; Bracebridge Garage, car repairs, 1.25; Bracebridge & Muskoka Lakes Telephone Co.,

Statutory—Continued

General Work, Unemployment Relief—Continued

long distance calls, 11.75; Dr. E. J. Brachen, services, examining men, 16.00; D. Bradford, gravel, 433.55; Andrew J. Brandon, trucking, 21.87; I. E. Brandrick, provisions, 26.16; F. Y. W. Brathwaite, hardware, explosives, kitchenware, gas, etc., 7,581.04; Ovila Brazeau, gravel, 191.80; Wm. Brazeau, board, 9.00; Fred R. Bray, car rental, travelling expenses, 134.50; Jas. Brennan, gravel, 381.85; Otto Bretzlaff, provisions, 149.85; Geo. L. Brewer, trucking, 40.00; Bridge Bros., hardware, explosives, tools, 2,734.57; Jas. Brigden, beef, 27.42; Ken Bridgman, hire of truck, 5.40; Percy Bridgeman, provisions, 5.00; A. C. Briggs, timber, 124.07; E. H. Briggs, glass for level, .65; C. Brigham, provisions, 7.42; Victor Brisebois, provisions, 60.50; Victor Brisson, gas, oil, transportation, hardware, 13.21; British America Express Co., Ltd., express, 8.20; British American Oil Co., Ltd., gas, oil, grease, 993.83; Elmer Broad, explosives, cartage, 12.15; P. Brock, gravel, 18.90; Geo. Brodie, gravel, 54.00; Henry Brock, gravel, 181.88; John Brook, posts, 2.10; Jos. Brook, Sr., provisions, 163.64; W. H. Brookbanks, travelling expenses, 8.85; Geo. W. Brooks, horse medicine, 1.10; Harold Brooks, timber, 2.24; Jos. Brooks, Sr., provisions, 27.70; J. Brooks, lumber, 9.10; A. Brosseau, cedar, 12.00; M. Brosseau, filling material, 93.75; P. O. Brosseau, provisions, 89.12; Dr. Wm. J. Brough, services, examining men, 22.00; Alf Brown, meat, 37.02; Alphonse Brown, meat, 24.00; Brown & Averell, provisions, 110.58; Brown & Co., hardware, provisions, roofing, gas, 381.96; Bert Brown, board, 72.60; C. Brown, grindstone, 4.00; Clarence Brown, car rental, 21.00; D. C. Brown, board, 48.00; L. E. Brown, meat, 45.12; W. Brown & Son, provisions, 1,154.37; Brown's Sales & Service, car repairs, 9.50; Milne H. Brownlee, travelling expenses, 44.36; Henry Bruijninck, provisions, 92.75; W. Brunelle, gravel, 3.30; P. J. Brunette, provisions, 3.80; A. H. Brunne, wood, 253.50; Brunne Apiaries, honey, 47.80; John D. Brunne, honey, 19.80; A. Brunton, travelling expenses, 3.85; S. Bryant, lumber, hardwood, 499.34; G. H. Bryson, travelling expenses, films, 31.32; A. Bryant, rent of wrench and jack, 15.00; Geo. Bucciarelli, oil, provisions, gas, 3,028.35; J. E. Buchanan, spikes, lumber, 3.49; E. Buckley, cedar, 18.50; Mrs. John Budge, board, 115.90; Eldridge Bull, wood, 60.00; Ed. Bullied, pork, wood, 49.10; Clem Bunn, lumber, gravel, 463.56; Mrs. F. Bunn, board, 4.50; W. Burch, stone, 3.40; R. P. Burchnall, travelling expenses, 13.10; John Burdynek, provisions, 53.10; A. Burford, repairs, gas, oil, 36.85; A. Burg, provisions, 16.75; F. A. Burgar, travelling expenses, 57.83; J. W. Burgess, Ltd., hardware, provisions, 41.28; A. A. Burk & Co., transportation, gas, oil, 21.73; G. Burk, provisions, 27.30; Ed. Burk, transportation, 28.00; Burk & Avery, hardware, provisions, gas, oil, oats, stationery, 7,183.77; Burks Falls Garage, gas, oil, repairs, 50.95; Burks Falls Hardware Co., hardware, tools, 292.01; Mrs. Ida Burman, rental of house and camp site, wood, gravel, poles, 339.41; S. J. Burnell, building for storehouse, 20.00; Burns & Co., Ltd. (Fort William), provisions, 15.42; Burns & Co., Ltd. (Winnipeg), provisions, 648.30; Adam Burnside, hardwood, 62.50; A. Busch, cedar, 45.40; Barney Busch, cedar, 27.00; Chas. Buschlen, board, 969.40; Barney Bush, cedar, 170.15; Jos. Bussineau, blacksmithing, 3.00; Wm. Bye, provisions, 23.40; Mrs. Wm. Bye, Sr., gravel, 12.75; Andrew Bynkoski, provisions, 17.36; Herb Caddell, gravel, 68.10; Stanislas Cadieux, gravel, 37.70; Cain Bros., provisions, 83.52; A. G. Cairncross, travelling expenses, 4.55; Boyd Caldwell, gravel, 48.05; H. Caldwell, provisions, 27.50; T. S. Caldwell, travelling expenses, 98.11; W. B. Caldwell, car rental, travelling expenses, 347.50; Albert Cameron, blacksmithing, 187.35; A. S. Cameron, gravel, 40.50; Dan Cameron, wood, 32.50; M. H. Cameron, lumber, provisions, hardware, 2,196.49; S. A. Cameron, travelling expenses, .75; Alex. Campbell, cedar, 10.08; Bert Campbell, gravel, 30.15; C. Campbell, transportation, 2.80; Geo. Campbell, creosote, ties, 8.25; Geo. Campbell, gravel, 127.80; Geo. E. Campbell, provisions, 44.65; The Campbell Heating Co., pipe, 10.75; Russell Campbell, oats, 30.43; Pat Campbell, gravel, 150.30; P. J. Campbell, provisions, hardware, timber, 34.38; Sandy Campbell, hay, wood, provisions, gravel, 241.10; G. D. Campeau, nails, 4.15 ; Canada Culvert Co., Ltd., culverts, 12,396.76; Canada Ingot Iron Co., Ltd., culverts, 9,031.73; Canadian Atlas Steels, Ltd., drill steel, 2,830.10; Canadian Industries, Ltd. (Montreal), explosives, 44,929.98; Canadian Industries, Ltd. (Toronto), explosives, wire, 35,992.95; Canadian Ingersoll Rand Co., Ltd., machinery parts, 1,613.57; Canadian National Express, express, 124.65; Canadian National Railways, freight, fares, protecting track, 1,821.33; Canadian National Telegraphs, telegrams, 4.00; Canadian Northern Hotel, board, 8.50; Canadian Oil Companies, Ltd. (Emo), oil, 28.80; Canadian Oil Companies, Ltd. (Fort Frances), gas, oil, grease, 176.12; Canadian Oil Companies, Ltd. (North Bay), gas, oil, grease, 3,420.89; Canadian Oil Companies, Ltd. (Port Arthur), gas, oil, 980.90; Canadian Oil Companies, Ltd. (Toronto), gas, oil, drums, 786.26; Canadian Oil Companies

Statutory—Continued

General Work, Unemployment Relief—Continued

(Winnipeg), gas, oil, grease, 604.92; Canadian Pacific Express Co., express, 73.30; Canadian Pacific Railway Co., fares, freight, fencing crossing, flagging protection, constructing new culvert, repairs to telegraph lines, 1,094.89; Canadian Pacific Railway Co's Telegraphs, telegrams, 128.26; Canadian Packing Co., Ltd., provisions, 11,816.51; Mrs. W. C. Canfield, butter, 11.04; D. Cardinal, gravel, 37.20; Geo. Carleton, provisions, 35.44; Gus Carlson, pork, 15.20; Fred Carlson, potatoes, 19.25; J. D. Carlyle, gravel, 9.00; A. A. Carmichael, travelling expenses, 21.70; W. Caron, provisions, hardware, fly tox, 74.32; Carpenter-Hixon Co., Ltd., lumber, hardware, explosives, oats, mattresses, gas, 3,358.23; H. Carr, cedar, 36.95; E. Carriere, lumber, 70.00; Ed. Carriere, blacksmithing, 4.70; Jos. Carriere, gravel, 27.90; Dr. F. B. Carron, services, examining men, 25.00; Carter Bros., provisions, 2,151.02; Melvin Carter, hardware, explosives, rent of community hall, transportation, cartage, 1,983.27; P. R. Carter, wood, 8.00; Robt. Carter, wood, 13.00; Jas. Case, timber, 21.76; E. Casey, storage rental and rent of barn, 50.00; E. A. Cash, travelling expenses, 85.14; E. O. Casselman Garage, gas, oil, car parts and repairs, 116.21; Frank Cassie, cable, wire, 569.32; E. Cassidy, gas, oil, 2.30; J. Cates, eggs, 7.68; J. C. Caughey, hay, oats, wagon parts, 59.85; A. M. Cauley, provisions, 10.80; F. H. Cavanagh, stationery, 9.45; Joe Cawthra, cedar, 1.32; Central Garage, gas, oil, trucking, car parts and repairs, installation of lights, 1,938.41; Central Hotel, board, 8.75; Central Meat Market, provisions, 923.19; Chadbourn Bros., cedar, 52.64; F. Chainey, cedar, 3.00; F. Chak, rent of store room, 20.00; Chalykoff & Co., Ltd., provisions, oil, 45.50; M. Chamberlain, gravel, 39.50; Jos. Chamberland, blacksmithing, 2.60; J. E. Chambers, posts, logs, 15.50; Jos. Chambers, timber, meat, 224.68; J. Champagne, provisions, 17.75; Chapleau Electric Light and Power Co., repairs, charging batteries, 16.46; Chapleau Meat Market, provisions, 2,027.78; L. Chapman, provisions, 7.59; Eli Charboneau, meat, 55.44; Sam Charette, cedar, 28.08; E. Chartrand, fill, gravel, 35.80; L. Chartrand, towing car, 2.00; Ed. Chauvin, car rental, 52.00; M. Cheaney, provisions, 974.89; J. B. Chenier, board, potatoes, 42.00; Alex. Cherkas, provisions, 87.17; D. R. Chester, clearing and grubbing land, 55.55; Alvin Chevalier, meat, 32.40; Albert Chevrefils, blacksmithing, 16.80; R. Chevrefils, gravel, 30.60; H. Cheyne, repairs, 3.90; Jas. Chillman, gravel, 6.30; John Christianson, gravel, blacksmithing, lumber, 821.28; Henry Christilaw, potatoes, 7.67; H. B. Christilaw, provisions, towelling, 828.82; W. W. Christopherson, travelling expenses, 75.20; Ciglen & Co., gravel, 51.75: City Meat Market, provisions, 1,302.60; E. W. Clairmont, declaration re report on accident, .50; Chas. Clark, provisions, 8.00; F. Clark, cedar posts, 36.40; J. Clark, towelling, 57.75; Clark, Howe, Waters & Knight Bros., Ltd., lumber, drafting board, 9.32; Thos. Clark, provisions, 261.86; W. E. Clark, travelling expenses, 6.00; D. W. Clayton, hardware, provisions, oil, hay, trucking, 6,378.42; Jerry Clayton, meat, 92.53; Wm. Clayton, trucking, 18.00; F. W. Clegg, provisions, 28.28; Wm. Clelland, provisions, 17.76; A. Clement, cedar, 6.00; Dr. S. R. Clemes, services, examining men, 38.00; Wm. Clink, meat, 35.76; J. E. Clipsham & Sons, Ltd., hardware, explosives, heater, gas, 1,028.78; A. Cloutier, provisions, 572.62; E. Cloutier, wood, provisions, 1,432.18; Jcs. Cloutier, provisions, 3.00; J. N. Cloutier, provisions, tools, 86.14; Nap Cloutier, wood, 39.52; Frank Clubbe, meat, 16.70; The Cobalt Foundry, steel plates, 11.44; C. Cochlin, provisions, 75.42; Cochrane Dunlop Hardware, Ltd. (North Bay), hardware, explosives, 1,992.40; Cochrane Dunlop Hardware, Ltd. (Pembroke), hardware, explosives, scraper, 258.06; Cochrane Dunlop Hardware, Ltd. (Sault Ste. Marie), hardware, explosives, 12,917.57; Cochrane Dunlop Hardware, Ltd. (Sudbury), hardware, explosives, steel, 3,817.84; The Cockshutt Plow Co., Ltd., plow, plow parts, 43.50; Abraham Code, gravel, 2.00; C. E. Code, travelling expenses, 4.85; Mike Cokoluk, provisions, 1.50; The Colbeck Clinic, services, examining men, 33.00; D. C. Cole & Son, oats, 128.00; Jas. A. Coles, nails, explosives, 2.00; Colledge Orchards, provisions, 6.00; W. S. Colledge, apples, 4.00; Isaac Collins, gravel, 48.60; Chas. Collison, provisions, 4.80; Dr. W. G. Collison, services, examining men, 16.00; Compressed Air Equipment, drill steel, 472.22; Conlin Bros., wood, 13.00; Conlin & Hogan, coal, 101.70; Donald Connelly, provisions, hardware, kitchenware, gas, oil, 8,522.09; R. Connolly, provisions, wood, 240.86; Ed. Conrad, provisions, 83.02; Construction Boarding Co., hardware, oil, board, matches, 8,026.07; Consumers Trading Co., provisions, lye, 1,337.17; Ernest Conway, meat, 61.60; Frank Cook (Emo), meat, 10.40; Frank Cook (Parry Sound), lumber, trucking, 2,544.07; Geo. Cook, meat, 13.20; Gordon S. Cook, blacksmithing, 17.65; John Cook, milk, 104.76; L. Cook, cedar, provisions, 249.40; N. W. Cook, blacksmithing, 5.70; Richard Cook, wood, 81.00; Roy Cooke, car rental, 52.00; Mrs. M. Cookson, meat, 69.05; A. Cooper, car rental, gas, oil, travelling expenses, 193.34; Mrs. A. Cooper,

Statutory—Continued

General Work, Unemployment Relief—Continued

board, 246.50; Angus Cooper & Son, lumber, 21.12; G. H. Cooper, car rental, travelling expenses, 194.00; H. J. Cooper, rental of transit and level, 30.00; Wm. Cooper, gas, oil, grease, car rental, hardware, wood, 356.30; Mrs. W. Cooper, board, 738.00; Chas. Corbett, oil, 3.00; Corbett's garage, gas, oil, repairs, 135.57; Mrs. Lena N. Corbiere, gravel, 10.50; E. B. Corbould, travelling expenses, 20.20; Corona Lumber Yards, Ltd., hardware, 18.00; Thos. Corpal, services, 2.00; Geo. Corrigan, potatotes, 12.50; Corrugated Pipe Co., Ltd., culverts, 19,677.84; Frank Coseo, provisions, towelling, matches, etc., 11,258.68; O. Cote, gravel, fill, 71.42; Tom Cottingham, meat, 10.72; Angus Coulter, transportation, 12.00; Wilfred Coultis, timber, 34.43; Jos. Coursol, plank, 10.00; Lorrain Courtemanche, repairs, 4.50; Mrs. C. Cousineau, lumber, 2.94; H. Cowan, travelling expenses, 11.40; Jas. Cowan, wood, 26.00; John Cowan, cedar, 55.00; Tom Cowan, gravel, 7.35; Geo. Cox, wood, cedar, 123.38; John Cox, gravel, 114.40; Victor Cox, wood, 487.00; Coynes Transport, trucking, 1.95; Craig Bros., lumber, cartage, 843.29; W. H. Craig, lumber, freighting, 1,458.93; Crane Lumber Co., Ltd., hardware, lumber, 222.55; A. W. Crawford, travelling expenses, 975.00; Alex. Crawford, elm poles, 2.40; L. G. Creasor, car rental, 50.00; Dr. W. H. K. Crehan, services, examining men, 1.00; E. Crespeau, gravel, 80.20; W. Crisp, hardware, provisions, gas, oil, 115.29; H. & G. Critchley, hardware, 42.55; L. A. Croghan, car rental, 92.00; D. Crossthwaite, gravel, 871.05; Chas. Crosswell, meat, 23.12; Mrs. W. Crowe, board, 47.20; Dr. L. E. Crowley, services, examining men, 64.00; Jack Crozier, wood, 112.50; Wm. Crozier, meat, wood, 43.39; Dr. W. W. Cruise, services, examining men, 43.00; Miss Lillie Cryderman, gravel, 36.50; H. Cuilleroer, livery, 6.50; A. G. Culbert, provisions, 1,276.31; R. Culin, gas, oil, grease, repairs, 128.41; A. G. Cumming, draughting supplies, 190.80; B. H. Cunningham, provisions, 62.55; John Currie, cedar poles, 7.20; Robt. Currie, meat, 79.40; Thos. Currie, hay, 95.45; Thos. Curtin, car hire, 6.00; J. Curtis, potatoes, 12.50; Geo. Cuthbertson, meat, 14.48; Armand Cyr, boat rental, 5.00; E. Cyr, blacksmithing, 16.85; Jas. Cyr, gravel, 115.50; F. Daigle, gravel, fill, 123.45; Victor Dalcourt, gravel, 157.60; Daley Bros., charging battery, 5.50; Herb Daley, cedar, 27.00; W. A. Dalgleish, car rental and travelling expenses, 220.40; J. H. Dallaire, hardware, provisions, stationery, 146.87; Andy Daly, oats, 30.60; O. Dambumont, gravel, 49.10; M. Daneff, hardware, explosives, stationery, 81.95; Felix Danis, cedar, 27.00; G. Daoust, rock, 104.10; Omer Daoust, earth fill, 26.25; Darling's Garage, transportation, 102.00; J. J. Darlington, provisions, soap, 1,969.24; R. M. Dart, lumber crayons, 1.00; Simon Dauphinois, hardware, 13.70; Geo. Davenport, travelling expenses, 3.25; H. Y. Davidson, towels, table cloth, 10.70; Jas. Davidson, posts, cedar, 64.99; John Davidson, blacksmithing, 2.70; Davies & Crosby, provisions, 192.94; R. J. Davies, timber, ties, 224.25; Ben Davis, hardwood, 18.00; Dr. D. Davis, services, examining men, 40.00; S. Davis, lumber, 31.50; Wilfrid Davison, lumber, 52.05; Harold Daw, provisions, 3.25; I. U. Dawkins, travelling expenses, 1.00; Mrs. Lorne Dawson, board, 18.80; Thos. Dawson, gravel, 88.25; Wallace Dawson, wood, 6.25; Annie Debassige, gravel, 30.00; David W. Debassige, posts, bags, 7.00; B. Debon, provisions, board, 117.44; Alfred Decasse, plank, 6.80; Frank Dellandrea, meat, 51.03; Mrs. John Dellandrea, meat, 67.85; Delongchamp Cartage Co., Ltd., trucking, .50; Deluxe Taxi & Transfer, livery, trucking, 1,142.75; D. Deneault, meals, 56.00; Mrs. Denhardt, provisions, 16.40; F. Denhardt, provisions, 12.60; Tony Denis, wood, 3.75; F. J. Dennie, travelling expenses, 190.52; W. C. Dennis, lath, blacksmithing, 8.00; John Dent, pork, 9.76; Desbarats Garage, barrels, 3.00; Jos. Desjardins, buggy, potatoes, 17.20; A. Deslauriers, wood, 36.00; S. Deslauriers, lumber, wood, 481.18; A. Derochers, wood, 44.00; Dr. A. Desrosiers, services, examining men, 22.00; A. Desrosiers, cement and lumber, 90.73; W. J. Detweiler, rubber boots, 61.00; H. Deyett, provisions, hardware, oil, oats, gas, 1,318.21; Diamond Taxi, cartage, taxi service, 154.50; H. E. Didier, gas, oil, grease, 146.95; A. Dignard, lumber, 17.30; Chas. Dillon, cartage, transportation, wood, cutting wood, 23.01; Dr. O. C. Dinniwell, services, examining men, 13.00; J. A. Dinsmore, car rental and travelling expenses, 84.42; Henry Disston & Sons, Ltd., tools, 295.34; Chas. J. Dix, livery, 106.00; C. Dixon, transportation, 10.20; P. E. Doal, mattresses, provisions, straw, taxi services, 83.55; Reg. Doal, car rental, 6.00; Dobbs Bros., lumber, rent of lot, 878.96; F. Dobbs, provisions, cedar poles, 116.24; Ira Dobbs, provisions, 43.61; J. A. Dobbs, provisions, hardware, oilcloth, paint, 512.26; Milner Dobbs, provisions, 37.65; W. Dobbs, provisions, board, 24.14; Geo. Dodds, car hire, 54.00; H. Doherty, cedar, 24.80; Miles Doherty, blacksmithing, 76.10; Peter Doig, oats, 495.60; Mrs. G. Dollar, board, 34.50; D. G. Doman, travelling expenses, 1.90; Dominion Equipment & Supply Co., Ltd., machinery parts, 712.32; Dominion

Statutory—Continued

General Work, Unemployment Relief—Continued

Government Dock, freight, 8.37; Dominion Hotel, board, 17.75; Dominion Road Machinery Co., Ltd., grader parts, 28.38; Dominion Rubber Co., Ltd. (Toronto), rubber boots, 46.64; Dominion Rubber Co., Ltd. (Winnipeg), rubber boots, 69.27; Dominion Tar & Chemical Co., Ltd., creosote, 15.50; Chas. Donald, gravel, 6.45; Wm. Donavon, gravel, 38.00; Chas. O. Donnell, hay, 7.00; E. Donnelly, wood, 9.00; Ivan Donnelly, hardwood, 75.00; Joe Donnelly's Taxi, transportation, 11.00; Boyd Dool, cedar, 21.50; Clayton Dormer, pork, 33.20; Wm. Dormer, meat, 37.95; Geo. Doucette, gravel, 70.00; J. A. Doust, car livery, 50.00; Paul Doust, cedar, 22.33; Estate of David Dover, gas, oil, hardware, stationery, telephone calls, 108.47; I. J. Downey & Sons, gravel, stone, 506.80; Geo. Draper, provisions, 16.24; H. C. Draper, travelling expenses, 144.00; John Draper, gravel, 24.50; Almer Driver, cedar, provisions, earth, poles, 112.24; E. Driver, provisions, rent of lot, cedar, 132.43; J. Driver, rent of lot, cedar, poles, 169.55; J. L. Driver & Son, cartage, 19.50; W. Driver, lumber, 139.64; Delphis Drolet, blacksmithing, 32.00; A. Drouin, wood, 25.50; Drummond, McCall & Co., Ltd., chain, 875.89; H. A. Drury Co., Ltd., drill steel, 95.40; Dryden Lumber Co., Ltd., lumber, hardware, 45.38; A. Dube, transportation, cartage, 106.75; Frank Dube, cedar, 30.00; Armand Dubois, gas, blacksmithing, 33.40; Paul H. Dubois, barrels, 1.00; Jos. Dubuc, gravel, 59.70; Cham. Ducharme, coal, hardware, 22.60; Maurice Ducharme, gravel, 8.20; Euchauste Dufour, gravel, 50.15; Paul Dufour, board, 281.73; Jas. Dugas, sand, stone, fill, 162.95; Jos. Dugas, twine, 1.02; Howard Duggan, fifty per cent. of work done on road, 81.50; Wm. Dumond, explosives, cedar, 22.24; Geo. Dunbar, lumber, 20.76; H. C. Dunbar, lumber, 161.80; John Dungey, meat, 33.60; Wm. Dungey, meat, 68.00; Geo. Dunker, gravel, 223.95; Dan Dunn, gravel, 60.70; David Dunn, hay, 108.77; R. Dunn, Jr., provisions, 12.65; R. Dunn, Sr., potatoes, 17.00; Dunn Hardware Co., Ltd., explosives, hardware, coal, 5,278.65; Thos. Dunn, gravel, 11.40; J. M. Dunsmore, travelling expenses, 3.25; A. J. Dupuis, blacksmithing, 2.05; Fred Dupuis, rent of blacksmith shop and tools, 16.15; Alan Durance, explosives, 40.35; Durance Brothers & Co., hardware, explosives, oil, 1,116.50; Ed. Dussault, cedar, 4.95; J. A. Dwyer, provisions, soap, 89.74; Robt. Eade, gravel, 391.30; J. Easson, oats, 32.40; Ecclestone & Bates, Ltd., pipe, hardware, soldering, 2.05; Jas. Eckford, cedar, 21.60; Arken Eddy, scrapers, 5.00; C. N. Eddy, plow parts, 3.00; Mrs. N. F. Eden, gravel, 78.00; Edgar & Co., provisions, 113.13; Henry Edgar, gravel, 16.40; E. Edwards, cartage, .25; Edwards Hardware, hardware, roofing, cement, kitchenware, pipe, 8,023.69; Hector Edwards, provisions, 98.27; Herb Edwards, provisions, hardware, coal, lumber, oil, 3,569.89; E. Einarson, travelling expenses, 7.80; V. Einarson, wood, board, making towels, 41.50; Elk Lake Garage & Machine Works, gas, oil, 59.46; Geo. E. Elliott, meat, 13.50; Elliott Hotel, board, 41.00; J. H. Elliott, stationery, .75; M. Elliott, provisions, 8.00; W. Elliott, provisions, 38.25; Elliott's Drug Store, stationery, sulphur, 2.20; Mark Ellis, gravel, 65.20; Warren Ellis, board, 17.30; Ellsmere Bros., wood, 5.30; Jas. Ellsmere, cedar poles, 89.30; J. W. Emberson, provisions, car rental, 142.19; Tyner Emberson, provisions, gravel, 45.36; Walker Emberson, provisions, 60.15; Geo. Emery, beef, 42.08; J. Emlan, wood, 20.00; J. E. Emmerson, trucking, 99.38; Emo Hotel, board, 44.00; J. Emond, hardware, oil, provisions, 166.93; D. J. Emrey, car rental, repair parts, travelling expenses, 315.37; Paul Enearson, cartage, 66.50; S. D. Eplett & Sons, Ltd., salt, 2.50; J. Erickson, gravel, 9.00; W. Erwin, wood, 55.00; Espanola Garage, gas, 45.77; Nels Espeland, gravel, 59.04; J. Ethier, gravel, 64.00; Henry Etler, wood, heater, gravel, 385.45; David Euler, gravel, 41.00; Henry Euler, provisions, 20.90; H. G. Everett, borax, veterinary supplies, 3.90; The Evans Co., Ltd., lumber, lath, 210.06; Albert Evans, car rental, 4.00; Dr. J. A. C. Evans, services, examining men, 48.00; Wilbert Evans, trucking, car rental, 118.00; W. A. Evans, car rental, travelling expenses, 283.25; W. H. J. Evans, rail posts, 37.80; Andrew Everett, wood, 2.40; D. Ewald, provisions, 72.42; Wm. Fairhall, gravel, 297.31; Falcon Oils, Ltd., gas, oil, 383.22; Fallis Foote Co., hardware, coal, steel, oil, 734.11; Frank Fancy, travelling expenses, 4.85; A. Farley, provisions, 348.60; Ezra Farley, provisions, 124.52; G. E. Farlinger, lumber, hay, oats, rental of blankets, 1,572.84; E. Farnsworth, provisions, 77.70; Nells Fasso, gravel, 105.80; A. J. Fawcett, board, 274.00; Fee Motors, car repairs, gas, oil, 155.53; Feldman Bros., provisions, matches, soap, 58.20; Fenn, Anderson & Co., roofing, provisions, hay, oats, explosives, hardware, 5,037.65; A. N. Fenn, hardware, coal, oil, cement, 2,962.79; Jno. Fenton, hardwood, 47.50; Arthur R. Ferguson, moving equipment, 9.00; Gordon Ferguson, transportation, snowmobile hire, 160.50; R. Ferguson, tent rental, 79.00; Wm. Ferguson, wood, 63.00; Fetterley & Bailey, gas, oil, grease, repairs, 117.16; R. Fiegehen, lumber, board, rent of camp ground, wood, 2,011.80; Field Hotel,

Statutory—Cont ı :

General Work, Unemployment e c—Continued

board, 246.50; Angus Cooper & Son, lumber, 21.1 (, H. Cooper, car rental travelling expenses, 194.00; H. J. Cooper, rental ı transit and level, 30.00 Wm. Cooper, gas, oil, grease, car rental, hardware. 356 30; Mrs. W. Cooper, board, 738.00; Chas. Corbett, oil, 3.00; Corbett's g gas, oil, repairs, 135.57; Mrs. Lena N. Corbiere, gravel, 10.50; E. B. C d, travelling expenses, 20.20; Corona Lumber Yards, Ltd., hardware, 1 00 Thos. Corpal, services, 2.00; Geo. Corrigan, potatoes, 12.50; Corrugat Pipe Co., Ltd., culverts, 19,677.84; Frank Cosco, provisions, towelling, matches, etc., 11,258.68; O. Cote, gravel, fill, 71.42; Tom Cottingham, 10.72; Angus Coulter, transportation, 12.00; Wilfred Coultis, timber, 34. Coursol, plank, 10.00; Lorrain Courtemanche, repairs, 4.50; Mrs. C. usneau, lumber, 2.94; H. Cowan, travelling expenses, 11.40; Jas. Cowan, wo , 26 00; John Cowan, cedar, 55.00; Tom Cowan, gravel, 7.35; Geo. Cox, wo cedar, 123.38; John Cox, gravel, 114.40; Victor Cox, wood, 487.00; Coxn Transport, trucking, 1.95; Craig Bros., lumber, cartage, 843.29; W. H. Cra umber, freighting, 1,458.93; Crane Lumber Co., Ltd., hardware, lumber, 222 5 A W. Crawford, travelling expenses, 975.00; Alex. Crawford, elm poles, 2 4(I Creasor, car rental, 50.00; Dr. W. H. K. Crehan, services, examining n 00 E. Crespeau, gravel, 80.20; W. Crisp, hardware, provisions, gas, oil, 11 H. & G. Critchley, hardware, 42.55; L. A. Croghan, car rental, 92.00; D rossthwaite, gravel, 871.05; Chas. Crosswell, meat, 23.12; Mrs. W. Crowe, bo. , 47 20; Dr. L. E. Crowley, services, examining men, 64.00; Jack Crozier, woo 112 50; Wm. Crozier, meat, wood, 43.39; Dr. W. W. Cruise, services, exam ng men, 43.00; Miss Lillie Cryderman, gravel, 36.50; H. Cuilleroer, livery, 6 ; A. G. Culbert, provisions, 1,276.31; R. Culin, gas, oil, grease, repairs, 128.41 , G. Cumming, draughting supplies, 190.80; B. H. Cunningham, provisions, 6 5; John Currie, cedar poles, 7.20; Robt. Currie, meat, 79.40; Thos. Currie, hay, 15; Thos. Curtin, car hire, 6.00; J. Curtis, potatoes, 12.50; Geo. Cuthbertson, 14 48; Armand Cyr, boat rental, 5.00; E. Cyr, blacksmithing, 16.85; Jas. C , gravel, 115.50; F. Daigl gravel, fill, 123.45; Victor Dalcourt, gravel, 157 60, les Bros., charging batter 5.50; Herb Daley, cedar, 27.00; W. A. Dalgleish, car ntal and travelling expen 220.40; J. H. Dallaire, hardware, provisions, statio s, 146.87; Andy Daly, c 30.60; O. Dambumont, gravel, 49.10; M. Danell, h. ware explosives, station 81.95; Felix Danis, cedar, 27.00; G. Daoust, rock 04 10, Omer Daoust, e fill, 26.25; Darling's Garage, transportation, 102 0 J. Darlington, provisi soap, 1,969.24; R. M. Dart, lumber crayons, 1 00; n n Dauphinois, hard 13.70; Geo. Davenport, travelling expenses, 3 H. Y. Davidson t table cloth, 10.70; Jas. Davidson, posts, cedar 64 9 John Davidson, blac ing, 2.70; Davies & Crosby, provisions, 192.94, R Davies, t mber, t Ben Davis, hardwood, 18.00; Dr. D. Davis, serv s, examining men Davis, lumber, 31.50; Wilfrid Davison, lumber, 5 5. Harold Daw 3.25; I. U. Dawkins, travelling expenses, 1 00; Mr orne Dawson Thos. Dawson, gravel, 88.25; Wallace Dawson, 6 25, Anni gravel, 30.00; David W. Debassige, posts, bags 00, B. Debon, board, 117.44; Alfred Decasse, plank, 6.80; Fr. Dellandrea, Mrs. John Dellandrea, meat, 67.85; Delongchamp artage Co., .50; Deluxe Taxi & Transfer, livery, trucking, 1 12.75; D. 56.00; Mrs. Denhardt, provisions, 16.40; F. Denl dt, provisions Denis, wood, 3.75; F. J. Dennie, travelling expe s, 190.52, lath, blacksmithing, 8.00; John Dent, pork, 9.7(Desbarats 3.00; Jos. Desjardins, buggy, potatoes, 17.20; . Deslauriers S. Deslauriers, lumber, wood, 481.18; A. Deroche, wood, 44 rosiers, services, examining men, 22.00; A. Desrosie, cement and W. J. Detweiler, rubber boots, 61.00; H. Deyett, provisions, h gas, 1,318.21; Diamond Taxi, cartage, taxi servic 154.50; H oil, grease, 146.95; A. Dignard, lumber, 17.30; Chs. Dillon, tation, wood, cutting wood, 23.01; Dr. O. C. Dinwell, men, 13.00; J. A. Dinsmore, car rental and travning expen Disston & Sons, Ltd., tools, 295.34; Chas. J. D ery, 10 transportation, 10.20; P. E. Doal, mattresses, prisions, stra 83.55; Reg. Doal, car rental, 6.00; Dobbs Bros., umber, re F. Dobbs, provisions, cedar poles, 116.24; Ira Dobs, provisi Dobbs, provisions, hardware, oilcloth, paint, 512.4 Milner D 37.65; W. Dobbs, provisions, board, 24.14; Geo Dodds, car Doherty, cedar, 24.80; Miles Doherty, blacksmithg, 76.10; 495.60; Mrs. G. Dollar, board, 34.50; D. G. Dorn, travelling Dominion Equipment & Supply Co., Ltd., machiry parts, 71

Statutory—Continued

General Wor Unemployment Relief—Cont

Government Dock, freight, 8.3; **Dominion Hotel**, board, Road Machinery Co., Ltd., grer parts, 28.38; Domini... (Torouto), rubber boots, 46.64; ominion Rubber Co., Ltd... boots, 69.27; Dominion Tar & Chmical Co., Ltd., creosote... **gravel, 6.45**; Wm. Donavon, gvel, 38.00; **Chas.** O. Do... **Donnelly, wood**, 9.00; Ivan Donelly, **hardwood**, 75.00; ... **transportation**, 11.00; Boyd Do, cedar, 21.50; Clayton D... **Wm. Dormer**, meat, 37.95; Geo.)oucette, **gravel**, 70.00; ... 50.00; **Paul Doust**, cedar, 22.3. **Estate of** David Dove... **stationery**, telephone calls, 108.4; I. J. **Downey** & Sons ... **Geo. Draper**, provisions, 16.24 H. C. Draper, travel... **John Draper**, gravel, 24.50; Amer **Driver**, cedar, p... 112.24; **E. Driver, provisions, rnt of lot**, cedar, 132.4... **cedar, poles**, 169.55; J. L. Dri r & Son, cartage, 19.5... 139.64; **Delphis Drolet**, blacksi hing, 32.00; A. Drou... **mond, McCall & Co., Ltd.**, ch 1, 875.89; H. A. Dru... 95.40; **Dryden Lumber** Co., L., lumber, hardware ... **portation, cartage**, 106.75; Fr. : Dube, cedar, 30.0... **blacksmithing**, 33.40; **Paul** H. I bois, barrels, 1.00; J... **Cham. Ducharme, coal**, har... e, 22.60; Maurice ... Euchauste Dufour, gravel, 50 ; Paul Dufour, bo... sand, stone, fill, 162.95; **Jos.** Du s, twine, 1.02; How... of work done on road, 81.50; Wm. Dumond, ex... Dunbar, lumber, 20.76; H. C. D oar, lumber, 161.8... **Wm. Dungey, meat**, 68.00; G. Dunker, gravel... **60.70; David Dunn, hay**, 10... R. Dunn, Jr., p... **potatoes, 17.00; Dunn** Har... Co., Ltd., expl... **Thos. Dunn, gravel**, 11.40; J. . Dunsmore, ... **Dupuis, blacksmithing**, 2.05; I. I Dupuis, rent... **16.15; Alan** Durance, exp... 40.35; Dur... **explosives**, oil, 1,116.50; I. I ssault, cedar, ... **soap, 89.74**; Robt. Eade, ... 391.30; J. ... **Bates, Ltd.**, pipe, hardware ... ring, 2.05; ... **Eddy**, scrapers, 5.00; C. N. ... plow ... **78.00**; Edgar & Co., provis... 3.13; H... cartage, .25; Edwards Har... hard... 8,023.69; Hector Edwards... ware, coal, **lumber, oil**. 3... Einarson, wood, board, ... Works, gas, oil, 59.46; G... J. H. Elliott, stationery... 38.25; Elliott's Drug St... Warren Ellis, board, 17... poles, 89.30; J. W. En... provisions, gravel, 45.3... beef, 42.08; J. Emlan, w... board, 44.00; J. Emor... rental, repair parts, travel... S. D. Eplett & Sons, Ltd., ... 55.00; Espanola Garage, ... gravel, 64.00; Henry Etle... 41.00; Henry Euler, provi... 3.90; The Evans Co., Ltd., ... Dr. J. A. C. Evans, servi... **car rental**, 118.00; W. A. E... Evans, rail posts, 37.80; ... 72.42; Wm. Fairhall, gravel ... Foote Co., hardware, coal, ... 4.85; A. Farley, provision... Farlinger, lumber, hay, oat... visions, 77.70; Nells Fasso, ... Motors, car repairs, gas, ... 58.20; Fenn, Anderson & ... ware, 5,037.65; A. N. Fen... hardwood, 47.50; Arthur ... transportation, snowmol... Ferguson, wood, 63.00; ... Fiegehen, lumber, boar...

... on & ... wood, ... ouve- ... ental, ... aham, ... gravel, ... Graham, ... Grainger, ... Grant, ... n, 23.00; ... Graven- ... rst Banner, ... ; Town of ... provisions, ... provisions, ... 0; S. Green, ... Green's Camp, ... o., steel pipe, 8.83; W. Green- ... , 16.80; Arthur ... r, 260.00; Thos. ... provisions, 10.80; Dr. J. B. Grieve, ... 6.76; T. C. Grieves, ... Griffith, trucking, ... ing expenses, 11.95; ... Grimm, timber, pro- ... gas, car parts, repairs, ... wood, 60.00; F. Grubbs ... oleon Guenard, gravel ... 5; E. Guenette, gravel ... red Guerin, chalk line, ... nt of camp site, 169.72; 84.32; John S. Gumley, ... Gustafson, meat, 16.64; ... ions, 62.40; H. Hackett, ... 0; Edwin Hagan, wood, ... John Hainchanan, wood, ... ar rental and taxi service, ... 234.99; S. Halverson, meat, ... Hall, repairs, 6.00; G. F. Hall, ... camp material, 5.00; Lloyd Hall, ... .15; **Wm. Hall, cedar**, 16.80; ... n, hay, 13.20; **Dr. C. J.** Hamilton, ... on, **lumber**, 514.71; Mrs. H. I. ... **provisions**, 24.7... H. P. ... ilton, pr... ... visions, 5... ; H. Hampel, ... , 38.0... arry Hands, ... travel... penses, 6.30; ... car ... avelling ... 364.95; ... tionery, ... , 63.14; ... visions, ... thing, ... Harris ... Co., ... ans- ... vel, ...

Statutory—Continued

General Work, Unemployment Relief—Continued

board, 35.50; A. T. Fife & Co., explosives, wire, 36.75; Fife Hardware Co., hardware, 106.53; A. Filheim, gravel, 30.75; Jos. Filiatreault, provisions, 47.20; H. Filliatreau, gravel, 34.10; V. T. Filion, ties, 72.50; Murray Fingland, cartage, 15.00; D. J. Finlan, gravel, 16.20; William Finlay, Sr., milk, 7.50; A. Fisher, provisions, 9.50; Art Fisher, meat, 24.96; Chas. Fisher, provisions, 15.44; F. H. Fisher, gravel, 9.00; Mrs. L. Fisher, provisions, 54.00; Wm. Fisher, hardwood, 50.00; Dick Fitz, wood, 40.00; L. Fitz, wood, poles, 63.20; Fitszimmons Fruit Co., Ltd., provisions, 1,193.01; O. L. Flanagan, travelling expenses, bedding, 189.94; R. Fleck, timber, 15.00; P. M. Fleming, gas, machinery parts, rent of drill, 192.32; John W. Fogg, Ltd. (Kirkland Lake), lumber, 2,123.24; JohnW. Fogg, Ltd. (Timmins), lumber, 192.96; John Fonk, wood, gravel, 41.60; Thos. Forbes, provisions, wood, 185.55; Presley Ford, repairs, 6.00; R. Ford, hardware, iron, coal, 220.04; J. Foreman, wood, 46.83; E. Forget, cedar, 42.80; Mrs. Elizabeth Forsythe, gravel, 52.30; Fort Frances Creamery Co., Ltd., provisions, 1,028.75; Fort Frances Pulp & Paper Co., Ltd., blue printing, 2.00; Fort Frances Service Station, gas, grease, 48.87; Fort Frances Wholesalers, Ltd., provisions, lye, etc., 7,147.62; City of Fort William, evidence at inquest, 3.50; H. Forth, provisions, barrels, 324.75; A. Fortier, provisions, 819.30; W. Fortier, wood, meat, 74.13; Emile Fortin, hay, 29.86; Jos. Fortin, beef, 15.68; J. L. Foster, spikes, cartage, 2.98; G. W. Foulkes, travelling expenses, 8.00; Pane Fournier, gravel, 50.20; Paul Fournier, fill, gravel, 33.75; E. Fowler, timber, 25.00; The Fowler Hardware Co., Ltd., tools, hardware, oil, 100.09; Jas. Fox, transportation, 5.00; The Milton Francis Lumber Co., Ltd., lumber, hardware, 588.38; L. Frappier, cedar, 31.90; Andrew Fraser, timber, 5.76; Dr. Donald Fraser, services, examining men, 1.00; D. Fraser, gravel, 30.60; G. L. Fraser, gravel, 206.20; W. Fraser, beef, 17.76; Herman Frederick, gravel, 29.70; Dr. J. S. Freeborn, wood, 125.00; Thos. A. Freeland, car rental, 324.00; F. Freeman, cedar, 12.50; R. M. French, travelling expenses, 9.90; A. Fry, provisions, 46.40; Harold Fry, wood, board, 98.60; Richard Fry, board, blacksmithing, 1,368.95; R. Fry, wood, straw, gravel, rent of camp site, 57.46; Robt. Fuller, gravel, 41.64; E. Fullerton, gravel, 40.00; John Funk, wood, 25.00; N. Gadoury, Sr., straw, 2.10; Narcisse Gadoury, logs, 35.00; Mrs. Rose Gagne, board, 7.00; D. Gagnon, gravel, 81.60; R. Gainor, wood, 21.00; L. Galipeau, transportation, 9.12; Napoleon Galipeau, car rental, gas, oil, 1,940.48; Paul Galipeau, car rental, 70.56; Thos. Gallagher, gravel, 392.40; Paul Gamache, blacksmithing, 21.85; Gamble-Robinson Cochrane, Ltd., provisions, 44.30; Gamble-Robinson Fort William, Ltd., provisions, 53.28; Gamble-Robinson Sault Ste. Marie, Ltd., provisions, 220.00; C. Gamsby, vegetables, 9.60; Thos. Ganton, gravel, 273.00; Allen Gardens, provisions, 18.00; A. Gardiner, oil, faucet, 1.35; W. Gareau, grease, tools, hardware, 34.25; Frank Gartshore, car rental, lumber, travelling expenses, 1,806.28; W. Gartshore, car rental, 35.00; D. Gascon, gravel, 32.40; Frank Gatty, hay, 17.31; L. Gaudette, gravel, 5.10; A. R. Gangion, yeast, 1.40; A. Gauthier, lumber, tube, 5.86; Jos. Gauthier (Blind River), provisions, 14.50; Joe Gauthier (Harty), wood, 33.00; O. Gauthier, gravel, 16.70; T. Gauthier, beef, 43.09; G. Gavin, car rental, 354.00; W. Geall, provisions, 81.21; F. Geauvreau, cedar, 32.75; E. W. Geddes, car rental, 53.70; D. Gee, provisions, 79.84; H. Gelinas, gravel, 31.80; Dr. W. T. Gemmell, services, examining men, 5.00; J. D. Gemmell, provisions, 222.65; General Steel Wares, Ltd., tools, hardware, 4,768.24; General Supply Co. of Canada, Ltd., machinery parts, 1,855.99; Harry Genno, cedar, 5.10; Leslie Genno, gravel, 10.00; E. George, meat, 30.54; M. George, wood, provisions, 39.67; George & Shamess, provisions, 326.40; Chris. Gerber, cedar, 21.13; Earl Gerber, provisions, 10.00; N. T. Gerhard, cedar, 11.00; Patrick Germain, provisions, 31.15; Albert J. Geroux, hardware, cedar, poles, 143.25; N. Geroux, trucking, 143.75; D. Gervais, provisions, 75.92; P. Gervais, gravel, 57.30; Dunn Gibbs, board, 101.60; A. B. Gibson, provisions, board, 485.64; Gibson Garage, gas, oil, 4.72; Robt. Gibson, provisions, 364.30; R. G. Gibson, provisions, 398.80; Wm. Gibson, hay, 87.83; Omer Gignac, rent of blacksmith shop, blacksmithing, 18.50; A. Gilbert, hay, 95.33; A. Gilchrist, cartage, 3.00; Mack Gillies, meat, 19.76; Gillmor & Noden, paint, hardware, 829.47; G. R. Gillon, rental of surveying instruments, 60.00; A. Gingrass, hardware, coal, repairs, 30.25; Jules Gingras, gravel, 254.80; Arthur Gionett, wood, 46.37; F. A. Giroux, cedar, 6.68; Mrs. F. A. Giroux, board, 34.40; Fred Gjos, hardware, sash, stoneboat repairs, 20.05; Dr. H. Glendinning, services, examining men, 47.00; Glengarry Dray, trucking, 471.92; M. S. Godfrey, provisions, tools, hardware, gas, oil, 3,100.59; M. Godin, transportation, 69.25; Albert A. Gohn, provisions, 42.00; A. C. Gohn, vegetables, 12.00; Steve Golec, blacksmithing, hardware, 9.15; C. E. Gooderham, transportation, 37.25; C. Goodman, board, 14.25; Goodman & Co., hardware, coal, explosives, rubber boots, 290.55; H. Goodman & Son, explosives, nails, 40.20;

Statutory—Continued

General Work, Unemployment Relief—Continued

Allen Goodwin, meat, 54.18; Norman Goodwin, cartage, 16.98; Geo. Gordon & Co., Ltd., lumber, 4,129.25; A. Gosselin, garage, rent 11.40; John Gostlin, wood, 120.00; Hector Goulard, explosives, 4.55; Irving Gouldie, livery, 4.00; F. Gouvereau, cedar, 32.75; Graham Bros., provisions, 3.35; Gordon Graham, car rental, transportation, 66.25; G. H. Graham, hay, provisions, 357.08; J. Graham, gyproc board, 9.60; Jas. N. Graham, wood, gravel, 30.90; Roy Graham, gravel, 29.50; R. L. Graham, posts, 11.25; Wm. Graham, gravel, 41.10; W. H. Graham, wood, 35.00; Graham's Garage, gas, car repairs, oil, 13.69; John H. Grainger, provisions, hardware, gas, oil, 1,922.07; Wm. Granger, gravel, 19.20; C. Grant, meat, 18.56; P. J. Grant, provisions, 512.40; R. Grant, transportation, 23.00; Eric A. Gratton, gravel, 54.00; S. Gratton, lumber, gravel, wood, 181.30; Gravenhurst Auto Repairs, gas, oil, car parts and repairs, 179.70; Gravenhurst Banner, advertisement, 6.50; Gravenhurst Service Station, gas, oil, 310.56; Town of Gravenhurst, installing lights to office, 4.79; Mrs. Wm. Grawbarger, provisions, 31.07; Geo. Gray, oats, 15.00; A. Green, lumber, 15.24; G. B. Green, provisions, 61.15; John F. Green & Son, provisions, towelling, brooms, 149.60; S. Green, meat, 33.48; Green's Tourist Camp, rent of boat, meals, 11.00; Green's Camp, gas, oil, 10.25; Ezra Greenier, meat, 18.48; B. Greenspoon & Co., steel pipe, 175.50; S. Greenwood & Son, oats, hay, provisions, hardware, 608.83; W. Greenwood & Son, cartage, hardware, 4.25; Greenwood's, provisions, 16.80; Arthur Greer, hardwood, 7.50; Jack Greer, gravel, 235.40; M. C. Greer, 260.00; Thos. Greer, wood, 37.50; Walter Greer, repairs, 3.60; S. Grenier, provisions, 10.80; E. Grennier, provisions, 12.16; David Grexton, gravel, 73.92; Dr. J. B. Grieve, services, examining men, 6.00; Grieve & Powell, provisions, 378.76; T. C. Grieves, cedar, 22.74; D. M. Griffith, blacksmithing, 91.18; W. T. Griffith, trucking, 90.00; Thos. Grigg, gas, oil, 8.72; Wm. Grimmer, travelling expenses, 11.95; Wm. Grimes, travelling expenses, car rental, 123.88; O. Grimm, timber, provisions, 286.75; Jos. Groulx, gravel, 88.80; Groves Motors, gas, car parts, repairs, storage, 7.35; Jno. Grozell, board, 10.20; C. Grubbs, wood, 60.00; F. Grubbs, wood, poles, 125.00; Lawrence Guay, cedar, 160.16; Napoleon Guenard, gravel, 53.50; Clo. Guenette, gas, oil, car parts and repairs, 310.75; E. Guenette, gravel, 70.60; Jos. Guenette, tools, hardware, repairs, 84.20; Wilfred Guerin, chalk line, 4.00; F. Guidotti, gas, 3.99; A. Gullberg, provisions, rent of camp site, 169.72; Gull River Lumber Co., Ltd., lumber, gravel, sash, 384.32; John S. Gumley, travelling expenses, 3.10; E. Gustafson, meat, 26.52; H. Gustafson, meat, 16.64; Alf. Guthrie, lumber, 5.04; Nicholas Hacker, provisions, 62.40; H. Hackett, transportation, 7.80; Ern Haerlen, blacksmithing, 1.50; Edwin Hagan, wood, provisions, 32.00; Township of Hagar, cedar, 75.60; John Hainchanan, wood, 62.50; Geo. Halcrow, posts, 54.00; Alfred Haley, car rental and taxi service, 51.00; Haliburton Lumber Co., Ltd., lumber, 1,234.99; S. Halverson, meat, 40.56; Adam Hall, Ltd., range parts, 1.36; F. G. Hall, repairs, 6.00; G. F. Hall, blacksmithing, 40.00; G. W. Hall, storage on camp material, 5.00; Lloyd Hall, provisions, wood, barrow, transportation, 109.15; Wm. Hall, cedar, 16.80; Albert Hambell, provisions, 32.88; Chas. Hamilton, hay, 13.20; Dr. C. J. Hamilton, services, examining men, 15.00; Geo. D. Hamilton, lumber, 514.71; Mrs. H. I. Hamilton, gravel, sand, 125.37; H. J. Hamilton, provisions, 24.75; Dr. H. P. Hamilton, services, examining men, 37.00; Jas. Hamilton, provisions, sand fill, 155.37; J. A. Hamilton, gas, 4.50; Thos. Hammell, provisions, 53.80; H. Hampel, Sr., provisions, 26.64; Hampshire's Taxi, taxi service, 38.00; Harry Hands, provisions, 17.00; Seth Hanes, repairs, 8.05; F. Haney, travelling expenses, 6.30; R. F. Haney, travelling expenses, 3.05; A. B. Hanna, car rental, travelling expenses, 208.22; C. Hanna, cedar, 18.40; H. Hanna, provisions, soap, 364.95; W. Hanna & Co., Ltd., roofing, hardware, provisions, oats, explosives, stationery, 584.18; John Hannikanen, wood, 78.75; Jos. Hannon, provisions, soap, 63.14; J. Hannsell, board, 79.70; O. Hansen, gravel, 30.00; Hare Bros., provisions, straw, oil, 426.91; L. Harney, trucking, 1.50; Horace G. Harper, blacksmithing, fencing, 66.27; Harris Abattoir (Western), Ltd., provisions, 1,731.04; Harris Abattoir Co., Ltd. (Sault Ste. Marie), provisions, 3,885.46; Harris Abattoir Co., Ltd. (Sudbury), provisions, 856.14; Fred Harris, fill, 44.25; Geo. Harris, transportation, 4.00; Rufus Harris, wood, provisions, fill, 49.55; Wm. Harris, gravel, 5.60; W. J. Harris, lath, gas, 7.89; Norman Harrison, wood, 25.00; Royce Harrison, livery, 3.00; Walter Harrison, wood, rental of tent, 48.00; Wm. B. Harrison, wood, gravel, 330.80; Mrs. Henry Harron, beef, 42.48; Arthur Harrow, cedar, 37.20; H. Hart, hay, 138.84; J. Harten, blacksmithing, 50.70; D. J. Hartle, tools, hardware, stationery, 861.63; Henry Hartman, hay, 74.31; A. T. Hartwick, provisions, board, 106.20; H. E. Hartwick, hay, 93.50; Ben Harvey, wood, 30.00; Mrs. E. J. Harvey, material from borrow pit, 25.00; Robt. Harvey, lumber, 744.40; J. Haterly, gravel, 12.90; A. Ernest Hatherley, gas, 24.91; Mrs.

Statutory—Continued

General Work, Unemployment Relief—Continued

H. Hatherley, provisions, 8.40; H. E. Hatherley, cedar, rental of pipes, 1.35; Jas. M. Hatherley, gravel, 7.35; Hugo Haufe, provisions, 4.12; Oscar Haufe, provisions, straw, 41.56; Alex. Hawa, meat, 40.00; Hawk Lake Lumber Co., Ltd., lumber, 3,324.21; Mrs. A. Hawke, Sr., provisions, 8.80; Claude Hawke, cartage, 22.31; Hawkins Bros., Ltd., hay, oats, 46.30; John Hawkins, provisions, towelling, 367.52; H. Hay, travelling expenses, 3.50; Geo. Hayes, cartage, transportation, barrels, 538.00; R. E. Hayes, oats, 60.00; Wm. Hayes, provisions, gravel, 76.84; W. J. Hayes, rental of camp site, 6.00; Eugene Hays, ploughshare, 1.25; Willis Hays, camp rental, 8.00; A. T. Hazelhurst, provisions, 38.20; W. L. Head, hardware, provisions, soap, 1,737.46; A. Heaney, transportation, 7.50; The Hearst Demonstration Farm, butter, 5.00; C. Heaslip, explosives, cartage, 64.87; E. Heaslip, gravel, 47.10; Mrs. Thos. Heaton, meat, 44.96; Narcisse Hebert, cedar, gravel, 114.49; Ernest Heidman, provisions, 64.27; Fred Heinbecker, gravel, 166.10; Frank Helmkay, trucking, 54.69; R. Hembruff, car rental, 199.40; F. Henry, tools, 4.90; Henry Motor Co., car repairs, 20.60; Geo. Herbert, hay, oats, 14.66; Narcisse Herbert, cedar, 52.50; E. J. Hermiston, gravel, 29.85; Mrs. F. T. Hermiston, gravel, 49.95; Hern Hardware, Ltd., hardware, coal, cement, 1,304.76; Mrs. Henry Herron, gravel, 103.60; C. Heslip, transportation, cartage, 24.25; Bruce E. Hewitson, travelling expenses, 2.05; F. Hewitt, cedar, 59.20; W. H. Hewitt, gas, oil, 9.29; F. Heyder, fill, 59.35; J. Heyder, fill, 4.35; T. A. Heye, gas, oil, car parts and repairs, 553.36; Wallace Hickie, rent of camp site, 4.00; J. Hicks, wood, 52.50; J. H. Hicks, rent of lot, gravel, wood, 112.80; Mrs. S. Hicks, provisions, 3.75; T. W. Hicks, gravel, 37.60; Jas. Hie, wood, 54.00; Mrs. E. Hiedman, provisions, 11.00; Higgins & Burke, Ltd., provisions, 2,574.04; Alex. Hill, posts, 55.50; Chris. Hill, provisions, 9.50; Frederick Hill, wood, cedar, 17.60; Harold H. Hill, trucking, 126.88; J. M. Hill, travelling expenses, 7.50; Randolph Hill, provisions, 33.84; S. J. Hill & Co., provisions, lumber, wood, oats, oil, 1,330.70; Toby Hill, cedar, meat, 54.78; Walter Hill, car rental, gas, oil, 175.55; Hill-Clark-Francis, Ltd., lumber, tile, 296.52; E. Hillman, car rental, gas, oil, 71.39; M. Hillman, gas, oil, 21.48; Chas. Hinsberger, meat, 32.16; Hinsperger Harness Co., Ltd., ticks, tent flys and repairs, 123.50; J. Hirch, fish, 9.50; Ernest Hobbs, provisions, 42.08; Allan Hobden, lumber, wood, 485.93; Hobson-Gauthier, Ltd., provisions, 2,186.67; J. W. Hocking, provisions, 8.00; Albert Hodges, hay, 62.70; Herbert Hodgson, milk, 6.80; A. Hodson, vegetables, 29.75; Herbert Hodgens, timber, 8.18; Alvin Hogg, gravel, 143.70; Mrs. Alvin Hogg, board, 104.60; Ralph Hogg, plank, 77.22; N. Hoggard, provisions, 12.80; Herbert Hodgson, provisions, 30.40; H. J. Hodgson, lumber, 10.22; F. J. Holliday, provisions, 137.03; Dr. Arthur B. Holme, services, examining men, 35.00; B. V. Holmes, kitchenware, 143.21; F. P. Holmes, travelling expenses, 37.50; John Holmes, meat, 38.48; Julius Holtz, hardwood, 30.00; D. Hood, travelling expenses, 16.05; H. Hook, gravel, 9.50; W. Hooper, sand, gravel, 82.70; O. A. Hoover, provisions, 33.32; C. Hopkins, tamarac, 7.50; David Hopkins, gravel, 49.50; Roy Hopkins, meat, 23.50; Lorne Horner, taxi service, 8.00; Harry Horner, gravel, 29.40; Hose Hardware Co., hardware, twine, 289.12; T. O. Hoskins, gravel, 30.00; Bert Houle, meat, hay, gravel, 60.20; Jos. Houle, fill, 124.60; L. Houle, iron, wagon repairs, 20.65; Hounsell Bros., lumber, 36.65; J. W. Hounsell, board, 105.80; Bazil Howe, wood, 37.50; Geo. Howell, piling, 10.00; Lucy K. Howell, replacing fencing, 25.00; H. S. Howland, Sons & Co., Ltd., tools, hardware, 1,081.65; P. Huard, timber, 4.20; A. Huber, gravel, 103.10; W. Huber, travelling expenses, 143.15; A. Hubner, gravel, 4.40; Hudon-Hebert-Chaput, provisions, 116.55; Hudson's Bay Co. (Dinorwic Post), provisions, hardware, gas, oil, 345.93; Hudson's Bay Co. (Gogama), gas, oil, 19.95; Hudson's Bay Co. (Mattice), hardware, roofing, provisions, towelling, 920.71; Hudson's Bay Co. (Sioux Lookout), provisions, towelling, 1,557.83; F. Huggert, provisions, oats, hay, 261.44; Geo. W. Hughes & Co., Ltd., plow part, lumber, 23.25; Hughes Owens Co., Ltd., draughting supplies, 396.09; W. Hughes, gas, 1.70; T. L. Hughson, travelling expenses, 5.05; John H. Hulbig, wood, 24.00; P. Humes, wood, 11.25; Wm. Hummel, blacksmithing, 18.15; Israel Humphrey, gravel, 51.70; Humphrey Municipal Telephone System, phone services, repairs to telephone lines, 54.50; T. H. Hungerford, provisions, 29.90; A. E. Hunt, cartage, 115.00; S. Hunt, explosives, hardware, 50.18; Hunt's Service Store, provisions, 2.00; John Hunter, cedar, gravel, 79.65; J. S. Hunter, provisions, 109.12; Louis Hunter, bricks, 4.76; S. F. Hunter, car rental, 75.00; The Huntsville Forester, printing, 2.40; Huntsville & Lake of Bays Telephone Co., Ltd., phone service, moving poles, 425.53; Huntsville, Lake of Bays & Lake Simcoe Navigation Co., Ltd., transportation, 184.15; Huntsville Planing Mills, lath, nails, lumber, 3.66; Huntsville Trading Co., tools, grain, cartage, hardware, 4,284.83; Mrs. E. Hurrell, provisions, 12.00;

Statutory—Continued

General Work, Unemployment Relief—Continued

Wm. Hurrell, Provisions, 12.00; H. M. Hurst, car rental, 8.00; Hussey, Ferrier Meat Co., Ltd., provisions, 548.24; Wm. Hutchins, cartage, 2,071.00; Dr. E. D. Hutchinson, services, examining men, 12.00; Hutchison Bros., provisions, soap, 753.22; R. J. Hutchison, gravel, 61.80; Dr. R. L. Hutton, services, examining men, 3.00; A. L. Hyre, cedar, 14.50; Hydro-Electric Power Commission of Ontario, relocating poles, cost of lineman during blasting, 452.80; Hy-Way Service Station, gas, oil, 426.00; M. Ibbitson, car rental, 60.00; John Ibbitson, ties, 9.00; Thos. Ibbitson, provisions, 8.50; Ideal Drug Co., Ltd., veterinary supplies, 9.40; Ideal Grocery, provisions, 666.64; Jos. Ikens, hardwood, 33.00; Imperial Bank of Canada, cheques, 9.00; Imperial Oil Ltd., (Toronto), gas, oil, grease, 4,038.10; Imperial Oil, Ltd. (Winnipeg), gas, oil, grease, 1,152.95; Department of Indian Affairs, gravel, wood, sand, 268.34; Instruments, Ltd., draughting supplies, 234.10; International Nickel Co. of Canada, Ltd., drill steel, 59.00; International Stores, hardware, provisions, transportation, gas, oil, 1,863.69; International Transit, Ltd., fares, 110.55; Gordon Ireland, transportation, 3.00; C. Ironmonger, gravel, 7.80; W. A. Ironsides, stone, 3.80; Mrs. Jos. Irvine, cleaning office, 54.05; Chas. W. Irwin, provisions, 25.65; Mrs. F. Irwin, laundry, 14.75; Samuel Irwin, wood, 67.18; J. A. Isaac, repairs, 14.75; Fred C. Ivy Co., provisions, 1,333.21; Charlie Jacklin, hay, gravel, provisions, cartage, 1,050.92; Jos. Jacklin, milk, hay, fill, provisions, wood, 286.95; Claud Jackson, rent of camp site, 59.00; Mrs. Elizabeth Jackson, provisions, 78.50; Geo. Jackson, borrow, 25.00; Jno. E. Jackson, gravel, 104.90; Jackson & Limbert, stationery, 9.70; R. C. Jackson, provisions, 7.15; R. S. Jackson, provisions, 11.00; Sam Jackson, provisions, 37.75; S. McT. Jackson, rental of cutter and robe, 7.50; Wm. Jackson, wood, 12.00; John Jacques, car rental, trucking, 323.50; S. Jacques, livery, 24.00; Mrs. R. Jalbert, lumber, wood, posts, 201.50; B. James, gravel, 175.00; C. James, cedar, 14.50; D. W. James, gas, 4.50; H. W. James, blacksmithing, 16.96; Thos. Jameus, tamarac, 13.00; Herb. Jamieson, gravel, 14.10; John Jarvi, fill, 21.60; H. P. Jarvis, travelling expenses, 10.35; Arthur Jeffery, wood, gravel, 91.53; Andrew Jenkins, provisions, wood, 748.32; Jos. Jenkins, gravel, 10.00; P. Jette, wood, 3.00; Geo. Jewell, meat, 17.36; V. J. Jewell, roofing, 40.50; S. W. Jewitt, gravel, cedar, 19.85; W. S. Jewett, provisions, 32.30; H. H. Joanisse, hardware, roofing, paint, tools, 134.19; Theo Jodoin, provisions, 67.26; Geo. Jodouin, earth, 38.45; Isidore Jodouin, cedar, 168.92; B. Johnson, gravel, 24.80; Ben Johnson, pork, 14.56; Johnson Bros., car parts, repairs, 31.75; Johnson & Co., lumber, blacksmithing, 16.18; Emil Johnson, provisions, 4.00; Ish. Johnson, gravel, 27.45; J. Johnson, provisions, 2.40; J. W. Johnson, gravel, 38.60; Johnson Municipal Telephone System, installing phone, rental of phone and services, 43.19; Peter Johnson, rental of batteries, 16.65; Johnson's Pharmacy, horse liniment, 1.15; A. E. Johnstone, provisions, hardware, 2,089.01; David Johnston & Son, blacksmithing, 16.11; D. Johnston, blacksmithing, 90.45; Don T. Johnston, car rental, 344.00; I. E. Johnston, oil, matches, netting, 2.93; Dr. J. A. Johnston, services, examining men, 10.00; Dr. T. J. Johnston, services, examining men, 30.00; Mrs. Rose Johnstone, board, 152.50; T. F. Johnston, lumber, 59.28; W. Johnston, gravel, 13.40; Nestor Jokinen, lumber, 15.28; Adelaire Jolin, wood, 43.81; C. Jonassen, provisions, 59.44; Chas. Joncas, gravel, sand, 46.25; Frank Jones, cedar, 246.50; Geo. Jones, trucking, slabs, 340.00; Peter Jones, fish, 12.75; T. Jones & Son, lumber, hardware, 1,063.54; John Jordon, transportation, 8.00; Dr. J. M. Jory, services, examining men, 8.00; N. Joseph, provisions, gas, oil, 637.40; Geo. Joudouin, gravel, 57.70; F. A. Kalar, repairs, 2.75; S. Kallio, gravel, 9.50; Kaministiquia Lumber Co., Ltd., lumber, 135.86; Richard P. Kanne, vegetables, 11.60; Kapuskasing Co-Operative Dairy Co., Ltd., butter, 40.38; Kapuskasing Supply Co., Ltd., provisions, pipe, heater, drygoods, machinery parts, 1,043.54; John Karlash, provisions, 96.83; Wm. Karlash, provisions, 45.56; Jacob Kaufmen, Ltd., lumber, 359.53; N. Kauffmann, wood, 68.00; Arnold Kause, sauerkraut, 14.95; J. S. Kaye, provisions, 177.94; Victor Kaye, straw, 6.00; Martin Kehoe, cedar, 42.24; John Kelly, Jr., provisions, 33.68; Kelly & Kimberley, coal, 202.60; N. A. Kelly, gas, car rental and repairs, cartage, 914.37; T. J. Kelly, provisions, 269.05; Geo. Kemp, gravel, 49.30; Mrs. Wm. Kemp, gravel, 7.80; Kena Store, explosives, hardware, oil, 132.45; Chas. Kennedy, provisions, oil, 60.28; T. J. Kennedy, travelling expenses, 40.50; Con. Kennelly, hauling, 14.00; The Kent House, board, 8.50; Guy H. Kenzett, cedar, 52.50; Bert Keown, meat, 29.50; Wm. Keown, provisions, cartage, hay, 114.89; Alex. Kernohan, wood, 23.25; Hugh and Mrs. Hugh Kernohan, board, 145.40; Albert Kerr, provisions, 50.00; Chas. D. Kerr, travelling expenses, 14.15; P. Kerr, travelling expenses, 172.15; Keyes Hardware, Ltd., explosives, 5.10; Cecil T. Kidd, hardware, provisions, oil, 1,983.65; D. R. Kidd, hardware, explosives, paint, tools, 1,767.18; Mrs.

Statutory—Continued

General Work, Unemployment Relief—Continued

Geo. Kidd, provisions, 1.71; Geo. Kidd, cedar, 131.00; Mason Kidd, provisions, 30.25; M. V. Kidd, provisions, 60.00; R. D. Kidd, shovels, 11.25; J. W. Kilburn, car rental and travelling expenses, 291.75; Jas. Kilby, wheelbarrows, 45.00; L. Kilpatrick, oats, 70.32; Mrs. A. J. Kimball, board, 43.50; G. Kimball, car rental, 30.00; Archie King, cedar, 85.70; Arthur King, wood, 120.62; C. F. King, travelling expenses, 52.20; Jas. King, gravel, 44.60; Leonard King, cedar, 30.35; Mrs. Lorne King, laundry, 10.45; Kingsboro & Baxter, coal, hardware, explosives, 49.68; Louis Kingsbury, gravel, 8.10; Mrs. Albert Kingshott, poles, rent of camp grounds, 18.55; Edward Kingshott, hardwood, 52.50; Wm. Kingshott, hay, 9.00; King's Printer, 4,248.59; L. R. Kinley, travelling expenses, 6.75; Harry Kinney, vegetables, 16.70; Robt. Kinney, provisions, 50.04; Kinzett Bros., cedar, 131.00; H. Kirby, rock, gravel, 177.30; N. W. Kirby, gas, oil, lumber, 83.15; Geo. Kirk, gravel, 49.00; Wm. Kirk & Son, oilcloth, towelling, 9.75; A. F. Kirkham, roofing, provisions, hardware, 911.50; I. Kirkham, travelling expenses, 5.25; Kirkland Lake Lumber Co., Ltd., lumber, 300.18; A. Kirkpatrick, gravel, 6.80; Geo. Kirkpatrick, provisions, 1,566.19; J. Kirkpatrick, transportation, 3.75; R. T. Kirkwood, car rental, 24.00; A. C. Kitchen, gas, oil, 32.64; E. A. Klose, hardware, tools, 376.44; Peter Kluke, lumber, 10.52; C. Knight, gravel, 39.10; Jas. Knight, blacksmithing, 12.65; Victor Knight, lumber, 15.96; I. Knowles, repairs, .55; John Koski, hay, 54.00; John Koski, meat, 11.96; H. Kotanen, potatoes, 3.75; Ernest Krauss, posts, 116.20; John Kron & Son, coal, 64.85; Mrs. J. Kunze, gravel, 49.86; Mrs. P. Kunze, potatoes, 12.75; Arthur Labbe, provisions, hardware, oats, gas, oil, 580.03; Lawrence Labbe, oats, 8.50; F. Labelle, logs, 2.00; D. Labbie, earth fill, 1.65; J. Labine, provisions, 59.58; O. Labonte, provisions, 133.68; A. Lachance, gravel, 18.40; O. Lachance, gravel, 34.80; Z. Lachappel, gravel, 13.50; L. Lacourisese, gravel, 93.50; Oscar Lacroix, timber, 36.80; Clarence Ladd, gravel, 61.50; Donat Laforge, car livery, 30.00; Wilfrid Laforge, hardware, tools, 10.35; Wm. Laforge, gas, oil, grease, car parts and repairs, transportation, 1,143.77; A. Lafortune, gravel, 116.20; A. Laframboise, blacksmithing, 61.50; H. & D. Lafrance, provisions, hardware, trucking, oil, 3,049.08; Art. Lafrenier, lumber, 112.90; C. H. Lafreniere, nails, 5.89; E. Lafreniere, gravel, 20.10; L. Lafreniere, gravel, .90; J. Lahti, gravel, 8.40; Frank Laine, timber, 44.64; Laing Bros., Ltd., hay, 325.12; Dr. Geo. F. Laing, services, examining men, 24.00; Patrick Lajeunesse, cedar, 6.35; Victor Lajoie, provisions, 23.25; Lake of Bays Bus & Mail Service, livery, 15.00; Lake of Bays & Haliburton Telephone System, phone services and rental, 29.05; Lake of the Woods Milling Co., Ltd., flour, 13.38; H. Lalonde, rental of barn, 25.00; Wm. Lalonde, hay, 62.44; A. Lamb, provisions, 35.00; Ray Lamb, provisions, 273.02; Alphonse Lambert, gravel, 67.00; Wm. F. Lamon, cartage, transportation, 13.00; Pierre Lamontagne, timber, 18.75; W. Lamontagne, blacksmithing, 9.73; Albert Landriault, cedar, 31.92; Eugene Landriault, wood, poatoes, 12.00; A. Landry, coal, repairs, 46.85; Felix Landry, pork, 18.96; Moise Landry, livery, 57.00; H. Lang, timber, 14.00; A. Langdon, lumber, 8.88; Henry Langford, lumber, gas. oil, repairs, trucking, 2,949.73; J. J. Langford, wood, 52.50; Mrs. J. Langford, board, 90.80; Thos. Langford, wood, 30.00; Samuel Langmaid, gravel, 85.70; Wm. Langmaid (Baysville), hardware, oats, hay, provisions, oil, transportation, 6,254.13; Wm. Langmaid (Brown's Brae), taxi service, 5.00; Langstaff, Schurg & Co., Ltd., lumber, 1.915.95; Langstaff Mercantile Co., provisions, oilcloth, grain, 58.84; Dr. Jurben Lannin, services, examining men, 21.00; J. A. Lapalme, tools, bread, 6.91; P. Lapointe, provisions, 36.40; Willey Laporte, timber, 12.75; Jos. Larabee, cedar, 15.10; Z. Larachapelle, gravel, 11.20; Art Larocque, gravel, 30.00; A. T. Larson, travelling expenses, 4.80; J. H. Latour, transportation, 5.00; Arsene Laurin, provisions, 45.40; Paul Lauzon, meals, 1.25; H. Lavallee, gravel, 13.10; J. D. Lavallee, travelling expenses, 1.90; A. Lavasseur, gravel, 94.00; J. W. Lavender, travelling expenses, 7.50; Donat Lavigne, provisions, cedar, 271.62; Frank Lavigne, earth, 20.00; Hermas Lavoie, wood, twine, 4.96; O. Lavoix, logs, 2.00; Ed. Lavrin, gravel, 19.80; Geo. Law, gravel, 87.60; Jos. Lawless, gravel, 119.80; Jim Larence, provisions, 103.00; Jos. Lawrence, provisions, office rental, 1,098.77; J. P. Lawrence, car rental, travelling expenses, 21.51; Thos. Lawrence, window sash, 3.00; Frank Lawson, gravel, rent of camp site, lumber, hay, provisions, 619.55; Alex. Laxo, provisions, 17.45; Mrs. Jno Laxo, meat, 14.40; J. A. Leach, oats, 58.88; Leslie Leader, provisions, 10.80; Jno. H. Learoyd, travelling expenses, 8.40; Nelson Leary, wood, 36.00; W. Leary, board, 48.80; Agnes Leblanc, cedar poles, 17.02; Eleda Leblanc, gravel, 39.30; J. A. Leblanc, lumber, 1.25; O. Leclaire, wood, 31.69; Raoul Lecompte, gravel, 30.20; A. Lecot, lumber, 1.59; John Ledingham, repairs, 18.75; Lecraw Bros., hardware, roofing, wood, 206.33; Jos. Leduc, rent of plow, 2.50; J. Leduc, provisions, 41.34; M. J. Leduc, provisions, 172.09; Arthur Lees,

Statutory—Continued

General Work, Unemployment Relief—Continued

provisions, 49.12; D. Lees, gravel, 616.40; F. Lees, provisions, 43.01; G. Lees, transportation, 149.28; A. Legault, gravel, 10.90; D. Legault, cedar, 12.00; I. Legault, gravel, 36.50; Jos. Legault, lumber, 6.78; Chas. H. Legge, posts, gravel, 260.95; J. Legrace, gravel, 50.35; T. Legros, meat, oats, 108.16; Carl Leif, coal, 9.00; J. Leishman, cartage, 3.00; L. Leizert, blacksmithing, 2.45; J. C. Lemake, cedar poles, 2.00; Lemaire & St. Germaine, gas, oil, 32.90; F. G. Lemeke, trucking, 10.00; D. Lemeux, gravel, 43.20; Jos. Lemieux, provisions, 68.89; Ed. Lemieux, gravel, 8.00; Roy Lendrun, transportation, 7.00; J. W. Leng, gas, provisions, 68.78; Chas. Lennox, cedar, 355.53; D. H. Lennox, wood, 31.00; Herb. Lennox, milk, 302.20; A. Leonard, provisions, 3.00; Jos. Lepage, provisions, 11.00; N. Lepage, gravel, 100.00; Z. R. Lepage, blacksmithing, 28.20; Edmond Lerose, cutting and grubbing land, 175.65; J. Leroux, rock, 15.35; W. Lesack, hay, 26.43; Luke Leslie, gravel, 147.70; W. W. Lethbridge, car rental, travelling expenses, 155.00; J. Lethorn, gravel, 282.40; Ralph Levesque, rental of house, 45.00; Fred Levert, cedar, 8.00; E. Levesques, potatoes, 7.50; J. A. Levis, travelling expenses, 69.33; J. H. Levis, travelling expenses, 177.22; L. Levis, gravel, 83.60; R. J. Lewis, gravel, 43.00; Loammi Leziert, blacksmithing, 2.95; Wm. Leziert, gravel, 35.85; C. Levy, logs, 15.36; Chas. Lick, 3.30; Mrs. Anna Liggins, provisions, 11.25; H. G. Liggins, provisions, hay, 142.18; V. Lind, provisions, 11.70; H. Lindley, timber, 10.35; W. A. Lindop, gas, oil, repairs, trucking, board, 1,015.52; E. Lindsay, meat, 30.42; Lindsay Coal Co., Ltd., coal, 201.82; Lindsay & McCluskey, Ltd., coal, 20.40; W. G. Lindsay, provisions, board, transportation, 39.50; Lindstrom & Nilson, lumber, hardware, roofing, 164.34; Mrs. Stanley Linklater, laundering towels, 27.20; C. Linquist, meat, 77.34; Dr. E. D. Linton, services, examining men, 15.00; Liskeard Laundry, washing blankets, 53.40; Wm. Litchfield, hardware, grease, oil, 120.10; D. S. Litster, provisions, cotton, 111.28; Alex. Little, wood, 51.50; Walter Little, Ltd., car rental, trucking, 287.00; Mrs. H. V. Littlefield, beef, 25.20; A. Littleton, gravel, 42.80; John Lloyd, lumber, provisions, 73.08; H. T. Lloyd, hardware, 1.15; W. E. Lobb, car rental, travelling expenses, 46.45; Geo. A. Lockerby, plow share, 8.50; E. A. Lockhart & Son, blacksmithing, 29.70; F. A. Lockhart, bolts, repairs, 108.85; Wm. Lockhart, oats, gravel, 325.65; C. W. Locking, plow parts, fly fluid, 38.30; Geo. Locking, provisions, 17.99; Gordon Lockman, wood, 4.00; Alex. Logan, table, chairs, desk, stool, 18.00; David Logan, provisions, 26.40; Mrs. Mildred Logan, board, 3.85; Ernest E. Long, meals, 8.10; John Long, wood, provisions, 117.95; V. H. Longstaffe, travelling expenses, 28.30; Fred Lorenzo, cedar poles, 50.50; Fred Loring, provisions, 5.50; Loring, Golden Valley, Powassan Telephone Co., telephone services, repairs to telephone line, 128.65; J. Lott, travelling expenses, 9.55; Henry Loucks, wood, 19.50; Loughead Bros., hardware, tools, 37.75; J. Loughead, pork, 32.56; N. Love, pork, 19.60; Mrs. C. Loveday, wood, 24.00; W. G. Lovegrove, wood, 212.50; N. F. Lovelave, blacksmithing, 23.25; Sam Lovett, board, 13.50; Albert Lowery, provisions, 57.60; Lufkin Rule Co. of Canada, Ltd., hardware, .28; Geo. Luidsell, oats, meat, 94.86; Ole Lundstrom, wood, 28.00; Forest Lundy, meat, oats, 49.00; W. T. Lundy, rent of camp site, gravel, timber, hay, 39.30; John Lupine, hardware, oil, 26.25; Clifford Luscombe, gravel, 20.20; Geo. Luttrel, meat, 20.16; J. L. Luxton, car rental, 196.96; Lynch Auto Sales Co., Ltd., car parts and repairs, 77.23; Robt. Lynch, car rental, shoeing team, 5.00; Jas. Lynett, lumber, 43.90; Earl Lyons, car rental, 14.00; E. J. Lyttle, clay, 30.30; John McAuley, hay, 103.85; N. McAuley, provisions, gravel, 97.88; Wm. McAuley, provisions, 7.50; J. C. McBride, provisions, 243.04; J. McCabe, trucking, transportation, board for horse, 42.50; R. M. McCaffrey, travelling expenses, 222.48; H. McCans, straw for ticks, 3.50; P. McCans, poplar poles, 7.60; R. McCans, maple poles, 4.48; D. McCauley, gravel, 30.50; Nelson McCauley, gravel, 15.00; A. McChristie, transportation, trucking, 80.00; Jas. McClocklin, timber, 3.00; L. McCloskey, roofing, hardware, kitchenware, explosives, 489.18; Capt, J. F. McColeman, coal, 115.00; Mrs. Ed. McColeman, board, 17.60; N. J. McColeman, lumber, 35.00; McColl-Frontenac Oil Co., Ltd., gas, oil, grease, 1,904.72; J. B. McCollom, provisions, 15.00; Chas. McConnell, cedar, 112.00; Jos. McConnell, gravel, 10.75; Wm. McConnell, provisions, 73.46; H. McCool, meat, 26.46; Dan McCormick, hay, 9.10; Dr. J. M. McCormack, services, examining men, 34.00; Roy McCoubrey, gravel, 340.10; The John McCrae Machine & Foundry Co., bolts and repairs, 213.66; J. P. McCrea, gravel, 218.00; Kenneth McCron, car rental, 118.00; Chas. McCulley, gravel, 74.50; Geo. McCulligh, gravel, 15.60; Clifford McCutcheon, gravel, 68.30; Dr. R. McDerment, services, examining men, 13.00; A. McDonald, blacksmithing, 12.00; Allan A. J. MacDonald, hardware, cement, coal, provisions, explosives, 1,762.44; Dr. A. R. MacDonald, services, examining men, 15.00; McDonald Bros., lumber, posts, 349.93; C.

Statutory—Continued

General Work, Unemployment Relief—Continued

McDonald, oats, 12.15; Charlie McDonald, gravel, 6.00; MacDonald's Consolidated, Ltd., provisions, soap, 2,542.54; David McDonald, gravel, 32.90; F. McDonald, lumber, 65.68; Mrs. J. MacDonald, gas, 46.56; J. A. McDonald, clay, 10.00; K. C. MacDonald, car rental, 8.00; McDonald's Garage, taxi service, transportation, 138.00; P. D. McDonald, gravel, 6.70; Roderick McDonald, timber, 1.00; Thos. McDonald (Footes Bay), provisions, gas, oil, 189.88; Thos. McDonald (Matheson), provisions, 14.25; Wm. McDonald (Emo), wood, 38.12; Wm. MacDonald, transportation, 42.00; Wm. McDonald (Meldrum Bay), gravel, plank, 24.00; M. E. McDougall, cedar poles, 65.70; W. T. McDougall, travelling expenses, 37.45; David W. McEachern, explosives, 6.00; John McEwen, wood, 25.00; Jos. McEwen, wood, 31.00; J. J. McFadden, Ltd., lumber, drawing board, cotton, oats, 909.32; R. H. McFarland, car rental, 238.00; Geo. McFarland, provisions, 25.80; R. H. McFarland, car rental, travelling expenses, 86.70; Jas. McFarlane, potatoes, 51.60; D. F. MacFie, provisions, 77.80; Dr. A. J. McGanity, services, examining men, 39.00; J. A. McGill, blacksmithing, 97.15; McGill Hardware, Ltd., hardware, kitchenware, tools, 1,167.54; Ed. McGilvery, provisions, 7.50; S. E. McGirr, hardware, roofing, 14.75; J. McGlashan, blacksmithing, 27.55; Clarence McGonigal, wood, 32.00; Malcolm McGregor, oil, cartage, felt paper, 4.10; Mrs. Leslie McGuire, board, 153.30; Dan McIlory, rent of camp site and buildings, 70.00; Gordon MacInnes, wood, 23.37; McIntosh Grain & Feed Co., Ltd., straw, 8.08 ; A. A. McIntosh, Ltd., provisions, 1,506.97; Duncan McIntyre, gravel, 205.40; John McIntyre, provisions, 118.55; Angus McIvor, spruce, earth fill, 21.27; Geo. McIvor, gravel, 16.90; Mrs. B. McKaig, making towels, .85; Angus McKay, timber, 1.00; Angus McKay & Sons, lumber, trucking, taxi service, 295.19; Ernest McKay, gravel, 60.90; J. A. McKay, hauling, 6.00; Sandy McKay, lumber, 41.41; Drs. McKay and Simpson, services, examining men, 20.00; Mrs. A. McKechnie, rental of shed, 10.00; Russell McKechnie, lumber, 61.09; R. McKee, cedar, 35.40; Robt. McKee, provisions, 111.20; Thos. McKee, provisions, 18.16; Hartley McKeen, horse killed by blasting, 50.00; McKellar Municipal Telephone System, telephone services, 33.95; Ernest McKelvie, gravel, 108.00; Geo. McKelvie, wood, 30.00; Herb McKelvie, rent of office, cleaning office, meals, 77.10; Norman McKelvey, wood, 30.00; Walter McKelvey, wood, 87.38; Alex. McKenzie, meat, 18.36; Dr. E. A. MacKenzie, services, examining men, 28.00; Noah McKenzie, meat, 31.20; W. McKenzie, provisions, 39.60; Mrs. M. F. McKey, roofing, provisions, hardware, oats, explosives, 4,525.09; J. H. McKinlay, freighting, transportation, 303.76; McKinley Hardware Co., hardware, gas, oil, 20.22; J. W. McKinley, trucking, 55.00; McKinnon Industries, Ltd., tools, 984.82; H. L. McKinnon Co., Ltd., provisions, 614.18; L. McKinnon, lumber, 21.99; McKinnon's Store, provisions, 25.34; A. H. MacLachlan, blacksmithing, 73.49; Jas. McLachlan, cedar, 60.00; Jas. A. McLachlan, lumber, 102.38; Robt. McLarty, lumber, gravel, 67.06; Capt. A. B. McLean & Sons, explosives, 212.40; G. A. McLean, gravel, 10.00; Mrs. W. J. McLean, pork, 15.04; McLellan Transportation Co. (Kirkland Lake), transportation, 937.50; McLellan Transportation Co. (Swastika), transportation, car rental, 841.00; A. McLennan, repairs, 5.00; Mrs. D. MacLennan, board, 36.20; D. D. MacLennan, lumber, 154.54; McLennans, Ltd., hardware, coal, roofing, 1,222.74; E. N. McLeod, tools, 6.00; The McLeod Garage, gas, installing radiator, 26.12; Geo. McLeod, timber, 6.00; J. C. McLeod, bolts, cedar, 15.60; K. McLeod, freight charges on blankets, 7.53; Norman McLeod, car rental, 34.00; McLeod's Transfer, cartage, 8.61; A. H. McLochlan, repairs, 3.00; P. MacMahon, wood, 8.00; H. McMaster, teaming, 5.00; Alex. McLennan, blacksmithing, 144.49; R. McMichael, travelling expenses, 7.15; D. McMillan, lumber, 147.52; F. M. McMillan, pork, 13.84; Gordon McMillan, meat, 67.28; G. E. McMillan, provisions, 30.00; Mrs. H. McMillan, barrow, 12.50; J. McMillan, travelling expenses, 2.70; Ben R. McMullin, earth fill, rebuilding, fence, 125.00; W. J. McNabb, travelling expenses, 8.90; Dan McNaughton, provisions, board, 1,970.48; John McNeill, lumber, poles, 54.66; McNeil & Norris, hardware, car parts, repairs, gas, oil, 231.44; Barney McNutt, wood, 164.50; J. McPhail, cedar posts, 25.10; Angus McPhee, gravel, 40.20; C. C. McPhee, hardware, lumber, towelling, 500.94; Dr. A. W. McPherson, services, examining men, 56.00; John McPherson, potatoes, 7.50; D. A. McQuarrie, provisions, 38.05; M. McRitchie, beef, 16.50; McTier Garage, car parts, repairs, gas, oil, grease, 24.24; J. H. McVeety, provisions, 11.84; Henry McVeety, provisions, 23.84; N. McVeety, lumber, 15.00; Thos. McVeety, blacksmithing, provisions, 118.08; John McVey, car repairs, gas, 78.70; A. H. Machlan, iron, 2.40; Everett Mackie, provisions, 69.29; John Machlain, wood, 33.31; Geo. Madigan, rent of camp site, 24.00; Herman Madigan, beets, 1.50; Jos. and Mr. Madigan, wood, milk, 227.35; Charlie Magahay, transportation, 5.00;

Statutory—Continued

General Work, Unemployment Relief—Continued

Mageau Lumber Co., Ltd. (Field), lumber, blacksmithing, 143.87; Mageau Lumber Co., Ltd. (Sturgeon Falls), lumber, 564.69; H. Magee, travelling expenses, 1.70; T. H. Magill & Co., trucking, hay, transportation, 220.09; Magnetawan Garage, gas, oil, car parts and repairs, 255.93; Magnetawan Municipal Telephone System, telephone services, moving telephone and poles, 114.91; Cyril Maheux, potatoes, wood, 10.50; Nazaire Maheux, wood, 14.25; Phillippe Maheux, wood, 37.50; Alfred Maille, trucking, 98.00; E. Mailloux, earth fill, gravel, 337.60; O. Mainville, cedar, backsmithing, 24.60; Alf. Maitland, blacksmithing, 77.40; R. Maitland, stamps, telephone calls, 2.34; Matti Makela, gravel, 12.00; E. Maki, wood, 10.00; John Maki, cedar, 10.00; E. F. Malleau, oats, 30.60; F. H. Malmloff, cartage, hardware, 16.20; Dr. G. W. Manning, services, examining men, 8.00; J. Mannister, drums, 4.00; Geo. Manser, fence posts, 22.50; Mansion House, board, 290.06; Mac. Mantha, transportation, 14.80; L. N. Manzuk, hardware, 47.82; Maple Leaf Milling Co., Ltd., flour, oats, 205.86; H. Maranda, stationery, .40; Marathon Lumber Co., gravel, 46.80; Albert Marchand, hardware, transportation, lumber, 341.47; M. Marchand, wood, 6.00; Albert Marcoux, posts, 52.50; T. Marion, gravel, 47.50; Dr. M. Markson, services, examining men, 4.00; P. J. Marrin, provisions, hardware, soap, 502.08; A. E. Marshall ,gas, 1.50; C. Marshall, travelling expenses, 5.35; Marshall-Ecclestone, Ltd., explosives, hardware, coal, machinery parts, 5,861.45; J. R. Marshall, provisions, oilcloth, wood, oil, 938.37; Pat Marshall, car rental, 7.00; R. Marshall, transportation, 10.00 Marshall-Wells Co., Ltd., provisions, iron, hardware, rubber boots, 4,037.01; Eugene Martin, wood, 25.50; H. K. Martin, provisions, 25.00; J. A. Martin, car rental, 296.00; Jas. Martin, hay, 267:29; Sandy Martin, gravel, fencing, 63.00; Mrs. S. Martin, board, 13.05; W. H. Martin, lumber, 78.99; T. H. Marwood, blacksmithing, .15; A. E. Mason, car rental and repairs, 31.60; Gilbert Mason, drygoods, 1.50; T. Mason, repairs to rod and tape, .75; W. Mason, car rental, 17.00; Massey-Harris Co., Ltd., machinery parts, 22.69; M. B. Mather, travelling expenses, 91.60; T. R. Mather, car rental and travelling expenses, 307.40; Matheson Co-operative Dairy Co., Ltd., provisions, 22.50; Mrs. F. Matheson, laundry, 15.50; Geo. Matheson, wood, gravel, 95.00; Jas. Matheson, gravel, 16.88; John Matheson, gravel, 126.45; Mrs. M. Matheson, rent of cabin for office, 22.50; John Mathews, gravel, 23.20; J. A. Mathieu, Ltd., sacks, 7.50; Matthews Sash & Door Co., lumber, 494.25; C. J. Mauer, wood, 27.00; Russell Mawhiney, provisions, cartage, 22.07; Maxwells, Ltd., scrapers, wheelbarrows, 2,391.91; Meaford Steel Products, Ltd., scrapers, 1,165.22; Mrs. Louis Meawaisage, washing blankets, 70.50; Medora & Wood Telephone System, telephone calls, .30; Kurt Meincke, provisions, wood, 503.56; N. Melford, cedar, 37.50; Mrs. A. Melin, provisions, 13.68; E. Melin, provisions, wood, 77.35; T. W. Mellors, wood, 55.00; Bill Melnyk, wood, 8.25; Henry Menard, car rental, 83.00; Menzies Bros., Ltd., flour, straw, hay, 697.98; Mrs. A. Merchant, use of house as camp, 5.00; T. Mercier, hardware, pipe, 6.20; Merrill, Rhind & Walmsley, tools, 13.40; Tom Merrylees, gravel, 18.80; Art Messenger, wood, transportation, 50.00; Metallic Roofing Co. of Canada, Ltd., culverts, iron, 15,188.94; H. Meyers, pork, 36.48; J. R. Meyers, meat, 31.68; R. Meyers, cartage, 35.75; Bernard Michaelis, provisions, 41.90; David Michaelis, transportation, 8.13; Michaud Bros., Ltd., hardware, roofing, cotton, 88.33; Michaud & Levesque, steel, 114.68; Alex. Michie, blacksmithing, 46.75; Mickle, Dyment & Son, Ltd., lumber, nails, 4,022.61; Dr. T. H. Middelbro, services, examining men, 25.00; G. E. Middleton, car hire, transportation, 272.61; Archie Miller, transportation, 15.05; Clifford Miller, wood, borrow, gravel, 63.90; Mrs. C. A. Miller, board, 12.00; Clive E. Miller, provisions, 2.40; D. J. Miller, travelling expenses, 6.25; Emery Miller, timber, 75.51; G. B. Miller, broom, .60; Geo. H. Miller, hardwood, 24.75; Harold Miller, milk, 259.20; H. R. Miller, wood, 12.38; H. S. Miller, hardware, provisions, wood, travelling expenses, car rental, 228.29; Joe Miller, hay, 107.80; J. T. Miller, provisions, wood, 73.57; Stewart Miller, transportation, trucking, 111.40; Walter Miller, cedar, gravel, 42.00; W. L. Miller, wood, 50.00; Miller's, towelling, oilcoth, 73.31; Miller's Service Station, gas, oil, 43.41; Millest & Fleming, blacksmithing, 265.30; H. Millette, provisions, 177.21; Chas. Milligan, trucking, 15.00; Frank Milligan, car rental, gas, oil, repairs, 298.30; Mills Bros., tools, hardware, 7.20; Geo. Mills, provisions, 30.00; Robt. Mills, provisions, hay, 125.66; Mrs. Sarah, mills, borrow, 12.50; Stanley Mills, cedar, gravel, wood, borrow, 252.98; W. Mills, gravel, 607.80; Robt. Millsap, wood, 45.00; Milne's Garage, gas, oil, repairs, 303.44; Wm. Milne & Sons, lumber, 391.52; Milner Turned Goods, tools, 231.39; Milton Francis Lumber Co., Ltd., lumber, 21.98; The Minden Echo, rental of typewriter, stationery, printing sheets, 60.47; Minden Municipal Telephone System, moving poles, telephone services, 223.63; N. Mironicks, gravel, 48.83; Bernard Mitchell,

Statutory—Continued

General Work, Unemployment Relief—Continued

provisions, 36.10; Geo. Mitchell provisions, posts, 38.20; Mitchell Hardware & Supply Co., Ltd., hardware, kitchenware, tools, towelling, 1,548.25; Thos. M. Mitchell, welding, .25; R. Mitchell, timber, 5.25; S. Mitchell, provisions, 123.15; Mitchell's Service Station, gas, oil, car parts and repairs, 455.74; W. Mitchell, piling timber, 18.00; Ed. Moffatt, provisions, 4.40; Henry Moffatt, cedar, 6.45; L. Moffatt, provisions, hardware, stationery, oil, 1,103.05; Mrs. T. M. Mohan, gravel, 19.80; Art Monahan, car rental, 13.00; P. Monnette, gravel, 20.30; Geo. Montgomery, cedar, 22.40; H. Montgomery, board, 135.00; A. Monthan, cedar, 6.40; R. J. Mooney, provisions, 45.68; Mrs. Alice Moore, gravel, 15.90; Allan Moore, cartage, 50; A. R. Moore, ripping and dressing lumber, lumber, 22.96; Moore Bros.. provisions, oil, explosives, hardware, 1,636.47; John Moore, provisions, 36.10; J. B. Moore, hardware, provisions, towelling, coal, 1,295.52; J. L. Moore, gravel, 22.28; O. W. Moore, cartage, 90.50; Mrs. R. K. Moore, provisions, 46.05; R. M. Moore, lumber, 256.00; W. A. Moore, blacksmithing, 48.00; Wallace Moore, gravel, 37.50; W. L. Moore, stationery, 1.45; Wendle Moore, board, 21.00; S. Moreau, transportation, 43.20; S. Moreau, gravel, 12.00; John Morel, provisions, 7.50; G. F. Morgan, gas, 1.40; Martin Morken, provisions, 30.00; J. G. Morphet, gravel, 176.10; W. Morphet, meat, 34.62; Geo. E. Morris, provisions, wood, 515.10; Stan Morris, gravel, 57.38; J. R. Morrish, keys, .50; Geo. K. Morrison, hardware, stationery, tools, 75.12; Jas. Morrison, provisions, 10.24; J. Morrison, gravel, 24.00; John Morrison, wood, 25.00; A. Morrissette, wood, pork, hay, 168.83; W. L. Morrissey, gas, 1.50; J. T. Morrow, travelling expenses, 3.95; Ora Morrow, wood, 12.00; J. H. Morrisette, meat, 31.14; Melvin Mosher, provisions, 2.24; Mosley's Garage, gas, oil, repairs, 109.97; Mount McKay Feed Co., Ltd., oats, bran, hay, coal, 3,311.46; John Moyer, potatoes, 4.80; J. B. Moyneur, board, hardware, lumber, provisions, 1,736.17; Leon Moyotte provisions, 7.50; Mrs. C. Mulveney, board, 9.40; Wesley Mumford, wood, gravel, borrow, 119.60; P. Munn, gravel, 15.20; Alex. Munroe, provisions, 96.26; D. Munroe, gravel, 4.00; Otto Munroe, meat, 62.01; K. Munro, cedar, 96.42; Mrs. R. Munro, board, 35.90; W. Munro, gravel, 28.80; Wm. Munroe, provisions, 23.04; Frank Murchison, meat, 31.80; J. Murish, repairs, 1.50; Sam Murray, pine, 10.08; Geo. Murray, travelling expenses, 74.85; Ken Murray, travelling expenses, 8.45; A. J. Murphy, beef, 38.57; T. Murtrough, cedar, 15.00; Muskoka Construction Co., explosives, 25.20; Muskoka Garage, gas, oil, repairs, 37.68; Muskoka Foundry, Ltd., plowshares, 7.00; J. B. Myers & Son, provisions, 788.35; Dr. E. R. Myles, services, examining men, 52.00; L. Nanne, coal, bags, rental of truck, 198.00; W. H. Nash, transportation, gravel, 181.30; National Grocers Co., Ltd. (Cochrane), provisions, cheesecloth, oilcloth, 3.512.30; National Grocers Co., Ltd. (New Liskeard), provisions, lye, 412.91; National Grocers Co., Ltd. (North Bay), provisions, 41.65; National Grocers Co., Ltd. (Sault Ste. Marie), provisions, 3,468.12; National Grocers Co., Ltd. (Sudbury), provisions, 560.13; J. W. Neelands, travelling expenses, 29.40; J. Neely, gravel, 216.30; V. E. Neely, borrow, 20.00; Neilson's, flanuel, 1.12; Albert Nelson, coal, hardware, 21.60; Dr. F. H. Nelson, services, examining men, 22.00; Dr. W. H. Nelson, services examining men, 48.00; Thos. Neolet, wood, 9.22; Dr. Jas. H. Nesbitt, services examining men, 35.00; Dr. J. Morris Nettleton, services, examining men, 15.00; Jos. Newburn, gravel, 6.30; Geo. Newell, provisions, 10.00; J. H. Newell & Co., provisions, hardware, oil, 2,593.79; Mrs. E. Newlove, cartage, 81.14; F. Newlove, teaming, 3.00; David Newman, gravel, 1.80; J. Newton, board, rent of residences, 741.50; P. F. Newton, meat, 69.93; Newton's Coal & Wood, coal, 7.00; New Windsor Hotel, board, 288.00; Alex. Nichols, blacksmithing, 29.50; Angus Nicholson, gravel, 42.00; Nickel City Service, gas, 412.16; Dr. H. R. Nicklin, services, examining men, 30.00; Antoine Niganawan, wood, 5.25; Nipissing Private Telephone Co., telephone calls, .70; Noelville Trading Co., lumber, 13.13; Thos. Nolet, wood, 9.22; Fred Nolting, provisions, 23.14; B. Nordin, pork, 41.84; Norfolk & Rochester Hardware Co., Ltd., lumber, hardware, 82.47; Alex. Norrie, wood, hay, 20.00; J. Norriss, pork, 12.00; North Country Supply Co., Ltd., cable, 3.00; Northern Development Department, cash accountable, 1,000.00; North Shore Bus Line, transportation, 124.95; North Star Garage, gas, oil, repairs, 15.42; North Star Oil, Ltd., gas, 59.13; North Star Publishing Co., Ltd., advertisement, 3.00; Northern Canada Supply Co., Ltd., hardware, explosives, towelling, kitchenware, 3,800.91; Northern Feed & Seed Co., Ltd., oats, hay, 687.39; Northern Foundry & Machine Co., Ltd., machinery parts, 105.49; Northern Metal Co., plates, screen, 15.16; Northern Ontario Power Co., Ltd., wire, 3.13; Northern Planing Mills, Ltd., lumber, 275.04; Northern Sand & Gravel Co., gravel, 1,125.50; Northern Telephone Co., Ltd., changing and repairs to line, telephone services, 150.96; Northland Grocers, Ltd., provisions, soap, hardware, hay, 2,027.43; Patsy Notter, transportation, 25.00; Bank of

Statutory—Continued

General Work, Unemployment Relief—Continued

Nova Scotia, interest on overdraft, 2.45; Cecil Nutt, car rental, 352.00; Mrs. C. Nutt, board, 20.80; Mrs. L. Nutt, board, 20.80; Levi Nutt, hay, 19.80; Cecil Nuttal, meat, 16.62; R. Nuttal, potatoes, 11.27; K. Nykolyohyn, gravel, 317.20; E. Nyman, explosives, wood, 94.50; Frank O'Brien, travelling expenses, 3.25; M. O'Connor, provisions, hardware, lumber, soap, 1,851.33; Chas. O'Donnell, rental of buildings, 60.00; G. Odorizzi, meat, 43.20; John Odorizzi, provisions, 235.26; Andrew Odrowski, provisions, lumber, 529.27; Henry Odrowski, cedar, 46.50; W. M. Oglestean, hardware, coal, blacksmithing, 92.61; J. O'Grady, travelling expenses, 32.50; John Ojala, gravel, pine, 39.48; E. H. Oldfield, drygoods, packing cases, 84.88; Harry Oldfield, wood, 9.90; Bill Olepik, hay, 32.31; Fred Oler, posts, 50.90; A. R. Oliver, car rental, 6.00; Bill Ollksuk, hay, 36.97; O. Olsen, provisions, 8.80; S. Olynuk, hay, 30.00; Ontario Forestry Branch, board, 335.30; Owens Cartage Co., trucking, 40.00; John O'Neill, pork, 35.44; Mrs. S. O'Neil, gravel, 320.66; M. Orchard, rental of camp ground, lumber, 70.58; John Orme, timber, 3.00; Dr. T. H. Orton, services, examining men, 86.00; Geo. Osborne, wood, 20.00; J. A. Osborn, gas, oil, grease, 27.50; John Osborne, provisions, 198.64; Melvin Osborne, wood, 19.50; Robt. Osborne, provisions, board, 83.26; Samuel Osborn (Canada), Ltd., steel, 174.80; John Oshell, provisions, rental of camp ground, 154.58; Ostrom & Andrews, provisions, 192.53; August Ouellette, gravel, 42.20; Eug. Ouellette, gravel, 42.20; E. Overholser, lumber, 172.47; P. & M. Navigation Co., trucking, 5.00; B. Paget, car rental, 24.00; Thos. Paget, gravel, 482.35; J. A. Paiment, cement, 40.00; Carl Palengio, gravel, 378.10; Cecil J. Palmer, provisions, 9.12; F. Palmer, Sr., cedar, 15.84; J. Palmer, gravel, 28.80; Cleve Panton, cartage, 3.75; J. Papilla, wood, 171.75; F. Papineau, travelling expenses, gas, oil, 155.14; K. Paquette, provisions, 13.50; E. Paradis, provisions, hardware, wood, rent of shacks, 513.59; Jno. Paris, car rental, travelling expenses, 92.27; E. Parisee, house rent, 20.00; J. H. Park travelling expenses, 5.05; Arthur Parker, timber, 4.50; E. J. Parker, cedar, 2.88; Geo. S. Parker, hardware, 35.59; Parkhill Gold Mines, Ltd., lumber, use of tractor, explosives, hardware, 1,062.51; Geo. Parlett & Son, lumber, 309.12; H. H. Parlier, gas, oil, rent of blacksmith shop and tools, 39.75; G. Parolin, butter, 10.00; W. Parolin, gravel, provisions, 45.85; Parry Sound Canadian, advertisement, 3.52; Town of Parry Sound, lighting, 10.70; Hugh Parslow & Co., Ltd., oats, hay, bran, 489.58; Alfred Parton, gravel, 7.88; Jas. Parton, wood, 35.63; Ted Pascall, travelling expenses, 5.35; L. Patry, wood, 42.00; Frank Patterson, gravel, 18.40; Patterson Garage, gas, 1.50; Leonard Patterson, wood, transportation, 15.50; R. Patterson, gravel, 54.50; T. G. Patterson, gas, oil, 11.35; Wm. Patterson, wood, 39.37; Joe Paul, posts, 6.00; S. Payne, cartage, 3.00; H. A. Peacock, rental of car, 140.00; Owen Pearcy, wood, 45.00; Carl Pearson, gravel, 66.00; Pearson Electric & Hardware Co., hardware, tools, 287.27; W. W. Pearson, provisions, 8.64; Wm. Peck, provisions, oil, 1,813.50; Pedlar People, Ltd. (Oshawa), machinery parts, culverts, 32,569.88; Pedlar People, Ltd. (Winnipeg), couplers, 19.60; Chas. Peel, wood, 12.00; Peerless Hardware, hardware, tools, 611.29; A. Peever, provisions, rent of camp site, 54.00; Albert Peever, provisions, rent of lot, 25.05; Jack Peever, timber, 122.95; Jas. Peever, provisions, 220.10; Jos Peever, potatoes, 5.00; T. Pekola, cedar, 10.50; Ed. Pelissier, blacksmithing, 29.86; E. Pellow, hardware, lumber, hay, oats, gas, oil, 3,225.70; Pellow's Garage & Taxi Service, gas, oil, repairs, 1,998.14; Gus Peltier, wood, 7.50; Pembroke Standard Observer, signs, 7.50; G. Pender, provisions, 18.98; Pen-Link Construction Co., trap rock, 1,690.50; W. Pennell, gravel, 10.80; T. C. Penno, gravel, 67.65; H. Penny, gravel, 146.25; John Pepila, wood, 46.50; F. D. Pepin & Co., provisions, broom, 224.36; N. Pera, wood, 31.30; Owen Percy, lumber, wood, 82.84; E. Periault, blacksmithing, 5.95; A. L. Perkins & Co., hardware, hay, stationery, 204.66; John Perks, provisions, soap, 84.80; Perkus, Ltd., hardware, kitchenware, oil, 288.49; Peter Perlin, tools, hardware, explosives, grease, 5,329.87; C. Perron, gravel, fill 174.75; Bert Perry, wood, 96.00; J. W. Perry, provisions, hay, oats, 1,787.94, Mrs. Peter Peterbaugh, clay, 44.25; Mat Peters, provisions, 100.16; P. J. Peterson, pork, 23.32; M. Phelan, vegetables, 6.40; Bill Phillips, gas, oil, 9.90; J. J. Phillips, travelling expenses, 7.70; Geo. Piche, cedar posts, 76.00; Chas. Pierce & Sons, Ltd., hardware, bed ticks, kitchenware, 961.45; Frank Pierce, gravel, 24.80; J. Piette, gravel, 251.20; Pigeon River Hotel, board, hay, 4,888.68; Frank Pilger, wood, 15.00; Jos. Pilon (Monetville), gravel, 35.20; Jos. Pilon (Noelville), cedar, 7.20; J. A. Pilon, tools, 21.30; Raoul Pilon, cedar, gravel, 47.96; Jos. Pilotte, gravel, 82.50; J. C. Pinch, Ltd., provisions, 555.43; Pine Grove Inn, board, gas, horse hire, 372.98; A. Pinion, gravel, 102.60; Piper Hardware Co., hardware, coal, heaters, explosives, 2,789.83; Alfred Pitt, Ltd., tools, 39.20; Ben Pittman, posts, 6.00; A. Plante, gravel, 50.70; E. Plante, gravel, 19.30; Martin Please, provisions, 67.59; A. W. Plowright, trucking, 10.75; John Pockailo,

Statutory—Continued

General Work, Unemployment Relief—Continued

potatoes, .50; Thos. Pocklington Co., chain, repairs to level, 58.25; A. Poitras, gravel, fill, 89.40; Thos. Pollard, gravel, 9.60; Thos. Poole, gravel, 1,394.20; Tom Poolton, beef, 47.70; J. Porco & Co., repairs, 9.00; Porcupine Hardware & Furniture, hardware, oil, 36.50; H. H. Porlier, hardware, lumber, gas, 95.95; Porquis Junction Garage, transportation, 129.00; Port Arthur Hardware, Ltd., hardware, tools, explosives, coal, 1,920.95; Port Carling Garage, gas, oil, grease, repairs, 186.55; Port Carling Livery, wood, 88.00; Felix Portelance, vegetables, 3.15; Porter & Co., provisions, 209.96; W. G. Porter, travelling expenses, 2.25; Postmaster (Baysville), stamps, 4.45; Postmaster (Bracebridge), stamps, registered letters, 6.14; Postmaster (Brown's Brae), stamps, 6.50; Postmaster (Callander), stamps, 2.08; Postmaster (Chapleau), stamps, 11.00; Postmaster (Cochrane), stamps, 13.00; Postmaster (Connaught Station), stamps, 2.00; Postmaster (Dorset), stamps, 11.08; Postmaster (Emsdale), stamps, 1.00; Postmaster (Espanola), stamps, 2.00; Postmaster (Footes Bay), stamps, 1.90; Postmaster (Gordon Bay), stamps, registration, 3.19; Postmaster (Hall's Lake), stamps, 1.00; Postmaster (Huntsville), stamps, 3.75; Postmaster (Iroquois Falls), stamps, 2.50; Postmaster (MacTier), stamps, registration, 4.57; Postmaster (Magnetawan), stamps, 8.40; Postmaster (Minden), stamps, rent of box, 201.20; Postmaster (Nipissing), stamps, 1.00; Postmaster (North Bay), stamps, 187.00; Postmaster (Parry Sound), stamps, registration, 39.14; Postmaster (Port Carling), stamps, 6.38; Postmaster (Port Cunningham), stamps, 3.00; Postmaster (Port Loring, stamps, registration, 3.55; Postmaster (Powassan), stamps, 35.00; Postmaster (Raymond), stamps. .60; Postmaster (Rousseau Road), stamps, 4.20; Postmaster (Severn Bridge), stamps, 3.95; Postmaster (Sioux Lookout), stamps, 14.00; Postmaster (South River), stamps, registration, 19.33; Postmaster Sundridge), stamps, 15.85; Postmaster, (Swastika), stamps, 3.00; Postmaster (Trout Creek), stamps, registration, 7.72; Postmaster (Warren), stamps, registration, 54.20; Postmaster (Waubamic), stamps, 4.50; John Pousette, rent of typewriter, 18.00; Powassan Garage, gas, oil, car parts and repairs, 711.65; Powassan Milk & Freight Transfer, transportation, 6.00; Powassan News, advertisment, 3.80; Mrs. Wm. Powell, board, 29.30; W. Powell (Keewatin), taxi service, 5.00; W. Powell (Tomstown P.O.), lumber, 134.16; Dr. M. Powers, services, examining men, 15.00; Geo. A. Powles, travelling expenses, 7.15; John Powley, posts, 11.00; W. E. Pratt, meat, 130.41; Leslie Prentice, teaming, 4.35; Thos. Prentice, wood, 43.50; W. W. Prentice, lumber, saw, lime, 9.50; Preston's Machine Shop, blacksmithing, 243.60; Jas. Pretsell, blacksmithing, 13.82; Percy Price, gravel, 148.96; J. A. Prieur, car parts and repairs, gas, oil, 229.42; Em. Primeaux, cedar, 20.04; Mrs. W. Pringle, board, 947.00; Frank Prior, potatoes, 7.00; Mrs. Alf. Pritchard, board, 269.50; Mrs. Earl Pritchard, hardwood, 125.73; Lawrence Pritchard, transportation, 10.00; Lewis Pritchard, lumber, car rental, trucking, 916.74; L. Pritchard, hardwood, 52.50; Producers' Co-operative Creamery Co., Ltd., provisions, 419.25; Provencher Bros., provisions, matches, 687.24; Dr. G. A. Publow, services, examining men, 6.00; P. Qualachuk, provisions, 11.10; Quality Meat Market, provisions, 50.50; Quality Meat & Grocery Co., Ltd., provisions, 379.19; Jos. Quenette, blacksmithing, 10.15; E. Quesnel, repairs, 8.25; Henry Quesnel, gravel, 28.70; J. Quesnell, provisions, 4.65; P. Quesnell, transportation, 109.08; P. Quesnel, gravel, transportation, 83.10; A. Quick, wood, 26.25; Quinlan & Co., roofing, 3.75; D. F. Quinlan & Co., provisions and soap, 18.75; Dr. P. F. Quinlan, services, examining men, 2.00; Andy Quinn, wood, 25.00; Fred and Mrs. Quinn, lumber, meat, cartage, 2,027.14; Mirvin Quinn, hardwood, 25.00; J. P. Quinn, rent for Orange Hall, 152.26; T. A. Quinn, films, prints, stationery, 12.00; E. M. Quirt, trucking, transportation, 587.50; A. J. Radbourne, meat, oats, 56.00; J. Radborne, beef, 21.36; Peter Radell, cedar, 5.00; Mark Radford, pine. 16.00; A. H. Radka, pork, 19.20; Alec Rahal, roofing, board, provisions, transportation, 396.08; Railway & Power Engineering Corporation, Ltd. (Toronto), steel, 148.66; Railway & Power Engineering Corporation, Ltd. (Winnipeg), steel, 171.81; E. Raincourt, wood, 14.08; L. Raincourt, firewood, 21.49; Max. Raincourt, firewood, 31.84; A.R. Rains, cartage, 4.00; Arsino Rainville, gravel, 44.00; Rainy Lake Hotel, board, 32.25; Rainy River Canners, hay, 82.11; Ramore Supply Store, provisions, hardware, 1,121.56; Wm. Randell, provisions, 14.25; B. H. Rands, gas, hardware, explosives, 91.65; Fred Rankin, timber, 1.98; Geo. Rankin, poles, 6.40; Jas. Rankin, wood, 185.00; Drs. J. P. Rankin and H. B. Kenner, services, examining men, 25.00; M. G. Ransford, travelling expenses, 5.55; Catherine Ranson, board, 339.84; Robt. Ranson, rental of storehouse, transportation, 25.70; W. Rattray, travelling expenses, 1.85; W. H. Ratz, provisions, 4.00; R. H. Raush, cedar, 67.60; J. Frank Raw Co., Ltd., draughting, supplies, 29.05; F. Ray, fill, reconstructing fence, 73.72; Reamsbottom & Edwards, Kirkland Co., Ltd., provisions, soap, hardware, 1,943.60; Sanford Reckie, wood,

Statutory—Continued

General Work, Unemployment Relief—Continued

butter, 136.75; Wallace Reckie, rental of camp site, provisions, 310.95; Chas. Reckin & Sons, provisions, 130.05; J. A. Redfern, gravel, 20.00; The Red & White Store, provisions, soap, blacksmithing, oil, 115.28; Harry Reechstein, wood, lumber, 320.25; L. Reed, lumber, 50.80; Tom Regan, gravel, 62.40; Fred Reickstein, provisions, 17.20; Harry Reickstein, wood, lumber, rental of lot, 52.00; A. R. Reid, pork, 25.84; Duncan Reid, provisions, 44.96; Geo. Reid, travelling expenses, telephone calls, express, 106.80; T. H. Reid & Co., cotton, 1.65; W. J. Reid, gravel, 98.80; W. Remillard, gravel, 12.00; Ben Renshaw, hay, 140.49; Chas. Resbeck, gravel, 73.20; John Reynolds Estate, tools, spikes, 8.00; Geo. R. Rhode &. Co., hardware, 42.00; Alfred Ribble, board, 207.75; Fred Ricard, surveying road, 1.00; Wm. J. Rice Co., blankets, 570.82; Anthony Rich, gravel, cedar, 92.45; Barney Rich, provisions, 25.28; Edmond Richard, provisions, 256.40; J. A. Richard, logs, 35.00; E. W. Richards, cartage, transportation, 1,290.25; Wilbert Richards, provisions, 495.78; Wm. Richards, provisions, 56.50; F. C. Richardson, provisions, bran, matches, hardware, 2,147.63; Stanley Richardson, clearing, grubbing, 80.40; Wallace Rickie, lumber, straw, 57.50; Barney Rick, provisions, 137.04; Cecil Ricker, hardware, .70; Fred Ricker, transportation, car rental, 58.00; Herb Ridout, board, 1,021.88; S. Rigby, trucking, transportation, 648.00; Medie Ritchie, Sr., clay, posts, 89.25; Orville Rivers, wood, 15.00; Jerry Rivet, poles, 76.32; C. W. Roark, travelling expenses, car rental, 251.70; J. O. Robert, gas, grease, 37.43; Cecil A. Roberts, trucking, 1,110.14; Donald Roberts, taxi service, 15.00; J. L. Roberts, gravel, 134.60; Nelson Roberts, lumber, 26.41; R. Roberts, poles, 76.80; Allan Robertson, gravel, 4.00; E. Robertson, repairs, 1.00; G. L. Robertson, gas, oil, provisions, repairs, 192.82; John Robertson, transportation, 5.00; Dr. Lorne Robertson, services, examining men, 12.00; Dr. W. A. Robertson, services, examining men, 10.00; Ian Robins, gravel, 770.40; Edward Robinson, gravel, 4.80; E. Robinson, hay, 86.64; Geo. Robinson, wood, 87.50; Joe Robinson, lumber, 3.00; Leslie Robinson, cartage, 3.84; Richard Robinson, meat, 13.44; S. N. Robinson, meat, 13.05; Dr. R. B. Robson, services, examining men, 10.00; P. Rocheford, travelling expenses, telephone account, 343.85; H. Rochon, gravel, 17.50; R. Rochon, gravel, 60.00; John W. Rodie, trucking, transportation, boat fares, 84.93; E. A. Rogers, hardware, roofing, telegrams, 312.99; Dr. Norman W. Rogers, services, examining men, 10.00; T. H. Rogers & Son, hardware, rent of tool shed, roofing, gas, grease, gravel, 213.67; W. E. Rogers, trucking, wood, 3,005.79; L. Romprey, lumber, 89.76; G. Rondeau, gravel, 5.70; G. Roque, transportation, 149.28; J. Roque, transportation, 55.19; L. V. Rorke, field notes, 2.00; G. Rosewan, valve, .50; A. Ross (Black Hawk), provisions, 3.50; A. Ross (WaWa), wood, rent of camp site, 84.00; L. Ross, car rental, 3.00; Rosseau Garage & Livery, taxi service, 2.75; Cliff Roszel, gravel, 7.50; D. Rousseau, gravel, 12.00; H. W. Rowdon, explosives, hardware, 149.57; J. W. Rowe, board, 8.00; W. Rowe, gravel, 58.50; S. Rowland, blacksmithing, 48.35; Richard Rowlandson, cedar, wood, 247.50; Robt. Rowlandson, cedar, 10.25; R. D. Rowlandson, board, 24.00; E. Rowley, cedar, 24.85; Alfred Roy, lumber, 25.00; D. Roy (Blind River), gravel, 22.30; D. Roy (Warren), 64.80; E Roy, travelling expenses, 4.30; Henry Roy, plank, 23.50; H. H. Roy (Warren), explosives, hardware, gas, grease, oil, 7,379.87; H. H. Roy (Markstay), coal, nails, 6.34; J. B. Roy, gravel, 93.00; Nap. and Mrs. Roy, gas, 239.22; O. Roy, gravel, 270.75; Dr. F. J. Rundle, services, examining men, 22.00; C. P. Rush, lettering signs, 3.00; Alfred Russell, gravel, 9.00; Joe Russell, meat, 38.70; Thos. R. Russell, gas, barrow, 6.24; S. Russell, posts, 7.50; Wm. Russell, gravel, 9.00; Dr. Gordon H. Rutherford, services, examining men, 32.00; Jas. Ruttan, steel blade, 1.50; Wm. Ruttan, blacksmithing, rent of blacksmith shop and tools, 13.05; Jos. Ryan (Blind River), meat, 73.92; Jos. Ryan (Raymond), wood, 8.00; T. F. Ryan, hardware, .93; Rydal Bank Garage, gas, oil, 237.11; D. St. Denis, gravel, 81.50; D. St. Germain, gravel, 4.00; E. St. Jacques, wood, 22.50; J. St. Laurent (Michipicoten River), provisions, car rental, tools, coal, 61.60; C. St. Laurent, board, hardware, 29.60; J. St. Laurent (WaWa), car rental, 100.00; St. Mary's Wood Specialty Co., Ltd., tools, 1,471.01; K. Saara, gravel, 12.00; Richard Sabourin, cedar, posts, 58.32; Sadowski & Co., provisions, hay, oats, 2,239.13; Thos. Salmon, meat, 67.57; J. W. Sanderson, trucking, 381.50; W. Sanderson, cartage, 32.00; Sanderson's Transport, cartage, 77.50; C. Sandrelli & Co., transportation, 42.00; S. Sanfrene, gravel, 6.00; F. Sanstrom, provisions, 4.76; E. Sarazen, gravel, 29.00; The Sault Daily Star, advertising, 2.25; Sault Ste. Marie Coal & Wood Co., Ltd., coal, 418.47; Stanley Sawickie, provisions, 91.08; Sawyer-Massey, Ltd., machinery parts, 165.89; Fred Saynor, travelling expenses, 110.50; Geo. Scace, transportation, trucking, 60.00; T. A. Scanlon, gravel, 89.85; L. B. Scannell, tools, explosives, hardware, 95.14; Henry Schaffner, Sr., gravel, 15.45; Frank Schmeler, hardwood, 27.00; Elmer Schmidt, wood, 28.13;

Statutory—Continued

General Work, Unemployment Relief—Continued

potatoes, .50; Thos. Pocklington Co., chain, repairs t level, 58.25; A. Poitras, gravel, fill, 89.40; Thos. Pollard, gravel, 9.60; Thos. Pole, gravel, 1,394.20; Tom Poolton, beef, 47.70; J. Porco & Co., repairs, 9.00 Porcupine Hardware & Furniture, hardware, oil, 36.50; H. H. Porlier, hardware, lumber, gas, 95.95; Porquis Junction Garage, transportation, 129.00; Port Arthur Hardware, Ltd., hardware, tools, explosives, coal, 1,920.95; Port Carling Garage, gas, oil, grease, repairs, 186.55; Port Carling Livery, wood, 88.00, Fct Portelance, vegetables, 3.15; Porter & Co., provisions, 209.96; W. G. Porter travelling expenses, 2.25; Postmaster (Baysville), stamps, 4.45; Postmaster (Bracebridge), stamps, registered letters, 6.14; Postmaster (Brown's Brae), stamps, 6.50; Postmaster (Callander), stamps, 2.08; Postmaster (Chapleau), stamps, 11.00; Postmaster (Cochrane), stamps, 13.00; Postmaster (Connaught Station), stamps, 2.00; Postmaster (Dorset), stamps, 11.08; Postmaster (madale), stamps, 1.00; Postmaster (Espanola), stamps, 2.00; Postmaster (Fotes Bay), stamps, 1.90; Postmaster (Gordon Bay), stamps, registration, 3.19, Postmaster (Hall's Lake), stamps, 1.00; Postmaster (Huntsville), stamps, 3.75; Postmaster (Iroquois Falls), stamps, 2.50; Postmaster (MacTier), stamps, registration 4.57, Postmaster (Magnetawan), stamps, 8.40; Postmaster (Minden), stamps rent of box, 201.20; Postmaster (Nipissing), stamps, 1.00; Postmaster (North Bay) stamps, 187.00; Postmaster (Parry Sound), stamps, registration, 39.14 Postmaster (Port Carling), stamps, 6.38; Postmaster (Port Cunningham), stamps 3.00 Postmaster (Port Loring, stamps, registration, 3.55; Postmaster (Powassan), stamps, 35.00, Postmaster (Raymond), stamps, .60; Postmaster (busseau Road), stamps, 4.20; Postmaster (Severn Bridge), stamps, 3.95, Postmaster (Sioux Lookout), stamps, 14.00; Postmaster (South River), stamps, registration, 19.33; Postmaster Sundridge), stamps, 15.85; Postmaster, (Swastika), stamps, 3.00, Postmaster (Trout Creek), stamps, registration, 7.72; Postmaster Warren), stamps, regis-), stamps, 4.50 John Pousette, rent of typewriter, 18.00; Powassan Garage, gas, oil, car parts and repairs, 711.65; Powassan Milk & Freight Transfer, transportation 6.00 Powassan News, advertisment, 3.80; Mrs. Wm. Powell, board, 29.30, W Powell (Keewatin), taxi service, 5.00; W. Powell (Tomstown P.O.), lumber, 34.16, Dr M. Powers, services, examining men, 15.00; Geo. A. Powles, travelling expenses, 7.15; John Powley, posts, 11.00; W. E. Pratt, meat, 130.41; Leal Prentice, teaming, 4.35; Thos. Prentice, wood, 43.50; W. W. Prentice, lumber, w, lime, 9.50; Preston's Machine Shop, blacksmithing, 243.60; Jas. Prutsell, blacksmithing, 13.82; Percy Price, gravel, 148.96; J. A. Prieur, car parts and repairs, gas, oil, 229.42; Em. Primeaux, cedar, 20.04; Mrs. W. Pringle, board, 947 , Frank Prior, potatoes, 7.00; Mrs. Alf. Pritchard, board, 269.50; Mrs Earl Pritchard, hardwood, 125.73; Lawrence Pritchard, transportation, 10.00; Lewis Pritchard, lumber, car rental, trucking, 916.74; L. Pritchard, hardwood, 52.50, Producers' Co-operative Creamery Co., Ltd., provisions, 419.25; Provencher Bros., provisions, matches, 687.24; Dr. G. A. Publow, services, examining men, 00, P. Qualachuk, provisions, 11.10; Quality Meat Market, provisions, 50.50 Quality Meat & Grocery Co., Ltd., provisions, 379.19; Jos. Quenette, blacksmithing, 10.15; E. Quesnel, repairs, 8.25; Henry Quesnel, gravel, 28.70; J. Quesnell, provisions, 4.65; P. Quesnell, transportation, 109.08; P. Quesnel, gravel, transportation, 83.10; A. Quick, wood, 26.25; Quinlan & Co., roofing, 3.75; D. F. Quinlan & Co., provisions and soap, 18.75; Dr. P. F. Quinlan, services, examining men, 2.00; Andy Quinn, wood, 25.00; Fred and Mrs. Quinn, lumber, meat, cartage, 2,027.14; Mirvin Quinn, hardwood, 25.00; J. P. Quinn, rent for Orange Hall, 152.26; T. A. Quinn, films, prints, stationery, 12.00; E. M. Quirt, trucking transportation, 587.50; A. J. Radbourne, meat, oats, 56.00; J. Radborne, beef, 2.36, Peter Radell, cedar, 5.00; Mark Radford, pine, 16.00; A. H. Radka, pork, .20; Alec Rahal, roofing, board, provisions, transportation, 396.08; Railway & Power Engineering Corporation, Ltd. (Toronto), steel, 148.66; Railway & Power Engineering Corporation, Ltd. (Winnipeg), steel, 171.81; E. Raincourt, wood, 14.0 L. Raincourt, firewood, 21.49; Max. Raincourt, firewood, 31.84; A.R. Rains, cartage, 4.00; Arsino Rainville, gravel, 44.00; Rainy Lake Hotel, board, 32.25; Rainy River Canners, hay, 82.11; Ramore Supply Store, provisions, hardware, 1,121.56; Wm. Randell, provisions, 14.25; B. H. Rands, gas, hardware, explosives, 91.65 Fred Rankin, timber, 1.98; Geo. Rankin, poles, 6.40; Jas. Rankin, wood, 185.6 Drs. J. P. Rankin and H. B. Kenner, services, examining men, 25.00; M. J. Ransford, travelling expenses, 5.55; Catherine Ranson, board, 339.84; Robt. Ranson, rental of storehouse, transportation, 25.70; W. Rattray, travelling expenses, 1.85; W. H. Ratz, provisions, 4.00; R. H. Raush, cedar, 67.60; J. Frank Ry Co., Ltd., draughting, supplies, 29.05; F. Ray, fill, reconstructing fence, 73.72; Ramsbottom & Edwards, Kirk

Statutory—Continued

General W k, Unemployment Relief—Continued

butter, 136.75; Wallace Recki rental of camp site, provisions, 310.95; Chas. Reckin & Sons, provisions, 130.5; J. A. Redfern, gravel, 20.00; The Red & White Store, provisions, soap, blacksmithing, oil, 115.28; Harry Reechstein, wood, lumber, 320.25; L. Reed, lumb, 50.80; Tom Regan, gravel, 62.40; Fred Reickstein, provisions, 17.20; Harry Reickstein, wood, lumber, rental of lot, 52.00; A. R. Reid, pork, 25.84; Duncan Reid, provisions, 44.96; Geo. Reid, travelling expenses, telephone calls, express, 106.8 T. H. Reid & Co., cotton, 1.65; W. J. Reid, gravel, 98.80; W. Remillard, gravel, 12.00; Ben Renshaw, hay, 140.49; Chas. Resbeck, gravel, 73.20; John Reynolds Estate, tools, spikes, 8.00; Geo. R. Rhode & Co., hardware, 42.00; Alfred Ribble, board, 207.75; Fred Ricard, surveying road, 1.00; Wm. J. Rice Co., blankets, 570.82; Anthony Rich, gravel, cedar, 92.45; Barney Rich, provisions, 25.28; Edmond Richard, provisions, 256.40; J. A. Richard, logs, 35.00, E. V. Richards, cartage, transportation, 1,290.25; Wilbert Richards, provisions, 95.78; Wm. Richards, provisions, 56.50; F. C. Richardson, provisions, bran, matches, hardware, 2,147.63; Stanley Richardson, clearing, grubbing, 80.40; Wallace Rickie, lumber, straw, 57.50; Barney Rick, provisions, 137.04; Cecil Ricker, hardware, .70; Fred Ricker, transportation, car rental, 58.00; Herb Ridout, board, 1,021.88; S. Rigby, trucking, transportation, 648.00; Medie Ritchie, Sr., cedar posts, 89.25; Orville Rivers, wood, 15.00; Jerry Rivet, poles, 76.32; C. W. Rock, travelling expenses, car rental, 251.70; J. O. Robert, gas, grease, 37.43; Cecil A. Roberts, trucking, 1,110.14; Donald Roberts, taxi service, 15.00; J. L. R[illegible], gravel, 134.60; Nelson Roberts, lumber, 26.41; R. Roberts, poles, 76.80; Allan Robertson, gravel, 4.00; E. Robertson, repairs, 1.00; G. L. Robertson, gas, provisions, repairs, 192.82; John Robertson, transportation, 5.00; Dr. Lo[illegible] Robertson, services, examining men, 12.00; Dr. W. A. Robertson, services examining men, 10.00; Ian Robins, gravel, 770.40; Edward Robinson, gravel, 4.80; E. Robinson, hay, 86.64; Geo. Robinson, wood, 87.50; Joe Robinson, lumber 3.00; Leslie Robinson, cartage, 3.84; Richard Robinson, meat, 13.44; S. Robinson, meat, 13.05; Dr. R. B. Robson, services, examining men, 10.00; P. Rocheford, travelling expenses, telephone account, 343.85; H. Rochon, gravel 150; R. Rochon, gravel, 60.00; John W. Rodie, trucking, transportation, box ares, 84.93; E. A. Rogers, hardware, roofing, telegrams, 312.99; Dr. N[illegible] W. Rogers, services, examining men, 10.00; T. H. Rogers & Son, hardware, rent of tool shed, roofing, gas, grease, gravel, 213.67; W. E. Rogers, trucking, wood, 3,005.79; L. Romprey, lumber, 89.76; G. Rondeau, gravel, 5.70; G. Roque, transportation, 149.28; J. Roque, transportation, 55.19; L. V. Rorke, old notes, 2.00; G. Rosewan, valve, .50; A. Ross (Black Hawk), provisions, 3.50; A. Ross (WaWa), wood, rent of camp site, 84.00; L. Ross, car rental, 3.00; Rosser Garage & Livery, taxi service, 2.75; Cliff Rossel, gravel, 7.50; D. Rousseau, gravel, 12.00; H. W. Rowdon, explosives, hardware, 149.57; J. W. Rowe, board .80; W. Rowe, gravel, 58.50; S. Rowland, blacksmithing, 48.35; Richard Rowndson, cedar, wood, 247.50; Robt. Rowlandson, cedar, 10.25; R. D. Rowlandson, board, 24.00; E. Rowley, cedar, 24.85, Alfred Roy, lumber, 25.00; D. Roy (Blind River), gravel, 22.50; D. Roy (Warren), 64.80; E Roy, travelling expenses, 4.30; Henry Roy, plank, 23.50, H. H. Roy (Warren), explosives, hardware, gas, grease, oil, 7,379.87; H. H. Roy (Markstay), coal, nails, 6.34; J. B. Roy, gravel, 93.00; Nap. and Mrs. Roy, gas, 239.22; O. Roy, gravel, 270.75; Dr. F. J. Rundle, services, examining men 22.00; C. P. Rush, lettering signs, 3.00 Alfred Russell, gravel, 9.00, Joe Russell, meat, 38.70 Thos. R. Russell, gas, barrow, .24; S. Russell, posts, 7.50, Wm. Russell, gravel, 9.00; Dr. Gordon H. Rutherford, services, examining men, 32.00; Jas. Ruttan, steel blade, 1.50; Wm. Ruttan, blacksmithing, rent of blacksmith shop and tools, 13.05; Jos. Ryan (Blind River) meat, 73.92; Jos. Ryan (Raymond) wood, [illegible] T. F. Ryan, hardware, .93 Rial Bank Garage, gas, oil, 237.11, D. St. [illegible] gravel, 81.50; D. St. Germain gravel, 4.00; E. St. Jacques, wood, 27.50, J. St. Laurent (Michipicoten River) provisions, car rental, tools, coal, 64.68, C. St. Laurent, board, hardware, 2.00; J. St. Laurent (WaWa) car rental, [illegible] St. Mary's Wood Specialty Co. Ltd., tools, 1,471.01; K. Saara, gravel, [illegible] Richard Sabourin, cedar, posts, 58.32; Sadowski & Co., provisions, [illegible] 2,239.13; Thos. Salmon, meat 67.57; J. W. Sanderson, trucking, [illegible] Sanderson, cartage, 32.00; Sanderson's Transport, cartage, 77.50; C. [illegible] Co., transportation, 42.00; [illegible] Sanfrene, gravel, 6.00; J. [illegible] 4.76; E. Sarazen, gravel, 20.00; The Sault Daily Star, advertising, [illegible] Ste. Marie Coal & Wood Co. Ltd., coal, 418.47; [illegible] 91.08; Sawyer-Massey, Ltd., machinery parts, [illegible] expenses, 110.50; Geo. Scott, transportation, trucking, [illegible] 89.85; L. B. Scannell, tools, explosives, hardware, [illegible]

Statutory—Continued

General Work, Unemployment Relief—Continued

M. Schmidt, earth fill, 110.25; F. H. Schoales, gravel, 503.05; W. E. Schraeder, provisions, 72.70; Chas. Schultz, hardware, 3.05; B. Schwartz, provisions, 26.86; Chas. Schwarze, wood, 92.00; Jno. Schwarze, wood, rent of camp site, 168.38; Geo. Schweitzer, provisions, 2.25; Scott Bros., cartage, 14.00; C. L. Scott, car rental, 28.00; C. P. Scott, provisions, rent of camp site, 186.51; Dr. H. R. Scott, services, examining men, 21.00; Reg. Scott, machinery parts, 2.00; Thos. A. Scott, welding, 66.00; Walter Scott, hardwood, sand, borrow, 120.00; Gordon Seabrook, gravel, 28.10; Pete Seager, meat, 19.20; Alfred Sear, cedar, 63.68; Searchmont Lumber Co., Ltd., lumber, blankets, hardware, tents, 338.57; Geo. Sears, rent of storehouse, board, 1,009.35; Isaac Sedgwick, lumber, 2,081.76; Mrs. R. Sedor, gas, oil, 65.28; Fred and Mrs. Seguin, truck and car rental, transportation, 81.00; Jos Seguin, gravel, 58.60; O. Seguin, gravel, 6.40; Henry Selin, timber, car rental, gas, oil, 459.43; John Selin, spruce, 15.00; Service Garage, gas, meals, 6.50; Service Market, provisions, 16.86; J. Sevigny, lumber, 340.20; Louis Shamas, beef, 18.30; Michael A. Shamas, provisions, towelling, oats, 482.79; Thos. Shamas, provisions, fill, gravel, 315.23; Estate of J. Shane, gravel, 42.40; Mrs. M. Sharp, gravel, stone, 1,238.05; John Shaughnessy, wire hardware, 47.28; Richard Shaughnessy, building power house, repairs, 31.50; Geo. Shaule, blacksmithing, gravel, 17.10; R. V. Shave, travelling expenses, 51.45; Alfred Shaw, provisions, gas, 10,838.53; Shaw & Co., oats, 1,220.50; C. V. Shaw, provisions, 47.16; E. Shaw, trucking, transportation, 446.05; Geo. M. Shaw, travelling expenses, 57.90; Geo. M. Shaw, photographs, 30.00; H. M. Shaw, provisions, 415.97; Thos. Shaw, provisions, 97.50; Wm. F. Shay, wood, pork, 40.88; D. Shea, trucking, 37.50; J. Sheedy, travelling expenses, 5.35; Shell Company of Canada, Ltd., gas, oil, 88.22; Otto Sherman, wood, 25.00; Alven Shevalier, provisions, 60.66; Shevlin-Clarke Co., Ltd., explosives, kitchenware, lumber, 963.85; W. B. Shewfelt, provisions, 222.17; Shiels Garage, gas, oil, repairs, 292.03; Wm. Shiels, gravel, 38.10; E. Shier, meat, 25.60; F. Shier, oats, 65.30; J. E. Shier, gas, 5.70; R. Shier, transportation, 7.50; Shier's Shoe Store, rubber boots, 17.34; Shillington General Store, provisions, hardware, 1,665.53; W. Shipman, provisions, 4.90; E. T. Shortland, gas, oil, repairs, 349.07; Wesley Shortreed, potatoes, 6.50; Adam Shoultz, pork, 22.24; F. Shrumm, provisions, 25.12; Wm. Shrumm, provisions, 19.08; Wilbur Shuttleworth, posts, 58.50; L. Silver, lumber, wood, 525.90; A. Silverman & Sons, rubber boots, 11.80; Geo. Simmons, travelling expenses, 20.20; T. Simpson & Co., hardware, provisions, oil, 186.52; Geo. Simpson, provisions, 27.36; Henry Simpson, meat, 35.20; Jas. I. Simpson, transportation, 15.01; Ralph Simpson, transportation, 4.75; T. Simpson & Son, provisions, soap, oil, 540.86; W. E. Simpson, office rental, 105.00; H. Sims, lath, 3.00; Daniel Sinclair, lumber, borrow, 61.20; Donald Sinclair, cedar, 20.80; Mrs. M. Sinclair, board, 10.75; Nelson Sinclair, cedar, borrow, 142.00; Sioux Lookout Bakery & Grocery, provisions, 644.03; A. Sirois, gravel, 92.10; E. J. Sirrett, poles, 5.32; Leigh Sissons, wood, gravel, car rental, 140.10; Mrs. Leigh Sissons, board, 103.20; Nelson Skelding, lumber, 32.50; H. A. Skene, hay, 40.00; A. J. Skjonsby, provisions, 20.09; Harold Skusky, wood, 25.46; Jas. Slater, wood, 14.00; N. Slater Co., Ltd., washer, bolts, 79.53; Walter Slater, travelling expenses, 3.25; Wm. Sloan, gravel, 142.05; Fred Sloman, shipping charges on relief clothing, 28.93; Wm. Sluman, cartage, 11.66; C. Smeeth, gravel, 9.00; Jessie Smeeth, gravel, 18.70; Tom Smeltzer, gravel, 6.30; Alex. Smith, provisions, 175.88; Smith & Chapple, Ltd., hardware, provisions, gas, 4,049.46; C. Smith, rental of camp site, 5.00; David Smith, wood, damage to house, 13.00; Dr. David Smith, services, examining men, 4.00; Mrs. Ed. Smith, board, 30.20; F. C. Smith, travelling expenses, 9.25; F. E. Smith, provisions, hardware, tools, oil, 3,692.35; G. Smith, cedar, 12.00; Mrs. Jas. Smith, Jr., board, 78.20; John Smith, wood, 322.00; John B. Smith & Sons, Ltd., lumber, 13.16; Leonard Smith, timber, 8.00; Oliver Smith, gravel, 117.80; Roy Smith, twine, gravel, sand, 5.53; Walter Smith, cedar poles, 189.95; Wm. Smith, lumber, 247.71; Mrs. W. Smith, fish, 5.00; Smith's Hardware & Grocery, hardware, provisions, gas, oil, 5,088.10; W. J. Snelgrove, provisions, 2,649.16; Con. Snider, travelling expenses, 7.10; Arvid Soderena, gravel, 54.10; C. Sohnlein, gravel, 18.40; Albert Solomon, provisions, oats, 828.91; Geo. Solomon, provisions, 219.95; Mrs. Geo. Solomon, washing blankets, 14.00; Isaac Solomon, gas, oil, provisions, 37.99; Moses Solomon, hardware, provisions, kitchenware, oil, 546.87; R. H. Somes, travelling expenses, 42.30; Otto Somes, board, 2,994.30; L. Sommacal, gravel, 5.00; Soo Business College, rent of typewriter, 22.91; Soo Lumber & Mill Co., lumber, 749.39; C. Souter, gravel, 35.70; Stan. Sowicki, beef, 34.14; Spanish Garage, gas, oil, car parts and repairs, car rental, 691.23; Spanish River Lumber Co., Ltd. (Skead), rent of blacksmith shop, boarding house, 72.90; Spanish River Lumber Co., Ltd. (Sudbury), lumber, rental of boarding house and building for stable, gas, 624.06;

Statutory—Continued

General Work, Unemployment Relief—Continued

Harry H. Sparks, gravel, sand, damages to cottage, 300.00; R. Sparks, cedar, 62.18; Speers Bros., stabling horses, 17.50; Dr. E. Spence, services, examining men, 29.00; Harold Spence, provisions, 18.00; Hugh Spence, cedar, 9.60; W. H. Spence, travelling expenses, 4.00; E. Spicer, oats, flax, 4.00; Thos. Spiers, transportation, 3.00; Paul Spooner, cedar, 14.56; Wm. Spreadborough, provisions, 44.10; E. Springhett, gravel, 323.70; Spruce Falls Power & Paper Co., Ltd., blacksmithing, explosives, 12.47; Joe Stadnisky, potatoes, 6.00; Dr. C. L. B. Stammers, services, examining men, 15.00; Mrs. Ellen Stamp, board, 39.10; Standard Chemical Co., Ltd., gravel, 30.25; Stanhope Municipal Telephone Co., telephone rent and services, repairs to telephone line, 118.00; Geo. Stanley, oats, hay, 9.85; Stanley Hotel, board, 11.20; Star Groceteria, provisions, 21.35; Star Taxi & Transfer, transportation, 4.50; A. Steed, blacksmithing, 1.00; Hugh Steed, pork, 11.52; A. L. Steele, blacksmithing, 47.25; The Steel Equipment Co., Ltd., filing cabinets, 24.50; Herb Steinburg, gravel, rent of blacksmithing equipment, 95.90; C. F. Steinke, provisions, 263.75; Peter Stepovay, timber, 18.00; Andy Stevens, board, 79.50; H. M. Stevens, travelling expenses, 3.60; Ed. Stevenson, wood, 21.25; M. G. Stevenson, wood, 50.00; Dave Stewart, wood, 6.25; Mrs. E. Stewart, gravel, 60.90; Frank Stewart, material from borrow pit, 20.00; H. C. Stewart, provisions, 14.19; J. A. Stewart, travelling expenses, 5.00; Jas. Stewart, wood, 60.00; L. D. N. Stewart, 5.50; Wm. Stewart, wood, 61.00; Mrs. E. Stillar, making towels, 4.56; Jack Still, cedar, 31.35; J. H. Still Manufacturing Co., tools, hardware, 1,082.45; Isaac Stiller, gravel, 2.40; Stirrett Lumber Co., lumber, 54.97; Stone Lumber Co., Ltd., lumber, 45.85; W. Stoneman, wood, 9.10; S. J. Storkson, oats, beef, 65.94; R. G. Storms, travelling expenses, 4.85; Robt. Strachan, meat, 36.00; Stroud Bros., lumber, 16.62; S. Stroud, provisions, 3.50; Mrs. S. C. Stroud, hay, 64.12; J. A. Strutt, blacksmithing, 6.50; E. Stubbington, gravel, 36.30; R. Stutvott, oats, 17.10; Sudbury Construction & Machinery Co., Ltd., machinery repairs, 16.60; Mrs. W. A. Suffern, board, 323.25; Sullivan Machinery Co., Ltd., machinery parts, 554.35; H. Sullivan, gravel, 55.20; W. Sullivan, gravel, 4.95; W. F. Sullivan, provisions, hardware, wood, oil, 572.14; Sundridge Garage, gas, oil, repairs, 219.51; Sundridge Meat Supply Co., provisions, 913.87; Wm. Suom, gravel, 21.00; Superior Iron & Steel Co. of Canada, Ltd., pipe, cable, 93.20; Thos. Swalwell, lumber, provisions, wood, 724.28; O. Swanson, wood, rent of house, 37.50; W. Swanstrom, provisions, poles, 153.30; B. Swantz, provisions, cedar, 29.10; Chas. Swartz, wood, 50.00; Swastika Drug Co., Ltd., fly oil, 11.10; Robt. Sweeney, blacksmithing, 27.20; Swift-Canadian Co., Ltd. (Sault Ste. Marie), provisions, 1,037.48; Swift-Canadian Co., Ltd. (Winnipeg), provisions, 659.91; P. D. Sword, hay, 65.75; J. L. Sylvester, gravel, 22.20; Ernest B. Symes, towelling, oilcloth, 17.40; P. V. Symes, towelling, oilcloth, 19.90; Richard Taillefer, posts, 30.30; Antti Tainio, rental of motor launch and operator, 6.00; Orson Tait, transportation, 4.00; R. N. Tait, cartage, 108.75; Jas. Taillon, travelling expenses, gravel, 117.70; Tally-Ho Inn, board, gas, oil, 92.05; Jos. Tapley, gravel, provisions, 201.24; B. W. Tardiff, explosives, 4.20; B. Tarricani, cedar, 39.41; Jos. Tassie, provisions, 8.00; Alex. Taylor, board, 12.30; Bert Taylor, travelling expenses, 1.25; C. Taylor, oats, 4.50; Mrs. C. H. Taylor, board, livery, 927.30; The Geo. Taylor Hardware, Ltd., explosives, wire, 24.91; Mrs. H. Taylor, board, 113.85; Jas. A. Taylor, gravel, wood, 83.30; Jim Taylor, 20.00; John Taylor, gravel, 99.10; Mark Taylor, lumber, provisions, transportation, posts, 2,852.41; Teck Fuel & Ice Co., coal, wood, 22.75; F Teeple, meat, 13.76; Temiskaming and Northern Ontario Railway, freight, fares, 2,868.34; Jas. A. Templeton, cartage, 2.00; Geo. Tennant, wood, 51.50; Wm Tennant, wood, 2.40; Walter Tessier, gravel, 91.00; Napoleon Tetreault, cedar, 7.70; Robt. Thaxter, meat, 54.48; W. I. Thayer, gravel, 447.40; Max. Thebault, stove, blankets, 140.00; Z. Theriault, wood, 11.25; D. Therien, wood, 4.00; Bondieuse Therrien, lumber, 21.25; Jos. Therrien, timber, 2.10; Arnold Thiel, lumber, 22.10; The Thomas Co., clock, advertisement, stationery, 5.70; Frank Thomas, wood, 57.60; Jas. Thomas, forge parts, 5.00; Mrs. Sarah Thomas, provisions, 58.48; Mrs. A. and A. Thompson, provisions, hay, oats, wood, 57.87; Austin Thompson, wood, 50.00; Chris. Thompson, timber, 37.80; Leo Thompson, gravel, 75.45; Thompson, Ltd., towelling, 36.60; Wm. A. Thompson, wood, 50.00; Wm. C. Thompson, light account, 13.35; W. G. Thompson, travelling expenses, 18.40; W. R. Thompson, car rental, 127.50; Frank Thomson, car rental, 50.00; K. E. Thomson, gas, repairs to car, 2.90; W. R. Thomson, travelling expenses, 5.50; Jesse Thorne, provisions, 15.36; C. J. Thornton, oil, 3.00; Frank Thornton, gas, oil, provisions, hay, 571.03; Thorpe Bros., mirror, 4.55; Thunder Bay Lumber Co., Ltd. (Fort William), lumber 858.08; Thunder Bay Lumber Co., Ltd. (Port Arthur), lumber, 307.91; Geo. Tibbel, poles, 45.57; Mrs. Geo. Tibbel, board, 1.90; S. O. Tickner, gas, repairs, 178.05; C. Tighe, travelling expenses, .70;

Statutory—Continued

General Work, Unemployment Relief—Continued

Chas. Tilson, gravel, wood, 85.00; Emil Tilvis, wood, 17.87; Timmins Laundry Co., washing blankets, 240.12; L. Tindall, cedar, transportation, 287.25; Arthur W. Tingey, provisions, 87.27; Fred Tiplady, provisions, 747.59; W. J. Tobin, blacksmithing, 29.96; H. Todd, lumber, gravel, poles, 105.73; W. Todd, hay, 87.85; W. C. Tomlinson, gravel, 54.30; Tompkins' Hardware, hardware, tools, roofing, oilcloth, 779.64; J. Toms, provisions, 27.20; O. V. Tontant, travelling expenses, 4.85; A. Topham, gravel, 132.80; Toronto Asphalt Roofing Manufacturing Co., Ltd., explosives, hardware, 1,433.69; Roy Torrance, wood, 13.53; Tourtellot Hardware Co., Ltd., hardware, 266.52; Wm. Towle, poles, 99.05; Oliver Towns, provisions, rent of camp site, 212.44; Wallace Towns, provisions, oats, cedar, hay, 2,024.61; Wm. Towns, provisions, soap, 190.49; Jos. Tranchemontagne, lumber, 18.72; Trap Rock, Ltd., trap rock, wheelbarrows, steel, coal, explosives, 1,860.65; Thos. Travers, travelling expenses, 58.35; A. Tremblay, transportation, 18.00; A. D. Tremblay, wood, 27.00; C. Tremblay, provisions, 52.56; D. Tremblay, wood, 106.48; Ed. Tremblay, wood, 50.25; J. Tremblay, wood, 48.00; J. F. Tremblay, rent of buildings, 45.00; J. J. Tremblay, board, 11.90; S. Tremblay, lunches, 8.25; W. E. Tremblay, straps, .80; T. S. Trenouth, nails, .16; L. S. Trepanier, hay, 353.85; Triangle Truck & Taxi Service, transportation, 29.00; Fred Tribe, potatoes, 9.37; Matt Trivers, hay, 100.00 Theodore Trotter, cedar, 14.50; A. Trottier, gravel, 2.50; G. Trottier, gravel, 40.50; Thos. Trottier, gravel, 65.25; A. E. Trousse, travelling expenses, 4.50; Trout Creek Garage, gas, oil, 38.41; Trout Creek Lumber Co., lumber, 1,266.96; Trout Creek Store, provisions, hardware, explosives, oil, 2,739.42; J. W. Troyer, provisions, hardware, gas, rent of office, transportation, 4,641.41; S. H. Troyer, provisions, 3,513.73; Albert Trowbridge, gravel, 25.35; A. E. Trowsse, travelling expenses, 6.00; G. Z. Trudeau, explosives, hardware, steel, 992.51; Albert Trudel, blacksmithing, 252.00; Mrs. Wm. Trumbull, board, 90.50; Donald Tucker, hay, 110.34; G. Tucker, wood, 7.50; Tudhope-Anderson, Ltd., stone boats, 157.90; Alex. Tulloch & Sons, hardware, 23.85; Fred Tummey, carrots, 5.17; John Turcotte, vegetables, 8.75; L. Turcotte, rental of cookery outfit, equipment, etc., 115.50; The Byron H. Turner Co., Ltd., rubber boots, 15.25; J. J. Turner & Sons, Ltd., tents, dunnage bags, 26.05; E. Turpin, wood, 13.50; Twin City Grain, Ltd., hay, oats, 241.76; P. T. Tyers, gravel, 46.90; Wm. Ullman, board, 1,198.10; Union Garage, gas, oil, repairs, car rental, 251.18; United Algoma Gold Mines, Ltd., rent of camp building, 650.00; United States and Dominion Transportation Co., Ltd., transportation, 461.73; United Typewriter Co., Ltd., typewriter parts, 1.08; John Urquahart, blacksmithing, 3.60; Robt. Urquahart, repairs, 7.90; S. Usiki, potatoes, 1.50; The Utterson Garage, car parts and repairs, 7.75; A. Vachon, gravel, 572.40; M.Vader, hardware, 50.40; A. B. Vaillancourt, hardware, lumber, explosives, cartage, 2,306.31; Louis Vaillancourt, gas, oil, hardware, trucking, 339,89; C. Valade, cedar, 24.16; J. Valland, beef, 53.64; Arthur Valley, taxi service, car rental, 132.00; Valley View Inn, board, 533.87; Thos. Vance, sand, gravel, 17.35; Fred Vanclieaf, window glass, putty, .35; Mrs. Fred Vanclieaf, board, 121.30; W. Vanclief, potatoes, lumber, gravel, 198.08; H. J. Vanderhorst, vegetables, 4.43; C. Vandrunen, provisions, 5.00; L. Vandrunen, provisions, 10.00; Phil Vanier, cedar, 32.16; Jno. Vaughan, gravel, 120.60; A. Vazant, gravel, 176.65; H. A. Veillette, repairs, 51.50; Narcisse Veilleux, wood, 12.00; P. Verbiski, trucking, car rental, 177.00; L. Viau, gravel, 176.30; I. Viau, gravel, 6.20; Viau Biscuit Corporation, Ltd., provisions, 19.80; Victoria Bakery, provisions, 295.69; P. J. Vigrass, provisions, hardware, gas, oil, 902.49; J. Z. Vinet, hardware, gas, provisions, 760.95; E. Vizeau, transportation, 43.21; Wm. Vizeau, transportation, 38.50; B. A. Vizena, stove, tent, parts, 126.00; Jas. Voicey, wood, 126.25; Thos. Voicey, wood, 76.50; Ed. Vowels, provisions, wood, 73.82; Mrs. E. Vowels, milk, 180.00; Walter Vowels, wood, 75.00; Wabi Iron Works, Ltd., machinery parts and repairs, repairs, 341.33; N. Wachnow, towelling, 14.08; Jas. W. Waddell, provisions, 14.64; Chas. Wadson, provisions, 49.76; A. A. and Mrs. Wagner, hardware, explosives, provisions, 122.76; D. D. Wagner, travelling expenses, 10.25; Mrs. W. Wagner, plumb bob, .40; E. J. Walden, travelling expenses, 9.90; G. Waldrif, gravel, 8.90; Bert Walker, board, 132.30; D. Walker, transportation, 156.97; Walker & Horne, blacksmithing, 693.65; John Walker, wood, 52.13; W. Walker & Son, Ltd., tools, cartage, 1,491.86; Ben H. Walsh, travelling expenses, 2.25; Ebert Walsh, gravel, timber, 9.16; Richard Walsh travelling expenses, 19.94; Swinburn Walton, hardware, plow parts, 11.40; E. A. Warburton, car rental, travelling expenses. 242.55; J. Ward, travelling expenses, 4.35; J. E. Ward, pork, 16.64; J. W. Ward, hardware, 3.55; Wardell & Co., rubber, boots, 169.44; John Wardell, provisions, 219.04; John Wardman, hay, 80.13; W. H. Wardrop, lumber, 5.60; Ware Bros., provisions, 3.40; F. A. Ware, potatoes, 39.00; E. C.

Statutory—Continued

General Work, Unemployment Relief—Continued

Warner, lumber, 58.50; E. Watkins, board, 2.25; C. Watkinson, towelling, 8.29; T. Watson, provisions, 85.78; Jas. Watt, blacksmithing, 18.25; Oliver Watt, lumber, 53.45; T. L. Watts, travelling expenses, 12.00; Watt Municipal Telephone System, telephone calls, 1.05; Edward Watts, clay fill, 111.00; Mrs. E. C. Watts, provisions, 12.00; Geo. Watts, wood, 5.00; Mrs. J. Watts, oats, provisions, 193.12; C. E. Weeks, sand fill, 155.02; Rev. E. Weeks, gravel, 31.20; H. Weeks, car rental, 160.00; Weismiller Bros., lumber, coal, 1,340.61; Jas. Weismiller, trucking, 117.00; D. H. Welch, provisions, wood, 3,328.48; Fred Welch, transportation, 10.00; John Welch, iron, steel, blacksmithing, 426.27; S. W. Welch, hardware, oil, lumber, 529.58; F. C. Wellar, lumber, tool box, 13.10; Wells Hardware Co., Ltd., coal, hardware, kitchenware, explosives, 13,593.36; Wells & Emerson, hardware, 169.47; C. Wench, plank, 59.76; E. Wendstrom, beef, 33.36; Lloyd T. Wesley, car rental, 254.00; Wesley Taxi & Transfer Co., rent of truck, trucking, transportation, 200.00; S. S. and Mrs. Wessell, board, 115.60; Geo. West, pork, 6.08; West & Co., provisions, oil, hardware, 433.46; Western Bakery, bread, 1.00; Western Engineering Service, Ltd., machinery parts, .62; Western Grocers, Ltd. (Fort Frances), provisions, soap, 3,635.67; Western Grocers, Ltd. (Fort William), provisions, soap, 5,019.05; Western Grocers, Ltd. (Kenora), matches, 4.93; Western Oil Co., Ltd., gas, oil, 311.67; W. H. Whalen, beef, 116.32; R. H. Whaley & Son, blacksmithing, 59.79; J. H. Whelen, blacksmithing, 13.25; A. C. White, lumber, 532.00; E. A. White, gas, hardware, explosives, cement, 374.21; Dave White, gravel, 22.90; White Drug Store, veterinary supplies, 33.32; Frank White, wood, 24.00; Geo. White, gravel, 41.60; G. L. White, film, prints, grease, 21.60; Thos. White, gravel, 8.25; W. A. White, livery, 76.10; S. Whitehead, beef, 17.92; Mrs. Phillip Whitelock, provisions, 4.50; Geo. Whitely, lumber, 26.00; John Whitely, board, 382.40; Drs. Whitely and Graham, services, examining men, 11.00; Albert Whitmill, hardwood, 38.75; John Whitmill, wood, 14.37; The Whitten Co., Ltd., hardware, tools, coal, 501.06; A. Wholgemuth, gravel, 62.85; H. Wigmore, stone boats, 15.30; Ben Wilcox, beef, 10.26; Mrs. Wm. Wilcox, wood, 186.00; Hiram Wilder, meat, 48.24; L. W. Wilder, meat, 41.40; R. Wilds, provisions, 24.21; Harvey Wilkin, posts, 13.75; C. L. Wilkinson, provisions, 23.20; Klint Wilkinson, timber, 140.70; Gordon Willard, hardwood, 25.00; Williams Hardware Co., hardware, tools, heaters, roofing, 2,281.05; L. F. Williams, travelling expenses, 18.45; Murdock Williams, gravel, 24.00; R. Williams, travelling expenses, 8.65; Williams & Scott, hardware, explosives, coal, gas, oil, 448.65; Tom Williams, gravel, 9.90; Jos. Williamson, stone lifters, 16.50; F. Willis, provisions, 7.50; John Willoughby, Sr., gravel, 31.80; Mrs. Elizabeth Wilman, gravel, 25.00; Wilson Bros., lumber, sash, 1,198.84; Wilson Bros. (Sundridge), hemlock, 187.20; Frank Wilson, 4.50; Henry Wilson, pork, 14.72; Jas. Wilson, cedar, 10.80; J. L. Wilson, lumber, 103.68; Ralph Wilson, wood, 16.00; R. H. Wilson, blacksmithing, 65.67; Tom Wilson, gravel, 124.45; W. Wilson, rental of camp site, provisions, wood, 49.15; W. B. Wilson, provisions, oil, gravel, rent of camp ground, 565.19; W. S. Wilson, travelling expenses, 40.64; Gordon Winch, plank, 45.45; W. G. Winch, lumber, 45.45; Windsor Hotel, board, 238.00; Geo. H. Winsor, hardware, tools, roofing, gas, 156.31; Ernest Windover, car rental, travelling expenses, 269.00; E. R. Windover, car rental, travelling expenses, 61.80; C. Wisman, transportation, 20.00; A. Witry, provisions, 15.00; Wolfe & Collins, hardware, provisions, oats, 5,293.81; Sam Wolsley, provisions, 36.56; Albert R. Wood, gas, oil, 2,993.91; Wood, Alexander & James, Ltd., tools, 628.39; Belford Wood, plank, 11.25; Fred Wood, provisions, 34.31; J. H. Wood, travelling expenses, 6.95; John Wood, plank, 11.00; A. R. Woodroffe, lumber, 16.00; Geo. Woodroffe, hay, 5.87; L. W. Woodruff & Son, cedar, 844.10; Wm. Woodruff, lumber, 555.65; W. L. Woodruff, cedar, 153.76; Wesley Woodruff, lumber, 596.16; Geo. Woods, gravel, 11.25; R. R. Woods, hardware, tools, explosives, towelling, 3,036.15; T. S. Woollings, gravel, 33.90; Colin Wright, gravel, 28.80; Mrs. Jas. Wright, board, 49.70; J. A. Wright, travelling expenses, 2.70; Tom Wright, gravel, 23.25; W. J. Wright, gravel, 6.50; Stanley Wurm, cedar, trucking, transportation, 329.54; David Wye, wood, 50.00; Geo. Wye, gravel, 21.60; Mrs. David Wylie, provisions, 8.00; Mrs. Encena Wylie, gravel, 20.00; John Wylie, borrow, 20.00; Yale & Towne Manufacturing Co., padlocks, 20.65; A. J. Yelle, provisions, 255.99; Yelle Co., Ltd., provisions, wheelbarrows, coal, 455.48; F. Yelle, gravel, 44.10; Hans Yensen, gravel, 240.00; Yen Yensen, gravel, 63.10; A. Young, travelling expenses, 2.40; Earl Young, provisions, 36.40; T. V. Young, wood, poles, cartage, 532.30; Bob Younge, gravel, 46.20; J. L. Yuill, travelling expenses, 98.51; Jos. Zettler, gravel, sand, 332.79; R. Zimmerman, wood, gravel, 438.10; Jos. Zoates, gravel, 69.90;

Statutory—Continued

General Work, Unemployment Relief—Continued

David Zurbrigg, wood, 10.00; Dr. Frank F. Zwick, services, examining men, 21.00	959,313 49
Pay lists, wages of men	3,817,820 73
Workmen's Compensation Board, compensation to injured workmen	56,614 68
Total	4,833,748 90
Less cash accountable, 1931	100,000 00
	4,733,748 90

Dam at Ivanoe Lake ($35,746.23)

Acme Timber Co., construction of a dam to restore the waters of Ivanhoe Lake, Schedules 1 B, 1 C	35,746 23

SUMMARY OF UNEMPLOYMENT EXPENDITURE

Trans-Canada Highway	6,070,193 61
General Work	4,733,748 90
Ivanhoe Dam	35,746 23
	10,839,688 74

Transferred to Labour Department for General Accounting and Dominion Government Refunds, see page N 19.

DEPARTMENT

OF

MINES

FISCAL YEAR, 1931-32

TABLE OF CONTENTS

GENERAL INDEX AT BACK OF BOOK

PART I—DEPARTMENT OF MINES

Statement of Expenditure Showing Amounts Expended, Unexpended and Overexpended for the Twelve Months Ended October 31st, 1932

Department of Mines	Page	Estimates	Expended			Un-expended	Over-expended	Treasury Board Minute
			Ordinary	Capital	Total Ordinary and Capital			
		$ c.	$ c.	$ c.	$ c.	$ c.	$ c.	$ c.
Main Office and Branches:								
Salaries	4	138,900 00	132,299 49	....	132,299 49	6,600 51	....	....
Contingencies	5	60,000 00	50,683 61	....	50,683 61	9,316 39	....	....
Main Office and Branches	..	198,900 00	182,983 10	....	182,983 10	15,916 90	....	....
Miscellaneous:								
Enforcement, Natural Gas Act, etc.	6	12,000 00	8,854 48	....	8,854 48	3,145 52	....	....
Fuel [illegible]oll [illegible]e.	..	2,500 00	....	....	....	2,500 00	....	....
Sul p[illegible]r Fumes [illegible]r.	7	5,000 00	....	....	....	5,000 00	....	....
Temiskaming Testing Laboratories	7	22,000 00	16,932 10	....	16,932 10	5,067 90	....	....
Mining Recorders, s[illegible]es a[illegible]d expenses	7	35,000 00	37,176 62	....	37,176 62	....	2,176 62	2,500 00
Inspector, Mining Recorder's Offices, salaries and expenses	8	3,500 00	3,110 15	....	3,110 15	389 85	....	....
Draughtsman, [illegible]h Bay	8	8,500 00	6,626 70	....	6,626 70	1,873 30	....	....
Legal assistance enforcing Acts	..	1,500 00	....	....	....	1,500 00	....	....
Salaries, etc., [illegible]ry Field and other assistants	8	40,000 00	35,783 71	....	35,783 71	4,216 29	....	....
Surveys in Mining Areas	..	4,000 00	....	....	....	4,000 00	....	....
Trails, clearing streams, [illegible]te.	9	5,000 00	....	995 88	995 88	4,004 12	....	....
Mineral [illegible]ds, [illegible]te.	9	10,000 00	2,575 58	....	2,575 58	7,424 42	....	....
Insurance	9	2,000 00	789 98	....	789 98	1,210 02	....	....
Moving [illegible]es of [illegible]	9	250 00	152 07	....	152 07	97 93	....	....
Research work	10	33,000 00	19,843 84	....	19,843 84	13,156 16	....	....
Grant, Canadian [illegible] of Mining	10	1,000 00	1,000 00	....	1,000 00	....	....	....
I[illegible]n [illegible]e Bounty Act, 1924	..	5,000 00	....	....	....	5,000 00	....	....
Maintenance, etc., [illegible]le testing machine	10	1,200 00	1,698 86	....	1,698 86	....	498 86	500 00
[illegible]se [illegible] [illegible]t of [illegible]es	10	3,000 00	193 59	....	193 59	2,806 41	....	....
Services and expenses [illegible]ded for	10	2,000 00	215 00	....	215 00	1,785 00	....	....

Diamond drilling, lignite and other deposits	10	50,000 00	13,971 28	....	13,971 28	36,028 72	....	....
Equipment, etc., in teaching Field Work, etc	10	1,329 63	1,252 41	....	1,252 41	77 22	....	....
Miscellaneous	..	247,779 63	150,176 37	995 88	151,172 25	99,282 86	2,675 48	....
Supply Bill	..	446,679 63	333,159 47	995 88	334,155 35	115,199 76	2,675 48	....
Statutory:								
Minister's Salary	10	....	10,000 00	....	10,000 00	....	....	....
Salaries not otherwise provided for	10	....	433 33	....	433 33	....	....	....
Statutory	..	....	10,433 33	....	10,433 33	....	....	....
Total	..	....	343,592 80	995 88	344,588 68	....	....	....
Less Salary Assessment	..	....	5,354 76	....	5,354 76	....	....	....
Department of Mines	..	....	338,238 04	995 88	339,233 92	....	....	....

SUMMARY

Department of Mines	Page	Ordinary	Capital	Fél
		$ c.	$ c.	$ c.
Main Office and Branches	4-6	182,983 10	....	182,983 D
Miscellaneous	6-10	150,176 37	995 88	151,172 25
Statutory	10	10,433 33	....	10,433 33
Total	..	343,592 80	995 88	344,588 68
Less Salary Assessment	..	5,354 76	....	5,354 76
Department of Mines	..	338,238 04	995 88	339,233 92

DEPARTMENT OF MINES

Hon. Chas. McCrea .... Minister (Statutory)............ $10,000.00

MAIN OFFICE AND BRANCHES

Salaries ($132,299.49)

Name	Position	Period		
T. W. Gibson	Deputy Minister..............(T)	12 months		4,000 00
T. F. Sutherland	Acting Deputy Minister	12 "		5,000 00
Malcolm McIntyre	Secretary to Minister and Departmental Secretary	12 "		2,700 00
Jno. Work	Head Clerk, Group 2	12 "		2,700 00
G. E. H. Graham	Supervisor of Dredging Operations	12 "		2,550 00
D. H. Barr	Senior Clerk	12 "		2,100 00
J. F. McFarland	" "	12 "		2,000 00
James Douglas	Draughtsman, Group 1	12 "		1,800 00
James P. Malone	Engrossing Clerk	12 "		1,600 00
H. W. Batchelor	Senior Clerk Stenographer	12 "		1,500 00
E. C. Bell	Clerk, Group 1	12 "		1,500 00
R. Eyre	" " 2	½ "		43 29
B. C. Lee	" " 3	12 "		975 00
A. Van Raalte	" " 3	12 "		900 00
C. F. Hamilton	" " 3	12 "		825 00
Isobel Wagar	Clerk Stenographer, Group 1	12 "		1,125 00
May L. Chenery	" " " 1	12 "		975 00
H. G. Matthews	Office Boy	12 "		675 00
Geo. T. Stevens	"	12 "		600 00
C. Freymond	Vault Caretaker	12		1,500 00

Geological Branch

Name	Position	Period		
A. G. Burrows	Provincial Geologist	12 months		5,400 00
Wm. S. Dyer	Assistant Geologist	12 "		3,600 00
M. E. Hurst	" "	12 "		3,600 00
Harold C. Rickaby	" "	12 "		3,450 00
J. L. McNaughton	Library Clerk	8⅔ "	1,164 40	
		3⅓ "	(T) 141 80	1,306 20
D. A. Lowry	Senior Clerk Stenographer	12 "		1,500 00

Publications and Statistics Branch

Name	Position	Period	
W. R. Rogers	Director	12 months	3,600 00
A. C. Young	Statistician	12 "	3,300 00
P. A. Jackson	Surveyor and Draughtsman	12 "	2,850 00
A. Braidwood	Senior Draughtsman, Group 1	12 "	2,700 00
J. Leddingham	" " " 1	12 "	2,700 00
John Jameson	" " " 1	12 "	2,400 00
D. J. Ferrier	Assistant Editor	12 "	2,100 00
Irene Williams	Clerk Stenographer, Group 1	12 "	1,125 00

Mines Inspection Branch

Name	Position	Period	
D. G. Sinclair	Chief Inspector of Mines	12 months	4,200 00
A. R. Webster	Inspector of Mines	12 "	3,600 00
Ralph H. Cleland	" "	12 "	3,450 00
E. C. Keeley	" "	12 "	3,450 00
D. F. Cooper	" "	12 "	3,300 00
D. J. Field	Senior Clerk Stenographer	12 "	1,500 00
R. Stewart	Laboratory Attendant	12	1,500 00

Mine Assessment Branch

Name	Position	Period	
G. R. Mickle	Mine Assessor	12 months	4,800 00
A. G. Scovell	Senior Clerk	12 "	2,000 00

Chemical and Assay Branch

Name	Position	Period	
W. K. McNeill	Provincial Assayer	12 months	3,800 00
T. E. Rothwell	Assistant Assayer	12 "	2,850 00
W. F. Green	" "	12 "	2,850 00
Wm. F. Ley	Junior Laboratory Attendant	12 "	900 00

Main Office and Branches—Continued

Salaries—Continued

Natural Gas Commissioner's Branch

R. B. Harkness	Natural Gas Commissioner	12 months		4,400 00
F. R. Saunders	Clerk Stenographer, Group 1	12 "		1,125 00

Mining Court of Ontario

T. E. Godson	Judge of Mining Court	12 months		6,000 00
W. H. Morris	Registrar and Reporter	2 "		500 00
F. L. Godson	Clerk, Group 2	12 "		1,250 00
Bessie C. Sefton	Senior Clerk Stenographer	12 "		1,500 00
M. M. Wilson	Clerk Stenographer, Group 1	12 "		1,200 00

Files Branch

A. M. Moffatt	Senior Clerk Stenographer	12 months		1,400 00
M. E. Clark	Clerk Stenographer, Group 1	12 "		1,050 00
M. B. Madden	Filing Clerk	12 "		975 00

Salaries not Provided for (Statutory) ($433.33)

Samuel G. Prescott	Mechanic	4 months	433 33	

Contingencies ($50,683.61)

Temporary Services, $8,157.25

Alfred Allen	Office Boy	12 months	525 00
J. E. Brown	Assistant in Vault	2½ "	215 38
F. H. Hart	Office Boy	12 "	525 00
Wm. Johnston	Assistant in Vault	½ "	30 29
Percy Logee	Office Boy	12 "	525 00
M. L. Madden	Clerk, Group 2	12 "	975 00
J. L. Milligan	Publicity Work	12 "	2,600 04
Peter Pickford	Office Boy	3⅛ "	141 35
J. B. Scanlon	Assistant Secretary	10 "	1,500 00
Martin A. Storey	Clerk, Group 2	12 "	975 00
W. V. Thompson	Office Boy	½ "	20 19
Jean G. Work	Clerk Stenographer	2 "	125 00

Travelling Expenses, $7,140.45.

A. G. Burrows, 250.00; R. H. Cleland, 783.74; D. F. Cooper, 862.77; W. C. Coo, 42.90; T. E. Godson, 329.05; E. C. Keeley, 754.39; Honourable Chas. McCrea, 975.00; J. F. McFarland, 751.15; G. R. Mickle, 63.50; J. L. Milligan, 99.30; S. G. Prescott, 38.65; H. C. Rickaby, 101.96; W. R. Rogers, 159.39; D. G. Sinclair, 375.02; R. Stewart, 37.65; T. F. Sutherland, 174.45; A. R. Webster, 1,038.25; J. Work, 270.83; A. C. Young, 32.45 .... 7,140 45

Advertising, $9,393.43.

Algoma Advocate, 5.00; Barron's, 196.00; Blind River Leader, 5.00; Border Cities Star, 61.60; British American Publishing Co., Ltd., 192.00; Bruce Mines Spectator, 109.00; Canadian Churchman, 243.60; Canadian Baptist, 311.64; Canadian Facts Publishing Co., 30.00; Canadian Geographical Society, 160.00; Canadian Holy Name Prefect, 36.00; Canadian Labour Press, Ltd., 728.00; Canadian Labour World, 100.00; Canadian Mining Journal, 600.00; Canadian Mining and Metallurgical Bulletin, 335.00; Canada Newspaper Co., Ltd., 170.33; Catholic Record, 270.00; Cochrane Northland Post, 10.00; Echoes, 130.00; Espanola Standard, 10.00; Evening Telegram, 27.60; Fort Frances Times, 45.00; Fort William Times-Journal, 45.00; Grand River Valley Booklet, 50.00; Haileyburian, 45.00; Journal Dailies, Ottawa, 72.00; Labour Leader Publishing Co., Ltd., 520.00; The Legionary, 247.50; Living Message, 90.00; Mail and Empire, 161.20; McLean Publishing Co., Ltd., 50.00; Manitoba Chamber of Mines, 50.00; Massey Tribune, 10.00; Miner Publishing Co., Kenora, 43.00; Mining Journal, 300.70; Mining & Industrial World, 34.50; Mining Magazine, 124.22; Mining World and Engineering Record, 149.03; Municipal Intelligence Bureau, 50.00; Monetary Times, 227.00; New Liskeard Speaker, 35.00; New Outlook, 270.00; Northern Miner, 797.20; The Nuggett, 30.00; Northern News, 105.00; Northern Observer, 150.00; Ottawa Danebrog, 45.00; Ottawa Catholic Times, 159.75; Porcupine Advance, 59.00; Record Publishing Co., Rainy River, 220.00; St. Joe Herald, 5.00; Scovil Bros. & Co., 375.00; Sault Daily Star, 65.00; Skillings Mining Review, 35.40; T. Skinner of Canada, Ltd., 135.00; Wilson Publishing Co., 195.00; Sudbury Star, 139.76; Temiskaming

Main Office and Branches—Continued

Contingencies—Continued

Advertising—Continued

Firemen's Association, 25.00; The News Chronicle Publishing Co., 39.00; The Sailor, 100.00; The Sentinel, 16.00; Toronto Globe Printing Co., 32.40; United Church Publishing House, 30.00; Westman Publication, Ltd., 285.00.......... 9,393 43

Maps and Plans, $6,118.54.

H. S. Crabtree, Ltd., 63.00; Harris Lithographing Co., Ltd., 416.73; Miller Lithographic Co., Ltd., 1,210.64; Richardson, Bond & Wright, Ltd., 76.90; Rolph-Clark-Stone, Ltd., 1,953.23; Thompson & Sons, Ltd., 2,390.73; petty disbursements, 7.31........ 6,118 54

Fees to Various Associations, $42.00.

American Institute of Mining and Metallurgical Engineering Society, 15.00; Association of Professional Engineers, 5.00; Association of Ontario Land Surveyors, 7.00; Canadian Institute of Chemistry, 10.00; National Tax Association, 5.00 42 00

Miscellaneous, $19,831.94.

Agent-General of Ontario, London, copies, papers, etc., 27.01; Angus Mack Co., map mounting, 49.05; Bell Telephone Co., rental, 6.00; M. Brunette, searches, 18.13; Bursar, University of Toronto, covers for reprints, prints, 12.00; Canadian Laboratory Supplies, Ltd., supplies, etc., 1,257.72; Canada Photo Copy Co., photostats, 336.69; Canadian Facts Publishing Co., copies, 16.25; Canada Press Clipping Service, clippings, 48.00 ; Carswell Co., Ltd., binding, etc., 29.00; Central Scientific Co., Ltd., radioscope, 13.50; W. C. Coo, reporting, 32.50; R. Davis, books, 30.00; Department of Highways, garage account, 483.27; Department of Public Works, blue prints, 119.25; Dominion Press Clipping Agency, service, 165.00; L. H. Ferguson, registration, 13.20; Field, Love & House, inspection, 30.00; J. F. Hartz Co., Ltd., repairs, 10.00; Herman & Co., reports, 57.50; International Press Clipping Bureau, service, 10.00; Instruments, Ltd., prints, etc., 21.72; P. S. King & Sons, Ltd., parliamentary paper, 24.11; King's Printer, 13,261.26; Ledoux & Co., Inc., analysis of ore, 20.00; Legge Bros., Engravers, Ltd., negative, etc., 24.80; McCann & Alexander, inspections, 12.00; A. L. McEwen, assay coupons, 1,015.50; J. J. Murphy, reports, 75.00; D. A. Mutch, mining services, 465.00; F. J. Nicholas, indexing books, 252.20; Northern Telephone Co., Ltd., rental, 41.50; tools, 1.40; T. Pocklington Co., repairs, 20.00; L. Pritzker, reports, 14.00; J. F. Raw Co., Ltd., tracings, etc., 23.35; Remington Typewriters, Ltd., inspection, 26.25; Richardson, Bond & Wright, Ltd., lithographing, 40.00; W. A. Stewart, rock sections, 47.50; Sundry persons, copies of evidence, 190.55; Toronto Transportation Commission, car tickets, 30.00; Typewriter Sales & Service Co., inspections, 14.50; United Typewriter Co., Ltd., repairs, etc., 185.50; University of Toronto, books, 17.90; Walker Metal Products, Ltd., assay tray, etc., 99.69; M. J. Watson, thermometer, 33.50; W. Wightman, rock sections, 23.00; W. A. Willison, revising bulletin, 125.00; J. T. Worden, reports, 14.00. Sundries—cartage, 1.05; express, 112.03; freight, 8.01; newspapers and periodicals, 390.30; postage, 4.00; telegrams, 364.97; petty disbursements, 74.28........ 19,837 94

Less fees........ 6 00

19,831 94

Main Office and Branches........ $182,983 10

GAS AND OIL WELL INSPECTORS

Gas and Oil Well Inspectors—Salaries, Equipment, etc. ($8,854.48)

Salaries, $5,700.00.

B. D. Burn	Inspector, Tillsonburg	12 months	2,200 00
Geo. F. Henderson	Natural Gas Referee, Ottawa	12 "	3,500 00

Temporary Services, $750.00.

John Scott	Inspector	12 months	750 00

Travelling Expenses, $1,374.28.

B. D. Burn, 490.96; A. R. Crozier, 36.32; R. B. Harkness, 349.95; G. F. Henderson, 106.30; John Scott, 390.75........ 1,374 28

Miscellaneous, $1,030.20.

American Association of Petroleum Geologists, dues, 15.00; B. C. Berry & Co., repairs, 30.00; F. Bulmer, boat hire, 23.00; Department of Highways, garage account, 453.35; King's Printer, 288.98; E. R. Reid, reporting, 11.00; F. Southcote, car repairs, 116.92; United Typewriter Co., Ltd., inspection, 12.00. Sundries—express, 51.22; newspapers and periodicals, 3.00; petty disbursements, 25.73. 1,030 20

SULPHUR FUMES ARBITRATOR

Salary, Travelling and other Expenses ($3,830.81)

R. H. Murray	Investigator, Sudbury	12 months	3,000 00	

Travelling Expenses, $88.43.

R. H. Murray	88 43	

Miscellaneous, $742.38.

Aikenhead Hardware, Ltd., blades, 1.50; Bell Telephone Co., rental, 41.25; tolls, .10; Gardner's Garage, auto repairs, gas, etc., 279.94; Get Gas, Ltd., gas, 81.36; P. L. Henderson, office and garage rent, 300.00; Smith & Ferry, insurance premium, 38.23 ..... 742 38

	3,830 31
Less refund from Smelters	3,830 31

TEMISKAMING TESTING LABORATORIES ($16,932.10)

Salaries, $6,533.28.

Geo. H. Dickson	Superintendent	12 months	3,000 00
Fred Mondoux	Assistant Assayer	12 "	2,400 00
Samuel G. Prescott	Senior Laboratory Assistant	8 "	1,133 28

Temporary Services, $5,601.16.

A. Cole	Manager	12 months	600 00
Z. Labelle	Millman and Watchman	12 "	1,508 10
J. Smith	" "	12 "	1,300 41
K. Lafrange	Night Watchman	12 "	1,248 55
P. A. Grozelle	Assay Helper and Watchman	6 "	512 00
Pay list, wages of mill helpers			432 10

Travelling Expenses, $41.10.

G. H. Dickson	41 10

Miscellaneous, $4,756.56.

Canadian General Electric Co., Ltd., lamps, 35.74; Cobalt Foundry, repairs, etc., 12.84; Cobalt Public Utilities, water, 30.17; B. Greening Wire Co., Ltd., wire cloth, 162.25; A. L. Herbert, coal, 1,302.50; Imperial Oil, Ltd., oil, 170.87; King's Printer, 27.01; La Rose-Rouyn Mines, Ltd., ground rent, 420.00; Liquor Control Board of Ontario, alcohol, 43.20; Nichols Chemical Co., Ltd., acid, 59.85; Northern Miner, advertising, 58.00; Northern Ontario Power Co., Ltd., power, light, etc., 1,601.73; Northern Telephone Co., Ltd., rental, 45.00; tolls, 6.85; Oliver Blais Co., Ltd., generator, 75.00; F. L. Smiley, legal services, 72.69; G. Taylor Hardware, Ltd., hardware, 389.42; Sundries—cartage, 48.05; customs, .87; express, 22.34; freight, 87.84; postage, 43.20; telegrams, 1.36; petty disbursements, 39.78 ..... 4,756 56

MINING RECORDERS ($37,176.62)

Salaries, $23,975.00.

J. A. Alexander	Recorder, Fort Frances	12 months	300 00
J. M. Coghill	" Elk Lake	12 "	1,800 00
Redvers Dixon	" South Porcupine	12 "	1,900 00
H. G. Ginn	" Swastika	12 "	2,200 00
H. E. Holland	" Goldpines	12 "	1,900 00
T. A. McArthur	" Sudbury	12 "	2,400 00
N. J. McAulay	" Haileybury	12 "	2,300 00
C. F. McGregor	" Port Arthur	12 "	1,900 00
M. M. McDonald	Assistant Recorder, Port Arthur	12 "	975 00
W. N. Miller	Recorder, Sault Ste. Marie	12 "	2,000 00
M. F. O'Rourke	" Tashota	12 "	1,800 00
J. D. C. Smith	" Kenora	12 "	600 00
M. Andrew	Clerk Stenographer, Group 2	12 "	975 00
G. M. Clements	" " "	12 "	975 00
I. McCauley	" " "	12 "	975 00
L. Tanner		12 "	975 00

Temporary Services, $4,506.50.

Dorothy I. Brown	Clerk Stenographer, Group 2	12 months	825 00
Ivan H. Fraser	" " "	9¾ "	674 28
Elfreda Harris	" " "	10½ "	713 95
Margaret C. McGregor	Clerk	12 "	750 00
Vina Ragan	Clerk Stenographer, Group 2	⅜ "	43 27
T. A. Wood	Assistant	12 "	1,500 00

Mining Recorders—Continued

Travelling Expenses, $477.90.

R. Dixon, 106.45; H. G. Ginn, 56.70; H. E. Holland, 54.75; M. A. Story, 260.00. 477 90

Miscellaneous, $8,217.22.

Mrs. S. Adair, rent, 360.00; Bank of Toronto, exchange, 34.71; Bell Telephone Co., rental, 99.40; tolls, 6.13; Mrs. L. Desmarais, rent, 1,080.00; J. V. Elliott, rent, 900.00; W. Gerrie, meals, etc., 260.00; Mrs. N. H. Hill, caretaker, 90.00; H. E. Holland, living allowance, 452.40; Imperial Bank, exchange, 18.92; King's Printer, 1,469.19; Mrs. M. Lowe, cleaning, 120.00; Northern Ontario Power Co., Ltd., light, 100.15; Northern Telephone Co., Ltd., rental, 142.50; tolls, 37.51; C. Parrott, janitor, 240.00; J. Pidgeon, wood, 20.00; Public Utilities Commission, Port Arthur, telephone rental 50.00; Remington Typewriters, Ltd., inspections, 28.00; H. M. Somerville, wood, 180.00; City of Sudbury, light, 36.06; Teck Fuel & Ice Co., coal, 258.00; Township of Teck, water and rent, 23.20; Township of Tisdale, rent of office, 660.00; tolls, 13.69; United Typewriter Co., Ltd., inspections, repairs, etc., 36.83; F. A. Wood, living allowance, 315.00; S. Ylinen, janitor, 30.00. Sundries—cartage, 18.10; express, 115.23; freight, 118.76; postage, 861.41; telegrams, 13.85; petty disbursements, 83.21.................................... 8,272 22

Less sale of old building..........................	10 00		
" " furniture..........................	45 00		
		55 00	
			8,217 22

Inspector of Mining Recorders' Offices ($3,110.15)

J. R. Moore, Inspector, 12 months, 2,000.00; travelling expenses, 1,110.15...... 3,110 15

Draughtsman, North Bay, Services and Expenses ($6,626.70)

Salaries, $975.00.

Hope Brookes..........	Clerk Stenographer, Group 2..............	12 months	975 00

Temporary Services, $3,347.60.

A. D. Williams.........	Draughtsman..........................	12 months	1,800 00
J. A. F. Stewart........	Assistant..............................	12 "	1,500 00
Gertrude McGonegal....	Clerk Stenographer.....................	⅔ "	47 60

Miscellaneous, $2,304.10.

Bell Telephone Co., rental, 45.00; tolls, .85; Hydro-Electric Power Commission, light, 157.14; King's Printer, 631.67; McMurchy Building, Ltd., rent, 900.00; Office Specialty Mfg. Co., Ltd., cases, etc., 405.00; Patton & Kennedy Insurance Agency, light, 18.00. Sundries—cartage, 5.00; express, 25.70; freight, 7.74; postage, 96.00; petty disbursements, 12.00................................ 2,304 10

Salaries, Equipment and Expenses of Temporary Field and Other Assistants, including Educational Work ($35,783.71)

Salaries, $975.00.

V. Kettle..............	Clerk Stenographer.....................	12 months	975 00

Services of Geologists and Field Men, $23,973.71.

W. L. Brown, field man at 125.00 per mo., 480.76; E. L. Bruce, geologist, at 300.00 per mo., 300.00; F. H. Burnaby, field man, at 125.00 per mo., 572.12; E. M. Burwash, instructor of prospectors' classes, at 225.00 per mo., 1,384.61; C. H. Charlewood, field man, at 200.00 per mo., 792.31; A. P. Coleman, geologist, at 300.00 per mo., 1,200.00; B. C. Coles, field man, at 125.00 per mo., 495.19; N. Colquhoun, stenographer, at 68.75 per mo., 137.50; A. R. Crozier, field man, at 200.00 per mo., 2,400.00; E. R. Davey, field man, at 150.00 per mo., 900.00; A. P. Forster, dredging inspector, at 150.00 per mo., 1,200.00; George D. Furse, geologist, at 250.00 per mo., 1,086.54; at 200.00 per mo., 200.00; Frank Gibson, caretaker, at 75.00 per mo., 75.00; A. R. Graham, geologist, at 225.00 per mo., 225.00; G. A. Harcourt, field man, at 150.00 per mo., 582.69; W. D. Harding, field man, at 200.00 per mo., 869.22; W. R. Hendrie, dredging inspector, at 150.00 per mo., 1,275.00; L. F. Kindle, geologist, at 200.00 per mo., 876.92; C. H. Knight, field man, at 125.00 per mo., 509.61; H. C. Laird, geologist, at 225.00 per mo., 225.00; at 200.00 per mo., 961.53; G. S. Mackenzie, field man, at 200.00 per mo., 830.77; Prof. A. McLean, geologist, at 250.00 per mo., 471.15; J. G. McMillan, geologist, at 250.00 per mo., 288.46; B. V. Meen, field man, at 125.00 per mo., 495.19; H. E. Purdy, assistant instructor of prospectors' classes, at 150.00 per mo., 1,130.77; H. Ross, laboratory assistant, at .40 per

Salaries, Equipment and Expenses of Temporary Field and Other Assistants, etc.—Continued

Services of Geologists and Field Men—Continued

hr., 12.00; Neil D. Runnalls, field man, at 200.00 per mo., 853.85; Bruce Russell, field man, at 110.00 per mo., 452.70; W. S. Savage, field man, at 150.00 per mo., 627.12; at 135.00 per mo., 93.46; J. E. Thomson, geologist, at 250.00 per mo., 1,173.08; at 225.00 per mo., 225.00; H. F. Zurbrigg, field man at 150.00 per mo., 571.16 .... 23,973 71

Travelling Expenses, $5,444.21.

W. L. Brown, 111.19; F. H. Burnaby, 84.20; A. G. Burrows, 6.36; E. M. Burwash, 976.77; A. P. Coleman, 474.06; B. C. Coles, 97.35; A. R. Crozier, 168.75; C. H. Charlewood, 98.65; E. R. Davey, 291.00; Dr. W. S. Dyer, 147.25; A. P. Forster, 110.69; G. D. Furse, 148.84; G. A. Harcourt, 120.95; W. D. Harding, 119.45; W. R. Hendrie, 74.30; M. E. Hurst, 414.01; C. H. Knight, 36.50; H. C. Laird, 95.45; G. S. MacKenzie, 96.85; A. McLean, 149.77; J. G. McMillan, 82.60; B. V. Meen, 97.50; H. E. Purdy, 663.95; H. C. Rickaby, 316.74; N. D. Runnalls, 127.05; B. Russell, 63.00; W. S. Savage, 46.95; J. E. Thomson, 154.62; T. F. Sutherland, 9.51; H. F. Zurbrigg, 59.90 .... 5,444 21

Miscellaneous, $5,390.79.

S. Bickett, typing, 15.00; H. A. Bishop, meals, 60.00; Canadian Airways, Ltd., fare, 484.60; Canadian Johnson Motor Co., Ltd., parts, 41.35; Dept. of Lands & Forests, aerial survey, 296.53; Dept. of Marine & Fisheries, Ottawa, maintenance, gas buoys, etc., 492.65; Dept. of Highways, garage account, 97.24; Dominion Machine & Tool Co., Ltd., grinding plate, etc., 70.00; T. Eaton Co., Ltd., photo, films, batteries, etc., 16.37; R. Fernell, compass, 15.00; Hamilton Potteries, Ltd., clay, 50.00; Hudson's Bay Co., provisions, 975.20; Hi Way Service Station, gas, 11.90; I.O.O.F., Kirkland Lake, rent of hall, 12.00; King's Printer, 191.72; J. Leckie, Ltd., bags, etc., 77.20; H. F. McLean, Ltd., provisions, 46.92; Merrill, Rhind & Walmsley, Ltd., provisions, 319.70; H. Moore, epidote, 20.00; Northern Transportation Co., transportation, 51.00; Peterboro Canoe Co., Ltd., canvas, 168.00; T. Pocklington Co., repairs, instruments, 203.98; C. Potter, slides, etc., 37.25; Smith & Chapple, Ltd., provisions, etc., 507.37; W. A. Stewart, rock sections, 219.50; Timmins Garage, gas, 21.20; University of Toronto, prints, 19.00. Sundries—cartage, 149.25; express, 437.23; freight, 197.37; postage, 5.86; telegrams, 23.82; petty disbursements, 146.41 .... 5,480 62

Less sale of canoes and tents 89 83

5,390 79

Trails, Clearing Streams, Opening Routes and Roads ($995.88).

Canadian Industries, Ltd., explosives, 13.53; J. Ledingham, gas, 12.00; M. O'Connor, provisions, 244.64; paylist, wages of men, 725.71 .... 995 88

Mineral Collections, including Cases and Displays at Exhibitions, also Services and Expenses ($2,575.58)

Travelling Expenses, $320.65.

C. Freymond, 28.10; W. K. McNeill, 35.22; D. G. Sinclair, 21.16; Percy C. Smith, 222.92; E. M. Tozer, 13.25 .... 320 65

Miscellaneous, $2,254.93.

E. Chamberlain, truck hire, 27.00; Albert Clark, display stand, 396.46; Robt. Fraser, services, 84.00; Goddard Bros., cartage, 175.40; House Bros., cartage, 458.31; King's Printer, 15.57; Madawaska Syndicate, cartage, etc., 70.00; T. Manton & Sons, rent of ferns, 91.50; W. H. Price, painting, 490.06; Safety Supply Co., flash light, 11.25; R. Simpson Co., Ltd., rent of chairs, 99.00; W. W. Stallworthy, lettering, etc., 33.25; Sudbury Construction & Machine Co., Ltd., car repairs, 29.58; E. M. Tozer, services, 144.00; Ward's Natural Science Establishment, Inc., mineral specimens, 117.34. Sundries—customs, 2.00; freight, .50; petty disbursements, 9.71 .... 2,254 93

Insurance ($789.98)

Smith & Ferry, Temiskaming Testing Laboratories, 700.00; Andrew E. Wright Agency, exhibits C.N.E., 89.98 .... 789 98

Moving Expenses of Officials ($152.07)

S. G. Prescott, Laboratory assistant, Cobalt to Toronto 152 07

Research Work, Salaries, Equipment and Expenses ($19,843.84)

Ontario Research Foundation, research work.................................. 19,843 84

Grant to Canadian Institute of Mining and Metallurgy ($1,000.00)

Canadian Institute of Mining and Metallurgy.................................. 1,000 00

Maintenance and Operation of Cable Testing Machine ($1,698.86)

Aikenhead Hardware, Ltd., hardware, 110.63; Anglo-Canadian Wire Rope Co., Ltd., wire rope, etc., 128.60; Canada Wire & Cable Co., Ltd., wire rope, 24.64; E. C. Clarke, services, 699.00; J. Inglis Co., Ltd., mould, 14.94; King's Printer, 52.70; Medicine Hat Pottery Co., crocks, 45.45; R. Stewart, travelling expenses, 119.10; Thompson & Sons, Ltd., certificates, 406.06. Sundries—customs, 1.10; express, 64.84; freight, 4.49; petty disbursements, 27.31.............................. 1,698 86

Purchase and Treatment of Gold and Silver Ores ($193.59)

W. Longworth, gold ore.. 193 59

Services, Salaries and Expenses not Otherwise Provided for ($215.00)

Estate of Geo. Henry, rental, gas well, 200.00; Margaret A. McColl, lease, oil and gas rights, 15.00.. 215 00

Expenses of Development, Mining Operations and Experimentation re Lignite and Other Deposits in Northern Ontario ($13,971.28)

Travelling Expenses, $322.53.

A. R. Crozier, 95.95; W. F. Fancy, 71.43; A. E. Hilder, 62.60; C. B. Jamieson, 46.60; G. Sutherland, 45.95.. 322 53

Miscellaneous, $13,648.75.

Canadian Johnson Motor Co., Ltd., parts, 36.66; Hobson Gauthier, Ltd., provisions, etc., 1,184.10; Imperial Oil, Ltd., coal oil, etc., 119.61; Liskeard Laundry, laundry, 25.00; McGill Hardware, Ltd., hardware, 41.87; H. F. McLean, Ltd., rental of siding, trucking, etc., 292.00; T. J. Montgomery, tests, 10.00; Dr. M. S. Paul, professional services, 200.00; Pay list, wages of men, 6,156.58; Smith & Travers Co., Ltd., diamond drilling, 5,256.90; Taylor Hardware, Ltd., hardware, 22.19; T. & N. O. Telephone, rental, 81.50; tolls, 101.54; Woods Manufacturing Co., Ltd., renovating sleeping robes, 30.00. Sundries—cartage, 142.00; express, 133.61; freight, 139.08; postage, 8.00; telegrams, 7.26; petty disbursements, 12.85.. 14,000 75

- Rebates on return of gas drums, sale of blankets, etc........... 352 00 | 13,648 75

Purchase of Equipment and Apparatus Required for Teaching Geophysical Prospecting and Field Work ($1,252.41)

Askania-Werke Aktiengesellschaft, magnet system, 160.00; R. H. Nichols, transformer, etc., 947.50; Rawson Electrical Instrument Co., melkammeter range, 90.91; University of Toronto, copper stakes, 49.42. Sundries—customs, 3.03; express, 1.55.. 1,252 41

Miscellaneous $151,172.25

STATUTORY

Minister's salary (see page I, 4).. 10,000 00
Salaries not otherwise provided for (see page I, 5) 433 33

Statutory..$10,433.33

Total.. 344,588 68
Less Salary Assessment... 5,354 76

Total Expenditure, Department of Mines.......................... **$339,233 92**

PART J

DEPARTMENT

OF

GAME AND FISHERIES

FISCAL YEAR, 1931-32

TABLE OF CONTENTS

GENERÁL INDEX AT BACK OF BOOK

PART J—DEPARTMENT OF GAME AND FISHERIES

Statement of Expenditure Showing Amounts Expended, Unexpended and Overexpended for the Twelve Months Ended October 31st, 1932

Department of Game and Fisheries	Page	Estimates	Expended			Un-expended	Over-expended	Treasury Board Minute
			Ordinary	Capital	Total Ordinary and Capital			
		$ c.	$ c.	$ c.	$ c.	$ c.	$ c.	$ c.
Main Office:								
Salaries	4	45,725 00	43,401 67	....	43,401 67	2,323 33	....	....
Contingencies	4	10,000 00	9,868 75	....	9,868 75	131 25	....	....
Main Office	..	55,725 00	53,270 42	....	53,270 42	2,454 58	....	....
Biological and Fish Culture Branch:								
Salaries	4	9,450 00	9,450 00	....	9,450 00	....	....	....
Contingencies	5	6,500 00	5,190 65	....	5,190 65	1,309 35	....	....
Services and expenses (hatcheries)	5	185,000 00	174,117 55	....	174,117 55	10,882 45	....	....
Biological and Fish Culture Branch	..	200,950 00	188,758 20	....	188,758 20	12,191 80	....	....
General:								
Erecting ponds and buildings, etc	12	90,000 00	....	66,967 61	66,967 61	23,032 39	....	....
Enforcement, Game and Fisheries Act	14	300,000 00	268,789 60	....	268,789 60	31,210 40	....	....
Moving expenses of officials	21	2,000 00	130 09	....	130 09	1,869 91	....	....
Purchase of and repairs to boats, boathouses, etc	21	25,000 00	15,559 47	115 00	15,674 47	9,325 53	....	....
Game animals and birds	24	15,000 00	10,197 51	....	10,197 51	4,802 49	....	....
Experimental Fur Farm	24	17,000 00	16,938 68	....	16,938 68	61 32	....	....
Services and expenses at MacDiarmid	25	7,300 00	5,016 03	....	5,016 03	2,283 97	....	....
Wild rice and celery seed, etc	25	2,500 00	704 36	....	704 36	1,795 64	....	....
Exhibits	25	5,000 00	2,391 26	....	2,391 26	2,608 74	....	....
Adjustment of Claims	..	1,000 00	....	....	....	1,000 00	....	....
Membership fees to associations	26	100 00	10 00	....	10 00	90 00	....	....
Unforeseen and unprovided	26	1,000 00	276 70	....	276 70	723 30	....	....
Sundry inquiries and investigations	26	5,000 00	4,616 38	....	4,616 38	383 62	....	....
Grants,								
Jack Miner	26	400 00	400 00	....	400 00	....	....	....
E. L. Marsh	26	300 00	300 00	....	300 00	....	....	....

T. N. Jones	26	200 00	200 00	....	200 00	....	....	....
Lake Erie Fishermen's Association	26	400 00	400 00	....	400 00	....	....	....
Lake Huron and Georgian Bay Fishermen's Association	26	100 00	100 00	....	100 00	....	....	....
General	..	472,300 00	326,030 08	67,082 61	393,112 69	79,187 31	....	....
Supply Bill	..	728,975 00	568,058 70	67,082 61	635,141 31	93,833 69	....	....
Total	..	....	568,058 70	67,082 61	635,141 31	....	....	....
Less Salary Assessment	..	....	5,965 29	....	5,965 29	....	....	....
Department of Game and Fisheries	..	....	562,093 41	67,082 61	629,176 02	....	....	....

SUMMARY

Department of Game and Fisheries	Page	Ordinary	Capital	Total
		$ c.	$ c.	$ c.
Main Office	4	53,270 42	....	53,270 42
Biological and Fish Culture Branch	4–12	188,758 20	....	188,758 20
General	12–26	326,030 08	67,082 61	393,112 69
Total	....	568,058 70	67,082 61	635,141 31
Less Salary Assessment	....	5,965 29	....	5,965 29
Department of Game and Fisheries	....	562,093 41	67,082 61	629,176 02

PART J—DEPARTMENT OF GAME AND FISHERIES

Statement of Expenditure Showing Amounts Expended, Unexpended and Overexpended for the Twelve Months Ended October 31st, 1932

Department of Game and Fisheries	Page	Estimates	Expended: Ordinary	Expended: Capital	Expended: Total Ordinary and Capital	Unexpended	Overexpended	Treasury Board Minute
		$ c.	$ c.	$ c.	$ c.	$ c.	$ c.	$ c.
[illegible]ain Office:								
Salaries	4	45,725 00	43,401 67		43,401 67	2,323 33		
Contingencies	4	10,000 00	9,868 75		9,868 75	131 25		
Main Office		55,725 [illegible]	[illegible]		[illegible]3,270 42	2,454 58		
[illegible]ological and Fish Culture Br.								
Salaries	[illegible]	[illegible]	[illegible] 00		[illegible] 00			
Contingencies	5	[illegible]	[illegible] 65		5,190 65	[illegible]		
[illegible]ervices [illegible]	5	[illegible]	[illegible] 17 [illegible]		74,117 55	10,[illegible]		
[illegible]		[illegible]	[illegible]		[illegible]	[illegible]		
[illegible]								
[illegible]								
[illegible]nforce[illegible]								
[illegible]oving expenses of [illegible]	[illegible]	[illegible]			[illegible]	[illegible]		
[illegible]urchase of and repa[illegible]	[illegible]	[illegible]	[illegible]		15,[illegible] 47	[illegible] 53		
[illegible]ame animals and birds	[illegible]	15,[illegible]	[illegible]		1[illegible] 51	[illegible] 49		
[illegible]xperimental Fur Farm	24	17,000 00	16,938 68		16,938 68	61 32		
[illegible]ervices and expenses at MacDiarmid	25	7,300 00	5,016 03		5,016 03	2,283 97		
[illegible]ild rice and celery seed, etc	25	2,500 00	704 36		704 36	1,795 64		
[illegible]xhibits	25	5,000 00	2,391 26		2,391 26	2,608 74		
[illegible]djustment of Claims		1,000 00				1,000 00		
[illegible]embership fees to associations	26	100 00	10 00		10 00	90 00		
[illegible]nforeseen and unprovided	26	1,000 00	276 70		276 70	723 30		
[illegible]undry inquiries and investigations	26	5,000 00	4,616 38		4,616 38	383 62		
[illegible]ants,								
Jack Miner	26	400 00	400 00		400 00			
E. L. Marsh	26	300 00	300 00		300 00			

T. N. Jones	26	200 00	200 00	....	200 00	....	....	....
Lake Erie Fishermen's Association	26	400 00	400 00	....	400 00	....	....	....
Lake Huron and Georgian Bay Fishermen's Association	26	100 00	100 00	....	100 00	....	....	....
General	..	472,300 00	326,030 08	67,082 61	393,112 69	79,187 31	....	....
Supply Bill	..	728,975 00	568,058 70	67,082 61	635,141 31	93,833 69	....	....
Total	..	....	568,058 70	67,082 61	635,141 31	....	....	....
Less Salary Assessn ent	..	....	5,965 29	....	5,965 29	....	....	....
Department f Game an F es	..	....	562,093 41	67,082 61	629,176 02	....	....	....

SUMMARY

Department of Game and Fisheries	Page	Ordinary	Capital	Total
		$ c.	$ c.	$ c.
Ma n Office	4	53,270 42	....	53,270 42
Bio ogi al an Fish Culture Branch	4–12	188,758 20	....	188,758 20
Genera	12–26	326,030 08	67,082 61	393,112 69
Total	....	568,058 70	67,082 61	635,141 31
Less Salary Assessment	....	5,965 29	....	5,965 29
Department of Game and Fisheries	.	562,093 41	67,082 61	629,176 02

DEPARTMENT OF GAME AND FISHERIES

Hon. Geo. H. Challies, Minister

Salaries ($43,401.67)

D. McDonald	Deputy Minister		12 months	6,000 00
James Farrington	Assistant to Deputy Minister		12 “	3,000 00
H. G. Cox	Inspector		12 “	2,400 00
G. P. Douse	Accountant, Group 3		12 “	2,400 00
Geo. Graham	Principal Clerk		12 “	2,400 00
C. G. Gladman	“ “		12 “	2,400 00
William Lee	“ “		12 “	2,200 00
Lorne Pelz	Senior Clerk		12 “	2,000 00
Eugene Langevin	Clerk, Group 1		12 “	1,700 00
J. M. Beaupre	“ “ 1		12 “	1,600 00
Jno. B. Bowman	“ “ 3		12 “	900 00
V. J. Doole	Secretarial Stenographer		12 “	1,600 00
Annie Newlands	Senior Clerk Stenographer		12 “	1,500 00
K. Campbell	“ “ “		12 “	1,500 00
Gertrude E. McAuley	“ “ “		12 “	1,300 00
Florabel McGill	Clerk Stenographer, Group 1		12 “	1,200 00
F. M. Sands	“ “ “ 1		12 “	1,200 00
Laura Turner	“ “ “ 1		12 “	1,125 00
Jean L. Brown	“ “ “ 1	1,050 00	12 “	
	Less Leave of Absence	22 78		1,027 22
J. F. Plummer	Clerk Stenographer, Group 1	1,050 00	12 “	
	Less Leave of Absence	5 75		1,044 25
Jessie A. Farintosh	Clerk Stenographer, Group 2		12 “	900 00
N. Lynch	Clerk Typist, Group 1	1,200 00	12 “	
	Less Leave of Absence	194 80		1,005 20
Madge Archer	Filing Clerk, Group 1		12 “	1,500 00
Lindow W. Huddart	Custodian of Furs and Confiscated Goods		12 “	1,500 00

Contingencies ($9,868.75)

Temporary Services, $4,998.80.

Jean L. Farewell	Clerk Stenographer, Group 2	12 months	825 00
M. Eva Gallivan	Filing Clerk, Group 2	12 “	900 00
Helen R. Gilchrist	Clerk, Group 3	2 “	123 80
Ruby Hague	Clerk Stenographer, Group 1	12 “	975 00
Amy C. Lee	Filing Clerk, Group 2	12 “	900 00
John B. Scanlon	Clerk, Group 1	2 “	300 00
Alex. B. Young	“ “ 2	12 “	975 00

Travelling Expenses, $159.42.

H. G. Cox, 39.50; J. Farrington, 34.70; D. McDonald, 85.22 .... 159 42

Miscellaneous, $4,710.53.

Ackerman Sportsmen's Guide, advertising, 200.00; Burroughs Adding Machine of Canada, Ltd., repairs, 37.85; Canadian Fairbanks-Morse Co., Ltd., truck, 12.41; Department of Highways, auto service, 17.88; Hygiene Products, Ltd., insecticide, 27.50; King's Printer, 3,646.06; Rice Lewis & Son, Ltd., hardware, 11.44; O. Spanner Co., Ltd., mounting birds, 48.25; Thomas & Corney Typewriter Co., Ltd., inspections, 15.00; Toronto Humane Society, advertising, 41.65; United Typewriter Co., Ltd., inspections and repairs, 239.95. Sundries—car tickets, 12.00; express, 4.50; postage, .45; newspapers and periodicals, 46.25; telegrams, 313.82; petty disbursements, 35.52 .... 4,710 53

Main Office $53,270.42

BIOLOGICAL AND FISH CULTURE BRANCH

Salaries ($9,450.00)

H. H. MacKay	Biologist and Director	12 months	3,150 00
A. W. McLeod	Supervisor of Hatcheries	12 “	2,850 00
Edna M. French	Clerk Stenographer, Group 1	12 “	1,200 00
Beulah Nesbitt	“ “ “ 1	12 “	1,200 00
Wm. Mulholland	Clerk, Group 2	12 “	1,050 00

Biological and Fish Culture Branch—Continued

Contingencies ($5,190.65)

Temporary Services, $2,574.96.

Margaret H. Wilton	Senior Laboratory Assistant	12 months	1,599 96
E. H. O'Neill	Clerk, Group 2	12 "	975 00

Travelling Expenses, $1,462.42.

H. H. MacKay, 555.16; A. W. McLeod, 882.31; Wm. Mulholland, 24.95....... 1,462 42

Miscellaneous, $1,153.27.

Department of Highways, gas, oil, etc, 68.44; J. F. Hartz Co., Ltd., drugs and chemicals, 80.74; King's Printer, 671.42; Puritan Laundry Co., Ltd., laundry, 16.42; S. J. Robertson, garage rent, 55.00; United Typewriter Co., Ltd., inspections and repairs, 41.69. Sundries—newspapers and periodicals, 6.00; telegrams, 207.71; petty disbursements, 5.85....... 1,153 27

Services and Expenses ($174,117.55)

Biological Surveys ($5,937.19)

W. H. R. Werner	Assistant Biologist	12 months	1,800 00	
	Less leave of absence		156 99	
				1,643 01

Travelling Expenses, $2,525.09.

R. F. Cain, 302.95; J. D. Detweiler, 338.64; E. O. Ebersole, 412.83; A. H. Louden, 320.22; P. W. Smith, 372.51; R. Strang, 8.96; W. H. R. Werner, 768.98. 2,525 09

Miscellaneous, $1,769.09.

Department of Highways, gas, oil, etc, 38.68; Pay list, wages of men, 1,723.39; Sundries—express, 1.56; petty disbursements, 5.46....... 1,769 09

Hatcheries

Belleville ($9,233.09)

Salaries, $3,000.00.

G. K. Manore	Manager	12 months	1,800 00
Elgin W. Hayes	Assistant	12 "	1,200 00

Temporary Services, $1,824.79.

William H. LaRue	Assistant	9¼ months	813 39
George E. Littles	"	11½ "	1,011 40

Travelling Expenses, $712.41.

E. W. Hayes, 77.45; H. Jordan, 113.30; A. Keene, 59.55; C. Kemsley, 40.85; W. LaRue, 64.55; G. La Brash, 84.20; C. LaRue, 70.85; W. H. LaRue, 107.35; G. Littles, 20.85; G. K. Manore, 73.46....... 712 41

Expenses, $3,695.89.

Bell Telephone Co., rentals, 64.55; tolls, 10.86; Berry Bros., paraffin, 18.00; M. J. Callaghan, ice, 29.25; Canadian Fish Net Co., Ltd., nets, 54.12; H. Hill, repairs, etc., 12.50; O. Johnson, meals, 38.71; Hyatt & Hart, fish boxes, 10.00; Hydro-Electric Power Commission, light, etc., 242.78; Imperial Oil, Ltd., gasolene and oil, 347.19; Mrs. E. Irwin, meals, 38.57; Pay list, spawn takers, 2,286.64; Mrs. J. W. Redner, meals, 15.00; Sundry persons, fish eggs, 73.98; White Hardware Co., Ltd., hardware, 193.36. Sundries—cartage, 172.00; express, 6.02; freight, 14.99; postage, 17.25; telegrams, 17.71; petty disbursements, 32.41..... 3,695 89

Codrington Trout Rearing Station ($4,952.87)

Salaries, $1,125.00.

George R. Ryckman	Assistant	12 months	1,125 00

Temporary Services, $437.50.

A. MacIver	Assistant	3 months	262 50
Edward Thurston	"	2 "	175 00

Travelling Expenses, $266.99.

F. J. Billett, 25.35; E. W. Hayes, 37.50; Geo. Little, 165.25; A. MacIver, 4.75; E. E. Persall, 34.14....... 266 99

Biological and Fish Culture Branch—Continued

Hatcheries—Continued

Codrington Trout Rearing Station—Continued

Expenses, $3,123.38.

W. Ames, gas, etc., 31.71; Berry Brothers, varnish, 23.52; E. W. Best, salt, 104.00; Brighton Garage, oil, etc., 13.68; Brighton Municipal Telephone System, tolls, 7.30; Canada Packers, Ltd., liver, 480.02; Mrs. W. Carr, meals, 181.28; B. Greening Wire Co., Ltd., zinc, etc., 40.10; R. P. Harper, hardware, etc., 105.40; Harris Abattoir Co., Ltd., liver, 518.10; C. Hough, gasolene, etc., 10.44; T. W. Martin, gasolene, 18.01; Pay list, wages of men, 691.00; J. E. Rinch, expenses operating truck, 25.78; G. A. Ryckman, expenses operating truck, 172.51; Mrs. R. B. Ryckman, meals, etc., 472.42; C. Todd, gasolene, 22.31; B. West, ice, 65.25. Sundries—cartage, 3.00; express, 16.19; freight, 2.66; postage, 11.25; telegrams, 31.54; petty disbursements, 75.91 .... 3,123 38

Collingwood ($11,217.54)

Salaries, $4,225.00.

John E. Turner	Manager	12 months	1,800 00
John D. Montgomery	Assistant	12 "	1,300 00
Geo. E. Andrews	"	12 "	1,125 00

Travelling Expenses, $88.17.

C. Clark, 12.45; J. D. Montgomery, 41.66; J. E. Turner, 34.06 .... 88 17

Expenses, $6,904.37.

Bell Telephone Co., rentals, 27.00; tolls, 14.38; Mrs. M. Burns, meals, 133.05; Berry Bros., paint, 18.00; J. W. Cauthers, provisions, 39.25; Collingwood Public Utilities Commission, light, 210.42; Collingwood Shipyards, Ltd., cutting of pipe, 15.33; J. H. Cornish, provisions, 10.50; F. W. Eldon, draying, 47.00; C. H. Gauthier, white fish eggs, 2,443.35; Gilpin Bros., hardware, 47.28; Imperial Oil, Ltd., gasolene, 346.79; Johnston Bros., hardware, 114.57; J. Leckie, Ltd., pump, 20.69; McFadyen & McQuade, furnace, 263.00; J. G. Peterman, lumber, 110.00; Pay list, wages of men, 2,178.55; A. Pomphrey, repairing and decorating house, 207.00; Prentice & Sproule, provisions, 104.06; C. J. Sandell, meat, 35.51; L. Sanderson, cans, 12.40; A. Staiman & Sons, iron pipe, 104.00; Sundry persons, fish eggs, 47.20; Trott's, mattresses, 13.00; C. Turner, laundry, 10.00; Wright Bros., provisions, 20.81; J. Wright, coal, 15.00. Sundries—cartage, 173.25; express, 31.53; freight, 27.33; postage, 6.00; telegrams, 8.72; petty disbursements, 49.40 .... 6,904 37

Dorion Trout Rearing Station ($6,215.42)

Salaries, $1,522.93.

James Garriock	Assistant	8 months	866 68
Harry Arvelin	"	8 "	656 25

Temporary Services, $1,312.50.

Harold C. Tester	Assistant	10 months	875 00
A. Gamble	" (night man)	5 "	437 50

Travelling Expenses, $492.52.

J. F. Atkinson, 66.61; H. Arvelin, 43.55; N. A. Barker, 58.91; N. Galbraith, 58.15; J. Garriock, 25.15; W. L. Hicks, 39.80; H. C. Tester, 200.35 .... 492 52

Expenses, $2,887.47.

P. Broughton, gas, 27.16; Canadian National Railways, coal and ice, 29.72; Dunn Hardware Co., Ltd., hardware, 38.35; T. Eaton Co., Ltd., window shades, 98.70; Fort William Public Utilities, tolls, 2.80; Fallis-Foote Co., hardware, 108.70; Mrs. A. Gamble, meals, 645.90; Grainport Motors, gas, 33.30; B. Greening Wire Co., Ltd., screen wire, 14.00; Harris Abattoir (Western), Ltd., liver, 615.70; Lampshire & Terry, strainers, 11.50; Rice Lewis & Son, Ltd., food chopper, etc., 34.38; A. McNichol, boat hire, 30.00; Marshall-Wells Co., Ltd., salt, 100.00; Pay list, wages of men, 423.13; E. E. Persall, expenses operating truck, 221.77; Jno. E. Rinch, expenses operating truck, 45.75; Swift Canadian Co., Ltd., meat, 28.11; Thunder Bay Lumber Co., Ltd., coal, 27.00; Wells & Emerson, hardware, 70.48. Sundries—cartage, 152.60; express, 9.66; freight, 51.13; postage, 9.20; telegrams, 11.41; petty disbursements, 47.02 .... 2,887 47

Fort Frances ($5,087.32)

Salaries, $2,900.00.

Neil Galbraith	Manager	12 months	1,600 00
Walter L. Hicks	Assistant	12 "	1,300 00

Biological and Fish Culture Branch—Continued

Hatcheries—Continued

Fort Frances—Continued

Travelling Expenses, $169.31.

R. Baillie, 6.00; G. Buckingham, 4.25; N. Galbraith, 32.95; W. L. Hicks, 126.11.	169 31

Expenses, $2,018.01.

Chapple Municipal Telephone System, tolls, 1.20; J. East Co., Ltd., coal, etc., 367.39; Gillmor & Noden, hardware, 41.33; Mac's Bluebird Groceterias, provisions, 179.31; North Star Oil, Ltd., gas, 72.10; Pay list, spawntakers, 975.68; Stratton Telephone Co., tolls, .45; S. M. Struve, boat hire, 24.00; Town of Fort Frances, telephone rental, 37.50; L. D. Traux, ice, 14.00. Sundries—cartage, 258.15; postage, 7.00; telegrams, 1.75; petty disbursements, 38.15...........	2,018 01

Glenora ($12,724.75)

Salaries, $2,925.00.

Norman H. Quinlan..........	Manager..........................	12 months	1,800 00
Harold E. Tyson.............	Assistant..........................	12 "	1,125 00

Temporary Services, $2,561.40.

John G. Barram..............	Net Foreman......................	12 months	1,200 00
Benson L. Dunn.............	Assistant..........................	10 "	1,050 00
Fred J. Billett................	"	3½ "	311 40

Travelling Expenses, $1,369.96.

J. G. Barram, 59.05; F. J. Billett, 195.20; L. E. Burns, 19.55; B. L. Dunn, 127.45; E. W. Hayes, 11.10; A. Keene, 22.00; G. La Brash, 42.55; W. H. La Rue, 147.40; J. G. Lighthall, 134.90; G. Littles, 84.60; B. Morris, 219.05; N. H. Quinlan, 74.70; E. Reader, 21.96; E. Thurston, 69.15; H. E. Tyson, 141.30..........	1,369 96

Expenses, $5,868.39.

C. Ackerman, meals, 10.00; Adams & Van Dusen Co., brooms, 11.21; Bell Telephone Co., rental, 25.35; tolls, 33.82; Berry Bros., varnish, 12.00; Canada Packers, Ltd., liver, 111.15; R. Chalk, Sr., rent of boathouse, 35.00; Cities Service Oil Co., Ltd., gas, 399.33; Mrs. J. B. Gould, meals, 106.25; Harris Abattoir Co., Ltd., liver, 35.90; Hepburn Bros., coal and ice, 536.03; Hogg & Lytle, salt, 15.00; Mrs. C. V. Howard, meals, 45.90; J. Leckie, Ltd., hardware, 70.59; McIntosh Meat Market, liver, 12.29; Ontario Shore Gas Co., Ltd., tar, 18.00; Pay list, wages of men, 3,947.56; A. M. Powers, hardware, 25.46; Sundry persons, fish eggs, 63.00. Sundries—cartage, 179.65; express, 17.46; freight, 13.70; postage, 19.41; telegrams, 97.28; petty disbursements, 27.05...............................	5,868 39

Ingersoll Bass Rearing Station ($367.00)

J. T. McCarthy, services as watchman, 366.00; Ingersoll Public Utilities Commission, rent of pond, 1.00..	367 00

Green Lake Bass Rearing Station ($659.15)

Temporary Services, $400.00.

John J. Carter...............	Watchman.......................	12 months	400 00

Expenses, $259.15.

Black Donald Graphite Co., Ltd., ice, 24.00; C. Kemsley, travelling expenses, 71.95; J. D. Montgomery, travelling expenses, 70.35; M. K. Mulvihill, rent, 10.00; J. B. Wilson, provisions, 32.08. Sundries—cartage, 46.60; telegrams, 4.17.	259 15

Kenora ($7,756.77)

Salaries, $3,100.00.

Fred W. Sole................	Manager..........................	12 months	1,800 00
Albert E. Openshaw..........	Assistant..........................	12 "	1,300 00

Temporary Services, $647.14.

George Millership............	Assistant.........................	6 months	539 60
G. Jamieson.................	" (night man).............	1¼ "	107 54

Expenses, $4,009.63.

J. T. Brett, gravel, 31.50; Canadian Fairbanks-Morse Co., Ltd., packing, 15.20; A. T. Fife & Co., furnace, etc., 361.10; R. Foster, provisions, 94.74; C. W. Fraser, travelling expenses, 57.40; Hudson's Bay Co., tent, 40.19; Imperial Oil, Ltd., gas, 178.77; J. V. Johnson, repairing furnace, 10.95; Kelley & Kimberley, gravel, 23.75; Town of Kenora, water and light, 453.00; telephone, rentals, 12.50; J. Kron & Son, coal, 302.03; J. A. Link, ice, 27.73; McKinnon & Ronen, provisions,

Biological and Fish Culture Branch—Continued

Hatcheries—Continued

Kenora—Continued

Expenses—Continued

22.71; A. E. Openshaw, travelling expenses, 70.05; Pay list, wages of men, 1,821.42; R. Peterson, boat hire, 13.00; H. Ritchie & Son, provisions, 98.17; Williams Hardware Co., hardware, 36.53. Sundries—cartage, 279.25; express, 17.78; postage, 7.75; telegrams, 3.76; petty disbursements, 30.35............ 4,009 63

Kingsville ($6,818.15)

Salaries, $2,800.00.

Samuel Adamson	Manager	10 months	1,500 00
Arthur E. Mouck	Assistant	12 "	1,300 00

Temporary Services, $2,155.75.

Samuel Adamson	Manager	2 months	300 00
W. Bowles	Engineer	5¼ "	560 00
Arthur C. Green	"	5¼ "	560 00
Alvin H. Scratch	"	5¼ "	560 00
R. Scratch	Assistant (night man)	2 "	175 75

Expenses, $1,862.40.

Bell Telephone Co., rentals, 33.00; tolls, 4.20; Co-operative Supply Co., Ltd., coal, 679.45; Cox Bros., gas, 11.95; Dearborn Chemical Co., Ltd., chemicals, 41.47; Chas. Kemsley, travelling expenses, 6.55; Kingsville Public Utilities Commission, light, 24.94; Lake Erie Coal Co., Ltd., coal, 274.43; A. G. Lashinger, travelling expenses, 22.72; M. Loop, boat hire, 80.00; M. McCormick, meals, 43.50; S. McCormick, meals, 33.00; F. Mains, gas tank, 13.00; Mrs. H. A. Messacar, board of men, 43.00; A. E. Mouck, travelling expenses, 13.55; Pay list, wages of men, 69.00; Sundry persons, fish eggs, 413.20; Windsor & Pelee Island Steamship Co., freight, 10.05. Sundries—cartage, 3.25; express, 7.43; freight, 9.51; postage, 14.00; telegrams, 1.10; petty disbursements, 10.10............ 1,862 40

Mount Pleasant ($7,496.53)

Salaries, $1,700.00.

John Neal	Manager	12 months	1,700 00

Temporary Services, $2,401.58.

Albert J. Bowler	Assistant	12 months	1,050 00
Ernest Swift	"	4 "	350 00
Albert Atkins	"	4⅔ "	413 29
Harold Rutherford	"	4⅔ "	413 29
Douglas R. Cutts	"	2 "	175 00

Travelling Expenses, $1,063.34.

A. Atkins, 295.40; A. M. Boughner, 21.02; A. Bowler, 30.90; D. R. Cutts, 15.35; J. Gall, 18.39; J. Neal, 66.92; H. Rutherford, 337.96; E. Swift, 277.40........ 1,063 34

Expenses, $2,331,61.

Bell Telephone Co., rentals, 44.70; tolls, 15.43; Berry Bros., paint, 24.00; Canada Packers, Ltd., liver, 896.09; Canadian National Railways, ice, 16.73; E. J. Devlin, hardware, 18.43; B. Greening Wire Co., Ltd., screen wire, etc., 98.47; Harris Abattoir Co., Ltd., liver, 329.09; Hydro-Electric Power Commission, light, 55.97; Mrs. J. McCarthy, meals, 16.00; G. McDonald, bass, 20.00; Mount Pleasant Coal & Fuel Co., salt, 37.00; Pay list, wages of men, 198.08; Sargeant Co., Ltd., ice, 45.00; Shultes Coal Co., coal, 112.00; Turnbull & Cutliffe, Ltd., soap, bulbs, etc., 24.22; C. Wetmore, gas and oil, 50.15. Sundries—cartage, 18.40; express, 7.65; freight, 144.93; postage, 6.43; telegrams, 113.61; petty disbursements, 39.23.... 2,331 61

Normandale ($8,600.47)

Salaries, $3,100.00.

William Kenefick	Manager	12 months	1,800 00
John W. Post	Assistant	12 "	1,300 00

Temporary Services, $2,550.00.

Wm. H. Derrick	Special Officer	12 months	1,500 00
J. Alex. Thompson	Assistant (night man)	12 "	1,050 00

Travelling Expenses, $567.47.

W. Kenefick, 10.00; A. E. Mouck, 96.15; J. Post, 258.72; C. Strowger, 40.71; J. A. Thompson, 161.89............ 567 47

Biological and Fish Culture Branch—Continued

Hatcheries—Continued

Normandale—Continued

Expenses, $2,383.00.

Canada Packers, Ltd., liver, 519.43; Canadian Pacific Railway Co., ice, 14.75; Dunlop Tire & Rubber Goods Co., Ltd., tubing, 35.59; A. S. Edmonds & Co., salt, 58.50; S. S. Edwards & Co., salt, 29.25; R. Ferris, oil, 31.64; Harris Abattoir Co., Ltd., liver, 419.00; Hydro-Electric Power Commission, light, 141.84; Hotel Norfolk, meals, 25.00; Pay list, wages of men, 459.49; Port Dover Coal & Supply Co., coal, 75.00; South Ontario Telephone System, rentals, 21.90; tolls, 9.63; Mrs. W. Stanley, board, 47.75; Sundry persons, fish eggs, 311.23; H. Swayze, gas, 14.66; Mrs. A. Thompson, milk, 11.40; Sundries—cartage, 99.75; express, .60; freight, 2.03; postage, 10.00; telegrams, 10.19; petty disbursements, 34.37	2,383 00

Normandale Trout Ponds ($7,202.53)

Salaries, $1,900.00.

Chas. Hartman	Manager	12 months	1,900 00

Temporary Services, $2,100.00.

Jno. B. Centeno	Assistant	10 months	1,050 00
Douglas R. Cutts	"	10 "	875 00
Harold C. Tester	"	2 "	175 00

Travelling Expenses, $298.58.

A. M. Boughner, 8.50; J. B. Centeno, 6.25; D. R. Cutts, 29.70; C. H. Hartman, 73.50; B. Morris, 70.50; A. E. Mouck, 16.55; J. Post, 9.88; H. C. Tester, 44.60; J. A. Thompson, 39.10	298 58

Expenses, $2,903.95.

W. A. Abbey, repairing pump, 18.70; Canada Packers, Ltd., liver, 852.75; E. Church, gas, 35.29; A. S. Edmonds & Co., salt, 106.47; B. Greening Wire Co., Ltd., wire cloth, 25.48; Harris Abattoir Co., Ltd., liver, 433.70; Pay list, wages of men, 777.82; H. F. Prelipp, hardware, 42.02; Quance Bros., Ltd., hay, salt, 218.26; Sargeant Co., Ltd., ice, 53.70; Southern Ontario Telephone Co., rentals, 26.28; tolls, 10.82; Mrs. W. Staley, meals, 28.75; H. Swayze, gas, 18.40; Sundries—express, 17.80; freight, 175.48; postage, 9.00; telegrams, 14.59; petty disbursements, 38.64	2,903 95

North Bay Distributing Station ($857.87)

Travelling Expenses, $308.45.

G. H. Gardiner, 19.30; O. Gehring, 3.70; C. Kemsley, 101.55; M. Laderoutte, 9.95; T. W. Mallory, 45.85; W. H. Quinn, 68.25; L. Schofield, 42.65; E. Swift, 17.20	308 45

Expenses, $549.42.

Mrs. H. D. Carroll, meals, 37.50; Cochrane-Dunlop Hardware, Ltd., hardware, 26.37; Continental Hotel, meals, 55.50; W. E. Kinsey, gas, 17.50; Pay list seasonal assistants, 294.51; H. Stockdale, ice, 15.28; T. Taylor & Co., tent, etc, 28.00; R. B. Tennant & Co., lumber 21.38. Sundries—express, 13.50; freight, 13.09; telegrams, 13.89; petty disbursements, 12.90	549 42

Pembroke Trout Rearing Station ($2,150.00)

Joseph Kreiger	Assistant (caretaker)	(T) 12 months	1,050 00

Travelling Expenses, $347.29.

F. J. Billett, 83.15; J. Gall, 80.10; E. W. Hayes, 70.64; J. J. Kreiger, 30.30; B. Morris, 83.10	347 29

Expenses, $752.71.

Berry Bros., paint, 23.52; Brash's Meat Market, liver, 15.40; Canada Packers, Ltd., liver, 230.18; Cockburn & Archer, hardware, 24.48; Fraser's Red Arrow Taxi, livery, 11.00; Mrs. A. Lindemann, board, 173.75; J. A. Moore, salt, 97.50; Pay list, wages of men, 50.00. Sundries—cartage, 50.35; express, 25.95; freight, 3.09; telegrams, 19.21; postage, 9.09; petty disbursements, 19.19	752 71

Port Arthur "P" ($7,510.09)

Salaries, $3,625.00.

John E. McKenzie	Manager	12 months	1,800 00
Samuel Craig	"	1 "	150 00
Duncan McAskill	Assistant	12 "	1,300 00
Harry Arvelin	"	4 "	375 00

Biological and Fish Culture Branch—Continued

Hatcheries—Continued

Port Arthur "P"—Continued

Expenses, $3,885.09.

E. Arvelin, travelling expenses, 8.90; Canadian National Railways, fares of men, 19.25; W. Doran, boat hire, 12.75; Fairway Stores, provisions, etc., 330.15; Fallis-Foote Co., Ltd., hardware, 52.70; F. Gerow, boat hire, etc., 297.75; Lampshire & Terry, plumbing, 10.50; D. McAskill, travelling expenses, 17.90; J. E. McKenzie, travelling expenses, 47.45; A. McLeod, boat hire, 223.00; Pay list, wages of men, 2,048.08; Port Arthur Public Utilities Commission, light and water, 160.24; telephone exchange, 24.00; Superior Ice Co., ice, 60.00; L. Walsh Coal Co., Ltd., coal, 297.00. Sundries—cartage, 135.50; car tickets, 36.00; express, 1.50; freight, 55.59; postage, 11.77; telegrams, 7.46; petty disbursements, 27.60............ 3,885 09

Port Arthur "F" ($1,944.05)

Salaries, $1,033.32.

Samuel Craig................	Manager.........................	6 months	600 00
James Garriock..............	Assistant.........................	4 "	433 32

Expenses, $910.73.

Austin, Chambers & Bradbury, coal, 52.00; Fallis Foote Co., Ltd., brooms, 10.22; Pay list, wages of men, 520.00; Port Arthur Public Utilities Commission, light and water, 45.21; telephone, 6.00; Sundry persons, fish eggs, 220.80. Sundries—cartage, 44.50; car tickets, 6.00; postage, 3.00; telegrams, 3.00...... 910 73

Port Carling ($560.93)

Travelling Expenses, $149.60.

J. S. Elliott, 20.95; F. A. Green, 19.05; E. Jermyn, 30.40; J. W. Post, 30.30; E. G. Snyder, 24.50; R. G. Trimble, 24.40............................... 149 60

Expenses, $411,33.

Mrs. C. A. Cannell, meals, 133.50; Hydro-Electric Power Commission, light, 15.00; Medora & Wood Municipal Telephone System, tolls, 6.50; Pay list, wages of men, 194.74; Sundries—cartage, 22.00; express, 1.30; telegrams, 12.31; postage, 2.00; freight, .65; petty disbursements, 23.33............... 411 33

Sarnia ($5,708.31)

Salaries, $3,100.00.

A. G. Laschinger.............	Manager.........................	12 months	1,800 00
Chas. D. Kemsley............	Assistant.........................	12 "	1,300 00

Temporary Services, $1,372.00.

J. W. Glass..................	Engineer.........................	6½ months	714 00
B. Tulett....................	"	6 "	658 00

Expenses, $1,236.31.

W. J. Barrie, boiler and fittings, 12.00; Bell Telephone Co., rentals, 35.60; tolls, 5.09; Canadian National Railways, rent, 20.00; Century Coal Co., Ltd., coal, 487.22; Hydro-Electric Power Commission, light, 24.28; Imperial Oil, Ltd., gas and oil, 118.23; Wm. Kemsley, repairing boiler, 12.80; Laidlaw Belton Co., Ltd., lumber, 23.56; A. G. Laschinger, travelling expenses, 65.89; Mackenzie Milne & Co., Ltd., hardware, 22.27; Pay list, wages of men, 286.00; Pelee Island Telephone Co., tolls, .35; Mrs. E. Randall, meals, 76.50. Sundries—cartage, 2.50; postage, 10.00; telegrams, 2.30; petty disbursements, 31.72.......................... 1,236 31

Sault Ste. Marie ($10,156.15)

Salaries, $4,400.00.

Joseph Oakes................	Manager.........................	12 months	1,800 00
Norman Miskimins...........	Assistant.........................	12 "	1,300 00
Wm. C. Sanders.............	"	12 "	1,300 00

Temporary Services, $1,035.89.

C. Hall......................	Assistant.........................	10 months	875 00
R. Chaput...................	"	1 5/6 "	160 89

Travelling Expenses, $1,665.31.

C. Hall, 411.25; N. Miskimins, 513.55; W. Rushton, 17.82; W. Sanders, 722.69; . 1,665 31

Expenses, $3,054.95.

Bell Telephone Co., rentals, 54.60; tolls, 6.80; Berry Bros., paint, 18.00; J. E. Buchanan, provisions, 40.20; Cochrane-Dunlop Hardware, Ltd., hardware, 31.67; Great Lakes Power Co., light, 36.00; Harris Abattoir Co., Ltd., liver, 143.71;

Biological and Fish Culture Branch—Continued

Hatcheries—Continued

Sault Ste. Marie—Continued

Expenses—Continued

Hussey Ferrier Meat Co., Ltd., liver, 146.80; Keyes Hardware, Ltd., hardware, 22.03; J. W. McDonald, coal, 450.00; Pay list, wages of men, 1,205.60; Purity Ice, Ltd., ice, 217.00; Sault Ste. Marie, Water and Light Dept., water, 24.97; Soo Tinsmiths & Roofers, repairs, cans, 27.25; H. Stockdale, ice, 13.00; Wesley Taxi & Transfer Co., livery, 12.70. Sundries—cartage, 390.33; express, 3.35; freight, 121.03; postage, 18.22; telegrams, 49.64; petty disbursements, 22.05............ 3,054 95

Sault Ste. Marie Trout Rearing Station ($17,489.71)

Salaries, $1,600.00.

Geo. E. Gerow	Manager	12 months	1,600 00

Temporary Services, $2,933.33.

James Savage	Biologist	1 month	133 33
I. M. McLean	Assistant	12 "	1,050 00
Edgar Porter	"	12 "	1,050 00
Francis Buck	"	8 "	700 00

Travelling Expenses, $2,343.03.

F. A. Buck, 296.20; R. J. Chaput, 49.45; H. Drackley, 141.70; J. Garriock, 15.05; G. E. Gerow, 32.45; D. H. Handley, 224.10; J. A. Johnston, 197.24; H. J. Lortie, 88.00; M. J. Oakes, 308.60; E. Porter, 325.77; W. Rushton, 399.83; J. Savage, 32.10; T. Snell, 90.34; M. Thibault, 142.20...................... 2,343 03

Expenses, $10,613.35.

E. L. Bedford, hardware, 17.95; Bell Telephone Co., tolls, 1.70; Canada Packers, Ltd., liver, 681.40; Cochrane-Dunlop Hardware, Ltd., hardware, 25.37; J. J. Downey & Sons, lime, 11.00; Edwards Hardware, hardware, 17.64; C. J. Fitzpatrick, ice, 290.08; B. Greening Wire Co., Ltd., wire cloth, 37.12; Harris Abattoir Co., Ltd., liver, 297.69; T. A. Heye, repairs, gas, etc., 18.84; Hussey Ferrier Meat Co., Ltd., liver, 5,021.06; Mrs. G. M. Johnston, board, 23.50; Keyes Hardware Co., Ltd., paint, etc., 77.15; Flockhart Bros., fry cans, etc., 23.35; J. H. McDonald, coal, 66.00; National Grocers Co., Ltd., salt, 309.75; Mrs. J. Oakes, board, 61.97; Pay list, wages of men, 2,970.31; Purity Ice, Ltd., ice, 104.00; Sault Water and Light Dept., light, 122.63; Soo Tinsmiths & Roofers, repairs, 11.05; H. Stockdale, ice, 22.10; Tallack Bros., towing, 19.00; Wesley Taxi & Transport Co., taxi, 21.00. Sundries—cartage, 75.50; express, 43.97; freight, 39.76; postage, 16.43; telegrams, 118.93; petty disbursements, 67.10.................................... 10,613 35

Southampton ($5,957.48)

Salaries, $3,000.00.

Alex. McDougall	Manager	12 months	1,800 00
Milne Oakes	Assistant	12 "	1,200 00

Temporary Services, $128.23.

John Sinclair	Engineer	5 months	128 23

Expenses, $2,829.25.

Bell Telephone Co., rentals, 29.70; tolls, 3.80; Mrs. Belrose, board, 29.25; Berry Bros., paint, 11.76; Canadian Fairbanks-Morse Co., Ltd., repairs, etc., 68.70; Commercial Hotel, board, 13.50; D. R. Cutts, travelling expenses, 10.80; Hydro-Electric Power Commission, light, 394.87; G. Knechtel, repairs, etc., 10.30; A. McDougall, travelling expenses, 4.20; J. McLellan, draying fry, 11.25; L. Matheson, hardware, 32.74; P. Matheson, tug hire, 142.00; Pay list, wages of men, 1,994.68; Trelford Bros., brooms, repairs to fish cans, etc., 13.17. Sundries—cartage, 20.60; express, 1.65; freight, 11.55; postage, 8.10; telegrams, 2.88; petty disbursements, 13.75.. 2,829 25

Wiarton ($10,206.38)

Salaries, $3,100.00.

William Colter	Manager	12 months	1,800 00
Henry A. Cheeseman	Assistant	12 "	1,300 00

Travelling Expenses, $451.54.

G. Capon, 18.00; H. A. Cheeseman, 76.75; G. Clemans, 22.00; W. Colter, 33.20; R. M. Crawford, 28.25; F. H. Eyre, 26.80; G. Hawke, 19.00; H. Kelly, 66.80; J. Lee, 39.00; G. Littles, 28.50; M. Meneray, 33.84; A. J. Reid, 22.40; E. Scott, 19.00; G. M. West, 18.00.. 451 54

Biological and Fish Culture Branch—Continued

Hatcheries—Continued

Wiarton—Continued

Expenses, $6,654.84.

Bell Telephone Co., rentals, 35.40; tolls, 18.24; L. Chapman & Sons, board, 11.00 C. Couture, boat hire, 480.00; J. Gildner & Son, liver, 66.00; G. E. C. Grant, rent, 10.00; B. Greening Wire Co., Ltd., screen, 23.16; Hunter Hardware Co., Ltd., hardware, 69.30; Hydro-Electric Power Commission, light, 46.27; S. Logan, ice, 46.10; Mrs. W. H. Oldfield, board, 10.50; Pay list, wages of men, 3,754.42; L. P. Ritchie, board, 57.00; G. H. Smith, ice, 10.50; Mrs. D. Sturgeon, board, 12.00; Town of Wiarton, water, 1,500.00; Wiarton Coal & Wood Co., coal, 231.00. Sundries—cartage, 96.10; express, 5.75; freight, 97.25; postage, 11.00; telegrams, 12.05; petty disbursements, 51.80........................ 6,654 84

Miscellaneous Hatcheries ($17,307.80)

John Gall......................Assistant Hatchery Supervisor......12 months 1,800 00

Travelling Expenses, $7,505.70.

G. Andrews, 63.35; J. Barram, 131.12; A. M. Boughner, 1,501.01; H. A. Cheeseman, 49.82; John Gall, 1,247.64; C. Kemsley, 58.52; J. D. Montgomery, 48.38; B. Morris, 55.85; M. J. Oakes, 22.45; A. E. Openshaw, 18.50; E. E. Persall, 1,663.46; A. Reader, 900.66; J. E. Rinch, 359.53; Fred W. Sole, 43.05; E. Tallon, 1,334.61; J. E. Turner, 7.75.. 7,505 70

General Expenses, $8,002.10.

Mrs. M. Andrew, board, 12.00; Mrs. J. Barram, board, 17.00; Bell Telephone Co., tolls, 5.52; Caledon Mountain Trout Club, fry, 1,875.00; Dept. of Highways, auto service, etc., 672.98; Exchange Hotel, meals, 17.50; French River Supply Post, provisions, 57.41; B. Greening Wire Co., Ltd., screen, 12.35; G. A. Hendry, gas, 10.39; King's Printer, 435.01; Mrs. T. McQuade, meals, 73.74; Pay list, wages of men, 4,623.25; Mrs. E. Pogue, board, ice, 10.65; H. Ritchie, provisions, 13.48. Sundries—cartage, 21.00; express, 95.25; postage, 1.00; telegrams, 4.33; freight, 16.55; petty disbursements, 27.69... 8,002 10

Biological and Fish Culture Branch.................... $188,758.20

GENERAL

Erecting Ponds and Buildings ($66,967.61)

Jno. W. Jones.................Superintendent of Construction.......12 months 2,700 00

Codrington Trout Rearing Station, $1,004.96.

Frost Steel & Wire Co., Ltd., fencing, 57.60; R. P. Harper, hardware, 26.20; M. Jex & Co., lumber, 93.15; J. W. Jones, travelling expenses, 1.25; Pay list, wages of men, 826.76.. 1,004 96

Codrington Bird Farm, $1,698.66.

B. Greening Wire Co., Ltd., netting, 46.30; R. P. Harper, hardware, 74.88; M. Jex & Co., lumber, 717.55; J. W. Jones, travelling expenses, 13.73; Pay list, wages of men, 846.20.. 1,698 66

Dorion Trout Rearing Station, $29,789.44.

Anthes Foundry, Ltd., pipe, 38.65; Bell Telephone Co., tolls, .40; P. Broughton, gas, 120.57; W. Brown, posts, 94.95; Canadian Fairbanks-Morse Co., Ltd., pipe, etc., 320.00; Canadian Steel Corporation, Ltd., wire, 443.06; J. M. Costonquay, plastering, 290.00; Crane, Ltd., pipe, 169.73; T. Crittall, chimney, etc., 61.00; Fallis-Foote Co., hardware, 2,400.16; Flaherty Manufacturing Co., faucets, 85.65; Frost Steel & Wire Co., Ltd., fencing, 116.80; Grain Port Motors, Ltd., gas, 166.74; B. Greening Wire Co., Ltd., screen wire, 263.53; J. W. Jones, travelling expenses, 536.00; Lakehead Engineering Co., troughs, roof, etc., 649.80; Lampshire & Terry, plumbing, 516.44; G. Lanktree, posts, 99.00; Rice Lewis & Son, Ltd., hardware, 46.78; McCall & Co., lumber, etc., 527.68; McLennan Lumber Co., lumber, 160.85; Pay list, wages of men, 19,251.21; Port Arthur Shipbuilding Co., Ltd., water wheel, etc., 349.64; Provincial Paper, Ltd., wire cloth, screening, 15.80; H. E. Stafford, wiring, etc., 409.90; Superior Brick & Tile Co., Ltd., brick, 19.24; Thunder Bay Lumber Co., Ltd., lumber, 2,085.78; Woodside Bros., stream grates, etc., 468.16. Sundries—express, 9.65; freight, 36.57; postage, 1.50; telegrams, 2.62; petty disbursements, 31.58.. 29,789 44

General—Continued

Erecting Ponds and Buildings—Continued

Experimental Fur Farm, $90.71.

J. Carew Lumber Co., Ltd., lumber, 77.21; Sundries—cartage, 13.50......... 90 71

Kingsville Hatchery, $1,791.84.

Canadian Fairbanks-Morse Co., Ltd., pump, motor engine, 1,776.46; J. W. Jones, travelling expenses, 15.38.. 1,791 84

Mount Pleasant Hatchery, $8,816.53.

R. H. Ballantyne, hardware, 249.24; A. D. Barton, repairs, 36.56; Brantford Novelties & Builders Supplies, Ltd., lumber, 362.48; B. Greening Wire Co., Ltd., wire cloth, 146.52; J. Guest, gravel, 378.55; Harold & Goetz, Ltd., cement, 710.64; Ingleby-Taylor Co., Ltd., cement, 32.41; W. H. Jones, travelling expenses, 202.85; Ker & Goodwin Machinery Co., Ltd., grating, 76.85; B. Mundy, frames, 10.00; Pay list, wages of men, 5,712.99; Soo Lumber & Mill Co., Ltd., lumber, 134.93; F. Strenkovsky, steel, 71.70; Turnbull & Cutcliffe, Ltd., pipe, etc., 82.46; West Brant Hardware, hardware, 14.52; Wetmore's Service, Ltd., gas, 459.10. Sundries—cartage, 105.75; petty disbursements, 28.98.............. 8,816 53

Normandale Trout Pond, $1,228.60.

Wm. H. Abbey, plumbing, wiring and supplies, 113.21; W. H. Jones, travelling expenses, 28.86; McCall & Co., lumber, 802.10; Pay list, wages of men, 248.70; H. F. Prelipp, cement, 26.78. Sundries—petty disbursements, 8.95 .... 1,228 60

Normandale Bird Farm, $4,071.52.

W. H. Abbey, eavestroughing, 120.00; Crosbie's Cooperage & Transport, trucking, 12.16; J. Elliott & Son, building chimney, 5.40; Frost Steel & Wire Co., Ltd., wire, 307.65; B. Greening Wire Co., Ltd., netting, 407.97; W. H. Jones, travelling expenses, 24.26; McCall & Co., lumber, 1,335.80; Pay list, wages of men, 1,647.85; H. F. Prelipp, hardware, etc., 210.43....................................... 4,071 52

Normandale Hatchery, $80.74.

McCall & Co., lumber.. 80 74

North Bay Distributing Station, $177.07.

Canadian Fairbanks-Morse Co., Ltd., gasket, 23.07; McCall & Co., tanks, 129.00; Tallman Brass & Metal, Ltd., faucets, 25.00.............................. 177 07

Pembroke Trout Rearing Station, $4,650.42.

Estate of L. S. Barrand, lumber, 820.38; Beatty & Beatty, surveying, 50.00; Cochrane-Dunlop Hardware, Ltd., hardware, 24.60; Flaherty Manufacturing Co., faucets, 21.88; J. W. Jones, travelling expenses, 59.11; Pay list, wages of men, 3,648.45. Sundries—cartage, 21.50; petty disbursements, 4.50......... 4,650 42

Sault Ste. Marie Trout Rearing Station, $9,657.06.

Anthes Foundry, Ltd., syphon, 38.65; Canadian Fairbanks-Morse Co., Ltd., water plant, 146.00; Edwards Hardware, hardware, 817.31; Flockhart Bros., trough, 37.38; B. Greening Wire Co., Ltd., trays and baskets, 1,008.32; Hesson Lumber Co., lumber, 470.00; G. M. Johnston, poles, gravel, 132.20; J. W. Jones, travelling expenses, 154.20; McCall & Co., lumber, 486.01; C. F. Mills, travelling expenses, 22.40; J. Nicholson, chimney, 22.00; Pay list, wages of men, 4,659.80; Soo Lumber & Mill Co., Ltd., lumber, 1,624.28. Sundries—cartage, 5.00; express, 6.07; freight, 26.44; postage, 1.00................................. 9,657 06

Southampton Hatchery, $993.73.

B. Greening Wire Co., Ltd., screen, 33.00; J. W. Jones, travelling expenses, 70.87; B. Knechtel, pump, 11.15; J. McLellan, teaming, 26.26; Pay list, wages of men, 483.55; Southampton Lumber Co., 187.10; Thompson Bros., belting, 30.57; Trelford Bros., hardware, 31.87; Walker House Hotel, meals, 74.00. Sundries—cartage, 17.00; petty disbursements, 28.36............................... 993 73

Miscellaneous, $216.33.

Mrs. H. Cooper, garage rent, 40.50; Department of Highways, garage accounts, 10.80; J. W. Jones, travelling expenses, 10.64; Jas. Teaham, purchase of log cabin, 150.00. Sundries—telegrams, 4.39................................ 216 33

General—Continued

Enforcement of the Ontario Game and Fisheries Act ($268,789.60)

District No. 1, Headquarters, London, $36,442.57.

Salaries, $22,067.74.

Col. R. Emmerton	District Superintendent	12 months		2,700 00
Donalda Leach	Clerk Stenographer	12 "		975 00
Harry Clark	Overseer	12 "		1,200 00
Arthur Cecile	"	12 "		1,200 00
John O. Hammond	"	12 "		1,200 00
Wm. B. Hare	"	12 "		1,300 00
Arthur C. Jensen	"	12 "		1,200 00
George H. Jolley	"	12 "	1,200 00	
		Less Leave of Absence	47 40	1,152 60
George A. Kay	"	12 months		1,300 00
Wm. Keller	"	12 "		1,600 00
Geo. L. Leedham	"	12 "		1,300 00
W. A. Mewhinney	"	12 "	1,500 00	
		Less Leave of Absence	59 86	1,440 14
Donald J. McRury	"	12 months		1,200 00
Oscar H. Robinson	"	12 "		1,500 00
Albert J. Rolston	"	12 "		1,300 00
Ira Toole	"	12 "		1,500 00

Temporary Services, $2,967.36.

Richard A. Duff	Overseer	12 months	1,200 00
Albert J. H. Hewer	"	12 "	1,125 00
C. J. Kerr	"	6 "	286 08
Robert Seymour	"	14/5"	170 80
E. B. Warren	Clerk Stenographer	1⅜ "	118 99
Doris E. Self	" "	1 "	66 49

Travelling Expenses, $7,624.92.

A. Cecile, 566.10; Harry Clark, 339.60; R. A. Duff, 68.00; R. Emmerton, 269.88; J. O. Hammond, 567.83; Wm. B. Hare, 428.56; A. J. H. Hewer, 378.54; A. C. Jensen, 355.57; Geo. H. Jolley, 464.90; Geo. A. Kay, 296.95; Wm. Keller, 339.35; C. J. Kerr, 243.25; G. L. Leedham, 402.97; D. J. McRury, 405.49; W. A. Mewhinney, 554.76; B. H. Robinson, 556.98; A. J. Ralston, 859.44; R. G. Seymour, 40.43; I. Toole, 486.32 .... 7,624 92

Allowances for use of Automobiles, $2,450.00.

A. Cecile, 200.00; H. Clark, 200.00; R. Emmerton, 250.00; W. B. Hare, 200.00; A. J. H. Hewer, 200.00; A. C. Jensen, 200.00; G. H. Jolly, 200.00; G. A. Kay, 200.00; W. Keller, 200.00; G. L. Leedham, 200.00; D. J. McRury, 200.00; I. Toole, 200.00 .... 2,450 00

Miscellaneous, $1,332.55.

Bell Telephone Co., rentals, 62.40; tolls, 45.38; J. Fowler, holsters, 47.85; E. Hogg, rent of garage, 48.00; W. G. Kearns, garage rent, 30.00; J. Parsons, counter, 10.00; Pay list, wages of men, 110.00; Rex Tailoring Co., Ltd., uniforms, 150.40; C. Rolston, garage rent, 38.00; Royal Bank of Canada, light and office rent, 492.99; United Typewriter Co., Ltd., inspections, 13.75. Sundries—cartage, .50; express, 22.57; postage, 241.00; telegrams, 7.96; petty disbursements, 11.75 .... 1,332 55

District No. 2, Headquarters, Orillia, $29,445.89.

Salaries, $16,195.88.

Peter Stevenson	District Superintendent	12 months	2,700 00
Muriel B. Wood	Clerk Stenographer	10 "	812 50
George F. Davies	Overseer	12 "	1,200 00
Bernard Gooderham	"	6 "	850 02
Robt. N. L. Hills	"	12 "	1,500 00
Neil MacNaughton	"	12 "	1,800 00
J. F. McGregor	Assistant Inspector	12 "	1,800 00
Geo. M. Richardson	Overseer	12 "	1,500 00
Edwin L. Skuce	"	12 "	1,200 00
R. D. Windsor	"	12 "	1,800 00
Albert J. Woodward	"	2 "	233 34
Alex E. Pennell	"	6 "	800 02

General—Continued

Enforcement of The Ontario Game and Fisheries Act—Continued

District No. 2—Headquarters, Orillia—Continued

Temporary Services, $3,871.89.

Robert W. Carson	Overseer	6 months		399 96
Norman L. Goldthorp	"	12 "		1,125 00
Michael P. Kennedy	"	12 "	1,125 00	
		Less Leave of Absence	78 99	1,046 01
Thos. J. Woods	"	12 months		1,125 00
Edythe W. Taylor	Clerk Stenographer	2½ "		175 92

Travelling Expenses, $7,585.82.

R. W. Carson, 38.85; Geo. F. Davies, 621.37; B. Gooderham, 288.48; N. L. Goldthorp, 671.88; R. N. L. Hills, 498.94; M. P. Kennedy, 595.66; N. MacNaughton, 663.98; J. F. McGregor, 617.69; A. E. Pennell, 254.18; G. M. Richardson, 428.11; E. L. Skuce, 779.65; P. Stevenson, 538.99; R. D. Windsor, 715.64; A. J. Woodward, 97.74; T. J. Woods, 774.66 .... 7,585 82

Allowances for use of Automobiles, $900.00.

J. F. McGregor, 250.00; E. L. Skuce, 200.00; P. Stevenson, 250.00; T. J. Woods, 200.00 .... 900 00

Miscellaneous, $892.30.

Bank of Montreal, exchange, 12.90; Mrs. A. Bartlett, cleaning, 24.60; Bell Telephone Co., rentals, 44.40; tolls, 27.51; Britton Bros., Ltd., rent of boathouse, 20.00; Cavana & Watson, light and rent, 366.00; Fee Motors, gas and oil, 16.99; J. Fowlie, belts, 21.75; Gordon Boat Works, gas, 39.85; T. E. Hall, garage rent, 35.00; Mrs. R. N. L. Hills, rent, garage, 23.00; Pay list, wages of men, 40.00; Stephenson Motor Sales, garage rent, 25.00; Mrs. R. D. Windsor, garage rent, 36.00. Sundries—cartage, 6.65; express, 6.54; postage, 110.00; telegrams, 2.06; petty disbursements, 34.05 .... 892 30

District No. 3, Headquarters, Ottawa, $37,406.77.

Salaries, $21,075.00.

J. W. Coffey	District Superintendent	12 months	2,700 00
Florida E. Goulet	Clerk Stenographer	12 "	975 00
Chas. W. Amey	Overseer	12 "	1,400 00
Royal Baker	"	12 "	1,600 00
James S. Code	"	12 "	1,200 00
Harold E. Costello	"	12 "	1,400 00
George M. Drew	"	12 "	1,300 00
George S. Leach	"	12 "	1,800 00
I. J. Lyons	"	12 "	1,700 00
Chas. E. Muffit	"	12 "	1,300 00
John W. J. Mundell	"	12 "	1,200 00
S. J. McClelland	"	12 "	1,700 00
Robt. G. Sheppard	"	12 "	1,500 00
Robt. G. Stringer	"	12 "	1,300 00

Temporary Services, $3,888.69.

John H. Boyd	Overseer	6 months		562 50
Wm. T. Clark	"	12 "	1,125 00	
		Less Leave of Absence	201 12	923 88
Patrick Dillon		12 months		1,125 00
Alex A. Kennedy	"	1½ "		152 31
Joseph S. Knapp	"	12 "		1,125 00

Travelling Expenses, $8,931.80.

Chas. W. Amey, 519.40; R. L. Baker, 754.92; J. H. Boyd, 185.42; W. T. Clark, 95.17; Jas. S. Code, 547.04; J. W. Coffey, 431.82; H. E. Costello, 507.17; Geo. M. Drew, 882.19; P. Dillon, 577.36; A. A. Kennedy, 59.41; J. S. Knapp, 525.19; Geo. S. Leach, 629.73; I. J. Lyons, 514.39; Chas. E. Muffit, 495.28; J. W. J. Mundell, 530.89; S. J. McClelland, 610.13; R. G. Sheppard, 712.91; R. G. Stringer, 353.38 .... 8,931 80

Allowance for Use of Automobiles, $1,910.00.

C. W. Amey, 200.00; J. H. Boyd, 100.00; W. T. Clark, 160.00; J. W. Coffey, 250.00; J. S. Code, 200.00; S. Knapp, 200.00; C. E. Muffitt, 200.00; J. W. J. Mundell, 200.00; R. G. Sheppard, 200.00; R. G. Stringer, 200.00 .... 1,910 00

General—Continued

Enforcement of The Ontario Game and Fisheries Act—Continued

District No. 3—Headquarters, Ottawa—Continued

Miscellaneous, $1,601.28.

Mrs. L. H. Baker, garage rent, 45.00; Bell Telephone Co. rentals, 68.40; tolls, 53.21; Cornwall Electric Service Co., garage rent, 23.75; Mrs. M. Costello, garage rent, 60.00; J. Fowlie, belts, 39.15; J. R. Gorra, garage rent, 24.00; G. Hamilton, garage rent, 48.00; Jackson Building, rent, 489.00; C. J. Jones, garage rent, 24.00; A. Leach, garage rent, 60.00; Mrs. C. A. McClelland, garage rent, 60.00; Ottawa Office Towel Supply, service, 18.00; Rex Tailoring Co., Ltd., uniforms, 198.80; B. Tremblay, janitor, 72.00. Sundries—express, 12.64; postage, 231.00; telegrams, 42.35; freight, 17.64; petty disbursements, 14.34 .... 1,601 28

District No. 4, Headquarters, North Bay, $37,100.80.

Salaries, $17,624.96.

George M. Parks	District Superintendent	12 months		2,700 00
Constance Cameron	Clerk Stenographer	12 "		975 00
Wm. G. Armstrong	Overseer	12 "		1,500 00
Geo. F. Charsley	"	12 "		1,600 00
Robert Edleston	"	12 "		1,300 00
Henry C. Haskins	"	12 "		1,200 00
Wm. H. Martin	"	12 "		1,700 00
Joseph Mulligan	"	12 "		1,800 00
Frank B. McKnight	"	12 "		1,600 00
Alex E. Pennell	"	6 "		799 98
Thos. Taylor	"	12 "		1,600 00
Bernard Gooderham	"	6 "		849 98

Temporary Services, $9,107.74.

A. G. Cook	Overseer	12 months		1,125 00
Thos. Foster	"	1 "		93 75
Wallace G. Hewson	"	12 "		1,125 00
John O'Donnell	"	12 "		1,125 00
J. Rielly	"	8 "		750 00
W. T. Raycraft	"	12 "		1,125 00
E. M. McLeod	"	⅔ "		53 12
R. W. C. Martin	"	4 "		377 22
Percy A. A. Schreiber	"	12 "		1,125 00
David Stewart	"	12 "		1,125 00
Robt. F. Thorne	"	12 "	1,125 00	
		Less Leave of Absence	41 35	1,083 65

Travelling Expenses, $6,576.69.

W. G. Armstrong, 579.33; G. F. Charsley, 630.81; A. G. Cook, 431.45; R. Edleston, 412.77; B. Gooderham, 379.00; H. C. Haskins, 521.99; W. G. Hewson, 181.00; E. McLeod, 61.21; F. B. McKnight, 311.85; W. H. Martin, 294.26; R. W. C. Martin, 69.40; J. Mulligan, 501.18; J. O'Donnell, 79.80; Geo. M. Parks, 352.18; A. E. Pennell, 180.35; W. T. Raycraft, 149.42; J. Reilly, 35.95; P. A. S. Schreiber, 245.54; D. Stewart, 330.15; T. Taylor, 613.98; R. T. Thorne, 215.07 .... 6,576 69

Allowances for Use of Automobiles, $1,000.00.

G. F. Charsley, 150.00; A. G. Cook, 200.00; B. Gooderham, 200.00; H. C. Haskins, 100.00; G. M. Parks, 250.00; R. F. Thorne, 100.00 .... 1,000 00

Miscellaneous, $2,791.41.

Bell Telephone Co., rentals, 66.60; tolls, 99.70; British American Oil Co., Ltd., gas, 11.93; Cochrane-Dunlop Hardware Ltd., snowshoes, etc., 89.18; T. Eaton Co., Ltd., provisions, 33.22; J. B. Fike, boat hire, 10.75; J. Fowlie, belts, 26.10; Mrs. Hickey, cleaning, 52.00; Hobson-Gauthier, Ltd., provisions, 85.06; M. Hurtubise, livery, 174.25; Hy-Way Service Station, gas, 34.84; W. E. Kinsey, gas, 130.32; Lindsay & McCluskey, rent, 540.00; J. Mulligan, garage rent, 50.00; New Liskeard Baptist Church, garage rent, 33.00; Pay list, wages of men, 68.41; A. E. Pennell, garage rent, 25.00; Perron & Marsh Navigation Co., boat hire, etc., 94.80; Rankin's Grocery, provisions, 208.54; F. F. Raycroft, rent of engine, 32.00; Rex Tailoring Co., Ltd., uniforms, 110.00; Royal Bank of Canada, exchange, 24.55; Robt. Simpson Co., Ltd., clock, 13.50; Muriel Sutherland, services, 47.60; T. Taylor, garage rent,

General—Continued

Enforcement of The Ontario Game and Fisheries Act—Continued

District No. 4—Headquarters, North Bay—Continued

Miscellaneous—Continued

50.00; S. O. Tickner, gas, 258.25; B. H. Turner & Co., Ltd., provisions 23.54; W. Windabie, toboggan, 12.00; Woods Manufacturing Co., Ltd., tent, 18.85. Sundries—cartage, 1.25; express, 50.70; freight, 9.83; postage, 221.00; telegrams, 33.87; petty disbursements, 50.77 .... 2,791 41

District No. 5, Headquarters, Sault Ste. Marie, $35,969.46.

Salaries, $16,400.00.

Name	Position	Period	Amount
Wm. A. Lyness	District Superintendent	12 months	2,200 00
Rita M. Crisp	Clerk Stenographer	12 "	900 00
John J. Bussineau	Overseer	12 "	1,200 00
R. R. Cockburn	"	12 "	1,600 00
H. T. Hare	"	12 "	1,200 00
Oliver Leblanc	"	12 "	1,400 00
Walter Leblanc	"	12 "	1,300 00
Ferdinand Legace	"	12 "	1,300 00
Orrin D. Lewis	"	12 "	1,500 00
Garnet Magill	"	12 "	1,400 00
Donald E. MacMillan	"	12 "	1,200 00
Fred Watson	"	12 "	1,200 00

Temporary Services, $7,875.00.

Name	Position	Period	Amount
James Barry	Overseer	12 months	1,125 00
J. Louis Berthelot	"	12 "	1,125 00
Patrick G. Dunne	"	12 "	1,125 00
Laurence S. Hemphill	"	12 "	1,125 00
Frank M. Kinahan	"	12 "	1,125 00
Jas. W. Maguire	"	12 "	1,125 00
John Thompson	"	12 "	1,125 00

Travelling Expenses, $8,793.55.

Jas. Barry, 940.20; J. L. Berthelot, 549.37; J. J. Bussineau, 421.29; R. R. Cockburn, 735.48; P. G. Dunne, 417.72; H. T. Hare, 655.91; L. S. Hemphill, 370.36; F. M. Kinahan, 528.07; O. Leblanc, 224.49; W. Leblanc, 427.08; F. Legace, 290.11; O. D. Lewis, 495.38; W. A. Lyness, 728.98; G. Magill, 557.26; J. W. Maguire, 357.38; D. E. MacMillan, 508.02; J. Thompson, 276.68; Fred Watson, 309.77 .... 8,793 55

Allowances for Use of Automobiles, $500.00.

R. R. Cockburn, 125.00; P. G. Dunne, 125.00; H. T. Hare, 125.00; J. W. Maguire, 125.00 .... 500 00

Miscellaneous, $2,400.91.

Algoma Central and Hudson Bay Railway, rent of land, 10.00; Bell Telephone Co., rentals, 44.95; tolls, 141.51; Blind River Garage, garage rent, 30.00; Mrs. W. A. Bridge, garage rent, 35.00; Geo. Bucciarelli, provisions, 68.99; T. Eaton Co., Ltd., stoves, 37.00; J. L. Elliott, services stenographer, 45.00; Mrs. J. Elliott, garage rent, 96.00; E. Fortin, snow shoes, 88.00; M. Foster, garage rent, 65.00; J. Fowlie, belts, 30.45; Flockhart Bros., eavestrough, 16.50; R. A. Gibson, oil, etc., 11.71; Hudson's Bay Co., provisions, 80.93; J. B. Lacroix, provisions, 81.38; Lang & Ross, Ltd., blue-printing, 13.65; Lynch Auto Sales, Ltd., oil, etc., 23.40; Rex Tailoring Co., Ltd., uniforms, 124.40; E. L. Ruddy Co., Ltd., signs, 65.00; J. Sandie, garage rent, 25.00; A. Shaw, provisions, 96.06; Smith & Chapple, provisions, 398.10; Spadoni Bros., provisions, 76.45; Wolfe & Collins, Ltd., provisions, 375.81; Woods Manufacturing Co., Ltd., sleeping bags and repairs, 49.50. Sundries—cartage, 2.10; express, 7.13; freight, 66.73; postage, 100.00; telegrams, 78.29; petty disbursements, 16.87 .... 2,400 91

District No. 6, Headquarters, Fort William, $25,044.99.

Salaries, $11,500.00.

Name	Position	Period	Amount
A. E. Fraser	District Superintendent	12 months	2,700 00
Claude H. Douglas	Overseer	12 "	1,600 00
Wilfred Faubert	"	12 "	1,400 00
Henry Harris	"	12 "	1,300 00
Walter Hawkins	"	12 "	1,500 00
John D. Jacob	"	12 "	1,200 00
Samuel E. Mills	"	12 "	1,800 00

General—Continued

Enforcement of The Ontario Game and Fisheries Act—Continued

District No. 6—Headquarters, Fort William—Continued

Temporary Services, $4,200.00.

C. N. Hendrickson	Overseer	12 months	1,125 00
Walter A. Horley	"	12 "	1,125 00
Chas. L. Perrie	"	12 "	1,125 00
Ethel Edwards	Clerk Stenographer	12 "	825 00

Travelling Expenses, $6,166.88.

C. H. Douglas, 46.79; W. Faubert, 864.68; A. E. Fraser, 772.06; H. Harris, 525.44; W. Hawkins, 651.63; C. N. Hendrickson, 836.51; W. A. Horley, 244.14; J. D. Jacob, 838.59; S. E. Mills, 984.03; C. L. Perrie, 393.71; T. Williams, 9.30 .... 6,166 88

Allowances for Use of Automobiles, $800.00.

W. Faubert, 200.00; H. Harris, 200.00; S. E. Mills, 200.00; C. L. Perrie, 200.00 800 00

Miscellaneous, $2,378.11.

Booth Fisheries, Canada, Ltd., fish, 37.00; L. Clark, meals, 10.75; Department of Lands and Forests, rent of cabin sites, 10.00; Mrs. J. Dickson, garage rent, 165.00; T. Edward, dog feed and provisions, 61.42; Fairway Stores, provisions, 13.59; Fort William Commercial Chambers, Ltd., rent, 546.00; Fort William Public Utilities, telephone rentals, 49.20; tolls, 1.55; J. Harju, provisions, 22.91; Hydro-Electric Power Commission, light, 11.06; Imperial Oil, Ltd., gasolene, 25.38; Leeper Store Co., provisions, 49.17; D. Legard, dog team, 60.00; Wm. McKirdy & Sons, rent of canoe, 15.50; D. A. McQuarrie, provisions, 79.64; Marshall-Wells Co., Ltd., provisions, 63.31; Mae Bros., provisions, 58.13; Moore Bros., provisions, 43.74; North Star Oil, Ltd., gas, 167.93; W. Polhill, janitor, 60.00; V. H. Pronger, provisions, 10.34; Proudman Rolls Motor Co., oil, etc., 17.50; Rex Tailoring Co., Ltd., uniform, 128.40; F. Sanderson, snowshoes, etc., 66.34; W. F. Sullivan, provisions, 113.17; Tomkins Hardware, hardware, 30.55; Watson & Lloyd, provisions, 79.46; Wells & Emmerson, cartridges, etc., 12.30; Woods Mfg. Co., Ltd., tents and sleeping bag, 93.00. Sundries—cartage, 10.00; express, 31.99; freight, 16.73; postage, 100.00; telegrams, 33.53; petty disbursements, 83.52 .... 2,378 11

District No. 7, Headquarters, Sioux Lookout, $13,711.95.

Salaries, $9,022.37.

Donald Ward	District Superintendent	12 months		2,400 00
Carl Fadden	Overseer	12 "		1,300 00
Ernest Farrington	"	12 "		1,500 00
Chas. D. Liddle	"	12 "	1,300 00	
		Less Leave of Absence	19 33	1,280 67
Arthur F. Spillett		12 months	1,500 00	
		Less Leave of Absence	125 00	1,375 00
A. J. Woodward		10 months		1,166 70

Travelling Expenses, $2,753.57.

Carl Fadden, 437.35; E. Farrington, 557.21; C. D. Liddle, 140.90; A. F. Spillett, 529.70; D. Ward, 727.65; A. J. Woodward, 360.76 .... 2,753 57

Miscellaneous, $1,936.01.

Mrs. L. Ahola, cleaning, etc., 80.25; U. Ahola, care of dogs, 12.00; A. Chenier, rent, dog team, 18.00; F. Cosco, provisions, 27.68; Day Realty Co., rent, 423.00; T. Eaton Co., Ltd., heater, 24.90; Falcon Oils, Ltd., gas, 100.19; Gastmeier & Co., dog meat, etc., 20.25; R. Grellier, gas, 40.05; L. Holst, provisions, 25.95; Hudson's Bay Co., canoe and provisions, 87.48; J. J. Jewell & Sons, provisions, 30.36; Kert & Co., straps, etc., 19.31; A. A. J. MacDonald, gas, 57.71; C. McDougall, provisions, 19.60; Minaki Boat House, gas, 17.25; H. L. Mundell, provisions, 57.43; Nakina Fur & Supply Co., supplies and provisions, 45.00; J. Porco & Co., gas and oil, 49.70; B. H. Rands, batteries, supplies, etc., 19.20; Rex Tailoring Co., uniform, 74.40; Sioux Electric Light Department, light, 23.45; Wm. Smith, caring for dogs, 20.00; Triangle Fish Co., provisions, 46.91; D. Ward, rent of boat house, 180.00; Mrs. West, care of dogs, 83.00; Western Oil Co., Ltd., gas, 11.96; Woods Mfg. Co., Ltd., tent, etc., 29.90. Sundries—cartage, 15.20; express, 41.94; freight, 17.16; postage, 101.00; telegrams, 25.01; petty disbursements, 90.77 .... 1,936 01

General—Continued

Enforcement of The Ontario Game and Fisheries Act—Continued

District Miscellaneous ($53,667.17)

Overseer, Toronto and Special Patrols ($22,356.34)

P. Revill, services as Inspector, 1,900.00; travelling expenses, 315.39; allowance for use of automobile, 200.00	2,415 39
Issuers of Special Export Permits and Collectors of Royalties.	
Temporary Services—J. W. Anderson, 200.00; P. Graves, 41.67; G. A. Hollands, 200.00; J. K. MacLennan, 200.00; J. McDonald, 200.00; R. H. Moore, 100.00; D. C. Saul, 58.33; H. A. Stewart, 100.00; J. F. Vance, 100.00	1,200 00
Seasonal Overseers.	
Hunting Season—Sundry persons, services, 2,649.13; travelling expenses, 179.14.	2,828 27
Spawning Season—Sundry persons, services, 1,404.00; travelling expenses, 93.80.	1,497 80
Advertising.	
Globe Printing Co., 25.20; Mail and Empire, 25.20; Sudbury Star, 4.20; Toronto Evening Telegram, 12.60; Toronto Hebrew Journal, 6.30	73 50
Legal Services.	
W. G. Atkin, 15.00; F. D. Boggs, 20.00; Boys & Boys, 20.00; B. C. Donnan, 72.00; R. F. Dynes, 7.75; F. G. Evans, 44.75; W. L. Fortier, 17.50; W. L. Haight, 40.00; W. D. Henry, 48.00; H. B. Johnson, 35.50; J. L. Lloyd, 12.00; M. MacDonald, 3.00; V. J. McElderry, 76.00; C. J. Moore, 100.00; F. Smiley, 10.00	521 50
Miscellaneous.	
Badge Speciality Co., Ltd., badges, 165.00; Department of Highways, insurance on cars, 430.13; A. Edwards, rent of boathouse, 25.00; E. C. Ford, badges, etc., 19.10; King's Printer, 11,309.47; A. A. Knapp, rent of boathouse, 25.00; David Montgomery, livery, 11.85; Ontario Provincial Police travelling expenses of constables, 23.15; R. J. Raycroft, rent of boathouse, 15.00; Rod and Gun, subscriptions, 61.00; Royal Canadian Mounted Police, expenses of constables, 408.97; R. B. Rye, storage of boats, 10.00; A. F. Schnaufer Co., Ltd., dressing pelts, 52.55. Sundries—express, 803.59; freight, 21.17; sundry persons, serving summonses, 2.50; sundry persons, witness fees, 84.15; sundry persons, bonuses for information, 300.00; petty disbursements, 52.25	13,819 88

Patrol Boats ($31,310.83)

"Athene," $3,551.85.	
Fuel and Oil.	
Imperial Oil, Ltd., 30.62; Midland Engine Works Co., 455.23; Richardson Motor Boat Garage, 200.69; Scott's Boat Livery, 40.15; P. V. Woodward, 56.96; J. M. Wallace, 13.00	796 65
Provisions.	
Geo. Brighty, 309.78; Kennedy Supply Boat, 12.49; W. J. Snelgrove, 24.58; petty disbursements, 9.07	355 92
Miscellaneous.	
Georgian Bay Shipbuilding & Wrecking Co., storage, etc., 128.25; T. Hill, laundry, 17.33; Pay list, wages of men, 2,222.74; petty disbursements, 30.96.	2,399 28
"Elsie Doris," $6,933.30.	
Fuel and Oil.	
Century Coal Co., Ltd., 701.50; Co-operative Supply Co., 4.50; Imperial Oil, Ltd., 60.94; R. McVittie, 3.90; Mullen Coal Co., Ltd., 52.25; Port Dover Coal & Supply Co., 72.68	895 77
Provisions.	
T. B. Coleman & Son, 54.97; W. E. Eastwick, 140.73; Goodall's Meat Market, 39.26; G. Kugler, 21.92; V. Leaney & Son, 22.60; W. E. McKibbon, 25.80; T. R. McMillan, 37.26; D. E. McVittie, 42.46; R. H. Mann, 12.69; G. M. Moffet, 10.34; F. C. Powell, 15.77; C. A. Quick & Son, Ltd., 201.86; Sanitary Meat Market, 53.22; W. E. Wicker, 133.77; petty disbursements, 16.87	829 52

General—Continued

Enforcement of The Ontario Game and Fisheries Act—Continued

Patrol Boats—Continued

"Elsie Doris"—Continued

Miscellaneous.

Bell Telephone Co., tolls, 2.95; Department of Marine and Fisheries, boiler inspection, 25.00; Captain Frewer, repairing compass, 39.75; M. R. Jones, travelling expenses, 9.30; Noble Laundry Co., Ltd., laundry, 21.30; Norfolk House, meals, 10.50; Pay list, wages of men, 5,050.44; G. A. Russell, travelling expenses, 2.85. Sundries—petty disbursements, 45.92.......... 5,208 01

"Hopewell," $2,467.94.

Fuel and Oil.

N. Trotter.......... 596 40

Provisions.

T. H. Jackson, .18; W. D. Ritchie & Son, 64.21; B. H. Turner & Co., Ltd., 59.51 123 90

Miscellaneous.

W. McGregor, meals, 13.00; Pay list, wages of men, 1,699.03; S. Smith, travelling expenses, 8.00; petty disbursements, 27.61.......... 1,747 64

"Marylyn," $3,504.41.

Fuel and Oil.

British American Oil, Ltd., .33; Deschamps Garage, 9.28; Ketchum & Co., Ltd., 4.50; Imperial Oil, Ltd., 480.16; McWain & Sherman, 146.31; Midland Engine Works, 174.49; St. Lawrence Engine Co., Ltd., 6.25.......... 821 32

Provisions.

H. G. Cooke, 38.15; F. J. Meyer, 31.50; Wallbridge & Clarke, 81.96; White Hardware Co., 16.55; petty disbursements, 5.17.......... 173 33

Miscellaneous.

Bell Telephone Co. tolls, 2.60; E. Hodgins, travelling expenses, 284.05; H. E. Hopperton, services, 67.74; expenses, 376.30; Pay list, wages of men, 1,661.93; Mrs. L. Sandford, laundry, 14.85; petty disbursements, 102.29.......... 2,509 76

"Mink," $155.95.

Fuel and Oil.

British American Oil Co., Ltd., 11.00; R. Dunlop, 123.84; R. Hill, 3.36; E. Mallett, 8.75.......... 146 95

Miscellaneous.

Sandwich Hydro-Electric, light.......... 9 00

"Miseford," $9,797.33.

Fuel and Oil.

Century Coal Co., Ltd., 543.00; Val Cottrill, 220.86; Fahner Lumber Co., 16.00; Falls & Son, 7.50; F. C. Kimmerley, 136.75; C. C. Lee, 115.78; MacKenzie, Milne & Co., Ltd., 63.65; E. R. McCay, 6.75; Mullen Coal Co., Ltd., 393.38; Sault Ste. Marie Coal & Wood Co., Ltd., 514.90; Wiarton Coal & Wood Co., 152.40; A. R. Wright & Son, 125.25.......... 2,296 22

Provisions.

C. T. Gildner, 17.79; D. E. MacVittie, 17.88; J. J. McEwen, 297.29; W. E. McKibbon, 78.03; R. H. McMann & Co., 31.19; J. F. Meyer, 81.26; J. C. Pinch, Ltd., 207.80; W. E. Preston & Co., Ltd., 113.31; C. A. Quick & Sons, Ltd., 338.63; T. Stephenson, 39.11; B. H. Turner Co., Ltd., 38.13; Wright Bros., 99.19; petty disbursements, 15.39.......... 1,375 00

Miscellaneous.

R. D. Black, travelling expenses, 3.95; S. Butters, travelling expenses, 17.00; W. Cooper, travelling expenses, 7.90; Department of Marine, inspection fee, 30.00; T. W. Ditson, travelling expenses, 15.90; Family Laundry, Ltd., laundry, 13.74; Mrs. J. Fick, meals, 15.75; G. D. Frewer, repairs to compass, 39.25; C. S. German, travelling expenses, 3.95; A. Henning, tug hire, 36.00; T. W. Ironsides, travelling expenses, 18.85; Lakeside Hotel, meals, 104.00; E. MacGillivray, fish boxes, 14.10; Marine Laundry, Ltd., laundry, 13.15; Midland Steam Laundry Co., Ltd., laundry, 17.44; Pay list, wages of men, 5,676.52; H. E. Tom, travelling expenses, 15.50; R. L. Williams, laundry, 21.55; J. A. Wilson, travelling expenses, 15.65. Sundries—petty disbursements, 45.91.......... 6,126 11

General—Continued

Enforcement of The Ontario Game and Fisheries Act—Continued

Patrol Boats—Continued

"Ogima," $3,334.63.

Fuel and Oil.

Canadian Oil Co., Ltd., 50.09; McColl-Frontenac Oil Co., Ltd., 125.11; J. H. McLennan Lumber Co., 15.50; J. Murphy Coal Co., 16.53; M. Sutherland, 146.75 .... 353 98

Provisions.

G. Benger, Ltd., 74.88; Climax Grocery, 37.92; Hudson's Bay Co., 107.30; Mrs. McLaren, .50; N. Salo, 511.92; 732 52

Miscellaneous.

W. L. Chisholm, travelling expenses, 86.75; Fairway Stores, 18.00; Pay list, wages of men, 2,014.67; Port Arthur Shipbuilding Co., Ltd., storage, 80.00; T. Sanderson, canoe rentals, 35.00; petty disbursements, 13.71 .... 2,248 13

"Skola," $433.20.

Fuel and Oil.

North Star Oil, Ltd 132 23

Provisions.

Mac's Bluebird Groceterias, 18.94; D. A. McQuarrie, 24.01; petty disbursement, 9.95 .... 52 90

Miscellaneous.

E. Farrer, boat repairs, 10.00; M. McLeod, travelling expenses, 12.00; Pay list, wages of men, 166.07; Preston's Machine Shop, repairs, 45.00; petty disbursements, 15.00 .... 248 07

"Snowbird," $1,132.22.

Fuel and Oil.

Imperial Oil, Ltd., 19.68; F. W. Peterson, 15.50; J. W. Stone Boat Mfg. Co., Ltd., 315.55 .... 350 73

Provisions.

A. L. Murray 206 65

Miscellaneous.

Pay list, wages of men 574 84

Moving Expenses of Officers of the Department ($130.09)

B. L. Dunn, Codrington to Picton, 3.70; H. C. Tester, Simcoe to Dorion, 76.98; A. E. Pennell, North Bay to Beaverton, 6.23; L. S. Hemphill, Chapleau to Missanabee, 43.18 .... 130 09

Purchase or Building of and Repairs to Boats, Boathouses, Machinery and Vehicles ($15,674.47)

Robert Strang .... Supervising Engineer .... 12 months 1,800 00

"Athene."

Auto Starter Co., Ltd., brushes and repairs, 25.00; A. Cross & Co., Ltd., repairs, 11.36; Foreman Motor & Machine Co., Ltd., repairs, 20.43; Georgian Bay Shipbuilding & Wrecking Co., repairs and painting, 72.59; Hartman & Sons, hardware, paint, etc., 72.29; Midland Engine Works, spark plugs, 11.95; National Automotive Parts, Ltd., plugs, etc., 11.24; Richardson Battery & Ignition Service, batteries, etc., 16.25; Thexton Machine Works, repair parts, 18.80; Sundries—cartage, 1.50; express, 1.76; freight, 27.65; petty disbursements, 23.31 .... 314 13

"Elsie Doris."

Finlay Fish & Storage Co., Ltd., castings, 10.00; E. R. Fish Co., towing boat, 50.00; John Leckie, Ltd., buoy, 18.92; E. R. McCay, paint, 36.93; Port Stanley Floating Dry Dock, repairs, 322.75; J. W. Schiltz, valves, paint, etc., 71.04; J. W. Sharpe, repairs, 41.12; W. B. Thompson, oilcloth, stair treads, mattress, 19.08; West Peachey & Sons, repairs, 33.45; petty disbursements, 30.95 .... 634 24

General—Continued

Purchase and Repairs of Boats, etc.—Continued

"Hopewell."

Auto Starter Co., Ltd., repairs, 17.38; O. T. Bennett, hardware, etc., 49.99; A. Cross & Co., Ltd., repairs, 20.13; National Automotive Parts, Ltd., plugs, 12.92; Richardson Battery & Ignition Service, battery, 16.95; Thexton Machine Works, rings, etc., 96.36. Sundries—cartage, 1.25; express, 2.25; freight, 30.59; petty disbursements, 29.51 .... 277 33

"Marylyn."

A. Chown Co., Ltd., hardware, 11.50; Fruit Machinery Co., Ltd., repairs, 10.35; Greenleaf Co., repairs, 23.85; C. Norsworthy Co., Ltd., repairs to boiler, 13.51; White Hardware Co., hardware, 38.15; A. K. M. Wright, paint, 52.00; petty disbursements, 43.06 .... 192 42

"Miseford."

Bryan Mfg. Co., Ltd., paint, 31.50; Carter's Wallpaper Shoppe, provisions, 35.48; Georgian Bay Shipbuilding & Wrecking Co., fenders, 25.06; T. W. Jeffrey & Sons, paint, 34.29; J. Leckie, Ltd., cover, 18.00; C. C. Lee, paint, 11.69; MacKenzie Milne & Co., Ltd., hardware, 13.60; J. Morrison Brass Mfg. Co., Ltd., gauge, brass pipe, etc., 172.33; C. Norsworthy Co., Ltd., repairs to pump, etc., 130.19; C. G. Turner, repairs, 15.90; A. R. Wright & Sons, rope, packing, etc., 240.81. Sundries—express, 4.87; petty disbursements, 5.30 .... 739 02

"Mink."

Foreman Motor & Machine Co., Ltd., propeller, 26.80; J. Leckie, Ltd., flag and compass 11.70; McKeough & Trotter, Ltd., propeller shaft, 10.82; Marentette Hardware, paint, 13.17; J. Sturdevant, repairs, 23.12; petty disbursements, 23.45 109 06

"Ogima."

Auto Starter Co., Ltd., repairs to generator, 33.51; Dow's Service Station, storage, etc., 26.25; Foreman Motor & Machine Co., propeller, etc., 37.50; National Automotive Parts, Ltd., plugs, etc., 11.08; Port Arthur Shipbuilding Co., Ltd., repairs, 59.12; T. Sanderson, canoe, 65.00; Thexton Machine Works, repairs, 134.58; Wells & Emmerson, paint, etc., 97.39. Sundries—cartage, 6.00; express, 5.80; freight, 30.93; petty disbursements, 13.45 .... 520 61

"Skola."

Gillmor & Noden, hardware, 11.25; G. S. Parker, paint, 30.98; petty disbursements, 3.00 .... 45 23

"Snowbird."

Williams Hardware Co., paint, 37.27; petty disbursements, 17.48 .... 54 75

Miscellaneous.

Anderson Boat Co., Ltd., repairs, 25.75; Canadian Fairbanks-Morse Co., Ltd., electric drill, etc., 86.20; Canadian Johnston Motor Co., Ltd., parts, 74.73; Central Motor Sales, repairs, 35.65; Cochrane-Dunlop Hardware, Ltd., canoe, paint, etc., 97.77; A. Cross & Co., Ltd., repairs, etc., 34.62; Cutten & Foster, paint, etc., 12.02; Department of Highways, garage accounts, etc., 10.50; Foreman Motor & Machine Co., Ltd., repairs, etc., 61.00; Gilpin Bros., chain, etc., 25.17; Greenleaf Co., shaft, etc., 11.06; Hannah's Garage, repairs, 14.95; Hudson's Bay Co., paint, etc., 36.15; Imperial Oil, Ltd., oil, 16.02; Johnson Bros., hardware, 10.10; J. H. Johnston, motor repairs, etc., 14.00; J. Leckie, Ltd., wood blocks, etc., 10.93; J. W. Magnus Co., outboard motor boat, repairs, etc., 637.89; Marshall-Ecclestone, Ltd., parts, etc., 13.39; J. Masscota, lumber, etc., 15.80; Pay list, wages of men, 262.00; B. H. Rands, hardware, etc., 14.65; A. E. Russell, paint, 14.90; St. Lawrence Engine Co., Ltd., hatch frame, 11.50; Smith & Chapple, paddles, etc., 29.82; Spadoni Bros., canvas, 22.95; J. W. Stone Boat Mfg. Co., Ltd., shaft and propellor, 31.10; Robt. Strang, travelling expenses, 190.93; G. Taylor Hardware Co., Ltd., nails and canoe, 82.70; C. L. Todd, battery, 10.50; Thexton Machine Works, repairs to engine etc., 110.82; White Hardware Co., hardware, 16.80. Sundries—cartage, 3.00; express, 4.40; freight, 67.28; petty disbursements, 204.98 .... 2,322 03

General—Continued

Purchase and Repairs of Boats, etc.—Continued

Parry Sound.

Town of Parry Sound, purchase of lots for boathouse site, 112.50; J. H. Tully, registration of deeds, 2.50 .... 115 00

District Automobiles, Repairs and Supplies.

No. 1, London.

R. D. Bryan & Co., repairs to car, etc., 16.10; Carmichael & Bell, car repairs, 22.90; Goodyear Tire & Rubber Co., Ltd., tires, 126.93; L. Mahler, car repairs, 31.21; petty disbursements, 51.71 .... 248 85

No. 2, Orillia.

Austin's Garage, repairs, tires and tubes, 34.95; Casselman Garage, chains and repairs, 98.91; Central Garage, repairs, 32.30; D. E. Charlton, tires, 25.00; Copping Marine Sales, auto repairs, 10.06; W. R. Curry & Son, car repairs, etc., 59.85; Davis & Charlton, repairs, 63.19; Department of Highways, car repairs, 30.33; Fee Motors, welding, car repairs, 422.41; Groves Motors, repairs, 41.45; T. E. Hall, oil rings, tires, etc., 92.19; Mitchell Service Station, repairs, etc., 30.85; Milne's Garage, tire, 12.90; Stephenson Motor Sales, car repairs, etc., 137.32; Woodman & Ross Motors, repairs, etc., 150.20; petty disbursements, 42.75 .... 1,284 66

No. 3, Ottawa.

Bank Street Garage, tires, 55.24; Carleton Motor Sales, Ltd., repairs, 14.50; City Battery Service, repairs, 24.47; Conklin Hepburn Motors, Ltd., car repairs, 36.34; Cornwall Electric Service Co., repairs, 44.07; Dominion Rubber Co., Ltd., tires, etc., 36.79; Department of Highways, repairs, 51.72; Frontenac Garage, Ltd., repairs, 72.06; Fursey Sales Service, repairs, 10.72; J. R. Gorru, repairs, battery, etc., 20.95; B. Hannah, repairs, 74.85; Killaloe Leading Garage, repairs, 31.00; Knight's Garage, repairs, 60.31; Kruger Bros., repairs, 10.38; McDonald Tire Shop, tires, etc., 10.69; R. McGarvey, repairs, etc., 219.60; I. G. Paul, repairs, 17.50; Pembroke Motor Sales, repairs, etc., 14.75; C. Smith, repairs, 14.72; petty disbursements, 127.73 .... 948 39

No. 4, North Bay.

W. H. Armstrong, repairs, etc., 64.60; Carrall's Service Station, repairs, 67.20; Doyle's Garage, repairs, 37.60; A. J. Grant, repairs, 75.80; J. Gutcher, repairs, 87.37; C. B. Hall, repairs, 106.64; W. E. Kinsey, tires, 60.60; Liskeard Garage, repairs, 11.40; Scott Motor Sales, repairs, 84.40; F. Suszek, tires, 41.50; Webbwood Garage, repairs, 96.54; T. Wood, painting 35.00; petty disbursements, 44.50 .... 813 15

No. 5, Sault Ste. Marie.

Blind River Garage, repairs, etc., 156.81; Department of Highways, car repairs, 211.93; A. P. Leclair, repairs, 32.17; Lynch Auto Sales Co., tire, repairs, etc., 285.47; Mills & Rouse, repairs, 16.84; Phillips Service Station, tire, etc., 60.81; petty disbursements, 21.44 .... 785 47

No. 6, Fort William.

T. Cordoni, wheel, 2.00; De Lamater & Milligan, Ltd., repairs, 72.85; Dow's Service Station, repairs, etc., 162.51; Kotanen Bros., repairs, 22.00; Proudman-Nolls Motor Co., repairs, etc., 61.95; Sid's Service Station, repairs, 130.10 .... 451 41

No. 7, Sioux Lookout.

J. Porco & Co., repairs, 187.51; petty disbursements, 10.89 .... 198 40

Miscellaneous re Cars.

Asselstine & Sons, repairs, 61.99; Battery Service Station, repairs, etc., 85.05; Blind River Garage, repairs, 24.25; Brantford Auto Parts, Ltd., springs, etc., 25.75; Central Garage, repairs, 15.90; Cheslock & Hones, repairs, 173.00; E. Church, battery, etc., 24.35; O. Casselman, tires, 53.53; Department of Highways, car repairs, 2,167.40; G. V. Dunn, repairs, etc., 90.45; Fallis Foote Co., chains, etc., 34.50; Fee Motors, repairs, 39.06; Goodyear Tire & Rubber Co., Ltd., tires, 19.57; Grain Port Motors, Ltd., repairs, 104.89; T. A. Heye, valves, etc., 13.95; Hudson Essex, York, Ltd., repairs, 76.57; W. E. Kinsey, tire, etc., 51.10; Lampton Motors, Ltd., repairs, 28.77; A. Leclair, bushing, 1.00; Livingston Bros., Ltd., repairs, 41.69; J. W.

General—Continued

Purchase and Repairs of Boats, etc.—Continued

Miscellaneous re Cars—Continued

McKinlay Auto Sales, tire, 31.95; Marshall Motor Car Co., Ltd., repairs, 19.26; Pembroke Motors, repairs, 3.30; C. E. Munro, repairs, 83.57; Palangios Service Station, bearing, etc., 45.52; Reo Motor Sales Co., of Toronto, Ltd., repairs, 72.99; Sarnia Tire Co., tires, 16.07; C. Todd, repairs, 19.21; G. Taylor, repairs, 16.00; Walker & Brown Motor Co., repairs, 33.51; White & McDowell, tires, 36.86; Willys-Overland Sales Co., Ltd., repairs, 16.06; Wright Bros., tires, 44.80; W. H. Young, repairs, 53.72; petty disbursements, 194.73 .... 3,820 32

Services and expenses in connection with Purchase, Importation, Rearing, Distribution of Game Animals and Birds and Equipment of Same, ($10,197.51)

Codrington Bird Farm, $4,936.80.

John H. Johnson	Manager	12 months	1,800 00

Temporary Services.

John D. MacDonald	12 months	1,200 00
Harry Shaw	12 "	1,200 00

Expenses.

Armitage Bros., Ltd., pheasant food, 51.98; Bell Telephone Co., tolls, .22; T. Eaton Co., Ltd., tape, etc., 43.20; Mrs. S. Finlay, hens, 22.00; R. P. Harper, hardware, 28.89; Hinde & Dauch Paper Co., Ltd., egg boxes, 56.96; J. H. Johnson, travelling expenses, .75; Kelly Feed & Seed Co., feed, 66.50; Rice Lewis & Son, Ltd., locks, etc., 26.21; Pay list, wages of men, 88.40; L. M. Puddephalt, hens, 24.00; Stoneburg's Service Station, gas, 26.71. Sundries—cartage, 2.50; customs, 14.78; express, 163.05; freight, 17.18; postage, 20.73; telegrams, .45; petty disbursements, 82.29 .... 736 80

Normandale Bird Farm, $4,841.63.

Wm. Chilton	Manager	12 months	1,500 00

Temporary Services.

Chas. A. May	Assistant	12 months	1,200 00
Lloyd K. Jackson	"	12 "	750 00

Expenses.

W. H. Abbey, repairs, etc., 12.69; Bell Telephone Co., rentals, 12.84; Brant Feed & Seed Co., Ltd., wheat, 37.50; T. Eaton Co., Ltd., tape, 15.45; A. S. Edmonds & Co., feed, etc., 73.85; O. J. Evans & Sons, signs, 28.00; Gilbertson & Page, Ltd., powder, etc., 64.79; J. F. Hartz Co., Ltd., drugs, etc., 12.92; Kelly Feed & Seed Co., feed, 282.30; Rice Lewis & Son, Ltd., mats, padlocks, etc., 89.82; Marchment Co., Ltd., manure, 325.08; Pay list, wages of men, 130.00; T. P. Pope, nails, etc., 10.74; Simcoe Hydro-Electric Commission, light, 85.00; R. E. Stacey, crates, 19.00; H. Thompson, teaming, 50.00. Sundries—customs, 16.08; express, 33.60; freight, 14.11; postage, 7.50; petty disbursements, 70.36 .... 1,391 63

Miscellaneous, $419.08.

J. Carew Lumber Co., Ltd., lumber, 26.64; Edwards Hardware, fencing, 30.50; King's Printer, 104.09; Owen Lewis, corn, 25.00; J. C. St. Laurent, milk, 25.00; Albert Sack, cutting hay, 100.00; Wolfe & Collins, Ltd., lumber, 35.24. Sundries—express, 47.75; petty disbursements, 24.86 .... 419 08

Services and Expenses in connection with Experimental Fur Farm ($16,938.68)

Salaries.

Ronald G. Law	Director	12 months	2,850 00
Chas. Brotherston	Attendant	12 "	1,200 00
Russell Hargrave	"	12 "	1,200 00

Temporary Services.

A. H. Kennedy	Veterinary Surgeon	12 months	1,900 00
Chas. Black	Attendant	12 "	900 00
Neil A. Jewell	Clerk Typist	12 "	750 00

General—Continued

Services and Expenses in Connection with Experimental Fur Farm—Continued

Expenses.

Abbott Laboratories, Ltd., drugs, 12.55; G. Bantam, fish, etc., 180.39; D. Bell, wood, etc., 11.00; Bell Telephone Co., rentals, 20.40; tolls, 51.35; Booth Fisheries Co., Canada, Ltd., herring, 67.50; Boxall & Matthie, Ltd., pipe, hardware, etc., 25.50; J. Brentnall, provisions, 41.70; Brigdens, Ltd., engravings, 16.70; British American Oil Co., Ltd., gas, 94.39; Chas. Brotherston, travelling expenses, 43.46; F. Brown, feed, etc., 33.12; Canadian Fairbanks-Morse Co., Ltd., engine, 120.00; Canadian Laboratory Supplies, Ltd., drugs, etc., 164.30; Canadian Packers, Ltd., meat, etc., 799.79; J. Carew Lumber Co., Ltd., shavings, lumber, etc., 251.19; Central Scientific Co., Ltd., corks, etc., 55.75; H. Clark, carrots, etc., 248.70; J. W. Coad, coal, 521.56; Delco Appliances Corporation, repairs to pump, etc., 62.08; Dominion Loose Leaf Co., Ltd., binders, 11.55; G. V. Dunn, gas, etc., 95.11; Eastman Kodak Stores, Ltd., camera, equipment and supplies, 454.13; A. G. Ewan, feed, 13.94; W. J. Ewers, oats, 14.10; F. I. Faed, drugs, 37.80; Grand & Toy, Ltd., binders, etc., 29.45; E. Gregory, drugs, 123.33; C. Hargrave, carrots, etc., 91.65; Harris Abattoir Co., Ltd., meat, etc., 513.17; J. F. Hartz Co., Ltd., supplies, 95.03; A. Hurron, horse meat, 10.00; Imperial Oil, Ltd., oil, 57.07; Ingram & Bell, Ltd., slides, etc., 84.02; W. Jewell, beef, etc., 40.00; Kelly Feed & Seed Co., wheat, etc., 64.30; A. N. Kennedy, travelling expenses, 56.83; King's Printer, 275.97; Kirkfield Hardware, oil, 16.96; R. G. Law, travelling expenses, 28.81; Liquor Control Board, alcohol, 30.64; J. McCrae Machine & Foundry Co., grates, etc., 19.10; J. A. McEachren, meat, etc., 528.25; J. O. McInnis, hardware, etc., 314.20; K. C. McKay, feed, etc., 63.46; McLennans, Ltd., hardware, 57.21; E. S. McNish, beef, 15.40; T. Meadows & Co., brokerage, 20.40; Morrison's Garage, gas, etc., 18.46; W. J. Neal, bread, feed, etc., 186.51; T. Nicholson, feed, 16.12; Peterborough Fox Supplies, flour, feed, etc., 414.11; V. Pfeffer, feed, 181.57; C. Potter, slides, 17.55; E. Poulson, meat, 10.00; E. Rea, feed, etc., 341.83; W. E. Rogers, feed, 87.30; Ross-Millar Biscuit Co., Ltd., biscuits, 204.50; R. B. Turner & Co., centrifuge machine and equipment, 82.49; United Typewriter Co., Ltd., repairs, 14.37; W. J. Wilson, cow, 10.00; W. L. Wood, Ltd., serum, 100.00. Sundries—express, 130.56; freight, 102.00; postage, 75.00; newspapers and periodicals, 37.15; petty disbursements, 125.85 .... 8,138 68

Services and Expenses, including Repairs, Maintenance and Equipment at MacDairmid ($5,016.03)

Temporary Services.

Oscar S. Lindstron........Teamster..............................12 months 1,140 00

Expenses.

Canadian National Railways, rent of siding, 24.33; Department of Lands and Forests, rent of land, 185.00; Fairway Stores, hay, hardware, etc., 1,216.94; King's Printer, 15.47; W. McKirdy & Sons, rent of canoe, 5.50; Pay list, wages of men, 2,422.19. Sundries—express, .60; postage, 6.00.................... 3,876 03

Purchase and Planting of Wild Rice Seed, Celery Seed and Plants ($704.36)

A. Bishop, rice, 10.50; W. J. Doolittle, celery plants, 130.00; J. Jessop, celery seed, 40.00; G. S. Taylor, celery plants, rice, 430.00. Sundries—express, 84.36; freight, 4.30; petty disbursements, 5.20.................................. 704 36

Exhibits ($2,391.26)

C. E. Brotherston, travelling expenses, 61.07; Brown Bros., Ltd., meat, 21.90; Canada Bread Co., Ltd., bread, 10.50; Clatworthy & Son, Ltd., rental of wax figures, 131.50; L. Corniffe, lettering, 57.00; D. G. Cowan, ice, 82.50; O. J. Evans & Son, painting, 254.40; S. A. Frost, moss, 64.90; R. F. Hargrave, travelling expenses, 16.06; C. Hartman, travelling expenses, 32.25; Holt, Renfrew Co., Ltd., making fur ties, 77.00; J. W. Jones, travelling expenses, 63.90; Kelly Feed & Seed Co., feed, 46.63; A. H. Kennedy, travelling expenses, 44.46; R. G. Law, travelling expenses, 38.41; Rice Lewis & Son, Ltd., paint, 61.32; J. Love, bear cubs, 25.00; J. McLeod, bear cubs, 20.00; Pay list, wages of men, 596.60; J. Prockisinko, services, 16.50; W. A. Rankin, Ltd., paint, 30.71; J. Robert, bear cubs, 20.00; W. E. Rogers, feed, 75.05; E. Sabourin, trees, 95.70; A. F. Schnaufer Co., Ltd., dressing pelts, 21.18; B. Slattery, Ltd., liver, 29.58; Smith & Walsh, Ltd., insurance, 20.40; P. Stevenson, travelling expenses, 59.02; R. Strang, travelling expenses, 17.12; J. A. Thompson, travelling expenses, 59.45; J. E. Turner, travelling expenses, 95.55; J. Valansky, bear cubs, 25.00. Sundries—cartage, 12.95; express, 23.69; freight, 15.52; petty disbursements, 68.44............................ 2,391 26

General—Continued

Annual Membership Fees to Associations ($10.00)

American Association for Advancement of Science, 5.00; American Fisheries Society, 3.00; International Association of Game and Fish Conservation Commissioners, 2.00	10 00

Unforeseen and Unprovided ($276.70)

Department of Fisheries, Ottawa, services Miss Demardy, 70.00; Edith L. Marsh, lectures, 201.70; Dr. J. J. Sheahan, professional services, 5.00	276 70

Sundry Inquiries and Investigations ($4,616.38)

Allowances to Members of Committee.

A. Z. Aubin, 30.00; W. D. Black, 1,065.00; F. E. Hollingsworth, 45.00; T. P. Lancaster, 165.00; A. C. McLean, 225.00; Jack Miner, 240.00; W. Newman, 165.00; T. Spence, 660.00; D. J. Taylor, 210.00	2,805 00

Travelling Expenses.

W. D. Black, 5.25; W. Cooper, 123.06; P. F. Cronin, 170.63; A. C. McLean, 5.25; Jack Miner, 83.35; D. J. Taylor, 5.25	392 79

Advertising.

Arnprior Chronicle, 5.60; Belleville Intelligencer, 3.45; Border Cities Star, 6.60; Brockville Recorder, 3.60; Espanola Standard, 2.50; Gananoque Reporter, 5.64; Guelph Daily Mercury, 10.00; Hamilton Herald, 13.50; Hamilton Spectator, 10.50; Kingston Whig-Standard, 4.20; Kingsville Reporter, 1.17; Kitchener News Record, 8.00; Leamington Post, 4.07; Le Droit, 3.90; London Advertiser, 10.50; London Free Press, 16.00; Manitoulin Expositor, 1.40; Massey Tribune, 2.50; Napanee Beaver, 4.60; Napanee Express, 4.80; North Bay Nugget, 8.40; Nickel City Press, 2.10; Ottawa Citizen, 7.00; Ottawa Journal, 6.60; Pembroke Standard-Observer, 2.64; Perth Courier, 3.00; Perth Expositor, 2.40; Peterborough Examiner, 5.04; Owen Sound Sun-Times, 6.00; Renfrew Mercury, 4.44; Smith's Falls Record, 2.00; Sudbury Star, 11.20	183 35

Miscellaneous.

Bell Telephone Co., tolls, 19.40; Margaret Cronin, services, 1,075.22; Dept. of Highways, auto services, 67.05; King's Printer, 38.95; Timmins Building Co., Ltd., rent of hall, 10.00; United Typewriter Co., Ltd., inspections, 9.00. Sundries—express, .12; postage, 3.50; telegrams, 12.00	1,235 24

Grants for Special Services re Crown Game Preserves ($900.00)

T. W. Jones, 200.00; E. L. Marsh, 300.00; J. Miner, 400.00	900 00

Grants ($500.00)

Lake Erie Fishermen's Association, 400.00; Lake Huron and Georgian Bay Fishermen's Association, 100.00		500 00
General	$393,112.69	
Total		$635,141 31
Less Salary Assessment		5,965 29
Total Expenditure, Department of Game and Fisheries		**$629,176 02**

PART K

DEPARTMENT

OF

PUBLIC WORKS

FISCAL YEAR, 1931-32

TABLE OF CONTENTS

GENERAL INDEX AT BACK OF BOOK

PART K—DEPARTMENT OF PUBLIC WORKS

Statement of Expenditure Showing Amounts Expended, Unexpended and Overexpended for the Twelve Months Ended October 31st, 1932

Department of Public Works	Page	Estimates	Expended			Un-expended	Over-expended	Treasury Board Minute
			Ordinary	Capital	Total Ordinary and Capital			
		$ c.	$ c.	$ c.	$ c.	$ c.	$ c.	$ c.
Main Office:								
Salaries	11	77,750 00	63,174 92	....	63,174 92	14,575 08	....	....
Contingencies	11	10,000 00	11,346 69	....	11,346 69	....	1,346 69	5,000 00
Travelling Expenses	12	3,500 00	3,238 72	....	3,238 72	261 28	....	....
Main Office	..	91,250 00	77,760 33	....	77,760 33	14,836 36	1,346 69	....
Maintenance and Repairs, Government Buildings:								
Government House,								
Salaries	12	16,950 00	14,516 66	....	14,516 66	2,433 34	....	....
Pay list, other help, repairs to grounds, etc	12	12,000 00	2,490 05	....	2,490 05	9,509 95	....	....
Water, fuel, light and power	12	10,000 00	4,568 23	....	4,568 23	5,431 77	....	....
Repairs, contingencies, etc	12	10,000 00	6,419 81	....	6,419 81	3,580 19	....	....
Furniture and furnishings	13	3,000 00	9 00	....	9 00	2,991 00	....	....
Uniforms for Messengers, etc	..	300 00	....	....	....	300 00	....	....
Telephone service	13	550 00	536 41	....	536 41	13 59	....	....
Government House	..	52,800 00	28,540 16	....	28,540 16	24,259 84	....	....
Parliament and Departmental Buildings,								
Salaries	13	178,250 00	145,480 66	....	145,480 66	32,769 34	....	....
Water and fuel	15	30,000 00	29,840 25	....	29,840 25	159 75	....	....
Electric power and light current and gas	15	14,500 00	18,326 16	....	18,326 16	....	3,826 16	7,500 00
Supplies, tools, etc	15	3,500 00	3,288 56	....	3,288 56	211 44	....	....
Caretakers of grounds and maintenance of grounds, drives and walks	15	5,000 00	4,564 85	....	4,564 85	435 15	....	....
Repairs and cleaning of buildings, etc	16	100,000 00	113,345 01	....	113,345 01	....	13,345 01	20,000 00
Shelving for Library	..	500 00	....	....	....	500 00	....	....
Alt Fittings and Shelving	17	5,000 00	4,072 76	....	4,072 76	927 24	....	....
Furniture ard furnishings for buildings	17	30,000 00	20,031 61	....	20,031 61	9,968 39	....	....
Interior alterati ons	18	10,000 00	8,843 97	....	8,843 97	1,156 03	....	....

Flowers, shrubs, plants, etc.	18	2,500 00	58 44	....	58 44	2,441 56	....	....
Uniforms for messengers, attendants, etc.	18	200 00	27 50	....	27 50	172 50	....	....
Painting outside and inside work	18	15,000 00	9,546 48	....	9,546 48	5,453 52	....	....
Telephone service	18	46,000 00	51,547 74	....	51,547 74	....	5,547 74	6,000 00
Fire protection	18	500 00	459 82	....	459 82	40 18	....	....
Rental of property and office space	18	10,000 00	930 00	....	930 00	9,070 00	....	....
Parliament and Departmental Buildings	..	450,950 00	410,363 81	....	410,363 81	63,305 10	22,718 91	....
Osgoode Hall,								
Salaries	19	23,965 00	17,925 66	....	17,925 66	6,039 34	....	....
Fuel, light, water and power	19	7,500 00	5,378 90	....	5,378 90	2,121 10	....	....
Furniture and furnishings	19	3,000 00	2,343 37	....	2,343 37	656 63	....	....
Telephone service	19	4,000 00	3,734 97	....	3,734 97	265 03	....	....
Cleaning of building	19	5,000 00	6,418 92	....	6,418 92	....	1,418 92	1,500 00
Fire protection	19	100 00	15 60	....	15 60	84 40	....	....
General repairs and alterations	19	5,000 00	4,989 21	....	4,989 21	10 79	....	....
Electric wiring and fixtures	20	200 00	16 00	....	16 00	184 00	....	....
Painting interior and exterior	20	2,000 00	1,996 03	....	1,996 03	3 97	....	....
Fittings for vaults and offices	20	500 00	305 50	....	305 50	194 50	....	....
Osgoode Hall	..	51,265 00	43,124 16	....	43,124 16	9,559 76	1,418 92	....
Normal and Model Schools,								
Toronto:								
Repairs and incidentals	20	5,000 00	4,526 62	....	4,526 62	473 38	....	....
Ottawa:								
Repairs and incidentals	20	2,000 00	671 36	....	671 36	1,328 64	....	....
London:								
Repairs and incidentals	20	600 00	494 60	....	494 60	105 40	....	....
Hamilton:								
Repairs and incidentals	20	600 00	90 00	....	90 00	510 00	....	....
Peterborough:								
Repairs and incidentals	20	600 00	70 57	....	70 57	529 43	....	....
Stratford:								
Repairs and incidentals	20	600 00	444 29	....	444 29	155 71	....	....
North Bay:								
Repairs and incidentals	21	700 00	461 50	....	461 50	238 50	....	....
Belleville School for the Deaf:								
Repairs and incidentals	21	3,000 00	1,921 46	....	1,921 46	1,078 54	....	....
Restoration of fireman's cottage	21	1,500 00	1,500 00	....	1,500 00	....	....	....
Brantford School for the Blind:								
Repairs and incidentals	21	2,000 00	554 13	....	554 13	1,445 87	....	....
Sandwich Training School:								
Repairs and incidentals	21	400 00	59 38	....	59 38	340 62	....	....

PART K—DEPARTMENT OF PUBLIC WORKS—Continued

Statement of Expenditure Showing Amounts Expended, Unexpended and Overexpended for the Twelve Months Ended October 31st, 1932

Department of Public Works	Page	Estimates	Expended: Ordinary	Expended: Capital	Expended: Total Ordinary and Capital	Un-expended	Over-expended	Treasury Board Minute
		$ c.	$ c.	$ c.	$ c.	$ c.	$ c.	$ c.
Normal and Model Schools—Continued								
Sturgeon Falls Training School:								
Repairs and incidentals	21	600 00	205 50	....	205 50	394 50	....	....
Monteith Northern Academy:								
Repairs and incidentals	21	700 00	500 00	....	500 00	200 00	....	....
Painting of building	21	1,700 00	1,400 00	....	1,400 00	300 00	....	....
Embrun Training School:								
Repairs and incidentals	..	400 00	....	....	....	400 00	....	....
General:								
To provide for repairs and incidentals to boilers	21	2,500 00	1,609 74	....	1,609 74	890 26	....	....
To provide for fire protection, etc.	22	500 00	85 25	....	85 25	414 75	....	....
Educational Buildings	..	23,400 00	14,594 40	....	14,594 40	8,805 60	....	....
Ontario Agricultural College:								
Repairs and incidentals	22	2,500 00	898 09	....	898 09	1,601 91	....	....
Repairs to Massey Dairy	22	1,500 00	678 06	....	678 06	821 94	....	....
Ontario Veterinary College:								
Repairs and incidentals	22	500 00	439 92	....	439 92	60 08	....	....
Horticultural Experimental Station, Vineland:								
Repairs and incidentals	22	2,000 00	1,907 08	....	1,907 08	92 92	....	....
Western Ontario Experimental Farm, Ridgetown:								
Repairs and incidentals	22	1,000 00	841 79	....	841 79	158 21	....	....
Agricultural School, Ridgetown:								
Repairs and incidentals	22	300 00	194 73	....	194 73	105 27	....	....
Eastern Dairy School, Kingston:								
Repairs and incidentals	23	1,000 00	30 00	....	30 00	970 00	....	....
Kemptville Agricultural School:								
Repairs and incidentals	23	1,000 00	811 64	....	811 64	188 36	....	....
Painting exterior	23	1,000 00	482 90	....	482 90	517 10	....	....
Turkey Experimental Farm:								
Repairs and incidentals	..	100 00	....	....	....	100 00	....	....

Vimy Ridge Farm:								
Repairs and incidentals	..	250 00	....	....	....	250 00	....	....
Demonstration Farm, New Liskeard:								
Repairs and incidentals	..	200 00	....	....	....	200 00	....	....
Agricultural Buildings	..	11,350 00	6,284 21	....	6,284 21	5,065 79	....	....
Welfare Buildings:								
Boys' Training School, Bowmanville:								
Repairs and incidentals, etc.	23	800 00	555 45	....	555 45	244 55	....	....
District Buildings:								
Algoma:								
Repairs and alterations, etc.	23	800 00	649 10	....	649 10	150 90	....	....
Furniture and furnishings	23	400 00	228 12	....	228 12	171 88	....	....
Cochrane:								
Repairs and alterations, etc.	23	1,000 00	684 04	....	684 04	315 96	....	....
Furniture and furnishings	23	300 00	90 98	....	90 98	209 02	....	....
Kenora:								
Repairs and alterations, etc.	24	1,000 00	646 83	....	646 83	353 17	....	....
Furniture and furnishings	24	300 00	299 75	....	299 75	.25	....	....
Manitoulin:								
Repairs to court house	24	500 00	289 43	....	289 43	210 57	....	....
Furniture and furnisings for district	24	300 00	58 35	....	58 35	241 65	....	....
Muskoka:								
Repairs, etc.	24	300 00	240 24	....	240 24	59 76	....	....
Furniture and furnishings	24	100 00	34 10	....	34 10	65 90	....	....
Nipissing:								
Repairs and alterations, etc.	24	1,000 00	781 44	....	781 44	218 56	....	....
Furniture and furnishings	24	300 00	141 36	....	141 36	158 64	....	....
Salary of caretaker, North Bay	24	1,200 00	1,200 00	....	1,200 00	....	....	....
Parry Sound:								
Repairs and alterations, etc.	24	800 00	425 24	....	425 24	374 76	....	....
Furniture and furnishings for district	25	300 00	64 20	....	64 20	235 80	....	....
Rainy River:								
Repairs and alterations, etc.	25	1,000 00	608 26	....	608 26	391 74	....	....
Furniture and furnishings	25	300 00	119 40	....	119 40	180 60	....	....
[illegible]:								
Repairs and alterations, etc.	25	1,000 00	832 90	....	832 90	167 10	....	....
Furniture and furnishings	25	300 00	293 55	....	293 55	6 45	....	....
Temiskaming:								
Repairs and alterations, etc.	25	800 00	517 31	....	517 31	282 69	....	....
Furniture and furnishings	25	600 00	464 37	....	464 37	135 63	....	....
Salary of caretaker, Government buildings, New Liskeard	25	720 00	720 00	....	720 00	....	....	....

PART K—DEPARTMENT OF PUBLIC WORKS—Continued

Statement of Expenditure Showing Amounts Expended, Unexpended and Overexpended for the Twelve Months Ended October 31st, 1932

Department of Public Works	Page	Estimates	Expended			Un-expended	Over-expended	Treasury Board Minute
			Ordinary	Capital	Total Ordinary and Capital			
		$ c.	$ c.	$ c.	$ c.	$ c.	$ c.	$ c.
District Buildings—Continued								
Thunder Bay:								
Repairs and alterations, etc.	25	1,100 00	1,061 20	....	1,061 20	38 80	....	....
Furniture and furnishings	26	400 00	305 44	....	305 44	94 56	....	....
General:								
To provide for repairs and installation of boilers, etc.	26	2,500 00	759 32	....	759 32	1,740 68	....	....
District Buildings	..	18,120 00	12,070 38	....	12,070 38	6,049 62	....	....
Miscellaneous:								
Salaries	26	27,750 00	26,049 31	....	26,049 31	1,700 69	....	....
Services, travelling and other expenses	26	8,000 00	7,721 33	....	7,721 33	278 67	....	....
Contingencies	26	100 00	39 10	....	39 10	60 90	....	....
Motion Picture Studio, Trenton,								
Repairs and incidentals	26	500 00	351 58	....	351 58	148 42	....	....
Government Building, Exhibition Park,								
Preparing exhibits, etc.	27	6,000 00	11,420 91	....	11,420 91	....	5,420 91	5,500 00
Insurance, including installation of lightning rods	27	9,000 00	9,886 78	....	9,886 78	....	886 78	1,000 00
Local improvement taxes	27	20,000 00	4,558 99	....	4,558 99	15,441 01	....	....
Labour Employment Offices, Toronto,								
Repairs and installations	..	600 00	....	....	....	600 00	....	....
Sewage Experimental Station, Toronto	27	150 00	129 05	....	129 05	20 95	....	....
110 University Avenue, Toronto,								
Repairs and installations, painting and alterations	27	800 00	7,932 01	....	7,932 01	....	7,132 01	15,800 00
Miscellaneous	..	72,900 00	68,089 06	....	68,089 06	18,250 64	13,439 70	....
Public Works and Bridges:								
Lockmasters, bridge tenders, etc.	28	5,500 00	4,769 00	....	4,769 00	731 00	....	....

[illegible], [illegible] docks, [illegible] [illegible], etc.	28	25,000 00	12,782 97		12,782 97	12,217 03		
Surveys and [illegible]	29	6,000 00	3,725 00		3,725 00	2,275 00		
Equipment, [illegible], [illegible], etc.	29	6,000 00	2,010 80		2,010 80	3,989 20		
Wages and [illegible] of supervising [illegible]	29	3,000 00	1,608 60		1,608 60	1,391 40		
Storage dams	..	10,000 00				10,000 00		
Cutting and [illegible] of ti[illegible] and [illegible]tion [illegible]	..	5,000 00				5,000 00		
Works in progress, 1930-31	..	17,000 00				17,000 00		
[illegible]	29	106,000 00		95,304 06	95,304 06	10,695 94		
[illegible] drainage	36	27,000 00		22,707 69	22,707 69	4,292 31		
Grants to Dominion [illegible] for [illegible] Grenville [illegible] bridge	37	26,067 87		26,067 87	26,067 87			
Grant to Bromley-Westmeath [illegible] bridge	37	100 00		100 00	100 00			
Grant to [illegible] and [illegible] for Bl[illegible] [illegible]	..	3,500 00				3,500 00		
Public Works and Bridges	..	240,167 87	24,896 37	144,179 62	169,075 99	71,091 88		
Public Buildings:								
Parliament and Departmental Buildings:								
To provide for additional accommodation	37	300,000 00		854,276 76	854,276 76		554,276 76	560,000 00
Purchase and installation of wire rope testing machine	38	17,500 00		15,744 88	15,744 88	1,755 12		
Painting East Block	39	5,000 00		4,998 30	4,998 30	1 70		
Parliament and Departmental Buildings	..	322,500 00		875,019 94	875,019 94	1,756 82	554,276 76	
[illegible] Hospitals:								
Additions, [illegible] and equipment	39	30,000 00		21,141 98	21,141 98	8,858 02		
[illegible] Hospitals:								
[illegible]:								
[illegible] for nurses	39	60,750 00		128,994 58	128,994 58		68,244 58	69,250 00
[illegible]:								
New Assembly Hall including furniture, furnishings and [illegible]	40	7,000 00		29,485 66	29,485 66		22,485 66	35,000 00
[illegible], including furniture	..	5,000 00				5,000 00		
Kingston:								
Purchase and installation, [illegible] storage plant	40	2,000 00		2,320 75	2,320 75		320 75	325 00
[illegible]:								
[illegible]s' [illegible], including furnishings	..	5,000 00				5,000 00		
[illegible]:								
[illegible], etc.	40	4,000 00		3,676 33	3,676 33	323 67		
To [illegible] new buildings	40	7,000 00		20,286 93	20,286 93		13,286 93	15,000 00
[illegible]:								
Nurses [illegible]	41	4,500 00		12,498 38	12,498 38		7,998 38	8,000 00
New tunnels and passageway to new buildings	41	500 00		429 48	429 48	70 52		

PART K—DEPARTMENT OF PUBLIC WORKS—Continued

Statement of Expenditure Showing Amounts Expended, Unexpended and Overexpended for the Twelve Months Ended October 31st, 1932

Department of Public Works	Page	Estimates	Expended: Ordinary	Expended: Capital	Expended: Total Ordinary and Capital	Un-expended	Over-expended	Treasury Board Minute
		$ c.	$ c.	$ c.	$ c.	$ c.	$ c.	$ c.
Public Buildings—Continued								
Orillia—Continued								
[illegible] installation, [illegible]	..	15,000 00	....	....	....	15,000 00	....	....
New building for [illegible]	41	110,000 00	....	180,923 17	180,923 17	....	70,923 17	71,000 00
[illegible] in connection therewith	41	8,000 00	....	104 73	104 73	7,895 27	....	....
[illegible]:								
Building for [illegible]ally insane prisoners	41	127,500 00	....	237,741 82	237,741 82	....	110,241 82	140,000 00
[illegible]ry machinery	..	2,000 00	....	....	....	2,000 00	....	....
Sewage [illegible]	42	18,000 00	....	15,550 23	15,550 23	2,449 77	....	....
[illegible]:								
Store [illegible]	42	2,000 00	....	1,595 22	1,595 22	404 78	....	....
[illegible]'s [illegible], including furnishings	..	7,500 00	....	....	....	7,500 00	....	....
[illegible]:								
New bui[illegible] to [illegible] 400 [illegible], etc.	42	6,500 00	....	33,459 70	33,459 70	....	26,959 70	27,000 00
N[illegible] building, [illegible]	43	60,000 00	....	89,975 78	89,975 78	....	29,975 78	30,000 00
N[illegible]tion	..	1,500 00	....	....	....	1,500 00	....	....
Ontario Hospitals	..	483,750 00	....	778,184 74	778,184 74	56,002 03	350,436 77	....
Ontario Reformatories:								
Ontario Reformatory, Guelph,								
Additions and alterations	43	6,000 00	....	570 00	570 00	5,430 00	....	....
Industrial Farm, Burwash,								
New reformatory buildings for men	43	100,000 00	....	32,324 51	32,324 51	67,675 49	....	....
Reformatories	..	106,000 00	....	32,894 51	32,894 51	73,105 49	....	....

Boys' Training School, Bowmanville:								
Construction of works and buildings	43	1,000 00	....	889 67	889 67	110 33	....	....
Girls' Training School, Galt:								
Construction of works and buildings	44	132,500 00	....	128,066 28	128,066 28	4,433 72	....	....
Welfare Buildings	..	133,500 00	....	128,955 95	128,955 95	4,544 05	....	....
[illegible]o Agricultural College:								
Administrative [illegible] Students' Residence, [illegible] [illegible] house, etc.	44	155,000 00	....	251,205 09	251,205 09	....	96,205 09	140,000 00
[illegible] with Horticultural [illegible]	45	2,175 00	....	6,172 36	6,172 36	....	3,997 36	4,000 00
[illegible] to [illegible] 43 students	45	2,275 00	....	5,946 84	5,946 84	....	3,671 84	3,950 00
Horticultural building	45	....	....	2,000 00	2,000 00	....	2,000 00	2,000 00
[illegible] Experimental Farm:								
Staff [illegible]	45	1,325 00	....	1,300 57	1,300 57	24 43	....	....
[illegible] Agricultural School:								
[illegible] well, [illegible], etc.	45	....	....	422 21	422 21	....	422 21	450 00
[illegible]	45	150 00	....	106 20	106 20	43 80	....	....
Agricultural Buildings	..	160,925 00	....	267,153 27	267,153 27	68 23	106,296 50	....
[illegible]s:								
Kenora:								
[illegible] [illegible]ments of gaoler's house	46	325 00	....	319 93	319 93	5 07	....	....
Mining [illegible] [illegible] and lock-up, Sioux [illegible]	46	6,000 00	....	22,671 77	22,671 77	....	16,671 77	20,000 00
[illegible] gaol, Kenora	46	....	....	303 50	303 50	....	303 50	350 00
Steel [illegible] at [illegible] Pines, Ontario, purchase and [illegible]	46	1,000 00	....	730 00	730 00	270 00	....	....
Nipissing,								
New gaol, [illegible]	46	....	....	7,575 77	7,575 77	....	7,575 77	7,938 88
[illegible] gaol	46	7,500 00	....	15,218 42	15,218 42	....	7,718 42	8,000 00
District Buildings	..	14,825 00	....	46,819 39	46,819 39	275 07	32,269 46	....
Miscellaneous:								
Government Building, Exhibition Park, grant to City of Toronto	46	50,000 00	....	50,000 00	50,000 00	....	....	....
Purchase of property	46	5,000 00	....	45,075 59	45,075 59	....	40,075 59	40,100 00
Public Buildings	..	1,276,500 00	....	2,224,103 39	2,224,103 39	135,751 69	1,083,355 08	....
Supply Bill	..	2,288,702 87	685,722 88	2,368,283 01	3,054,005 89	356,976 28	1,122,279 30	....

PART K—DEPARTMENT OF PUBLIC WORKS—Continued

Statement of Expenditure Showing Amounts Expended, Unexpended and Overexpended for the Twelve Months Ended October 31st, 1932

Department of Public Works	Page	Estimates	Expended			Un-expended	Over-expended	Treasury Board Minute
			Ordinary	Capital	Total Ordinary and Capital			
		$ c.	$ c.	$ c.	$ c.	$ c.	$ c.	$ c.
Statutory:								
Minister's salary	47	....	10,000 00	....	10,000 00	....	....	....
Drainage aid work	47	....	....	98,143 00	98,143 00	....	....	....
Statutory	..	....	10,000 00	98,143 00	108,143 00	....	....	....
Special Warrants:								
Payment for portrait of Hon. W. D. Ross	47	....	5,000 00	....	5,000 00	....	....	....
For construction boys' camp, Lake Couchiching	47	....	....	427 12	427 12	....	....	....
To pay for provisions for the Government House	47	....	278 97	....	278 97	....	....	....
Ontario Hospital, Orillia, reconstruction of barns	47	....	....	19,497 58	19,497 58	....	....	....
Special Warrants	..	....	5,278 97	19,924 70	25,203 67	....	....	....
Total	..	....	701,001 85	2,486,350 71	3,187,352 56	....	....	....
Less Salary Assessment	..	....	7,966 98	....	7,966 98	....	....	....
Department of Public Works	..	....	693,034 87	2,486,350 71	3,179,385 58	....	....	....

SUMMARY

Department of Public Works	Page	Ordinary	Capital	Total
		$ c.	$ c.	$ c.
Main Office	11-12	77,760 33	....	77,760 33
Maintenance and Repairs, Government Buildings	12-27	583,066 18	....	583,066 18
Public Works and Bridges	28-37	24,896 37	144,179 62	169,075 99
Buildings	37-46	....	2,224,103 39	2 224,103 39
Statutory	47	10,000 00	98,143 00	108,143 00
Special Warrants	47	5,278 97	19,924 70	25,203 67
Total	..	701,001 85	2,486,350 71	3,187,352 56
Less Salary Assessment	..	7,966 98	....	7,966 98
Department of Public Works	..	693,034 87	2,486,350 71	3,179,385 58

DEPARTMENT OF PUBLIC WORKS

Hon. Dr. J. D. Monteith....Minister (Statutory)..........10,000 00

MAIN OFFICE

Salaries ($63,174.92)

Geo. Hogarth	Deputy Minister	12 months	5,200 00
Digby Horrell	Head Clerk	12 "	3,200 00
E. Purvis	Secretary to Minister	12 "	2,000 00
A. J. Halford	Engineer (T)	12 "	1,999 92
J. W. Hackner	Assistant Engineer	12 "	3,300 00
J. A. Michaud	Senior Draughtsman	12 "	2,400 00
Geo. White	Assistant Architect	12 "	3,600 00
E. M. Allen	Senior Architectural Draughtsman	12 "	2,700 00
A. C. B. Nicol	" " "	12 "	2,700 00
E. H. Russell	" " "	12 "	2,700 00
W. B. Hackett	" " "	12 "	2,700 00
F. I. M. Owen	" " "	12 "	2,400 00
A. Grant	" " "	12 "	2,550 00
A. Blyth	" " "	12 "	2,300 00
R. J. Roberts	Architectural Draughtsman	12 "	2,200 00
A. M. Taylor	" "	12 "	2,000 00
L. G. Odam	Office Appliance Operator	12 "	1,500 00
Sydney Wood	Principal Clerk	12 "	2,100 00
C. Kentleton	Accountant	12 "	2,300 00
A. C. Smith	Senior Clerk	12 "	1,900 00
M. St. Charles	Secretarial Stenographer	12 "	1,600 00
F. Wiley	" "	12 "	1,600 00
W. Tobin	Senior Clerk Stenographer	12 "	1,500 00
D. B. Gillis	" " " Group 1	12 "	1,400 00
M. G. Dundas	Clerk Stenographer, " 1	12 "	1,200 00
Margaret Creswick	" " " 1	12 "	975 00
M. D. Ross	Clerk Typist, Group 1	12 "	1,200 00
Edward Meagher	Clerk Stenographer, Engineer's Branch	12 "	1,200 00
Abie Zelden	Clerk, Group 3, Architect's Branch	12 "	750 00

Contingencies ($11,346.69)

Temporary Services, $5,428.85.

E. L. Crowley	Filing Clerk, Group 1	12 "		900 00
M. Dunseith	Clerk Stenographer, Group 2	12 "		825 00
H. L. M. Dymond	Draughtsman, Group 2	12	1,200 00	
	Less Leave of Absence		46 15	1,153 85
E. F. Haines	Clerk Stenographer, Group 2	12 months		825 00
Ruby Nelson	Clerk Typist	12 "		750 00
Eva Whitehead	Clerk Stenographer, Group 1	12 "		975 00

Advertising, $388.06.

Ayr News, 4.50; Beacon-Herald of Stratford, Ltd., 6.30; Border Cities Star, 6.75; Brantford Expositor, 5.40; British American Publishing Co., Ltd., 6.75; Canadian Engineer, 17.00; Canadian Statesman, 5.40; Cochrane Northland Post, 3.96; Contract Record and Engineering Review, 17.00; Daily Commercial News and Building Record, 12.75; Daily Times Journal, 4.00; Fort Frances Publishing Co., Ltd., 4.00; Free Press, 9.00; Galt Daily Reporter, 5.40; Globe Printing Co., 52.50; The Haileyburian, 4.80; Hamilton Herald, 6.75; Hamilton Review, 4.50; Hamilton Spectator, Ltd., 6.75; Journal Dailies, 9.00; Mail and Empire, 52.50; Miner Publishing Co., 4.80; News-Chronicle Publishing Co., Ltd., 4.00; The Nuggett, 8.50; Ontario Intelligencer, 6.75; Parry Sound Canadian, 4.00; Peterborough Examiner, Ltd., 6.30; The Recorder, 2.40; Sault Daily Star, 4.80; Smallpiece Advertising, 18.00; Standard Weekly Publishings Ltd., 20.25; Sudbury Star, 4.00; Evening Telegram, 39.00; Toronto Daily Hebrew Journal, 20.25... 388 06

Miscellaneous, $5,529.78.

Art Metropole, blueprint paper, cloth, etc., 1,209.82; Boiler Inspection Branch, inspection, 30.00; Bourne & Towse, map, 12.50; Burroughs Adding Machine of Canada, Ltd., maintenance service, etc., 21.60; H. S. Crabtree, Ltd., blueprint paper, etc., 408.86; A. G. Cumming, Ltd., blue print paper, etc., 542.59; Dept. of Trade and Commerce, expenses re inquiry, 22.32; W. H. Hoidge, inspection and valuation, 45.00; Instruments, Ltd., blue print paper, 977.40; International Business Machine Co., Ltd., time cards, etc., 31.55; King's Printer, 2,952.90;

Main Office—Continued

Contingencies—Continued

Miscellaneous—Continued

McCann & Alexander, inspections, etc., 26.00; Morris & Bale, registration fees, 31.50; National Drug & Chemical Co., Ltd., chemicals, 33.75; J. Frank Raw Co., Ltd., blue print paper, 1,193.31; The Robert Simpson Co., Ltd., films, books, etc., 22.68; Taylor Typewriter Co., reconditioning machine, 15.00; United Typewriter Co., Ltd., inspections, repairs to type, etc., 158.74. Sundries—car tickets, 180.00; express, 36.10; freight, 41.85; newspapers and periodicals, 83.30; postage, 1.00; telegrams, 137.60; petty disbursements, 24.37 .... 8,329 74

Less repayment of blueprints supplied .... 2,709 96 | 5,529 78

Travelling Expenses ($3,238.72)

E. M. Allen, 72.55; Dept. of Highways, 691.04; Allen Grant, 23.40; W. B. Hackett, 13.85; J. W. Hackner, 359.29; A. J. Halford, 312.20; Geo. Hogarth, 35.10; J. A. Michaud, 373.50; Hon. Dr. J. D. Monteith, 1,000.00; R. J. Roberts, 41.10; E. H. Russell, 37.60; Allen M. Taylor, 72.49; Geo. White, 183.40; S. Wood, 23.20 .... 3,238 72

Main Office $77,760.33

Maintenance and Repairs of Government Buildings

GOVERNMENT HOUSE

Salaries ($14,516.66)

Thos. Lymer	Steward	(T)	1 month	66 66
T. Vine	Assistant Steward		12 months	1,400 00
H. Johnston	Head Gardener		12 "	1,600 00
J. Hornby	Gardener		12 "	1,400 00
A. Lindow	"		12 "	1,400 00
A. Brehurt	"		12 "	1,400 00
W. J. Jackson	Stationary Engineer		12 "	2,000 00
T. Ellaby	Cleaner and Helper		12 "	1,400 00
Mrs. E. Deans	Housekeeper		12 "	1,050 00
H. Cate	Fireman		12 "	1,400 00
J. Lauder	"		12 "	1,400 00

Pay List for Other Help, Repairs to Grounds, etc. ($2,490.05)

Dale Estate, Ltd., plants and bulbs, 154.68; Dept. of Highways, auto service, 29.00; Pay list, wages of men, 1,991.54; D. Spence, Ltd., bulbs, 161.10; Steele, Briggs Seed Co., Ltd., seedlings, bamboo stalks, 149.75; petty disbursements, 3.98 .... 2,490 05

Water, Fuel, Light and Power ($4,568.23)

Consumers' Gas Co., gas, 205.95; Corporation City of Toronto, water, 520.54; Doan Coal Co., Ltd., wood, coal, etc., 164.00; Milnes Coal Co., Ltd., coal, 2,585.91; Toronto Hydro Electric System, electric light and power, 1,091.83... 4,568 23

Repairs, Contingencies, etc. ($6,419.81)

Advance Window Cleaning Co., cleaning windows, etc., 168.70; Aikenhead Hardware, Ltd., repairs to lawn mower, etc., 30.35; Brunswick-Balke-Collender Co. of Canada, Ltd., removing tables, 25.85; H. C. Burton & Co., lamps, 124.14; Canada Bread Co., Ltd., bread, 26.81; Mrs. M. Chambers, fish, 25.60; City Dairy Co., Ltd., milk, etc., 57.21; Geo. Coles, Ltd., provisions, 20.19; Consolidated Plate Glass Co., Ltd., glass, 10.24; H. G. Cook, meat, 159.42; Cudahy Packing Co., oil, soap, 11.76; Dept. of Highways, labour, oxygen, rent of trucks, etc., 37.18; The T. Eaton Co., Ltd., soap, etc., 25.94; Empire Brass Manufacturing Co., Ltd., plumbing, etc., 924.47; M. Hollingshead, provisions, 164.50; International Varnish Co., Ltd., paint, turpentine, etc., 24.22; King's Printer, 357.96; Langley's, Ltd., cleaning curtains and blankets, etc., 196.10; A. S. Leitch Co., Ltd., iron fireman, 73.20; Luxfer Prism Co., Ltd., floor lights, 1,688.00; Michie & Co., Ltd., provisions, 266.95; Monastery of Our Lady of Charity, laundry, 323.51; Pay list, wages of men, 1,328.55; The Robert Simpson Co., Ltd., washboards, repairs and supplies, 100.80; G. F. Sterne & Sons, Ltd., soda, 12.84; Taylor-Forbes Co., Ltd., plumbing supplies, 51.75; W. Walker & Sons, Ltd., sash chain, wire cable, etc., 71.66; Whirlwind Carpet Cleaners, Ltd., cleaning rugs, 47.10; W. Williamson Lumber Co., Ltd., lumber, 19.23; petty disbursements, 45.58 .... 6,419 81

Maintenance and Repairs of Government Buildings—Continued

Government House—Continued

Furniture and Furnishings ($9.00)

The Robert Simpson Co., Ltd., kitchen utensils 9 00

Telephone Service ($536.41)

The Bell Telephone Co., exchange service 536 41

Government House $28,540.16

PARLIAMENT AND DEPARTMENTAL BUILDINGS

Salaries ($145,480.66)

Walter Blackwell	Housekeeper	12 months		2,700 00
W. P. Thompson	Assistant Housekeeper	12 "		1,600 00
Wm. Campbell	Messenger, Prime Minister's Department	12 "		1,700 00
J. A. Henry	Cleaner and Helper	12 "		1,400 00
J. Whyte	" "	12 "		1,400 00
T. Fenwick	" "	12 "		1,400 00
T. Durkin	" "	12 "		1,400 00
M. Bryan	" "	12 "		1,400 00
J. Carroll	" "	12 "		1,400 00
J. Johnston	" "	12	1,400 00	
	Less leave of absence		25 51	1,374 49
T. Buttress	" "	12 months		1,400 00
A. R. Sherwood	" "	12 "		1,400 00
J. Wallace	" "	12 "		1,400 00
Peter Harrison	" "	12 "		1,400 00
T. Jones	" "	12 "		1,400 00
J. Brown	" "	12 "		1,400 00
R. S. Young	" "	12 "		1,400 00
P. Benzies	" "	12 "		1,400 00
A. Graham	" "	12 "		1,400 00
W. J. Heaney	" "	12	1,400 00	
	Less leave of absence		47 66	1,352 34
G. Currell	" "	12 months		1,400 00
W. G. Clarke	" "	12 "		1,400 00
J. Doig	" "	12 "		1,400 00
W. Mason	" "	12 "		1,400 00
J. Miles	" "	12 "		1,400 00
R. Nidd	" "	12 "		1,400 00
R. J. Swanton	" "	12 "		1,400 00
F. Stent	" "	5½ "		637 00
W. Seddon	" "	2 "		233 32
J. Thomson	" "	12 "		1,400 00
H. Short	" "	12 "		1,400 00
R. Urquhart	" "	12 "		1,400 00
C. Collins	" "	12 "		1,400 00
I. Whittaker	" "	12 "		1,300 00
J. W. Welch	" "	12 "		1,300 00
A. E. Doran	" "	12 "		1,300 00
F. Hilliard	" "	12 "		1,300 00
C. H. Jefferson	" "	12 "		1,300 00
Wm. J. Kane	" "	12 "		1,200 00
Geo. F. McCaig	" "	12 "		1,200 00
T. G. Goulding	" "	12 "		1,200 00
Wm. Petrie	" "	12 "		1,125 00
George Mullen	" "	12 "		1,125 00
C. Carlyle	Porter and Messenger	12 "		1,350 00
Jesse S. Day	" "	12 "		1,200 00
J. Bennett	Elevator Attendant	12 "		1,600 00
S. McKenzie	" "	12 "		1,400 00
T. L. Cordell	" "	12 "		1,400 00
George Anderson	" "	12 "		1,400 00
M. Button	" "	12 "		1,400 00
J. W. Smith	" "	12 "		1,400 00
G. P. Saunders	" "	12 "		1,400 00
G. Sowray	" "	12 "		1,400 00

Maintenance and Repairs of Government Buildings—Continued

Parliament and Departmental Buildings—Continued

Salaries—Continued

P. M. J. Gavin	Elevator Attendant	12 months		1,300 00
S. Pears	Watchman	12 "		1,400 00
M. J. Dodds	"	12 "		1,400 00
H. W. Watson	"	12 "		1,400 00
C. C. Knox	"	12 "		1,400 00
W. Marwood	Clerk, Group 2	12 "		1,125 00
E. Longstaff	Speaker's Messenger	12 "		750 00
H. G. Walsh	Stationary Engineer, East Block	12 "		2,100 00
S. T. Pearson	Assistant Engineer	12 "		1,600 00
Wm. J. Sheridan	" "	12 "		1,600 00
S. J. Bredin	" "	12 "		1,600 00
J. Stitt	Fireman	12 "		1,400 00
G. F. Pownall	"	12 "		1,400 00
F. Cope	"	12 "		1,400 00
James Gillespie	"	12 "		1,400 00
J. Scriven	"	12 "		1,400 00
N. Pellow	"	12 "		1,400 00
W. Edmonds	"	12 "		1,400 00
Fred Hirst	"	12 "		1,125 00
H. McKinnon	"	12 "		1,125 00
E. C. Kelly	"	12 "		1,125 00
J. J. Meagher	Head Gardener	12 "		1,600 00
W. Pierce	Assistant Gardener	12 "		1,400 00
T. Goulding	" "	12 "		1,400 00
R. Fish	" "	12 "		1,400 00
Robert McLaren	" "	12 "		1,125 00
Edward Stanley	Assistant Mason	12 "		1,200 00
C. E. I. Dean	Head Telephone Operator	12 "		1,400 00
E. Devlin	Telephone Operator	12 "		1,200 00
Marion Wale	" "	12 "		1,200 00
Irene Penrose	" "	12 "		1,200 00
Maud M. Connolly	" "	12 "		1,125 00
Ada M. Hazard	" "	12 "		1,125 00
E. M. Sexsmith	Telegraph Operator	12 "		1,600 00
S. W. Lowe	Assistant Telegraph Operator	12 "		1,200 00
Elizabeth Turner	Charwoman	12 "		825 00
Annie Brown	"	12 "		775 00
Elizabeth Beck	"	12 "		775 00
Edith R. Clarke	"	12 "		775 00
Mary Clark	"	12 "		775 00
Isabella Connell	"	12 "		775 00
Elizabeth Craik	"	4 months	258 32	
		(T) 8 "	250 64	508 96
Lily G. Dursley	"	12 months		775 00
Annie Grant	"	12 "		775 00
Mary Gordon	"	12 "		775 00
Florence Lee	"	12 "		775 00
Florence McKay	"	12 "		775 00
Margaret Morrant	"	12 "		775 00
Ellen Power	"	12 "		775 00
A. Burton	"	12 "		775 00
A. Cookes	"	12 months	775 00	
		Less leave of absence	149 15	625 85
M. Sloman	"	12 months		775 00
Mary L. Edgar	"	12 "		775 00
E. Fairacre	"	12 "		775 00
Helen Kilbride	"	12 "		775 00
Elizabeth Perkins	"	12 "		775 00
Agnes McFaul	"	12 "		775 00
Johan White	"	12 "		775 00
C. Stewart	"	12 "		775 00
B. Cotton	"	12 "		775 00
I. Dickson	"	12 "		775 00
A. Atkinson	"	12 "		775 00
M. Budd	"	12 "		775 00
E. Havelin	"	12 "		775 00
M. Wilson	"	12 "		775 00
J. Wood	"	12 "		775 00

Maintenance and Repairs of Government Buildings—Continued

Parliament and Departmental Buildings—Continued

Salaries—Continued

Emily Phypers	Charwoman	12 months	775 00
J. M. Ringham	"	12 "	775 00
Bessie A. Stephenson	"	4¼ "	248 70
Lillian M. Williams	"	12 "	700 00

Water and Fuel ($29,840.25)

Corporation City of Toronto, water, 4,728.45; Doan Coal Co., Ltd., coal, 1,513.89; Lake Simcoe Ice and Fuel, Ltd., ice, 10.40; Milnes Coal Co., Ltd., coal, 38,674.73.

		44,927 47	
Less Refunds:			
Board of Governors, University of Toronto, cost of heating Pathological building	6,500 00		
Department of Health, cost of heating Psychiatric Hospital	2,500 00		
Dominion Government subventions re Nova Scotia Coal.	6,087 22		
		15,087 22	
			29,840 25

Electric Power and Light Current and Gas ($18,326.16)

Consumer's Gas Co., Ltd., 2,750.77; Toronto Hydro-Electric System, 15,575.39.. 18,326 16

Supplies, Tools, etc., for Engine Room and General Repairs ($3,288.56)

Aikenhead Hardware, Ltd., ash cans, etc., 91.30; F. Armstrong Co., Ltd., plumbing supplies, 215.00; Babcock-Wilcox & Goldie-McCulloch, Ltd., repairs to crank shaft, etc., 151.80; Beldam's Asbestos & General Manufacturing Co., Ltd., packing, 56.55; Bond Engineering Works, new key and keyway shaft and pulley, 119.13; Canadian Blower and Forge Co., Ltd., fan shaft, 110.25; Canadian Fairbanks-Morse Co., Ltd., wheelbarrow pans, 18.20; Canadian Gasket Co., gaskets, 45.11; Canadian Industries, Ltd., paint, ammonia, etc., 36.49; Canadian Johns-Manville Co., Ltd., pipe covering, etc., 97.70; Combustion Engineering Co., Ltd., valve spindle, dump grates, bars, etc., 117.24; Darling Bros., Ltd., webster traps, etc., 503.65; Dept. of Highways, motor car service, etc., 243.30; Dominion Bridge Co., Ltd., plates, 62.03; Dominion Oxygen Co., Ltd., steel, oxygen, etc., 29.26; C. A. Dunham Co., Ltd., repairs to valve and pump, etc., 70.50; Empire Brass Manufacturing Co., Ltd., boiler, 25.18; Factory Equipment, Ltd., packing, boxes, 73.01; Grimmer-Wilson Engineering Co., welding, 13.50; Hamilton Gear & Machine Co., Ltd., boiler parts, 22.00; J. Inglis Co., Ltd., boiler tubes, 18.48; Instruments, Ltd., recording thread, charts, 27.00; International Varnish Co., Ltd., paint and oil, etc., 16.68; Johnson Temperature Regulating Co., Ltd., valve parts, 60.20; A. S. Leitch Co., Ltd., baffle plates, etc., 34.25; McColl-Frontenac Oil Co., Ltd., oil, 349.86; G. B. Meadows, Ltd., shovels, 37.80; Minneapolis-Honeywell Regulator Co., Ltd., pressure rolls, 26.36; H. Morris Crane & Hoist Co., Ltd., cable, 45.90; Jas. Morrison Brass Manufacturing Co., Ltd., vacuum seal, bronze pieces, 26.45; National Silicates, Ltd., silicate of soda, 35.40; Nichols Chemical Co., Ltd., calcium chloride, 20.00; Otis-Fensom Elevator Co., Ltd., brushes, etc., 34.08; W. R. Perrin, Ltd., valves, 23.65; Price & Burton, calcium chloride, 18.44; Pyrene Manufacturing Co. of Canada, Ltd., pyrene, brackets, extinguishers, etc., 21.25; Smart-Turner Machine Co., Ltd., brass liners, 11.50; Steele, Briggs Seed Co., Ltd., flax seed, 58.40; G. F. Sterne & Sons, silicate of soda, 21.38; Supplies & Insulation, Ltd., sheet rubber, cement, etc., 102.47; Taylor-Forbes Co., Ltd., plumbing supplies, 93.18; Turnbull Elevator Co., Ltd., brushes, 10.00. Sundries—cartage, 9.50; freight, 6.89; petty disbursements, 78.24 3,288 56

Caretakers of Grounds and Maintenance of Grounds, Drives and Walks ($4,564.85)

W. G. Boag, pruning trees, 64.00; Canadian Building Materials, Ltd., gravel, 190.04; Dale Estate, Ltd., bulbs, 201.86; Dept. of Highways, truck rentals, etc., 188.78; Dominion Rubber Co., Ltd., hose, 17.97; Dunlop Tire & Rubber Goods Co., Ltd., hose, etc., 31.23; Goodyear Tire & Rubber Co., Ltd., hose, etc., 20.97; W. Graham, turf, 46.50; Gutta Percha & Rubber, Ltd., hose, etc., 23.29; S. McCord & Co., Ltd., screenings, 11.79; Pay list, wages of men, 2,247.60; Powerlite Devices, Ltd., globes, 13.36; Price & Burton, calcium chloride, 37.42; The Robert Simpson Co., Ltd., rakes and spades, 20.10; D. Spence, Ltd., bulbs, 188.63; Steele, Briggs Seed Co., Ltd., tobacco stems, etc., 24.65; Taylor-

Maintenance and Repairs of Government Buildings—Continued

Parliament and Departmental Buildings—Continued

Caretakers of Grounds, etc.—Continued

Forbes Co., Ltd., mowers, 60.48; J. G. Tickell & Sons, cleaning statues, 775.00; A. N. Walker, repairing and cleaning monument 386.00; petty disbursements, 15.18.......... 4,564 85

Repairs and Cleaning of Buildings, ($113,345.01)

The A. C. Co., Ltd., soap, paste, etc., 341.02; Acme Caretakers' Supply Co., dust pans, soap, etc., 127.34; Acme Lighting Products, Ltd., electric supplies, 12.00; Advance Window Cleaning Co., cleaning windows and doors, 871.70; Aikenhead Hardware, Ltd., door closers and springs, etc., 423.76; Allanson Armature Exchange Co., armature, 16.00; American Tent and Awning Co., Ltd., awnings, 187.44; Armour & Emmons Co., cleaning supplies, 41.75; F. Armstrong Co., Ltd., plumbing supplies, 697.28; Armstrong Cork and Insulation Co., Ltd., cement, 12.20; Atlas Chemical Co., marvello, 12.00; Baines & David, Ltd., angle iron, 15.39; Bates Products, Ltd., cleaning supplies, 78.30; Beldam's Asbestos Packing & General Manufacturing Co., Ltd., packing, 28.67; Belleville-Sargent & Co., Ltd., keys, cylinders, etc., 32.68; Biggar Lock & Key Co., keys and repairs, 29.00; A. M. Bitzer, electric panels, 340.00; Booth Signs, Ltd., lettering door, 38.25; Brantford Roofing Co., Ltd., roofing materials, 103.56; H. C. Burton & Co., lamps, 1,188.26; Canadian Elevator Equipment Co., Ltd., springs, etc., 671.15; Canadian Fairbanks-Morse Co., Ltd., compressor, couplings, etc., 17.45; Canadian General Electric Co., Ltd., lamps, etc., 3,098.40; Canadian Germicide Co., Ltd., washers, etc., 36.57; Canadian Johns-Manville Co., Ltd., asbestos wool, pipe covering, etc., 427.88; Canadian Laboratory Supplies, Ltd., elements, 19.00; Canadian Laco Lamps, Ltd., lamps, 550.82; Canada Metal Co., Ltd., sheet lead, 38.20; Canada Packers, Ltd., soap, 60.00; Canadian Westinghouse Co., Ltd., lamps, repairs to motor, etc., 330.77; Canada Wire & Cable Co., Ltd., cable, 199.21; Chicago Hardware Foundry Co., Ltd., parts for drier, 53.16; Church Engineering Co., radiator handles, 54.00; Consolidated Plate Glass Co., Ltd., glass, 308.48; Geo. Cooke Co., Ltd., CC&B cleaner, wax, etc., 244.50; M. Corcoran, metal polish, 50.00; Corporation of the City of Toronto, elevator license, 70.00; Coulter Copper & Brass Co., Ltd., pipe, 67.15; Cudahy Packing Co., cleanser, 72.78; D'Arcy Manufacturing Co., cleaning supplies, toilet flush, 27.00; Darling Bros., Ltd., radiator valves, etc., 1,001.35; Dept. of Highways, gasolene, acetyline, 177.56; Diamond Cleanser, Ltd., soap powder, 399.00; Diamond State Fibre Co. of Canada, Ltd., fibre tube, etc., 35.07; Dictograph Products Co. of Canada, Ltd., inspections, 24.50; W. E. Dillon & Co., Ltd., dampers, cabinets, etc., 168.52; Dominion Oxygen Co., Ltd., acetylene, oxygen, etc., 648.25; Dominion Radiator & Boiler Co., Ltd., boiler grates, etc., 28.86; Durant Tile & Marble Co., patching marble, 30.00; Dustbane Products, Ltd., repairs to scrubber, etc., 149.81; The T. Eaton Co., Ltd., repairs to lantern, etc., 137.50; E. B. Eddy Co., Ltd., toilet paper, 1,264.73; Empire Brass Manufacturing Co., Ltd., plumbing supplies, etc., 457.54; J. Ennis' Wonder Polish Co., floor oil, etc., 57.50; Evans Co., Ltd., chamois, sponges, etc., 44.86; Excelsior Brushes, Ltd., mop handles, etc., 1,119.59; Factory Equipment, Ltd., jointing, etc., 72.03; Fairbanks Products, insect powder, etc., 71.54; Ferranti Electric, Ltd., electric supplies, 83.04; Flexo Cotton Products, wringers, 35.64; R. Fowler, cleaning chimneys, 50.00; A. Frank, repairing pans, etc., 93.25; Galt Brass Co., Ltd., washers, 16.00; General Sound Equipment, Ltd., electric supplies, 40.00; General Steel Wares, Ltd., pails, etc., 70.34; Good Specialties, Ltd., washers, etc., 188.54; Grand & Toy, Ltd., repairs to furniture, etc., 39.35; J. Graybill, repairs to vacuum cleaner, 16.55; B. Greening Wire Co., Ltd., steel rope, 170.40; A. J. Grigg, repairs to clock, 31.25; Griswold Machine Works, film splicers, etc., 113.94; Guaranteed Exterminating Co., fumigating No. 7 Queen's Park, 216.00; G. A. Hardie & Co., Ltd., cheesecloth, 33.00; Harris Abattoir Co., Ltd., soap, 40.00; Hospital & Kitchen Equipment Co., Ltd., steel, 17.50; Huntington Laboratories of Canada, Ltd., wax, 226.46; Instruments, Ltd., repairs to indicator, 34.00; Interlake Tissue Mills Co., Ltd., towels, toilet rolls, etc., 1,493.80; Italian Mosaic & Tile Co., Ltd., repairs to marble, etc., 31.50; King's Printer, 76.88; R. Laidlaw Lumber Co., Ltd., lumber, 1,060.22; Langley's, Ltd., cleaning curtains, etc., 67.46; Leatherdale Studio, replacing frame, 25.00; Lavoline Cleanser Co., Ltd., cleaning compound, 181.59; A. S. Leitch Co., Ltd., check valve, 326.00; Lever Bros., Ltd., soap, 344.52; Rice Lewis & Son, Ltd., hardware, 194.17; Jas. Lumbers Co., Ltd., soap, 71.00; McColl-Frontenac Oil Co., Ltd., soap, 307.87; S. McCord & Co., Ltd., sand, etc., 600.17; C. A. McLellan, cabinets, 20.64; Mahaffy Iron Works, Ltd., rubber tires, etc., 55.47; Mrs. C. Marwood, repairing flags, etc., 30.65; Masco Co., Ltd., electric supplies, 1,069.32; Thos. Meredith & Co., Ltd., nails, roofing, etc., 145.62; Midland Wood Products,

Maintenance and Repairs of Government Buildings—Continued

Parliament and Departmental Buildings—Continued

Repairs and Cleaning of Buildings—Continued

Ltd., lumber, 360.69; Jas. Morrison Brass Manufacturing Co., Ltd., plumbing supplies, 184.32; New York Window Cleaning Co., Ltd., cleaning windows, 198.63; Nicholls Chemical Co., Ltd., sal soda, 77.00; Ontario Reformatory, Mimico, tile, 25.20; Otis Fensom Elevator Co., Ltd., springs, etc., 141.02; Pay list, wages of men, attendants and charwomen, 82,927.12; W. R. Perrin, Ltd., repairing ice machine, 60.67; E. F. Phillips Electric Works, Ltd., electric supplies, 47.13; Powerlite Devices, Ltd., compound, 10.85; Geo. Rathbone Lumber Co., Ltd., lumber, 59.77; Riverdale Lumber Co., Ltd., lumber, 20.00; Jas. Robertson Co., Ltd., plumbing supplies, 197.68; Roofers Supply Co., Ltd., sheet metal, etc., 602.96; Township of Scarborough, collecting Bon Air garbage, 50.00; K. Schiff, wipers, 90.93; The Robert Simpson Co., Ltd., felt, cushions, rental of chairs, etc., 1,282.25; John B. Smith & Sons, lumber, 14.40; Soclean, Ltd., soclean, 493.47; Estate of George Sparrow & Co., repairs, etc., 28.65; Sure-Way Products, cleaning compound, 48.04; Taylor-Forbes Co., Ltd., plumbing supplies, 108.80; J. & J. Taylor, Ltd., moving safe, etc., 21.39; Textan Co., Ltd., soap, 141.52; Toronto Hydro-Electric System, replacing transformers, 23.18; Toronto Lock Manufacturing Co., cylinders, locks, etc., 16.45; Trelco, Ltd., sponges, etc., 16.25; Turnbull Elevator Co., Ltd., buzzers, etc., 111.00; United Typewriter Co., Ltd., inspections, repairs, etc., 177.63; Utility Products, Ltd., bleach, 14.00; Wagner Electric Manufacturing Co., Ltd., repairs to motor, etc., 39.05; W. Walker & Son, Ltd., hardware, 221.51; Wentworth Radio & Auto Supply Co., Ltd., soldering, radiotrons, etc., 15.27; Whirlwind Carpet Cleaners, Ltd., cleaning carpets, etc., 131.70; W. Williamson Lumber Co., Ltd., lumber, 133.72; Wonder Products, cleanser, 151.58; G. H. Wood & Co., Ltd., glass, water bottles, etc., 1,656.26. Sundries—cartage, 15.36; customs, 47.90; express, 10.85; freight, 41.43; petty disbursements, 155.09 .... 114,669 19

Less Repayments Liquor Control Board	258 05		
" " Public Welfare	8 50		
" " Labour	59 83		
" " Civil Service Association	200 00		
" " Ontario Athletic Commission	797 80		
		1,324 18	
			113,345 01

Vault Fittings and Shelving ($4,072.76)

Department of Lands and Forests, shelving, lumber, etc., 997.00; Grand & Toy, Ltd., steel shelving, etc., 2,385.63; R. Laidlaw Lumber Co., Ltd., making pigeon holes, 246.51; Pay list, wages of men, 192.60; Geo. Rathbone Lumber Co., Ltd., shelving, 25.00; J. & J. Taylor, Ltd., door for vault, 150.00; W. Williamson Lumber Co., Ltd., shelving, 76.02 .... 4,072 76

Furniture and Furnishings for Buildings ($20,031.61)

Addressograph-Multigraph of Canada, Ltd., cabinet of drawers, 27.10; Aikenhead Hardware, Ltd., card holders, locks, etc., 24.65; Booth Signs, Ltd., sign, 20.00; Burroughs Adding Machine of Canada, Ltd., chair, 31.65; B. Cairns, Ltd., sign, 29.50; Canadian Beaver Co., turnstile, 50.00; Canadian Flag Manufacturing Co., union jacks, 18.00; Canadian General Electric Co., Ltd., telechron, electric supplies, 89.23; Canadian Office and School Furniture, Ltd., benches, cabinets, etc., 257.35; Canadian Westinghouse Co., Ltd., fan, 40.49; Cassidy's, Ltd., syrup jugs, trays, etc., 513.47; Continental Sound Equipment Co., lamps, etc., 135.00; Dept. of Lands and Forests, cupboards, 338.00; The T. Eaton Co., Ltd., linoleum, placing drapes, etc., 1,224.43; Excelsior Brushes, Ltd., dusting mops, etc., 15.44; Ferranti Electric, Ltd., rectifier voltmeter, 26.88; Grand & Toy, Ltd., guides, chairs, etc., 8,353.20; Haynes Art Gallery, framing photos, etc., 44.25; B. M. & T. Jenkins, Ltd., furniture, 650.00; R. Laidlaw Lumber Co., Ltd., gate, lumber, etc., 128.50; Bert Lofts, curtains and rods, etc., 25.03; Mahaffy Iron Works, Ltd., truck, 10.50; Mitchell & McGill, chairs, etc., 215.50; A. Moody, chairs, etc., 74.75; Office Specialty Manufacturing Co., Ltd., office furniture, 855.60; Ontario Reformatory Industries, office furniture, 252.85; Province of Ontario Pictures, frames, 407.20; Geo. Rathbone Lumber Co., Ltd., stands, cupboards, etc., 689.75; The Robert Simpson Co., Ltd., clock, mirror, etc., 781.94; Geo. Sparrow & Co., kitchen utensils, etc., 62.08; Steel Equipment Co., Ltd., cabinets, etc., 523.75; Stratford Chair Co., desks, chairs, etc., 3,033.90; C. Tarling Co., map case, mounting maps, etc., 57.00; J. & J. Taylor, Ltd., exchange of safes, 455.00; Toronto Hydro-Electric System, vacuum cleaner, 57.50; C. L. Turnbull Co., Ltd., files, 20.40; Vetcraft Industries, wreaths, 41.25; W. Walker & Son, Ltd., bronze,

Maintenance and Repairs of Government Buildings—Continued

Parliament and Departmental Buildings—Continued

Furniture and Furnishings—Continued

castings, lantern, etc., 19.62; W. Williamson Lumber Co., Ltd., shelves, etc., 296.50. Sundries—cartage, 16.08; express, 1.40; freight, 104.67; petty disbursements, 12.20 ... 20,031 61

Interior Alterations ($8,843.97)

Aikenhead Hardware, Ltd., hardware, 25.24; Fred Armstrong Co., Ltd., plumbing supplies, 39.96; Baines & David, Ltd., steel, etc., 31.98; Bond Engineering Works, Ltd., shaft, etc., 79.05; Canada Building Material Co., Ltd., building supplies, 148.24; Canadian Allis-Chalmers, Ltd., rope drive, etc., 203.36; Darling Bros., Ltd., valve, 37.80; Dominion Oxygen Co., Ltd., welding, 18.60; Empire Brass Manufacturing Co., Ltd., plumbing supplies, 513.93; Geo. M. Hendry Co., Ltd., asbetolate, 51.20; R. Laidlaw Lumber Co., Ltd., lumber, doors, etc., 828.31; S. McCord & Co., Ltd., sand, etc., 125.10; J. C. McLaren Belting Co., Ltd., repairs to belts, 12.67; Masco Co., Ltd., electric supplies, 38.17; Geo. B. Meadows, Ltd., repairing cashier's cage, 30.00; The James Morrison Brass Manufacturing Co., Ltd., brass end posts, etc., 174.88; Pay list, wages of men, 5,058.48; W. H. Price, lettering doors, etc., 52.48; Geo. Rathbone Lumber Co., Ltd., pedestals, 241.24; Reid & Brown Structural Steel and Iron Works, Ltd., beams, 30.00; Roofers' Supply Co., Ltd., roofing materials, 145.53; The Robert Simpson Co., Ltd., wallpaper, 113.38; W. Williamson Lumber Co., Ltd., lumber, 823.90; petty disbursements, 20.47 ... 8,843 97

Flowers, Shrubs, Plants, etc. ($58.44)

Miller & Sons, flowers, 28.50; D. Spence, Ltd., plants, etc., 20.00; H. Waters Co., flowers, 9.94 ... 58 44

Uniforms for Messengers, Attendants, etc. ($27.50)

Rex Tailoring Co., Ltd., uniform ... 27 50

Painting Outside and Inside Work ($9,546.48)

Atlas Chemical Co., marvello, 36.00; Aulcraft Paints, Ltd., paint, etc., 38.86; Canada Paint Co., Ltd., white lead, 158.74; Excelsior Brushes, Ltd., sash tools and brushes, 133.73; G. A. Hardie & Co., Ltd., cheesecloth, etc., 13.65; Imperial Varnish & Color Co., Ltd., paint, 22.05; International Varnish Co., Ltd., shellac, varnish, etc., 413.80; Lowe Bros. Co., Ltd., varnish, 56.41; Pay list, wages of men, 8,275.71; K. Schiff, cotton waste, etc., 12.54; Malcolm Sinclair Co., Ltd., paint supplies, 173.42; Trelco, Ltd., paint, brushes, etc., 160.10; Tremco Manufacturing Co., paint supplies, 38.22; petty disbursements, 13.25 ... 9,546 48

Telephone Service ($51,547.74)

Bell Telephone Co. of Canada, rental, 28,110.41; tolls, 19,945.14 ... 48,055 55

Temporary Services of Operators, $3,416.95.

Anna Afford at 62.50 per month, 125.00; M. E. Elder at 81.25 per month, 975.00; Clarice G. Locke at 62.50 per month, 2.40; Ailsa F. Linge at 62.50 per month, 750.00; Johan McLagan at 62.50 per month, 225.95; G. D. Quince at 2.50 per night, 80.00; Aileen D. Sharpe, at 81.25 per month, 975.00; E. L. Sporle at 62.50 per month, 283.60 ... 3,416 95

Miscellaneous, $75.24.

King's Printer ... 75 24

Fire Protection ($459.82)

Coleman Electric Co., fire extinguishers, 47.80; Dominion Rubber Co., Ltd., fire hose, 58.24; Dunlop Tire & Rubber Goods Co., Ltd., fire hose, 86.08; Goodyear Tire & Rubber Co., Ltd., fire hose, 86.08; Gutta Percha & Rubber Ltd., fire hose, 57.38; Pyrene Manufacturing Co. of Canada, Ltd., refills, extinguishers, etc., 108.66. Sundries—petty disbursements, 15.58 ... 459 82

Rental of Property and Office Space ($930.00)

Dept. of Lands and Forests, License of Occupation, Goldpines, 30.00; Lady Gage, 358 Bloor St. W., Toronto, for Poppy Fund, 900.00 ... 930 00

Parliament and Departmental Buildings ... $410,363.81

Maintenance and Repairs of Government Buildings—Continued

OSGOODE HALL

Salaries ($17,925.66)

N. J. Harrison	Housekeeper	11 1/6 months	1,860 66
J. H. Best	Assistant Housekeeper	12 "	1,400 00
A. Britton	Elevator Attendant	12 "	1,400 00
J. T. Lister	Cleaner and Helper	12 "	1,400 00
M. Ruddock	" "	12 "	1,400 00
J. C. Spratley	" "	12 "	1,400 00
T. McPortland	" "	12 "	1,400 00
J. Faragher	"	12 "	1,400 00
A. McCann	Janitress	12 "	940 00
F. Harrison	Laundress	(T) 12 "	400 00
S. Paquin	Fireman	12 "	1,400 00
B. M. Freestone	Telephone Operator	12 "	1,200 00
J. Priest	Charwoman	12 "	775 00
Margaret Clark	"	12 "	775 00
E. Webber	"	12 "	775 00

Fuel, Light, Water and Power ($5,378.90)

Belle Ewart Ice Co., ice, 270.06; Consumers' Gas Co., gas, 86.60; Corporation of City of Toronto, water, 207.03; Doan Coal Co., Ltd., coal, 195.73; Milnes Coal Co., Ltd., coal, 2,902.22; Toronto Hydro-Electric System, power and light, 2,435.09 .... 6,096 73
Less refunded by Law Society of Upper Canada 717 83
5,378 90

Furniture and Incidentals ($2,343.37)

American Tent and Awning Co., Ltd., awnings, 39.50; H. C. Burton & Co., lamps, 85.01; B. Cairns, Ltd., sign, 16.00; Canadian Flag Mfg. Co., union jack, 17.00; Canadian Laco Lamps, Ltd., lamps, 95.82; T. Eaton Co., Ltd., linoleum, 101.00; E. B. Eddy Co., Ltd., toilet paper, 27.00; Evans & Co., Ltd., chamois, etc., 11.22; Grand & Toy, Ltd., cabinets, etc., 784.40; G. A. Hardie & Co., Ltd., cheesecloth, 24.00; Interlake Tissue Mills Co., Ltd., towels, toilet paper, 209.42; George B. Meadows, Ltd., screens, 50.00; Pay list, wages of men, 130.95; The Robert Simpson Co., Ltd., flag, mirror, etc., 618.64; Taylor Typewriter Co., repairs, 18.75; G. H. Wood & Co., Ltd., paper cups, soap, 90.80; Sundries—freight, .75; petty disbursements, 23.11 .... 2,343 37

Telephone Service ($3,734.97)

Bell Telephone Co. of Canada, 3,499.22; salary of relief operator, 235.75 .... 3,734 97

Cleaning of Building ($6,418.92)

Cudahy Packing Co., cleanser, 14.55; Evans & Co., Ltd., chamois, sponges, 11.22; Excelsior Brushes, Ltd., chamois, etc., 102.23; Interlake Tissue Mills Co., Ltd., towels, 19.60; Lavoline Cleanser Co., Ltd., lavoline, 28.66; Ontario Gasoline & Oils, Ltd., soap, 132.02; Ontario Soap & Oil Co., soap, 31.99; Pay list, wages of charwomen, etc., 5,925.29; The Robert Simpson Co., Ltd., soap, etc., 95.90; Soclean, Ltd., mop wringers, etc., 43.85. Sundries—petty disbursements, 13.61 .... 6,418 92

Fire Protection ($15.60)

Pyrene Manufacturing Co. of Canada, Ltd., repairs to extinguisher 15 60

General Repairs and Alterations ($4,989.21)

Aikenhead Hardware, Ltd., hardware, etc., 20.10; F. Armstrong Co., Ltd., plumbing supplies, 94.76; Beatty Bros., Ltd., repairing washing machine, 38.00; Beldam's Asbestos Packing & General Manufacturing Co., Ltd., gaskets, 15.05; H. C. Burton & Co., lamps, 18.58; Canadian Elevator Equipment Co., Ltd., cable, 23.00; Canadian Johns-Manville Co., Ltd., pipe covering, 40.49; Canadian Laco Lamps, Ltd., lamps, 19.34; Darling Bros., Ltd., traps, air vents, 33.15; Dennisteel, Ltd., window guards, 36.63; A. J. Grigg, repairs to clock, 32.25; F. Hankin & Co., Ltd., repairs to boiler, 70.00; Interlake Tissue Mills Co., Ltd., towels, 55.11; A. S. Leitch Co., Ltd., repairs, etc., 115.20; S. McCord & Co., Ltd., wood fibre, 175.56; Masco Co., Ltd., conduit, 12.26; Thos. Meredith & Co., Ltd., rope, files, 59.57; James Morrison Brass Manufacturing Co., Ltd., tube cleaner, charts, 24.49; Pay list, wages of men, 3,922.90; G. F. Sterne & Sons, Ltd., cement, 28.84; Taylor-Forbes Co., Ltd., plumbing supplies, 13.29; G. H. Wood & Co., Ltd., drinking cups, 52.00. Sundries—petty disbursements, 88.64 .... 4,989 21

Maintenance and Repairs of Government Buildings—Continued

Osgoode Hall—Continued

Electric Wiring and Fixtures ($16.00)

Pay list, wages of men.. 16 00

Painting Interior and Exterior ($1,996.03)

Aulcraft Paints, Ltd., paint, 12.58; Canada Paint Co., Ltd., paint, 12.63; Canadian Industries, Ltd., paint and turpentine, 14.26; Lowe Bros. Co., Ltd., paint, etc., 15.86; Pay list, wages of men, 1,853.60; Malcolm Sinclair & Co., Ltd., paint, 71.92. Sundries—petty disbursements, 15.18.................................... 1,996 03

Fittings for Vaults and Offices ($305.50)

A. B. Ormsby Co., Ltd., steel shutters, 185.00; J. & J. Taylor, Ltd., vault door, 120.00; petty disbursements, .50.. 305 50

Osgoode Hall.......................................$43,124.16

EDUCATIONAL BUILDINGS

Toronto Normal and Model Schools

Repairs and Incidentals ($4,526.62)

Fred Armstrong Co., Ltd., plumbing supplies, 20.03; Aulcraft Paints, Ltd., paint, etc., 19.95; Canada Paint Co., Ltd., paint, 19.66; Consolidated Plate Glass Co., Ltd., glass, 57.18; W. E. Dillon & Co., Ltd., repairs to roof, 40.00; T. Eaton Co., Ltd., painting, 350·00; Empire Brass Manufacturing Co., Ltd., heater, 10.79; International Varnish Co., Ltd., paint, etc., 23.20; S. McCord & Co., Ltd., sand, etc., 68.37; Pay list, wages of men, 3,836.75; Roofers' Supply Co., Ltd., paint, etc., 49.97; Robert Simpson Co., Ltd., shades, 12.80. Sundries—petty disbursements, 17.92... 4,526 62

Ottawa Normal and Model Schools

Repairs and Incidentals ($671.36)

A. Eagles, repairing bells, 64.17; McKelvey & Birch, Ltd., repairs to furnace, roof, etc., 447.00; W. A. Rankin, Ltd., blackboards, 136.50; Stromberg Time Recorder of Canada, Ltd., repairs to armature, 14.49. Sundries—petty disbursements, 9.20.. 671 36

London Normal School

Repairs and Incidentals ($494.60)

Wm. C. Dace, work on floors, 34.00; W. T. Mortimer, repairs to steps, 22.00; Pay list, wages of men, 7.60; I. Quick & Son, painting, 431.00.................. 494 60

Hamilton Normal School

Repairs and Incidentals ($90.00)

Staunton & Mitchell, blow-off pipe, etc.................................... 90 00

Peterborough Normal School

Repairs and Incidentals ($70.57)

Thos. C. Ephgrave, repairing floor, 10.25; F. O. Goodfellow, repairing tank and plumbing, 27.85; G. H. Hutchinson, plumbing supplies, 14.60. Sundries—petty disbursements, 17.87.. 70 57

Stratford Normal School

Repairs and Incidentals ($444.29)

J. G. Armstrong, removing trees, 25.00; W. C. Berry, plumbing supplies, 322.29; George W. Fink, tile drain, 97.00....................................... 444 29

Maintenance and Repairs of Government Buildings—Continued

Educational Buildings—Continued

North Bay Normal School

Repairs and Incidentals ($461.50)

Canadian Powers Regulator Co., Ltd., thermostats, 437.00; Davidson & South, painting flag pole, 12.00; Electric Supply Co., electric supplies, 12.50........	461 50

Belleville School for the Deaf

Repairs and Incidentals ($1,921.46)

Aikenhead Hardware, Ltd., hardware, etc., 84.32; Beaver Laundry Machinery Co., Ltd., parts for ironer, 64.68; Canada Wire & Cable Co., Ltd., wire, etc., 20.89; Canadian General Electric Co., Ltd., switches, etc., 24.94; T. Eaton Co., Ltd., brass spannings, 22.00; Ferranti Electric, Ltd., electric supplies, 50.24; Hibbard Bros., installing irons, 260.00; Charles L. Hyde, boiler, 130.00; International Resistance Co., Ltd., electric supplies, 18.04; Masco Co., Ltd., electric supplies, 21.56; Northern Electric Co., Ltd., card tips, reproducer, etc., 25.74; Pay list, wages of men, 230.00; C. N. Reid, repairs to building, 70.00; Riley Engineering Supply Co., Ltd., repairs to heating plant, 212.80; Charles G. Roos, microphone parts, 100.00; Robert Simpson Co., Ltd., curtains, 187.20; Trimm Radio Manufacturing Co., headphones, 91.60; Utah-Carter Radio, Ltd., radio parts, 33.40; E. P. White, lumber, 255.79. Sundries—duty, 1.03; petty disbursements, 17.23.	1,921 46

Restoration of Fireman's Cottage Destroyed by Fire ($1,500.00)

Hibbard Electric, electric wiring, 79.95; Ontario Intelligencer, advertising re tenders, 6.75; J. E. Parkes & James Owens, contract reconstruction, 1,413.30..........	1,500 00

Brantford School for the Blind

Repairs and Incidentals ($554.13)

C. C. Bowden, shingling, 380.00; R. Feely, repairing eavestroughs, 98.00; Ingleby-Taylor Co., Ltd., lumber, 36.37; Pay list, wages of men, 16.00. Sundries—petty disbursements, 23.76..........	554 13

Sandwich Training School

Repairs and Incidentals ($59.38)

Sandwich Lumber Co., Ltd., lumber, 15.63; George Thornton, repairing roof, 41.60. Sundries—petty disbursements, 2.15..........	59 38

Sturgeon Falls Training School

Repairs and Incidentals ($205.50)

Aikenhead Hardware, Ltd., hardware, 16.25; J. F. Demers, retubing boiler, 182.00. Sundries—petty disbursements, 7.25..........	205 50

Monteith Northern Academy

Repairs and Incidentals ($500.00)

Hill-Clark-Francis, Ltd., contract repairs to roof, etc..........	500 00

Painting of Building ($1,400.00)

W. E. Deforge, contract painting..........	1,400 00

Repairs and Incidentals to Boilers and Heating Plants in Educational Buildings ($1,609.74)

Belleville School for the Deaf—Darling Bros., Ltd., bellows, 96.00; C. A. Dunham Co., Ltd., heating supplies, 99.96; C. L. Hyde, pipe, fittings, etc., 103.00; Paterson Construction Co., Ltd., repairs to boiler, 365.00..........	663 96
Brantford School for the Blind—Boiler Repair & Grate Bar Co., grate bars.......	93 67
Hamilton Normal School—J. H. Buscombe, repairs to boilers, 73.75; Canadian Johns-Manville Co., Ltd., gaskets, 3.02; Adam Clark, Ltd., repairing pipes, 15.00..........	91 77
London Normal School—Noble & Rich, repairing valves..........	30 08
North Bay Normal School—G. H. Hockchull, repairing boilers, 70.87. Sundries—cartage, 3.76; freight, 16.20; petty disbursements, 4.69..........	95 52

Maintenance and Repairs of Government Buildings—Continued

Educational Buildings—Continued

Boilers and Heating Plants—Continued

Ottawa Normal & Model Schools—Campbell Steel & Iron Works, Ltd., repairs to boilers, 210.00; McKinley & Northwood, Ltd., grate, 8.00.................. 218 00

Peterborough Normal School—J. L. P. Smith, repairs to heating plant........... 72 00

Stratford Normal School—George W. Fink, building arches.................... 30 00

Sturgeon Falls Training Schools—John Inglis Co., Ltd., boiler tubes............ 58 49

Toronto Normal and Model Schools—Fred Armstrong Co., Ltd., pipe and fittings, 10.84; Beldam's Asbestos Packing & General Manufacturing Co., Ltd., rope, 8.10; Boiler Repair & Grate Bar Co., bar, 8.75; Pay list, wages of men, 37.60.. 65 29

General—Baines & David, Ltd., boiler tubes held in storage for Educational buildings 190 96

To Provide for Fire Protection and Fire Equipment in Educational Buildings ($85.25)

Belleville School for the Deaf—Gutta Percha & Rubber, Ltd., hose............. 85 25

Educational Buildings.................................$14,594.40

AGRICULTURAL BUILDINGS

Ontario Agricultural College

Repairs and Incidentals ($898.09)

Canadian Ice Machine Co., Ltd., repairs, etc., 120.36; J. Erskine, repairs to steps, 20.25; Hydro-Electric Power Commission of Ontario, labour, etc., construction of track, 32.60; Jackson-Lewis Co., Ltd., repairing stonework, etc., 54.28; H. Occomore, repairs to roof, etc., 240.00; O. Smith, steps, 60.00; Vulcan Asphalt & Supply Co., Ltd., flooring, 365.00. Sundries—petty disbursements, 5.60... 898 09

Repairs to Massey Library ($678.06)

R. E. Christie Co., Ltd., electric wiring, 590.66; Sundry newspapers, advertisements re tenders, 87.40.. 678 06

Ontario Veterinary College

Repairs and Incidentals ($439.92)

McArthur Engineering & Construction Co., Ltd., laying sidewalk, etc., 250.00; H. Occomore, repairs to roof, 30.00; Otis-Fensom Elevator Co., Ltd., brake and coil, 64.71; Pay list, wages of men, 87.00. Sundries—petty disbursements, 8.21.. 439 92

Horticultural Experimental Station, Vineland

Repairs and Incidentals ($1,907.08)

Beamsville Lumber & Supply Co., Ltd., lumber, 111.63; Canadian Westinghouse Co., Ltd., lamps, 58.15; T. Eaton Co., Ltd., window shades, 52.50; W. G. Fletcher, syphon, plumbing, etc., 135.15; Lincoln Art Glass, light, 10.00; McNamara & Reynolds, wallpaper, 43.97; Pannill Door Co., Ltd., sash, 76.76; Paterson Engineering Co. of Canada, Ltd., chloronome complete, 1,075.00; Pay list, wages of men, 261.45; C. Stewart, weatherstrip, 32.18; Vineland General Store, Ltd., oil, etc., 35.09. Sundries—petty disbursements, 15.20................. 1,907 08

Western Ontario Experimental Farm, Ridgetown

Repairs and Incidentals ($841.79)

Canadian Blower & Forge Co., Ltd., ball float, etc., 18.00; W. H. Goodhue, paint, etc., 139.40; Pay list, wages of men, 23.00; George Poag & Son, repairing house foundation, 163.00; A. J. Silcox, painting, etc., 358.65; Watson & Taylor, lumber, etc., 139.74... 841 79

Agricultural School, Ridgetown

Repairs and Incidentals ($194.73)

Pay list, wages of men, 22.50; A. J. Silcox, oil, 76.00; Warwick & Son, sashes, 35.00; Watson & Taylor, lumber, 48.10; petty disbursements, 13.13................. 194 73

Maintenance and Repairs of Government Buildings—Continued

Agricultural Buildings—Continued

Eastern Dairy School, Kingston

Repairs and Incidentals ($30.00)

Geo. C. Wright, repairs to window	30 00

Agricultural School, Kemptville

Repairs and Incidentals ($811.64)

Acme Lighting Products, Ltd., globes, 38.51; Anderson & Langstaff Co., Ltd., window shades, etc., 71.33; Geo. Appleton, repairs to boiler, 246.00; W. A. Barnes & Son, repairs to roof, 87.00; H. C. Burton & Co., lamps, 126.36; Canadian Laco Lamps, Ltd., lamps, 64.16; Kemptville Hydro-Electric Commission, wiring motor, etc., 115.00; McKinley & Northwood, Ltd., plumbing supplies, 18.48; Ontario Wind Engine & Pump Co., Ltd., tank, etc., 27.60; Reid & Brown Structural Steel & Iron Works, Ltd., manhole, etc., 17.20	811 64

Painting Exterior ($482.90)

Pay list, wages of men		482 90
Agricultural Buildings	$6,284 21	

BOYS' TRAINING SCHOOL, BOWMANVILLE

Repairs and Incidentals, including Drives and Walks ($555.45)

W. L. Elliott, repairing eavestroughs, coils in greenhouse, 243.00; Dan. Goodwin, ties, 204.75; Pay list, wages of men, 107.70	555 45

DISTRICT BUILDINGS

District of Algoma

Repairs and Alterations ($649.10)

A. Attle, repairs to locks, etc., 18.90; Bailey & McMaster, shelving, 18.00; Alex. Brechin, repairs to doors, 69.03; Wm. Calvert, making tables, 35.92; O. C. Carney, lamps, electric supplies, 22.32; Cochrane-Dunlop Hardware, Ltd., hayfork, etc., 82.43; Dunseath & McClary, plumbing, 83.65; Keyes Hardware, Ltd., hardware, 24.25; Lowe Bros. & Co., Ltd., boiled oil, etc., 18.95; J. McLeod, plumbing supplies, etc., 30.95; C. L. Mason, installing water meter, 18.00; Northern Foundry & Machine Co., Ltd., grate bars, 13.65; Corporation of City of Sault Ste. Marie, repairing water service, 38.57; Taylor Bros., electric supplies and repairs to elevator, 124.40; Alex. Wray, plumbing supplies, 16.10; petty disbursements, 33.98	649 10

Furniture and Furnishings ($228.12)

O. C. Carney, lamps, 47.10; Cochrane-Dunlop Hardware, Ltd., kitchen utensils, 46.68; Grand & Toy, Ltd., supplies, 15.00; J. F. Hartz Co., Ltd., scales, 19.00; Keyes Hardware, Ltd., pails, kitchen utensils, etc., 69.03; Taylor Bros., lamps, 20.59; Sundries—express, 3.65; freight, 2.82; petty disbursements, 4.25	228 12

District of Cochrane

Repairs and Alterations ($684.04)

Cochrane Machine Works, drilling, etc., 58.80; Delco Appliance Corporation, cylinder head, battery, 214.30; Chas. MacKenzie, cleaning boiler, overhauling generator, 14.25; McGill Hardware, Ltd., hardware, etc., 28.95; A. B. Ormsby Co., Ltd., bolts, 41.60; W. G. Theobald, lowering platform, 28.00; H. Tremblay, painting, 225.00; Wilson Bros., steel frame, etc., 39.70; Sundries—express, 1.60; freight, 18.85; petty disbursements, 12.99	684 04

Furniture and Furnishings ($90.98)

H. C. Burton & Co., lamps, 26.55; Grand & Toy, Ltd., chair, shelving, 29.25; McGill Hardware, Ltd., lawn mower, etc., 22.25; Sundries—express, .75; petty disbursements, 12.18	90 98

Maintenance and Repairs of Government Buildings—Continued

District Buildings—Continued

District of Kenora

Repairs and Alterations ($646.83)

J. G. Brown, plumbing supplies, repairing boiler, 93.35; Canada Wire & Iron Goods Co., hinges, 12.00; Hose Hardware Co., paint, etc., 26.85; International Varnish Co., Ltd., paint, 125.68; Kelly & Kimberley, plastering, repairing roof, etc., 221.68; Lindstrom & Nilson, putting on storm windows, 13.00; S. Prosick, cleaning chimneys, 11.00; Williams Hardware Co., glass, etc., 69.40. Sundries—cartage, 1.00; express, 2.00; freight, 15.02; petty disbursements, 55.85	646 83

Furniture and Furnishings for the District ($299.75)

H. Cheyne, lamps, etc., 35.80; Grand & Toy, Ltd., steel cabinet, 28.25; A. A. J. Macdonald, garbage cans, etc., 26.75; Steel Equipment Co., Ltd., files, 49.00; Taylor & Tackaberry, shades, 51.45; Williams Hardware Co., lamps, etc., 101.30; petty disbursements, 7.20	299 75

District of Manitoulin

Repairs to Court House, etc. ($289.43)

F. W. Baxter, plumbing supplies, hardware, etc., 258.05; J. L. McKenzie, hardware, etc., 29.13; petty disbursements, 2.25	289 43

Furniture and Furnishings for the District ($58.35)

George & Riching, lumber, 27.70; J. F. Hartz Co., Ltd., scales, 20.50; petty disbursements, 10.15	58 35

District of Muskoka

Repairs to Court House, etc. ($240.24)

Corporation of Bracebridge Power, Light and Water Commission, electric supplies, 17.63; Ecclestone & Bates, Ltd., plumbing repairs, etc., 49.12; Rice Lewis & Son, Ltd., padlocks, 32.90; A. H. Waltenberg, vault floor, 107.00; R. A. Whaley, repairing roof, 14.25; The Whitten Co., Ltd., paint, etc., 11.84; petty disbursements, 7.50	240 24

Furniture and Furnishings ($34.10)

Ontario Reformatory Industries, Guelph, pails, 16.90; petty disbursements, 17.20	34 10

District of Nipissing

Repairs and Alterations, etc. ($781.44)

Bay Electric, wiring, 96.90; Canada Wire & Iron Goods Co., Ltd., steel grills, 42.00; Cochrane-Dunlop Hardware, Ltd., culvert pipes, etc., 101.49; A. N. Fenn, lamps, 25.65; E. Finnigan, placing grilles over windows, 27.00; H. Gomoll, repairs to steps, 65.00; A. G. Hume, decorating, 112.70; Jeffrey & Stevens, doors, iron grille, 100.06; J. M. MacPherson, plumbing repairs, 142.00; Mason & Campbell, plumbing supplies, 34.01; Sime Plumbing Co., grates, etc., 16.00; petty disbursements, 18.63	781 44

Furniture and Furnishings ($141.36)

Cochrane-Dunlop Hardware, Ltd., hardware, etc., 113.46; V. K. Polk, lamps, etc., 23.76. Sundries—cartage, 1.00; express, 1.40; freight, 1.74	141 36

Salary of Caretaker, North Bay ($1,200.00)

Geo. Hooey	1,200 00

District of Parry Sound

Repairs and Alterations, etc. ($425.24)

A. N. Fenn, hardware, 30.01; W. H. Ferrar, contract, wall and steps, 30.00; Hardie Bros., plumbing supplies, etc., 126.93; Geo. Hull, repairs to ceiling, 18.00; International Varnish Co., Ltd., paint, 16.17; J. C. Moffatt, plumbing supplies, etc., 17.75; J. D. Ryder, repairing lights, etc., 23.75; A. Wright, shingling, 111.00. Sundries—cartage, 5.80; express, 1.35; petty disbursements, 44.48	425 24

Maintenance and Repairs of Government Buildings—Continued

District Buildings—Continued

District of Parry Sound—Continued

Furniture and Furnishings ($64.20)

A. N. Fenn, hardware, etc., 24.15; A. Logan, shades, 11.35; McFarlane Manufacturing Co., Ltd., ladder, 10.80; A. W. Wood, tables and benches, 17.00. Sundries—freight, .90 .... 64 20

District of Rainy River

Repairs and Alterations ($608.26)

J. East Co., Ltd., plumbing supplies and repairs, 577.12; Fort Frances Pulp & Paper Co., Ltd., manhole gaskets, 15.84; petty disbursements, 15.30 .... 608 26

Furniture and Furnishings ($119.40)

Canadian Flag Manufacturing Co., flag, 16.00; John East Co., Ltd., heater, lamps, 68.00; Gillmor & Noden, pails, 10.05; Wells Hardware Co., Ltd., hardware, lamps, etc., 25.35 .... 119 40

District of Sudbury

Repairs and Alterations ($832.90)

Cochrane-Dunlop Hardware, Ltd., paint, scales, etc., 163.91; Duncan Construction Co., Ltd., repairing steps, etc., 40.00; Edward Grain Co., fertilizer, 120.00; Evans Co., Ltd., cement, etc., 93.59; D. S. Humphrey, repairs, electric supplies, etc., 297.58; Steele-Briggs Seed Co., Ltd., grass seed, etc., 73.90; Sudbury Construction Co., Ltd., furnace grates, 40.00. Sundries—cartage, 2.46; freight, 1.46 .... 832 90

Furniture and Furnishings ($293.55)

Cochrane-Dunlop Hardware, Ltd., dishes, etc., 140.72; Grand & Toy, Ltd., book cases, etc., 22.00; J. F. Hartz Co., Ltd., scales, etc., 59.60; D. S. Humphrey, ash cans, etc., 52.30; Taylor-Forbes Co., Ltd., lawn mower, 10.60. Sundries—cartage, 1.33; freight, 7.00 .... 293 55

District of Temiskaming

Repairs and Alterations ($517.31)

Canada Wire & Iron Goods Co., screens, 79.00; Canadian General Electric Co., Ltd., electric supplies, etc., 20.92; Canadian Industries, Ltd., floor paint, 56.84; Hill-Clark-Francis, Ltd., lumber, etc., 26.60; International Varnish Co., Ltd., wall paint, 101.18; Jas. Isherwood, shelving, 36.60; Norfolk and Rochester Hardware Co., Ltd., hardware, etc., 121.67; Porcupine Hardware & Furniture, hardware, 19.15; Geo. Taylor Hardware, Ltd., drip trap, 11.50. Sundries—freight, 8.32; petty disbursements, 35.53 .... 517 31

Furniture and Furnishings ($464.37)

J. F. Hartz Co., Ltd., glass, etc., 19.00; Norfolk and Rochester Hardware Co., Ltd., hardware, etc., 27.73; Northern Ontario Power Co., Ltd., lamps, etc., 16.78; Ontario Reformatory Industries, Guelph, cots, 360.00. Sundries—express, 1.50; freight, 28.43; petty disbursements, 10.93 .... 464 37

Salary of Caretaker, Ontario Government Building, New Liskeard ($720.00)

Horace Royce 720 00

District of Thunder Bay

Repairs and Alterations ($1,061.20)

Dunn Hardware Co., Ltd., paint, etc., 40.69; Fallis-Foote Co., hardware, etc., 262.11; Fort William Window Cleaning Co., cleaning sash, etc., 26.22; H. Kalliner, lumber, 18.00; Lakehead Engineering Co., plumbing repairs, 28.25; A. MacFadyen, repairing windows, etc., 19.55; J. C. McRae, plumbing repairs, 16.25; Mahon Electric Co., Ltd., repairs to lights, etc., 35.07; Port Arthur Public Utilities Commission, telephone service, 50.00; Port Arthur Shipbuilding Co., Ltd., heater, 192.62; Sime Plumbing Co., repairs to toilet, shower, etc., 96.29; Steele-Briggs Seed Co., Ltd., seed, plants, 31.95; Thunder Bay Lumber Co., Ltd., lumber, 13.60; Wells & Emmerson, explosives, 20.70; Western Engineering Service Co., Ltd., repairing railing, 80.00. Sundries—cartage, 76.50; express, 4.05; petty disbursements, 49.35 .... 1,061 20

Maintenance and Repairs of Government Buildings—Continued

District Buildings—Continued

District of Thunder Bay—Continued

Furniture and Furnishings ($305.44)

Dunn Hardware Co., Ltd., spoons, lamps, etc., 15.10; Fallis-Foote Co., hardware, etc., 122.06; Grand & Toy, Ltd., desk, etc., 36.50; Ingram & Bell, Ltd., surgical supplies, 78.50; Mahon Electric Co., Ltd., lamps, 53.28........ 305 44

To Provide for Repairs and Installation of Boilers and Heating Plants etc., in Districts ($759.32)

Algoma.

Keyes Hardware, Ltd., repairing boilers, etc., 83.60; J. McLeod, repairing steam main, 21.50; Northern Foundry & Machine Co., Ltd., grate bars, 13.13; Jas. Robertson Co., Ltd., steam heating supplies, 13.81; petty disbursements, 1.00... 133 04

Kenora.

Taylor-Forbes Co., Ltd., grates........ 7 64

Sudbury.

Duncan Construction Co., Ltd., erection of brick chimney, 180.00; D. S. Humphrey, repairs to water pump, etc., 37.03, petty disbursements, 7.40....... 224 43

Thunder Bay.

T. Critall, repairing boilers, 176.45; Fallis-Foote Co., fire bars, etc., 18.00; J. C. McRae, repairing boiler, etc., 157.26; Mahon Electric Co., Ltd., installing lightning rods, 40.50; petty disbursements, 2.00........ 394 21

District Buildings........$12,070 38

MISCELLANEOUS

Salaries ($26,049.31)

Name	Position	Period	Amount
S. J. Spall	Superintendent of Construction	12 months	3,000 00
John M. Philip	" "	12 "	2,700 00
C. B. Medley	" "	12 "	2,550 00
F. E. Joselin	Clerk of Works	12 "	2,000 00
S. J. Vance	" "	12 "	2,000 00
George Moses	" "	12 "	1,900 00
F. W. Norman	Clerk and Timekeeper	12 "	1,600 00
L. D. Brown	Plumber	12 "	2,000 00
A. Pellow	"	11⅓ "	1,699 31
A. Chandler	"	12 "	1,800 00
F. G. Stroud	Head Electrician	12 "	2,400 00
J. Sharp	Inspector of Steam Boilers and Heating Engineer	12 "	2,400 00

Services, Travelling and Other Expenses ($7,721.33)

Travelling Expenses, $5,475.81.

L. D. Brown, 70.74; M. J. Brown, 6.85; H. Conlan, 6.20; P. Colter, 534.24; D. M. Hughes, 104.90; W. Johnston, 19.93; E. R. Livingston, 470.20; C. B. Medley, 453.64; F. Meigh, 159.32; G. Moses, 10.80; J. M. Philip, 589.86; A. E. Putsey, 388.20; C. Radford, 555.58; Jas. Robertson, 14.05; J. Sharp, 713.55; T. Sims, 328.67; S. J. Spall, 520.96; A. Stevenson, 14.58; F. G. Stroud, 398.24; H. Walsh, 80.95; F. C. Whatmough, 9.75; S. Wood, 24.60........ 5,475 81

Miscellaneous $2,245.52.

Department of Highways, auto and truck service, 2,243.52; Postmaster, 2.00.. 2,245 52

Contingencies ($39.10)

Aikenhead Hardware, Ltd., vises, 20.16; Architectural Bronze & Iron Works, belt hooks, 16.00. Sundries—petty disbursements, 2.94........ 39 10

Motion Picture Studio, Trenton, Repairs and Incidentals ($351.58)

Allore Lumber Co., lumber, 13.50; Canada Wire & Cable Co., Ltd., wire, 32.76; Canadian General Electric Co., Ltd., electric supplies, 20.38; Pyrene Manufacturing Co. of Canada, Ltd., extinguishers, 24.30; Robbins & Meyers Co. of Canada, Ltd., motor, 49.68; J. S. Stacey, repairing boiler, 49.00; H. Strong, wire, lath, etc., 150.00. Sundries—petty disbursements, 11.96........ 351 58

Maintenance and Repairs of Government Buildings—Continued

Miscellaneous—Continued

Government Building, Exhibition Park, Preparing and Installing Exhibits, etc. ($11,420.91)

Acton Tool & Stamping Co., Ltd., boxes, 29.40; Aulcraft Paints, Ltd., paints, 29.63; Aikenhead Hardware, Ltd., hardware, 26.15; Bell Telephone Co., rental, 22.21; tolls, .60; H. C. Burton & Co., lamps, 159.36; Canadian Laboratory Supplies, Ltd., electric supplies, 77.00; Treasurer, Canadian National Exhibition, electrical services, wages, etc., 1,156.60; Consolidated Plate Glass Co., Ltd., glass, 10.23; Hydro-Electric Power Commission, inspection of electrical work, 16.00; International Varnish Co., Ltd., paint, 10.82; R. Laidlaw Lumber Co., Ltd., lumber, 207.83; Masco Co., Ltd., electric supplies, 413.83; Pay list, wages of men, 1,946.85; W. H. Price, painting, 524.40; Ramsay Contracting Co., floor, 332.00; Noble Scott Co., Ltd., booklets, 6,000.00; The Robert Simpson Co., Ltd., removing and packing decorations, etc., 441.26. Sundries—freight, 2.45; petty disbursements, 14.29 .... 11,420 91

Insurance, Including Installation of Lightning Rods ($9,886.78)

Sundry Insurance Premiums—Canadian Fire Insurance Co., 84.00; Central Agencies, 33.00; M. M. Clancy & Sons, 400.00; Consolidated Fire & Casualty Insurance Co., 75.00; Davidson's Agency, Ltd., 172.48; K. R. Galbraith, 342.50; John Gouinlock & Son, 70.00; J. F. Gray, 132.25; Grenville Patrons Mutual Fire Insurance Co., 43.50; S. H. Guest & Son, 786.00; W. N. Harrison, 180.00; M. Hook, 93.75; Jones & Johnston, Ltd., 252.00; McKee & Farrar, 84.00; E. L. McLean, Ltd., 142.88; P. S. Maule, 131.50; Elliott Maynard & Co., 555.84; Mitchell & Ryerson, 91.48; Jno. Moon, 77.00; H. A. Morine, 49.00; Muntz & Beattie, Ltd., 123.60; Murray & Co., 468.75; Mutual Life Assurance Co. of Canada, 163.16; Thos. R. Orr, 967.98; G. F. Perley & Co., 210.00; Perth Mutual Fire Insurance Co., 66.00; Portage la Prairie Mutual Insurance Co., 75.00; Prudential Assurance Co., Ltd., 1,827.00; Royal Insurance Co., Ltd., 93.75; L. J. Salter and H. Watson, 218.50; Alfred W. Smith, Son & Ridout, Ltd., 132.25; Smith & Walsh, Ltd., 491.85; Walter Stewart, 170.75; Sun Insurance Office, Ltd., 252.00; Jno. Sutherland & Sons, Ltd., 376.66; A. E. Wilson & Co., Ltd., 460.15 .... 9,893 58

Less refund, H. A. Stringer & Co., Ltd. 6 80

9,886 78

Local Improvement Taxes ($4,558.99)

Town of Cochrane, 200.00; City of Peterborough, 227.16; Township of Scarborough, 4,131.83 .... 4,558 99

Sewage Experimental Station, Toronto ($129.05)

Consumers' Gas Co., installing boiler, etc., 12.00; Pay list, wages of men, 65.45; Rice Wire Works, wire guards, 12.00; W. Williamson Lumber Co., Ltd., lumber, 39.60 .... 129 05

No. 110 University Avenue, Toronto, Repairs, Alterations, Painting and Incidentals ($7,932.01)

F. Armstrong Co., Ltd., plumbing supplies, 370.28; Baines & David, Ltd., iron, 112.98; Canada Paint Co., Ltd., paint, etc., 17.28; Canada Wire & Cable Co., Ltd., wire rope, 63.90; Canadian Elevator Equipment Co., Ltd., brake coils, 15.60; Canadian General Electric Co., Ltd., electrical supplies, 24.36; Canadian Johns-Manville Co., Ltd., wire, etc., 56.78; W. E. Dillon Co., Ltd., repairs to windows, 30.00; Dominion Oxygen Co., Ltd., oxygen, 20.10; Empire Brass Manufacturing Co., Ltd., plumbing supplies, 13.93; Factory Equipment, Ltd., insulation, 11.15; W. J. Hynes, plastering, 587.00; John Inglis Co., Ltd., contract re boilers, etc., 1,814.62; A. S. Leitch Co., Ltd., plates, 32.60: S. McCord & Co., Ltd., sand, stone and cement, etc., 419.38; Thos. Meredith & Co., Ltd., nails, etc., 28.24; Pay list, wages of men, 3,817.79; Malcolm Sinclair & Co., Ltd., paint, etc., 24.93; Sundry newspapers, advertising re tenders, 88.70; Teagle & Son, rental of tarpaulin, 39.50; Turnbull Elevator Co., Ltd., cables, 115.78; W. Williamson Lumber Co., Ltd., lumber, 202.17. Sundries—petty disbursements, 24.94 .... 7,932 01

Miscellaneous $68,089.06

Total Repairs and Maintenance, Government Buildings.... $583,066 18

PUBLIC WORKS AND BRIDGES

Lockmasters, Bridge Tenders, Caretakers, Etc.

Salaries ($4,769.00)

E. M. Davidson	Lockmaster, Port Carling	12 months	600 00
R. Rowe	" Huntsville	12 "	480 00
F. Stewart	" Magnetawan	12 "	480 00
Ronald Brown	Assistant Lockmaster, Port Carling	4 5/6 "	272 00
John McClintock	" " " "	2 1/6 "	112 00
W. Gray	Bridge Tender, Ryerson	12 "	600 00
J. Lewis	" " Huntsville	12 "	480 00
E. Cox	" " Port Sandfield	12	400 00
Colin Campbell	" " Indian Point	12 "	75 00
T. Mason	Caretaker, Bala	12	300 00
D. J. McRae	" Deer Lake Dam	12	300 00
Chas. Tilson	" Ahmic	12	160 00
C. Crawford	" Port Sydney	12	150 00
R. Richards	" Baysville	12	150 00
A. J. Bowland	" Wahnapitae	12	100 00
D. Hutcheson	" Dryden Dam	12 "	75 00
F. VanKoughnet	" Crane Lake	12	25 00
H. Ditchburn	Gauge Reader, Gravenhurst	12	10 00

Maintenance of Locks, Dams, Bridges, Dredging, etc. ($12,782.97)

Camp Supplies and Equipment.

Bracebridge Garage, gas, etc., 159.91; Burton's Service Station, gas and oil, 247.35; Captain J. H. Campbell, wood slabs, 204.75; Canadian Industries, Ltd., paint, 50.00; Clark & Brown, electrical supplies, 110.99; J. E. Clement, gas and oil, 23.40; Cochrane-Dunlop Hardware, Ltd., hardware, battery, etc., 10.96; Dept. of Highways, gas, etc., 11.90; V. Einarson, gas and oil, 46.76; W. Fowler, cordwood, 200.25; Gravenhurst Hardware Co., Ltd., hardware, 36.21; Hare Bros., provisions, 49.04; Hern Hardware, Ltd., hardware, 46.19; Kahshe Service Station, gas, etc., 39.99; P. A. Kellar, gas, etc., 25.28; Wm. Kennedy & Sons, Ltd., gear, 15.35; Jno. Lupien, hardware, 27.06; Geo. McCulley, provisions, 58.86; McJannett Ltd., provisions, 108.76; H. Martin, milk and butter, provisions, etc., 55.80; Milne's Garage, gas, oil, etc., 130.04; Mosley's Garage, gas and oil, 54.14; Muskoka Foundry, Ltd., frames and clamp covers, etc., 35.10; Muskoka Garage, gas, oil, etc., 92.37; W. J. Passmore, provisions, 136.56; W. Richards, provisions, 91.15; J. Robinson, hardwood, 35.00; Jas. I. Simpson, gas, etc., 16.89; A. Stephen, provisions, 24.99; Sundridge Garage, gas, etc., 18.80; The Whitten Co., Ltd., hardware, lime, etc., 173.56. Sundries—petty disbursements, 149.29 .... 2,486 70

Lumber and Timber.

Claude J. Austin, 133.00; Barry's Bay Lumber Co., Ltd., 42.60; Bates Bros., 16.58; Lake of Bays Bus and Mail Service, Baysville, 36.36; Geo. Boyle, 24.75; Canadian Timber Co., Ltd., 65.16; F. Cherney, 13.79; Jos. Degagne, Jr., 20.16; C. R. Dunne, 13.15; Fassett Lumber Corporation, 10.92; J. E. Finlay & Sons, 117.03; T. J. Gorra, 44.00; B. M. Gray, 31.50; Alex. Guillemette, 10.80; Hawke Lake Lumber Co., Ltd., 230.09; Huntsville Planing Mills, 17.09; L. Hutchinson, 57.00; J. Ilan, 53.57; Wm. F. Krieger, 20.00; H. Langford, 52.00; P. Losch, 12.20; Thos. Madigan, 23.00; Mickle, Dyment & Son, Ltd., 27.25; W. M. Miller, 46.50; Northern Planing Mills, Ltd., 465.03; Ontario Hospital, Penetanguishene, 400.00; Fred Quinn, 38.10; J. Rankin, 36.00; Ed. Roy, 24.00; J. W. Sanderson, 31.68; J. T. Shaw & Son, 15.00; Standard Chemical Co., Ltd., 12.02; Mark Taylor, 77.00; W. G. Tough, 79.75; Utterson Lumber Co., 11.50; A. H. Vigrass, 63.84; Thos. White, 42.30; L. W. Woodruff, 20.30. Sundries—petty disbursements, 26.89.... 2,461 91

Structural Steel, Wages, etc.

The B. Greening Wire Co., Ltd., 655.76; Pay list, wages of men, 6,161.43........ 6,817 19

Travelling Expenses.

W. Lowe, 28.92; T. J. Paget, 17.70 .... 46 62

Miscellaneous.

D. A. Barker, repairs to truck, 23.03; E. S. Barr & Sons, rental of car and truck, 16.85; The Bell Telephone Co. of Canada, tolls, 14.71; E. Brewer, repairs to truck, 24.50; W. G. Callacott, removing logs, 73.50; Daley Bros., electric light, 28.00; D. Davis, sawing, 16.00; Dept. of Highways, towing truck, 25.11; Gravenhurst Electric Light and Water Commission, light service, etc., 37.72; Gordon Hill, board of men, 11.90; Hydro-Electric Power Commission of Ontario, lighting

Public Works and Bridges—Continued

Maintenance of Locks, Dams, Bridges, Dredging, etc.—Continued

Miscellaneous—Continued

locks, etc., 361.53; Kahshe Lake Hotel, board of men, 50.40; Milne's Garage. repairs to car, etc., 24.16; Pakesley Lumber Co., Ltd., repairs to dam, 121.46; Sundries—cartage, 9.25; express, 2.56; freight, 57.06; postage, 11.00; petty disbursements, 61.81 .... 970 55

Surveys and Inspections ($3,725.00)

Services and Travelling Expenses.

Wm. Anderson, services, 84.50; C. H. Jermey, services, 130.00; expenses, 31.51; Wm. Lowe, expenses, 53.47; J. A. Michaud, expenses, 16.50; W. C. Millar, services, 424.20; expenses, 2.25; D. Mitchell, services, 301.05; J. J. Morris, services, 32.50; T. J. Paget, services, 24.75; expenses, 14.91; W. W. Pringle, services, 395.35; expenses, 104.17; L. A. Pritchard, services, 705.50; J. O. Rochefort, services, 423.40; expenses, 95.99; W. E. Wiggins, services, 725.50; expenses, 66.10 .... 3,631 65

Miscellaneous.

The Bell Telephone Co. of Canada, tolls, 2.40; Canadian Inspection & Testing Co., Ltd., testing cement, 64.00. Sundries—postage, 25.50; telegrams, 1.45 .... 93 35

Equipment, Instruments, Machinery, Scows, Boats, Rubber Boots, Motor Trucks and Cars ($2,010.80)

Blackburn Auto Electric Service, battery, 11.95; Bracebridge Garage, repairs to truck, etc., 35.53; Canadian Fairbanks-Morse Co., Ltd., parts for meter, pulley, etc., 91.62; Dept. of Highways, auto service, etc., 479.22; Dominion Rubber Co., Ltd., rubber boots, etc., 81.42; Thos. E. Henry, truck, 1,000.00; London Concrete Machinery Co., Ltd., piston rings, repairs to gas engine, hose, etc., 46.40; Milne's Garage, repairs to truck, 17.03; Mussen's, Ltd., button head snaps, 19.80; S. W. Revell, rubber boots, 17.90; Jas. I. Simpson, repairing truck, 18.65; Sterling Bros., Ltd., rubber boots, 67.07; Wettlaufer Machine Co., pinion, 12.00; The Whitten Co., Ltd., spark plugs, etc., 15.70; Woodman & Ross, repairs to truck, 43.59. Sundries—petty disbursements, 52.92 .... 2,010 80

Wages and Expenses of Supervising Foreman ($1,608.60)

Wm. Lowe, wages, 1,578.50; travelling expenses, 30.10 .... 1,608 60

MUNICIPAL BRIDGES ($95,304.06)

Astorville Culvert, Nipissing—Burlington Steel Co., Ltd., steel, 14.63; Canadian Timber Co., Ltd., lumber, 25.50; pay list, wages of men, 212.50; Mrs. H. Rochefort, board, 50.00; A. Rogers, Ltd., cement, 149.33. Sundries—freight, 8.94; petty disbursements, 4.50 .... 465 40

Balsam Road Culvert, Hagerman—The B. Greening Wire Co., Ltd., guard rail wire 15 35

Barry's Bay Culvert, Renfrew—Pedlar People, Ltd., culvert 352 00

Beard's Creek, Medonte—Dominion Bridge Co., Ltd., posts, 18.18; Pay list, wages of men, 21.00; Steel Co. of Canada, Ltd., steel, 20.66 .... 59 84

Beaudry, Mayo—Freight 9 10

Beaumaris, Muskoka.—Northern Planing Mills, Ltd., lumber 316 75

Beaver Creek—Pay list, wages of men 250 00

Beckett's, Tay.—H. Beckett, gravel, 26.70; Mrs. H. Beckett, board, 10.85; Imperial Oil, Ltd., gasolene, etc., 59.50; MacNab & Sons, hardware, 29.09; Pay list, wages of men, 829.99; Alfred Rogers, Ltd., cement, 369.25; Steel Co. of Canada, Ltd., steel and wire, 87.41; Switzer Planing Mills, lumber, 57.34; Sundries—express, 1.30; freight, 15.28; petty disbursements, 12.75 .... 1,499 46

Bentley, Dungannon.—M. Churcher, cedar, 28.00; Pay list, wages of men, 224.65 .... 252 65

Black Creek, Strong.—S. Cottrell, rent, etc., 31.71; Dominion Bridge Co., Ltd., tees, 33.00; H. Genna, timber, etc., 21.00; A. E. Johnston, provisions, etc., 78.66; W. J. Kent Estate, lumber, 36.25; D. R. Kidd, cement, etc., 315.06; W. Lang, provisions, 37.27; Pay list, wages of men, 467.19; Sundridge Garage, gas, etc., 34.63. Sundries—freight, 3.77; petty disbursements, 7.65 .... 1,066 19

Public Works and Bridges—Continued

Municipal Bridges—Continued

Black Donald Road Culvert.—Pay list, wages of men, 97.00; Pedlar People, Ltd., culvert, 571.24	668 24
Blythfield Culvert, Renfrew.—Canada Ingot Iron Co., Ltd., culvert, 214.80; Pay list, wages of men, 120.55	335 35
Britannia Culvert, Brunel.—Canada Ingot Iron Co., Ltd., culvert, 179.00; Pay list, wages of men, 252.20	431 20
Boardbent, McKellar.—Canadian Industries, Ltd., paint, 25.00; A. N. Fenn, hardware, 28.55; Gibson Garage, gas and oil, 31.60; David Magee, gravel, 12.75; Pay list, wages of men, 693.50; Pedlar People, Ltd., steelcrete, 44.56; Alfred Rogers, Ltd., cement, 357.50; petty disbursements, 4.14	1,197 60
Brown Creek, Abinger.—Pay list, wages of men, 362.25; J. A. Pringle, cement, 85.85; V. Wienecke, lumber, 20.00; petty disbursements, 16.40	484 50
Brudenell, Killaloe Road Culverts.—Pay list, wages of men	201 00
Bucks, Sherwood.—S. Matcheski, lumber, 20.00; Pay list, wages of men, 331.50	351 50
Buck River, Stisted.—Pay list, wages of men, 368.00; Steel Co. of Canada, Ltd., wire, 153.96. Sundries—freight, 29.80; petty disbursements, 5.56	557 32
Byers, Hagarty.—Burlington Steel Co., Ltd., steel, 17.63; Dominion Bridge Co., Ltd., tees, 22.00; Imperial Oil, Ltd., gasoline, 10.80; Pay list, wages of men, 672.41; Pedlar People, Ltd., culvert, 70.46; J. Price, lumber, 109.51; J. M. Roche, cement, 338.40; Scott Hardware, wire and nails, 10.75; A. Shulist, lumber, 40.00. Sundries—freight, 21.62	1,313 58
Callendar Culvert, Parry Sound.—Geo. K. Morrison, hardware	17 76
Cardwell Township, Culverts.—H. Middlebrook, lumber, 31.20; Northern Planing Mills, Ltd., lumber 23.27; Pay list, wages of men, 608.80; Alfred Rogers, Ltd., cement, 239.63; Steel Co. of Canada, Ltd., steel, 26.93; petty disbursements, 14.00	943 83
Christie Road, Foley.—Dominion Bridge Co., Ltd., steel, 122.00; A. N. Fenn, hardware, 28.66; J. R. Harrop, travelling expenses, 22.00; T. C. McNaught, timber, 89.60; Mrs. J. McRoberts, board, 167.00; Pay list, wages of men, 544.29; M. Rogers, lumber, 38.00; petty disbursements, 17.24	1,028 79
Coburn Bridge, Alice.—Pay list, wages of men	45 50
Cole's, Anglesea.—John Bishop, gravel, 16.60; Burlington Steel Co., Ltd., steel, 14.89; Canada Cement Co., Ltd., cement, 239.63; Dominion Bridge Co., Ltd., tees, 37.14; J. D. Flake, lumber, 53.75; Pay list, wages of men, 453.75; J. A. Pringle, gasolene, etc., 47.50; Steel Co. of Canada, Ltd., steel, 33.19; Geo. W. Wood, gas, repairs, 47.65. Sundries—freight, 11.58; petty disbursements, 5.47	961 15
Cole, Hagarty.—J. G. Kuehl, lumber, etc., 22.67; Pay list, wages of men, 251.00; R. G. Reinke, Ltd., cement, 83.50; petty disbursements, 5.00	362 17
Cole, Mayo.—Thomas Bronson, lumber, 45.50; Burlington Steel Co., Ltd., steel, 29.97; George Caldwell, gas, 35.61; Dominion Bridge Co., Ltd., tees, 18.81; Pay list, wages of men, 615.80; Sundries—freight, 7.49	753 18
Commanda, Gurd.—D. R. Kidd, hardware, etc., 11.88; G. H. Kinzett, lumber, 52.06; Pay list, wages of men, 237.00; petty disbursements, 19.08	320 02
Coulter Creek, Minden.—H. Coulter, gravel, 36.96; Pay list, wages of men, 171.40; J. Welch, spikes, 30.92; petty disbursements, 8.70	247 98
Dean's, Faraday.—Canada Cement Co., Ltd., cement, 369.25; U. A. Hubbell, lumber, 88.27; P. A. Kellar, gas, etc., 141.49; Pay list, wages of men, 1,335.70	1,934 71
Dennison Creek.—Jas. Dennison, lumber, 43.50; Pay list, wages of men, 437.80; E. A. Rogers, spikes, 2.43	483 73

Public Works and Bridges—Continued

Municipal Bridges—Continued

Dorset Road Culverts, Haliburton.—W. A. Lindop, livery, 12.00; Pedlar People, Ltd., culverts, 558.00	570 00
Doyle's, Brudenell.—P. Doyle, lumber	48 56
Duck Creek, Macauley.—S. Gaido, board, etc., 14.00; Northern Planing Mill, Ltd., lumber, 21.00; Pay list, wages of men, 119.50; Whitten Co., Ltd., nails, 3.45	157 95
Eighteenth Concession, Cardiff.—U. A. Hubbell, lumber, 36.05; E. F. Landry, hardware, 12.00; Pay list, wages of men, 178.80; T. J. Watson, lumber 15.84	242 69
Eighth Line, Bexley.—A. E. Bryant, gas, etc., 53.87; S. Bryant, posts, 12.00; Canada Cement Co., Ltd., cement, 186.75; Dominion Bridge Co., Ltd., tees, 18.20; Kirkfield Hardware, hardware, 11.64; Mrs. W. Olsen, board, 25.00; Pay list, wages of men, 521.50; Steel Co. of Canada, Ltd., steel, 31.66. Sundries—freight, 9.13; petty disbursements, 9.10	878 85
Eleventh Concession, Humphrey.—Burlington Steel Co., Ltd., steel, 33.55; T. J. Paget, travelling expenses, 23.74; Pay list, wages of men, 243.50; Alfred Rogers, Ltd., cement, 190.00	490 79
Enty, Brunel.—Burlington Steel Co., Ltd., steel, 17.46; Pay list, wages of men, 280.40; Alfred Rogers, Ltd., cement, 142.00. Sundries—freight, 11.57	451 43
Factory Hill, Bangor.—Jas. A. Boyle, timber, 42.30; Pay list, wages of men, 216.80	259 10
Fall River, Oso.—W. Balfour, lumber. 216.43; Pay list, wages of men, 256.05; J. A. Pringle, hardware, 6.05	478 53
Ferronia, Chisholm.—Pay list, wages of men	710 70
Ferronia, Widdifield.—Cochrane-Dunlop Hardware, Ltd., hardware, 16.71; Dominion Bridge Co., Ltd., tees, 25.62; N. Falconi, gas, etc., 36.66; L. Kennedy, board, 60.00; Lindsay & McCluskey, Ltd., cement, 62.50; H. Perron, cartage, 24.00. Sundries—freight, 6.50; petty disbursements, 6.16	238 15
Fifth Concession, Eldon.—Pay list, wages of men	45 66
Fifth Concession, Oakley.—Burlington Steel Co., Ltd., steel, 17.37; Canada Cement Co., Ltd., cement, 177.50; Dominion Bridge Co., Ltd., tees, etc., 11.00; Pay list, wages of men, 296.20; Alfred Rogers, Ltd., cement, 142.00; T. Sampson, lumber, 34.26; Whitten Co.,Ltd., hardware, 4.16	682 49
Fork's, Wicklow.—H. Davis, lumber, 16.50; W. J. Davis, lumber, 39.00; P. A. Kellar, provisions, etc., 133.25; C. W. Mullett, explosives, 111.35; Wm. Nieman, lumber, 61.00; Pay list, wages of men, 2,931.55; Pedlar People, Ltd., steelcrete, 10.65; Alfred Rogers, Ltd., cement, 372.75; Steel Co. of Canada, Ltd., steel, 164.87. Sundries—freight, 40.95	3,881 87
Forsyth, Christie.—R. Ford, bolts and wire, 32.02; J. R. Harrop, travelling expenses, 29.83; Pay list, wages of men, 516.02; Reid & Brown Structural Steel Works, Ltd., steel, 188.50; M. Rogers, lumber, 56.90; A. J. Watkinson, lumber, 114.18; Mrs. W. Wilcox, board, etc., 121.00; petty disbursements, 13.71	1,072 16
Fourteenth Concession, Machar.—Pay list, wages of men	102 00
Fourth Concession, Brunel.—Pay list, wages of men	81 20
Fourth Concession Culvert, Draper.—Canada Culvert Co., Ltd., culvert, 260.50; A. McCraken, gravel, 19.50; Pay list, wages of men, 233.00	513 00
Galway Culverts, Peterborough.—Pedlar People, Ltd., culverts	164 40
Gin Creek, Ashby.—B. Barker, lumber, 34.72; E. Brewer, repairs to truck, 13.25; C. H. Caverley, gas, 48.40; J. Demore, gas, etc., 37.40; Dominion Bridge Co., Ltd., tees, 24.72; R. Hannah, gravel, etc., 23.80; Pay list, wages of men, 1,340.50; J. A. Pringle, gas, etc., 39.68; Mrs. R. S. Ready, cartage, 15.00; Steel Co. of Canada, Ltd., wire steel, etc., 64.16. Sundries—freight, 13.58	1,655 21

Public Works and Bridges—Continued

Municipal Bridges—Continued

Grey's Creek, Watt.—Dominion Bridge Co., Ltd., tees, 24.19; Northern Planing Mills, Ltd., lumber, 126.48; Pay list, wages of men, 717.00; Alfred Rogers, Ltd., cement, 239.62; Steel Co. of Canada, Ltd., steel, 29.10; Whitten Co., Ltd., hardware and oil, 12.85	1,149 24
Griffith-Matawatchan Culverts, S. Renfrew.—A. Adams, lumber, 30.00; F. Hiderman, lumber, 20.00; B. Kelly, lumber and gravel, 21.40; J. King, lumber, 48.00; Alex. McPherson, lumber, 12.40; A. Marchand, lumber, 33.10; Pay list, wages of men, 274.00	438 90
Himsworth, Nipissing.—C. McConnell, lumber, 21.20; Pay list, wages of men, 165.50; Purdon's Service Station, gas, 20.30; H. Toeppner, lumber, 14.40; Trout Creek Lumber Co., lumber, 26.06	247 46
Honey Harbor Road Culvert, Baxter.—Pedlar People, Ltd., culvert	53 28
Hurdville, McKellar.—Burlington Steel Co., Ltd., steel, 90.77; A. N. Fenn, hardware, 13.61; R. Ford, hardware, etc., 13.00; A. Hardie, provisions and lumber, 197.05; A. C. Keetch, gasoline, 30.04; Pay list, wages of men, 871.90; Wm. Peck, provisions, 83.64; Mrs. A. Phillips, milk and butter, 11.81; Alfred Rogers, Ltd., cement, 177.50; Taylor-Mark, meat, 26.25. Sundries—freight, 17.55; petty disbursements, 15.25	1,548 37
Hurren, Eldon.—S. Bryant, lumber, 12.00; A. Hurren, board and gravel, 14.00; Kirkfield Garage, gas, oil, etc., 11.24; Pay list, wages of men, 150.75; petty disbursements, 15.58	203 57
Hyde Creek, Denbigh.—Dominion Bridge Co., Ltd., tees, 16.50; J. A. Glaeser, gas and oil, 35.75; Pay list, wages of men, 550.88; J. A. Pringle, cement, etc., 349.31; Steel Co. of Canada, Ltd., 29.68; L. Thompson, gravel, 13.50; petty disbursements, 10.00	1,005 62
Ingoldsby, Minden.—Pay list, wages of men, 243.20; T. Pogue, lumber, 70.00; I. Snell, lumber, 75.60	388 80
Johns, Denbigh.—Dominion Bridge Co., Ltd., tees, 16.50; Pay list, wages of men, 173.75	190 25
Jones, Calvin.—E. Amyot, lumber, 50.83; Burlington Steel Co., Ltd., steel, 37.89; Dominion Bridge Co., Ltd., tees, 18.95; Mrs. E. R. Jones, board, 16.00; J. H. Mulligan, gas, oil, etc., 24.03; Pay list, wages of men, 411.50; H. Perron, gas and cartage, 132.12; Mrs. H. Rochefort, board, 21.25; P. A. Valois, trucking, 37.50	750 07
Kelusky's, Monteagle.—Pay list, wages of men	214 40
Kingston Road, Sheffield.—Burlington Steel Co., Ltd., steel, 41.06; Canada Cement Co., Ltd., cement, 241.87; Carscallen Mills, cement, 24.50; Dominion Bridge Co., Ltd., tees, 18.44; Pay list, wages of men, 650.25; J. A. Pringle, gas, etc., 66.99; W. Redden, gas, etc., 8.54; John Stinson, lumber, 100.80	1,152 45
Lake Dove Culvert, Wilberforce.—Estate of K. S. Barrand, lumber, 13.00; Dominion Bridge Co., Ltd., tees, 18.70; Pay list, wages of men, 669.15; R. G. Reinke, Ltd., explosives, 21.91; Steel Co. of Canada, Ltd., steel, 18.91; petty disbursements, 12.59	754 26
Lake St. Peter, McClure.—D. K. Card, sawing wood, 35.00; Pay list, wages of men, 460.40	495 40
Latchford, Raglan.—Burlington Steel Co., Ltd., steel, 108.22; Canada Cement Co., Ltd., cement, 385.00; Geo. Chisan, lumber, 26.50; Coulas Garage, supplies, 14.20; Dominion Bridge Co., Ltd., angles and bolts, 33.80; P. Gruntz, wood, 32.00; Mrs. P. Helferty, board, 290.00; Imperial Oil, Ltd., gas, 11.16; A. Jessup, lumber, 18.00; D. R. Kidd, gas, etc., 12.06; F. Kreiger & Son, lumber, 104.18; A. E. Lidkie, gas, etc., 10.50; T. J. Paget, travelling expenses, 57.21; V. Lidke, lumber, 10.00; Pay list, wages of men, 1,963.49; J. E. Phanenhaur, lumber, rent of boiler, 86.25; Jas Pilgrim, lumber, 237.60; J. A. Proudfoot, hardware, 79.76; Jas. Sullivan, gravel, 19.30; M. Sullivan, lumber, 151.45; P. J. Windle, lumber, 48.00. Sundries—freight, 109.11; petty disbursements, 36.67	3,844 46

Public Works and Bridges—Continued

Municipal Bridges—Continued

Little Madawaska, Richards.—F. Belaskie, lumber, 68.85; Estate of J. Hazelton, bolts, 12.78; S. J. Kruger, hardware, 11.86; F. Lasenski, lumber, 14.40; I. Smith, lumber, 11.47; petty disbursements, 19.04	138 40
Little Madawaska, Sherwood.—C. D. Murray, explosives, 20.25; Pay list, wages of men, 628.60	648 85
Longchamp.—B. Inkster, lumber, 41.00; Pay list, wages of men, 152.75; petty disbursements, 6.77	200 52
Louis Light, Hungerford.—Burlington Steel Co., Ltd., steel, 64.67; P. A. Hellar, gas, oil, etc., 76.71; petty disbursements, 9.84	151 22
Loveless.—T. P. Dafoe, lumber, 27.15; Pay list, wages of men, 139.40; J. H. Sprackett, lumber, 33.20	199 75
McCue's Creek, Monmouth.—Burlington Steel Co., Ltd., steel, 17.64; Canada Cement Co., Ltd., cement, 186.38; Mrs. C. L. Carey, board, 24.80; Dominion Bridge Co., Ltd., tees, 18.00; J. R. Falconer, gas, 41.37; L. H. Hunter, lumber, 23.85; Pay list, wages of men, 570.25	882 29
McKean's, Strong.—Burlington Steel Co., Ltd., steel, 87.96; A. B. Caldwell, gravel, 20.00; E. M. Caldwell, lumber, 22.00; Canada Cement Co., Ltd., cement, 440.00; Canada Culvert Co., Ltd., culvert, 128.50; D. R. Kidd, hardware, 60.04; E. M. Lueck, lumber, 158.89; T. J. Paget, travelling expenses, 16.82; Pay list, wages of men, 1,878.00; Sundridge Garage, gas and oil, 89.01. Sundries, freight, 69.60; petty disbursements, 12.88	2,983 70
Madill Creek, Glamorgan.—E. S. Barr & Son, gas, 7.35; Burlington Steel Co., Ltd., steel, 20.44; Canada Cement Co., Ltd., cement, 186.37; Dominion Bridge Co., Ltd., tees, 17.99; J. R. Falconer, gas, etc., 55.76; Mrs. A. Hunter & Sons, lumber, 29.76; L. H. Hunter, lumber, 72.83; Pay list, wages of men, 671.25; Mrs. J. Pickens, board, 24.80; Jas. I. Simpson, repairs to truck, 22.07; petty disbursements, 4.50	1,113 12
Malone, Marmora.—G. B. Airhart, lumber, 126.19; Burlington Steel Co., Ltd., steel, 163.03; Canada Cement Co., Ltd., cement, 369.25; Pay list, wages of men, 54.50; Pedlar People, Ltd., steelcrete, 14.77; R. A. Sager, hardware, 27.44. Sundries—freight, 36.65	791 83
Malone, Sheffield.—Pay list, wages of men	783 25
Matchedash, East Simcoe.—Pedlar People, Ltd., culvert, 174.80. Sundries—freight, 32.56	207 36
Medora Culvert.—Canada Culvert Co., Ltd., culvert	465 14
Miller.—F. Kingyens, timber, etc	44 30
Mink Creek, Effingham.—J. D. Flake, lumber, 50.00; Pay list, wages of men, 892.50; J. A. Pringle, hardware, etc., 29.38; S. A. Wheeler, gas, 31.62. Sundries—freight, 6.54	1,010 04
Mississippi, Clarendon.—Canada Cement Co., Ltd., cement, 535.00; W. A. Geddes & Son, lumber, 257.50; E. Olmstead, lumber, 36.00; Pay list, wages of men, 1,835.25; Pedlar People, Ltd., steelcrete, 56.62; J. A. Pringle, steel, etc., 167.62; petty disbursements, 6.75	2,894 74
Mississippi, Mayo.—Pay list, wages of men	1,055 75
Mississippi, Palmerston.—Pay list, wages of men	966 25
Mitchell Creek, Minden.—H. Camen, timber, 30.00; Pay list, wages of men, 145.30	175 30
Monmouth.—J. E. Finlay & Sons, timber, 49.52; M. McCrea, timber, 38.80; Pay list, wages of men, 310.70	399 02

Public Works and Bridges—Continued

Municipal Bridges—Continued

Moore's Falls, Lutterworth.—O. J. Austin & Sons, lumber, 100.00; Canada Paint Co., Ltd., paint, 94.00; S. Bryant, lumber, 196.29; Baines & David, Ltd., steel, 22.38; Canada Cement Co., Ltd., cement, 1,318.75; S. Bryant, lumber and cartage, 135.68; Hopkins Mark Co., Ltd., explosives, 18.45; Dominion Bridge Co., Ltd., tees, 27.50; Mrs. N. Leary, board, 137.00; Le Craw Bros., hardware, gravel, 266.60; S. Martin, meals and gravel, 87.00; Pay list, wages of men, 4,283.75; Pedlar People, Ltd., steelcrete, 86.93; Isaac Sedgewick, lumber, 33.00; J. T. Simpson, repairs to truck, 44.98; Standard Steel Construction Co., Ltd., spans, 2,615.00; J. R. Umphrey, cart hooks, 10.50. Sundries—express, 7.00; freight, 3.34; petty disbursements, 28.46	9,516 61
Morden, Spence.—Dominion Bridge Co., Ltd., tees, 18.44; Pay list, wages of men, 283.50; Alfred Rogers, Ltd., cement, 180.00; Steel Co. of Canada, Ltd., steel bars, 35.53	517 47
Murphy, Spence.—J. H. Blackmore, lumber, 74.24; Burk's Falls Garage, gas, 22.79; Burlington Steel Co., Ltd., steel, 29.52; A. G. Culbert, provisions, 39.51; R. S. Doherty, rent of boiler, 25.00; Dominion Bridge Co., Ltd., tees, 16.50; Jas. E. Glass, gravel, etc., 29.66; Estate of W. G. Kent, lumber, 38.25; Pay list, wages of men, 1,046.89; W. Peck, provisions, 82.70; Alfred Rogers, Ltd., cement, 385.00; J. Spears, lumber, 34.44; R. Tard, hardware, 47.33. Sundries—express, 9.43; petty disbursements, 31.69	1,912 95
Murray, Huntington.—J. Benson, lumber, 11.90; Burlington Steel Co., Ltd., freight, 19.17; Dominion Bridge Co., Ltd., tees, 24.07; Pay list, wages of men, 370.75; J. Robson, lumber, 15.00; R. A. Sager, hardware, 12.13	453 02
Nesbitt's, Minden.—R. Hogg, lumber, 122.71; L. McKnight, lumber, 25.62; Pay list, wages of men, 174.30	322 63
Ninth Concession, Chisholm.—Rochefort Hotel, board	42 50
Ninth Concession, Eldon.—Mrs. R. Bell, board, 15.00; Dominion Bridge Co., Ltd., steel girder bridge, 480.00; Kirkfield Hardware Co., cement, etc., 35.78; D. McDonald, gravel, 14.00; Pay list, wages of men, 254.88; Pedlar People, Ltd., steelcrete, 27.12; petty disbursements, 3.28	830 06
Norway Point, Ridout.—Burlington Steel Co., Ltd., steel, 45.08; Canada Cement Co., Ltd., cement, 355.00; Dominion Bridge Co., Ltd., tees, 38.50; Pay list, wages of men, 500.00; Steel Co. of Canada, Ltd., steel, 161.95. Sundries—freight, 39.59	1,140 12
Oelkie, Alice.—Cochrane-Dunlop Hardware, Ltd., hardware, 13.16; E. J. Foster, spikes and iron, 31.60; B. Greening Wire Co., Ltd., guard rail cable, 14.59; Hamilton Bridge Co., Ltd., steelwork, 813.00; M. Howard, lumber, 74.20; Imperial Oil, Ltd., 37.94; Pay list, wages of men, 733.15; petty disbursements, 19.88	1,737 52
Otter Creek, Huntington.—Dominion Bridge Co., Ltd., structural steel	1,398 00
Paudash, Faraday.—D. Davis, sawing lumber, 28.00; P. A. Kellar, gas, etc., 73.53; C. Maschke, sawing lumber, 12.00; Pay list, wages of men, 780.70; petty disbursements, 6.74	900 97
Raglan Township Culvert, South Renfrew.—Wallace Beaudrie, lumber, 38.95; Corrugated Pipe Co., Ltd., culvert, 596.74; Pay list, wages of men, 144.70; J. Pilgrim, lumber, 35.00	815 39
Rawdon Creek, Huntington.—Dominion Bridge Co., Ltd., tees	24 06
Ryde-Draper, Muskoka.—Northern Planing Mills, Ltd., lumber, 11.01; Mrs. S. Ruttan, board, 20.00; Mrs. W. Ruttan, board, 19.95; petty disbursements, 3.66.	54 62
Salmon River, Sheffield.—Barrett & Sons, rods, etc., 26.30; Carscallen Mills, cement, etc., 214.55; P. J. Hopkins, hardware, 13.79; Pay list, wages of men, 511.50; Pedlar People, Ltd., steelcrete, 40.17; W. B. Richardson, gas, 10.95; Standard Steel Construction Co., Ltd., steelwork, 665.00; J. E. Woodcock, lumber, 55.20; petty disbursements, 19.61	1,557 07

Public Works and Bridges—Continued

Municipal Bridges—Continued

School, Cardiff.—O. Canert, lumber, etc., 17.05; Metallic Roofing Co., of Canada, Ltd., culverts, 96.90; Pay list, wages of men, 352.97	466 92
Scoot River, Anglesea.—J. Demore, cement, etc., 177.11; Dominion Bridge Co., Ltd., structural steel, 259.00; Pay list, wages of men, 886.50; J. A. Pringle, gas, etc., 24.20; C. C. Thompson, gas, etc., 11.17. Sundries—freight, 5.37	1,363 35
Scoot River, Kaladar.—Hamilton Bridge Co., Ltd., steelwork	419 00
Scotch Line, Anson.—Pay list, wages of men, 315.00; L. Pritchard, lumber, 67.38; O. Stamp, lumber, 50.88; petty disbursements, 14.03	447 29
Sebastopol Culvert, South Renfrew.—John Irving, lumber, 23.60; F. Kellar, lumber, 30.00; J. J. Kelly, lumber, 15.00; Pay list, wages of men, 465.50	534 10
Seguin River, Spence.—M. Brown, lumber, 16.00; Burk's Falls Garage, gas, 11.11; Mrs. O. Farrow, meals, etc., 77.08; R. Ford, hardware, 70.16; E. E. Harrop, beef, 32.40; Thos. Hughes, car hire, 18.00; Pay list, wages of men, 1,384.01; W. Peck, provisions, 76.76; Mrs. E. J. Pletzer, provisions and board, 20.78; M. Rogers, lumber, 26.88; J. Stewart, cartage, 18.00; A. H. Vigrass, lumber, 186.34; H. A. Vigrass, provisions, 31.36; petty disbursements, 14.45	1,983 33
Seventh Concession, Oro.—Freight	2 13
Seventh Line, Laxton.—S. Bryant, lumber, etc., 28.32; Canada Cement Co., Ltd., cement, 186.00; Central Garage, trucking, 50.00; Dominion Bridge Co., Ltd., tees, 12.14; H. Hogg, board account, 17.00; Le Craw Bros., hardware, etc., 30.26; Pay list, wages of men, 321.50; Steel Co. of Canada, Ltd., steel, 16.14. Sundries—freight, 2.84; petty disbursements, 5.20	669 40
Sherwood, South Renfrew.—Peter Gutoski, lumber, 35.00; Jno. Norlock, lumber, 27.00; Thos. Norlock, lumber, 27.75; Pay list, wages of men, 589.60; V. Pyslenski, lumber, 24.50; M. Rekaskie, lumber, 15.00; A. Yantha, lumber, 24.50	743 35
Sixteenth Concession, East Ferris.—O. Carriere, lumber, 60.50; Pay list, wages of men, 136.50; T. Turcotte, lumber, 42.60; petty disbursements, 3.80	243 40
Sixth Concession, Orillia.—Pay list, wages of men, 73.35; Amos Train, travelling expenses, 23.80; petty disbursements, 14.99	112 14
Slater's Creek, Brunel.—B. Cottrill & Son, lumber, 43.27; Hern Hardware, Ltd., hardware, 33.67; Northern Planing Mills, Ltd., lumber, 19.45; Ware Bros., provisions, etc., 47.22; petty disbursements, 1.50	145 11
Snake Creek, Raglan.—Adolph Liedje, lumber, spikes, etc., 304.01 Pay list, wages of men, 406.65	710 66
Springtown, Bagot.—Mrs. J. H. Hayward, board, 44.00; A. E. McCrae, burning and cleaning approach, 250.00; A. N. Mousseau, gas, oil, etc., 17.15; M. J. O'Brien, Ltd., boom chains, etc., 24.00; Pay list, wages of men, 237.50. Sundries—freight, 10.20; petty disbursements, 27.07	609 92
Sprucedale, McMurrich.—Dominion Bridge Co., Ltd., steelwork, 124.00; R. Ford, hardware, 11.53; B. Greening Wire Co., Ltd., bolts, etc., 22.98; D. Hall, lumber, 54.40; A. C. Keetch, gas, etc., 16.66; Pay list, wages of men, 474.08; M. Rogers, lumber, 28.00; Sprucedale Garage, bolts, 18.75; Thos. White, lumber and gas, 27.75	778 15
Stormy Lake, Glamorgan.—Freight	1 42
Swamp Creek, Clarendon.—Jas. Derue, gas, etc.	12 20
Tenth Concession, Chisholm.—R. W. Butler, hardware, 26.18; T. A. Butler, trucking, 28.40; Dominion Bridge Co., Ltd., tees, 33.00; W. F. Graff, gravel, 50.00; Pay list, wages of men, 169.75; H. Perron, gas, etc., 57.40; A. Rogers, Ltd., cement, 149.34; Steel Co., of Canada, Ltd., steel, 17.64	531 71

Public Works and Bridges—Continued

Municipal Bridges—Continued

Tenth Concession, Stephenson.—Burlington Steel Co., Ltd., steel, 19.19; Pay list, wages of men, 208.80; Alfred Rogers, Ltd., cement, 142.00; Utterson Lumber Co., lumber, 49.92; petty disbursements, 2.94 .... 422 85

Third Concession, Admaston.—Canada Cement Co., Ltd., cement, 374.50; Dominion Bridge Co., Ltd., tees, 12.65; Herman Kallies, gravel, 17.90; Pay list, wages of men, 654.10; Scott Hardware, Ltd., hardware, 15.10; K. M. Sharp, lumber, 102.00; Steel Co. of Canada, Ltd., steel, 65.02; Sundries—freight, 20.47 .... 1,261 74

Third River Bridge, Carden.—S. Bryant, posts, 12.00; Burlington Steel Co., Ltd., steel, 15.30; Dominion Bridge Co., Ltd., tees, 11.00; S. H. Fox, gasoline, 11.01; Kirkfield Garage, cartage, 10.00; J. A. McGillivray, lumber, 33.38; Pay list, wages of men, 187.00. Sundries—freight, 8.79; petty disbursements, 6.75 .... 295 23

Townline Bridge, Parry Sound.—Pay list, wages of men 99 00

Twelfth Concession, Chisholm.—Dominion Bridge Co., Ltd., tees, 16.50; H. R. Owens, gravel, 50.00; Pay list, wages of men, 225.00; A. Rogers, Ltd., cement, 149.33; Steel Co. of Canada, Ltd., steel, 17.64 .... 458 47

Twin Sisters.—B. Inkster, lumber, 41.00; Pay list, wages of men, 151.80; petty disbursements, 6.50 .... 199 30

Veitches, Watt.—H. Longhurst, gravel 31 50

Walsh Creek, Sebastopol.—H. O'Connor, lumber and gravel, 9.40; Pay list, wages of men, 399.15; R. G. Reinke, lumber and cement, 288.69 .... 697 24

Waubamic, McKellar.—S. Campbell, gravel, 11.90; Burlington Steel Co., Ltd., steel, 64.14; C. Collison, milk and timber, 13.14; A. N. Fenn, hardware, 26.28; Dominion Bridge Co., Ltd., tees, 24.73; A. Hardie, lumber, 16.74; A. F. Kirkham, hardware, etc., 106.53; Pay list, wages of men, 1,041.53; Mrs. A. Phillips, butter and eggs, 22.01; Alfred Rogers, Ltd., cement, 177.50; M. Taylor, provisions, 120.98. Sundries—express, 1.15; freight, 17.23; petty disbursements, 24.80 .... 1,668 66

Wilberforce Culvert.—Pay list, wages of men, 23.40; Pedlar People, Ltd., culvert, 129.20 .... 152 60

Willow Creek, Vespra.—British American Oil Co., Ltd., gas, 16.90; Dominion Bridge Co., Ltd., girder span, 360.00; F. Francom, lumber, 87.00; MacNab & Sons, hardware, etc., 32.02; Pay list, wages of men, 1,217.63; Scott Bros., unloading steel, 17.50; Shell Oil Co. of Canada, Ltd., gas, 16.90; Mrs. Geo. Smith, board, 42.00; Switzer Planing Mills, lumber, 102.84. Sundries—express, .95; petty disbursements, 6.60 .... 1,900 34

Yerkie, Pringle.—G. H. Keinzett, lumber, 23.48; Pay list, wages of men, 219.50; Sundridge Garage, gas, etc., 30.09; Trout Creek Lumber Co., lumber, 32.84; petty disbursements, 7.10 .... 313 01

95,694 46

Repayment on empty sacks returned to Canada Cement Co., Ltd. 390 40

95,304 06

MUNICIPAL DRAINAGE ($22,707.69)

Addington ($2,482.31)
J. Brothers, dynamite, 13.66; Corporation of County of Frontenac, tile, 53.90; Pay list, 2,261.15; J. A. Pringle, cement, etc., 137.42; petty disbursements, 16.18. 2,482 31

Bruce, North ($907.48)
S. Munn, drilling, blasting, etc., 480.23; Pay list, wages of men, 427.25 .... 907 48

Haliburton ($2,492.80)
J. Noble, gravel, 10.70; Pay list, wages of men, 2,470.10; petty disbursements, 12.00 .... 2,492 80

Hastings, North ($2,497.25)
C. W. Mullett, explosives, 16.50; Pay list, wages of men, 2,473.75; petty disbursements, 7.00 .... 2,497 25

Public Works and Bridges—Continued

Municipal Drainage—Continued

Muskoka, ($2,030 96)
Canada Culvert Co., Ltd., culvert, 44.40; J. Kingsborough, explosives, 14.50; Pay list, wages of men, 1,926.16; Whitten Co., Ltd., explosives, 45.90........ 2,030 96

Nipissing ($2,228.43)
Pay list, wages of men........ 2,228 43

Ontario North ($1,497.85)
Pay list, wages of men........ 1,497 85

Parry Sound ($2,372.37)
Pay list, wages of men, 2,358.60; petty disbursements, 13.77........ 2,372 37

Peterborough ($748.25)
M. Allen, lumber, 16.25; Pay list, wages of men, 732.00........ 748 25

Renfrew, North ($900.01)
Pay list, wages of men, 883.01; F. Roney, lumber, 17.00........ 900 01

Renfrew, South ($1,751.35)
C. W. Mullett, explosives, 13.25; Pay list, wages of men, 1,738.10........ 1,751 35

Simcoe, Centre ($1,017.74)
Pay list, wages of men........ 1,017 74

Simcoe, East ($1,396.89)
Pay list, wages of men, 1,384.85; petty disbursements, 12.04........ 1,396 89

Simcoe, West ($384.00)
R. H. Boyd, blacksmithing, 13.00; Pay list, wages of men, 371.00........ 384 00

Grant to the Dominion Government for Hawkesbury-Grenville Inter-Provincial Bridge ($26,067.87)

Department of Public Works, Canada, third and final payment........ 26,067 87

Grant to Bromley-Westmeath Townline Bridge, North Renfrew ($100.00)

Treasurer Township of Bromley........ 100 00

Public Works and Bridges........$169,075.99

PUBLIC BUILDINGS

PARLIAMENT AND DEPARTMENTAL

To Provide Additional Accommodation ($854,276.76)

Acton Tool & Stamping Co., Ltd., box, 14.70; Chas. Adamson, contract, stone figures, 5,350.00; Aikenhead Hardware, Ltd., contract, finishing hardware, drills, 3,868.11; The Alcor Co., electric supplies, 100.32; H. A. J. Aldington, shores, 10.15; Anaconda American Brass, Ltd., copper, 112.30; Architectural Bronze & Iron Works, window sash, 21,017.60; F. Armstrong Co., Ltd., pumbing supplies, etc., 397.06; Art Metrople, tracing cloth, 24.88; Aulcraft Paints, Ltd., paint supplies, 21.41; Baines & David, Ltd., steel, iron, angles, etc., 2,793.62; Balmer & Blakely, plastering, 481.76; Belleville-Sargent Co., Ltd., lock cylinders, 80.00; Jas. Black, hinges and clamps, 99.00; Block Supply Co., Ltd., cinder tile, 8,573.88; Bond Hardware Co., Ltd., lock cylinders, 69.44; Burlington Steel Co., Ltd., steel, 892.88; H. W. Calkins, Ltd., plaster of paris, etc., 94.39; Canada Building Materials, Ltd., grey hydrate, etc., 7,226.97; Canada Cement Co., Ltd., cement, 89.10; Canada Metal Co., Ltd., sheet lead, 1,049.28; Canada Paint Co., Ltd., paint supplies, 29.25; Canada Wire & Cable Co., Ltd., electric supplies, 345.00; Canadian Bridge Co., Ltd., contract, structural steel, 21,549.54; Canadian General Electric Co., Ltd., cutouts and fuses, etc., 4,453.31; Canadian Industries, Ltd., paint, 58.81; Canadian Ornamental Iron Co., Ltd., contract, steel stairs, 8,550.00; Canadian Westinghouse Co., Ltd., cable, 20.87; Chemical Protection Co., contract, installing hold-up equipment, 1,200.00; Clarke, Howe, Waters & Knight Bros., Ltd., doors, trim, etc., 24,400.00; Colville Cartage Co., Ltd., moving machine, 225.00; Concrete Column Clamps, Ltd., shores, 1,468.95; Cooksville Co., Ltd., haydite, lumber, etc., 6,234.51; Corporation of City of Toronto, drain, 390.52; Darling Bros., Ltd., pump repairs, 55.00; Dept. of Highways, gasoline, rental of trucks, etc., 2,710.32; Diamond State Fibre Co. of Canada, Ltd., fibre tube, etc.,

Public Buildings—Continued

Parliament and Departmental—Continued

To Provide Additional Accommodation—Continued

57.82; Dictograph Products Co., Ltd., cable, 23.94; W. E. Dillon Co., Ltd., galvanized iron sleeves, etc., 217.35; Doan Coal Co., Ltd., coal and coke, 240.60; Dominion Bridge Co., Ltd., tees, etc., 167.30; Drummond & Reeves, Ltd., ty-spreaders, etc., 125.35; Dual Mixed Concrete & Materials, Ltd., paristone, 156.49; Dunlop Tire & Rubber Good Co., Ltd., hose, 33.87; T. Eaton Co., Ltd., linoleum, etc., 5,004.05; English Electric Co., transformers, etc., 6,755.00; Fairbank Block & Supply Co., cinderblox, 61.91; Fibre Conduits, Canada, Ltd., electric supplies, 1,009.46; Fiddes & Hogarth, heating contract, 29,193.27; Fox Bros., sand, 110.32; Goldie & McCulloch Co., Ltd., contract vault doors, 13,257.00; W. Graham, manure, 48.00; Francis Hankin & Co., Ltd., contract chimney, 10,527.07; Harkness & Hertzberg, contract, engineering services, 4,052.35; H. S. Howland Sons Co., Ltd., anchors and bolts, etc., 274.46; R. W. Hunt & Co., Ltd., testing cement, 36.00; W. J. Hynes, Ltd., rent of plastering equipment, etc., 709.79; Interlocking Tile Co., Ltd., tile, 416.58; International Varnish Co., Ltd., paint supplies, 106.29; Italian Mosaic & Tile Co., Ltd., contract flooring, 5,396.16; Jackson, Lewis Co., Ltd., contract stone work and supervising services, 150,871.59; King's Printer, 27.44; R. Laidlaw Lumber Co., Ltd., lumber, 2,077.42; Leaside Block & Tile, Ltd., cinder block, 2,462.86; J. Leckie, Ltd., tarpaulins, 117.20; Rice Lewis & Son, Ltd., screws, etc., 12.95; Lowe Bros. Co., Ltd., paint, 21.10; S. McCord Co., Ltd., grey hydrate, etc., 3,741.76; McGregor-McIntyre Iron Works, Ltd., plate covers, etc., 316.00; Alex McKay Co., Ltd., paristone, etc., 197.65; Masco Co., Ltd., electric supplies, etc., 1,623.40; Metallic Roofing Co. of Canada, Ltd., metal lath, etc., 460.59; Milton Brick, Ltd., brick, 1,260.05; W. A. Moffatt & Sons, Ltd., contract roofing, 3,338.00; James Morrison Brass Manufacturing Co., Ltd., plumbing supplies, 83.39; Alex. Murray & Co., Ltd., asphalt, 21.00; National Fireproofing Co., wall fillers, etc., 770.99; Northern Electric Co., Ltd., electric supplies, 203.86; Ontario Reformatory, Mimico, tile, 4,498.84; Ontario Wind Engine & Pump Co., Ltd., galvanized anchors, 245.58; A. B. Ormsby Co., Ltd., fire door, 19.50; Otis-Fensom Elevator Co., Ltd., contract tower elevator, etc., 6,817.00; Patterson Electric, Ltd., contract installing, electric equipment, 400.00; Pay list, wages of men, 247,869.36; Peckover's, Ltd., steel, 76.60; Pedlar People, Ltd., rib fabric, etc., 745.76; W. E. Phillips Co., contract glass, 7,500.00; Powerlite Devices, Ltd., pothead, 11.27; Price & Burton, calcium chloride, 277.84; W. H. Price, lettering doors, 274.65; Provincial Glass Co., contract chipped glass, 1,616.02; Rayner Construction Co., Ltd., contract marble, 50.000,00; Reid & Co., Ltd., lumber, 494.62; Riverdale Lumber Co., Ltd., lumber, 877.87; J. Robertson, travelling expenses, 258.45; The Jas. Robertson Co., Ltd., plumbing supplies, 51.91; A. Rogers, Ltd., cement, 3,880.90; Roofers Supply Co., Ltd., roofing materials, 193.53; Robt. Simpson Co., Ltd., cotton, flashlight, etc., 298.91; Malcolm Sinclair Co., Ltd., paristone, etc., 74.30; H. E. Smith, Ltd., paristone, etc., 857.27; J. B. Smith & Sons, Ltd., lumber, etc., 64.08; C. Smythe, Ltd., sand, 4,018.40; Standard Electric Co., contract electric wiring, 14,100.00; Arthur Stead Cut Stone Co., Ltd., contract stone for tower, 127,884.62; Steel Co. of Canada, Ltd., steel, 1,028.83; Sternson Structural Specialties, Ltd., asphalt waterproofing, etc., 69.96; Sturgeon's, Ltd., hydro salignum, 16.33; Supplies & Insulation, Ltd., cement, 42.73; Sundry newspapers, advertising re tenders, 717.25; D. Telfer, contract inspection of steel, 55.80; travelling, 13.60; Toronto Brick Co., Ltd., brick, etc., 5,011.50; Toronto Hydro-Electric System, removing transformers, etc., 433.03; Trelco, Ltd., paste, 53.25; Tremco Manufacturing Co. of Canada, Ltd., calking compound, 63.69; Truscon Steel Co. of Canada, Ltd., lath and nails, etc., 274.91; Valley City Seating Co., Ltd., contract picture moulding, 2,637.50; Vulcan Asphalt & Supply Co., Ltd., contract floor, 218.40; W. Walker & Son, Ltd., wire, etc., 449.11; W. R. Watson, sanding floors, 72.58; W. Williamson Lumber Co., Ltd., lumber, 137.00. Sundries—cartage, 5.90; express, 7.14; freight, 37.71; petty disbursements, 50.55.................................... 854,449 56

Less refund:

Board of Governors, University of Toronto................ 172 80

854,276 76

Purchase and Installation of Wire Rope Testing Machine, East Block ($15,744.88)

Aikenhead Hardware, Ltd., rope, etc., 21.30; W. T. Avery & Co., Ltd., contract supplying and erecting machine, 13,464.78; Baines & David, Ltd., steel plates, etc., 15.00; Canadian Industries, Ltd., carbon tetrachloride, 69.25; Canadian Laboratory Supplies, Ltd., distillation apparatus, 39.50; Dept. cf Mines, rope test, 10.00; W. E. Dillon Co., Ltd., sliding canopy and cooling tank, 283.00; Flexible Shaft Co., Ltd., furnace, 260.00; Hendrie & Co., Ltd., contract delivering and placing machine, 392.98; Hospital & Kitchen Equipment, Ltd., container,

Public Buildings—Continued

Parliament and Departmental Buildings—Continued

Purchase and Installation of Wire Rope Testing Machine—Continued

25.00; Hoyt Metal Co. of Canada, Ltd., metal, 155.93; Imperial Oil, Ltd., oil, 71.75; John Inglis Co., Ltd., cable babbiting frame, weights, etc., 229.99; R. Laidlaw Lumber Co., Ltd., lumber, 15.33; W. A. Moffatt & Sons, Ltd., bolt seats, etc., 89.94; Herbert Morris Crane & Hoist Co., Ltd., trolley, etc., 170.50; Reid & Brown Structural Steel & Iron Works, Ltd., flooring, etc., 349.00; W. Williamson Lumber Co., Ltd., bench, etc., 73.50; petty disbursements, 8.13	15,744 88

Painting East Block ($4,998.30)

Aulcraft Paints, Ltd., paint, 36.08; Canada Paint Co., Ltd., varnish, etc., 39.03; International Varnish Co., Ltd., paint supplies, 77.58; Lowe Bros. Co., Ltd., paint, 48.97; Pay list, wages of men, 4,614.83; Malcolm Sinclair Co., Ltd., paint supplies, 170.44; petty disbursements, 11.37	4,998 30

Parliament and Departmental Buildings $875,019 94

ONTARIO HOSPITALS

Additions, Alterations and Equipment ($21,141.98)

Cobourg.	
Acme Lighting Products, Ltd., electric fixtures	67 70
Hamilton.	
Empire Brass Manufacturing Co., Ltd., caulking lead	3 25
Kingston.	
S. Hamilton, hose and coupling	7 30
London.	
Bell Telephone Co. of Canada, tolls, 1.80; Canada Culvert Co., Ltd., sewer pipe, 575.00; Clatworthy Lumber Co., Ltd., lumber, 24.67; Dyment-Baker Lumber Co., lumber, 642.91; Gartshore-Thomson Pipe & Foundry Co., Ltd., pipe, 57.00; Hayman & Mills, pipe and cement, 831.75; Hobbs Hardware Co., Ltd., shovels, etc., 160.89; W. J. Howlett, explosives, 45.00; Imperial Oil, Ltd., gasoline, 19.24; G. N. Kernohan Lumber Co., Ltd., lumber, 57.33; Wm. Liley, sand and gravel, 70.00; London Structural Steel Co., Ltd., steel, etc., 16.25; Ontario Farmers Drainage Co., Ltd., claim re artesian well, 736.39; Pay list, wages of men, 16,664.91; A. Train, travelling expenses, 195.13; Jas. Wright & Co., iron, 15.17. Sundries—cartage, 4.00; express, 4.24; petty disbursements, 40.08	20,161 76
Mercer Reformatory.	
Pay list, wages of men	253 40
Mimico.	
Grand & Toy, Ltd., lockers	40 00
Penetanguishene.	
Canada Wire & Cable Co., Ltd., copper wire, 72.72; Canadian Fairbanks-Morse Co., Ltd., gauges, 10.50; Canadian General Electric Co., Ltd., heaters, 4.77; J. E. Desroches, plumbing, 18.68; Empire Brass Manufacturing Co., Ltd., valves, 52.50	159 17
Toronto.	
Sundry newspapers, advertising re tenders	64 80
Whitby.	
Northern Electric Co., Ltd., cable and conduit	384 60

Ontario Hospital, Brockville

Addition to Home for Nurses ($128,994.58)

Adams Furniture Co., Ltd., contract linoleum, etc., 3,462.93; Brockville Public Utilities Commission, electrical supplies, 176.08; H. S. Brown, plumbing supplies, 10.50; Cameron-Borthwick, Ltd., kitchen equipment, 585.00; Canadian Elevator Equipment Co., Ltd., elevator, 3,500.00; Canadian General Electric Co., Ltd., electric supplies, 130.76; Cooksville Co., Ltd., brick, 1,087.50; W. E. Dillon & Co., Ltd., grilles, 34.50; T. Dochart, brick, 98.00; T. Eaton Co., Ltd., kitchen equipment, etc., 5,125.49; J. F. Hartz Co., Ltd., hospital equipment, 215.50; Ingram & Bell, Ltd., surgical supplies, 228.85; C. E. Johnston & Co., shades,

Public Buildings—Continued

Ontario Hospitals—Continued

Brockville—Addition to Home for Nurses—Continued

222.72; McGregor & McIntyre Iron Works, Ltd., coal covers and rings, 31.02; McKinley & Northwood, contract plumbing, 10,395.00; Mercer Reformatory Industries, sheets, etc., 1,666.50; Metal Craft Co., Ltd., hospital equipment, 529.40; Mueller, Ltd., valves, 99.12; National Fireproofing Co. of Canada, Ltd., tile, 903.00; National Sewer Pipe Co., Ltd., pipe, 157.60; Ontario Reformatory, Mimico, tile, etc., 4,060.00; Ontario Hospital, Orillia, Industries, bath towels, 219.00; Ontario Reformatory Industries, Guelph, blankets, 4,942.50; Pay list, wages of men, 2,242.30; J. R. Scalland, travelling expenses, 35.64; Standard Brick Co., Ltd., brick, 2,450.50; Stevens Companies, hospital equipment, 135.07; M. Sullivan & Son, general contract, 72,085.61; Sundry newspapers, advertising re tenders, 108.90; Toronto Lock Manufacturing Co., contract hardware, 2,511.41; Toronto Brick Co., Ltd., brick, 362.50; Vokes Hardware Co., Ltd., hardware, 41.30; P. W. Wilson, contract electric work, 3,300.00; Wright Bros., contract heating etc., 7,594.73; freight, 245.65 .... 128,994 58

Ontario Hospital, Hamilton

New Assembly Hall, including Furniture, Furnishings and Equipment and Expenses in Connection therewith ($29,485.66)

Cassidy's, Ltd., chinaware, etc., 407.23; A. Clark, Ltd., contract plumbing and heating, 7,368.43; Culley Electric Co., contract wiring, 2,627.39; T. Eaton Co., Ltd., table cloths, etc., 1,092.50; Garvin Hardware Co., Ltd., contract hardware, 882.39; General Steel Wares, Ltd., electric range and shelf, 82.85; Heintzman & Co., Ltd., piano and bench, 350.00; Metal Studios, Ltd., contract electrical fixtures, 1,030.47; Wm. Murray, bookcase shelving, 123.00; Ontario Reformatory, Mimico, tile, 474.90; Ontario Reformatory Industries, Guelph, furniture, 1,304.85; Pay list, wages of men, 546.00; G. W. Robinson Co., Ltd., linoleum, 1,030.06; Tope Construction Co., general contract, 9,604.31; Valley City Seating Co., Ltd., benches, 1,965.00; Wright & Noxon, contract preparing drawings, etc., 121.03; Wrought Iron Range Co. of Canada, Ltd., urns and stands, 395.00. Sundries—cartage, 61.00; petty disbursements, 19.25 .... 29,485 66

Ontario Hospital, Kingston

Purchase and Installation of Cold Storage Plant, Machinery, Remodelling of Existing Kitchen Sculleries and Adjacent Rooms and Expenses in Connection therewith ($2,320.75)

Jas. Harris, installing switches, 62.80; Lemon & Sons, contract alterations, 148.90; Simmons Bros., Ltd., contract kitchen equipment, 117.00; Geo. C. Wright, contract alterations, 1,986.00; petty disbursements, 6.05 .... 2,320 75

Ontario Hospital, Mimico

Nurses' Residence, Water Mains, Furniture, Furnishings and Expenses in Connection therewith ($3,676.33)

Adams Furniture Co., Ltd., curtains, 524.50; Canada Building Materials, Ltd., cement, etc., 18.49; J. H. Doughty, Ltd., contract plumbing and heating, 537.99; T. Eaton Co., Ltd., furniture, radio, etc., 1,249.37; Ingram & Bell, Ltd., bed, etc., 266.45; Kelvinator of Canada, Ltd., refrigerator, 315.00; Metal Craft, Ltd., table, etc., 39.50; Pay list, wages of men, 40.20; Robt. Simpson Co., Ltd., shades, etc., 600.40; D. Spence, Ltd., plants, 75.00; petty disbursements, 9.43 .. 3,676 33

Ontario Hospital, Orillia

New Buildings for Patients, Furniture, Furnishings, equipment, etc., and Expenses in Connection therewith ($20,286.93)

Canada Crushed Stone Corporation, Ltd., stone, 27.92; Canadian General Electric Co., Ltd., electric supplies, 36.54; Canadian Westinghouse Co., Ltd., rewinding motor, 52.00; T. Eaton Co., Ltd., toasters, thermos, etc., 1,416.30; General Steel Wares, Ltd., frames for counter, etc., 292.20; A. D. Gibson, quilts, 528.00; Hospital & Kitchen Equipment Co., Ltd., dish wagons, 292.00; Lundy Fence Co., Ltd., contract steel railing, 960.05; MacNab & Sons, hardware, etc., 367.66; Masco Co., Ltd., electric supplies, 16.96; Midland Wood Products, Ltd., screens, 742.62; Geo. B. Meadows, Ltd., hat and coat racks, 325.00; National Locks, Ltd., contract hardware, 511.93; Newton Croxall, Ltd., shades, 1,374.03; Ontario Reformatory Industries, Guelph, benches, etc., 200.00; Pay list, wages of men,

Public Buildings—Continued

Ontario Hospitals—Continued

Orillia—New Buildings for Patients, etc.—Continued

947.30; Ritchie & Mould, connecting dish washer, 44.50; Jas. Robertson Co., Ltd., plumbing supplies, 136.47; Sheppard & Abbott, contract plumbing and heating, 1,921.53; Estate of Geo. Sparrow & Co., food conveyors, etc., 2,197.00; Valley City Seating Co., Ltd., shelving, 1,857.50; E. Webb & Son, contract erection of boys' dormitory, 3,498.03; Wrought Iron Range Co. of Canada, Ltd., warming cabinets, etc., 2,470.00. Sundries—cartage, 38.55; express, 2.87; freight, 19.47; petty disbursements, 10.50 .... 20,286 93

To Complete Nurses' Residence, Furniture, Furnishings and Expenses in Connection therewith ($12,498.38)

T. Eaton Co., Ltd., furniture, linoleum, etc., 4,162.24; Grand & Toy, Ltd., desk, etc., 44.75; MacNab & Sons, electric range, 41.00; Midland Wood Products, Ltd., screens, 434.50; E. N. Moyer Co., Ltd., blackboard, 10.13; Newton-Croxall, Ltd., furniture, etc., 2,352.45; Ontario Electric Construction Co., electric wiring, 179.75; Partridge Sanitary & Heating Engineers, grilles, 46.00; Pay list, wages of men, 390.00; Ritchie & Mould, electric wiring, 10.50; Roelofson Elevator Works, contract electric passenger elevator, 110.00; Ruddy Manufacturing Co., Ltd., cupboard, etc., 490.75; Sheppard & Abbott, contract plumbing and heating, 1,223.81; Standard Garage, kelvinators, 358.00; E. Webb & Son, general contract nurses' residence, 2,534.84. Sundries—cartage, 60.60; express, 4.17; freight, 43.89; postage, 1.00 .... 12,498 38

New Tunnels and Connecting Passageways to New Buildings ($429.48)

E. Webb & Son, contract 429 48

New Buildings for Patients, Furniture, Furnishings and Other Expenses in Connection therewith ($180,923.17)

Dennisteel, Ltd., coat racks, 279.00; T. Eaton Co., Ltd., stoves, dishwashing machines, etc., 962.00; H. S. Fenton, coke, etc., 1,374.69; General Steel Wares, Ltd., counter, etc., 1,902.74; Grand & Toy, Ltd., lockers, 111.00; Grinnell Co. of Canada, Ltd., inserts, 70.00; Italian Mosaic & Tile Co., Ltd., tile, 1,500.00; Lundy Fence Co., Ltd., contract railing, 2,000.00; McGibbon Lumber Co., Ltd., shelving, 1,335.19; Mercer Reformatory Industries, linens, 929.38; Midland Wood Products, Ltd., screens, 797.50; Newton-Croxall, Ltd., pillows, rugs, etc., 1,540.50; Ontario Reformatory, Mimico, brick, etc., 16,462.93; Ontario Electrical Construction Co., contract electric wiring, 185.53; Ontario Reformatory Industries, Guelph, blankets, etc., 8,144.50; Orillia Water, Light & Power Commission, removing poles, 19.33; Partridge Sanitary & Heating Engineers, contract heating, etc., 33,550.00; Pay list, wages of men, 7,008.90; H. A. Raney & Co., bends, 17.60; Ritchie & Mould, laying conduit, 97.00; Stratford Chair Co., desks and chairs, 67.10; Sundry newspapers, advertising re tenders, 99.45; Turnbull Elevator Co., Ltd., contract dumb waiter, 1,200.00; Vokes Hardware Co., Ltd., contract hardware, 1,843.62; E. Webb & Son, contract sidewalks and girls' dormitory, 89,106.86; G. S. Whelpton, contract electric wiring, 8,824.45; Wrought Iron Range Co. of Canada, Ltd., warmers, 1,030.00. Sundries—cartage, 449.15; express, 1.70; postage, 2.00; petty disbursements, 11.05 .... 180,923 17

Water Service, etc. ($104.73)

Orillia Water, Light and Power Commission, testing lines, etc., ... 104 73

Ontario Hospital, Penetanguishene

Building for Criminally Insane Prisoners, Furniture and Furnishings and Other Expenses in Connection therewith ($237,741.82)

C. Beck Co., Ltd., coke, 438.51; Callander Foundry & Manufacturing Co., Ltd., contract fixtures, 950.00; Canada Building Materials, Ltd., salamanders and covers, 98.32; Canadian General Electric Co., Ltd., electric supplies, 387.31; Cassidys, Ltd., dishes, 100.49; T. Eaton Co., Ltd., knives, etc., 369.24; Empire Brass Manufacturing Co., Ltd., plumbing supplies, 29.69; Gartshore-Thomson Pipe & Foundry Co., Ltd., pipe, etc., 75.77; Garvin Hardware Co., contract finishing hardware, 600.00; General Steel Wares, Ltd., mixer, etc., 1,707.74; C. E. Greenan & Co., contract plumbing, 36,566.23; J. F. Hartz Co., Ltd., floor lamp, 13.50; H. G.

Public Buildings—Continued

Ontario Hospitals—Continued

Penetanguishene—Building for Criminally Insane Prisoners, etc.—Continued

Holman, contract, preparing plans, 820.00; Hospital & Kitchen Equipment Co., Ltd., dishwasher, 450.00; A. R. McDonald, stove pipes, etc., 273.07; Mercer Reformatory Industries, sheets, etc., 1,351.90; B. J. Miller & Co., Ltd., contract heating, etc., 13,618.05; Moloney Electric Co. of Canada, Ltd., transformer, 229.51; National Sewer Pipe Co., Ltd., pipe, 736.56; Northern Electric Co., Ltd., electric supplies, 740.25; Ontario Reformatory, Mimico, tile, etc., 15,986.12; Ontario Reformatory Industries, Guelph, chairs, etc., 7,206.36; Patterson Electric Co., contract wiring, 4,897.60; Pay list, wages of men, 14,440.17; Corporation Town of Penetanguishene, gravel, 258.50; Alfred Rogers, Ltd., cement, 512.50; Scholey Construction Co., contract construction of building, 89,416.53; W. F. Smith, architect's fees, 1,750.00; Spencer Foundry Co., Ltd., manhole covers and frames, 137.50; Steel Co. of Canada, Ltd., steel, 150.99; Sundry newspapers, advertising re tenders, 236.20; J. & J. Taylor, Ltd., contract steel cells, 41,500.00; Tessier Planing Mill, sash, etc., 352.85; Toronto Brick Co., Ltd., brick, 57.50; A. Train, travelling expenses, 49.53; Wrought Iron Range Co. of Canada, Ltd., steamtable, etc., 736.00. Sundries—cartage, 249.60; express, 11.47; freight 206.01; postage, 5.33; petty disbursements, 24.92..... 237,741 82

Sewage Disposal Works ($15,550.23)

Burlington Steel Co., Ltd., steel, 111.38; Canada Cement Co., Ltd., cement, 372.75; Gartshore-Thomson Pipe & Foundry Co., pipe, etc., 322.51; Kerr Engine Co., Ltd., valve boxes, 204.60; A. R. McDonald hardware, 558.26; McGibbon Lumber Co., Ltd., lumber, 1,098.93; Midland Engine Works, cutting pipe, etc., 12.13; Midland Wood Products Co., pike pole handles 11.25; National Sewer Pipe Co., Ltd., pipe, 1,349.08; Pay list, wages of men, 8,908.67; Pedlar People, Ltd., steelcrete, 301.61; Penetanguishene Water & Light Commission, lead, 19.00; Alfred Rogers, Ltd., cement, 410.00; Spencer Foundry Co., Ltd., ladder rungs, manhole covers, etc., 422.80; Steel Co. of Canada, Ltd., steel wire, 148.69; Taylor-Forbes Co., Ltd., pipe, etc., 857.96; Tessier Planing Mill, lumber and cement, 221.10; A. Train, travelling expenses, 95.25; Victaulic Co. of Canada, Ltd., couplings, 152.22; J. M. Wallace, cement, etc., 126.20; The E. Dean Wilkes Co., sewage syphon, 126.00. Sundries—cartage, 6.00; express, 3.78; freight, 95.40; petty disbursements, 14.66.............................. 15,950 23

Less lumber sold to Public Works Department for maintenance purposes.. 400 00

15,550 23

Ontario Hospital, Whitby

Storehouse Building, including Equipment ($1,595.22)

Bowra Electric, contract wiring, 176.00; Carew Lumber Co., Ltd., lumber, 68.60; Dept. of Highways, rent of roller, 48.00; T. Eaton Co., Ltd., shades, etc., 400.77; Grand & Toy, Ltd., desks, 53.50; Gurney Scale Co., Ltd., scales, 58.85; Linde Canadian Refrigeration Co., Ltd., refrigeration equipment, 370.00; Estate of Geo. Sparrow & Co., meat hooks, 27.00; J. S. Stacey, contract erection of building, 392.50.. 1,595 22

Ontario Hospital, Woodstock

New Buildings to Accommodate 400 Patients, Furniture, Furnishings and Other Expenses in Connection therewith ($33,459.70)

Bennett & Wright Co., Ltd., contract plumbing, etc., 2,193.37; Boiler Repair & Grate Bar Co., castings, 250.00; Canadian Comstock Co., contract electric wiring, 339.81; Canadian General Electric Co., Ltd., electric supplies, 14.21; Canadian Ice Machine Co., Ltd., contract installation of refrigerating plant, 247.29; E. J. Canfield, dishes, 75.60; Canada Wire & Iron Goods Co., Ltd., fly screens, 983.00; Cassidys Ltd., dishes, etc., 131.65; Clatworthy & Son, Ltd., hangers, 103.50; Darling Bros., Ltd., heating element, 75.00; DeLaval Co., contract steam pasturizer, 80.49; Dennisteel, Ltd., coat racks, 628.65; T. Eaton Co., Ltd., tables, etc., 2,156.20; General Steel Wares, Ltd., bake oven, etc., 2,452.69; Grinnell Co. of Canada, Ltd., plumbing supplies, 18.37; T. Harris, installing stoker equipment, 64.75; Hobart Manufacturing Co., dish rack, 18.13; Jones Bros. & Co., Ltd., barber chairs, 130.00; F. W. Karn, aluminum trays, 36.00; E. Leonard & Son, contract boilers, etc., 454.00; Masco Co., Ltd., electric supplies, 86.98; G. B. Meadows, Ltd., contract coat hangers, 150.00; Ontario Reformatory

Public Buildings—Continued

Ontario Hospitals—Continued

Woodstock—New Buildings to Accommodate 400 Patients, etc.—Continued

Industries, Guelph, furniture, 98.00; Pay list, wages of men, 415.00; Pounder Bros., contract construction of sidewalks, 5,586.03; Rice Wire Works, wire partition, 45.75; Roelofson Elevator Works, contract elevator, 90.00; Schultz Construction Co., contract, general, 7,300.00; Sheppard & Abbott, contract connecting kitchen equipment, 617.95; Robt. Simpson Co., Ltd., kitchen equipment, etc., 1,537,75; Estate of Geo. Sparrow & Co., food trucks, etc., 3,922.90; Stratford Chair Co., desks, etc., 241.00; Sundry newspapers, advertising re tenders, 27.00; Valley City Seating Co., Ltd., shelving, 2,600.00; W. Walker & Son, Ltd., hardware, 160.25. Sundries—cartage, 65.97; freight, 47.31; petty disbursements, 15.10 .... 33,459 70

New Laundry Building, Machinery, Equipment and Expenses Connected therewith ($89,975.78)

Beaver Laundry Machinery Co., Ltd., contract laundry machinery, 12,534.00; Canada Baker-Perkins, Ltd., extractors, etc., 1,068.00; Canadian Laundry Machinery Co., Ltd., ironers, 1,000.00; Cooksville Co., Ltd., tile, 274.05; Long Hardware Co., Ltd., hardware, 616.40; F. B. McFarren Co., Ltd., brick, 250.85; Milton Brick Co., Ltd., brick, 290.00; Ontario Reformatory, Mimico, brick, 6,316.72; Pay list, wages of men, 2,555.00; Pedlar People, Ltd., contract steel shelving, 300.00; Pounder Bros., contract general construction, 40,488.25; Premier Laundry Equipment Co., extractors, 3,600.00; Purdy, Mansell, Ltd., contract plumbing, 5,188.00; Sheppard & Abbott, contract heating, 9,829.25; Sundry newspapers, advertising re tenders, 90.00; Toronto Brick Co., Ltd., brick, 63.08; Turnbull Elevator Co., Ltd., contract dumb waiter, 1,485.00; W. Walker & Son, Ltd., hardware, etc., 27.18; P. W. Wilson, contract electric wiring, 4,000.00 89,975 78

Ontario Hospitals $778,184 74

Reformatories

Ontario Reformatory, Guelph

Additions and Alterations ($570.00).

Laundry, Dairy & Textile Machinery Co., contract laundry equipment 570 00

Industrial Farm, Burwash

New Reformatory Buildings for Men ($32,324.51)

H. Barlow, services as office assistant, 104.17; Burwash Industrial Farm, lumber, 1,712.69; Canada Cement Co., Ltd., cement, 730.00; Canada Paint Co., Ltd., paint, etc., 148.82; Canadian General Electric Co., Ltd., electric supplies, 232.95; Cochrane-Dunlop Hardware, Ltd., hardware, etc., 2,549.09; Dept. of Highways, 3-ton truck, 1,700.00; Dunlop Tire & Rubber Goods Co., Ltd., belting, etc., 173.26; Empire Brass Manufacturing Co., Ltd., bar, plumbing supplies, 162.67; Evans Co., Ltd., lime, etc., 30.65; Fowler Hardware Co., Ltd., beaver board, etc., 23.70; Goodyear Tire & Rubber Co., Ltd., belting, 79.82; International Varnish Co., Ltd., paint, 201.90; King Paving Co., Ltd., pipe, etc., 1,776.00; D. C. Merrill, travelling expenses, 17.50; services as office assistant, 94.62; J. H. Morin & Co., Ltd., paint, 57.20; Ontario Reformatory, Mimco, brick, etc., 11,325.15; Peckover's, Ltd., iron, 107.81; Pedlar People, Ltd., lath, etc., 110.34; Alfred Rogers, Ltd., cement, 1,123.00; John E. Russell, hoist, etc., 1,100.00; Sawyer-Massey, Ltd., screen, 30.25; Steel Co. of Canada, Ltd., wire, 14.94; G. F. Sterne & Sons, Ltd., cement, 91.55; Sundry newspapers, advertising re tenders, 50.75; J. Sutherland & Sons, Ltd., insurance premiums, 25.00; Taylor-Forbes Co., Ltd., pipe, 41.10; Wettlaufer Machinery Co., elevator, etc., 1,073.70. Sundries—cartage, 9.00; express, 19.46; freight, 7,358.32; postage, 4.40; telegrams, 1.43; petty disbursements, 43.27 32,324 51

Reformatories $32,894 51

Welfare Buildings

BOYS' TRAINING SCHOOL, BOWMANVILLE

Construction of Works and Buildings ($889.67)

Canadian Pacific Railway Co., rental of siding, 65.00; R. H. Hamley, services, plowing, 20.00; Lord & Burnham Co., Ltd., bench material, etc., 784.51; Jas. Morrison Brass Manufacturing Co., Ltd., plumbing supplies, 20.16 .... 889 67

Public Buildings—Continued

Welfare Buildings—Continued

GIRLS' TRAINING SCHOOL, GALT

Construction of Works and Buildings ($128,066.28)

Aikenhead Hardware, Ltd., hardware, 109.13; David Anderson, manhole steps, 11.20; Anthes Foundry, Ltd., pipe, 36.45; Anguish & Whitfield, contract plumbing, 1,000.00; Art Electric, contract electric work, 550.00; P. Atkinson, contract plumbing, 1,445.00; Baines & David, Ltd., iron, 73.47; R. H. Ballantyne, contract plumbing, 1,360.00; Bell Telephone Co., rental, 33.70; tolls, 121.00; connection charges, 5.00; Caledon Shale Brick Co., brick, 464.00; Canadian National Railways, rent of siding, etc., 63.62; Canadian Pacific Railway Co., installing temporary deck, etc., 170.04; Chapman Bros., brick, 638.00; Combustion Engineering Corporation, Ltd., contract boiler equipment, 5,000.00; Cooksville Co., Ltd., brick, etc., 1,687.62; R. Fitzsimmons Co., Ltd., contract heating, 595.00; Francis-Hankin & Co., Ltd., contract chimney, 1,496.00; Fraser Hardware Co., Ltd., hardware, 62.03; Corporation of City of Galt, tile, etc., 11.20; Galt Fuel & Supply Co., sewer pipe, etc., 249.00; Galt Public Utilities Commission, watermain, etc., 100.45; P. W. Gardiner & Son, Ltd., lumber, 241.41; James Gillies & Son, lumber, etc., 89.12; Grand River Railway Co., labour, 96.32; C. E. Greenan Co., Ltd., contracting installing watermains, 1,500.00; Homer Grimm, fencing, 71.50; Guelph Tent & Awning Co., rent of marquee, 20.00; Interlocking Tile Co., Ltd., tile, 1,605.28; Interprovincial Brick Co., Ltd., brick, 464.00; W. Kidd, sharpening picks, etc., 51.30; F. B. McFarren, Ltd., brick, 478.50; C. Martin, stone, 39.62; B. J. Miller Co., Ltd., contract heating, school building, 1,500.00; Milton Brick, Ltd., tile-brick, 1,136.00; National Fireproofing Co., Ltd., tile, 1,276.03; National Sewer Pipe Co., Ltd., pipe, 1,027.62; Ontario Reformatory, Mimico, tile and brick, 4,693.15; Orillia Heaters & Plumbers, contract plumbing, 658.75; Pay list, wages of men, 19,743.49; Pounder Bros., contract, administration building, 7,470.43; Schultz Construction Co., Ltd., contract, general construction, dormitories, 36,851.75; Schweitzer Electric Co., contract, electric work, 585.61; Sheldon's, Ltd., manhole covers, 81.00; Smart Turner Machine Co., Ltd., sump pump, 150.94; Standard Brick Co., Ltd., brick, 725.01; Standard Electric, contract electric work, 467.50; A. Stevenson, travelling expenses, 23.34; W. Stobbs, contract, heating, 933.30; Sundry newspapers, advertising re tenders, 200.77; Taylor-Forbes Co., Ltd., plumbing supplies, 87.44; G. H. Thomas & Son, Ltd., contract, construction power house, etc., 27,722.93; Richard Tope Brick Works, brick, 507.50; Toronto Brick Co., Ltd., brick, 812.00; P. W. Wilson, contract, electric wiring, 201.79; Wood, Alexander & James, Ltd., hardware, 102.54; Wright Bros., Ltd., contract, heating dormitory, 1,041.37. Sundries—cartage, 28.79; express, .30; freight, 32.13; petty disbursements, 65.84........................ 128,066 28

Welfare Buildings..$128,955.95

Agricultural Buildings

Ontario Agricultural College

Administrative Building, etc., Electric Sub-station, Water Tank and Water Mains, and Power House, including Furniture, Furnishings and Equipment ($251,205.09)

T. R. Barber, numbering doors, etc., 51.50; Battler & Freiburger, setting sleeves and inserts, 747.68; Bell Telephone Co., tolls, 71.25; A. H. Bennett, repairing glass, etc., 31.75; Bennett & Wright Co., Ltd., contract, electric wiring, 3,635.86; Bond Hardware Co., Ltd., coal oil, etc., 2,302.42; Canada Ingot Iron Co., Ltd., culvert pipe, 33.28; Canadian General Electric Co., Ltd., conduit, etc., 2,161.43; Canadian Westinghouse Co., Ltd., lamps, etc., 1,733.50; Cassidys, Ltd., chinaware, 510.27; J. Coulter Co., Ltd., contract, kitchen equipment, 122.00; Creswell-Pomeroy, Ltd., fly screens, 441.30; Diamond State Fibre Co. of Canada, Ltd., tube, 40.22; Dominion Bridge Co., Ltd., beams, etc., 36.74; T. Eaton Co., Ltd., dish towels, dish washer, etc., 11,695.53; English Electric Co., transformer station, etc., 8,816.22; Geo. Fairley, wiring, etc., 4,340.00; Federal Wire & Cable Co., Ltd., wire, etc., 477.06; Ferranti Electric, Ltd., transformers, 1,392.99; Robt. Fitzsimmons Co., Ltd., contract, heating, 3,532.50; W. L. Forsythe, locks, etc., 85.00; Frigidaire Sales Corporation, refrigerator equipment, 2,200.00; Frost Steel & Wire Co., contract, fence, 328.55; Gartshore-Thomson Pipe & Foundry Co., Ltd., bends, etc., 53.74; General Steel Wares, Ltd., kitchen equipment, 3,429.46; Gowdy Bros., sewer pipe, 415.88; Grand & Toy, Ltd., waste baskets, etc., 746.67; Griffin Foundry Co., grates and frames, 34.00; Guelph Board of Heat & Light Commissioners, electric supplies, 94.64; Corporation City of Guelph, valve, etc., 82.20; Guelph Sand & Gravel, Ltd., sand, etc., 25.57; Harkness & Hertzberg, preparing plans, 852.20; Hospital & Kitchen Equipment Co., Ltd., contract, kitchen equipment, 102.30; Hydro-Electric Power Com-

Public Buildings—Continued

Agricultural Buildings—Continued

Ontario Agricultural College—Administrative Building, etc.—Continued

mission, electric supplies, 14.82; Jackson-Lewis Co., Ltd., contract, construction of section 3, 113,395.23; Jones Bros. of Canada, Ltd., barber chairs, 360.00; M. Lasby, gravel, 135.00; McArthur Engineering Co., contract, tunnels, etc., 22,841.08; J. A. McFarlane, cedar poles, 32.50; F. B. McFarren, Ltd., brick, 580.00; McGlashan Clarke Co., Ltd., spoons, etc., 1,240.60; Masco Co., Ltd., electric supplies, 1,336.81; Milton Brick, Ltd., brick, 217.50; National Sewer Pipe Co., Ltd., pipe, 46.56; Northern Electric Co., Ltd., electric supplies, etc., 2,667.48; Office Specialty Manufacturing Co., Ltd., contract, office equipment, 734.95; Ontario Reformatory, Mimico, tile, etc., 6,624.41; Ontario Reformatory Industries, Guelph, beds, etc., 4,989.20; A. B. Ormsby Co., Ltd., installing doors, etc., 341.00; Otis-Fensom Elevator Co., Ltd., contract, elevator and dumb waiter, 500.00; Pay list, wages of men, 25,206.48; E. F. Phillips Electrical Works, Ltd., cable, 295.98; Powerlite Devices, Ltd., electric supplies, 172.33; Roelofson Elevator Works, contract, freight elevator, 1,768.00; G. B. Ryan & Co., Ltd., window shades, 635.00; Schreiters, Ltd., draperies, 1,104.00; Schweitzer Electric Co., Ltd., contract electric wiring, 3,561.60; Sheppard & Abbott, welding, 2,873.28; Robt. Simpson Co., Ltd., contract, linoleum, etc., 5,780.38; Geo. Sparrow & Co., kitchen equipment, 238.30; Steel Equipment Co., Ltd., contract, fittings, 76.70; Sundry newspapers, advertising re tenders, 93.60; Stratford Chair Co., desks, etc., 320.00; Taylor-Forbes Co., Ltd., plumbing supplies, 57.66; J. & J. Taylor, Ltd., safes, 1,200.00; L. Taylor, dishes, 716.98; Vokes Hardware Co., Ltd., hardware, 19.16; Wrought Iron Range Co. of Canada, Ltd., cooking utensils, 206.41. Sundries—cartage, 67.28; express, 15.61; freight, 64.47; postage, .50; telegrams, .36; petty disbursements, 50.16..................	251,205 09
Greenhouses in Connection with Horticultural Building ($6,172.36)	
Bond Hardware Co., Ltd., hardware, etc., 169.25; R. E. Christie Electric Co., Ltd., contract, electric work, 1,097.65; Gowdy Bros., sewer pipe, etc., 42.55; Guelph Lumber Co., Ltd., screen doors, 265.00; Jackson-Lewis Co., Ltd., general trade contract, 1,112.69; King Construction Co., contract, erecting greenhouse, 695.73; Masco Co., Ltd., electric supplies, 11.85; Sheppard & Abbott, contract, plumbing and heating, 2,651.84; Taylor-Forbes Co., Ltd., sprocket rims and chain, 118.80. Sundries—cartage, .50; petty disbursements, 6.50...........................	6,172 36
Girls' Residence to Accommodate 43 Students ($5,946.84)	
Adams Furniture Co., Ltd., dressers, 842.50; Battler & Freiburger, covering steam pipes, 52.00; Bond Hardware Co., Ltd., door checks, etc., 113.95; Canadian Laundry Machinery Co., Ltd., ironing board, 192.39; T. Eaton Co., Ltd., chairs, etc., 1,571.40; R. Fitzsimmons Co., Ltd., changing radiators, 12.61; Grand & Toy, Ltd., waste paper baskets, 16.67; C. W. Greenan, contract, plumbing and heating, 215.69; Harris & Marson, contract, electric wiring, 1,343.00; Hayes Wheel & Forgings, Ltd., refrigerator, 170.40; Jackson-Lewis Co., Ltd., contract, construction, 270.59; M. Lasby, gravel, 20.25; Masco Co., Ltd., electric supplies, 16.96; Jas. Morrison Brass Manufacturing Co., Ltd., towel bars, 26.66; National Locks, Ltd., contract, hardware, 197.95; Pay list, wages of men, 305.80; Penfold Hardware Co., cement, 88.11; Schreiters, Ltd., curtains, 307.25; Robt. Stewart, Ltd., cupboards and tables, 118.00; Sundry newspapers, advertising re tenders, 22.50; J. A. Wilson Co., Ltd., electric supplies, 26.40. Sundries—cartage, .90; freight, 1.10; petty disbursements, 13.76...................................	5,946 84
Horticultural Building ($2,000.00)	
E. P. Muntz Co., claims re delay in approval of sub-trades, etc..................	2,000 00
Turkey Experimental Farm Staff House ($1,300.57)	
Hydro-Electric Power Commission, pole spans, 210.97; The McCaul Co., contract, construction of superintendent's residence, 1,000.00; Robt. Simpson Co., Ltd., electric fixtures, 89.60..	1,300 57
Kemptville Agricultural School	
Water Supply, Drilling Well, etc. ($422.21)	
Dominion Concrete Co., Ltd., pipe, 107.75; McMaster Lumber Co., Ltd., lumber, etc., 36.30; Pay list, wages of men, 270.00; petty disbursements, 8.16..........	422 21
Western Ontario Experimental Farm, Ridgetown	
Chicken House ($106.20)	
A. Warwick & Son, roofing..	106 20
Agricultural Buildings.................................$267,153.27	

Public Buildings—Continued

DISTRICTS

Kenora District

Alterations and Improvements to Existing House for Gaoler ($319.93)

J. G. Brown, contract plumbing 319 93

Mining Recorder's Office and Lock-up, Sioux Lookout ($22,671.77)

Callander Foundry & Manufacturing Co., Ltd., ceiling fixtures, 16.25; Canada Hardware, Ltd., hardware, 459.34; Canadian National Railways, connecting water main, etc., 67.72; Day Lumber Co., coal, 60.65; H. Cheyne, contract, electric wiring, 825.00; Grand & Toy, Ltd., chairs, settees, etc., 216.45; L. A. Greene & Co., contract, plumbing, etc., 4,928.37; R. Laidlaw Lumber Co., Ltd., lumber, 447.51; A. A. J. MacDonald, coal, etc., 583.90; Mueller, Ltd., valves, 78.75; Neptune Meter Co., Ltd., meter, 52.00; Pay list, wages of men, 1,156.10; Robt. Simpson Co., Ltd., blinds, 57.60; Town of Sioux Lookout, sidewalk, etc., 662.70; J. & J. Taylor Co., Ltd., contract, steel cells, 2,964.31; W. Walker & Son, Ltd., hardware, 12.48; R. E. Wright & Co., general contract, etc., 10,123.62. Sundries—express, 6.40; freight, 72.56; petty disbursements, 34.06 .. 22,825 77

Less refund, Criminal Justice Department for coal 154 00

22,671 77

New Gaol ($303.50)

Corporation of Town of Kenora, installing power and light service 303 50

Payment of Purchase and Installation of Steel Cells at Gold Pines Patricia Portion ($730.00)

Goldie & McCulloch Co., Ltd., prison cells, etc., 475.00; R. E. Wright & Co., contract, putting up cells, 255.00 ..... 730 00

Nipissing

New Gaol, North Bay ($7,575.77)

R. R. Foster, wire fence, 168.00; Jeffrey & Stevens, work on garage and stable, 168.89; Corporation Town of North Bay, part cost of sewer, 7,238.88 ..... 7,575 77

Wall around Gaol, North Bay ($15,218.42)

Estate of J. H. Bell, explosives, 18.00; J. W. Billington, rock, 448.25; Canada Cement Co., Ltd., cement, 960.40; Cochrane-Dunlop Hardware, Ltd., hardware, etc., 488.76; Hydro-Electric Power Commission, machinery parts, 196.16; Lindsay & McCluskey, Ltd., lime, 54.00; Ontario Reformatory, Mimico, brick, 300.00; Pay list, wages of men, 5,906.77; E. M. Quirt, unloading steel, 25.00; Standard Planing Mills & Lumber Co., lumber, 1,491.23; Steel Co. of Canada, Ltd., steel, 2,033.74; H. Stockdale, lumber, gravel, etc., 1,382.92; J. & J. Taylor, Ltd., steel door and gate, 500.00; Geo. Thompson, gravel, 1,102.50. Sundries—cartage, 139.50; freight, 144.74; petty disbursements, 26.45 ..... 15,218 42

District Buildings $46,819 39

MISCELLANEOUS ($95,075.59)

Ontario Government Building, Exhibition Park, Toronto, Grant to City of Toronto ($50,000.00)

Corporation of the City of Toronto, annual grant 50,000 00

Purchase of Property ($45,075.59)

Departments of Northern Development and Public Works—

Executors of Batten Estate, house and lot No. 113 in Village of Port Carling for approach to Port Carling swing bridge, 2,000.00; Thos. Johnson, legal fees, 16.78 2,016 78

Fort William Industrial Farm—

J. R. Elliott, west half of lot 22 in 4th Concession, Township of Neebing 700 00

Ontario Agricultural College—

H. E. LeDrew, commission on purchase price of Graesser property 625 00

Ontario Hospital, Cobourg—

Armstrong and Willmott, legal expenses re purchase of Heaslip property, 61.89; Benjamin R. Heaslip, purchase of north parts of lots 10 and 11 in block "F" on south side of University Avenue, in the Town of Cobourg, for residence of physician in charge, 4,500.00 ..... 4,561 89

Ontario Hospital, Whitby—

J. Pearse, payment of mortgage and interest on Annis property 1,253 86

Ontario Provincial Police—

Imperial Bank of Canada, purchase of two buildings on lot 34, Gold Pines, Ontario, for use as police post 900 00

Miscellaneous—

Trustees of Toronto General Hospital, purchase of No. 2 Queen's Park 35,018 06

Public Buildings $2,224,103.39

Supply Bill $3,054,005.89

STATUTORY

Minister's salary (see page K 11).......... 10,000 00

Drainage Aid Work, R.S.O. 1927, Chap. 63, Section 4 ($98,143.00)

Treasurer, Township of—Caledonia, 2,169.00; Colchester, South, 3,049.00; Culross, 2,353.00; Dover. 3,580.00; Drummond, 21,040.00; Harwich, 10,100.00; Howard, 2,169.00; Kinloss, 2,172.00; McGillivray, 2,695.00; Nepean, 8,172.00; Osgoode, 3,943.00; Raleigh, 2,051.00; Sombra, 3,716.00; Usborne, 2,435.00; Wallace, 3,581.00; Westminster, 4,214.00; Yonge Front, 3,940.00; Essex Border Utilities Commission, 16,764.00.......... 98,143 00

Statutory.......... $108,143 00

SPECIAL WARRANTS

For the Payment of Portrait of the Honourable William Donald Ross, Lieutenant-Governor of Ontario ($5,000.00)

John Russell, portrait.......... 5,000 00

Boys' Camp, Lake Couchiching, Erection of Building, Water Supply, etc. ($427.12)

Canadian Westinghouse Co., Ltd., lamps, 38.59; Department of Public Works, furniture, 86.50; Globe Printing Co., advertising, 13.50; Jones & Bolton, plumbing supplies, 141.69; Ritchie & Mould, electric supplies, 146.84.......... 427 12

To pay for Provisions for Government House ($278.97)

Canada Bread Co., Ltd., bread, 19.51; Mrs. M. Chambers, fish, 10.23; City Dairy Co., Ltd., milk and cream, 38.61; H. G. Cook, meat, 62.12; M. Hollingshead, groceries, 147.40; petty disbursements, 1.10.......... 278 97

Ontario Hospital, Orillia, Reconstruction of Barns Destroyed by Fire ($19,497.58)

M. H. Braden, construction and equipping of barns, 15,545.90; Canadian General Electric Co., Ltd., electrical supplies, 126.46; Sundry newspapers, advertising re tenders, 172.70; E. Webb & Son, contract re silos, 3,652.52.......... 19,497 58

Special Warrants.......... $25,203.67

Total.......... $3,187,352 56
Less Salary Assessment.......... 7,966 98

Total Expenditure, Department of Public Works.......... $3,179,385 58

PART L

DEPARTMENT OF HIGHWAYS

FISCAL YEAR, 1931-32

TABLE OF CONTENTS

GENERAL INDEX AT BACK OF BOOK

PART L—DEPARTMENT OF HIGHWAYS

Statement of Expenditure Showing Amounts Expended, Unexpended and Overexpended for the Twelve Months Ended October 31st, 1932

Department of Highways	Page	Estimates	Expended			Un-expended	Over-expended	Treasury Board Minute
			Ordinary	Capital	Total Ordinary and Capital			
		$ c.	$ c.	$ c.	$ c.	$ c.	$ c.	$ c.
Main Office:								
Salaries	4	209,325 00	174,125 00	24,816 66	198,941 66	10,383 34		
Contingencies	5	90,000 00	99,068 19	4,768 87	103,837 06		13,837 06	15,000 00
Telephone Accounts	6	500 00	153 73		153 73	346 27		
Main Office	..	299,825 00	273,346 92	29,585 53	302,932 45	10,729 61	13,837 06	
Miscellaneous:								
Salaries, Garage Foreman, Chauffeurs, etc	7	24,600 00	23,100 00		23,100 00	1,500 00		
Automobiles, purchase, repairs, maintenance, etc	7	18,000 00	16,912 73		16,912 73	1,087 27		
Exhibits	7	5,000 00	5,349 17		5,349 17		349 17	500 00
Grants:								
Ontario Good Roads Association	7	400 00	400 00		400 00			
Canadian Good Roads Association	7	2,000 00	2,000 00		2,000 00			
Membership Fee, Association of Road Congress	..	50 00				50 00		
Road Surveys, etc	7	40,000 00	28,680 85	2,749 06	31,429 91	8,570 09		
Taxes now due or accruing on Properties, etc	8	500 00	283 60		283 60	216 40		
Unforeseen and unprovided	8	3,500 00	54 00		54 00	3,446 00		
Miscellaneous	..	94,050 00	76,780 35	2,749 06	79,529 41	14,869 76	349 17	
Motor Vehicles Branch:								
Salaries	8	93,250 00	87,414 20		87,414 20	5,835 80		
Contingencies	9	60,000 00	70,360 82		70,360 82		10,360 82	25,000 00
Motor Vehicles Branch	..	153,250 00	157,775 02		157,775 02	5,835 80	10,360 82	
Miscellaneous:								
Traffic Supervisor and Inspectors	10	10,200 00	5,400 00		5,400 00	4,800 00		
Services and Expenses re Traffic Act, etc	10	10,000 00	8,389 72		8,389 72	1,610 28		

Automobile markers and supplies	10	65,000 00	62,194 41	....	62,194 41	2,805 59	....	....
Testing automobile headlights	10	400 00	75 00	....	75 00	325 00	....	....
Safety Committee to pay cost of advertising, etc	10	35,000 00	30,544 22	....	30,544 22	4,455 78	....	....
Educational work, etc	10	3,000 00	130 50	....	130 50	2,869 50	....	....
Miscellaneous	..	123,600 00	106,733 85	....	106,733 85	16,866 15	....	....
Supply Bill	..	670,725 00	614,636 14	32,334 59	646,970 73	48,301 32	24,547 05	....
Statutory:								
Minister's salary	11	....	10,000 00	....	10,000 00	....	....	....
Provincial Highways construction	11	....	725,664 88	3,603,531 13	4,329,196 01	....	....	....
County Roads construction	55	....	1,280,735 88	2,389,598 84	3,670,334 72	....	....	....
Township Roads construction	55	....	1,236,209 60	641,195 95	1,877,405 55	....	....	....
Connecting Links	56	....	2,615 44	43,962 70	46,578 14	....	....	....
Indian Reserve Roads	56	....	11,129 12	2,115 89	13,245 01	....	....	....
Statutory	..	....	3,266,354 92	6,680,404 51	9,946,759 43	....	....	....
Total	..	....	3,880,991 06	6,712,739 10	10,593,730 16	....	....	....
Less Salary Assessment	..	....	15,144 04	....	15,144 04	....	....	....
Department of Highways	..	....	3,865,847 02	6,712,739 10	10,578,586 12	....	....	....

SUMMARY

Department of Highways	Page	Ordinary	Capital	Total
		$ c.	$ c.	$ c.
Main Office	4-6	273,346 92	29,585 53	302,932 45
Miscellaneous, Main Office	7-8	76,780 35	2,749 06	79,529 41
Motor Vehicles Branch	8-10	157,775 02	....	157,775 02
Miscellaneous, Motor Vehicles Branch	10	106,733 85	....	106,733 85
Statutory	11-56	3,266,354 92	6,680,404 51	9,946,759 43
Total	....	3,880,991 06	6,712,739 10	10,593,730 16
Less Salary Assessment	....	15,144 04	....	15,144 04
Department of Highways	....	3,865,847 02	6,712,739 10	10,578,586 12

DEPARTMENT OF HIGHWAYS

Hon. Leopold Macaulay......Minister (Statutory)......$10,000 00

MAIN OFFICE

Salaries ($198,941.66)

Name	Position	Period		Amount
R. M. Smith	Deputy Minister	12	months	6,000 00
A. A. Smith	Chief Engineer	12	"	4,800 00
G. G. Creig	Assistant Chief Engineer	12	"	3,800 00
C. H. Nelson	Location and Equipment Engineer	12	"	275 00
R. G. Muir	Chief Engineer of Municipal Roads	12	"	4,000 00
W. H. Brown	Chief Accountant	12	"	3,300 00
J. A. P. Marshall	Municipal Road Engineer	12	"	3,000 00
J. M. MacInnes	" " "	12	"	3,000 00
A. N. Fellows	" " "	12	"	3,000 00
J. H. Hawes	" " "	12	"	3,000 00
H. A. Smail	" " "	12	"	3,000 00
H. T. Eaton	" " "	12	"	3,000 00
P. Higgins	" " "	12	"	2,850 00
H. L. Schermerhorn	" " "	12	"	2,850 00
W. H. Keith	" " "	12	"	2,850 00
W. S. Cook	" " "	12	"	2,550 00
W. G. Gibson	" " "	12	"	2,550 00
W. A. MacLachlan	Assistant Highway Engineer	12	"	3,000 00
Adam Hay	" " "	12	"	3,000 00
H. N. Lamont	" " "	12	"	2,550 00
A. Sedgwick	Bridge Engineer	12	"	3,300 00
D. Barclay	Senior Draughtsman, Group 2	12	"	2,300 00
L. Loch	Draughtsman, Group 1	12	"	2,100 00
J. F. Cassidy	" "	12	"	2,000 00
John F. Hill	" " 2	12	"	1,600 00
D. S. Spence	" "	12	"	1,600 00
R. N. McLagan	" "	12	"	1,600 00
W. L. Jackson	" "	12	"	1,600 00
W. A. Skinner	" "	12	"	1,600 00
C. J. Carson	" "	½	"	66 66
Geo. Stockdale	" "	12	"	1,500 00
W. Kitson	Testing Engineer	12	"	2,200 00
W. Braggins	Senior Laboratory Assistant	12	"	1,800 00
J. L. Zoller	Principal Clerk and Assistant Accountant	12	"	2,400 00
N. W. Cosby	Principal Clerk	12	"	2,200 00
J. Smith	" "	12	"	2,100 00
N. W. Hallett	Senior Clerk	12	"	2,000 00
H. Allen	" "	12	"	2,000 00
F. Martin	" "	12	"	2,000 00
Wm. Spence	" "	12	"	1,900 00
E. A. Mitchell	" "	12	"	1,900 00
A. R. Kennedy	" "	12	"	1,900 00
N. W. Hainesworth	" "	12	"	1,900 00
W. A. Anderson	" "	12	"	1,900 00
M. F. Cross	" "	12	"	1,800 00
M. Kennedy	" "	12	"	1,800 00
C. A. Saunders	" "	12	"	1,800 00
H. H. Knight	" "	12	"	1,800 00
S. J. Burstow	Clerk, Group 1	12	"	1,600 00
W. Coomber	" "	12	"	1,600 00
A. V. Rochemont	" "	12	"	1,600 00
C. Hoover	" "	12	"	1,500 00
C. Gorman	" "	12	"	1,400 00
J. Pogue	" "	12	"	1,400 00
C. Hewitt	" "	12	"	1,400 00
D. Chambers	" " 2	12	"	1,200 00
L. Lindsay	" "	12	"	1,200 00
E. C. Morley	" "	12	"	1,125 00
M. E. Murray	" "	12	"	1,125 00
E. E. Brown	" "	12	"	1,125 00
R. N. Page	" " 3	12	"	900 00
L. Rooker	" "	12		900 00
G. C. Rudback	" "	12	"	825 00
D. H. Talbot	" "	12	"	750 00

Main Office—Continued

Salaries—Continued

Name	Position	Time	Amount
J. Fraser	Head Automobile Mechanic	12 months	2,000 00
W. M. Johnson	Automobile Mechanic	12 "	1,800 00
F. Porter	Stock Clerk	12 "	1,500 00
J. H. Morris	" "	12 "	1,500 00
M. H. Woods	Senior Audit Clerk	12 "	2,000 00
J. H. Robinson	" " "	12 "	1,900 00
A. H. Foley	" " "	12 "	1,800 00
W. G. Allen	" " "	12 "	1,700 00
Geo. Brown	Audit Clerk	12 "	1,600 00
L. B. Teetzell	" "	12 "	1,500 00
P. H. Jory	" "	12 "	1,500 00
H. M. Beemer	Secretarial Stenographer	12 "	1,600 00
B. Bradley	Senior Clerk Stenographer	12 "	1,500 00
E. M. James	" " "	12 "	1,500 00
E. K. Reid	" " "	12 "	1,400 00
I. H. Bradley	Clerk Stenographer, Group 1	12 "	1,200 00
M. Crumpton	" " "	12 "	1,200 00
E. Moffitt	" " "	12 "	1,200 00
P. M. Griffin	" " "	12 "	1,200 00
A. M. Boisseau	" " "	12 "	1,200 00
L. Wicks	" " "	12 "	1,200 00
H. Farewell	" " "	12 "	1,125 00
M. J. Wilson	" " "	12 "	1,125 00
R. E. Beaupre	" " "	12 "	1,050 00
Lillian E. Leeson	" " "	12 "	1,050 00
E. D. Morgan	" " "	12 "	1,050 00
M. Walker	" " "	12 "	975 00
Isabel L. Hayden	" " " 2	12 "	900 00
M. Carson	Clerk Typist, " 1	12 "	1,200 00
S. Simpson	" " "	12 "	1,200 00
H. E. Milligan	" " "	12 "	1,200 00
C. McCoy	" " "	12 "	1,200 00
Esme Banning	" " " 2	12 "	900 00
H. F. Brown	" " "	12 "	900 00
Mrs. W. Adams	Senior Filing Clerk	12 "	1,600 00
K. Lindsay	Filing Clerk, Group 1	12 "	1,200 00
N. Rapson	" " "	12 "	1,200 00
J. Mason	Office Appliance Operator, Group 1	12 "	1,600 00
A. E. Luck	" " " " 2	12 "	1,300 00
B. Edwards	" " " " 3	12 "	900 00
N. H. Richardson	Property Valuator	12 "	3,000 00
N. Crew	Cheque Writer, Group 2	12 "	1,200 00
G. Saul	" " " 3	12 "	975 00
K. A. Cockburn	Secretary to Minister	12 "	2,400 00
R. W. Bond	Office Boy	12 "	675 00
J. Rule	" "	12 "	675 00
Frank H. Smith	" "	12 "	750 00
W. H. Ramsay	Tracer	12 "	900 00

Contingencies ($103,837.06)

Temporary Services, $18,343.67:

Name	Position	Time	Amount
M. K. Barchard	Clerk Typist, Group 2	12 months	750 00
A. W. Bradbury	Clerk, " 1	12 "	1,200 00
A. J. Brown	Clerk Stenographer, " 2	12 "	825 00
F. W. Burch	Clerk, " 3	12 "	750 00
Dora A. Doe	Clerk Typist " 2	7 "	437 50
M. Fawcett	Filing Clerk, " 1	12 "	900 00
Mary Fice	Clerk Typist, " 2	12 "	750 00
M. D. Fralick	Clerk Stenographer, " 2	12 "	825 00
T. D. Gordon	Clerk " 2	12 "	975 00
K. Rae Green	Clerk Stenographer, " 2	1 "	68 75
C. Hewson	" " " 2	12 "	825 00
W. H. Jarvis	Office Boy	12 "	525 00
J. A. Leslie	Inspector of Signs and Gasoline Pumps	12 "	2,299 92
D. E. Manchester	Municipal Road Engineer	12 "	2,400 00
H. MacGregor	Office Boy	12 "	525 00
J. D. Millar	Acting Municipal Road Engineer	3 "	450 00
C. A. Poynton	Municipal Road Engineer	12 "	2,400 00

Main Office—Continued

Contingencies—Continued

Temporary Services—Continued.

Ross Roberts	Office Boy	12 months	525 00
M. A. Sheppard	Clerk Typist, Group 2	12 "	750 00
W. R. C. Warren	Draughtsman, " 2	1 "	100 00
Elmere Williams	Clerk Typist, " 2	1 "	62 50

Travelling Expenses, $32,747.40.

H. Allen, 68.95; W. G. Allen, 1,127.58; W. A. Anderson, 259.03; George Brown, 1,491.00; W. H. Brown, 1,123.01; C. J. Carson, 9.30; K. A. Cockburn, 51.73; W. S. Cook, 493.56; H. T. Eaton, 648.19; A. N. Fellows, 622.71; A. H. Foley, 1,213.61; W. G. Gibson, 548.62; C. Gorman, 1,558.08; T. D. Gordon, 1,215.65; N. W. Hallett, 28.05; J. H. Hawes, 575.37; A. Hay, .90; P. M. Higgins, 524.85; P. H. Jory, 1,805.30; W. H. Keith, 536.93; T. L. Kennedy, 53.40; A. R. Kennedy, 29.45; H. H. Knight, 18.75; Hon. L. Macaulay, 700.00; D. E. Manchester, 1,339.98; J. A. P. Marshall, 934.86; W. A. MacLachlan, 36.13; J. B. Mason, 2.90; J. M. MacInnes, 563.11; J. D. Miller, 425.00; E. A. Mitchell, 333.20; R. C. Muir, 780.46; R. N. Page, 144.25; J. Pogue, 1,316.65; C. A. Poynton, 735.45; J. H. Robinson, 1,430.77; A. V. Rochemont, 24.90; C. A. Saunders, 1,856.97; H. L. Schermerhorn, 1,324.26; H. A. Smail, 751.19; J. Smith, 426.02; R. M. Smith, 1,465.99; D. H. Talbot, 183.00; L. B. Teetzel, 1,556.37; M. H. Woods, 1,892.43; J. L. Zoller, 519.49 .... 32,747 40

Advertising, $1,008.96.

J. J. Gibbons Co., Ltd., 868.96; F. Smily, 140.00 .... 1,008 96

Advisory Board, $1,800.00.

J. F. Hill, 510.00; F. V. Laughton, 585.00; T. G. Mahoney, 705.00 .... 1,800 00

Miscellaneous, $49,937.03.

Addressograph Multigraph of Canada, Ltd., rolls, repairs, etc., 2,022.68; American Society for Testing Materials, 15.00; Anglo Traders, Ltd., bunting, 75.00; Angus-Mack Co., census, 31.40; Art Metropole, books, etc., 1,003.76; Bourne & Towse, maps, 12.50; Burroughs Adding Machine of Canada, Ltd., inspections, repairs, etc., 17.93; Buscombe & Dodds, Ltd., wipers, 32.75; Canadian Colortype, Ltd., gas pump markers, etc., 664.20; Canadian Photo Copy Co., photostats, 83.03; Copp-Clark Co., Ltd., road maps, etc., 3,702.47; Corona Typewriters, Ltd., inspections, 12.00; H. L. Crabtree, Ltd., maps, 76.65; A. G. Cumming, Ltd., blueprinting, 957.28; Department of Public Works, blueprint paper, etc., 439.01; Diver Electrotype Co., repairs, etc., 239.44; Employers Liability Assurance Corp., Ltd., premiums, 30.00; Engineering Institute of Canada, fees, etc., 10.00; Field, Love & House, inspections, etc., 109.00; General Office Equipment Corp., Ltd., maintenance, 36.00; Heaton Publishing Co., books, 5,000.00; Instruments, Ltd., blueprinting, etc., 152.31; King's Printer, 26,939.09; Leatherdale Studios, prints, 12.00; McCann & Alexander, inspections, 12.00; McAdam & Langstaff, bond, 150.00; Might Directories, Ltd., maps, 29.50; Miller Lithographic Co., Ltd., maps, 935.00; Ocean Accident and Guarantee Corp., Ltd., gas tax bond, 30.00; Province of Ontario Pictures, pictures, etc., 294.75; J. F. Raw Co., Ltd., blueprinting, etc., 368.19; Reed, Shaw & McNaught, gas tax bond, 100.00; Reliance Engravers, Ltd., designing layout, etc., 106.54; Remington Typewriters, Ltd., inspection, etc., 86.74; Roneo Co. of Canada, Ltd., cabinet, 118.64; Russell & Russell, surety bonds, 2,454.37; R. M. Smith, services as consulting engineer, 1,500.00; Stewart Ray Motors, gas, etc., 11.93; Stratford Chair Co., table, 18.00; J. R. Summers Co., premium on bond, 25.00; Typewriter Sales & Service Co., inspections, etc., 65.00; Thayers, Ltd., gas, 28.22; Thomas & Corney Typewriters, Ltd., inspections, 17.00; United Typewriter Co., Ltd., inspections, etc., 93.24; Watson & McVittie, premium on bonds, 75.00. Sundries—cartage, .50; car tickets, 60.00; excise stamps, 49.00; express, 972.38; newspapers and periodicals, 180.25; telegrams, 417.33; petty disbursements, 64.95 .... 49,937 03

Telephone Account ($153.73)

Bell Telephone Co. of Canada, Ltd., tolls 153 73

Main Office $302,932.45

Miscellaneous—Continued

Garage

Salaries ($23,100.00)

T. Johnston	Garage Foreman	12 months	2,700 00
Owen Pope	Chauffeur	12 "	1,600 00
D. Neave	"	12 "	1,600 00
C. G. Knight	"	12 "	1,600 00
W. McCallum	"	12 "	1,600 00
G. Treadway	"	12 "	1,600 00
J. Dollery	"	12 "	1,600 00
H. Coleman	"	12 "	1,600 00
Frank Law	"	12 "	1,600 00
Douglas Best	"	12 "	1,600 00
M. Rutherford	"	12 "	1,600 00
W. Gordon	"	12 "	1,400 00
C. H. G. Peto	Automobile Mechanic, Group 2	12 "	1,600 00
W. McGrath	Garage Attendant	12 "	1,400 00

Automobile, Purchase, Repairs, Maintenance, Equipment and Service for all Departments of Government ($17,981.48)

Barker Bros., Ltd., cleaning uniforms, 12.00; Department of Highways, gas, oil, etc., 17,903.29; The Suititorium, cleaning uniforms, 66.19 .... 17,981 48
Less Refunds, Rentals, etc 1,068 75
16,912 73

Highways Exhibits ($5,349.17)

H. Allen, travelling expenses, 404.43; T. H. Burton, travelling expenses, 114.40; Canadian General Electric Co., bulbs, 15.34; J. Carew Lumber Co., Ltd., lumber, 13.09; C. J. Carson, travelling expenses, 99.20; K. A. Cockburn, travelling expenses, 686.32; Day Sign Co., Ltd., glass, etc., for sign, 43.50; Department of Lands and Forests, erecting cabins, 144.60; Detroit Exposition Co., building floor, etc., 205.00; Downer Pattern Works, constructing cabin, labour, etc., 582.70; O. J. Evans & Sons, rent of drapes, 19.00; T. D. Gordon, travelling expenses, 78.85; Grand Central Palace Electric Corp., electric service, 65.34; E. A. Mitchell, travelling expenses, 18.17; Ottawa Hydro-Electric Commission, electric current, 25.10; W. F. Petry, shipping cases, 139.10; Province of Ontario Pictures, transparencies, 44.00; L. Rooker, travelling expenses, 13.10; Royal Agricultural Winter Fair, electrical service, etc., 59.84; W. W. Stallworthy, repairs to models, 1,461.84; E. Stockdale, travelling expenses, 2.00; George Stockdale, travelling expenses, 250.18; Treasurer, Canadian National Exhibition, electrical work, 67.67; W. Winters, cartage, 600.00. Sundries—customs, 129.45; freight, 2.62; petty disbursements, 64.33 .... 5,349 17

Grants ($2,400.00)

Canadian Good Roads Association, grants, 2,000.00; Ontario Good Roads Association, grants, 400.00 .... 2,400 00

Road Surveys, Inspections, etc. ($31,429.91)

Temporary Services, $25,923.26.

R. S. Code, surveyor, at 208.00 per month, 2,496.00. Pay list, wages of men taking traffic census, 23,427.26 .... 25,923 26

Travelling Expenses, $253.06.

W. Kitson 253 06

Conferences of Superintendents, Counties and Townships, $3,021.40.

Sundry Superintendents 3,021 40

Miscellaneous, $2,232.19.

Art Metropole, blueprint paper, 48.82; Bursar, University of Toronto, tinsmith and carpenter's time, etc., 60.18; Canadian Foresters' Hall, Ltd., rent, 70.00; Canadian Laboratory Supplies, Ltd., flasks, etc., 95.09; A. G. Cumming, Ltd., blueprint paper, 247.63; Department of Public Works, blueprinting, paper, etc., 713.19; Canadian Fairbanks-Morse Co., Ltd., scale, weights, etc., 55.75; M. J. Galvin, resetting drill, 21.00; Instruments, Ltd., blueprint paper, 137.86; J. F. Raw & Co., Ltd., blueprint paper, etc., 112.82; C. J. Tagliabue Mfg. Co., thermometers, 33.84; The Levis, wipers and waste, 12.50. Sundries—express, 544.37; freight, 7.02; telegrams, 5.13; petty disbursements, 66.99 .... 2,232 19

Miscellaneous—Continued

Road Surveys, Inspections, etc.—Continued

Taxes on Gravel Pits, etc. ($283.60)

Treasurer, Township of Scarboro, taxes.. 283 60

Unforeseen and Unprovided For ($54.00)

Coles Florist, wreath, 12.00; Gore Park Floral Co., Ltd., wreath, 12.00; McKenna's House of Flowers, wreath, 20.00; R. M. Smith, meals for engineers, publishers, etc., 10.00.. 54 00

Miscellaneous.. $79,529.41

MOTOR VEHICLES BRANCH

Salaries ($87,414.20)

Name	Position	Time		Amount
J. P. Bickell	Registrar of Motor Vehicles	12 months		4,200 00
H. Kelly	Head Clerk, Group 1	12 "		2,850 00
A. A. Townley	" " "	12 "		2,700 00
T. E. Burkitt	" " " 2	12 "		2,400 00
J. S. Tatton	Senior Clerk	12 "		2,000 00
G. C. Evans	" "	12 "		1,900 00
Alfred G. Hovey	" "	12 "		1,700 00
James Jackson	" "	12 "		1,700 00
W. E. Laxton	Chauffeur Examiner	12 "		1,600 00
W. Arnold	Clerk, Group 1	12 "		1,700 00
C. Miller	" "	12 "		1,600 00
C. C. Ware	" "	12 "		1,600 00
R. G. Baker	" "	12 "		1,700 00
E. Smith	" "	12 "		1,500 00
Mrs. H. Nicholls	" "	12 "		1,500 00
W. Boughner	" "	12 "		1,500 00
Wm. S. Verner	" "	12 "		1,400 00
A. G. McNab	" "	12 "		1,400 00
Richard J. Taylor	" "	12 "		1,400 00
Wm. Keddy	" " 2	12 "		1,300 00
J. F. MacLean	" "	12 "	1,200 00	
	Less Leave of Absence		250 00	950 00
L. Wingfield	" "	12 "		1,125 00
A. H. Rowan	" "	12 "		1,200 00
B. F. Moses	" "	12 "		1,050 00
M. Cocker	" "	12 "		1,050 00
W. M. Earl	" "	12 "		1,050 00
E. L. Mortimer	" " 3	12 "		900 00
A. H. Saunders	Stock Clerk, Group 2	12 "		1,050 00
M. Howard	Senior Clerk Stenographer	12 "		1,500 00
I. G. Smith	Clerk Stenographer, Group 1	12 "		1,125 00
O. Fraser	" " "	12 "		1,125 00
N. C. F. Brown	" " "	12 "		1,125 00
N. Kirby	" " "	12 "		1,050 00
R. B. Sharland	" " "	12 "		1,050 00
C. M. Creswell	" " " 2	12 "		975 00
M. I. Gillies	" " " 2	12 "		900 00
H. E. Kelly	Clerk Typist " 1	12 "	1,200 00	
	Less Leave of Absence		53 97	1,146 03
F. J. O'Connor	" " "	12 "		1,125 00
M. Folger	" " "	12 "		1,125 00
K. Loughrin	" " "	12 "		1,125 00
Mrs. C. H. Kerfoot	" " "	12 "		1,125 00
L. McNabb	" " "	12 "		1,125 00
I. E. Madden	" " "	12 "	1,050 00	
	Less Leave of Absence		87 50	962 50
B. Tilston	" " "	12 "		1,050 00
M. B. Evans	" " "	12 "		1,050 00
J. Judd	" " "	12 "		1,050 00
M. Netterfield	" " "	12 "		1,050 00
L. V. Lott	" " "	12 "		1,050 00
N. Geddes	" " "	12 "		1,050 00

Motor Vehicles Branch—Continued

Salaries—Continued

Name	Position	Group	Time	Amount
E. E. Secker	Clerk Typist	Group 1	12 months	1,050 00
R. Riches	“ “	“	12 “	975 00
E. M. Flavelle	“ “	“	12 “	975 00
D. E. Holmes	“ “	“	12 “	975 00
H. E. Lyons	“ “	“ 2	12 “	825 00
B. Scott	Senior Filing Clerk		3¼ “	430 67
N. Griffiths	Filing Clerk,	“ 1	12 “	1,125 00
E. M. Eldridge	“ “	“	12 “	1,125 00
O. Hammett	“ “	“	12 “	1,050 00
P. Peers	“ “	“	12 “	975 00
E. Jones	“ “	“	12 “	975 00
G. Manning	“ “	“	12 “	975 00
L. M. Morrison	“ “	“	12 “	975 00
D. K. Weir	“ “	“	12 “	975 00
C. Craig	“ “	“ 2	12 “	900 00
M. Edmund	“ “	“	12 “	900 00
F. Godfrey	“ “	“	12 “	900 00
D. Kerns	“ “	“	12 “	900 00
E. E. Durham	“ “	“	12 “	825 00
Wm. E. Brown	Office Boy		12 “	675 00

Contingencies ($70,360.82)

Temporary Services, $32,356.12.

Name	Position	Group	Time		Amount
M. Aitken	Filing Clerk,	Group 2	12 months		750 00
H. J. Arnott	Clerk Typist	“ 2	12 “		750 00
J. Bain	Filing Clerk,	“ 2	12 “		750 00
F. Banks	Clerk Typist,	“ 2	12 “		750 00
F. J. Biette	Filing Clerk,	“ 2	12 “		750 00
K. Bradley	Clerk,	“ 3	12 “		750 00
H. C. Brown	Office Boy		10½ “		462 74
F. Bruce	Clerk Typist,	“ 2	12 “		750 00
E. M. Cockin	Inspector		12 “		1,200 00
M. E. Crowley	Clerk Stenographer,	“ 2	12 “		825 00
G. M. Crozier	Filing Clerk,	“ 2	12 “		750 00
T. S. Cumber	Inspector		12 “		1,200 00
M. Daniel	Clerk Typist,	“ 2	12 “		750 00
G. R. Duncan	Clerk,	“ 2	12 “		750 00
M. Dunn	Clerk Stenographer,	“ 2	12 “		825 00
R. B. Galna	Clerk Typist	“ 2	12 “		750 00
J. L. Gardiner	Clerk,	“ 2	12 “		975 00
R. Hanna	Filing Clerk,	“ 3	12 “		750 00
C. J. Higgins	Clerk,	“ 2	12 “		975 06
N. Holdsworth	Filing Clerk,	“ 2	12 “		750 00
U. Hodge	Clerk Typist,	“ 2	12 “		750 00
G. A. Hodgson	Special Examiner		12 “		2,199 90
G. Huffman	Filing Clerk,	“ 2	12 “		750 00
A. K. M. Little	Clerk Typist,	“ 1	12 “		750 00
L. G. Madill	“ “	“	12 “		900 00
J. Miller	Filing Clerk,	“ 2	12 “		750 00
J. M. McGarrie	“ “	“ 2	12 “		750 00
W. J. Nelson	Chauffeur Examiner		12 “		1,980 00
Jeana C. Painter	Clerk,	“ 2	12 “		975 00
P. S. Pedlar	Special Examiner		12 “		2,199 96
M. Quinn	Clerk Typist,	“ 1	12 “		900 00
J. J. Smith	Inspector,		12 “	1,200 00	
	Less Leave of Absence			211 54	988 46
G. M. Tibbetts	Filing Clerk,	“ 2	12 “		750 00
A. E. J. Rumley	Clerk Typist,	“ 2	12 “		750 00
E. Watson	Filing Clerk,	“ 2	12 “		750 00

Travelling Expenses, $1,316.12.

J. P. Bickell, 552.54; W. M. Earl, 72.15; G. A. Hodgson, 11.90; A. G. Hovey, 143.20; P. S. Pedlar, 48.69; S. J. Tatton, 394.77; A. A. Townley, 92.87.......... 1,316 12

Motor Vehicles Branch—Continued

Contingencies—Continued

Miscellaneous, $36,688.58.

B. P. Branham Co., automobile reference books, 170.84; Canadian Photo Copy Co., photostats, 160.60; Commercial Reproducing Co., Ltd., photostats, etc., 91.50; Diver Electrotype Co., Ltd., type, composition, etc., 249.87; Dominion Press Clipping Agency, clippings, 180.00; Eastern Conference of Motor Vehicle Administrators, membership, 25.00; Hydro-Electric Power Commission, tests, 110.00; King's Printer, 29,153.67; Might Directories, Ltd., listing registrations, etc., 2,658.32; National Safety Council, Inc., dues, 20.00; J. F. Raw Co., Ltd., blueprint paper, 21.87; Recording & Statistical Corp., Ltd., monthly statistics, 780.00; Remington Typewriters, Ltd., inspections, 19.75; L. C. Smith & Corona Typewriters of Canada, Ltd., index platen, inspections, 128.50; Society of Automotive Engineers, Inc., dues, 22.00; Wm. Stockdale, car repairs, 12.35; Sundry—persons, meals re overtime, 176.78; Toronto Transportation Commission, car tickets, 60.00; United Typewriter Co., Ltd., inspections, etc., 728.67. Sundries—Canadian customs, 21.88; excise stamps, 50.00; express, 1,701.70; newspapers and periodicals, 17.00; telegrams, 108.53; petty disbursements, 19.75.............. 36,688 58

Motor Vehicles Branch.................................$157,775.02

MISCELLANEOUS

Special Officers for Enforcement of Highway Traffic Act ($5,400.00)

A. J. Gamble.............	Inspector...............................	12 months	1,800 00
C. McKelvie..............	"	12 "	1,800 00
W. Stockdale.............	"	12 "	1,800 00

Services and Expenses re Traffic Act, etc. ($8,389.72)

Travelling Expenses, $6,261.75.

W. Arnold, 1,103.79; T. E. Burkett, 40.75; E. M. Cockin, 1,610.09; A. Cordery, 3.80; T. S. Cumber, 1,478.55; W. F. Fenton, 3.00; A. Gamble, 100.40; G. A. Hodgson, 37.55; A. G. Hovey, 15.35; W. E. Laxton, 156.32; W. J. Nelson, 142.21; P. S. Pedlar, 204.89; J. J. Smith, 990.47; Wm. Stockdale, 59.99; S. J. Tatton, 314.59.. 6,261 75

Serving Summonses, Legal Services and Legal Fees, $1,853.68.

F. D. Boggs, 37.80; L. J. C. Bull, 70.00; S. A. Caldbeck, 42.75; J. A. Chambers, 32.46; W. M. Charlton, 15.00; T. K. Creighton, 3.00; F. G. Evans, 212.65; J. G. Harkness, 20.00; F. H. Herman, 777.00; J. M. Kearns, 25.00; R. W. Lent, 46.40; C. W. A. Marion, 45.70; H. Mehr, 38.40; W. C. Mickel, 25.00; J. Murray, 20.00; G. T. Puffer, 16.09; P. Smith, 66.18. Sundry persons, witness fees, 360.25...... 1,853 68

Miscellaneous, $274.29.

Commissioner of Police for Ontario, board and room of constables, 131.70; Hydro-Electric Power Commission, tests on signals, 80.00; Dr. A. W. Keane, professional services, 22.00; E. Williams, services as Court Reporter, 20.00; petty disbursements, 20.59.. 274 29

Automobile Markers and Supplies, $62,194.41.

Canadian Colortype, Ltd., plates, 2,934.00; Ontario Reformatory Industries, auto markers, 55,538.80. Sundries—cartage, 1,975.94; express, 67.30; freight, 1,678.37.. 62,194 41

Testing Automobile Headlights, $75.00.

Hydro-Electric Power Commission.. 75 00

Safety Committee to Pay Cost of Advertising, etc., $30,544.22.

J. J. Gibbons, Ltd., 23,754.22; E. L. Ruddy Co., Ltd., 6,775.00; Wellesley School Old Boys' Association, 15.00.. 30,544 22

Educational Work, Conference, Membership Fees, Advertising, etc., $130.50.

E. Langstaff, catering.. 130 50

Miscellaneous, Motor Vehicles Branch $106,733.85

STATUTORY

Minister's salary (see page L 4)			10,000 00

KING'S HIGHWAYS CONSTRUCTION ($4,329,196.01)

(7 Geo. V, Chap. 16, Sec. 5)

Residency No. 1		555,275 80	
Residency No. 2		400,526 38	
Residency No. 3		587,536 79	
Residency No. 4		1,334,681 39	
Residency No. 5		938,178 90	
Residency No. 6		1,032,115 31	
Residency No. 7		753,280 32	
Residency No. 8		755,353 21	
Residency No. 9		444,498 59	
Actinolite-Perth Project		1,609,553 53	
Automobile and Road Equipment Branch		168,672 74	
General		519,473 11	
		9,099,146 07	
Less Federal and Provincial Unemployment Relief Fund contribution	1,000,000 00		
Automobile rentals, repairs and services	46,686 98		
Municipal repayments for materials	346,809 37		
		1,393,496 35	
		7,705,649 72	
Accountable outstanding, 1931-32		55,716 70	
		7,761,366 42	
Less advanced, 1930-31		11,366 42	
		7,750,000 00	
Less repayment by counties, suburban areas, etc. (see page L 54)		3,420,803 99	
		4,329,196 01	

Residency No. 1 ($555,275.80)

Highway No. 2—Windsor to Lambeth via Belle River.
Highway No. 2a—Windsor to Tilbury.
Highway No. 3—Talbotville to Windsor (Ambassador Bridge).
Highway No. 3a—Highway No. 3 to Windsor (Tunnel).
Highway No. 7—Sarnia to junction with Highway No. 22.
Highway No. 18—Sandwich to Leamington.
Highway No. 21—Morpeth to Wyoming.

Engineer, C. K. S. Macdonell, Chatham

Blacksmithing, $69.95.

F. C. Kimmerley, 18.80; Shanks Garage, 25.50; Sundries—25.65 .... 69 95

Board of Men, $59.00.

Chatham Hotel Co., Ltd., Chatham 59 00

Cement, Calcium Chloride and Bituminous Materials, $42,294.12.

Barrett Co., Ltd., 1,084.76; Canada Cement Co., Ltd., 21.944.65; Canada Colors & Chemicals, Ltd., 739.79; Colas Roads, Ltd., 4,166.20; Dow Chemical Co., 3,597.00; Hadley's Chatham, Ltd., 165.00; Imperial Oil, Ltd., 2,874.72; Alexander Murray & Co., Ltd., 92.48 (credit); Non-Skid Pavement, Ltd., 3,443.78; Ontario Amiesite, Ltd., 379.60; Alfred Rogers, Ltd., 6,032.75; Simrall Refining Corp. of Canada, Ltd., 1,212.75; miscellaneous cement sack credits, 3,254.40 .... 42,294 12

Coal, $346.32.

F. S. Crow, 224.50; Falls & Son, 32.00; Hadleys' Chatham, Ltd., 26.30; J. W. Kerr, 15.55; Oldcastle Farmers' Co-operative Association, 44.72. Sundries, 3.25 .... 346 32

Contracts, $198,013.45.

Bituminous Spraying & Contracting Co., Ltd., No. 633, surface treatment, Ekfrid twp., Thamesville-Delaware project, 3,210.79; Cadwell Sand & Gravel Co., Ltd., No. 31-46, concrete pavement, Sandwich West twp., Amherstburg-

Statutory—Continued

King's Highway Construction—Continued

Residency No. 1—Continued

Contracts—Continued.

Windsor project, 26,289.41; Canada Paving & Supply Corporation, Ltd., No. 31-59, concrete pavement, Rochester & Maidstone twp., Windsor-Tilbury project, 26,023.39; Canada Paving & Supply Corporation, Ltd., No. 31-03; concrete pavement, Rochester and Maidstone twps., Tilbury-Windsor project, 13,963.85; Canada Paving & Supply Corporation, Ltd., No. 31-43, Warwick Bridge, Warwick twp., Sarnia-Strathroy project, 3,729.50; John Chick, Nos. 913, 1041 and 1092, spreading stone, Malden and Gosfield twps., Amherstburg-Kingsville project, 12,824.38; Colautti Bros., Ltd., No. 31-42, Big Creek Bridge, Tilbury twp., Belle River-Tilbury project, 4,950.79; Hadleys' Chatham, Ltd., No. 31-52, Blenheim Overhead Bridge, Harwich twp., Blenheim-Ridgetown project, 12,657.92; Hadleys' Chatham, Ltd., No. 31-83, Petrolia Bridges, Enniskillen twp., Dresden-Petrolia project, 10,608.94; Johnson Bros. Co., Ltd., No. 31-04, concrete pavement, Dawn twp., Dresden-Lambton Line project, 21,314.99; Keystone Construction, Ltd., No. 32-16, culverts, Malden twp., Amherstburg-Windsor project, 6,461.18; W. A. Mackey, No. 32-08, grading, Gosfield and Malden twps., Kemptville-Amherstburg project, 9,296.45; Frank W. Nicholls, No. 32-35; Ekfrid Bridge, Ekfrid twp., Wardsville-Deleware project, 2,052.76; Ontario Bridge Co., Ltd., No. 31-72, Oil Springs and Oil City bridges, Enniskillen twp., Dresden-Petrolia project, 9,936.83; John Patterson Co., Ltd., Nos. 497 and 571, Puce River bridge, Maidstone and Rochester twp., Windsor-Tilbury project, 13,165.18; Ryan Construction, Ltd., No. 32-11, Cedar Creek bridge, S. Colchester twp., Amherstburg-Kingsville project, 10,934.66; James Vance, No. 32-10, Knapp Island bridge, Malden twp., Amherstburg-Kingsville project, 5,981.18; Waltham and Fuller, No. 32-15, culverts, Gosfield and Colchester twps., Kingsville-Malden project, 4,611.25.......................... 198,013 45

Drainage Materials (culverts, tile, etc.), $9,202.32.

Canada Culvert Co., Ltd., 4,463.82; Canada Ingot Iron Co., Ltd., 10.95; Concrete Pipe, Ltd., 262.50; Corrugated Pipe, Ltd., 936.72; Crane, Limited, 21.18; Joseph Dalton, 10.00; Denison Tile Co., Ltd., 64.01; Dominion Wheel & Foundries, Ltd., 336.00; C. R. Gammage, 61.60; Hadleys' Chatham, Ltd., 1,368.80; Aaron Hill, 21.20; D. A. Hitch, 504.00; Katzman Pipe Supply Co., 91.20; Keystone Contractors, Ltd., 82.99; London Rolling Mills, Ltd., 198.74; Thos. E. Martin, 241.62; Meretsky, Burnstine & Meretsky, 16.90; Oil Springs Tile & Cement Co., 403.63; Pedlar People, Ltd., 62.61; Rebidoux Bros., 15.00; Union Natural Gas Co. of Canada, Ltd., 12.00. Sundries—16.85......................... 9,202 32

Fence and Guard Rail Materials, $18,877.56.

Benson-Wilcox Electric Co., 78.68; Canadian Steel Corporation, Ltd., 12,583.22; Conklin Planing Mills, 402.66; Frost Steel & Wire Co., Ltd., 95.89; Hadleys' Chatham, Ltd., 3,472.01; Harrow Farmers' Co-operative Association, Ltd., 19.00; Lundy Fence Co., Ltd., 1,020.00; O'Brien Lumber Co., Ltd., 372.74; Archibald Park, 588.40; P. G. Piggott Lumber Co., Ltd., 244.96............ 18,877 56

Gas and Lubricants, $6,667.40.

Bailey Bros., 135.70; Roswell Bondy, 28.77; Bothwell Manufacturing Co., Ltd., 48.57; British American Oil Co., Ltd., 81.92; Brush's Tire & Battery Shop, 171.61; Canadian Oil Companies, Ltd., 58.19; M. A. Cornwall, 174.89; James Cowan & Co. of Windsor, Ltd., 26.77; Dresden Service Station, 76.47; Gammage & Co., 73.96; William Goold, 13.72; Geo. Harvey, 27.29; Harvey's Service Station, 48.97; S. Hues, 47.58; Imperial Oil, Ltd., 77.44; Johnston Garages & Motors, Ltd., 68.68; F. Kendall, 391.71; J. W. Kerr, 14.76; L. J. Lacey, 54.71; Ladouceur Bros., 50.27; Eli Malefant, 55.34; Merritt's Garage, 125.49; J. E. Moffatt, 32.77; J. E. McDonald & Sons, 37.72; McIrvine's Garage, 79.06; G. McMaster, 12.24; John O'Neil, 522.03; J. A. Parsons, 51.42; Rebidoux Bros., 208.75; Royal Windsor Garage, 38.18; C. S. Sheldon, 60.44; James Stansworth, 42.75; Stodgell & Symes Motor Sales, Ltd., 383.83; Thayers, Ltd., 2,519.35; N. S. Wade, 93.93; C. C. Wakefield & Co., Ltd., 654.67. Sundries—77.45...................... 6,667 40

Hardware, $2,483.65.

W. A. Barr & Co., 15.15; L. T. Ferris, 25.66; Harry Harvey, 10.20; E. S. Hubbell & Sons, 59.94; S. J. Jackson, 32.43; J. W. Kerr & Sons, 28.49; McKeough & Trotter, Ltd., 886.02; John O'Neil, 34.90; Rice Lewis & Son, 50.00; Shillington Bros., 150.43; A. J. Silcox, 15.85; Howard Warren, 13.93; Willard Hardware Co., 1,107.61. Sundries—53.04.. 2,483 65

Statutory—Continued

King's Highway Construction—Continued

Residency No. 1—Continued

Lumber, $3,385.34.

Conklin Planing Mills, 195.14; Hadleys' Chatham, Ltd., 2,744.34; Chas. Hubbell, Planing Mill, 25.60; S. G. Jackson, 61.56; O'Brien Lumber Co., Ltd., 68.79; Smith Planing Mill, 250.26; D. E. Wallace, 33.85. Sundries—5.80.... 3,385 34

Miscellaneous, $41,905.36.

F. Ackerman Co., bulbs, 17.50; Geo. Adkins, car hire, 57.89; O. J. Ball, car hire, 180.46; Harry Bell, office rent, 16.00; Bell Telephone Co. of Canada, moving poles and aerials, 1,516.34; messages, 886.21; rentals, 139.55; Boeckh Co., Ltd., brushes, 19.42; Border Cities Star, printing and advertising, 37.00; British-Canadian Seed Co., grass seed, 343.45; Building Products, Ltd., expansion joints, 14.48; Burlington Steel Co., Ltd., steel, 1,362.15; Burroughs Adding Machine of Canada, Ltd., rentals and inspections, 25.00; Camden Township, drain assessment, 174.24; Canada Dominion Sugar Co., Ltd., chain, 10.72; Canadian Department Stores, Ltd., turkey red, etc., 21.60; Canadian Inspection & Testing Co., Ltd., tests, 26.70; Canadian National Railways, freight, 1,962.00; sidings and wigwags, etc., 1,584.41; Canadian National Telegraphs, moving poles, 60.07; services, 28.64; Canadian Pacific Railway Co., freight, 352.52; sidings and wigwags, etc., 997.92; Canadian Pacific Railway Company's Telegraphs, services, 10.75; H. Cartier Electric Co., Ltd., electrical supplies, 16.32; Chatham Gas Co., Ltd., pipe and services, 76.64; Chatham Public Utilities Commission, services, 189.93; Chatham Water Works, services, 38.56; Copeland's Book Store, office supplies, 11.15; Cooper's Novelty Store, office supplies, 13.24; M. A. Cornwall, car hire, 500.01; W. J. Coutts, sidings, 150.00; Dawn Municipal Telephone System, moving poles, 146.11; Dawn Township, detour, etc., 500.00; Dominion Bridge Co., Ltd., structural steel, 357.53; J. T. Donald & Co., Ltd., sampling, 187.44; Dresden Service Station, kerosene, 38.78; Echo Printing Co., Ltd., printing, 28.25; Town of Essex, road paving, 1,383.36; Essex Border Utilities Commission, culverts and drain benefits, 2,732.90; Essex Stamp Co., Ltd., badges, 227.50; Essex Terminal Railway Company, freight, 156.31; maintenance of gates, 2,183.72; Gasaccumulator Co., Canada, Ltd., reflectors, 344.90; General Office Equipment Corporation, Ltd., office equipment, rental, 105.34; General Steel Wares, Ltd., signs, 358.76; Hadleys' Chatham, Ltd., truck and trailer hire, etc., 1,858.24; E. Harris Co. of Toronto, Ltd., drafting supplies, 11.45; Harwick Township, drain assessment, 22.90; Horticultural Society, trees, 75.00; Howard Township, drain assessment, 364.78; Robert W. Hunt & Co., Ltd., cement inspections, 42.68; Hydro-Electric Power Commission of Ontario, moving poles, 1,597.27; services and lamps, 114.59; Inspector of Weights and Measures, services, 14.00; Instruments, Ltd., surveying instruments and repairs, 35.40; Everett Jones, moving hedge, 10.00; G. Jones, office rent, 40.00; Ernest Kimbell, removing hedge, 22.00; King's Printer, office supplies, 31.59; C. T. Laidlaw, car hire, 61.11; London Rolling Mills, Ltd., steel, 1,880.13; Lowe Brothers Co., Ltd., paint, 682.05; Lufkin Rule Co. of Canada, Ltd., tapes, 31.47; Maidstone Township, drain assessment, 430.88; H. N. Merritt, car hire, 198.73; S. B. Arnold in trust re Merritt & Co., Ltd., property rental, 540.00; Metallic Roofing Co. of Canada, Ltd., expansion strips and signs, etc., 1,473.75; Michigan Central Railroad, sidings and wigwags, 98.98; freight, 945.52; W. J. Moore, surveying instruments and repairs, 16.50; Municipal Road Spraying & Oiling Co., Ltd., material and services, 1,368.98; E. P. Muntz, Ltd., services, 27.00; McKeough & Trotter, Ltd., steel bars, etc., 47.64; H. R. McKim, Ltd., snowplow hire, 88.25; Archibald Park, bars, 52.39; Pedlar People, Ltd., steelcrete, 170.31; Pere Marquette Railway Co., freight, 1,354.95; sidings and wigwags, 264.63; Plympton Township, repairing culverts, 30.00; Thos. Pocklington Co., surveying instruments and repairs, 11.21; Robt. T. Purves & Co., expansion joints, 203.38; J. Frank Raw Co., Ltd., surveying instruments and repairs, 48.60; Remington Typewriters, Ltd., inspections and ribbons, etc., 14.40; Romney Township, drain assessment, 20.60; Shepherd Printing Co., office supplies, 26.15; M. H. Sher, car hire, 658.42; Southern Ontario Gas Co., pipe, 79.12; Steel Company of Canada, Ltd., structural steel, 1,285.61; Sulman's, office supplies, 26.15; Gordon Summers, car hire, 338.59; Sundry Registry Fees, services, 268.97; Tilbury E. Township, drain assessment, 45.00; Truscon Steel Co. of Canada, Ltd., steel, 4,729.18; Union Natural Gas Co., Ltd., office rent and services, 423.00; United Typewriters Co., Ltd., machine rentals and services, 40.50; R. J. Warnock, sodium chlorate, 14.58. Sundries, 76.96........ 41,905 36

Pay Lists, $176,598.92.

Wages of men.. 176,598 92

Statutory—Continued

King's Highway Construction—Continued

Residency No. 1—Continued

Purchase of Property, Right-of-Way, $21,058.23.

Colchester South twp., James Girard, 267.10; John McLean, 1,128.00; Mrs. Chloe Readman, 63.50; School Section No. 6, V. F. McLean, 50.00; Mrs. Myrtle Scott and Carrie Crichton, 125.00; Dawn twp., Margaret Nurse, 48.60; Geo. A. Webster, 475.00; Enniskillen twp., D. Wallace, 104.70; Harwick twp., Mr. and Mrs. E. Eade, 225.00; Wm. R. McGregor, 1,650.00; W. J. Holmes, 2,500.00; Wm. N. Young, 52.75; Maidstone twp., George Beckett, 172.00; Amedie Bellaire, 249.10; Mrs. E. Bellaire, 49.70; Leon Bellaire, 164.80; N. V. Chavin, 29.00; D. Durocher, 1,106.00; Huron & Erie Mortgage Corporation, re J. H. Price, 242.00; H. W. Maisonville, 59.20; Rena Mero, 333.50; Mrs. T. M. Pohl, 433.30; Malden twps., Agriculture Development Board, 218.25; Silas Beaudoin, 552.80; Francis G. Brush, 22.20; Fred Deneau, 64.50; Oliver Deneau, 94.25; Ross B. Deneau, 21.95; L. A. Eldridge and J. B. Swan, 100.00; Bertha Fleming, 400.00; John Gibb, 173.45; S. A. Honor, 242.50; Daniel La Ferte, 100.00; Demos Langlois, 69.10; Stanley W. Langlois, 46.10; Forest Lockwood, 400.00; Malden United Church, 200.00; James Martin, 80.85; C. R. Mickle, 100.00; Thos. S. Mickle, 142.50; Mullen Investments, Ltd., 2,200.00; Chas. E. Park, 10.00; John Parks, 275.00; Nettie Patterson, 30.00; E. A. Patton Estate, 200.00; A. Hazen Price, 150.00; Anne Reaume, 75.00; Eugene Reaume, 175.00; Mrs. M. St. Onge, 60.00; School Section No. 1, 25.00; Alfred J. Sellers, 12.75; Ernest R. Sellars, 17.80; Forrest Sellars, 476.75; Gordon W. Sellars, 214.65; Arthur J. Welch, 10.00; John T. Williams, 25.00; Mrs. E. J. Wood, 106.00; Harry J. Wood, 75.00; Levi Wright, 906.90; Rochester twp., Leo. J. Girard, 359.50; Sandwich East twp., A. Andrews, 60.00; Sandwich South twp., B. H. Warner, 1,530.66; Sandwich West twp., S. W. Dumouchel, 31.80; Messrs. Page & Chappus, 650.00; Tilbury East twp., A. R. Bell, 33.00; Tilbury North twp., Mrs. Alphonsine Mailloux, 365.12; John Palmer, 416.50. Sundries, 10.10.................... 21,058 23

Property, Miscellaneous, $4,658.25.

Silas Beaudoin, Malden twp., borrow pit, 200.00; T. G. Brush, Malden twp., borrow pit, 129.75; Basil Burns, Dawn twp., removing fence, 60.00; Albert Crowder, Secretary-Treasurer School Section No. 5, Maidstone twp., new well, 75.00; James A. Currie, Dawn twp., borrow pit, 75.00; Noah Dame, Maidstone twp., borrow pit, 100.00; Alfred Dupuis, Rochester twp., borrow pit, 787.80; James Eaton, Maidstone twp., borrow pit, 75.00; William Eden, Dawn twp., moving fence, 28.50; John Gibb, Malden twp., borrow pit, 138.90; V. and Maude Grayer, Colchester twp., fill, removal of house and damages, 450.00; Samuel Gyde, Dawn twp., borrow pit, 200.00; Frederick Irwin, Colchester twp., loss of well, 150.00; Mrs. Bertha Keats, Raleigh twp., removal of barn, 50.00; A. W. Kennedy, Maidstone twp., fruit trees, 30.00; Ernest Kimball, Mersea twp., removal of hedge, 21.90; W. H. Lecocq, Enniskillen twp., borrow pits, 37.50; Fred Mickle, Malden twp., crop damages, 25.00; Caroline Miller, Colchester twp., borrow pits, 225.00; James Martin, Malden twp., borrow pits, 400.00; John F. McLean, Colchester S. twp., borrow pit, 427.60; C. J. McTaggart, Ekfrid twp., borrow pit, 30.00; Adolard Plante, Maidstone twp., damages to drainage, 150.00; Forrest Sellars, Malden twp., borrow pit, 269.80; J. W. Sutherland, Enniskillen twp., borrow pit, 37.50; Ernest Thomson, Colchester S. twp., wells, 400.00; T. W. Wride, Colchester S. twp., removal of buildings, 75.00. Sundries, 9.00.. 4,658 25

Road Equipment and Supplies, $1,732.86.

Frank Ackerman, 19.52; Biddell's Tire & Battery Service, 27.75; Canada Ingot Iron Co., Ltd., 221.58; Chatham Auto Wreckers, 31.50; Chatham Foundry, 16.39; Chatham Malleable & Steel Manufacturing Co., Ltd., 62.97; James Cowan & Co. of Windsor, Ltd., 166.62; Peter Ennett, 10.00; Albert G. Hill, 200.00; Levy & Westwood Machinery Co., 125.35; Massey-Harris Co., 27.70; McKeough & Trotier, Ltd., 59.53; H. R. McKim, Ltd., 15.00; Oldcastle Farmers' Co-operative Association, 13.33; Archibald Park, 52.09; Sawyer-Massey, Ltd., 205.15; Charles Scarlett, 27.72; Thompson & Smith, 264.76; West End Garage, 100.05. Sundries, 85.85.. 1,732 86

Stone, Gravel and Screenings, $21,670.99.

Brunner Mond Canada, Ltd., 7,450.19; Cadwell Sand & Gravel Co., Ltd., 6,485.60; Canada Crushed Stone Corporation, Ltd., 1,358.45; Colautti Bros., Ltd., 811.25; Consolidated Sand & Gravel, Ltd., 243.80; Gordon Crushed Stone Co., Ltd., 239.16; Hadleys' Chatham, Ltd., 722.40; Hagersville Quarries, Ltd., 4,257.02; Sherman & Hubbell, 76.62; Sundries, 26.50........................... 21,670 99

Statutory—Continued

King's Highway Construction—Continued

Residency No. 1—Continued

Travelling Expenses and Disbursements, $6,252.08.

George Adkins, 458.80; Wm. G. Almas, 191.70; James Asquith, 191.75; O. J. Ball, 204.85; Ira Brisco, 187.10; F. W. Burch, 187.95; James Calder, 40.00; C. J. Carson, 12.80; Louis A. Desjardins, 84.10; A. F. Flintoff, 479.07; Wm. Garrod, 31.30; L. Gelina, 81.92; H. Harrison, 564.11; W. M. Henry, 78.00; W. R. Jackson, 13.06; C. R. Kendall, 189.76; C. T. Laidlaw, 184.73; Garfield Light, 15.40; David H. P. Low, 236.50; C. K. S. MacDonell, 878.88; H. N. Merritt, 182.65; Reginald D. McLean, 135.75; R. N. Page, 58.15; R. M. Perkins, 156.25; Nat. Phipps, 17.00; Gerald Poisson, 72.50; M. H. Sher, 408.50; Gordon L. Summers, 121.35; Chas. Taymon, 13.05; F. Watson, 537.45; Keah West, 194.85. Sundries, 42.80 .... 6,252 08

Residency No. 2 ($400,526.38)

Highway No. 2—Lambeth to Brantford.
Highway No. 3—Talbotville to Simcoe.
Highway No. 4—Port Stanley to Clinton.
Highway No. 7—Junction of Highway No. 22 to Stratford.
Highway No. 19—Port Burwell to Ingersoll; Woodstock to Tavistock.
Highway No. 22—Highway No. 7 to Highway No. 4.
Highway No. 24—Brantford to Simcoe.

Engineer, H. E. Macpherson, London.

Blacksmithing, $76.42.

Beaver Foundry & Furnace Works, 16.17; R. J. Henderson, 25.50. Sundries, 34.75 76 42

Bonus for Wire Fencing, $100.00.

Geo. Wenig, Bayham twp., 100.00 .... 100 00

Cement, Calcium Chloride and Bituminous Materials, $44,793.69.

Barrett Company, Ltd., 631.56; Colas Roads, Ltd., 13,250.92; Copp Builder's Supply Co., Ltd., 14.65; Dow Chemical Co., 621.50; Imperial Oil, Ltd., 24,414.61; S. F. Lawrason & Co., Ltd., 243.98; Alexander Murray & Co., Ltd., 676.00; Non-Skid Pavement, Ltd., 665.28; Ontario Amiesite, Ltd., 365.30; R. M. Pincombe & Sons, 21.60; Alfred Rogers, Ltd., 3,882.75; Solvay Sales Corporation, 1,261.00; B. C. Turville, 22.50. Sundries, 18.82; miscellaneous cement sack credits, 1,296.78 .... 44,793 69

Coal, $82.75.

Beachville Co-operative Association, 13.25; W. J. Kennedy, 14.75; J. G. Orchard & Sons, 32.50; Wm. Gordon Patrick, 16.00. Sundries, 6.25 .... 82 75

Contracts, $122,011.60.

Canada Paving & Supply Corporation, Ltd., No. 31-20, mixed macadam pavement, Oxford and Durham twps., London-Ingersoll project, 2,058.06; Wm. Clark & Son, No. 31-53, Clinton bridge over Bayfield river, Goderich and Stanley twps., Clinton-Goderich project, 14,805.77; Dufferin Paving & Crushed Stone, Ltd., No. 32-28, mixed macadam pavement, E. Zorra twp., Woodstock-Tavistock project, 59,647.32; W. E. Hayes, No. 515, spreading gravel, Biddulph and London twps., Clinton-London project, 5,036.75; King Paving Co., Ltd., No. 509, Waterford Bridge approaches, Townsend twp., Simcoe-Brantford project, 1,624.46; E. P. Muntz, Ltd., No. 30-75, Paris bridge over Grand River, Dumfries S. twp., Paris-Brantford project, 27,037.50; Towland Construction Co., Ltd., No. 30-77, concrete pavement, Yarmouth twp., Port Stanley-St. Thomas project, 11,801.74 .... 122,011 60

Drainage Materials (culverts, tile, etc.), $4,794.54.

Brick Manufacturing & Supply Co., Ltd., 49.52; Canada Culvert Co., Ltd., 3,010.39; Canada Ingot Iron Co., Ltd., 392.90; Concrete Pipe, Ltd., 668.78; Geo. Coultis & Son, 16.63; Wm. H. Deller, 10.00; Dominion Wheel & Foundries, Ltd., 119.20; T. Hitch, 17.55; Hollier & Son, 31.25; Fred Kerr, 94.34; London Rolling Mills, Ltd., 84.15; Chester McComb, 13.65; McCormick Brothers, 21.00; Phinu Brick Co., 12.60; E. R. Seabrook & Co., 136.31; Steel Co. of Canada, Ltd., 105.27. Sundries, 11.00 .... 4,794 54

Fence and Guard Rail Materials, $29,494.81.

D. C. Baird, 3,772.00; Wray Bee, 150.00; M. D. Berdan, 23.10; Canada Wire & Iron Goods Co., 149.85; Carroll & Thompson, 19.92; Exeter Lumber Co.,

Statutory—Continued

King's Highway Construction—Continued

Residency No. 2—Continued

Fence and Guard Rail Materials—Continued.

Ltd., 614.31; Frost Steel & Wire Co., Ltd., 16,823.78; W. N. Gilroy, 169.00; B. Greening Wire Co., Ltd., 279.40; E. A. Guest, 30.00; Laidlaw, Belton lumber Co., Ltd., 242.25; Lambeth Farmers' Co-operative Co., Ltd., 15.00; Theodore Legault, 132.00; Line & Cable Accessories, Ltd., 10.24; Lundy Fence Co., Ltd., 2,621.99; John Morrow Screw & Nut Co., Ltd., 215.04; R. M. McKay, 299.84; Sarnia Fence Co., Ltd., 3,211.50; Steel Company of Canada, Ltd., 288.50; Stoney Lake Hotels, Ltd., 379.80; Strathroy Hardware, 19.65. Sundries, 27.64.. 29,494 81

Gas and Lubricants, $6,164.53.

Wm. Aberdein, 12.98; T. W. Atkinson, 15.93; A. Baechler & Son, 24.98; Barnard's Service Station and Tourist Camps, 33.86; Beachville Garage, 343.87; Burgess & Shipway, 34.04; W. G. Caines, 417.87; Canadian Oil Companies, Ltd., 27.78; Chevrolet Garage, Exeter, 84.84; Cities Service, Oil Co., Ltd., 47.82; Leo Conner, 30.28; Jas. Cowan & Co., Ltd., 43.94; L. E. Davidson, 20.83; J. M. Elliott, 130.18; Sandy Elliot, 17.04; Geo. W. Ewer, 195.77; Ford Garage, Delhi, 384.85; Haley's Service Station, 39.60; F. J. Henshaw, 10.89; Hobbs Garage, 236.17; Imperial Oil, Ltd., 1,957.37; S. Lundy, 499.00; Mann Bros., 52.50; Chas. Martin, 21.20; Ray Morningstar, 10.26; Murray's Service, 39.38; W. J. McLachlan, 13.25; Angus McLean, 22.50; Milton M. Napper, 163.74; Nediger's Garage, 56.13; Oxford Garage, 11.43; Paris Motors, Ltd., 17.12; J. A. Parsons, 520.61; J. E. Stedelbauer, 29.16; Supertest Petroleum Corporation, Ltd., 331.39; Tench Bros., 33.41; Thedford Garage, 29.60; Ira Truefitt, 12.10; C. A. Walsh, 11.00; A. J. Ward, 28.76; J. E. Wilkinson, 52.27; Sundries, 98.83.................. 6,164 53

Hardware, $798.00.

Brooks & Barrie, 10.53; Carroll & Thompson, 33.99; W. A. Clarke Hardware, 14.60; Cowan Hardware, Ltd., 10.77; G. A. Hawkins, 90.48; Hobbs Hardware Co., Ltd., 10.34; D. H. Howden & Co., Ltd., 242.01; Lambeth Farmer Co-operative Co., Ltd., 19.01; Lindenfield Bros., 13.51; J. F. Meyers, 32.11; H. S. Morgan, 17.31; C. B. Munn, 11.63; Fred McLeod, 11.30; Sinclair's Hardware, Ltd., 11.05; Stanley Hardware, 62.74; Strathroy Hardware Co., 15.24; Erle Taylor, 21.51; E. I. Torrens, 113.21. Sundries, 56.66...................... 798 00

Lumber, $2,753.59.

B. V. Bailey, 67.32; D. C. Baird, 33.45; Barrett & Young, 58.25; Jas. R. Boque, 20.67; Ella M. Burwell, 96.59; Geo. Coultis & Son, 38.50; Matthew Cowper, 21.96; Exeter Lumber Co., Ltd., 1,247.40; Wm. Gerry & Sons, 11.79; Green Lumber Co., Ltd., 10.50; E. A. Guest, 33.00; O. A. Hepburn & Son, 630.00; County of Huron, 13.50; W. H. Jackson, 12.00; Geo. N. Kernohan Lumber Co., Ltd., 409.64; Robert Quance Co., Ltd., 28.02. Sundries, 21.00.......... 2,753 59

Miscellaneous, $53,786.93.

J. H. Back & Co., drafting supplies, 106.91; C. F. Barron & Acme Motor Truck Co., Ltd., truck hire, 596.00; Bell Telephone Co. of Canada, moving poles and aerials, 219.87; messages, 265.22; rentals, 107.40; Fred Blayney, pulling hedge, 131.00; Wm. J. Boss, equipment rental, 60.00; Boss & Brazier Construction Co., Ltd., material and services, 85.00; Brant County, equipment rental, 25.00; Canadian Industries, Ltd., paint and soda, 85.75; Canadian National Railways, freight, 25,945.50; sidings and wigwags, etc., 362.14; subways, 13,063.49; Canadian Pacific Railway Co., freight, 998.11; George Dale, drain assessment, 17.00; Dennisteel, Ltd., garage, rent, etc., 108.25; Dereham Township, drain assessment, 13.94; Dominion Bridge Co., Ltd., structural steel, 116.50; J. T. Donald & Co., Ltd., sampling, 45.24; J. M. Elliott, garage rent, 10.00; Norman Epps, snowplow rental, 186.00; Gasaccumulator Co., Canada, Ltd., reflectors, 62.50; General Steel Wares, Ltd., signs, 98.30; G. M. Hubbell, car hire, 23.45; Hydro-Electric Power Commission of Ontario, moving poles, 624.41; Instruments, Ltd., surveyor's instruments and repairs, 40.45; King Paving Co., Ltd., material and services, 71.76; Lake Erie and Northern Railway Co., sidings, 12.00; Law Construction Co., Ltd., material and services, 319.15; London Bolt & Hinge Works, bolts, etc., 44.56; London Paint Service, Ltd., paint, 20.03; London Structural Steel Co., Ltd., steel and rods, etc., 45.84; London Towel Supply Co., rent of towels, 15.00; Lowe Brothers Co., Ltd., paint, 149.42; Machine & Tool Co., Ltd., drilling signs, etc., 10.85; Mann Bros., garage rent, 60.00; Metallic Roofing Co. of Canada, Ltd., expansion strips and signs, etc., 420.17; Michigan Central Railroad, freight, 186.24; Benjamin Moore & Co., Ltd., paint, 15.68; E. W. G. Moore, office rent, 780.00; E. P. Muntz, Ltd., building shed, 30.00; Colin McCallum, storage, 14.00; Mrs. Emma Nelles, storage, 10.00;

Statutory—Continued

King's Highway Construction—Continued

Residency No. 2—Continued

Miscellaneous—Continued.

Oxford County, grader hire, 278.00; Corporation of Paris, taxes, 99.32; J. A. Parsons, garage rent, 75.00; Reflex Sign Co., Ltd., signs and signals, 164.43; Remington Typewriters, Ltd., inspections and ribbons, etc., 14.00; Sanderson Pearcy-Marietta, Ltd., paint, 19.21; E. Smith, sawing trees, 19.94; Mrs. M. R. Smith, garage rent, 35.00; Southern Ontario Gas Co., moving gas-line, 4,673.75; Stanley Township, drain assessment, 40.00; Steel Company of Canada, Ltd., structural steel, 349.89; Sundry Registry Fees, services, 44.00; Superior Transportation & Shipping Co., Ltd., snowplow hire, 543.32; Toronto, Hamilton & Buffalo Railway Co., freight, 88.74; Towland Construction Co., Ltd., material and services, 177.78; E. L. Townsend, truck hire, 451.43; Ira Truefitt, garage rent, 10.00; J. E. Wainwright, snow clearing, 706.43; Westminster Township, drain assessment, 154.20; Mrs. C. Whelchan, crop damages, 12.00; Ozar Wilson, services on drain, 52.00; Roy Wilson, mower rental, 12.00; James Wright, iron bars, 14.30. Sundries, 150.06 .... 53,786 93

Pay Lists, $98,919.38.

Wages of men 98,919 38

Purchase of Property, Right-of-Way, $4,914.80.

Biddulph twp., Oscar F. Mead, 500.00; Brantford twp., Gordon Gill, 35.00; David Lee Estate, 2,900.00; C. A. McCormick, 47.00; A. E. Thurman, 300.00; G. A. Traut, 300.00; Dereham twp., Wm. Ostrander, 100.00; London twp., Geo. McComb, 54.00; Nelson and Lorne Kirk, 62.00; John Shannon, 100.00; Middleton twp., Canadian National Railways, 20.00; J. W. Sanders, 246.80; Townsend twp., Dr. F. H. Massecar, 250.00 .... 4,914 80

Property, Miscellaneous, $1,788.33.

Jos. and Chas. Allison, Goderich, Stanley and Tuckersmith twps., damages, 95.00; Chas. A. Campbell, Caradoc twp., damages, 50.00; Wm. W. Cooper, Stanley twp., removing fence, 80.00; Chas. Crossett, Bayham, twp. drainage damages, 100.00; E. A. Edwards, Bosanquet twp., damages to trees, 50.00; Fred Elmes, Brantford twp., arbitration fees, 60.00; E. Evoy, Adelaide twp., removing fence, 13.00; C. E. Hallowell, Brantford twp., arbitration fee, 60.00; Knowles Studio, Dumfries S. twp., photos re arbitration, 12.00; Lawson & Stratton, Dumfries S. twp., arbitration fees, 190.00; John McLeod, Townsend twp., removal of fence, 18.75; Roy Palen, Middleton twp., fill, 40.00; Robert Patterson, Adelaide twp., removal of fence, 60.00; Albert E. Peaslee, Adelaide twp., removal of fence, 30.00; Henry Reinhardt, Adelaide twp., removal of fence, 15.00; Evelyn S. Roberts, Dumfries S. twp., damages, 348.58; School Section No. 7, Adelaide twp., moving fence, 14.00; Helen M. Shaw, London twp., damages, 500.00; Byron Waldron, Stanley twp., removal of fence, 40.00. Sundries, 12.00 .... 1,788 33

Road Equipment and Supplies, $1,259.15.

J. D. Adams (Can.), Ltd., 146.42; Canada Ingot Iron Co., Ltd., 13.12; James Cowan & Co., Ltd., 18.03; Dennisteel, Ltd., 59.65; Dominion Road Machinery Co., Ltd., 122.05; R. G. Dowding, 11.35; Frost & Wood Co., Ltd., 51.77; International Harvester Co. of Canada, Ltd., 126.03; Machine & Tool Co., Ltd., 13.65; Massey-Harris Co., 441.15; Geo. Penfound, 23.65; Sawyer-Massey, Ltd., 157.64; Otto Schmidt, 10.48; W. F. Thurlow, 16.60. Sundries, 47.56 .... 1,259 15

Stone, Gravel and Screenings, $26,102.65.

Chas. Brown, 322.50; W. E. Buttery, 10.50; Canada Crushed Stone Corporation, Ltd., 1,576.93; S. B. Chambers, 38.95; Consolidated Sand & Gravel, Ltd., 2,610.65; Ellis Cutler, 61.00; Gordon Crushed Stone Co., Ltd., 674.12; Gypsum, Lime & Alabastine, Canada, Ltd., 18.51; Hagersville Quarries, Ltd., 18,695.87; John Hill, 151.30; Innerkip Lime & Stone Co., Ltd., 1,112.50; Harry Murphy, 266.25; Peter McCormick, 330.00; M. G. McLaws, 119.00; Robert Quance Co., Ltd., 43.25; Austin Springett, 19.00. Sundries, 52.32 .... 26,102 65

Travelling Expenses and Disbursements, $2,685.21.

Thomas Ayres, 146.39; J. A. Coombs, 189.37; N. H. Crowe, 187.50; A. Evans, Jr., 17.25; A. Evans, Sr., 154.09; A. H. Foley, 103.25; George Gibb, 18.43; O. Hardy, 221.40; H. Harrison, 11.40; G. U. Howell, 236.00; G. M. Hubbell, 248.60; W. J. Lachey, 26.95; A. E. Long, 96.92; A. MacPherson, 108.99; H. E. MacPherson, 208.25; Hugh MacVicar, 19.42; N. McLean, 15.00; Milfred Nichols, 11.10; W. Randall, 57.25; W. F. Smith, 225.90; S. Vankoughnett, 82.25; A. G. Vining, 216.35; W. T. Waller, 10.80; George E. Walsh, 56.00. Sundries, 16.35... 2,685 21

Statutory—Continued

King's Highway Construction—Continued

Residency No. 3 ($587,536.79)

Highway No. 5—Paris to Highway No. 24.
Highway No. 6—Clappison's Corners to Arthur.
Highway No. 7—Kitchener to Highway No. 10, north of Brampton.
Highway No. 8—Goderich to Highway No. 5.
Highway No. 9—Arthur to Orangeville.
Highway No. 10—Junction with Highway No. 7, north of Brampton, to Orangeville.
Highway No. 23—Mitchell to Listowel.
Highway No. 24—Guelph south to Highway No. 5 (St. George Road).
Highway No. 24a—Paris to Galt.

Engineer, S. A. Cummiford, Stratford

Blacksmithing, $30,75.

A. Reid, 19.25. Sundries, 11.50 .... 30 75

Bonus for Wire Fencing, $1,886.97.

Edward Bald, Fullarton twp., 30.00; John Burke, Amaranth twp., 22.80; R. C. Cronin, Beverly twp., 24.00; Harry Davidson, Beverly twp., 57.00; Errett Dickson, W. Luther twp., 150.75; Herbert Duffey, E. Luther twp., 32.10; A. W. L. Graham, N Dumfries twp., 18.00; John Haley, W. Luther twp., 17.10; T. H. Hillis, Garafraxa E. twp., 88.80; Herbert Irvine, E. Garafraxa twp., 24.00; Samuel Irvine, E. Luther twp., 72.36; W. J. Irvine, E. Luther twp., 29.40; J. Kirby, S. Dumfries twp., 58.92; G. H. Lane, Dumfries S. twp., 156.60; A. E. Livingston, S. Dumfries twp., 57.84; Geo. Mair, Goderich twp., 84.00; Robert Miller, Luther E. twp., 72.60; Chas. McCurdy, E. Garafraxa twp., 135.60; M. Plumstead, S. Dumfries twp., 58.98; J. C. Reid, E. Garafraxa twp., 57.78; Geo. W. Rounding, W. Garafraxa twp., 53.28; W. R. Stringer, E. Garafraxa twp., 111.00; A. Taylor, E. Garafraxa twp., 92 70; David Taylor, E. Garafraxa twp., 46.20; J. Taylor, N. Dumfries twp., 11.40; W. E. Thompson, E. Luther twp., 145.20; W. J. Thompson, Beverly twp., 72.00; John White, W. Luther twp., 43.20; Herbert Woods, Garafraxa twp., 63.36 .... 1,886 97

Cement, Calcium Chloride and Bituminous Materials, $84,393.46.

Barrett Company, Ltd., 261.05; Canada Cement Co , Ltd., 56,032.14; Canadian Bitumuls Co., Ltd., 1,935.03; Dow Chemical Co., 1,875.90; Wm. Hogg Coal Co., Ltd., 141.60; Imperial Oil, Ltd., 12,834.32; Merck & Co., Ltd., 35.00; Alexander Murray & Co., Ltd., 355.80 credit; Non-Skid Pavement, Ltd., 2,048.39; Ontario Amiesite, Ltd., 2,110.27; Alfred Rogers, Ltd., 7,975.76; Miscellaneous cement sack credits, 500.20 .... 84,393 46

Coal, $823.07.

W. J. Baker, 70.51; Alex. Chambers & Co., 96.60; Galt Fuel & Supply Co., 89.47; Henderson Coal Co., 148.45; J. M Roach Co., 25.38; Elias Rogers Co., Ltd., 303.21; Geo. Schrader, 19.05; Fred Thomas, 62.40. Sundries, 8.00 ...... 823 07

Contracts, $263,567.80.

Archibald-Birdsall, Ltd., No. 31-11, concrete pavement, Amaranth & Garafraxa E. twps., Orangeville-Arthur project, 16,753.38; Frank Barber & Associates, Ltd., No. 30-45, Breslau Bridge supervision, Waterloo twp., Stratford-Guelph project, 12,208.17; Bergman Construction Co., Ltd., No. 32-48, concrete pavement, Guelph and Waterloo twps., Guelph-Waterloo project, 11,151.15; H. J. Clark, No 997, curbs and gutters, N. and S. Dumfries twps., Paris-Galt project, 1,486.35; H. J. Clark, No. 32-18, curbs and gutters, Vespra twp., Midhurst-Elmvale project, 1,287.00; Alfred and Milton Denstedt, No. 30-81, grading and culverts, Luther and Garafraxa twps., Orangeville-Arthur project, 7,685.03; Dufferin Paving & Crushed Stone, Ltd., No. 30-45, Breslau Bridge approaches, Waterloo twp., Kitchener-Guelph project, 18,871.46; John Gaffney, No. 30-44, three bridges, Garafraxa twp., Arthur-Orangeville project, 12,531.05; John Gaffney, No. 32-12, Maitland River Bridge, Elma twp., Mitchell-Listowel project, 8,331.79; Godson Contracting Co., No. 31-17, mixed macadam pavement, Guelph and Eramosa twps., Guelph-Rockwood project, 12,936.37; W. A. Mackey No. 31-37, grading and culverts, Garafraxa and E. Luther twps., Arthur-Orangeville project, 20,240.47; Municipal Road Spraying & Oiling Co., Ltd., No. 1112, surface treatment, Eramosa twp., Georgetown-Guelph project, 1,938.23; Municipal Road Spraying & Oiling Co., Ltd., No. 964, surface treatment, Gainsboro twp., Bismarck-Wellandport project, 913.60; McArthur Engineering & Construction Co., Ltd., No. 31-45, concrete pavement, Dumfries S. twp., Galt-Paris project, 43,904.04; Ontario Ready Mix Concrete, Ltd., No. 31-07, concrete pavement, Logan and Elma twps., Mitchell-Listowel project, 16,947.82; Sam

Statutory—Continued

King's Highway Construction—Continued

Residency No. 3—Continued

Contracts—Continued.

Russell, No. 710, gravelling, Dumfries S. twp., Galt-St. George project, 2,625.00; Thomas Shenton, No. 30-19, grading and culverts, Guelph twp., Galt-Guelph project, 863.00; Standard Paving, Ltd., Nos. 970 and 1102, concrete repairs, Waterloo twp., Stratford-Guelph project, 1,939.50; Standard Paving, Ltd., No. 31-49, mixed macadam pavement, S. Dumfries twp., Galt-Paris project, 48,664.33; W. E. Taylor, No. 30-61, grading and culverts, Dumfries N. and S. twps., Galt-Brantford project, 14,780.06; Wm. Yundt, Nos. 72 and 761, gravelling, Garafraxa W. twp., Orangeville-Arthur project, 5,510.00; Wm Yundt, No. 668, gravelling, Wallace and Elma twps., Atwood-Listowel project, 2,000.00. . 263,567 80

Drainage Materials (culverts, tile, etc.), $3,884.51.

Burlington Steel Co., Ltd., 229.06; Canada Culvert Co., Ltd., 907.44; Canada Ingot Iron Co , Ltd., 1,240.86; Corrugated Pipe Co., Ltd., 10.40; Cunningham & Co., 29.15; Dominion Wheel & Foundries, Ltd., 168.00; National Sewer Pipe Co., Ltd., 1,251.60; Ernest Robinson, 41.29. Sundries, 6.71................ 3,884 51

Fence and Guard Rail Materials, $13,541.00.

D. C. Baird, 5,774.68; Canada Wire & Iron Goods Co., 205.82; Canadian Steel Corporation, Ltd., 66.81; Frost Steel & Wire Co., Ltd., 4,242.46; B. Greening Wire Co., Ltd., 417.47; John Morrow Screw & Nut Co., Ltd., 150.00; J. A. McFarlane, 864.25; Railway Power Engineering Corporation, Ltd., 630.68; Steel Company of Canada, Ltd., 1,183.78. Sundries, 5.05................... 13,541 00

Gas and Lubricants, $5,787.11.

Clarence Campbell, 1,016.76; Canadian Oil Companies, Ltd., 1,717.48; James Cowan & Co., Ltd., 165.25; Daubs Garage, 24.28; W. England, 26.25; Imperial Oil, Ltd., 1,997.15; Lewis Menary, 80.85; Model Tire Service, Ltd., 19.08; McColl-Frontenac Oil Co., Ltd., 69.85; J. A. McMillan, 25.46; J. H. McNally, 130.78; People's Fuel Co., Ltd., 416.30; W. S. Stuckey, 18.46; G. E. Swire, 43.09. Sundries, 36.07.. 5,787 11

Hardware, 409.64.

Bond Hardware Co., Ltd., 100.61; H. B. Douglas, 17.00; C. M. MacDonald, 22.29; Thos. Meredith, 47.75; J. R. Myers & Sons, Ltd., 62.64; R. Nicholson, 16.35; Rice Lewis & Son, Ltd., 65.15; Sebringville Hardware Co., 29.74; Tait & Kitchen, 19.39; R. H. Thompson & Co., 18.30. Sundries, 10 42............ 409 64

Lumber, $1,075.65.

Boake Manufacturing Co., Ltd., 37.50; Brampton Lumber Co., 553.92; Dufferin Paving & Crushed Stone, Ltd., 140.58; John L. Forler, 16.80; L. Hoffmeyer, 38.47; Kalbfleisch Bros., Ltd., 46.11; Longfield Brothers, Ltd., 16.19; W. B. McCulloch, 90.93; Nagel's Upholstery Works, 100.00; W. I. Reid & Co., 30.20. Sundries, 4.95.. 1,075 65

Miscellaneous, $95,957.70.

Bell Telephone Co. of Canada, moving poles and aerials, 364.45; messages, 436.42; rentals, 101.80; Norman Bellman, storage, 330.00; Bennington Electric Co., Ltd., electrical wiring, 23.16; Blanshard Municipal Telephone System, services, 32.70; Burlington Steel Co , Ltd., steel, 1,244.91; Canada Paint Co., Ltd., paint, 58.80; Canadian Inspection & Testing Co., Ltd., tests, 39.45; Canadian Johns-Manville Co. Ltd., expansion joints, 62.52; Canadian National Express Co., services, 11.60; Canadian National Railways, freight, 3,464.98; sidings and wigwags, etc., 219.19; subways, 72,700.94; Canadian National Telegraphs, services, 28.26; Canadian Pacific Railway Co., freight, 1,137.22; sidings and wigwags, etc., 107.18; Canadian Steel Corporation, Ltd., steel, 955.30; A. E. Dockrill, cleaning windows, 10.50; Dominion Bridge Co., Ltd., structural steel, 180.00; J. T. Donald & Co., Ltd., sampling, 457.52; Dufferin Paving & Crushed Stone, Ltd., laying amiesite, 333.16; Fouse & Brobst, truck hire, 42.50; Gasaccumulator Co., Canada, Ltd., reflectors, 45.42; General Steel Wares, Ltd., signs, 64.80; F. A. Gilbert, expense account, 31.68; Goderich Water & Light Commission, power and lamps, 58.00; Samuel Greenwood, truck hire, 18.20; Robert W. Hunt & Co., Ltd., cement inspections, 17.46; W. J. Hyatt, safety devices, 700.00; Hydro-Electric Power Commission of Ontario, moving poles, 41.78; B. L. Irwin, car hire, 135.52; Lake Erie & Northern Railway Co., freight, 72.00; London Structural Steel Co., Ltd., steel and rods, etc., 15.32; Lowe Brothers Co., Ltd., paint, 260.07; Metallic Roofing Co. of Canada, Ltd., expansion strips and signs, etc., 1,380.45; W. J. McCully, office rent, 564.00;

Statutory—Continued

King's Highway Construction—Continued

Residency No. 3—Continued

Miscellaneous—Continued.

R. O'Brien, car hire, 453.32; Pedlar People, Ltd., steelcrete, 17.96; People's Fuel Co., Ltd., garage rent, 21.00; Thos. Pocklington Co., surveying instruments and repairs, 14.36; Prince Edward County, snowplow hire, 18.00; Public Utilities Commission, Clinton, services, 50.00; Public Utilities Commission of Galt, Canada, lighting crossing, 48.00; Robt. T. Purves & Co., expansion joints, 271.23; Reflex Sign Co., Ltd., signs and signals, 100.84; Malcolm Sinclair Co., Ltd., paint, 1,032.74; Southern Ontario Gas Co., moving gas-line, 3,166.25; Standard Paving, Ltd., equipment rental, 279.50; Steel Company of Canada, Ltd., structural steel, 220.31; Stratford Public Utilities Commission, services, 44.91; Sundry Registry Fees, services, 38.27; Truscon Steel Co. of Canada, Ltd., steel, 3,081.38; E. G. Tyler Cartage, truck hire, 926.86; United Typewriter Co., Ltd., rent and services on machines, 18.00; F. B. Whiteley, car hire, 379.82. Sundries, 27.69 .... 95,957 70

Pay Lists, $90,553.03.

Wages of men 90,553 03

Purchase of Property, Right-of-Way, $3,512.37.

Dumfries N. twp., Archie McLellan, 400.00; Neil McPherson, 36.75; John Wilson, 50.00; Dumfries S. twp., Gordon E. Swire, 730.00; Dumfries W. twp., W. C. Turnbull, 50.00; Eramosa twp., Robert Williamson, 891.50; Garafraxa E. twp., Neil Farrell, 109.00; J. C. Reid, 13.00; Walter Shaw, 53.00; Archie Smith, 341.6?; Guelph twp., Alfred C. Crane, 50.00; Luther W. twp., Everett Dickson, 153.00; John Haley, 16.00; John W. Saunders, 188.00; George Shaw, 53.00; John H. White, 45.00; Nichol twp., James Robb, 160.00; Waterloo twp., Fred W. Bagg, 30.00; Isaac Harmer, 75.00; A. L. Shantz, 60.00. Sundries, 7.50. 3,512 37

Property, Miscellaneous, $780.00.

Oliver Betzner, Waterloo twp., borrow pit, 258.00; James Carney, Garafraxa twp., damages, etc., 75.00; Miss Jennie Carrick, Dumfries, N. twp., trees and damages, 37.00; Raymond Engliss, Wilmot twp., crop damages, 10.00; A. Gillies, Waterloo twp., building steps, 25.00; John Kirkby, Dumfries S. twp., damages, 250.00; Harry Smith, Guelph twp., right to enter property and clear land, 125.00. 780 00

Road Equipment and Supplies, $592.62.

David Anderson, 17.65; Aaron W. Ash, 32.24; Canada Ingot Iron Co., Ltd., 172.44; Dominion Road Machinery Co., Ltd., 40.81; George Forwell, 26.44; E. T. Hicks, 15.60; International Harvester Co., of Canada, Ltd., 239.75; B. J. McCabe, 11.77; James T. Omand, 10.25. Sundries, 25.67 .... 592 62

Stone, Gravel and Screenings, $19,159.21.

Canada Crushed Stone Corporation, Ltd., 293.85; Consolidated Sand & Gravel, Ltd., 8,889.47; Harold Glew, 21.00; Guelph Sand & Gravel, Ltd., 5,392.26; Gypsum, Lime & Alabastine, Canada, Ltd., 123.37; C. Martin, 400.00; David Miller, 40.00; A. C. Misener, 25.00; Oliver R. Pannabecker, 24.00; W. M. Reid, 15.40; Windmill Point Crushed Stone Co., Ltd., 550.96; Wm. Yundt, 3,371.00. Sundries, 12.90 .... 19,159 21

Travelling Expenses and Disbursements, $1,581.90.

G. Alison, 46.56; Thomas Ayres, 82.90; John G. Bradley, 49.30; S. A. Cummiford, 476.76; H. W. Dennison, 31.60; Harold Down, 92.40; G. J. Foster, 90.65; D. R. Gordon, 167.95; B. L. Irwin, 10.00; Leslie F. Marsh, 49.30; Sam Moore, 19.45; H. Murray, 39.70; Frank O'Brien, 10.55; R. O'Brien, 131.90; S. E. Paisley, 24.70; A. H. Pitt, 20.25; George E. Poyner, 15.10; L. Sandy, 15.80; Frank Soulsby, 19.55; F. B. Whiteley, 101.85; D. Youngs, 43.65. Sundries, 41.98.... 1,581 90

RESIDENCY No. 4 ($1,334,681.39)

Highway No. 2—Brantford to Toronto.
Highway No. 3—Simcoe to Fort Erie.
Highway No. 3a—Chambers' Corners to Thorold.
Highway No. 5—Clappison's Corners to Highway No. 24.
Highway No. 6—Clappison's Corners to Hamilton to Port Dover.
Highway No. 8—Niagara Falls to Hamilton; Binkley's Corner to Highway No. 5.
Highway No. 20—Niagara Falls to Burlington via Smithville.

Statutory—Continued

King's Highway Construction—Continued

Residency No. 4—Continued

Highway No. 24—Brantford to Highway No. 5 (St. George Road).
St. David's to Queenston.
Burlington Beach to Hamilton.
Bismarck to Wellandport.
Hamilton to Elfrida at Highway No. 20.

Engineer, G. F. Hanning, Grimsby

Blacksmithing, $185.90.

Peter Banks, 43.25; N. R. Ford, 11.60; J. W. Hoffman, 17.40; H. Richards, 60.55. Sundries, 53.10 .... 185 90

Bonus for Wire Fencing, $475.99.

James N. Allen, Canboro twp., 44.64; Gunner Dosser, Walpole twp., 67.20; Ernest L. Egger, Canboro twp., 25.80; J. Folville, Cayuga twp., 13.02; L. Jacobs, Saltfleet twp., 30.00; Leslie Keen, Walpole twp., 109.86; A. H. Kitchen, S. Dumfries, twp., 86.40; Thomas McNeill, Walpole twp., 29.04; William Piper, Canboro twp., 63.60. Sundries, 6.43 .... 475 99

Cement, Calcium Chloride and Bituminous Materials, $238,717.98.

Earl H. Baird, 27.85; Barrett Company, Ltd., 976.44; E. Builder, 16.25; Canada Cement Co., Ltd., 163,464.96; Canadian Bitumuls Co., Ltd., 10,631.77; Fred Carson & Sons, 644.00; Colas Roads, Ltd., 10,457.00; C. C. Cornell, 285.00; Currie Products, Ltd., 5,744.68; Doolittle, Ltd., 162.01; Dow Chemical Co., 612.25; Imperial Oil, Ltd., 34,536.21; Alexander Murray & Co., Ltd., 7,822.71; Near's Coal Yard, 225.55; Non-Skid Pavement, Ltd., 1,509.10; Ontario Amiesite, Ltd., 1,687.95; Alfred Rogers, Ltd., 771.00; Sturgeons, Ltd., 205.95; Texas Co. of Canada, Ltd., 72.00; L. B. Tufford, 20.30. Sundries, 22.20; Miscellaneous cement sack credits, 1,177.20 .... 238,717 98

Coal, $278.71.

P. Burns & Co., Ltd., 63.87; W. Cowper & Co., 21.38; S. M. Culp & Co., 97.72; Hillmer Fuel & Ice Co., 13.70; Johnston Coal Co., 14.50; J. A. Lottridge, 38.17; Fred Thomas, 19.25. Sundries, 10.12 .... 278 71

Contracts, $400,896.60.

Archibald & Birdsall, Ltd., No. 32-23, concrete pavement, Saltfleet and Binbrook twps., Hannon-St. Ann's project, 53,907.51; Bituminous Spraying & Contracting Co., Ltd., No. 32-46, surface treatment, Walpole twp., Hagersville-Jarvis-Nelles Corners project, 3,740.66; R. F. Booth, No. 936, overhead bridge, Louth twp., St. Catharines-Jordan project, 405.18; R. F. Booth, No. 31-68, grading and culverts, Pelham twp., Bismarck-Thorold project, 9,169.30; Brennan Paving Co., Ltd., No. 31-36, mixed macadam pavement, Thorold twp., Black Horse Corners-Turner's Corners project, 15,641.10; Brennan Paving Co., Ltd., No. 32-30, mixed macadam pavement, Saltfleet and Binbrook twps., Hannon-Smithville project, 44,614.53; W. G. Campbell Engineering & Construction Co., Ltd., No. 31-35, Cainsville Bridge, Brantford twp., Cainsville-Alberton project, 3,266.83; A. Cope & Sons, Ltd., No. 31-28, grading and culverts, etc., Garafraxa and Gainsboro twps., Smithville-Wellandport project; 13,622.48; Curran & Briggs, Ltd., No. 32-20, concrete pavement, Pelham and Gainsboro twps., Thorold-Bismarck project, 50,549.40; Gordon Crushed Stone Co., Ltd., No. 31-16, mixed macadam pavement, Canboro and Cayuga N. twps, Canboro-Cayuga project, 26,444.46; Roy Honsberger, No. 32-22, concrete pavement, S. Grimsby and Gainsboro twps., Hannon-St. Ann's project, 38,585.88; Law Construction Co., Ltd., No. 30-87, grading, penetration and overhead bridge, Saltfleet twp., Toronto-Hamilton-Beamsville project, 50,312.40; Law Construction Co., Ltd., No. 30-37, macadam pavement, Wainfleet twp., Chamber's Corners-Welland County Line project, 234.17; Municipal Road Spraying & Oiling Co., No. 944, surface treatment, Gainsboro twp., Bismarck-Wellandport project, 1,180.85; J. W. McBurney, No. 682, Extension to bridge, Townsend twp., Jarvis-Simcoe project, 594.49; Standard Paving, Ltd., No. 32-06, mixed macadam pavement, Beverly & S. Dumfries twps., St. George-Rockton project, 82,005.75; W. E. Taylor, No. 602, grading, Beverly twp., Woodstock-Hamilton project, 6,022.01; W. E. Taylor, No. 718, bridge at Cainsville, Brantford twp., Brantford-Alberton project, 599.60 .... 400,896 60

Drainage Materials (culverts, tile, etc.), $29,592.50.

Brantford Metal Co., Ltd., 14.00; Burlington Steel Co., Ltd., 1,126.67; Bernard Cairns, Ltd., 24.00; Canada Culvert Co., Ltd., 3,434.24; Canada Ingot Iron

Statutory—Continued

King's Highway Construction—Continued

Residency No. 4—Continued

Drainage, Materials, etc.—Continued.

Co., Ltd., 4,606.04; Concrete Pipe, Ltd., 5,781.44; Corrugated Pipe Co., Ltd., 471.60; Crane, Ltd., 19.72; D. Dashwood & Sons, 23.10; Dominion Wheel & Foundries, Ltd., 978.00; Metallic Roofing Co. of Canada, Ltd., 624.00; National Sewer Pipe Co., Ltd., 9,919.68; Harold Oliver, 15.00; Pedlar People, Ltd., 2,225.46; Steel Co. of Canada, Ltd., 133.11; T. Tomlinson Foundry Co., Ltd., 186.24. Sundries, 10.20 .... 29,592 50

Fence and Guard Rail Materials, $14,280.11.

A. Bailey, 32.67; Barton Lumber & Supply Co., 18.82; Beamsville Lumber & Supply Co., Ltd., 441.32; The Bowman Lumber Co., 21.40; O. L. Brewer, 12.15; Canada Wire & Cable Co., Ltd., 64.37; Canada Wire & Iron Goods Co., 240.29; Clark Machine Co., 53.00; Consumers Lumber Co., Ltd., 21.60; Davis Lumber Company, 46.11; Drummond & Reeves, Ltd., 15.00; H. Fonger, 205.80; Frost Steel & Wire Co., Ltd., 4,745.55; B. Greening Wire Co., Ltd., 1,702.84; The Ideal Lumber & Supply Co., Ltd., 27.02; Lambert-Rogers Co., 90.44; Line & Cable Accessories, Ltd., 331.72; Lundy Fence Co., Ltd., 3,739.15; W. P. Purdy, 830.80; William Shirton Co., Ltd., 27.90; N. Slater Co., Ltd., 652.06; Standard Underground Cable Co. of Canada, Ltd., 107.04; Steel Company of Canada, Ltd., 797.30; Wood, Alexander & James, Ltd., 39.49. Sundries, 16.27 .... 14,280 11

Gas and Lubricants, $11,023.29.

Fred Bier, 58.63; Bitner's Auto Service, 14.66; British American Oil Co., Ltd., 10.55; A. A. Carey, 189.37; Cities Service Oil Co., Ltd., 799.43; G. Coleman, 25.77; A. E. Corman, 368.52; F. W. Cresswell, 96.99; V. Crispe, 584.65; Raymond Dean, 133.44; D. Edwards, 54.34; English's Garage, 792.39; Fenwick Garage, 68.57; Gibson Garage, 499.27; Grimsby Garage, 35.67; W. H. Harrington, 41.20; Heaslip Service, 61.67; Imperial Oil, Ltd., 1,034.33; Kitchen's Garage, 334.80; Knights, Bronte, 468.19; Laidlaw Garage, 527.83; V. G. Leavey Service Station, 105.16; Le Page's Garage, 48.50; Lynn's Red Indian Service Station, 14.45; Maple Leaf Garage, 321.51; Mount Hope Garage, 41.74; McColl-Frontenac Oil Co., Ltd., 134.94; Allen McLean, 37.78; J. McNeice, 18.50; F. W. Reicheld, 340.76; C. Roberts, 65.73; W. A. Schoenburn, 300.46; Scott & Edgecombe, 110.81; W. E. Shepherd & Son, 1,015.49; O. L. Teal, 51.78; A. S. Teeft, 491.12; Transport Oil, Ltd., 47.91; Mahlon I. Tufford, 224.16; Turner's Corners Bar-B-Q, 19.85; Vail & Wilcox, 13.28; M. A. Walker, 12.66; West End Motors, 727.44; Winger Garage, 626.07. Sundries, 52.92 .... 11,023 29

Hardware, $1,228.00.

E. T. Carter, 46.54; H. V. Guest, 15.12; Graham McKee, 24.64; J. W. McMaster, Ltd., 10.14; Notman Hardware Co., Ltd., 51.89; Sims Hardware, 78.37; Vallance, Brown & Co., Ltd., 16.17; W. Walker & Son, Ltd., 64.83; Wood, Alexander & James, Ltd., 878.48. Sundries, 41.82 .... 1,228 00

Lumber, $1,007.19.

W. J. Bailey, 31.26; Beamsville Lumber & Supply Co., Ltd., 816.36; Boake Manufacturing Co., Ltd., 37.50; The Bowman Lumber Co., 22.67; The Ideal Lumber & Supply Co., Ltd., 17.30; Lambert-Rogers Co., 33.24; Port Dover Planing Mills, 17.50; Chas. Reichman & Son, 14.95; William Shirton Co., Ltd., 16.41 .... 1,007 19

Miscellaneous, $276,320.16.

S. Aiken, kerosene, 11.60; A. Anderson, making well, 15.40; Anglo Traders, Ltd., turkey red, 10.00; Arco Co., Ltd., paint, 93.89; Art Metropole, surveyors' instruments and repairs, 32.95; Aulcraft Paints, Ltd., paint, 107.80; Geo. Bell, car hire, 184.31; Bell Telephone Co. of Canada, moving poles and aerials, 2,921.47; tolls, 530.72; rentals, 143.95; Chas. R. Bilger, office rent, 66.00; Bituminous Spraying & Contracting Co., Ltd., material and services, 531.19; C. Boose, car hire, 141.12; Brennan Paving Co., Ltd., material and services, 12,386.09; British-Canadian Seed Co., grass seed, 50.00; Brown Brothers Co. Nurserymen, Ltd., trees and planting, 1,837.50; John A. Bruce Seed Co. Ltd., grass seed, 30.60; Burlington Steel Co., Ltd., steel, 242.98; W. G. Campbell Engineering & Construction Co., Ltd., maintenance of detour, 421.30; Canada Culvert Co., Ltd., centre joints, 2,177.50; Canada Paint Co., Ltd., paint, 539.00; Canadian Industries Ltd., soda and paint, 269.50; Canadian Inspection & Testing Co., Ltd., tests, 10.02; Canadian Johns-Manville Co., Ltd., expansion joints, 1,447 94; Canadian National Railways, sidings and wigwags, etc., 1,562.95; freight, 23,090.42;

Statutory—Continued

King's Highway Construction—Continued

Residency No. 4—Continued

Miscellaneous—Continued.

Canadian National Telegraphs, services, 15.11; moving poles, 97.84; Canadian Pacific Railway Co., subways, 360.66; sidings and wigwags, etc., 31.87; Canadian Steel Corporation, Ltd., steel, 16,120.74; Clark Blanket Co., Ltd., rent of storehouse, 55.00; Wm. A. Clarke, car hire, 94.99; Clark Machine Co., steps, 16.10; J. C. Collard, removal of gas pump, 50.00; A. Cope & Sons, Ltd., material and services, 269.78; Robert F. Cowan, car hire, 429.66; Dominion Bridge Co., Ltd. structural steel, 114.97; Dominion Natural Gas Co., Ltd., moving gas line, 22.32; J. T. Donald & Co., Ltd., sampling, 73.72; Jas. A. Donaldson, installation of lights, etc., 10.95; John Durham, storage and garage rent, 20.00; C. J. Eames, office rent, 900.00; T. J. Ewen, locating well, 10.00; Fonthill Village, changing water line, 228.36; Frost Steel & Wire Co., Ltd., screens, 18.35; Gordon Fry, explosives, 13.28; Gasaccumulator Co., Canada, Ltd., reflectors, 182.20; J. Ghent, sinking of well, 125.00; A. Gill, drilling well, 388.41; A. F. Gilmore, rent of mower and storage, 37.50; A. Glenney, car hire, 22.68; Grimsby Natural Gas Co., Ltd., moving lines, 38.79; South Grimsby Township, storage, 75.00; D. J. Guilfoil, car hire, 379.82; Hamilton Cataract Power, Light & Traction Co., Ltd., services, 819.90; W. Huber, car hire, 34.93; Robert W. Hunt & Co., Ltd., cement inspections, 389.94; Hydro-Electric Power Commission of Ontario, moving poles, 2,645.37; service and lamps, 470.32; Imperial Varnish & Color Co., Ltd., paint, 176.40; Inspector of Weights and Measures, services, 28.00; Instruments, Ltd., surveying instruments and repairs, 60.55; Irish & Maulson, Ltd., insurance, 60.00; Frank H. James, car hire, 102.62; E. S. Kerr, explosives, 12.50; Kett Brothers, truck hire, 190.38; Kilmer & Barber, Ltd., freight, 104.48; material and services, 166.38; King's Printer, office supplies, 20.06; Laidlaw Garage, garage rent, 15.00; W. O. Langs, rent of barn, 60.00; Law Construction Co., Ltd., material and services, equipment, rental, 1,639 54; Leaney Transport, services, 643.48; Le Page's Garage, garage rent, 17.00; Lincoln Oil Co., Ltd., kerosene, 21.10; W. Lofts, sinking wells, 101.92; Lorne Park, Nurseries Ltd., plants, 50.00; Lorraine Floral Gardens, plants, etc., 34.00; Lowe Brothers Co., Ltd., paint, 85.36; A. & J. Lunness, siding fees, 14.00; A. V. Mason, truck hire, 786.86; Metallic Roofing Co. of Canada, Ltd., expansion strips, signs, etc., 6,427.51; Michigan Central Railroad, sidings and wigwags, 285.54; Henry J. Moore, forestry services, 72.17; W. J. Moore, surveying instruments and repairs, 42.75; Hugh McDonald, truck hire, 561.69; Niagara, St. Catharines & Toronto Rly. Co., sidings and wigwags, 43.31; freight, 11,429.15; W. G. Perks, car hire, 1,456.00; Arthur Philipps, rent of mower, 24.00; J. A. Purcell, sinking wells, 91.87; Robt. T. Purves & Co., expansion joints, 2,609.21; S. A. Purvis, car hire, 135.52; J. Frank Raw Co., Ltd., surveying instruments and repairs, 36.35; Rayner Construction, Ltd., material and services, 1,683.25; Reflex Sign Co., Ltd., signs and signals, 356.26; Remington Typewriters, Ltd., inspections and ribbons, etc., 43.50; W. B. Ronald, rent of snowplow, 480.00; St. Lawrence Transports, Ltd., services, 11.55; Sanderson, Pearcy-Marietta, Ltd., paint, 144.06; C. A. Scharfe, car hire, 161.25; Scharfe & Co., Ltd., paint, 161.25; James Scott, car hire, 16.80; Scott & Edgecombe, garage rent, 17.00; Sherwin-Williams Co. of Canada, Ltd., paint, 46.57; Malcolm Sinclair Co., Ltd., paint, 510.76; W. Morgan Smith, oakum, 37.50; Southern Ontario Telephone Co., Ltd., moving poles, 123.50; Standard Brands, Ltd., soda, 35.80; Steel Company of Canada, Ltd., structural steel, 454.76; Steele, Briggs Seed Co., Ltd., grass seed, 70.30; J. Edward Stubbs, legal services, 27.35; Sundry Registry Fees, services, 358.91; W. E. Taylor, moving water trough, 13.31; Thorold Township, repairs to road, 200.00; Toronto, Hamilton & Buffalo Rly. Co., freight, 32,646.05; Silverdale subway, 125,507.51; Toronto Transportation Commission, paving, 72.13; Truscon Steel Co. of Canada, Ltd., steel, 9,483.31; Village Inn, office rent, 60.00; J. Villetorte, car hire, 371.86; W. W. Vyse, rent of snow plow, 652.00; Walpole Chalmers Church, rent of shed, 20.00; A. A. Webster, car hire, 18.48; City of Welland, rent of roller, 49.70; County of Wentworth, retread and rent of equipment, 323.00; Wentworth Explosives, Ltd., explosives, 324.45; W. Westlake, car hire, 585.27; H. K. Whyte, garage rent, 20.00; Lewis Wilson, storage, 20.00; Jonathan Winger, rent of mower, 46.25; Geo. M. Wood, rent of tractor, 18.00. Sundries, 124.01 .... 276,320 16

Pay Lists, $151,320.93.

Wages of men 151,320 93

Purchase of Property, Right-of-Way, $93,191.41.

Bertie twp., Henry Benner, 125.00; Beverly twp., Wm. B. Cleland, 29.70; A. E. Copeman, 50.00; Robt. B. Parks, 55.00; Troy United Church, 25.00; Geo. M.

Statutory—Continued
King's Highway Construction—Continued
Residency No. 4—Continued

Purchase of Property, Right-of-Way—Continued.

Wood, 50.00; Cayuga North twp., John A. Gasby, 496.87; Dumfries South twp., Earl H. Baird, 2,537.50; Mrs. S. G. Kitchen, 5,000.00; Etobicoke twp., F. McMahon, 935.26; Provincial Improvement Corporation, Ltd., 54,452.00; Gainsborough twp., Hilary Bryce, 150.00; John E. Fester, 600.00; James A. Ross, 200.00; School Section No. 6, 15.00; Cirvilla A. Shrumm, 10.00; Grimsby South twp., Geo. Adams, 15.00; W. B. Davis, 1,100.25; Stephen Fisher, 353.50; A. Manuel, 774.25; C. A. Merritt, 32.00; W. Podivinski, 277.50; Niagara twp., A. Henderson, 75.00; Pelham twp., B. J. Berg, 75.00; George L. Berg, 3,500.00; E. Boyes, 700.00; J. F. Bravin, 250.00; Frank Misener, 40.00; Frank Rounds, 6,000.00; Mrs. A. Sharp, 25.00; Saltfleet twp., Charlotte A. Brooks, 2,807.63; C. P. Carpenter & Son, 1,700.00; D. A. Felker, 24.70; Mary Grieve, 574.00; O. M. Mackie, 69.00; Jas. Milne, 67.50; John Ernest Payne, 247.50; James Reid, 515.00; Fred Y. Stevenson, 243.00; D. F. Tait, 200.50; Jessie E. Townsend, 7,250.00; Harvey Twiss, 600.00; Nathan Utter, 10.00; J. A. Walker, 221.25; Thorold twp., E. H. Bouk, 594.00; H. P. Landry, 20.00; Walpole twp., H. A. Johnson, 84.00. Sundries, 14.50 .... 93,191 41

Property, Miscellaneous, $24,992.22.

Thos, H. Bardwell, Etobicoke twp., damages, 2,500.00; Chester Benner, Bertie twp., digging well, 50.00; B. J. Berg, Pelham twp., damages, 105.00; Geo. L. Berg, Pelham twp., damages, 95.00; Wm. Berry, Glanford twp., removal of buildings, 50.00; Hugh Bertram, Saltfleet twp., arbitration fees, 50.00; Messrs. Bogart and Kennedy and J. R. L. Starr, Etobicoke twp., arbitrations, 3,303.20; F. Bravin, Pelham twp., damages, 95.00; Chartered Trust & Executor Co., Ltd., Etobicoke twp., evidence, 550.00; Wm. C. Coo, Etobicoke twp., arbitration fee, 180.00; Coo and Thompson, Etobicoke twp., arbitration fee, 30.00; Alfred E. Copeman, Beverly twp., damages, 400.00; Rutherford Cumming, Etobicoke twp., arbitration fees, 1,000.00; Walter Davidson & Co., Etobicoke twp., arbitration fee, 75.00; F. E. Davidson, Pelham twp., damages, 111.80; Walter Dean, Etobicoke twp., arbitration fees, 75.00; A. H. Davis, South Grimsby twp., fruit trees, 40.00; Dunnville County House Committee, Moulton twp., land for fill, 65.00; John A. Fegan, Pelham twp., removal of buildings, 100.00; R. J. Fuller, Etobicoke twp., services rendered, 186.30; Wm. Gibbons, Pelham twp., valuating property, 10.00; I. S. Havens, Louth twp., lease on land, 10.00; Chas. E. Horton and James Chambers, Gainsborough twp., removal of buildings, 225.00; William Julian, Pelham twp., damages, 225.00; Kilmer, Irving & Davis, Etobicoke twp., legal services, 4,012.63; Fred Kager, Pelham twp., valuing buildings, 10.00; C. H. Knopton, Etobicoke twp., arbitration fee, 75.00; Henry E. Kramer, Humberstone twp., borrow pit, 100.00; M. R. Lahey, West Flamboro twp., land for storage, 25.00; Lawson & Stratton, South Dumfries twp., arbitration fees, 200.35; Geo. A. Lister, Etobicoke twp., witness fee, 1,000.00; Wm E. Lister, Pelham twp., damages, 118.80; J. F. Louch, Pelham twp., damages, 75.00; Annie and Edwin Lounsbury, Clinton twp., damages, 750.00; J. Kellier MacKay, Saltfleet twp., arbitration fee, 225.00; Manufacturers Life Insurance Co., Beverly twp., fruit trees, 40.00; A. Marshall, Pelham twp., damages, 100.00; Chas. A. Mathewson, Beverly twp., damages to property and lawn, 35.00; George Milne, Saltfleet twp., arbitration fee, 20.00; John N. Misener, Gainsborough twp., fruit trees, 10.00; H. M. Mosby, Thorold twp., trees, 18.50; G. McKenzie, South Dumfries twp., storage, 135.60; Wm. and Elizabeth Newnham, South Grimsby twp., fruit trees, 35.00; Ontario Railway Board, Saltfleet twp., arbitration fees, 15.00; A. C. Patrick, Beverly twp., removal of fence, 20.00; C. C. Pettit, Saltfleet twp., arbitration fee, 40.00; E. Pollitt, Etobicoke twp., arbitration fee, 75.00; Annie C. Reder, Beverly twp., damages, 500.00; W. H. Rudolph, Gainsborough twp., trees and grape vines, 30.00; Harry B. Smith, Saltfleet twp., damages, 4,517.79; Saul Solman, Etobicoke Twp., witness fee, 50.00; Nathan Utter, Saltfleet twp., trees and damages, 2,820.00; Geo. Weatherston, Beverly twp., fence, 10.00; Wellington & Davidson, Thorold twp., trees, 375.00. Sundries, 22.25 .... 24,992 22

Road Equipment and Supplies, $1,355.62.

J. D. Adams (Canada), Ltd., 101.12; Forrest Arnold, 40.20; W. D. Beath & Son, Ltd., 26.08; Canadian Laboratory Supplies, Ltd., 10.35; Samuel Edmonds, 13.40; Steve Evans, 30.00; General Steel Wares, Ltd., 48.19; Goold, Shapely & Muir Co., Ltd., 135.92; Rupert Greenwood, 13.10; Gurney Scale Co., Ltd., 17.40; International Harvester Co., of Canada, Ltd., 216.60; Lakewood Engineering Co., 16.34; T. R. McCaw, 78.30; H. Richards, 17.35; Sawyer-Massey, Ltd., 58.27; Taylor-Forbes Co., Ltd., 10.54; Truck & Tractor Equipment Co., Ltd., 253.00; A. E. Wilkinson, 143.05; Wilkinson-Kompass, Ltd., 23.04. Sundries, 103.37 .... 1,355 62

Statutory—Continued

King's Highway Construction—Continued

Residency No. 4—Continued

Stone, Gravel and Screenings, $84,566.50.

Benson & Patterson, 62.48; Alfred Best, 50.00; A. D. Brown, 14.75; Miss Helen Brown, 10.00; Canada Crushed Stone Corporation, Ltd., 34,678.81; Consolidated Sand & Gravel, Ltd., 16,820.29; Frank Cooks, 54.25; Gainsborough twp., 256.76; The Gallagher Lime & Stone Co., Ltd., 17.25; Gordon Crushed Stone Co., Ltd., 10,735.85; A. W. Green, 10.00; Wm. Grief, 97.00; Hagersville Quarries, Ltd., 6,655.40; Hamilton Wrecking Co., Ltd., 79.20; I. S. Havens, 40.00; E. F. Henderson, 22.50; F. A. Howell, 59.25; Lejeune Bros., 1,212.00; M. Mallory, 36.75; Sidney Merritt, 528.50; John Pirson, 58.39; Queenston Quarries, Ltd., 23.01; Samuel Russell, 129.90; Saltfleet twp., 15.00; Standard Quarries, Ltd., 1,742.62; W. D. Taylor, 43.00; James Thompson, 32.00; Walker Bros., Ltd., 1,901.68; Windmill Point Crushed Stone Co., Ltd., 9,170.46. Sundries, 9.40............ 84,566 50

Travelling Expenses and Disbursements, $5,248.28.

H. C. Anderson, 32.50; Guy R. Ballock, 16.80; Charles Bier, 19.85; C. Boose, 26.85; Lorne Bradt, 149.15; Wm. A. Clarke, 54.70; E. Collins, 126.05; H. Consitt, 19.75; Robert F. Cowan, 165.00; J. S. Davis, 99.85; H. R. Dickson, 125.05; E. D. Fairbrother, 134.40; Chas. Garlett, 188.90; D. R. Garlett, 59.85; A. Glenney, 122.70; G. F. Hanning, 681.78; H. Harrison, 21.15; Willmoth B. Henry, 41.10; Jas. M. Howland, 10.95; W. Huber, 83.90; Tudor Hughes, 453.90; Frank H. James, 82.80; R. Jarden, 33.75; J. W. Kilburn, 73.50; J. Long, 549.51; Fred W. Male, 23.90; R. N. Page, 38.35; H. C. Patterson, 17.50; W. G. Perks, 187.93; S. A. Purvis, 87.25; Wm. Rankin, 36.00; I. C. Rasberry, 37.75; E. D. Ray, 92.50; Robt. C. Ripley, 32.25; J. Ruttledge, 105.75; W. A. Schoenburn, 11.45; James Scott, 87.05; F. Simmonds, 36.60; Wm. Taylor, 14.55; J. H. Thompson, 58.45; J. Villetorte, 114.85; M. B. Watson, 19.15; C. W. Webster, 366.11; W. Westlake, 124.05; H. C. Williams, 143.45; W. Harry Williams, 43.15; F. Yarwood, 139.05. Sundries, 57.45.. 5,248 28

RESIDENCY No. 5 ($938,178.90)

Highway No. 4—Clinton to junction with Highway No. 9; Walkerton to Durham.
Highway No. 6—Arthur to Owen Sound.
Highway No. 9—Kincardine to Arthur; Primrose Corner to Cookstown.
Highway No. 10—Orangeville to Chatsworth.
Highway No. 23—Listowell to Teviotdale.
Highway No. 26—Owen Sound to Stayner.

Engineer, W. R. Alder, Durham

Blacksmithing, $440.82.

H. Atkin, 17.20; Mark P. Currie, 13.90; Wm. P. Dey, 158.77; H. L. Dexter, 10.15; I. R. Elder, 12.95; David Ewan, 28.80; Thos. Henderson, 14.90; W. J. Lawrence, 16.75; James Lynes, 12.40; A. F. Merrett, 27.25; A. Selfe, 25.50; Neil Smith, 22.65; Henry Wilson, 26.95. Sundries, 52.65......................... 440 82

Board of Men, $17.00.

Collison House, Harriston, 10.00. Sundries, 7.00............................ 17 00

Bonus for Wire Fencing, $1,041.31.

William Baker, Bentinck twp., 24.03; J. Becker, Carrick twp., 28.56; J. B. Blackwell, Minto twp., 23.70; H. Brown, Wallace twp., 30.36; George Button, Culross twp., 83.23; Thos. Congram, Morris twp., 68.05; John Dickson, Normanby twp., 24.00; Harold Farr, Brant twp., 24.24; Conrad Felzing, Brant twp., 38.40; Walter Hoggard, Collingwood twp., 38.52; David Holmes, Turnberry twp., 38.76; Adam Hossfield, Carrick twp., 51.60; John Hunter, Morris twp., 35.84; Mrs. E. Ann James, Wawanosh twp., 23.31; R. Lamont, Sydenham twp., 27.12; John Leach, Brant twp., 24.60; Jake McClanahan, Minto twp., 26.52; D. McLosh, Melancthon twp., 24.60; Geo. McVittie, St. Vincent twp., 55.44; O. C. Nesbitt, Wallace twp., 32.10; James Porter, Turnberry twp., 48.40; Francis Sadlo, Greenock twp., 156.77; Wm. Shoebottom, East Wawanosh twp., 48.78; Chester Smith, Wallace twp., 33.00; Herbert Wells, Wallace twp., 18.12. Sundries, 13.26.. 1,041 31

Cement, Calcium Chloride and Bituminous Materials, $258,267.64.

H. A. J. Aldington, 776.40; Barrett Company, Ltd., 533.41; Canada Building Materials, Ltd., 1,096.00; Canada Cement Co., Ltd., 108,565.60; Canada Colors & Chemicals, Ltd., 2,649.16; Canadian Bitumuls Co., Ltd., 7,954.75; Christie

Statutory—Continued

King's Highway Construction—Continued

Residency No. 5—Continued

Cement, Calcium, Chloride, etc.—Continued.

Bros. Co., Ltd., 115.94; Colas Roads, Ltd., 918.75; Cross & Sutherland Hardware Co., Ltd., 265.63; Dow Chemical Co., 2,846.10; Imperial Oil, Ltd., 11,532.59; W. Elmore Mahood, 272.15; Alexander Murray & Co., Ltd., 522.73; Non-Skid Pavement, Ltd., 113.58; Alfred Rogers, Ltd., 115,204.70; Schultz Pump & Tile Co., 303.26; Solway Sales Corporation, 5,400.60; Wilson, Paterson, Gifford, Ltd., 1,149.39. Sundries, 11.70; miscellaneous cement sack credits, 1,964.80.... 258,267 64

Coal, $260.70.

W. Calder Estate, 43.43; A. J. Creighton, 18.00; Alex. George, 10.36; D. A. Hogg, 34.27; John Howes & Sons, Ltd., 11.17; J. N. Murdock, 66.05; Teeswater Creamery, 72.69. Sundries, 4.73........ 260 70

Contracts, $394,438.16.

F. Bell & Bros., No. 32-09, bridge north of Teeswater, Culross twp., Teeswater-Walkerton project, 2,842.23; Cardiff and McNabb, No. 30-86, grading and culverts, Hullett twp., Clinton-Wingham project, 9,940.71; C. C. Cornell, No. 32-41, surface treatment, Kincardine twp., Kincardine-Kinloss project, 2,588.55; Town of Collingwood, Nos. 732 and 821, crushed stone, Collingwood twp., Thornbury-Stayner project, 16,274.11; John Densteadt and Wm. Yundt, No. 30-64, grading and culverts, Brant twp., Hanover-Walkerton project, 10,578.88; Dufferin Paving & Crushed Stone, Ltd., No. 32-03, concrete pavement, Wallace twp., Palmerston-Listowel project, 64,067.42; Dufferin Paving & Crushed Stone, Ltd., No. 31-21, mixed macadam pavement, Egremont and Normanby twps., Mount Forest-Durham project, 45,762.91; John Gaffney, No. 32-36, bridges north of Arthur, Arthur twp., Arthur-Kenilworth project, 3,007.30; G. A. Gibson and Robt. Mowbray, No. 32-55, Londesboro bridge, Hullett twp., Londesboro-Blyth project, 540.82; Highway Paving Co., Ltd., No. 31-32, concrete pavement, Minto and Wallace twps., Palmerston-Teviotdale project, 2,694.94; Holdcroft Construction Co., Ltd., No. 32-34, Williamsford bridge, Holland and Sullivan twps., Durham-Owen Sound project, 5,618.25; Johnson Bros. Co., Ltd., No. 31-09, concrete pavement, Brant and Greenock twps., Kincardine-Walkerton project, 13,283.21; Keys Brothers, No. 31-27, bridge and culverts, Kincardine twp., Kincardine-Greenock project, 6,467.49; Duncan Keys, No. 32-17, bridge and culverts, Morris twp., Blyth-Wingham project, 3,022.65; King Paving Co., Ltd., No. 32-05, concrete pavement, Nottawasaga twp., Collingwood-Stayner project, 105,988.83; King Paving Co., Ltd., No. 547, concrete paving, Artemesia twp., Orangeville-Owen Sound project, 10,947.34; Law Construction Co., Ltd., No. 29-58, grading and retread, Nottawasaga and Sydenham twps., Collingwood-Owen Sound project, 31,871.41; Wm. E. Macke, No. 31-51, repairs to Orchardville bridge, Egremont twp., Walkerton-Clifford project, 2,254.85; Municipal Road Spraying & Oiling Co., No. 32-42, surface treatment, Collingwood twp., Meaford-Thornbury project, 7,228.33; R. H. McGregor Construction Co., No. 32-25, concrete pavement, Melancthon North twp., Shelburne-Flesherton project, 26,742.60; F. R. Wilford, No. 29-77, grading and culverts, Collingwood twp., Barrie-Owen Sound project, 1,759.18; Wingham Construction Co., No. 31-23, grading and culverts, Turnberry and Culross twps., Wingham-Teeswater project, 19,162.65; Wingham Construction Co., No. 32-58, grading, Wawanosh East twp., Wingham-Belgrave project, 1,793.50........... 394,438 16

Drainage Materials (culverts, tile, etc.), $8,214.23.

L. H. Bosman, 511.60; Burlington Steel Co., Ltd., 526.70; Canada Culvert Co., Ltd., 49.40; Canada Ingot Iron Co., Ltd., 737.32; W. A. Coleman, 79.70; Corrugated Pipe Co., Ltd., 473.80; Crane, Ltd., 21.54; Cross & Sutherland Hardware, Co., Ltd., 21.80; Dominion Wheel & Foundries, Ltd., 34.80; Wm. Elliott & Son, 133.50; F. A. Harrison, 67.00; Metallic Roofing Co. of Canada, Ltd., 1,874.13; A. McQueen, 20.40; Pedlar People, Ltd., 1,339.80; Schultz Pump & Tile Co., 2,009.15; Wm. M. Sproat, 162.98; Steel Co. of Canada, Ltd., 128.86. Sundries, 21.75........ 8,214 23

Fence and Guard Rail Materials, $29,302.04.

W. A. Armstrong & Son, 36.90; Fred Bender, 14.00; Benson-Wilcox Electric Co., 310.01; N. Blough, 11.70; J. Breckenridge, 21.90; Joshua Brinkman, 132.00; Canada Wire & Cable Co., Ltd., 351.98; Canada Wire & Iron Goods Co., 173.62; Canadian Steel Corporation, Ltd., 2,457.76; L. Conn, 21.00; S. C. Daniels Co., Ltd., 5,642.00; E. B. Dargavel, 54.15; Dominion Wire Rope Co., Ltd., 47.52; Donaldson Bros., 32.00; S. Farley, 33.00; W. G. Firth, 64.20; Andrew Frieberger, 18.00; Frost Steel & Wire Co., Ltd., 8,306.15; Conrad Goll, 24.30; Albert Gower,

Statutory—Continued

King's Highway Construction—Continued

Residency No. 5—Continued

Fence and Guard Rail Materials—Continued.

71.40; B. Greening Wire Co., Ltd., 739.81; John Harrison & Sons Co., Ltd., 291.95; Jas. Heffron, 18.00; Joe Kerr, 19.25; W. Kraemer, 13.80; Line & Cable Accessories, Ltd., 84.28; Lundy Fence Co., Ltd., 6,776.69; Andrew Moore, 14.50; Peter Morrison, 30.00; John Morrow Screw & Nut Co., Ltd., 159.25; A. Parsons, 11.00; Harold Pearce, 20.00; Mrs. V. Pinder, 47.45; W. O. Pinder, 17.40; W. P. Purdy, 152.50; Chas. Rahn, 38.40; Sarnia Fence Co., Ltd., 1,628.30; Robt. Smith, 35.00; Standard Underground Cable Co. of Canada, Ltd., 100.78; Steel Company of Canada, Ltd., 887.90; Jos. P. Weiler, 70.90; Jake Willits, 100.55; W. T. Wilson, 17.85; Fred Zettle, 105.70. Sundries, 97.19.................... 29,302 04

Gas and Lubricants, $4,162.01.

D. G. Albrecht, 21.86; Alliston Garage, 14.76; Wm. T. Atchison, 92.01; Leslie Ball, 53.82; G. F. Brackenbury, 18.25; Brack's Garage, 22.95; T. Brooks & Son, 51.14; Canadian Oil Companies, Ltd., 12.28; Checkerboard Garage, 10.50; Chevrolet Garage, Teeswater, 79.09; Geo. G. Collinson, 30.97; Ed. Connor, 13.92; Cooksville Motors, 11.75; A. Down, 56.49; Eagle's Garage & Service Station, 24.58; Edgar's Service Station, 24.61; A. M. Ewing, 38.80; H. M. Hazlitt, 15.10; J. C. Howell, 10.97; Imperial Oil, Ltd., 306.70; A. S. Inkley, 12.80; Dalton Keeling's Service Station, 45.97; Wm. Keller, 495.86; Robert H. Laking, 15.99; Chas. E. Lemon & Son, 35.66; Markdale Garage Co., 146.00; Milligan's Garage, 20.96; W. J. Molson, 10.64; Mrs. A. Morrice, 13.38; Wm. McConnell, 24.87; D. B. McFadden, 19.87; McLeod & Arthur, 46.52; D. McTavish & Son, 16.55; Noble's Service Station, 615.23; Archie Park, 69.96; John Reavie, 49.88; E. S. Reid, 69.88; H. Ross, 58.78; S. J. Scharback, 49.40; George Scott & Son, 52.44; Shelburne Garage, 14.85; Smith Bros., 592.09; South End Garage, 126.90; George Stafford, 41.20; J. J. Stinson, 40.42; W. S. Stuckey, 104.30; G. E. Swire, 15.75; Tanner & Zister, 51.38; Walker Bros., 52.93; J. L. Walsh, 35.21; E. C. William's Garage, 66.35; B. H. Willis, 70.69; Young's Garage, 15.28. Sundries, 153.47.. 4,162 01

Hardware, $1,214.50.

J. W. Armstrong, 13.35; Chalmers Bros., 14.57; Cleland Bros., 129.37; Collingwood Hardware Co., 22.26; Cross & Sutherland Hardware Co., Ltd., 98.11; Frank W. Duncan, 51.52; Eastland's, 17.95; John G. Ellenton, 35.32; Gillespie Brothers, 44.78; J. H. Harding, 89.68; H. L. Hawthorne, 50.90; O. B. Henry Hardware Co., Ltd., 65.50; H. S. Howland Sons & Co., Ltd., 24.99; Jeffery Hardware, 22.89; Moffat's Hardware, 10.44; Munro Bros., 46.75; Padfield's Hardware, 78.20; W. S. Perkins & Sons, 14.45; Rae & Thompson, 24.40; Russell Bros., 29.82; J. J. Stinson, 62.23; S. W. Vogan, 47.41; Geo. E. Wright, 110.08. Sundries, 109.53.. 1,214 50

Lumber, $525.45.

Roland Beattie Estate, 60.70; W. R. F. Clark, 30.26; Walter Dixon, 26.60; The Durham Furniture Co., Ltd., 132.15; John Harrison & Sons Co., Ltd., 91.38; George Kerr, 11.10; Leggatt Bros., 33.94; J. N. Murdock, 67.39; C. H. Seim, 14.30. Sundries, 57.63.. 525 45

Miscellaneous, $67,268.94.

Bell Telephone Co. of Canada, moving poles and aerials, 149.09; tolls, 303.64; rentals, 52.25; Bergman Construction Co., Ltd., detour, 140.00; Bituminous Spraying & Contracting Co., Ltd., material and services, 135.00; Village of Blythe, filling cracks, 113.57; Blyth Telephone System, moving poles, 51.70; Brant twp., spreading gravel, 160.00; J. A. Bremner, car hire, 54.88; South Bruce Rural Telephone Co., Ltd., moving poles, 37.75; Burlington Steel Co., Ltd., steel, 290.20; Alex. Campbell, garage rent, 35.00; Roy Campbell, car hire, 57.67; Canadian Industries, Ltd., soda and paint, 17.15; Canadian Inspection & Testing Co., Ltd., tests, 18.99; Canadian Johns-Manville Co., Ltd., expansion joints, 1,148.84; Canadian National Railways, sidings and wigwags, etc., 98.08; freight, 4,173.46; Canadian Pacific Railway Co., freight, 4,119.86; sidings and wigwags, etc., 194.72; M. L. Cardiff and J. McNab, truck hire, 1,341.40; H. S. Crabtree, Ltd., surveying supplies, 13.70; Culross twp., drain assessment, 149.40; T. G. Davis, rent of shop, 93.00; Wilbert Dinsmore, rent of mixer, 12.00; Dirstein Transports, Ltd., truck hire, 795.00; Dominion Bridge Co., Ltd., structural steel, 10.81; J. T. Donald & Co., Ltd., sampling, 64.32; Durham Road Telephone Co., moving poles, 12.60; The Durham Furniture Co., Ltd., moving poles, 61.70; I. W. Elvidge, car hire, 123.76; Fouse & Brobst, truck hire, 172.50; General Steel Wares, Ltd., signs, 15.50; George Gibb, car hire, 27.37; Joseph Gibbons,

Statutory—Continued

King's Highway Construction—Continued

Residency No. 5—Continued

Miscellaneous—Continued.

car hire, 53.41; Geo. C. Godard, car hire, 108.36; Robert W. Hunt & Co., Ltd., cement inspections, 708.10; Hydro-Electric Power Commission of Ontario, moving poles, 2,895.35; Instruments, Ltd., surveying instruments and repairs, 18.85; Corporation of the Town of Kincardine, gravelling, 314.20; King's Printer, office supplies, 13.69; Law Construction Co., Ltd., material and services, equipment rental, 84.10; Lowe Brothers Co., Ltd., paint, 21.38; Metallic Roofing Co. of Canada, Ltd., expansion strips, signs, etc., 3,759.49; W. J. Moore, surveying instruments and repairs, 47.50; Municipal Road Spraying & Oiling Co., Ltd., material and services, 1,643.12; McFadden's Drug Store, office supplies and drugs, 42.00; James McLachlan, car hire, 1,064.49; Northern Paint & Varnish Co., Ltd., paint, 857.30; Owen Sound Quarries, Ltd., rent of siding, 12.00; Pedlar People, Ltd., steelcrete, 26,637.54; Thos. Pocklington Co., surveying instruments and repairs, 12.30; Robt. T. Purves & Co., expansion joints, 4,067.63; Reflex Sign Co., Ltd., signs and signals, 148.55; C. L. Robertson, car hire, 31.71; D. M. Saunders, office rent, 300.00; Frank Simmonds, car hire, 110.74; Standard Brands Ltd., soda, 12.17; N. A. Stauffer, car hire, 14.98; Steel Company of Canada, Ltd., structural steel, 1,791.19; Sundry Registry Fees, services, 170.01; Truscon Steel Co. of Canada, Ltd., steel, 7,869.87; Mrs. I. Vickers, cleaning office, 96.00; E. L. Webster, typewriter repairs, 15.10; Edward Weiler, explosives, 17.37. Sundries, 85.53 .... 67,268 94

Pay Lists, $152,068.61.

Wages of men 152,068 61

Purchase of Property, Right-of-Way, $4,449.05.

Arthur twp., Henry Wilkie, 114.90; Bentinck twp., Elmer Baker, 24.37; Wm. Baker, 16.50; Wm. Hoerle, 33.12; Wm. J. Switzer, 112.40; Brant twp., Richard Wm. Burrell, 50.00; Henry Koening, 24.00; Louis J. Lambertus, 684.25; Thos. H. O'Neil, 322.00; Culross twp., Wm. Andrew Colvin, 19.25; Glenelg twp., James Lawrence, 595.35; Mrs. Elizabeth C. Murdock, 100.00; McKechnie Estate, 35.00; James Vessie Estate, 307.65; Greenock twp., Jesse C. Baechler, 32.50; George Brindley, 66.87; J. A. Cunningham, 50.37; Joseph Freiburger, 17.18; Albert Heidmiller, 33.12; Stephen Kraemer, 100.00; Wm. Joseph Kraemer, 60.62; Neil McKinnon, 43.37; George Winters, 66.87; Hullett twp., Ernest A. Adams, 41.51; Harold Adams, 65.15; Stanley Carter, 101.81; John Hutton, 56.40; Kincardine twp., John McGinnis, 49.12; Nottawasaga twp., W. J. Best, 11.00; Amos Girdwood, 184.50; Fred Girdwood, 187.50; John Mullen, 35.00; St. Vincent twp., Carnahan Estate, E. H., Geo. B. and Susan M. Carnahan, 250.00; Sydenham twp., Wm. Best, 50.00; Dennis Hatton, 150.00; Turnberry twp., David Holmes, 61.60; Mrs. Elizabeth Jenkins, 36.70; Wallace twp., O. C. Nesbitt, 14.90; Wawanosh twp., Collinson & Glousher, 232.70. Sundries, 11.47 4,449 05

Property, Miscellaneous, $2,528.12.

R. W. Clarmount, Egremont twp., damages, 25.00; Mrs. Annie Gabel, Kincardine twp., borrow pit, 100.00; A. Hanley, Ancaster twp., storage, 15.00; Alexander Herd, Bentinck twp., moving fence, 100.62; E. B. Knight, St. Vincent twp., fruit trees, 10.00; Louis Lambertus, Brant twp., damages, 15 00; Mrs. W. E. Moffatt, Nottawasaga twp., damages, 125.00; James McLurg, Sydenham twp., damages, 500.00; David McNabb, Arthur twp., damages, 100.00; Ed. and W. J. McNaughton, Brant twp., borrow pit, 100.00; T. H. O'Neil, Brant twp., damages, 35.00; J. B. Peters, Sydenham twp., construction and maintenance of ditch, 50.00; W. G. Robinson, Nottawasaga twp., damages, 150.00; Wilfred L. Roy, Hullett twp., gravel pit, 500.00; Albert Wesson, Tecumseh twp., gravel pit, 700.00. Sundries, 2.50 .... 2,528 12

Road Equipment and Supplies, $1,700.88.

Forrest Arnold, 634.50; W. D. Beath & Son, Ltd., 26.08; Canada Carriage & Body Co., Ltd., 18.70; Canada Ingot Iron Co., Ltd., 33.02; G. Caslick, 21.70; Davis & Bell, 19.00; Dominion Road Machinery Co., Ltd., 185.70; W. F. Jackson, 29.30; W. H. Kerr, 20.50; J. Wesley Leggatt, 15.00; Levy & Westwood Machinery Co., 367.00; L. McCracken, 44.35; P. J. McLean, 21.91; Harold Phillips, 25.95; R. J. Robinson, 13.60; Frank I. Rogers, 21.40; Sawyer-Massey, Ltd., 41.90; S. J. Scharback, 19.65; South End Garage, 25.21. Sundries, 116.41 .... 1,700 88

Stone, Gravel and Screenings, $8,301.80.

Earl Brett, 70.20; F. Brock, 42.00; George Carbert, 17.40; Town of Collingwood, 472.68; Consolidated Sand & Gravel, Ltd., 2,346.42; Norman Dowling, 233.14;

Statutory—Continued

King's Highway Construction—Continued

Residency No. 5—Continued

Stone, Gravel and Screenings—Continued.

Dufferin Paving & Crushed Stone, Ltd., 1,587.20; John Gonder, 94.30; John Heslip, 239.16; Emerald Ludlow, 242.29; Ontario Rock Co., Ltd., 2,182.10; Owen Sound Quarries, Ltd., 418.51; Austin Paterson, 239.31; James Quinlan, 13.80; Wallace twp., 60.30. Sundries, 42.99 .... 8,301 80

Travelling Expenses and Disbursements, $3,977.64.

W. R. Alder, 416.33; A. L. Baldwin, 162.81; Donald J. Black, 249.35; David Burns, 89.45; Roy Campbell, 69.35; I. W. Elvidge, 153.30; D. J. Emry, 15.40; Wm. Fitzsimmons, 221.05; George Gibb, 19.79; Joseph Gibbons, 198.03; James Hilton, 22.85; Tom Johnston, 11.23; George Jones, 15.00; J. K. Lettner, 12.70; G. W. Littlejohns, 92.00; Kenneth Long, 79.15; R. A. Low, 29.70; E. Morrison, 11.65; A. D. McAuliffe, 106.85; James McLachlan, 160.25; H. Calder Noble, 290.85; R. N. Page, 57.05; A. E. Rudd, 263.42; James Seed, 14.05; F. Simmonds, 212.48; Jas. D. Smith, 17.60; J. M. Smith, 319.19; Raymond Snowe, 247.50; N. A. Stauffer, 40.10; R. J. Stewart, 30.75; Lawrence Whitmore, 214.65; Percy Willis, 100.80. Sundries, 32.96 .... 3,977 64

RESIDENCY No. 6 ($1,032,115.31)

Highway No. 2—Toronto to Oshawa.
Highway No. 5—Toronto to Clappison's Corners.
Highway No. 7—Brampton to Thornhill; Langstaff to Brooklin; Highway No. 12 to East limit Brock Township.
Highway No. 10—Port Credit to Highway No. 7, north of Brampton.
Highway No. 11—Toronto to Severn; Yonge Blvd; Avenue Road.
Highway No. 12—Whitby to Midland (via Orillia).
Highway No. 25—Nelson to Highway No. 2; Palermo to Milton.
Highway No. 26—Barrie to Stayner.
Highway No. 27—Midhurst to Midland and Penetanguishene.
Middle Road (Queen Street) to Highway No. 10.

Engineer, C. A. Robbins, Toronto

Blacksmithing, $174.03.

Alex. Cleland, 82.00; Cameron Cotton, 33.50; J. D. Lamont, 11.75; F. Woodward, 27.63. Sundries, 19.15 .... 174 03

Board of Men, $8.50.

Sundries 8 50

Bonus for Wire Fencing, $331.50.

G. W. Atkinson, Oro twp., 25.80; Delbert Bryans, Brock twp., 42.00; Thos. Carnaby, Brock twp., 24.00; A. Conner, Pickering twp., 23.16; J. J. Cummings, Floss twp., 21.60; C. O. Lawton, Pickering twp., 36.96; Cliff McMaster, Brock twp., 28.20; Murdock McRae, Thorah twp., 33.96; C. Richardson, Pickering twp., 19.20; Harry Rowell, Vespra twp., 74.22. Sundries, 2.40 .... 331 50

Cement, Calcium Chloride and Bituminous Materials, $150,498.54.

H. A. J. Aldington, 508.95; Barrett Co., Ltd., 8,406.20; Bowden Lumber Co., Ltd., 31.89; Canada Cement Co., Ltd., 55,632.05; Canada Colors & Chemicals, Ltd., 3,302.05; Canadian Bitumuls Co., Ltd., 1,618.06; Colas Roads, Ltd., 100.00, credit; Imperial Oil, Ltd., 29,726.50; C. L. Mackey, & Son, 35.10; Merck & Co., Ltd., 744.80; Milne Coal & Supply Co., 40.25; Alexander Murray & Co., Ltd., 267.60; S. McCord & Co., Ltd., 3,115.77; McKenzie Bros., 59.15; Non-Skid Pavement, Ltd., 11,282.32; Ontario Amiesite, Ltd., 5,630.18; H. A. Raney & Co., 77.04; Alfred Rogers, Ltd., 30,407.45; Sarjeant Co., Ltd., 67.58; Solvay Sales Corporation, 3,380.25; Stiver Bros., 70.00; Wilson, Paterson, Gifford, Ltd., 1,438.97; Winn & Holland, Ltd., 718.75; miscellaneous cement sack credits, 5,962.37 .... 150,498 54

Coal, 724.76.

J. E. Coombs, 39.30; H. S. Fenton, 166.75; James Grant, 14.35; B. B. Grose, 43.88; Thos. Law, 90.00; Lindsay Coal Co., Ltd., 71.63; Arthur O. Mix, 14.60; McLaughlin Coal & Supplies, Ltd., 34.65; D. S. Pratt, 30.90; J. D. Ramer & Son, 30.45; F. F. Sayers & Son, 15.50; J. G. Scott, 15.00; Sarjeant Co., Ltd., 29.51; Simone Coal Co., Ltd., 36.40; H. J. Thomson & Co., 74.98; A. S. Willmott, 16.86 .... 724 76

Statutory—Continued

King's Highway Construction—Continued

Residency No. 6—Continued

Contracts, $350,942.53.

Wm. Birmingham & Son, No. 31-29, Greenwood bridge, Pickering twp., Langstaff-Brooklin project, 3,535.39; Bituminous Spraying & Contracting Co., Ltd., No. 32-38, surface treatment, Mara twp., Langstaff-Markham project, 6,468.92; W. G. Campbell Engineering & Construction Co., Ltd., No. 31-82, grading and culverts, Etobicoke and Toronto twps., Port Credit-Toronto project, 55,046.76; W. G. Campbell Engineering & Construction Co., Ltd., No. 30-70, bridges, Beaverton and Gamebridge, Thorah and Mara twps., Beaverton-Gamebridge project, 605.40; W. G. Campbell Engineering & Construction Co., Ltd., No. 1030, bridge, Vespra and Floss twps., Barrie-Elmvale project, 782.00; H. I. Clarke Construction Co., Ltd., No. 32-18, curbs and gutters, Floss twp., Barrie-Elmvale project, 1,147.50; Curran & Briggs, Ltd., No. 31-48, concrete pavement, Pickering twp., Langstaff-Brooklin project, 6,222.84; Gamebridge Limestone Products, No. 835, spreading stone, Thorah twp., Beaverton-Atherly project, 8,100.12; Godson Contracting Co., Ltd., No. 32-51, asphalt mixed macadam, King and East Gwillimbury twps., Eagle St.-Holland Landing project, 14,930.51; Holdcroft Construction Co., Ltd., No. 31-39, bridges and culverts, Vespra and Floss twps., Barrie-Collingwood project, 26,638.57; A. E. Jupp Construction Co., Ltd., No. 32-19, concrete pavement, Brock twp., Sunderland-Brock town-line project, 46,315.44; A. E. Jupp Construction Co., Ltd., No. 31-66, grading, culverts and amiesite pavement, Scarborough, North York and King twps., Barrie-Toronto-Whitby project, 44,832.21; King Paving Co., Ltd., No. 30-06, concrete pavement, Vespra and Oro twps., Barrie-Orillia project, 2,028.85; Mara Township, Nos. 769 and 747, relief work, crushing stone, Mara twp., Brechin-Atherly project, 13,500.00; Municipal Road Spraying & Oiling Co., Ltd., Nos. 963 and 1090, surface treatment, Sunnidale, Vespra and Floss twps., Stayner-Midhurst-Waverley project, 2,380.15; McNamara Construction Co., Ltd., No. 31-12, storm sewers and concrete pavement, York, Orillia and Oso twps., Hoggs Hollow-Orillia project, 3,467.16; Non-Skid Pavement Co., Ltd., No. 1109, approaches to Scarborough Overhead, Scarborough twp., Toronto-Scarborough project, 1,937.49; Ontario Bridge Co., Ltd., No. 31-39, bridge, Floss and Vespra twps., Collingwood-Stayner project, 19,525.34; John Patterson Construction Co., Ltd., No. 31-41, Orillia Overhead, Orillia twp., Barrie-Orillia project, 17,044.21; John Pirson, No. 30-89, grading and culverts, Pickering and Whitby West twps., Langstaff-Brooklin project, 7,575.60; Ryan Contracting Co., Ltd., No. 32-31, concrete pavement, York twp., Avenue Road-Wilson Ave. project, 51,798.12; C. B. Stewart, No. 30-90, Severn River bridge, North Orillia twp., Gravenhurst-Orillia project, 300.00; Storms Contracting Co., Ltd., No. 31-34, culverts and mixed macadam pavement, Vaughan twp., Woodbridge-Thornhill project, 5,814.61; J. K. Stout Haulage Co., No. 30-82, grading and culverts, Pickering twp., Langstaff-Greenwood project, 5,445.34; Warren Bituminous Paving Co., Ltd., No. 930, repairs to pavement, York and King twps., Toronto-Schomberg Jct. project, 5,500.00 .... 350,942 53

Drainage Materials (culverts, tile, etc.), $22,684.49.

Bowden Lumber Co., Ltd., 29.46; Canada Ingot Iron Co., Ltd., 1,168.20; Concrete Pipe, Ltd., 5,584.27; Crane, Ltd., 220.06; Norman L. Daniels, 275.00; W. J. Devitt, 41.00; Dominion Wheel & Foundries. Ltd., 1,014.80; J. H. Doughty, Ltd., 31.30; W. H. Johnson & Son, 25.65; Maw Bros., 400.00; Metallic Roofing Co. of Canada, Ltd., 6,557.53; National Sewer Pipe Co., Ltd., 5,547.57; Ontario Brick & Tile Plant, 249.85; Town of Orillia, 12.00; Pedlar People, Ltd., 1,406.70; Sarjeant Co., Ltd., 11.43; F. F. Sayers & Son, 12.60; W. H. Thomson, 76.32; T. Tomlinson Foundry Co., Ltd., 12.00. Sundries, 8.75 .... 22,684 49

Fence and Guard Rail Materials, $7,961.87.

Canada Wire & Cable Co., Ltd., 266.44; Canada Wire & Iron Goods Co., 134.16; Copeland Milling Co., 92.64; S. C. Daniels Co., Ltd., 1,424.38; Drummond & Reeves, Ltd., 476.00; Frost Steel & Wire Co., Ltd., 1,231.17; Levi Hopkins, 378.15; Herb. Justin, 17.10; Lundy Fence Co., Ltd., 2,612.24; John Morrow Screw & Nut Co., Ltd., 641.65; G. F. Mulvihill, 10.65; W. T. Reed, 56.00; Steel Co. of Canada, Ltd., 244.42; Stoney Lake Hotels, Ltd., 233.75; Frank Strachan, 13.75; E. Turpin, 17.50; Harry Wilson, 70.00; Woodbridge Farmers Co., Ltd., 10.25. Sundries, 31.62 .... 7,961 87

Gas and Lubricants, $9,070.68.

Joseph Allin, 29.69; Bannerman & Hunter, 12.64; Beauchamp Garage, 52.31; British American Oil Co., Ltd., 22.25; Brown Bros. & Eplett, 277.60; L. G. Bugg, 251.28; Harold Bunt, 615.60; Chittick Motor Sales, 91.53; Coldwater

Statutory—Continued

King's Highway Construction—Continued

Residency No. 6—Continued

Gas and Lubricants—Continued.

Garage, 276.71; Cooksville Motors, 640.46; H. R. Cooper, 15.94; Cameron W. Cotton, 210.36; Davidson Motor Co., Ltd., 21.24; P. W. Drake Service Station, 162.97; Fee Motors, 12.90; S. R. Goodwin, 525.62; W. J. Gracey, 29.94; J. M. Graham, 14.29; Imperial Oil, Ltd., 1,410.08; James Kingsborough, 281.66; Gordon Law, 86.59; Chas. E. Lemon & Son, 10.13; R. Lytton, 22.59; Maynard's Garage, 153.19; W. D. Mercer, 582.23; C. R. Miller, 33.70; J. A. Mills, 277.80; I. K. Milne, 479.50; R. J. Moore, 152.40; George Muir, 367.19; McColl-Frontenac Oil Co., Ltd., 14.00; Ontario Motor Sales, 10.50; C. C. Parker, 160.36; R. E. Sculthorpe, 162.91; Shell Co. of Canada, Ltd., 636.24; G. E. Swire, 103.27; L. R. Taylor, 339.04; Oliver Wilson, 70.11; Wilson's Garage, 212.41; Woodman & Ross, 15.01; Wyant Garage, 22.19; J. C. Young, 32.22. Sundries, 172.03........ 9,070 68

Hardware, $1,663.31.

Joseph Allin, 16.50; Armstrong & Rainford, 13.80; John S. Balsdon, 315.11; Cameron W. Cotton, 51.75; Dempsey Bros., 25.00; H. F. S. Gardner, 87.50; S. R. Goodwin, 36.10; Knapps Hardware, 14.90; Jas. Mahoney, 10.50; Manning Hardware, 21.85; Thos. Meredith & Co., Ltd., 196.00; Rice Lewis & Son, Ltd., 29.24; W. W. Sadler, 29.49; Charles Sargent, 11.10; H. H. Smith, 467.54; George W. Turner, 18.30; W. Walker & Son, Ltd., 128.77; G. S. Wood, 34.59; Wood Hardware, 114.38. Sundries, 40.89.. 1,663 31

Lumber, $1,595.84.

Ball Planing Mill Co., Ltd., 15.76; Boake Manufacturing Co., Ltd., 18.75; Walter Borland, 63.60; Bowden Lumber Co., Ltd., 67.08; Comrie Lumber Company, Ltd., 206.57; Cameron W. Cotton, 33.75; Dominion Lumber Co., 42.64; Freeman Lumber Co., Ltd., 34.50; Mickle, Dyment & Son, Ltd., 16.28; Milmine & Son, 30.00; Reid & Co., Lumber, Ltd., 15.30; O. W. Rhynas & Son, Ltd., 17.64; F. F. Sayers & Son, 422.68; W. H. Thomson, 73.21; Welsh Lumber Co., Ltd., 506.91. Sundries, 31.17.. 1,595 84

Miscellaneous, $116,147.69

The Ardtrea Telephone Co., Ltd., moving poles, 116.13; Art Metropole, surveyors' instruments and repairs, 62.43; Baines & David, Ltd., iron and steel supplies, 506.13; Mrs. J. Bell, rent of equipment, 10.50; Bell Telephone Co. of Canada, moving of poles and aerials, 614.99; messages, 267.32; rentals, 112.14; Charles Bier, rent of mower, 39.00; Bituminous Spraying & Contracting Co., Ltd., material and services, 4,389.18; Boeckh Co., Ltd., brushes, 73.96; Brandram-Henderson, Ltd., paint, 111.62; A. Brown, car hire, 21.35; E. L. Brown, storage, 10.00; Brown Bros. & Eplett, garage rent, 15.00; Harold Bunt, garage rent, 36.00; Burlington Steel Co., Ltd., steel, 1,173.38; Canadian General Electric Co., Ltd., lamps and services, 1,235.73; Canadian Industries, Ltd., soda and paint, 968.46; Canadian Inspection & Testing Co., Ltd., tests, 94.31; Canadian National Railways, sidings and wigwags, etc., 862.34; freight, 28,117.12; Canadian National Telegraphs, moving poles, 145.93; Canadian Pacific Railway Co., subways, 9,756.39; freight, 5,952.78; sidings and wigwags, etc., 599.88; R. Cavotti, truck hire, 26.00; G. H. Chalmers, car hire, 300.02; H. J. Clark Construction Co., removal of concrete, 33.20; Coldwater Garage, garage rent, 12.00; Coville Transport Co., Ltd., services, 18.14; Daily Commercial News & Building Record, advertising, 12.00; J. A. Dillane, car hire, 217.14; Dominion Bridge Co., Ltd., structural steel, 670.24; J. T. Donald & Co., Ltd., sampling, 252.44; Eastman Kodak Stores, Ltd., films, 27.21; S. J. Ellery, rent of shed, 16.65; Fouse & Brobst, truck hire, 55.00; Gasaccumulator Co., Canada, Ltd., reflectors, 162.40; General Steel Wares, Ltd., signs, 630.02; Globe Printing Co., advertising, 12.00; John S. Grandy, rent of land, 12.00; Hogg & Lytle, Ltd., grass seed, 47.00; Home Telephone Co., Ltd., moving poles, 305.00; Hubbard's Hardware, paint, 44.00; Robert W. Hunt & Co., Ltd., cement inspections, 232.80; Hydro-Electric Power Commission of Ontario, moving poles, 2,331.20; service and lamps, 92.29; Inspector of Weights & Measures, services, 12.00; Instruments, Ltd., surveying instruments and repairs, 39.10; H. P. Jones, car hire, 208.60; A. E. Jupp Construction Co., Ltd., equipment rental and services, 2,393.85; King's Printer, office supplies, 24.68; Thos. Law, rent of sidings, 15.00; Law Construction Co., Ltd., material and services, equipment rental, 307.28; Livingston Bros., Ltd., garage rent, 18.00; Lowe Brothers Co., Ltd., paint, 30.74; R. MacLennan, car hire, 33.88; Mail and Empire, advertising, 12.00; Metallic Roofing Co. of Canada, Ltd., expansion strips, signs, etc., 3,621.71; Wm. J. Mitchell, storage, 12.00; W. J. Moore, surveying instruments and repairs, 44.05; Municipal Road Spraying & Oiling Co., Ltd., material and services,

Statutory—Continued

King's Highway Construction—Continued

Residency No. 6—Continued

Miscellaneous—Continued.

138.00; McNamara Construction Co., material and services, 4,731.15; J. P. McRae, road markers, 50.00; H. E. McTear, car hire, 603.40; Ontario Bridge Co., Ltd., structural steel, 268.26; Oshawa Fire Department, use of fire truck, 52.00; Oshawa Public Utilities Commission, moving poles, 418.33; C. M. Palmer & Sons, garage rent, 230.00; Patterson Electric, Ltd., installing conduit boxes, 552.00; Pedlar People, Ltd., steelcrete, 2,223.40; Peterborough Examiner, Ltd., advertising, 11.13; Thos. Pocklington Co., surveying instruments and repairs, 47.75; Public Works Dept., Ontario, paper, 73.62; Robt. T. Purves & Co., expansion joints, 477.53; D. G. Ramsay, car hire, 116.62; J. Frank Raw Co., Ltd., surveying instruments and repairs, 46 01; Reflex Sign Co., Ltd., signs and signals, 102.00; Remington Typewriters, Ltd., inspections and ribbons, etc., 26.50; W. J. Robertson, car hire, 1,276.45; Sanderson Pearcy-Marietta, Ltd., paint, 1,169.83; Scarborough Public Utilities Commission, 12.99; C. A. Scharfe, car hire, 1,164.52; Sherwin-Williams Co. of Canada, Ltd., paint, 99.48; A. E. Smith, bed springs, 10.50; Steel Company of Canada, Ltd., structural steel, 7,105.61; G. F. Sterne & Sons, paint, 32.50; Walter Stewart, insurance, 60.00; C. J. Stevenson, rent of shed, 10.00; Robert Stiver, shed rental, 24.00; Storms Contracting Co., Ltd., services, 2,513.38; Sundry Registry Fees, services, 152.45; Taylor Instruments Co. of Canada, Ltd., thermometers, 26.40; Corporation of the City of Toronto, water main, Havergal College, 648.37; City of Toronto, Treasurer, cutting weeds and water, 34.65; Toronto Transportation Commission, Bowden's Siding, 801.27; Toronto & York Roads Commission, grading and paving, 4,236.17; Truscon Steel Co. of Canada, Ltd., steel, 3,559.63; United Typewriter Co., Ltd., machine rentals and services, 12.00; Warren Bituminous Paving Co., Ltd., repairs to Yonge Blvd., 1,259.36; F. R. Wilford & Co., Ltd., use of crushing plant, 120.00; Clarence Wood, rental of shed, 36.00; Woodbridge & Vaughan Telephone Co., moving poles, 429.65; North York Twp., lowering main and moving poles, 13,484.53. Sundries, 126.54 .... 116,147 69

Pay Lists, $257,065.55.

Wages of men 257,065 55

Purchase of Property, Right-of-Way, $43,552.71.

Brock Twp., Wm. J. H. Philip, 20.00; Etobicoke Twp., Mrs. M. J. Alderson, 1,300.00; Thos. Bryans, 3,630.10; Bertram Craven, 804.00; Thos. and Sid. Goudge, 1,534.00; J. T. Hutson, 506.00; Margaret I. Mercer, 1,445.00; J. O'Brien and Robt. A. Montgomery, 1,698.00; Geo. Munden, 313.00; Archie Primrose, 3,000.00; Samuel Shields, 25.00; Soldier Settlement Board and C. E. Boyd, 7,750.00; Floss Twp., W. H. Archer, 17.10; Fred Richardson, 17.80; J. H. Ritchie, 136.60; W. Kerr Ritchie, 198.80; King Twp., City of Toronto, 10.00; Mara Twp., Russell Barbour, 125.00; W. B. and F. J. Kelly, 150.00; Orillia S. Twp., C. E. Calvert, 2,500.00; R. Curran, 30.00; Pickering Twp., Chas. Crew, 11.55; W. J. Devitt, 500.00; Alex. Moore, 130.00; Ross Raine, 10.35; Scarborough Twp., Dr. H. C. Brown, 2,200.00; Florence H. Carter, 2,792.76; Eleanor Ellis, 2,258.21; Harry and Eleanor F. Sweeny, 2,047.38; United Church of Canada, 248.00; C. White & Co., 1,200.00; Toronto twp., C. F. Cavin, 17.90; W. H. Cawthra, 47.90; M. Gardiner, 20.00; J. J. Goldthorpe and J. B. Thomson, 82.70; W. R. Gummerson, 33.90; Ida A. and J. H. Jones, 2,100.00; Frederick W. Mead, 10.10; F. J. Paskak, 73.30; Jas. P. Robinson, 25.24; School Section No. 23, 31.16; Viola G. Turner, 175.00; Fred J. Watson, 1,472.20; Willard's Chocolates, Ltd., 17.20; Vaughan twp., Donald McKenzie, 800.00; Vespra twp., Chas. Robertson, 1,750.00; Harry Rowell, 82.50; Whitby twp., Elizabeth Lawrence, 13.35; F. Lewis, 49.50; James Routley, 12.83; J. W. Stephenson, 11.88; Whitchurch twp., W. J. Knowles, 23.20; City of Toronto, 40.00. Sundries, 54.20 .. 43,552 71

Property, Miscellaneous, $5,662.85.

Mrs. M. J. Alderson, Etobicoke twp., removal of buildings, etc., 800.00; James Annand, Tiny twp., damages, 10.00; W. J. Bigham, Toronto twp., moving buildings and arbitration fee, 875.20; W. A. Brown, J. P., Scarborough twp., arbitration fee, 35.00; E. J. Campbell, Brock twp., gravel pit, 653.80; Coo & Thompson, Toronto twp., arbitration fee, 13.50; Wm. Crosby, Mara twp., piling ground, 252.00; Dept. of Lands & Forests, Orillia twp., rental of land, 15.00; James Devins, Vaughan twp., damages, 25.00; Fahey Estate, Markham twp., damages and rent of land, 35.00; R. J. N. Faulkner, Toronto twp., valuating property, 75.00; Mrs. Rosella Gettings, Mara twp., fencing, 26.40; H. J. Howell, Trafalgar twp., injury to cow and damages, 50.00; George Kallen, N. York twp., fill, 50.00; Kilmer, Irving & Davis, Toronto, Pickering and Scarborough

Statutory—Continued

King's Highway Construction—Continued

Residency No. 6—Continued

Property, Miscellaneous—Continued.

twps., legal services, 566.80; Mr. and Mrs. E. Lawrence, Whitby twp., crop damages and borrow pit, 101.65; F. Lewis, Whitby twp., rose bushes, trees and damages, 10.00; Wm. Moody, Toronto twp., land for fill and damages, 300.00; J. W. McCormick, Whitby twp., stock damages, 45.00; Mrs. Addie H. McLean, Vespra twp., fill, 25.00; J. H. Nawton, Vaughan twp., damages, and rent of land, 35.00; Chas. O'Neil, Thorah twp., rental of land and damages, 225.00; R. Parton, Toronto twp., fill 15.00; R. R. Patterson, Scarborough twp., arbitration fee, 20.00; Frank Poucher, Scarborough twp., valuating land, 100.00; Roy Salisbury, Tiny twp., damages and trees, 50.00; J. Skeleton, Scarborough twp., damages, 350.00; Ellis Spurgeon, Scarborough twp., damages, 200.00; W. W. Stallworthy, Etobicoke twp., plaster model at Humber Bridge, 225.00; C. J. Stevenson, Whitby twp., damages, 250.00; Henry Thurlow, Floss twp., crop damages, 10.00; Frank Walterhouse, Toronto twp., damages to trees, 10.00; Willard's Chocolates, Ltd., Toronto twp., fill, 200.00. Sundries, 8.50.. 5,662 85

Road Equipment and Supplies, $1,900.55.

J. D. Adams (Can.), Ltd., 245.41; Canada Ingot Iron Co., Ltd., 31.55; Cameron W. Cotton, 17.50; Crane, Ltd., 83.66; Garf. Durnford, 19.00; Albert G. Hill, 200.00; Levy & Westwood Machinery Co., 758.25; R. G. Manning, 21.20; J. H. McCaw, 14.20; J. E. Nesbitt, 28.17; J. M. Robertson & Son, 14.25; A. C. Robinson, 222.40; Sawyer-Massey, Ltd., 196.39; F. Woodward, 10.80. Sundries, 37.77 1,900 55

Stone, Gravel and Screenings, $56,132.82.

Mrs. Annie Andross, 10.50; W. Bell, 35.00; William Bermingham & Son, 43.34; Canada Crushed Stone Corporation, Ltd., 259.96; H. J. Clark Construction Co., Ltd., 33.00; Coldwater Crushed Stone, Ltd., 2,069.81; Herbert L. Conlin, 816.50; Consolidated Sand & Gravel, Ltd., 2,357.08; Mrs. Edward Cook, 129.30; Cooksville Co., Ltd., 52.50; Alex. Constable, 45.00; Edmund Duncan, 39.00; Ed. Dutton, 18.00; E. W. French, 12.60; Gordon Crushed Stone Co., Ltd., 4,873.75; F. Goss, 13.25; Hagersville Quarries, Ltd., 339.01; J. W. Johnstone, 28.20; Kirkfield Crushed Stone, Ltd., 1,875.02; Limestone Products, Ltd., 19,424.90; E. C. Lockyer, 381.25; Longford Crushed Stone, Ltd., 1,173.40; Milne Coal & Supply Co., 106.60; Chas. Morris, 85.00; S. McCord & Co., Ltd., 18,268.23; William McDonald, 281.25; Ontario Rock Co., Ltd., 2,899.10; John Parr, 175.50; Mary H. Price, 228.20; J. H. Robbins, 13.25; Sarjeant Co., Ltd., 54.37; Henry Sawdon, 32.70; William Sheridan, 42.00; C. Smythe, Ltd., 2,336.00; John F. Soden, 644.90; Chas. K. Stevenson, 432.75; James Thompson, 111.75. Sundries, 53.25; Miscellaneous credits, 3,662.40.......................... 56,132 82

Travelling Expenses and Disbursements, $5,997.09.

Ross Andrews, 18.00; Chas. Aylward, 13.60; Morris Booth, 26.30; J. C. Boyes, 31.65; A. Brown, 246.85; Fred M. Brown, 20.96; G. H. Chalmers, 190.16: E. H. Coates, 61.10; N. H. Crowe, 16.00; Jas. L. Cuttell, 42.45; Ben Davidson, 104.56; J. A. Dillane, 21.55; John R. Downer, 34.42; A. R. Duffin, 112.65; Daniel Dyer, 20.68; G. W. Fields, 84.80; B. A. Gordon, 29.66; George L. Harris, 29.89; Mansfield Harrison, 13.75: J. J. Hopkins, 347.44; I. I. Johnston, 92.12; Tom Johnston, 27.40; Humphrey P. Jones, 36.85; J. E. King, 10.65; F. W. Kitching, 25.81; V. Kitching, 265.68; Alex. Larkin, 38.68; R. Leigh, 24.32; Anson Lucas, 86.78; Duncan MacDonald, 13.65; Thomas Maguire, 11.55; L. Middleton, 12.70; John Morris, 15.15; T. F. Mulvihill, 17.88; F. C. McKenna, 13.80; T. A. McNeill, 344.54; H. E. McTear, 112.04; R. B. Newbery, 46.50; S. E. Paisley, 26.60; D. G. Ramsay, 391.75; H. Ransford, 32.25; W. Randall, 28.40; I. C. Rasberry, 127.80; C. A. Robbins, 1,208.46; R. L. Robertson, 26.31; W. J. Robertson, 377.15; C. W. Rymal, 24.00; C. A. Scharfe, 470.65; George Shriner, 211.50; H. K. Siddall, 17.15; Chas. Snooks, 126.95; Aubrey Stephenson, 12.00; J. W. Stevenson, 53.15; L. Stewart, 10.00; R. J. Stewart, 11.00; S. Vankoughnett, 29.70; Leonard Westlake, 37.65; Ed. Wiggins, 12.65; W. Harry Williams, 15.60. Sundries, 83.80.. 5,997 09

RESIDENCY No. 7 ($753,280.32)

Highway No. 2—Oshawa to west limit of Frontenac County.
Highway No. 7—West limit of Victoria County to Madoc.
Highway No. 14—Picton to Marmora.
Highway No. 28—Port Hope to Peterborough.
Highway No. 30—Brighton to Campbellford.
Highway No. 33—Trenton to Stirling.

Statutory—Continued

King's Highway Construction—Continued

Residency No. 7—Continued

Highway No. 35—Lindsay to Fenelon Falls.
Highway No. 36—Lindsay to Bobcaygeon.
Highway No. 37—Belleville to Actinolite.
Welcome to Dale.

Engineer, W. L. Saunders, Port Hope

Blacksmithing, $267.05.

James R. Baskin, 10.00; Bruce Cassidy, 15.00; Robert Chalk, 13.50; Crosby & Simpson, 11.05; Earl M. Cuthbertson, 17.15; S. J. Elliott, 27.00; George Hall, 33.35; H. Lummiss, 17.60; J. M. O'Dette, 12.80; J. H. Pallin, 10.10; W. C. Spry, 47.60. Sundries, 51.90 .... 267 05

Board of Men, $768.40.

Armstrong House, Havelock, 22.00; Clarendon Hotel, Brighton, 315.00; Globe Hotel, Picton, 27.15; Huyck House, Tweed, 81.00; King's Hotel, Norwood, 93.75; King's Hotel, Peterborough, 12.00; Mansion House, Fenelon Falls, 46.00; Mrs. E. Milne, Frankford, 93.25; Hotel Paisley, Napanee, 11.25; Royal Hotel, Marmora, 51.00; White House, Peterborough, 16.00 .... 768 40

Bonus for Wire Fencing, $1,269.97.

James Anderson, Smith twp., 24.06; Palmer Andress, Hope twp., 24.58; Harold Archer, Smith twp., 19.80; Jess. Barlow, Rawdon twp., 11.28; Mike Brant, Tyendinaga twp., 12.72; William Broadworth, Rawdon twp., 75.54; W. Noble Brown, Hope twp., 30.51; M. S. Burnham, Otonabee twp., 66.42; G. Coombs, Brighton twp., 27.00; W. J. Detlor, Sidney twp., 102.60; Ira J. Falls, Emily twp., 31.80; Isaac Fee, Emily twp., 14.40; Lewis S. Fife, Asphodel twp., 10.14; Eliza J. Hendren, Asphodel twp., 45.48; Chris. Howson, Otonabee twp., 34.20; Andrew Jamieson, Hope twp., 31.98; John Lang, Otonabee twp., 68.82; W. E. Lewis, Hope twp., 97.02; Miss M. Livingston, Rawdon twp., 72.54; Robert Martin, Clarke twp., 79.80; Bernard McGinnis, Tyendinaga twp., 26.16; F. T. McMillan, Belmont twp., 30.48; Roy Parker, Asphodel twp., 59.34; Clayton Sanderson, Smith twp., 22.20; C. W. Sine, Rawdon twp., 48.03; K. B. Thompson, Rawdon twp., 58.08; T. J. Thompson, Rawdon twp., 64.29; West Wilson, Emily twp., 68.46. Sundries, 12.24 .... 1,269 97

Cement, Calcium Chloride and Bituminous Materials, $66,657.91.

H. A. J. Aldington, 825.00; Barrett Co., Ltd., 4,107.01; George Butterfield, 550.00; Canada Building Materials, Ltd., 696.62; Canada Cement Co., Ltd., 12,967.37; Canada Colors & Chemicals, Ltd., 1,073.66; Canada Creosoting Co., Ltd., 135.00; Canadian Bitumuls Co., Ltd., 1,453.37; Colas Roads, Ltd., 7,534.79; Currie Products, Ltd., 3,915.43; Dow Chemical Co., 3,142.80; Thomas Garnett & Sons, 207.15; E. S. Hubbell & Son, 325.80; Imperial Oil, Ltd., 22,124.15; Merck & Co., Ltd., 185.00; Murray & Fitzgerald, 15.40; Non-Skid Pavement, Ltd., 2,754.64; Ontario Amiesite, Ltd., 356.63; Alfred Rogers, Ltd., 675.00; Schofield-Donald, Ltd., 514.17; Solvay Sales Corporation, 2,234.34; Wilson, Paterson, Gifford, Ltd., 1,661.58; miscellaneous, cement sack credits, 797.00 .... 66,657 91

Coal, $751.45.

Canadian Canners, Ltd., 16.65; A. G. Dawson, in trust, G. N. Patterson, 252.50; J. E. A. Fitzgerald, 64.80; H. M. Fowlds & Son, 43.50; W. H. Peacock & Co., 206.00; A. E. Phillips, 13.00; B. W. Powers & Sons, 155.00 .... 751 45

Contracts, $384,436.11.

Wm. Birmingham, No. 32-56, Omemee Bridge, Emily twp., Peterborough-Lindsay project, 497.08; Brennan Paving Co., Ltd., No. 30-79, grading and culverts, Otonabee twp., Peterborough-Madoc project, 24,295.40; Canadian Pacific Railway Co., No. 957, Norwood Subway, Asphodel twp., Peterborough-Marmora project, 12,234.60; Curran & Briggs, Ltd., No. 32-14, concrete culverts, Brighton twp., Brighton-Campbellford project, 7,400.62; John Denstedt and Wm. Yundt, No. 32-57, grading and culverts, Fenelon twp., Cameron-Fenelon Falls project, 2,271.32; Fletcher & Springer, No. 1096, grading, Otonabee twp., Peterborough-Norwood project, 1,481.85; Frontenac Dredging Co., Ltd., No. 30-26, Belleville Bay Bridge, Ameliasburg twp., Belleville-Picton project, 7,891.52; Johnson Bros. Co., Ltd., No. 32-33, grading and culverts, Thurlow twp., Belleville-Tweed project, 14,634.20; A. E. Jupp Construction Co., Ltd., No. 31-14, concrete pavement, Emily twp., Fowlers' Corners-Omemee project, 5,119.12; Kilmer & Barber, Ltd., No. 31-44, concrete pavement, Sidney and Thurlow twps., Trenton-Belleville Bay Bridge project, 9,564.37; Edward Lansfield, No. 670, gravelling, Emily and

Statutory—Continued
King's Highway Construction—Continued
Residency No. 7—Continued

Contracts—Continued.

Ops twps., Cameron-Fenelon Falls project, 925.00; L. B. Miles, No. 32-37, surface treatment, Ops and Fenelon twps., Lindsay-Bobcaygeon-Fenelon Falls project, 3,294.03; E. P. Muntz, Ltd., No. 1067, Norwood Subway, Asphodel twp., Peterborough-Marmora project, 589.41; Municipal Road Spraying & Oiling Co., Ltd., No. 32-39, surface treatment, Ameliasburg and Hallowell twps., Belleville-Picton project, 6,474.68; McGinnis & O'Connor, No. 31-35, mixed macadam pavement, Ernesttown twp., Napanee-Kingston project, 16,067.07; McNamara Construction Co., Ltd., No. 30-80, grading and culverts, Brighton twp., Brighton-Campbellford project, 42,244.27; McNamara Construction Co., Ltd., No. 31-38, grading and culverts, Marmora twp., Marmora-Stirling project, 26,260.09; Ontario Construction Co., Ltd., No. 31-71. Ops Bridge, Trent Canal, Otonabee twp., Lindsay-Peterborough project, 28,704.54; Rayner Construction, Ltd., No. 30-84, grading, culverts and crushed stone, Asphodel, Belmont, Seymour and Brighton twps., Peterborough-Madoc-Brighton project, 104,823.23; Routly Construction Co., No. 31-24, grading, culverts and crushed stone, Thurlow, Rawdon, Marmora and Sidney twps., Belleville-Marmora and Stirling-Trenton project, 65,734.82; F. R. Wilford & Co., No. 671, crushed stone, Ops and Emily twps., Lindsay-Bobcaygeon project, 3,928.89 .... 384,436 11

Drainage Materials (Culverts, Tile, etc.), $8,727.57.

Burlington Steel Co., Ltd., 752.16; Bernard Cairns, Ltd., 14.50; Canada Culvert Co., Ltd., 267.20; Canada Ingot Iron Co., Ltd., 225.80; Corrugated Pipe Co., Ltd., 52.08; Dominion Wheel & Foundries, Ltd., 53.90; Jas. C. Kingsborough, 117.75; Metallic Roofing Co. of Canada, Ltd., 727.10; Pedlar People, Ltd., 5,848.72; Steel Co. of Canada, Ltd., 627.24. Sundries, 41.12.................. 8,727 57

Fence and Guard Rail Materials, $30,924.56.

G. B. Airhart, 75.00; D. C. Baird, 1,120.00; Roy Baker, 12.10; Jas. R. Baskin, 155.45; Benson-Wilcox Electric Co., 159.94; A. E. Bottum & Sons, 17.21; Canada Creosoting Co., Ltd., 133.00; Canada Wire & Cable Co., Ltd., 402.51; John Carew Lumber Co., Ltd., 93.51; A. Clapperton, 11.75; Thos. E. Colby, 17.05; Wm. Cross, 20.00; Joseph Danford, 23.25; S. C. Daniels Co., Ltd., 8,750.00; J. F. Dauncey, 24.16; Austin Dingman, 50.50; Frost Steel & Wire Co., Ltd., 10,613.68; R. P. Harper, 10.20; Harry Herrington, 120.80; F. B. Hill, 100.00; Samuel Jones, 10.00; Peter Kilbank, 29.65; G. S. Langdon, 43.25; Robert Light, 13.75; Line & Cable Accessories, Ltd., 180.63; Lundy Fence Co., Ltd., 3,650.46; C. H. Mallory, 10.80; S. T. Matthews, 25.00; Morgan Car Exchange, 21.60; John Morrow Screw & Nut Co., Ltd., 477.70; C. B. McCoy, 23.40; Lorne McDonald, 46.00; W. A. McMurray, 300.75; Cecil Palmer, 32.50; Pedlar People, Ltd., 54.81; Peoples Bros., 12.50; R. M. Potter, 30.60; Railway Power Engineering Corporation, Ltd., 70.54; H. M. Reddon, 67.15; Andrew Runciman, 30.00; Sarnia Fence Co., Ltd., 139.50; Morley R. Simpson, 51.80; Standard Underground Cable Co. of Canada, Ltd., 99.35; Steel Co. of Canada, Ltd., 2,792.16; Stirling Cheese Box and Basket Co., 245.98; Stoney Lake Hotels, Ltd., 60.00; Edward Strong, 12.00; G. H. Switzer, 26.22; Joe Tackabury, 22.50; Glen Thompson, 17.40; Gregory Towns, 32.50; Joseph Tully, 27.00; Arthur Walker, 20.00; C. E. Way, 233.25. Sundries, 103.70... 30,924 56

Gas and Lubricants, $6,618.23.

E. G. Bailey, 581.68; Bloomfield Garage, 29.22; J. A. Bovay, 11.32; British American Oil Co., Ltd., 28.33; F. C. Burgess, 30.28; Casson Bros., 42.44; Cities Service Oil Co., Ltd., 18.10; Cooksville Motors, 11.31; J. D. Dale, 41.64; Richard Ennis, 82.93; Fee Motors, 658.85; G. H. Fletcher, 230.16; Lloyd S. Gerow Garage Co., 17.93; J. M. Graham, Napanee, 517.41; Graham's Garage, Trenton, 149.00; A. F. Hall, 185.79; Hood & Cumming Motors, Ltd., 417.30; Imperial Garage, 347.36; Imperial Oil, Ltd., 519.28; H. Jackett, 17.08; E. W. Jones, 168.10; John Lloyd, 23.84; Marysville Garage & Service Station, 10.15; McColl-Frontenac Oil Co., Ltd., 277.00; Robt. McCutcheon, Jr., 53.70; Riggs Motor Sales, 118.54; R. E. Sculthorpe, 750.06; Shannonville Garage, 29.70; Shell Co. of Canada, Ltd., 23.37; Springbrooke Garage & Service Station, 130.81; Springville Garage, 181.98; Stephenson & Lent Motor Sales, 472.95; Vallance Bros., 38.23; Wellman's Garage, 91.63; J. A. Whelan, 234.67; A. F. Whimsett, 38.88. Sundries, 37.21.......... 6,618 23

Hardware, $1,433.58.

Boxall & Matthie, Ltd., 26.89; Boyle & Son, 20.36; Chas. C. Brown, 13.00; M. W. Connor & Son, 24.43; R. P. Harper, 10.55; Higgins Hardware Co., 18.81; Jones & Potts, 58.28; L. & R. W. Meiklejohn, 151.54; Thos. Meredith & Co., Ltd., 417.31; Murray & Fitzgerald, 43.78; Myles & Son, 48.24; McClung Hard-

Statutory—Continued

King's Highway Construction—Continued

Residency No. 7—Continued

Hardware—Continued.

ware, Ltd., 13.33; McLennans, Ltd., 95.20; G. A. Outram, 283.23; W. Reynolds, 71.70; Rice Lewis & Son, Ltd., 43.85; J. W. Rork & Son, 21.78; W. Walker & Son, Ltd., 23.77; Walker Hardware Co., Ltd., 18.56. Sundries, 28.97............. 1,433 58

Lumber, $1,280.69.

Brighton Lumber Mills, 22.00; John Carew Lumber Co., Ltd., 135.13; J. F. Dauncey, 66.71; Martin Jex & Co., 13.41; J. Marshall, 605.37; Ontario Cheese Box Co., 84.00; W. F. Petry, 106.70; William Robb, 14.00; S. B. Rollins, 16.42; A. Spencer & Son, 12.50; R. E. Stacey, 85.50; Stirling Cheese Box & Basket Co., 73.05; W. Whytock, 22.50. Sundries, 23.40.............................. 1,280 69

Miscellaneous, $42,661.35.

George Allen & Co., paint, 38.22; Art Metropole, surveyor's instruments and repairs, 10.70; Asphodel twp., detour, 179.03; Bell Telephone Co. of Canada, moving poles and aerials, 3,550.13; messages, 495.22; rentals, 48.20; Belmont Municipal Telephone System, moving poles, 33.00; Bituminous Spraying & Contracting Co., Ltd., material and services, 3,589.26; Boeckh Co., Ltd., brushes, 119.12; Ed. Brandwood, car hire, 11.20; Brennan Paving Co., Ltd., material and services, 186.67; C. H. Brenton, lighting lanterns, 28.60; Brighton Municipal Telephone Co., moving poles, 751.44; W. H. Bruce, signs, 85.90; Burlington Steel Co., Ltd., steel, 1,380.49; Canada Paint Co., Ltd., paint, 215.60; Canadian Industries, Ltd., paint and soda, 71.34; Canadian Inspection & Testing Co., Ltd., tests, 29.63; Canadian National Railways, freight, 6,843.09; office rent, 360.00; sidings and wigwags, etc., 949.00; Canadian Pacific Railway Co., freight, 2,968.77; sidings and wigwags, 1,532.09; Robert Chalk, signs, 32.50; Arthur Clazier, shed rent, 10.00; M. W. Connor & Son, explosives, 30.95; Daily Commercial News & Building Record, advertising, 20.25; G. M. Darwin, car hire, 421.29; J. W. Devereux, snow plow, rental 650.00; J. T. Donald & Co., Ltd., sampling, 178.12; E. E. Down, car hire, 777.42; Dunsford Telephone Co-Operative Association, Ltd., moving poles, 49.25; H. V. Fox, brackets, 174.88; Gasaccumulator Co., Canada, Ltd., reflectors, 202.80; General Steel Wares, Ltd., signs, 252.00; Gliddon Co., Ltd., paint, 20.98; Globe Printing Co., advertising, 28.50; Geo. C. Godard, car hire, 20.37; Godson Contracting Co., Ltd., paving, 235.55; E. Harris Co., of Toronto, Ltd., drafting supplies, 20.53; V. A. Huffman, legal services, 10.00; Robert W. Hunt & Co., Ltd., inspections of cement, 19.40; Hydro-Electric Power Commission of Ontario, moving poles, 3,374.17; services and lamps, 354.81; Instruments, Ltd., surveying instruments and repairs, 39.80; R. A. Johnston, truck hire, 40.00; Kilmer & Barber, Ltd., material and services, 54.50; King's Printer, office supplies, 27.18; William A. Logan, car hire, 717.57; Lowe Brothers Co., Ltd., paint, 312.49; John W. Lowery, car hire, 20.16; Mail & Empire, advertising, 28.50; Metallic Roofing Co. of Canada, Ltd., expansion strips and signs, etc., 1,402.49; L. B. P. Miles, cartage, 49.40; W. H. Montgomery, work on well, 10.00; W. J. Moore, surveying instruments and repairs, 43.25; Mountain View Church, shed rental, 10.00; Municipal Road Spraying & Oiling Co., Ltd., material and services, 873.50; Harry McCreary, truck hire, 545.00; McGinnis & O'Connor, snow plow hire, 120.00; J. Wm. McLeod, signs, 59.95; McNamara Construction Co., material and services, 676.99; Corporation of the Town of Napanee, roller rental, 130.00; Ontario Rock Co., Ltd., explosives, 143.74; Otonabee Municipal Telephone System, moving poles, 118.80; Frank Owens, mower rental, 46.50; Pedlar People, Ltd., steelcrete, 165.78; Peterborough Examiner, Ltd., advertising, 16.29; Peterborough Utilities Commission, moving poles, 15.60; Robt. T. Purves & Co., expansion joints, 72.44; Reflex Sign Co., Ltd., signs and signals, 225.80; Remington Typewriters, Ltd., inspections and ribbons, etc., 26.00; Riggs Motor Sales, garage rent, 16.00; Routley Construction Co., material and services, 286.35; Sanders Hardware & Electric Co., electric installation, 215.11; Sanderson Pearcy-Marietta, Ltd., paint, 290.27; Sherwin-Williams Co. of Canada, Ltd., paint, 178.76; Sidney Township Road System, maintenance and equipment rentals, 356.00; L. A. Smallwood, car hire, 14.42; Fred Smith, truck hire, 652.00; Frank A. Sparkes, truck hire, 746.86; Standard Brands, Ltd., soda, 11.86; Steel Company of Canada, Ltd., structural steel, 3,120.34; Sundry Registry Fees, services, 144.76; "T. & G." Engineering Sales Co., chemical tank, 39.50; Tremco Mfg. Co., Canada, Ltd., paint, 26.95; R. Wade, car hire, 14.70; R. A. Webb, car hire, 12.18; H. B. Zavitz, car hire, 16.45. Sundries, 166.64.. 42,661 35

Pay Lists, $173,213.77.

Wages of men.. 173,213 77

Statutory—Continued

King's Highway Construction—Continued

Residency No. 7—Continued

Purchase of Property, Right-of-Way, $9,607.39.

Asphodel twp., Elizabeth A. Andrews, 50.00; Fletcher Buck, 100.00; Joe Dickens, 50.00; John F. Elliott, 65.00; Lewis Fife, 115.00; Geo. A. Graham, 125.00; John Graham, 277.75; Ernest Haigh, 125.00; Mrs. E. J. Hendren, 160.00; David T. Kelly, 20.00; Kenneth Kempt, 75.00; John N. McKay, 145.00; Norwood Milling Co., Ltd., 2,000.00; Belmont twp., Hector Bannon, 30.00; Canadian Pacific Railway Co., 125.00; J. A. Cochrane, 246.75; C. W. Coon, 40.00; Susanna Daniels, 104.32; Miss Mary Gilbert, 255.00; Wm. H. King, 176.00; F. T. MacMillan, 101.17; Walter Wilde, 182.50; Brighton twp., Thos. Hatton, 131.50; H. W. Hodges Estate, 362.00; Joe Megginson, 316.50; James W. Moir, 250.00; John Rowley, 50.00; Mrs. Jessie Seguire, 29.25; Haldimand twp., James Walsh, 14.70; Albert Wills, 50.00; Hope twp., Joseph Harcourt, 100.00; W. E. Lewis, 141.00; Marmora twp., George R. Aunger, 157.48; William R. Aunger, 12.75; Joseph Fletcher, 21.96; W. G. Mackecknie, 67.88; Ops twp., B. Tully, 10.00; Otonabee twp., M. S. Burnham, 163.00; Thos. Hefferman, 113.00; Christopher A. Houson, 37.00; John Lang, 67.50; James C. Petrie, 215.00; Percy twp., R. B. Nelson, 82.00; Andrew Runciman, 107.50; Fred Simmons, 15.75; Rawdon twp , Wm. Broadworth, 409.50; A. V. Brown, 150.00; John Farrell, 79.35; Wm. H. Heath, 138.15; Warren Reid, 226.50; C. M. Sine, 14.85; Karl I. Sine, 124.20; George Snarr, 170.92; J. B. Thompson, 125.92; Thos. J. Thompson, 113.62; Earl and David Wallace, 104.70; James Warren, 70.60; George Wellman, 132.95; John Wellman, 68.55; Thurlow twp., H. Elvidge, 190.00; Fred Gray, 60.00; Chas. Lloyd, 150.00; Absolom Parks, 150.00; Ellen Tummon, 25.00. Sundries, 18.32.. 9,607 39

Property, Miscellaneous, $5,149.27.

F. C. Burgess, Otonabee twp., trees and damages, 50.00; John Christie, Asphodel twp., gravel pit, 500.00; T. E. and E. G. Colby, Asphodel twp., damages, 96.00; Blake Collins, Thurlow twp., borrow pit, 50.00; Richard J. Cornwall, Emily twp., damages, etc., 75.00; Mrs. S. Daniels, Belmont twp., trees, 15.00; Chas. W. Dracup, Rawdon twp., moving of buildings, 75.00; Harry L. Dunning, Thurlow twp., trees, 20.00; Thos. C. Ephgrave, Belmont twp., valuating fee, 19.00; S. E. Flindall, Brighton twp., stream diversion and damages, 25.00; John Graham, Asphodel twp., damages, 10.00; Jos. S. Graham, Asphodel twp., damages to lawn, 75.00; W. B. Graham, Mariposa twp., crop damages, 25.00; Carl M. Haynes, Brighton twp., digging well, 156.00; Mrs. Jessie Lancaster, Otonabee twp., trespassing and cutting trees, 50.00; W. J. Langdon, Brighton twp., apple tree, 10.00; Leo. Logan, Dummer twp., fill and damages, 202.50; Charles Mackie, Whitby East twp., damages, 35.00; Mrs. Alice Mullin, Asphodel twp., damages, 100.00; L. E. Neal, Marmora twp., borrow pit, 75.00; R. Neal, Rawdon twp., trees and borrow pit, 167.87; R. B. Nelson, Percy twp., crop damages and trees, 27.00; Norwood Milling Co., Ltd., Asphodel twp., stone house, 2,500.00; Overton E. Powley, Ernesttown twp., quarry, 164.00; Mrs. Hugh Simpson, Brighton twp., diversion of stream and tree, 35.00; Morley B. Simpson, Brighton twp., borrow pit, 50.00; Miss Agnes Stark, Asphodel twp., fruit trees, 30.00; B. Tully, Ops twp., fill, 150.00; Allen, Walbridge twp., crop damages and borrow pit, 138.90; Geo. W. Young, Murray twp., damages, 200.00. Sundries, 23.00.............. 5,149 27

Road Equipment and Supplies, $1,806.13.

J. D. Adams (Canada), Ltd., 604.67; Boyle & Son, 31.95; F. B. Carscallen, 13.20; D. W. Church, 25.00; J. Leslie Finlay, 10.00; J. M. Graham, 69.66; International Harvester Co. of Canada, Ltd., 408.00; J. H. Isbister, 16.30; Meaford Steel Products, Ltd., 17.67; John McCrae Machine & Foundry, 22.99; R. D. Robson, 25.80; Sawyer-Massey, Ltd., 495.68. Sundries, 65.21........................ 1,806 13

Stone, Gravel and Screenings, $14,474.05.

Wm. Anderson, 21.15; Norman Andrew, 160.57; Albin Arnott, 33.75; William Arnott, 34.20; Roy Baker, 31.50; Elwood Beavis, 33.75; N. E. Bellyou, 16.75; Stanley Brien, 138.30; Walter Brien, 164.40; George Burgess, 33.75; David Burley, 33.75; John Christie, 153.15; Consolidated Sand & Gravel, Ltd., 2,831.20; Charles Conger, 14.50; Ernest Corley, 12.80; Ronald Devitt, 33.86; Hubert Elliott, 33.75; John Elliott, 57.09; Cecil English, 41.10; Wm. Frise, 27.00; George Gay, 23.63; Ernest Germyn, 162.90; County of Hastings, 1,120.00; John Herr, 74.78; Ellsworth Hogg, 98.83; Joseph Hunter, 33.75; John Hutchinson, 15.00; Wes. Irwin, 123.45; Boyd Johnstone, 31.50; George Kennedy, 190.95; Lloyd Kennedy, 183.86; Tom Kennedy, 84.90; Jas. C. Kingsborough, 126.23; Kirkfield Crushed Stone, Ltd., 4,285.56; E. Lansfield, 11.25; C. Lindsay, 17.25; J. H. Little, 34.30; Patrick Maguire, 14.20; John Maiers, 129.30; Geo. Mitchell, 34.43; Laverne Mitchell, 33.75; Ralph Murdock, 33.75; Wm. Murdock, 33.75; Ross

Statutory—Continued

King's Highway Construction—Continued

Residency No. 7—Continued

[illegible]—Continued

[illegible] McCoy, 163.90; Sam O'Brien [illegible]; Ontario Rock [illegible] Parker, 37.00; A. Patterson, .60; Norman Robertson [illegible] Robertson, 34.00; [illegible] Rolls, 12.00; [illegible] Sheehey, 31.50; [illegible] Mrs. Jeanette Sine, 163.55; Addie [illegible], 38.75; Albert [illegible] Thurston, 133.00; Alvin Thurston, 59.78; Carmen [illegible] Thurston, 13.75; Irwin Thurston, 92.60; James A. [illegible] Thurston, 119.10; J. R. Thurston, 7.[illegible]; [illegible] Thurston [illegible] Thurston, 89.10; Mrs. Newton Thurston, 35.80; Vern [illegible] Thurston, 37.21; Rankin Thurston, [illegible]; Albert Wallace, [illegible] 33.96; Lee Wilson, 135.15. Sundries, 102.[illegible] 14,474 05

[illegible], $3,232.84

[illegible] W. A. Anderson, 296.71; W. [illegible], 56.77; G. V. [illegible], 89.33; Jas. Campbell, [illegible]; Walter Carr, [illegible] 27.14; Albert Connor, 41.97; [illegible], 55.34; G. M. [illegible], 133.11; Emlyn Edwards, 13.[illegible]; [illegible] Fitzpatrick, [illegible]; George H. Graham, 16.23; [illegible] Hancock, 154.04; [illegible], 15.86; Harry A. [illegible]; [illegible] Kewley, [illegible]; William A. Logan, 67.[illegible]; [illegible], 25.90; [illegible], 69.15; H. Murray, [illegible]; [illegible] McCracken, [illegible] Morrow, 69.15; [illegible] Queen, 19.30; W. Randall, [illegible]; W. L. Saunders, [illegible], 64.90; Aubrey Stephenson, [illegible]; [illegible] Vankoughnett, [illegible] 36.30; Robert Wright, 20.40; [illegible] Yates, 59.40 ..... 3,232 84

RESIDENCY No. 8 ($[illegible])

[illegible] & Frontenac County to [illegible] boundary.

[illegible] Place.

[illegible] River.

[illegible] Falls.

[illegible] limit of Dundas County.

[illegible] Highway No. 15.

[illegible] limit of Glengarry County.

Engineer, W. F. [illegible]

[illegible], 19.35; A. [illegible], 39.55; A. R. Jacob, [illegible] Reid & Son, 17.55; [illegible] Coal Co., Ltd., [illegible] Sundries, 89.00 ..... 345 76

[illegible], 18.20; Hotel Frontenac, Kingston, 12.25; Mrs. H. [illegible], Alexandria, 147.[illegible]; Sundries, 3.00 ..... 207 95

[illegible], 185.80; Stewart [illegible] twp., 16.20; [illegible] 30.80; Wilfred [illegible] Edwardsburg twp., [illegible] Edwardsburg twp., [illegible] 91.20; Claude [illegible]; E. H. Mills, [illegible] McLennan, [illegible] McKinnon, [illegible] Leeds twp.,

Statutory—Continued
King's ighway Construction—Continued
Isidency No. 8—Continued

Coal, $178.00.

G. T. Bishop, 10.74; Ellison Bradley, 15.90; James Buckley Estate, 12.81; Sampson Coal Co., Ltd., 136.3 Sundries, 2.24 .... 178 00

Contracts, $446,106.41.

W. H. Harvey & Son, No. 31-. concrete pavement, Winchester and Mountain twps., Morrisburg-Carlton Ccity Line project, 27,536.21; M. G. Henniger, No. 31-81, mixed macadam pa ment, South Elmsley and Kitley twps., Smith's Falls-Brockville project, 26,463 1; Holdcroft Construction Co., Nos. 616 and 961, culverts and Crosby brid. rosby and Elmsley South twps., Gananoque-Smith's Falls project, 7,4. 7 Edgar Irvine Co., Ltd., No. 31-67, grading, gravelling and concrete stru ures, Lochiel and Kenyon twps., Lancaster-Hawkesbury project, 39,4 .7 Johnson Bros. Co., Ltd., No. 30-12, mixed macadam pavement, Corn wa and Charlottenburg twps., Cornwall-Quebec Boundary project, 54,556. ; mark County, Nos. 1040, 663, 629, spreading stone, Drummond and Elm twps., Wemyso-Carlton Place project, 11,673.00; McGinnis and O'Connor, N 32-26, mixe l macadam pavement, Kingston twp., Nigger Hill-Cataraqu oject, 61,064.00; Municipal Road Spraying & Oiling Co., Ltd., No. 32-45 urface treatment, Morrisburg and Winchester twps., Perth-Carleton Pl . oject, 7,505.75; Municipal Road Spraying & Oiling Co., Ltd., No. 32-4 rface treatment, Pittsburgh twp., Barriefield-Seeley's Bay project, 2,200 49 R. Murphy, No. 551, crushed stone, Verulam twp., Lindsay-Duns or l pro e 505.80; Routley Construction, Ltd., County Road No. 8, surface treatment Augusta twp., Maitland-North Augusta project, 82,294.15; Routly Constr. Co., Nos. 1045 and 1070, grading and crushed stone, South Elmsley twp. r y-Smith's Falls project, 11,220.00; F. Stidwill, No. 32-13, bridge, Kenyo Lochiel twps., Lancaster-Hawkesbury project, 4,078.33; F. Stidwill, No. 31 73 oncrete pavement, Prescott-Morrisburg project, 2,164.38; V. H. Woodland N 30-88, grading and culverts, Leeds twp., Gananoque-Smith's Falls proje t 10 349.87 .... 446,106 41

Drainage Materials (Culverts, Tile, et , $6,616.81.

A. Anderson, 23.65; Atchis & o., Ltd., 58.63; A. W. Beach, 641.90; W. Bingley & Son, 507.20; Canada C l r o., Ltd., 191.64; Canada Foundries & Forgings, Ltd., 88.40; Canada Ingot I o o., Ltd., 266.40; John Dillon, 92.50; Dominion Concrete Co., Lt l., 19.50 C oration of the County of Frontenac, 670.35; Harry Hayley, 1,276.50; J l. ee ler, 24.00; Metallic Roofing Co. of Canada, Ltd., 1,421.66; National S r ipe Co., Ltd., 180.00; Peck Rolling Mills, Ltd., 151.97; Pedlar People, Lt l 7 76; Joseph Seabrooke, 20.00; Geo. S. Stanley, 206.13. Sundries, 24.62 .... 6,616 81

Fence and Guard Rail Materials, $10, .41.

Alexandria Broom Ham le s, 12.37; David Allison, 117.40; S. Anglin Co., Ltd., 40.00; Anglo-Canadi n W Rope Co., Ltd., 221.75; D. C. Baird, 1,344.00; Robert Barton, 91.60; W. a n, 91.20; I. W. Bennett & Son, Ltd., 16.50; Benson-Wilcox Electric C 631; E. H. Bolton, 62.48; Browne Brothers, 86.82; Canada Creosoting Co., L. 9.50; Canada Wire & Cable Co., Ltd., 456.89; Canada Wire & Iron Good C , 261.77; R. H. Cowan, 921.60; C. Crampton, 12.00; Crescent Wire & Ir orks, Ltd., 59.66; W. B. Dalton & Sons, Ltd., 189.66; S. C. Daniels Co l t 2,240.00; J. L. Dietrich, 25.02; Frost Steel & Wire Co., Ltd., 2,211.46 W Fraser, 44.30; E. Hutchings, 11.40; Milton Johnston, 420.00; Allan J n ly, 100.85; Alex. Lacombe, 12.25; Line & Cable Accessories, Ltd., 55.62; l 'y ence Co., Ltd., 14.73; Myles Mac-Millan, 20.00; Mitchell & Wilson, 51.72 J r Iorrow Screw & Nut Co., Ltd., 305.20; John J. McDonald, 20.00; W. W. K on, 12.00; N. J. Newman, 35.00; John Noonan, 38.30; J. Peters & Son, 23. m A. Shaver, 14.00; Steel Company of Canada, d., 396.43; A. Sweet & 110; W. F. Tate, 21.00. Sundries, 92.99 .... 10,432 41

nd Lubricants, $12,160.80.

W. Bain, 3,624.45; B. o Garage, 418.54; George Cain, 373.45; Clark Lewis, Ltd., 38.81; J. l D ich, 344.83; Dietrich Garage, 21.80; H. Earl, 3.23; Fursey Sales i 11.25; F. J. Gates, 316.77; Glengarry Livery, ; Harback's Garage 18 ; Imperial Oil, Ltd., 606.07; James Brothers, Loney Bros., 555.2 D. MacPherson, 21.72; James E. Miller, 805.70; rris, 381.49; R. Mur 129.05; L. H. McAuley, 102.07; T. A. McLellan, W. F. Neal, 10.6 n d Bros., 20.80; W. R. Roach, 11.40; St. Law-l & Supply Co. , 57.57; Albert E. Seguin, 228.20; Shannonville 12.40; Spencer L s, 42.16; Square Deal Garage, 194.61; Ray 184.18; Chas. J Iol, 13.65; Van Luvan Bros., Ltd., 82.04; Webb 13.38; Well's ra , Cardinal, 36.51. Sundries, 107.28 .... 12,160 80

Statutory—Continued

King's Highway Construction—Continued

Residency No. 7—Continued

Stone, Gravel and Screenings—Continued.

McCallum, 33.75; Wm. McCoy, 163.50; Sam O'Brien, 28.95; Ontario Rock Co., Ltd., 1,413.39; Clinton Parker, 27.00; A. Patterson, 19.60; Norman Robertson, 31.50; Walter Robertson, 34.09; Ivy Rolin, 12.00; Cecil Sheehey, 31.50; Chas. Shire, 28.50; Mrs. Jennette Sine, 161.55; Addie Stickle, 18.75; Albert Thurston, 113.10; Alex. Thurston, 155.10; Alvin Thurston, 59.70; Carmen Thurston, 27.00; Delmar Thurston, 33.75; Irwin Thurston, 93.60; James A. Thurston, 199.05; J. J. Thurston, 116.10; J. R. Thurston, 78.00; Milburn Thurston Estate, 111.00; W. J. Thurston, 89.10; Mrs. Newton Thurston, 85.80; Vern Thurston, 152.10; Neil Thurston, 27.23; Rankin Thurston, 27.45; Albert Wallace, 27.00; Stanley Wallace, 33.90; Lee Wilson, 135.15. Sundries, 102.20........... 14,474 05

Travelling Expenses and Disbursements, $3,232.84.

N. C. Anderson, 247.67; W. A. Anderson, 296.71; W. H. Atkins, 56.77; G. V. Bradburn, 17.15; Ed. Brandwood, 89.33; Jas. Campbell, 167.62; Walter Carr, 13.53; Geo. C. Chisholm, 17.14; Albert Connor, 41.93; H. Consitt, 55.34; G. M. Darwin, 85.35; E. E. Down, 323.11; Emlyn Edwards, 13.70; John T. Fitzpatrick, 12.75; Thos. Gimblett, 11.40; George H. Graham, 16.23; D. M. Hancock, 154.04; George Hartin, 39.88; Jno. J. Heaslip, 15.86; Harry A. Ingram, 13.50; R. Kewley, 82.15; Charles D. Logan, 10.00; William A. Logan, 67.85; W. A. Millen, 25.30; Alex. Moon, 74.20; Earl A. Morrow, 69.15; H. Murray, 190.95; B. McCracken, 21.57; G. Nantel, 22.25; Frank Ovens, 19.30; W. Randall, 21.10; W. L. Saunders, 519.14; Leo. A. Smallwood, 64.50; Aubrey Stephenson, 36.45; S. Vankoughnett, 68.50; Wilson M. Webb, 14.20; Robert Wright, 20.40; J. Munroe, Yates 59.40. Sundries, 157.42.. 3,232 84

RESIDENCY No. 8 ($755,353.21)

Highway No. 2—West limit of Frontenac County to Ontario-Quebec boundary.
Highway No. 15—Barriefield to Carleton Place.
Highway No. 16—Johnstown to Rideau River.
Highway No. 29—Brockville to Smith's Falls.
Highway No. 31—Morrisburg to north limit of Dundas County.
Highway No. 32—Gananoque to Highway No. 15.
Highway No. 34—Lancaster to north limit of Glengarry County.

Engineer, W. F. Noonan, Brockville

Blacksmithing, $345.76.

E. Blackman, 91.20; James Emberg, 10.35; A. Gordon, 50.55; A. R. Jacob, 35.20; Chas. McKinnon, 20.95; Jas. Reid & Son, 17.15; Sampson Coal Co., Ltd., 20.50; L. P. Shortall, 10.85. Sundries, 89.01............................... 345 76

Board of Men, $207.95.

Hotel Cornwallis, Cornwall, 35.10; Hotel Frontenac, Kingston, 11.25; Mrs. H. Monger, Brockville, 10.85; Ottawa House, Alexandria, 147.75. Sundries, 3.00.. 207 95

Bonus for Wire Fencing, $1,291.40.

Earl Adams, Edwardsburg twp., 103.80; Stewart Atcheson, Bastard twp., 16.20; Thos. Burns, Edwardsburg twp., 31.80; Wilfred Dukelow, Edwardsburg twp., 36.95; Joseph Fillion, Lancaster twp., 110.40; James Gore, Edwardsburg twp., 30.60; Alfred Guay, Lochiel twp., 93.00; Geo. Hope, Lochiel twp., 91.20; Claude Johnson, Kitley twp., 180.00; Geo. Lalonde, Lochiel twp., 63.60; E. H. Mills, Edwardsburg twp., 39.90; Ben McNilage, Oxford twp., 34.80; John McLennan, Lochiel twp., 125.40; James McGovern, Oxford twp., 67.20; Angus McKinnon, Lochiel twp., 70.20; D. N. McLeod, Lochiel twp., 12.00; M. O'Neil, Leeds twp., 25.74; E. Westlake, Elizabethtown twp., 141.81. Sundries, 16.80............. 1,291 40

Cement, Calcium Chloride and Bituminous Materials, $46,666.24.

Barrett Company, Ltd., 9,856.19; Canada Building Materials, Ltd., 851.23; Canada Cement Co., Ltd., 973.00; Canada Colors & Chemicals, Ltd., 1,715.10; Canadian Bitumuls Co., Ltd., 3,151.57; Clark & Lewis, Ltd., 19.50; Colas Roads, Ltd., 4,240.95; Currie Products Ltd., 1,384.83; H. G. Dean, 38.25; Dow Chemical Co., 1,440.08; Imperial Oil, Ltd., 12,664.75; Merkley & Barclay, 81.00; Alexander Murray & Co., Ltd., 6,283.75; McCurdy-Looser Chemical Co., 688.05; Non-Skid Pavement, Ltd., 1,400.29; Solvay Sales Corporation, 1,848.30; F. Stidwill, B.Sc., 100.00; R. M. Wallace, 39.00. Sundries, 13.10; miscellaneous cement sack credits, 122.70.. 46,666 24

Statutory—Continued
King's Highway Construction—Continued
Residency No. 8—Continued

Coal, $178.00.

G. T. Bishop, 10.74; Ellison Bradley, 15.90; James Buckley Estate, 12.81; Sampson Coal Co., Ltd., 136.31. Sundries, 2.24 .... 178 00

Contracts, $446,106.41.

W. H. Harvey & Son, No. 31-31, concrete pavement, Winchester and Mountain twps., Morrisburg-Carlton County Line project, 27,536.21; M. G. Henniger, No. 31-81, mixed macadam pavement, South Elmsley and Kitley twps., Smith's Falls-Brockville project, 26,463.34; Holdcroft Construction Co., Nos. 616 and 961, culverts and Crosby bridge, Crosby and Elmsley South twps., Gananoque-Smith's Falls project, 7,471.77; Edgar Irvine Co., Ltd., No. 31-67, grading, gravelling and concrete structures, Lochiel and Kenyon twps., Lancaster-Hawkesbury project, 39,432.73; Johnson Bros. Co., Ltd., No. 30-12, mixed macadam pavement, Cornwall and Charlottenburg twps., Cornwall-Quebec Boundary project, 54,556.59; Lanark County, Nos. 1040, 663, 629, spreading stone, Drummond and Elmsley twps., Wemyso-Carlton Place project, 11,673.00; McGinnis and O'Connor, No. 32-26, mixed macadam pavement, Kingston twp., Nigger Hill-Cataraqui project, 61,064.00; Municipal Road Spraying & Oiling Co., Ltd., No. 32-45, surface treatment, Morrisburg and Winchester twps., Perth-Carleton Place project, 7,505.75; Municipal Road Spraying & Oiling Co., Ltd., No. 32-43, surface treatment, Pittsburgh twp., Barriefield-Seeley's Bay project, 2,290.49; R. Murphy, No. 551, crushed stone, Verulam twp., Lindsay-Dunsford project, 505.80; Routley Construction, Ltd., County Road No. 8, surface treatment, Augusta twp., Maitland-North Augusta project, 82,294.15; Routly Construction Co., Nos. 1045 and 1070, grading and crushed stone, South Elmsley twp., Crosby-Smith's Falls project, 11,220.00; F. Stidwill, No. 32-13, bridge, Kenyon and Lochiel twps., Lancaster-Hawkesbury project, 4,078.33; F. Stidwill, No. 31-73, concrete pavement, Prescott-Morrisburg project, 2,164.38; V. H. Woodland, No. 30-88, grading and culverts, Leeds twp., Gananoque-Smith's Falls project, 107,849.87 .... 446,106 41

Drainage Materials (Culverts, Tile, etc.), $6,616.81.

A. Anderson, 23.65; Atchison & Co., Ltd., 58.63; A. W. Beach, 641.90; W. Bingley & Son, 507.20; Canada Culvert Co., Ltd., 191.64; Canada Foundries & Forgings, Ltd., 88.40; Canada Ingot Iron Co., Ltd., 266.40; John Dillon, 92.50; Dominion Concrete Co., Ltd., 19.50; Corporation of the County of Frontenac, 670.35; Harry Hayley, 1,276.50; J. L. Leeder, 24.00; Metallic Roofing Co. of Canada, Ltd., 1,421.66; National Sewer Pipe Co., Ltd., 180.00; Peck Rolling Mills, Ltd., 151.97; Pedlar People, Ltd., 751.76; Joseph Seabrooke, 20.00; Geo. S. Stanley, 206.13. Sundries, 24.62 .... 6,616 81

Fence and Guard Rail Materials, $10,432.41.

Alexandria Broom Handle Works, 12.37; David Allison, 117.40; S. Anglin Co., Ltd., 40.00; Anglo-Canadian Wire Rope Co., Ltd., 221.75; D. C. Baird, 1,344.00; Robert Barton, 91.60; W. Barton, 91.20; I. W. Bennett & Son, Ltd., 16.50; Benson-Wilcox Electric Co., 63.91; E. H. Bolton, 62.48; Browne Brothers, 86.82; Canada Creosoting Co., Ltd., 199.50; Canada Wire & Cable Co., Ltd., 456.89; Canada Wire & Iron Goods Co., 261.77; R. H. Cowan, 921.60; C. Crampton, 12.00; Crescent Wire & Iron Works, Ltd., 59.66; W. B. Dalton & Sons, Ltd., 189.66; S. C. Daniels Co., Ltd., 2,240.00; J. L. Dietrich, 25.02; Frost Steel & Wire Co., Ltd., 2,211.46; Wm. Fraser, 44.30; E. Hutchings, 11.40; Milton Johnston, 420.00; Allan J. Kennedy, 100.85; Alex. Lacombe, 12.25; Line & Cable Accessories, Ltd., 55.62; Lundy Fence Co., Ltd., 14.73; Myles Mac-Millan, 20.00; Mitchell & Wilson, 51.72; John Morrow Screw & Nut Co., Ltd., 305.20; John J. McDonald, 20.00; W. W. McKinnon, 12.00; N. J. Newman, 35.00; John Noonan, 38.30; J. Peters & Son, 23.93; Glenn A. Shaver, 14.00; Steel Company of Canada, Ltd., 396.43; A. Sweet & Co., 17.10; W. F. Tate, 21.00. Sundries, 92.99 .... 10,432 41

Gas and Lubricants, $12,160.80.

Jas. W. Bain, 3,624.45; Bigford's Garage, 418.54; George Cain, 373.45; Clark & Lewis, Ltd., 38.81; J. L. Dietrich, 344.83; Dietrich Garage, 21.80; H. Earl, 1,168.23; Fursey Sales & Service, 11.25; F. J. Gates, 316.77; Glengarry Livery, 14.11; Harback's Garage, 348.15; Imperial Oil, Ltd., 606.07; James Brothers, 18.80; Loney Bros., 555.28; D. J. MacPherson, 21.72; James E. Miller, 805.70; W. Morris, 381.49; R. Murdock, 29.05; L. H. McAuley, 102.07; T. A. McLellan, 45.41; W. F. Neal, 10.64; Olmstead Bros., 20.80; W. R. Roach, 11.40; St. Lawrence Oil & Supply Co., Ltd., 657.57; Albert E. Seguin, 228.20; Shannonville Garage, 12.40; Spencer & Evans, 42.16; Square Deal Garage, 194.61; Ray Stewart, 1,484.18; Chas. L. Todd, 13.65; Van Luvan Bros., Ltd., 82.04; Webb Motor Sales, 13.38; Well's Garage, Cardinal, 36.51. Sundries, 107.28 .... 12,160 80

Statutory—Continued

King's Highway Construction—Continued

Residency No. 8—Continued

Hardware, $6,405.23.

H. E. Baker & Co., 18.19; I. W. Bennett & Son, Ltd., 2,667.79; James F. Boyle, 147.20; R. H. Bradfield & Co., 15.38; J. B. Bunt, 27.36; Antoine Chenier, 34.32; Clark & Lewis, Ltd., 494.49; R. H. Cowan, 1,693.18; W. B. Dalton & Sons, Ltd., 462.00; J. R. Dargavel, 11.55; A. G. Dobbie & Co., 51.28; C. W. Gibson, 11.05; S. L. Heath, 25.71; James Brothers, 309.69; J. P. Lawrence & Son, 20.15; C. D. Martin, 14.65; C. R. Robinson, 23.31; Jas. L. Sanders, 17.75; R. H. Smart, Ltd., 45.84; Spencer & Evans, 28.35; Steacy & McKinley, 185.41; A. Sweet & Co., 17.91; R. M. Wallace, 22.17. Sundries, 60.50 .... 6,405 23

Lumber, $1,508.85.

Roy Barton, 60.94; Brockville Lumber Corporation, Ltd., 38.83; C. W. Hartley & Son, 274.57; Mallory Lumber Co., 65.46; Mitchell & Wilson, Ltd., 979.14; T. A. Thompson Estate, 33.98. Sundries, 55.93 .... 1,508 85

Miscellaneous, $36,238.53.

M. Andress, mower rental, 54.40; Art Metropole, surveying instruments and repairs, 17.29; Wm. Ault, rent of mower, 32.00; W. E. Austin, camp supplies, 117.38; Bernard Baker, rent of ground, 10.00; George Baker, mower rental, 10.50; W. F. Barker, mower rental, 32.00; Bathurst Township, grader rental, 32.37; C. Baxter, building rental, 26.00; Bell Telephone Co. of Canada, moving poles and aerials, 214.04; messages, 617.38; rentals, 53.40; Bituminous Spraying & Contracting Co., Ltd., material and services, 2,608.55; Boeckh Co., Ltd., brushes, 47.03; Burlington Steel Co. of Canada, Ltd., steel, 376.81; Wm. Burnside, mower rental, 22.00; Canada Paint Co., Ltd., paint, 193.12; Canadian National Railways, freight, 5,407.99; sidings and wigwags, etc., 343.46; Canadian National Telegraphs, services, 15.27; Canadian Pacific Railway Co., freight, 6,761.87; sidings and wigwags, etc., 14.33; Canadian Steel Foundries, Ltd., steel, 458.22; W. Cardiff, mower rental, 25.60; Geo. H. Chambers, garage rent, 33.00; D. S. Clow, mower rental, 27.00; C. Crampton, barn rent, 30.00; James Crawford & Son, Ltd., camp supplies, 16.00; Ed. Danby, mower rental, 26.00; John Davis, barn rent, 18.00; Dominion Bridge Co., Ltd., structural steel, 120.05; Dominion Oxygen Co., Ltd., oxygen, 92.09; J. T. Donald & Co., Ltd., sampling, 72.80; H. A. Drury Co., Ltd., steel, 238.40; Elmsley North Township, drain assessment, 14.50; James Everett, building rental, 25.00; Fidelity Lodge, A.F. & A.M., sheds rental, 24.00; Fouse & Brobst, truck hire, 830.50; John W. Gardiner, barn and mower rental, 37.30; Gasaccumulator Co., Canada, Ltd., reflectors, 46.40; F. J. Gates, mower rental, 94.00; General Steel Wares, Ltd., signs, 504.00; Mrs. Eva Gibson, building rental, 24.00; J. Giles, mower rental, 62.40; Glengarry Telephone Co., Ltd., moving poles, 100.55; A. C. Gore, building rental, 36.00; Ogle R. Gowan Memorial Temple Board, office rent, 1,080.00; Grant-Holden-Graham, Ltd., camp supplies, 268.97; W. E. Gray, mower rental, 35.00; J. Haggerty, snow plow rental, 1,801.40; E. Halladay, barn rent, 20.00; W. H. Harvey & Son, services and equipment rental, 433.50; Henry's Machine Shop, tripods repaired, etc., 39.34; A. E. Holmes, barn rent, 24.00; Hydro-Electric Power Commission of Ontario, moving poles, 1,244.53; Instruments, Ltd., surveying instruments and repairs, 20.00; R. Jackson, mower rent, 11.80; C. G. Johnston, storage, 27.00; W. P. Judson, car hire, 1,680.70; J. P. Kavanagh, building rental, 25.00; Kelly's Bakery, bread, 16.05; J. H. Kenny, repairs and rent of building, 124.35; W. J. Kingston Machine Co., iron and steel, 112.15; City of Kingston, labour, materials and equipment rental, 924.93; Wm. Lackie, mower rental, 19.40; Lancaster Lodge, No. 207, barn rental, 35.00; Law Construction Co., Ltd., material, services and equipment rental, 342.00; Leeds Farmers' Co-Operative Co., Ltd., barn rent, 24.00; Leeds & Frontenac Rural Telephone Co., moving poles, 194.27; South Leeds & Pittsburgh Rural Telephone Co., Ltd., moving poles, 141.70; Lowe Brothers Co., Ltd., paint, 369.07; Mahoney & Rich, Ltd., moving shovel, 150.00; Metallic Roofing Co., of Canada, Ltd., expansion strips and signs, etc., 286.54; Metropolitan Transport, Ltd., services, 10.80; R. A. Michea, piling ground rental, 14.17; Walter Moffat, building rental, 30.00; Mountain Township, drain assessment, 497.25; Thomas Murphy, camp supplies, 11.40; A. McArthur Estate, shed rental, 16.00; D. A. McArthur, snow plow rental, 62.50; W. F. McBroom, storehouse rental, 48.00; D. J. McConnell, barn rental, 10.50; Mrs. Edith McCrea, barn rental, 18.00; R. McCurdy, mower rental, 16.00; John Hugh McDonald, building rental, 36.00; McGinnis & O'Connor, snow plow hire, 96.25; Robert McGregor, mower rental, 14.00; N. J. Newman, mower rental, 26.00; New York Central Railroad Co., freight, 54.78; Leo. O'Neill, camp supplies, 28.54; W. T. O'Neil, mower rental, 56.00; Ontario Steel Products Co., Ltd., steel, 91.42; Osgoode Township, damages to roads, 350.00; Isaiah Parker,

Statutory—Continued

King's Highway Construction—Continued

Residency No. 8—Continued

Miscellaneous—Continued.

barn rental, 20.00; Pedlar People, Ltd., steelcrete, 15.20; Ernest Perrin, building rental, 16.00; John Phillips, ground rental, 15.00; M. G. Phillips, mower rental, 10.00; George Pike, mower rental, 31.00; Thos. Pocklington Co., surveying instruments and repairs, 95.50; Charles Polk, barn rental, 15.00; Prest-O-Lite Co., Ltd., acetylene, 53.89; Robt. T. Purves & Co., expansion joints, 37.82; J. Frank Raw Co., Ltd., surveying instruments and repairs, 166.80; Reflex Sign Co., Ltd., signs and signals, 37.09; G. J. Reid, mower rental, 54.00; Robertson Grocery Co., camp supplies, 921.89; J. S. Robinson, mower rental, 19.00; R. C. Runions, building rental, 36.00; Rural Telephone Co., of Kitley, Ltd., moving poles, 50.50; J. E. Safford, mower and garage rentals, 93.00; Sanderson, Pearcy-Marietta, Ltd., paint, 636.17; F. E. Saunders, car hire, 590.59; Scott & Curry, building rental, 18.00; Sherwin-Williams Co., of Canada, Ltd., paint, 87.09; Henry Shennett, barn rental, 24.00; Ben Simzer, mower rental, 17.00; Wilfred Sproule, barn rental, 20.00; Standard Brands, Ltd., soda, 30.11; Ray Stewart Motors, garage rent, 164.00; Sundry Registry Fees, services, 90.16; Clarence Taylor, building rental, 16.00; Thousand Islands Railway Co., siding and wigwags, 89.93; Arthur Trottier, building rental, 22.00; George L. Walker, drugs, 13.70; James Walker, truck hire, 1,157.70; George F. Walsh, car hire, 37.10; Webster Typewriter Service, repairs to machine, 15.95; Williamsburg Township, drain assessment, 141.00; William Wills, building rental, 18.00; Winchester Township, road damages, 200.00; Harry Winstanley, car hire, 78.00. Sundries, 183.03..... 36,238 53

Pay Lists, $154,102.21.

Wages of men.......... 154,102 21

Purchase of Property, Right-of-Way, $11,546.07.

Charlottenburg twp., Mrs. Daniel Fraser, 100.00; Elzaer Levert, 90.62; Donald D. Macdonnell, 340.00; Crosby South twp., Sarah J. Laming, 400.00; Drummond twp., Nellie Robinson, 765.00; Elizabethtown twp., E. M. Westlake, 43.00; Kenyon twp., Wm. Campbell, 22.75; Neil MacLeod, 200.00; D. E. Markson, 162.50; Lancaster twp., Joseph Filion, 268.35; Dan H. McDonald, 330.00; St. Andrews Presbyterian Church, 1,001.40; Leeds twp., W. B. Green, 114.00; John E. Murphy, 1,350.00; Lochiel twp., Robert Barton, 596.25; William Barton, 591.75; J. H. Charlebois, 67.18; Malcolm Fraser, 911.00; Alfred Guay, 109.00; George Hope, 80.00; Oseas Lacombe, 335.50; George Lalonde, 151.20; Mrs. Susan MacDonald, 456.50; Angus A. MacMillan, 496.00; Peter Massie, 250.00; J. N. McIntosh, 332.75; Angus H. McKinnon, 60.00; John McLennan, 138.75; Norman D. McNeil, 366.02; Mrs. Flora McPhee, 351.25; Wm. and T. H. Proulx, 16.00; Alphonse Sabourin, 350.00; Joseph Vachon, 40.25; Mountain twp., W. J. Poole, 46.50; Olden twp., Daniel McDonald, 60.00; Winchester twp., Mrs. J. W. Durant, 120.00; Coleman Hutchinson, 318.75; Mrs. Marcia Strader, 107.80. Sundries, 6.00.......... 11,546 07

Property, Miscellaneous, $1,442.20.

R. J. Empey, Winchester twp., damages and inconveniences, 75.00; George Lalonde, Lochiel twp., borrow pit, 257.20; Frank Morley, Kingston twp., crop damages, 25.00; Mrs. J. B. Morley, Kingston twp., stone quarry, 500.00; George Murray, Kingston twp., crop damages, 30.00; Hester A. McNairn, Cornwall twp., rent of piling ground, 30.00; T. A. McRae, Lochiel twp., borrow pit, 75.00; Salem United Church, Charlottenburg twp., removal of buildings, etc., 250.00; Wm. Summers, Winchester twp., damage and inconveniences, 100.00; Alex. Watson, Edwardsburg twp., well, 100.00.......... 1,442 20

Road Equipment and Supplies, $3,667.06.

J. D. Adams (Canada), Ltd., 150.59; M. Bailey, 16.10; W. N. Barton, 19.45; Hugh Carson, 668.72; Wm. Cleary, 13.65; G. O. Emery, 47.56; Albert G. Hill, 200.00; A. R. Jacob, 19.12; W. J. Kingston Machine Co., 21.75; Millard & Lumb, 303.40; F. A. Mulligan & Co., 1,699.74; L. H. McAuley, 73.14; J. Alex. McDonald, 20.75; Niagara Brand Spray Co., Ltd., 39.73; F. H. Plant, Ltd., 201.90; Jas. Reid & Son, 11.80; Sawyer-Massey, Ltd., 111.11. Sundries, 48.55.......... 3,667 06

Stone, Gravel and Screenings, $13,677.55.

Corporation of the Town of Alexandria, 75.00; J. Andre, 115.97; Rupert Avery, 120.00; George Baldock, 10.00; Allen Ball, 30.00; J. F. Boyle, 343.05; John M. Casselman, 16.25; Harold Churchill, 17.25; Consolidated Sand & Gravel, Ltd., 2,879.20; Ernest Cotnam, 22.00; S. Delorme, 10.50; S. Duval, 21.25; R. H. Fair, 3,518.16; R. G. Freeman, 12.50; Grenville Crushed Rock Co., Ltd., 1,366.45;

Statutory—Continued

King's Highway Construction—Continued

Residency No. 8—Continued

Stone, Gravel and Screenings—Continued.

R. E. Harpell, 28.00; Holdcroft Construction Co., Ltd., 30.00; D. Hudson, 42.00; Harry Jackson, 26.00; Johnson Bros. Co., Ltd., 475.51; Kirkfield Crushed Stone, Ltd., 529.48; John Mallory, Jr., 62.50; Kenneth Merkley, 46.00; Fred Dan McCrimmon, 10.00; Angus H. McKinnon, 15.90; H. C. McLean, 599.45; Harry W. McLean, 78.00; N. J. Newman, 15.00; Michael O'Neil, 302.10; Ontario Rock Co., Ltd., 1,586.40; Charles Proctor, 24.25; Rayner Construction, Ltd., 260.05; St. Lawrence Sand & Gravel Co., 10.00; H. South, 16.25; Kenneth Steacy, 62.50; Wright Builders Supply, Ltd., 834.28. Sundries, 66.30........................ 13,677 55

Travelling Expenses and Disbursements, $2,759.73.

M. A. Buell, 51.15; N. H. Crowe, 14.55; A. H. Dale, 70.13; F. J. Gates, 13.65; S. H. Griffin, 12.00; W. P. Judson, 262.35; W. J. Latimer, 118.40; Charles E. Logan, 53.45; C. D. Lyon, 433.67; J. D. Millar, 71.63; K. E Miller, 101.40; H. E. Monger, 210.90; Cecil McMachen, 21.95; W. T. Noonan, 494.00; Levi Perrin, 21.95; W. Randall, 10.45; F. E. Saunders, 102.80; D. M. Thomson, 14.20; A. F. Vincent, 311.55; W. T. Waller, 20.05; George F. Walsh, 133.25; Harry Winstanley, 17.75; Elmer F. Woodcock, 116.05. Sundries, 82.45........ 2,759 73

RESIDENCY No. 9 ($444,498.59)

Highway No. 15—Carleton Place to Britannia.
Highway No. 16—Ottawa to Rideau River.
Highway No. 17—Pembroke to Ottawa to Point Fortune (Ontario-Quebec boundary).
Highway No. 29—Carleton Place to Arnprior.
Highway No. 34—Hawkesbury to south limit of Prescott County.

Engineer, J. Sears, Ottawa

Blacksmithing, $438.48.

Alex. Clarke, 54.20; T. W. Cotie, 13.95; R. J. Hickey, 29.45; W. A. Hunt, 18.40; Wilfred Lavoie, 16.46; S. Murray, 63.30; F. Pouliatte, 24.99; A. G. Preen, 28.27; H. Pulcine & Son, 54.66; Albert Seguin, 54.60; James Warren & Son, 51.10. Sundries, 29.10.. 438 48

Board of Men, $105.00.

Casa Inn, L'Orignal, 42.00; Windsor Hotel, Vankleek Hill, 63.00............... 105 00

Bonus for Wire Fencing, $60.75.

Gordon Lavallee, McNab twp., 15.45; J. G. Morgan, March twp., 22.80; Eber Pettipiece, North Gower twp., 22.50.. 60 75

Cement, Calcium Chloride and Bituminous Materials, $39,876.82.

George Butterfield, 562.50; Cadieux & Frere, 30.00; Canada Cement Co., Ltd., 2,298.46; Canadian Bitumuls Co., Ltd., 1,180.47; Canadian Industries, Ltd., 953.15; Cochrane-Dunlop Hardware, Ltd., 13.00; Colas Roads, Ltd., 1.115.75; Currie Products, Ltd., 3,334.70; Devine & Legree, 22.40; Dow Chemical Co., 3,427.12; Imperial Oil, Ltd., 22,798.93; Independent Coal Co., Ltd., 37.48; Rodrigue Lalonde, 32.50; Alexander Murray & Co., Ltd., 3,591.73; J. R. McQuigge, 50.40; L. P. Pattee, 30.95; Stephen Pilon, 45.50; Solvay Sales Corporation, 949.20; Taylor Hardwares, Ltd., 17.16. Sundries, 3.72; miscellaneous cement sack credits, 618.30.. 39,876 82

Coal, $157.25.

M. N. Cummings, 19.78; Wm. R. Cummings, 64.85; Hawkesbury Dairy Co., 17.03; Leafloor Brothers, 26.45; Renfrew Textiles, Ltd., 20.84. Sundries, 8.30... 157 25

Contracts, $241,691.15.

Almonte Township, No. 1009, crushed stone, Ramsay and Pakenham twps., Carleton Place-Arnprior project, 10,710.00; Bituminous Spraying & Contracting Co., Ltd., No. 32-40, surface treatment, Nepean and Gloucester twps., Ottawa approaches project, 12,080.15; Ed. Brunet & Son, No. 31-26, L'Orignal C.N.R. overhead, Longuiel twp., Ottawa-Port Fortune project, 13,036.06; Dibblee Construction Co., Ltd., No. 31-19, mixed macadam pavement, Nepean, Cloucester and Beckwith twps., Ashton-Carleton Place and Ottawa approaches project, 23,063.73; Grant Bros. Construction Co., Ltd., Nos. 510, 568, 620 and 896, mixed macadam pavement, etc., Nepean and Gloucester twps., Ottawa-Pembroke project, 19,309.28; Holmes & Jamieson, Nos. 593 and 611, retread pavement, Nepean twp., Carleton Place-Arnprior project, 4,278.71; Johnson

Statutory—Continued

King's Highway Construction—Continued

Residency No. 9—Continued

Contracts—Continued.

Bros. Co., Ltd., No. 32-27, mixed macadam pavement, Almonte twp., Carleton Place-Arnprior project, 93,750.30; McAlpine & Belanger, No. 30-83, grading and culverts, Longuiel and Hawkesbury West twps., Ottawa-Port Fortune project, 24,251.07; Peter McKenzie, Nos. 698 and 1065, stone, Longuiel and Hawkesbury West twps., Hawkesbury-Vankleek Hill project, 20,746.08; J. R. McQuigge, No. 30-68, culverts, Clarence twp., Ottawa-Port Fortune project, 4,679.31; McNamara Construction Co., Ltd., No. 30-08, grading and concrete pavement, Horton, McNab and Ross twps., Pembroke-Arnprior project, 15,786.46 .... 241,691 15

Drainage Materials (Culverts, Tile, etc.), $3,581.85.

Geo. E. Baker, 86.95; Ernest Bertrand, 92.50; Canada Culvert Co., Ltd., 1,691.54; Dochart Brick, Tile & Terra-Cotta Works, 62.37; Dominion Concrete Co., Ltd., 20.00; Harry Hayley, 142.00; T. Hunault, 55.00; Jamieson Lime Co., 65.00; Metallic Roofing Co. of Canada, Ltd., 950.93; Pedlar People, Ltd., 130.36; Geo. S. Stanley, 236.63; Steel Co. of Canada, Ltd., 44.57. Sundries, 4.00 ...... 3,581 85

Fence and Guard Rail Materials, $6,755.76.

Anglo-Canadian Wire Rope Co., Ltd., 1,074.25; John G. Barton, 100.05; Robert Besharah, 15.00; Alek. Boyd, 92.80; Byron A. Boyd, 18.00; Jas. E. Caldwell, 40.00; J. W. Caldwell, 54.65; S. C. Daniels, Co. Ltd., 2,450.00; Oliver Dezell, 50.00; Dominion Bridge Co., Ltd., 114.00; D. Doyle, 13.79; Lloyd Farnell, 210.60; Hubert Fee, 37.50; Frost Steel & Wire Co., Ltd., 1,394.25; R. J. Gault, 15.60; W. H. Goth, 30.00; B. Greening Wire Co., Ltd., 62.33; Gilbert Lemay, 15.90; Line & Cable Accessories, Ltd., 24.05; Lundy Fence Co., Ltd., 20.25; Mooney & Wood, 68.50; John Morrow Screw & Nut Co., Ltd., 171.60; H. McCurdy, 57.60; McKay Brothers, 12.00; W. H. Neilson, 55.00; Greig Presley, 55.20; Adelar Rouleau, 88.95; Melvile Royce, 31.25; Steel Company of Canada, Ltd., 90.21; John Somerville, 40.50; S. D. Stevens, 21.90; Douglas Stewart, 33.65; Kenneth A. Wallace, 15.30; Cecil Wier, 62.50; A. Workman & Co., Ltd., 54.75. Sundries, 63.83 .... 6,755 76

Gas and Lubricants, $7,463.99.

Wm. T. Baker, 295.81; G. F. W. Barton, 15.99; Thos. A. Bradley, 19.36; Geo. E. Brannan, 28.05; Campbell Motor Sales, 242.13; Colonial Coach Lines, Ltd., 72.71; Crozier's Garage, 47.04; R. Gamble & Son, 49.28; Gamble Motors, 38.98; Hawkesbury Tire Sales & Vulcanizing Co., 433.22; Jos. Houle, Jr., 12.77; Imperial Oil, Ltd., 1,805.00; R. Lytton, 160.60; C. A. Martin, 219.25; Mooney & Wood, 18.19; Mulvihill Garage & Machine Shop, 128.00; McMullen-Perkins, Ltd., 22.10; Ottawa Electric Railway Co., 89.01; Pakenham Garage, 78.83; Peever's Garage, 22.20; Pembroke Service Garage, 18.62; Powell's Auto Service, 458.53; Stephenson & Lent Motor Sales, 10.12; Stewart's Service Station, 377.71; Ray Stewart Motors, 191.59; Supertest Petroleum Corporation, Ltd., 1,317.98; Taylor Hardwares, Ltd., 25.93; Teskey's Service Station, 41.32; C. O. Thacker, 137.10; Thibeau & Weedmark, 30.08; Westboro Garage, 462.74; H. H. Wright, 10.76; Young's Service Station, 402.73. Sundries, 180.26 .... 7,463 99

Hardware, $2,011.28.

Fred J. Bradley, 12.91; Buckham & Vance, 101.75; Cochrane-Dunlop Hardware, Ltd., 47.31; Geo. Craig Sons & Co., 45.45; Walter Crooks, 35.93; Devine & Legree, 301.31; D. Doyle, 61.94; W. W. Dunning & Son, 32.06; H. H. Falls, 60.40; Gray-Harvey Co., Ltd., 32.06; D. Hagan, 12.60; N. S. Lee, 313.80; Leegree Hardware, 63.19; Charles McFaul, 52.89; D. A. McRae, 17.10; Needham & Sneddon, 31.43; Geo. S. Stanley, 239.98; Stevenson's Hardware, 57.15; Taylor Hardwares, Ltd., 168.23; Arthur E. Wilson, 14.45; A. Workman & Co., Ltd., 283.25. Sundries, 26.09 .... 2,011 28

Lumber, $1,171.12.

Barrett Bros., 25.98; A. F. Campbell & Son, 40.15; Duplantie Freres, 29.73; D. Kemp Edwards, Ltd., 549.38; Hugh Gilmour, 151.80; Hawkesbury Lumber Co., Ltd., 76.82; P. A. Lauzon, 87.92; W. A. Nichols, 116.20; Philias Quimet, 35.28; Renfrew Manufacturing Co., Ltd., 42.39. Sundries, 15.47 .... 1,171 12

Miscellaneous, $16,225.27.

George Allen Co., paint, 22.93; Bell Telephone Co. of Canada, moving poles and aerials, 747.52; messages, 579.17; rentals, 144.90; Bituminous Spraying & Contracting Co., Ltd., material and services, 271.66; Thos. A. Bradley, barn

Statutory—Continued

King's Highway Construction—Continued

Residency No. 9—Continued

Miscellaneous—Continued

rental, 15.00; Burroughs Adding Machine, of Canada, Ltd., machine rentals and inspections, 24.55; Campbell Steel & Iron Works, Ltd., signs, 120.09; Canada Paint Co., Ltd., paint, 129.36; Canadian Industries, Ltd., paint and soda, 156.06; Canadian National Railways, freight, 1,034.89; Canadian National Telegraphs, moving poles, 238.01; services, 17.85; Canadian Pacific Railway Co., sidings and wigwags, etc., 173.19; freight, 2,008.32; Wm. Clarke, explosives, 20.33; D. Clermont, shop rent, 132.00; Continental Paper Products, Ltd., sanitary supplies, 11.30; Wm. R. Cummings, Ltd., lime, 11.00; Dibblee Construction Co., Ltd., services, 506.00; Dominion Reinforcing Steel Co., Ltd., steel, 75.55; J. T. Donald & Co., Ltd., sampling, 58.84; John Fitzpatrick, straw, 19.90; Geo. C. Godard, car hire, 78.75; J. Haggerty, snow plow hire 546.00; Higginson & Stevens, explosives, 19.88; Hill Construction Co., equipment, 14.00; Hydro-Electric Power Commission of Ontario, moving poles, 37.81; Inspector of Weights & Measures, services, 18.00; Instruments, Ltd., surveying instruments and repairs, 211.51; Keyes Supply Co., Ltd., light and office rent, 1,290.22; King's Printer, office supplies, 14.28; L. Lavigne, garage rent, 42.00; Leo. Levigne, garage rent, 35.00; Lowe Brothers Co., Ltd., paint, 242.32; R. W. MacBey, office and car rentals, 132.01; Harold May, car hire, 28.28; Metallic Roofing Co. of Canada, Ltd., expansion strips and signs, etc., 732.80; T. M. Milligan, storage, 15.00; John Minogue, straw, 16.34; Henry J. Moore, forestry services, 67.15; Geo. Mulligan, storage, 15.00; McFarlane-Douglas Co., Ltd., signs, 60.75; P. W. McKenzie, warehouse rental, 10.00; McNamara Construction Co., material and services, 1,350.00; Corporation of the Township of Nepean, drain assessment, 1,230.20; Ottawa Electric Co., services, 39.25; Ottawa Electric Railway Co., storage, 173.26; Ottawa Suburban Roads Commission, snow plow hire, 201.00; Pedlar People, Ltd., steelcrete, 27.93; F. Perry, car hire, 531.53; Powell's Auto Service, garage rent, 11.00; Pritchard-Andrews Co., scale repairs, 31.00; Public Utilities Commission, Carleton Place, services, 89.75; Robert T. Purves & Co., expansion joints, 20.20; James Ragan, shed rental, 12.00; John T. Rothwell, car hire, 165.06; C. W. Rymal, car hire, 30.80; Lawrence St. Denis, straw, 43.88; Sanderson, Pearcy-Marietta, Ltd., paint, 182.29; R. D. Scott, rubber boots, 14.20; E. W. Sheehan, car hire, 164.85; Sherwin-Williams Co., of Canada, Ltd., paint, 315.90; John Spratt, snow plow hire, 21.50; Steel Company of Canada, Ltd., structural steel, 703.25; S. C. Stevenson, garage rent, 160.00; Sundry Registry Fees, services, 155.51; H. Totten, mixer hire, 73.00; United Typewriter Co., Ltd., machine rentals and services, 10.63; Nap. Vachon, steel, 18.54; L. C. Wilde, car hire, 140.14; Wright Builders Supply, Ltd., explosives, 59.89. Sundries, 103.19 .... 16,225 27

Pay Lists, $102,274.86.

Wages of men 102,274 86

Purchase of Property, Right-of-Way, $10,885.57.

Clarence twp., Elmer Tucker, 352.10; Cumberland twp., Octave Fortier, 20.00; Emanuel Lavatorie, 250.00; Gloucester twp., Mrs. James Fox, 673.28; Hawkesbury West twp., Thos. Barton, 519.75; Amidi Cadieux and Defrid Theoret, 74.12; Mrs. Hormesdas Charbonneau, 1,532.70; George P. Cooper, 76.25; Joseph Cousineau, 10.75; Leo. Cusson, 48.00; Edward Desjardins, 311.25; Wilfrid Desjardins, 154.50; Joseph Deslauriers, 50.75; Wm. Deslauriers, 71.62; Chas. H. Green, 52.81; J. J. Johnstone, 350.00; Thos. P. Kerr, 210.00; Alfred Kirby, 69.12; S. W. Kirby, 187.50; John A. McIlwain, 78.75; Mary A. McKinnon, 215.00; N. H. McRae, 112.25; Leslie Nixon, 300.00; W. J. Nixon, 150.00; Jno. A. Sinclair and J. R. MacLaurin, 51.62; Mrs. E. C. Smith, 100.00; Robert Sproule, 186.62; Edwin Steele, 196.25; Richard Willis, 24.50; Longueil twp., James B. O'Brian and Colin G. O'Brian, 114.81; McNabb twp., John J. McCallum, 271.25; Nepean twp., A. A. Dupont, 42.15; Mrs. Annie Morris, 75.00; Paul Sanders, 45.00; Plantagenet twp., Albert Fitzgerald, 559.80; Ramsay twp., F. A. C. Darling, 20.00; E. D. Devine, 50.00; John J. Johnston, 20.00; William Munro, 37.72; Thomas Rollins, 25.00; A. G. Rosamond, 65.00; Soldier's Settlement, and N. K. Simons, 27.50; Ross twp., Mrs. E. Church, 25.00; Arnold Dale, 1,400.00; Robert Quast, 150.00; Ed. Roach, 1,400.00; Westmeath twp., William Nelson, 100.00. Sundries, 27.85 .... 10,885 57

Property, Miscellaneous, $867.55.

Mathias Cusson, Hawkesbury West twp., damages, 300.00; Victor Dault, Longueil twp., borrow pit, 182.25; Chas. H. Green, Hawkesbury West twp.,

Statutory—Continued

King's Highway Construction—Continued

Residency No. 9—Continued

Property, Miscellaneous—Continued.

damages and borrow pit, 55.30; John Hudson, Nepean twp., moving garage, 35.00; John J. McCallum, McNabb twp., crop damages, 45.00; Tucker Estate, Clarence twp., damages, 250.00 .... 867 55

Road Equipment and Supplies, $1,055.85.

J. D. Adams (Canada), Ltd., 13.12; G. A. Ellis, 21.00; Albert G. Hill, 200.00; International Harvester Co. of Canada, Ltd., 629.49; McKeough & Trottier, Ltd., 102.31; Sawyer-Massey, Ltd., 59.03. Sundries, 30.90 .... 1,055 85

Stone, Gravel and Screenings, $5,438.27.

E. D. Brule & Sons, Ltd., 115.16; Mrs. Ethel Church, 73.80; Couch & Sands, 66.00; Milton Craig, 10.00; Clifford Crozier, 72.00; Jno. J. Davidson, 54.45; R. R. Foster, 21.91; Frazer Duntile Co., Ltd., 749.08; S. A. Fraser, 18.00; Arthur Griese, 77.25; W. A. Hare, 14.50; J. Henderson, 106.88; Hill Construction Co., 192.89; Holmes & Jamieson, 1,676.32; Harry John, 52.65; T. Sidney Kirby Co., Ltd., 45.24; Omer Lalonde, 20.00; D. A. McPhee, 197.70; E. O'Leary, 13.95; Ontario Rock Co., Ltd., 1,346.20; H. Robillard & Son, 445.59; Standard Lime Co., Ltd., 56.95. Sundries, 11.75 .... 5,438 27

Travelling Expenses and Disbursements, $4,437.77.

Albert Argue, 207.75; John Ball, 17.18; J. R. Bell, 73.05; N. D. Bennett, 45.96; Wm. A. Clarke, 62.25; L. M. Clayton, 77.45; W. Davis, 199.45; Jas. H. Garlick, 23.35; Geo. C. Godard, 11.15; Sam Godin, 288.50; S. H. Griffin, 128.95; Wesley Hewitt, 211.60; P. A. Keenan, 324.31; J. H. Lord, 77.34; R. W. MacBey, 16.45; E. F. Marston, 586.16; Philip B. Martin, 17.25; B. A. Matheson, 423.00; H. May, 69.80; R. N. Page, 155.40; F. Perry, 420.08; Fred Quigg, 20.80; John T. Rothwell, 187.20; Lawrence St. Denis, 47.25; J. Sears, 568.89; E. W. Sheehan, 81.60; L. C. Wild, 30.30; J. E. Williams, 33.00; R. Williams, 27.30. Sundries, 5.00 .... 4,437 77

Actinolite-Perth Project ($1,609,553.53)

Less Dominion Government contribution	400,000 00		
Provincial Government contribution	600,000 00	1,000,000 00	
(For further accounting see page N 19).		609,553 53	

Engineer, C. H. Nelson, Toronto, ($609,553.53)

Blacksmithing, $122.14.

Wm. DeWitt, 57.00; W. J. Kirkham, 34.15; F. L. Wormworth, 13.39. Sundries, 17.60 .... 122 14

Board of Men, $20,550.48.

Angus & Taylor, North Bay, 156.00; C. V. Billie, Sharbot Lake, 3,107.70; A. Blair, Perth, 80.00; Mrs. Daniel Brady, Perth, 13.00; Mrs. D. Buchanan, Sharbot Lake, 11.50; Campbell Construction Co., Ltd., Kaladar, 2,453.40; H. A. Conboy, Maberly, 404.10; Mrs. Freeburn Cronk, Mountain Grove, 14.00; Empire Hotel, Arden, 3,331.15; Mrs. Robert Halley, Sharbot Lake, 22.00; M. G. Henniger, Arden, 1,245.00; Hillcrest Hotel, Sharbot Lake, 1,450.00; Huyck House, Tweed, 306.00; Kendall Brothers (Ontario), Ltd., Sharbot Lake, 1,495.50; Hotel La Salle, Kingston, 10.65; Hotel Maberley, Maberley, 115.00; Mrs. J. E. Marsh, Actinolite, 194.00; Mrs. John Moss, Maberley, 77.00; F. O'Neill, Madoc, 301.00; Hotel Perth, Perth, 484.75; Sim. Rowley, Tweed, 1,186.81; Mrs. R. M. Rudsdale, Perth, 30.00; St. Lawrence Hall, Madoc, 31.50; Mrs. Annie Scott, Arden, 1,127.00; H. J. Thomson & Co., Sharbot Lake, 36.00; W. W. Villneff, Kaladar, 2,018.17; Mrs. J. E. Warren, Oso, 105.00; Mrs. J. C. Wilson, Perth, 30.00; York Construction Co., Ltd., Actinolite, 694.20. Sundries, 20.05 .... 20,550 48

Cement, Calcium Chloride and Bituminous Materials, $16,036.22.

Barrett Company, Ltd., 12.83; Dow Chemical Co., 965.65; Canada Cement Co., Ltd., 10,834.80; Imperial Oil, Ltd., 3,541.97; Merck & Co., Ltd., 14.97; Solvay Sales Corporation, 666.00 .... 16,036 22

Coal, $377.48.

J. T. Kleinstuber, 10.00; J. A. Marshall, 25.00; John Price, 12.00; D. W. Reid, 75.86; H. J. Thomson & Co., 142.12; C. W. Thornton, 80.00. Sundries, 32.50 .. 377 48

Contracts, $1,248,322.71.

Angus & Taylor, Ltd., No. 31-77, grading and culverts, Kaladar twp., Actinolite-Perth project, 202,352.14; Chas. V. Billie, No. 31-80, grading and culverts,

Statutory—Continued

King's Highway Construction—Continued

Actinolite-Perth Project—Continued

Contracts—Continued

Kaladar twp., Actinolite-Perth project, 201,185.84; Chas. V. Billie, No. 31-81, grading and culverts, Bathurst twp., Madoc-Perth project, 127,599.54; Campbell Construction Co., Ltd., No. 31-75, grading and culverts, Kaladar twp., Madoc-Perth project, 168,912.78; Campbell Construction Co., Ltd., No. 31-76, grading and culverts, Kaladar twp., Madoc-Perth project, 105,292.01; M. G. Henniger, No. 31-78, grading and culverts, Kaladar twp., Madoc-Perth project, 143,695.31 M. G. Henniger, No. 31-74, grading and culverts, Kaladar twp., Actinolite-Perth project, 67,005.70; Kendall Bros., No. 31-79, grading and culverts, Oso West twp., Madoc-Perth project, 163,866.11; York Construction Co., Ltd., No. 31-74, grading and culverts, Kaladar twp., Actinolite-Perth project, 68,413.28 .... 1,248,322 71

Drainage Materials (Culverts, Tile, etc.), $40,527.87.

Burlington Steel Co., Ltd., 284.52; Bernard Cairns, Ltd., 160.00; Canada Culvert Co., Ltd., 10,394.66; Canada Ingot Iron Co., Ltd., 5,053.60; Crane, Limited, 105.79; Metallic Roofing Co. of Canada, Ltd., 10,647.30; National Sewer Pipe Co., Ltd., 630.00; Pedlar People, Ltd., 13,128.40; J. A. Pringle, 120.00. Sundries, 3.60 .... 40,527 87

Fence and Guard Rail Materials, $34,765.37.

Angus & Taylor, Ltd., 110.50; Aubrey Benn, 60.00; W. M. Both, 10.20; E. B. Buell, 887.95; Canada Wire & Cable Co., Ltd., 924.68; Canada Wire & Iron Goods Co., 103.22; C. J. Casey, 330.20; W. B. Dalton & Sons, Ltd., 470.65; J. L. Dietrich, 20.52; Frost Steel & Wire Co., Ltd., 6,852.71; General Supply Co., of Canada, Ltd., 204.21; B. Greening Wire Co., Ltd., 306.00; Damon Hoover, 11.00; R. Jackson, 24.64; James Bros., 186.00; Lundy Fence Co., Ltd., 4,887.51; A. Miller, 42.50; Elmer Miller, 11.00; G. A. Miller, 14.10; John Morrow Screw & Nut Co., Ltd., 2,000.36; Myles & Son, 29.00; C. McEwen, 60.98; John Noonan, 1,152.90; J. A. Pringle, 3,659.01; Railway Power Engineering Corporation, Ltd., 538.03; Russell Sedore, 243.55; Keith Smith, 72.30; Standard Underground Cable Co., of Canada, Ltd., 286.80; Steel Company of Canada, Ltd., 9,731.80; Nelson Tryon, 10.00; Jas. J. Vogan, 127.21; W. Walker & Son, Ltd., 237.71; C. E. Way, 1,126.86. Sundries, 31.27 .... 34,765 37

Gas and Lubricants, $5,226.60.

D. A. Barker, 264.40; Imperial Oil, Ltd., 3,770.03; James Brothers, 27.07; E. W. Jones, 13.83; Kendall Brothers (Ontario), Ltd., 115.01; Le Sage Motor Sales, 21.34; F. Milligan, 150.08; A. L. Perkins, 37.14; J. A. Perkins & Son, 197.14; J. A. Pringle, 33.54; Ray Stewart Motors, 93.83; H. J. Thomson & Co., 259.04; C. W. Thornton, 26.60; W. W. Villneff, 151.21; C. W. Wood, 10.46. Sundries, 55.88 .... 5,226 60

Hardware, $2,855.39.

E. B. Buell & Son, 554.72; H. A. Conboy, 33.69; Frank Dafoe, 44.23; W. B. Dalton & Sons, Ltd., 43.77; P. E. Fitzpatrick, 25.49; House & Maunder, 16.40; James Brothers, 293.02; Thos. Meredith & Co., Ltd., 117.50; Myles & Son, 202.50; R. W. McVeigh & Sons, 259.66; G. A. Outram, 111.15; J. A. Perkins & Son, 40.01; J. A. Pringle, 865.47; C. C. Thompson, 106.75; H. J. Thomson & Co., 91.93; Tweed Hardware, 15.48; W. Walker & Son, Ltd., 19.34. Sundries, 14.28 .... 2,855 39

Lumber, $2,012.31.

J. E. Barker & Son, 820.45; P. W. Clement, 476.28; A. E. Kirkham, Jr., 15.00; J. A. Marshall, 33.28; Rashotte Brothers, 456.28; J. R. Robertson, 159.94; Jas. J. Vogan, 37.88. Sundries, 13.20 .... 2,012 31

Miscellaneous, $59,112.55.

J. M. Airth, car hire, 71.61; T. J. Alexander, car hire, 1,081.81; Dr. H. H. Alger, services, 15.00; Arden & Long Lake Telephone System, rentals, 139.04; calls, 451.14; Art Metropole, surveyor's instruments and repairs, 396.84; T. Ayres, car hire, 263.83; A. E. Bailey, rent of camp site, 18.25; D. A. Barker, car hire, and storage, 113.46; M. A. Becksted, car hire, 40.11; Bell Telephone Co. of Canada, moving poles and aerials, 5,459.97; rentals, 20.25; N. D. Bennett, car hire, 172.48; Dr. Grant Berry, services, 62.00; Chas. V. Billie, material and services, 1,616.33; Bituminous Spraying & Contracting Co., Ltd., material and services, 1,073.32; J. Blair, garage rent, 15.00; E. C. Boag, car hire, 210.91; Drs. Bogart and Boucher, services, 12.00; Dr. Gordon E. Booth, services, 22.00;

Statutory—Continued
King's Highway Construction—Continued
Actinolite-Perth Project—Continued

Miscellaneous—Continued.

J. G. Both, car hire, 146.51; Dr. H. Austin Boyce, services, 11.00; Dr. E. J. Bracken, services, 13.00; M. C. Britt, car hire, 19.60; Dr. Wm. J. Brough, services, 27.00; E. B. Buell, camp supplies, 2,997.96; Burlington Steel Co., Ltd., steel, 1,906.33; Dr. J. C. Byers, services, 18.00; Dr. G. Calder, services, 17.00; Robert Cameron, car hire, 15.40; Dr. W. N. Campbell, services, 11.00; Campbell Construction Co., Ltd., camp construction, 2,456.33; material and services, 1,775.03; Canadian Inspection & Testing Co., Ltd., tests, 179.95; Canadian National Railways, freight, 12.27; Canadian Pacific Railway Co., freight, 2,827.32; sidings and wigwags, etc., 562.53; Dr. H. G. Carleton, services, 14.00; Wm. A. Clark, car hire, 222.04; Dr. W. G. Collison, services, 20.00; Conboy Telephone Co., services, 40.32; Dr. J. T. Courtice, services, 15.00; Dr. J. S. Crawford, services, 37.00; A. W. Crawford, escorting workmen, 481.30; Dr. M. G. Dales, services, 212.00; J. D. Davidson, car hire, 52.36; J. A. Dillane, car hire, 141.40; J. R. C. Dobbs & Co., office equipment rental, 19.00; Dominion Oxygen Co., Ltd., oxygen, 148.86; J. T. Donald & Co., Ltd., sampling, 16.64; Dr. W. Ritchie Dowd, services, 10.00; Dr. S. Eagleson, services, 13.00; G. J. Edwards, car hire, 16.10; Dr. C. D. Farquharson, services, 23.00; Dr. J. Albert Faulkner, services, 14.00; P. E. Fitzpatrick, team work, 125.60; Dr. Howard Price Folger, services, 10.00; J. G. Frost, ambulance services, 34.00; Jas. H. Garlick, car hire, 73.85; General Steel Wares, Ltd., signs, 40.32; General Supply Co. of Canada, Ltd., steel, 468.49; Dr. H. Glendinning, services, 48.00; Geo. C. Godard, car hire, 455.42; Dr. M. K. Gordon, services, 10.00; Grand & Toy, Ltd., office supplies, 53.95; Great War Memorial Hospital of Perth District, services, 18.00; Dr. F. T. Green, services, 10.00; G. G. Greig, planimeter, 45.00; Hamilton Bridge Co., Ltd., structural steel, 4,802.00; C. J. Hamilton, M.D., services, 10.00; W. A. Hare, equipment rental, 814.00; J. F. Hartz Co., Ltd., drugs, 861.48; Mrs. C. E. Hayes, laundry, 103.75; M. G. Henniger, camp supplies, etc., 507.08; Dr. D. J. Holdcroft, services, 36.00; C. H. Hopper, Jr., car hire, 210.35; A. E. Hughes, house rental, 95.16; E. Hughes, camp cots, 10.00; Robert W. Hunt & Co., Ltd., cement inspections, 25.22; James Hutcheon, surveyor's instruments, 30.00; Hydro-Electric Power Commission of Ontario, camp building, 207.16; Instruments, Ltd., surveying instruments and repairs, 91.98; F. T. James Co., Ltd., camp supplies, 12.50; Frank H. James, car hire, 833.49; James Brothers, explosives, 479.60; Dr. A. Jamieson, services, 11.00; Fred Johnston, office and garage rent, 101.50; Dr. J. A. Johnston, services, 21.00; Dr. W. J. Johnston, services, 27.00; H. P. Jones, car hire, 333.83; Kaladar & Northern Telephone System, installation and services, 165.22; Kendall Brothers (Ontario), Ltd., camp supplies, 1,246.49; culverts, etc., 1,505.73; Mrs. T. T. Killingbeck, laundry, 20.98; King's Printer, office supplies, 499.62; Kingston General Hospital, services, 69.70; D. D. Kirk, car hire, 42.84; H. L. Kirkwood, car hire, 37.45; C. T. Laidlaw, car hire, 42.63; Dr. Jurben Lannin, services, 30.00; T. W. Lee, car hire, 126.56; Dr. A. C. Locke, services, 167.50; C. E. Logan, car hire, 43.61; William A. Logan, car hire, 46.62; Dr. W. F. Loucks, services, 40.00; Mrs. W. E. Loyst, laundry, 40.20; Dr. S. S. Lumb, services, 14.00; Maberley Telephone Co., Ltd., installation and toll tickets, 54.40; Dr. P. M. Macdonnell, services, 79.00; A. J. Maynes, camp supplies, 46.53; Dr. W. A. Meighen, services, 26.00; Metallic Roofing Co., of Canada, Ltd., expansion strips and signs, etc., 665.43; Dr. A. A. Metcalfe, services, 13.00; Anna T. Mieske, services, 25.00; Dr. T. H. Middlebro, services, 10.00; J. D. Millar, car hire, 345.03; W. J. Moore, surveying instruments and repairs, 150.66; D. I. Murray, car hire, 99.96; James Murray, map tubs, etc., 12.00; Dr. S. R. McCleary, services, 12.00; J. S. McKeown, drugs, 34.25; Dr. A. W. McPherson, services, 31.00; J. R. McQuigge, truck hire, 244.00; H. E. McTear, car hire, 42.00; Dr. James H. Nesbitt, services, 189.00; R. B. Newbery, car hire, 121.45; Mrs. Claude Nugent, laundry, 136.72; Mrs. George Nugent, laundry, 227.32; Dr. D. A. Parkhill, services, 16.00; Thos. Pocklington Co., surveying instruments and repairs, 348.53; J. A. Pringle, camp supplies and explosives, 2,370.72; Provincial Treasurer of Ontario, transportation of men, 1,222.83; Robt. T. Purves & Co., expansion joints, 265.96; S. A. Purvis, car hire, 13.72; A. H. Rabb, car hire, 100.73; W. E. Rainboth, car hire, 323.40; J. Frank Raw Co., Ltd., surveying instruments and repairs, 360.73; Dr. Clyde H. Robertson, services, 24.00; Dr. William A. Robertson, services, 199.00; T. D. K. Rooney, car hire, 202.44; C. W. Rymal, car hire, 253.96; W. V. Sargent, M.D., car hire, 574.28; F. E. Saunders, car hire, 207.13; A. J. Scott, car hire, 21.77; John Scott, camp supplies, 117.38; L. Sedore, car hire, 15.68; Dr. T. H. Seldon, services, 2,115.00; Dr. J. Cameron Smith, services, 16.00; Dr. Warren Snyder, services, 71.00; Dr. C. L. B. Stammers, services, 31.00; Steel Company of Canada, Ltd., structural steel, 2,380.54; F. Stewart, tractor rental, 117.50; Ray Stewart Motors, garage rent, 28.00; Dr. C. K. Stevenson, services, 10.00; Sundry Registry

Statutory—Continued

King's Highway Construction—Continued

Actinolite-Perth Project—Continued

Miscellaneous—Continued.

Fees, services, 181.65; Dr. Robert W. Tennent, services, 15.00; B. Tett, car hire, 48.72; Lavern Thomlinson, car hire, 15.00; Dr. A. S. Thompson, services, 11.00; C. C. Thompson, camp supplies, 100.85; Dr. D. Thomson, services, 13.00; D. M. Thomson, car hire, 355.11; H. J. Thomson & Co., camp supplies, 626.21; C. W. Thornton, camp supplies, 2,925.72; Dr. T. J. C. Tindle, services, 385.00; W. Treadgold, car hire, 14.00; Tweed Hospital, services, 88.00; Tweed News, cards, 18.89; J. Villetorte, car hire, 551.53; J. J. Vogan, telephone messages, 19.05; Dr. R. P. Walker, services, 10.00; Peter Walters, explosives, 48.50; Roy W. Ware, car hire, 743.75; W. R. C. Warren, car hire, 487.55; C. E. Way, car and truck hire, 447.37; David Webster, camp supplies, 272.56; A. R. Westcott, car hire, 10.08; L. C. Wild, car hire, 22.68; Dr. J. B. Willoughby, services, 87.00; W. B. Wing, car hire, 58.17; H. B. Zavitz, car hire, 1,160.11. Sundries, 161.75; miscellaneous credits for camp supplies, 4,641.23 .... 59,112 55

Pay Lists, $164,353.93.

Wages of men 164,353 93

Purchase of Property, Right-of-Way, $6,584.61.

Bathurst twp., Robert G. Perkins, 75.00; Mrs. Robert Taylor, 250.00; Elzevir twp., The Canada Co., 275.00; Francis Kleinsteuber, 32.50; Stewart Marsh, 111.00; Chas. Minnie, 101.75; M. McGeachy, 38.00; Andrew Oliver, 188.00; Fred Oliver, 18.25; Joseph F. Plue, 75.00; Donald Simmons, Jr., 62.50; Clara H. and C. K. Wallbridge, 93.50; Kaladar twp., Frank Baalin and Robert Phillips, 147.50; John Beatty, 241.45; Mrs. Oscar Huffman, 82.50; Oake Parks, 76.00; Olive and Oakie Parks, 200.00; Murney Simmons, 83.75; T. J. C. Tindle, 67.50; Kenneth Tryon, 186.80; Nelson Tryon, 147.50; Walter Villneff, 93.07; Kennebec twp., Bertha I. Hannah, 75.00; Fred Hartwick, 57.50; Frank Knight, 153.12; G. A. Miller, 61.50; G. R. Miller, 26.50; James Parks, 77.10; Garnet Scott, 65.75; Miles Wood, 50.00; Samson Wood, 57.75; Olden twp., P. E. Barr, 41.00; Roy W. Barr, 92.50; Robert Bertrim, 135.00; Barton Bradley, 111.00; Frank Cox, 125.00; Robert Cox, 25.00; George F. Flynn, 108.00; Wm. Johnston, 150.75; H. J. Thomson, 50.00; Oso twp., Henry Chambers, 28.40; Wm. G. England, 289.50; F. H. Giddings, 275.00; Mrs. Elizabeth Kimberley, 97.00; J. J. McPherson, 137.20; Alex. McVeigh, 61.20; Wilfred Wesley, 105.00; Sherbrooke twp., John Blair, 43.77; Thomas Briggs, 250.00; Alex. England, 250.00; Robert Marks, 37.50; W. H. Moore, 27.05; W. H. C. Munro, 100.00; Mrs. A. Robertson, 43.25; Wm. Robertson, 92.45; Leslie Strong, 164.00; Burton Wesley, 158.20; Wilfred Wesley, 302.05. Sundries, 14.00 .... 6,584 61

Property, Miscellaneous, $1,745.94.

Frank Baalin and Robert M. Phillips, Kaladar twp., erecting fences, 100.00; John Blair, Sherbrooke South twp., borrow pit, 25.00; Thos. Briggs, Sherbrooke South twp., damages and borrow pit, 225.00; H. J. Buchanan, Sherbrooke South twp., damages, 25.00; John J. England, Oso twp., rock, 35.00; W. G. England, Oso twp., gravel and borrow pit, 53.25; J. E. Hughes, Kennebec twp., damages to cow, 15.00; Wm. Johnston, Olden twp., damages, 25.00; W. G. Kirkham, Bathurst twp., borrow pit, 100.00; G. R. Miller, Kennebec twp., permission to dig ditch, 25.00; Robert Monds, Kennebec, twp. damages, 50.00; Mrs. Edna Moss, Sherbrooke South twp., diversion of stream and damages, 65.00; Robert McCharles, Oso twp., rock and damages, 125.00; James H. Parks, Kennebec twp., inconveniences by blasting, 100.00; Mary Ann Parks, Kennebec twp., damages and removal of buildings, 600.00; Murney Simmons, Kaladar twp., damages, 25.00; Leslie Strong, Sherbrooke South twp., borrow pit, 40.00; Robert Blair, Bathurst twp., fill, 75.00; Wilfred Wesley, Oso twp., borrow pit, 16.50. Sundries, 21.19 .... 1,745 94

Road Equipment and Supplies, $1,573.33.

J. D. Adams (Canada), Ltd., 28.36; General Supply Co., of Canada, Ltd., 713.60; W. Gordon Steel Products, Ltd., 39.05; W. A. Hare, 650.59; International Harvester Co., of Canada, Ltd., 19.38; Sawyer-Massey, Ltd., 60.00; Fred Vanmeer, 14.00; Waterous, Ltd., 24.00. Sundries, 24.35 .... 1,573 33

Stone, Gravel and Screenings, $481.95.

Grenville Crushed Rock Co., Ltd., 374.75; John McLaren, 50.00; T. Wesley, 23.60. Sundries, 33.60 .... 481 95

Statutory—Continued
King's Highway Construction—Continued
Actinolite-Perth Project—Continued

Travelling Expenses and Disbursements, $4,904.65.

G. Alison, 60.85; M. A. Becksted, 15.93; N. D. Bennett, 76.20; E. C. Boag, 87.20; Morris Booth, 12.75; S. G. Booth, 52.50; Charles W. Boyd, 15.35; R. Brisco, 12.66; R. Cameron, 22.50; J. Chambers, 28.50; Geo. Chenery, 26.10; R. E. Clark, 55.90; Wm. A. Clark, 54.95; R. S. Code, 605.17; A. H. Dale, 46.55; J. D. Davidson, 26.80; J. A. Dillane, 31.40; W. J. Fulton, 13.90; Geo. C. Godard, 115.80; F. E. Hindson, 16.80; C. H. Hopper, Jr., 23.80; H. S. Howden, 16.50; Hugh Hughes, 10.90; Frank H. James, 188.33; Humphrey P. Jones, 166.65; C. T. Laidlaw, 17.45; Thos. W. Lee, 34.05; Chester Ley, 15.30; Howard Lloyd, 43.28; Charles W. Magwood, 13.00; J. D. Millar, 107.51; H. E. Monger, 11.00; Duncan Murray, 171.77; V. Murray, 21.30; Alex. McLennan, 14.00; H. E. McTear, 60.10; C. H. Nelson, 577.43; R. B. Newbery, 18.89; A. A. Outram, 362.10; R. N. Page, 27.75; Gerald Poisson, 17.30; Arthur H. Rabb, 22.05; W. P. Rae, 10.50; W. E. Rainboth, 63.82; T. D. K. Rooney, 68.82; C. W. Rymal, 50.00; W. V. Sargent, M.D., 60.05; A. J. Scott, 129.76; James Scott, 19.45; K. H. Siddall, 11.05; H. J. Simmons, 21.00; B. Tett, 57.00; D. M. Thomson, 34.95; Geo. Treadway, 14.90; J. Villetorte, 145.71; Roy W. Ware, 165.20; W. R. C. Warren, 302.61; C. E. Way, 66.10; F. C. White, 16.65; W. B. Wing, 74.57; H. B. Zavitz, 142.69. Sundries, 131.55 .... 4,904 65

Actinolite-Perth Project $1,609,553.53

Automobile and Road Equipment Branch

Automobile and Road Equipment Branch	168,672 74
Less automobile rentals, repairs and services	46,686 98
	121,985 76

Automobile Supplies and Repairs, $48,191.93.

Frank Ackerman & Co., 72.38; Advance Glass & Mirror Co., Ltd., 58.25; Aikenhead Hardware, Ltd., 105.65; T. J. Alexander, 80.75; Allatt Machine & Tool Co., 1,193.67; H. G. Allen, 49.02; Architectural Bronze & Iron Works, 258.00; Auto Electric Service Co., Ltd., 406.20; Auto Glass Suppliers, 82.16; Auto Ignition & Battery Service, 24.50; Auto Starter Co., Ltd., 25.44; E. G. Bailey, 22.50; Bailey Bros., 23.20; Baker Bros., Ltd., 72.35; Bannerman & Hunter, 28.40; D. A. Barker, 224.08; Beacock & Co., 296.82; Bear Equipment Co., 36.57; W. D. Beath & Son, Ltd., 34.96; Bennett & Elliott, Ltd., 682.22; B. C. Berry & Co., 266.55; Biddell's Tire & Battery Service, 118.34; Bitner's Auto Service, 18.70; Bloomfield Garage, 47.55; S. F. Bowser Co., Ltd., 10.37; Brake Service Station, Ltd., 13.00; Breay-Nash Motors, Ltd., 28.67; Breuls Mfg. Co., 94.41; British American Motors, Ltd., 65.78; Brockville Auto Shop, 45.25; Brockville Battery & Ignition Service, 72.95; T. Brooks & Son, 18.85; Brown Bros. & Eplett, 334.56; Cadillac Motor Car Co. of Canada, Ltd., 227.62; Clarence Campbell, 15.65; Campbell Motor Sales, 268.10; Canada Auto Top & Trimming Co., 26.70; Canada Carriage & Body Co., Ltd., 243.30; Canadian Fairbanks-Morse Co., Ltd., 1,856.95; Canadian Industries, Ltd., 42.50; Canadian Johns-Manville Co., Ltd., 27.10; Hugh Carson Co., Ltd., 255.28; Carter & Thompson Welding & Supplies, Ltd., 55.86; Carters, Ltd., 26.35; Central Garage, Kemptville, 14.85; Chambers & Cooke, 714.69; Chatham Battery & Electric Service, 208.41; A. J. Christie, 41.83; Chrysler Motor Parts Corporation of Canada, Ltd., 104.97; City Storage, Ltd., 35.00; Clark's Garage, 38.62; Cleveland Pneumatic Tool Co., of Canada, Ltd., 77.88; Cooks Body & Fender Repair, 161.00; Cooksville Motors, 33.16; James Cowan & Co., Ltd., 725.29; James Cowan & Co. of Windsor, Ltd., 248.97; John Cowley, 261.53; Cozens Spring Service Co., Ltd., 472.63; A. Cross & Co., Ltd., 127.20; Crown Tailoring Co., Ltd., 831.00; Cutten & Foster, Ltd., 405.17; Daley's Motor Service, 19.65; Dell's, 25.25; Dennisteel, Ltd., 20.72; Devitts Duco Shop, 35.00; J. L. Dietrich, 39.26; Dietrich's Garage, 271.99; Dominion Oxygen Co., Ltd., 462.96; A. Down, 42.19; Noble Duff, 25.98; Durant Motor Sales, 35.09; H. Earl, 26.05; Robert Elder Carriage Works, Ltd., 285.79; Ellis-McIntyre Motors, Ltd., 22.90; English's Garage, 13.85; Evans & Co., Ltd., 36.86; A. M. Ewing, 11.95; Exide Batteries of Canada, Ltd., 203.79; Fairs Garage, 12.80; Fee Motors, 134.58; Maurice Ferrier, 14.12; Plater's Auto Top Shop, 12.43; Flexo Piston Ring Agency, 55.95; Ford Garage, Delhi, 11.58; Four-Wheel Drive Auto Co., Ltd., 290.12; Frisby the Vulcanizer, 69.03; Frontenac Garage, Ltd., 64.49; Fursey Sales & Service, 21.11; S. H. Gallagher, 60.67; Garage Supply Co., Ltd., 761.19; Giles, Rice & Peters, Ltd., 11.79; Golightly Bros., 28.93; Goodyear Tire & Rubber Co. of Canada, Ltd., 362.87; Gordon Auto Parts Co., 10.77; A. D. Gorrie & Co., Ltd., 586.88; J. M. Graham, 109.12; Graham's Garage, 14.30; A. B. Greer & Son, Ltd., 17.00; Geo. Green Welding Co., 14.25; Grimsby Garage, 35.44; Guarantee Motor Co., Ltd., 209.83; Guelph Spring & Axle Co., Ltd., 18.45; Guide Motor Manf. Co., 536.25; A. J.

Statutory—Continued

King's Highway Construction—Continued

Automobile and Road Equipment Branch—Continued

Automobile Supplies and Repairs—Continued.

Gurry, 22.35; Gutta Percha & Rubber, Ltd., 2,266.49; Hall Gear & Machine Co., Ltd., 113.13; Hall & McKie, 169.41; B. Hannah, 11.60; Hannon Tire & Rubber Co., Ltd., 35.70; Harback's Garage, 10.95; G. A. Hardie & Co., Ltd., 67.65; A. H. Harker, Ltd., 13.48; Harpham Brothers, 1,584.35; Hart Battery Co., Ltd., 274.04; Hawkesbury Tire Sales & Vulcanizing Co., 17.90; Albert Henry, 15.33; Henry's Machine Shop, 49.75; Hobbs Mfg. Co., Ltd., 17.60; G. W. Hogan, Ltd., 24.23; Hood & Cumming Motors, Ltd., 74.75; T. Hopkins Auto Top Co., 60.15; Hoskins Bros., 40.25; Ideal Welding Co., Ltd., 32.45; J. S. Innes, Ltd., 1,237.29; James Brothers, 68.78; M. & H. Jerome, 16.68; Johnston-Deane, Ltd., 81.50; Johnston Motor Sales, 89.30; Jolley Motor Car Co., Ltd., 10.88; E. W. Jones, 48.39; Kari-Keen & Auto Trunks, Ltd., 82.23; Wm. Keller, 205.58; Kennedy Auto Top & Body Repairs, 25.75; Kent Bros., 42.71; Kent Motors, 16.13; J. D. Kerr, Ltd., 290.58; Keyes Supply Co., Ltd., 96.05; Kitchener Auto Electric, 10.10; Laidlaw Garage, 24.62; Fred Lake & Co., 18.40; Gordon Law, 22.85; James Lawson, 11.00; Lea & Hawley, Ltd., 34.10; A. G. Leonard Tire Service, 14.25; Le Page's Garage, 57.17; J. Leroux, 15.75; Le Sage Motor Sales, 41.47; Levi's, 81.15; Lillico Motors, 16.32; Geo. Lister Co., 54.40; Litt's Garage, 17.85; Jos. A. Lobraico, 2,202.72; London Chevrolet Co., 22.52; Machine & Tool Co., Ltd., 34.00; Maple Leaf Garage, 10.50; Melvin's Garage, 14.23; Middlesex Motors, Ltd., 796.54; R. J. Mitchell, 1,194.07; Model Tire Service Ltd., 260.23; Monarch Battery Mfg. Co., Ltd., 125.26; Moore Motors, 17.93; W. Morris, 26.75; John Morrow Screw & Nut Co., Ltd., 42.95; Motor Accessory & Supply Co., Ltd., 16.00; Motor & Coach, Ltd., 53.00; McCann & Houghton, Ltd., 70.75; P. McCarthy, 12.00; McCord Radiator & Mfg. Co., 14.00; John McCrea Machine & Foundry Co., 16.14; J. C. McLaren Belting Co., Ltd., 38.49; McLaughlin Motor Car Co., Ltd., 766.78; McLeod & Son, 401.00; McMullen Supplies, Ltd., 56.64; McMullen-Perkins, Ltd., 397.58; J. H. McNally, 30.52; Nagel's Upholstery Works, 52.95; National Automotive Parts, Ltd., 493.23; National Chevrolet Sales, Ltd., 12.11; National Motors, Ltd., 416.81; New Haven Clock Co., 15.94; Noble's Service Station, 15.05; R. Nurse & Son, 14.57; Obey's Garage, 47.37; Ontario Automobile Co., Ltd., 63.46; Ontario Motor Sales, Ltd., 19.25; Ontario Steel Products Co., Ltd., 24.00; Ontario Tire System, 772.47; Ottawa Electric Railway Co., 37.01; Ottawa Motor Sales, Ltd., 38.48; Ed. Ovens, 15.00; Packard-Ontario Motor Co., Ltd., 302.29; Padfield's Hardware, 12.20; Archibald Park, 16.75; Pearson Batteries, Ltd., 63.95; W. F. Petry, 21.56; Pilkington Brothers (Canada), Ltd., 35.22; Fred Powell Motors, Ltd., 474.20; J. A. Pringle, 10.35; Provincial Tire Corporation, Ltd., 913.51; Pryal & Nye, 61.91; Reflex Sign Co., Ltd., 160.00; Reliable Radiator Co., 52.88; Reliable Tire & Vulcanizing Co., 73.70; Reo Motor Sales Co., of Toronto, Ltd., 356.68; Rice Lake Garage, 10.00; Rice Lewis & Son, Ltd., 36.73; Richardson Battery & Ignition Service, 41.98; Riggs Motor Sales, 10.40; N. A. Rondeau, 27.95; Roode Brothers, Ltd., 66.04; Roy Bros., Garage, 73.52; Rudecal Transfers, Ltd., 64.93; Russell, Willis & Crispo, Ltd., 483.79; John Rydall, 10.00; George Scott & Son, 11.00; Scott & Edgecombe, 16.57; Scragg's Studio, 48.00; R. E. Sculthorpe, 512.90; Scythes & Co., Ltd., 33.05; See & Duggan Motors, Ltd., 312.01; Service Station Equipment Co., Ltd., 15.75; J. B. Sheppard, 35.64; Sherwin-Williams Co. of Canada, Ltd., 18.18; Simplex Piston Ring Sales Co., of Ontario, 50.84; Smith Bros., 375.82; South End Garage, 18.25; Spring Service, Ltd., 39.43; Square Deal Garage, 16.40; Standard Engineering Co., 16.00; Stephenson & Lent Motor Sales, 77.98; Stewart-Warner Alemite Sales, 70.56; Ray Stewart Motors, 287.87; Stodgell & Symes Motor Sales, Ltd., 19.87; Stittsville Garage, 42.00; Fred Stratford, Ltd., 19.50; Stratford Auto Hospital, 12.00; Stratford Motor Transport, 11.20; G. H. Strawbridge & Son, 27.70; W. S. Stuckey, 10.73; Sullivan Machinery Co., Ltd., 67.35; Suititorium, 62.34; Swayze's Artcraft Top & Trimming Division, 1,265.41; Taylor Hardwares, Ltd., 20.43; J. A. M. Taylor Tool Co., Ltd., 13.49; H. J. Thomson & Co., 28.55; Tiverton Tire Repair, 1,571.08; Toronto Battery & Electric, Ltd., 190.40; Toronto Bearings & Parts Co., 863.06; Toronto Durant Co., Ltd., 576.17; Trelco, Ltd., 329.38; Truck & Tractor Equipment Co., Ltd., 38.50; United Motors Service, Inc., 459.75; Universal Ignition & Battery Co., 125.02; Valspar Corporation, Ltd., 33.89; Van Luvan Bros., Ltd., 11.39; Virtue Motors, Ltd., 23.45; Charlie H. Waghorne, 14.25; Walker Bros., 12.05; W. C. Warburton & Co., Ltd., 282.15; Watkins Rebabbiting, 13.22; Welch & Johnston, Ltd., 48.38; Wellington Auto Trimming, 46.50; Wentworth Motors, Ltd., 157.25; Westboro Garage, 14.43; West End Motors, 583.48; Wheel & Rim Co., of Canada, Ltd., 190.17; White & Thomas, 126.55; White & Co., Ltd., 77.31; Leo. Wildgen, 138.07; E. C. Williams, 32.07; Willys-Overland Sales Co., Ltd., 681.44. Sundries, 821.08.................................. 48,191 93

Statutory—Continued
King's Highway Construction—Continued
Automobile and Road Equipment Branch—Continued

Automobile and Truck Purchases, $3,816.69.

McLaughlin Motor Car Co., Ltd., 1,316.69; Mrs. Wm. Taylor, 350.00; Toronto Durant Co., Ltd., 1,350.00; Willys-Overland Sales Co., Ltd., 800.00........... 3,816 69

Gas and Lubricants, $16,523.18.

British American Oil Co., Ltd., 409.13; Harold Bunt, 11.85; Canadian Oil Companies, Ltd., 3,668.68; Colloid Oil Co., 35.85; Cooksville Motors, 60.82; Electric Furnace Products Co., 10.91; Gordon's Garage, 19.58; Geo. W. Grant & Co., 76.64; Haley's Service Station, 19.95; High Grade Oil Co., Ltd., 395.71; Huston Oil Co., 725.49; Imperial Oil, Ltd., 79.32; Donald F. Johnston, Ltd., 58.00; F. Kendall, 93.04; Leed's Motor Sales, 21.35; R. J. Moore, 10.80; McColl-Frontenac Oil Co., Ltd., 3,687.57; McMillan's Service Station, 13.02; Nymoc Products Co., 19.25; Ottawa Car Mfg. Co., Ltd., 18.77; Paramount Petroleum Co., Ltd., 2,480.68; Pyroil Sales, 11.19; Ray Stewart Motors, 124.13; J. A. Stinson, 17.58; Supertest Petroleum Corporation, Ltd., 23.07; Supreme Oil Co., Ltd., 4,040.53; G. E. Swire, 138.06; Sykes Auto Service, 40.17; L. R. Taylor, 30.68; Chas. L. Todd, 18.14. Sundries, 163.22.......................... 16,523 18

Miscellaneous, $12,324.92.

Canadian National Express Co., services, 671.09; Canadian National Railways, freight, 173.86; Canadian Pacific Express Co., services, 318.10; Russell & Russell, Ltd., insurance, 11,064.87; Ray Stewart Motors, garage rent, 13.00; Walter Stewart, insurance, 60.00. Sundries, 24.00.............................. 12,324 92

Pay Lists, $60,930.85.

Wages of men... 60,930 85

Road Equipment and Supplies, $19,179.77.

J. D. Adams (Canada), Ltd., 1,530.06; Aikenhead Hardware, Ltd., 17.06; Allatt Machine & Tool Co., 39.58; Forrest Arnold, 650.00; D. F. Ashley, 191.00; Auto Electric Service Co., Ltd., 12.45; Barrett & Young, 48.35; J. Beleskey, 14.75; Brown Bros. & Eplett, 34.70; H. E. Burrows & Son, 60.96; Clarence Campbell, 49.43; Campbell Motor Sales, 13.25; Campbell Steel & Iron Works, Ltd., 42.09; Canada Ingot Iron Co., Ltd., 16.45; Canadian Fairbanks-Morse Co., Ltd., 13.63; Canadian Ingersoll-Rand Co., Ltd., 441.11; Carters, Ltd., 25.25; Clark & Lewis, Ltd., 21.85; Alex. Cleland, 19.60; Cockshutt Plow Co., Ltd., 375.66; James Cowan & Co., Ltd., 14.74; James Cowan & Co. of Windsor, Ltd., 17.66; Crane, Ltd., 30.84; A. Cross & Co., Ltd., 50.19; Cross, Purser, Bull, Ltd., 14.86; Cutten & Foster, Ltd., 37.34; Dominion Bridge Co., Ltd., 21.73; Dominion Road Machinery Co., Ltd., 463.40; John Downey, 11.00; Drummond McCall & Co., Ltd., 93.74; Noble Duff, 14.42; G. Durnford, 10.85; Durham Furniture Co., Ltd., 12.80; Robert Elder Carriage Works, Ltd., 1£0.00; Fee Motors, 11.85; Garage Supply Co., Ltd., 35.05; General Supply Co., of Canada, Ltd., 63.47; Golightly Bros., 30.74; Goodyear Tire & Rubber Co. of Canada, Ltd., 35.07; W. Gordon Steel Products, Ltd., 16.05; Greenleaf Co., 13.03; Grimmer-Wilson Engineering Co., 62.65; Guaranty Motor Co., Ltd., 86.50; Guide Motor Mfg. Co., 92.46; Gurney Scale Co., Ltd., 1,650.00; Gutta Percha & Rubber, Ltd., 97.47; Hall Gear & Machine Co., Ltd., 20.00; Hall & McKie, 60.74; William Hamilton, Ltd., 41.66; Harpham Bros., 647.98; Henry's Machine Shop, 54.75; J. S. Innes, Ltd., 2,896.58; International Harvester Co. of Canada, Ltd., 47.12; James Bros., 28.85; Kilmer & Barber, Ltd., 48.00; Kitchen's Garage, 13.80; Knight Bros., 21.06; La Salle Lead Products, Ltd., 70.06; Leeds Motor Sales, 12.52; J. Leroux, 12.00; Lyman Tube & Supply Co., Ltd., 12.80; Machine & Tool Co., Ltd., 42.00; Mackie Equipment Co., 999.50; Markdale Garage Co., 15.10; Massey-Harris Co., 1,882.76; Middlesex Motors, 23.86; R. J. Mitchell, 363.24; Model Tire Service, Ltd., 243.25; Mulvihill Garage & Machine Shop, 15.90; J. H. McGowan, 11.20; D. G. McKinnon, 10.00; McMullen-Perkins, Ltd., 122.02; J. H. McNally, 23.35; Nagel's Upholstery Works, 13.15; National Automotive Parts, Ltd., 12.64; Archibald Park, 28.75; Peckover's Ltd., 64.62; B. Pennington & Son, 325.00; Ernest W. Perkins, 52.00; Port Colborne Iron Works, Ltd., 25.48; Roode Bros., Ltd., 17.58; Ross Garage, 12.25; C. Rumble, 92.40; Rumble & Son, 247.72; Sawyer-Massey, Ltd., 158.60; Charles Schissler, 53.74; Scott & Sangster, 14.25; Smith Bros., 20.00; Steel Company of Canada, Ltd., 181.93; Stephens-Adamson Mfg. Co. of Canada, Ltd., 18.65; Ray Stewart Motors, 12.49; Sullivan Machinery Co., Ltd., 102.28; L. R. Taylor, 14.30; Mrs. Wm. Taylor, 200.00; Toronto Bearings & Parts Co., 11.20; Toronto & Hamilton Electric Co., Ltd., 10.08; Truck & Tractor Equipment Co., Ltd., 226.30; W. C. Warburton Co., Ltd., 389.03; Waterous, Ltd., 1,848.41; E. Webster, 27.30; West End Motors, 14.64; A. R. Williams Machinery Co., Ltd., 42.92; Wilson's Garage, 14.65; Wood, Alexander & James, Ltd., 41.57. Sundries, 360.60 19,179 77

Statutory—Continued

King's Highway Construction—Continued

Automobile and Road Equipment Branch—Continued

Travelling Expenses and Disbursements, $7,705.40.

Thomas Ayres, 55.65; O. J. Ball, 141.17; F. J. Barry, 133.99; D. Best, 368.13; J. C. Boyes, 19.62; Jas. Campbell, 239.42; L. M. Clayton, 38.45; R. S. Code, 53.35; H. Coleman, 107.35; H. Constitt, 135.49; William Cooper, 257.51; A. H. Dale, 105.00; J. E. Dollery, 500.98; A. R. Duffin, 19.30; C. G. Fairs, 1,217.02; J. J. Haigh, 10.02; G. F. Hanning, 17.30; Tom Johnston, 991.20; Frank Law, 368.45; A. E. Long, 68.90; J. Long, 450.99; J. H. Lord, 86.88; Fred Lucy, 451.90; C. D. Lyon, 17.40; Wm. MacCallum, 582.16; D. Neave, 110.80; C. H. Nelson, 11.45; W. F. Noonan, 12.00; A. A. Outram, 24.44; Owen Pope, 30.38; W. Randall, 41.34; N. H. Richardson, 12.21; M. Rutherford, 393.02; W. L. Saunders, 15.34; F. Simmons, 18.22; F. T. Smith, 12.89; Chas. Snooks, 13.18; Geo. Stewart, 56.00; Geo Treadway, 201.61; F. T. Webster, 34.35; Leonard Westlake, 113.05; W. Harry Williams, 14.88. Sundries, 152.61 .... 7,705 40

GENERAL

General	519,473 11	
Less municipal repayments for materials	346,809 37	
	172,663 74	

Board of Men, $6,026.00.

Alexander Hotel, Ottawa, 576.70; Arlington Hotel, Collingwood, 42.00; Campbell House, Cayuga, 87.00; Clarendon Hotel, Brighton, 42.00; Copeland Hotel, Pembroke, 21.00; Dexter-Reeta Hotels, Welland, 19.50; O. R. Edwards, Norwood, 61.50; Empress Hotel, Peterborough, 96.00; Georgian Hotel, Midland, 150.05; Hotel Gilbert, Trenton, 114.00; Grand Central Hotel, St. Thomas, 116.25; Hahn House, Durham, 18.00; Jordan Inn, Jordan, 126.00; King's Hotel, Norwood, 220.00; King Edward Hotel, Niagara Falls, 502.50; Hotel Lincoln, St. Catharines, 56.00; Mrs. Wm. Macdonald, Windsor, 400.00; Hotel Mississippi, Carleton Place, 57.50; New Queen's Hotel, Belleville, 230.00; Palmer House, Orillia, 159.00; Paul's Hotel, Meaford, 65.00; Hotel Perth, Perth, 98.00; Queen's Hotel, Barrie, 24.00; Queen's Hotel, Palmerston, 102.00; Hotel Renfrew, Renfrew, 35.00; Royal Hotel, Marmora, 166.50; St. Lawrence Hall, Morrisburg, 20.00; Village Inn, Grimsby, 2,398.00; Westcott Hotel, Dresden, 22.50 .... 6,026 00

Cement, Calcium Chloride and Bituminous Materials, $239,667.45.

Barrett Co., Ltd., 11,318.88; Canada Cement Co., Ltd., 61,208.31; Canadian Bitumuls Co., Ltd., 21,418.80; Canadian Industries, Ltd., 2,070.87; Colas Roads, Ltd., 3,276.70; Currie Products, Ltd., 735.00; Dow Chemical Co., 21,506.96; Eaton-Clark Co., 1,994.65; Imperial Oil, Ltd., 35,496.49; S. F. Lawrason & Co., Ltd., 1,245.75; Alexander Murray & Co., Ltd., 56,476.93; Alfred Rogers, Ltd., 19,278.91; Solvay Sales Corporation, 3,639.20 .... 239,667 45

Drainage Materials (Culverts, Tile, etc.), $5,208.74.

Canada Cement Co., Ltd., 1,540.51; Canada Ingot Iron Co., Ltd., 1,254.52; Corrugated Pipe Co., Ltd., 122.32; Metallic Roofing Co. of Canada, Ltd., 520.44; National Sewer Pipe Co., Ltd., 1,161.90; Pedlar People, Ltd., 609.05 .... 5,208 74

Fence and Guard Rail Materials, $16,033.50.

D. C. Baird, 1,115.80; Canada Ingot Iron Co., Ltd., 1,347.92; Canada Wire & Cable Co., Ltd., 18.34; Canadian Steel Corporation, Ltd., 117.68; S. C. Daniels Co., Ltd., 1,105.00; Frost Steel & Wire Co., Ltd., 3,982.45; Lundy Fence Co., Ltd., 6,286.77; Pedlar People, Ltd., 2,059.54 .... 16,033 50

Gas and Lubricants, $416.92.

K. S. Duncan, 14.71; Chas. Durham, 25.86; Hood & Cumming Motors, Ltd., 22.62; F. Kendall, 16.15; Knights, Bronte, 17.73; McColl-Frontenac Oil Co., Ltd., 184.34; J. A. Perkins & Son, 11.40; Russell's Service Station, 17.66; F. J. Stewart, 14.30; West End Motors, 43.75; Wm. Whitaker, Sr., 12.66. Sundries, 35.74 .... 416 92

Hardware, 8.39.

Sundries 8.39

Lumber, $191.59.

Midland Wood Products, Ltd., 13.05; R. E. Stacey, 14.00; Welsh Lumber Co., Ltd., 158.54. Sundries, 6.00 .... 191 59

Statutory—Continued
King's Highway Construction—Continued
General—Continued

Miscellaneous, $119,784.94.

Geo. Adkins, car hire, 35.00; Art Metropole, surveyors' instruments and repairs, 90.61; Village of Beachville, sidewalk, 38.99; N. D. Bennett, car hire, 1,363.32; Municipality of Bertie, sidewalk, 4,094.05; Brennan Paving Co., Ltd., material and services, 10,606.82; P. D. Brown, car hire, 27.86; Burlington Steel Co., Ltd., steel, 881.97; Canadian Engineer, advertising, 193.20; Canadian Industries, Ltd., soda and paint, 167.52; Canadian National Railways, freight, 193.07; Canadian Pacific Railway Co., sidings and wigwags, etc., 79.20; Contract Record & Engineering Review, advertising, 91.00; William C. Coo, services, 24.63; A. G. Cumming, Limited, surveying instruments and repairs, 46.15; Daily Commercial News & Building Record, advertising, 142.50; J. T. Donald & Co., Limited, sampling, 208.72; John J. Dyer & Son, insurance, 42.75; T. Eaton Co., Ltd., rubber boots, etc., 11.85; Lawrence Edmonds, damages, 25.00; Elliott Brothers, damage to truck, 73.65; Etobicoke twp., cost of sidewalk and land, 867.77; Municipality of West Flamboro, taxes, 115.62; Gazette Printing Co., Ltd., advertising, 17.70; J. J. Gibbons, Ltd., advertising, 2,843.94; W. D. Gilmore, car hire, 21.00; Municipality of Glanford, sidewalk, 114.80; Globe Printing Co., advertising, 136.50; Grantham twp., sidewalk, 415.49; J. J. Haigh, car hire, 82.95; Howard twp., sidewalk at Morpeth, 88.72; G. M. Hubbell, car hire, 26.25; Robert W. Hunt & Co., Ltd., cement inspections, 81.48; Instruments, Ltd., surveying instruments and repairs, 68.50; John E. Jackson, car hire, 947.03; Journal Dailies, advertising, 12.00; King's Printer, office supplies, 36.00; Kingston Whig-Standard Co., Ltd., advertising, 24.00; D. B. Kirby, car hire, 526.05; London Free Press Printing Co., advertising, 12.00; Lowe Bros. Co., Ltd., paint, 38.86; Messrs. MacKay & McKay, blueprint, 15.00; Mail and Empire, advertising, 136.50; Metallic Roofing Co. of Canada, Ltd., expansion strips, signs, etc., 31.46; Montreal Star Co., Ltd., advertising, 18.00; W. J. Moore, surveying instruments and repairs, 185.40; Municipal Intelligence Bureau, advertising, 50.00; W. J. McCully, office rent, 180.00; Frank McLaughlin, expert evidence re Palace Pier arbitration, 500.00; W. F. Neelin, car hire, 1,431.40; Ontario Provincial Police, payroll investigations, 27.75; Pedlar People, Ltd., steelcrete, 709.29; F. Perry, car hire, 59.01; Thos. Pocklington Co., surveying instruments and repairs, 45,80; Provincial Treasurer of Ontario, superannuation fund, 4,060.65; Ralph Auto & Radio Sales Co., damage to truck, 68.59; J. Frank Raw Co., Ltd., surveying instruments and repairs, 60.04; J. Ross Robertson Estate, advertising, 48.00; H. Sargent, car hire, 1,665.86; W. V. Sargent, M.D., car hire, 20.51; W. A. Schoenburn, car hire, 83.23; Arthur Sedgwick, car hire, 661.08; Seneca twp., sidewalk, 657.53; K. H. Siddall, car hire, 1,251.95; G. F. Skinner, funeral expenses, 27.80; J. S. Slater, car hire, 1,222.83; Smallpeice Advertising, advertising, 78.00; L. A. Smallwood, car hire, 20.02; Steel Co. of Canada, Ltd., stakes and structural steel, 2,266.92; Sundry Registry Fees, services, 349.07; J. G. Tickell & Sons, bronze tablet, 80.00; D. R. Townley, car hire, 677.74; John and Mildred Truesdale and The Saltfleet & Binbrook Mutual Fire Insurance Co., insurance, 1,650.00; Union Gas Co. of Canada, Ltd., office rent and services, 180.00; A. F. Vincent, car hire, 70.14; R. S. Whitton, car hire, 113.12; Whittemore Publications, Ltd., advertising, 137.66; W. P. Wilgar, car hire, 1,098.44; J. Williams, painting out signs, 55.00; A. E. Wilson & Co., Ltd., insurance, 9,082.51; Municipality of Woodbridge, taxes, 25.50; Workmen's Compensation Board, compensation, 24,112.25; North York twp., lowering main and moving poles, 41,549.62. Sundries, 106.75 .... 119,784 94

Pay Lists, $79,615.15.

Wages of men, bridge painting and core drill, 1,724.70; County Roads Department, 5,343.43; Head Office, 7,321.09; Head Office, miscellaneous labour, 3,052.58; Head Office, engineering, 18,332.30; Property Department, 9,197.99; Road Surveys, 29,163.56; Sign Inspection Department, 4,062.00; Testing Laboratory, 1,417.50 .... 79,615 15

Purchase of Property, Right-of-Way, $4,400.00.

York North twp., Gordon Bros., 1,800.00; The Trusts & Guarantee Co., Ltd., 2,600.00 .... 4,400 00

Property, Miscellaneous, $1,025.00.

W. J. Ground, North York twp., arbitration fees, 15.00; Kilmer, Irving & Davis, North York twp., legal services, 160.00; Thos. A. and Helen Osborne, North York twp., damages, 800.00; W. H. Patchell, York twp., arbitration fees, 50.00 .. 1,025 00

Road Equipment and Supplies, $1,856.74.

Canadian Ingersoll-Rand Co., Ltd., 13.37; William Kennedy & Sons, Ltd., 154.56; Sawyer-Massey, Ltd., 613.56; Truck & Tractor Equipment Co., Ltd., 830.00; Waterous, Ltd., 245.25 .... 1,856 74

Statutory—Continued
King's Highway Construction—Continued
General—Continued

Stone, Gravel and Screenings, $28,930.95.

Canada Crushed Stone Corporation, Ltd., 1,891.00; Canadian Aggregates, Ltd., 1,261.61; Coldwater Crushed Stone, Ltd., 8,975.04; Consolidated Sand & Gravel, Ltd., 374.33; Guelph Sand & Gravel, Ltd., 3,191.42; Innerkip Lime & Stone Co., Ltd., 470.92; Kirkfield Crushed Stone, Ltd., 2,585.88; Limestone Products, Ltd., 10,180.75 .... 28,930 95

Travelling Expenses and Disbursements, $16,307.74.

Chas. Beldam, 614.62; N. D. Bennett, 804.50; P. D. Brown, 1,465.26; R. S. Code, 1,090.44; Stanley Cooke, 11.90; A. Cordery, 156.86; N. B. Dickson, 1,524.85; W. J. Fulton, 183.76; A. J. Gamble, 503.61; W. D. Gilmore, 160.50; G. G. Greig, 158.73; J. J. Haigh, 214.04; H. S. Howden, 223.00; John E. Jackson, 1,633.43; D. B. Kirby, 185.50; H. N. Lamont, 55.25; John A. Leslie, 311.49; A. MacPherson, 111.85; V. Murray, 28.45; F. W. Neelin, 637.73; F. Perry, 16.35; J. Powers, 84.94; J. T. Ransom, 436.78; W. Randall, 18.20; N. H. Richardson, 304.61; H. Sargent, 712.65; W. A. Schoenburn, 14.65; Arthur Sedgwick, 240.69; K. H. Siddall, 825.65; J. S. Slater, 326.75; A. A. Smith, 707.21; F. T. Smith, 316.58; D. R. Townley, 589.91; W. T. Waller, 12.70; F. T. Webster, 129.96; R. S. Whitton, 33.40; W. P. Wilgar, 814.95; W. Harry Williams, 610.04. Sundries, 35.95 .... 16,307 74

			9,099,146 07
Accountable outstanding, 1931-32, 55,716.70 less 1930-31 advance accounted for 11,366.42			44,350 28
			9,143,496 35
Less Federal Provincial Unemployment Relief Fund contribution		1,000,000 00	
Automobile rentals, repairs and services		46,686 98	
Municipal repayments for materials		346,809 37	
			1,393,496 35
			7,750,000 00
Less Repayment by Counties		2,837,497 82	
Repayments by Cities and Towns		404,786 09	
Board of Railway Commissioners—			
Proportion of cost of,			
Scarborough Overhead	24,248 21		
Owen Sound Overhead	5,986 19		
Trenton Overhead	366 71		
L'Orignal Overhead	16,003 38		
		46,604 49	
Canadian Pacific Railway Company—			
Proportion of cost of,			
Raising grade at Stittsville	975 00		
Whitby Pedestrian Subway	3,000 00		
Orillia Overhead	10,000 00		
Trenton Overhead	25,000 00		
		38,975 00	
Canadian National Railways—			
Proportion of cost of,			
Raising grade at Stittsville	2,204 97		
Breslau Diversion and Subway	10,000 00		
Scarborough Overhead	41,411 06		
		53,616 03	
Pere Marquette Railway Company—			
Proportion of cost of,			
Lowering grade at Blenheim Overhead		4,124 26	
Department of Northern Development—			
Proportion of cost of Severn Bridge		29,861 95	
Sale of bridges		1,866 62	
Damage to guard rail and fences		645 88	
Installation of tile drains		1,063 23	
Freight and demurrage		1,210 74	
Surface treatment		364 39	
Miscellaneous		187 49	
			3,420,803 99
King's Highway Construction			**$4,329,196 01**

Statutory—Continued

County Road Construction ($3,670,334.72)

Brant, 52,445.07; Bruce, 96,655.54; Carleton, 131,917.90; Dufferin, 37,711.42; Dundas, Stormont and Glengarry, 96.888.15; Elgin, 49,605.03; Essex, 144,135.83; Frontenac, 34,850.24; Grey, 77,234.59; Haldimand, 41.564.50; Halton, 29,319.26; Hastings, 76,950.15; Huron, 64,089.41; Kent, 82,855.55; Lambton, 78,952.61; Lanark, 47,501.23; Leeds and Grenville, 416,959.63; Lennox and Addington, 77,431.56; Lincoln, 38,821.03; Middlesex, 111,905.18; Norfolk, 85,703,56; Northumberland and Durham, 187,315.30; Ontario, 80,716.64; Oxford, 79,572.96; Peel, 106,832.47; Perth, 44,557.36; Peterborough, 42,577.02; Prescott and Russell, 68,576.51; Prince Edward, 44,175.97; Renfrew, 72,230.49; Simcoe, 115,252.29; Victoria, 60,772.58; Waterloo, 106,427.44; Welland, 36,669.93; Wellington, 59,163.09; Wentworth, 94,140.80; York, 597,856.43 .... 3,670,334 72

Township Road Construction ($1,877,405.55)

Adelaide, 1,112.10; Adjala, 3,973.01; Adolphustown, 612.31; Albemarle, 10,992.01; Albion, 7,220.63; Aldborough, 5,171.60; Alfred, 2,174.28; Alnwick, 2,760.73; Amabel, 2,690.65; Amaranth, 6,169.64; Ameliasburg, 2,499.53; Ancaster, 7,270.91; Anderdon, 5,235.98; Arran, 3,277.73; Artemesia, 5,904.45; Arthur, 3,255.57; Ashfield, 4,067.19; Asphodel, 1,542.82; Augusta, 3,684.70; Barton, 2,631.64; Bastard and Burgess, 2,426.88; Bathurst, 3,193.48; Bayham, 5,341.31; Beckwith, 2,474.68; Belmont and Methuen, 8,185.58; Bentinck, 4,281.92; Bertie, 19,130.76; Beverley, 5,627.59; Biddulph, 2,977.82; Binbrook, 3,793.21; Blandford, 2,500.89; Blanchard, 3,551.13; Blenheim, 5,646.09; Bosanquet, 924.97; Brant, 5,947.90; Brantford, 9,108.47; Brighton, 4,113.90; Brock, 5,278.00; Brooke, 3,883.70; Bruce, 4,300.84; Burgess North, 1,526.30; Burford, 1,248.64; Caistor, 1,373.16; Caledon, 5,449.94; Caledonia, 7,347.13; Cambridge, 2,171.83; Camden, 6,015.02; Camden East, 6,006.68; Canboro, 972.41; Caradoc, 6,677.54; Carrick, 4,285.77; Cartwright, 4,017.59; Cavan, 3,855.27; Cayuga North, 4,189.99; Cayuga South, 1,841.13; Charlotteville, 4,061.93; Charlottenburg, 6,838.82; Chatham, 23,166.54; Chinquacousy, 12,607.99; Clarence, 2,650.00; Clarke, 3,548.40; Clinton, 5,343.69; Colborne, 1,867.94; Colchester North, 4,662.96; Colchester South, 5,872.63; Collingwood, 4,039.64; Cornwall, 5,440.31; Cramahe, 3,794.64; Crowland, 7,625.78; Culross, 3,587.29; Cumberland, 16,301.45; Dalhousie and North Sherbrooke, 6,752.40; Darlington, 7,961.89; Dawn, 8,912.80; Delaware, 2,720.26; Derby, 2,690.48; Dereham, 6,169.43; Dorchester North, 4,018.50; Dorchester South, 4,847.45; Douro, 3,277.76; Dover, 13,103.64; Downie, 3,387.33; Drummond 2,641.00; Dumfries North, 5,049.81; Dumfries South, 2,436.96; Dummer, 5,949.32; Dunwich, 5,631.70; Dunn, 3,196.50; Easthope North, 3,347.94; Easthope South, 1,686.89; Eastnor, 6,431.65; Edwardsburg, 2,661.73; Egremont, 4,998.68; Ekfrid, 3,446.12; Elderslie, 2,886.97; Elizabethtown, 6,352.61; Ellice, 4,296.78; Elma, 7,123.17; Elmsley North, 1,670.65; Elmsley South, 1,761.12; Emily, 2,262.69; Enniskillen, 7,402.93; Ennismere, 721.44; Eramosa, 3,591.49; Erin, 6,078.45; Ernesttown, 5,141.22; Escott Front, 1,264.09; Esquesing, 10,811.34; Essa, 5,501.75; Etobicoke, 41,692.70; Euphemia, 2,394.09; Euphrasia, 4,700.20; Fenelon, 3,840.69; Finch, 3,102.52; Fitzroy, 4,503.67; Flamboro East, 3,391.28; Flamboro West, 3,921.26; Flos, 7,984.33; Fredericksburg North, 2,680.48; Fredericksburg South, 2,573.33; Fullarton, 2,851.84; Gainsboro, 2,411.85; Garafraxa East, 3,063.43; Garafraxa West, 5,222.48; Georgina, 2,987.00; Glanford, 3,982.84; Glenelg, 4,143.38; Gloucester, 13,589.18; Goderich, 2,396.35; Gosfield North, 2,685.01; Gosfield South, 5,636.90; Goulburn, 2,999.85; Gower North, 2,347.29; Gower South, 2,187.83; Grantham, 9,016.65; Greenock, 2,704.15; Grey, 5,321.11; Grimsby North, 3,866.41; Grimsby South, 1,680.55; Guelph, 4,343.06; Gwillimbury East, 5,006.73; Gwillimbury North, 4,873.43; Gwillimbury West, 2,625.88; Haldimand, 5,223.53; Hallowell, 4,805.41; Hamilton, 4,997.08; Harwich, 10,456.83; Hawkesbury East, 4,051.95; Hawkesbury West, 1,623.54; Hay, 2,714.39; Hibbert, 2,934.56; Hillier, 2,928.88; Holland, 4,447.12; Hope, 2,214.65; Horton, 1,400.95; Houghton, 2,324.13; Howard, 6,532.16; Howe Island, 709.94; Howick, 4,667.80; Hullett, 3,458.81; Humberstone, 9,384.15; Huntley, 1,529.74; Huron, 4,862.20; Innisfil, 7,249.67; Kenyon, 2,314.46; Kippell, 6,327.85; Kin cardine, 3,835.20; King, 12,147.06; Kingston, 4,217.28; Kinloss, 2,087.28; Kitley 4,768.45; Lancaster, 3,604.22; Leeds and Lansdowne Front, 4,011.28; Leeds and Lansdowne Rear, 3,303.17; Lindsay, 6,286.80; Lobo, 3,105.42; Lochiel, 7,412.90; Logan, 4,163.83; London, 8,689.90; Longueuil, 693.06; Loughborough, 5,183.97; Louth, 8,551.90; Luther East, 2,478.47; Luther West, 2,047.01; Maidstone, 6,044.06; Malahide, 4,093.57; Malden, 4,205.63; Manvers, 4,657.91; Mara, 4,618.54; March, 1,709.04; Mariposa, 5,121.06; Markham, 12,837.96; Marlborough, 1,345.83; Marysborough, 4,204.88; Marysborough North, 1,236.32;

Statutory—Continued

Township Road Construction—Continued

Matilda, 2,688.26; Melancthon, 5,295.03; Mersea, 5,295.83; Metcalf, 2,954.65; Middleton, 2,632.05; Minto, 5,187.91; Mono, 6,382.29; Monohan North, 2,939.42; Moore, 6,137.67; Mornington, 3,684.25; Morris, 1,681.84; Mosa, 3,813.97; Moulton, 2,720.60; Mountain, 3,318.67; Mulmer, 5,857.34; Murray, 4,508.52; McGillivray, 4,377.32; McKillop, 2,817.41; McNabb, 1,740.02; Nassagaweya, 4,876.83; Nelson, 5,843.69; Nepean, 9,508.05; Niagara, 3,100.76; Nichol, 2,431.15; Nissouri East, 2,456.88; Nissouri West, 3,477.41; Normanby, 3,596.95; Norwich North, 2,992.71; Norwich South, 2,304.89; Nottawasaga, 7,114.97; Oakland, 489.11; Oneida, 2,793.28; Onondaga, 2,930.17; Ops, 3,616.92; Osgoode, 11,719.17; Osnabruck, 2,374.80; Osprey, 3,567.32; Otonabee, 5,186.15; Oxford, 3,819.27; Oxford East, 4,474.23; Oxford North, 2,138.84; Oxford West, 3,440.70; Oxford on Rideau, 6,318.96; Peel, 5,002.17; Pelee Island, 1,373.96; Pelham, 5,348.89; Percy, 6,559.79; Pickering, 8,563.55; Pilkington, 3,012.94; Pittsburgh, 1,683.19; Plantagenet North, 4,207.41; Plantagenet South, 2,781.41; Portland, 4,045.51; Presqu'Ile Park Commission, 887.58; Proton, 6,877.67; Puslinch, 4,353.81; Rainham, 2,047.14; Raleigh, 9,755.75; Ramsay, 2,378.15; Rawdon, 3,321.73; Reach, 4,839.90; Richmond, 2,952.84; Rochester, 2,290.61; Romney, 2,152.34; Roxborough, 2,953.71; Russell, 3,849.40; St. Edmunds, 7,751.58; St. Vincent, 3,070.36; Saltfleet, 8,956.29; Sandwich East, 3,550.98; Sandwich South, 3,267.12; Sarawak, 1,262.66; Sarnia, 6,148.34; Saugeen, 5,247.29; Scarborough, 76,510.99; Scott, 2,287.41; Seneca, 4,547.72; Seymour, 5,306.61; Sherbrooke, 310.41; Sherbrooke South, 2,483.09; Sidney, 5,002.52; Smith, 3,742.23; Sombra, 4,500.36; Sophiasburgh, 3,793.98; Southwold, 6,126.80; Stamford, 49,611.00; Stanley, 2,306.79; Stephen, 4,025.05; Storrington, 3,754.30; Sullivan, 4,808.57; Sydenham, 5,239.72; Tecumseh, 2,593.39; Thorah, 1,584.53; Thorold, 6,765.23; Thurlow, 8,277.49; Tilbury East, 9,582.76; Tilbury North, 4,781.04; Tilbury West, 1,805.45; Torbolton, 2,233.12; Toronto, 20,570.19; Toronto Gore, 2,280.92; Tossorontio, 3,205.61; Townsend, 7,556.28; Trafalgar, 7,986.97; Tuckersmith, 5,926.16; Turnberry, 1,751.22; Tyendinaga, 5,411.92; Usborne, 2,197.71; Uxbridge, 4,109.79; Vaughan, 12,161.61; Verulam, 5,115.44; Wainfleet, 7,082.07; Wallace, 5,976.29; Walpole, 9,798.17; Walsingham North, 3,672.04; Walsingham South, 2,134.27; Warwick, 4,563.27; Waterloo, 8,138.72; Wawanosh East, 2,559.18; Wawanosh West, 2,154.99; Wellesley, 6,687.75; Westminster, 8,555.99; Whitby, 2,833.01; Whitby East, 6,182.24; Whitchurch, 8,111.05; Williams East, 2,209.19; Williams West, 1,617.12; Williamsburg, 2,902.44; Willoughby, 3,538.23; Wilmot, 4,950.42; Winchester, 4,376.48; Windham, 4,309.48; Wolfe Island, 5,063.34; Wolford, 2,413.20; Woodhouse, 3,494.89; Woolwich, 8,637.18; Yarmouth, 7,959.66; Yonge and Escott Rear, 1,479.57; Yonge Front, 1,847.43; York, 86,851.26; York North, 48,538.29; York East, 48,328.48; Zone, 1,501.98; Zorra East, 7,882.39; Zorra West, 3,639.27 .... 1,877,405 55

Grants to Municipalities Linking Up Provincial Highways ($46,578.14)

Alliston, 524.40; Aurora, 6,656.79; Brampton, 3,868.42; Etobicoke, 2,126.98; Flesherton, 6,651.07; Hagersville, 159.61; Hespeler, 93.69; Leamington, 2,218.04; Markdale, 10,254.21; Meaford, 90.34; Mitchell, 1,418.29; Port Credit, 1,598.43; Sandwich, 10,384.00; Tillsonburg, 533.87 .... 46,578 14

Grants to Indian Reserve Roads ($13,245.01)

Cape Crocker, 2,730.07; Caradoc, 231.48; Kettle and Stoney Point, 299.08; Moravian, 65.41; Mud Lake, 650.68; Rice Lake, 391.28; Sarnia, 192.05; Saugeen, 775.66; Six Nations, 7,051.03; Tyendinaga, 360.00; Walpole, 498.27 .... 13,245 01

Statutory	**$9,946,759.43**	
Total		**$10,593,730.16**
Less Salary Assessment		15,144.04
Total Expenditure, Department of Highways		**$10,578,586.12**

PART M

DEPARTMENT OF HEALTH

FISCAL YEAR, 1931-32

TABLE OF CONTENTS

GENERAL INDEX AT BACK OF BOOK

PART M—DEPARTMENT OF HEALTH

Statement of Expenditure Showing Amounts Expended, Unexpended and Overexpended for the Twelve Months Ended October 31st, 1932

Department of Health	Page	Estimates	Expended			Un-expended	Over-expended	Treasury Board Minute
			Ordinary	Capital	Total Ordinary and Capital			
		$ c.	$ c.	$ c.	$ c.	$ c.	$ c.	$ c.
Main Office:								
Salaries	13	33,825 00	32,225 00		32,225 00	1,600 00		
Contingencies	13	12,000 00	8,677 50		8,677 50	3,322 50		
Library Fees, etc.	13	2,500 00	1,624 18		1,624 18	875 82		
Grant to Connaught Laboratories	13	18,000 00	18,000 00		18,000 00			
Grant to St. Johns Ambulance Association	13	2,000 00	2,000 00		2,000 00			
Main Office	..	68,325 00	62,526 68		62,526 68	5,798 32		
Branches:								
District Health Officers:								
Salaries	14	32,975 00	32,975 00		32,975 00			
Services and Expenses, etc.	14	12,000 00	9,194 57		9,194 57	2,805 43		
Annual Conference of Health Officers	14	300 00	962 00		962 00		662 00	662 00
District Health Officers Branch	..	45,275 00	43,131 57		43,131 57	2,805 43	662 00	
Maternal and Child Hygiene:								
Salaries	14	35,325 00	33,216 67		33,216 67	2,108 33		
Contingencies	14	5,000 00	3,447 27		3,447 27	1,552 73		
District Nurses, Services and Expenses	15	47,000 00	43,988 77		43,988 77	3,011 23		
Maternal and Child Hygiene Branch	..	87,325 00	80,652 71		80,652 71	6,672 29		
Dental Service:								
Salaries	15	6,100 00	6,100 00		6,100 00			
Contingencies	15	10,000 00	896 23		896 23	9,103 77		
Services and Expenses, etc.	16	10,000 00	7,892 84		7,892 84	2,107 16		
Dental Service Branch	..	26,100 00	14,889 07		14,889 07	11,210 93		

Inspection of Training Schools for Nurses:								
Salaries	16	7,575 00	7,575 00		7,575 00			
Services and Expenses	16	4,000 00	4,230 16		4,230 16		230 16	1,000 00
Inspection of Training Schools for Nurses	..	11,575 00	11,805 16		11,805 16		230 16	
Preventable Diseases:								
Salaries	17	24,675 00	23,750 01		23,750 01	924 99		
Contingencies	17	6,000 00	2,289 90		2,289 90	3,710 10		
Outbreaks of Diseases	17	192,000 00	187,877 93		187,877 93	4,122 07		
Treatment of Patients	17	100,000 00	94,984 17		94,984 17	5,015 83		30,000 00
Payment of Board, etc., Tuberculosis Patients	18	45,000 00	16,011 71		16,011 71	28,988 29		
Grant Canadian Social Hygiene Council	18	7,500 00	4,000 00		4,000 00	3,500 00		
Preventable Diseases Branch	..	375,175 00	328,913 72		328,913 72	46,261 28		
Industrial Hygiene:								
Salaries	18	35,300 00	35,300 00		35,300 00			
Services and Expenses	18	20,000 00	11,845 07		11,845 07	8,154 93		
Industrial Hygiene Branch	..	55,300 00	47,145 07		47,145 07	8,154 93		
Sanitary Engineering:								
Salaries	19	30,225 00	27,858 34		27,858 34	2,366 66		
Services and Expenses	19	20,000 00	19,915 24		19,915 24	84 76		
Sanitary Engineering Branch	..	50,225 00	47,773 58		47,773 58	2,451 42		
Main Laboratory:								
Salaries	20	56,975 00	55,350 00		55,350 00	1,625 00		
Services and Expenses	20	40,000 00	35,192 15		35,192 15	4,807 85		
Establishment, etc., re Clinical Laboratory Centres	..	15,000 00				15,000 00		
Main Laboratory Branch	..	111,975 00	90,542 15		90,542 15	21,432 85		
Public Health Laboratories:								
Salaries	22	21,275 00	21,275 00		21,275 00			
Services and Expenses	22	18,000 00	13,313 61		13,313 61	4,686 39		
Grants:								
Queen's University	22	3,300 00	3,300 00		3,300 00			
Peterborough	23	2,000 00	2,000 00		2,000 00			
Peterborough (Equipment, etc.)	23	500 00	311 38		311 38	188 62		

PART M—DEPARTMENT OF HEALTH—Continued

Statement of Expenditure Showing Amounts Expended, Unexpended and Overexpended for the Twelve Months Ended October 31st, 1932

Department of Health	Page	Estimates	Expended: Ordinary	Expended: Capital	Expended: Total Ordinary and Capital	Un-expended	Over-expended	Treasury Board Minute
		$ c.	$ c.	$ c.	$ c.	$ c.	$ c.	$ c.
Public Health Laboratories—Continued								
Grants—Continued								
Institute of Public Health, Western University, London	23	6,000 00	6,000 00	....	6,000 00	....	....	....
Public Health Laboratories	..	51,075 00	46,199 99	....	46,199 99	4,875 01	....	....
Public Health Education:								
Salaries	23	8,625 00	8,625 00	....	8,625 00	....	....	....
Public Health Exhibits	23	13,000 00	2,029 00	....	2,029 00	10,971 00	....	....
Services and Expenses	23	25,000 00	10,675 52	....	10,675 52	14,324 48	....	....
Advertising	23	1,000 00	583 50	....	583 50	416 50	....	....
Public Health Education Branch	..	47,625 00	21,913 02	....	21,913 02	25,711 98	....	....
Main Office and Branches	..	929,975 00	795,492 72	....	795,492.72	135,374 44	892 16	....
Hospitals Branch:								
Salaries	24	90,375 00	80,635 41	....	80,635 41	9,739 59	....	....
Contingencies	24	36,350 00	49,159 88	....	49,159 88	....	12,809 88	14,000 00
Hospitals Branch	..	126,725 00	129,795 29	....	129,795 29	9,739 59	12,809 88	....
General Hospitals and Charities:								
Salaries	25	10,350 00	7,500 00	....	7,500 00	2,850 00	....	....
General Hospitals	25	1,093,000 00	1,100,834 83	....	1,100,834 83	....	7,834 83	10,000 00
Homes for Incurables	26	153,500 00	163,202 00	....	163,202 00	....	9,702 00	10,000 00
Maintenance of patients in Municipal Sanitoria	26	590,000 00	620,238 62	....	620,238 62	....	30,238 62	31,000 00
To pay travelling expenses, etc., of Indigent Patients	26	1,000 00	60 65	....	60 65	939 35	....	....
Grant to Victorian Order of Nurses	27	2,500 00	2,250 00	....	2,250 00	250 00	....	....
Grant, Hospital for Sick Children re Out Patients	27	7,000 00	6,811 00	....	6,811 00	189 00	....	....

Grant, Hospital for Sick Children to erect a 100-bed Country Hospital	27	11,500 00	11,350 00	....	11,350 00	150 00	....	....
Contingencies	25	4,950 00	4,348 99	....	4,348 99	601 01	....	....
General Hospitals and Charities	..	1,873,800 00	1,916,596 09	....	1,916,596 09	4,979 36	47,775 45	....
General:								
Printing examination papers, etc., School for Nurses	27	500 00	385 05	....	385 05	114 95	....	....
Board of Examiners, School for Nurses	27	600 00	497 62	....	497 62	102 38	....	....
Removal of patients	27	10,000 00	12,102 88	....	12,102 88	....	2,102 88	2,500 00
Clothing for Bailiffs, escorting patients	27	500 00	299 95	....	299 95	200 05	....	....
Printing and Stationery for Public Institutions	27	22,000 00	14,836 74	....	14,836 74	7,163 26	....	....
Medical advice, etc., re employees	27	650 00	601 70	....	601 70	48 30	....	....
Treatment of Patients and Inmates	27	1,300 00	114 50	....	114 50	1,185 50	....	....
Fees, removal expenses, re Indigent Patients	27	600 00	494 38	....	494 38	105 62	....	....
Travelling Expenses of Social Service Workers	27	1,000 00	356 61	....	356 61	643 39	....	....
Minor Comforts for Indigent Patients	..	1,500 00	....	....	....	1,500 00	....	....
Legal Costs re Sundry Investigations	27	1,000 00	7 00	....	7 00	993 00	....	....
Expenses re Conventions at Institutions	27	3,000 00	15 20	....	15 20	2,984 80	....	....
Removal Expenses, other than Patients	27	1,000 00	1,497 00	....	1,497 00	....	497 00	500 00
Unforeseen and Unprovided	28	1,500 00	1,003 90	....	1,003 90	496 10	....	....
Expenses in connection with Exhibit	28	2,000 00	3,628 61	....	3,628 61	....	1,628 61	1,650 00
Payment to Ontario Research Foundation	28	3,000 00	2,955 26	....	2,955 26	44 74	....	....
General	..	50,150 00	38,796 40	....	38,796 40	15,582 09	4,228 49	....
Mental Hospitals:								
Brockville,								
Salaries,								
Superintendent, physicians and dentists	28	22,300 00	17,934 00	....	17,934 00	4,366 00	....	....
Steward and assistants	28	12,300 00	11,775 00	....	11,775 00	525 00	....	....
Matron and assistants, domestic help	28	23,850 00	26,081 26	....	26,081 26	....	2,231 26	2,600 00
Engineers and assistants	28	15,575 00	15,462 50	....	16,462 50	....	887 50	1,000 00
Artisans not domestic	28	12,700 00	12,670 00	....	12,670 00	30 00	....	....
Farm and garden	28	11,000 00	10,175 00	....	10,175 00	825 00	....	....
Attendants and nurses	28	117,550 00	112,106 27	....	112,106 27	5,443 73	....	....
Expenses	28	150,000 00	160,095 93	....	160,095 93	....	10,095 93	14,000 00
Repairs to buildings	31	25,000 00	15,354 58	....	15,354 58	9,645 42	....	....
	..	390,275 00	382,654 54	....	382,654 54	20,835 15	13,214 69	....
Less Patients' maintenance, perquisites, etc.	31	....	103,601 70	....	103,601 70	103,601 70	....	....
Brockville	..	390,275 00	279,052 84	....	279,052 84	124,436 85	13,214 69	....

PART M—DEPARTMENT OF HEALTH—Continued

Statement of Expenditure Showing Amounts Expended, Unexpended and Overexpended for the Twelve Months Ended October 31st, 1932

Department of Health	Page	Estimates	Expended			Un-expended	Over-expended	Treasury Board Minute
			Ordinary	Capital	Total Ordinary and Capital			
		$ c.	$ c.	$ c.	$ c.	$ c.	$ c.	$ c.
Mental Hospitals—Continued								
Cobourg,								
Salaries,								
Superintendent, physicians and dentists	31	10,800 00	8,720 00	....	8,720 00	2,080 00	....	....
Steward and assistants	31	4,000 00	3,972 90	....	3,972 90	27 10	....	....
Matron and assistants, domestic help	31	10,800 00	11,755 63	....	11,755 63	....	955 63	1,000 00
Engineer and assistants	31	8,250 00	7,900 00	....	7,900 00	350 00	....	....
Artisans not domestic	31	1,300 00	1,300 00	....	1,300 00	....	....	....
Farm and garden employees	31	2,350 00	2,250 00	....	2,250 00	100 00	....	....
Attendants and nurses	31	25,350 00	22,868 82	....	22,868 82	2,481 18	....	....
Expenses	32	60,000 00	67,132 18	....	67,132 18	....	7,132 18	8,000 00
Repairs to buildings	33	15,000 00	17,103 60	....	17,103 60	....	2,103 60	7,000 00
	..	137,850 00	143,003 13	....	143,003 13	5,038 28	10,191 41	....
Less Patients' maintenance, perquisites, etc.	33	....	28,216 23	....	28,216 23	28,216 23	....	....
Cobourg	..	137,850 00	114,786 90	....	114,786 90	33,254 51	10,191 41	....
Hamilton,								
Salaries,								
Superintendent and physicians	34	23,350 00	24,147 30	....	24,147 30	....	797 30	797 30
Steward and assistants	34	12,375 00	12,980 62	....	12,980 62	....	605 62	1,000 00
Matron and assistants, domestic help	34	28,475 00	26,867 90	....	26,867 90	1,607 10	....	....
Engineers and assistants	34	20,475 00	20,300 00	....	20,300 00	175 00	....	....
Artisans not domestic	34	15,025 00	15,675 00	....	15,675 00	....	650 00	800 00
Farm and garden [illegible]	34	17,275 00	16,010 00	....	16,010 00	1,265 00	....	....
Attendants and nurses	34	131,850 00	128,773 80	....	128,773 80	3,076 20	....	....
Expenses	34	215,000 00	187,215 45	....	187,215 45	27,784 55	....	....
Repairs to buildings	36	40,000 00	36,650 86	....	36,650 86	3,349 14	....	....
	..	503,825 00	468,620 93	....	468,620 93	37,256 99	2,052 92	....

Less Patients' maintenance, Perquisites, etc.	37	....	174,361 27	....	174,361 27	174,361 27	....	....
Hamilton	..	503,825 00	294,259 66	....	294,259 66	211,618 26	2,052 92	....
Kingston,								
Salaries,								
Superintendent, physicians and dentists	37	22,987 50	23,461 37	....	23,461 37	....	473 87	650 00
Steward and assistants	37	10,325 00	9,971 58	....	9,971 58	353 42	....	....
Matron and assistants, domestic help	37	17,125 00	18,419 95	....	18,419 95	....	1,294 95	1,500 00
Engineer and assistants	37	16,375 00	15,950 00	....	15,950 00	425 00	....	....
Artisans not domestic	37	8,300 00	8,100 00	....	8,100 00	200 00	....	....
Farm and garden employees	37	9,200 00	9,075 00	....	9,075 00	125 00	....	....
Attendants and nurses	37	124,300 00	120,218 17	....	120,218 17	4,081 83	....	....
Expenses	38	135,000 00	154,965 43	....	154,965 43	....	19,965 43	20,000 00
Repairs to buildings	40	25,000 00	28,820 58	....	28,820 58	....	3,820 58	7,000 00
	..	368,612 50	388,982 08	....	388,982 08	5,185 25	25,554 83	....
Less Patients' maintenance, perquisites, etc.	41	....	97,968 34	....	97,968 34	97,968 34	....	....
Kingston	..	368,612 50	291,013 74	....	291,013 74	103,153 59	25,554 83	....
London,								
Salaries,								
Superintendent, physicians and dentists	41	25,237 50	24,470 46	....	24,470 46	767 04	....	....
Steward and assistants	41	14,975 00	16,479 17	....	16,479 17	....	1,504 17	1,600 00
Matron and assistants, domestic help	41	47,425 00	42,140 61	....	42,140 61	5,284 39	....	....
Engineer and assistants	41	24,725 00	21,917 00	....	21,917 00	2,808 00	....	....
Artisans not domestic	41	8,425 00	9,237 22	....	9,237 22	....	812 22	950 00
Farm and garden employees	41	18,650 00	18,550 00	....	18,550 00	100 00	....	....
Attendants and nurses	41	151,575 00	144,934 24	....	144,934 24	6,640 76	....	....
Expenses	41	180,000 00	175,094 20	....	175,094 20	4,905 80	....	....
Repairs to buildings	43	75,000 00	69,645 50	....	69,645 50	5,354 50	....	....
	..	546,012 50	522,468 40	....	522,468 40	25,860 49	2,316 39	....
Less Patients' maintenance, perquisites, etc.	44	....	184,102 77	....	184,102 77	184,102 77	....	....
London	..	546,012 50	338,365 63	....	338,365 63	209,963 26	2,316 39	....
Mimico,								
Salaries,								
Superintendent, physicians and dentists	44	24,787 50	23,814 16	....	23,814 16	973 34	....	....
Steward and assistants	44	10,025 00	9,506 71	....	9,506 71	518 29	....	....
Matron and assistants, domestic help	44	17,500 00	17,890 44	....	17,890 44	....	390 44	750 00
Engineer and assistants	44	14,600 00	14,600 00	....	14,600 00	....	....	....
Artisans not domestic	44	9,125 00	8,974 50	....	8,974 50	150 50	....	....
Farm and garden employees	44	7,075 00	5,969 58	....	5,969 58	1,105 42	....	....
Attendants and nurses	44	112,475 00	105,464 29	....	105,464 29	7,010 71	....	....

PART M—DEPARTMENT OF HEALTH—Continued

Statement of Expenditure Showing Amounts Expended, Unexpended and Overexpended for the Twelve Months Ended October 31st, 1932

Department of Health	Page	Estimates	Expended			Un-expended	Over-expended	Treasury Board Minute
			Ordinary	Capital	Total Ordinary and Capital			
		$ c.	$ c.	$ c.	$ c.	$ c.	$ c.	$ c.
Mental Hospitals—Continued								
Mimico—Continued								
Expenses	44	135,000 00	147,885 00	....	147,885 00	....	12,885 00	13,000 00
Repairs to buildings	47	100,000 00	89,675 08	....	89,675 08	10,324 92	....	....
	..	430,587 50	423,779 76	....	423,779 76	20,083 18	13,275 44	....
Less Patients' maintenance, perquisites, etc.	48	....	99,330 88	....	99,330 88	99,330 88	....	....
Mimico	..	430,587 50	324,448 88	....	324,448 88	119,414 06	13,275 44	....
Orillia,								
Salaries,								
Superintendent, physicians and dentists	48	27,150 00	25,573 60	....	25,573 60	1,576 40	....	....
Stewards and assistants	48	14,500 00	15,247 91	....	15,247 91	....	747 91	1,000 00
Matron and assistants, domestic help	48	30,600 00	28,886 61	....	28,886 61	1,713 39	....	....
Engineers and assistants	48	16,175 00	17,025 00	....	17,025 00	....	850 00	1,200 00
Artisans not domestic	48	11,525 00	10,572 00	....	10,572 00	953 00	....	....
Farm and garden employees	48	13,000 00	12,875 00	....	12,875 00	125 00	....	....
Attendants and nurses	48	132,425 00	125,903 98	....	125,903 98	6,521 02	....	....
Teachers and industrial instructors	48	15,350 00	15,535 00	....	15,535 00	....	185 00	300 00
Expenses	48	240,000 00	207,149 58	....	207,149 58	32,850 42	....	....
Repairs to buildings	51	35,000 00	33,825 92	....	33,825 92	1,174 08	....	....
Industries, salaries, operating expenses, etc.	52	25,000 00	8,038 65	....	8,038 65	16,961 35	....	....
	..	560,725 00	500,633 25	....	500,633 25	61,874 66	1,782 91	....
Less Patients' maintenance, perquisites, etc.	52	....	114,757 50	....	114,757 50	114,757 50	....	....
Orillia	..	560,725 00	385,875 75	....	385,875 75	176,632 16	1,782 91	....
Penetanguishene,								
Salaries,								
Superintendent, physicians and dentists	52	7,800 00	7,776 66	....	7,776 66	23 34	....	....

Steward and assistants	52	3,900 00	3,875 00	....	3,875 00	25 00	....	....
Matron and assistants, domestic help	52	9,000 00	8,753 59	....	8,753 59	246 41	....	....
Engineer and assistants	52	6,450 00	6,345 75	....	6,345 75	104 25	....	....
Artisans not domestic	52	4,400 00	4,234 70	....	4,234 70	165 30	....	....
Farm and garden employees	52	6,200 00	6,000 00	....	6,000 00	200 00	....	....
Attendants and nurses	52	40,225 00	41,440 96	....	41,440 96	....	1,215 96	1,400 00
Expenses	52	50,000 00	60,159 61	....	60,159 61	....	10,159 61	12,000 00
Repairs to buildings	54	30,000 00	36,867 09	....	36,867 09	....	6,867 09	12,000 00
	..	157,975 00	175,453 36	....	175,453 36	764 30	18,242 66	....
Less Patients maintenance, perquisites, etc.	55	....	29,943 37	....	29,943 37	29,943 37	....	....
Penetanguishene	..	157,975 00	145,509 99	....	145,509 99	30,707 67	18,242 66	....
Toronto,								
Salaries,								
Superintendent, physicians and dentists	55	17,550 00	17,241 18	....	17,241 18	308 82	....	....
Steward and assistants	55	10,400 00	9,586 20	....	9,586 20	813 80	....	....
Matron and assistants, domestic help	55	19,225 00	18,631 25	....	18,631 25	593 75	....	....
Engineer and assistants	55	14,050 00	15,475 00	....	15,475 00	....	1,425 00	1,500 00
Artisans not domestic	55	7,550 00	5,999 96	....	5,999 96	1,550 04	....	....
Farm and garden employees	55	2,600 00	2,525 00	....	2,525 00	75 00	....	....
Attendants and nurses	55	98,500 00	100,714 13	....	100,714 13	....	2,214 13	3,800 00
Expenses	55	140,000 00	131,293 98	....	131,293 98	8,706 02	....	....
Repairs to buildings	57	25,000 00	27,935 23	....	27,935 23	....	2,935 23	8,000 00
	..	334,875 00	329,401 93	....	329,401 93	12,047 43	6,574 36	....
Less Patients' maintenance, perquisites, etc.	58	....	92,607 13	....	92,607 13	92,607 13	....	....
Toronto	..	334,875 00	236,794 80	....	236,794 80	104,654 56	6,574 36	....
Whitby,								
Salaries,								
Superintendent, physicians and dentists	58	31,500 00	31,062 50	....	31,062 50	437 50	....	....
Steward and assistants	58	17,800 00	16,991 78	....	16,991 78	808 22	....	....
Matron and assistants, domestic help	58	34,900 00	33,503 86	....	33,503 86	1,396 14	....	....
Engineer and assistants	58	20,450 00	21,350 00	....	21,350 00	....	900 00	1,000 00
Artisans not domestic	58	9,000 00	8,900 00	....	8,900 00	100 00	....	....
Farm and garden employees	58	18,950 00	18,341 24	....	18,341 24	608 76	....	....
Attendants and nurses	58	177,468 75	169,914 22	....	169,914 22	7,554 53	....	....

PART M—DEPARTMENT OF HEALTH—Continued

Statement of Expenditure Showing Amounts Expended, Unexpended and Overexpended for the Twelve Months Ended October 31st, 1932

Department of Health	Page	Estimates	Expended: Ordinary	Expended: Capital	Expended: Total Ordinary and Capital	Un-expended	Over-expended	Treasury Board Minute
		$ c.	$ c.	$ c.	$ c.	$ c.	$ c.	$ c.
Mental Hospitals—Continued								
Whitby—Continued								
Expenses	58	255,000 00	254,065 11	....	254,065 11	934 89	....	....
Repairs to buildings	61	25,000 00	15,260 27	....	15,260 27	9,739 73	....	....
	..	590,068 75	569,388 98	....	569,388 98	21,579 77	900 00	....
Less Patients' maintenance, Perquisites, etc.	62	....	259,621 00	....	259,621 00	259,621 00	....	....
Whitby	..	590,068 75	309,767 98	....	309,767 98	281,200 77	900 00	....
Woodstock,								
Salaries,								
Superintendent, physicians and dentists	62	14,050 00	13,964 50	....	13,964 50	85 50	....	....
Steward and assistants	62	7,275 00	7,977 39	....	7,977 39	....	702 39	900 00
Matron and assistants, domestic help	62	9,050 00	11,241 39	....	11,241 39	....	2,191 39	4,000 00
Engineers and assistants	62	6,450 00	7,129 88	....	7,129 88	....	679 88	800 00
[illegible]	62	3,900 00	2,232 81	....	2,232 81	1,667 19	....	....
Farm and garden employees	62	9,475 00	8,550 58	....	8,550 58	924 42	....	....
Attendants and nurses	62	47,331 25	56,231 24	....	56,231 24	....	8,899 99	9,700 00
Expenses	62	76,000 00	66,428 01	....	66,428 01	9,571 99	....	....
Repairs to buildings	64	7,000 00	11,786 03	....	11,786 03	....	4,786 03	6,000 00
	..	180,531 25	185,541 83	....	185,541 83	12,249 10	17,259 68	....
Less Patients' maintenance, Perquisites, etc.	64	....	79,154 57	....	79,154 57	79,154 57	....	....
Woodstock	..	180,531 25	106,387 26	....	106,387 26	91,403 67	17,259 68	....
Toronto Psychiatric,								
Salaries,								
Superintendent, physicians and dentists	65	23,000 00	20,603 30	....	20,603 30	2,396 70	....	....
Steward and assistants	65	9,500 00	10,975 00	....	10,975 00	....	1,475 00	1,500 00
Matron and assistants, domestic help	65	20,800 00	18,417 70	....	18,417 70	2,382 30	....	....

Engineer and assistants	65	1,650 00	1,300 00	....	1,300 00	350 00	....	....
Attendants and nurses	65	40,775 00	39,292 47	....	39,292 47	1,482 53	....	....
Expenses	65	30,000 00	34,733 73	....	34,733 73	....	4,733 73	5,000 00
Repairs to buildings	66	3,000 00	2,056 48	....	2,056 48	943 52	....	....
	..	128,725 00	127,378 68	....	127,378 68	7,555 05	6,208 73	....
Less Patients' maintenance, Perquisites, etc.	66	....	30,218 79	....	30,218 79	30,218 79	....	....
Toronto Psychiatric	..	128,725 00	97,159 89	....	97,159 89	37,773 84	6,208 73	....
Mental Hospitals	..	4,330,062 50	2,923,423 32	....	2,923,423 32	1,524,213 20	117,574 02	....
Supply Bill	..	7,310,712 50	5,804,103 82	....	5,804,103 82	1,689,888 68	183,280 00	....
Statutory:								
Minister of Health, salary	66	....	10,000 00	....	10,000 00	....	....	....
Salaries not otherwise provided for	66	....	925 00	....	925 00	....	....	....
Statutory	..	....	10,925 00	....	10,925 00	....	....	....
Special Warrants:								
[illegible] and [illegible] [illegible] re [illegible] Commission	67	....	3,635 84	....	3,635 84	....	....	....
[illegible] [illegible], Mimico, [illegible] and [illegible]	66	....	72,907 73	....	72,907 73	....	....	....
Grant for [illegible] Dental [illegible] for entertaining [illegible] from Great Britain and the United States	67	....	1,000 00	....	1,000 00	....	....	....
Bursar, [illegible] University, for furnishing School of Nursing, No. 7 Queen's Park	67	....	1,000 00	....	1,000 00	....	....	....
Reimbursing Village of Portsmouth, [illegible] of payment for repairing and oiling King Street	67	....	250 00	....	250 00	....	....	....
[illegible] Reformatory, [illegible], to [illegible] [illegible], [illegible] of [illegible] Patients	67	....	25,005 17	....	25,005 17	....	....	....
Special Warrants	..	....	103,798 74	....	103,798 74	....	....	....
Total	..	....	5,918,827 56	....	5,918,827 56	....	....	....
Less Salary Assessment	..	....	48.557 03	....	48,557 03	....	....	....
Department of Health	..	....	5,870,270 53	....	5,870,270 53	....	....	....

SUMMARY

Department of Health	Page	Ordinary	Capital	Total
		$ c.	$ c.	$ c.
Main Office and Branches	13-23	795,492 72	....	795,492 72
Statutory—Minister's Salary	66	10,000 00	....	10,000 00
Special Warrants	67	5,635 84	....	5,635 84
Total	....	811,128 56	....	[illegible]128 56
Less Salary Assessment	....	7,539 20	....	7,539 20
Main Office and Branches	....	803,589 36	....	803,589 36
Hospitals Branch	25-27	168,591 69	....	[illegible]591 69
General Hospitals and Charities	25-27	1,916,596 09	....	1,916,596 09
Mental Hospitals	28-66	2,923,423 32	....	2,923,423 32
Statutory—Salaries not otherwise provided for	66	925 00	....	925 00
Special Warrants	66-67	98,162 90	....	[illegible]162 90
Total	....	5,107,699 00	....	5,107,699 00
Less Salary Assessment	....	41,017 83	....	41,017 83
Hospitals Branch	....	5,066,681 17	....	5,066,681 17
Department of Health	....	5,870,270 53	....	[illegible]70 53

DEPARTMENT OF HEALTH

Hon. John M. Robb, Minister (Statutory)............$10,000.00

MAIN OFFICE

Salaries (32,225.00)

W. J. Bell	Deputy Minister	12 months	6,000 00
J. W. S. McCullough	Chief Inspector of Health	12 "	5,700 00
C. J. Telfer	Secretary to Minister	12 "	3,300 00
J. M. Coates	Accountant, Group 3	12 "	2,200 00
C. C. Chambers	Senior Clerk	12 "	2,000 00
A. Ward	Clerk, Group 1	12 "	1,500 00
S. Hindley	" " 2	12 "	1,125 00
G. M. Bowman	Secretarial Stenographer	12 "	1,600 00
E. R. Boggis	Senior Clerk Stenographer	12 "	1,500 00
D. Hamlin	" " "	12 "	1,500 00
F. Wright	Library Clerk	12 "	1,500 00
May J. McGernon	Senior Filing Clerk	12 "	1,500 00
A. Wood	Office Appliance Operator, Group 1	12 "	1,600 00
A. Tumber	Senior Clerk Messenger	12 "	1,200 00

Contingencies ($8,677.50)

Temporary Services, $4,058.75.

G. Beckett	Office Appliance Operator, Group 2	6 months	375 00
Marjory Brockway	Clerk Stenographer " 2	2/3 "	40 00
M. C. Darroch	" " " 2	12 "	975 00
E. LeMesurier	" " " 3	5 "	343 75
Marion Scott	" " 2	12 "	975 00
J. Sheldrake	Office Boy	12	525 00
M. Stewart	Clerk Stenographer " 2	12 "	825 00

Travelling Expenses, $979.64.

W. J. Bell, 879.64; Hon. J. M. Robb, 500.00		1,379 64	
Less Refund Accountable Warrants, 1931:			
C. J. Telfer	200 00		
C. C. Chambers	200 00		
		400 00	
			979 64

Miscellaneous, $3,639.11.

Bourne & Ironside, maps, 24.70; Burroughs Adding Machine of Canada, Ltd., inspections, etc., 13.80; Department of Highways, auto service, etc., 35.00; Field, Love & House, inspections, 65.00; Grand & Toy, Ltd., indexes, 10.55; J. F. Hartz Co., Ltd., tablets, etc., 10.80; Imperial Oil, Ltd., gasoline, etc., 150.00; King's Printer, 2,657.03; R. J. Mitchell, tires and tubes, etc., 17.70; Remington Typewriters, Ltd., ribbon, inspections, etc., 41.50; C. L. Turnbull Co., Ltd., files, 16.60; United Typewriter Co., Ltd., rentals, inspections, etc., 156.38. Sundries—car tickets, 90.00; customs, 12.67; excise stamps, 11.00; telegrams, 315.35; petty disbursements, 11.03 .... 3,639 11

Library and Medical Fees, Journals and Publications ($1,624.18)

Fees, $28.50.

American Social Hygiene Council, 2.50; College of Physicians and Surgeons, 6.00; Conference of State and Provincial Health Authorities of North America, 20.00 .... 28 50

Journals and Publications, $1,595.68.

American Journal of Hygiene, 13.00; American Medical Association, 48.30; British Medical Journal, 16.30; Canadian Medical Association, 74.00; Canadian Public Health Association, 735.13; Wm. Dawson Subscription Service, Ltd., 266.30; H. M. Stationery Office, 11.16; King's Printer, 84.75; Library of Congress, Washington, 11.20; J. B. Lippincott Co., 14.00; McAinsh & Co., Ltd., 26.50; McGraw-Hill Publishing Co., Inc., 11.50; C.W. Mosby Publishing Co., 37.10; T. Nelson & Sons, 20.00; E. Tobin, 12.00; Williams & Wilkins Co., 17.50. Sundries—petty disbursements, 196.94 .... 1,595 68

Grant to Connaught Laboratories ($18,000.00)

Grant 18,000 00

Grant to St. John's Ambulance Association ($2,000.00)

Grant 2,000 00

Main Office $62,526.68

Main Office and Branches—Continued

DISTRICT OFFICERS OF HEALTH

Salaries ($32,975.00)

W. E. George	District Officer	12 months	4,000 00
D. A. McClenahan	" "	12 "	4,000 00
T. J. McNally	" "	12 "	4,000 00
P. J. Moloney	" "	12 "	4,000 00
G. L. Sparks	" "	12 "	4,000 00
H. W. Johnston	" "	12 "	4,000 00
J. J. Fraser	" "	12 "	4,000 00
Norman H. Sutton	" "	12 "	4,000 00
N. Smythe	Clerk Stenographer, Group 2	12 "	975 00

Services, Equipment and Expenses ($9,194.57)

Travelling Expenses, $5,391.38.

J. J. Fraser, 929.15; W. E. George, 683.44; H. W. Johnston, 895.89; D. A. McClenahan, 546.22; T. J. McNally, 823.90; P. J. Moloney, 447.03; G. L. Sparks, 372.47; N. H. Sutton, 693.28 ..... 5,391 38

Miscellaneous, $3,803.19.

Bank St. Garage, auto repairs, 100.33; C. W. Barker, office rent, 20.00; The Bell Telephone Co. of Canada, rentals, 62.40; tolls, 125.75; Better Battery Service, Ltd., repairs, 11.00; J. Blount, gas, auto repairs, etc., 68.28; Canada Steamship Lines, 12.95; Cannon Service Station, gas, etc., 27.64; Mrs. R. Cockburn, scrubbing, cleaning office, etc., 10.00; Department of Highways, auto service, 37.57; J. J. Fraser, office rent, etc., 260.00; M. George, garage rent, 72.00; Goodyear Tire & Rubber Co. of Canada, Ltd., tubes, tires, etc., 192.32; Grain Port Motors, Ltd., gas, etc., 250.02; Dr. A. R. Hanks, medical services, 100.00; H. W. Johnston, garage rent, 72.50; D. A. McClenahan, office and garage rent, 308.00; T. J. McNally, office and garage rent, 234.00; L. McNally, clerical services, 90.00; Marshall Motor Car Co., Ltd., repairs, etc., 161.83; P. J. Moloney, office and garage rent, 330.00; North Bay Garage, gasoline, etc., 242.06; K. O'Brien, typing, 250.00; Parker's Garage, Ltd., repairs, 17.95; Pine Cove Garage, gas, etc., 51.41; Richardson Battery and Ignition Service, battery, etc., 19.50; J. B. Ross, Ltd., oil, gas, etc., 81.95; Slater & Kelly, Ltd., gas and oil, etc., 200.64; B. Smith, typing, 25.00; N. H. Sutton, garage rent, 30.00; A. L. Torgis & Son, supplies, 32.57; F. Tuggey, garage rent, 10.00. Sundries, express, 12.60; postage, 182.40; telegrams, 36.45; petty disbursements, 64.07 ..... 3,803 19

Annual Conference of Health Officers ($962.00)

Royal York Hotel, Dinners re Annual Conference 962 00

District Officers of Health $43,131 57

MATERNAL AND CHILD HYGIENE AND PUBLIC HEALTH NURSING

Salaries ($33,216.67)

J. T. Phair	Director, Division of Child Hygiene	12 months	4,400 00
Elizabeth Kiteley	Medical Inspection Officer	12 "	2,400 00
Mary McKenzie Smith	" " "	12 "	2,000 00
E. S. Sumner	Senior Clerk Stenographer	12 "	1,500 00
L. K. Nichols	Clerk Stenographer, Group 1	12 "	1,125 00
E. L. Moore	Chief Public Health Nurse	11 "	2,291 67
H. E. Smith	Public Health Nurse	12 "	1,500 00
K. E. Osborne	" " "	12 "	1,500 00
I. U. Grenville	" " "	12 "	1,500 00
E. M. Squires	" " "	12 "	1,500 00
R. Hally	" " "	12 "	1,500 00
E. Bagshaw	" " "	12 "	1,500 00
H. G. Pennock	" " "	12 "	1,500 00
L. V. Vrooman	" " "	12 "	1,500 00
H. D. Shearer	" " "	12 "	1,500 00
H. Lunn	" " "	12 "	1,500 00
M. E. Howey	" " "	12 "	1,500 00
B. E. Johnson	" " "	12 "	1,500 00
D. H. Mickleborough	" " "	12 "	1,500 00

Travelling Expenses ($3,447.27)

E. L. Kiteley, 1,046.94; E. L. Moore, 446.00; J. T. Phair, 553.93; M. McK. Smith, 1,400.40 ..... 3,447 27

Main Office and Branches—Continued

Maternal and Child Hygiene—Continued

District Nurses, Services and Expenses, Grants, Purchase and Maintenance of Motor Cars ($43,988.77)

Temporary Services, $4,299.96.

M. E. Hopper	Public Health Nurse	12 months	1,500 00
Ora A. Lefler	" " "	12 "	1,299 96
E. R. Wheler	" " "	12 "	1,500 00

Grants, $22,699.96.

Ayr and North and South Dumfries, 500.00; Blind River, 333.33; Bowmanville, 250.00; Brantford, 800.00; Burlington, 500.00; Capreol, 500.00; Chapleau, 333.32; Cobalt, 500.00; Cornwall, 500.00; East Whitby Township, 249.99; East York Township, 800.00; Elmira, 458.33; Forest Hill, 500.00; Gananoque, 500.00; Haileybury, 500.00; Ingersoll, 500.00; Kenora, 250.00; Kitchener, 950.00; Lindsay, 500.00; New Toronto, 500.00; North Bay, 600.00; North York Township, 500.00; Oakville, 500.00; Orillia, 600.00; Oshawa, 900.00; Paris, 500.00; Penetanguishene, 41.66; Perth, 500.00; Port Arthur, 400.00; Port Colborne, 500.00; Renfrew, 500.00; Richmond Hill, 100.00; Simcoe, 500.00; St. Mary's, 500.00; St. Thomas, 600.00; Stratford, 600.00; Strathroy, 550.00; Sturgeon Falls, 500.00; Swansea, 333.33; Township of Teck, 500.00; Tecumseh and Sandwich East, 500.00; Timmins, 550.00; Township of Vaughan, 400.00; Wallaceburg, 500.00; Weston, 500.00; Woodstock, 600.00 .... 22,699 96

Travelling Expenses, $14,887.18.

E. Bagshaw, 904.62; I. Grenville, 1,005.03; R. Hally, 1,166.87; M. E. Hopper, 916.98; M. E. Howey, 1,683.70; B. E. Johnson, 872.30; O. R. Lefler, 849.49; H. Lunn, 791.10; D. H. Mickleborough, 1,409.35; K. E. Osborne, 964.25; H. G. Pennock, 625.85; H. D. Shearer, 570.05; H. E. Smith, 760.86; E. M. Squires, 632.52; L. V. Vrooman, 886.94; E. R. Wheler, 847.27 .... 14,887 18

Miscellaneous $2,101.67.

Alfred Garage, gas, 14.15; Bell Telephone Co. of Canada, tolls, 5.60; A. A. Burke & Co., auto repairs, etc., 60.44; Canadian Press Clipping Service, clippings, 90.00; Central Storage Garage, storage, 30.60; Chas. Dale, gas, 20.33; Dept. of Highways, auto service, 351.41; Dominion Transport Co., Ltd., cartage, 15.15; Forbes Bros., gas, 25.18; Goodyear Tire & Rubber Co., Ltd., tube, etc., 130.03; A. D. Gorrie & Co., Ltd., gas, 14.65; J. F. Hartz Co., Ltd., plasters, gauze, etc., 74.50; Harvey & Evans, auto repairs, 42.54; King's Printer, 383.07; Marshall Motor Car Co., Ltd., auto repairs, etc., 41.51; Chas. McFee, gas, 13.48; McGill Hardware, Ltd., repairs to car, etc., 68.64; J. W. McKinlay Auto Sales, gas, 14.55; John McVey, auto repairs, etc., 94.55; National Auto Sales, gas, etc., 64.49; G. S. Richardson Battery & Ignition Service, battery, 31.40; See & Duggan Motors, Ltd., radiator, etc., 25.85; Straight Service Stations, Ltd., gas, etc., 10.66; Sundry Persons, anti-freeze, 27.06; S. O. Ticknor, gas, 133.38; United Typewriter Co., Ltd., repairs, 26.65; Victorian Order of Nurses, Ontario, nurses' equipment, 17.50; M. Welden, garage rent, 30.00; Wentworth Motors, gas, 55.08; M. Young, rental of office, 80.00. Sundries—express, 41.20; postage, 9.50; petty disbursements, 71.30 .... 2,114 45

Less Auto Insurance 12 78

2,101 67

Maternal and Child Hygiene $80,652 71

DENTAL SERVICE

Salaries ($6,100.00)

F. J. Conboy	Director	12 months	4,000 00
Ralph N. Brownlow	Dentist	12 "	2,100 00

Contingencies ($896.23)

E. E. Inkster, services, clerk stenographer, 806.48; F. J. Conboy, travelling expenses, 191.30; King's Printer, 37.88; Price Foran, Ltd., insurance, 70.00. Sundries—petty disbursements, 13.00 .... 1,118 66

Less Refund T. Eaton Co., Ltd 22 43

" " Accountable Warrant, 1931, J. M. McIntyre 200 00

222 43

896 23

Main Office and Branches—Continued

Dental Service—Continued

Services and Expenses and for the Payment of Such Grants to Municipalities, etc. ($7,892.84)

Board of Education and School Boards, $5,698.10.

Barrie, 49.67; Belleville, 100.80; Braeside, 16.25; Brantford, 137.42; School Section No. 16, Etobicoke, 55.00; School Section No. 15, Fairbank, 691.69; Fort Frances, 90.00; London, 726.04; Long Branch, 65.00; New Toronto, 107.50; Ottawa, 40.32; Owen Sound, 300.00; Peterborough, 123.22; Port Arthur, 159.84; St. Catharines, 257.96; Thorold, School Section No. 2, 231.59; Thorold Township, Section No. 2, 56.04; Toronto, 500.00; Walkerville, 947.50; Windsor East, 231.20; Windsor, 398.50; Windsor East, Separate School, 360.56; Woodstock, 52.00	5,698 10

Boards of Health, $2,709.04.

Fairbank, School Section No. 15, 146.65; Hamilton, 750.00; Midland, 137.72; New Toronto, 142.50; North Bay, 100.00; Stamford, 60.00; Stamford Township, 135.00; St. Thomas, 186.74; Stratford, 247.72; Toronto, 500.00; Woodstock, 60.00; York Township, School Section Nos. 29, 32, 33, Medical Committee, 242.71	2,709 04

Miscellaneous, $985.70.

Ash-Temple Co., Ltd., dental supplies, etc., 172.53; R. N. Brownlow, drugs, travelling expenses, 141.15; Canadian Pacific Railway Co., repairs to dental car and supplies, 612.29; T. Eaton Co., Ltd., mops, etc., 33.48; Vortex Manufacturing Co., cups, etc., 13.35. Sundries—express, 7.95; petty disbursrments, 4.95		985 70
Total	9,392 84	
Less Repayments, Rosedale Chapter I.O.D.E., re equipment Dental car	1,500 00	
	7,892 84	
Dental Service	$14,889 07	

INSPECTION OF TRAINING SCHOOLS FOR NURSES

Salaries ($7,575.00)

A. Munn	Inspector of Training Schools for Nurses	12 months	2,700 00
I. H. Bray	Senior Clerk Stenographer	12 "	1,500 00
F. Gleed	Clerk, Group 2	12 "	1,125 00
Maude Dunlop	" " 2	12 "	1,125 00
A. Mason	Clerk Typist, Group 1	12 "	1,125 00

Services and Expenses ($4,230.16)

Temporary Services, Examiners, $1,683.50.

L. D. Acton, 216.00; E. Clarke, 284.00; B. Jeffrey, 216.00; E. L. Racicot, 37.50; Sister St. Elizabeth, 214.00; K. Scott, 250.00; G. Sharpe, 216.00; M. Thompson, 250.00	1,683 50

Travelling Expenses, $726.47.

L. D. Acton, 29.60; E. M. Elliott, 11.70; S. B. Hallman, .88; E. M. Hodgins, 2.02; B. Jeffrey, 20.05; J. K. McArthur, 3.85; E. M. McKee, 39.75; A. Munn, 481.61; S. A. Price, 4.21; F. C. Ritchie, 3.80; Sister M. Gonzaga, 1.25; Sister Madeleine of Jesus, 11.00; Sister St. Elizabeth, 48.05; F. M. Smith, 8.25; M. Thompson, 48.35; O. Waterman, 12.10	726 47

Miscellaneous, $1,820.19.

King's Printer, 1,185.81; A. Mason, stenographic services, 18.75; Remington Typewriters, Ltd., inspections, etc., 21.00; United Typewriter Co., Ltd., inspections, etc., 12.00; A. E. Venables, certificates, etc., 473.23. Sundries—postage, 1.59; express, 82.55; petty disbursements, 25.26		1,820 19
Inspection of Training Schools for Nurses	$11,805 16	

Main Office and Branches—Continued

PREVENTABLE DISEASES

Salaries ($23,750.01)

A. L. McKay	Director	12 months	4,400 00
Geo. C. Brink	Clinical Specialist	12 "	4,000 00
D. G. Wilson	" "	8 "	3,000 01
R. P. Hardman	" "	12 "	3,800 00
Agnes H. Haygarth	Nurse	12 "	1,500 00
K. C. Bricker	"	12 "	1,500 00
A. Poole	Clerk Stenographer, Group 1	12 "	1,200 00
C. Gazey	" " " 1	12 "	1,125 00
A. Keith	" " " 1	12 "	1,200 00
M. K. Ross	" " " 2	12 "	975 00
E. J. O'Brien	Laboratory Assistant " 2	12 "	1,050 00

Contingencies ($2,289.90)

Travelling Expenses.

K. C. Bricker, 64.80; A. H. Haygarth, 1,389.78; R. P. Hardman, 482.82; A. L. McKay, 352.50 ..... 2,289 90

Outbreaks of Diseases, Sanitary Investigations, etc., ($187,877.93)

Purchase of Anti-toxins $187,714.38.

Connaught Laboratories, antitoxin and insulin, 185,127.38; Sundry persons, blood donations, 2,587.00 ..... 187,714 38

Medical and Nursing Services, $82.00.

Dr. R. F. Malo, re James Deschamps, 24.00; Dr. J. K. McBane, 58.00 ..... 82 00

Miscellaneous, $81.55.

Canadian National Railways, fares, 26.50; J. E. Genley, travelling expenses, 27.00; Revillion Freres Trading Co., Ltd., provisions, 23.05; petty disbursements, 5.00 ..... 81 55

Treatment of Patients in Hospitals and Clinics, etc., and Grants and Equipment to Clinics ($94,984.17)

Services, $1,000.00.

N. F. W. Graham	Clinician	12 months	500 00
C. B. Waite	Clinical Specialist	12 "	500 00

Travelling Expenses, $29.45.

R. P. Hardman 29 45

Grants, $11,291.63.

Brantford General Hospital, 625.00; Hamilton General Hospital, 520.83; Kingston General Hospital, 250.00; City of Kitchener, 500.00; London Victoria Memorial Hospital, 1,000.00; Ottawa Board of Health, 416.66; Owen Sound Board of Health, 666.66; Peterborough Board of Health, 250.00; Port Arthur Board of Health, 166.66; St. Catharines General Hospital, 500.00; Sault Ste. Marie Board of Health, 125.00; Sudbury Board of Health, 2,000.00; Toronto General Hospital, 583.33; Toronto Grace Hospital, 625.00; Toronto Sick Children's Hospital, 520.83; Toronto St. Michael's Hospital, 500.00; Toronto Western Hospital, 1,000.00; Toronto Women's College Hospital, 625.00; Windsor Board of Health, 416.66 ..... 11,291 63

Treatment of Patients in Clinics $97,054.00.

Brantford General Hospital, 1,121.50; Fort William McKellar Hospital, 1,627.00; Hamilton General Hospital, 7,020.50; Kingston Board of Health, 232.00; Kingston General Hospital, 2,995.00; Kitchener and Waterloo Hospital, 1,279.00; London Victoria Memorial Hospital, 4,056.00; Ottawa Board of Health, 13,565.50; Owen Sound Board of Health, 1,944.00; St. Catharines General Hospital, 3,812.50; Sudbury Board of Health, 2,262.00; Toronto General Hospital, 18,367.00; Toronto Grace Hospital, 3,905.50; Toronto Sick Children's Hospital, 1,689.00; Toronto St. Michael's Hospital, 13,199.50; Toronto Western Hospital, 8,394.00; Toronto Women's College Hospital, 2,128.00; Windsor Board of Health, 9,456.00 ..... 97,054 00

Qualified Medical Practitioners, $33.50.

Dr. R. F. Malo, Field, Ont. 33 50

Miscellaneous, $18,001.52.

Beeton Dickenson & Co., needles, 125.00; Canadian Laboratory Supplies, Ltd., supplies, etc., 879.03; Collett-Sproule, Ltd., tubes, etc., 1,206.90; Connaught Laboratories, tuberculin, 16.25; Diarsenol Co., Inc., cylinders, 35.00; W. Erdman, cleaning clinic, 120.00; Fanning Steam Laundry, laundry, 84 30; Field, Love &

Main Office and Branches—Continued

Treatment of Patients in Hospitals and Clinics, etc.—Continued

Miscellaneous—Continued.

House, overhauling machine and inspection, 23.00; J. F. Hartz Co., Ltd., tablets, etc., 305.81; Honeywell-Lailey, Ltd., bismuth, 47.50; King's Printer, 1,033.11; Chas. Lee, laundry, 60.15; Main Laboratory, supplies, 81.20; Northrop & Lyman, Co., Ltd., seal oil, etc., 51.15; Parke Davis & Co., Ltd., chloroform, 24.00; Remington Typewriters, Ltd., inspection, 10.00; Richards Glass Co., Ltd., mercury, etc., 1,267.03; Synthetic Drug Co., Ltd., drugs, etc., 12,573.50. Sundries—customs, 17.18; express, .75; postage, 3.00; petty disbursements, 37.66 — 18,001 52

Total	127,410 10	
Less Dominion Government Grant	32,425 93	
Treatment of Patients in Hospitals and Clinics	$94,984 17	

Services and Expenses for Payment of Board for Tuberculosis Patients, etc. ($16,011.71)

Services, $4,050.00.

E. R. Harris	Clinical Specialist	2 months	450 00
K. M. Shorey	" "	12 "	3,600 00

Travelling Expenses, $5,303.20.

K. C. Bricker, 711.57; Geo. C. Brink, 894.50; E. R. Harris, 305.37; E. J. O'Brien, 1,657.40; K. M. Shorey, 1,104.90; D. G. Wilson, 629.46 — 5,303 20

Maintenance of Patients, $221.30.

Hamilton Health Association, 93.00; Toronto Hospital for Consumptives, 128.30 — 221 30

Miscellaneous, $6,437.21.

Burke Electric X-ray Co., Ltd., films, lamps, etc., 5,129.17; Connaught Laboratories, tuberculin, 21.25; Corbett-Cowley, Ltd., medical gowns, 24.00; King's Printer, 89.91; Lewis Mfg. Co. of Canada, Ltd., gauze, 36.54. Sundries—express, 1,107.33; petty disbursements, 29.01 — 6,437 21

Grant to Canadian Social Hygiene Council ($4,000.00)

Canadian Social Hygiene Council — 4,000 00

Preventable Diseases — $328,913 72

INDUSTRIAL HYGIENE

Salaries ($35,300.00)

J. Grant Cunningham	Director	12 months	4,400 00
A. R. Riddell	Clinical Specialist	12 "	4,000 00
Dr. F. M. R. Bulmer	Research Specialist	12 "	4,000 00
H. E. Rothwell	Assistant Chemist, Group 1	12 "	2,400 00
W. C. Millar	Chief Sanitary Inspector	12 "	2,700 00
R. B. McCauley	Sanitary Inspector	12 "	2,200 00
J. Richardson	" "	12 "	2,200 00
D. McKee	" "	12 "	2,200 00
H. McIntyre	" "	12 "	2,100 00
A. O'Hara		12 "	1,900 00
J. Sime	" "	12 "	1,900 00
Geo. Williams	Clerk, Group 1	12 "	1,300 00
Vera V. Harrison	" " 1	12 "	1,300 00
G. M. Jose	Senior Clerk Stenographer	12 "	1,400 00
H. L. Spereman	" " "	12 "	1,300 00

Services and Expenses, ($11,845.07)

Temporary Services, $2,149.98

J. D. Leitch	Physicist	6 months	1,249 98
M. McBride	Clerk Typist, Group 2	12 "	900 00

Travelling Expenses, $7,090.19.

F. M. R. Bulmer, 214.10; J. G. Cunningham, 530.24; J. L. Leitch, 84.70; R. B. McCauley, 896.93; H. McIntyre, 760.16; D. McKee, 828.70; W. C. Millar, 1,077.41; A. O'Hara, 752.86; J. Richardson, 756.51; A. R. Riddell, 612.40; H. E. Rothwell, 26.80; J. Sime, 1,042.33; Geo. Williamson, 7.05 — 7,590 19

Less Refund Accountable Warrant, H. E. Rothwell	200 00		
" " " " A. R. White	300 00		
		500 00	
			7,090 19

Main Office and Branches—Continued

Industrial Hygiene—Continued

Miscellaneous, $2,604.90.

Acme Block Co., rent of office, 225.00; Bell Telephone Co. of Canada, rentals, 50.50; tolls, 20.97; Canadian Laboratory Supplies, Ltd., calcium, etc., 40.52; Canadian Press Clipping Service, clippings, 36.00; Central Scientific Co. of Canada, Ltd., benzoil, etc., 23.19; Dr. W. J. Cook, rent, 150.00; T. N. Dean, tabulation, 76.38; Department of Highways, auto service, 23.76; L. E. Dodson, posters, 15.00; T. G. Dowling, sketch, 25.00; A. Duke, rent, 180.00; T. Eaton Co., Ltd., coats, 11.40; B. Green, posters, 30.00; Hudson's Bay Co., rent, 90.00; King's Printer, 539.52; Main Laboratory, supplies, 223.95; A. G. Newell & Co., folios, 38.25; Photo Engravers & Electrotypers, Ltd., bulletins, 86.70; A. M. Proctor, posters, 15.00; Royal Sanitary Institute, fees, 15.00; Sundry persons, cleaning offices, 58.00; E. Vincent, typing, 190.00; Norah Wilson, services as stenographer, 200.00. Sundries—cartage, 2.45; car tickets, 5.25; express, 13.70; postage, 85.19; telegrams, 38.41; petty disbursements, 95.76........................ 2,604 90

Industrial Hygiene.................................. $47,145 07

SANITARY ENGINEERING ($47,773.58)

Salaries ($27,858.34)

A. E. Berry	Provincial Sanitary Engineer		12 months		4,200 00
A. V. DeLaporte	Chemist		12 "		3,300 00
D. H. Matheson	Assistant Chemist,	Group 1	12 "		2,000 00
G. A. H. Burn	Assistant Sanitary Engineer	" 1	12 "		2,700 00
O. V. Ball	" " "	" 1	12 "		2,550 00
E. W. Johnston	" " "	" 1	12 "		2,550 00
A. T. Byram	" " "	" 1	12 "		2,400 00
Geo. M. Galimberti	" " "	" 1	12 "		2,200 00
H. G. Tyler	Sanitary Investigator		12 "		1,600 00
L. R. Ridgeway	Laboratory Attendant		12 "	1,400 00	
			Less Leave of Absence	116 66	1,283 34
G. Kinsella	Senior Clerk Stenographer		12 months		1,500 00
M. E. Craig	Clerk Stenographer, Group 2		12 "	900 00	
			Less Leave of Absence	150 00	750 00
M. MacBeth	Clerk Typist	" 2	12 months		825 00

Services and Expenses ($19,915.24)

Temporary Services, $9,265.67.

W. S. R. Edmunds	Assistant Sanitary Engineer, Group	1	12 months	1,200 00
R. A. Irwin	" " " "	1	7½ "	1,125 00
L. A. Kay	" " " "	1	12 "	1,200 00
A. McLaren	" " " "	1	12 "	1,800 00
W. B. Webster	" " " "	1	12 "	1,800 00
R. C. Williamson	" " " "	1	7½ "	1,125 00
M. G. McMillan	Clerk Typist	1	12 "	900 00
E. L. LeMesurier	Clerk Stenographer	2	2 "	115 67

Travelling Expenses, $8,188.32.

O. V. Ball, 343.50; A. E. Berry, 783.61; G. A. H. Burn, 548.57; A. T. Byram, 486.41; A. V. DeLaporte, 507.71; W. L. Edmunds, 573.84; G. M. Galimberti, 1,161.61; R. A. Irwin, 496.62; E. W. Johnston, 414.90; L. A. Kay, 266.41; J. A. McLaren, 500.27; D. H. Matheson, 473.76; H. G. Tyler, 623.84; L. Ridgeway, 99.45; W. B. Webster, 771.32; R. C. Williamson, 136.50...................... 8,188 32

Miscellaneous, $2,461.25.

Art Metropole, pens, etc., 10.22; Artists' Supply Co., Ltd., cards, 11.75; Bell Telephone Co. of Canada, tolls, 1.35; Canadian Laboratory Supplies, Ltd., flasks, etc., 173.92; Canadian Milk Products, Ltd., powder, 18.20; Central Scientific Co. of Canada, Ltd., thermometers, etc., 66.77; Collett-Sproule, Ltd., bottles, 72.58; Cherry-Burrell Co. of Canada, Ltd., sterilizer, etc., 44.12; Department of Highways, auto service, 66.55; Department of Public Works, blue prints, etc., 33.23; Eastman Kodak Stores, Ltd., films, etc., 11.36; T. Eaton Co., Ltd., soap, etc., 31.24; Dorothy E. Farr, nets, 28.00; Firstbrook Boxes, Ltd., boxes, 24.20; J. F. Hartz Co., Ltd., tablets, etc., 33.05; Johnson Matthey & Co., dishes, 12.43; King's Printer, 682.24; Liquid Carbonic Canadian Corp., Ltd., carbonic

Main Office and Branches—Continued

Sanitary Engineering—Continued

Miscellaneous—Continued.

gas, 10.00; Main Laboratory, supplies, 11.64; Merck & Co., Ltd., chloride, 17.06; Nichols Chemical Co., Ltd., chloride of lime, etc., 27.06; Province of Ontario Pictures, photographs, 15.00; J. F. Raw Co., Ltd., cotton, map mounting, etc., 127.45; Richards Glass Co., Ltd., jars, etc., 135.85; United Typewriter Co., Ltd., inspections, etc., 27.62; Wilson Scientific Co., Ltd., boards, etc., 216.21. Sundries—cartage, .80; customs, 3.00; express, 472.74; freight, 3.33; telegrams, .65; postage, 7.35; petty disbursements, 64.28 .... 2,461 25

Sanitary Engineering $47,773 58

LABORATORIES

Main Laboratory

Salaries ($55,350.00)

Name	Position	Period	Amount
A. L. McNab	Director of Provincial Laboratories	12 months	4,200 00
W. M. Wilson	Pathologist and Bacteriologist	12 "	3,600 00
A. R. Bonham	Chemist	12 "	3,300 00
J. E. Fasken	Assistant Chemist, Group 1	12 "	2,700 00
P. F. Morley	" " " 1	12 "	2,400 00
W. Pratt	" " " 2	12 "	2,000 00
A. D. McClure	Assistant Bacteriologist	12 "	2,100 00
G. J. Morrison	Senior Clerk	12 "	2,000 00
G. Matthews	Senior Laboratory Assistant	12 "	1,800 00
V. Crossley	" " "	12 "	1,800 00
R. E. Packham	Laboratory Assistant, Group 1	12 "	1,600 00
H. G. Killham	" " " 1	12 "	1,600 00
M. D. Ward	" " " 1	12 "	1,600 00
W. Fenton	" " " 1	12 "	1,600 00
Jean Harrison	" " " 1	12 "	1,400 00
A. M. Chew	" " " 1	12 "	1,300 00
M. E. Locke	" " " 1	12 "	1,300 00
H. Wright	" " " 1	12 "	1,300 00
M. Fields	" " " 2	12 "	1,200 00
B. Baycroft	" " " 2	12 "	1,125 00
R. W. Hollinger	Laboratory Clerk Attendant	12 "	1,600 00
E. Jewel	Laboratory Attendant, Group 1	12 "	1,500 00
John Cogle	" " " 1	12 "	1,300 00
Jas. R. Buchanan	" " " 1	12 "	1,200 00
L. Brydson	" " " 2	12 "	1,050 00
Evelyn F. Tuft	" " " 2	12 "	825 00
Ruby I. Hughes	" " " 2	12 "	825 00
M. J. Benning	Clerk Group 1	12 "	1,600 00
I. Crew	Clerk Stenographer " 1	12 "	1,125 00
Theresa M. Sullivan	" " " 1	12 "	1,050 00
O. D. Teasdale	" " " 2	12 "	900 00
H. M. Heustis	" " " 2	8 "	650 00
R. Schiff	Clerk Typist " 1	12 "	975 00
D. Price	" " " 2	12 "	825 00

Services and Expenses ($35,192.15)

Temporary Services, $14,762.02.

Name	Position	Period	Amount
J. E. Bates	Pathologist	12 months	3,600 00
M. H. Brockway	Clerk Typist Group 2	⅜ "	43 27
M. E. Copp	Laboratory Assistant " 1	12 "	1,200 00
D. Dow	" " " 1	12 "	1,200 00
M. Harrison	Laboratory Attendant " 2	12 "	750 00
W. B. McClure	Bacteriologist	5 "	1,125 00
E. E. McNally	Laboratory Attendant, Group 2	9 "	675 00
M. Mercer	" " " 2	12 "	825 00
W. A. Murphy	" " " 2	12 "	750 00
E. M. Parsons	" " " 1	12 "	1,200 00
C. R. Smith	Assistant Bacteriologist	12 "	1,800 00
I. Stephen	Clerk Stenographer, Group 1	12 "	975 00
W. G. Stewart	Junior Laboratory Assistant	3½ "	218 75
T. J. Wright	Laboratory Assistant, Group 1	4 "	400 00

Main Office and Branches—Continued

Laboratories—Continued

Main Laboratory—Continued

Winery Inspectors at $5.00 per diem, $90.00.

E. A. Bedell, 20.00; F. F. Guscott, 20.00; S. F. Ward, 20.00; G. A. Wiggins, 30.00 — 90 00

Extra Services, $1,990.70.

B. Baycroft, 44.00; A. R. Bonham, 12.00; L. Brydson, 214.00; J. R. Buchanan, 123.25; A. M. Chew, 7.00; J. Cogle, 238.03; M. Copp, 34.00; V. Crossley, 52.00; W. Fenton, 246.78; E. Jewell, 185.14; A. McClure, 79.50; A. L. MacNab, 80.00; E. E. McNally, 12.00; M. Mercer, 6.00; W. Murphy, 190.25; R. E. Packham, 123.75; C. L. Smith, 213.00; G. Stewart, 9.00; E. Tuft, 7.00; M. D. Ward, 52.00; W. M. Wilson, 60.00; H. Wright, 2.00 .... 1,990 70

Travelling Expenses, $510.43.

L. Backus, 39.67; E. A. Bedell, 28.56; A. R. Bonham, 39.80; J. E. Faskin, 14.20; J. J. Freed, 5.50; F. F. Guscott, 8.10; P. Labasco, 2.45; A. L. MacNab, 163.95; A. D. McClure, 107.20; S. F. Ward, 58.24; A. C. Watts, 8.76; Geo. A. Wiggins, 11.25; W. Wilson, 22.75 .... 510 43

Laboratory Supplies and Equipment, $20,106.27.

Associated Chemical Co. of Canada, 13.72; J. & A. Aziz, 70.50; Beeton Dickenson & Co., 253.20; Bureau of Laboratories, 11.00; M. C. Burns, 20.30; Canadian Charmalax Co., 198.90; Canadian Industries, Ltd., 200.15; Canadian Industrial Alcohol Co., Ltd., 45.00; Canadian Laboratory Supplies, Ltd., 5,939.97; Canadian Packers, Ltd., 24.25; Carning Glass Works, 421.83; A. Carpento, 371.15; B. Caren, 16.80; Central Scientific Co., Ltd., 993.06; R. H. Choppel, 67.04; G. A. Chater, 30.00; A. R. Clark & Co., 26.24; F. Cogo, 64.50; Collett-Sproule, Ltd., 1,178.82; H. G. Cook, 144.12; Corrugated Paper Box Co., Ltd., 176.55; Cross Paper Products Corporation, 50.71; Geo. Crouse, Jr., 20.40; E. Cullen, 40.70; F. H. Dance, 39.60; Mrs. A. E. Davidson, 25.20; Dominion Rubber Co., Ltd., 40.90; K. W. Duncan, 35.40; E. B. Eddy Co., Ltd., 31.50; C. Emmett, 512.55; Firstbrook Boxes, Ltd., 30.00; L. Fleming, 16.95; W. Garden, 68.50; Gooderham & Worts, Ltd., 163.98; Mrs. Alex. Gordon, 10.50; Gunn's, Ltd., 14.40; J. F. Hartz Co., Ltd., 1,581.66; Honeywell-Lailey, Ltd., 23.20; Imperial Oil, Ltd., 19.01; Johnson Matthey & Co., of Canada, Ltd., 91.72; Ingram & Bell, Ltd., 663.48; Kelley Feed & Seed Co., 391.37; Lever Bros., Ltd., 41.54; Lewis Manufacturing Co., Ltd., 310.07; Liquor Control Board of Ontario, 87.38; Mallingskrodt Chemical Works, Ltd., 91.50; Michigan Department of Health, 11.00; New York State Department of Health, 24.14; Ontario Cork Co., Ltd., 666.00; Parke Davis & Co., 1,122.52; F. A. Past, 10.80; G. Pearce, 98.40; C. Pickering, 33.80; Richards Glass Co., Ltd., 1,992.49; Robbins & Myers Co., 28.66; Simpson Planing Mills Co., 191.25; Geo. Sparrow & Co., 52.05; Standard Chemical Co., Ltd., 115.25; Superior Wire Works, 148.40; University of Michigan, 22.00; West Company, 24.08; T. C. Wheaton Co., 380.16; White & Thomas, 416.15; Wilson Scientific Co., Ltd., 27.29; G. H. Woods & Co., 23.25; petty disbursements, 49.26 .... 20,106 27

Miscellaneous, $6,728.28.

Beach Laundry, laundry, 82.69; Canadian General Electric Co., Ltd., fuses, etc., 11.40; Department of Highways, auto service, 591.34; Diamond Cleanser, Ltd., compound, 21.00; Dictaphone Sales Corporation, Ltd., inspection, 30.00; T. Eaton Co., Ltd., steps, etc., 31.34; E. B. Eddy Co., Ltd., towels, 61.80; Field, Love & House, inspections, 12.00; Improved Mailing Case Co., cases, 305.85; King's Printer, 4,175.50; Rice Lewis & Son, Ltd., paint, etc., 45.16; Queen City Laundry, laundry, 519.73; Ratcliffe Paper Co., Ltd., paper, 94.52; Remington Typewriters, Ltd., inspections, etc., 20.00; Rogers Electric Co., Ltd., lamps, 13.46; Scales & Roberts, Ltd., matches, 34.41; Thomas & Corney Typewriters, Ltd., repairs and inspections, 11.75; United Typewriter Co., Ltd., inspections, 45.00; University of Toronto, binding records, etc., 20.80; Wesco Paint Products Co., soap, 196.00; The West Co., exchange on cheques, etc., 37.36; White & Thomas, iron, etc., 133.37. Sundries—customs, 83.24; cartage, 2.15; express 62.80; freight, 46.92; petty disbursements, 38.69 .... 6,728 28

Total Services and Expenses		44,187 70	
Less Sundry supplies transferred to Public Health Laboratories		8,995 55	
		35,192 15	
Main Laboratory	$90,542 15		

Main Office and Branches—Continued

PUBLIC HEALTH LABORATORIES

Salaries ($21,275.00)

Name	Position	Period	Amount
N. F. W. Graham	Director, Sault Ste. Marie	12 months	2,900 00
W. A. R. Michell	" North Bay	12 "	2,800 00
J. H. Lawson	Laboratory Assistant, Group 1, North Bay	12 "	1,500 00
J. W. Bell	Director, Fort William	12 "	3,000 00
W. J. Thompson	Laboratory Assistant, Group 1, Ft. William	12 "	1,600 00
Rhoda M. Gordon	Clerk Stenographer " 2, "	12 "	900 00
F. L. Letts	Director, Ottawa	12 "	3,300 00
J. Barron	Senior Laboratory Assistant, Ottawa	12 "	1,700 00
A. White	Laboratory Assistant, Group 1 "	12 "	1,400 00
N. Martin	" " " 2 "	12 "	1,050 00
J. McKinnon	Clerk Stenographer " 1 "	12 "	1,125 00

Services and Expenses ($13,313.61)

Fort William.

J. W. Bell, travelling expenses, 98.50; Mrs. M. Barrynowski, pigs, 64.80; Mrs. R. Cockburn, cleaning office, 14.00; Fitzsimmon's Fruit Co., Ltd., carrots, 59.15; Fort William Ice Co., ice, 72.00; B. Hardy, services, 900.00; Main Laboratory, supplies, 973.27; Mount McKay Feed Co., oats, 12.35; Municipal Hospital, pigs, 11.70; Mrs. S. Whittaker, care of sheep, 30.00. Sundries—cartage, 2.75; freight, 38.31; express, 53.20; postage, 120.00; telegrams, 5.75; petty disbursements, 26.49 .... 2,482 27

Kingston.

Dr. Jas. Miller, travelling expenses, 21.20; Main Laboratory, supplies, 749.47. Sundries—express, 31.83; postage, 80.00 .... 882 50

London.

Main Laboratory, supplies, 2,839.61; Dr. A. J. Slack, 21.35. Sundries—express, 181.12; freight, 3.33; postage, 549.61; petty disbursements, 1.00 .... 3,596 02

North Bay.

Mrs. J. Allen, laundry, 34.97; Bay Electric Co., repairs, 24.70; Bell Telephone Co., of Canada, rental, 104.60; tolls, 45.64; Thomas Comba, repairs to cages, 48.92; J. Conray, services, 790.63; Main Laboratory, supplies, 789.50; W. A. R. Michell, travelling expenses, 52.95; Rankin's Grocery, groceries, etc., 112.06; J. Richardson, care of animals, 10.00; E. J. Roche, garage, 24.00; D. Shepherd, services, 62.00; H. Stockdale, ice, 90.00; United Typewriter Co., Ltd., inspections, 11.00. Sundries—cartage, 5.00; express, 77.72; postage, 132.00; telegrams, 2.30; petty disbursements, 9.12 .... 2,427 11

Ottawa.

W. R. Argue, hay and feed, 42.96; Bell Telephone Co., of Canada, rental, 69.41; tolls, .82; Mrs. E. Jeleniuk, cleaning office, 345.00; G. E. Kingsburgy, ice, 120.00; Dr. F. L. Letts, travelling expenses, 25.90; Main Laboratory, supplies, 2,342.54; J. MacAlpine, services, 1,200.00; F. MacAlpine, services, 162.00; E. E. McNally, services, 225.00; travelling expenses, 11.45; United Typewriter Co., Ltd., ribbons, etc., 11.00; Vail's Laundry, laundry, 62.27; Mrs. M. Zoholsky, vegetables, 187.05 Sundries—express, 35.70; freight, 33.43; postage, 352.00; telegrams, 1.60; petty disbursements, 25.15 .... 5,253 28

Sault Ste. Marie.

N. F. W. Graham, travelling expenses, 55.10; Main Laboratory, supplies, 429.12; Sundries—express, 65.33; postage, 55.50 .... 605 05

Peterborough.

Main Laboratory, supplies 92 38

Total services and expenses		15,338 61
Less contributions, City of Ottawa	900 00	
" " Sault Ste. Marie	1,125 00	
		2,025 00
		13,313 61

Grants

Grant to Public Health Laboratory, Queen's University ($3,300.00)

Queen's University 3,300 00

Main Office and Branches—Continued

Public Health Laboratories—Continued

Grant to Public Health Laboratory, Peterborough ($2,000.00)

City Treasurer, Peterborough 2,000 00

Grant to Public Health Laboratory, Peterborough, for Equipment, Maintenance and Supplies ($311.38)

City Treasurer, Peterborough 311 38

Grant to Public Health Laboratory, Institute of Public Health, Western University, London, Ontario ($6,000.00)

Western University 6,000 00

Public Health Laboratories $46,199 99

PUBLIC HEALTH EDUCATION

Salaries (8,625.00)

M. Power	Director of Publicity	12 months	2,550 00
B. Knox	Senior Clerk	12 "	1,900 00
E. Jones	Attendant in charge of Health Exhibit	12 "	2,000 00
E. Butt	Clerk Stenographer, Group 1	12 "	1,200 00
C. Crown	Filing Clerk, " 1	12 "	975 00

Public Health Exhibit, Services and Expenses ($2,029.00)

Travelling Expenses.

M. Power 45 10

Miscellaneous.

F. Bracken, services as helper, 84.00; Canadian National Exhibition, electrical work, 401.07; R. F. Collins, displays, etc., 403.50; Cox & Andrews, posters, 61.80; Department of Highways, auto service, 211.79; T. Eaton Co., Ltd., towelling, flanellette, etc., 75.37; Film & Slide Co., of Canada, Ltd., lamps, etc., 33.10; Abbot Graham, services as helper, 80.00; Geo. Kline, decorations, 13.75; E. May, services as nightwatchman, 72.00; Province of Ontario Pictures, prints, 25.00; Rapid Grip & Batten, Ltd., photos, 204.70; W. W. Stallworthy, exhibit, etc., 30.25; Sundry clerks, meals, 127.28; H. C. Tugwell & Co., Ltd., tracings, etc., 11.60; J. J. Turner & Sons, Ltd., repairs, 25.00; H. Wainwright, rental of furniture, 50.00. Sundries—cartage, 13.50; customs, 5.00; express, 9.55; petty disbursements, 45.64 .... 1,983 90

Services and Expenses ($10,675.52)

Temporary Services.

G. Vale .... Clerk, Group 3 .... 12 months 750 00

Travelling Expenses.

E. Jones, 126.48; Mary Power, 516.59; G. M. Vale, 6.65 .... 649 72

Miscellaneous.

Addressograph-Multigraph of Canada, Ltd., inspections, etc., 24.61; Brighton Laundry, laundry, 33.07; Mrs. A. Diplock, making clothing, 15.90; Dairymen's League Co-operative Association, posters, etc., 19.26; Department of Highways, auto service, 59.71; Department of Public Works, blue prints, 14.18; T. Eaton Co., Ltd., rental of torcheries, etc., 16.35; Merle Foster, nut animals, 10.00; Fleurette Studios, posters, 2,263.48; King's Printer, 5,465.88; W. S. Larkin, posters, 14.83; E. Le Boeuf, posters, 10.17; Main Laboratory, medical supplies, 28.30; Peake & Whittingham, prints, 15 00; Province of Ontario Pictures, prints, 88.80; Rapid Grip & Batten, Ltd., photos, 22.75; Mrs. M. Smith, sweaters, etc., 51.60; S. Towers, posters, 15.00; J. J. Turner & Sons, tent, 71.45; United Typewriter Co., Ltd., card clips, etc., 19.56; University of Toronto, programmes, 158.17; Ruth Webb, posters, services teaching, 188.50; F. W. Woolworth & Co., Ltd., jars, 13.35. Sundries—cartage, 57.43; customs, 35.60; express, 485.27; freight, 4.53; newspapers and periodicals, 5.28; petty disbursements, 67.77 .... 9,275 80

Advertising ($583.50)

Academy of Medicine, 144.00; Canadian Public Health Association, 360.00; Mrs. W. A. Quibell, 50.00; The Canadian Nurse, 12.00; The Swimmer, 17.50 .... 583 50

Public Health Education $21,913 02

Main Office and Branches $795,492.72

HOSPITALS BRANCH

Salaries ($80,635.41)

Name	Position	Period			Amount
H. M. Robbins	Deputy Minister of Hospitals	12	months		5,400 00
B. T. McGhie	Chief Director, Hospital Services for the Province	12	"	10,000 00	
	Less voluntary reduction			1,562 50	8,437 50
D. R Fletcher	Senior Assistant Physician, Ontario Hospitals	1	"		316 66
F. G. Beardall	Chief Clerk	12	"		3,300 00
I. R. Aikens	Head Clerk	12	"		3,000 00
Chas. W. Anderson	" "	12	"		2,550 00
Jas. Lonergan	Principal Clerk	12	"		2,400 00
Edward Hill	" "	12	"		2,300 00
J. P. Sharp	Senior Clerk	12	"		2,000 00
Arthur W. Ward	" "	12	"		1,700 00
C. D. Gourlie	" "	12	"		1,800 00
Phillip M. Till	Clerk, Group 1	12	"		1,500 00
Cecilia Clementi	" " 1	12	"		1,400 00
Bruce F. Anderson	" " 1	12	"		1,200 00
Viola Webster	Secretarial Stenographer	12	"		1,300 00
Gladys Courtney	Senior Clerk Stenographer	12	"		1,500 00
Sadie Scott	" " "	12	"		1,400 00
Kathleen Towers	" " "	12	"		1,400 00
Dorothy E. Wilson	" " "	12	"		1,200 00
Evelyn MacKay	Clerk Stenographer, Group 1	12	"		1,200 00
Rose Hargrave	" " " 1	12	"		1,125 00
Freda Jones	" " " 1	11	"		1,031 25
Enid B. Rickman	" " " 2	12	"		975 00
Mary E. Welsh	" " " 2	12	"		975 00
Isobel C. M. Kennedy	" " " 2	12	"		900 00
Edna Porte	Senior Filing Clerk	12	"		1,600 00
Vera G. Peterson	Clerk Typist, Group 1	12	"		975 00
Archibald L. McPherson	Inspector of Hospitals and Charitable Institutions	12	"		4,000 00
Robert Beatty	Farm Director	12	"		2,300 00
George N. Williams	Maintenance Architect	12	"		3,450 00
T. P. Bellinger	Clerk of Works	12	"		2,000 00
Chas. J. Fox	Provincial Bailiff	12	"		2,000 00
Agnes Porter	" "	12	"		1,600 00
Thomas W. Barnard	Heating Engineer	12	"		2,200 00
W. F. Shepherd	Senior Draughtsman	12	"		2,400 00
Victor L. Gladman	" "	12	"		2,200 00
C. B. Janes	Placement Officer	12	"		2,800 00
John A. Wilkinson	" "	12	"		2,800 00

Salaries Not Provided for (Statutory), ($925.00)

Name	Position	Period			Amount
Eva R. Little	Clerk Stenographer, Group 1	9		843 75	
Grace H. Evans	Clerk Typist, " 1	1		81 25	

Contingencies ($49,159.88)

Temporary Services ($24,379.96).

Name	Position	Period		Amount
Andrew A. Allan	Assistant	12	months	1,800 00
William J. Annand	Senior Clerk	12	"	1,599 96
Grace A. Bland	Clerk Stenographer	12	"	825 00
George Bray	Office Boy	12	"	525 00
R. Ross Burrows	Orchardist	10	"	1,083 30
Velma G. J. Caven	Clerk, Group 3	10	"	625 00
Anna M. Duncan	Clerk Stenographer, " 2	2⅔	"	192 50
George A. Firby	Senior Clerk	12	"	1,599 96
Jack Fish	Errand Boy	1	"	35 43
Jason A. Hannah	Neuro Pathologist	12	"	3,000 00
Margaret Irwin	Clerk Stenographer, Group 1	11 5/6	"	965 63
Emma Le Mesurier	Clerk Stenographer	1	"	68 75
Henry J. Mattocks	Clerk Stenographer, Group 1	12	"	975 00
George A. Morell	Senior Clerk	12	"	1,599 96
C. Roger Myers	Consultant Psychologist	12	"	1,200 00
Delphina O'Neill	Clerk Stenographer, Group 2	11⅓	"	780 05
Daniel H. Presho	Clerk, " 1	12	"	1,177 78
Joan E. I. Read	Clerk Stenographer, " 2	4¾	"	811 78

Hospitals Branch—Continued

Contingencies—Continued

Temporary Services—Continued.

William T. Roberts	Senior Clerk	12 months	1,599 96
Margaret S. Thompson	Laboratory Assistant, Group 1	4 "	400 00
Betty M. Wallace	Clerk Stenographer, " 2	3½ "	237 98
Chester C. Woods	Senior Draughtsman	12 "	2,100 00
Effie I. Woolley	Clerk Typist, Group 1	12 "	900 00
Margaret J. Wright	Filing Clerk	3⅓ "	276 92

Travelling Expenses, $7,407.61.

A. A. Allan, 9.45; C. W. Anderson, 14.50; T. W. Barnard, 889.82; F. G. Beardall, 86.72; R. Beatty, 596.98; T. P. Bellinger, 401.17; R. R. Burrows, 162.40; E. C. Clark, 104.49; F. J. Conboy, 12.85; K. Day, 19.53; D. R. Fletcher, 33.80; V. L. Gladman, 16.90; T. M. Gourlay, 66.05; J. A. Hannah, 163.89; J. Hillock, 7.10; C. B. Janes, 1,075.59; H. P. LeVesconte, 36.60; B. T. McGhie, 677.15; W. L. McJannet, 366.17; C. R. Myers, 157.65; H. M. Robbins, 370.96; M. Rose, 5.65; F. Ruston, 7.65; W. F. Shepherd, 80.75; W. K. Siddall, 7.10; A. M. Smith, 600.44; J. Vance, 93.62; A. W. Ward, 3.45; J. A. Wilkinson, 1,162.61; G. N. Williams, 11.15; C. C. Woods, 165.42 .... 7,407 61

Miscellaneous, $17,372.31.

Addressograph-Multigraph of Canada, Ltd., inspections, etc., 32.48; Burroughs Adding Machine of Canada, Ltd., inspections, etc., 15.75; Canadian Inspection & Testing Co., Ltd., analysis of boiler compound, 170.00; Corrugated Paper Box Co., Ltd., boxes, 24.50; Department of Highways, auto service, 1,508.27; Department of Public Works, building paper, 113.04; Goodyear Tire & Rubber Co., Ltd., tires, etc., 83.56; Hamilton Spectator, advertising, 75.00; J. F. Hartz & Co., Ltd., drugs, etc., 48.80; King's Printer, 13,950.95; Rice Lewis & Son, Ltd., handcuffs, 10.50; Province of Ontario Pictures, frames, prints, 12.70; See & Duggan Motors Ltd., auto repairs, 39.88; Sentinel Review, advertising, 64.00; Smith & Walsh, insurance premiums, 23.34; The Stevens Co., sphygmomanometer, 22.50; Swayze's, auto repairs, 49.00; A. L. Torgis & Co., auto repairs, 56.78; E. M. Tozer, grinding coal samples, 94.50; United Typewriter Co., Ltd., rental, repairs, etc., 334.67. Sundries—cartage, 4.18; car tickets, 177.00; express, 9.75; freight, .80; newspapers and periodicals, 143.67; postage, 20.00; telegrams, 247.46; petty disbursements, 39.23 .... 17,372 31

Hospitals Branch **129,795.29**

HOSPITALS AND CHARITIES BRANCH

Salaries ($7,500.00)

Bertram K. Coulson	Principal Clerk	12 months	2,400 00
Cecil W. Garthwaite	" "	12 "	2,200 00
J. Buchan Hardie	Clerk, Group 1	12 "	1,500 00
Nellie M. Simpson	" " 1	12 "	1,400 00

Contingencies ($4,348.99)

Travelling Expenses, $4,208.83.

A. A. Allan, 838.78; C. W. Garthwaite, 1,515.62; A. L. McPherson, 445.17; C. A. Morrell, 1,324.81; H. M. Robbins, 84.45 .... 4,208 83

Miscellaneous, $140.16.

King's Printer, 130.41. Sundries, newspapers and periodicals, 9.75 .... 140 16

Hospitals ($1,100,834.83)

General Hospitals, $1,083,438.43.

Alliston Stevenson Memorial, 1,803.60; Almonte Rosamond Memorial, 1,330.00; Barrie Royal Victoria, 2,395.50; Belleville, 6,602.50; Bowmanville, 1,063.80; Brampton Peel Memorial, 3,180.70; Brantford, 21,253.80; Brockville St. Vincent de Paul, 3,405.10; Brockville, 3,680.20; Chapleau Lady Minto, 2,122.70; Chatham, 7,775.60; Chatham St. Joseph's, 2,043.60; Clinton Public, 187.80; Cobalt Mines, 1,394.70; Cobourg, 2,000.50; Cochrane, Lady Minto, 7,017.60; Collingwood, 3,962.10; Cornwall, 8,022.30; Cornwall Hotel Dieu, 8,400.10; Durham Red Cross Memorial, 1,188.40; Fergus Groves Memorial, 575.30; Fergus Royal Alexandra, 558.30; Fort Erie Douglas Memorial, 302.70; Fort William McKellar, 20,008.30; Galt, 5,733.40; Goderich General and Marine, 1,401.70; Guelph, 6,077.10; Guelph St. Joseph's, 7,882.90; Haileybury Misericordia, 3,306.10;

Hospitals and Charities Branch—Continued

Hospitals—Continued

General Hospitals—Continued.

Hamilton, 69,158.50; Hamilton, Mount Hamilton, 10,551.60; Hamilton St. Joseph's, 6,152.20; Hanover Memorial, 1,350.80; Hawkesbury Notre Dame, 2,476.80; Hearst, St. Paul's, 2,602.85; Ingersoll Alexandra, 966.90; Iroquois Falls Anson, 3,344.35; Kenora, 1,612.10; Kenora St. Joseph's, 2,255.40; Kincardine, 1,427.60; Kingston, 20,508.60; Kingston, Hotel Dieu, 10,677.10; Kitchener and Waterloo, 4,751.00; Kitchener and Waterloo St. Mary's, 10,924.00; Lindsay Ross Memorial, 2,812.80; Listowel Memorial, 1,356.90; London Victoria 32,144.00; London St. Joseph's, 6,353.10; Matheson Rosedale War Memorial, 1,307.50; Mattawa, 3,204.20; Midland, St. Andrew's, 3,371.80; Mindemoya, 483.70; Mount Forest Louise Marshall, 1,054.40; Newmarket York County, 3,664.10; Niagara Falls, 6,941.10; Niagara-on-the-Lake Cottage, 278.10; North Bay St. Joseph's, 1,320.90; North Bay Queen Victoria Memorial, 3,683.00; Orangeville Lord Dufferin, 1,294.00; Orillia Soldiers' Memorial, 5,506.80; Oshawa, 5,127.10; Ottawa, 25,174.50; Ottawa, Protestant, 5,937.20; Ottawa Salvation Army, 7,942.40; Ottawa Misericordia, 8,649.30; Ottawa Civic, 80,315.40; Owen Sound, 4,344.70; Palmerston, 574.80; Paris Willett, 3,972.70; Parry Sound St. Joseph's, 3,065.00; Parry Sound, 2,979.40; Parry Sound John R. Stone, 225.55; Pembroke, 4,671.30; Pembroke Cottage, 1,827.10; Penetanguishene, 947.30; Perth Great War Memorial, 4,010.50; Peterborough St. Joseph's, 7,740.30; Peterborough Nicholl's, 6,676.00; Petrolia Charlotte Englehart, 1,202.10; Picton Prince Edward County, 363.00; Port Arthur, 9,521.90; Port Arthur St. Joseph's, 11,179.30; Port Hope, 2,477.60; Renfrew Victoria, 6,333.00; Sault Ste. Marie, 6,309.40; Sault Ste. Marie, Plummer, 6,231.08; Sarnia, 3,388.90; Seaforth, 169.80; Simcoe Norfolk, 6,086.90; Sioux Lookout, 5,793.10; Smith's Falls Public, 2,824.50; Smith's Falls St. Frances, 1,758.90; South Porcupine Presbyterian, 1,169.80; St. Catharines, 9,787.00; St. Thomas Memorial, 10,815.30; Strathroy, 1,751.50; Stratford, 5,259.00; Sturgeon Falls, Brebeuf, 2,449.90; Sudbury St. Joseph's, 19,265.90; Toronto, 120,683.05; Toronto Sick Children's, 67,550.15; Toronto St. Michael's, 68,373.10; Toronto Western, 37.600.70; Toronto Grace, 14,600.10; Toronto St. Joseph's, 31,426.30; Toronto St. John's, 3,911.90; Toronto Orthopedic, 2,394.70; Toronto Lockwood Clinic, 115.20; Toronto Eastern, 23,325.00; Toronto Women's College, 7,389.40; Toronto Salvation Army Women's, 3,116.10; Toronto Mount Sinai, 5,233.20; Toronto Wellesley, 1,156.50; Tillsonburg Soldier's Memorial, 3,011.20; Timmins St. Mary's, 10,402.40; Walkerton, 1,059.30; Walkerville Metropolitan, 15,112.80; Welland County, 4,082.30; Windsor Salvation Army Grace, 5,132.40; Windsor Hotel Dieu, 7,025.90; Wingham, 409.80; Woodstock, 3,795.90........ 1,083,438 43

Red Cross Hospitals, $17,396.40.

Apsley, 137.40; Atikoken, 42.20; Bancroft, 451.20; Blind River, 144.60; Bonfield, 48.90; Bracebridge, 2,448.90; Coe Hill, 145.50; Dryden, 3,001.00; Ellis, 14.00; Englehart, 1,011.35; Hornepayne, 193.80; Kakabeka Falls, 114.50; Kirkland Lake, 4,612.90; Lions Head, 138.00; Loring, 219.60; Nakina, 480.00; New Liskeard, 395.05; Nipigon, 5.40; Quibell, 192.90; Rainy River, 1,149.60; Redditt, 92.70; Richard's Landing, 319.50; St. Joseph's Island, 486.60; Thessalon, 1,317.60; Whitney, 83.20; Wilberforce, 150.00........ 17,396 40

Homes for Incurables ($163,202.00)

Hamilton, St. Peters, 4,533.00; London, Parkwood, 18,819.60; Ottawa, Perley, 17,187.60; Ottawa, St. Vincent, 26,053.40; Toronto, Hospital for Incurables, 66,921.00; Toronto, Mercy, 22,076.40; Toronto, Home for Incurable Children, 7,611.00........ 163,202 00

Maintenance of Patients in Municipal Sanitoria for Consumptives ($620,238.62)

Brant, 27,537.00; Essex County, 34,651.50; Freeport, 23,192.25; Mountain, 119,647.50; Muskoka, 94,980.62; Niagara Peninsula, 22,083.00; Queen Alexandra, 102,261.00; Royal Ottawa, 34,801.50; The Preventorium, 30,118.50; Toronto and Queen Mary, 120,168.75; Windsor East, 10,797.00........ 620,238 62

Travelling and Other Expenses of Indigent Patients ($60.65)

Canadian Pacific Railway Co., fares........ 60 65

Hospitals and Charities Branch—Continued

Grants ($20,411.00)

Hospital for Sick Children (Toronto), out patients, 6,811.00; Hospital for Sick Children (Toronto), to erect 100-bed Country Hospital, 11,350.00; Victorian Order of Nurses, 2,250.00 ..... 20,411 00

General Hospitals and Charities $1,916,596.09

GENERAL

Training School for Nurses, Printing Examination Papers, etc. ($385.05)

V. G. Allison, graduation pins, 309.10; T. Eaton Co., Ltd., presentation case, 11.30; E. E. Shaw, certificates, 62.00; Robert Simpson Co., Ltd., ribbon, 2.65 ..... 385 05

Board of Examiners, Training School for Nurses, Ontario Hospitals ($497.62)

E. A. James, services, 100.00, expenses, 35.80; G. W. Kells, services, 100.00; expenses, 66.55; Lillian Palmer, services as stenographer, 25.00; C. H. Pratt, expenses, 30.97; J. N. Senn, services, 100.00; expenses, 39.30 ..... 497 62

Removal of Patients ($12,102.88)

C. J. Fox, 4,648.19; Miss A. Porter, 3,414.70; Sundry Hospitals, transportation of patients, 4,039.99 ..... 12,102 88

Clothing for Bailiffs, Removing Patients ($299.95)

A. A. Allan & Co., Ltd., 7.50; R. H. Bond, 56.00; Exclusive Ladies Wear, 23.90; R. B. Hutchinson Co., Ltd., 68.60; A. Porter, 16.45; Robert Simpson Co., Ltd., 36.50; Springer & Son, 75.00; Wylie's Shoe Store, 16.00 ..... 299 95

Printing and Stationery for Public Institutions ($14,836.74)

King's Printer 14,836 74

Medical Attendance, Funeral Transportation and Burial Expenses, Officials and Employees of Public Institutions ($601.70)

I. A. Angus, 19.00; Brockville General Hospital, 15.00; W. J. Brown, 225.00; H. O. Fancar, 150.00; A. H. Judson, 95.00; J. M. Nettleton, 9.00; Sinclair, Stevens & Black, 20.00; B. Stewart, 12.95; Toronto General Hospital, 49.00; Woodstock General Hospital, 6.75 ..... 601 70

Treatment of Patients and Inmates of Public Institutions ($114.50)

Hospital Services.

Kingston General Hospital, 26.50; R. J. Reid, 8.00; E. F. Richardson, 25.00; St. Michaels Hospital, Toronto, 34.25; Toronto Western Hospital, 19.00; Woodstock Hospital, 1.75 ..... 114 50

Grants to Recovered Indigent Patients from Ontario Hospitals and Removal Expenses to their legal domicile ($494.38)

Ontario Hospitals.

Brockville, 84.80; Cobourg, 116.96; Hamilton, 4.55; Kingston, 10.55; London, 8.62; Mimico, 138.25; Toronto, 116.30; Whitby, 9.15; Woodstock, 5.20 ..... 494 38

Travelling Expenses of Social Service Workers at Ontario Hospitals ($356.61)

K. Day, 209.83; M. S. Polson, 146.78 ..... 356 61

Legal Costs and Expenses Covering Sundry Investigation ($7.00)

Ontario Provincial Police 7 00

Provision for Expenses in Connection with Conventions Held at Various Institutions ($15.20)

Travelling Expenses.

W. C. Herriman, 7.60; E. A. James, 7.60 ..... 15 20

Removal Expenses (Other than Patients) in Connection with the Public Institutions ($1,497.00)

H. A. Abraham, 27.35; H. L. Batstone, 2.95; S. Ballantyne, 15.10; J. Barrister, 3.85; L. Bell, 4.95; J. Black, 2.75; K. Black, 6.20; Bezley's Transport, 130.00; J. Campbell, 2.75; C. A. Cleland, 38.20; R. Y. Close, 2.60; J. Canning, 53.25; F. B.

Hospitals and Charities—Continued

Removal Expenses (Other than Patients), etc.—Continued

Dixon Co., 73.00; A. Dodd, 23.60; M. Ferguson, 5.45; D. R. Fletcher, 17.40; R. G. Goodwin, 5.15; W. H. Gould, 7.90; J. D. Grieve, 3.60; C. H. Gundry, 12.90; Hartford Fire Insurance Co., 3.00; M. Hunt, 26.60; J. Hunter, 2.75; W. Jubb, 12.80; G. C. Kidd, 36.45; J. E. Laughrey, 6.90; T. J. Lennon, 6.30; I. Little, 2.40; D. O. Lynch, 30.20; Martin Transport, Ltd., 23.00; J. C. Marriott, 12.65; N. B. McAuley, 40.20; C. McClenahan, 108.61; E. McIntyre, 6.30; D. C. McKerracher, 3.45; J. Moore, 4.65; W. Mosley, 39.42; S. C. Parsons, 4.50; O. Foad, 7.90; M. Polson, 5.30; Pridmares Eastern Express, 43.50; D. S. Reynolds, 1.50; J. Stewart, 2.90; M. B. Stott, 4.65; G. Strachan, 1.60; R. Trott, 5.35; C. A. Ward, Ltd., 362.00; Wedge, The Mover, 31.00; R. Wright, 4.60; D. S. Wright, 4.60; C. Wright, 8.80. Sundries—freight, 178.89; express, 14.53; cartage, 10.75 .... 1,497 00

Unforeseen and Unprovided ($1,003.90)

L. A. Ball, funeral expenses, 75.00; D. Bradd, board, 76.25; Canadian National Railways, fares, 16.00; Canadian Pacific Railway Co., fares, 22.05; Children's Aid Society, maintenance of patients, 519.00; G. Frinland, board, 30.15; Rev. A. Jackson, travelling expenses, 6.65; F. T. Jones, travelling expenses, 20.00; F. J. Kuill, auto repairs, 6.00; F. J. Martyn & Son, ambulance service, 10.00; Orillia Anti Mosquito Campaign, oil, 190.80; A. Warren, clothes, 18.00; A. Watson, board, 14.00 .... 1,003 90

Expenses in Connection with Exhibit of the Department of Health, Hospitals Branch, at the Canadian National and Other Exhibitions ($3,628.61)

Day Sign Co., Ltd., signs, 515.86; Dyment-Baker Lumber Co., lumber, 10.98; D. M. Fraser, Ltd., electrical supplies, 332.79; Kingsmill's, Ltd., decorating display, 15.00; R. Laidlaw Lumber Co., Ltd., lumber, 495.08; Rice Lewis & Son, Ltd., hardware, 15.16; Macey Sign Co., signs, etc., 623.14; The C. E. Marley, Ltd., painting, 11.00; The Masco Co., Ltd., cable, lamps, etc., 63.89; Mimico Planing Mills, lumber, 15.04; Province of Ontario Pictures, negatives, etc., 64.70; Pay list, wages of men, 1,134.40; Rogers Electric Co., Ltd., fuses, etc., 14.27; The Robert Simpson Co., Ltd., dust sheet, curtains, etc., 271.10; Toronto Lock Manufacturing Co., hinges, 12.15; H. Waters & Co., flowers, 35.25. Sundries—petty disbursements, 2.80 .... 3,632 61

Less salvage material C.N.E. 4 00

3,628 61

Provision for Payment to Ontario Research Foundation in Connection with Contagious Abortion in Farm Herds ($2,955.26)

Ontario Research Foundation, testing herds 2,955 26

General $38,796.40

BROCKVILLE

Salaries ($207,204.03)

Superintendent, Physicians and Dentists	17,934 00
Steward and Assistants	11,775 00
Matron and Assistants, including domestic help	26,081 26
Engineers and Assistants	16,462 50
Artisans, not domestic	12,670 00
Farm and Garden employees	10,175 00
Attendants and Nurses	112,106 27

Expenses ($160,095.93)

Medicines and Medical Comforts, $7,604.44.

Abbot Laboratories, Ltd., 165.59; Ash-Temple Co., Ltd., 20.05; Ayerst, McKenna, Harrison, Ltd., 91.06; Brockville General Hospital, 12.00; Burroughs Wellcome & Co., 94.42; Canadian National Express, 27.04; Canadian National Railways, 20.63; Canadian Pacific Express, 20.38; Colgate-Palmolive-Peet Co., Ltd., 18.19; Connaught Laboratories, 161.37; Denver Chemical Mfg. Co., 12.51; Dominion Dental Co., Ltd., 23.05; Dominion Rubber Co., Ltd., 12.60; Chas. E. Frosst & Co., Ltd., 506.21; Fullerton's Drug Stores, 186.88; A. D. Gibson, 111.37; Gooderham & Worts, Ltd., 113.09; J. F. Hartz Co., Ltd., 1,190.59; K. R. Haskett, 12.00; Hygiene Products, 40.65; Imperial Tobacco Co., Ltd., 482.40; Ingram & Bell, Ltd., 663.44; Kincaid's Drug Store, 129.80; V. P. Lawless,

Ontario Hospitals—Continued

Brockville—Continued

Expenses—Continued

Medicines—Continued.

45.11; Lemieux Drug Store, 92.15; Lewis Mfg Co. of Canada, Ltd., 54.34; Liquor Control Board, 37.99; Mallinckrodt Chemical Works, Ltd., 54.89; R. E. Mitchell, 176.40; G. W. Morrison, cigars, 42.75; Parke Davis & Co., 73.44; Recorder Printing Co., Ltd., 15.00; Richards Glass Co., Ltd., 21.44; Ritchie's Cigar Store, 497.13; The Robert Simpson Co., Ltd., 14.00; Standard Tobacco Co., 23.84; The Stevens Co., Ltd., 247.32; Synthetic Drug Co., Ltd., 261.12; Textile Products Co., Ltd., 116.60; Tuckett Tobacco Co., Ltd., 779.22; The Vi-Tone Co., 27.93; Henry K. Wampole Co., Ltd., 281.61; Wark's Drug Store, 270.98; West Disinfecting Co., 61.44; White X-ray Surgical Supply Co., 66.30; Chas. R. Will & Co., Ltd., 68.34; William's Drug Store, 80.05; Drs. Woodrow and Mallory, 40.50; petty disbursements, 39.23 .... 7,604 44

Groceries and Provisions, $52,942.45.

J. Belfoi, 336.25; G. C. Bellamy, 153.13; Brockville Fruit Market, 1,611.69; T. Burns & Son, 128.11; H. A. Campbell, 208.81; Canadian National Railways, 164.56; Canadian Pacific Railway Co., 200.46; Canada Packers, Ltd., 3,108.79; Copeland Flour Mills, Ltd., 3,805.00; W. J. Crothers Co., Ltd., 30.72; R. Davis, 124.20; Fullerton's Drug Store, 16.56; Gilmour & Co., Ltd., 8,317.25; T. J. Gilpin, 176.09; James Glazier, 230.53; Gunn's, Ltd., 2,610.63; F. E. Hammond, 286.00; J. R. Hayden & Co., 267.30; J. J. Henderson & Sons, 3,026.60; W. R. Henderson & Sons, 264.50; Higgins & Burke, Ltd., 189.75; The Harry Horne Co., Ltd., 34.56; G. C. Howison, 83.16; Johnson & Clark, 446.59; James Lumbers Co., Ltd., 227.70; N. Manhard, 278.10; Mrs. C. A. Markell, 178.02; John McConkey, 488.92; McDougall Bros., 196.65; A. B. McInnes, 181.02; John Moore, 102.50; Morrison Ice Co., 1,242.70; Ontario Hospital, London, 206.25; Ontario Reformatory Industries, 8,479.77; W. Paterson, Ltd., 90.12; G. C. Reynolds, 249.67; T. T. Shaw, 171.19; T. D. Spence, 253.07; Standard Brands, Ltd., 364.02; J. J. Tierney, 60.00; F. P. West, 439.08; Whyte Packing Co., Ltd., 13,645.87; H. B. Wright & Co., 242.30; petty disbursements, 24.26 .... 52,942 45

Fuel, Light and Water, $38,213.14.

Brockville Public Utilities Commission, 7,506.49; H. C. Burton & Co., 44.11; Eddy Match Co., Ltd., 194.89; Hydro-Electric Power Commission, 375.55; W. B. Reynolds & Co., 30,084.50; petty disbursements, 7.60 .... 38,213 14

Clothing, $18,513.18.

G. F. Adamson, 51.00; Bell Thread Co., Ltd., 15.41; Canadian National Express, 20.34; Canadian National Railways, 74.23; Circle Bar Knitting Co., Ltd., 252.00; The Coghill Tailoring Co., 1,495.45; Robert Craig & Co., Ltd., 52.60; A. D. Currie, 285.65; W. L. Dailey, 10.60; Dominion Rubber Co., Ltd., 41.34; John M. Garland, Son & Co., Ltd., 37.00; A. D. Gibson, 238.32; W. H. Gilhooley, 30.60; Greenshields, Ltd., 47.50; Jackson & Kerr, 33.70; J. A. Johnston & Co., 1,610.05; Lailey, Trimble Co., Ltd., 961.48; The Leverette Store, 881.36; Mercer Reformatory Industries, 9,151.61; Ontario Hospital, Orillia, Industries, 757.00; Ontario Reformatory Industries, 972.00; Penman's, Ltd., 48.60; Smith Glove Co., 78.75; Storey's Glove Works, 106.63; Superior Cloak Co., Ltd., 468.00; Wiseman Bros., 510.06; Woods Mfg Co., Ltd., 179.50; Robert Wright & Co., 91.20; petty disbursements, 11.20 .... 18,513 18

Laundry and Cleaning, $6,942.56.

Alpha Chemical Co., Ltd., 38.86; Associated Chemical Co., Ltd., 760.69; Beaver Laundry Machinery Co., Ltd., 110.16; J. Belfoi, 22.10; G. C. Bellamy, 57.61; Thos. Burns & Son, 49.10; Caldwell Linen Mills, Ltd., 129.50; H. A. Campbell, 49.85; Canada Colors & Chemicals, Ltd., 65.60; Canadian Industries, Ltd., 47.37; Canadian National Institute for the Blind, 330.00; Canadian National Railways, 140.78; Diamond Cleansers, Ltd., 689.19; V. Dionne & Sons, 422.24; E. B. Eddy Co., Ltd., 65.00; Gilmour & Co., 215.25; T. J. Gilpin, 19.78; F. E. Hammond, 34.30; Hatch Specialty Co., 28.00; Lavoline Cleanser Co., Ltd., 23.89; N. Manhard, 44.40; Mrs. C. A. Markell, 57.71; A. B. McInnes, 31.90; Ontario Reformatory Industries, 28.80; Rexo Chemical Cleaner Co., Ltd., 1,157.80; Ritchie's Cigar Store, 112.50; T. A. Shaw, 40.00; R. H. Smart & Co., Ltd., 114.00; T. D. Spence, 53.90; St. Croix Soap Mfg. Co., Ltd., 1,045.53; Syrett Paper Co., Ltd., 145.95; Victoria Paper & Twine Co., Ltd., 83.40; V. P. West, 53.13; Williams Drug Store, 385.95; G. H. Wood & Co., Ltd., 247.79; petty disbursements, 40.53 6,942 56

Ontario Hospitals—Continued

Brockville—Continued

Expenses—Continued

Furniture and Furnishings, $18,127.98.

Caldwell Linen Mills, Ltd., 288.20; Cameron-Borthwick, Ltd., 92.20; Canadian Industries, Ltd., 56.85; Canadian National Express, 14.01; Canadian National Railways, 169.80; Cassidy's, Ltd., 1,650.27; W. L. Dailey, 66.00; W. B. Dalton & Sons, Ltd., 19.25; Delany & Pettit, 77.40; Desmarais & Robitaille, Ltd., 85.30; Dionne & Sons, 15.75; A. G. Dobbie & Co., Ltd., 99.97; Dr. W. M. English, 50.00; John Garde & Co., Ltd., 128.75; A. D. Gibson, 2,809.55; Gilmour & Co., 10.50; Grand & Toy, Ltd., 40.00; C. E. Johnston Co., 1,135.07; The Leverette Store, 290.96; Mrs. C. A. Markell, 11.00; Martin Transport, 49.00; McGlashan, Clarke & Co., Ltd., 131.16; Mercer Reformatory Industries, 6,286.21; A. H. Ness, 10.85; Ontario Reformatory Industries, 3,629.30; Pridmore Eastern Express, 32.25; Singer Sewing Machine Co., 123.90; R. H. Smart, Ltd., 206.18; R. E. Stewart, 28.37; Textile Products, Ltd., 34.82; R. G. Venn, 55.86; G. H. Wood & Co., Ltd., 392.00; petty disbursements, 37.25 .... 18,127 98

Office expenses, $1,518.93.

Bell Telephone Co., rentals, 417.80; tolls, 95.89; Canadian National Express, 13.91; Canadian National Railways, 31.71; Canadian National Telegraphs, 24.92; Canadian Pacific Express, 19.92; Office Specialty Mfg. Co., 183.40; Postmaster, 725.00; petty disbursements, 6.38 .... 1,518 93

Farm Expenses, $10,438.64.

Associated Chemical Co., Ltd., 220.15; John Borthwick, 770.00; Brockville Corporation, 43.60; H. Brown & Sons, 1,470.97; Canada Foundry & Forgings, Ltd., 68.25; Canada Mineral Products, Ltd., 140.00; Canadian National Railways, 313.73; G. F. Cook, 61.00; W. L. Dailey, 389.05; V. Dionne & Sons, 31.50; A. G. Dobbie & Co., 329.34; Edwards Florists, 89.64; Fullarton's Drug Store, 102.44; Gilmour & Co., 55.80; Hay Floral & Seed Co., 27.15; Holstein-Friesian Association, 44.00; Imperial Oil, Ltd., 680.36; International Harvester Co., Ltd., 21.85; McArthur's Beltings, Ltd., 23.03; McDougall Bros., 2,038.80; McDougall & Sheridan, 177.34; Frank Murray, 167.50; O'Hara Motor Supply Co., 13.30; Parrish & Heimbecker, Ltd., 2,143.31; D. M. Robertson, 292.00; Scottish Fertilizers, Ltd., 336.00; W. J. Sheridan, 30.00; R. H. Smart, 148.03; T. G. Waghorn, 94.00; Wm. Watson, 10.00; G. H. Wood & Co., Ltd., 83.30; petty disbursements, 23.20 .... 10,438 64

Contingencies, $5,794.61.

Beacock & Co., repairs, 70.84; J. Belfoi, paper bags, 15.50; T. Burns & Son, paper bags, 20.68; Canada Foundries & Forgings, Ltd., 12.29; Canadian National Express, 127.85; Canadian Pacific Express, 42.09; Dr. Cleland, travelling expenses, 429.36; M. Davidson, travelling expenses, 178.75; A. G. Dobbie & Co., hardware, 15.20; Easter Sales & Service, gas, etc., 385.32; The T. Eaton Co., Ltd., books, 97.72; Dr. W. M. English, travelling expenses, 10.96; Dr. Fletcher, travelling expenses, 27.65; Gilmour & Co., paper bags, 47.71; T. J. Gilpin, paper bags, 13.21; James Glazier, paper bags, 24.05; Gooderham & Worts, Ltd., spirits, 23.23; Dr. F. M. Goodfellow, travelling expenses, 17.25; Goodyear Tire & Rubber Co., Ltd., tubes, 19.39; Joseph Grier, taxi services, 46.00; F. E. Hammond, paper bags, 20.83; Hay Floral & Seed Co., flowers, 55.00; Imperial Oil, Ltd., oil, 76.88; C. E. Johnston, funeral fees, 250.00; Dr. A. H. Judson, operations, 150.00; Fred H. Kay, music, etc., 37.10; Dr. G. W. Kells, travelling expenses, 219.75; V. P. Lawless, dental services, 19.60; Leverette's Store, notions, etc., 70.50; M. A. Lunan, travelling expenses, 37.05; K. A. MacAskill, repairs, 36.50; Macmillan Co. of Canada, Ltd., books, 42.84; Mrs. C. A. Markell, bags, 32.51; McAinsh & Co., Ltd., books, 153.95; Dr. C. A. McClenahan, travelling expenses, 17.95; M. McCormick, travelling expenses, 221.95; Dr. H. C. Moorhouse, travelling expenses, 68.35; Geo. W. Morrison, subscriptions to newspapers and magazines, 137.50; Moving Picture Operator, 36.00; Musical Services, 150.00; O'Hara Motor Supply Co., repairs, 14.33; Ontario Reformatory, Guelph, haulage, 37.91; Thos. Plunkett, travelling expenses, 13.10; Ray Stewart Motors, gas, etc., 18.76; Recorder Printing Co., printing, 75.73; Regal Films, Ltd., films, 187.50; Religious Services, 555.00; J. H. Reynolds, bags, etc., 39.37; Ritchie's Cigar Store, subscriptions to newspapers and magazines, etc., 402.80; R. Shaw, repairs, 16.00; T. T. Shaw, twine, 22.00; A. Shiells, Christmas trees, 20.00; J. M. Short, travelling expenses, 46.20; R. H. Smart, bags, 16.70; Smith & Walsh, car insurance, 31.98; T. D. Spence, paper bags, 20.69; R. E. Stewart, vocational supplies, 181.24; R. T. Stratton, operating picture machine, 363.00; A. L. Targis & Son, anti-freeze, 13.52; Drs. Woodrow and Mallory, X-ray, 40.00; F. W. Woolworth Co., Ltd., Christmas decorations, etc., 118.56; petty disbursements, 100.91 .... 5,794 61

Ontario Hospitals—Continued

Brockville—Continued

Repairs to Buildings ($15,354.58)

Maintenance and Repairs of all Buildings, Roads, Walks, Grounds and Fences $5,718.10.

Aulcraft Paints, Ltd., 14.70; Corporation, Town of Brockville, 33.75; Cameron-Borthwick, Ltd., 132.15; Canada Foundries & Forgings, Ltd., 24.00; Canada Paint Co., Ltd., 202.00; Canada Varnish Co., Ltd., 24.70; Canadian Durex Abrasives, Ltd., 18.16; Canadian National Railways, 17.23; Dennisteel, Ltd., 19.30; A. G. Dobbie & Co., 1,132.00; Eastern Sales Service Co., 32.15; Hippo-Weir Co., Ltd., 83.24; Imperial Varnish & Color Co., Ltd., 85.62; C. E. Johnston Co., 42.07; Lowe Bros. Co., Ltd., 189.14; Lundy Fence Co., Ltd., 74.57; The Mallory Lumber Co., 1,593.12; Metallic Roofing Co., Ltd., 51.92; J. A. Morin Co., Ltd., 125.00; Ontario Reformatory, Mimico, 415.25; Pay list, wages of men, 168.00; The Pedlar People, Ltd., 24.82; W. E. Phillips Co., Ltd., 74.22; Sanderson, Pearcy-Marietta, Ltd., 149.35; Sherwin-Williams Co., Ltd., 65.12; J. H. Simpson & Sons, 54.25; R. H. Smart, Ltd., 431.83; Trelco, Ltd., 15.60; Tremco Co., Ltd., 14.72; Vokes Hardware Co., Ltd., 263.50; Williams Drug Store, 12.25; George Wilson, 122.94; petty disbursements, 11.43.. 5,718 10

Maintenance and Repairs of Plumbing, Steam and Electric Plants, $8,448.38.

Beaver Laundry Machinery Co., Ltd., 46.21; Boiler Repair & Grate Bar Co., 229.09; Brockville Public Utilities Commission, 30.55; H. S. Brown, 515.92; Bull Dog Electric Products, Ltd., 94.87; H. C. Burton & Co., 450.84; Canadian Allis-Chalmers, Ltd., 15.23; Canada Foundries & Forgings, Ltd., 74.14; Canadian General Electric Co., Ltd., 42.53; Canadian Johns-Manville Co., Ltd., 38.46; Canadian Laundry Machinery Co., Ltd., 31.43; Canadian National Express, 26.25; Canadian National Railways, 116.78; Canadian Powers Regulator Co., Ltd., 335.00; Dearborn Chemical Co., Ltd., 47.76; A. G. Dobbie & Co., 149.72; Dominion Oxygen Co., Ltd., 79.51; F. J. Downes & Co., 1,003.61; Drummond-McCall & Co., Ltd., 432.10; Empire Brass Manufacturing Co., Ltd., 382.38; Garlock Packing Co., Ltd., 142.71; Goodyear Tire & Rubber Co., Ltd., 48.39; Gurney Foundry Co., Ltd., 118.86; Gutta Percha & Rubber, Ltd., 48.39; Imperial Oil, Ltd., 158.48; Insulation Manufacturing Co., 70.12; Jenkins Bros., Ltd., 26.70; Arthur S. Leitch Co., Ltd., 70.40; Link-Belt Co., 47.03; McArthur Beltings, Ltd., 12.39; Northern Electric Co., Ltd., 15.60; O'Hara Motor Supply Co., 35.40; Oshawa Electric Supply Co., Ltd., 29.11; Pay list, wages of men, 1,077.90; Premier Laundry Equipment Co., Ltd., 106.47; Pridmore Eastern Express, 99.89; The Jas. Robertson Co., Ltd., 283.95; Roelofson Elevator Works, 500.00; Sheridan & Power, 45.00; R. H. Smart, Ltd., 734.30; Standard Sales Service, 16.50; G. F. Sterne & Sons, 13.03; Superior Electric Supply Co., 19.90; Taylor-Forbes Co., Ltd., 92.15; Trane Co. of Canada, Ltd., 160.72; Watrous, Ltd., 40.00; George Wilson, 34.82; Wolverine, Ltd., 191.23; petty disbursements, 66.56.. 8,448 38

Live Stock, Vehicles and Farm Implements, $1,188.10.

A. B. Brubacker, 115.00; Canadian National Railways, 33.10; T. J. Devlin, 100.00; McDougall & Sheridan, 109.00; Harold Percival, 156.00; H. Skinner, 25.00; L. C. Snowden, 650.00.. 1,188 10

Total		382,654 54	
Less Maintenance of Patients	74,230 64		
Perquisites	27,752 84		
Sale of Produce	1,618 22		
		103,601 70	
Brockville		279,052 84	

COBOURG

Salaries ($58,767.35)

Superintendent, Physicians and Dentists	8,720 00
Steward and Assistants	3,972 90
Matron and Assistants, including domestic help	11,755 63
Engineer and Assistants	7,900 00
Artisans, not domestic	1,300 00
Farm and Garden employees	2,250 00
Attendants and Nurses	22,868 82

Ontario Hospitals—Continued

Cobourg—Continued

Expenses ($67,132.18)

Medicines, $1,950.90.

Ash, Temple Co., Ltd., 80.79; Canadian National Express, 32.30; Cobourg General Hospital, 75.00; Dr. A. L. Erskine, 22.64; J. F. Hartz Co., Ltd., 83.35; Hygiene Products, Ltd., 35.12; Ingram & Bell, Ltd., 771.64; O. G. Johns, 322.05; Kerr Dental Laboratory, 73.92; Lewis Manufacturing Co., Ltd., 26.97; Parke Davis Co., 14.60; H. Powell Chemical Co., 39.44; Dr. A. R. Richards, 15.00; Richards Glass Co., 35.34; Dr. T. Samis, services, 15.00; Smith & Nephew, Ltd., 43.42; Squibb & Sons, Ltd., 11.66; Stevens Companies, 48.75; Textile Products Co., 34.00; Vi-Tone Co., 27.93; H. K. Wampole & Co., Ltd., 12.57; A. Wander, Ltd., 20.33; Dr. W. E. Wilkins, 30.00; Chas. R. Will & Co., Ltd., 21.07; G. H. Wood & Co., Ltd., 24.50; petty disbursements, 33.51........................ 1,950 90

Groceries and Provisions, $29,978.78.

W. T. Bates, 1,074.15; Bowes Co., Ltd., 3,778.06; Canadian National Railways, 22.93; Canadian Pacific Railway Co., 80.40; Thos. Cann, 16.83; Cobourg City Dairy Co., 4,684.99; F. J. Cochrane, 40.40; Copeland Flour Mills, Ltd., 1,619.75; John J. Fee, 166.60; S. B. Gray, 58.00; J. W. Hayden, 312.30; The Harry Horne Co., Ltd., 410.39; Higgins & Burke, Ltd., 229.68; Hoar Transport, 19.38; F. W. Humphrey Co., 252.96; W. C. Hugh, 338.37; F. W. Krause & Sons, 30.00; Frank M. Love, 60.64; James Lumbers Co., Ltd., 2,662.24; T. Mitchell & Sons, 4,747.74; Ontario Hospital, Kingston, 55.00; Ontario Reformatory, 31.20; Ontario Reformatory Industries, 5,479.89; Ontario Hospital, Whitby, 77.50; S. E. H. Rorabeck, 1,804.06; Standard Brands, Ltd., 260.17; Stiver's, 17.30; F. W. Stull Transport, 77.40; H. O. Taylor, 1,199.32; J. S. Walden, 342.60; petty disbursements, 28.53.. 29,978 78

Fuel, Light and Water, $14,609.68.

Eddy Match Co., Ltd., 11.15; J. M. Harrison, 11,059.23; Milnes Coal Co., Ltd., 173.54; Hydro-Electric Power Commission, 3,167.99; Northern Electric Co., Ltd., 192.77; petty disbursements, 5.00.................................. 14,609 68

Clothing, $6,123.98.

Canadian National Railways, 10.11; Circle Bar Knitting Co., Ltd., 336.00; A. D. Gibson, 1,202.85; Greenshields, Ltd., 277.95; Gutta Percha & Rubber, Ltd., 68.92; Hamburg Felt Boot Co., Ltd., 361.20; Hamilton & Johnston, 851.34; G. Killock, 33.40; Mercer Reformatory Industries, 2,540.04; Mercury Mills, Ltd., 89.77; Morris Shoe & Slipper Co., 200.00; Ontario Reformatory Industries, 20.00; Superior Cloak Co., 117.00; petty disbursements, 15.40............... 6,123 98

Laundry and Cleaning, $3,022.16.

Alpha Chemical Co., 13.65; Associated Chemical Co., Ltd., 780.20; Beaver Laundry Machinery Co., Ltd., 392.53; Canadian National Railways, 32.50; Colgate-Palmolive-Peet Co., Ltd., 135.56; Diamond Cleansers, Ltd., 357.20; Dundas Bros., 52.35; Electric Boiler Compound Co., Ltd., 71.17; Excelsior Brushes, Ltd., 109.30; J. Gillard, 17.95; Hamilton & Johnston, 130.13; Hoar Transport, 19.87; S. F. Lawrason Co., 157.20; James Lumbers Co., Ltd., 51.60; Mackinnon Sales, 126.00; Martin Transport, 11.36; Ontario Reformatory Industries, 14.40; Oshawa Electric Supply, Ltd., 14.11; Parke Davis & Co., 11.60; St. Croix Soap Manufacturing Co., Ltd., 186.04; Swift Canadian Co., Ltd., 265.00; H. O. Taylor, 51.29; petty disbursements, 21.15................ 3,022 16

Furniture and Furnishings, $8,293.78.

Adams Furniture Co., Ltd., 286.88; Canadian Fairbanks-Morse Co., Ltd., 18.47; Canadian General Electric Co., Ltd., 12.57; Caldwell Linen Mills, 517.27; Canadian National Railways, 36.84; Cassidy's, Ltd., 692.62; Cobourg Matting & Carpet Co., Ltd., 17.55; Dundas Bros., 287.26; Empire Brass Manufacturing Co., Ltd., 10.00; A. D. Gibson, 1,307.69; J. Gillard, 180.96; Greenshields, Ltd., 679.98; Hamilton & Johnston, 80.42; Martin Transport, 27.77; Mercer Reformatory Industries, 2,191.93; Metal Craft Co., Ltd., 38.00; Ontario Reformatory, 21.84; Ontario Reformatory Industries, 1,746.25; H. S. Pierce, 38.50; Stull Transport Co., 14.60; Textile Products Co., 38.16; petty disbursements, 48.23.......... 8,293 78

Office Expenses, $697.94.

Bell Telephone Co., rental, 132.20; tolls, 70.12; Canadian National Express, 15.21; King's Printer, 60.00; Office Specialty Manufacturing Co., Ltd., 215.70; Postmaster, 184.50; petty disbursements, 20.21................................ 697 94

Ontario Hospitals—Continued
Cobourg—Continued
Expenses—Continued

Farm Expenses, $393.50.

Edw. Cavanagh, 80.55; D. Denton & Son, 263.90; J. Gillard, 20.60; Ontario Reformatory Industries, 10.70; petty disbursements, 17.75.................. 393 50

Contingencies, $2,061.46.

American Psychiatric Association, subscription, 10.00; Brunswick-Balke-Collendar Co., Ltd., bowls, 51.33; Canadian National Express, 225.94; Dr. W. A. Cardwell, travelling expenses, 12.45; Consolidated Optical Co., Ltd., 24.91; J. Davidson, operating picture machine, 36.00; Dawson Subscription Service, 48.40; E. L. Delaney, repairs, 27.75; Dominion Reed Supplies, reed, 66.65; General Board of Religious Education, subscription, 10.00; A. D. Gibson, decorations, 14.26; Hamilton & Johnston, wool, tinsel, etc., 587.00; Dr. W. C. Herriman, travelling expenses, 25.05; Hudson Taxi Service, 19.00; Dr. J. C. Kidd, travelling expenses, 11.35; James Lumbers Co., Ltd., 10.74; McAinsh Co., Ltd., books, 52.53; M. Melville, room rent, 15.00; Mail and Empire, subscription, 15.00; Geo. Mitchell, orchestra, 12.00; Thos. Nelson & Sons, books, 15.00; Ontario Medical Association, fees, 10.00; H. S. Pierce, burial fees, 88.00; Religious Services, 280.00; Dr. A. R. Richards, services, 15.00; School Loom Company, loom, 13.30; Smith & Walsh, insurance, 22.69; Sparling & Reeson, Ltd., gas and repairs, 28.78; Stevenson & Lent Motor Sales, repairs, 11.44; Stevens Orchestra, 42.60; Syrett Paper Co., paper, 20.36; Victoria Paper & Twine Co., Ltd., bags, 12.30; Vivian Bros., books, 18.00; W. C. Waller, travelling expenses, 31.45; Wilson Motors, gas, 41.76; Dr. W. E. Wilkins, services, 10.00; G. H. Wood & Co., Ltd., cups, 13.08; petty disbursements, 112.34.................................. 2,061 46

Repairs to Buildings ($17,103.60)

Maintenance and Repairs of All Buildings, Roads, Walks, Grounds and Fences, $10,565.22.

W. L. Allen & Co., 130.04; Aulcraft Paints, Ltd., 35.47; Austin & Bradbury, 130.81; P. Bradbury, 173.99; Brantford Roofing Co., Ltd., 167.35; Canada Paint Co., Ltd., 136.61; Canada Varnish Co., Ltd., 102.75; Canadian Fairbanks-Morse Co., Ltd., 47.50; Canadian Pacific Express Co., 61.69; Canadian Rogers Sheet Metal Roofing, Ltd., 389.00; Cobourg, town of, 38.25; Dundas Bros., 109.41; J. Gillard, 108.80; Hoar Transport, 27.25; J. Martin & Co., 1,851.54; Martin Transport, 11.30; J. H. Morin & Co., 103.12; Ontario Reformatory, Mimico, 15.45; Ontario Reformatory Industries, 22.91; A. B. Ormsby Co., Ltd., 232.00; Pilkington Bros., Ltd., 29.40; Pay list, wages of men, 6,480.30; W. Walker & Son, Ltd., 127.10; petty disbursements, 33.18............................ 10,565 22

Maintenance and Repairs of Plumbing, Steam and Electric Plants, $6,538.38.

W. L. Allen & Co., 25.60; Beardmore Leathers, Ltd., 23.13; Beaver Laundry Machinery Co., Ltd., 89.18; Beldam's Asbestos Packing & General Manufacturing Co., Ltd., 31.55; Bird & Archer Co., Ltd., 86.87; Boiler Repair & Grate Bar Co., 26.73; Bolton Machine Works, 92.06; Bowden Machine Co., 52.00; Bull Dog Electric Products, 53.50; Canadian General Electric Co., Ltd., 145.96; Canadian National Express, 30.65; Canadian National Railways, 15.72; Canadian Powers Regulator Co., 120.50; Duncan Bros., 90.86; C. A. Dunham Co., Ltd., 88.89; Dominion Wheel & Foundries, Ltd., 19.74; F. J. Downes & Co., 76.72; Empire Brass Manufacturing Co., Ltd., 552.88; Everlasting Valve Co., 42.75; D. M. Fraser, Ltd., 22.13; Garlock Packing Co., Ltd., 26.94; Good Specialties, Ltd., 18.46; Gurney Foundry Co., Ltd., 16.83; Gutta Percha & Rubber, Ltd., 15.49; J. T. Hepburn, 124.18; Hoar Transport, 21.35; Hydro-Electric Power Commission, 38.38; Industrial Farm, Burwash, 23.35; A. S. Leitch Co., Ltd., 560.69; Martin's Transport, 11.87; The Masco Co., Ltd., 12.33; Mitchell's Electric Shop, 96.41; Moffat's, Ltd., 12.11; Montgomery Hose Reel Co., 120.00; Jas. Morrison Brass Manufacturing Co., Ltd., 82.98; McColl-Frontenac Oil Co., Ltd., 18.00; National Meter Co., Ltd., 50.50; Northern Electric Co., Ltd., 123.53; Oshawa Electric Supply Co., Ltd., 243.29; Pay lists, wages of men, 2,566.97; Pridmore Express, 25.50; Regent Electric Supply Co., Ltd., 41.88; The James Robertson Co., Ltd., 91.53; Rogers Electric Co., Ltd., 53.77; J. A. Sexauer Manufacturing Co., Ltd., 26,10; Smart-Turner Machine Co., Ltd., 144.00; Standard Sales Service, 16.50; Taylor-Forbes Co., Ltd., 17.63; Toronto-Peterborough Transport, 23.58; Waterous, Ltd., 132.55; Wilson Illumination Co., Ltd., 48.51; petty disbursements, 45.75.. 6,538 38

Total		143,003 13
Less Maintenance of Patients	21,566 37	
Perquisites	6,187 72	
Sale of Produce, etc.	462 14	
		28,216 23
Cobourg		114,786 90

Ontario Hospitals—Continued

HAMILTON

Salaries ($244,754.62)

Superintendent, Physicians and Dentists	24,147 30
Steward and Assistants	12,980 62
Matron and Assistants, including domestic help	26,867 90
Engineers and Assistants	20,300 00
Artisans, not domestic	15,675 00
Farm and Garden employees	16,010 00
Attendants and Nurses	128,773 80

Expenses ($187,215.45)

Medicines, $8,050.00.

Ash-Temple Co., Ltd., 95.00; Ayerst, McKenna & Harrison, 51.54; Balfours, Ltd., 30.00; Bisodol Co., 14.54; Burroughs Welcome & Co., 108.83; Burke Electric & X-Ray Co., Ltd., 310.26; Cameron Surgical Specialty Co., 13.88; Cheney Chemicals, Ltd., 67.30; Ciba Co., Ltd., 40.79; A. C. Drewery Co., Ltd., 185.37; Dental Co. of Canada, 19.96; The T. Eaton Co., Ltd., 88.75; C. E. Frosst & Co., Ltd., 98.91; J. F. Hartz & Co., Ltd., 394.64; Hargraft Bros., 512.50; Hygiene Products, Ltd., 26.25; Imperial Tobacco Co., Ltd., 76.47; Ingram & Bell, Ltd., 555.46; Johnes Box Label Co., Ltd., 11.14; A. D. Keeble, 96.41; James Kirk, Ltd., 40.69; Liquor Control Board, 141.66; Lewis Manufacturing Co., Ltd., 222.12; R. E. Mitchell, 468.75; National Drug & Chemical Co., Ltd., 671.95; Parke & Parke, Ltd., 312.88; Parke Davis & Co., Ltd., 111.73; Petrolager Laboratories, Ltd., 72.00; Powell Chemical Co., Ltd., 301.66; Queen City Dental Manufacturing Co., Ltd., 18.15; Rolls & Darlington, Ltd., 40.52; Standard Tobacco Co., 103.32; The Stevens Co., Ltd., 350.41; E. R. Squibb & Sons, Ltd., 81.58; Synthetic Drug Co., Ltd., 241.91; Textile Products Co., Ltd., 164.30; Tucketts Tobacco Co., Ltd., 1,684.11; Vanzant, Ltd., 48.94; Henry K. Wampole & Co., Ltd., 10.86; A. Wander, Ltd., 17.49; West Disinfecting Co., 10.90; Chas.. R. Will & Co., Ltd., 152.34; Walter Woods, Ltd., 16.90; petty disbursements, 91.11. Less refunds for dental work, 124.28 .... 8,050 00

Groceries and Provisions, $83,038.85.

Balfours, Ltd., 2,735.60; Cabot Macaroni Manufacturing Co., 151.51; Canada & Dominion Sugar Co., Ltd., 3,003.79; Canadian Pacific Railway Co., 88.50; Canada Packers, Ltd., 538.20; Central Fish & Poultry Market, 1,073.15; Christie, Brown & Co., Ltd., 36.11; Copeland Flour Mills, Ltd., 922.50; Cross & Blackwell, Ltd., 27.33; Edward A. Downey, 144.30; The James Dunlop Co., Ltd., 256.80; Ellis Canning Co., 15.00; Fearman Bros., Ltd., 55.00; F. W. Fearman Co., Ltd., 52.20; John J. Fee, 6,946.75; Finlay Fish Co., 106.53; K. C. Freeman, 602.25; W. H. Freeman, 24.30; Hamilton Dairies, Ltd., 81.10; The Harris Abattoir Co., Ltd., 565.25; H. J. Heinz Co., Ltd., 553.66; Higgins & Burke, Ltd., 379.50; The Harry Horne Co., Ltd., 103.36; F. W. Humphrey Co., Ltd., 451.42; Imperial Coffee & Spice Co., Ltd., 915.81; Individual Tea Bag Co., Ltd., 247.50; J. G. Jowett, 24.00; Kerr Milling Co., Ltd., 2,995.93; Laing & Sons, Ltd., 93.37; Lake Ontario Fish Co., Ltd., 1,581.62; Lake of the Woods Milling Co., Ltd., 316.50; James Lumbers Co., Ltd., 2,325.34; Lumsden Bros., 3,318.63; Maple Leaf Milling Co., Ltd., 78.25; Mara Lodge Poultry Farms, 563.64; A. W. Milne, 14.85; Ontario Butter Grading Station, 5,102.24; Ogilvie Flour Mills, Ltd., 149.00; Ontario Hospital, London, 275.00; Ontario Reformatory Industries, 34,936.78; D. S. Perrin & Co., Ltd., 142.79; Pure Gold Manufacturing Co., Ltd., 62.50; Standard Brands, Ltd., 768.70; Standard Wholesalers, Ltd., 87.50; G. T. Scott, Ltd., 479.82; Silverwoods, Ltd., 132.00; Stevens & Soloman, 168.05; Stevenson Fruit Co., Ltd., 1,683.95; St. Lawrence Starch Co., Ltd., 917.32; Sunera Cereals, Ltd., 104.50; Sutherlands, Ltd., 32.14; Bert Smith, 40.25; Tavistock Milling Co., Ltd., 765.00; Tillsonburg Creamery, 324.23; Tip Top Canners, Ltd., 217.45; Wagstaffe, Ltd., 24.25; Geo. Weston, Ltd., 90.78; Wilson's Produce, 1,024.55; Whyte Packing Co., Ltd., 2,371.43; Unxld Products Co., 30.80; Young-Winfield, Ltd., 1,676.85; petty disbursements, 41.52 .... 83,038 85

Fuel, Light and Water, $36,948.98.

H. C. Burton & Co., 305.67; Canadian Oil Cos., Ltd., 35.88; Dominion Natural Gas Co., Ltd., 64.80; Eddy Match Co., Ltd., 83.57; Gillies, Guy & Co., Ltd., 18,414.39; Hamilton Hydro-Electric Co., Ltd., 4,770.63; Corporation, City of Hamilton, 12,234.08; Hydro-Electric Power Commission of Ontario, 132.66; United Gas & Fuel Co., Ltd., 861.75; Wilkinson-Kompass, Ltd., 44.09; petty disbursements, 1.46 .... 36,948 98

Ontario Hospitals—Continued

Hamilton—Continued

Expenses—Continued

Clothing, $18,036.20.

Anglo-Canadian Leather Co., Ltd., 285.83; A. Bradshaw & Sons, Ltd., 69.54; Canadian National Railways, 16.31; Circle Bar Knitting Co., Ltd., 95.00; Coppley, Noyes & Randall, Ltd., 1,693.15; Dunham & Duggan, Ltd., 929.10; Eisman & Co., Ltd., 191.07; W. Farrar & Co., Ltd., 526.98; A. D. Gibson, 583.23; Gordon Mackay & Co., Ltd., 2,475.51; Greenshields, Ltd., 214.69; Gutta Percha & Rubber, Ltd., 162.54; Hamilton & Johnston, 1,009.24; Ingram & Bell, Ltd., 19.10; W. J. Leacock, 114.75; Barnet Lipman, 22.33; Martin's Transport, 16.28; Mercury Mills, Ltd., 98.00; Mercer Reformatory Industries, 3,633.97; Nisbet & Auld, Ltd., 15.00; Ontario Reformatory Industries, 1,691.05; Ontario Hospital, Orillia, Industries, 658.50; Penman's, Ltd., 187.50; Schofield Woollen Co., Ltd., 240.00; Smith Glove Co., 65.00; Sterling Bros. Co., Ltd., 1,339.08; Storey Glove Co., Ltd., 89.00; Superior Cloak Co., 1,080.60; Victoria Cap Co., 135.00; Wilkinson-Kompass, Ltd., 25.50; Woods Manufacturing Co., Ltd., 319.00; petty disbursements, 34.35 .... 18,036 20

Laundry and Cleaning, $7,111.40.

Alpha Chemical Co., Ltd., 45.00; Associated Chemical Co., Ltd., 1,506.54; Balfours, Ltd., 58.58; Beaver Laundry Machinery Co., Ltd., 70.56; Joseph Burns, 229.93; Canadian National Railways, 30.14; Canadian National Institute for the Blind, 350.90; Canadian Industries, Ltd., 39.60; Bernard Cairns, Ltd., 36.00; Capo Polishes, 230.00; Colgate-Palmolive-Peet Co., Ltd., 591.79; Diamond Cleansers, Ltd., 172.26; Dominion Soap Co., Ltd., 17.82; Electric Boiler Compound Co., Ltd., 32.18; Excelsior Brushes, Ltd., 113.68; G. T. French, 513.14; General Steel Wares, Ltd., 29.59; Hoar Transport, 58.17; Ingram & Bell, Ltd., 71.50; The Judd Soap Co., Ltd., 38.22; S. F. Lawrason & Co., Ltd., 302.40; Lavoline Cleanser Co., Ltd., 52.56; James Lumbers Co., Ltd., 21.80; Lumsden Bros., 67.34; Meakins, Sons, Ltd., 294.05; David Morton & Sons, Ltd., 372.25; Ontario Reformatory Industries, 76.80; Procter & Gamble, Ltd., 55.21; Rexo Cleansers Co., Ltd., 1,082.57; St. Lawrence Starch Co., Ltd., 12.00; Sunclo Products, 12.50; Taylor Bros., Cutlery Co., Ltd., 24.60; Wood, Alexander & James, Ltd., 120.34; G. H. Wood & Co., Ltd., 346.63; petty disbursements, 34.75 .... 7,111 40

Furniture and Furnishings, $18,068.55.

Alderman Transport, 12.00; John W. Almas, 16.13; Aluminum VI, Ltd., 114.12; Harold Bates, 16.50; Caldwell Linen Mills, Ltd., 389.88; Canadian Industries, Ltd., 698.91; Canadian National Railways, 23.33; Cassidy's, Ltd., 737.58; Delaney & Pettit, Ltd., 757.00; The T. Eaton Co., Ltd., 17.82; John Garde & Co., Ltd., 100.00; General Steel Wares, Ltd., 142.67; A. D. Gibson, 2,340.11; Gordon Mackay & Co., Ltd., 607.56; Greenshields, Ltd., 405.17; Hamilton & Johnston, 52.56; Hobart Manufacturing Co., Ltd., 12.53; Hospital & Kitchen Equipment Co., 453.96; International Silver Co., Ltd., 74.52; Johnson & Barbour, Ltd., 451.02; Kelvinator of Canada, Ltd., 168.27; Martin Transports, Ltd., 18.14; Mercer Reformatory Industries, 4,503.24; Henry Mendes & Co., 198.83; McMahon, Grainger & Co., Ltd., 37.64; Ontario Reformatory Industries, 3,908.50; Pendrith Machinery Co., Ltd., 10.00; G. W. Robinson Co., Ltd., 217.09; John E. Riddell & Sons, Ltd., 60.89; George Sparrow & Co., Ltd., 11.09; Spencer-Turner Co., Ltd., 16.66; Stauffer-Dobbie, Ltd., 132.75; F. W. Stull Transport Co., Ltd., 49.90; Sully Brass Foundry Co., Ltd., 523.95; Taylor Brothers Cutlery Co., Ltd., 20.65; Textile Products Co., 255.65; Watson & Co., 21.00; Thomas C. Watkins, Ltd., 26.44; White Supply Co., Ltd., 86.94; Wilkinson-Kompass, Ltd., 252.37; Wood, Alexander & James, Ltd., 65.85; petty disbursements, 59.33 .... 18,068 55

Office Expenses, $2,031.87.

Bell Telephone Co., rentals, 579.23; tolls, 236.97; Canadian National Express, 15.83; Canadian National Telegraphs, 13.63; Canadian Pacific Express, 19.30; Grand & Toy, Ltd., 276.50; Postmaster, 647.00; Remington Typewriters, Ltd., 77.00; Victor Smith & Co., 145.70; Vernon Directories, 12.00; petty disbursements, 8.71 .... 2,031 87

Farm Expenses, $8,652.00.

Adams Bros., Ltd., 11.64; The Aldridge Co., 58.00; T. A. Blacklock, 106.00; Blatchford Calf Meal Co., Ltd., 238.31; Geo. A. Bowman, 38.00; J. A. Bruce & Co., Ltd., 985.52; Caledonia Milling Co., Ltd., 821.50; Caledonia Creamery Co., Ltd., 180.00; Canada Mineral Products Co., Ltd., 140.00; J. T. Casson,

Ontario Hospitals—Continued

Hamilton—Continued

Expenses—Continued

Farm Expenses—Continued

45.00; Cities Service Oil Co., Ltd., 235.85; Commercial Oil Co., 80.80; Consumers Lumber Co., 88.91; B. Coles, 19.20; W. Deakin, 42.50; James Dunlop & Co., Ltd., 894.56; Foster Pottery Co., 75.50; Frost Steel & Wire Co., Ltd., 94.86; Gallagher Stone & Lime Co., Ltd., 24.66; Gunn's, Ltd., 68.40; Hamilton Dairies, Ltd., 117.00; Holstein-Friesian Association, 44.00; Jamesway, Ltd., 118.33; Kerr Milling Co., Ltd., 1,663.68; Lake of the Woods Milling Co., Ltd., 913.74; Edward Lowden, 55.85; Lumsden Bros., 15.00; Merritt Bros., 49.05; Ralph Moore & Sons, 40.80; T. R. McCaw, 65.43; Niagara Brand Spray Co., Ltd., 29.18; C. H. Nix, 58.85; Ontario Reformatory, Guelph, 40.00; Parke, Davis & Co., 15.00; Ralston Purina Co., 65.32; Ressors-Marmill, Ltd., 253.25; John E. Riddell & Sons, 77.01; Taylor Bros. Cutlery Co., Ltd., 14.75; Taylor-Forbes Co., Ltd., 33.87; Watts Brothers, 11.90; Wentworth County Hunt Club, 231.25; A. E. Wilkinson, 104.85; Wilkinson-Kompass, Ltd., 264.35; Wood, Alexander & James, Ltd., 63.58; petty disbursements, 56.75.................................... 8,652 00

Contingencies, $5,277.60.

Bell Thread Co., Ltd., thread, 27.73; Belding-Corticelli, Ltd., wool, 54.44; G. W. Boag, travelling expenses, 33.87; J. B. Boyd, travelling expenses, 25.95; Brown Bros., interment, 30.00; Carters, Ltd., auto repairs, 179.78; M. E. Carson, travelling expenses, 14.25; Clarke & Clarke, Ltd., leather, 21.38; Dr. E. A. Clark, travelling expenses, 27.45; Clokes Book Shop, books, etc., 38.95; Commercial Engravers, Ltd., photos, 77.00; Commercial Oil Co., Ltd., oil, 63.90; S. Cotterell, burials, 228.00; A. M. Cunningham & Son, photos, 18.50; Connaught Motor Sales Co., Ltd., repairs, 18.90; W. Dawson Subscription Service, 190.29; Dodsworth, Marlatt & Brown, burials, 44.00; Dominion Reed Supplies, reed, 20.55; D. & R. Garage, auto repairs, 100.87; James Dwyer Estate, burials, 22.00; The T. Eaton Co., Ltd., smallwares, 15.79; Ellis-McIntyre Motors, auto repairs, 48.29; G. T. French, kraft bags, etc., 303.83; Gordon Mackay & Co., Ltd., felt, 56.80; Hamilton & Barton Incline Railway, rent, 118.65; Hamilton Cemetery Board, burials, 56.00; Hamilton & Johnston, wool, etc., 300.85; Hamilton Herald, advertising, 16.00; Hamilton Spectator, advertising, 20.00; Hargraft Brothers, pipes, etc., 36.00; Holy Sepulchre Cemetery, burials, 32.00; Robert Hyslop Co., Ltd., smallwares, 37.20; Imperial Oil, Ltd., gas and oil, 244.05; James Kirk, Ltd., pipes, etc., 80.85; Dr. J. H. Kreiner, travelling expenses, 127.02; Lewis Manufacturing Co., Ltd., kotex pads, 16.66; McColl-Frontenac Oil Co., Ltd., gas, 214.88; McKay & Co., flowers, 61.00; D. G. McKerrocher, travelling expenses, 67.15; Musical Services, 321.75; National Drug & Chemical Co., Ltd., chemicals, 27.01; Lilian Oliver, travelling expenses, 124.35; J. D. Patterson & Co., auto repairs, 23.70; Province of Ontario Pictures, reels, 50.75; Robert Raw & Co., printing, 134.75; religious services, 540.00; G. W. Robinson & Co., Ltd., smallwares, 82.37; Sherwin-Williams & Co., Ltd., paint, 13.98; Silverwood-Burke Dairy, dixies, 50.00; Smith & Walsh, insurance premiums, 100.65; Stevenson Fruit Co., Ltd., wreaths, 14.40; Supertest Petroleum Corporation, Ltd., gas, 329.70; C. V. Syrett Paper Co., tissue, 54.98; Victoria Paper & Twine Co., Ltd., twine, 24.20; Wilkinson-Kompass, Ltd., heater, etc., 27.40; Dr. J. J. Williams, travelling expenses, 86.10; Walter Woods, Ltd., pins, etc., 8.55; Wood, Alexander & James, Ltd., hardware, 50.52; petty disbursements, 121.61............................... 5,277 60

Repairs to Buildings, etc. ($36,650.86)

Maintenance and Repairs of all Buildings, Walks, Grounds and Fences, $18,248.23

Alliance Lumber Co., Ltd., 883.59; Aulcraft Paints, Ltd., 424.84; The Berryman Co., 74.64; Builders Supplies, Ltd., 218.03; Canada Crushed Stone Corporation, 88.21; Canadian Durex Abrasives, Ltd., 20.89; Canadian Metal Window and Steel Products, Ltd., 13.50; Canadian National Railways, 195.07; Canadian Pacific Railway Co., 98.18; Canada Paint Co., Ltd., 74.00; Canadian Rogers Sheet Metal & Roofing, Ltd., 206.06; Canada Varnish Co., Ltd., 73.50; Canada Wire & Iron Goods Co., Ltd., 120.90; Consumers Lumber Co., Ltd., 2,092.68; Crane, Ltd., 10.35; Dennisteel, Ltd., 95.04; Dominion Lumber & Coal Co., 203.89; Doolittle, Ltd., 394.06; Frost Steel & Wire Co., Ltd., 838.15; Gallagher Stone & Lime Co., Ltd., 168.39; Garvin Hardware Co., Ltd., 45.08; Goldie & McCulloch Co., Ltd., 246.00; M. E. Goodale & Son, 225.00; Hamilton Bridge Co., Ltd., 328.51; Hamilton Paint & Varnish Works, 79.63; Sackville Hill, 860.26; Dept. of Public Highways, 946.94; N. H. Howard, 86.25; Imperial Varnish & Color Co., Ltd., 183.21; Kent Tile & Marble Co., Ltd., 30.00; Martin-Senour Co., Ltd., 238.39; Meakins & Son, Ltd., 22.32; M. V. McLean, 38.00; National Sewer Pipe

Ontario Hospitals—Continued

Hamilton—Continued

Repairs to Buildings, etc.—Continued

Maintenance and Repairs of all Buildings, etc.—Continued

Co., Ltd., 22.79; Olmstead Iron Works, 887.65; Ontario Reformatory, Mimico, 928.15; Ontario Plate Glass Co., Ltd., 115.52; Ontario Reformatory Industries, 60.16; The A. B. Ormsby Co., Ltd., 392.00; Pay list, wages of men, 1,:27.96; Peckover's, Ltd., 18.08; The Pedlar People, Ltd., 61.73; Pilkington Bros., Ltd., 48.00; J. E. Riddell & Sons, Ltd., 1,017.20; Ritchie Cut Stone Co., Ltd., 53.00; Roberts & Deacon Saw Co., 20.13; Alfred Rogers, Ltd., 472.50; Scarfe & Co., Ltd., 155.70; Sherwin-Williams & Co., Ltd., 497.61; Malcolm Sinclair & Co., Ltd., 222.12; Steel Co. of Canada, Ltd., 11.04; Richard Tope Brick Works, 58.58; Toronto Lock & Mfg. Co., 141.79; Trelco, Ltd., 616.00; Tremco Mfg. Co., Ltd., 18.03; Wallie Moore Paint Co., 257.50; W. A. Ward, 11.25; Weights and Measures Inspector, 11.75; Wilkinson-Kompass, Ltd., 308.72; Wood, Alexander & James, Ltd., 943.37; petty disbursements, 46.34 .... 18,248 23

Maintenance and Repairs of Plumbing, Steam and Electric Plants, $16,857.61.

Aluminum, Ltd., 11.41; James Bain & Sons, 1,415.93; The Berryman Co., 73.50; Boiler Repair & Grate Bar Co., 215.66; Bull Dog Electric Products Co., Ltd., 105.11; H. Burnison, 260.00; H. C. Burton & Co., 67.72; The Brooks Oil Co., 393.96; Canadian National Express, 11.17; Canadian National Railways, 17.48; Canadian General Electric Co., Ltd., 11.33; Canadian Industries, Ltd., 89.31; Canadian Johns-Manville Co., Ltd., 456.68; Canadian Line Materials, 51.89; Canadian Westinghouse Co., Ltd., 122.07; Champion Oil & Varnish Co., 231.85; Commercial Oil Co., Ltd., 152.35; W. H. Cunningham & Hill, Ltd., 249.19; Crane, Ltd., 404.92; Dominion Radiator & Boiler Co., Ltd., 139.20; F. J. Downes & Co., 39.11; C. A. Dunham & Co., Ltd., 714.72; Drummond-McCall & Co., Ltd., 49.60; Empire Brass Mfg. Co., Ltd., 455.23; George Farrow & Son, 37.00; W. Fraser, 19.80; Garlock Packing Co., Ltd., 88.94; M. E. Goodale & Son, 41.10; Gurney Foundry Co., Ltd., 29.92; Gutta Percha & Rubber, Ltd., 34.92; Hamilton City Corporation, 22.86; Hamilton Engine Packing Co., 162.40; Hamilton Welding Co., 22.30; Imperial Oil, Ltd., 66.99; S. F. Lawrason & Co., Ltd., 144.80; The Arthur S. Leitch Co., Ltd., 76.90; Masco Co., Ltd., 26.89; McColl-Frontenac Oil Co., Ltd., 40.50; Northern Electric Co., Ltd., 1,183.23; Otis-Fensom Elevator Co., Ltd., 12.50; Pay liscs, wages of men, 3,672.53; The Pedlar People, Ltd., 10.08; Powerlite Devices, 29.11; John E. Riddell & Son, Ltd., 18.44; Regent Electric Supply Co., Ltd., 34.79; Roelofson Elevator Works, 3,546.85; Geo. Sparrow & Co., Ltd., 22.95; Standard Sanitary Mfg. Co., Ltd., 35.91; Standard Underground Cable Co., Ltd., 97.64; Supplies & Insulation Co., 132.30; Taylor-Forbes Co., Ltd., 142.92; Trane Co., Ltd.; 150.57; Vallance, Brown & Co., 38.54; Wilkinson-Kompass, Ltd., 739.65; Williams Tool Corporation, 21.25; A. R. Williams Machinery Co., Ltd., 43.00; Wilson Illumination Co., Ltd., 205.21; Wood, Alexander & James, Ltd., 82.15; petty disbursements, 83.28 .... 16,857 61

Live Stock, Vehicles and Farm Implements, $1,545.02.

A. B. Brubecker, 765.00; James Bain & Son, 11.20; R. J. Cole, 300.00; International Harvester Co., Ltd., 143.35; Garfield McDennett, 125.00; Ontario Hospital, Whitby, 25.00; H. Sturch, 170.00; petty disbursements, 5.47 .... 1,545 02

Total		468,620 93
Less Maintenance of Patients	118,906 98	
Perquisites	43,724 73	
Sale of Produce	11,729 56	
		174,361 27
Hamilton		294,259 66

KINGSTON

Salaries ($205,196.07)

Superintendent, Physicians and Dentists	23,461 37
Steward and Assistants	9,971 58
Matron and Assistants, including Domestic Help	18,419 95
Engineer and Assistants	15,950 00
Artisans, not Domestic	8,100 00
Farm and Garden Employees	9,075 00
Attendants and Nurses	120,218 17

Ontario Hospitals—Continued

Kingston—Continued

Expenses ($154,965.43)

Medicines, $5,637.46.

Ash-Temple Co., Ltd., 43.50; Austin's Drug Store, 239.94; Ayerst, McKenna & Harrison, Ltd., 77.92; Burroughs Wellcome & Co., 87.54; Dr. Clarence Buck, 75.00; Canadian National Express, 21.54; Connaught Laboratories, 26.88; Denver Chemical Mfg. Co., 12.51; C. E. Frosst & Co., 380.36; A. D. Gibson, 123.75; F. J. Hoag, 150.64; Hargraft Bros., Ltd., 311.50; J. F. Hartz Co., Ltd., 1,044.04; Imperial Tobacco Co., Ltd., 450.00; Ingram & Bell, Ltd., 483.92; Jackson Press, 10.00; Jury & Peacock, 40.95; Kingston General Hospital, 10.00; Lewis Mfg. Co., Ltd., 190.39; Liquor Control Board, 156.96; McCall's Drug Store, 148.80; W. C. MacDonald, 251.00; R. E. Mitchell, 220.50; Parke Davis & Co., 17.79; W. J. Peters, 302.41; Standard Tobacco Co., Ltd., 17.32; Stevens Co., 58.02; Synthetic Drug Co., Ltd., 27.06; Textile Products Co., 35.00; Tuckett, Ltd., 178.74; G. S. Trudell & Co., 82.00; H. K. Wampole & Co., Ltd., 196.09; Ward & Hamilton Drugs, Ltd., 20.16; G. H. Wood & Co., Ltd., 82.00; petty disbursements, 63.23 .... 5,637 46

Groceries and Provisions, $64,981.67.

Amodoe Bros., 208.06; Anderson Bros., Ltd., 4,596.68; W. A. Babcock, 78.75; Beaver Food Products, Ltd., 84.00; A. Birrell, 206.50; Booth Fisheries, Ltd., 3,091.97; Bowes Co., Ltd., 8,705.25; T. F. Burke, 3,898.95; E. Campbell, 111.25; Canada & Dominion Sugar Co., Ltd., 467.56; Canada Packers, Ltd., 188.00; Canada Vinegars, Ltd., 82.12; Canadian National Railways, 79.06; Canadian Pacific Railway Co., 13.77; H. G. Cooke, 4,997.50; Copeland Flour Mills, Ltd., 3,039.25; W. J. Crothers, Ltd., 447.66; Dalton Bros., Ltd., 41.60; C. Ellerbeck, 28.13; Everready Tea Bag Co., 97.02; D. Freeman, 150.40; K. C. Freeman, 874.64; Higgins & Burke, Ltd., 189.75; S. Hisey & Son, 504.75; W. Hughes, 16.20; F. W. Humphrey Co., Ltd., 589.15; G. Johnston, 14.50; F. Krouse, 142.80; E. Lazenby & Sons, Ltd., 33.07; J. A. McFarlane & Son, 895.10; J. Marshall, 3,498.28; G. Mascud, 20.68; A. W. Milne, in trust, 10.00; Moreland Coffee Co., 67.20; National Grocers Co., Ltd., 612.01; Newmarket Flour Mills, 945.50; Ontario Hospital, London, 206.25; Ontario Reformatory Industries, 19,191.17; Ontario Reformatory, 40.00; Ontario Boys' Training School, Bowmanville, 182.25; Price's Dairy, 11.20; Robertson Grocery Co., Ltd., 4,176.87; W. Sloan, 32.50; A. E. Smith, 43.88; Smithfield Milling Co., 19.60; Standard Brands, Ltd., 432.79; F. W. Stull Transport, 582.84; R. H. Toye & Co., 897.90; T. H. Watson, 100.40; petty disbursements, 36.91 .... 64,981 67

Fuel, Light and Water, $42,035.40.

British American Oil Co., Ltd., 17.40; Canadian Laco Lamps, Ltd., 149.68; Canadian General Electric Co., 21.66; W. B. Dalton & Sons, Ltd., 33.12; Eddy Match Co., Ltd., 66.85; Kingston Public Utilities Commission, 3,692.81; Simmons Bros., Ltd., 12.50; J. Sowards Coal Co., 38,040.13; petty disbursements, 1.25 .... 42,035 40

Clothing, $14,433.00.

Bibbys, Ltd., 12.75; Canadian National Express, 19.76; Canadian National Railways, 32.93; The Circle Bar Knitting Co., Ltd., 356.25; Coghill Tailoring Co., 1,580.00; W. B. Dalton & Sons, Ltd., 452.18; J. M. Garland, Son & Co., Ltd., 265.09; A. D. Gibson, 343.68; Greenshields, Ltd., 497.93; Johnston, Crossley & McComb, Ltd., 49.50; J. Laidlaw & Son, 69.75; B. Lipman, 465.90; Mercer Reformatory Industries, 4,818.42; Midland Shoe Co., Ltd., 1,121.21; Moodie's Underwear, Ltd., 592.50; Ontario Reformatory Industries, 1,011.63; Ontario Hospital, Orillia, Industries, 422.30; A. M. Reid, 41.00; D. A. Shaw, Ltd., 1,131.49; Shaw's Men's Wear, 101.50; Storey Glove Co., 89.00; Superior Cloak Co., 585.00; Woods Manufacturing Co., Ltd., 322.50; York Manufacturing Co., Ltd., 17.50; petty disbursements, 33.23 .... 14,433 00

Laundry and Cleaning, $5,626.20.

Associated Chemical Co., Ltd., 525.47; The Beaver Laundry Machinery Co., Ltd., 215.02; Canada Colours & Chemical Co., Ltd., 51.50; Canadian National Institute for the Blind, 58.50; Canadian National Railways, 76.87; Cherry-Burrell Corporation, 24.20; The Colgate-Palmolive-Peet Co., Ltd., 36.74; W. B. Dalton & Sons, Ltd., 1,647.92; Diamond Cleanser, Ltd., 179.50; Electric Boiler Compound Co., Ltd., 168.82; Excelsior Brushes, Ltd., 43.56; Guelph Soap Co., Ltd., 55.00; P. S. Graham, 49.10; G. A. Hardie & Co., 18.20; F. J. Hoag, 113.29; Imperial Oil, Ltd., 41.15; A. Jergens Co., Ltd., 206.32; S. C. Johnson & Son, Ltd., 14.03; C. W. Langworth, 27.50; Lavoline Cleanser Co., Ltd., 47.77;

Ontario Hospitals—Continued

Kingston—Continued

Expenses—Continued

Laundry and Cleaning—Continued

H. W. Marshall, 44.40; Martin's Transport, 26.37; Metropolitan Transport, 11.38; National Grocers Co., Ltd., 48.50; Premier Laundry Equipment Co., 79.24; Rexo Chemical Cleaner Co., Ltd., 1,058.05; Robertson Grocery Co., Ltd., 234.22; Saunders Electric Co., 15.10; Simmons Bros., Ltd., 348.50; G. H. Wood & Co., Ltd., 122.01; petty disbursements, 37.97.................... 5,626 20

Furniture and Furnishings, $10,475.65.

Aluminum Goods, Ltd., 108.05; W. Anderson, 11.25; S. Anglin Co., Ltd., 52.50; Beaver Laundry Machinery Co., Ltd., 23.52; Bond Engineering Works, 390.00; Caldwell Linen Mills, Ltd., 163.13; Canadian National Express, 10.39; Canadian National Railways, 50.48; Cassidy's, Ltd., 107.38; Clatworthy & Son, Ltd., 56.10; Crescent Wire & Iron Works, 85.91; W. B. Dalton & Sons, Ltd., 2,140.38; Delaney & Pettit, Ltd., 113.10; General Steel Wares, Ltd., 10.77; A. D. Gibson, 634.20; J. Garde & Co., Ltd., 175.57; Graves Bros., 244.71; Greenshield, Ltd., 277.94; S. Hamilton, 40.15; F. W. Harold, 73.56; Hobart Manufacturing Co., 15.40; W. Junor, Ltd., 133.38; King Paper Sales Co., 12.26; Mahood Bros., 12.85; The Masco Co., Ltd., 11.11; Martin Transports, Ltd., 12.54; H. Mendes & Co., 81.00; Mercer Reformatory Industries, 2,386.03; North American Bent Chair Co., 47.50; Ontario Reformatory Industries, 1,624.20; Pendrith Machinery Co., 65.70; J. Reid 174.15; D. A. Shaw, 793.02; Simmons Bros., Ltd., 68.93; The Robert Simpson Co., Ltd., 65.00; Singer Sewing Machine Co., 20.86; F. W. Stull Transport, 94.65; R. G. Venn, 11.17; B. O. Whitney, 44.00; petty disbursements, 32.81.. 10,475 65

Office Expenses, $1,212.71.

The Bell Telephone Co., rentals, 474.36; tolls, 69.28; Canadian National Express, 15.35; Canadian National Railways, 12.51; Canadian National Telegraphs, 29.22; Canadian Pacific Railway Co., 13.15; Canadian Pacific Telegraphs, 31.45; J. R. C. Dobbs & Co., 11.95; Jackson Press, 39.90; Murdoch Stationery, 16.00; Postmaster, 490.00; petty disbursements, 9.54.. 1,212 71

Farm Expenses, $5,025.85.

Andrewes Mountain Seed Co., Ltd., 162.00; Associated Chemical Co., Ltd., 32.44; British American Oil Co., Ltd., 306.68; Brookdale Nurseries, 66.30; J. B. Bunt & Co., 84.45; Canada Mineral Products, Ltd., 140.00; Canadian National Railways, 16.21; J. F. Cramer, 41.80; W. B. Dalton & Sons, Ltd., 290.21; Foster Pottery Co., 11.00; C. Giddy, 15.00; N. Graham, 100.00; S. Hamilton, 12.03; Holstein-Friesian Association, 12.50; Kingston Milling Co., Ltd., 55.60; Kingston Penitentiary, 154.12; Lakeside Milling Co., Ltd., 502.50; McConnell Nursery Co., 35.90; J. A. McFarlane & Son, 711.91; R. Moore & Sons, 18.20; National Fertilizer, Ltd., 192.30; W. Nicholls, 98.75; J. M. Patrick, 56.75; W. P. Peters Seed Co., Ltd., 403.40; Simmons Bros., Ltd., 89.45; J. C. Spence, 45.00; Steele, Briggs Seed Co., Ltd., 90.02; H. Swaffield, 152.70; J. J. Taugher, 211.02; Taylor-Forbes Co., Ltd., 22.32; Toronto Elevators, Ltd., 790.00; John Trudell, 61.25; petty disbursements, 44.04.. 5,025 85

Contingencies, $5,537.49.

American Psychiatric Association, subscription, 10.00; Atlantic Service Co., Ltd., repairs, 11.24; L. E. Austin, services, 200.00; British American Oil Co., Ltd., oil, 15.00; C. A. Buck, travelling expenses, 333.75; Canadian National Express, 18.05; K. Carscallen, travelling expenses, 38.95; H. Collins, travelling expenses, 10.25; C. Compeau, subscriptions, 23.40; S. S. Corbett, interments, 70.00; J. Cornelius, interments, 875.00; C. M. Crawford, travelling expenses, 28.90; T. D. Cumberland, travelling expenses, 82.60; W. B. Dalton & Sons, Ltd., paper bags, etc., 243.09; M. A. Davis, travelling expenses, 124.60; H. Dine, auto repairs, 11.75; Douglas & Dunlop Garage, gas, 323.46; J. F. Doyle, gas, 160.91; Edwards & Edwards, leather, 24.24; Frontenac Battery Service, repairs, 11.25; Goodyear Tire & Rubber Co., Ltd., tubes, 149.30; J. G. Graham, travelling expenses, 58.90; R. S. Graham, travelling expenses, 29.05; R. Greenlees, repairs, 47.45; Grinham's Book Shop, books, etc., 172.35; S. W. Houston, medical services, 50.00; Imperial Optical Co., glasses, 62.80; Jackson Press, printing, 47.70; Dr. S. J. Keyes, services, 10.00; Kingston City Coach Lines, transportation, 33.90; Kingston General Hospital, medical services, 67.50; G. H. Kirkpatrick, flowers, 54.00; J. Laidlaw & Son, supplies, 78.21; C. H. Lewis, travelling expenses, 419.59; M. Lewis, travelling expenses, 21.00; H. F. Lumb, travelling expenses, 30.10; Musical Services, 307.00; T. Nelson & Sons, books, 15.00; Ontario Medical

Ontario Hospitals—Continued

Kingston—Continued

Expenses—Continued

Contingencies—Continued

Association, subscription, 10.00; J. Reid, ambulance, 12.00; Religious Services, 785.00; B. Sears, travelling expenses, 27.37; D. A. Shaw, Ltd., supplies, 163.86; Simmons Bros., Ltd., supplies, 57.54; Smith & Walsh, car insurance, 36.20; C. T. Stewart, travelling expenses, 14.65; A. L. Torgis & Son, auto supplies, 44.51; Treadgold Sporting Goods Co., lawn bowls, etc., 28.20; Wickett & Craig, buffings, 19.05; petty disbursements, 126.65 .... 5,595 32
Less refund Dental Services for patients 57 83
5,537 49

Repairs to Buildings, etc. ($28,820.58)

Maintenance and Repairs of all Buildings, Walks, Grounds and Fences, $13,952.22.

S. Anglin & Co., Ltd., 221.03; Aulcraft Paints, Ltd., 29.40; The Barrett Co., Ltd., 470.72; Belleville-Sargent Co., Ltd., 651.29; Canada Paint Co., Ltd., 39.50; Canada Varnish Co., Ltd., 116.38; Canadian General Electric Co., Ltd., 25.46; Canadian National Railways, 507.02; Carr Chromatox Co., Ltd., 11.47; W. B. Dalton & Sons, Ltd., 2,021.03; Disher Steel Construction Co., Ltd., 112.00; W. Drury, 250.31; L. G. Freeman, 368.40; Graves Bros., 91.21; Gurney Foundry Co., Ltd., 34.76; S. Hamilton, 129.14; Imperial Varnish & Colour Co., Ltd., 90.93; Italian Mosaic & Tile Co., Ltd., 39.50; City of Kingston, 27.00; Kingston Sand & Gravel Co., Ltd., 42.50; J. Laird & Sons, 223.61; Lowe Bros. Co., Ltd., 209.18; G. McGill, 28.50; Metropolitan Transport, 33.90; J. H. Morin, 520.00; Ontario Reformatory, Mimico, 1,164.14; Ontario Hospital, Mimico, 40.00; J. M. Patrick, 33.95; Pay list, wages of men, 4,479.00; Peckovers, Ltd., 91.13; The Pedlar People, Ltd., 36.09; Pembroke Lumber Co., Ltd., 683.73; W. E. Phillips Co., 83.05; J. Robertson Co., Ltd., 21.58; C. H. Rodden, 268.03; Sanderson, Pearcy & Marietta, Ltd., 248.00; The Sherwin-Williams Co., Ltd., 70.29; Simmons Bros., Ltd., 167.12; G. Sparrow & Co., 17.00; J. J. Taugher, 14.09; The Tremco Manufacturing Co., Ltd., 150.64; petty disbursements, 90.14 .... 13,952 22

Maintenance and Repairs of Plumbing, Steam and Electric Plants, $12,293.13.

Anderson Bros., 17.70; A. Bain, 13.60; Beaver Laundry & Machinery Co., Ltd., 26.02; T. G. Bishop, 157.20; Boiler Repair & Grate Bar Co., 28.51; Boyd Electric Co., 220.96; Canada Colours & Chemicals, Ltd., 63.86; Canadian Asbestos Ontario, Ltd., 16.50; Canadian Foundry Supplies & Equipment, Ltd., 635.20; Canadian Ice Machine Co., Ltd., 72.34; Canadian Industries, Ltd., 73.12; Canadian National Express, 33.25; Canadian National Railways, 76.84; Canadian Powers Regulator Co., Ltd., 336.00; Canadian Westinghouse Co., Ltd., 14.34; Clarence St. Garage, 20.25; Crane Co., Ltd., 52.20; W. H. Cunningham & Hill, Ltd., 72.44; W. B. Dalton & Sons, Ltd., 187.00; Dearborn Chemical Co., Ltd., 801.83; R. Dewsbury, 17.17; Dictograph Products Co., Ltd., 93.00; Dominion Oxygen Co., Ltd., 30.03; Drury's, 23.00; Empire Brass Manufacturing Co., Ltd., 349.41; Everlasting Valve Co., 64.13; Findlay Bros. & Co., Ltd., 11.60; E. T. Flanagan, 131.67; Garlock Packing Co., Ltd., 417.27; P. S. Graham, 165.34; Graves Bros., 34.49; S. Hamilton, 753.00; J. Harris, 150.08; F. J. Hoag, 17.15; Huston Oil Co., Ltd., 161.00; Imperial Oil, Ltd., 91.70; King Refractories, Ltd., 471.15; Kingston Public Utilities Commission, 23.40; Kingston Shipbuilding Co., Ltd., 42.59; La France Fire Engine & Foamite Co., 16.98; A. S. Leitch & Co., Ltd., 722.22; Lernon & Son, 20.34; Martin Transports, Ltd., 21.11; The Masco Co., Ltd., 71.62; Matthews Cartage, 121.59; G. B. Meadows, Ltd., 12.00; Metropolitan Transport, 33.38; Jas. Morrison Brass Manufacturing Co., Ltd., 488.27; Northern Electric Co., Ltd., 21.01; Oshawa Electric Supply Co., Ltd., 58.38; Pay list, wages of men, 2,540.20; H. W. Petrie, Ltd., 50.14; Premier Laundry Equipment Co., 65.77; Pridmore's Eastern Express, 76.64; Pyrene Manufacturing Co., Ltd., 143.57; Radio Den, 14.30; Regent Electric Supply Co., Ltd., 49.54; Robertson Grocery Co., 171.60; The G. Robertson Co., Ltd., 50.90; Rogers Electric Co., Ltd., 45.14; Saunders Electric Co., Ltd., 10.80; Simmons Bros., Ltd., 114.11; Smart-Turner Machine Co., Ltd., 81.35; Standard Sales Service, 16.50; Standard Underground Cable Co., Ltd., 16.39; G. F. Sterne & Sons, 286.75; J. J. Taugher, 134.63; Trane Co. of Canada, Ltd., 20.58; Turnbull Elevator Co., Ltd., 406.05; Wallace & Tiernan, Ltd., 126.91; W. J. Westaway Co., Ltd., 95.00; R. Williamson, 22.05; Wilson Illumination Co., Ltd., 101.63; petty disbursements, 99.34 .... 12,293 13

Live Stock, Vehicles and Farm Implements, $2,575.23.

Canadian National Railways, 38.72; C. H. Doering, 875.00; R. H. Fair, 200.00;

Ontario Hospitals—Continued

Kingston—Continued

Repairs to Buildings, etc.—Continued

Live Stock, Vehicles and Farm Implements—Continued

Frost & Wood Co., Ltd., 249.05; A. D. Gorrie Co., Ltd., 763.46; J. E. Siddell, 375.00; Trout Electric Hatchery, 74.00 .... 2,575 23

Total		388,982 08	
Less Maintenance of Patients	66,540 82		
Perquisites	29,302 28		
Sale of Produce	2,125 24		
		97,968 34	
Kingston		291,013 74	

LONDON

Salaries ($277,728.70)

Superintendent, Physicians and Dentists	24,470 46
Steward and Assistants	16,479 17
Matron and Assistants, including domestic help	42,140 61
Engineers and Assistants	21,917 00
Artisans, not domestic	9,237 22
Farm and Garden Employees	18,550 00
Attendants and Nurses	144,934 24

Expenses ($175,094.20)

Medicines, $8,420.27.

Ash-Temple Co., Ltd., 190.05; Bovinine Co., 31.42; Burroughs, Wellcome & Co., Ltd., 191.45; Connaught Laboratories, 34 10; Canadian Pacific Express, 17.19; Dental Co. of Canada, Ltd., 98.73; Difco Laboratories, 110.66; Chas. E. Frosst & Co., 250.46; Charles Gyde & Sons, Ltd., 12.00; J. F. Hartz Co., Ltd., 256.26; Hygiene Products, Ltd., 13.80; Ingram & Bell, Ltd., 729.45; Imperial Tobacco Co., 50.50; Lewis Mfg Co., Ltd., 537.04; Liquor Control Board, 82.20; London Optical Co., 97.20; W. C. Macdonald, 1,218.60; R. E. Mitchell, 140.50; National Drug & Chemical Co., Ltd., 686.21; National Grocers Co., Ltd., 104.95; Parke Davis & Co., Ltd., 118.99; Petrolagar Laboratories, 12.00; W. E. Saunders & Co., Ltd., 498.91; A. M. Smith & Co., 61.84; Strong's Drug Store, 242.19; B. Shuttleworth & Co., Ltd., 45.85; Smith & Nephew, 154.43; The Stevens Co., 87.62; Standard Tobacco Co., 103.32; Synthetic Drug Co., Ltd., 78.20; Geo. S. Trudell & Co., 539.31; Textile Products Co., 31.50; Tuckett, Ltd., 1,029.17; Victor X-ray Corporation, 76.67; Charles R. Will & Co., Ltd., 318.41; Henry K. Wampole & Co., Ltd., 41.76; petty disbursements, 127.33 .... 8,420 27

Provisions, $70,228.27.

Acadia Sugar Refining Co., Ltd., 73.89; American Can Co., 1,873.70; G. Bartman, 25.40; Bowes & Co., Ltd., 11,486.97; Canadian National Railways, 479.81; Coleman & Co., 996.55; Connor Bros., 101.02; Christie Brown & Co., Ltd., 23.42; Crosse & Blackwell, Ltd., 59.28; Dominion Linseed Oil Co., Ltd., 33.83; T. Dexter & Son, 837.00; T. B. Escott, 746.13; K. C. Freeman, 624.25; J. R. Hayden Co., 89.10; Jack Hamilton, 71.40; Hunt Milling Co., Ltd., 3,521.78; Harry Horne Co., Ltd., 142.56; F. W. Humphrey Co., Ltd., 99.66; I. X. L. Spice & Coffee Mills, Ltd., 1,769.80; Langford & Edwards, 119.30; E. Lazenby & Son, 292.00; London Cold Storage & Warehouse Co., Ltd., 91.35; James Lumbers Co., Ltd., 379.50; A. Leff, 15.00; W. Marsh, 274.05; Marshall Bros. & Co., 282.10; C. A. Mann & Co., 33.00; Maple Leaf Milling Co., Ltd., 41.94; McCormick Mfg. Co., Ltd., 260.10; National Grocers Co., Ltd., 5,981.18; Mrs. Geo. Nyman, 45.00; Onns Meat Market, 2,993.75; Ontario Reformatory Industries, 21,673.68; Ontario Creamery, Ltd., 326.16; D. S. Perrin & Co., Ltd., 265.71; W. Paterson, Ltd., 48.69; Silverwoods, Ltd., 1,335.11; Saul's Dairy, 1,173.60; Silversteins, 85.50; A. M. Smith & Co., 8,437.91; Silverwoods Milk Products, Ltd., 226.96; Smith Creamery, 832.28; Sargeant Co., Ltd., 101.61; Standard Brands, Ltd., 650.63; Swift-Canadian Co., Ltd., 1,081.67; Alfred Tune, 53.00; W. Waddell, 24.00; Young Winfield, Ltd., 18.51; petty disbursements, 29.43 .... 70,228 27

Fuel, $28,420.72.

H. C. Burton & Co., 402.60; Canadian Coal Co., Ltd., 16,954.70; City Gas Co., 274.20; Catholic Record, 19.32; Chantler Bros., 66.00; Eddy Match Co., Ltd., 139.26; D. H. Howden & Co., Ltd., 27.42; Hunt Coal Co., 133.00; Hobb's Hardware Co., Ltd., 13.60; Public Utilities Commission, 10,232.23; Towe & Towe, 136.80; petty disbursements, 21.59 .... 28,420 72

Ontario Hospitals—Continued

London—Continued

Expenses—Continued

Clothing, $20,915.80.

Canadian National Railways, 25.94; Circle Bar Knitting Co., Ltd., 280.00; Dominion Rubber Co., Ltd., 13.31; W. Farrar & Co., Ltd., 572.00; W. H. Graham, 520.62; Greene Swift Co., Ltd., 1,590.35; Greene & Moule, 772.40; Johnstone's Hat Shop, 186.25; Johnston, Crossley, McComb, Ltd., 199.50; Kingsmill's, Ltd., 391.25; Barnet Lipman, 37.22; McMahon, Grainger & Co., Ltd., 2,771.13; Mercer Reformatory Industries, 5,044.36; Mocdie's Underwear, Ltd., 271.50; Martin Transports, Ltd., 41.15; W. L. Mara, 146.71; C. R. Moule, 262.50; Northern Rubber Co., Ltd., 295.68; Ontario Reformatory Industries, 2,357.38; Ontario Hospital, Orillia, Industries, 564.97; Penmans, Ltd., 220.20; Schofield Woollen Co., Ltd., 975.00; Sterling Bros., Ltd., 2,609.14; R. W. Wray & Co., 568.20; Woods Mfg. Co., Ltd., 127.65; F. W. Woolworth Co., Ltd., 10.05; petty disbursements, 61.34 .... 20,915 80

Laundry, $9,540.83.

Alpha Chemical Co., Ltd., 129.60; Associated Chemical Co., Ltd., 689.54; Aulcraft Paints, Ltd., 21.17; Brantford Willow Works, 10.80; Joseph Burns, 78.97; Canadian National Institute for the Blind, 440.91; Canadian Colors & Chemicals, Ltd., 59.00; Canadian National Railways, 34.20; Diamond Cleansers, Ltd., 40.00; J. A. Darrow, 16.75; Dominion Linseed Oil Co., Ltd., 62.87; T. B. Escott & Co., Ltd., 22.00; Guelph Soap Co., Ltd., 77.60; A. Graham Scott, 20.64; Hay Stationery Co., Ltd., 79.80; G. A. Hardie & Co., Ltd., 105.69; Hobbs Hardware Co., Ltd., 246.47; D. H. Howden & Co., Ltd., 437.81; Edward Hawes & Co., Ltd., 30.00; Imperial Oil, Ltd., 37.72; International Trading Co., 28.00; S. F. Lawrason & Co., Ltd., 851.18; Lavoline Cleanser Co., Ltd., 20.58; London Soap Co., Ltd., 2,300.18; London Cleansers Supply House, 83.40; Paint Service, 12.25; London Stencil & Stamp Works, 15.60; The Levis, 90.00; McMahon, Grainger Co., Ltd., 107.98; Mercer Reformatory Industries, 120.50; MacKinnon Sales, 69.00; National Grocers Co., Ltd., 332.14; National Drug & Chemical Co., Ltd., 29.24; Ontario Reformatory Industries, 21.60; Roxo Chemical Cleanser Co., Ltd., 40.79; Reckitts (Oversea), Ltd., 529.23; Scott Paint & Varnish Co., Ltd., 187.69; A. M. Smith & Co., Ltd., 1,211.23; Swift Canadian Co., Ltd., 450.00; Sunclo Products, 16.25; G. H. Wood & Co., Ltd., 272.43; West Disinfecting Co., 60.88; petty disbursements, 49.14 .... 9,540 83

Furniture and Furnishings, $17,546.52.

J. A. Brownlee, 100.72; Canadian National Railways, 21.73; Canadian Pacific Railway Co., 14.62; Continental Salvage Corporation, 331.50; Canadian National Institute for the Blind, 27.00; Caldwell Linen Mills, Ltd., 363.29; S. B. Clark, 22.00; Canadian Speedo Co., 36.00; Dennisteel, Ltd., 79.20; Delany & Pettit, Ltd., 182.20; Gutta Percha & Rubber, Ltd., 42.56; Hay Stationery Co., Ltd., 84.38; Hobbs Hardware Co., Ltd., 352.04; D. H. Howden & Co., Ltd., 306.39; Interlake Tissue Mills Co., Ltd., 207.30; Johnson & Barbour, 257.43; Kingsmill's, Ltd., 694.62; A. A. Langford Co., Ltd., 80.22; McMahon, Grainger & Co., Ltd., 387.87; Martin Transports, Ltd., 25.69; Mercer Reformatory Industries, 4,676.76; Henry Mendes & Co., 212.85; National Grocers Co., Ltd., 15.99; Ontario Crockery Co., Ltd., 1,185.52; Ontario Reformatory Industries, 4,926.54; Public Utilities Commission, 45.00; Red Star News Co., 25.00; Smallman & Ingram, Ltd., 54.00; A. M. Smith & Co., 37.97; F. W. Stull Transport Co., 114.20; Sully Brass Foundry, Ltd., 375.01; Super Health Aluminum Co., Ltd., 132.53; Textile Products Co., 568.17; R. G. Venn, 44.68; James Wright & Co., 1,409.32; Wyatt Furniture Co., 61.96; petty disbursements, 44.26 .... 17,546 52

Office Expenses, $1,837.93.

Bell Telephone Co., rentals, 560.71; tolls, 143.38; Canadian National Express, 16.55; Canadian National Telegraphs, 66.53; Canadian Pacific Express, 26.80; Grand & Toy, Ltd., 45.00; Hay Stationery Co., 33.63; Postmaster, 879.00; Smith Typewriter Service, 23.80; Vernon Directories, Ltd., 18.00; petty disbursements, 24.53 .... 1,837 93

Farm Expenses, $13,025.08.

Alpha Chemical Co., Ltd., 61.20; Associated Chemical Co., Ltd., 78.40; Beatty Bros., Ltd., 18.93; Canadian Oil Cos, Ltd., 538.18; Canada Mineral Products, Ltd., 260.00; Cowan Hardware, Ltd., 27.38; Charcoal Supply Co., Ltd., 10.00; Canadian Pacific Railway Co., 182.59; Frank Dunn, 147.00; Dominion Linseed Oil Co., Ltd., 42.65; T. Dexter & Son, 30.00; Eureka Planter Co., Ltd., 15.00; Forest Basket Co., Ltd., 66.75; John Garlick, 108.80; E. Girvan, 54.07; John

Ontario Hospitals—Continued

London—Continued

Expenses—Continued

Farm Expenses—Continued

Goodison Thresher Co., Ltd., 33.12; Hayman Mills, 1,006.17; Hobbs Hardware Co., Ltd., 170.06; D. H. Howden & Co., Ltd., 217.59; Hayman & Mills, 279.30; Hunt Milling Co., Ltd., 1,406.45; John Joynt, 100.00; Jenkins Manufacturing Co., Ltd., 2,338.58; Kellogg Co. of Canada, Ltd., 1,845.00; A. G. Karn, 27.60; John Labatt, Ltd., 160.21; London Township, 35.14; Maple Leaf Milling Co., Ltd., 1,430.50; W. McDonald, 187.00; Morgans Supply House, 139.43; Ralph Moore & Sons, 42.70; Marchment Co., Ltd., 73.20; W. J. Mihm, 41.72; Murdock Seed Co., Ltd., 324.05; Robert Marshall, 63.51; E. McCarthy, 56.31; Massey-Harris Co., Ltd., 35.44; Niagara Brand Spray Co., Ltd., 120.58; National Grocers Co., Ltd., 38.93; Ontario Reformatory Industries, 290.00; Geo. Penfound, 55.00; W. Pickell, 140.00; W. A. Piper, 169.89; Ralston Purina Co., Ltd., 41.00; Silverwoods, Ltd., 15.08; Silverwoods Milk Products, Ltd., 54.88; H. E. Smith, 13.05; Spraymotor Co., Ltd., 13.70; Stull Transport Co., 42.00; John Tack, 185.70; Tudhope Anderson Co., Ltd., 19.80; James Wright & Co., 108.28; petty disbursements, 63.16 .... 13,025 08

Contingencies, $5,158.78.

American Psychiatric Association, fees, 10.00; Canadian National Express, express, 34.34; Canadian Oil Cos, Ltd., gas, 582.51; Catholic Record, printing, 18.85; S. G. Chalk, travelling expenses, 831.20; Dominion Rubber Co., Ltd., casings, 36.96; Dennisteel, Ltd., guards, 17.82; Dicks Flowers, bouquets, 49.00; Erskine Bros., repairs, 126.88; English Auto Wreckers, 35.57; F. S. Fisher, travelling expenses, 24.69; General Motors Products, Ltd., parts, 19.68; Gray's Book Store, periodicals, 216.45; Gutta Percha & Rubber, Ltd., cover, etc., 48.10; Wendell Holmes, Ltd., books, 77.62; Ingram & Bell, Ltd., books, 19.34; R. Jeffrey, travelling expenses, 12.40; E. C. Killingsworth, burial, 45.00; E. Kennedy, travelling expenses, 14.90; T. Kirkland, travelling expenses, 23.90; G. E. Logan, burials, 157.50; London Billiard Table & Supply House, supplies, 34.20; London Advertiser, advertising, 68.46; London Tent & Awning Co., Ltd., rent of tent, 12.00; London Battery & Tire Repair Co., repairs, 38.76; London Free Press Printing Co., advertising, 127.79; Dr. D. O. Lynch, travelling expenses, 10.05; A. R. Lewis, travelling expenses, 15.10; London Printing & Litho Co., Ltd., printing, 101.25; London Technical & Commercial High School fees, 26.00; London Hudson-Essex Sales, repairs, 14.50; McMahon, Grainger & Co., Ltd., wool, floss, etc., 282.55; M. McArthur, travelling expenses, 62.38; A. Morphy, repairs, 23.00; Ruth McConnell, travelling expenses, 21.50; Musical Services, 485.50; Macmillan Co., Ltd., books, 56.08; National Grocers Co., Ltd., 22.99; John A. Nash, repairs, 91.70; Ontario Medical Association, fee, 10.00; People's Electric Co., tubes, 11.28; Religious Services, 430.00; Dr. G. A. Ramsey, service, 10.00; Rapid Grip & Batten, Ltd., photos, 25.00; Red Star News Co., services re mail bag, 24.00; A. M. Smith & Co., bags, twine, etc., 206.34; C. H. Stoelting Co., tests, 17.70; Smith & Walsh, car insurance, 49.94; Supertest Petroleum Corporation, motor oil, 31.15; George S. Trudell Co., skeleton, 100.00; Dr. F. S. Vrooman, travelling expenses, 65.95; Victoria Hospital, lectures, 45.00; M. Wilson & Son, auto repairs, 10.25; petty disbursements, 225.65 .... 5,158 78

Repairs to Buildings, $69,645.50.

Maintenance and Repairs of all Buildings, Roads, Walks, Grounds and Fences, $43,955.15.

Ault & Wiborg Co., Ltd., 13.72; Aulcraft Paints, Ltd., 306.64; Brick Mfg. Supply Co., Ltd., 1,737.90; J. A. Brownlee, 721.83; Brooks Oil Co., 66.15; John Bowman, 20.00; Canadian National Railways, 40.23; Canadian Pacific Railway Co., 601.74; Cowan Hardware Co., Ltd., 48.33; Canadian Oil Cos., Ltd., 12.60; Canadian Paint Co., Ltd., 54.65; Clatworthy Lumber Co., Ltd., 420.12; Corporation of the City of London, 26.24; Colerick Bros., 28.85; F. W. Crispo & Co., 10.80; Dennisteel, Ltd., 1,204.28; Dyment Baker Lumber Co., Ltd., 3,054.16; Edwards Bros. Glass Co., 51.24; John Fredin & Son, 10.00; General Steel Wares, Ltd., 241.60; Hayman & Mills, 2,703.57; Hobbs Hardware Co., Ltd., 835.09; Hobbs Mfg. Co., 121.10; D. H. Howden & Co., Ltd., 620.81; J. H. Howard, 33.65; Italian Mosaic & Marble Co., Ltd., 4,250.55; Imperial Varnish Co., Ltd., 72.85; W. Jefferies, 179.00; Kernohan Lumber Co., Ltd., 456.41; Kilpatrick Bros., 36.20; W. Liley, 652.00; London Structural Steel Co., Ltd., 2,397.62; London Paint Service, 294.48; Lowe Bros., Ltd., 265.48; Metal Craft Co., Ltd., 30.00; McMahon, Grainger & Co., Ltd., 84.88; Martin Senour Co., Ltd., 113.54; Ontario Reformatory, Mimico, 646.29; Ontario Reformatory Industries, 389.96; A. B. Ormsby Co., Ltd., 632.00; Pay list, wages of men, 17,973.95; Pedlar People, Ltd., 260.51; Phinn Brick Co., 802.40; Public Utilities Commission, 45.00; W. A. Reid, 21.25; Richards-Wilcox Canadian Co., Ltd., 14.24; Scott Paint & Varnish

Ontario Hospitals—Continued

London—Continued

Repairs to Buildings, etc.—Continued

Maintenance and Repairs of all Buildings, etc.—Continued

Co., Ltd., 584.48; Sanderson Pearcy-Marietta, Ltd., 319.44; Shirley-Dietrich Co., Ltd., 20.32; F. W. Stull Transport Co., 50.60; Sherwin-Williams Co., Ltd., 96.98; F. B. Smith & Co., 121.63; Malcolm Sinclair Co., Ltd., 37.15; Trelco, Ltd., 39.00; Tremco Mfg. Co., Ltd., 46.31; Valspar Corporation, Ltd., 18.50; petty disbursements, 17.23 .... 43,955 15

Maintenance and Repairs of Plumbing, Steam and Electric Plants, $22,917.82.

American Can Co., 11.65; Atlas Engineering Machine Co., Ltd., 76.00; J. A. Brownlee, 126.29; Beaver Laundry Machinery Co., Ltd., 14.11; H. C. Burton & Co., 276.77; Canadian National Railways, 189.52; Canadian General Electric Co., Ltd., 37.53; Canadian National Express, 18.70; Canadian Laundry Machinery Co., Ltd., 65.64; Canadian Pacific Railway Co., 1,371.62; Canadian Johns-Manville Co., Ltd., 579.68; Canadian Colortype, Ltd., 356.50; Canadian Oil Cos, Ltd., 100.95; Combustion Service Co., 63.97; Canadian Powers Regulator Co., Ltd., 150.10; Canadian Fairbanks-Morse Co., Ltd., 270.00; Canadian Westinghouse Co., Ltd., 13.12; Crane, Ltd., 1,604.25; Dearborn Chemical Co., Ltd., 514.58; Dominion Radiator & Boiler Co., Ltd., 120.63; Dunlop Tire & Rubber Goods Co., Ltd., 255.45; C. A. Dunham Co., Ltd., 244.99; Drummond McCall Co., Ltd., 183.54; Dennisteel, Ltd., 151.52; Empire Brass Mfg. Co., Ltd., 1,657.34; E. T. Flanagan, 84.66; Garlock Packing Co., Ltd., 180.98; General Steel Wares, Ltd., 302.26; Good Specialties, Ltd., 70.66; Gurney Foundry Co., Ltd., 65.96; Hayman & Mills, 253.51; Sam Harris, 50.00; Hobbs Hardware Co., Ltd., 196.60; John Hooper, 30.00; Huston Oil Co., 29.25; D. H. Howden & Co., Ltd., 252.20; Instruments, Ltd., 36.71; Insulation Mfg. Co., Ltd., 158.76; Jefferson Glass Co., 36.34; Arthur S. Leitch Co., Ltd., 123.90; London Structural Steel Co., Ltd., 67.78; London Brokerage Co., 14.35; London Concrete Machinery Co., Ltd., 175.10; La France Fire Engine Co., Ltd., 14.15; London Bolt & Hinge Works, 19.93; Masco Co., Ltd., 32.71; Metal Craft Co., Ltd., 11.70; B. H. Montgomery Hose Reel Co., 568.40; Mueller, Ltd., 15.25; Northern Electric Co., Ltd.. 869.02; Ontario Hospital, Brockville, 11.75; Pay list, wages of men, 4,702.99; Public Utilities Commission, 614.96; Peckover's, Ltd., 197.01; Pendrith Machinery Co., Ltd., 20.00; People's Electric Co., 1,113.84; Sayles Transport, 25.38; Square D Co. of Canada, Ltd., 232.60; Stewart & Morkin, 17.15; G. F. Sterne & Sons, 450.93; Standard Sales Service, 16.50; Stabler & Baker, 15.00; Taylor-Forbes Co., Ltd., 436.95; A. L. Torgis & Son, 33.32; Tremco Co., Ltd., 170.00; Trane Co., Ltd., 322.81; Truscon Steel Co. of Canada, Ltd., 555.39; Toronto Coppersmithing Co., 446.29; Williams Tool Corporation, 10.20; Warren Bros., 186.20; Wilson Illumination Co., Ltd., 38.81; James Wright & Co., Ltd., 1,068.98; petty disbursements, 116.13 .... 22,917 82

Live Stock, Vehicles and Farm Implements, $2,772.53.

Canadian Pacific Railway Co., 34.40; Howe Bros., 221.20; Byron Jenvey, 690.00; Ontario Hospital, Whitby, 25.00; Ontario Hospital, Woodstock, 1,275.00; George Penfound, 193.00; Roe's Poultry Ranch, 126.00; W. Rivers, 80.00; Robert Woods, 110.00; petty disbursements, 17.93 .... 2,772 53

Total		522,468 40	
Less Maintenance of Patients	140,604 48		
Perquisites	35,292 05		
Sale of Produce	8,206 24		
		184,102 77	
London		338,365 63	

MIMICO

Salaries ($186,219.68)

Superintendent, physicians and dentists	23,814 16
Steward and assistants	9,506 71
Matron and assistants, including domestic help	17,890 44
Engineers and assistants	14,600 00
Artisans, not domestic	8,974 50
Farm and garden employees	5,969 58
Attendants and nurses	105,464 29

Expenses ($147,885.00)

Medicines, $6,922.82.

Allan & Rollaston Dental Laboratories, 71.37; Art Metropole, 54.90; Burroughs, Wellcome & Co., 19.98; Caldwell Pharmacy, 104.11; Canada Foils, Ltd., 48.61;

Ontario Hospitals—Continued

Mimico—Continued

Expenses—Continued

Medicines—Continued

Dominion Dental Co., 133.83; A. D. Gibson, 17.08; Grand & Toy, Ltd., 115.00; Chas. Gyde & Son, Ltd., 15.65; Gooderham & Worts, Ltd., 95.45; J. F. Hartz Co., Ltd., 123.08; Hargraft Bros., Ltd., 1,008.70; F. W. Humphrey Co., Ltd., 67.10; Ingram & Bell, Ltd., 1,190.47; Imperial Tobacco Co., Ltd., 147.52; Liquor Control Board, 84.11; Landan & Cormack, Ltd., 312.00; R. E. Mitchell, 88.20; J. A. MacDonald, 44.55; National Grocers Co., Ltd., 54.00; Ontario Hospital, Toronto, 40.00; Parke, Davis & Co., 300.15; E. B. Shuttleworth Chemical Co., Ltd., 607.13; W. E. Saunders, Ltd., 239.70; The Stevens Co., 768.69; Standard Tobacco Co. of Canada, 24.12; Tuckett, Ltd., 368.60; Textile Products Co., 262.20; Victor X-ray Corporation, Ltd., 102.78; Vi-Tone Co., 167.58; Chas. R. Will & Co., Ltd., 183.61; petty disbursements, 62.55 .... 6,922 82

Provisions, $53,396.84.

H. J. Ash, 283.76; Beaver Food Products, Ltd., 399.00; Bowes Co., Ltd., 166.42; Canada Vinegars, Ltd., 10.12; Caulfield & Sons, Ltd., 2,196.42; H. J. Cook, 100.00; Canada Packers, Ltd., 92.00; Canada Milk Products, Ltd., 18.43; Copeland Flour Mills, Ltd., 823.50; Dalton Bros., 184.20; Elder Flour Mills Co., Ltd., 108.75; Everist Bros., Ltd., 678.53; John J. Fee, 10,051.18; K. C. Freeman, 365.96; Graham's Bread, 166.04; Higgins & Burke, Ltd., 1,820.38; F. W. Humphrey Co., Ltd., 2,670.82; J. R. Hayden Co., 161.70; The Harry Horne Co., Ltd., 39.00; Ideal Bread Co., Ltd., 870.14; F. T. James Co., Ltd., 1,839.30; Kipling Farms Dairy, 826.80; James Lumbers Co., Ltd., 1,457.98; E. Lazenby & Son, Ltd., 24.95; Loblaw Groceterias, Ltd., 523.45; Joe Lowe Corporation, 161.90; Maple Leaf Milling Co., Ltd., 1,810.72; Mara Lodge Poultry Farms, 427.52; Morland Coffee Co., 210.00; McCormack Mfg. Co., Ltd., 25.31; J. S. Moore, 45.00; National Grocers Co., Ltd., 1,069.07; W. Neilson, Ltd., 68.25; Donald Nicolson & Son, 408.60; Newmarket Flour Mills, 861.00; Ontario Reformatory, Mimico, 5,953.48; Ontario Reformatory Industries, Guelph, 11,495.81; Ogilvie Flour Mills Co., Ltd., 92.50; Ontario Honey Producers, Ltd., 79.05; D. S. Perrin & Co., Ltd., 128.37; H. M. Pallett, 150.00; W. G. Patrick & Co., Ltd., 23.00; Silverwood's Milk Products, Ltd., 57.23; Sunera Cereals, Ltd., 134.02; Standard Brands, Ltd., 514.42; St. Lawrence Fish Market, 1,950.05; F. W. Stull Transport, Ltd., 119.84; Tavistock Milling Co., Ltd., 739.50; Whyte Packing Co., 845.29; Young-Winfield, Ltd., 126.96; petty disbursements, 21.12 .... 53,396 84

Fuel, Light and Water, $35,347.10.

P. Burns & Co., Ltd., 28,861.94; E. B. Eddy Match Co., Ltd., 83.57; Hydro-Electric Power Commission, 1,996.25; New Toronto Public Utilities Commission, 3,806.87; Wadsworth Coal Co., Ltd., 592.70; petty disbursements. 5.77 .... 35,347 10

Clothing, $17,912.46.

Anderson-MacBeth & Co., Ltd., 126.00; A. Bradshaw & Sons, Ltd., 116.58; Big 88 Shoe Store, 29.25; Canadian National Railways, 17.49; Canadian National Express, 15 63; Canada Panama & Straw Hats, Ltd., 68.00; Coghill Tailoring Co., 1,562.00; Circle Bar Knitting Co., Ltd., 147.80; A. D. Gibson, 362.25; Greenshields & Co., Ltd., 245.46; Hamilton & Johnston, 2,251.16; Johnston, Crossley & McComb, 199.50; G. T. Lanning, 18.50; J. A. McLaren Co., Ltd., 991.40; Mercury Mills, Ltd., 129.36; Midland Whitewear Costume Co., Ltd., 158.25; Mercer Reformatory Industries, 6,406.72; Morris Shoe Co., 226.80; Ontario Reformatory Industries, 2,339.15; Ontario Hospital, Orillia, Industries, 1,004.60; The Robert Simpson Co., Ltd., 230.36; Superior Cloak Co., Ltd., 292.50; Schofield Woollen Co., Ltd., 562.50; Storey Glove Co., Ltd., 89.00; Textile Products Co., 14.25; Woods Manufacturing Co., Ltd., 297.00; petty disbursements, 10.95 .... 17,912 46

Laundry and Cleaning, $7,437.21.

Acme Caretakers Supply Co., 125.00; Aikenhead Hardware, Ltd., 43.80; Alpha Chemical Co., Ltd., 84.65; Associated Chemical Co., Ltd., 1,789.70; Beaver Laundry Manufacturing Co., Ltd., 176.40; Canada Blade Co., 102.16; Canadian Colors & Chemicals, Ltd., 58.99; Canadian National Railways, 18.17; Canadian National Institute for the Blind, 324.00; Consolidated Sales Book & Wax Paper Co., Ltd., 25.00; W. H. Cunningham & Hill, Ltd., 30.38; Diamond Cleansers, Ltd., 553.15; A. B. Drake & Co., 35.28; Electric Boiler Compound Co., Ltd., 138.10; Ennis Wonder Polish Co., 16.00; Excelsior Brushes, Ltd., 394.45; Philip C. Garratt, 33.60; R. S. Gillan, 65.17; A. Scott Graham, 17.80; Grand & Toy, Ltd., 35.00; Guelph Soaps, 52.50; Hamilton & Johnston, 176.32; Hatch Specialty Co., 66.60; Higgins & Burke, Ltd., 124.30; Hoar Transport, 25.52; H. S. Howland Sons & Co., Ltd., 105.10; International Trading Co.,

Ontario Hospitals—Continued

Mimico—Continued

Expenses—Continued

Laundry and Cleaning—Continued

10.00; Ingram & Bell, Ltd., 143.00; The Andrew Jergens Co., Ltd., 500.27; W. H. Lake, 291.95; Lavoline Cleanser Co., Ltd., 83.06; James Lumbers Co., Ltd., 27.99; Nonsuch, Ltd., 34.00; National Grocers Co., Ltd., 11.00; W. J. Oliphant, Ltd., 74.25; Premier Laundry Equipment Co., Ltd., 53.40; Ratcliffe Paper Co., Ltd., 126.61; Rexo Chemical Cleaner Co., Ltd., 887.41; The Robert Simpson Co., Ltd., 10.50; Scott Paper Co., Ltd., 17.35; St. Croix Soap Manufacturing Co., Ltd., 167.42; Standard Wax Co., 43.12; Sunclo Products, 16.63; C. V. Syrett Paper Co., Ltd., 89.82; Toronto Salt Works, Ltd., 28.60; Victoria Paper & Twine Co., Ltd., 95.00; G. H. Wood & Co., Ltd., 82.46; petty disbursements, 26.23........ 7,437 21

Furniture and Furnishings, $17,658.30.

Aluminum Goods, Ltd., 94.92; Associated Chemical Co., Ltd., 12.74; A. Bradshaw & Sons, Ltd., 203.78; British & Colonial Trading Co., Ltd., 83.43; Canadian National Railways, 14.76; Caldwell Linen Mills, Ltd., 485.90; Canadian National Institute for the Blind, 139.00; Cassidy's, Ltd., 251.99; Delaney & Pettit, Ltd., 565.95; A. D. Gibson, 570.23; Grand & Toy, Ltd., 53.80; Gordon MacKay & Co., Ltd., 121.00; Greenshields, Ltd., 128.12; Hamilton & Johnston, 154.04; Geo. M. Hendry Co., Ltd., 15.00; Hospital and Kitchen Equipment Co., Ltd., 135.00; William Junor, Ltd., 1,093.44; King Paper Sales Co., 70.00; W. H. Lake, 801.35; Mercer Reformatory Industries, 4,567.20; A. B. McArthur, 25.00; Metal Craft Co., Ltd., 267.00; Ontario Reformatory Industries, 6,311.16; Ontario Hospital, Orillia, Industries, 175.20; Ratcliffe Paper Co., Ltd., 137.35; H. Renaud, 11.98; The Robert Simpson Co., Ltd., 212.08; Stainless Tablecloth Co., 51.74; Stull Transport Co., Ltd., 205.67; C. V. Syrett Paper Co., Ltd., 37.50; Sully Aluminum Co., Ltd., 52.50; Sewsure Garment Co., Ltd., 21.00; Textile Products Co., Ltd., 296.65; Toronto Feather & Down Co., Ltd., 169.60; Victoria Paper & Twine Co., Ltd., 66.00; R. G. Venn, 22.34; petty disbursements, 33.88.......... 17,658 30

Office Expenses, $1,591.73.

Bell Telephone Co., rentals, 831.60: tolls, 33.04: Grand & Toy, Ltd., 125.20; A. E. McLean, 17.50; Postmaster, 496.00; Remington Typewriters, Ltd., 20.75; United Typewriter Co., Ltd., 36.00; petty disbursements, 31.64.............. 1,591 73

Farm Expenses, $3,887.09.

Paul Adams, 195.06; Adams Bros., Ltd., 23.41; A. Armstrong, 225.79; Andrewes Mountain Seed Co., Ltd., 359.18; Canadian National Railways, 593.56; Canada Crushed Stone Corporation, 44.76; H. J. Cook, 1,075.20; Cockshutt Plow Co., Ltd., 16.00; The Foster Pottery Co., 44.00; R. J. Fenwick, 18.00; A. Gibson, 20.35; Gunns, Ltd., 102.60; H. S. Howland Sons & Co., Ltd., 123.49; W. H. Lake, 49.18; Marchment Co., Ltd., 244.19; Massey-Harris Co., Ltd., 21.40; Ontario Reformatory Industries, 403.06; Sheridan Nurseries, Ltd., 141.03; Steele, Briggs Seed Co., Ltd., 156.35; petty disbursements, 30.48.............. 3,887 09

Contingencies, $3,731.45.

Aikenhead Hardware, Ltd., hardware, 17.01; Vernon G. Allison, medals, 12.35; American Psychiatric Association, subscriptions, 10.00; M. Boyd, Christmas trees, 16.25; W. E. Baycroft & Son, interments, 257.00; Brown & Tawse, map, 12.50; Canada Universal Film Co., Ltd., service, 158.25; Cozens Spring Service, repairs, 16.00; Dawson Subscription Service, books, etc., 138.50; Dominion Reed Supplies, reed, 105.10; Geo. Elliott, confectionery, 33.00; Epworth Press, printing, 33.00; Fairview Chemical Co., Ltd., 27.60; Grand & Toy, Ltd., ink, 19.25; Goodyear Tire & Rubber Co., Ltd., repairs, 66.75; Hamilton & Johnston, wool, etc., 760.16; Hargraft Bros., pipes, 108.00; Highways Department, repairs, 108.15; Ingram & Bell, Ltd., medical books, 634.66; Lake Shore Flower Shop, flowers, 17.00; Mason Service Station, gas, 377.95; McAinsh & Co., Ltd., books, 35.40; E. McTavish, newspapers, 84.90; Musical Services, 225.50; Dr. H. A. McKay, travelling expenses, 10.84; New Toronto Tailoring Co., suspenders, 19.00; D. Pike Co., Ltd., rent of tent, 20.00; Prager Paper Sales Co., napkins, etc., 135.10; Pulman Garage, gas, 34.92; Ratcliffe Paper Co., Ltd., napkins, etc., 177.23; The Robert Simpson Co., Ltd., hampers, tables, etc., 111.63; Smith & Walsh, car insurance, 50.33; J. M. Sutherland, travelling expenses, 24.71; Stewart & Wood, Ltd., varnish, 10.15; C. V. Syrett Paper Co., Ltd., paper, 11.04; A. L. Torgis & Son, heater, repairs, etc., 59.41; Victoria Paper & Twine Co., Ltd., twine, etc., 12.63; Harold A. Wilson Co., Ltd., sporting goods, etc., 26.31; Dr. D. E. Wishart, services, 60.00; petty disbursements, 114.75; Less refunds, sale of books, 420.88.. 3,731 45

Ontario Hospitals—Continued

Mimico—Continued

Repairs to Buildings, etc. ($89,675.08)

Maintenance and Repairs of all Buildings, Roads, Walks, Grounds and Fences, $60,489.41.

Aikenhead Hardware, Ltd., 297.52; Aulcraft Paints, Ltd., 224.72; Advance Products, Ltd., 40.98; Biggar Lock & Key Co., 24.45; Builders Supplies, Ltd., 5,197.31; T. A. Bush, 15.00; Canadian National Railways, 113.44; Canada Varnish Co., Ltd., 110.25; Canada Paint Co., Ltd., 456.82; Canadian Metal Window & Steel Products Co., Ltd., 14.00; Consumers Oil Co., Ltd., 68.54; Dennisteel, Ltd., 2,281.08; Disher Steel Construction Co., Ltd., 98.80; Dominion Bridge Co., Ltd., 107.95; J. H. Doughty, Ltd., 707.94; Faultless Caster Co., 44.85; Ferrier Wire Goods Co., Ltd., 156.40; Grand & Toy, Ltd., 98.80; General Products, Ltd., 889.00; B. Greening Wire Co., Ltd., 57.86; Joseph Grimshaw, 28.59; Heathcote Hardware, 43.15; Howland Investments, 235.08; Italian Mosaic & Tile Co., Ltd., 1,281.73; Iron's Hardware, 27.00; R. Laidlaw Lumber Co., Ltd., 856.00; Lowes Construction Co., Ltd., 150.00; Lowe Bros. Co., Ltd., 176.07; Lundy Fence Co., Ltd., 48.50; Lake Shore Builders Supplies, Ltd., 251.33; Rice Lewis & Son, Ltd., 50.10; Mimico Planing Mills, 3,202.95; J. H. Morin & Co., Ltd., 31.15; Alex. Murray & Co., Ltd., 16.02; McFarlane Manufacturing Co., Ltd., 12.00; National Sewer Pipe Co., Ltd., 376.63; Ontario Reformatory, Mimico, 15,299.54; Pay list, wages of men, 25,283.17; Pedlar People, Ltd., 196.49; H. W. Petrie, Ltd., 15.15; W. E. Phillips Co., Ltd., 105.84; Pilkington Bros., 129.76; Roelofson Elevator Works, 544.00; Sanderson, Pearcy-Marietta, Ltd., 18.52; Sun Oil Co., Ltd., 48.95; Toronto Lock Manufacturing Co., Ltd., 534.81; Toronto Asphalt Roofing Manufacturing Co., 61.74; Tremco Manufacturing Co., Ltd., 52.06; Truscon Steel Co. of Canada, Ltd., 26.00; W. Walker & Son, Ltd., 310.37; Wilkinson-Kompass, Ltd., 22.78; petty disbursements, 48.22.................. 60,489 41

Maintenance and Repairs of Plumbing, Steam and Electric Plants, $29,185.67.

Art Metropole, 26.25; Beaver Laundry Machinery Co., Ltd., 10.31; Bull Dog Electric Products, Ltd., 27.15; Bickle Fire Engines, Ltd., 17.93; Beldam's Asbestos Packing Co., Ltd., 104.63; H. C. Burton & Co., 744.81; Joseph Burns, 22.09; Boiler Repair & Grate Bar Co., 622.29; British American Oil Co., Ltd., 32.54; Bawden Machine Co., Ltd., 114.75; Canadian General Electric Co., Ltd., 221.29; Cactizona Products Co., 72.25; Canada Ice Machine Co., Ltd., 12.91; Canadian Chemical Co., 56.76; Canadian National Railways, 15.04; Canadian Westinghouse Co., Ltd., 20.47; Canadian Powers Regulator Co., Ltd., 285.00; Coulter Copper & Brass Co., Ltd., 199.68; Canada Foils, Ltd., 13.23; Canadian Laundry Machinery Co., Ltd., 50.06; Crane, Ltd., 98.20; W. H. Cunningham & Hill, Ltd., 198.64; Dearborn Chemical Co., Ltd., 255.37; Dominion Wheel & Foundries, Ltd., 42.00; J. H. Doughty, 77.00; C. A. Dunham & Co., Ltd., 112.81; Dunlop Tire & Rubber Goods Co., Ltd., 286.94; Empire Brass Manufacturing Co., Ltd., 2,119.67; Everlasting Valve Co., Ltd., 723.80; Geo. Farrow & Son, 134.11; Garlock Packing Co., Ltd., 77.24; Gurney Foundry Co., Ltd., 174.71; General Steel Wares, Ltd., 919.85; Goodyear Tire & Rubber Co., Ltd., 297.43; Good Specialties, Ltd., 42.03; Garratt Callaghan Co., Ltd., 132.82; Heathcote Hardware, 15.15; G. A. Hardie & Co., Ltd., 73.16; Herod Construction Co., Ltd., 36.00; Hobart Manufacturing Co., 54.39; Huston Oil Co., Ltd., 69.80; Hubbard Portable Oven Co., 42.47; Hospital & Kitchen Equipment Co., Ltd., 37.50; John Inglis Co., Ltd., 13.90; Instruments, Ltd., 12.87; Kerr Engine Co., Ltd., 421.14; W. Lake, 12.65; LaFrance Fire Engine Foamite, Ltd., 300.96; A. S. Leitch & Co., Ltd., 37.34; Rice Lewis & Son, Ltd., 24.00; Long Branch Village, 811.69; The Masco Co., Ltd., 643.88; Mercer Reformatory Industries, 19.09; Moffats, Ltd., 84.73; J. H. Morin & Co., Ltd., 49.00; B. H. Montgomery Hose Reel Co., 200.00; Jas. Morrison Brass Manufacturing Co., Ltd., 665.09; Mimico Planing Mills, 16.92; National Silicates, Ltd., 32.69; Northern Electric Co., Ltd., 133.99; Ontario Wind Engine & Pump Co., Ltd., 17.35; Ontario Hospital, Woodstock, 75.00; Pay lists, wages of men, 12,487.10; H. W. Petrie, Ltd., 181.02; Pendell Boiler, Ltd., 75.00; Premier Laundry Equipment Co., 181.20; Public Utilities Commission, 65.00; Robert T. Purves Co., 160.86; Pyrene Manufacturing Co., Ltd., 17.28; Regent Electric Supply Co., Ltd., 129.94; Reid & Brown, Ltd., 13.50; James Robertson Co., Ltd., 921.09; Rogers Electric Co., Ltd., 51.62; Sheldons, Ltd., 54.32; Smart-Turner Machine Co., 936.27; Shur-Line Automatic Fire Protection System, 29.29; Geo. Sparrow & Co., 16.00; Standard Underground Cable Co., Ltd., 56.22; G. F. Sterne & Sons, 20.91; Supplies and Insulation, Ltd., 338.39; Taylor-Forbes Co., Ltd., 297.46; Toronto Salt Works, Ltd., 71.50; Trane Co., Ltd., 65.07; Walker-Wallace, Ltd., 173.94; Wilkinson-Kompass, Ltd., 53.34;

Ontario Hospitals—Continued

Mimico—Continued

Repairs to Buildings, etc.—Continued

Maintenance and Repairs of Plumbing, etc.—Continued

R. Willett, 18.50; J. A. Wilson & Co., Ltd., 50.00; Wilson Scale & Machinery Corporation, 159.99; Wilson Illumination Co., Ltd., 175.18; Wrought Iron Range Co., Ltd., 18.00; petty disbursements, 104.88 ... 29,185 67

Total		423,779 76	
Less Maintenance of Patients	81,024 83		
Perquisites	17,318 21		
Sale of Produce	987 84		
		99,330 88	
Mimico		324,448 88	

ORILLIA

Salaries ($251,619.10)

Superintendent, Physicians and Dentists	25,573 60
Steward and Assistants	15,247 91
Matron and Assistants, including domestic help	28,886 61
Engineer and Assistants	17,025 00
Artisans, not domestic	10,572 00
Farm and Garden employees	12,875 00
Attendants and Nurses	125,903 98
Teachers and Industrial Instructors	15,535 00

Expenses ($207,149.58)

Medicines, $6,638.53.

Abbott Laboratories, Ltd., 73.16; Ash-Temple Co., Ltd., 78.06; Ayerst, McKenna & Harrison, Ltd., 12.93; Bauer & Black, Ltd., 714.00; British Drug House, Ltd., 11.33; Burk's Electric X-Ray Co., Ltd., 176.04; Canadian National Express, 19.00; Canadian National Railways, 15.77; Consolidated Optical Co., Ltd., 12.68; Dominion Dental Co., 92.94; Faichney Instrument Corporation, 23.87; Charles E. Frosst & Co., 361.02; W. C. George, 596.42; Gooderham & Worts, Ltd., 98.45; Hargraft Bros., 142.84; J. F. Hartz Co., Ltd., 179.82; John A. Huston Co., 35.86; Ingram & Bell, Ltd., 1,003.56; H. L. Jebb, 81.60; Lewis Manufacturing Co., Ltd., 107.51; L. G. Liggett Co., Ltd., 43.70; W. C. Macdonald, 51.40; Northrop & Lyman Co., Ltd., 63.50; Parke Davis & Co., 35.93; W. L. Pratt, 11.50; B. H. Price, 105.30; Richards Glass Co., Ltd., 31.18; W. E. Saunders, Ltd., 71.88; E. B. Shuttleworth Chemical Co., Ltd., 505.00; George Sinclair, 1,033.48; Smith & Nephew, Ltd., 226.51; E. R. Squibb & Sons, Ltd., 26.40; Standard Tobacco Co. of Canada, 17.32; Strathdee Transport Co., 18.80; Clifton H. Stewart, 18.00; G. S. Trudell Co., 23.05; Wallace's Drug Store, 138.49; H. K. Wampole & Co., 29.89; A. Wander, Ltd., 34.98; C. R. Will & Co., Ltd., 57.83; Winthrop Chemical Co., 25.25; J. Woods, 172.18; petty disbursements, 60.10... 6,638 53

Groceries and Provisions, $73,663.02.

Art Allan, 36.12; Balfours, Ltd., 1,095.47; Barrie Flour Mills, 315.13; Barrie Wholesale, 34.71; Battalia & Son, 100.25; M. Beard, 10.00; A. G. Beaton, 44.00; L. F. Beatty, 768.98; J. Beaupre, 18.00; Beaver Food Products, Ltd., 56.00; W. Berryman, 36.75; The Borden Co., Ltd., 62.46; Bowes & Co., Ltd., 10,626.77; R. J. Cairns, 317.55; Canada & Dominion Sugar Co., Ltd., 124.99; Canada Packers, Ltd., 130.76; Canadian Milk Products, 18.43; Canadian National Express, 25.88; Canadian National Railways, 40.92; Carter's Cafe, 99.25; L. A. Coleman Co., Ltd., 59.40; Cooke's Fish Market, 159.62; Copeland's Flour Mills, Ltd., 3,564.00; T. B. Cramp, Ltd., 369.40; Frank Crawford, 37.50; Cunningham & Ferguson, 102.00; Dalton Bros., 234.89; Drimilk Co., Ltd., 37.24; Dumarts, Ltd., 425.19; T. A. Dwinnell, 294.76; Walter E. Esdon Co., 261.83; A. Evans, 19.60; Flavelle's, Ltd., 1,149.01; K. C. Freeman, 336.93; S. Gentile, 1,363.36; Amos B. Gordon Co., Ltd., 50.20; C. Graham, 18.00; Gunn's, Ltd., 37.80; J. Hamilton, 90.00; Harris Abattoir Co., Ltd., 165.00; Hatley's, 45.60; J. J. Hatley, 243.68; H. Hawke, 53.90; H. J. Heintz Co., Ltd., 559.09; Hewitt Bros., 59.25; L. C. Hise, 76.50; The Harry Horne Co., Ltd., 390.39; F. W. Humphrey Co., Ltd., 4,433.51; J. A. Huston Co., 20.98; F. T. James Co., Ltd., 1,380.25; J. Kells, 15.00; E. A. Kenny, 90.05; F. W. Krouse, 105.00; A. Lang, 12.00; J. Lowe Corporation, Ltd., 86.90; J. Lumbers Co., Ltd., 5,187.41; T. A. Macdonald, 33.88; M. E. Mahoney, 45.81; Mara Lodge Poultry Farms, 320.32; A. W. May, 13.13; Martindale Farm, 15.40; A. W. Milne, 24.87; National Grocers Co., Ltd., 7,872.55; Ontario Reformatory, 21.20; Ontario Reformatory Industries, 16,569.30;

Ontario Hospitals—Continued

Orillia—Continued

Expenses—Continued

Groceries and Provisions—Continued

Orillia Creamery Co., Ltd., 1,995.31; Orillia Dairy Co., 2,876.29; S. G. Pack, 600.03; S. Passmore, 727.29; Pure Gold Manufacturing Co., Ltd., 343.05; J. Regan, 24.66; Royal Manufacturing Co., 46.50; R. J. Sanderson Marble Co., 27.00; St. Lawrence Fish Market, 480.55; Scott Bros., 32.97; Silverwood's Milk Products, Ltd., 171.71; G. Sinclair, 696.49; Standard Brands, Ltd., 874.64; Strathdee Transport, 65.38; Stull Transport, 148.05; Swift Canadian Co., Ltd., 908.25; Sunera Cereals, Ltd., 24.87; J. Tesky, 16.70; D. C. Thomson, 59.85; Turner's Dairy, 2,203.78; A. Wanders, Ltd., 100.00; Waupoos Canning Co., 18.00; E. Webb & Son, 60.00; George Weston, Ltd., 243.78; White's Fish Co., 55.00; Whyte Packing Co., Ltd., 159.60; L. C. Wise, 112.20; Young-Winfield Co., Ltd., 98.12; petty disbursements, 78.83 .... 73,663 02

Fuel, Light and Water, $58,694.41.

H. C. Burton & Co., 1,146.74; H. S. Fenton, 491.25; Amos B. Gordon & Co., 121.60; Orillia Water, Light and Power Commission, 4,663.37; D. S. Pratt, 52,188.71; Richie & Mould, 43.20; Wilkinson-Kompass, Ltd., 25.42; petty disbursements, 14.12 .... 58,694 41

Clothing, $26,225.02.

Arch-Aid Boot Shop, 10.50; Arrow Stores, 13.50; Moses Boyd, 57.60; A. Bradshaw & Sons, Ltd., 699.24; Brown's Boot Shop, 94.15; Burnet's Men's Shop, 441.59; Canadian National Express, 22.58; Canadian National Railways, 79.07; Carss Mackinaw Co., Ltd., 2,634.25; Circle Bar Knitting Co., Ltd., 245.00; Corbett-Cowley, Ltd., 10.40; Dick Bros., 80.46; A. D. Gibson, 1,361.60; Greenshields, Ltd., 4,139.40; Hague & Hague, 48.00; Hamilton & Johnston, Ltd., 2,692.88; J. T. Heath, 169.70; Johnston's Clothes Shop, 195.00; Johnston, Crossley & McComb, 370.50; B. Lipman, 45.12; Mason & Co., 2,856.30; Mercer Reformatory Industries, 1,578.13; Miller's Ready-to-Wear, 39.50; Moodie's Underwear, Ltd., 166.75; Northern Rubber Co., Ltd., 399.11; Ontario Footwear Co., 236.11; Ontario Hospital, Orillia, Industries, 2,897.37; Ontario Reformatory Industries, 1,542.78; Penman's, Ltd., 20.00; J. Samuels & Sons, 110.25; Schofield Woollen Co., Ltd., 187.50; Singer Sewing Machine Co. (Inc.), 41.34; Steacy's Dry Goods, 88.36; Strathdee Transport, 28.59; Textile Products, Ltd., 76.42; A. Weatherwax, 45.00; J. C. Weir, 21.00; J. P. Wells, 1,460.26; E. A. Woods, Ltd., 63.00; Woods Manufacturing Co., Ltd., 937.48; petty disbursements, 19.23 .... 26,225 02

Laundry, $11,003.82.

Alpha Chemical Co., Ltd., 113.70; Applegate Chemical Co., Ltd., 65.50; Associated Chemical Co., Ltd., 1,836.86; Ault & Wiborg, Ltd., 54.56; Balfour's, Ltd., 74.69; Beaver Laundry Machinery Co., Ltd., 77.62; Canada Customs, 18.42; Canada Paint Co., 45.61; Canadian Colours & Chemicals Co., Ltd., 178.49; Canadian National Institute for the Blind, 294.84; Canadian National Railways, 165.69; Canadian Westinghouse Co., Ltd., 46.78; Colgate-Palmolive-Peet Co., Ltd., 175.71; Coville Transport Co., Ltd., 64.87; Diamond Cleansers, Ltd., 384.80; Dominion Soap Co., 24.75; Dustbane Products, Ltd., 10.81; Dye & Chemical Co., Ltd., 15.52; E. B. Eddy Co., Ltd., 36.00; Electric Boiler Compound Co., Ltd., 248.74; Excelsior Brushes, Ltd., 291.58; W. C. George, 285.50; A. S. Graham, 82.20; Greenshields, Ltd., 16.20; Guelph Soap Co., 55.00; Hamilton & Johnston, 77.61; N. C. Hayner Co., 34.65; F. W. Humphrey Co., Ltd., 123.55; Imperial Oil, Ltd., 26.55; Imperial Varnish & Colour Co., Ltd., 323.61; Ingram & Bell, Ltd., 323.51; Jones Bros. of Canada, Ltd., 28.25; King Paper Sales Co., 37.50; S. F. Lawrason & Co., Ltd., 604.80; J. Leckie, Ltd., 119.48; A. A. Lord, 490.05; Lowe Bros. Co., Ltd., 38.50; J. Lumbers Co., Ltd., 147.93; Meyer Bros. Laundry & Machinery Co., Ltd., 49.87; J. H. Morin & Co., Ltd., 80.86; D. Morton & Sons, Ltd., 68.75; National Grocers Co., Ltd., 146.11; W. J. Oliphant, Ltd., 27.19; Ontario Reformatory Industries, 36.00; Oshawa Electrical Supply, Ltd., 25.48; Pratt's Drug Store, 50.20; B. H. Price, 326.48; Rexo Chemical Cleaner Co., Ltd., 2,101.64; St. Croix Soap Manufacturing Co., Ltd., 566.27; Safety Silent Policeman Co., 30.24; Scott Paper Co., Ltd., 48.02; J. B. Sheppard, 27.35; Strathdee Transport Co., Ltd., 17.40; Wallace's Drug Store, 53.85; G. H. Wood & Co., Ltd., 206.49; F. W. Woolworth Co., Ltd., 38.10; petty disbursements, 63.09 11,003 82

Furniture and Furnishings, $13,324.08.

Acme Scales Service, 12.50; Aikenhead Hardware, Ltd., 29.60; Beatty Bros., Ltd., 11.17; Beaver Laundry Machinery Co., Ltd., 47.04; G. A. Blakeslee & Co., 18.00; British & Colonial Trading Co., 106.39; W. R. Brock & Co., Ltd., 85.23; Caldwell Linen Mills, Ltd., 144.10; Canadian National Railways, 27.31; Canadian

Ontario Hospitals—Continued

Orillia—Continued

Expenses—Continued

Furniture and Furnishings—Continued

W. A. Rogers, Ltd., 56.80; Canadian Wood Specialty Co., 46.30; Cassidy's, Ltd., 1,259.59; Coville Transport, 35.79; The T. Eaton Co., Ltd., 147.29; John Garde & Co., 18.15; General Steel Wares, Ltd.. 195.03; A. D. Gibson, 563.50; Greenshields, Ltd., 909.91: Hamilton & Johnston, 288.15; Geo. M. Hendry Co., Ltd., 212.93; Hospital & Kitchen Equipment Co., Ltd., 128.00; Hygiene Products, Ltd., 11.55; Ingram & Bell, Ltd., 57.00; Johnston & Barbour, 106.99; Kelvinator of Canada, Ltd., 170.00; MacNab & Sons, 33.34; Marshall Ventilated Mattress Co., 46.06; Matchett Bros., 24.00; McGlashan, Clarke Co., 90.54; Mercer Reformatory Industries, 5,009.12; Modern Kitchen Equipment Co., 525.28: Moffats, Ltd., 79.83; Newton-Croxall, Ltd., 33.48; Ontario Hospital, Orillia, Industries, 334.87; Ontario Reformatory Industries, 1,060.50; Orillia Hardware Co., Ltd., 16.07; Phillips & Co., 66.25; Geo. Sparrow & Co., Ltd., 525.06; G. Street & Sons, 50.00; F. W. Stull Transport, 47.20; Strathdee Transport Co., 43.90; W. M. Swinton & Sons, 207.14; C. V. Syrett Paper Co., Ltd., 45.00; R. G. Venn, 89.38; Victoria Paper & Twine Co., Ltd., 66.25; Wilkinson-Kompass, Ltd., 27.93; G. H. Wood & Co., Ltd., 152.12; petty disbursements, 62.44.................. 13,434 08

Office Expenses, $2,098.53.

Bell Telephone Co., rentals, 790.92; tolls, 278.85; Canadian National Express, 41.28; Canadian National Telegraphs, 51.92; W. C. George, 11.90; Grand & Toy, Ltd., 140.05; Postmaster, 711.00; United Typewriter Co., Ltd., 26.03; petty disbursements, 46.58.. 2,098 53

Farm Expenses, $8,759.20.

Acme Scale Service, 113.50; Aikenhead Hardware, Ltd., 42.63; J. Allan, 17.38; Barrie Flour Mills, 162.15; F. Beatty, Ltd., 469.30; J. Beaupre, 75.00; M. Boyd, 212.00; British American Oil Co., Ltd., 54.83; Dr. Caley, 223.75; Canada Mineral Products, Ltd., 200.00; Canadian National Railways, 104.15; J. T. Cassin, 42.50; Copeland Flour Mills, Ltd., 775.79; T. B. Cramp, 333.20; Deloro Chemical Co., 35.89; R. Doolittle, 22.00; D. Dunn, 330.00; J. R. Eaton & Sons, Ltd., 16.38; H. L. Fenton, 15.50; Fountain Bros., 125.10; Galt Chemical Products, Ltd., 178.91; S. A. Geach, 344.25; Gunn's, Ltd., 439.39; J. M. Haley, 94.38; Hayman & Mills, 285.00; Hewitt Bros., 80.00; Holstein-Friesan Association, 16.50; J. James, 30.81; F. W. Jones, 19.12; H. Justin, 62.50; D. M. Kean, 15.70; Macnab & Sons, 39.54; C. Macpherson & Son, 47.00; A. McEachren, 16.80; D. McFadden, 21.80; G. L. Milligan Co., 11.00; Modern Hardware Co., 35.47; R. Moore & Sons, 34.05; Motherwell Grain Co., Ltd., 92.50; E. Murphy, 52.19; Orillia Creamery Co., Ltd., 17.75; Orillia Hardware Co., Ltd., 35.90; D. T. Parker, 59.50; Parrish & Heimbecker, Ltd., 695.60; Quaker Oats Co., 731.25; Ralston Purina Co., 417.20; D. Regan, 305.00; Reid Lumber Co., Ltd., 152.10; T. D. Robinson, 175.00; G. Sinclair, 50.60; Stone & Wellington, 84.75; G. H. Street, 18.00; G. Street & Sons, 105.30; Steele-Briggs Seed Co., Ltd., 379.19; J. Thompson, 35.64; D. C. Thomson, 51.30; E. Webb & Sons, Ltd., 10.00; Wilkinson-Kompass, Ltd., 61.03; Young & Young, 15.00; petty disbursements, 71.13.................. 8,759 20

Contingencies, $6,742.97.

E. Bacon, plants, 65.65; T. Bartlett, travelling expenses, 29.38; Blackburn Bros., repairs, 12.90; V. A. Brazier, travelling expenses, 304.45; British American Oil Co., Ltd., gas and oil, 1,401.35; Brown Bros. & Eplett, auto repairs, 57.12; Canada Customs, 10.74; Canadian National Express, 121.66; Canadian Universal Film Co., films, 45.00; Canada Wood Specialty Co., Ltd., basswood, 46.45; Cassidy's, Ltd., toys, 101.79; Chicago Medical Book Co., books, 52.26; The Misses Collings, craft supplies, 78.80; K. Day, travelling expenses, 17.11; Dominion Toy Co., toys, 42.46; J. R. Eaton & Sons, Ltd., basswood, 113.28; East Simcoe Agricultural Exhibition, admissions, 12.00; M. Ferguson, travelling expenses, 76.89; J. H. Forrester, travelling expenses, 46.45; W. C. George, small wares, 228.38; R. M. Goodfellow, travelling expenses, 286.50; Goodyear Tire & Rubber Co., Ltd., tubes, 58.47; Greenshields, Ltd., toys, 119.30; Dr. J. G. Grieve, travelling expenses, 35.05; N. M. Hand, ink, etc., 26.53; Hargraft Bros., Ltd., paper, 18.00; G. M. Hendry Co., Ltd., kindergarten supplies, 172.13; Dr. S. J. Horne, travelling expenses, 52.70; Hewitt Bros., cartage, 10.00; Heywood-Wakefield Co., reed, etc., 11.30; Department of Public Highways, gas., 71.33; E. M. Hill, newspapers, 16.50; Jones Music Stores, records, 10.05; King Paper Sales Co., paper bags, 39.33; L. K. Liggett Co., Ltd., paper, 12.16; J. B. Lippincott Co., books, 14.00; Love & Bennett, Ltd., sporting goods, 79.70; Macnab & Sons, Ltd., hardware, 108.10; G. F. Madden, repairs, 30.50; B. S. Marshall, fees, 20.00; G. W. Martin, travelling expenses, 12.80; Matchett Bros., prizes, 44.75; McAinsh

Ontario Hospitals—Continued

Orillia—Continued

Expenses—Continued

Contingencies—Continued

& Co., Ltd., books, 97.78; A. N. McKaughan, paper, 20.00; A. McKerrol, rental, 385.00; W. N. Millar, musical services, 25.00; Musson Book Co., music, 42.17; Nerlich & Co., toys and games, 213.98; H. R. Niebel, films, etc., 14.40; Northway-Dempsey Co., stool, etc., 20.74; Orillia Hardware Co., Ltd., supplies, 63.36; Packet Times & Press, Ltd., printing, etc., 36.24; A. Porter, travelling expenses, 12.90; Pratt's Drug Store, stationery, 63.60; J. H. Ross Boat Co., tent rent, 12.50; G. Sinclair, tobacco supplies, 37.40; Singer Sewing Machine Co., Inc., repairs, 17.63; M. R. Smith, travelling expenses, 13.55; Smith & Walsh, Ltd., car insurance, 377.28; C. H. Stoelting Co., tests, 15.59; G. H. Street & Sons, skates, etc., 53.23; Sykes Auto Service, gasoline, 13.20; C. V. Syrett Paper Co., Ltd., bags, 30.30; J. Thompson, travelling expenses, 22.18; A. L. Torgis & Son, auto supplies, 34.88; United Shoe Machinery Co., Ltd., skate holder, 11.76; Universal Films, films, 67.50; Victoria Paper & Twine Co., Ltd., towels, etc., 49.11; Walker's Stores, Ltd., oilcloth, 41.73; H. A. Wilson Co., Ltd., sporting goods, 30.59; Woodman & Ross, auto repairs, 103.78; F. W. Woolworth Co., Ltd., fancy goods, 225.95; J. A. Zarfas, travelling expenses, 119.20; petty disbursements, 227.65.............. 6,742 97

Repairs to Buildings, etc. ($33,825.92)

Maintenance and Repairs of all Buildings, Roads, Walks, Grounds and Fences, $12,979.76.

Ault & Wiborg, Ltd., 14.11; Boeckh Co., Ltd., 20.12; Brantford Roofing Co., Ltd., 543.79; Canadian Johns-Manville Co., Ltd., 14.45; Canada Paint Co., Ltd., 1,234.45; Canada Varnish Co., Ltd., 255.68; Canada Wood Specialty Co., Ltd., 33.25; Canadian National Express, 12.62; Canadian National Railways, 77.93; Canadian Pacific Railway Co., 452.87; The Cooksville Co., Ltd., 44.00; Colville Transport, 39.27; Dominion Cement Paint Co., 35.35; Dominion Bridge Co., Ltd., 919.74; H. S. Fenton, 96.50; Graham Nail Wire Products, Ltd., 35.23; Dept. of Public Highways, 58.78; Hospital & Kitchen Equipment Co., Ltd., 165.00; Imperial Varnish & Color Co., Ltd., 24.34; Italian Mosaic & Tile Co., Ltd., 83.35; Lasby's Transport, 48.00; Longford Quarry Co., 42.50; Lowe Bros. Co., Ltd., 346.82; Lundry Fence Co., Ltd., 26.04; Macnab & Sons, 97.85; Meakins & Sons, Ltd., 65.84; Modern Hardware, 167.52; J. H. Morin & Co., 80.38; Oliver Machinery & Lumber Co., 56.24; Ontario Reformatory, Mimico, 1,040.35; Ontario Reformatory Industries, 168.21; Orillia Hardware Co., Ltd., 226.15; Orillia Motor Supply, 17.14; Patterson & Heward, 22.00; Pay list, wages of men, 2,946.70; The Pedlar People, Ltd., 226.87; Pilkington Bros., Ltd., 53.85; W. E. Phillips Co., Ltd., 232.94; H. A. Raney & Co., 886.18; The Roofers Supply Co., Ltd., 224.17; Sherwin-Williams Co., Ltd., 62.95; Strathdee Transport, 100.55; Switzer Planing Mills, 84.50; Toronto Lock Mfg. Co., Ltd., 240.87; Truscon Steel Co. of Canada, Ltd., 97.02; W. Walker & Son, Ltd., 24.12; Wilkinson-Kompass Co., Ltd., 150.25; Wrought Iron Range Co., Ltd., 220.50; petty disbursements, 67.65. Total, 13,004.11. Less refunds— Canada Colors & Chemicals, Ltd., 9.50; Imperial Oil Ltd., 6.85; McColl-Frontenac Oil Co., Ltd., 8.00.......................... 12,979 76

Maintenance and Repairs of Plumbing, Steam and Electric Plants, $16,945.66.

The Alcor Co., 28.50; Beldam's Asbestos Packing Co., Ltd., 237.60; Bickle Fire Engines, Ltd., 107.80; Bird, Archer Co., Ltd., 172.38; Blackburn Auto Electric Service, 89.20; Boiler Repair & Grate Bar Co., 496.32; Bowden Machine Co., 25.00; F. L. Buchanan, 21.67; Bull Dog Electric Products, 11.87; Burke Electric X-ray Co., Ltd., 409.91; Canadian Fairbanks-Morse Co., Ltd., 219.23; Canadian General Electric Co., Ltd., 491.45; Canadian Johns-Manville Co., Ltd., 124.34; Canadian Laundry Machinery Co., Ltd., 11.58; Canadian Liquid Air Co., Ltd., 400.40; Canadian National Express, 38.55; Canadian National Railways, 92.14; Canadian Powers Regulator Co., Ltd., 708.50; Canadian Westinghouse Co., Ltd., 118.88; Cansfield Electric Works, 16.45; Crane, Ltd., 187.73; Crown Electric Mfg. Co., 10.78; Coville Transport Co., 172.70; W. H. Cunningham & Hill, Ltd., 33.87; Dearborn Chemical Co., Ltd., 263.55; J. Downes & Co., 561.08; C. A. Dunham Co., Ltd., 655.28; Empire Brass Mfg. Co., Ltd., 2,847.95; E. T. Flanagan, 869.34; Garlock Packing Co., Ltd., 225.45; General Steel Wares, Ltd., 180.51; Goodyear Tire & Rubber Co., Ltd., 116.49; Gurney Foundry Co., Ltd., 119.12; Gutta Percha & Rubber, Ltd., 118.81; J. F. Hartz Co., Ltd., 110.00; Hospital & Kitchen Equipment Co., Ltd., 188.16; Huston Oil Co., Ltd., 69.30; Jones Bros. of Canada, Ltd., 12.50; La France Fire Engine Co., Ltd., 121.60; A. S. Leitch Co., Ltd., 171.95; Rice Lewis & Son, Ltd., 49.98; Macnab & Sons, 44.33; Mahaffy Iron Works, 15.48; Master Plumber Products, 14.25; T. McAvity & Sons, 25.48; James Morrison Brass Mfg. Co., Ltd., 801.07; The Music Co., Ltd.,

Ontario Hospitals—Continued

Orillia—Continued

Repairs to Buildings, etc.—Continued

Maintenance and Repairs of Plumbing, etc.—Continued

33.33; National Silicates, Ltd., 12.18; Northern Electric Co., Ltd., 204.75; Northrop & Lyman Co., Ltd., 12.70; Orillia Hardware Co., Ltd., 94.25; Ontario Hospital, Orillia, Industries, 210.76; Orillia Water, Light and Power Commission, 74.71; Pay list, wages of men, 802.57; H. W. Petrie, Ltd., 198.82; Phillips & Co., 91.12; Powerlite Devices, Ltd., 12.17; Premier Laundry Equipment Co., Ltd., 28.17; R. T. Purves & Co., 151.03; H. A. Raney & Co., 35.05; Regent Electric Supply Co., Ltd., 98.65; R. Richardson & Co., 32.30; Ritchie & Mould, 44.65; The James Robertson Co., Ltd., 287.69; Roelofson Elevator Works, 32.05; Rogers Electric Co., Ltd., 11.46; Shur-Line Auto Tire Systems, 93.79; Square D Co., Ltd., 30.40; Sternson Structural Specialties, 47.30; Strathdee Transport Co., Ltd., 90.78; Superior Electric Supply Co., Ltd., 17.50; Supplies & Insulation, Ltd., 263.31; Taylor-Forbes Co., Ltd., 983.60; T. W. Terry, 15.60; Trane Co., Ltd., 266.60; G. S. Whelpton, 195.00; Wilkinson-Kompass, Ltd., 101.10; Wilson Illumination Co., Ltd., 107.50; Wrought Iron Range Co., Ltd., 373.38; petty disbursements, 82.56 .... 16,945 66

Live Stock, Vehicles and Farm Implements, $3,900.50.

S. G. Burns, 88.00; S. A. Geach, 100.00; A. D. Gorrie & Co., Ltd., 685.00; McLeod Garage, 1,000.00; C. McPherson & Son, 19.50; W. J. Murphy, 1,900.00; Ontario Hospital, Hamilton, 108.00 .... 3,900 50

Industries ($8,038.65)

Anglo-Canadian Leather Co., Ltd., 3,106.08; Beardmore Leathers, Ltd., 500.40; Bennett, Ltd., 29.27; Canada Customs, 11.25; Canadian National Railways, 23.31; Connecticut Web & Buckle Co., 22.50; Coville Transport Co., 37.78; Frank & Bryce, Ltd., 123.00; J. Garde & Co., Ltd., 40.03; Goodyear Tire & Rubber Co., Ltd., 79.48; A. E. Long & Co., Ltd., 140.76; C. Parsons & Sons, Ltd., 251.23; Quality Button & Trimming Co., 219.88; Robson Leather Co., Ltd., 2,638.64; A. Stein & Co., Ltd., 237.59; Toronto Heel Co., 250.50; United Shoe Machinery Co., Ltd., 269.08; petty disbursements, 57.87 .... 8,038 65

Total		500,633 25
Less Maintenance of Patients	51,578 89	
Perquisites	43,731 06	
Sale of Produce	19,447 55	
		114,757 50
Orillia		385,875 75

PENETANGUISHENE

Salaries ($78,426.66)

Superintendent, Physicians and Dentists	7,776 66
Steward and Assistants	3,875 00
Matron and Assistants, including domestic help	8,753 59
Engineers and Assistants	6,345 75
Artisans, not domestic	4,234 70
Farm and Garden employees	6,000 00
Attendants and Nurses	41,440 96

(Expenses $60,159.61)

Medicines, $2,613.18.

Ash-Temple Co., Ltd., 16.56; Ayerst, McKenna & Harrison, Ltd., 54.49; Burroughs, Wellcome & Co., 54.56; Canadian National Express, 23.15; Dental Company of Canada, Ltd., 42.83; C. V. Donaldson, 76.94; Charles E. Frosst & Co., 87.58; A. D. Gibson, 28.86; J. F. Hartz Co., Ltd., 189.10; Herald Printing Co., 15.00; Hargraft Bros., Ltd., 148.04; Ingram & Bell, Ltd., 230.76; Lewis Manufacturing Co., Ltd., 108.82; Liquor Control Board, 37.00; Macmillan Co. of Canada, Ltd., 22.91; Nettleton's Drug Store, 293.10; Richardson & Beaulieu, 633.37; Richards Glass Co., Ltd., 16.94; W. E. Saunders, Ltd., 155.30; E. B. Shuttleworth Chemical Co., Ltd., 93.80; Synthetic Drug Co., Ltd., 10.15; The Stevens Companies, 36.00; Textile Products Co., 32.50; George S. Trudell & Co., 49.40; Standard Tobacco Co., 17.32; Henry K. Wampole & Co., Ltd., 60.96; Chas. R. Will & Co., Ltd., 37.44; petty disbursements, 40.30 .... 2,613 18

Ontario Hospitals—Continued

Penetanguishene—Continued

Expenses—Continued

Groceries and Provisions, $19,837.73.

Balfours, Ltd., 177.82; Bowes Co., Ltd., 2,673.52; Canadian National Railways, 58.71; Canada Dominion Sugar Co., Ltd., 143.40; Canadian National Express, 96.72; Canada Packers, Ltd., 818.08; Copeland Flour Mills, Ltd., 960.00; E. T. Copeland, 75.00; L. A. Coleman Co., Ltd., 118.84; Dalton Bros., 188.80; Walter W. Esdon Co., Ltd., 80.92; K. C. Fruman, 538.32; H. A. Hornsby, 520.05; The Harry Horne Co., Ltd., 47.82; H. J. Heinz Co., 35.68; F. W. Humphrey Co., Ltd., 1,430.60; F. T. James & Co., Ltd., 1,219.48; F. W. Krouse, 15.00; Laing Produce Sales Co., Ltd., 67.86; James Lumbers Co., Ltd., 891.61; J. M. Lowes Co., Ltd., 50.50; D. McArthur, 150.00; Edgar J. Moreen, 24.00; National Grocers Co., Ltd., 765.09; Ontario Reformatory Industries, 6,431.24; E. H. Price, 443.39; Penetang Dairy, 13.50; D. S. Perrin & Co., 10.18; Standard Brands, Ltd., 274.21; W. M. Thompson & Co., Ltd., 970.87; Whyte Packing Co., Ltd., 361.76; Young-Winfield, Ltd., 168.73; petty disbursements, 16.03 .... 19,837 73

Fuel, Light and Water, $16,314.45.

C. Beck Co., Ltd., 37.66; Canadian General Electric Co., Ltd., 114.80; Eddy Match Co., Ltd., 27.87; H. S. Fenton, 11,780.90; Amos B. Gordon Co., Ltd., 30.40; Penetang Water and Power Commission, 4,315.20; petty disbursements, 7.62 .... 16,314 45

Clothing, $7,419.22.

Anderson & McBeth, Ltd., 85.00; Canadian National Railways, 29.93; Circle Bar Knitting Co., Ltd., 114.00; Miss Chalue, 36.00; Dominion Rubber Co., Ltd., 104.28; Victor G. Edwards, 15.00; The J. D. Flynn Shoe Store, 14.90; A. D. Gibson, 94.05; Gendron Penetang Shoe Pack Co., 399.77; Hamburg Felt Boot Co., Ltd., 237.60; Hamilton & Johnston, 1,733.64; J. A. Johnston Co., 129.00; Mercer Reformatory Industries, 1,593.60; McArthur Beltings, Ltd., 35.00; National Textiles, Ltd., 70.00; Ontario Reformatory Industries, 1,683.33; Ontario Hospital, Orillia, Industries, 476.34; Penman's, Ltd., 106.25; W. M. Thompson & Co., Ltd., 72.28; J. P. Wells, 348.48; F. W. Woolworth Co., Ltd., 11.35; petty disbursements, 29.42 .... 7,419 22

Laundry and Cleaning, $2,798.65.

Associated Chemical Co., Ltd., 389.83; Aikenhead Hardware, Ltd., 19.61; Beaver Laundry & Machinery Co., Ltd., 99.01; Canadian National Railways, 96.35; Canadian National Institute for the Blind, 32.50; Capo Po.ishers, Ltd., 21.44; Canada Colors & Chemicals, Ltd., 45.60; Colgate-Palmolive-Peet Co., Ltd., 51.54; Diamond Cleansers, Ltd., 107.50; Durham Duplex Razor Co., 38.81; Excelsior Brushes, Ltd., 113.40; Electric Boiler Compound Co., Ltd., 267.56; The E. B. Eddy Co., Ltd., 19.69; Philip C. Garratt Co,. 84.00; General Steel Wares, Ltd., 17.38; Guelph Soaps, 35.10; Hamilton & Johnston, 15.39; James Lumbers Co., Ltd., 21.57; S. F. Lawrason & Co., Ltd., 210.00; A. R. McDonald, 25.95; National Grocers Co., Ltd:, 30.00; Procter & Gamble Co., Ltd., 64.18; Rexo Chemical Cleaner Co., Ltd., 804.12; Ratcliffe Paper Co., Ltd., 81.35; W. M. Thompson & Co., Ltd., 16.24; G. H. Wood & Co., Ltd., 61.25; petty disbursements, 29.28 .... 2,798 65

Furniture and Furnishings, $4,902.82.

A. Bradshaw & Sons, Ltd., 105.60; J. A. Brownlee, 36.00; Canadian National Railways, 76.60; Cassidy's, Ltd., 295.91; Delaney & Pettit, Ltd., 185.00; Victor G. Edwards, 64.60; A. D. Gibson, 64.35; General Steel Wares, Ltd., 28.85; Hamilton & Johnston, 258.29; A. R. Macdonald, 23.30; John McGuire Estate, 128.08; Metal Craft Co., Ltd., 33.68; Mercer Reformatory Industries, 1,414.20; J. E. Nettleton, 67.20; Ontario Reformatory Industries, 1,686.75; Pendrith Machinery Co., 277.63; Singer Sewing Machine Co., Inc., 68.65; W. M. Thompson & Co., Ltd., 19.21; Toronto Feather & Down Co., Ltd., 37.55; petty disbursements, 31.37 .... 4,902 82

Office Expenses, 496.20.

Bell Telephone Co., rentals, 251.35; tolls, 27.85; Canadian National Express, 13.21; Canadian National Telegraphs, 25.86; Postmaster, 172.60; petty disbursements, 5.33 .... 496 20

Farm Expenses, $4,410.42.

Andrewes Mountain Seed Co., Ltd., 246.66; British American Oil Co., Ltd., 172.80; Jos. Beaupre, 236.23; A. M. Bell, 38.25; Canadian National Railways, 23.67; D. R. Caley, 175.00; Copeland Flour Mills, Ltd., 1,959.08; D. Currie, 19.00; A. Clark, 31.60; Canada Mineral Products, Ltd., 140.00; Foster Pottery Co.,

Ontario Hospitals—Continued

Penetanguishene—Continued

Expenses—Continued

Farm Expenses—Continued

18.11; John Fowell & Son, 23.00; M. A. Gendron, 22.50; N. Grier, 10.00; Goodyear Tire & Rubber Co., Ltd., 46.59; J. W. Hollister & Son, 115.45; Holstein-Friesian Association, 18.50; Kerr Woodworkers, 358.63; A. R. McDonald, 239.00; Ralph Moore & Sons, 27.30; Bert Mason, 66.55; R. W. Ney, 105.95; D. T. Parker, 33.00; F. Phillips, 23.90; Alfred Robitaille, 50.00; Jos. Robillard, 22.00; Spramotor Co., 27.35; W. M. Thompson & Co., Ltd., 68.79; Taylor-Forbes Co., Ltd., 38.75; H. G. Todd, 30.20; petty disbursements, 22.56 .... 4,410 42

Contingencies, $1,366.94.

American Psychiatric Association, subscription, 15.00; Dr. B. A. Blackwell, services, 80.00; A. M. Bell, travelling expenses, 22.50; Canadian National Express, 24.91; N. J. Cole, travelling expenses, 99.10; G. Chisholm, travelling expenses, 11.00; Dominion Reed Supplies, Ltd., reed, 15.35; Dawson Subscription Service, Ltd., subscriptions, 76.50; Fire Brigade, Penetanguishene, for services, 50.00; Gray Coach Lines, hire, 45.00; Hamilton & Johnston, floss, 17.45; Herald Printing Co., subscription and printing, 10.00; Hargraft Bros., Ltd., pipes and cards, 51.90; F. W. Humphrey Co., Ltd., bags, 10.14; J. W. Hollister & Son, valve, 31.51; Ingram & Bell, Ltd., books, 10.24; Dr. G. C. Kidd, travelling expenses, 44.25; Love & Bennett, Ltd., sporting goods, 23.75; Dr. D. O. Lynch, travelling expenses, 66.10; Jos. Murphy, travelling expenses, 12.90; The Macmillan Co., Ltd., books, 20.40; Dr. J. Morris Nettleton, services, 36.34; Mary Neal, travelling expenses, 10.55; Ontario Medical Association, subscription, 10.00; E. J. Parker, newspapers, 41.00; Religious Services, 195.50; Richardson & Beaulieu, pipes, 16.98; C. V. Syrett Paper Co., Ltd., bags, 25.57; Smith & Walsh, car insurance, 22.69; J. Walsh, travelling expenses, 16.00; Harold A. Wilson Co., Ltd., sporting goods, 31.01; petty disbursements, 223.30 .... 1,366 94

Repairs to Buildings, etc. ($36,867.09)

Maintenance and Repairs of all Buildings, Roads, Walks, Grounds and Fences, $17,968.76.

Aikenhead Hardware, Ltd., 103.69; Arco Co., Ltd., 135.00; Associated Chemical Co., Ltd., 25.33; Burke Electric & X-Ray Co., Ltd., 96.19; Burke Towing & Salvage Co., Ltd., 125.00; Builders Supplies, Ltd., 347.19; Canadian National Railways, 264.33; Canadian Johns-Manville Co., Ltd., 1,098.72; Canadian Rogers Sheet Metal & Roofing, Ltd., 213.36; Canada Paint Co., Ltd., 626.60; Coville Transport Co., Ltd., 24.29; Canada Varnish Co., Ltd., 173.71; Dennisteel, Ltd., 59.40; Disher Steel Construction Co., Ltd., 34.00; W. E. Dillon Co., Ltd., 39.16; Dow Chemical Co., 29.39; Excelsior Brushes, Ltd., 33.74; V. G. Edwards, 46.90; M. A. Gendron, 194.50; Italian Mosaic & Marble Co., Ltd., 97.00; Louden Machinery Co., Ltd., 103.39; Rice Lewis & Son, Ltd., 26.05; A. R. McDonald, 365.65; J. H. Morin & Co., Ltd., 85.64; The McGibbon Lumber Co., Ltd., 442.34; Ontario Reformatory, Mimico, 182.47; Ontario Reformatory Industries, 60.26; Pay list, wages of men, 7,069.85; Peckover's, Ltd., 93.37; W. E. Phillips Co., Ltd., 11.76; Robert T. Purves & Co., 257.50; Pilkington Bros., Ltd., 15.08; Penetang Planing Mill, 276.55; Roofers Supply Co., Ltd., 629.16; H. E. Smith, Ltd., 244.51; Spencer Foundry Co., Ltd., 1,845.15; Alfred Tessier, 2,079.99; Toronto Lock Mfg. Co., Ltd., 126.29; H. G. Todd, 77.50; Truscon Steel Co., Ltd., 129.21; W. Walker & Son, Ltd., 39.17; petty disbursements, 40.37 .... 17,968 76

Maintenance and Repairs of Plumbing, Steam and Electric Plants, $17,740.43.

Associated Chemical Co., Ltd., 25.85; Bull Dog Electric Products, Ltd., 76.25; Bennett & Wright, Ltd., 28.91; Canadian National Railways, 80.52; Canadian Chemical Co., 55.60; T. J. Campbell Co., Ltd., 23.36; Canadian National Express, 90.21; Canadian General Electric Co., Ltd., 106.68; Crown Electrical Mfg. Co., Ltd., 12.25; Coville Transport Co., 77.31; Canadian Industries, Ltd., 14.25; Crane, Ltd., 124.02; Canadian Powers Regulator Co., Ltd., 16.50; C. A. Dunham & Co., Ltd., 229.35; J. E. Desroches, 58.49; Drummond-McCall & Co., Ltd., 324.80; F. J. Downes & Co., 316.06; Dearborn Chemical Co., Ltd., 33.71; Empire Brass Mfg. Co., Ltd., 856.54; E. T. Flanagan, 47.02; D. M. Fraser, Ltd., 44.26; Garlock Packing Co., Ltd., 134.92; Gurney Foundry Co., Ltd., 194.56; Gutta Percha & Rubber, Ltd., 61.66; Huston Oil Co., Ltd., 12.50; Hardinge Bros., Ltd., 10.50; Ingram & Bell, Ltd., 1,012.22; Arthur J. Leitch Co., Ltd., 367.07; A. R. Donald, 43.65; McArthur Beltings, Ltd., 28.33; T. McAvity & Sons, Ltd., 229.78; The Masco Co., Ltd., 184.02; James Morrison Brass Mfg. Co., Ltd., 267.94; B. H. Montgomery Hose Reel Co., Ltd., 365.00; Mueller, Ltd., 13.58; National Meter Co., Ltd., 39.00; Northern Electric Co., Ltd., 242.14; Pay lists, wages of men, 8,301.06; Penetang Water and Light Commission, 525.59; H. W. Petrie, Ltd., 88.12; P. Payette Co., 231.45; The James Robertson Co., Ltd., 380.30; C. Richard-

Ontario Hospitals—Continued

Penetanguishene—Continued

Repairs to Buildings, etc.—Continued

Maintenance and Repairs of Plumbing, etc.—Continued

son & Co., Ltd., 12.13; Regent Electric Supply Co., Ltd., 183.37; Rogers Electric Co., Ltd., 29.87; Supplies & Insulation, Ltd., 887.39; Smart-Turner Machine Co., Ltd., 269.18; J. A. Sexauer Mfg. Co., Ltd., 70.54; Standard Underground Cable Co., Ltd., 25.91; Standard Sales & Service, 16.50; Spencer Foundry Co., Ltd., 40.70; Stabler & Baker, 15.00; Taylor-Forbes Co., Ltd., 181.27; Trane Co., Ltd., 141.44; T. W. Terry, 196.60; Tools & Hardware, Ltd., 22.40; Wilson Illumination Co., Ltd., 163.08; Wrought Iron Range Co., Ltd., 15.63; petty disbursements, 94.09 .... 17,740 43

Live Stock, Vehicles and Farm Implements, $1,157.90.

Canadian National Express, 38.90; Hewitt Bros., 50.00; Ontario Hospital, Orillia, 922.00; Ontario Hospital, Woodstock, 42.00; Ontario Hospital, Hamilton, 90.00; Ontario Hospital, Whitby, 15.00 .... 1,157 90

Total		175,453 36	
Less Maintenance of Patients	12,322 88		
Perquisites	17,034 50		
Sale of Produce	585 99		
		29,943 37	
Penetanguishene		$145,509.99	

TORONTO

Salaries ($170,172.72)

Superintendent, Physicians and Dentists	17,241 18
Steward and Assistants	9,586 20
Matron and Assistants, including domestic help	18,631 25
Engineers and Assistants	15,475 00
Artisans, not domestic	5,999 96
Farm and Garden Employees	2,525 00
Attendants and Nurses	100,714 13

Expenses ($131,293.98)

Medicines, $5,356.70.

Ash-Temple Co., Ltd., 53.69; A. Bradshaw & Sons, Ltd., 13.20; Bovinine Co., 16.34; The British Drug Houses, Ltd., 48.87; Burroughs Welcome & Co., 57.64; Consolidated Optical Co., Ltd., 12.20; Dominion Dental Co., 59.15; C. E. Frosst & Co., 55.53; The Hargraft Bros., Ltd., 152.08; J. F. Hartz Co., Ltd., 525.66; Dr. H. J. Hodgins, 82.25; Horlick's Malted Milk, 36.00; Hygiene Products, Ltd., 12.00; Ingram & Bell, Ltd., 1,001.53; F. T. James Co., Ltd., 94.50; Lewis Manufacturing Co., Ltd., 201.19; Liquor Control Board, 40.48; Mallinckrodt Chemical Works, Ltd., 58.51; R. E. Mitchell, 677.71; National Drug & Chemical Co., Ltd., 154.46; Parke-Davis & Co., 206.30; Petrolager Laboratories, 60.00; Princess Jewellers, 33.70; Richards Glass Co., Ltd., 73.60; Rolls & Darlington, Ltd., 200.34; W. E. Saunders, Ltd., 58.56; Standard Tobacco Co., 213.95; The Stevens Co., Ltd., 400.25; E. B. Shuttleworth Chemical Co., Ltd., 20.61; Textile Products, Ltd., 274.90; Tuckett, Ltd., 212.91; Van Zant's, Ltd., 18.77; Vi-Tone Co., 27.43; H. K. Wample Co., Ltd., 134.19; A. Wander, Ltd., 15.91; petty disbursements, 52.29 .... 5,356 70

Groceries and Provisions, $64,801.29.

H. J. Ash, 540.73; Barry & Hamilton, 350.20; Bowes Co., Ltd., 474.66; S. Campbell, 826.70; Canada Dominion Sugar Co., Ltd., 2,449.90; Canadian National Railways, 87.73; L. A. Coleman Co., 118.95; Copeland Flour Mills, Ltd., 816.00; Crosse & Blackwell, Ltd., 33.49; Dalton Bros., 22.80; Department of Horticulture, O.A.C., 20.00; Dominion Linseed Oil Co., Ltd., 24.50; Economy Tea & Coffee Co., 884.24; W. W. Esdon Co., Ltd., 24.75; Everest Bros., 1,287.18; W. Everton, 10.15; John J. Fee, 10,055.81; K. C. Freeman, 1,045.95; H. Hand, 31.25; J. R. Hayden Co., 378.51; H. J. Heinz Co., 56.29; Higgins & Burke, Ltd., 1,329.94; The Harry Horne Co., Ltd., 392.55; F. W. Humphreys Co., Ltd., 2,358.77; F. T. James & Co., Ltd., 1,050.00; Kademay Co., 28.00; Lakeside Milling Co., Ltd., 775.25; Loblaw Groceterias Co., Ltd., 51.10; Lowe Corporation, 112.05; James Lumbers Co., Ltd., 1,404.34; G. A. Lyons, 566.85; Maple Leaf Milling Co., Ltd., 1,243.96; Mara Lodge Poultry Farms, 455.08; J. S. Moore, 85.00; D. McArthur, 750.00; L. McTague, 45.40; National Grocers Co., Ltd., 40.91; W. Neilson, Ltd., 310.75; Newmarket Flour Mills, 903.00; Ontario Reformatory, Mimico, 754.33; Ontario

Ontario Hospitals—Continued

Toronto—Continued

Expenses—Continued

Groceries and Provisions—Continued

Honey Producers Co., Ltd., 79.05; Ontario Hospital, Hamilton, 182.19; Ontario Reformatory Industries, 26,664.48; W. M. Pace Co., Ltd., 72.50; W. G. Patrick & Co., 23.75; People's Produce Co., 530.70; D. S. Perrin & Co., 122.27; Pure Gold Manufacturing Co., Ltd., 386.27; Geo. E. Rees, 50.48; Rose Marie Farms, 32.34; St. Lawrence Fish Market, 1,455.24; St. Lawrence Starch Co., Ltd., 414.78; H. Sarson, 67.55; Standard Brands, Ltd., 634.48; Standard Wholesale Grocery Co., Ltd., 558.50; Sunera Cereals, Ltd., 22.25; J. Stearn, 25.00; Stull Transport Co., 90.44; Swift Canadian Co., Ltd., 317.93; Toronto Dairy, Ltd., 513.86; Toronto Municipal Farm, 10.00; Toronto Salt Works, 155.01; Vi-Tone Co., 27.93; Geo. Weston Ltd., 51.72; Whyte Packing Co., Ltd., 108.65; petty disbursements, 6.85 .... 64,801 29

Fuel, Light and Water, $27,009.88.

P. Burns & Co., Ltd., 18,583.96; H. C. Burton & Co., 481.02; City of Toronto Water Department, 5,142.10; Consumers' Gas Co., 471.76; Eddy Match Co., Ltd., 55.69; Toronto Hydro-Electric System, 2,269.95; petty disbursements, 5.40 27,009 88

Clothing, $10,594.19.

Anderson-MacBeth, Ltd., 173.50; Big 88 Shoe Store, 24.00; Billie Burke Dress Co., 70.00; A. Bradshaw & Sons, Ltd., 370.72; W. A. Brophy Co., Ltd., 22.80; Canadian Panama & Straw Hats, Ltd., 25.50; Circle Bar Knitting Co., Ltd., 475.00; Corbett, Cowley, Ltd., 81.55; Eisman & Co., Ltd., 25.24; John Garde & Co., Ltd., 11.83; A. D. Gibson, 590.49; Gordon MacKay & Co., Ltd., 24.78; Greenshields, Ltd., 15.13; Hamilton Carhartt Manufacturing Co., Ltd., 52.69; Hamilton & Johnston, 1,305.60; Lailey-Trimble, Ltd., 735.00; Lyman Barnet, 37.22; J. A. McLaren & Co., Ltd., 750.42; Mercer Reformatory Industries, 3,883.44; Midland Whitewear Costume Co., 62.00; Morris Shoe and Slipper Co., 73.80; Ontario Hospital, Orillia, Industries, 34.62; Ontario Reformatory Industries, 528.90; C. Parson & Sons, Ltd., 214.37; Penmans, Ltd., 30.00; Rex Tailoring Co., Ltd., 636.80; I. Rovansky, 34.42; Schofield Woolen Co., Ltd., 72.00; J. R. Siberry, Ltd., 39.54; Textile Products, 53.07; Welman Dress & Skirt Co., 121.00; petty disbursements, 18.76 .... 10,594 19

Laundry and Cleaning, $6,398.20.

Acme Caretakers Supply Co., 706.84; Aikenhead Hardware, Ltd., 42.12; Alpha Chemical Co., Ltd., 32.03; Associated Chemical Co., Ltd., 689.59; Aulcraft Paints, Ltd., 26.73; Bates Products, Ltd., 31.36; Beaver Laundry Machinery Co., Ltd., 175.31; The John Bull Manufacturing Co., 85.53; Canadian Germicide Co., Ltd., 16.83; Canadian National Institute for the Blind, 104.30; Copeland & Bonner, 15.00; Diamond Cleansers, Ltd., 580.75; A. B. Drake & Co., 423.36; Dye & Chemical Co., Ltd., 33.66; Electric Boiler Compound Co., Ltd., 35.39; P. C. Garratt & Co., 487.20; R. S. Gillan, 88.20; A. S. Graham, 34.70; Gutta Percha & Rubber, Ltd., 14.24; G. A. Hardie Co., Ltd., 329.22; Higgins & Burke, Ltd., 45.68; Hoar Transport Co., 11.49; F. W. Humphreys Co., Ltd., 40.54; The Andrew Jergens Co., Ltd., 446.88; Jones Bros., Ltd., 22.75; Kilgours, Ltd., 293.25; W. H. Lake, 78.45; Lever Bros., Ltd., 142.56; The Levis, 42.00; James Lumbers Co., Ltd., 33.60; H. Mendes & Co., 28.00; Ontario Reformatory Industries, 12.00; Parke-Davis & Co., 40.32; Procter & Gamble Co., Ltd., 38.33; Rexo Chemical Cleanser Co., Ltd., 149.06; St. Croix Soap Manufacturing Co., Ltd., 433.62; St. Lawrence Starch Co., Ltd., 68.00; Standard Wax Co., 57.20; J. B. Sheppard, 27.35; Sure Way Products, 22.49; John Taylor & Co., 154.44; Toronto Salt Works, 100.10; Victoria Paper & Twine Co., Ltd., 81.45; Wonder Products, 22.93; petty disbursements, 53.35 .... 6,398 20

Furniture and Furnishings, $12,265.83.

Acme Caretakers Supply Co., 21.60; Aikenhead Hardware, Ltd., 46.35; A. Bradshaw & Sons, Ltd., 18.21; Caldwell Linen Mills, 186.08; Canadian Fairbanks-Morse Co., Ltd., 15.60; Canadian Industries, Ltd., 75.26; Canadian Speedo Co., 10.00; Cassidy's, Ltd., 29.98; H. Druiffe & Co., 82.35; The T. Eaton Co., Ltd., 13.84; Empire Brass Manufacturing Co., Ltd., 13.99; John Garde & Co., Ltd., 21.81; Gendron Manufacturing Co., Ltd., 60.30; General Steel Wares, Ltd., 36.19; A. D. Gibson, 713.83; Gold Medal Furniture Co., Ltd., 132.43; Grand & Toy, Ltd., 202.40; H. Grimshaw, 167.95; Hamilton & Johnston, 312.03; G. A. Hardie & Co., Ltd., 226.57; G. H. Hees Son & Co., Ltd., 23.74; Johnson Office Furniture Co., 48.00; Wm. Junor, Ltd., 407.25; Kilgours, Ltd., 35.00; W. H. Lake, 1,128.69; McGlashan-Clarke & Co., Ltd., 24.75; Mercer Reformatory Industries, 3,892.56; Ontario Reformatory Industries, 3,088.15; Ontario Rubber Co., Ltd., 20.00;

Ontario Hospitals—Continued

Toronto—Continued

Expenses—Continued

Furniture and Furnishings—Continued

C. Parsons & Sons, Ltd., 19.06; Simmons, Ltd., 35.50; The Robt. Simpson Co., Ltd., 20.39; Singer Sewing Machine Co., 13.46; Sully Aluminum, Ltd., 292.50; F. W. Stull Transport, 30.36; Textile Products, Ltd., 403.19; Thermos Bottle Co., Ltd., 39.98; R. G. Venn, 22.34; Victoria Paper & Twine Co., Ltd., 181.60; G. H. Wood & Co., Ltd., 50.96; petty disbursements, 101.58 .... 12,265 83

Office Expenses, $1,094.06.

Bell Telephone Co., rentals, 767.06; tolls, 1.30; Bourne & Towse, map, 12.50; Grand & Toy, Ltd., supplies, 55.35; Postmaster, 209.60; Remington Typewriters, Ltd., inspections, 32.00; Seitz Typewriter Co., repairs, 13.75; petty disbursements, 2.50 .... 1,094 06

Farm Expenses, $856.18.

Andrewes Mountain Seed Co., 234.43; John Castor, 34.70; Knox & Patterson, 29.55; G. A. Lyons, 140.81; Marchment Co., Ltd., 361.39; J. W. Peacock, 24.15; W. Walker & Son, Ltd., 22.36; petty disbursements, 8.79 .... 856 18

Contingencies, $2,917.65.

Aikenhead Hardware, Ltd., hardware, 77.46; Bates & Dodds, Ltd., interments, 130.00; J. W. Benson, printing, 89.25; Canadian Colortype, Ltd., tube sets, 184.00; Canadian National Exhibition, admissions, 32.00; Robt. Clarke, entertainment, 15.00; Dawson Subscription Service, 154.50; The T. Eaton Co., Ltd., notions, 21.37; Ellis Bros., medals, 19.75; Goodyear Tire & Rubber Co., Ltd., tubes, 41.28; Gordon MacKay & Co., Ltd., notions, 20.09; Gray Coach Lines, bus hire, 28.00; Hargraft Bros., Ltd., pipes, etc., 27.60; Department of Public Highways, auto service, 302.16; E. Hogan, trees, 12.00; Dr. A. J. Hodgins, services, 19.00; F. W. Humphrey Co., Ltd., cards, 11.00; Ingram & Bell, Ltd., medical books, 209.14; Dr. E. A. James, travelling expenses, 19.10; Kilgours, Ltd., paper bags, 105.42; W. H. Lake, gas, 358.28; J. B. Lippincott & Co., books, 11.40; J. Malacarne & Son, repairs, 84.15; Mail and Empire, subscriptions, 12.00; N. L. Martin, books, 20.17; Might Directories, directory, 18.00; McAinsh & Co., Ltd., medical books, 92.00; Musical Services, 173.00; Nerlich & Co., decorations, 19.05; New Cambridge Book Shop, books, 20.52; Ontario Motion Picture Bureau, films, 47.95; Ontario Rubber Co., Ltd., hose, 11.10; Princess Jewellers, repairs, 28.15; The Robt. Simpson Co., Ltd., notions, 65.56; Slichters, Ltd., flowers, 33.10; Smith & Walsh, car insurance, 53.91; A. L. Torgis & Son, anti-freeze, 13.53; Victoria Paper & Twine Co., Ltd., 48.07; Wilkins Smallwares Co., Ltd., decorations, 84.30; F. W. Woolworth Co., Ltd., prizes, 15.25; petty disbursements, 190.04 .... 2,917 65

Repairs to Buildings, etc. ($27,935.23)

Maintenance and Repairs of all Buildings, Roads, Walks, Grounds and Fences, $22,446.35.

Aikenhead Hardware, Ltd., 291.12; American Hardware Corporation, Ltd., 89.42; Aulcraft Paints, Ltd., 684.53; Ault & Wiborg Co., Ltd., 201.47; The Barrett Co., Ltd., 12.42; Bigger Lock & Key Co., 77.75; Canada Metal Co., Ltd., 22.00; Canada Building Materials, Ltd., 272.10; Canadian Fairbanks-Morse Co., Ltd., 15.60; Canadian Johns-Manville Co., Ltd., 15.00; Canadian Pacific Railway Co., 94.55; Canada Paint Co., Ltd., 303.00; Canadian Rogers Sheet Metal Roofing, Ltd., 22.50; W. E. Dillon Co., Ltd., 18.02; Disher Steel Construction Co., Ltd., 19.00; Dominion Bridge Co., Ltd., 21.00; Frankel Bros., 14.00; Imperial Varnish & Color Co., Ltd., 98.83; R. Laidlaw Lumber Co., Ltd., 1,771.08; W. H. Lake, 43.24; Rice Lewis & Son, Ltd., 43.24; Lowe Bros. Co., Ltd., 30.22; Mathews Bros., Ltd., 44.19; S. McCord & Co., 27.44; J. H. Morin & Co., Ltd., 1,521.47; Montgomery Hose Reel Co., 117.60; Alex. Murray & Co., Ltd., 25.61; Ontario Reformatory, Mimico, 24.50; Ontario Reformatory Industries, 55.87; Pay lists, wages of men, 13,695.10; J. W. Peacock, 26.19; The Pedlar People, Ltd., 104.27; Pilkington Bros., Ltd., 94.48; Roofers Supply Co., Ltd., 252.34; Sanderson, Pearcy, Marietta Co., Ltd., 152.00; Sherwin-Williams Co., Ltd., 93.42; Simons Canadian Saw Co., Ltd., 13.86; The Robt. Simpson Co., Ltd., 19.70; Malcolm Sinclair Co., Ltd., 540.00; J. B. Smith & Sons, Ltd., 282.06; R. E. Smith, Ltd., 490.14; Toronto Brick Co., 11.64; Toronto Lock Manufacturing Co., Ltd., 212.39; Tremco Manufacturing Co., Ltd., 26.99; Trelco, Ltd., 31.20; Truscon Steel Co., Ltd., 37.70; W. Walker & Son, Ltd., 79.74; W. Williamson Lumber Co., Ltd., 233.90; petty disbursements, 72.46 .... 22,446 35

Maintenance and Repairs of Plumbing, Steam and Electric Plants and Machinery, $5,488.88.

Aikenhead Hardware, Ltd., 45.98; Beardmore Leathers, Ltd., 10.59; Canadian Asbestos Co., Ltd., 56.68; Canadian Chemicals Co., 416.00; Canadian Foundry

Ontario Hospitals—Continued

Toronto—Continued

Repairs to Buildings, etc.—Continued

Maintenance and Repairs of Plumbing, etc.—Continued

Supplies & Equipment, Ltd., 288.60; Canadian General Electric Co., Ltd., 110.71; Canadian Powers Regulator Co., Ltd., 477.68; Canadian Rumley Co., Ltd., 18.43; Canadian Westinghouse Co., Ltd., 11.04; W. H. Cunningham & Hill, Ltd., 23.22; Dearborn Chemical Co., Ltd., 11.88; Darnell Corporation, Ltd., 10.58; Dominion Bridge Co., Ltd., 19.50; C. A. Dunham, Ltd., 121.91; Dunlop Tire & Rubber Goods Co., Ltd., 48.43; Empire Brass Manufacturing Co., Ltd., 345.74; Everlasting Valve Co., 21.38; Garlock Packing Co., Ltd., 64.74; Good Specialties, Ltd., Ltd., 94.49; Grinnell Co., Ltd., 19.44; Gurney Foundry Co., Ltd., 15.27; Gutta Percha & Rubber, Ltd., 35.85; Huston Oil Co., Ltd., 25.40; The John Inglis Co., Ltd., 24.48; Knox & Patterson, 14.30; La France Fire Engine & Foamite, Ltd., 21.28; W. H. Lake, 10.55; A. S. Leitch Co., Ltd., 407.37; Rice Lewis & Sons, Ltd., 34.77; Linde Canadian Refrigeration Co., Ltd., 14.95; The Masco Co., Ltd., 226.86; Jas. Morrison Brass Manufacturing Co., Ltd., 135.15; Northern Electric Co., Ltd., 28.80; The A. B. Ormsby Co., Ltd., 206.91; Pay lists, wages of men, 1,393.08; J. W. Peacock, 11.70; Pedlar People, Ltd., 58.68; Premier Laundry Equipment Co., Ltd., 141.94; James Robertson Co., Ltd., 26.49; Regent Electric Supply Co., Ltd., 31.89; Rogers Electric Co., Ltd., 40.85; Smart-Turner Machine Co., Ltd., 14.95; W. Walker & Son, Ltd., 51.69; W. J. Westaway Co., Ltd., 28.50; A. Wilson, 68.75; Wilson Illumination Co., Ltd., 136.12; petty disbursements, 65.28 .... 5,488 88

Total		329,401 93	
Less Maintenance of Patients	69,199 03		
Perquisites	22,399 00		
Sale of Produce, etc	1,009 10		
		92,607 13	
Toronto		236,794 80	

WHITBY

Salaries ($300,063.60)

Superintendent, Physicians and Dentists	31,062 50
Steward and Assistants	16,991 78
Matron and Assistants, including Domestic Help	33,503 86
Engineers and Assistants	21,350 00
Artisans, not domestic	8,900 00
Farm and Garden Employees	18,341 24
Attendants and Nurses	169,914 22

Expenses ($254,065.11)

Medicines, $9,425.18.

Abbott Laboratories, Ltd., 132.49; A. H. Allin, 462.50; American Psychiatric Association, 10.00; Ash-Temple, Ltd., 70.93; Ayerst, McKenna & Harrison, Ltd., 247.93; Burke Electric & X-Ray Co., Ltd., 22.40; Canadian Fairbanks-Morse Co., Ltd., 18.25; Canadian National Express, 35.76; Canadian National Railways, 14.27; Canadian Pacific Express, 31.20; Dominion Dental Co., Ltd., 44.65; Dominion Rubber Co., Ltd., 95.18; Eastman Kodak Stores, Ltd., 452.41; Chas. E. Frosst & Co., 144.85; General Steel Wares, Ltd., 32.74; A. D. Gibson, 360.51; Gooderham & Worts, Ltd., 65.07; Jas. C. Goodwin, 160.00; Chas. Gyde & Son, Ltd., 45.55; Hargraft Bros., Ltd., 356.00; J. F. Hartz Co., Ltd., 522.13; Hygiene Products, Ltd., 60.20; Imperial Optical Co., 48.86; Imperial Tobacco Co. of Canada, Ltd., 1,083.60; Ingram & Bell, Ltd., 514.64; Liquor Control Board of Ontario, 185.00; Mercer Reformatory Industries, 58.63; R. E. Mitchell, 480.90; National Committee for Mental Hygiene, 12.50; E. L. Odlum, 88.46; Parke-Davis & Co., 485.16; E. C. Platt, 10.00; Polusterine Products Co. of Canada, Ltd., 49.28; The Record Press, 38.60; Dr. E. F. Richardson, 46.00; Seiberling Rubber Co., 12.68; E. B. Shuttleworth Chemical Co., Ltd., 128.46; Smith & Nephew, Ltd., 167.41; E. R. Squibb & Sons of Canada, Ltd., 46.21; Standard Tobacco Co. of Canada, 47.52; The Stevens Companies, 274.95; A. E. Sturgess, 28.50; Synthetic Drug Co., Ltd., 352.84; Wm. Taylor, 149.85; Textile Products Co., 181.79; Tuckett, Ltd., 956.80; Van Zant, Ltd., 22.79; Victor X-Ray Corporation of Canada, 15.75; Chas. R. Will & Co., Ltd., 514.88; petty disbursements, 38.10 .... 9,425 18

Groceries and Provisions, $99,259.53.

American Can Co., 1,543.83; Beaton's Dairy Products, Ltd., 691.20; Beaver Food Products, Ltd., 58.00; Canada & Dominion Sugar Co., 2,631.00; Canadian Frosted Foods, Ltd., 35.64; Canadian National Railways, 174.61; Crosse &

Ontario Hospitals—Continued

Whitby—Continued

Expenses—Continued

Groceries and Provisions—Continued

Blackwell, Ltd., 91.11; John W. Crozier, 47.10; Dalton Bros., Ltd., 1,373.85; Egg-O Baking Powder Co., Ltd., 90.88; Everready Tea Bag Co., 66.64; John J. Fee, 17,032.90; Fletcher Manufacturing Co., Ltd., 94.20; K. C. Freeman, 1,202.70; F. L. Green, 1,129.33; J. R. Hayden & Co., 371.42; Higgins & Burke, Ltd., 1,513.02; Hillcrest Dairy, 458.52; Harry Horne Co., Ltd., 83.16; F. W. Humphrey & Co., Ltd., 3,742.60; Mrs. A. Jeffery, 26.25; S. T. Kempthorne, 187.50; E. Lazenby & Son, Ltd., 99.00; Little Covent Garden, 5,855.64; Joe Lowe Corporation, 85.70; Jas. Lumbers Co., Ltd., 4,782.29; Mara Lodge Poultry Farms, 246.12; J. S. Moore, 106.92; Morland Coffee Co., 33.49; National Grocers Co., Ltd., 6,928.03; Wm. Neilson, Ltd., 108.00; Ontario Reformatory Industries, 22,490.90; Oshawa Wholesale, Ltd., 1,872.69; Oxo, Ltd., 96.29; D. S. Perrin & Co., Ltd., 1,699.73; Pure Gold Manufacturing Co., Ltd., 138.00; Standard Brands, Ltd., 33.06; St. Lawrence Fish Market, 4,837.82; St. Lawrence Starch Co., Ltd., 679.70; F. W. Stull Transport, 37.06; A. E. Sturgess, 16,166.68; The Whyte Packing Co., Ltd., 72.22; Young-Winfield, Ltd., 232.93; petty disbursements, 11.80 .... 99,259 53

Fuel, Light and Water, $56,232.16.

P. Burns & Co., Ltd., 33,925.69; H. C. Burton & Co., 1,131.22; Eddy Match Co., Ltd., 224.13; H. M. Fowlds & Son, 2,506.39; Whitby Hydro-Electric System, 8,026.44; Whitby Public Utilities, 10,410.89; petty disbursements, 7.40 .... 56,232 16

Clothing, $26,346.57.

Anderson & Macbeth, Ltd., 361.00; A. Bradshaw & Sons, Ltd., 128.72; Canadian National Express, 22.03; Canadian National Railways, 33.26; Chester Cleaners & Dyers, Ltd., 13.00; Circle-Bar Knitting Co., Ltd., 997.50; The Coghill Tailoring Co., 2,024.00; Corbett & Cowley, 328.77; Dominion Rubber Co., Ltd., 82.94; A. D. Gibson, 965.87; Greenshields, Ltd., 368.24; Gutta Percha & Rubber, Ltd., 83.26; Hamburg Felt Boot Co., Ltd., 1,227.60; Hamilton & Johnston, 1,387.38; Hoar Transport, Ltd., 11.35; Philip B. Jacobi, Ltd., 606.89; Johnston, Crossley & McComb, 270.75; Lailey-Trimble, Ltd., 5,228.57; B. Lipman, 44.67; F. T. McIntyre Hardware, 12.00; Mercer Reformatory Industries, 6,965.82; Mercury Mills, Ltd., 970.41; National Textiles, Ltd., 61.52; Nisbet & Auld, Ltd., 19.50; Ontario Hospital, Orillia, Industries, 443.70; Ontario Reformatory Industries, 1,560.19; J. Peel & Son, 17.60; Penmans, Ltd., 642.00; Quality Glove Co., Ltd., 145.53; Schofield Woollens Co., Ltd., 232.50; Singer Sewing Machine Co., Inc., 45.30; The T. Sisman Shoe Co., Ltd., 674.10; W. G. Walters, 333.49; petty disbursements, 37.11 .... 26,346 57

Laundry and Cleaning, $13,683.36.

A. H. Allin, 299.15; Alpha Chemical Co., Ltd., 123.20; Associated Chemical Co. of Canada, Ltd., 2,524.99; Beaver Laundry Machinery Co., Ltd., 306.40; J. Blight Transport, 14.20; Canada Colors & Chemicals, Ltd., 17.25; Canadian Laundry Machinery Co., Ltd., 376.80; Canadian National Institute for the Blind, 424.80; Chester Cleaners & Dyers, Ltd., 22.00; Diamond Cleanser, Ltd., 1,184.89; A. B. Drake & Co., 62.93; Dustbane Products, Ltd., 138.17; Dye & Chemical Co. of Canada, Ltd., 169.97; E. B. Eddy Co., Ltd., 1,332.50; Electric Boiler Compound Co., Ltd., 398.32; Excelsior Brushes, Ltd., 398.90; Philip C. Garratt & Co., Ltd., 462.00; General Steel Wares, Ltd., 39.73; Scott A. Graham, 161.78; Guelph Soaps, 70.63; Hamilton & Johnston, 18.71; Hatch Specialty Co., 117.00; Hoar Transport, Ltd., 14.72; D. H. Howden & Co., 569.22; Jones Bros. of Canada, Ltd., 89.50; Lavoline Cleanser Co., Ltd., 52.92; F. T. McIntyre Hardware, 51.60; National Drug & Chemical Co. of Canada, Ltd., 40.00; Ontario Laundry Co., Ltd., 235.33; Ontario Reformatory Industries, 271.50; Oshawa Wholesale, Ltd., 400.83; Procter & Gamble Co. of Canada, Ltd., 828.62; Rogers Transport, 76.90; J. A. Sexauer Manufacturing Co., Ltd., 10.04; St. Croix Soap Manufacturing Co., 2,089.81; St. Lawrence Starch Co., Ltd., 110.94; F. W. Stull, 10.00; John Taylor Co., Ltd., 47.52; Utility Products, Ltd., 50.00; G. H. Wood & Co., Ltd., 41.65; petty disbursements, 27.94 .... 13,683 36

Furniture and Furnishings, $26,784.49.

Aluminum Goods, Ltd., 36.42; Associated Chemical Co. of Canada, Ltd., 72.74; A. Bradshaw & Sons, Ltd., 418.50; Brantford Oven & Rack Co., 130.43; Canadian National Express, 19.69; Canadian National Railways, 14.12; Cassidy's, Ltd., 3,322.63; Chester Cleaners & Dyers, Ltd., 10.00; Coulter Manufacturing Co., Ltd., 16.00; Delaney & Pettit, Ltd., 632.00; R. Dewsbury, 528.55; E. B. Eddy Co., Ltd., 2,565.65; Gendron Manufacturing Co., Ltd., 51.35; General Steel

Ontario Hospitals—Continued

Whitby—Continued

Expenses—Continued

Furniture and Furnishings—Continued

Wares, Ltd., 144.97; A. D. Gibson, 2,615.62; Greenshields, Ltd., 69.15; Hamilton & Johnston, 139.74; Geo. H. Hees Sons & Co., Ltd., 129.71; Hoar Transport, Ltd., 36.55; Hobart Manufacturing Co., 11.94; D. H. Howden & Co., Ltd., 31.60; Hygiene Products, Ltd., 57.60; Wm. Junor, Ltd., 67.50; Mahaffany Iron Works, Ltd., 11.10; Martin Transports, Ltd., 33.92; McFarlane Manufacturing Co., Ltd., 11.52; F. T. McIntyre Hardware, 90.91; Mercer Reformatory Industries, 7,826.74; North American Bent Chair Co., 13.72; Ontario Hospital, Orillia, Industries, 70.08; Ontario Reformatory Industries, 5,659.75; Oshawa Lumber Co., Ltd., 205.00; Oshawa Wholesale, Ltd., 10.04; E. Pullan, Ltd., 21.75; G. Rogers Transport, 54.05; Scott Paper Co. of Canada, Ltd., 161.21; The Shipper's Supply Co., 63.70; The Robt. Simpson Co., Ltd., 157.96; Geo. Sparrow & Co., Ltd., 68.00; F. W. Stull Transport, 79.68; Toronto Coppersmithing Co., 282.24; W. C. Town, 18.00; Samuel Trees & Co., Ltd., 75.90; R. G. Venn, 11.17; W. G. Walters, 18.50; G. H. Wood & Co., Ltd., 363.85; Wrought Iron Range Co. of Canada, Ltd., 293.19; petty disbursements, 60.05 .... 26,784 49

Office Expenses, $2,781.29.

Bell Telephone Co. of Canada, rentals, 415.80; tolls, 429.58; Canadian National Express, 26.61; Canadian National Telegraphs, 42.99; Canadian Pacific Express, 11.70; Canadian Pacific Railway Co.'s Telegraphs, 22.57; Dictaphone Sales Corporation, Ltd., 68.09; Grand & Toy, Ltd., 149.00; King's Printer, 119.28; Pay list, wages of men, 234.65; Postmaster, 1,228.00; United Typewriter Co., Ltd., 20.90; petty disbursements, 12.12 .... 2,781 29

Farm Expenses, $11,907.46.

A. H. Allin, 46.65; Associated Chemical Co. of Canada, Ltd., 535.08; M. Atkinson, 78.56; Geo. Bedding, 397.45; H. W. Boys, 28.25; British American Oil Co., Ltd., 722.40; W. A. Broughton & Son, 72.00; Canada Mineral Products, Ltd., 260.00; Canadian National Express, 16.15; Canadian National Railways, 106.59; Canadian Pacific Railway Co., 88.00; G. A. Canning, 2,206.40; Cooper, Smith Co., 201.60; General Steel Wares, Ltd., 27.14; Bruce Glover, 20.00; F. L. Green, 304.00; Holstein-Friesian Association, 18.00; D. H. Howden & Co., Ltd., 12.25; Huston Oil Co., Ltd., 46.40; J. George Jones, 209.60; J. Lewington, 489.98; W. J. Luke, 55.75; Marchment Co., Ltd., 47.14; G.E. Mason, 30.50; Lorne McCoy, 27.30; The F. J. McIntyre Hardware, 435.81; W. J. Murphy, 28.00; National Fertilizers, Ltd., 203.25; J. J. O'Connor, 116.20; Ontario Training School for Boys, 190.00; D. T. Parker, 30.00; Parrish & Heimbecker, Ltd., 1,254.03; Ralston Purina Co., Ltd., 928.00; Geo. M. Rice, 530.07; R. R. Richardson, 143.00; Scottish Fertilizers, Ltd., 420.00; E. J. Shirley, 519.00; E. D. Smith & Sons, Ltd., 163.45; Steele, Briggs Seed Co., Ltd., 413.11; Taylor-Forbes Co., Ltd., 32.56; D. Turner, 22.95; W. G. Walters, 111.15; Whitby Coal & Wood Yard, 283.58; petty disbursements, 36.11 .... 11,907 46

Contingencies, $7,645.07.

Gertrude W. Aikenhead, travelling expenses, 127.10; A. H. Allin, stationery, 17.37; American Can Co., rental, closing machine, 161.50; Bates & Dodds, Ltd., funeral expenses, 40.00; Bennett & Elliott, Ltd., battery, 11.95; W. J. Bird, travelling expenses, 12.90; British American Oil Co., Ltd., oil, etc., 19.75; R. G. Bryan, piano, 125.00; Canadian National Express, charges, 63.20; Canadian Universal Film Co., Ltd., films, 200.00; Collacutt Coach Lines, rent of coach, 28.00; Collins Motor Sales, Ltd., repairs, 259.73; The Davidson Motor Co., Ltd., repairs, 438.65; Wm. Dawson Subscription Service, Ltd., subscriptions, 168.68; Department of Public Highways, gas, repairs, etc., 269.26; E. H. Ditchburn, travelling expenses, 10.00; Dominion Reed Supplies, Ltd., reed, 82.00; Irene Doucette, travelling expenses, 10.00; Anne M. Duff, travelling expenses, 10.10; Kathleen Ferguson, travelling expenses, 13.30; N. D. Fidler, travelling expenses, 11.30; Dr. Jas. C. Goodwin, professional services, 115.00; Goodyear Tire & Rubber Co. of Canada, Ltd., tubes, etc., 54.11; Groveside Cemetery, interments, 20.00; Leonard Harris, travelling expenses, 14.20; Dr. Stuart W. Houston, professional services, 50,00; F. W. Humphrey Co., Ltd., Christmas supplies, 144.44; Imperial Oil, Ltd., gas, oil, etc., 1,000.00; J. J. Liernan, travelling expenses, 108.31; J. Lewington, rent of plants, 12.50; Robt. Lowden, music, 120.00; The Macmillan Co. of Canada, Ltd., books, 83.61; Jean Margueratt, travelling expenses, 96.90; Vera Marshall, travelling expenses, 13.95; J. S. McCurdy, travelling expenses, 34.65; F. J. McIntyre Hardware, hardware, 27.10; Mental Hygiene Institute, Inc., subscription, 15.00; Mary B. Millburn, travelling expenses, 10.80; Dr. S. R. Montgomery, travelling expenses, 445.68;

Ontario Hospitals—Continued

Whitby—Continued

Expenses—Continued

Contingencies—Continued

Mundy-Goodfellow Printing Co., printing, 352.53; National Drug & Chemical Co., Ltd., crepe paper, etc., 107.31; Nicholson & Seldon, funeral expenses, 206.00; E. L. Odlum, Christmas decorations, 13.17; Ontario Medical Association, fees, 10.00; Ontario Motor Sales, Ltd., gas, etc., 97.68; Oshawa Fire Department, services of inhalator, 13.50; Oshawa Wholesale, Ltd., paper bags, twine, etc., 360.36; Chas. Peebles, papers, 28.80; John H. Perry, trees, 69.30; M. Polson, travelling expenses, 30.90; Province of Ontario Pictures, films, 21.95; Jas. Rainnie, orchestra, 106.00; Ratcliffe Paper Co., Ltd., paper, etc., 183.68; Scythes & Co., Ltd., tarpaulin, 24.93; Dr. J. N. Senn, travelling expenses, 26.15; The Robt. Simpson Co., Ltd., flag, 13.00; Smith & Walsh, Ltd., insurance, 67.97; Dr. G. H. Stevenson, travelling expenses, 123.12; Sundry Ministers, religious services, 340.00; Florence Thomas, travelling expenses, 10.55; Chas. Tod, flowers, 60.00; A. L. Torgis & Son, battery, etc., 79.83; W. C. Town, funeral expenses, 176.30; N. I. Truax, interments, 24.00; E. G. Van Horn, interments, 42.00; W. G. Walters, bunting, 12.62; Elizabeth Walton, travelling expenses, 97.70; Whitby Citizens' Band, services, 75.00; Whitby Gazette & Chronicle, subscriptions, 18.50; Wilkins Smallware Co., Ltd., fancy goods, 133.47; Harold A. Wilson Co., Ltd., sporting goods, 62.21; petty disbursements, 210.50 .... 7,645 07

Repairs to Buildings, etc. ($15,260.27)

Maintenance and Repairs of all Buildings, Roads, Walks, Grounds and Fences, $8,191.27.

Adams Furniture Co., Ltd., 420.08; Aulcraft Paints, Ltd., 11.27; Belleville-Sargent Co., Ltd., 101.35; Boiler Repair & Grate Bar Co., 271.02; Canada Paint Co., Ltd., 97.98; Canada Varnish Co., Ltd., 228.77; Canadian Chromalax Co., 73.74; Canadian Foundry Supplies & Steel Equipment, Ltd., 15.84; Canadian Johns-Manville Co., Ltd., 246.28; Canadian National Railways, 514.16; Canadian Pacific Railway Co., 133.17; Carew Lumber Co., Ltd., 1,261.70; E. M. Deverell, 349.15; W. A. Dewland, 14.00; Dunlop Tire & Rubber Goods Co., Ltd., 29.17; Empire Brass Mfg. Co., Ltd., 88.41; B. Greening Wire Co., Ltd., 50.96; Joseph Heard & Sons, 27.50; Geo. H. Hees Son & Co., Ltd., 352.14; Hoar Transport, Ltd., 33.78; D. H. Howden & Co., Ltd., 300.67; Imperial Varnish & Color Co., Ltd., 24.93; LaFrance Fire Engine & Foamite, Ltd., 22.95; The Arthur S. Leitch Co., Ltd., 33.00; F. J. McIntyre Hardware, 326.17; Mueller, Ltd., 23.82; Alexander Murray & Co., Ltd., 145.09; Ontario Reformatory, Mimico, 11.79; Ontario Hospital, Orillia, 190.00; Ontario Reformatory Industries, 65.70; Oshawa Electric Supply, Ltd., 26.02; Oshawa Lumber Co., Ltd., 601.61; Pay list, wages of men, 758.10; Pease Foundry Co., Ltd., 64.38; The Pedlar People, Ltd., 78.09; Pilkington Bros., Ltd., 205.75; A. Ramsay & Son Co., Ltd., 284.98; George M. Rice, 182.40; Jas. Robertson Co., Ltd., 30.47; Sanderson, Pearcy-Marietta, Ltd., 189.00; Sherwin-Williams Co., Ltd., 24.45; Smith Transport, 24.96; Geo. Sparrow & Co., 13.50; Toronto Lock Mfg. Co., Ltd., 19.21; Toronto Paint Co., 104.53; W. C. Town, 14.55; Valspar Corporation, Ltd., 39.51; petty disbursements, 65.17 .... 8,191 27

Maintenance and Repairs of Plumbing, Steam and Electric Plants, $5,497.02.

Anaconda American Brass, Ltd., 52.00; Beardmore Leathers, Ltd., 12.48; Geo. Bedding, 10.50; Beldam's Asbestos Packing & General Mfg. Co., Ltd., 107.75; The Boeckh Co., Ltd., 77.11; Boiler Repair & Grate Bar Co., 15.89; British American Oil Co., Ltd., 99.96; Canada Colors & Chemicals, Ltd., 24.59; Canadian Ice Machine Co., Ltd., 97.75; Canadian Industries, Ltd., 37.98; Canadian Laundry Machinery Co., Ltd., 600.80; Canadian National Express, 25.90; Canadian National Railways, 26.51; Canadian Powers Regulator Co., Ltd., 616.88; Coleman Electric Co., 11.20; W. H. Cunningham & Hill, Ltd., 471.29; Dearborn Chemical Co., 189.78; Dominion Oxygen Co., Ltd., 62.04; C. A. Dunham Co., Ltd., 73.50; Dunlop Tire & Rubber Goods Co., Ltd., 73.96; Economic Products, Ltd., 74.80; Empire Brass Mfg. Co., Ltd., 361.06; Fittings, Ltd., 124.39; Garlock Packing Co., Ltd., 34.09; General Steel Wares, Ltd., 50.83; Hoar Transport, Ltd., 19.03; The Hobart Mfg. Co., 226.30; D. H. Howden & Co., Ltd., 185.67; The Huston Oil Co., Ltd., 67.35; Linde Canadian Refrigeration Co., Ltd., 11.00; Masco Co., Ltd., 22.38; F. J. McIntyre Hardware 40.36; Herbert Morris Crane & Hoist Co., Ltd., 12.94; Jas. Morrison Brass Mfg. Co., Ltd., 33.09; Northern Electric Co., Ltd., 165.70; Oshawa Electric Supply, Ltd., 358.79; Oshawa Wholesale, Ltd., 19.04; Page-Hersey Tubes, Ltd., 132.08; Pay list, wages of men, 590.60; The Pedlar People, Ltd., 16.01; Jas. Robertson Co., Ltd., 122.15; Supplies & Insulation, Ltd., 32.97; Whitby Malleable Iron & Brass Co., Ltd., 28.33; petty disbursements, 80.19 .... 5,497 02

Ontario Hospitals—Continued

Whitby—Continued

Repairs to Buildings, etc.—Continued

Live Stock, Vehicles and Farm Implements, $1,571.98.

Cockshutt Plow Co., Ltd., implement parts, 48.98; W. J. Murphy, cattle, 985.00; Oak Lodge Stock Farm, boar, 35.00; Ontario Hospital, Hamilton, poultry, 328.00; Ontario Training School for Boys, Bowmanville, boar, 12.50; Alex. Peacock, horses, 162.50 ..... 1,571 98

Total		569,388 98	
Less Maintenance of Patients	211,015 74		
Perquisites	42,694 35		
Sale of Produce, etc	5,910 91		
		259,621 00	
Whitby		$309,767.98	

WOODSTOCK

Salaries ($107,327.79)

Superintendent, Physicians and Dentists	13,964 50
Steward and Assistants	7,977 39
Matron and Assistants, including domestic help	11,241 39
Engineers and Assistants	7,129 88
Artisans, not domestic	2,232 81
Farm and Garden employees	8,550 58
Attendants and Nurses	56,231 24

Expenses ($66,428.01)

Medicines, $4,707.20.

Abbott Laboratories, Ltd., 108.92; Ash-Temple Co., Ltd., 24.01; Ayerst, McKenna & Harrison, Ltd., 56.03; Burroughs-Wellcome & Co., 109.84; Canadian National Express, 20.37; Canadian National Railways, 13.24; A. W. Cole, 73.15; Denver Chemical Manufacturing Co., 12.51; Dominion Dental Co., Ltd., 40.21; Chas. E. Frosst & Co., 189.84; Chas. Gyde & Son, 47.57; The J. F. Hartz Co., Ltd., 1,198.54; Dr. V. L. Heath, 141.30; Imperial Oil, Ltd., 231.00; Ingram & Bell, Ltd., 1,157.80; Keith's Drug Store, 20.25; Lewis Manufacturing Co., of Canada, Ltd., 70.87; W. C. Macdonald, 384.40; Martin Transports, Ltd., 11.66; R. E. Mitchell, 45.00; Parke, Davis & Co., 174.21; Polusterine Products Co. of Canada, Ltd., 28.22; Rolls & Darlington, Ltd., 13.40; Smith & Nephew, Ltd., 270.35; E. R. Squibb & Sons, Ltd., 12.89; The Standard Tobacco Co. of Canada, Ltd., 60.32; Geo. S. Trudell Co., 10.15; Tuckett, Ltd., 158.30; VanZant, Ltd., 10.21; Vi-Tone Co., 27.93; Chas. R. Will & Co., Ltd., 27.03; Winthrop Chemical Co., Incorporated, 15.20; G. H. Wood & Co., Ltd., 13.08; W. Lloyd Wood, Ltd., 16.81; Woodstock Hospital, 23.00; petty disbursements, 86.34; Less refund for Dental Services, 196.75 ..... 4,707 20

Provisions, $19,890.31.

Balfours, Ltd., 1,236.25; Bowes Co., Ltd., 1,817.81; E. J. Canfield, 397.25; Christie Brown & Co., Ltd., 130.27; Daily Bread Co., Ltd., 3,373.93; Geo. A. Despond, 342.53; K. C. Freeman, 149.82; Malcolm Hall, 70.00; Jack Hamilton, 37.80; J. R. Hayden Co., 44.55; Higgins & Burke, Ltd., 79.86; Harry Horne Co., Ltd., 327.05; The T. A. King Estate, 33.30; Geo. Kirk, 244.15; Jas. Lumbers. Co., Ltd., 151.80; National Grocers Co., Ltd., 165.00; Onn's, 435.51; Ontario Hospital, London, 75.00; Ontario Reformatory, Guelph, 108.40; Ontario Reformatory Industries, 6,290.47; Ontario Reformatory, Mimico, 113.70; Poole & Co., 50.20; F. W. Stull, 42.21; W. N. Thornton, 37.50; Geo. Watt & Sons, Ltd., 3,224.19; Whyte Packing Co., Ltd., 849.21; Woodstock Produce Co., 10.50; Young-Winfield, Ltd., 28.82; petty disbursements, 23.23 ..... 19,890 31

Fuel, Light and Water, $17,814.99.

H. C. Burton & Co., 55.73; The Henderson Coal Co., 13,159.61; Hydro-Electric Power Commission, 2,485.99; Towe & Towe, 275.97; Geo. Watt & Sons, Ltd., 108.67; Woodstock Public Utilities Commission, 41.70; Woodstock Water Works, 1,668.53; petty disbursements, 18.79 ..... 17,814 99

Clothing, $7,056.95.

Canadian National Express, 17.39; Coghill Tailoring Co., 682.00; A. D. Gibson, 19.01; Grafton & Co., Ltd., 10.82; Greenshields, Ltd., 496.05; Gutta Percha & Rubber, Ltd., 52.72; Hamilton & Johnston, 282.01; Hamburg Felt Boot Co., Ltd., 277.20; Harvey Knitting Co., Ltd., 30.25; Hersee Bros., 23.00; Hosiers,

Ontario Hospitals—Continued

Woodstock—Continued

Expenses—Continued

Clothing—Continued

Ltd., 14.40; Martin Transports, Ltd., 30.32; Mercer Reformatory Industries, 1,931.60; Morris Shoe & Slipper Co., 55.20; W. R. Murray, 156.60; Ontario Hospital, Orillia, Industries, 1,468.40; Ontario Reformatory Industries, 983.50; Penmans, Ltd., 12.50; Schofield Woollen Co., Ltd., 156.00; Storey Glove Co., Ltd., 18.03; Superior Cloak Co., Ltd., 117.00; W. Teeft, 43.10; Tower Canadian, Ltd., 36.48; Woods Manufacturing Co., Ltd., 72.00; Woodstock Rubber Co., Ltd., 16.85; petty disbursements, 54.52 .... 7,056 95

Laundry and Cleaning, $6,003.42.

Archer & Dobbin, 14.45; Associated Chemical Co. of Canada, Ltd., 647.28; Balfours, Ltd., 84.05; Beaver Laundry Machinery Co., Ltd., 20.09; The Boeckh Co., Ltd., 32.94; Canada Colors & Chemicals, Ltd., 63.03; Canadian Department Stores, Ltd., 12.00; Canadian Industries, Ltd., 15.81; Canadian National Institute for the Blind, 167.76; E. J. Canfield, 57.50; Capo Polishes, Ltd., 27.00; Colgate-Palmolive-Peet Co., Ltd., 303.72; Cudahy Packing Co., 20.58; Diamond Cleanser, Ltd., 74.76; Electric Boiler Compound Co., Ltd., 15.00; Eaton-Clark Co., 130.68; Excelsior Brushes, Ltd., 118.90; Guelph Soap Co., 23.40; J. F. Hartz Co., Ltd., 56.24; Holmes Hardware, 124.05; Imperial Oil, Ltd., 15.92; Industrial Farm, Burwash, 336.04; Interlake Tissue Mills Co., Ltd., 159.00; Fred W. Karn, 30.13; Keith's Drug Store, 92.00; King Paper Sales Co., 61.00; S. F. Lawrason & Co., Ltd., 208.10; MacKinnon Sales, 468.00; Martin Transports, Ltd., 37.90; McArthur Chemical Co., 10.64; Ontario Reformatory, Guelph, 138.01; Ontario Reformatory Industries, 1,105.11; Oshawa Electric Supply, Ltd., 20.10; The Rexo Chemical Cleanser Co., Ltd., 31.83; St. Lawrence Starch Co., Ltd., 27.25; F. W. Stull, 563.00; Sunclo Products, 82.50; W. Walker & Son, Ltd., 26.95; White Mop Wringer Co. of Canada, 24.50; Victoria Paper & Twine Co., Ltd., 60.45; Geo. Watt & Sons, Ltd., 289.90; G. H. Wood & Co., Ltd., 139.16; petty disbursements, 66.69 .... 6,003 42

Furniture and Furnishings, $2,981.84.

Associated Chemical Co. of Canada, Ltd., 18.37; British & Colonial Trading Co., Ltd., 125.76; Canadian Department Stores, Ltd., 244.54; Canadian National Institute for the Blind, 32.00; Cassidy's, Ltd., 62.91; Dennisteel, Ltd., 262.35; E. B. Eddy Co., Ltd., 10.80; Empire Brass Manufacturing Co.. Ltd., 14.11; Hobbs Hardware Co., Ltd., 22.05; Holmes Hardware, 51.20; Interlake Tissue Mills Co., Ltd., 19.00; J. C. Jaimet & Co., Ltd., 55.55; Johnson & Barbour, 146.90; Fred W. Karn, 85.42; King Paper Sales Co., 32.00; Marshall Ventilated Mattress Co., Ltd., 26.25; Mercer Reformatory Industries, 856.58; Noble's Stores, 16.00; Ontario Reformatory, Guelph, 14.28; Ontario Reformatory Industries, 482.58; Raymond Bros., 37.70; Geo. Sparrow & Co., 22.66; F. W. Stull, 23.05; Tools & Hardware, Ltd., 11.06; Victoria Paper & Twine Co., Ltd., 85.35; W. Walker & Son, Ltd., 10.82; John White Co., Ltd., 100.84; G. H. Wood & Co., Ltd., 29.15; Wrought Iron Range Co. of Canada, Ltd., 21.56; petty disbursements, 61.00 .... 2,981 84

Office Expenses, $1,455.89.

Bell Telephone Co. of Canada, 536.15; Canada Furniture Manufacturers, Ltd., 58.80; Canadian National Telegraphs, 23.03; Canadian Pacific Express Co., 13.20; Canadian Pacific Railway Co., 18.67; King's Printer, 117.73; Office Specialty Manufacturing Co., Ltd., 102.00; Postmaster, 540.00; United Typewriter Co., Ltd., 26.25; petty disbursements, 20.06 .... 1,455 89

Farm Expenses, $4,704.27.

Andrewes Mountain Seed Co., Ltd., 64.30; Avery's Sales & Service, 66.70; W. M. Bickell, 93.00; W. A. Bull, 40.00; Canada Mineral Products, Ltd., 260.00; Canadian National Railways, 17.70; Canadian Pacific Railway Co., 45.71; S. J. Cherry & Sons, Ltd., 575.00; Frank Cronin, 85.65; James Cullen & Sons, Ltd., 187.01; Arthur Davis, 71.75; Dominion Rubber Co., Ltd., 16.03; Eureka Planter Co., Ltd., 119.60; John Fowell & Son, 29.20; F. W. Goble, 68.00; Holmes Hardware, 38.77; Holstein-Friesian Association, 25.50; H. J. Hudon, 22.60; A. G. Karn, 14.40; Fred W. Karn, 302.88; George Kirk, 918.50; E. Lefler & Son, 75.90; Albert Mather, 190.50; Ralph Moore & Sons, 18.20; Murdock Seed Co., 101.64; National Fertilizers, Ltd., 213.80; Ontario Reformatory Industries, 65.10; D. T. Parker, 58.75; Dr. B. G. Parker, 15.50; Parrish & Heimbecker, Ltd., 527.94; R. Patrick, 52.00; W. A. Sawdon, 51.49; Silverwood's Milk Products, Ltd., 11.76; E. D. Smith & Sons, Ltd., 89.23; West End Chopping & Feed Mill, 130.94; petty disbursements, 39.22 .... 4,704 27

Ontario Hospitals—Continued

Whitby—Continued

Repairs to Buildings, etc.—Contin l

Live Stock, Vehicles and Farm Implements, $1,571.98.

Cockshutt Plow Co., Ltd., implement parts, 48.98; W. J. Mi hy cattle, 985.00; Oak Lodge Stock Farm, boar, 35.00; Ontario Hospital, Hami n, poultry, 328.00; Ontario Training School for Boys, Bowmanville, boar 12); Alex. Peacock, horses, 162.50 .... 1,571 98

Total		569,388 98	
Less Maintenance of Patients	[illegible]		
Perquisites	[illegible]		
Sale of Produce, etc	[illegible]	259,621 00	
Whitby		$309,767.98	

WOODSTOCK

Salaries ($107,327.79)

Superintendent, Physicians and Dentists	13,964 50
Steward and Assistants	7,977 39
Matron and Assistants, including domestic help	11,241 39
Engineers and Assistants	7,129 88
Artisans, not domestic	2,232 81
Farm and Garden employees	8,550 58
Attendants and Nurses	56,231 24

Expenses ($66,428.01)

Medicines, $4,707.20.

Abbott Laboratories, Ltd., 108.92; Ash-Temple Co., Ltd., 21 [illegible] McKenna & Harrison, Ltd., 56.03; Burroughs-Wellcome & Co., 109.8 [illegible] National Express, 20.37; Canadian National Railways, 13.24; A. W [illegible] Denver Chemical Manufacturing Co., 12.51; Dominion Dental Co. [illegible] Chas. E. Frosst & Co., 189.84; Chas. Gyde & Son, 47.57; The J. F. H [illegible] 1,198.54; Dr. V. L. Heath, 141.30; Imperial Oil, Ltd., 231.00; Ingram [illegible] 1,157.80; Keith's Drug Store, 20.25; Lewis Manufacturing Co [illegible] Ltd., 70.87; W. C. Macdonald, 384.40; Martin Transports, Ltd., 11 [illegible] E. Mitchell, 45.00; Parke, Davis & Co., 174.21; Polusterine Products [illegible] Canada, Ltd., 28.22; Rolls & Darlington, Ltd., 13.40; Smith & Nephew [illegible] 270.35; E. R. Squibb & Sons, Ltd., 12.89; The Standard Tobacco C [illegible] Canada, Ltd., 60.32; Geo. S. Trudell Co., 10.15; Tuckett, Ltd., 158 [illegible] VanZant, Ltd., 10.21; Vi-Tone Co., 27.93; Chas. R. Will & Co., Ltd., 27.03 [illegible] Chemical Co., Incorporated, 15.20; G. H. Wood & Co., Ltd., 13.08; [illegible] Wood, Ltd., 16.81; Woodstock Hospital, 23.00; petty disbursements, 8 [illegible] Less refund for Dental Services, 196.75 .... 4,707 20

Provisions, $19,890.31.

Balfours, Ltd., 1,236.25; Bowes Co., Ltd., 1,817.81; E. [illegible] 397.25; Christie Brown & Co., Ltd., 130.27; Daily Bread Co., Lt [illegible] 3,473.93; Geo. A. Despond, 342.53; K. C. Freeman, 149.82; Malcolm Hall, 7 [illegible]; Jack Hamilton, 37.80; J. R. Hayden Co., 44.55; Higgins & Burke, Ltd., [illegible]; Harry Horne Co., Ltd., 327.05; The T. A. King Estate, 33.30; Geo. Kirk, [illegible] Jas. Lumbers. Co., Ltd., 151.80; National Grocers Co., Ltd., 165.00; [illegible] 135.51; Ontario Hospital, London, 75.00; Ontario Reformatory, Guelph, 8.40; Ontario Reformatory Industries, 6,290.47; Ontario Reformatory, Min [illegible] 113.70; Poole & Co., 50.20; F. W. Stull, 42.21; W. N. Thornton, 37.50; Geo. Watt & Sons, Ltd., 3,224.19; Whyte Packing Co., Ltd., 849.21; Woodstock [illegible] Co., 10.50; Young-Winfield, Ltd., 28.82; petty disbursements, 23.23 .... 19,890 31

Fuel, Light and Water, $17,814.99.

H. C. Burton & Co., 55.73; The Henderson Coal Co., 13,1[illegible]61; Hydro-Electric Power Commission, 2,485.99; Towe & Towe, 275.97; Geo. Watt & Sons, Ltd., 108.67; Woodstock Public Utilities Commission, 41.70; Woodstock Water Works, 1,668.53; petty disbursements, 18.79 .... 17,814 99

Clothing, $7,056.95.

Canadian National Express, 17.39; Coghill Tailoring Co., 6[illegible].00; A. D. Gibson, 19.01; Grafton & Co., Ltd., 10.82; Greenshields, Ltd., 4965; Gutta Percha & Rubber, Ltd., 52.72; Hamilton & Johnston, 282.01; Hamburg Felt Boot Co., Ltd., 277.20; Harvey Knitting Co., Ltd., 30.25; Hersee Bros., 23.00; Hosiers,

[illegible]ntario Hospitals—Continued

Woodstock—Continued

Expenses—Continued

Clothing—Continued

Ltd., 14.40; Martin Tran[illegible], Ltd., 30.32; Mercer Reformatory Industries,
1,931.60; Morris Shoe & [illegible] Co., 55.20; W. R. Murray, 156.60; Ontario
Hospital, Orillia, Industr[illegible] 168.40; Ontario Reformatory Industries, 983.50;
Penmans, Ltd., 12.50; S[illegible] Woollen Co., Ltd., 156.00; Storey Glove Co.,
Ltd., 18.03; Superior Cloak Co. Ltd., 117.00; W. Teeft, 43.10; Tower Canadian,
Ltd., 36.48; Woods Man[illegible]ing Co., Ltd., 72.00; Woodstock Rubber Co.,
Ltd., 16.85; petty disburse[illegible], 54.52 ... 7,056 9[illegible]

Laundry and Cleaning, $6,[illegible]

Archer & Dobbin, 14.45; [illegible]ated Chemical Co. of Canada, Ltd., 647.3[illegible];
Balfours, Ltd., 84.05; Beaver [illegible]ndry Machinery Co., Ltd., 20.09; The Bosch[illegible]
Co., Ltd., 32.94; Canada Co[illegible] Chemicals, Ltd., 63.0[illegible]; Canadian Department
Stores, Ltd., 12.00; Canadian [illegible]stries, Ltd., 15.81; Canadian National Institute
for the Blind, 167.76; F. J. [illegible]ll, 57.50; Cape Polishes, Ltd., 27.00; Colgate-
Palmolive-Peet Co., Ltd., [illegible] [illegible]dahy Packing Co., 20.3[illegible]; Diamond Cleanser
Ltd., 74.76; Electric Boiler [illegible]und Co., Ltd., 15.00; Eaton-Clark Co., 130.6[illegible];
Excelsior Brushes, Ltd., [illegible] [illegible]uelph Soap Co., 23.40; J. F. Hartz Co., Ltd.,
56.24; Holmes Hardware, [illegible]; Imperial Oil, Ltd., 15.92; Industrial Farm,
Burwash, 336.04; Interlake [illegible] Mills Co., Ltd., 159.00; Fred W. Kurn, 30.1[illegible];
Keith's Drug Store, 92.00; [illegible] Sales Co., 61.00; S. F. Lawrason & Co.,
Ltd., 208.10; MacKinnon [illegible] [illegible].00; Martin Transports, Ltd., 37.90; McArthur
Chemical Co., 10.94; Ontario [illegible]matory, Guelph, 118.01; Ontario Reformatory
Industries, 1,105.11; Oshawa El[illegible]ic Supply, Ltd., 20.10; The Rexo Chemical
Cleanser Co., Ltd., 31.8[illegible]; St. [illegible] Starch Co., Ltd., 27.2[illegible]; F. W. Staff,
563.00; Sunds Products, 67.[illegible] [illegible] Walker & Son, Ltd., 26.95; White Map[illegible]
Wringer Co. of Canada, 24.[illegible] [illegible]toria Paper & Twine Co., Ltd., 68.43; Geo.
Watt & Sons, Ltd., 299.9[illegible]; G. [illegible] [illegible]ood & Co., Ltd., 139.36; petty disbursements,
66.69 ... 6,003 42

Furniture and Furnishings, $[illegible]

Associated Chemical Co. of Ca[illegible], Ltd., 19.[illegible]; British & Colonial Trading
Co., Ltd., 125.[illegible]; Canadian De[illegible]ment Stores, Ltd., 344.54; Canadian National
Institute for the Blind, [illegible]; [illegible]y's, Ltd., 42.9[illegible]; Dominion[illegible], Ltd., [illegible];
E. B. Eddy Co., Ltd., [illegible]; [illegible] Brass Manufacturing Co., Ltd., 14.[illegible];
Hobbs Hardware Co., Ltd., [illegible]; Holmes Hardware, [illegible]; Interlake Tissue
Mills Co., Ltd., [illegible]; J. C. [illegible] & Co., Ltd., [illegible]; Johnson & Barbour,
146.90; Fred W. Kurn, [illegible]; [illegible] Paper Sales Co., [illegible]; Marshall Ventilated
Mattress Co., Ltd., [illegible]; [illegible] Reformatory Industries, [illegible]; Noble's
Stores, 16.00; Ontario Re[illegible], Guelph, 14.[illegible]; Ontario Reformatory
Industries, 482.58; Raymond [illegible] 37.[illegible]; Geo. Sparrow & Co., [illegible]; F. W.
Staff, 23.[illegible]; Tools & Hardware [illegible] 11.00; Victoria Paper & Twine Co., Ltd.,
85.[illegible]; W. Walker & Son, Ltd., [illegible]; John White Co., Ltd., [illegible]; G. H. Wood
& Co., Ltd., 29.[illegible]; Wringer [illegible] Co. of Canada, Ltd., [illegible]; petty
disbursements, [illegible] ... 2,[illegible] [illegible]

Office Expenses, $[illegible]

Bell Telephone Co. of Can[illegible]; Canada Furniture Manufacturers, Ltd.,
5[illegible]; Canadian National Tele[illegible]; Canadian Pacific Express Co., [illegible];
Canadian Pacific Railway Co., [illegible]; King's Printer, 117.[illegible]; Office Specialty
Manufacturing Co., Ltd., [illegible]; [illegible]master, [illegible]; United Typewriter Co.,
Ltd., 20.25; petty disbursements, [illegible]

Farm Expenses, $[illegible] ... [illegible]

Ontario Hospitals—Continued

Woodstock—Continued

Expenses—Continued

Contingencies, $1,813.14.

Balfours, Ltd., paper, 25.42; Harvey J. Cooke, newspapers, etc., 25.60; Frost Steel & Wire Co., Ltd., chain link fabric, 31.12; Grafton & Co., Ltd., prizes for sports day, 15.30; Imperial Oil, Ltd., oil, grease, etc., 34.26; Instruments, Ltd., charts, 13.11; Jones Bros., pipes, 15.05; Journal of Nervous and Mental Disease, subscriptions, 10.00; Fred W. Karn, whiting, etc., 15.45; E. Lefler & Son, repairs, etc., 66.52; Barbara E. McAllister, orchestra, 186.00; McColl-Frontenac Oil Co., Ltd., gasoline, 493.06; John W. McLevin, funeral expenses, 197.00; Ontario Medical Association, fees, 10.00; Religious Services, 250.00; Scythes & Co., Ltd., tarpaulin, 13.56; Sentinel-Review Co., Ltd., subscriptions, 12.60; Smith & Walsh, Ltd., insurance, 33.98; Supertest Petroleum Corporation, Ltd., gas, 53.78; J. & J. Sutherland, Ltd., paper napkins, etc., 51.68; J. A. Tapson, tuning pianos, 15.00; Dr. C. S. Tennant, travelling expenses, 48.50; Geo. Watt & Sons, Ltd., paper bags, etc., 41.21; John White Co., Ltd., prizes for sports day, 17.26; petty disbursements, 137.68 .... 1,813 14

Repairs to Buildings, etc. ($11,786.03)

Maintenance and Repairs to all Buildings, Roads, Walks, Grounds and Fences, $4,077.96.

The American Hardware Corporation of Canada, Ltd., 48.42; Wm. Baird & Son, 13.44; Canadian Industries, Ltd., 136.27; W. J. Chipperfield, 19.40; Department of Public Works, 37.50; Dennisteel, Ltd., 64.35; Empire Brass Manufacturing Co., Ltd., 14.85; Frost Steel & Wire Co., Ltd., 143.17; Gypsum Lime & Alabastine, Ltd., 28.97; Harvey & Wilson, 12.33; A. Hastings & Son, 243.20; Holmes Hardware, 182.96; Hutcheson Lumber Co., Ltd., 1,034.55; Imperial Varnish & Color Co., Ltd., 22.93; Italian Mosaic & Marble Co., Ltd., 80.25; Fred W. Karn, 109.82; Malcolm Sinclair Co., Ltd., 32.01; The McIntosh Coal Co., Ltd., 31.20; McKinney Lumber Co., Ltd., 179.09; J. H. Morin & Co., Ltd., 36.00; Ontario Reformatory, Mimico, 46.04; Pay list, wages of men, 1,410.70; W. E. Phillips Co., Ltd., 18.43; Sherwin-Williams Co., Ltd., 21.45; J. & J. Sutherland, Ltd., 10.75; Twisswire Brushes, Ltd., 21.05; petty disbursements, 78.83 .... 4,077 96

Maintenance and Repairs of Plumbing, Steam and Electric Plants and Machinery, $5,520.37.

Allen-Bradley Co., 23.41; Wm. Baird & Son, 137.06; Beldam's Asbestos Packing Co., Ltd., 32.72; Bell Telephone Co. of Canada, 73.35; Wm. Brown, 10.20; Cactizona Products Co. of Canada, 72.25; Canadian Fairbanks-Morse Co., Ltd., 60.14; Canadian General Electric Co., Ltd., 31.19; Canadian Ice Machine Co., Ltd., 37.46; Canadian National Express, 22.10; Canadian Powers Regulator Co., Ltd., 205.88; Combustion Service Co., 24.00; E. S. Coppins, 536.13; W. F. Craig & Co., Ltd., 48.73; Crane, Ltd., 68.47; W. H. Cunningham & Hill, Ltd., 58.85; Davison & McInnis, 56.58; Dearborn Chemical Co., 89.54; Empire Brass Manufacturing Co., Ltd., 544.71; Garlock Packing Co., Ltd., 196.86; Good Specialties, Ltd., 31.67; Gurney Foundry Co., Ltd., 13.35; Harvey & Wilson, 21.43; Holmes Hardware, 32.26; The Huston Oil Co., Ltd., 96.10; Fred W. Karn, 15.30; Arthur S. Leitch Co., Ltd., 459.77; E. Leonard & Sons, Ltd., 53.81; Link-Belt, Ltd., 48.00; Martin Transports, Ltd., 19.78; Jas. Morrison Brass Manufacturing Co., Ltd., 48.76; Northern Electric Co., Ltd., 157.54; H. W. Petrie, Ltd., 63.58; Regent Electric Supply Co., Ltd., 54.85; Jas. Robertson Co., Ltd., 13.05; Rogers Electric Co., Ltd., 15.46; Standard Underground Cable Co. of Canada, Ltd., 88.22; Taylor-Forbes Co., Ltd., 388.18; Trane Co. of Canada, Ltd., 25.17; Tremco Manufacturing Co., Ltd., 18.55; Universal Cover Co. of Canada, Ltd., 18.06; Van Camp, Ltd., 469.54; Wagner Electric Manufacturing Co., Ltd., 87.55; Western Foundry Co., Ltd., 55.88; R. Whitelaw Estate, 62.75; Wilson Illumination Co., Ltd., 33.22; Woodstock Electric Co., Ltd., 51.38; City of Woodstock, 610.00; petty disbursements, 137.53 .... 5,520 37

Live Stock, Vehicles and Farm Implements, $2,187.70.

A. B. Brubacher, 370.00; Canadian Pacific Express Co., 11.20; George Fallowfield, 10.00; Byron Jenvey, 1,512.50; Ontario Hospital, Hamilton, 54.00; W. A. Sawdon, 155.00; Frank M. Tobin, 75.00 .... 2,187 70

Total		185,541 83
Less Maintenance of Patients	53,875 34	
Perquisites	21,865 47	
Sale of Produce, etc	3,413 76	
		79,154 57
Woodstock		$106,387.26

Ontario Hospitals—Continued

TORONTO PSYCHIATRIC

Salaries ($90,588.47)

Superintendent, Physicians and Dentists	20,603 30
Steward and Assistants	10,975 00
Matron and Assistants, including domestic help	18,417 70
Engineers and Assistants	1,300 00
Attendants and Nurses	39,292 47

Expenses ($34,733.73)

Medicines, $4,002.52.

Abbott Laboratories, Ltd., 24.74; The Art Metropole, 1,848.23; Associated Chemical Co., of Canada, Ltd., 31.85; Cameron Surgical Specialty Co., 14.94; Canadian Laboratory Supplies, Ltd., 124.50; Carnahan's, Ltd., 24.36; Central Scientific Co. of Canada, Ltd., 28.30; Department of Health, 109.30; Dominion Oxygen Co., Ltd., 13.00; Charles E. Frosst & Co., 25.38; Gendron Mfg. Co., Ltd., 23.72; J. F. Hartz Co., Ltd., 351.36; F. J. Hind Chemical Co., Ltd., 23.52; Ingram & Bell, Ltd., 491.06; Lewis Mfg. Co. of Canada, Ltd., 31.36; Moffats, Ltd., 14.10; Ontario Hospital, Toronto, 128.00; Parke, Davis & Co., Ltd., 10.00; W. E. Saunders, Ltd., 43.36; Scales & Roberts, Ltd., 159.80; The Stevens Companies, 418.76; Toronto General Hospital (Dept. of Radiology), 12.00; petty disbursements, 50.88 .... 4,002 52

Groceries and Provisions, $11,694.38.

Jas. Bamford & Sons, Ltd., 1,030.28; Barker's Bread, Ltd., 535.04; Canada Dry Ginger Ale, Ltd., 27.35; Canada Packers, Ltd., 131.69; Doyle Produce, 16.70; Everist Bros., Ltd., 342.59; John J. Fee, 1,716.20; K. C. Freeman, 286.60; H. J. Heinz Co., 226.22; F. W. Humphrey Co., Ltd., 421.92; E. Lazenby & Son, 17.50; Loblaw Groceterias Co., Ltd., 778.17; Jas. Lumbers & Co., Ltd., 305.47; Mara Lodge Poultry Farms, 64.58; Oak Vale Dairy, 39.69; Ontario Reformatory Industries, 4,420.28; Ontario Reformatory, Mimico, 192.35; Payne & Freeland, 12.19; Sid. Perkins, 53.25; D. S. Perrin & Co., Ltd., 72.04; Pure Gold Mfg. Co., Ltd., 401.44; Purity Bread, Ltd., 24.84; St. Lawrence Fish Market, 138.43; F. W. Stull, 12.40; Toronto Dairies, Ltd., 286.13; Western Bakeries, 76.50; petty disbursements, 64.53 .... 11,694 38

Fuel, Light and Water, $6,372.26.

H. C. Burton & Co., 75.82; Canadian General Electric Co., Ltd., 235.94; Department of Public Works, 2,500.00; City of Toronto, 649.93; Toronto Hydro-Electric System, 2,899.37; petty disbursements, 11.20 .... 6,372 26

Clothing, $199.19.

Corbett-Cowley, Ltd., 37.19; Gordon MacKay & Co., Ltd., 121.20; Hamburg Felt Boot Co., Ltd., 37.80; petty disbursements, 3.00 .... 199 19

Laundry and Cleaning, $7,103.07.

Acme Caretakers Supply Co., 12.25; Associated Chemical Co. of Canada, Ltd., 201.59; Colgate-Palmolive-Peet Co., Ltd., 121.67; Cudahy Packing Co., 21.36; Dearborn Chemical Co., Ltd., 11.88; Diamond Cleanser, Ltd., 36.50; T. Eaton Co., Ltd., 22.74; E. B. Eddy Co., Ltd., 85.00; Guelph Soaps, Ltd., 44.10; Hatch Specialty Co., 68.85; Interlake Tissue Co., Ltd., 177.19; Andrew Jergens Co., Ltd., 59.78; C. L. Johnston & Co., 39.98; Lavoline Cleanser Co., Ltd., 52.55; Herbert L. Lugsdin, 12.50; Mercer Reformatory, 5,695.40; Mercer Reformatory Industries, 56.32; National Drug & Chemical Co., Ltd., 16.86; Ontario Laundry Co., Ltd., 23.16; Procter & Gamble Co., of Canada, Ltd., 26.55; Scott Paper Co. of Canada, Ltd., 101.93; J. B. Sheppard, 25.24; Standard Wax Co., 81.01; Sure-Way Products, 13.30; Tarbox Bros., Ltd., 13.06; Wonder Products, 26.99; petty disbursements, 55.31 .... 7,103 07

Furniture and Furnishings, $1,942.58.

Aikenhead Hardware, Ltd., 10.53; Aluminum Goods, Ltd., 66.12; Cassidy's, Ltd., 324.93; T. Eaton Co., Ltd., 55.17; Federal Electric Appliance Co., Ltd., 441.00; General Steel Wares, Ltd., 71.73; A. D. Gibson, 157.73; Gold Medal Furniture Mfg. Co., Ltd., 12.94; Gordon MacKay & Co., Ltd., 37.38; Grand & Toy, Ltd., 290.80; Hamilton & Johnston, 15.75; R. G. Kirby & Sons, Ltd., 52.35; The Masco Co., Ltd., 14.57; Mercer Reformatory Industries, 133.60; Office Specialty Mfg. Co., Ltd., 36.75; Ontario Hospital, Toronto, 96.60; Ontario Reformatory Industries, 47.00; J. A. Wilson Co., Ltd., 20.58; petty disbursements, 57.05 1,942 58

Ontario Hospitals—Continued

Toronto Psychiatric—Continued

Expenses—Continued

Office Expenses, $2,020.28

Bell Telephone Co. of Canada, rentals, 762.60; tolls, 179.48; T. Eaton Co., Ltd., 12.93; Grand & Toy, Ltd., 313.70; King's Printer, 150.06; Office Specialty Mfg. Co., Ltd., 117.20; Postmaster, 162.00; Steel Equipment Co., Ltd., 69.30; Toronto Transportation Commission, 132.00; United Typewriter Co., Ltd., 98.77; petty disbursements, 22.24 .... 2,020 28

Lawn Expenses, $120.30.

Canada Building Materials, Ltd., 26.14; Slichter's, Ltd., 61.64; petty disbursements, 32.52 .... 120 30

Contingencies, $1,279.15.

American Hospital Association, dues, 10.00; Andrew H. Baird, educational supplies, 23.41; Canada Customs, duty charges, 10.31; Clarke & Clarke Co., Ltd., leather, etc., 111.83; Wm. Dawson Subscription Service, Ltd., subscriptions, 140.13; Dominion Reed Supplies, Ltd., reed, 44.66; T. Eaton Co., Ltd., crepe paper, etc., 23.40; Dr. C. B. Farrar, travelling expenses, 87.34; N. D. Fidler, travelling expenses, 89.43; Graham Magazine Agency, subscriptions, 46.20; Hamilton & Johnston, knitting yarns, 34.01; Ed. R. Lewis, Leather Co. Ltd., leather patches, etc., 42.98; The Robt. Simpson Co., Ltd., fancy goods etc., 197.81; C. H. Stoelting Co., picture texts, etc., 17.45; Students' Book Department, U. of T., 235.20; Ed. Tobin, subscriptions, 12.00; petty disbursements, 152.99 .... 1,279 15

Repairs to Buildings, etc. ($2,056.48)

Maintenance and Repairs to all Buildings, Walks, Roads, Grounds and Fences, $707.00.

Aikenhead Hardware, Ltd., 45.89; Empire Brass Mfg. Co., Ltd., 96.81; Italian Mosaic & Tile Co., Ltd., 63.00; R. G. Kirby & Sons, Ltd., 56.20; Rice Lewis & Son, Ltd., 20.70; Pay lists, wages of men, 96.20; Toronto Lock Mfg. Co., 19.56; Trelco, Ltd., 263.65; W. Williamson, Lumber Co., Ltd., 19.00; petty disbursements, 25.99 .... 707 00

Maintenance and Repairs of Plumbing, Steam and Electric Plants, $1,349.48.

Allanson Armature Exchange Co., 20.40; Fred Armstrong Co., Ltd., 55.41; Atlas Engineering & Machine Co., Ltd., 12.00; Canadian Fairbanks-Morse Co., Ltd., 23.36; Canadian Powers Regulator Co., Ltd., 60.20; Dictograph Products Co. of Canada, 83.27; Electrical Maintenance & Repairs Co., 18.80; Empire Brass Mfg. Co., Ltd., 138.18; Hobart Mfg. Co., 11.18; Hospital & Kitchen Equipment Co., Ltd., 101.18; Rice Lewis & Son, Ltd., 38.95; The Masco Co., Ltd., 32.56; Northern Electric Co., Ltd., 32.82; Pay lists, wages of men, 540.37; Jas. Robertson Co., Ltd., 47.64; Turnbull Elevator Co., Ltd., 34.20; Wrought Iron Range Co., Ltd., 52.49; petty disbursements, 46.47 .... 1,349 48

Total		127,378 68
Less Maintenance of Patients	24,492 84	
Perquisites	4,925 95	
Sale of Products	800 00	
		30,218 79
Toronto Psychiatric		97,159 89

Mental Hospitals $2,923,423.32

STATUTORY

Minister's salary (see page M 13) 10,000 00
Salaries not otherwise provided for (see page M 24) 925 00

Statutory $10,925.00

SPECIAL WARRANTS

Ontario Hospital, Mimico, to Cover the Cost Incurred in Reconstruction, Alterations, Additions on Cottages ($72,907.73)

Barnett Lumber Co., lumber, 120.69; Bennett & Wright, Ltd., elbows, 1,270.72; Brantford Roofing Co., Ltd., slates, 209.17; Builders' Supplies, Ltd., cement, lime, etc., 4,000.48; Canadian General Electric Co., Ltd., conduit, etc., 201.64;

Special Warrants—Continued

Ontario Hospital, Mimico, Reconstruction, etc., re Cottages—Continued

Canada Metal Window & Steel Products, Ltd., steel sash, etc., 57.22; Crane, Ltd., plumbing supplies, 605.87; Disher Steel Construction Co., Ltd., lintels, steel, etc., 848.52; Dominion Bridge Co., Ltd., beams and angles, 2,700.18; Dominion Wheel & Foundries, Ltd., manhole tops, 44.00; J. H. Doughty, Ltd., sheet iron, 171.96; C. A. Dunham Co., Ltd., valves, etc., 71.26; Empire Brass Manufacturing Co., Ltd., wheels, guard rail, etc., 1,061.83; Fenestra Canada Metal Products, Ltd., sash, 18.81; Fittings, Ltd., plumbing supplies, 10.85; Heathcote Hardware, hardware, 401.87; John T. Hepburn, Ltd., steel, 1,656.00; Lake Shore Builders' Supplies, Ltd., stone, cement, etc., 1,215.05; Rice Lewis & Son, Ltd., shovels, hardware, etc., 127.74; Mason's Service Station, gasoline, 61.28; The Masco Co., Ltd., lock nuts, 36.85; Mimico Planing Mills, lumber, etc., 1.993.20; Northern Electric Co., Ltd., conduit, 42.16; Ontario Reformatory, Mimico, brick and tile, 5,819.25; Pay list, wages of men, 46,409.65; The Pedlar People, Ltd., steel, etc., 971.31; Regent Electric Supply Co., Ltd., boxes, 21.91; Ritchie Cut Stone Co., Ltd., stone, 60.00; The James Robertson Co., Ltd., plumbing supplies, 16.74; Rogers Electric Co., Ltd., conduit, etc., 24.14; Sun Oil Co., Ltd., hydrolene, 14.12; Taylor-Forbes Co., Ltd., pipe, 1,117.03; Truscon Steel Co., Ltd., steel, sash, etc., 138.60; W. Walker & Son, Ltd., water bar, hardware, 95.62; Wilkinson-Kompass, Ltd., steel, 30.28; W. Williamson Lumber Co., Ltd., lumber, 148.00. Sundries—cartage, 1,103.10; petty disbursements, 10.63 .... 72,907 73

Grant for the Ontario Dental Association for Expenses of Entertaining Distinguished Guests from Great Britain and United States at the Annual Meeting of the Ontario Dental Association and Canadian Dental Association ($1,000.00)

Ontario Dental Association 1,000 00

Bursar, University of Toronto for Furnishing School of Nursing No. 7, Queen's Park ($1,000.00)

Bursar, University of Toronto, Grant 1,000 00

Reimbursing the Village of Portsmouth as Proportionate Payment for the Repairing and Oiling of King Street Approaching the Ontario Hospital, Kingston, ($250.00)

Village of Portsmouth 250 00

Ontario Reformatory, Guelph to Cover Cost of Maintenance of Insane Patients from November 1st, 1931 to October 13th, 1932 ($25,005.17)

Treasurer of Ontario for Ontario Reformatory, Guelph 25,005 17

Travelling and Other Expenses re Cancer Commission ($3,635.84)

W. T. Connell, travelling expenses, 139.75; W. D. Beath & Son, Ltd., trays, 3.00; Central Scientific Co., of Canada, Ltd., pump, 97.75; Department of Highways, auto service, 41.90; A. R. Ford, travelling expenses, 77.50; Professor Ireton, services preparing report, 30.00; King's Printer, 2,340.89; Kingston Whig-Standard, advertising, 3.36; J. D. Leitch, travelling expenses, 103.95; J. W. S. McCullough, travelling expenses, 270.59; Province of Ontario Pictures, pictures and enlargements, etc., 513.24; J. F. Raw Co., Ltd., prints, 2.04;. Sundries—customs, 2.32; express, 9.55 .... 3,635 84

Special Warrants **$103,798.74**

Total 5,918,827 56
Less Salary Assessment 48,557 03

Total Expenditure, Department of Health **$5,870,270.53**

PART N

DEPARTMENT OF LABOUR

FISCAL YEAR, 1931-32

TABLE OF CONTENTS

GENERAL INDEX AT BACK OF BOOK

PART N—DEPARTMENT OF LABOUR

Statement of Expenditure Showing Amounts Expended, Unexpended and Overexpended for the Twelve Months Ended October 31st, 1932

Department of Labour	Page	Estimates	Expended			Un-expended	Over-expended	Treasury Board Minute
			Ordinary	Capital	Total Ordinary and Capital			
		$ c.	$ c.	$ c.	$ c.	$ c.	$ c.	$ c.
Main Office:								
Salaries	6	23,400 00	17,771 50		17,771 50	5,628 50		
Insurance Premium, Caisson Inspector	6	266 50	266 50		266 50			
Contingencies	6	12,000 00	10,095 03		10,095 03	1,904 97		
Labour Exhibit, services and expenses	6	3,000 00	1,986 38		1,986 38	1,013 62		
Investigations	6	2,000 00	223 09		223 09	1,776 91		
Main Office	..	40,666 50	30,342 50		30,342 50	10,324 00		
General:								
Educational Work, Conferences, etc.	7	7,000 00	5,902 55		5,902 55	1,097 45		
Litigation of Constitutional and other questions	7	200 00	85 75		85 75	114 25		
General	..	7,200 00	5,988 30		5,988 30	1,211 70		
Branches:								
Apprenticeship,								
Salaries	7	25,475 00	20,481 25		20,481 25	4,993 75		
Contingencies	7	10,000 00	5,955 02		5,955 02	4,044 98		
	..	35,475 00	26,436 27		26,436 27	9,038 73		
Less Fees	8		1 00		1 00	1 00		
Apprenticeship	..	35,475 00	26,435 27		26,435 27	9,039 73		
Boiler [illegible]in,								
Salaries	8	29,250 00	19,773 04		19,773 04	9,476 96		
Contingencies	8	10,000 00	4,353 12		4,353 12	5,646 88		
	..	39,250 00	24,126 16		24,126 16	15,123 84		
Less Fees	8		12,623 66		12,623 66	12,623 66		
Boiler Inspection	..	39,250 00	11,502 50		11,502 50	27,747 50		

Factory Inspection,								
Salaries	8	61,875 00	58,775 00	....	58,775 00	3,100 00	....	....
Contingencies	9	15,000 00	15,604 69	....	15,604 69	....	604 69	1,200 00
Factory Inspection	..	76,875 00	74,379 69	....	74,379 69	3,100 00	604 69	....
Building Trades Protection Act,								
Contingencies, Salaries, etc.	..	1,000 00	....	....	....	1,000 00	....	....
Building Trades Protection Act	..	1,000 00	....	....	....	1,000 00	....	....
Stationary Engineers Board,								
Salaries	9	21,175 00	21,100 00	....	21,100 00	75 00	....	....
Contingencies	9	10,000 00	7,221 55	....	7,221 55	2,778 45	....	....
	..	31,175 00	28,321 55	....	28,321 55	2,853 45	....	....
Less Fees	10	....	25,383 11	....	25,383 11	25,383 11	....	....
Stationary Engineers Board	..	31,175 00	2,938 44	....	2,938 44	28,236 56	....	....
Ontario Government Employment Offices,								
Salaries	10	135,800 00	134,028 11	....	134,028 11	1,771 89	....	....
Contingencies	10	75,000 00	85,332 41	....	85,332 41	....	10,332 41	15,000 00
	..	210,800 00	219,360 52	....	219,360 52	1,771 89	10,332 41	....
Less Dominion Government Subventions	11	....	66,618 34	....	66,618 34	66,618 34	....	....
Ontario Government Employment Offices	..	210,800 00	152,742 18	....	152,742 18	68,390 23	10,332 41	....
Travelling Expenses, etc.,								
Employment Service Council	..	5,000 00	....	....	....	5,000 00	....	....
Administration of Employment,								
Service Councils	..	1,000 00	....	....	....	1,000 00	....	....
Minimum Wage Board,								
Salaries	14	3,800 00	3,400 00	....	3,400 00	400 00	....	....
Administration of the Act	14	15,000 00	12,186 69	....	12,186 69	2,813 31	....	....
Minimum Wage Board	..	18,800 00	15,586 69	....	15,586 69	3,213 31	....	....
Supply Bill	..	467,241 50	319,915 57	....	319,915 57	158,263 03	10,937 10	....

PART N—DEPARTMENT OF LABOUR—Continued

Statement of Expenditure Showing Amounts Expended, Unexpended and Overexpended for the Twelve Months Ended October 31st, 1932

Department of Labour	Page	Estimates	Expended			Un-expended	Over-expended	Treasury Board Minute
			Ordinary	Capital	Total Ordinary and Capital			
		$ c.	$ c.	$ c.	$ c.	$ c.	$ c.	$ c.
Statutory:								
Salaries not otherwise provided for	12	....	100 00	....	100 00	....	....	....
Unemployment Relief Act, 22 Geo. V, Chap. 4,								
Administration	14	....	5,721 81	....	5,721 81	....	....	....
Municipal Works and Direct Relief	15	....	511,995 46	5,284,141 67	5,796,137 13	....	....	....
Lands and Forests Department,								
Removing Fire Hazards	18	....	....	55,270 81	55,270 81	....	....	....
Highway, Madoc to Perth	19	....	....	600,000 00	600,000 00	....	....	....
Northern Development Department,								
Trans-Canada Highway	19	....	....	3,047,242 15	3,047,242 15	....	....	....
General work	19	....	....	2,811,103 02	2,811,103 02	....	....	....
Construction, Ivanhoe Dam	19	....	....	17,873 12	17,873 12	....	....	....
Statutory	..	....	517,817 27	11,815,630 77	12,333,448 04	....	....	....
Special Warrants:								
Unemployment Relief,								
Administration	19	....	17,811 40	....	17,811 40	....	....	....
Direct Relief	20	....	272,942 01	1,416,245 02	1,689,187 03	....	....	....
Ottawa Office of the Provincial Employment Service	22	....	1,200 00	....	1,200 00	....	....	....
Trades and Labour Council re Convention	22	....	500 00	....	500 00	....	....	....
Special Warrants	..	....	292,453 41	1,416,245 02	1,708,698 43	....	....	....
Total	..	....	1,130,186 25	13,231,875 79	14,362,062 04	....	....	....
Less Salary Assessment	..	....	6,275 44	....	6,275 44	....	....	....
Total Expenditure, Department of Labour	..	....	1,123,910 81	13,231,875 79	14,355,786 60	....	....	....

SUMMARY

Department of Labour	Page	Ordinary	Capital	Total
		$ c.	$ c.	$ c.
Main Office and Branches	6	319,915 57	....	319,915 57
Statutory	14	517,817 27	11,815,630 77	12,333,448 04
Special Warrants	19	292,453 41	1,416,245 02	1,708,698 43
Total	..	1,130,186 25	13,231,875 79	14,362,062 04
Less Salary Assessment	..	6,275 44	....	6,275 44
Department of Labour	..	1,123,910 81	13,231,875 79	14,355,786 60

DEPARTMENT OF LABOUR

Hon. Dr. J. D. Monteith, Minister

MAIN OFFICE

Salaries ($17,771.50)

Name	Position	Group	Period	Amount
A. W. Crawford	Deputy Minister		12 months	5,100 00
Wm. Burns	Mechanical and Safety Engineer		12 "	2,400 00
F. Swarbrick	Inspector of Caisson Work		12 "	2,400 00
M. C. Findlay	Senior Investigator		12 "	2,000 00
A. D. Harpell	Accountant,	Group 4	12 "	2,000 00
Daniel Smyth	Clerk,	" 1	12 "	1,300 00
R. F. Tait	Stock Clerk,	" 1	1½ "	171 50
H. Davis	Clerk Stenographer,	" 1	12 "	1,200 00
C. Trewin	" "	" 1	3 "	300 00
M. J. Thomas	" "	" 2	12 "	900 00

Insurance Premium, Caisson Inspector ($266.50)

Empire Life Insurance Co 266 50

Contingencies ($10,095.03)

Temporary Services, $5,783.90.

Name	Position	Group	Period		Amount
W. W. Allison	Clerk,	Group 1	12 months		1,200 00
J. E. Burch	"	" 2	12 "	975 00	
		Less leave of absence		15 62	959 38
R. Bush	Clerk Stenographer,	" 2	11 "		756 25
H. T. Kelleher	Clerk Typist,	" 2	12 "		750 00
G. E. Mason	Clerk,	" 1	12 "		1,200 00
M. W. Murphy	Filing Clerk,	" 2	8½ "		512 02
H. K. Patton	Clerk,	" 2	5 "		406 25

Travelling Expenses, $681.29.

Wm. Burns, 117.58; A. W. Crawford, 83.24; F. A. Swarbrick, 480.47 .... 681 29

Miscellaneous, $3,629.84.

Ediphone Co., Ltd., inspections, 11.93; King's Printer, 3,392.49; Remington Typewriters, Ltd., inspections, etc., 26.25; Taylor Typewriter Co., repairs, etc., 23.25; United Typewriter Co., Ltd., inspections, 61.50. Sundries—car tickets, 2.25; customs, .11; newspapers and periodicals, 63.17; telegrams, 8.80; petty disbursements, 40.09 .... 3,629 84

Exhibits ($1,986.38)

Temporary Services, $229.82.

Name	Position	Period	Amount
Thos. A. Blakely	Watchman	½ month	47 12
Joseph Gibson	Caretaker	½ "	53 85
Chas. A. Smith	Assistant	1¼ months	128 85

Travelling Expenses, $93.73.

Wm. Burns, 91.63; C. A. Smith, 2.10 .... 93 73

Miscellaneous, $1,662.83.

Aikenhead Hardware, Ltd., staples, etc., 16.16; Armstrong Bros., machine work, etc., 84.00; Bertram & Cumming, arranging exhibits, etc., 62.40; Canadian General Electric Co., Ltd., lamps, 11.20; City Pattern Works, patterns, 20.50; Department of Highways, auto service, 19.30; Josephine De Witt Co., artificial flowers, 20.58; Ferranti Electric, Ltd., transformer, 12.00; Florentine Co., Ltd., repairing and repainting figures, 15.00; Garage Supply Co., Ltd., services re air compressor, 10.25; King's Printer, 366.12; K. Patton, meals, etc., 11.50; W. H. Price, painting booth, 88.00; Province of Ontario Pictures, prints, films, etc., 498.74; Root, Neal & Co., gears, 21.87; W. J. Scott, meals, 16.20; Slichters, Ltd., flowers, 13.50; T. Taylor & Co., curtains, 22.50; Wells Bros. Amusement Co., rent of moving picture equipment, 175.00. Sundries—cartage, 107.10; customs, 3.00; express, .84; freight, 1.75; petty disbursements, 65.32 .... 1,662 83

Investigations, Library, Publications, Journals, Subscriptions, etc. ($223.09)

Travelling Expenses, $132.99.

W. C. Ferris, 132.24; H. K. Patton, .75 .... 132 99

Main Office and Branches—Continued

Investigations, Library, Publications, etc.—Continued

Publications, Subscriptions, etc., $90.10.

American Association for Labour Legislation, book, .75; Canadian Political Science Association, subscription, 3.00; Daily Commercial News, subscription, 20.00; Imperial Publishing Co., book, 2.00; International Labour Office, subscription, 40.00; King's Printer, 22.35; Saturday Night, subscription, 2.00...... 90 10

Main Office.. $30,342 50

General ($5,988.30)

Educational Work, Conference, Advertising, etc. ($5,902.55)

Advertising, $5,579.95.

Age Publications, Ltd., 90.00; All-Canadian Congress of Labour, 225.00; Canadian Brotherhood of Railway Employees, 150.00; Canadian Congress Publishing Co., Ltd., 228.00; Canadian Engineers, 253.43; Canadian Jewish Review, 21.60; Canadian Labour Press, 360.00; Canadian Labour World, 37.50; Canadian Manufacturers Association, 540.00; Canadian Trade Unionist, 176.00; Canadian Yardmaster's Association, 245.00; Contract Record & Engineering Review, 554.00; Daily Commercial News, 240.00; Federated Railwaymen, 96.00; Fisher Publishing Co., Ltd., 195.00; Hamilton Trade and Labour Council, 215.00; Labour Educational Association of Ontario, 100.00; Labour Directory, 20.00; Labour Leader Publishing Co., Ltd., 520.00; Labour News, 150.00; Labour Temple Co., Ltd., 25.00; The Legionary, 123.42; MacLean Publishing Co., Ltd., 752.50; Postal Journal of Canada, 150.00; Toronto Daily Hebrew Journal, 112.50 5,579 95

Membership Fees, $76.05.

American Chemical Society, 17.25; American Society of Mechanical Engineers, 18.80; Association of Government Officials in Industry, 15.00; Dominion Association of Fire Chiefs, 5.00; National Safety Council, 20.00...................... 76 05

Legal Fees, $23.30.

J. E. Anderson, K.C., 5.00; Jno. Bruce, 18.30.............................. 23 30

Miscellaneous, $223.25.

King's Printer, 185.00; Newall & Co., folios, 38.25.......................... 223 25

Litigation of Constitutional and Other Questions, $85.75.

B. N. Davis, Grass and Timmins, legal costs re case of Grant vs. Kenny and Saunders.. 85 75

General.. $5,988 30

APPRENTICESHIP BRANCH

Salaries ($20,481.25)

George Chambers	Assessment Officer		12 months		2,550 00
J. R. Johnson	District Inspector		12 "		2,000 00
F. J. Hawes	" "		12 "		2,000 00
Chas. E. Needham	" "		12 "		2,000 00
Walter Thorne	" "		12 "		2,000 00
Harold Skelton	Assistant District Inspector		12 "		1,500 00
Geo. B. Evans	Senior Clerk		12 "		2,000 00
L. Cummins	Clerk,	Group 2	12 "	1,125 00	
		Less leave of absence		93 75	1,031 25
M. Haveland	"	Group 2	12 "		1,050 00
S. B. Burgess	Senior Clerk Stenographer		12 "		1,500 00
B. J. MacDonald	Clerk Stenographer,	" 2	12 "		975 00
Hazel M. J. Smith	" "	" 2	12 "		975 00
Villa Bayes	" "	" 2	12 "		900 00

Contingencies ($5,955.02)

Temporary Services ($900.00).

L. H. Kingerley........Assistant..................................6 months 900 00

Main Office and Branches—Continued

Apprenticeship Branch—Continued

Contingencies—Continued

Members of Committee, per Diem Allowance, $880.00.

H. J. Ball, 60.00; J. W. Bruce, 30.00; J. B. Carswell, 390.00; E. Ingles, 110.00; W. Jenoves, 60.00; P. Mansell, 50.00; J. F. Marsh, 50.00; J. M. Pigott, 50.00; F. S. Rutherford, 80.00 .... 880 00

Travelling Expenses, $2,538.15.

H. J. Ball, 24.55; J. B. Carswell, 148.20; G. Chambers, 285.61; G. B. Evans, 21.71; F. J. Hawes, 314.14; E. Ingles, 116.60; J. R. Johnson, 427.24; L. H. Kingerley, 168.79; C. E. Needham, 614.46; J. M. Pigot, 26.60; F. S. Rutherford, 13.30; H. Skelton, 27.44; W. Thorne, 349.51 .... 2,538 15

Miscellaneous, $1,636.87.

Bell Telephone Co., rental, 172.00; tolls, 32.83; C.O.L.C. No. 97, Hall Board, office rent, 240.00; Stewart Chambers, office rent, 312.00; Guaranty Trust Co. of Canada, office rent, 180.00; King's Printer, 258.36; Norton-Palmer, Ltd., office rent, 120.00; Province of Ontario Pictures, prints, 24.00; Remington Typewriters, Ltd., inspections, 10.00; R. Trevor, lettering certificates, 102.00; United Typewriter Co., Ltd., inspections, repairs, etc., 70.10. Sundries—express, 9.25; cartage, 2.50; newspapers and periodicals, 40.00; postage, 39.64; telegrams, 2.49; petty disbursements, 21.60 .... 1,636 87

Total	26,436 27	
Less fees	1 00	
Apprenticeship Branch	$26,435 27	

BOILER INSPECTION BRANCH

Salaries ($19,773.04)

Name	Position	Period	Amount
D. M. Medcalf	Chief Inspector of Steam Boilers	12 months	3,300 00
E. T. Urquhart	Examiner of Reports and Designs	12 "	2,700 00
J. M. Kelly	Inspector of Steam Boilers	12 "	2,400 00
N. S. Smith	" " "	12 "	2,300 00
J. A. MacKenzie	" " "	12 "	2,100 00
J. N. Briggs	" " "	12 "	2,200 00
W. H. Barrett	" " " (T)	5½ "	923 04
D. Roberts	Clerk, Group 1	12 "	1,600 00
Helen Brown	Clerk Stenographer, " 1	12 "	1,200 00
A. Christie	" " " 1	12 "	1,050 00

Contingencies ($4,353.12)

Travelling Expenses, $3,348.32.

W. H. Barrett, 264.57; J. N. Briggs, 910.75; J. M. Kelly, 309.48; J. A. MacKenzie, 634.21; D. M. Medcalf, 304.35; N. S. Smith, 881.49; E. T. Urquhart, 43.47 .... 3,348 32

Miscellaneous, $1,004.80.

Bell Telephone Co., tolls, 4.08; King's Printer, 880.63; James Morrison Brass Manufacturing Co., Ltd., repairs to gauge, 15.40; United Typewriter Co., Ltd., inspections, 52.00. Sundries—customs, 5.24; express, 1.20; freight, 1.00; newspapers and periodicals, 15.50; postage, 1.00; telegrams, 20.25; petty disbursements, 8.50 .... 1,004 80

Total	24,126 16	
Less Fees	12,623 66	
Boiler Inspection Branch	$11,502 50	

FACTORY INSPECTION BRANCH

Salaries ($58,775.00)

Name	Position	Period	Amount
T. J. Burke	Chief Inspector of Factories	12 months	3,600 00
J. P. West	Examiner of Reports and Designs	12 "	2,700 00
H. A. Clark	Inspector	12 "	2,200 00
S. J. Mallion	"	12 "	2,200 00
W. S. Forester	"	12 "	2,200 00
W. T. E. Brennagh	"	12 "	2,200 00

Main Office and Branches—Continued

Factory Inspection Branch—Continued

Salaries—Continued

Name	Position	Group	Period		Amount
H. Stevenson	Inspector		12	months	2,200 00
R. Albrough	"		12	"	2,200 00
H. Bourne	"		12	"	2,200 00
J. R. Prain	"		12	"	2,200 00
J. H. Ainsborough	"		12	"	2,200 00
J. Monteith	"		12	"	2,200 00
H. A. Winnett	"		12	"	2,100 00
J. P. Ferguson	"		12	"	1,900 00
William C. Crozier	"		12	"	1,800 00
J. W. Ogilvie	"		12	"	1,600 00
E. Gurnett	"		12	"	1,600 00
N. Hamilton	"		12	"	1,600 00
G. E. Hornell	"		12	"	1,600 00
E. Scott	"		12	"	1,600 00
Nina B. Garden	"		12	"	1,400 00
M. Pettit	Clerk,	Group 1	12	"	1,600 00
E. H. Gilbert	"	" 1	12	"	1,600 00
L. Longthorne	"	" 2	12	"	1,200 00
K. E. Reesor	"	" 2	12	"	1,200 00
D. Marriott		" 2	12	"	1,200 00
H. Cummings	"	" 3	12	"	975 00
A. M. Buckler	Clerk Stenographer,	" 1	12	"	1,200 00
Gladys Brown	" "	" 2	12	"	975 00
Aileen M. Burley	" "	" 2	12	"	900 00
Louise Hannah	" "	" 2	12	"	900 00
E. L. Sylvester	" "	" 2	(T) 12	"	825 00
D. Tew	Clerk Typist	1	12	"	1,200 00
Lorna Jennett	" "	" 2	(T) 12	"	750 00
M. M. McLaughlin	" "	2	(T) 12	"	750 00

Contingencies ($15,604.69)

Travelling Expenses, $14,398.57.

J. H. Ainsborough, 1,113.50; R. Albrough, 1,151.32; H. Bourne, 1,236.18; W. T. Brennagh, 627.63; T. J. Burke, 11.25; H. A. Clark, 195.38; W. C. Crozier, 1,136.43; J. P. Ferguson, 201.31; W. S. Forester, 1,080.78; N. B. Garden, 530.80; E. Gurnett, 335.80; N. Hamilton, 836.57; G. E. Hornell, 514.22; S. J. Mallion, 1,593.61; J. Monteith, 1,011.20; J. W. Ogilvie, 1,047.64; E. Scott, 449.30; H. Stevenson, 60.13; H. A. Winnett, 1,251.67; J. P. West, 13.85 .... 14,398 57

Miscellaneous, $1,206.12.

King's Printer, 1,055.65; United Typewriter Co., Ltd., inspections, etc., 111.80. Sundries—express, 12.00; newspapers and periodicals, 22.50; telegrams, 4.17 .... 1,206 12

Factory Inspection $74,379 69

STATIONARY AND HOISTING ENGINEERS' BOARD

Salaries ($21,100.00)

Name	Position	Group	Period		Amount
J. M. Brown	Chairman		12	months	3,000 00
W. J. Scott	Member of Board		12	"	2,400 00
S. G. Rose	" "		12	"	2,400 00
Edward J. Everett	Inspector		12	"	2,000 00
Wm. J. Jordan	"		12	"	1,900 00
Wm. Robertson	Senior Clerk		12	"	1,800 00
M. T. Waizman	Clerk,	Group 1	12	"	1,300 00
S. McComb	"	" 2	12	"	1,200 00
Nellie E. R. Watts	"	" 3	12	"	825 00
M. L. Bowerman	Clerk Stenographer,	" 1	12	"	1,200 00
Eileen R. O'Connor	" "	" 3	12	"	825 00
C. I. McGhie	Clerk Typist,	1	12	"	1,200 00
M. A. McCrary	" "	1	12	"	1,050 00

Contingencies ($7,221.55)

Temporary Services, $256.12.

Name	Position	Period		Amount
R. Bush	Clerk Stenographer, Group 2	1	month	68 75
M. McAvoy	" " " 3	3	"	187 37

Main Office and Branches—Continued

Stationary and Hoisting Engineers' Board—Continued

Contingencies—Continued

Travelling Expenses, $3,001.36.

J. M. Brown, 56.19; E. J. Everett, 141.01; W. J. Jordan, 893.44; W. Robertson, 6.24; S. G. Rose, 1,163.55; W. J. Scott, 740.93 ... 3,001 36

Miscellaneous, $3,964.07.

King's Printer, 3,790.54; United Typewriter Co., Ltd., inspections, 80.40. Sundries—newspapers and periodicals, 80.65; telegrams, 12.48 ... 3,964 07

Total	28,321 55	
Less Fees	25,383 11	
Stationary and Hoisting Engineers Board	$2,938 44	

ONTARIO GOVERNMENT EMPLOYMENT OFFICES

Salaries ($134,028.11)

Head Office and Clearing House:					
H. C. Hudson	General Superintendent		12 months		3,000 00
R. Davids	Senior Clerk Stenographer		12 "	1,500 00	
	Less Leave of Absence			24 66	1,475 34
G. Law	Clerk Stenographer, Group	1	9 "		787 50
W. C. Ferris	Clerk,	" 1	12 "		1,500 00
Belleville:					
L. F. Green	Superintendent,	" 3	12 "		1,600 00
I. Keeler	Clerk Stenographer,	" 2	12 "	900 00	
	Less Leave of Absence			14 80	885 20
Brantford:					
M. H. MacBride	Superintendent,	" 3	12 "		1,800 00
M. Corcoran	Clerk Stenographer.	" 2	12 "		900 00
Chatham:					
G. W. Wands	Superintendent,	" 3	12 "	1,800 00	
	Less Leave of Absence			29 58	1,770 42
Cobalt:					
T. E. Dowse	Superintendent,	" 3	8 "		1,066 66
Fort William:					
A. H. Power	Superintendent,	" 3	12 "		1,500 00
J. T. Foxton	Clerk,	" 1	12 "		1,500 00
Fort Frances:					
D. Murphy	Clerk,	" 1	12 "		1,500 00
Guelph:					
A. W. Taylor	Superintendent,	" 3	12 "		1,700 00
M. I. Sinclair	Clerk Stenographer,	" 2	12 "	900 00	
	Less Leave of Absence			14 79	885 21
Hamilton:					
W. A. Selkirk	Superintendent,	" 2	12 "		2,100 00
P. J. McCabe	Senior Clerk,	" 1	12 "		1,700 00
W. Hamilton	Clerk,	" 1	12 "		1,500 00
I. Johnson	"	" 1	12 "		1,400 00
M. S. MacMillan	"	" 2	12 "		1,050 00
A. Christmas	"	" 2	12 "	1,200 00	
	Less Leave of Absence			19 73	1,180 27
Kingston:					
W. A. Stroud	Superintendent,	" 3	12 "		1,800 00
M. Lennox	Clerk Stenographer,	" 2	12 "		975 00
Kitchener:					
M. H. Phillips	Superintendent,	" 3	12 "	1,800 00	
	Less Leave of Absence			223 14	1,576 86
T. H. Scott	Acting Superintendent		7 "		991 66
Doris Youngblut	Clerk Stenographer,	" 2	12 "		900 00
London:					
H. Wray	Superintendent,	" 2	12 "		2,000 00
E. M. McKay	Clerk,	" 2	12 "		1,125 00

Main Office and Branches—Continued

Ontario Government Employment Offices—Continued

Salaries—Continued

Name	Position	Group	Period		Amount
Niagara Falls:					
H. P. Hanan	Superintendent,	Group 3	12 months		1,800 00
J. Newport	Clerk Stenographer,	" 2	5½ "		412 50
Mildred A. Cole	" "	" 2 (T)	6½ "		444 23
North Bay:					
H. A. Desjardins	Superintendent,	" 3	12 "		1,800 00
D. Lowe	Clerk Stenographer,	" 2	4 "		325 00
Oshawa:					
R. G. Hamilton	Superintendent,	" 3	12 "		2,100 00
N. M. Robinson	Clerk Stenographer,	" 2	10½ "		853 12
Bessie Wilcox	" "	" 2 (T)	1¾ "		118 99
Ottawa—Men's Division:					
R. Halliday	Superintendent,	" 2	12 "		2,000 00
F. Turner	Senior Clerk,	" 1	12 "		1,700 00
W. J. Palen	" "	2	12 "		1,500 00
C. E. Levy	Clerk Stenographer,	" 2	12 "		975 00
Ottawa—Women's Division:					
E. Appleton	Clerk,	" 1	12 "	1,600 00	
		Less Leave of Absence		26 30	1,573 70
L. M. Currie	Clerk Stenographer,	" 2	12 "	900 00	
		Less Leave of Absence		14 80	885 20
Pembroke:					
G. H. Ross	Superintendent,	" 3	12 "		1,800 00
I. Brown	Clerk Stenographer,	" 2	12 "	900 00	
		Less Leave of Absence		14 80	885 20
Peterboro:					
H. Robertson	Superintendent,	" 3	12 "		1,700 00
M. I. Ruth	Clerk Stenographer,	" 2	12		975 00
Port Arthur:					
A. C. Wood	Superintendent,	" 2	12 "		2,100 00
H. O. Taylor	Clerk,	" 1	12 "		1,600 00
J. Kerr	"	" 1	12 "		1,400 00
St. Catharines:					
L. P. Cunningham	Superintendent,	" 3	12 "		1,800 00
D. Lowe	Clerk Stenographer,	" 2	2¼ "		173 18
Alice N. Cheshire	" "	" 2 (T)	6½ "		444 23
Sault Ste. Marie:					
W. E. Hunt	Superintendent,	" 3	12 "	1,800 00	
		Less Leave of Absence		29 58	1,770 42
St. Thomas:					
W. J. Peacock	Superintendent,	" 3	12 "		1,800 00
Sarnia:					
A. E. Palmer	Superintendent,	" 3	12		1,600 00
E. Gracy	Clerk Stenographer,	" 2	12 "		975 00
Sudbury:					
E. H. Manor	Superintendent,	" 3	5 "		750 00
A. E. Woods	"	(T)	7½ "		932 70
A. H. Carmichael	Clerk,	" 1	12 "	1,600 00	
		Less Leave of Absence		26 30	1,573 70
Timmins:					
H. C. Garner	Superintendent,	" 3	12 "	1,800 00	
		Less Leave of Absence		29 58	1,770 42
T. E. Dowse	"	" 3	4 "	533 34	
		Less Leave of Absence		26 30	507 04
Toronto—Women's Division:					
L. O. R. Kennedy	Superintendent,	Group 3	12 "		1,800 00
E. Tompkins	Clerk,	" 1	12 "		1,400 00
M. MacMillan	"	" 2	12 "		1,200 00
N. Corcoran	"	" 2	12 "		1,200 00
E. VanKoughnet	"	" 2	12 "		1,200 00
V. Stewart		" 2	12 "		1,050 00

Main Office and Branches—Continued

Ontario Government Employment Offices—Continued

Salaries—Continued

Name	Position	Group	Months		Amount
Toronto—Women's Division—Continued.					
B. D. Friend	Clerk	Group 2	12 months		1,125 00
K. Keenan	"	" 2	12 "		1,125 00
M. Lane	"	" 2	12 "		975 00
G. M. Firth	Clerk Stenographer,	" 2	12 "		975 00
M. Owen	" "	" 2	12 "		975 00
P. Mathieson	Caretaker,	" 2	12 "		1,400 00
E. Bond	Telephone Operator		12 "		975 00
Toronto—Men's Division:					
W. S. Dobbs	Superintendent,	" 1	12 "		2,500 00
J. F. Marsh	Deputy Superintendent		12 "		2,200 00
R. C. Eakins	Senior Clerk,	" 1	12 "		1,800 00
F. C. Butt	" "	" 1	12 "		1,800 00
W. Ruddick	" "	" 1	12 "		1,700 00
T. G. Mill	" "	" 1	12 "	1,700 00	
		Less Leave of Absence		27 95	1,672 05
W. H. Cameron	" "	" 1	12 "		1,700 00
G. C. Warner	Scout		12 "		1,800 00
T. H. Scott	"		5 "		708 34
C. W. King	Clerk,	" 1	12 "		1,600 00
F. W. McGregor	"	" 1	12 "		1,600 00
J. F. Stewart	"	" 1	12 "		1,600 00
F. Kelly	"	" 1	12 "		1,600 00
J. H. Kerr	"	" 1	12 "		1,500 00
H. C. Shelton	"	" 1	12 "		1,500 00
A. C. White	"	" 1	12 "		1,400 00
J. A. Villeneuve	"	" 1	12 "		1,300 00
H. Alley	Senior Clerk Stenographer		12 "		1,400 00
J. Vickers	Cleaner and Helper		12 "		1,400 00
New Toronto:					
H. N. Reid	Superintendent,	" 3	12		1,600 00
Windsor:					
A. J. Cooper	Superintendent,	" 2	12 "	2,100 00	
		Less Leave of Absence		115 07	1,984 93
W. J. Fitzgerald	Clerk,	" 1	12 "	1,600 00	
		Less Leave of Absence		26 30	1,573 70
S. K. Doherty	"	" 1	12 "	1,500 00	
		Less Leave of Absence		24 66	1,475 34

Salaries not Provided for (Statutory) ($100.00)

Name	Position	Group	Months	Amount
Toronto—Women's Division:				
C. Trewin	Clerk Stenographer,	Group 1	1 "	100 00

Contingencies ($85,332.41)

Temporary Services, $31,813.15.

Name	Position	Group	Months	Amount
Head Office:				
G. Marsh	Clerk Typist,	Group 2	12 months	750 00
H. K. Patton	Clerk,	" 2	7 "	568 75
Arden, Kaladar, Maberly and Sharbot Lake:				
J. A. Wood	Acting Superintendent		1⅓ "	134 62
R. Gendall	Clerk,	" 1	3¾ "	384 61
J. D. Davidson	"	" 1	5 "	488 45
Brantford:				
E. W. Porteous	Clerk Stenographer,	" 2	½ "	34 37
M. E. Vanfleet	Clerk Typist,	" 2	3 "	187 50
Chatham:				
B. Garment	Clerk Stenographer,	" 2	12	825 00
Fort William:				
E. G. Fummerton	Clerk,	1	1½ "	146 15
C. B. Rennie	"	" 1	11 "	1,096 15
Hamilton:				
W. B. Drysdale	Caretaker,	1	12	1,200 00
London:				
W. E. Onion	Clerk,	1	12 "	1,200 00
J. E. Brooks	Clerk Typist,	" 2	10¼ "	649 04

Main Office and Branches—Continued

Ontario Government Employment Offices—Continued

Contingencies—Continued

Temporary Services—Continued.

Name	Position	Group	Months		Amount
North Bay:					
J. W. Butler	Clerk,	Group 2	3 months		243 75
S. McGuire	Clerk Stenographer,	" 2	6½ "		441 59
I. Nelson	" "	" 2	3 "		208 90
Oshawa:					
D. M. Douglas	Clerk,	" 1	12 "		1,200 00
Ottawa—Men's Division:					
A. L. Greene	Clerk,	" 1	12 "		1,200 00
Ottawa—Women's Division:					
E. K. McGiffen	Clerk,	2	12		975 00
Sault Ste. Marie:					
A. Fisher	Clerk,	" 1	2 "		200 01
M. I. Routledge	Clerk Stenographer,	" 2	5¾ "		396 64
M. E. Gaffney	Clerk Typist,	" 2	7 "		432 70
St. Catharines:					
A. N. Cheshire	Clerk Stenographer,	" 2	4		267 07
St. Thomas:					
H. Price	Clerk Stenographer,	" 2	12 "	825 00	
		Less Leave of Absence		15 86	809 14
Stratford:					
F. M. Higgins	Superintendent,	" 3	12 "		1,500 00
M. I. Perry	Clerk Stenographer,	" 2	12 "		825 00
J. Gibson	Clerk,	" 1	1 "		100 00
Toronto Veterans':					
Col. W. Rhoades	Director		1 "		250 00
P. S. Robinson	Clerk,	Group 1	1 "		100 00
Toronto—Women's Division:					
C. Houston	Clerk,	" 2	½ "		40 62
E. C. Kennedy	Filing Clerk,	" 1	12 "		900 00
M. Salyerds	Clerk,	" 2	12 "		975 00
Toronto—Men's Division:					
C. H. Biscoe	Clerk,	" 1	12 "		1,599 96
J. F. Bray	"	" 1	12 "		1,200 00
A. L. Dann	Scout		12 "		1,599 96
A. C. Fenning	Clerk,	" 1	12 "		1,200 00
G. Harrington	Telephone Operator,	" 1	12 "		975 00
J. E. Kennedy	Clerk,	" 1	12 "		1,200 00
P. Lanchbury	"	" 1	8½ "		842 30
J. Laraway	Clerk Stenographer,	" 2	2 "		137 50
P. MacKellar	Clerk,	" 1	12 "		1,200 00
M. J. Murphy	"	1	3½ "		369 23
New Toronto:					
G. W. Janes	Clerk,	2	12 "		975 00
H. P. Mills	"	" 2	12 "		975 00
Windsor:					
E. O'Donoghue	Clerk Stenographer		12 "	825 00	
		Less Leave of Absence		15 86	809 14

Travelling Expenses, $1,013.76.

R. Davids, .70; W. C. Ferris, 186.96; H. C. Hudson, 826.10 ..... 1,013 76

Branches, $52,505.50.

Arden, 624.50; Belleville, 698.28; Brantford, 1,257.99; Chatham, 779.07; Cobalt, 389.34; Fort Frances, 892.05; Fort William, 1,303.34; Guelph, 651.57; Hamilton, 3,182.17; Kaladar-Maberley, 166.46; Kingston, 583.16; Kitchener, 1,282.32; London, 1,576.29; New Toronto, 1,532.49; Niagara Falls, 1,178.43; North Bay, 1,472.38; Oshawa, 1,032.13; Ottawa, Women, 1,153.56; Ottawa, Men, 3,661.78; Pembroke, 861.31; Peterborough, 792.11; Port Arthur, 1,259.96; Sarnia, 981.35; Sharbot Lake, 186.12; Sault Ste. Marie, 114.16; St. Catharines, 1,159.00; St. Thomas, 467.01; Stratford, 804.37; Sudbury, 1,188.69; Timmins, 1,114.19; Toronto, Head Office, 777.11; Toronto, Men, 11,657.51; Toronto, Women, 4,937.11; Toronto, Eglinton, 5.00; Toronto, Veterans', 36.12; Windsor, 2,747.07 ..... 52,505 50

Total	219,360 52
Less Dominion Government subventions	66,618 34
Ontario Government Employment Offices	$152,742 18

Main Office and Branches—Continued

ADMINISTRATION OF THE MINIMUM WAGE ACT

Salaries ($3,400.00)

R. Mearns	Clerk,	Group 1	12 months	1,400 00
M. R. Heakes	"	" 2	12 "	1,200 00
C. Trewin	Clerk Stenographer,	" 1	8 "	800 00

Administration of the Act ($12,186.69)

Temporary Services, $553.85.

Beatrice M. Sauriol	Senior Clerk Stenographer	5½ "	553 85

Allowances to Members of the Board, $10,248.41.

H. G. Fester, 5,470.00; J. W. MacMillan, 1,410.93; R. A. Staples, 2,010.00; M. Stephen, 1,357.48 .... 10,248 41

Travelling Expenses, $864.33.

H. G. Fester, 538.96; J. W. MacMillan, 88.62; R. A. Staples, 211.45; M. Stephen, 25.30 .... 864 33

Miscellaneous, $520.10.

W. D. Henry, legal services, 10.25; King's Printer, 299.79; M. Lancaster, legal services, 20.00; Mail and Empire, advertising, 16.80; B. Mullen, reporting, etc., 19.40; J. A. Ritchie, legal services, 24.00; M. Stephen, meals at C.N.E., etc., 12.44; Taylor Typewriter Co., repairs, etc., 17.50; United Typewriter Co., Ltd., inspections, 33.07; N. M. Wilson, legal services, 10.00. Sundries—car tickets, 3.00; newspapers and periodicals, 6.00; telegrams, 8.26; petty disbursements, 39.59 .... 520 10

Minimum Wage Board $15,586 69

Main Office and Branches 319,915.57

STATUTORY

Salaries not otherwise provided for (see page 12) 100 00

UNEMPLOYMENT RELIEF

(21 Geo. V, Chap. 4)

Administration ($5,721.81)

Temporary Services, $3,842.29.

T. M. Birkett	Inspector	6 months	1,249 98
H. L. Grasswell	"	5⅔ "	859 62
Jas. L. Malcolm	"	1½ "	225 00
J. D. Kneitl	Accounts Clerk	3 1/6 "	315 38
T. Cooper	Clerk Stenographer	2 "	137 51
M. Devlin	" "	⅔ "	42 30
E. M. Ellis	" "	6 "	600 00
N. Thane	" "	6 "	412 50

Travelling Expenses, $2,509.35.

J. Allan, 43.00; T. M. Birkett, 1,556.17; W. M. Clendening, 64.82; J. A. Ellis, 169.55; H. L. Grasswell, 500.53; accountable, 100.00; J. L. Malcolm, 32.18; W. A. Train, 43.10 .... 2,509 35

Miscellaneous, $305.69.

King's Printer, 255.10; telegrams, 50.59 .... 305 69

Total	6,657 33
Less refund Dominion Government, proportion T. M. Birkett's salary and expenses	935 52
	5,721 81

Statutory—Continued

UNEMPLOYMENT RELIEF

(21 Geo. V, Chap. 4)

($5,796,137.13)

	Direct Relief	Relief Works
Cities:		
Belleville	19,141 86	31,435 81
Brantford	103,879 18	113,674 88
Chatham	19,258 63	28,624 27
East Windsor	198,136 46	....
Fort William	36,177 93	125,000 00
Galt	62,736 32	12,083 76
Guelph	22,570 93	74,926 87
Hamilton	499,434 05	906,009 47
Hamilton (Mountain Hospital)	....	50,000 00
Kingston	134,104 96	50,000 00
Kitchener	62,496 79	100,000 00
London	136,465 31	250,000 00
Niagara Falls	83,698 29	91,995 34
North Bay	47,772 79	33,285 00
Oshawa	67,481 73	143,091 26
Ottawa	211,719 61	330,550 00
Owen Sound	15,982 23	30,000 00
Peterborough	42,635 09	49,966 89
Port Arthur	41,607 05	....
St. Catharines	64,795 19	45,000 00
St. Thomas	18,266 57	31,747 86
Sarnia	19,380 96	75,000 00
Sault Ste. Marie	34,218 11	886 24
Stratford	20,586 78	45,000 00
Sudbury	61,467 54	125,000 00
Toronto	1,186,224 13	1,056,741 66
Welland	25,757 97	44,287 76
Windsor	343,746 09	....
Woodstock	13,072 05	40,000 00
Towns:		
Alexandria	1,888 11	5,000 00
Almonte	282 49	4,982 94
Amherstburg	1,637 27	....
Arnprior	3,812 80	12,500 00
Aurora	130 12	7,500 00
Aylmer	1,550 05	....
Barrie	2,248 78	14,462 53
Blenheim	1,785 43	....
Blind River	1,364 25	....
Bowmanville	2,982 12	1,945 35
Bracebridge	835 33	1,868 64
Brampton	2,851 68	11,752 42
Bridgeburg	1,558 16	669 48
Brockville	17,662 33	20,000 00
Burlington	649 19	7,500 00
Cache Bay	479 47	788 75
Campbellford	938 87	1,745 65
Capreol	573 02	266 12
Carleton Place	191 30	15,000 00
Cobalt	....	4,000 00
Cobourg	3,916 83	6,920 22
Cochrane	3,260 99	12,428 42
Collingwood	6,582 82	25,000 00
Cornwall	6,776 55	30,000 00
Deseronto	280 79	2,468 72
Dresden	479 99	....
Dundas	3,113 20	25,000 00
Dunnville	899 75	....
Eastview	9,113 25	19,397 50
Elmira	1,298 46	3,500 00

	Direct Relief	Relief Works
Towns:		
Essex	1,773 76	1,504 73
Fort Erie	14,539 34	10,000 00
Fort Frances	6,110 68	10,893 17
Gananoque	3,886 43	10,000 00
Georgetown	804 78	....
Goderich	986 12	7,500 00
Gore Bay	....	499 39
Gravenhurst	1,350 83	10,000 00
Grimsby	1,783 24	....
Haileybury	....	10,000 00
Hanover	....	7,500 00
Hawkesbury	11,196 87	13,193 26
Hearst	....	100 00
Hespeler	1,730 34	7,486 15
Huntsville	8,373 06	17,500 00
Ingersoll	3,821 13	10,000 00
Kapuskasing	6,782 67	....
Keewatin	....	1,000 00
Kenora	600 77	5,413 74
Kincardine	1,145 36	....
Kingsville	273 73	....
LaSalle	439 72	....
Latchford	....	459 43
Leamington	3,748 03	790 71
Leaside	2,299 62	....
Lindsay	8,487 25	11,257 80
Meaford	3,786 68	2,500 00
Merritton	1,964 53	7,500 00
Midland	83,739 07	35,000 00
Milton	2,315 28	....
Mimico	35,978 15	60,000 00
Mitchell	517 57	....
Mount Forest	93 05	....
Napanee	2,645 14	2,969 41
New Liskeard	601 43	5,000 00
Newmarket	2,468 15	8,000 00
New Toronto	59,948 24	60,000 00
Niagara	246 84	2,000 00
Oakville	3,886 42	7,500 00
Orillia	56,844 71	24,995 78
Palmerston	370 10	2,474 85
Paris	2,106 94	5,000 00
Parkhill	156 26	....
Parry Sound	2,921 95	2,500 00
Pembroke	5,755 52	30,000 00
Penetanguishene	8,780 46	18,000 00
Perth	668 80	....
Petrolia	1,427 89	1,574 34
Picton	793 32	4,998 70
Port Colborne	9,811 05	4,022 71
Port Hope	1,944 66	5,000 00
Prescott	7,089 20	5,000 00
Preston	10,074 74	15,000 00
Rainy River	843 56	....
Renfrew	753 95	14,107 99
Ridgetown	866 29	434 73
Riverside	29,008 24	37,913 02
Rockland	15,308 29	10,850 00
St. Mary's	238 26	2,618 49
Sandwich	37,853 54	2,253 81
Simcoe	....	5,792 78
Sioux Lookout	16,326 39	3,999 00

Statutory—Continued

UNEMPLOYMENT RELIEF—Continued

	Direct Relief	Relief Works
Towns:		
Smith's Falls	8,054 74	20,000 00
Southampton	....	4,000 00
Strathroy	2,061 22	2,246 68
Sturgeon Falls	22,424 69	65,720 00
Tecumseh	21,130 00	....
Thessalon	370 30	....
Thorold	4,051 79	22,807 43
Tilbury	1,784 05	10,000 00
Tillsonburg	1,247 18	....
Timmins	25,875 89	20,000 00
Trenton	1,298 73	14,737 75
Walkerton	1,297 39	880 15
Walkerville	76,265 17	....
Wallaceburg	1,311 57	1,907 90
Waterloo	7,417 01	24,999 99
Weston	4,002 35	2,500 00
Whitby	2,292 05	2,500 00
Wingham	413 74	2,500 00
Villages:		
Acton	1,355 44	....
Arthur	....	2,500 00
Bancroft	436 26	....
Beamsville	317 37	....
Bobcaygeon	....	1,250 00
Bolton	37 45	....
Bradford	537 74	....
Braeside	396 87	....
Brighton	....	1,750 00
Burk's Falls	105 39	350 00
Caledonia	371 14	....
Cardinal	....	750 00
Casselman	980 22	2,500 00
Chesterville	1,015 84	....
Chippawa	1,334 87	668 40
Cobden	64 01	....
Coldwater	102 40	2,000 00
Crystal Beach	491 91	....
Elora	256 69	....
Fenelon Falls	....	2,064 26
Fergus	1,936 49	25,000 00
Finch	10 33	....
Fonthill	214 39	....
Forest Hill	4,567 01	....
Hastings	68 04	....
Havelock	672 82	1,419 93
Humberstone	1,682 63	849 83
Kemptville	352 72	....
Killaloe Station	....	112 16
Lakefield	....	2,433 59
Lancaster	431 29	....
Long Branch	4,622 34	3,750 00
L'Orignal	197 16	....
Lucan	90 85	....
Magnetawan	....	1,000 00
Markdale	....	2,500 00
Marmora	....	5,375 00
Maxville	215 08	....
Newcastle	56 25	....
New Hamburg	....	1,164 01
Norwich	16 12	....
Norwood	359 39	....
Omemee	617 53	....
Point Edward	794 99	1,577 61
Port Credit	235 55	4,000 00

	Direct Relief	Relief Works
Villages:		
Port Dalhousie	2,681 04	5,000 00
Port Dover	....	690 05
Port Elgin	17 73	1,665 59
Portsmouth	131 85	....
Rockcliffe Park	39 85	....
Stoney Creek	232 54	....
Sundridge	335 42	....
Swansea	1,368 72	7,500 00
Thedford	....	200 00
Tweed	....	6,374 94
Victoria Harbour	202 37	2,000 00
Waterford	90 89	1,250 00
Wellington	514 95	....
Winchester	130 88	....
Townships:		
Asphodel	47 13	....
Atwood	15 79	....
Bangor, Wicklow and McClure	107 63	....
Barton	8,465 50	....
Belmont and Methuen	80 43	....
Bertie	1,325 62	....
Beverly	246 04	....
Bexley	499 83	2,201 07
Binbrook	19 07	....
Blandford	....	834 43
Blenheim	123 06	....
Brantford	4,233 39	1,050 55
Burleigh and Anstruther	64 88	....
Caldwell	572 60	....
Cambridge	480 59	....
Cardiff	16 12	2,999 81
Chandos	130 02	....
Chapleau	1,139 30	....
Chapple	204 54	....
Charlottenburgh	711 06	....
Clarence (for Police Village of Bourget)	2,889 55	2,500 00
Clarence (for Police Village of Clarence Creek)	259 24	5,000 00
Clinton	1,126 82	....
Colchester, North	124 60	....
Cornwall	1,723 50	2,500 00
Crowland	6,510 71	35,000 00
Dereham	210 16	....
Dilke	10 00	....
Douro	96 25	....
Dummer	72 16	....
Dungannon	111 07	....
Dysart	....	29,899 95
Elizabethtown	180 49	....
Emily	29 02	....
Emo	234 23	....
Eramosa	299 27	....
Etobicoke	12,986 26	25,000 00
Faraday	185 56	....
Finch	149 37	....
Fitzroy	226 78	....
Flamboro, East	1,470 50	....
Foley	120 15	....

Statutory—Continued

UNEMPLOYMENT RELIEF—Continued

	Direct Relief	Relief Works
Townships:		
Fredericksburg	819 59	....
Galway and Cavendish	42 36	1,995 66
Glamorgan	....	2,993 84
Gloucester (for Police Village of Overbrook)	440 89	15,000 00
Goulburn	8 51	....
Grantham	6,113 49	4,268 39
Grimsby, North	624 32	....
Guelph	1,040 07	....
Hagar	61 08	....
Hallowell	317 62	....
Harvey	....	1,000 00
Hillier	76 15	....
Himsworth, North	1,922 08	....
Korah	111 48	....
Lancaster	168 66	....
Leeds and Lansdowne Front	409 67	....
London	658 86	2,000 00
Louth	696 58	....
Lutterworth	....	1,500 00
Matilda	48 64	....
Mayo	172 87	....
McDougall	1,444 09	....
McIrvine	329 46	1,411 57
McMurrich	1,064 88	....
McNab	177 63	....
Minden	....	1,404 08
Monaghan, North	1,465 52	2,000 00
Monck	98 24	....
Monmouth	....	4,402 31
Montague	289 30	....
Monteagle and Herschel	68 78	....
Morley	304 89	....
Morson	37 75	....
Nepean	10,726 95	40,000 00
Niagara	497 07	....
Nichol	74 45	....
Nipigon	648 93	10,000 00
Norwich, South	68 54	....
Orillia	....	2,500 00
Oxford, West	111 65	....
Percy	76 85	....
Plantagenet, N.	662 39	....
Prince	147 54	....
Rama	5,151 70	....
Rayside	261 68	....
Richmond	54 24	....
Roxborough	317 32	....
Russell	303 99	....
Ryerson	44 02	....
Saltfleet	11,790 37	6,400 00
Sandwich East	42,024 66	....
Sandwich West	18,495 68	500 00
Sarnia	1,768 53	....
Scarborough	84,873 51	65,465 84
Shuniah	510 74	....
Snowdon	12 22	3,000 00
Sombra (for Police Village of Sombra)	....	1,701 40
Somerville	610 80	3,747 39

	Direct Relief	Relief Works
Townships:		
Springer	2,622 80	....
Stafford	86 14	....
Stamford	51,658 00	15,000 00
Stanhope	....	1,500 00
Tay	1,181 33	....
Teck	20,041 55	50,000 00
Thorold	3,808 14	1,359 51
Thurlow	487 42	....
Tilbury North	264 40	....
Tilbury West	140 60	....
Tisdale	11,702 54	....
Toronto	974 20	15,000 00
Trafalgar	344 07	901 96
Vaughan	1,109 60	....
Verulam	....	1,000 00
Waterloo	2,213 88	....
Westminster	1,813 53	486 89
Whitby, East	7,967 90	5,853 01
Whitney	198 20	....
Woolwich (for Police Village of St. Jacobs)	....	627 73
York	231,368 39	231,961 85
York, East	77,421 26	83,489 96
York North	54,289 40	20,000 00
Provincial Direct Relief—Unorganized areas in the vicinity of:		
Capreol	72 80	....
Chapleau	2,504 39	....
Chisholm	6,303 45	....
Connaught Station	200 00	....
Foleyet	1,993 86	....
French River	200 00	....
Gogama	2,746 09	....
Hearst	199 90	....
Henwood	940 95	....
Nakina	500 00	....
Pickerel River	697 96	....
Rainy River	608 85	....
Sault Ste. Marie	1,315 61	....
Spragge	1,299 92	....
Sudbury	480 18	....
Wabigoon	21 80	....
Wallbridge	2,984 99	....
Miscellaneous:		
Brant Sanatorium, Brantford	....	5,124 10
Freeport Sanitarium, Kitchener	....	35,000 00
Haileybury Sanitorium	....	37,450 00
Mountain Sanitarium, Hamilton	....	105,000 00
Queen Alexandra Sanitarium, London	....	98,728 34
National Sanitorium Association	....	113,065 47

Statutory—Continued

UNEMPLOYMENT RELIEF—Continued

	Direct Relief	Relief Works			
Miscellaneous:			Direct Relief...	....	5,119,960 73
RoyalOttawaSanitarium, Ottawa	....	40,250 00	Relief Works...	....	6,063,678 18
Navy League of Canada.......	9,235 96	....	Less:		11,183,638 91
			Dominion Government refunds...	5,384,217 95	....
	5,119,960 73	6,063,678 18	Dominion Government refunds (1931).........	3,283 83	5,387,501 78
				....	5,796,137 13

Removing Fire Hazards about Settlements along Roads and Trails, etc. ($55,270.81)

Pay lists, wages of men.. 94,138 47

Travelling Expenses, $1,520.35.

L. Acheson, 134.00; H. S. Anderson, 183.75; F. Belmore, 24.60; R. H. Bliss, 11.80; A. C. Bouchey, 13.95; W. Cleaveley, 26.25; W. D. Cram, 66.15; N. A. Cross, 38.55; W. H. Fayle, 24.50; J. A. Gillespie, 47.44; F. Hamilton, 35.40; M. H. Hearn, 54.72; A. Holinshead, 40.25; H. A. Hooper, 52.16; D. J. Kennedy, 19.00; C. W. Macdonald, 5.20; V. Mawn, 36.90; Thos. McCormick, 5.37; J. A. Nelson, 28.95; M. Patterson, 7.10; F. R. Parmeter, 5.95; E. E. Potter, 8.25; V. H. Prewer, 161.79; M. Rabbits, 82.61; Jas. Ruxton, 197.60; J. H. Strain, 83.85; L. Swardflager, 16.65; A. G. Taylor, 91.31; M. E. Walker, 16.30...................... 1,520 35

Camp Supplies, Provisions, etc., $14,376.87.

J. Boeckler, 163.19; Barnes & Oliver, 11.25; Beauchesne Bros., 183.96; A. Beauparlant, 378.86; Mrs. A. Bourgeois, 34.50; E. Bliss, 11.85; Blind River Garage, 207.87; I. B. Bradley, 77.22; F. Y. W. Brathwaite, 120.89; Canadian Oil Co.'s, Ltd., 81.28; M. S. Campbell, 18.80; Carpenter-Hixon Co., Ltd., 151.14; Cascade Laundry, Ltd., 12.00; A. Chenier, 52.31; H. B. Christelaw, 429.49; Cochrane-Dunlop Hardware, Ltd., 106.62; D. Connelly, 405.22; Coulter's Pharmacy, 15.30; D. Denault, 24.40; Dominion Stores, Ltd., 69.29; J. L. Driver, 14.10; Dunn Hardware Co., Ltd., 36.70; Durrance Bros. & Co., 23.94; J. East Co., Ltd., 76.79; Fairway Stores, 47.18; Falcon Oils, Ltd., 25.92; R. Foster, 266.22; S. A. Foster, 22.08; Fowler Hardware Co., Ltd., 89.40; D. Giroux, 18.60; N. G. Gough, 41.93; J. O. Gough, 190.08; J. A. Hawkins, 246.34; Hesson Lumber Co., Ltd., 15.00; Hose Hardware Co., 119.56; Hudson's Bay Co., 646.03; Imperial Oil, Ltd., 184.35; Keewatin Lumber Co., Ltd., 37.46; Keyes Hardware, Ltd., 119.53; L. Laderoute, 55.52; J. A. Lapalme, 52.06; O. Larocque & Sons, 145.27; Lee Bros., 23.80; Lynch Auto Sales Co., Ltd., 169.83; A. A. J. MacDonald, 127.20; Marine Laundry, Ltd., 44.95; Marshall Motor Car Co., Ltd., 27.80; Marshall-Ecclestone, Ltd., 73.80; McColl-Frontenac Oil Co., Ltd., 136.50; S. Mitchell, 124.06; Monarch Oil Co., Ltd., 270.30; W. L. Morrisey, 128.98; National Grocers, Co., Ltd., 215.96; Neale & Heath, 359.63; Nipissing Laundry Co., Ltd., 33.60; Northern Canada Supply Co., Ltd., 34.76; J. Parco & Co., 162.23; C. R. Parker, 2,100.25; P. Perlin, 40.70; Porter & Co., 177.43; O. E. Post, 50.59; Pratt & Shanacy, 12.80; Provencher Bros., 114.27; B. H. Rands, 34.00; J. Robert Co., 139.39; T. R. Robertson, 123.62; Geo. Roque, 21.60; Sadowski & Co., 692.33; A. Shaw, 1,177.03; Shevlin-Clarke Co., Ltd., 54.53; Sudbury Steam Laundry, 16.00; Soo Garage, 41.38; Star Grocery, 163.74; Sullivan's Grocery, 134.82; Taylor's Grocery, 44.81; F. Tiplady, 206.96; Victoria Bakery, 25.12; Watson & Lloyd, 474.93; Western Oil Co., Ltd., 23.92; White Drug Co., 12.75; Williams Hardware Co., 328.91; Wells Hardware Co., 17.70; Wolfe & Collins, Ltd., 17.20; A. R. Wood, 778.03; Yuill's Auto Electric Service, 14.95. Sundries—freight, 94.19; express, 39.12; telegrams, 4.36; cartage and livery, 405.56; postage, 6.19; petty disbursements, 170.09.. 14,722 17

Less Scott Bros., damage to truck..........	10 00		
Department Northern Development, meals supplied men................	335 30		
		345 30	
			14,376 87
			110,035 69
Less refunded by Dominion Government..........................			54,764 88
			55,270 81

Statutory—Continued

Actinolite—Perth Project
($600,000.00)

(For details see page L 45 and 54, Highways Department)	1,000,000 00	
Less Dominion Government refund	400,000 00	
		600,000 00

Trans-Canada Highway
($3,047,242.15)

(For details see page H 44, Department of Northern Development)	6,070,193 61	
Less Dominion Government refund	3,022,951 46	
		3,047,242 15

General Work, Northern Development Department
($2,811,103.02)

(For details see page H 54, Department of Northern Development	4,733,748 90	
Less Dominion Government refund	1,922,645 88	
		2,811,103 02

Construction of Ivanhoe Dam
($17,873.12)

Acme Timber Co. (for details see page H 80 Department of Northern Development)	35,746 23	
Less Dominion Government refund	17,873 11	
		17,873 12
Statutory	**$12,333,448.04**	

SPECIAL WARRANTS

Unemployment Relief

Administration ($17,811.40)

Temporary Services, $9,185.09.

Name	Position	Period	Amount
D. B. Harkness	Special Investigator	2 months	500 00
T. M. Birkett	Inspector	6 "	1,249 98
Neil C. Campbell	"	3½ "	346 15
M. S. Clapp	"	1⅔ "	173 08
H. L. Grasswell	"	6 "	900 00
W. J. Laforest	"	6 "	900 00
Jas. L. Malcolm	"	4⅔ "	703 84
W. Martin	"	4½ "	442 30
Geo. J. McArthur	"	4 "	411 54
Jas. McCluskey	"	⅔ "	65 39
H. J. McNenly	"	1 ⅔ "	173 08
J. A. Nelson	"	1 1/6 "	119 23
W. A. Robertson	"	1 ⅔ "	173 08
L. Spence	"	1 ⅔ "	173 08
F. H. Wolfe	"	⅓ "	19 23
Albert Philion	Assistant Inspector	3½ "	194 23
W. A. Webster	" "	3½ "	173 08
J. D. Kneitl	Accounts Clerk	6 "	600 00
R. L. Clarke	" "	1½ "	150 00
E. A. Torrance	" "	⅔ "	65 39
M. Devlin	Clerk Stenographer	6½ "	446 88
E. M. Ellis	" "	6 "	600 00
C. Stewart	" "	3¾ "	193 03
N. Thane	" "	6 "	412 50

Extra Services, $700.00.

A. Becker, 100.00; W. J. Crawford, 200.00; J. J. Hoolihan, 200.00; G. D. Kennedy, 200.00 .... 700 00

Travelling Expenses and Disbursements, $6,693.49.

F. Anderson, 14.00; L. M. Balmer, 48.00; H. S. Beattie, 2.07; T. M. Birkett, 163.11; J. Brown, 113.90; Neil Campbell, 203.64; accountable, 200.00; W. S. Carruthers, 26.65; Chairman, Essex Border Relief Board, accountable, 300.00; J. E. Davidson, 120.13; E. M. Ellis, 53.70; J. A. Ellis, 112.95; Jas. Forbes, 5.17; Hector Goulard, 44.03; H. L. Grasswell, 552.55; Rev. Jos. E. Gravelle, 13.34; A. Grigg, 60.84; E. G. Hagen, 174.90; R. B. Harkness, 54.55; Rev. A. Jackson, 23.10; M. Johnston, 46.60; Geo. D. Kennedy, 105.26; W. J. Laforest

Special Warrants—Continued

Unemployment Relief—Continued

Administration—Continued

Travelling Expenses and Disbursements—Continued.

716.15; accountable, 300.00; J. A. Lapalme, 5.70; J. S. Lowe, 28.95; J. L. Malcolm, 622.89; R. MacKenzie, 485.00; Wm. Martin, 763.19; accountable, 50.00; Geo. J. McArthur, 163.28; J. R. McCracken, 89.74; J. McIntosh, 19.15; H. J. McNenly, 3.00; J. A. Nelson, accountable, 100.00; E. W. Rasene, 3.75; A. M. Robertson, 198.55; accountable, 100.00; L. Spence, 163.40; accountable, 100.00; J. C. Sylvain, 1.10; C. Tackaberry, 325.05; T. H. Wolfe, 216.10........ 6,893 49

Less refund accountable, 1931, T. M. Birkett.......... 200 00

6,693 49

Miscellaneaus ($1,232.82)

King's Printer, 1,133.12; telegrams, 99.70.................................. 1,232 82

SPECIAL WARRANTS

Unemployment Relief

($1,689,187.03)

	Direct Relief		Direct Relief
Cities:		Towns:	
Belleville	4,812 78	Carleton Place	257 86
Brantford	55,209 49	Chelmsford	5,053 54
Chatham	8,245 09	Cochrane	1,967 00
East Windsor	133,539 87	Cornwall	151 00
Fort William	18,557 36	Dundas	800 30
Galt	11,718 50	Dunnville	320 93
Guelph	8,868 92	Durham	20 28
Hamilton	264,151 96	Eastview	1,419 55
Kingston	52,916 16	Elmira	967 10
Kitchener	44,883 93	Fort Erie	4,398 31
London	63,305 07	Fort Frances	2,896 00
Niagara Falls	41,314 01	Georgetown	168 62
North Bay	47,866 51	Goderich	9 50
Oshawa	55,463 80	Gravenhurst	404 31
Ottawa	85,921 22	Haileybury	1,020 68
Owen Sound	6,164 20	Hawkesbury	9,166 09
Peterborough	41,540 73	Hespeler	30 65
Port Arthur	20,429 29	Huntsville	4,806 16
St. Catharines	30,252 81	Ingersoll	2,115 90
St. Thomas	7,983 17	Kapuskasing	2,761 28
Sarnia	7,348 63	Kenora	1,316 64
Sault Ste. Marie	21,879 57	Kincardine	138 96
Stratford	18,984 42	Kingsville	219 58
Sudbury	76,868 40	La Salle	56 43
Sudbury (Settlers' Account)	3,305 74	Leamington	157 09
Toronto	485,653 39	Leaside	2,153 20
Welland	8,593 86	Lindsay	2,080 86
Windsor	165,968 20	Massey	747 65
Woodstock	7,508 47	Meaford	595 89
		Merritton	1,164 74
Towns:		Midland	23,442 09
Almonte	199 22	Mimico	38,239 02
Amherstburg	626 11	New Toronto	28,873 35
Arnprior	2,355 12	Niagara	51 08
Aylmer	90 54	Orillia	14,179 93
Barrie	708 86	Paris	228 32
Blenheim	253 28	Parkhill	37 19
Blind River	11,733 52	Parry Sound	457 45
Bowmanville	250 03	Penetanguishene	4,386 16
Bracebridge	989 11	Perth	428 47
Brampton	205 92	Petrolia	411 40
Brockville	15,146 86	Port Colborne	8,103 37
Bruce Mines	99 63	Port Hope	475 75
Cache Bay	1,482 05	Prescott	3,443 36
Capreol	1,217 94	Preston	3,316 59

Special Warrants—Continued

Unemployment Relief—Continued

	Direct Relief
Towns:	
Rainy River	391 53
Riverside	13,950 54
Rockland	11,328 72
Sandwich	19,689 86
Sioux Lookout	16,395 55
Smith's Falls	4,394 54
Sturgeon Falls	19,571 87
Tecumseh	11,507 39
Thessalon	863 07
Thorold	1,465 52
Tilbury	806 60
Timmins	14,596 53
Trenton	2,144 39
Walkerton	93 85
Walkerville	27,584 72
Wallaceburg	254 48
Waterloo	3,373 08
Webbwood	475 91
Weston	1,231 60
Whitby	1,620 07
Villages:	
Acton	82 71
Bancroft	353 04
Braeside	120 89
Casselman	391 54
Chesterville	182 61
Chippawa	853 40
Cobden	40 15
Fergus	162 63
Humberstone	1,949 94
Lakefield	1,652 44
Long Branch	2,342 04
L'Orignal	273 55
Maxville	31 09
Port Credit	25 08
Port Dalhousie	265 04
Swansea	223 37
Victoria Harbour	126 42
Townships:	
Baldwin	117 52
Balfour	1,422 02
Barton	1,255 89
Beverly	32 07
Bexley	181 52
Blezard	350 77
Brantford	633 23
Bucke	921 83
Caldwell	244 26
Cambridge	85 20
Camden	32 78
Casimer, Jennings and Appleby	374 20
Chandos	13 24
Chapleau	2,090 28
Charlottenburg	70 94
Clinton	83 25
Cornwall	135 72
Cosby and Mason	15 89
Crowland	4,636 67
Dereham	17 21
Dowling	218 40
Drury, Denison and Graham	290 40
Dungannon	74 00
Townships:	
Elizabethtown	18 76
Emily	13 33
Eramosa	94 63
Etobicoke	9,062 49
Fauquier	283 19
Field	2,726 32
Fitzroy	130 41
Flamboro, East	365 82
Foley	196 74
Freeman	2,143 37
Glackmeyer	898 18
Gloucester	12 89
Grantham	1,628 26
Guelph	215 85
Hallowell	45 75
Hanmer	212 12
Lancaster	37 03
London	332 57
Marmora and Lake	67 01
Martland	57 79
Matilda	46 15
McDougall	25 48
McIrvine	444 95
McKim	269 15
McMurrich	263 71
McNab	323 90
Minden	72 18
Minto	25 86
Monaghan, North	102 66
Montague	41 79
Morson	28 20
Neelon and Garson	2,062 95
Nepean	1,478 25
Norwich, South	28 33
Orillia	232 62
Oxford, West	84 28
Prince	98 03
Rama	519 22
Rayside	1,257 14
Richmond	3 86
Russell	20 61
Saltfleet	1,735 65
Sandwich, East	20,101 54
Sandwich, West	10,623 65
Scarborough	50,820 59
Shackleton and Machin	109 24
Shuniah	423 22
Somerville	837 49
Springer	202 88
Stamford	34,157 15
Tay	182 58
Teck	7,744 49
Thorold	1,680 21
Tilbury North	109 29
Tisdale	3,408 49
Toronto	681 23
Trafalgar	102 82
Vaughan	183 45
Whitby, East	5,469 08
Widdifield	240 37
York	137,870 05
York, East	54,614 30
York, North	19,570 46

Special Warrants—Continued

Unemployment Relief—Continued

	Direct Relief
Provincial Direct Relief:	
Unorganized Areas, in the vicinity of:	
Ardberg	998 72
Blind River	2,457 78
Brent	203 69
Bruce Mines	1,356 69
Burk's Falls	60 88
Canoe Lake	24 22
Capreol	1,977 55
Chapleau	3,891 46
Chisholm	4,437 65
Cochrane, North	16,974 76
Cochrane, South	711 84
Conger	289 58
Connaught Station	2,813 71
Corbeil	189 60
Espanola	6,975 27
Foleyet	1,392 92
French River	1,250 91
Gogama	4,665 02
Haliburton	269 72
Hearst	28,773 52
Henry	3,285 48
Henwood	499 13
Hudson	91 29
Kapuskasing	2,425 81
Kenora	611 86
Levack Mines	1,996 26
Markstay	9,031 14
Massey	1,318 88

	Direct Relief
Provincial Relief:	
Maynooth	417 43
Muskoka	24 49
Nakina	207 22
Nipissing	4,512 39
Normand and Wismer	2,633 57
Osaquan	253 75
Pickerel River	500 47
Port Arthur	39 81
Rainy River	957 93
River Valley	3,099 78
Sault Ste. Marie	3,626 58
Shining Tree	75 50
Spragge	412 01
Sudbury	20,958 04
Sudbury (Settlers' Account)	2,806 95
Temiskaming	1,372 62
Thessalon	3,121 27
Timmins	398 21
Wallbridge	6,233 38
Whitney	1,597 19
Miscellaneous:	
Navy League of Canada	1,844 74
	2,713,075 15
Less proportion refunded by Dominion Government	1,023,888 12
	1,689,187 03

Ottawa Office of the Provincial Employment Service ($1,200.00)

Laura Chartrand................Clerk, Group 1......................12 months 1,200 00

Hamilton District Trades and Labour Council to Assist in the Convention of the All-Canada Congress of Labour ($500.00)

Hamilton District Trades and Labour Council, grant............................ 500 00

Special Warrants.................................$1,708,698.43

Total	14,362,062 04
Less Salary Assessment	6,275 44
Total Expenditure, Department of Labour	**$14,355,786.60**

SUMMARY OF UNEMPLOYMENT RELIEF

1931-1932

		Total Payments	Payable by Ontario	Payable by Dominion
		$ c.	$ c.	$ c.
ADMINISTRATION:				
Statutory	Page N 14	5,721 81	5,721 81	....
Special Warrant	" N 19	17,811 40	17,811 40	....
		23,533 21	23,533 21	....
DIRECT RELIEF:				
Statutory	Page N 18	$5,119,960 73	$2,559,977 32	$2,559,983 41
Special Warrant	" N 22	2,713,075 15	1,364,710 03	1,348,365 12
		7,833,035 88	3,924,687 35	3,908,348 53
RELIEF WORKS—Statutory:				
Municipal Works and Sanitaria	Page N 18	6,063,678 18	3,032,081 09	3,031,597 09
Removing Fire Hazards about Settlements	" N 18	110,035 69	55,270 81	54,764 88
Actinolite-Perth Highway	" N 19	1,000,000 00	600,000 00	400,000 00
Trans-Canada Highway	" N 19	6,070,193 61	3,047,242 15	3,022,951 46
General Work—Northern Ontario	" N 19	4,733,748 90	2,811,103 02	1,922,645 88
Ivanhoe Dam	" N 19	35,746 23	17,873 12	17,873 11
		18,013,402 61	9,563,570 19	8,449,832 42
Total Disbursements during Year		25,869,971 70	13,511,790 75	12,358,180 95
REPAYMENTS BY DOMINION:				
On account of current year		11,826,341 40	....	11,826,341 40
" " " 1930-31		3,283 83	3,283 83	....
		11,829,625 23	3,283 83	11,826,341 40
Net Disbursements during Year		14,040,346 47	13,508,506 92	531,839 55

	ORDINARY	CAPITAL
	$ c.	$ c.
Administration	23,533 21	....
Direct Relief, payable by Ontario (write off over 5 years)	784,937 47	3,139,749 88
Relief Works, payable by Ontario	....	9,563,570 19
Dominion Government:		
Balance due	....	531,839 55
	808,470 68	13,235,159 62
Less—Dominion Government — Repayment on account 1930-31	....	3,283 83
	808,470 68	13,231,875 79

DEPARTMENT

OF

PUBLIC WELFARE

FISCAL YEAR, 1931-32

TABLE OF CONTENTS

GENERAL INDEX AT BACK OF BOOK

PART O—DEPARTMENT OF PUBLIC WELFARE

Statement of Expenditure Showing Amounts Expended, Unexpended and Overexpended for the Twelve Months Ended October 31st, 1932

Department of Public Welfare	Page	Estimates	Expended			Un-expended	Over-expended	Treasury Board Minute
			Ordinary	Capital	Total Ordinary and Capital			
		$ c.	$ c.	$ c.	$ c.	$ c.	$ c.	$ c.
Main Office:								
Salaries	5	12,600 00	12,400 00	....	12,400 00	200 00	....	....
Contingencies	5	12,000 00	13,214 03	....	13,214 03	....	1,214 03	1,500 00
Expenses of Exhibits	5	1,000 00	999 65	....	999 65	35	....	....
Main Office	..	25,600 00	26,613 68	....	26,613 68	200 35	1,214 03	....
Refuges	5	120,000 00	83,889 45	....	83,889 45	36,110 55	....	....
Orphanages	6	60,000 00	58,693 20	....	58,693 20	1,306 80	....	....
Grants:								
Salvation Army for Prison Gate Work	6	5,500 00	4,000 00	....	4,000 00	1,500 00	....	....
Infants Home and Infirmary	..	500 00	....	....	....	500 00	....	....
Ontario Society for Prevention of Cruelty to Animals	6	2,000 00	1,500 00	....	1,500 00	500 00	....	....
Canadian Girl Guides' Association	6	3,000 00	2,000 00	....	2,000 00	1,000 00	....	....
Boy Scouts' Association	6	3,500 00	2,500 00	....	2,500 00	1,000 00	....	....
Royal Canadian Humane Society Association	6	250 00	250 00	....	250 00	....	....	....
Maintenance, Indigents in Unorganized Territory	6	1,000 00	1,218 00	....	1,218 00	....	218 00	218 00
Soldiers' Aid Commission:								
Grants re Expenses of Soldiers' Aid Commission	6	87,500 00	55,000 00	....	55,000 00	32,500 00	....	....
Assisting re claims for Ex-Service Men	6	5,000 00	136 00	....	136 00	4,864 00	....	....
Grants, Refuges and Orphanages	..	288,250 00	209,186 65	....	209,186 65	79,281 35	218 00	....
Children's Aid Branch:								
Salaries	6	53,625 00	51,565 72	....	51,565 72	2,059 28	....	....
Contingencies	7	10,000 00	8,756 13	....	8,756 13	1,243 87	....	....
Administration of Act, services and expenses	7	91,000 00	85,886 71	....	85,886 71	5,113 29	....	....
Industrial Schools	9	110,000 00	121,127 00	....	121,127 00	....	11,127 00	11,251 50

Grant to Association of Children's Aid Societies	9	1,000 00	1,000 00	....	1,000 00	....	....	....
Children's Aid Branch	..	265,625 00	268,335 56	....	268,335 56	8,416 44	11,127 00	....
Boys' Training School, Bowmanvile:								
Salaries,								
Superintendent	10	4,500 00	4,383 34	....	4,383 34	116 66	....	....
Academic and Vocational	10	11,850 00	13,700 00	....	13,700 00	....	1,850 00	1,950 00
Bursar and Staff	10	3,925 00	3,890 14	....	3,890 14	34 86	....	....
Farm Dir and Assistants	10	5,700 00	7,074 37	....	7,074 37	....	1,374 37	1,375 00
Chef and Assistants	10	3,325 00	3,325 00	....	3,325 00	....	....	75 00
Engineer and Fi emen	10	5,425 00	4,700 00	....	4,700 00	725 00	....	....
Supervisors	10	10,775 00	9,374 92	....	9,374 92	1,400 08	....	....
Expenses	10	55,600 00	44,689 84	....	44,689 84	10,910 16	....	....
Repairs to buildings, te	11	20,000 00	9,786 66	....	9,786 66	10,213 34	....	....
Allowance to Superintendent for use of car	12	200 00	200 00	....	200 00	....	....	....
Gratuities, etc	12	2,500 00	2,040 28	....	2,040 28	459 72	....	....
Assistance to graduates	..	1,000 00	....	....	....	1,000 00	....	....
Boys' Club, Toronto	12	3,500 00	3,499 11	....	3,499 11	89	....	....
	..	128,300 00	106,663 66	....	106,663 66	24,860 71	3,224 37	....
Less Maintenance, Perquisites, etc	12	....	67,783 79	....	67,783 79	67,783 79	....	....
Boys' Training School	..	128,300 00	38,879 87	....	38,879 87	92,644 50	3,224 37	....
Mothers' Allowances Commission:								
Salaries	12	47,550 00	47,550 00	....	47,550 00	....	....	....
Contingencies	13	45,000 00	35,535 00	....	35,535 00	9,465 00	....	....
Allowances	13	2,250,000 00	1,455,102 44	121,165 00	1,576,267 44	673,732 56	....	....
Mothers' Allowances Commission	..	2,342,550 00	1,538,187 44	121,165 00	1,659,352 44	683,197 56	....	....
Old Age Pensions Commission:								
Salaries	14	18,800 00	18,272 51	....	18,272 51	527 49	....	....
Contingencies	14	45,000 00	52,058 24	....	52,058 24	....	7,058 24	28,500 00
Allowances	15	2,500,000 00	2,010,382 57	687,403 17	2,697,785 74	....	197,785 74	2,580,000 00
Old Age Pensions Commission	..	2,563,800 00	2,080,713 32	687,403 17	2,768,116 49	527 49	204,843 98	....
Supply Bill	..	5,614,125 00	4,161,916 52	808,568 17	4,970,484 69	864,267 69	220,627 38	....
Statutory:								
Minister's Salary	16	....	10,000 00	....	10,000 00	....	....	....
Statutory	..	....	10,000 00	....	10,000 00	....	....	....

PART O—DEPARTMENT OF PUBLIC WELFARE—Continued

Statement of Expenditure Showing Amounts Expended, Unexpended and Overexpended for the Twelve Months Ended October 31st, 1932

Department of Public Welfare	Page	Estimates	Expended			Un-expended	Over-expended	Treasury Board Minute
			Ordinary	Capital	Total Ordinary and Capital			
		$ c.	$ c.	$ c.	$ c.	$ c.	$ c.	$ c.
S[illegible]ial W[illegible]:								
[illegible]s of [illegible]ts at [illegible]s.	16	......	6 05	......	6 05	......	......	......
[illegible]e of Patients [illegible]d to Houses of Refuge	16	......	133 00	......	133 00	......	......	......
G[illegible]t to [illegible]ity Welfare Council	16	......	2,000 00	......	2,000 00	......	......	......
" G[illegible]o Society f[illegible]r [illegible]d Children	17	......	8,000 00	......	8,000 00	......	......	......
" Soldiers' Aid Commission	17	......	2,000 00	......	2,000 00	......	......	......
[illegible]s of V[illegible]s re War [illegible]ls	17	......	1,065 00	......	1,065 00	......	......	......
G[illegible]t to [illegible]n [illegible]ncil on Child and Family W[illegible]e	17	......	1,000 00	......	1,000 00	......	......	......
Special Warrants	..	......	14,204 05	......	14,204 05	......	......	......
Total	..	......	4,186,120 57	808,568 17	4,994,688 74	......	......	......
Less Salary Assessment	..	......	5,621 64	......	5,621 64	......	......	......
Department of Public Welfare	..	......	4,180,498 93	......	4,989,067 10	......	......	......

SUMMARY

Department of Public Welfare	[illegible]ry	Capital	Total
	$ c.	$ c.	$ c.
Main Office	26,613 68	......	26,613 68
Grants	209,186 65	......	209,186 65
Children's Aid Branch	268,335 56	......	268,335 56
Boys' Training School, Bowmanville	38,879 87	......	38,879 87
Mothers' Allowances Commission	1,538,187 44	121,165 00	1,659,352 44
Old Age Pensions Commission	2,080,713 32	687,403 17	2,768,116 49
Statutory	10,000 00	......	10,000 00
Special Warrants	14,204 05	......	14,204 05
	4,186,120 57	808,568 17	[illegible]88 74
Deduct—Transferred to Loans and Special Funds (see Part U)	......	808,568 17	808,568 17
Total	4,186,120 57	......	4,186,120 57
Less Salary Assessment	5,621 64	......	5,621 64

DEPARTMENT OF PUBLIC WELFARE

Honourable W. G. Martin........Minister (Statutory)......$10,000.00

MAIN OFFICE

Salaries ($12,400.00)

Milton A. Sorsoleil	Deputy Minister	12 months	4,600 00
W. George Pifher	Secretary to Minister and Departmental Secretary	12 "	2,400 00
John M. McCullough	Accountant	12 "	3,000 00
M. Hutton	Senior Clerk Stenographer	12 "	1,200 00
Elizabeth W. Best	" " "	12 "	1,200 00

Contingencies ($13,214.03)

Temporary Services, $7,727.88.

George C. Clegg	Medical Officer	12 months	3,000 00
Kathleen N. Dale	Clerk Stenographer Group 2	¾ "	52 88
Phyllis Nevison	" " " 2	12 "	825 00
William Rhoades	Director of Veterans Employment Service	11 "	2,750 00
Phillip S. Robinson	Clerk, Group 1	11 "	1,100 00

Travelling Expenses, $1,880.81.

C. H. Buckland, 66.75; C. G. Clegg, 67.61; J. Hannah, 5.64; M. Hutton, 13.60; Honourable W. G. Martin, 925.00; W. G. Pifher, 17.50; W. Rhoades, 346.36; M. A. Sorsoleil, 438.35 .... 1,880 81

Miscellaneous, $3,605.34.

Bell Telephone Co., rentals, 92.95; tolls, 28.71; Canadian Press Clipping Service, clippings, 269.56; Commissioner of Police for Ontario, operating cost of car, 113.25; Dept. of Highways, auto service, 65.15; King's Printer, 2,629.49; McCann & Alexander, typewriter inspection, 18.00; National Stationers, Ltd., printing, 32.00; Ontario School Trustees' and Ratepayers' Association, pictures, 18.00; Province of Ontario Pictures, prints, etc., 37.25. Sundries—cartage, 35.00; car tickets, 15.00; newspapers and periodicals, 53.35; telegrams, 114.53; postage, 60.00; petty disbursements, 23.10 .... 3,605 34

Expenses of Exhibits at Canadian National and Other Exhibitions ($999.65)

Dept. of Highways, truck rental, 3.50; T. Eaton Co., Ltd., books, etc., 4.40; A. J. Evans & Sons, building and painting exhibit, 920.20; A. G. Munroe, expenses, Ottawa exhibit, 23.05; Province of Ontario Pictures, film rental, 6.50; Mrs. W. C. Tilley, services as attendant at C.N.E., 42.00 .... 999 65

Main Office........$26,613.68

GRANTS

Refuges ($83,889.45)

Belleville, Home for the Aged, 353.80; Brantford, The Widows' Home, 157.50; Chatham, Home for the Friendless, 1,023.50; Cornwall, St. Paul's Home for the Aged, 1,132.50; Dundas, House of Providence, 2,844.60; Guelph, Elliott Home, 777.30; Guelph, House of Providence, 701.90; Haileybury, Misericordia Refuge, 335.55; Hamilton, Aged Women's Home, 1,857.20; Hamilton, Home for Aged and Infirm, 4,576.20; Hamilton, St. Peter's Infirmary, 167.80; Hospital Branch, Dept. of Health, Ontario, 120.80; Kingston, Home for Friendless Women and Infants, 664.60; Kingston, House of Providence, 3,721.00; Kingston, House of Refuge, 610.30; London, House of Providence, 3,928.10; London, McCormack Home for the Aged, 1,445.10; North Bay, House of Refuge, 693.30; Ottawa, Bronson Memorial Home, 206.80; Ottawa, Elizabeth Residence for Elderly Ladies, 742.50; Ottawa, Home for Friendless Women, 1,236.05; Ottawa, May Court Club Convalescent Home, 302.80; Ottawa, Monastery of Our Lady of Charity, 4,892.45; Ottawa, Protestant House for the Aged, 555.60; Ottawa, St. Charles Hospice, 6,153.10; Ottawa, St. Patrick's Asylum, Refuge Branch, 2,587.80; Peterborough, Anson House, 873.20; Peterborough, St. Joseph's House of Providence, 1,561.95; Powasson House of Refuge, 317.80; St. Thomas, Thomas Williams House, 330.00; Sault Ste. Marie, House of Refuge, 2,489.90; Toronto, Aged Men's Home, 970.70; Toronto, Aged Women's Home, 1,828.10 ; Toronto, Church Home for the Aged, 890.10; Toronto, Good Shepherd Female Refuge, 6,036.60; Toronto, Haven and Prison Gate Mission, 1,238.20; Toronto, Hillcrest

Grants—Continued

Refuges—Continued

Convalescent Home, 843.80; Toronto, House of Industry, 3,527.80; Toronto, House of Providence, 10,428.60; Toronto, Humewood House Association, 785.80; Toronto, Industrial Refuge, 3,108.55; Toronto, Jewish Old Folk's Home, 1,519.30; Toronto, Julia Greenshields Home, 855.20; Toronto, Pentecostal Bethel, 150.05; Toronto, Salvation Army Rescue Home, 1,699.20; Toronto, St. Mary's Convalescent Home, 574.15; Toronto, Victor Home for Young Women, 927.60; Windsor, Home for the Friendless, 1,144.70 .... 83,889 45

Orphanages ($58,693.20)

Cobourg, St. Joseph's Orphanage, 643.15; Cornwall, Nazareth, 847.30; Fort William, St. Joseph's, 1,909.85; Hamilton, Boys' Home, 689.65; Hamilton, Girls' Home, 861.65; Hamilton, Home for Friendless and Infants, 1,837.85; Hamilton, St. Mary's Orphan Asylum, 2,360.35; Hamilton, Salvation Army Rescue Home, 796.55; Hearst, St. Joseph's Orphanage, 1,578.50; Kingston, Orphan's Home and Widows' Friend Society, 305.05; Kingston, St. Mary's-on-the-Lake, 1,983.45; Kitchener, Orphanage, 527.65; London, Mount St. Joseph's, 2,777.70; London, Protestant House, 739.15; London, Ronald Gray Memorial Home, 522.15; London, Salvation Army Rescue Home and Children's Shelter, 965.55; Ottawa, Misericordia Refuge and Orphans' Home, 3,184.55; Ottawa, Protestant Children's Village, 666.85; Ottawa, St. Joseph's, 4,954.90; Ottawa, St. Patrick's Infants' Home, 1,049.35; Ottawa, Salvation Army Rescue Home, 1,795.90; Peterborough, St. Vincent's, 563.30; Richmond Hill Loyal True Blue, 2,724.30; St. Agatha, Orphanage, 1,219.30; St. Catharines, Protestant Orphans' Home, 576.00; Sudbury, Orphelinat d'Youville, 1,021.75; Toronto, Boys' Home, 813.50; Toronto, Carmelite Orphanage, 957.10; Toronto, Catholic Welfare Bureau, 2,707.15; Toronto, Infants' Home and Infirmary, 7,073.80; Toronto, Jewish Children's Home, 1,047.05; Toronto, Protestant Children's Home, 4,410.15; Toronto, St. Mary's Infants' Home, 1,820.40; Toronto, Sacred Heart, 1,367.50; Toronto, Working Boys' Home, 1,394.80 .... 58,693 20

Grants ($10,250.00)

Salvation Army for Prison Gate Work, 4,000.00; Society for Prevention of Cruelty to Animals, 1,500.00; Royal Canadian Humane Society, 250.00; Canadian Girl Guides' Association, 2,000.00; Boy Scouts' Association, 2,500.00 .... 10,250 00

To Provide for Maintenance of Indigents from Unorganized Territory ($1,218.00)

North Bay, Home of the Aged, 792.00; Parry Sound, House of Refuge, 426.00 .... 1,218 00

Soldiers' Aid Commission ($55,000.00)

Grant 55,000 00

Assisting in Presentation of Claims for Ex-Service Men ($136.00)

Sundry doctors, fees for medical examinations 136 00

Grants $209,186.65

CHILDREN'S AID BRANCH

Salaries ($51,565.72)

Name	Position	Period		Amount
J. J. Kelso	Superintendent	12	months	4,000 00
J. A. Blakey	Principal Clerk	12	"	2,400 00
Wm. O'Connor	Inspector	12	"	2,400 00
C. H. Buckland	"	12	"	2,400 00
A. E. Boys	Assistant Inspector	12	"	1,800 00
John Longmoor	" "	12	"	1,800 00
L. E. Lowman	" "	12	"	1,600 00
A. A. Rogers	Senior Clerk	12	"	2,000 00
M. B. Finlay	" "	12	"	1,700 00
V. Carscadden	" "	12	"	1,800 00
H. E. MacKenzie	"	12	"	1,800 00
L. McMahon	" "	12	"	1,700 00
H. L. McKay	Clerk, Group 1	12	"	1,600 00
I. Pethick	" " 1	12	"	1,200 00
R. Montgomery	" " 2	12	"	1,200 00

Children's Aid Branch—Continued

Salaries—Continued

Name	Position	Period	Amount
M. E. Hamilton	Clerk, Group 2	12 months	1,200 00
F. Price	" " 2	12 "	1,125 00
L. W. Jinks	" " 2	12 "	1,050 00
F. Lightwood	Senior Clerk Stenographer	12 "	1,500 00
M. E. Case	" " "	⅔ "	71 97
M. Wingate	Clerk Stenographer, Group 1	12 "	1,300 00
J. I. Burden	" " " 1	12 "	1,200 00
S. Christie	" " " 1	12 "	1,200 00
K. Frampton	" " " 1	12 "	1,200 00
V. Taverner	" " " 1	12 "	1,125 00
M. Jeffrey	" " " 1	12 "	1,125 00
M. Dennis	" " " 1	12 "	1,125 00
E. Carr	" " " 1	12 "	1,125 00
I. Griffiths	" " " 1	10½ "	918 75
I. Anderson	Clerk Typist " 1	12 "	1,050 00
E. Montgomery	" " " 1	12 "	1,050 00
M. Little	" " " 1	12 "	975 00
I. Webb	Filing Clerk " 1	12 "	1,050 00
D. Soady	" " " 1	12 "	975 00
R. Wilson	" " " 1	12 "	900 00
A. Paisley	" " " 1	12 "	900 00

Contingencies ($8,756.13)

Temporary Services, $4,993.86.

Name	Position	Period	Amount
H. Carr	Filing Clerk, Group 2	12 months	750 00
A. C. Cross	Clerk " 1	12 "	1,200 00
J. Ferris	Filing Clerk " 2	12 "	750 00
L. Martin	Clerk Stenographer " 1	1⅔ "	97 84
E. W. Porteous	" " " 2	11 "	753 70
S. T. Simpson	Assistant Inspector	12 months 1,500 00	
	Less leave of absence	57 68	1,442 32

Travelling Expenses, $862.17.

C. H. Buckland, 8.70; J. J. Kelso, 17.25; W. O'Connor, 833.22; Dr. S. T. Simpson, 3.00 .... 862 17

Car Allowances, $800.00.

A. E. Boys, 400.00; L. E. Lowman, 400.00 .... 800 00

Miscellaneous, $2,100.10.

King's Printer, 1,405.07; United Typewriter Co., Ltd., inspections, etc., 345.37. Sundries—car tickets, 270.00; customs, 12.00; express, 3.25; newspapers and periodicals, 19.50; telegrams, 13.41; petty disbursements, 31.50 .... 2,100 10

Enforcement of The Children's Protection Act of Ontario and The Children of Unmarried Parents Act, 1921 ($85,886.71)

Salaries ($38,483.34)

Name	Position	Period	Amount
Orra M. Alger	Agent, Oshawa	12 months	600 00
Frank Appleyard	" Chatham	12 "	600 00
T. W. Ault	" Cornwall	12 "	600 00
J. L. Axford	" Brantford	12 "	600 00
W. F. Barrett	" Napanee	12 "	600 00
G. Batman	" Sheguindah	12 "	200 00
Chas. R. Bilger	" Dunnville	12 "	600 00
Rev. Wm. Black	" Kingston	12 "	600 00
Frank Blain	" Fort William	12 "	1,000 00
John Brown	" North Bay	12 "	1,000 00
W. S. Carruthers	" Toronto	8½ "	708 34
A. G. Carson	" Timmins	12 "	1,000 00
H. A. Carter	" Simcoe	12 "	600 00
Mrs. E. Caughell	" St. Thomas	12 "	600 00
Alex. Clark	" Lindsay	12 "	600 00
James Clark	" Dundas	12 "	300 00
C. H. Claus	" St. Catharines	10 "	500 00
J. T. Daley	" Port Hope	12 "	600 00
J. S. Davidson	" Sudbury	12 "	1,000 00
J. H. Devlin	" Perth	12 "	600 00

Enforcement of The Children's Protection Act, etc.—Continued

Salaries—Continued

L. C. Ecker	Agent, Woodstock	12 months		600 00
John Edgar	" Peterborough	12 "		600 00
H. T. Edwards	" Goderich	12 "		600 00
M. P. Everett	" Toronto	12 "		1,000 00
Rev. H. Ferguson	" Stratford	12 "		600 00
H. Fonger	" St. Catharines	1		75 00
W. D. Forrest	" Huntsville	12 "		1,000 00
Geo. Gibbon	" Port Arthur	12 "		600 00
John Hartill	" Burks Falls	12 "		1,000 00
B. W. Heise	" Hamilton	12 "		1,000 00
R. W. Hubbs	" Picton	12 "		600 00
E. A. Johnson	" L'Orignal	12 "		600 00
Wm. E. Jones	" Niagara Falls	12 "		400 00
W. J. Justice	" Barrie	12 "		600 00
W. E. Kelly	" London	12 "		1,000 00
G. B. Little	" Toronto	12 "		600 00
Alex. MacKenzie	" Rainy River	12 "		1,000 00
J. R. McCracken	" Haileybury	12 "		1,000 00
A. G. Munroe	" Ottawa	12 "		1,000 00
Hiram Pearson	" Gore Bay	12 "		300 00
Rev. R. Perdue	" Walkerton	12 "		600 00
G. M. Pool	" Welland	12 "		400 00
Dr. W. J. Price	" Orangeville	8 "		400 00
A. Pullam	" Kitchener	12 "		600 00
Rev. W. M. H. Quartermaine	" Renfrew	12 "		600 00
J. P. Reed	" Sault Ste. Marie	12 "		1,000 00
T. D. Ruston	" Belleville	12 "		600 00
Jos. Ryder	" Parry Sound	12 "		1,000 00
W. J. Sample	" Essex	12 "		600 00
A. G. Schofield	" Haliburton	12 "		1,000 00
Robt. Teakle	" Fenwick	12 "		400 00
G. F. Thompson	" Milton	12 "		600 00
Rev. A. Tovell	" Guelph	12 "		600 00
A. E. Trout	" Owen Sound	12 "		600 00
H. F. Tuck	" Orangeville	4 "		200 00
John Wilkinson	" Sarnia	12 "		600 00
M. R. Winters	" Windsor	12 "		1,000 00
G. A. Wright	" Brockville	12 "		600 00

Travelling Expenses, $7,395.70.

O. M. Alger, 69.17; F. Appleyard, 56.85; T. W. Ault, 55.20; J. L. Axford, 52.93; W. F. Barrett, 56.37; G. Bateman, 31.50; C. R. Bilger, 47.55; W. Black, 198.76; J. Brown, 302.65; W. S. Carruthers, 153.80; E. H. Caughill, 56.00; A. G. Carson, 51.40; A. Clark, 153.90; J. Clark, 27.72; C. H. Claus, 49.00; F. Christall, 23.23; J. T. Daley, 213.57; J. S. Davidson, 176.35; J. H. Devlin, 71.26; L. C. Ecker, 38.71; J. Edgar, 82.53; H. T. Edwards, 208.98; H. Ferguson, 61.78; H. Fonger, 13.79; W. D. Forrest, 297.30; D. T. Foster, 8.54; C. J. Fox, 8.25; G. Gibbon, 11.90; J. Hartell, 638.91; B. W. Heise, 250.54; R. W. Hubbs, 22.94; E. A. Johnson, 565.48; W. E. Jones, 28.01; W. J. Justice, 428.75; G. H. Keith, 39.93; G. B. Little, 194.76; Alex. MacKenzie, 264.50; J. R. McCracken, 151.10; H. Pearson, 17.36; R. Perdue, 207.13; W. J. Price, 98.78; A. Pullam, 207.09; J. P. Reed, 405.40; T. D. Ruston, 285.76; J. Ryder, 61.45; W. J. Sample, 63.49; A. G. Scofield, 47.70; R. Teakle, 84.98; G. F. Thompson, 297.96; A. Tovell, 151.75; A. E. Trout, 174.19; H. F. Tuck, 21.21; J. Wilkinson, 36.21; G. A. Wright, 71.33 .... 7,395 70

Maintenance of Children, $39,194.18.

Children's Aid Societies—Algoma District, 2,429.20; Cochrane District, 2,307.50; Dufferin County, 1,191.58; Fort William Electoral District, 1,868.00; Muskoka District, 189.17; Nipissing District, 3,782.00; Parry Sound East, 2,559.80; Parry Sound West, 2,280.50; Port Arthur Electoral District, 1,088.25; Saint Vincent de Paul, 193.70; Sault Ste. Marie and Algoma District, 2,301.20; Sudbury District, 10,079.34; Temiskaming District, 1,062.75; Toronto, 31.00; Waterloo County, 36.00; Weston Consumptive Hospital, 499.50; York County, 25.00; Mrs. D. Benjamin, 287.00; B. F. Boake, 315.00; Mrs. L. Bowman, 264.70; Mrs. E. J. Brooks, 51.00; Mrs. E. Brown, 294.75; Mrs. M. C. Casserley, 18.00;

Enforcement of The Children's Protection Act, etc.—Continued

Maintenance of Children—Continued

Mrs. R. Feddery, 879.12; Mr. and Mrs. T. Fiola, 180.00; Mr. and Mrs. T. Fisher, 80.00; Mrs. A. E. Fisher, 1,693.55; Mrs. T. J. Frawley, 25.40; A. J. Giroux, 15.63; I. Hanley, 76.40; Mrs. K. Healey, 230.75; Home for Incurable Children, 75.80; Mrs. R. Hood, 144.00; Hospital for Sick Children, Toronto, 13.50; Mrs. C. A. Hutton, 182.00; Mrs. E. Isabelle, 228.84; Mrs. G. Keith, 74.35; Mrs. A. Ledger, 264.00; Lord Dufferin Hospital, 22.00; McKellar General Hospital, 15.00; Mrs. H. Matthews, 154.90; John MacDonald, 12.00; Mrs. P. Miller, 53.25; Mrs. M. Mulock, 274.50; E. Murphy, 6.00; Neighbourhood Workers' Association, 5.00; Mrs. J. O'Dea, 27.75; Presbyterian Redemptive Home, 92.00; Mrs. C. Robinson, 75.00; Mrs. W. Roulston, 396.00; St. Joseph's Orphanage, 224.00; St. Vincent's Orphanage, 96.00; W. M. Sinclair, 175.00; Mrs. J. Smith, 126.00; D. Thompson, 24.00; M. Williamson, 97.50 .... 39,194 18

Legal Services, Witness Fees, etc., $4,093.96.

J. E. Anderson, 19.00; H. Atkinson, 30.00; H. Arrell, 12.00; R. N. Ball, 35.00; A. E. Baker, 12.50; F. D. Boggs, 25.00; T. J. Bourke, 18.00; R. B. Burns, 12.00; S. A. Caldbick, 24.20; D. A. Carey, 84.45; R. S. Clark, 22.25; F. Christall, 12.75; C. H. Curran, 22.00; Dalzel & Stewart, 20.00; Day, Revelle & Rankin, 58.50; Doctor & Hughes, 34.00; B. C. Donnan, 141.00; D. E. Douglas, 21.50; E. Dufresne, 29.50; J. Edgar, 16.35; W. W. Fair, 14.50; F. Fasker, 11.50; G. R. Foster, 209.00; Goodwin & Andrew, 35.00; J. E. Hays, 12.90; Harrington & Slater, 10.00; C. C. Hahn, 42.50; W. L. Height, 50.55; B. W. Herse, 10.92; G. Henderson, 10.00; Hugill & Hesson, 30.00; G. T. Inch, 153.50; J. M. Kearns, 65.00; John A. Kerr, 40.00; Le Sueur, Le Sueur & Dawson, 99.35; L. J. Long, 47.00; MacCracken, Fleming & Schroeder, 10.00; J. Mackay, 85.00; H. A. McColl, 11.00; W. McCue, 30.00; P. McDonald, 23.50; J. A. McKibbon, 98.00; A. A. McKinnon, 27.00; W. F. McRae, 16.50; M. G. Manders, 10.00; L. C. Mason, 35.45; S. T. Medd, 60.50; G. M. Miller, 37.00; C. F. Moore, 933.00; E. E. Petrimoulx, 10.00; S. R. Pearson, 16.00; C. R. Penfold, 16.55; D. J. Rankin, 40.00; H. J. Reynolds, 130.00; Riddell & Murray, 22.75; W. T. Robb, 19.50; T. D. Ruston, 18.26; Sanders & Sanders, 29.50; Smith & Smith, 10.00; Slemin & Slemin, 24.50; E. C. Spereman, 15.00; F. H. Thompson, 34.00; Treleaven, Biggar & Treleaven, 382.50; Williams & Williams, 11.50; Wilson, Pike & Stewart, 46.00; C. H. Wood, 48.10, Sundry persons, 351.13 .... 4,093 96

Miscellaneous, $824.13.

T. Eaton Co., Ltd., clothing, 211.33; Dr. G. D. Gordon, professional services, 11.00; G. H. Keith, provisions, 79.47; E. Longstaffe, meals for C.A.S. delegates, 50.00; F. H. Malmloff, provisions, 65.21; Merrill, Rhind & Walmsley, provisions, 106.81; W. H. Miller, provisions, 78.29; Miller's Departmental Store, clothing, 63.27; Dr. E. W. Nolan, professional services, 10.00; W. J. Poulson, auto livery, 12.50; E. C. Rhehume, rental of house, 30.00; Wm. Sinclair, groceries, 25.00; Dr. W. J. Wesley, professional services, 15.00; Dr. C. S. Wright, professional services, 15.00; Dr. M. A. Wittick, professional services, 10.00; petty disbursements, 41.25 .... 824 13

Total Children's Aid	89,991 31	
Less refund legal services	4,104 60	
		85,886 71

Industrial Schools ($121,127.00)

Alexandra Industrial School, 25,251.25; St. John's Industrial School, 32,291.50; St. Mary's Industrial School, 15,401.75; Victoria Industrial School, 48,182.50 .. 121,127 00

Association of Children's Aid Societies of the Province of Ontario ($1,000.00)

Grant 1,000 00

Children's Aid Branch $268,335.56

BOYS' TRAINING SCHOOL, BOWMANVILLE

Salaries ($46,447.77)

Superintendent	4,383 34
Academic and Vocational	13,700 00
Bursar and Office Staff	3,890 14
Farm Director and Assistants	7,074 37
Chef and Assistants	3,325 00
Engineer and Firemen	4,700 00
Supervisors	9,374 92

Expenses ($44,689.84)

Medicines, $1,863.88.

Dr. G. C. Bonnycastle, 576.00; Bowmanville Hospital, 229.25; Frances Cryderman, 126.00; Jury & Lovell, 203.68; R. M. Mitchell Co., 27.65; Dr. Louis J. Sebert, 36.00; Dr. C. W. Slemon, 40.00; Dr. V. H. Storey, 625.00; petty disbursements, .30 ... 1,863 88

Provisions, $11,280.11.

Harry Allin, 3,212.42; W. J. Bagnall, 14.80; Bowes Co., Ltd., 1,670.64; Geo. Coles, Ltd., 12.25; W. P. Corbett, 1,726.05; Dalton Bros., Ltd., 241.30; G. A. Edmonstone, 203.06; H. J. Heinz Co., Ltd., 60.78; Harry Horne Co., Ltd., 88.65; Thos. J. Lipton, Ltd., 64.35; Ontario Reformatory Industries, 3,922.93; A. J. Reid, 15.48; Etta Willmott, 12.25; petty disbursements, 35.15 ... 11,280 11

Fuel, Light and Water, $7,345.43.

Canada Coal, Ltd., 3,021.91; John A. Holgate & Son, 46.50; Hydro Electric Power Commission of Ontario, 2,931.55; Sheppard & Gill Lumber Co., Ltd., 10.15; Blake Wilkins, 1,333.25; petty disbursements, 2.07 ... 7,345 43

Clothing, $5,026.05.

Anderson, MacBeth, Ltd., 72.25; A. Bradshaw & Son, Ltd., 104.09; S. Burnett, 12.25; John Catto Co., Ltd., 206.36; E. & S. Currie, Ltd., 60.50; Dominion Rubber Co., Ltd., 150.76; T. Eaton Co., Ltd., 842.85; Grafton & Co., Ltd., 829.20; Hamilton & Johnston, 209.59; J. A. Haugh Manufacturing Co., 18.00; Mrs. H. Hooper, 14.90; Fred Knox, 10.25; Mercer Reformatory Industries, 149.15; National Textiles, Ltd., 54.00; Ontario Reformatory Industries, 246.00; Quality Glove Co., Ltd., 15.84; The Robt. Simpson Co., Ltd., 645.00; T. Sisman Shoe Co., Ltd., 803.75; Toronto Radio & Sports, Ltd., 183.50; Victoria Industrial School, 375.96; petty disbursements, 21.85 ... 5,026 05

Laundry and Cleaning, $5,288.78.

Harry Allin, 99.71; Associated Chemical Co. of Canada, Ltd., 301.78; Geo. H. Bickell, 280.00; Canada Colors & Chemicals, Ltd., 18.51; Canadian Fairbanks-Morse Co., Ltd., 106.90; Canadian National Institute for the Blind, 81.00; Colgate-Palmolive-Peet Co., Ltd., 59.21; Mrs. W. Crossey, 10.78; Diamond Cleanser, Ltd., 29.75; Dustbane Products, Ltd., 147.47; T. Eaton Co., Ltd., 29.10; Excelsior Brushes, Ltd., 18.37; Guelph Soaps, 17.60; Hamilton & Johnston, 13.96; S. C. Johnson & Son, Ltd., 25.48; Jury & Lovell, 48.60; Lever Bros., Ltd., 165.37; Mercer Reformatory Industries, 3,044.26; J. W. Miller, 499.17; W. J. Oliphant, Ltd., 23.42; St. Croix Soap Manufacturing Co., 61.38; Scott Paper Co. of Canada, Ltd., 54.29; G. H. Wood & Co., Ltd., 132.30; petty disbursements, 20.37 ... 5,288 78

Furniture and Furnishings, $1,316.67.

A. Bradshaw & Son, Ltd., 20.90; Canadian Pacific Express Co., 13.30; Couch, Johnston & Cryderman, Ltd., 14.05; Wm. Duncan Co., Ltd., 30.86; Dustan's Cash Hardware, 190.50; T. Eaton Co., Ltd., 54.70; Foster Pottery Co., 63.79; General Steel Wares, Ltd., 55.56; Goodyear Tire & Rubber Co. of Canada, Ltd., 32.80; Wm. Junor, Ltd., 340.13; Jury & Lovell, 34.20; Mason & Dale, 52.00; Mercer Reformatory Industries, 113.20; Ontario Reformatory Industries, 54.00; Robert Simpson Co., Ltd., 40.05; Steel Equipment Co., Ltd., 24.50; L. B. Tapson, 40.00; Textile Products Co., Ltd., 44.40; petty disbursements, 97.73 ... 1,316 67

Office Expenses, $3,193.49.

W. J. Bagnell, 25.00; Bell Telephone Co., rental, 270.00; tolls, 328.94; Canadian National Telegraphs, 21.31; Canadian Pacific Railway Co.'s Telegraph, 10.30; The Canadian Statesman, 49.75; T. Eaton Co., Ltd., 221.14; J. W. Jewell, 12.05; King's Printer, 1,312.50; Postmaster, 558.25; Province of Ontario Pictures, 25.00; Ernest Reynolds, 74.85; United Typewriter Co., 65.55; petty disbursements, 218.85 ... 3,193 49

Boys' Training School, Bowmanville—Continued

Expenses—Continued

Farm Expenses, $3,078.36.

Aikenhead Hardware, Ltd., 13.00; D. R. Alldread, 58.35; Harry Allin, 128.38; Andrewes Mountain Seed Co., Ltd., 287.85; Geo. H. Bickell, 50.00; Canada Colours & Chemicals, Ltd., 17.10; Canada Mineral Products, 70.00; Canadian Fairbanks Morse Co., Ltd., 28.75; Canadian National Live Stock Records, 21.00; Cryderman & Morrow, 145.50; S. T. Dowson, 323.00; Dustan's Cash Hardware, 27.76; T. Eaton Co., 43.20; Fred C. Hoar, 75.00; C. E. Horn, 90.00; Mason & Dale, 33.90; R. E. Osborne, 36.00; Pay list, wages of men, 32.10; Wm. C. Parsons, 34.00; Ralston Purina Co., Ltd., 161.80; Wm. Rennie Seeds, Ltd., 21.25; Reesor's, Marmill, Ltd., 785.07; St. Vincent de Paul Penitentiary, 13.65; Sheppard & Gill Lumber Co., Ltd., 55.87; Steele Briggs Seed Co., Ltd., 123.42; F. T. Tighe, 88.50; Turnbull & Cutliffe, Ltd., 54.30; F. C. Vanstone, 233.59; petty disbursements, 26.02 .... 3,078 36

Contingencies, $6,297.07.

John Allan, travelling expenses, 96.10; The Art Metropole, drawing materials, 23.85; Reuben J. Ashton, drilling well, 927.00; Bennett & Elliott, Ltd., auto supplies, 25.99; Geo. H. Bickell, travelling expenses, 10.00; Dorothy Bonnycastle, services, 42.50; Gus Bownsall, wages, 98.00; E. P. Bradt, travelling expenses, 42.30; British American Oil Co., Ltd., gas, etc., 45.88; J. J. Brown, travelling expenses, 1,104.13; Canadian Fairbanks Morse Co., Ltd., repairs, 15.60; Canadian National Express, 68.42; Canadian National Railways, 37.00; Canadian Pacific Express, 20.28; Canadian Pacific Railway Co., 18.89; Geo. E. Carr, travelling expenses, 11.32; Carruther's Garage Service Station, gas, 92.95; Chapman, Ward Co., Ltd., auto repairs, 13.00; Chesley Enterprise, books, 14.40; Cities Service Oil Co., Ltd., gas, oil, 28.59; City Service Garage, gas, etc., 26.16; Commercial Text Book Co., books, 21.60; R. L. Corbett, travelling expenses, 40.00; Cox Motor Sales, gas, 308.93; J. C. Coyle, wages, 51.00; Crown Dominion Oil Co., Ltd., oil, 60.68; W. E. Davidson, travelling expenses, 15.10; Wm. Dawson Subscription Service, subscriptions, 50.75; T. Eaton Co., Ltd., footballs, etc., 58.20; Evening Telegram, copies, 13.28; R. J. Fenton, travelling expenses, 22.67; Goodyear Tire & Rubber Co. of Canada, Ltd., rubber mats, tires, etc., 48.77; Gregg Publishing Co., printing, etc., 16.80; W. H. Hill, car allowance, 200.00; Hoar Transport, Ltd., cartage, 27.55; Jury & Lovell, repairing band instruments, 85.00; King's Printer, 184.36; E. Longstaffe, luncheon, Advisory Committee, 21.50; The Mail and Empire, subscriptions, 30.00; J. G. Martin, repairing plaster, 35.00; Mason & Dale, supplies, 13.80; Metropolitan Transport, Ltd., cartage, 11.37; F. V. Ott, travelling expenses, 48.68; Parsons' Auto Wreckers, auto, 30.00; Ralph Pearce, wages, 90.00; Province of Ontario Pictures, films, 53.15; G. E. Reaman, travelling expenses, 59.55; Ross & Weir, cartage, 25.00; Royal Theatre, admissions, 21.55; Robert Simpson Co., Ltd., books, etc., 101.89; Frank Converse Smith, violin tuition, 253.50; Stedman's Bookstore, Ltd., books, 10.60; Toronto Daily Star, subscriptions, 30.00; Toronto Star Weekly, subscriptions, 25.00; Toronto Radio & Sports Co., Ltd., sporting goods, 76.95; United Church Publishing House, books, 132.30; United Typewriter Co., inspections, 26.08; A. R. Virgin, travelling expenses, 244.17; services, 633.32; West End Garage, gas, 22.57; Arthur Woolley, wages, 50.00; petty disbursements, 284.04 .... 6,297 07

Repairs to Buildings, etc. ($9,786.66)

Maintenance and Repairs of all Buildings, Walks, Grounds and Fences, $7,925.15.

Auto Specialty Manufacturing Co., 21.72; Arthur Balfour & Co., Ltd., 13.74; Bowmanville Foundry Co., Ltd., 58.10; Canadian Durex Abrasives, Ltd., 28.84; Canadian Fairbanks-Morse Co., Ltd., 1,920.12; Canadian General Electric Co., Ltd., 22.67; Canadian Liquid Air Co., Ltd., 18.26; Dustan's Cash Hardware, 341.68; W. Len Elliott, 505.42; General Steel Wares, Ltd., 10.82; John A. Holgate & Son, 214.35; Kingsway Nurseries, 28.90; Mason & Dale, 16.80; J. H. Morin & Co., 33.50; W. B. Mutton, 15.00; Ontario Reformatory Industries, 372.23; Pay list, wages of men, 1,342.61; H. W. Petrie, Ltd., 1,196.40; Sheppard & Gill Lumber Co., Ltd., 883.08; Stucco Products, Ltd., 82.90; Turnbull & Cutcliffe, Ltd., 50.15; A. R. Williams Machinery Co., Ltd., 715.27; petty disbursements, 32.59 .... 7,925 15

Maintenance and Repairs of Plumbing, Steam and Electric Plants, $1,710.51.

Fred Armstrong Co., Ltd., 47.40; Beldam's Asbestos Packing Co., Ltd., 68.65; Gus Bounsall, 34.27; Canadian General Electric Co., Ltd., 108.70; Canadian Industries, Ltd., 145.68; Crown-Dominion Oil Co., Ltd., 71.19; Darling Bros., Ltd., 33.15; Dearborn Chemical Co., Ltd., 91.37; W. Len Elliott, 761.32; Ever-

Boys' Training School, Bowmanville—Continued

Repairs to Buildings—Continued

Maintenance and Repairs of Plumbing, etc.—Continued

lasting Valve Co., Ltd., 28.80; Garratt-Callahan Co., Ltd., 43.56; General Supply Co. of Canada, 144.25; A. Holt, 20.00; Hydro-Electric Power Commission of Ontario, 19.40; Jas. Morrison Brass Manufacturing Co., Ltd., 14.12; Oshawa Electric Supply, Ltd., 10.26; Safety Supply Co., 25.00; J. A. Sexauer Manufacturing Co., Ltd., 17.24; petty disbursements, 26.15 ..... 1,710 51

Live Stock, Vehicles and Farm Implements, $151.00.

H. S. Barrie, 35.00; Bell City Hatchery, 56.00; Irwin R. Bragg, 60.00 ..... 151 00

Gratuities to Boys ($2,040.28)

Sundry boys 2,040 28

Allowances to Superintendent for Use of Motor Car ($200.00)

G. E. Reaman 200 00

Club House in Toronto in Connection with Boys' Training School at Bowmanville ($3,499.11)

Acme Farmers' Dairy, milk, etc., 171.82; Bell Telephone Co., rental, 90.75; tolls, 84.53; J. J. Brown, provisions, 18.00; Canada Bread Co., Ltd., bread, 247.31; Canada Packers, Ltd., provisions, 208.37; A. E. Collins, rent, 1,500.00; Consumers Gas Co., gas, 99.33; Doan Coal Co., Ltd., coal, 205.75; T. Eaton Co., Ltd., utensils, rug, etc., 44.72; Gunn's, Ltd., provisions, 122.05; F. W. Humphrey Co., Ltd., groceries and provisions, etc., 319.98; Lake Simcoe Ice & Fuel Co., ice, 33.90; Singer Sewing Machine Co., machine, 44.62; Stronach & Sons, provisions, 12.35; City of Toronto, water rates, 17.33; Toronto Hydro-Electric System, light, 77.10; Mrs. M. Watson, services as supervisor, 129.00; E. Wright, plumbing supplies, etc., 29.20. Sundries—newspapers and periodicals, 22.56; petty disbursements, 20.44 ..... 3,499 11

Total		106,663 66
Less Maintenance	59,081 17	
Perquisites	6,430 50	
Stock and Equipment	98 23	
Sale of Produce	1,919 89	
Club Fees	254 00	
		67,783 79
Boys' Training School, Bowmanville		38,879 87

MOTHERS' ALLOWANCES COMMISSION

Administration of Mothers' Allowances Act ($47,550.00)

Name	Position	Period		Amount
Harry Bentley	Chief Investigator	12	months	2,550 00
A. G. Bruce	Senior Investigator	12	"	1,700 00
E. A. Rogers	Investigator	12	"	1,500 00
R. M. Graham	"	12	"	1,500 00
M. M. Abernethy	"	12	"	1,500 00
A. E. Lawrence	"	12	"	1,500 00
A. M. Fraser	"	12	"	1,500 00
H. Bapty	"	12	"	1,500 00
E. McMullen	"	12	"	1,500 00
E. Storms	"	12	"	1,500 00
B. Genin-Preston	"	12	"	1,500 00
C. L. Steward	"	12	"	1,500 00
M. J. D. Kennedy	"	12	"	1,500 00
M. F. Bennetts	"	12	"	1,500 00
A. E. Hindley	"	12	"	1,500 00
John Walter	"	12	"	1,500 00
Norah E. Smyth	"	12	"	1,500 00
Norman R. Wilson	"	12	"	1,500 00
C. A. Twidale	"	12	"	1,400 00
C. G. Boyle	"	12	"	1,300 00
C. Folkard	"	12	"	1,400 00
Alex. Patterson	Senior Clerk	12	"	1,900 00

Mothers' Allowances Commission—Continued

Administration of Mothers' Allowances Act—Continued

F. L. Duff	Clerk, Group 1	12 months	1,200 00
B. Mayes	" " 2	12 "	1,050 00
E. V. McKechnie	Secretarial Stenographer	12 "	1,600 00
D. Pleasants	Clerk Stenographer, Group 1	12 "	1,050 00
N. McIldoon	" " " 1	12 "	1,050 00
B. Aston	" " " 2	12 "	975 00
F. Lanchbury	" " " 2	12 "	975 00
M. Beatty	" " " 2	12 "	975 00
D. Brooks	" " " 2	12 "	900 00
C. Smith	" " " 2	12 "	900 00
C. Cook	" " " 2	12 "	900 00
H. Hopkins	" " "	12 "	900 00
E. Francis	Filing Clerk, Group 2	12 "	825 00

Contingencies ($35,535.00)

Allowances to Members of Commission, $1,478.00.

A. J. Reynolds, 470.00; Minnie Singer, 480.00; Belle Thompson, 528.00........ 1,478 00

Temporary Services, $6,025.00.

Madeline Barker	Investigator	12 months	1,200 00
M. Constance Hennessey	Clerk, Group 2	12 "	975 00
M. A. U. Johnstone	Clerk Stenographer, Group 1	12 "	975 00
E. M. Periers	" " " 2	12 "	900 00
E. Riddell	" " " 2	12 "	825 00
Mary Telfer	Investigator	12 "	1,150 00

Travelling Expenses, $19,555.25.

M. M. Abernethy, 876.96; H. Bapty, 1,035.30; M. Barker, 1,218.60; M. F. Bennetts, 221.43; C. G. Boyle, 1,090.24; H. I. Cannon, 9.87; G. G. Clegg, 866.76; C. A. Folkard, 1,696.86; A. M. Fraser, 542.62; B. Genin-Preston, 1,498.57; R. M. Graham, 632.08; A. E. Hindley, 731.27; M. J. D. Kennedy, 742.55; A. E. Lawrence, 777.07; R. G. Leggett, 6.60; F. E. Lyons, 5.15; E. V. McKechnie, 13.10; E. H. McMullen, 494.76; E. M. Metcalfe, 39.80; E. W. Rogers, 347.88; N. E. Smyth, 386.38; C. L. Steward, 422.15; E. M. Storms, 344.75; A. M. Telfer, 1,314.25; C. A. Twidale, 760.54; John Walter, 1,634.60; Norman R. Wilson, 1,845.11.. 19,555 25

Local Board Expenses, $3,721.39.

Algoma, 22.64; Brant, 52.61; Brantford, 10.00; Bruce, 66.37; Carleton, 42.60; Dundas, 6.00; Durham, 54.12; Elgin, 128.29; Essex, 125.80; Frontenac, 77.05; Galt, 2.00; Glengarry, 204.85; Grenville, 102.75; Grey, 286.58; Haldimand, 6.05; Hamilton, 21.15; Hastings, 103.97; Kenora, 4.00; Kent, 61.09; Lambton, 112.55; Lanark, 38.55; Leeds, 145.00; Lennox and Addington, 42.60; Lincoln, 48.70; Muskoka, 85.25; Norfolk, 97.00; Northumberland, 14.78; Ontario, 50.99; Oshawa, 6.00; Ottawa, 76.00; Owen Sound, 4.20; Parry Sound, 22.92; Peel, 101.40; Perth, 47.45; Peterborough City, 79.67; Peterborough County, 164.00; Prescott, 14.00; Prince Edward, 34.57; Rainy River, 26.95; Renfrew, 403.45; Russell, 100.72; Simcoe, 66.14; Stormont, 105.19; Sudbury, 2.00; Temiskaming, 21.09; Toronto, 28.00; Victoria, 5.90; Waterloo, 68.84; Welland County, 35.24; Wellington, 111.32; Wentworth, 17.70; Windsor East, 6.95; Woodstock, 2.50; York, 155.85.. 3,721 39

Miscellaneous, $4,755.36.

Grand & Toy, Ltd., fitting lock, steel cabinet, etc., 45.50; Ingram & Bell, Ltd., beaumanometer, 33.75; King's Printer, 4,218.98; McAinsh & Co., Ltd., supplies, 19.50; Might Directories, Ltd., maps, 12.50; Muskoka Hospital for Consumptives, chest examination and report re W. R. Wood, 10.00; Remington Typewriters, Ltd., inspections, etc., 51.25; United Typewriter Co., Ltd., inspections, etc., 216.91. Sundries—car tickets, 110.00; express, 1.80; freight, .78; newspapers and periodicals, 6.00; postage, 8.00; telegrams, 12.37; petty disbursements, 8.02. 4,755 36

Allowances in Connection with the Mothers' Allowances Act ($1,576,267.44)

Counties, $968,340.00.

Brant, 12,205.00; Bruce, 17,495.00; Carleton, 26,750.00; Dufferin, 7,440.00; Elgin, 9,630.00; Essex, 33,695.00; Frontenac, 8,885.00; Grey, 26,955.00; Haldimand, 10,075.00; Haliburton, 5,675.00; Halton, 16,110.00; Hastings, 29,490.00; Huron, 22,605.00; Kent, 23.020,00; Lambton, 10,030.00; Lanark, 20,095.00;

Mothers' Allowances Commission—Continued

Allowances in connection with The Mothers' Allowances Act—Continued

Counties—Continued

Leeds and Grenville, 20,265.00; Lennox and Addington, 9,500.00; Lincoln, 17,535.00; Middlesex, 31,705.00; Norfolk, 13,990.00; Northumberland and Durham, 29,110.00; Ontario, 19,295.00; Oxford, 11,460.00; Peel, 11,275.00; Perth, 6,780.00; Peterborough, 17,850.00; Prescott and Russell, 55,610.00; Prince Edward, 10,195.00; Renfrew, 58,815.00; Simcoe, 64,427.00; Stormont, Dundas and Glengarry, 68,975.00; Victoria, 19,530.00; Waterloo, 21,230.00; Welland, 35,405.00; Wellington, 14,600.00; Wentworth, 15,535.00; York, 135,098.00.... 968,340 00

Cities, $1,472,652.50.

Belleville, 20,065.00; Brantford, 36,990.00; Chatham, 13,590.00; East Windsor, 20,145.00; Fort William, 22,660.00; Galt, 10,760.00; Guelph, 18,770.00; Hamilton, 162,030.00; Kingston, 26,225.00; Kitchener, 27,125.00; London, 76,020.00; Niagara Falls, 15,415.00; North Bay, 21,230.00; Oshawa, 20,355.00; Ottawa, 148,210.00; Owen Sound, 12,330.00; Peterborough, 22,659.00; Port Arthur, 23,770.00; St. Catherines, 32,372.00; St. Thomas, 12,555.00; Sarnia, 13,645.00; Sault Ste. Marie, 17,915.00; Stratford, 20,220.00; Sudbury, 13,835.00; Toronto, 600,307.00; Welland, 11,969.50; Windsor, 44,940.00; Woodstock, 6,545.00..... 1,472,652 50

Towns, $32,220.00.

Brockville, 7,365.00; Gananoque, 2,790.00; Ingersoll, 3,375.00; Prescott, 5,280 00; St. Marys, 2,195.00; Smiths Falls, 2,975.00; Trenton, 4,975.00; Walkerville, 3,265.00.......... 32,220 00

Indian Reserves, $4,865.00.

Indian Reserves.......... 4,865 00

Districts, $216,145.00.

Algoma, 12,570.00; Kenora, 8,390.00; Manitoulin, 5,175.00; Muskoka, 15,290.00; Nipissing, 38,655.00; Parry Sound, 22,920.00; Rainy River, 12,825.00; Sudbury, 25,850.00; Temiskaming, 65,455.00; Thunder Bay, 9,015.00.......... 216,145 00

Lacking Municipal Residence.......... 4,566 00

Total Allowances..........			2,698,788 50	
Less Cash refunds..........		9,061 19		
Repayments by Municipalities....	1,220,805 37			
Less on account of 1930-1931...	107,345 50			
		1,113,459 87		
			1,122,521 06	
				1,576,267 44

Mothers' Allowances Commission..........1,659,352.44

OLD AGE PENSIONS COMMISSION

Salaries ($18,272.51)

D. J. Jamieson..........	Chairman..........	12 months		6,000 00
Charles Green..........	Inspector..........	12 "		2,500 00
T. J. Lancaster..........	"	8½ "		1,204 15
O. G. Clarke..........	Senior Clerk..........	12 "		1,800 00
Wilfred W. Boyce..........	" "	12 "		1,700 00
Percival G. Robson..........	Office Appliance Operator, Group 1......	12 "		1,500 00
P. Baker..........	Clerk, Group 3..........	12 months	825 00	
		Less leave of absence	31 64	
				793 36
M. Manion..........	Clerk Stenographer, Group 1..........	12 months		1,125 00
C. Strong..........	" " " 2..........	12 "		825 00
E. Stevenson..........	Filing Clerk " 2..........	12 "		825 00

Contingencies ($52,058.24)

Temporary Services, $25,052.54.

R. G. Ashbury..........	Inspector..	12 months	1,725 00	
		Less leave of absence	34 62	
				1,690 38
Jesse Bradford..........	Solicitor..........	12 months		3,500 00

Old Age Pensions Commission—Continued

Contingencies—Continued

Temporary Services—Continued

Name	Position	Group	Months	Amount
Lily Brown	Office Appliance Operator,	Group 2	12 months	975 00
Winnifred Brown	" " "	" 2	12 "	975 00
H. Bernice Cameron	Clerk	" 3	12 "	750 00
Dorothy M. Coghlan	Office Appliance Operator	" 2	12 "	975 00
William Cowan	Clerk	" 3	12 "	825 00
P. Dontigny	Inspector		12 "	1,725 00
Meredith Egan	"		12 "	1,725 00
J. K. Fairfull	"		11 "	1,600 00
John R. Finlay	Clerk,	Group 2	12 "	1,800 00
F. W. Forde	Inspector		12 "	1,725 00
Elizabeth V. French	Clerk Typist	Group 2	12 "	750 00
Harry Hollingshead	Office Boy		12 "	525 00
Ida M. McBride	Clerk Stenographer,	Group 2	12 "	825 00
Emerie Moncion	Inspector		12 "	1,725 00
H. L. Scace	Clerk Stenographer,	Group 2	12 "	825 00
Henrietta Scotland	Clerk	" 3	12 "	825 00
J. R. Vaughan	Inspector		7 "	908 32
Alfred F. Wright	"		3 1/5	403 84

Travelling Expenses, $15,434.09.

R. Ashbury, 1,999.80; J. Bradford, 2.95; P. Dontigny, 2,500.02; M. Egan, 1,933.18; J. K. Fairfull, 1,713.94; J. R. Finlay, 556.66; F. W. Forde, 2,254.92; C. H. Green, 33.70; D. J. Jamieson, 10.65; T. J. Lancaster, 1,068.94; E. Moncion, 2,739.62; J. R. Vaughan, 153.35; A. F. Wright, 466.36.................... 15,434 09

Local Board Expenses, $2,760.95.

Algoma, 328.50; Cochrane, 191.26; Haliburton, 160.80; Kenora, 150.00; Manitoulin, 271.41; Muskoka, 245.32; Nipissing, 217.40; Parry Sound, 282.26; Rainy River, 150.00; Sault Ste. Marie, 283.30; Sudbury, 156.00; Temiskaming, 174.70; Thunder Bay, 150.00.. 2,760 95

Miscellaneous, $8,810.66.

Addressograph-Multigraph of Canada, Ltd., inspections and ribbons, 251.54; Corona Typewriters of Canada, Ltd., inspections, 9.00; King's Printer, 8,397.65; Remington Typewriters, Ltd., inspections, 22.00; United Typewriter Co., Ltd., repairs, 86.25. Sundries—express, 18.90; freight, .86; postage, 14.30; telegrams, 10.16.. 8,810 66

Allowances in Accordance with The Old Age Pensions Act ($2,697,785.74)

Counties, $4,203,355.81.

Brant, 56,989.05; Bruce, 84,488.08; Carleton, 127,648.29; Dufferin, 33,873.18; Elgin, 124,931.34; Essex, 123,321.49; Frontenac, 83,569.69; Grey, 120,959.09; Haldimand, 48,711.35; Halton, 63,096.34; Hastings, 148,317.91; Huron, 138,817.25; Kent, 84,210.15; Lambton, 93,084.62; Lanark, 90,456.96; Leeds and Grenville, 137,488.96; Lennox and Addington, 67,121.50; Lincoln, 65,821.87; Middlesex, 141,359.44; Norfolk, 112,481.61; Northumberland and Durham, 194,791.28; Ontario, 127,409.70; Oxford, 74,676.58; Peel, 69,094.09; Perth, 69,084.89; Peterborough, 60,787.99; Prescott and Russell, 145,793.19; Prince Edward, 82,700.92; Renfrew, 152,013.93; Simcoe, 281,198.68; Stormont, Dundas and Glengarry, 197,249.52; Victoria, 74,478.52; Waterloo, 110,939.78; Welland, 94,496.88; Wellington, 100,136.99; Wentworth, 69,492.78; York, 352,261.92...4,203,355 81

Cities, $3,969,517.82.

Belleville, 41,367.75; Brantford, 119,835.79; Chatham, 43,230.82; East Windsor, 13,125.96; Fort William, 25,604.12; Galt, 43,871.45; Guelph, 58,033.05; Hamilton, 423,474.69; Kingston, 94,975.40; Kitchener, 37,483.32; London, 247,913.04; Niagara Falls, 23,238.86; North Bay, 37,706.52; Oshawa, 36,618.81; Ottawa, 399,607.91; Owen Sound, 42,779.05; Peterborough, 79,008.26; Port Arthur, 30,546.51; St. Catharines, 64,124.76; St. Thomas, 55,748.56; Sarnia, 43,115.26; Sault Ste. Marie, 42,913.98; Stratford, 55,720.48; Sudbury, 24,643.91; Toronto, 1,736,595.36; Welland, 16,362.89; Windsor, 100,955.56; Woodstock, 30,915.75..3,969,517 82

Towns, $180,588.45.

Brockville, 46,149.66; Gananoque, 20,473.99; Ingersoll, 16,066.40; Prescott, 9,004.53; St. Marys, 18,460.00; Smiths Falls, 21,863.85; Timmins, 8,052.85; Trenton, 27,460.35; Walkerville, 13,056.82.................................. 180,588 45

Old Age Pensions Commission—Continued

Allowances in accordance with The Old Age Pensions Act—Continued

Districts, $727,133.39.

Algoma, 96,727.56; Cochrane, 44,734.46; Haliburton, 37,375.48; Kenora, 37,172.72; Manitoulin, 21,013.06; Muskoka, 82,178.19; Nipissing, 101,722.81; Parry Sound, 111,685.98; Pelee Island, 1,555.33; Rainy River, 41,407.75; Sudbury, 61,634.04; Thunder Bay, 19,493.08; Temiskaming, 64,027.94; Province of Ontario, 6,404.99 .... 727,133 39

Other Provinces, $27,632.44.

Alberta, 5,334.37; British Columbia, 3,578.93; Manitoba, 4,060.00; Saskatchewan, 14,659.14 .... 27,632 44

Inter-Provincial Accounts, $33,994.29.

Alberta, 8,437.61; British Columbia, 10,511.03; Manitoba, 7,847.64; Saskatchewan, 14,632.47			41,428 75	
Less Cash Refunds			7,434 46	
				33,994 29
Total Pensions Paid			9,142,222 20	
Less Cash Refunds by Estates, etc.			52,160 24	
Net Pensions Paid during the year			9,090,061 96	
Deduct Repayments:				
Dominion Government		6,420,517 78		
Municipalities		965,124 10		
Other Provinces		22,413 84		
		7,408,055 72		
Less—On account of 1930-31		1,015,779 50		
			6,392,276 22	
				2,697,785 74

Note:	Total	Payable by Ontario	Payable by other Authorities
Net Pensions Paid	9,090,061 96	1,443,262 32	7,646,799 64
Repayment on account of Current Year	6,392,276 22	....	6,392,276 22
	2,697,785 74	1,443,262 32	1,254,523 42
Adjustment of 75% charged to Dominion as from August 1st, 1931; agreement became effective only from November 1st, 1931	....	567,120 25	567,120 25
	2,697,785 74	2,010,382 57	687,403 17

Old Age Pensions Commission $2,768,116.49

STATUTORY

Minister's Salary (see page O 5) 10,000 00

Statutory $10,000.00

SPECIAL WARRANTS

Expenses in Connection with the Exhibit of the Department of Public Welfare at the Canadian National and other Exhibitions ($6.05)

Department of Highways, auto service 6 05

Maintenance of Patients Transferred from Public Hospitals to Houses of Refuge ($133.00)

Parry Sound District House of Refuge, maintenance of children 133 00

Grant to Assist the Community Welfare Council of Ontario in Developing Public Interest in Social Work ($2,000.00)

Community Welfare Council of Ontario 2,000 00

Special Warrants—Continued

Grant to Ontario Society for Crippled Children to Assist in Providing or or Arranging for the Care of Handicapped Children ($8,000.00)

Ontario Society for Crippled Children	8,000 00

Soldiers' Aid Commission in Payment of a Grant to Provide Direct Relief to Destitute Families of War Veterans ($2,000.00)

Soldiers' Aid Commission	2,000 00

For the Purchase of Sufficient Wreaths to be Placed on the War Memorials of the Province where Services are Held ($1,065.00)

Provincial Command Canadian Legion B.E.S.L.	1,065 00

Grant to The Canadian Council on Child and Family Welfare to Assist in the Carrying on of its Work in the Province of Ontario ($1,000.00)

Canadian Council on Child and Family Welfare		1,000 00
Special Warrants	**$14,204.05**	
Total		4,994,688 74
Less Salary Assessment		5,621 64
Total **Expenditure, Department of Public Welfare**		**$4,989,067 10**

PART P

DEPARTMENT OF PROVINCIAL TREASURER

FISCAL YEAR, 1931-32

TABLE OF CONTENTS AND SUMMARY OF EXPENDITURE

	Page	Amount	Total
MAIN OFFICE	8		82,016 73
CONTROLLER OF REVENUE	9		147,511 75
SUCCESSION DUTY BRANCH	11		55,492 41
BOARD OF CENSORS OF MOVING PICTURES	12		19,445 49
MOTION PICTURE BUREAU	12		79,627 70
PUBLIC RECORDS AND ARCHIVES	14		20,318 83
HOUSE POST OFFICE	15		121,035 65
STATUTORY:			
Distribution to Municipalities—Corporations Tax Act	15	40,758 74	
Interest on Assurance Fund—Land Titles Act	16	7,500 00	
Assurance Fund under Land Titles Act	16	765 15	
Drainage Debentures, Tile	16	99,096 40	
" " Municipal	16	8,055 50	
Municipal Sinking Fund	16	153,198 13	
Debenture Guarantee Act	16	42,168 56	
Common School Fund	16	4,246 65	
Banting and Best Medical Research	16	10,000 00	
Banting Research Aid Act	16	10,000 00	
Northern Ontario Fire Relief	17	7,809 34	
Ontario Public Service Superannuation Fund	17	304,606 36	
Agricultural Development Finance Act:			
Province of Ontario Savings Offices	17		
Debentures	18	8,500,000 00	
Farm Loans	18	33,790 00	
Miscellaneous	16	20,864 56	9,242,859 39
			9,768,307 95
Less:			
Salary Assessment			9,990 82
			9,758,317 13
Public Debt, Principal, Interest, etc.			151,562,660 35
			161,320,977 48
Deduct:			
Public Debt Maturities, Loans Advanced and Repayment on Account of Special Funds transferred to Part "U"			144,460,288 18
			16,860,689 30

PART P—DEPARTMENT OF PROVINCIAL TREASURER

Statement of Expenditure Showing Amounts Expended, Unexpended and Overexpended for the Twelve Months Ended October 31st, 1932

Department of Provincial Treasurer	Page	Estimates	Expended			Un-expended	Over-expended	Treasury Board Minute
			Ordinary	Capital	Total Ordinary and Capital			
		$ c.	$ c.	$ c.	$ c.	$ c.	$ c.	$ c.
Main Office:								
Salaries	8	71,825 00	65,158 26	....	65,158 26	6,666 74	....	....
Contingencies	8	20,000 00	16,858 47	....	16,858 47	3,141 53	....	....
Main Office	..	91,825 00	82,016 73	....	82,016 73	9,808 27	....	....
Controller of Revenue:								
Salaries	9	90,925 00	86,875 00	....	86,875 00	4,050 00	....	....
Contingencies	10	50,000 00	46,645 01	....	46,645 01	3,354 99	....	....
Stock Transfer Stamps	..	2,000 00	....	....	....	2,000 00	....	....
Law Stamps, printing, etc.	10	15,000 00	13,976 74	....	13,976 74	1,023 26	....	....
Membership and Annual Fees in various Associations	10	50 00	15 00	....	15 00	35 00	....	....
Controller of Revenue	..	157,975 00	147,511 75	....	147,511 75	10,463 25	....	....
Succession Duty Branch:								
Salaries	11	42,600 00	40,799 78	....	40,799 78	1,800 22	....	....
Contingencies	11	13,500 00	11,626 62	....	11,626 62	1,873 38	....	....
Valuator, use of motor car	11	250 00	250 00	....	250 00	....	....	....
Legal expenses, etc.	11	10,000 00	2,816 01	....	2,816 01	7,183 99	....	....
Repayments under Succession Duty Act	..	20,000 00	....	....	....	20,000 00	....	....
Succession Duty Branch	..	86,350 00	55,492 41	....	55,492 41	30,857 59	....	....
Board of Censors of Moving Pictures:								
Salaries	12	19,925 00	15,591 60	....	15,591 60	4,333 40	....	....
Contingencies	12	9,000 00	3,853 89	....	3,853 89	5,146 11	....	....
Board of Censors	..	28,925 00	19,445 49	....	19,445 49	9,479 51	....	....

Motion Picture Bureau:								
Salaries	12	43,425 00	42,399 76	....	42,399 76	1,025 24	....	....
Contingencies	12	8,000 00	5,778 46	....	5,778 46	2,221 54	....	....
Circulation of films, etc.	13	8,500 00	3,839 07	....	3,839 07	4,660 93	....	....
Equipment, machines, etc.	13	50,000 00	27,610 41	....	27,610 41	22,389 59	....	....
Motion Picture Bureau	..	109,925 00	79,627 70	....	79,627 70	30,297 30	....	....
Public Records and Archives:								
Salaries	14	18,975 00	12,712 50	....	12,712 50	6,262 50	....	....
Contingencies	15	6,000 00	5,854 07	....	5,854 07	145 93	....	....
Purchase of Documents, Paintings, Relics, etc.	15	3,000 00	1,752 26	....	1,752 26	1,247 74	....	....
Public Records and Archives	..	27,975 00	20,318 83	....	20,318 83	7,656 17	....	....
House Post Office:								
Salaries	15	11,925 00	11,925 00	....	11,925 00	....	....	....
Postage and cost of House Post Office	15	125,000 00	109,110 65	....	109,110 65	15,889 35	....	....
House Post Office	..	136,925 00	121,035 65	....	121,035 65	15,889 35	....	....
Supply Bill	..	639,900 00	525,448 56	....	525,448 56	114,451 44	....	....

Statutory:	Page						
Salary of Minister	15	10,000 00	....	10,000 00	....	....	....
Salaries unprovided for	15	4,650 00	....	4,650 00	....	....	....
Distribution to Municipalities under Corporations Tax Act	15	40,758 74	....	40,758 74	....	....	....
Assurance Fund under Land Titles Act	16	....	765 15	765 15	....	....	....
Interest—Assurance Fund under Land Titles Act	16	7,500 00	....	7,500 00	....	....	....
Drainage Debentures—Tile	16	....	99,096 40	99,096 40	....	....	....
" " —Municipal	16	....	8,055 50	8,055 50	....	....	....
Provincial Sinking Fund	16	52,735 90	100,462 23	153,198 13	....	....	....
Seagram Bequest to Galt Hospital	16	200 00	....	200 00	....	....	....
McLellan Bequest, School for the Blind	16	25 00	....	25 00	....	....	....
Annie E. Cullen Bequest to Toronto Model School	16	25 00	....	25 00	....	....	....
Jno. Livingstone, Bequest, School for the Blind	16	183 57	....	183 57	....	....	....
Adamson Memorial Scholarship	16	50 00	....	50 00	....	....	....
Robt. McKay Bequest to Guelph Collegiate	16	163 29	....	163 29	....	....	....
Hon. J. R. Cooke Scholarship	16	150 00	....	150 00	....	....	....
Debenture Guarantee Act	16	....	42,168 56	42,168 56	....	....	....
Common School Fund	16	4,246 65	....	4,246 65	....	....	....
Banting and Best Medical Research Act	16	10,000 00	....	10,000 00	....	....	....

PART P—DEPARTMENT OF PROVINCIAL TREASURER—Continued

Statement of Expenditure Showing Amounts Expended, Unexpended and Overexpended for the Twelve Months Ended October 31st, 1932

Department of Provincial Treasurer	Page	Expended			Un-expended	Over-expended	Treasury Board Minute
		Ordinary	Capital	Total Ordinary and Capital			
		$ c.	$ c.	$ c.	$ c.	$ c.	$ c.
Statutory—Continued							
Banting Research Aid Act	16	10,000 00	....	10,000 00	....	....	....
Audit of Teachers' and Inspectors' Superannuation Fund	17	1,750 00	....	1,250 00	....	....	....
Ontario Government Contribution to Public Service Superannuation Fund	17	304,606 36	....	304,606 36	....	....	....
Northern Ontario Fire Relief	17	7,809 34	....	7,809 34	....	....	....
R.S.O. 19, Chpter 22, Seion 5	17	4,000 00	....	4,000 00	....	....	....
Compensation—blind [illegible]rs for injuries, etc.	17	167 70	....	167 70	....	....	....
Province of Ontario Savings Office:—(Details)	17	....	....	....	....	....	....
Agricultural Development Finance Act:							
Debentures	18	....	8,500,000 00	8,500,000 00	....	....	....
Farm Loans	18	....	33,790 00	33,790 00	....	....	....
Statutory	..	458,521 55	8,784,337 84	9,242,859 39	....	....	....
Total	..	983,970 11	8,784,337 84	9,768,307 95	....	....	....
Less Salary Assessment	..	9,990 82	....	9,990 82	....	....	....
Total, Treasury Department	..	973,979 29	8,784,337 84	9,758,317 13	....	....	....
Public Debt (Statutory), see itemized statement next page.							
Loans and Treasury Bills, matured and paid	18	....	130,351,168 14	130,351,168 14	....	....	....
Interest	7	13,526,821 66	....	13,526,821 66	....	....	....
Commission and Exchange	7	2,354,128 26	....	2,354,128 26	....	....	....
Engraving, advertising, insurance, postage, etc	7	5,760 09	....	5,760 09	....	....	....
Debt Redemption Investment	26	....	5,324,782 20	5,324,782 20	....	....	....
Total, Public Debt	..	15,886,710 01	135,675,950 34	151,562,660 35	....	....	....
Total—Treasury and Public Debt	..	16,860,689 30	144,460,288 18	161,320,977 48	....	....	....
Deduct:							
Public Debt maturities, Loans advanced and repayments on account of Special Funds (see Part "U")	..	....	144,460,288 18	144,460,288 18	....	....	....
Department of Provincial Treasurer	..	16,860,689 30	....	16,860,689 30	....	....	....

Public Debt Charges

Department of Provincial Treasurer	Outstanding Oct. 31st, 1931	ORDINARY Interest	ORDINARY Commission and Exchange	ORDINARY Eng. and Advtg.	ORDINARY Total	CAPITAL Principal	Grand Total
Gto Stock and Debentures:	$ c.	$ c.	$ c.	$ c.	$ c.	$ c.	$ c.
£422, 59- 4-10 1⁄3%	2,056,406 30	71,974 18	59 90	37 16	72, 31 24	....	72, 31 24
317 912-. ,0- 4 4 %	1,547,175 70	61,887 00	09 44	44 54	62,240 98	....	62,240 98
542- 8 1⁄2%	834,412 54	37,548 56	87 74	33 07	, 69 37	....	, 69 37
$3,000, .00 1⁄2%	348,000 00	12,188 75	....	....	12, 88 75	....	12, 88 75
1,150, .00 4 %	1,150,000 00	45,920 00	19 11	....	45, 99 11	....	45, 99 11
3 , .00 4 % A	665,950 00	26,558 00	16 57	....	26,574 57	....	26,574 57
, .00 4 % B	224,000 00	8,960 00	1 58	....	, 91 58	....	, 91 58
3,000, 00.00 4 % CD	1,188,400 00	47,496 00	34 11	....	47, 30 11	....	47, 30 11
3,000, 00.00 6 % TU	....	3 00	....	....	3 00	....	3 00
4,000, .00 6 % VWX	....	24 00	03	....	24 03	100 00	124 03
2,000, 00.00 6 % KK	1,981,000 00	117,720 00	71 96	....	117, 91 96	....	17, 91 96
6,800, 00.00 6 % LL	....	30 00	1 67	....	31 67	2,000 00	2, 31 67
8,000, 00.00 6 % MM	....	00 00	....	....	00 00	1,500 00	1, 00 00
16,000, 00.00 6 % RR	15,233, 00 00	916,500 00	267 24	....	, 67 24	....	96, 67 24
10,000, .00 6 % SS	9. 63, 00 00	570,120 00	132 16	....	50,252 16	....	50,252 16
15,000, 00.00 6 % TT	14, , 00 00	861,450 00	192 71	....	61,642 71	....	61,642 71
15,000, 00.00 6 % XK	14,912, 00 00	888,650 88	, 65 76	....	, 06 64	....	, 06 64
15,000, 00.00 6 % WWYY	14,612, 00 00	873,566 71	328 18	....	83,894 89	....	83,894 89
15,000, 00.00 5½% ZZ	15, , 00 00	825,825 00	,028 66	....	826, 83 66	....	826, 83 66
15,000, .00 5 % B	15, , 00 00	750,875 00	95 39	....	51, 80 39	....	51, 80 39
20,000, .00 5 % AC	20, 00, 00 00	997,025 00	1,242 16	....	98,267 16	....	98, 67 16
20,000, .00 5½% AD	18, 69, 00 00	1,028, 90 12	340 13	....	1, 09,320 25	....	1,029,320 25
40,000, .00 5 % AF	38, , 00 00	1,912,300 00	31 02	....	1,912, 61 02	....	1,912, 61 02
20,000, .00 1⁄2% AG	19,200, 00 00	861,345 00	97 53	....	862,142 53	....	862,142 53
21,000, .00 1⁄2% AH	17, , 00 00	772,020 00	1, 08 51	....	73,028 51	....	73,028 51
24,000, 00.00 1⁄2% AJ	20, , 00 00	917,685 00	1, 39 80	....	98,824 80	....	98,824 80
24,000, .00 1⁄2% AK	21, , 00 00	953 07,7 50	1,293 96	....	954, 31 46	....	954, 31 46
30,000, .00 4 % AL	28,982, 00 00	1, 90 00	, 66 84	....	1, 60, 66 84	....	1, 60, 66 84
35,000, 00.00 5 % AM	35, , 00 00	1,728, 30 18	2, 06 58	....	1, 30,747 06	....	1, 30, 47 06
35,000, .00 5 % AN	35, , 00 00	1,730,038 41	1,994 95	....	1,732, 03 36	....	1,732, 03 36
30,000, .00 4½% AP	29, 01, 00 00	1,339,717 50	1, 66 58	....	1,341,394 08	....	1,341,394 08
2,000, 00.00 1⁄2% AQ	2, 00, 00 00	90,000 00	....	....	, 00 00	....	90, 00 00
30,000, .00 4½% R	, , 00 00	1,335,577 50	1, 88 01	....	1, 37, 65 51	....	1, 37, 65 51
30,000, 00. 0 4 % AS	, , 00 00	1,197,600 00	, 17 86	....	1, , 97 86	....	1, , 97 86
20,000, .00 1⁄2% AT	....	521,748 36	2,020 53	....	523, 68 89	....	523, 68 89

PART P—DEPARTMENT OF PROVINCIAL TREASURER—Continued
Public Debt Charges—Continued

Department of Provincial Treasurer	Outstanding Oct. 31st, 1931	ORDINARY				CAPITAL	Grand Total
		Interest	Commission and Exchange	Eng. and Advtg.	Total	Principal	
Ontario Stock and Debentures—Continued	$ c.	$ c.	$ c.	$ c.	$ c.	$ c.	$ c.
5,000,000.00 6 % AU		143,595 78	48 46		143,644 24		143,644 24
2,000,000.00 5½% ZA-AT		55,000 00		15 50	55,015 50		55,015 50
20,000,000.00 5½% AW		365 41			65 41		65 41
500,000.00 5 %		12,500 00			12,500 00		12,500 00
150,000.00 5 %		3,750 00			3,750 00		3,750 00
		22,878,093 14	23,665 13	130 27	22,901,888 54	3,600 00	22,905,488 54
Treasury Bills:							
$940,000.00 5 % BG 21-25		46,125 00			46,125 00	35,000 00	81,125 00
5,000, 00.00 2½% BW 11-115		42,708 33			42,708 33	5,000, 00 00	5,042,708 33
5,000, 00.00 2½% CF 6-55		32,291 75			32,291 75	5,000,000 00	5,032,291 75
5,000, 00.00 2½% CG [illegible]		52,430 55			52,430 55	5,000, 00 00	5,052,430 55
5,000, 00.00 2½% CH		28,437 50			28,437 50	5,000,000 00	5,028,437 50
5,000, 00.00 5 % CI 1-5						5,000,000 00	5,000,000 00
5,000, 00.00 5½% CI 11-15		23,356 15			23,356 15	5,000,000 00	5,023,356 15
5,000, 00.00 ½% CI -0		67,808 20			67,808 20	5,000,000 00	5,067,808 20
5,000, 00.00 5½% CI 21-25		45,958 90			45,958 90	5,000,000 00	5,045,958 90
4,000 000.00 6 % CJ		62,246 58		275 33	62,521 91	4,000,000 00	4,062,521 91
00, 00.00 ½% CJ		4,500 00			4,500 00		4,500 00
5, 00, 00.00 6 % CK		76,666 66		281 67	76,948 33	5,000,000 00	5,076,948 33
5, 00, 00.00 6 % CL 1-10		75,000 00		353 01	75,353 01	5,000,000 00	5,075,353 01
5, 00, 00.00 6 % CL 11-20		87,500 00		368 80	87,868 80	5,000,000 00	5,087,868 80
2, 60, 00.00 6 % CL 21-25		38,333 33		183 66	38,516 99	2,500,000 00	2,538,516 99
2, 60, 00.00 6 % CL 26-30				17 00	17 00		17 00
20, 00, 00.00 ½% CM		183,994 26		90 48	184, 84 74	19,000,000 00	19, 184,084 74
4, 00, 00.00 6 % CN 1-10		60,000 00		402 76	60,402 76	4,000,000 00	4,060,402 76
4, 00, 00.00 6 % CN 11-18		71,333 33		418 45	71,751 78	4,000,000 00	4,071,751 78
2, 00, 00.00 6 % CN 9-22				165 67	165 67		165 67
800, 00.00 ½% CO		7,112 32			7,112 32	80, 00 00	807,112 32
3, 60, 00.00 5½% CO 1-7		16,349 35			16,349 35	3,500, 00 00	3,516, 349 35
3, 60, 00.00 ½% CO 8-14		15,294 59			15,294 59	3,500, 00 00	3,515,294 59
3, 60, 00.00 ½% CO 15-21		48,520 56			48,520 56	3,500, 00 00	3,548,520 56
7, 00, 00.00 6 % CP 1-70		105,000 00		330 00	105,330 00	7,000, 00 00	7,105,330 00
3, 60, 00.00 6 % CP 1-105		52,500 00		381 97	52,881 97	3,500, 00 00	3,552,881 97
3, 60, 00.00 6 % CP 201-235				390 05	390 05		390 05

10,000,000.00 5½% CQ 1-10					10,000,000 00	10,000,000 00
3,000,000.00 5 % CR 1-73			397 95	397 95		397 95
5,000,000.00 5½% CS 1-5					5,000,000 00	5,000,000 00
100,000.00 5½% CT 1	2,169 86			2,169 86	100,000 00	102,169 86
2,000,000.00 5½% CT 2-9			18 25	18 25		18 25
15,000,000.00 5⅝% CU 1-150			75 00	75 00		75 00
5,000,000.00 6 % CV 1-5000			1,077 71	1,077 71		1,077 71
1,950,000.00 5½% HY 1-4	11,610 27			11,610 27	1,950,000 00	1,961,610 27
	1,257,247 49		5,227 76	1,262,475 25	127,385,000 00	128,647,475 25
Miscell ea						
Province of Ontario Savings Office, withdrawals					2,924,143 14	2,924,143 14
" " " " tiat on l s	942,535 80			942,535 80		942,535 80
I t t on bank s	165,546 81			165,546 81		165,546 81
" Teachers' l Inspectors' Superannuation Fund s	43,824 84			43,824 84		43,824 84
" lic Service p ation Fund	198,104 20			198,104 20		198,104 20
Exchange on ir s		2,330,463 13		2,330,463 13		2,330,463 13
e, s, ge, te., on ds and securities			402 06	402 06		402 06
Premiums on Debentures r l r Sinking Fund and t					38,425 00	38,425 00
Di ct on s l y Bills	282,882 73			282,882 73		282,882 73
	1,632,894 38	2,330,463 13	402 06	3,963,759 57	2,962,568 14	6,926,327 71
Total Payments, Public Debt	25,768,235 01	2,354,128 26	5,760 09	28,128,123 36	130,351,168 14	158,479,291 50
Deduct:						
t received on Loans to various commissions, etc.	12,201,892 01			12,201,892 01		12,201,892 01
c l interest received on bond issues	39,521 34			39,521 34		39,521 34
al Repayments received	12,241,413 35			12,241,413 35		12,241,413 35
Total Stock, Debentures, and Treasury Bills, etc.	13,526,821 66	2,354,128 26	5,760 09	15,886,710 01	130,351,168 14	146,237,878 15
Debt Redemption Investments:						
Matured Loans, Certificates, etc., paid					4,450,618 94	4,450,618 94
Series AM n, Sinking Fund					388,000 00	388,000 00
" AN " " "					353,000 00	353,000 00
% Inscri l Stock, Sinking Fund					59,932 60	59,932 60
% " " " "					53,385 71	53,385 71
4½% " " " "					19,844 95	19,844 95
					5,324,782 20	5,324,782 20
Total Public Debt	13,526,821 66	2,354,128 26	5,760 09	15,886,710 01	[illegible] 34	151,562,660 35

DEPARTMENT OF PROVINCIAL TREASURER

Honourable E. A. Dunlop.....Provincial Treasurer.......$10,000 00

MAIN OFFICE

Salaries ($65,158.26)

Name	Position	Period	Amount
F. Martin Turnbull	Assistant Treasurer and Financial Controller	12 months	6,600 00
G. J. L. Jones	Deputy Assistant Treasurer	12 "	3,600 00
F. M. Irwin	Secretary to Minister and Dept. Secretary	1½ "	250 00
H. J. Chater	" " " " "	11½ "	2,300 00
H. C. Phair	Head Clerk	12 "	2,700 00
R. T. Regan	Head Cashier	12 "	3,000 00
H. J. Chater	Principal Clerk	½"	100 00
L. B. Fisher	" "	12 "	2,200 00
A. C. MacKay	Senior Clerk	12 "	2,250 00
E. Cosgrove	" "	12 "	2,000 00
G. Harris	" "	12 "	2,000 00
H. L. Austin	" "	11 "	1,833 26
R. E. Lee	" "	12 "	2,000 00
W. H. Callaghan	" " (T)	12 "	1,000 00
F. M. Watson	" "	12 "	1,900 00
A. W. Davies	" "	12 "	1,800 00
P. B. McLaughlin	Clerk, Group 1	12 "	1,600 00
J. A. Greenwood	" " 1	12 "	1,600 00
W. J. Cafley	" " 1	12 "	1,600 00
G. Millar	" " 1	12 "	1,600 00
B. Sheriff	" " 1	12 "	1,600 00
L. W. Orchard	" " 1	12 "	1,400 00
J. A. Russell	" " 2	12 "	1,200 00
G. E. Wilkinson	" " 2	12 "	1,125 00
L. H. Trivett	" " 2	12 "	1,050 00
M. E. Readman	" " 2	12 "	1,050 00
W. P. Gill	Cheque Writer, Group 1	12 "	1,500 00
Geo. M. Inman	" " " 2	12 "	1,125 00
C. G. King	" " " 2	12 "	1,125 00
W. G. Carter	Senior Filing Clerk	12 "	1,600 00
P. V. Goold	Junior Clerk	12 "	825 00
J. G. Malloy	Senior Clerk Stenographer	12 "	1,500 00
V. Harris	" " "	12 "	1,300 00
E. Madill	Clerk Stenographer, Group 1	12 "	1,200 00
E. J. Carr	" " " 1	12 "	1,125 00
Margaret P. Mack	" " " 1	12 "	1,125 00
O. M. Lawrence	" " " 1	12 "	975 00
Allene M. Ditchfield	" " " 1	12 "	975 00
R. A. Groves	Office Boy	12 "	750 00
R. Roberts	" "	12 "	675 00

Contingencies ($16,858.47)

Temporary Services, $3,630.63.

Name	Position	Period	Amount
H. M. Adamson	Office Boy	1 month	43 75
H. Boal	" "	12 "	525 00
T. W. Graham	Clerk, Group 2	12 "	975 00
J. Keith Harvard	Office Boy	10⅜ "	474 38
F. A. Jardine	" "	11 "	481 25
W. W. Lothrop	Clerk, Group 3	2½ "	156 25
E. M. Murphy	Clerk Stenographer	12 "	975 00

Travelling Expenses, $1,394.53.

H. J. Chater, 78.20; Hon. E. A. Dunlop, 1,000.00; G. Harris, 30.80; G. J. L. Jones, 285.53 ..... 1,394 53

Advertising, $1,812.29.

American Banker, 10.36; Beacon-Herald of Stratford, Ltd., 56.35; Border Cities Star, 123.00; Chatham Daily News, 30.00; Consolidated Press, Ltd., 110.00; Galt Daily Reporter, 42.50; Globe Printing Co., 281.52; Guelph Daily Mercury, Ltd., 42.56; Journal Dailies, 124.00; Lakefield News, 5.00; London Free Press, 144.00; MacLean Publishing Co., Ltd., 370.00; Mail and Empire, 145.60; Monetary Times, 187.50; St. Thomas Times Journal, 49.50; Sarnia Canadian Observer, Ltd., 50.40; Woodstock Sentinel Review, 40.00 ..... 1,812 29

Main Office—Continued

Contingencies—Continued

Miscellaneous, $10,021.02.

Burroughs Adding Machine of Canada, Ltd., inspections and repairs, 83.10; Dept. of Highways, auto service, 379.12; General Office Equipment Corporation, Ltd., maintenance service of equipment, 18.00; King's Printer, 8,758.46; McCann & Alexander, typewriter inspections, 15.75; Remington Typewriters, Ltd., inspections, 24.96; Todd Sales Co., repairs, etc., to cheque signer, 128.50; Underwood, Elliott, Fisher Co., maintenance service, 54.00; United Typewriter Co., Ltd., inspections and repairs, 170.16; Western Union Telegraph Co., registration of cable address, 25.00. Sundries—car tickets, 60.00; newspapers and periodicals, 184.74; telegrams, 87.11; petty disbursements, 32.12........................ 10,021 02

Main Office... $82,016.73

CONTROLLER OF REVENUE'S OFFICE

Salaries ($86,875.00)

Name	Position	Period		Amount
J. T. White	Controller of Revenue	12	months	5,400 00
W. A. Orr	Assistant Controller of Revenue	12	"	3,600 00
Thomas Scott	Director, Amusement Branches	12	"	2,700 00
John H. Carnegie	Law Stamp Distributor	12	"	2,500 00
W. W. McKinlay	Head Clerk, Group 1	12	"	2,850 00
H. R. Boal	Head Inspector, Office of Controller of Revenue	12	"	2,400 00
R. C. Buckley	Chief Inspector of Theatres	12	"	2,500 00
G. E. Burtt	Principal Clerk	12	"	2,200 00
J. A. Kennedy	Senior Clerk	12	"	2,000 00
A. J. Ferguson	" "	12	"	2,000 00
A. R. Terhune	" "	12	"	2,000 00
A. W. Thompson	" "	12	"	1,900 00
W. J. Jones	" "	12	"	1,800 00
A. Stevenson	" "	12	"	1,700 00
B. T. Smith	Senior Audit Clerk	12	"	2,000 00
L. Kemp	" " "	12	"	1,800 00
John McDonald	" " "	12	"	1,900 00
W. H. Gleed	" " "	12	"	1,800 00
F. H. Cable	" " "	12	"	1,800 00
O. R. Dew	" " "	12	"	1,700 00
M. T. Moorby	" " "	12	"	1,700 00
R. H. Burns	" " "	12	"	1,700 00
A. F. C. Hotson	" " "	12	"	1,600 00
A. Hill	Inspector of Amusements Tax	12	"	1,600 00
E. Woodburn	Inspector of Theatres	12	"	2,200 00
J. McNamara	" "	12	"	2,200 00
H. T. Dobson	" "	12	"	2,100 00
W. R. B. McKay	" "	12	"	1,900 00
E. J. Sheridan	Clerk, Group 1	12	"	1,600 00
R. Wilson, Jr.	" " 1	12	"	1,600 00
R. G. Stevenson	" " 1	12	"	1,600 00
R. S. Kerr	" " 1	12	"	1,500 00
G. R. McMillen	" " 1	12	"	1,400 00
Eldon Hamilton	" " 1	12	"	1,300 00
J. Wallace	" " 3	12	"	825 00
Albert E. Prince	" " 3	10	"	625 00
N. Scott	" " 3	12	"	825 00
G. Mogan	Senior Clerk Stenographer	12	"	1,500 00
B. Brown	" " "	12	"	1,300 00
K. Reaume	Clerk Stenographer, Group 1	12	"	1,200 00
E. M. Tidy	" " " 1	12	"	1,200 00
J. Robertson	" " " 1	12	"	1,200 00
J. L. Pearson	" " " 1	3	"	300 00
F. E. Bell	" " " 1	12	"	1,200 00
B. M. Nichols	" " " 1	12	"	1,050 00
Dorothy Susands	" " " 2	12	"	975 00
H. M. Gilmour	" " " 2	12	"	900 00
M. M. Leslie	" " " 2	12	"	900 00
Asta Larsen	" " " 2	9	"	675 00
A. M. E. Spence	Filing Clerk " 1	12	"	1,050 00
G. C. Chapman	Office Boy	12	"	600 00

Controller of Revenue's Office—Continued

Contingencies ($46,645.01)

Temporary Services, $21,463.34.

Name	Position	Period		Amount
H. S. Adam	Senior Audit Clerk	12 months	1,599 96	
		Less leave of absence	61 53	1,538 43
H. Adamson	Office Boy	1 month		45 43
H. D. Bayne	Senior Audit Clerk	12 months		1,599 96
A. L. Beatty	Clerk Stenographer, Group 2	2½ "		177 16
M. E. Boyle	" " " 2	12 "		825 00
H. W. Coo	" " 1	7 "		692 31
C. Cote	" " 3	5 "		326 92
P. J. McDermott	" " 1	2⅔ "		280 77
M. J. Garfunkel	Clerk Typist " 2	12 "		750 00
Wm. F. Garrow	Senior Clerk	5 "		799 98
E. T. Gosnell	Audit Clerk	4½ "		453 85
H. Hunter	Clerk Stenographer, Group 1	6 "		503 13
F. Jardine	Office Boy	1 "		43 75
Wm. R. Jones	Audit Clerk	12 "		1,200 00
T. R. Kerr	Assistant in Law Stamp Office	2¼ "		167 31
Mae V. Lake	Clerk Stenographer, Group 2	7¼ "		497 12
V. I. Lynes	Clerk Typist " 2	12 "		750 00
E. J. McDougall	Senior Clerk	6 "		799 98
T. H. McKee	" "	7 "		912 80
W. K. Morris	Office Boy	2 "		90 87
H. E. Munro	Senior Audit Clerk	12 "		1,599 96
G. G. Pinfold	Clerk Stenographer, Group 2	12 "		825 00
L. B. Richardson	Clerk Typist, " 2	7 "		432 69
J. C. Ruddy	Clerk, " 1	9 1/5		919 23
J. L. St. Jean	" " 2	12 "		975 00
S. C. Southgate	" " 1	6½ "		650 00
D. A. Swan	Senior Audit Clerk	12 "		1,599 96
R. Thomas	Clerk Stenographer, Group 1	2 "		162 50
Thomas C. Tinline	Clerk " 1	1 1/5		119 23
M. L. Wilcox	Clerk Stenographer " 2	12 "		825 00
E. F. M. White	Clerk " 2	12 "		900 00

Temporary Inspectors, $8,245.37.

Temporary Inspectors, services, 4,781.81; expenses, 3,463.56.................. 8,245 37

Travelling Expenses, $8,639.38.

H. S. Adam, 6.80; H. R. Boal, 784.83; R. C. Buckley, 357.53; R. H. Burns, 195.73; F. H. Cable, 630.88; H. T. Dobson, 660.63; W. F. Garrow, 501.38; W. H. Gleed, 73.47; A. Hill, 91.26; A. C. F. Hotson, 279.00; W. R. Jones, 84.85; L. Kemp, 36.55; P. J. McDermott, 610.15; J. McDonald, 543.92; J. McNamara, 1,006.26; I. A. Markowitz, 13.00; W. A. Orr, 545.39; J. L. St. Jean, 115.85; T. Scott, 50.35; E. J. Sheridan, 6.20; A. Stevenson, 292.43; A. G. Smith, 94.97; D. A. Swan, 359.34; J. T. White, 233.74; E. Woodburn, 1,064.87............ 8,639 38

Miscellaneous, $8,296.92.

Bryant Press, Ltd., amusement tax tickets, 1,086.50; Burroughs Adding Machine of Canada, Ltd., inspections and repairs, 30.93; S. A. Caldbick, legal services, 93.00; E. Frisby, witness fees, 15.00; A. W. Hornby, witness fees, 48.00; King's Printer, 5,247.13; McCann & Alexander, inspections of typewriters, 36.00; Smith & Walsh, robbery insurance, 182.12; Southam Press, Ltd., amusement tax tickets, 202.50; A. R. Terhune, meals of staff, working overtime, 489.00; United Typewriter Co., Ltd., inspections and repairs, 271.50; W. H. Wilson, legal fees, 14.20. Sundries—car tickets, 387.00; express, 38.43; newspapers and periodicals, 29.00; telegrams, 123.02; petty disbursements, 3.59.............. 8,296 92

Law Stamps, Printing and Other Expenses ($13,976.74)

Sundry law stamp distributors, commissions.................................. 13,976 74

Membership and Annual Fees in Various Associations ($15.00)

Citizens' Research Institute of Canada, 10.00; National Tax Association, 5.00.... 15 00

Controller of Revenue $147,511.75

SUCCESSION DUTY BRANCH

Salaries ($40,799.78)

R. E. M. Meighan	Solicitor under Succession Duty Act		12 months		4,400 00
F. M. Devine	Senior Assistant Solicitor under Succession Duty Act		12 "		3,600 00
H. G. MacBeth	Asst. Solicitor under Succession Duty Act		7½ "		1,840 40
J. D. O'Brien	" " " " " "		12 "		3,000 00
W. Turner	Property Valuator		12 "		3,000 00
E. H. Curry	Principal Clerk		12 "		2,400 00
F. S. Quinn	Succession Duty Clerk,	Group 1	12 "		2,200 00
A. G. Smith	" " "	" 1	12 "		2,100 00
Edward J. Danby	" " "	" 2	12 "		1,700 00
A. G. A. Nelson	Senior Clerk		12 "		2,000 00
W. C. Larmouth	" "		12 "		1,900 00
G. E. Johnston	Clerk	" 1	12 "		1,600 00
W. W. Engall	"	" 1	12 "		1,300 00
C. A. Donley	Senior Clerk Stenographer		12 "		1,500 00
G. Heagens	Clerk Stenographer	" 1	12 "		1,200 00
Areta Toms	" "	" 1	12 "		1,200 00
E. K. Keenan	" "	" 1	12 "		1,125 00
E. McGill	" "	" 2	12 "		1,050 00
A. I. Rothwell	" "	" 2	12 months	975 00	
	Less leave of absence			40 62	934 38
K. Graham	Clerk Typist	Group 1	12 months		1,050 00
V. Cooper	Office Appliance Operator	" 2	12 "		1,200 00
M. A. MacKenzie	Consulting Actuary		12 "		500 00

Contingencies ($11,626.62)

Temporary Services, $8,415.14.

G. A. S. Allan	Office Boy		12 months	525 00
K. Boyd	Clerk Typist,	Group 2	12 "	750 00
L. R. Bradley	Office Boy		6 "	262 50
T. M. Dittrick	Clerk Stenographer	" 1	12 "	975 00
M. M. Denholm	" "	" 1	4½ "	375 00
A. Dolen	Clerk Typist	" 2	12 "	750 00
A. M. Hawthorne	Clerk	" 1	12 "	1,200 00
C. H. Hewgill	Succession Duty Clerk,	" 1	6 "	900 00
A. G. Hocking	Office Boy		6⅓ "	277 64
M. O. Mason	Clerk	" 3	12 "	750 00
K. W. Naylor	Filing Clerk	" 2	12 "	750 00
L. A. Richard	Succession Duty Clerk	" 1	6 "	900 00

Travelling Expenses, $48.57.

A. G. Smith, 23.17; W. Turner, 25.40 .... 48 57

Miscellaneous, $3,162.91.

Houston's Standard Publications, reports, 84.29; King's Printer, 2,227.51; L. A. Philip & Co., inspection of calculating machine, 40.00; Poors' Publishing Co., manual, 100.00; Standard Statistics Co., Inc., reports, 192.00; Sundry Banks and Trust Companies, services re opening of safety deposit boxes, 310.75; Trustees and Managers of the Stock Exchange, daily lists, 19.46; United Typewriter Co., Ltd., inspections and repairs, 102.50. Sundries—customs, 13.15; newspapers and periodicals, 38.50; telegrams, 18.05; petty disbursements, 16.70. 3,162 91

Valuator, Use of Motor Car ($250.00)

W. Turner 250 00

Legal Expenses, Valuations, Arbitrations, etc. ($2,816.01)

Bain, Bicknell, White & Bristol, 1,000.00; T. Brown, 12.00; G. N. Dickson, 10.00; N. B. Gash, 60.00; V. G. Hector, 34.90; V. Jackson, 10.00; Lucas, Henry & Lucas, 56.20; M. D. MacPhail, 39.98; Mason, Foulds, Davidson, Carter & Kellock, 616.30; A. A. May, 84.80; J. A. N. Mercier, 60.00; J. A. McEvoy, 500.00; W. H. McKeon, 183.75; G. A. Scroggie, 20.00; T. W. Thomas, 84.80; Thompson & Thompson, 43.28 .... 2,816 01

Repayments Under The Succession Duties Act

Sundry Estates	198,005 54
Less deducted from revenue	198,005 54
Succession Duty Branch	$55,492 41

BOARD OF CENSORS OF MOVING PICTURES

Salaries ($15,591.60)

J. C. Boylen	Chairman	12 months	3,300 00
L. Phillips	Member	12 "	2,500 00
E. Joseph Byrne	"	12 "	2,000 00
E. Moran	"	12 "	1,900 00
M. Elliott	Projectionist	12 "	2,000 00
P. Ristow	"	10 "	1,666 60
M. Canning	Senior Clerk Stenographer	12 "	1,400 00
G. Belcher	Clerk, Group 3	12 "	825 00

Salaries not provided for (Statutory) ($4,650.00)

P. Thornloe	Member	12 months	1,900 00
J. Norris	Projectionist	12 "	2,000 00
W. Eden	Clerk, Group 3	12 "	750 00

Contingencies ($3,853.89)

Temporary Services, $2,550.00.

J. B. Hardwicke	Member	12 months	1,800 00
E. Young	Clerk, Group 3	12 "	750 00

Miscellaneous, $1,303.89.

J. C. Boylen, travelling expenses, 315.29; H. Cosens, typing, 6.00; King's Printer, 604.31; W. T. King, film cement, 10.00; Dr. M. Lyon, eye examination, 15.00; Dr. A. L. Morgan, eye examinations, 12.50; F. Shorney, Ltd., eye glasses, 87.75; United Typewriter Co., Ltd., inspections and repairs, 36.00. Sundries—car tickets, 36.00; newspapers and periodicals, 153.04; telegrams, 12.54; petty disbursements, 15.46 .... 1,303 89

Board of Censors $19,445.49

MOTION PICTURE BUREAU

Administration and Distribution

Salaries ($22,412.48)

G. E. Patton	Director	12 months	3,000 00
H. M. Blake	Film Editor	12 "	2,000 00
J. V. Curran	Senior Clerk (T)	12 "	1,599 98
A. H. Gray	Motion Picture Operator	12 "	1,900 00
R. O'Connor	Cameraman (T)	12 "	1,800 00
P. W. Bull	Field Man	12 "	1,800 00
J. R. Grant	Clerk Group 1	12 "	1,600 00
E. D. Conway	" " 1	12 "	1,500 00
G. McCabe	" " 1	12 "	900 00
J. B. Monk	" " 1	12 "	750 00
A. K. Sprague	Clerk Typist " 1 (T)	1 "	75 00
C. T. Mitten	Laboratory Attendant (T)	11 "	687 50
T. A. Bristow	Clerk Stenographer	12 "	1,125 00
D. Parker	" "	12 "	1,125 00
G. Shute	Filing Clerk	12 "	1,200 00
G. Morris	Film Rewinder	12 "	750 00
H. C. Chamberlain	" " (T)	12 "	600 00

Contingencies ($5,778.46)

Temporary Services, $2,100.00.

G. Moore	Film Rewinder	12 "	1,200 00
J. Travers	Assistant	12 "	900 00

Travelling Expenses, $623.00.

T. A. Bristow, 14.95; P. W. Bull, 502.87; H. C. Chamberlain, 12.40; J. V. Curran, 13.00; J. R. Grant, 9.82; G. Morris, 10.85; D. Parker, 8.00; G. E. Patton, 36.11; G. Shute, 8.00; M. Webster, 7.00 .... 623 00

Miscellaneous, $3,055.46.

Department of Highways, auto service, 657.97; Dominion Press Clipping Agency, press clippings, 50.00; King's Printer, 1,660.85; Manufacturers Life Insurance Co., garage rent, 96.00; J. W. McLaren, colour proofing catalogue cover, 60.00; Ontario Laundry Co., Ltd., laundry, 22.11; E. Pullen, Ltd., dusters, 10.25; E. Skinner, smocks, 14.00; Smith & Walsh, Ltd., accident and auto insurance,

Motion Picture Bureau—Continued

Contingencies—Continued

Miscellaneous—Continued

125.80; Sterling Laundry Co., Ltd., laundry, 23.52; United Typewriter Co., Ltd., inspections and repairs, 97.12. Sundries—car tickets, 60.00; newspapers and periodicals, 80.11; telegrams, 87.91; petty disbursements, 9.82.......... 3,055 46

Express and Customs Charges, Circulation of Films ($3,839.07)

Customs and brokerage, 826.66; cartage, 206.75; express, 2,803.10; freight, 2.56... 3,839 07

Laboratory

Salaries ($19,987.28)

Name	Position	Period		Amount
B. J. Bach	Superintendent	12	months	2,700 00
A. R. Tuite	Laboratory Foreman	12	"	1,800 00
A. E. Hider	Laboratory Assistant	12	"	1,599 84
J. A. Finnegan	" "	12	"	1,500 00
H. R. Smith	" "	12	"	1,200 00
M. B. Burtt	" "	(T) 12	"	1,200 00
T. Brown	Junior Laboratory Assistant	12	"	1,125 00
J. G. Rutherford	Cameraman	12	"	2,100 00
F. H. Severn	Senior Clerk (Still Pictures)	12	"	2,200 00
R. Watson	Lantern Slide Laboratory Foreman	12	"	1,900 00
K. Simpson	Clerk Stenographer, Group 2	12	"	975 00
M. E. Webster	" " " 2	12	"	900 00
G. H. Edwards	Clerk " 3	6	"	412 44
R. Waite	" " 3	(T) 6	"	375 00

Purchase and Maintenance of Equipment, Motion Picture Machines, Films, etc. ($27,610.41)

Temporary Services, $10,649.48.

Name	Position	Period		Amount
J. C. Coutts	Night Watchman and Engineer (Trenton Studio)	12	months	1,098 00
A. W. Galbraith	Senior Laboratory Assistant	12	"	1,599 96
W. H. Graham	Cameraman	12	"	1,800 00
A. Hopkins	Gardener and Day Watchman (Trenton Studio)	12	"	1,189 50
F. J. Lee	Laboratory Assistant, Group 1	12	"	1,200 00
G. Miller	" " " 1	12	"	1,200 00
K. Johnson	Title Artist	12	"	1,200 00
C. L. Mitten	Laboratory Attendant	1/5	"	12 02
E. Stone	Colour Artist	12	"	975 00
R. Waite	Junior Laboratory Attendant	6	"	375 00

Extra Services, $804.75.

P. W. Bull, 292.50; A. H. Gray, 199.50; A. E. Hider, 246.00; R. O'Connor, 66.75. 804 75

Travelling Expenses, $2,536.35.

B. J. Bach, 615.77; H. M. Blake, 26.40; T. Brown, 60.47; A. W. Galbraith, 29.15; W. H. Graham, 231.78; A. H. Gray, 24.35; A. E. Hider, 148.63; F. J. Lee, 1.50; E. R. Livingston, 101.50; G. Miller, 21.62; R. O'Connor, 189.92; J. G. Rutherford, 381.37; F. H. Severn, 695.20; K. Simpson, 10.00; H. R. Smith, 100.68; A. R. Tuite, 120.75; R. Watson, 27.26................. 2,786 35

Less refund 1931 Accountable F. H. Severn................... 250 00

2,536 35

Equipment and Maintenance, $22,680.76.

Acton Tool & Stamping Co., Ltd., 46.22; Agfa Anso, Ltd., 29.94; Aikenhead Hardware, Ltd., 400.43; Akeley Camera, Inc., 355.00; Allcock, Laight & Westwood Co., Ltd., 85.00; American Baptist Publication Society, 18.00; American Hardware Corporation of Canada, Ltd., 20.24; Art Metropole, 19.51; Armstrong Bros., 40.53; Associated Screen News, Ltd., 126.00; Atkins & Hoyle, 59.36; A. Baker, 78.00; Bass Camera Co., 65.00; Bausch & Lomb Optical Co., 10.36; Bell & Howell Co., 94.00; Blue Seal Sound Service, Inc., 63.00; Bodine Electric Co., 34.65; Booth Studio, 27.40; Boston Gear Works Sales Co., 59.49; E. F. Brayham, 47.00; L. Burford, 25.00; Campbell's Paint Shop, 14.00; C. Campbell, 37.50; Canadian General Electric Co., Ltd., 476.36; Canadian Government Motion Picture Bureau, 40.98; Canadian Kodak Co., Ltd., 7,337.28; Canadian Laboratory Supplies, Ltd., 50.00; Canadian National Carbon, Ltd., 26.49; Canadian Universal Film Co., 100.00; Canadian Westinghouse Co., Ltd., 30.77;

Motion Picture Bureau—Continued

Laboratory—Continued

Purchase and Maintenance of Equipment, etc.—Continued

Equipment and Maintenance—Continued

Canada Wire & Cable Co., Ltd., 48.40; City Pattern Works, 58.00 Coleman Electric Co., 29.22; Continental Sound Equipment Co., 12.00; Cork Insulation Co., Ltd., 23.40; Coulter Copper & Brass Co., Ltd., 25.22; Courian's Oriental Rugs, 10.80; C. De Grave, 55.21; Dennison Manufacturing Co. of Canada, Ltd., 68.78; Diamond State Fibre Co. of Canada, Ltd., 24.59; Duplex Motion Picture Industries, 500.00; Dupont Film Manufacturing Corporation, 218.13; T. Eaton Co., Ltd., 44.37; Eastman Kodak Stores, Ltd., 1,774.48; Engravers Metal Co., Ltd., 211.22; O. J. Evans & Sons, 96.38; Fairgrieve & Son, Ltd., 40.20; Ferranti Electric, Ltd., 112.45; Filmart Motion Pictures, 65.83; Film Laboratories of Canada, Ltd., 158.52; Film & Slide Co. of Canada, Ltd., 3,319.30; W. T. Freeland, 19.00; Fruit Machinery Co., Ltd., 22.57; General Sound Equipment, Ltd., 48.00; Gevaert Co. of America, 759.35; G. M. Laboratories, Inc., 38.25; W. H. Graham, 52.00; Graham's Garage, 10.00; Greenleaf Co., 123.12; Griswold Machine Works, 25.10; A. E. Hagen, 125.00; Hamilton Gear & Machine Co., 135.94; Hans Renold of Canada, Ltd., 50.74; Hardinge Bros. of Canada, Ltd., 37.80; E. Harris Co., Ltd., 10.20; Hollywood Camera Exchange, Ltd., 25.00; House & Maunder, 138.08; Ilex Optical Co., 20.19; Imperial Optical Co., Co., 13.75; International Resistance Co., Ltd., 16.17; A. Jackson Machine Tool Co., 20.55; Jarrett Printing & Publishing Co., Ltd., 11.55; A. J. Johnson, 88.25; G. La Brash, 12.00; H. S. Langdon, 103.75; M. Langmuir Manufacturing Co., Ltd., 293.50; W. G. Lendrum, 35.00; Lockhart's Camera Exchange, 61.37; Mallinckrodt Chemical Works, 24.00; D. Marshall, 88.00; Matthews Bros., Ltd., 524.95; McClung Hardware, Ltd., 115.57; McDonald Hardware, 15.08; McIntyre & Taylor, Ltd., 17.04; F. McKissock, 32.00; Mitchell Camera Corporation, 140.00; J. Morrison Brass Manufacturing Co., Ltd., 21.30; Neal's Flower Shop, 20.31; Northern Electric Co., Ltd., 38.79; Perkins Electric Co., Ltd., 91.25; Photographic Stores, Ltd., 55.53; Pilkington Bros., Ltd., 288.62; T. Pocklington Co., 118.50; Powerlite Devices, Ltd., 13.05; Prescott & Co., 63.58; Pringle & Booth, 370.00; Racon Electric Co., Inc., 16.17; Robbins & Myers Co. of Canada, Ltd., 31.83; C. G. Roos, 32.00; A. Schustek & Co., 375.00; H. V. Shaw, 55.25; M. Sheppard, 35.00; E. A. Simmons, 151.45; G. Sneyd, 83.25; R. E. Stacey, 24.27; A. H. Tallman Bronze Co., 33.03; Tarling Map Mounting Co., 10.50; W. G. Tugwell & Co., 427.35; United Projector & Film Corporation, 211.98; Utah-Carter Radio, Ltd., 59.00; Wells Bros. Amusement Co., 45.00; J. Whitehouse, 12.50; Wholesale Radio Co., 13.36; A. R. Williams Machinery Co., Ltd., 16.01 .... 22,680 76

Miscellaneous, $3,350.01.

Bell Telephone Co., rentals, 33.75; tolls, 80.96; Day Sign Co., signs, 92.25; Dept. of Highways, auto service, 517.89; Kerns, Peron & Stockwell, Ltd., insurance on apparatus, 135.52; Hydro-Electric Power Commission, light, 167.17; King's Printer, 255.99; Thos. Laird, services as watchman, 14.65; La Morre Bros., ice, 10.19; W. MacWaters, services as watchman, 135.00; B. W. Powers & Son, coal, 666.35; E. Pullan Co., Ltd., dusters, 30.75; Smith & Walsh, Ltd., accident insurance, 70.00; Sundry persons, re making of film, etc., 547.50; Trenton Public Utilities Commission, light, 118.59; Trenton Water Works, water, 130.57; Mrs. M. Westlake, cleaning studio, 50.00; G. E. Wilson, cleaning material, 12.72. Sundries—postage, 25.00; telegrams, 15.01; petty disbursements, 240.15. 3,350 01

Purchase and maintenance of equipment		40,021 35		
Less sale of supplies	813 80			
Rent of films, etc.	11,597 14			
		12,410 94		
			27,610 41	

Motion Picture Bureau $79,627.70

DEPARTMENT OF PUBLIC RECORDS AND ARCHIVES

Salaries ($12,712.50)

Alexander Fraser	Provincial Archivist (T)	12 months		2,000 00
A. E. Lavell	Historian	9 "		2,925 00
J. J. Talman	Specialist, Historical Documents	12 "		2,100 00
H. McClung	Senior Clerk	12 "		1,900 00
C. C. Creed	Clerk, Group 2	12 "		1,125 00
William D. Reid	" " 3	12 "		900 00
M. Gadway	Senior Clerk Stenographer	12 "		1,500 00
H. Egerton	Clerk Typist, Group 2	6½ months	487 50	
	Less leave of absence		225 00	
				262 50

Department of Public Records and Archives—Continued

Contingencies ($5,854.07)

Temporary Services, $5,250.00.

John S. Carstairs	Specialist in Historical and Biological Records	12 months	1,800 00
L. H. Irving	Assistant	12 "	1,500 00
Murdoch McLeod	Senior Clerk Messenger	12 "	1,125 00
J. Silverthorne	Clerk, Group 3	12 "	825 00

Miscellaneous, $604.07.

King's Printer, 433.97; A. E. Lavell, travelling expenses, 108.75; Remington Typewriters, Ltd., inspections and repairs, 24.00; United Typewriter Co., Ltd., inspections and repairs, 24.00. Sundries—car tickets, 12.00; petty disbursements, 1.35 .... 604 07

Purchase of Documents, Paintings, Relics, etc. ($1,752.26)

Mrs. M. Badgerow, 20.00; J. Bale, Sons & Danielson, Ltd., 1.70; Barrie Examiner, 2.00; A. E. Brown, 4.00; Bulletin des Recherches Historiques, 2.00; Canadian Churchman, .50; Canadian Forum, 2.00; Canadian Geographical Society, 3.00; Canadian Historical Review, 2.00; Catholic Truth Society of Canada, 1.10; Champlain Society, 20.00; Church of England in Canada, General Board of Religious Education, 1.00; W. Dawson Subscription Service, Ltd., 1.25; J. Dougall & Son, 3.50; Eastman Kodak Stores, Ltd., 4.50; Farmers Publishing Co., Ltd., 1.50; H. Fraser, 10.00; Gazette Printing Co., Ltd., 4.00; Wm. George's Sons, Ltd., 1.01; Globe Printing Co., 9.30; Grey County Historical Commission, 4.00; C. E. Haight, 17.50; Herman & Co., 12.50; M. A. Hipson, 1.25; Historical Association, 1.21; Dora Hood's Book Room, 29.50; L. H. Irving, 4.50; R. Jocelyn, 45.00; King's Printer, 1,152.05; La Societe des Nations, 22.70; W. G. Lendrum, 100.00; The Librarian, 25.48; Lowe Bros., Ltd., 27.50; Macmillan Co. of Canada, Ltd., 6.00; Mail and Empire, 19.44; R. S. Mortley, 3.60; T. Nelson & Sons, Ltd., 5.25; Nova Scotia Historical Society, 10.39; J. Orr, 11.47; F. H. Page, 5.00; Planet Book Service, 5.00; Photostat Corporation, 56.20; Province of Ontario Pictures, 1.50; Receiver-General of Canada, 2.50; Rectigraph Co. of Canada, Ltd., 17.00; Review Publishing Co., Ltd., 2.00; G. Routledge & Sons, Ltd., 6.37; Ryerson Press, 8.00; J. M. Snyder, 25.00; Society for Army Historical Research, 5.10; H. Stevens, Son & Stiles, 2.43; C. Tarling Map Mounting Co., 10.00; Times Publishing Co., Ltd., 4.46; E. Tobin, 6.00; F. I. Weaver, 2.00 ... 1,752 26

Public Records and Archives $20,318.83

HOUSE POST OFFICE

Salaries ($11,925.00)

D. D. MacMillan	Postmaster	12 months	2,400 00
A. B. Gillies	Postal Clerk	12 "	1,800 00
W. T. Gray	" "	12 "	1,800 00
S. McLean Grant	" "	12 "	1,800 00
W. J. Barber	Junior Postal Clerk	12 "	1,200 00
R. J. Jewell	" " "	12 "	1,200 00
R. P. Sirman	Postal Clerk, Group 3	12 "	1,050 00
Alfred Booth	Office Boy	12 "	675 00

Postage and Cost of House Post Office ($109,110.65)

Addressograph Multigraph of Canada, Ltd., inspections and repairs, 26.95; Dept. of Highways, auto service, 14.48; King's Printer, 205.40; C. A. McEachern, inspection of seals, 3.00; Postmaster, postage, 108,315.48; Postage Meter Co., repairs, 78.66; rentals, 451.55; G. F. Rogers, repairs to cash register, 7.63; Toronto Railway & Steamboat Guide, subscription, 7.50 .... 109,110 65

Postage and Cost of House Post Office $121,035.65

Main Office and Branches $525,448.56

STATUTORY

Minister's salary (see page P 8) 10,000 00

Salaries, not otherwise provided for (see page P 12) 4,650 00

Distribution to Municipalities under Corporations Tax Act ($40,758.74)
R.S.O. 1927, Chap. 29, Sec. 24

Sundry municipalities 40,758 74

Statutory—Continued

Assurance Fund under Land Titles Act ($765.15)
R.S.O. 1927, Chap. 158, Sec. 130

A. Turgeon, compensation and interest	765 15

Interest—Assurance Fund under Land Titles Act ($7,500.00)
R.S.O. 1927, Chap. 158, Sec. 130

Accountant, Supreme Court of Ontario, interest charges at 2½ per cent. on $300,000.00; July 15th, 1931 to July 15th, 1932	7,500 00

Drainage Debentures (Tile) ($99,096.40)
R.S.O. 1927, Chap. 65

Sundry municipalities	99,096 40

Drainage Debentures (Municipal) ($8,055.50)
R.S.O. 1927, Chap. 64

Sundry municipalities	8,055 50

Municipal Sinking Fund ($153,198.13)
8 Edw. VII, Chap. 51

Treasurer, Municipality of.—Barton, 56,466.91; Beaverton, 4,272.50; Brockville, 9,980.78; Ingersoll, 6,409.83; Lincoln, 28,935.58; Prescott, 5,873.82; St. Mary's, 41,258.71	153,198 13

Edward F. Seagram Bequest to Galt Hospital ($200.00)
5 Geo. V, Chap. 20, Sec. 25

Treasurer, Galt Hospital, interest, 1932	200 00

Jesse McLellan Bequest to Ontario School for the Blind, Brantford ($25.00)
5 Geo. V, Chap. 20

Bursar, Ontario School for the Blind	25 00

Annie E. Cullen, Bequest to Toronto Model Schools ($25.00)
10 Edw. VII, Chap. 26, Sec. 47

V. Tremaine (Scholarship)	25 00

John Livingstone Bequest to Ontario School for the Blind, Brantford ($183.57)
10 Edw. VII, Chap. 26, Sec. 47

Superintendent, Ontario School for the Blind, interest, 1931	183 57

Peter Adamson Memorial Scholarship ($50.00)
10 Edw. VII, Chap. 26, Sec. 47

Goderich Collegiate Institute, interest, 1932	50 00

Robert McKay Bequest to Goderich Collegiate Institute Board ($163.29)
5 Geo. V, Chap. 20, Sec. 25

Board of Trustees, Goderich Collegiate Institute, interest, 1931	163 29

Hon. J. R. Cooke Scholarship ($150.00)
R.S.O. 1927, Chap. 22, Sec. 6

M. E. Walt, 50.00; S. Bulback, 50.00; D. Fox, 50.00	150 00

Debenture Guarantee Act ($42,168.56)
9 Geo. V, Chap. 14

Town of Matheson, 5,170.29; Town of Riverside, 16,168.02; City of East Windsor, 20,830.25	42,168 56

Common School Fund ($4,246.65)

Dominion Government, amount accountable by Ontario re sale of school lands during year ended October 31st, 1932	4,246 65

Banting and Best Medical Research Act ($10,000.00)
13-14 Geo. V, Chap. 56, Sec. 2

University of Toronto, grant, 1932	10,000 00

Banting Research Aid Act, 1927 ($10,000.00)
17 Geo. V, Chap. 94, Sec. 2

Banting Research Foundation, grant, 1932	10,000 00

Statutory—Continued

Audit of Teachers' and Inspectors' Superannuation Fund ($1,250.00)
R.S.O. 1927, Chap. 331, Sec. 2

Clarkson, Gordon, Dilworth, Guilfoyle & Nash 1,250 00

Ontario Government Contribution to the Public Service Superannuation Fund ($304,606.36)

Public Service Superannuation Fund 304,606 36

Northern Ontario Fire Relief ($7,809.34)
13-14 Geo. V, Chap. 7, Sec. 2

Town of Haileybury 7,809 34

R.S.O. 1927, Chap. 22, Sec. 5 ($4,000.00)

Ancient, Illustrious and Military Order, Knights of Malta, settlement of judgment... 4,000 00

Compensation to Blind Workers for injuries, etc., contracted in the course of their employment ($167.70)
2 Geo. V, Chap. 38, Sec. 3

Workmen's Compensation Board 167 70

THE PROVINCE OF ONTARIO SAVINGS OFFICE

Salaries, Head Office ($18,868.70)

Name	Position	Period	Amount
M. E. McKenzie	Director	12 months	6,000 00
R. M. Rattray	Chief Accountant	12 "	3,300 00
S. C. Patton	Inspector	12 "	2,000 00
O. J. McCullough	"	12 "	2,100 00
E. McGee	Clerk Stenographer, Group 2	5 "	468 70
M. Kingston	Clerk Typist " 2	12 "	900 00
H. Hanmer	Clerk, " 1	12 "	1,600 00
C. Houston	Office Appliance Operator, " 3	12 "	900 00
F. Mason	Secretarial Stenographer	12 "	1,600 00

Contingencies ($37,620.68)

Travelling Expenses.—M. E. McKenzie 427 36

Advertising.—Canadian Holy Name Banner, 15.00; Canadian Legion British Service League, 25.00; Canadian Street Car Advertising Co., 2,098.75; Labor Temple Co., Ltd., 50.00; Clarke E. Locke, Ltd., 19,386.75; Royal Agricultural Winter Fair, 100.00; Geo. Sheppard, 200.00; Toronto Women's Organization Directory, 50.00 .... 21,925 50

Miscellaneous.—Bell Telephone Co., tolls, 109.75; W. Black, insurance premiums, 202.50; Burroughs Adding Machine of Canada, Ltd., inspections and repairs, 14.10; Canadian Laco Lamps, Ltd., lamps, 15.88; Canadian Surety Co., insurance premiums, 791.85; Canadian Westinghouse Co., Ltd., fan, 39.02; R. F. Collins, construction of booth for exhibit, 365.00; Dept. of Highways, auto service, 198.60; Field, Love & House, typewriter inspections and repairs, 20.25; Flexlume Sign Co., Ltd., sign, 199.65; Goldie & McCulloch Co., Ltd., vault doors, safety deposit boxes, 916.00; King's Printer, 9,720.17; London Canada Insurance Co., insurance premiums, 258.65; F. & T. McMulkin, insurance premiums, 292.50; W. H. Price, signs, 32.50; J. & J. Taylor, storage on safe, 18.00; safe, 1,000.00; Typewriter Sales & Service Co., inspections, 3.50; United Typewriter Co., Ltd., inspections and repairs, 18.50. Sundries—postage, 825.00; newspapers and periodicals, 183.00; telegrams, 43.40 .... 15,267 82

Salaries and Expenses of Branch Offices ($160,189.56)

Permanent Salaries.—Aylmer, 3,525.00; Brantford, 7,300.00; Hamilton, 8,975.00; Hamilton East End, 4,150.00; Newmarket, 2,225.00; Ottawa, 11,353.84; Owen Sound, 3,825.00; Pembroke, 5,050.00; Seaforth, 2,600.00; St. Catharines, 5,375.00; St. Mary's, 3,300.00; Toronto—University and Dundas, 10,387.40; Bay and Adelaide, 18,040.59; Danforth and Fenwick, 8,425.00; Woodbine, 7,115.68; Walkerton, 2,975.00; Woodstock, 3,175.00 .... 107,797 51

Statutory—Continued

Province of Ontario Savings Office—Continued

Salaries and Expenses of Branch Offices—Continued

Temporary Salaries.—Brantford, 1,500.00; Hamilton, 1,650.00; Ottawa, 632.69; Pembroke, 525.00; Toronto—University and Dundas, 2,555.28; Bay and Adelaide, 3,151.44; Danforth and Fenwick, 1,725.00; Woodbine, 1,275.00; Woodstock, 750.00	13,764 41	
Expenses.—Aylmer, 550.35; Brantford, 1,984.98; Hamilton, Market Branch, 2,605.00; Hamilton, East End, 1,300.00; Newmarket, 730.00; Ottawa, 3,900.00; Owen Sound, 1,349.92; Pembroke, 1,665.11; Seaforth, 525.00; St. Catharines, 1,682.00; St. Mary's, 866.42; Toronto—Bay and Adelaide, 10,089.96; University and Dundas, 2,500.00; Danforth and Fenwick, 4,200.00; Danforth and Woodbine, 3,022.50; Walkerton, 836.40; Woodstock, 820.00	38,627 64	
	216,678 94	
Less refunded by Province of Ontario Savings Office	216,678 94	

Agricultural Development Finance Act ($8,500,000.00)
11 Geo. V, Chap. 31, Sec. 4B and 4C

Agricultural Development Board, debentures	8,500,000 00

Farm Loans Act ($33,790.00)

Ekfrid Farm Loan Association	2,350 00
Glanford Farm Loan Association	900 00
Howard Farm Loan Association	1,300 00
Mosa Farm Loan Association	4,450 00
Nassagaweya Farm Loan Association	3,550 00
Nelson Farm Loan Association	4,750 00
North Grimsby Farm Loan Association	1,200 00
Sault Ste. Marie Farm Loan Association	240 00
Seneca Farm Loan Association	900 00
Toronto Township Farm Loan Association	2,300 00
Trafalgar Farm Loan Association	11,850 00

Statutory	**$9,962,101 05**
Total	9,242,859 39
Less Salary Assessment	9,990 82
Total Treasury Department (excluding Public Debt)	**$9,232,868 57**

PUBLIC DEBT—PRINCIPAL, INTEREST, ETC. (STATUTORY)
Stock and Debentures

3½% Registered Stock, £422,549-4-10 ($72,371.24)

Bank of Montreal, interest	71,974 18
" " commission charges	359 90
" " advertising, cable charges, etc.	37 16

4% Registered Stock £317,912-16-4 ($62,240.98)

Bank of Montreal, interest	61,887 00
" " commission charges	309 44
" " advertising, cable charges, etc.	44 54

4½% Registered Stock, £171,454-12-8 ($37,769.37)

Bank of Montreal, interest	37,548 56
" " commission charges	187 74
" " advertising, cable charges, etc.	33 07

3½% Stock and Debentures, $3,000,000.00 ($12,188.75)

Interest on $348,000.00 outstanding	12,188 75

4% Stock and Debentures, $1,150,000.00 ($45,939.11)

Interest on $1,150,000.00 outstanding	45,920 00
Commission charges, Bank of Montreal	19 11

4% Stock and Debentures, $3,500,000.00 ($26,574.57)

Series A

Interest on $665,950.00 outstanding	26,558 00
Commission charges, Bank of Montreal	16 57

Public Debt (Statutory)—Continued

Stock and Debentures—Continued

4% Stock and Debentures, $500,000.00 ($8,961.58)

Series B

Interest on $224,000.00 outstanding	8,960 00
Commission charges, Bank of Montreal	1 58

4% Stock and Debentures, $3,000,000.00 ($47,530.11)

Series C and D

Interest on $1,188,400.00 outstanding	47,496 00
Commission charges, Bank of Montreal	34 11

6% Debentures, $3,000,000.00 ($3.00)

Series T and U

Interest, outstanding coupon paid	3 00

6% Debentures, $4,250,000.00 ($124.03)

Series V, W and X

Principal on $4,250,000.00 loan—outstanding debentures paid	100 00
Interest—outstanding coupons paid	24 00
Commission charges, Bank of Montreal	03

6% Debentures, $3,000,000.00 ($117,791.96)

Series K.K.

Interest on $1,981,000.00 outstanding	117,720 00
Commission charges, Bank of Montreal	71 96

6% Debentures, $6,800,000.00 ($2,331.67)

Series L.L.

Principal on $6,800,000.00 loan—outstanding debentures paid	2,000 00
Interest—outstanding coupons paid	330 00
Commission charges, Bank of Montreal	1 67

6% Debentures, $8,000,000.00 ($1,800.00)

Series M.M.

Principal on $8,000,000.00 loan—outstanding debentures paid	1,500 00
Interest—outstanding coupons paid	300 00

6% Debentures, $16,000,000.00 ($916,767.24)

Series R.R.

Interest on $15,233,000.00 outstanding	916,500 00
Commission charges, Bank of Montreal	267 24

6% Debentures, $10,000,000.00 ($570,252.16)

Series S.S.

Interest on $9,503,500.00 outstanding	570,120 00
Commission charges, Bank of Montreal	132 16

6% Debentures, $15,000,000.00 ($861,642.71)

Series T.T.

Interest on $14,390,000.00 outstanding	861,450 00
Commission charges, Bank of Montreal	192 71

6% Debentures, $15,000,000.00 ($889,706.64)

Series U.U. and X.X.

Interest on $14,912,000.00 outstanding	888,650 88
Commission charges, Bank of Montreal	1,055 76

6% Debentures, $15,000,000.00 ($873,894.89)

Series W.W. and Y.Y.

Interest on $14,612,500.00 outstanding	873,566 71
Commission charges, Bank of Montreal	328 18

Public Debt (Statutory)—Continued

Stocks and Debentures—Continued

5½% Debentures, $15,000,000.00 ($826,853.66)

Series Z.Z.

Interest on $15,000,000.00 outstanding	825,825 00
Commission charges, Bank of Montreal	1,028 66

5% Debentures, $15,000,000.00 ($751,810.39)

Series A.B.

Interest on $15,000,000.00 outstanding	750,875 00
Commission charges, Bank of Montreal	935 39

5% Debentures, $20,000,000.00 ($998,267.16)

Series A.C.

Interest on $20,000,000.00 outstanding	997,025 00
Commission charges, Bank of Montreal	1,242 16

5½% Debentures, $20,000,000.00 ($1,029,320.25)

Series A.D.

Interest on $18,639,500.00 outstanding	1,028,980 12
Commission charges, Bank of Montreal	340 13

5% Debentures, $40,000,000.00 ($1,912,671.02)

Series A.F.

Interest on $38,306,500.00 outstanding	1,912,300 00
Commission charges, Canadian Bank of Commerce	371 02

4½% Debentures, $20,000,000.00 ($862,142.53)

Series A.G.

Interest on $19,200,000.00 outstanding	861,345 00
Commission charges, Bank of Montreal	797 53

4½% Instalment Debentures, $21,000,000.00 ($773,028.51)

Series A.H.

Interest on $17,500,000.00 outstanding	772,020 00
Commission charges, Bank of Montreal	1,008 51

4½% Instalment Debentures, $24,000,000.00 ($918,824.80)

Series A.J.

Interest on $20,800,000.00 outstanding	917,685 00
Commission charges, Bank of Montreal	1,139 80

4½% Instalment Debentures, $24,000,000.00 ($954,371.46)

Series A.K.

Interest on $21,600,000.00 outstanding	953,077 50
Commission charges, Bank of Montreal	1,293 96

4% Instalment Debentures, $30,000,000.00 ($1,160,506.84)

Series A.L.

Interest on $28,982,000.00 outstanding	1,159,140 00
Commission charges, Bank of Montreal	1,366 84

5% Debentures, $35,000,000.00 ($1,730,747.06)

Series A.M.

Interest on $35,000,000.00 outstanding	1,728,730 48
Commission charges, Bank of Montreal	2,016 58

5% Debentures, $35,000,000.00 ($1,732,033.36)

Series A.N.

Interest on $35,000,000.00 outstanding	1,730,038 41
Commission charges, Bank of Montreal	1,994 95

Public Debt (Statutory)—Continued

Stock and Debentures—Continued

4½% Annuity Debentures, $30,000,000.00 ($1,341,394.08)

Series A.P.

Interest on $29,701,000.00 outstanding	1,339,717 50
Commission charges, Bank of Montreal	1,676 58

4½% Debentures, $2,000,000.00 ($90,000.00)

Series A.Q.

Interest on $2,000,000.00 outstanding	90,000 00

4½% Instalment Debentures, $30,000,000.00 ($1,337,465.51)

Series A.R.

Interest on $30,000,000.00 outstanding	1,335,577 50
Commission charges, Bank of Montreal	1,888 01

4% Instalment Debentures, $30,000,000.00 ($1,199,117.86)

Series A.S.

Interest on $30,000,000.00 outstanding	1,197,600 00
Commission charges, Bank of Montreal	1,517 86

5½% Debentures, $20,000,000.00 ($523,768.89)

Series A.T.

Interest on $20,000,000.00 outstanding (half year)	521,748 36
Commission charges, Bank of Montreal	2,020 53

6% Debentures $5,000,000.00 ($143,644.24)

Series A.U.

Interest on $5,000,000.00 outstanding (half year)	143,595 78
Commission charges, Bank of Nova Scotia	48 46

5½% Debentures, $2,000,000.00 ($55,015.50)

Series Z.A.-A.T.

Interest on $2,000,000.00 outstanding (half year)	55,000 00
Engraving debentures, British American Bank Note Co., Ltd	15 50

5½% Debentures, $20,000,000.00 ($365.41)

Series A.W.

Interest on $15,000.00 (purchased for Sinking Fund)	365 41

5% Debentures, $500,000.00 ($12,500.00)

Interest on $500,000.00 outstanding (half year).....a	12,500 00

5% Debentures, $150,000.00 ($3,750.00)

Interest on $150,000.00 outstanding (half year)		3,750 00
Stock and Debentures	$22,905,488.54	

TREASURY BILLS

Series B.G., $940,000.00 at 5% ($81,125.00)

Bills Nos. 21 to 25

Principal	35,000 00
Interest on $940,000.00	46,125 00

Series B.W., $5,000,000.00 at 2½% ($5,042,708.33)

Bills Nos. 111 to 115

Principal	5,000,000 00
Interest on $5,000,000.00	42,708 33

Public Debt (Statutory)—Continued

Treasury Bills—Continued

Series C.F., $5,000,000.00 at 2½% ($5,032,291.75)

Bills Nos. 6 to 55

Principal	5,000,000 00
Interest on $5,000,000.00	32,291 75

Series C.G., $5,000,000.00 at 2½% ($5,052,430.55)

Renewal

Principal	5,000,000 00
Interest on $5,000,000.00	52,430 55

Series C.H., $5,000,000.00 at 2½% ($5,028,437.50)

Principal	5,000,000 00
Interest on $5,000,000.00	28,437 50

Series C.I., $5,000,000.00 at 5% ($5,000,000.00)

Bills Nos. 1 to 5

Principal	5,000,000 00

Series C.I., $5,000,000.00 at 5½% ($5,023,356.15)

Bills Nos. 11 to 15

Principal	5,000,000 00
Interest on $5,000,000.00	23,356 15

Series C.I., $5,000,000.00 at 5½% ($5,067,808.20)

Bills Nos. 16 to 20

Principal	5,000,000 00
Interest on $5,000,000.00	67,808 20

Series C.I., $5,000,000.00 at 5½% ($5,045,958.90)

Bills Nos. 21 to 25

Principal	5,000,000 00
Interest on $5,000,000.00	45,958 90

Series C.J., $4,000,000.00 at 6% ($4,062,521.91)

Principal	4,000,000 00
Interest on $4,000,000.00	62,246 58
Printing Bills, British American Bank Note Co., Ltd.	25 33
Legal opinion, Long & Daly	250 00

Series C.J., $100,000.00 at 4½% ($4,500.00)

Interest on $100,000.00	4,500 00

Series C.K., $5,000,000.00 at 6% ($5,076,948.33)

Principal	5,000,000 00
Interest on $5,000,000.00	76,666 66
Printing Bills, British American Bank Note Co., Ltd.	31 67
Legal opinion, Long & Daly	250 00

Series C.L., $5,000,000.00 at 6% ($5,075,353.01)

Bills Nos. 1 to 10

Principal	5,000,000 00
Interest on $5,000,000.00	75,000 00
Printing Bills, British American Bank Note Co., Ltd.	2 26
Legal opinion, Long & Daly	250 00
Postage and insurance	100 75

Series C.L., $5,000,000.00 6% ($5,087,868.80)

Bills Nos. 11 to 20

Principal	5,000,000 00
Interest on $5,000,000.00	87,500 00
Printing Bills, Britsh American Bank Note Co., Ltd.	18 50
Legal opinion, Long & Daly	250 00
Postage and insurance	100 30

Public Debt (Statutory)—Continued

Treasury Bills—Continued

Series C.L., $2,500,000.00 6% ($2,538,516.99)

Bills Nos. 21-25

Principal	2,500,000 00
Interest on $2,500,000.00	38,333 33
Printing Bills, British American Bank Note Co., Ltd.	17 00
Legal opinion, Long & Daly	166 66

Series C.L., $2,500,000.00 6% ($17.00)

Bills Nos. 26-30

Printing Bills, British American Bank Note Co., Ltd.	17 00

Series C.M., $20,000,000.00 5½% ($19,184,084.74)

Principal	19,000,000 00
Interest on $20,000,000.00	183,994 26
Printing Bills, British American Bank Note Co., Ltd.	90 48

Series C.N., $4,000,000.00 6% ($4,060,402.76)

Bills Nos. 1 to 10

Principal	4,000,000 00
Interest on $4,000,000.00	60,000 00
Printing Bills, British American Bank Note Co., Ltd.	2 26
Legal opinion, Long & Daly	250 00
Postage and insurance	150 50

Series C.N., $4,000,000.00 6% ($4,071,751.78)

Bills Nos. 11 to 18

Principal	4,000,000 00
Interest on $4,000,000.00	71,333 33
Printing Bills, British American Bank Note Co., Ltd.	18 25
Legal opinion, Long & Daly	250 00
Postage and insurance	150 20

Series C.N., $2,000,000.00 6% ($165.67)

Bills Nos. 19 to 22

Printing Bills, British American Bank Note Co., Ltd.	15 50
Legal opinion, Long & Daly	100 00
Postage and insurance	50 17

Series C.O., $800,000.00 5½% ($807,112.32)

Principal	800,000 00
Interest on $800,000.00	7,112 32

Series C.O., $3,500,000.00 5½% ($3,516.349 35)

Bills Nos. 1 to 7

Principal	3,500,000 00
Interest on $3,500,000.00	16,349 35

Series C.O., $3,500,000.00 5½% ($3,515,294.59)

Bills Nos. 8 to 14

Principal	3,500,000 00
Interest on $3,500,000.00	15,294 59

Series C.O., $3,500,000.00 5½% ($3,548,520.56)

Bills Nos. 15 to 21

Principal	3,500,000 00
Interest on $3,500,000.00	48,520 56

Series C.P., $7,000,000.00 6% ($7,105,330.00)

Bills Nos. 1 to 70

Principal	7,000,000 00
Interest on $7,000,000.00	105,000 00
Printing Bills, British American Bank Note Co., Ltd.	80 00
Legal opinion, Long & Daly	250 00

Public Debt (Statutory)—Continued

Treasury Bills—Continued

Series C.P., $3,500,000.00 6% ($3,552,881.97)

Bills Nos. 71 to 105

Principal	3,500,000 00
Interest on $3,500,000.00	52,500 00
Printing Bills, British American Bank Note Co., Ltd.	39 50
Legal opinion, Long & Daly	166 67
Postage and insurance	175 80

Series C.P., $3,500,000.00 6% ($390.05)

Bills Nos. 201 to 235

Printing Bills, British American Bank Note Co., Ltd.	39 50
Legal opinion, Long & Daly	175 00
Postage and insurance	175 55

Series C.Q., $10,000,000.00 5½% ($10,000,000.00)

Bills Nos. 1 to 10

Principal	10,000,000 00

Series C.R., $3,000,000.00 5% ($397.95)

Bills Nos. 1 to 73

Printing Bills, British American Bank Note Co., Ltd.	80 00
Legal opinion, Long & Daly	166 67
Postage and insurance	151 28

Series C.S., $5,000,000.00 5½% ($5,000,000.00)

Bills Nos. 1 to 5

Principal	5,000,000 00

Series C.T., $100,000.00 5½% ($102,169.86)

Bill No. 1

Principal	100,000 00
Interest on $100,000.00	2,169 86

Series C.T., $2,000,000.00 5½% ($18.25)

Bills Nos. 2 to 9

Printing Bills, British American Bank Note Co., Ltd.	18 25

Series C.U., $15,000,000.00 5⅝% ($75.00)

Bills Nos. 1 to 150

Printing Bills, British American Bank Note Co., Ltd.	75 00

Series C.V., $5,000,000.00 6% ($1,077.71)

Bills Nos. 1 to 5,000

Printing Bills, British American Bank Note Co., Ltd.	1,075 00
Express charges	2 71

Series H.Y., $1,950,000.00 5½% ($1,961,610.27)

Bills Nos. 1 to 4

Principal	1,950,000 00
Interest on $1,950,000.00	11,610 27

Treasury Bills $128,647,475.25

MISCELLANEOUS

Province of Ontario Savings Office ($2,924,143.14)

Deposit withdrawals during year	2,924,143 14

Province of Ontario Savings Office ($942,535.80)

Interest on deposits at 4 per cent.	942,535 80

Public Debt (Statutory)—Continued

Miscellaneous—Continued

Interest Charges on Bank Overdrafts ($165,546.81)

Bank of Montreal	102,122 98
Bank of Nova Scotia	61,637 51
Canadian Bank of Commerce	1,652 39
Royal Bank of Canada	133 93

Interest Charges on Teachers' and Inspectors' Superannuation Fund ($43,824.84)

Teachers' and Inspectors' Superannuation Fund, interest on contributions	43,824 84

Interest Charges on Public Service Superannuation Fund ($198,104.20)

Public Service Superannuation Fund, interest on fund	198,104 20

Exchange on Transfer of Foreign Moneys ($2,330,463.13)

Bank of Montreal	3,460,775 32		
Bank of Nova Scotia	441,687 49		
Imperial Bank of Canada	487 50		
Manufacturers Mutual Fire Insurance Co.	504 00		
Mercantile Trust Co.	337 50		
		3,903,791 81	
Less refund:			
Hydro-Electric Power Commission of Ontario:			
Amount applicable to funds advanced		1,573,328 68	
			2,330,463 13

Insurance, Express, Postage, etc., on Bonds and Securities ($402.06)

Queen Insurance Co. of Canada, insurance	402 06

Premiums on Debentures Purchased for Sinking Funds ($38,425.00)

Loan AM—Sinking Fund (see page 26)	10,140 00	
" AN— " " (see page 26)	28,285 00	
		38,425 00

Discount on Debentures and Treasury Bills issued on account of "Old Debt" Refunding ($282,882.73)

Debentures—			
Series A.J.	22,132 00		
A.K.	5,536 08		
A.L.	14,618 00		
A.M.	2,705 83		
A.P.	12,400 00		
A.R.	9,754 00		
		67,145 91	
Treasury Bills—			
Series C.I.	42,009 13		
C.Q., Bills Nos. 1 to 5	68,561 65		
C.Q., Bills Nos. 6 to 10	45,959 00		
C.R.	13,494 72		
C.S.	22,602 75		
		192,627 25	
Premiums on Debentures purchased for Retirement and Sinking Funds		25,909 57	
		285,682 73	
Less premium received on Series A.N. Debentures		2,800 00	
			282,882 73
Miscellaneous		$6,926,327 71	

Public Debt (Statutory)—Continued

Stock and Debentures, Total, page 21			22,905,488 54
Treasury Bills, " " 24			128,647,475 25
Miscellaneous, " " 25			6,926,327 71
			158,479,291 50
Deduct:			
Interest received on loans advanced, etc.,			
Hydro-Electric Power Commission	9,870,112 54		
Settlers' Loan Commission	15,505 94		
Agricultural Development Board	1,601,966 11		
Farm Loans' Associations	6,015 56		
T. & N. O. Railway Commission	400,000 00		
Housing Commission	199,922 27		
Sundry Banks, special deposits	81,333 55		
Farm Loans Reserve	27,036 04		
		12,201,892 01	
Accrued interest received on,			
Series A.V. Debentures	1,416 43		
A.W. "	33,150 60		
C.R. Treasury Bills	1,666 66		
C.V. " "	3,287 65		
		39,521 34	
			12,241,413 35
Total Stock, Debentures, Treasury Bills and Miscellaneous			**146,237,878.15**

DEBT REDEMPTION INVESTMENTS

Matured Debentures, Certificates, etc ($4,450,618.94)

Railway Aid Certificates, due 1932	127,918 94	
Annuities, due 1932	36,700 00	
University of Toronto Certificates, due 1932	30,000 00	
Series A.H. Debentures—Instalment due 1932	700,000 00	
" A.J. " " " "	800,000 00	
" A.K. " " " "	800 000 00	
" A.L. " " " "	367,000 00	
" A.P. " " " "	312,000 00	
" A.R. " " " "	961,000 00	
" A.S. "	316,000 00	
		4,450,618 94

Series A.M. Debentures, Sinking Fund ($388,000.00)

Debentures Purchased

Sundry Investment Houses:	Par Value	Cost	
Series A.T 5½% due 1947	30,000 00	31,620 00	
" W.W. & Y Y. 6 % " 1943	23,000 00	23,895 00	
" A.M. 5 % " 1959	300,000 00	305,850 00	
" A.D. 5½% " 1942	10,000 00	10,425 00	
" A.W. 5½% " 1946	25,000 00	26,350 00	
	388,000 00	398,140 00	
Less—Premium paid on purchase (see page P 25)		10,140 00	
			388,000 00

Series A.N. Debentures—Sinking Fund ($353,000.00)

Debentures Purchased

Sundry Investment Houses:	Par Value	Cost	
Series A.N., 5 %, due 1960	353,000 00	381,285 00	
Less—Premium paid on purchase (see page P 25)		28,285 00	
			353,000 00

3½% Inscribed Stock Sinking Fund ($59,932.60)

	Par Value £ s. d.	Book Value $ c.	
British War Loan, 5% stock, 1947	5,808- 3- 2	28,449 40	
Commonwealth of Australia, 5% stock, 1975	4,637- 6-10	24,191 98	
Province of Ontario, 3½% stock, 1946	1,498- 3-11	7,291 22	
			59,932 60

4% Inscribed Stock Sinking Fund ($53,385.71)

	Par Value £ s. d.	Book Value $ c.	
British War Loan, 5% stock, 1947	7,366-16- 3	35,661 91	
Commonwealth of Australia, 5% stock, 1975	2,611- 9- 5	13,624 09	
Province of Ontario, 4% stock, 1947	842- 8- 1	4,099 71	
			53,385 71

4½% Inscribed Stock Sinking Fund ($19,844.95)

	Par Value £ s. d.	Book Value $ c.	
British War Loan, 5% stock, 1947	1,748- 8- 2	8,509 57	
Commonwealth of Australia, 5% stock, 1975	1,437-10- 2	7,499 65	
Province of Ontario, 3½% stock, 1946	538- 3- 3	2,619 06	
" " 4½% " 1965	250- 0- 0	1,216 67	
			19,844 95

Total—Debt Redemption Investments $5,324,782.20

Public Debt—Principal, Interest, etc. ($151,562,660.35)

SUMMARY

Treasury Department and Branches		9,768,307 95
Less Salary Assessment		9,990 82
		9,758,317 13
Public debt		151,562,660 35
		161,320,977 48
Deduct—Transferred to Part "U":		
Public Debt—Principal Payments	135,675,950 34	
Loans Advanced and Special Funds Repayments	8,784,337 84	
		144,460,288 18
Total Expenditure, Department of Provincial Treasurer		**$16,860,689 30**

PART Q

PROVINCIAL AUDITOR'S OFFICE

FISCAL YEAR, 1931-32

GENERAL INDEX AT BACK OF BOOK

PART Q—PROVINCIAL AUDITOR'S OFFICE

Statement of Expenditure Showing Amounts Expended, Unexpended and Overexpended for the Twelve Months Ended October 31st, 1932

Provincial Auditor's Office	Page	Estimates	Expended			Un-expended	Over-expended	Treasury Board Minute
			Ordinary	Capital	Total Ordinary and Capital			
		$ c.	$ c.	$ c.	$ c.	$ c.	$ c.	$ c.
Salaries	3	94,725 00	91,350 36	....	91,350 36	3,374 64	....	....
Contingencies	3	15,000 00	17,366 73	....	17,366 73	....	2,366 73	4,000 00
Supply Bill	..	109,725 00	108,717 09	....	108,717 09	3,374 64	2,366 73	....
Statutory: Salary of Auditor	4	....	6,500 00	....	6,500 00	....	....	....
Total	..	....	115,217 09	....	115,217 09	....	....	....
Less Salary Assessment	..	....	2,194 13	....	2,194 13	....	....	....
Total Expenditure, Provincial Auditor's Office	..	....	113,022 96	....	113,022 96	....	....	....

PROVINCIAL AUDITOR'S OFFICE

Gordon A. Brown.......Provincial Auditor (Statutory).......6,500 00

Salaries ($91,350.36)

T. R. Jennings	Assistant Provincial Auditor	12 months		4,200 00
W. A. Glocking	Chief Audit Clerk	12 "		3,450 00
W. M. Clendening	" " "	12 "		3,450 00
H. H. MacFadyen	Head Audit Clerk	12 "		2,850 00
J. A. Jackes	Principal Clerk	12 "		2,400 00
W. H. Hewitt	" "	12 "		2,400 00
L. J. Leigh	" "	12 "		2,400 00
J. H. Dignam	" "	12 "		2,300 00
W. B. Starratt	" "	12 "		2,300 00
C. F. Harris	" "	12 "		2,200 00
R. J. L. Boyd	" "	12 "		2,200 00
W. A. Train	" "	12 "		2,100 00
J. E. Maclean	Senior Audit Clerk	12 "		2,100 00
C. E. O'Reilly	" " "	3 months	548 00	
		(T) 9 "	777 41	1,325 41
M. De B. Sillifant	" " "	12 months		2,100 00
J. Scott	" " "	12 "		2,000 00
J. Milne	" " "	12 "		2,000 00
C. V. Watson	" " "	12 "		2,000 00
T. W. McEachern	" " "	12 "		2,000 00
A. H. Hawkins	" " "	12 "		2,000 00
F. Howard Lee	" " "	12 "		2,000 00
J. D. Laing	" " "	12 "		2,000 00
W. A. Little	" " "	12 "		2,000 00
T. J. O'Connor	" " "	12 "		2,000 00
J. A. Milling	" " "	12 "		2,000 00
R. J. Davidson	" " "	12 "		2,000 00
H. L. Cheeseman	" " "	12 "		2,000 00
J. H. Adamson	" " "	12 "		1,900 00
W. McLachlan	" " "	12 "		1,900 00
H. G. Cochran	" " "	12 "		1,900 00
W. E. Crampton	" " "	12 "		1,900 00
M. D. Rankin	" " "	12 "		1,900 00
T. J. Ingoldsby	" " "	12 "		1,900 00
J. Allan	" " "	12 "		1,800 00
A. S. Dickson	" " "	12 "		1,700 00
G. C. Mackay	" " "	12 "		1,700 00
C. G. Duggan	" " "	(T) 12 "		1,599 96
R. H. Aitken	" " "	12 "		1,300 00
A. W. Portch	" "	(T) 12 "		1,599 99
C. Tomlin	Clerk, Group 2	12 "		900 00
J. Varney	" " 3	12 "		675 00
J. Robinson	" " 3	12 "		600 00
F. Delves	Clerk Stenographer, " 1	12 "		1,200 00
M. I. Curran	Clerk Typist, " 1	12 "		1,050 00
J. Kruspe	" " " 1	(T) 12 "		900 00
S. Mordan	" " " 2	12 "		825 00
E. Mason	Clerk Stenographer " 2	12 "		900 00
M. A. Hunt	" " " 2	12 "		900 00
Frank Boyd	Office Boy	(T) 12 "		525 00

Contingencies ($17,366.73)

Temporary Services, $12,004.66.

M. Capling	Clerk Typist, Group 1	12 months	900 00
R. L. Cowan	Senior Audit Clerk	11 "	1,456 76
J. A. Cuthbert	" " "	12 "	1,599 96
W. A. Geddes	" " "	12 "	1,599 96
H. C. Jackson	Audit Clerk	12 "	1,200 00
J. G. McKeddie	Senior Audit Clerk	12 "	1,599 96
R. B. Morgan	Audit Clerk	12 "	1,200 00
Frances E. Ross	Clerk Typist, Group 1	10 "	750 00
Sundry Clerks on Interest Coupon Audit at $1,200.00 per annum			1,698 02

Contingencies—Continued

Travelling Expenses, $2,985.55.

J. Allan, 365.15; R. J. L. Boyd, 8.49; W. M. Clendening, 913.82; R. L. Cowan, 229.30; A. S. Dickson, 255.40; J. H. Dignam, 662.58; H. H. MacFayden, 247.10; J. G. McKeddie, 282.81; W. A. Train, 20.90 .... 2,985 55

Miscellaneous, $2,376.52.

Burroughs Adding Machine of Canada, Ltd., repairs, 23.77; Dept. of Highways, auto service, 19.63; King's Printer, 1,748.13; Geo. C. Mackay, books, 84.00; Monotype Co. of Canada, Ltd., rental, 43.05; Remington Typewriters, Ltd., inspections, 20.00; Todd Sales Co., Ltd., inspections and repairs, 123.00; United Typewriter Co., Ltd., rentals and repairs, 206.89. Sundries—newspapers and periodicals, 94.74; telegrams, 3.36; petty disbursements, 9.95 .... 2,376 52

STATUTORY

Auditor's salary 6,500 00

Total	$115,227.09	
Less Salary Assessment	2,194 13	
Total Expenditure, Provincial Auditor's Office	**$113,022.96**	

PART R

DEPARTMENT OF PROVINCIAL SECRETARY

FISCAL YEAR, 1931-32

TABLE OF CONTENTS

GENERAL INDEX AT BACK OF BOOK

PART R—DEPARTMENT OF PROVINCIAL SECRETARY

Statement of Expenditure Showing Amounts Expended, Unexpended and Overexpended for the Twelve Months Ended October 31st, 1932

Department of Provincial Secretary	Page	Estimates	Expended			Un-expended	Over-expended	Treasury Board Minute
			Ordinary	Capital	Total Ordinary and Capital			
		$ c.	$ c.	$ c.	$ c.	$ c.	$ c.	$ c.
Main Office:								
Salaries	6	51,700 00	46,832 48	....	46,832 48	4,867 52	....	....
Contingencies	6	15,000 00	11,869 12	....	11,869 12	3,130 88	....	....
Enforcement, Real Estate Brokers' Act	6	10,000 00	7 75	....	7 75	9,992 25	....	....
Main Office	..	76,700 00	58,709 35	....	58,709 35	17,990 65	....	....
Bureau of Municipal Affairs:								
Grant, Ontario Municipal Association	7	500 00	400 00	....	400 00	100 00	....	....
Registrar General:								
Salaries	7	49,275 00	49,043 75	....	49,043 75	231 25	....	....
Contingencies	7	15,000 00	5,457 32	....	5,457 32	9,542 68	....	....
District Registrar's fees	7	600 00	399 50	....	399 50	200 50	....	....
Registrar General	..	64,875 00	54,900 57	....	54,900 57	9,974 43	....	....
Public Institutions Branch:								
Salaries	8	34,950 00	23,532 04	....	23,532 04	11,417 96	....	....
Contingencies	8	7,650 00	8,850 14	....	8,850 14	....	1,200 14	2,000 00
Main Office	..	42,600 00	32,382 18	....	32,382 18	11,417 96	1,200 14	....
General:								
Travelling and other expenses of Bailiff and prisoners	8	20,000 00	15,402 96	....	15,402 96	4,597 04	....	....
Railway fares and clothing discharged prisoners	8	16,700 00	11,999 25	....	11,999 25	4,700 75	....	....
Removal expenses (other than patients)	9	500 00	323 31	....	323 31	176 69	....	....
Printing and stationery, Public Institutions	9	7,000 00	5,880 70	....	5,880 70	1,119 30	....	....
Medical attendance, funeral expenses, etc., of officials	9	350 00	5 00	....	5 00	345 00	....	....
Treatment of patients in hospitals and sanitoria	9	700 00	419 75	....	419 75	280 25	....	....
Exhibit at Canadian National Exhibition	9	3,000 00	2,968 70	....	2,968 70	31 30	....	....
Compassionate Allowances	..	1,700 00	....	....	....	1,700 00	....	....

Legal costs and expenses	9	500 00	81 35	....	81 35	418 65	....	....
Unforeseen and unprovided	9	500 00	15 20	....	15 20	484 80	....	....
General	..	50,950 00	37,096 22	....	37,096 22	13,853 78	....	....
Board of Parole:								
Salaries	9	14,875 00	10,450 01	....	10,450 01	4,424 99	....	....
Contingencies	9	6,000 00	6,255 96	....	6,255 96	....	255 96	500 00
Allowances and expenses for Parole Board	10	3,600 00	4,097 45	....	4,097 45	....	497 45	700 00
Prisoners' Assistance Fund	10	500 00	100 65	....	100 65	399 35	....	....
Expenses returning to prison parole violators	10	1,000 00	892 09	....	892 09	107 91	....	....
Board of Parole	..	25,975 00	21,796 16	....	21,796 16	4,932 25	753 41	....
Ontario Reformatory, Guelph:								
Salaries,								
Executive staff	10	16,230 00	14,400 00	....	14,400 00	1,830 00	....	....
Clerks and stenographers	10	7,375 00	7,748 54	....	7,748 54	....	373 54	450 00
Guards, etc	10	122,975 00	126,640 43	....	126,640 43	....	3,665 43	4,000 00
Expenses	10	210,000 00	178,339 90	....	178,339 90	31,660 10	....	....
Repairs to buildings, etc	13	30,000 00	16,675 22	....	16,675 22	13,324 78	....	....
Industrial operations	14	40,000 00	....	10,000 00	10,000 00	30,000 00	....	....
	..	426,580 00	343,804 09	10,000 00	353,804 09	76,814 88	4,038 97	....
Less perquisites, maintenance, etc	13	....	129,841 48	....	129,841 48	129,841 48	....	....
Ontario Reformatory, Guelph	..	426,580 00	213,962 61	10,000 00	223,962 61	206,656 36	4,038 97	....
Mimico Reformatory:								
Salaries	16	47,125 00	46,232 42	....	46,232 42	892 58	....	....
Expenses	16	60,000 00	53,698 95	....	53,698 95	6,301 05	....	....
Repairs to buildings	16	10,000 00	6,159 63	....	6,159 63	3,840 37	....	....
Purchase of materials	18	30,000 00	....	....	....	30,000 00	....	....
	..	147,125 00	106,091 00	....	106,091 00	41,034 00	....	....
Less miscellaneous sales, perquisites, etc	18	....	92,374 50	....	92,374 50	92,374 50	....	....
Ontario Reformatory, Mimico	..	147,125 00	13,716 50	....	13,716 50	133,408 50	....	....
Mercer Reformatory:								
Salaries,								
Executive staff	19	19,050 00	16,516 90	....	16,516 90	2,533 10	....	....
Engineering staff, etc	19	5,800 00	4,950 00	....	4,950 00	850 00	....	....

PART R—DEPARTMENT OF PROVINCIAL SECRETARY—Continued

Statement of Expenditure Showing Amounts Expended, Unexpended and Overexpended for the Twelve Months Ended October 31st, 1932

Department of Provincial Secretary	Page	Estimates	Expended			Un-expended	Over-expended	Treasury Board Minute
			Ordinary	Capital	Total Ordinary and Capital			
		$ c.	$ c.	$ c.	$ c.	$ c.	$ c.	$ c.
Mercer Reformatory—Continued								
Salaries—Continued								
Attendants, etc.	19	23,250 00	20,229 63	....	20,229 63	3,020 37	....	....
Temporary assistants	20	1,200 00	666 87	....	666 87	533 13	....	....
Expenses	20	40,000 00	35,039 50	....	35,039 50	4,960 50	....	....
Repairs to buildings, etc.	21	10,000 00	9,888 40	....	9,888 40	111 60	....	....
Industrial operations	..	10,000 00	....	....	....	10,000 00	....	....
	..	109,300 00	87,291 30	....	87,291 30	22,008 70	....	....
Less miscellaneous sales, etc.	21	....	27,717 35	....	27,717 35	27,717 35	....	....
Mercer Reformatory	..	109,300 00	59,573 95	....	59,573 95	49,726 05	....	....
Burwash Industrial Farm:								
Salaries,								
Executive staff	22	25,375 00	18,147 00	....	18,147 00	7,228 00	....	....
Clerks, etc.	22	8,950 00	6,612 50	....	6,612 50	2,337 50	....	....
School teachers	22	3,100 00	2,350 00	....	2,350 00	750 00	....	....
Engineering staff	22	6,900 00	6,642 50	....	6,642 50	257 50	....	....
Guards	22	110,031 25	94,705 56	....	94,705 56	15,325 69	....	....
Temporary help	22	2,500 00	1,125 00	....	1,125 00	1,375 00	....	....
Expenses	23	180,000 00	166,637 96	....	166,637 96	13,362 04	....	....
Repairs to buildings, etc.	25	25,000 00	32,417 56	....	32,417 56	....	7,417 56	10,000 00
	..	361,856 25	328,638 08	....	328,638 08	40,635 73	7,417 56	....
Less miscellaneous sales, etc.	26	....	55,590 13	....	55,590 13	55,590 13	....	....
Burwash Industrial Farm	..	361,856 25	273,047 95	....	273,047 95	96,225 86	7,417 56	....

Fort William Industrial Farm:								
Salaries,								
Executive staff	26	8,500 00	5,315 00		5,315 00	3,185 00		
Guards, etc.	26	13,100 00	15,569 57		15,569 57		2,469 57	
Temporary assistants		500 00				500 00		
Expenses	26	20,000 00	20,563 24		20,563 24		563 24	1,500 00
Repairs to buildings, etc.	27	10,000 00	9,428 12		9,428 12	571 88		
		52,100 00	50,875 93		50,875 93	4,256 88	3,032 81	
Less miscellaneous sales, etc.	28		4,801 37		4,801 37	4,801 37		
Fort William Industrial Farm		52,100 00	46,074 56		46,074 56	9,058 25	3,032 81	
Supply Bill		1,358,561 25	811,660 05	10,000 00	821,660 05	553,344 09	16,442 89	
Statutory:								
Minister's Salary	28		10,000 00		10,000 00			
Special Warrants:								
Citizens' Service Association	28		3,500 00		3,500 00			
Payment to Dr. W. C. Morrison, Sudbury Gaol	28		100 00		100 00			
Special Warrants			3,600 00		3,600 00			
Total			825,260 05	10,000 00	835,260 05			
Less Salary Assessment			10,771 57		10,771 57			
Department of Provincial Secretary			814,488 48	10,000 00	824,488 48			

SUMMARY

Department of Provincial Secretary	Page	Ordinary	Capital	Total
		$ c.	$ c.	$ c.
Main Office and Branches	6-7	114,009 92		114,009 92
Public Instititutions Branch	8-10	91,274 56		91,274 56
Ontario Reformatory, Guelph	10-16	213,962 61	10,000 00	223,962 61
Ontario Reformatory, Mimico	16-19	13,716 50		13,716 50
Mercer Reformatory	19-22	59,573 95		59,573 95
Burwash Industrial Farm	22-26	273,047 95		273,047 95
Fort William Industrial Farm	26-28	46,074 56		46,074 56
Statutory	28	10,000 00		10,000 00
Special Warrants	28	3,600 00		3,600 00
Total		825,260 05	10,000 00	835,260 05
Less Salary Assessment		10,771 57		10,771 57
Department of Provincial Secretary		814,488 48	10,000 00	824,488 48

PROVINCIAL SECRETARY'S DEPARTMENT

Hon. Geo. H. Challies....Provincial Secretary (Statutory)....10,000 00

MAIN OFFICE

Salaries ($46,832.48)

F. V. Johns	Assistant Provincial Secretary		12 months		4,800 00
A. E. Semple	Secretary to Minister and Departmental Secretary		12 "		3,300 00
F. Costello	Deputy Registrar		12 "		2,000 00
F. A. Hicks	Head Clerk	Group 2	12 "		2,700 00
A. E. Venables	Engrossing Clerk		12 "		1,600 00
R. M. Predam	Senior Clerk		12 "		1,900 00
J. D. Law	" "		12 "		1,700 00
E. M. Rice	Clerk	Group 1	12 "		1,600 00
Irene Edmunds	"	" 1	12 "		1,400 00
E. M. Rice	"	" 1	12 "		1,400 00
E. M. Rooney	"	" 1	12 "		1,300 00
N. S. Arnall	"	" 1	12 "		1,200 00
F. T. Jennings	"	" 2	12 "		1,125 00
G. R. Baker	"	" 2	12 "		1,125 00
E. Laister	"	" 2	12 "		1,050 00
A. Thompson	"	" 2	12 "		975 00
Violet I. Couling	Secretarial Stenographer		12 "		1,400 00
Elsie Graham	Clerk Stenographer,	Group 1	12 "		1,125 00
M. U. Johnson	" "	" 1	12 "		1,125 00
G. M. Duffy	" "	" 1	12 "		1,125 00
L. M. Lalonde	" "	" 1	12 "		1,125 00
Vera M. Crawford	" "	" 1	12 "	1,050 00	
	Less Leave of Absence			392 52	657 48
A. W. Edgar	" "	" 2	12 "		975 00
Annie Wallwin	" "	" 2	12 "		975 00
Mabel Mitchell	" "	" 2	12 "		900 00
Grace C. Dunsford	" "	" 2	12 "		900 00
T. C. Fleming	Clerk Typist,	" 1	12 "		1,125 00
A. M. Henderson	" "	" 1	12 "		1,050 00
G. C. F. Meredith	Senior Filing Clerk		12 "		1,500 00
G. Hopper	Filing Clerk,	" 1	12 "		1,125 00
J. Cooper-Mason	" "	" 2	12 "		975 00
R. D. Strange	" "	2	12 "		900 00
G. Gordon	Office Boy		12 "		675 00

Contingencies ($11,869.12)

Temporary Services, $5,355.74.

W. F. Carpenter	Clerk Stenographer,	Group 1	12 months	975 00
R. J. Cudney	Assistant		3½ "	149 99
Winifred E. Darke	Clerk Stenographer,	" 1	12 "	975 00
Jack D. Frazer	Office Boy		12 "	525 00
Clara Hanlon	Junior Filing Clerk		12 "	900 00
C. H. Henderson	Office Boy		12 "	525 00
N. E. Johns	Clerk Stenographer,	" 2	12 "	825 00
G. E. Webb	Clerk,	" 3	7⅔ "	480 75

Travelling Expenses, 650.00.

Hon. G. H. Challies 650 00

Miscellaneous, $5,863.38.

Canada Law Book Co., Ltd., law reports, 36.00; Dept. of Highways, auto service, 33.08; Field, Love & House, typewriter inspections, 20.00; King's Printer, 5,091.36; Remington Typewriters, Ltd., inspections and repairs, 36.95; Sundry persons, meals re overtime, 13.00; United Typewriter Co., Ltd., inspections and repairs, 307.05. Sundries—car tickets, 19.00; customs and excise, 6.60; newspapers and periodicals, 154.65; postage, 8.70; telegrams, 87.86; petty disbursements, 49.13 .... 5,863 38

Travelling and other expenses re Administration and Enforcement of the Real Estate Brokers Act, 1930 ($7.75)

Commissioner of Police for Ontario, travelling expenses re investigation 7 75

Main Office **$58,709.35**

BUREAU OF MUNICIPAL AFFAIRS

Grant to Ontario Municipal Association ($400.00)

Secretary, Ontario Municipal Association	400 00

REGISTRAR-GENERAL'S BRANCH

Salaries ($49,043.75)

Name	Position	Group	Period	Amount
S. J. Manchester	Registrar of Vital Statistics		12 months	2,500 00
E. G. Smith	Senior Clerk		12 "	2,000 00
G. W. Jones	" "		12 "	2,000 00
C. S. Horrocks	Clerk	Group 1	12 "	1,800 00
J. E. Latimer	"	" 1	12 "	1,600 00
C. H. Johnston	"	" 1	12 "	1,600 00
C. H. George	"	" 1	12 "	1,600 00
I. W. Curry	"	" 1	12 "	1,600 00
Geo. Routcliffe	"	" 1	12 "	1,600 00
W. Kell	"	" 1	12 "	1,600 00
R. B. Wallace	"	" 1	12 "	1,600 00
F. H. Binden	"	" 1	12 "	1,400 00
G. F. Avis	"	" 1	12 "	1,300 00
E. Fowler	"	" 2	12 "	1,200 00
F. M. Port	"	" 2	12 "	1,200 00
M. White	"	" 2	12 "	1,200 00
L. McDonald	"	" 2	12 "	1,200 00
F. E. Stout	"	" 2	12 "	1,200 00
K. McLeod	"	" 2	12 "	1,200 00
C. Snetzinger	"	" 2	12 "	1,050 00
R. LeRoy	"	" 2	10½ "	918 75
S. A. Quillman	"	" 2	12 "	1,050 00
V. Willoughby	"	" 2	12 "	1,050 00
D. Hally	Senior Clerk Stenographer		12 "	1,500 00
O. Leaf	Clerk Stenographer,	" 1	12 "	1,050 00
Alma D. Barrett	" "	" 3	12 "	975 00
F. M. Dion	" "	" 2	12 "	975 00
M. Gray	Clerk Typist,	" 1	12 "	1,200 00
N. W. Sherman	" "	" 1	12 "	1,200 00
Esther R. Scott	" "	" 1	12 "	1,200 00
A. E. McDonnell	" "	" 1	12 "	1,050 00
M. McLean	" "	" 1	12 "	1,050 00
L. Greer	" "	" 2	12 "	900 00
M. M. Jardine	Filing Clerk.	" 1	12 "	1,125 00
G. Hughes	" "	" 1	12 "	1,050 00
Isabel S. Bethune	" "	" 1	12 "	900 00
A. B. Holmes	Senior Clerk Messenger		12 "	1,400 00

Contingencies ($5,457.32)

Temporary Services, $3,450.00.

Name	Position	Group	Period	Amount
Marion Fessey	Clerk Stenographer,	Group 2	12 months	825 00
G. Hill	" "	" 2	12 "	825 00
Jos. M. Judson	Clerk,	" 2	12 "	975 00
P. Moore	Clerk Stenographer,	" 2	12 "	825 00

Miscellaneous, $2,007.32.

Field, Love & House, inspections, 29.00; E. Harley, certificate re divorce actions, 42.00; King's Printer, 5,935.75; Remington Typewriters, Ltd., inspections, 57.80; Sundry persons, registrations of divorces, 270.00; Typewriter Sales & Service Co., repairs and ribbon, 14.55; United Typewriter Co., Ltd., inspections and repairs, 13.37; R. B. Wallace, commissions on money orders, 92.81. Sundries—express, 19.65; telegrams, 18.79; petty disbursements, 1.00 .... 6,494 72

Less Dominion Government subventions 4,487 40

2,007 32

District Registrars' Fees ($399.50)

Sundry persons	399 50

Registrar General $54,900.57

Public Institutions

MAIN OFFICE

Salaries ($23,532.04)

Name	Position	Group	Period		Amount
Clarence F. Neelands	Deputy Provincial Secretary		12 months		5,200 00
James Hillock	Accountant	Group 4	12 "		1,800 00
James Masterson	Clerk,	" 1	3½ "		466 67
William K. Siddall	"	" 1	8½ "		850 00
Franklin J. Jeffs	"	" 2	12 "		1,050 00
Nora V. Noble	Clerk Stenographer,	" 1	12 "		1,200 00
Eva R. Little	" "	" 1	3 "		281 25
Adelaide McIldoon	" "	" 1	12 "		1,125 00
Jean J. McAdam	" "	" 1	12 "		1,125 00
Elma Lafferty	" "	" 1	12 "		1,050 00
James A. Norris	Inspector of Prisons and Public Charities		12 "		2,700 00
Jno. H. Fisk	Provincial Bailiff		12 "		1,600 00
Thos. M. Gourlay	Supervisor of Industries		12 "		2,300 00
J. L. McJannett	Supervising Electrician		12 "		2,200 00
Donald Ross	Office Boy		12 "	675 00	
	Less Leave of Absence			90 88	584 12

Contingencies ($8,850.14)

Temporary Services, $3,160.95.

Name	Position	Group	Period		Amount
Gwynneth P. Davy	Clerk Stenographer,	Group 1	12 months		975 00
Gabrielle Kelly	Filing Clerk,	" 1	12 "	900 00	
	Less Leave of Absence			20 00	880 00
Lindsay J. Pitt	Clerk,	Group 2	1 "		81 25
Della M. Shaver	Clerk Typist,	" 2	7 "		444 70
Nathaniel Topping	" "	" 2	12 "		780 00

Travelling Expenses, $2,491.95.

T. W. Barnard, 21.40; R. Beatty, 49.65; John J. Dundas, 5.05; V. L. Gladman, 38.45; T. M. Gourlay, 286.76; J. Hillock, 517.73; B. T. McGhie, 37.04; W. L. McJannet, 582.69; J. H. Masterson, 13.23; C. F. Neelands, 395.50; Nora V. Noble, 5.90; J. A. Norris, 463.70; H. M. Robbins, 19.45; J. Vance, 55.40........ 2,491 95

Miscellaneous, $3,197.24.

Burroughs Adding Machine of Canada, Ltd., inspections, 15.57; Department of Highways, auto service, 187.93; Lionel Godson, auto insurance, 31.74; King's Printer, 2,412.51; Thomas & Corney Typewriters, Ltd., rental and inspections, 15.75; United Typewriter Co., Ltd., rental and inspections, 173.56. Sundries—car tickets, 68.00; express, 3.03; freight, .90; newspapers and periodicals, 25.50; telegrams, 220.39; petty disbursements, 42.36........ 3,197 24

Main Office........ $32,382.18

GENERAL

Travelling and Other Expenses of Bailiffs and Prisoners ($15,402.96)

Travelling Expenses, $15,228.36.

W. A. Baker, 56.40; R. H. Craig, 5.00; J. H. Fell, 43.85; J. H. Fisk, 12,070.85; C. J. Fox, 75.10; A. Irving, 44.45; A. J. Johnston, 21.00; W. McGhee, 14.00; A. Morris, 34.85; Agnes Porter, 1,799.68; E. J. Ryan, 30.00; Superintendent, Industrial Farm, Fort William, 142.85; Superintendent, Industrial Farm, Burwash, 699.25; Superintendent, Mercer Reformatory, 14.44; Superintendent, Ontario Reformatory, Guelph, 49.04; E. J. Turner, 58.10; R. F. Vair, 67.00; J. Weymouth, 2.50........ 15,228 36

Miscellaneous, $174.60.

A. A. Allan & Co., Ltd., hat, 4.50; R. H. Bond, making and trimming suit and overcoat, 56.00; R. B. Hutchinson & Co., cloth for suit and overcoat, 43.10; Rice Lewis & Sons, Ltd., handcuffs, 63.00; James Wylie, boots, 8.00........ 174 60

Railway Fares and Clothing of Discharged Prisoners ($11,999.25)

Fares.

Canadian National Railways, 5,723.00; Canadian Pacific Railway Co., 1,653.55. 7,376 55

Clothing.

A. Bradshaw & Son, Ltd., print, 15.91; Hamilton & Johnston, flannel, cotton, etc., 76.95; J. A. McLaren Co., Ltd., shoes, 34.80; Mercer Reformatory Industries, print, etc., 9.91; E. Newbird, damage to clothing, 20.00; Ontario Reformatory Industries, Guelph, clothing, 4,416.53; A. Saywell, suit cases, 48.60........ 4,622 70

Public Institutions—Continued

General—Continued

Removal Expenses (Other than Patients) in Connection with the Public Institutions ($323.31)

J. Buckley, Fort William to Guelph, 115.66; I. C. Florence, Fort William to Burwash and return, 48.05; G. Graham, Ontario Reformatory, Mimico to Burwash, 8.15; H. Hollingshead, Burwash to Guelph Reformatory, 13.60; J. E. Hunter, Guelph City to Ontario Reformatory, 9.60; J. H. Masterson, Guelph to Toronto, 38.50; J. Reeves, W. Bush and E. Loper, Fort William to Burwash, 73.60; V. Savage and J. Quinn, Guelph to Burwash, 5.50; C. Zinger, Ontario Reformatory, Mimico to Burwash, 10.65 .... 323 31

Printing and Stationery for Public Institutions ($5,880.70)

King's Printer 5,880 70

Medical Expenses, Funeral Transportation, etc., of Officials and Employees of Public Institutions ($5.00)

Dr. A. B. Ritchie, professional services re R. Barry 5 00

Treatment of Patients and Inmates of Public Institutions in Hospitals and Sanatoria ($419.75)

Guelph General Hospital, 22.50; St. Joseph's Hospital, Guelph, 52.50; St. Joseph's Hospital, Toronto, 344.75 .... 419 75

Expenses in Connection with the Exhibit of the Provincial Secretary's Department at the Canadian National and Other Exhibitions ($2,968.70)

Travelling Expenses, $314.32.

E. J. Gonyeau, 3.75; T. M. Gourlay, 13.40; J. J. Kirvan, 43.75; J. A. Livingston, 87.09; W. L. McJannet, 25.70; M. Marquess, 26.35; A. M. Richardson, 16.75; Wm. Roulston, 15.95; A. Smith, 57.23; T. Warden, 24.35 .... 314 32

Miscellaneous, $2,654.38.

Associated Chemical Co. of Canada, Ltd., mystic gloss, etc., 18.81; Bariger & Ritchie, painting stand and railing, 43.00; Barrett Bros., lumber, 37.39; H. C. Burton & Co., lamps, 25.94; City Signs, lettering booth, 32.50; Day Sign Co., Ltd., map and card, 850.60; D. K. Edwards, Ltd., lumber, 65.49; Grant-Holden-Graham, Ltd., wool jacks, 16.20; R. Laidlaw Lumber Co., Ltd., beaver board, etc., 10.56; Masco Co., Ltd., electric supplies, 30.60; J. H. Morin & Co., Ltd., duresco, etc., 92.20; Pay list, wages of men, 437.76; Province of Ontario Pictures, negatives, prints, 748.18; The Robt. Simpson Co., Ltd., decorating panels, 139.65. Sundries—cartage, 85.00; petty disbursements, 20.50 .... 2,654 38

Legal Costs and Expenses Covering Sundry Investigations ($81.35)

J. A. Hanrahan, services reporting, 46.25; Velma Hill, copies of evidence, 35.10 .... 81 35

Unforeseen and Unprovided ($15.20)

E. J. Turner, refund of expenses, Burwash to New Brunswick and return 15 20

General $37,096.22

BOARD OF PAROLE

Salaries ($10,450.01)

Name	Position	Months		Amount
A. E. Lavell	Parole Officer	3 months		1,075 00
Thomas D. Bell	Parole Inspector	3 "	675 00	
	Acting Parole Officer	9 "	2,025 00	2,700 00
Edward J. Etherington	Parole Inspector	12 "		2,400 00
Grant Potter	Senior Clerk	9 "		1,200 01
Velma Moore	Clerk Stenographer, Group 1	12 "		1,050 00
Marjorie Morrison	" " " 2	12 "		975 00
Merle Latimer	Filing Clerk " 1	12 "		1,050 00

Contingencies ($6,255.96)

Temporary Services, $1,950.00.

Name	Position	Months	Amount
Florence C. Bellingham	Clerk, Group 2	12 months	975 00
Nora Hollings	Clerk Stenographer, " 1	12 "	975 00

Public Institutions—Continued

Board of Parole—Continued

Contingencies—Continued

Travelling Expenses.

T. D. Bell, 1,414.70; E. J. Etherington, 1,846.99; A. E. Lavell, 159.35; G. Potter, 10.75 ..... 3,431 79

Miscellaneous.

King's Printer, 724.85; United Typewriter Co., Ltd., inspections and repairs, 57.00. Sundries—express, 2.05; newspapers and periodicals, 24.00; telegrams, 62.27; petty disbursements, 4.00 ..... 874 17

Allowances and Expenses for Parole Board ($4,097.45)

G. A. Brodie, allowance, 15.00; Judge Coatsworth, allowance, 105.00; expenses, 153.00; W. A. Evans, allowance, 120.00; expenses, 206.20; F. C. Greenside, allowance, 90.00; expenses, 128.20; P. Kerwin, allowance, 240.00; expenses, 182.60; J. F. McKinley, allowance, 420.00; expenses, 608.10; G. S. Matthews, allowance, 270.00; expenses, 441.65; J. B. Tudhope, allowance, 285.00; expenses, 270.50; G. B. Woods, allowance, 300.00; expenses, 256.80; petty disbursements, 5.40 ..... 4,097 45

Prisoners' Assistance Fund ($100.65)

T. D. Bell, sundry persons 100 65

Expenses of Returning to Prison, Parole and Permit Violators ($892.09)

Canadian National Railways, fares, 39.60; Canadian Pacific Railway Co., fares, 513.66; Commissioner of Police for Ontario, expenses, 167.38; J. Jamieson, travelling expenses, 71.00; Superintendent, Ontario Reformatory, Guelph, travelling expenses of guards, 100.45 ..... 892 09

Board of Parole $21,796.16

ONTARIO REFORMATORY, GUELPH

Permanent Salaries ($140,417.08)

J. Hunter	Superintendent		12 months	3,600 00
Norman Wallace	Physician		12 "	3,000 00
James H. Masterson	Senior Clerk		8½ "	1,344 50
William F. Holloway	Clerk,	Group 1	12 "	1,600 00
Edmund J. Downey	"	" 1	12 "	1,500 00
Edward Murray	"	" 1	3½ "	465 50
John P. Evans	"	" 3	12 "	825 00
Sadie A. Melrose	Clerk Stenographer,	" 1	12 "	1,200 00
Earl Hogan	Storekeeper		12 "	1,800 00
W. G. Buskin	Store Assistant		12 "	1,400 00
Alfred Crossley	Teacher		12 "	2,000 00
E. A. Hammond	Stationary Engineer		12 "	2,100 00
H. Evans	Farmer		12 "	1,500 00
Rob Roy	Chef		12 "	1,600 00
William Waterhouse	Mason		12 "	1,600 00
George Roberts	Gardener		12 "	1,400 00
Engineering Staff, including assistant engineers, electrical engineers, plumbers and blacksmiths				6,200 00
Guards and Attendants				107,282 08

Temporary Salaries ($8,371.89)

Henry O. Howitt	Surgeon (part time)	1,000 00
Guards and Attendants		7,371 89

Expenses ($178,339.90)

Medicines, $8,347.74.

The Ash-Temple Co., Ltd., 68.09; F. Bogardus, 76.59; Bogardus & Barton, 113.61; Dr. E. S. Burrows, 532.00; N. S. Burrows, 10.00; Canadian Pacific Express, 44.80; Guelph General Hospital, 10.00; The Guelph Paper Co., 10.50; J. F. Hartz Co., Ltd., 43.95; J. Hillis, 100.80; Ingram & Bell, Ltd., 42.41; W. C. Macdonald, Inc., 6,170.00; R. E. Mitchell, 124.50; The H. Powell Chemical Co., Ltd., 548.47; Dr. W. A. Proud, 20.00; W. E. Saunders, 25.19; A. D. Savage, 120.65; E. B. Shuttleworth Chemical Co., Ltd., 153.40; Dr. L. M. Stuart, 35.00; F. W. Stull, 19.50; Chas. R. Will & Co., Ltd., 40.65; petty disbursements, 37.63 ..... 8,347 74

Public Institutions—Continued

Ontario Reformatory, Guelph—Continued

Expenses—Continued

Groceries and Provisions, $79,837.29.

Acton Creamery, 26.17; Balfours, Ltd., 697.45; Black & Ferrie, 1,792.98; Bowes Co., Ltd., 1,254.80; Cabot Macaroni Manufacturing Co., 175.33; Canada Packers, Ltd., 41.25; The Canada Starch Co., Ltd., 133.14; Canadian & Dominion Sugar Co., Ltd., 2,022.36; Canadian Milk Products, Ltd., 448.90; Cook Bros. Milling Co., 168.40; Crosse & Blackwell, Ltd., 28.51; E. A. Downey and C. H. Cummins, 82,89; Empire Tea Co., 36.00; J. L. Fielding & Co., 1,073.25; Amos B. Gordon Co., Ltd., 156.89; The Guelph Creamery, 72.80; The Harris Abattoir Co., Ltd., 21.74; The Hicks-Groom Co., 4,881.88; Harry Horne Co., Ltd., 532.38; Individual Tea Bag Co., Ltd., 330.00; The F. T. James Co., Ltd., 110.76; Mrs. G. Kean, 170.01; Lever Bros., Ltd., 23.02; Thos. J. Lipton, Ltd., 76.87; Maple Leaf Milling Co., Ltd., 2,898.54; McCarthy Milling Co., Ltd., 752.25; Muratori's Macaroni Manufacturing Co., 38.25; National Grocers Co., Ltd., 2,614.86; Chas. S. Ogg, 16.00; Ontario Agricultural College, Dept. of Apiculture, 85.20; Dairy Dept., 712.95; Trent Institute, 1,036.15; Ontario Hospital, London, 50.55; Ontario Reformatory Industries, 48,473.87; G. E. Rees, 2,426.44; Rowntree Co., Ltd., 48.30; J. Rider, 10.00; Silverwood's Milk Products, Ltd., 19.40; Standard Brands, Ltd., 631.68; Steep's Meat Market, 3,137.59; J. B. Stringer & Co., 95.00; Swift Canadian Co., Ltd., 245.26; Tavistock Milling Co., Ltd., 915.00; Hugh Walker & Son, Ltd., 726.80; Western Canada Flour Mills Co., Ltd., 286.88; J. Wilson & Sons, 60.00; Wright Fruit Co., 17.85; Chas. Yeates Co., Ltd., 16.06; Young-Winfield, Ltd., 119.43; petty disbursements, 45.20 .... 79,837 29

Fuel, Light and Water, $25,704.74.

P. Burns & Co., Ltd., 2,032.75; H. C. Burton & Co., 470.25; Canada Coal, Ltd., 240.59; Conger Lehigh Coal Co., Ltd., 8,100.91; Dalyte Electric, Ltd., 13.99; Amos B. Gordon Co., Ltd., 30.40; Gowdy Bros., 13.20; Hydro-Electric Power Commission, 3,125.91; Standard Fuel Co., Ltd., 10,829.91; Wadsworth Coal Co., Ltd., 844.33; petty disbursements, 2.50 .... 25,704 74

Clothing, $22,983.93.

A. A. Allen Co., Ltd., 254.85; J. Armstrong, Ltd., 23.00; Beardmore Leathers, Ltd., 322.01; Canadian National Express, 10.94; Canadian National Railways, 41.64; The Coghill Tailoring Co., 1,584.00; Dominion Rubber Co., Ltd., 166.84; The Dotzert Glove Co., Ltd., 327.88; Dunham & Duggan, Ltd., 421.05; Wm. Farrar Co., Ltd., 356.00; Goodyear Tire & Rubber Co. of Canada, Ltd., 213.05; Gutta Percha & Rubber, Ltd., 167.55; Jeffray & Taylor, 116.60; Lang Tanning Co., Ltd., 227.01; D. E. Macdonald & Bros., Ltd., 225.16; H. B. McCarthy, Ltd., 228.00; F. C. McCordick, 77.40; Mercer Reformatory Industries, 750.78; Northern Rubber Co., Ltd., 376.41; Ontario Hospital, Orillia, 3,200.00; Ontario Reformatory Industries, 10,432.23; Roden Bros., Ltd., 58.50; Scythes & Co., Ltd., 37.16; T. Sisman Shoe Co., Ltd., 340.00; Storey Glove Co., Ltd., 816.10; Taylor-Forbes Co., Ltd., 11.87; Tip Top Tailors, 420.00; C. Turnbull Co., Ltd., 897.90; J. J. Turner & Sons, Ltd., 87.26; United Shoe Machinery Co. of Canada, Ltd., 395.59; Woods Manufacturing Co., Ltd., 373.14; petty disbursements, 24.01 .... 22,983 93

Laundry and Cleaning, $5,010.58.

The Alpha Chemical Co., Ltd., 24.00; John Armstrong, Ltd., 10.00; Associated Chemical Co. of Canada, Ltd., 587.90; Beaver Laundry Machinery Co., Ltd., 69.34; The Bond Hardware Co., Ltd., 49.70; Canada Colors & Chemicals, Ltd., 197.13; Canadian Germicide Co. Ltd., 288.40; Canadian National Institute for the Blind, 84.67; Canadian Pacific Railway Co., 10.13; Electric Boiler Compound Co., Ltd., 730.00; J. R. Elliott, 97.50; Guelph Paper Box Co., Ltd., 16.00; A. J. Hawkins, 65.00; Hicks-Groom Co., 73.47; Interlake Tissue Mills Co., Ltd., 375.25; P. J. Jacobi, Ltd., 32.40; Jones Bros. of Canada, Ltd., 14.50; Lavoline Cleanser Co., Ltd., 143.33; S. F. Lawrason & Co., Ltd., 210.00; Lever Bros., Ltd., 61.30; Ontario Hardware Co., of Guelph, 52.75; Ontario Reformatory Industries, 28.85; The Penfold Hardware, 30.16; The St. Croix Soap Manufacturing Co., 565.69; R. E. Smith, 14.32; H. Spring & Sons, 53.25; Standard Brands, Ltd., 436.25; Stevens-Hepner Co., Ltd., 132.27; Tarbox Bros., Ltd., 218.28; J. J. Turner & Sons, 36.38; United Shoe Machinery Co. of Canada, Ltd., 13.00; Utility Products, Ltd., 19.50; J. B. Williams Co., Ltd., 29.12; J. C. Wilson, Ltd., 121.12; G. H. Wood & Co., Ltd., 99.52; petty disbursements, 20.10 .... 5,010 58

Furniture and Furnishings, $4,987.94.

Aluminum Goods, Ltd., 408.18; John Armstrong, Ltd., 99.59; The Ash-Temple Co., Ltd., 12.90; G. S. Blakeslee & Co., Ltd., 14.04; The Bond Hardware Co., Ltd., 40.31; J. Burns & Co., 21.33; Casings, Ltd., 18.25; T. Eaton Co., Ltd.,

Public Institutions—Continued

Ontario Reformatory, Guelph—Continued

Expenses—Continued

Furniture and Furnishings—Continued

29.50; General Steel Wares, Ltd., 202.93; Guelph Paper Co., 104.45; Gurney Foundry Co., Ltd., 25.28; Interlake Tissue Mills Co., Ltd., 118.40; D. E. Macdonald & Bros., Ltd., 20.63; Mercer Reformatory Industries, 1,494.52; Ontario Reformatory Industries, 2,011.65; Pendrith Machinery Co., Ltd., 23.50; Pilkington Bros., Ltd., 18.08; The Ratcliffe Paper Co., Ltd., 13.00; E. B. Shuttleworth Chemical Co., Ltd., 21.95; Geo. Sparrow & Co., 125.60; Standard Brands, Ltd., 49.22; R. G. Venn, 33.52; Victoria Paper & Twine Co., Ltd., 24.61; Wrought Iron Range Co. of Canada, Ltd., 10.00; petty disbursements, 46.50............ 4,987 94

Office Expenses, $2,451.57.

C. Anderson & Co., 13.83; Bell Telephone Co., rentals, 322.20; tolls, 473.07; B. Cairns, Ltd., 11.38; Canadian National Express, 12.17; Canadian National Telegraphs, 40.65; Canadian Pacific Express, 16.75; Chapple's, Guelph, 15.03; Guelph Paper Co., 13.00; King's Printer, 142.36; Pay list, wages of men, 105.00; Postmaster, 1,108.00; United Typewriter Co., Ltd., 141.75; petty disbursements, 36.38............ 2,451 57

Farm Expenses, $14,710.40.

Acton Creamery, 192.91; The Alpha Chemical Co., Ltd., 29.50; Associated Chemical Co. of Canada, Ltd., 297.60; Beatty Bros., Ltd., 33.87; Geo. J. Bell, 28.13; F. Bogardus, 29.80; The Bond Hardware Co., Ltd., 223.34; British American Oil Co., Ltd., 16.50; Canada Paint Co., Ltd., 292.94; Canadian Industrial Alcohol Co., Ltd., 65.80; Canadian National Express, 10.96; Canadian National Railways, 1,007.67; Canadian Oil Companies, Ltd., 65.91; Canadian Pacific Railway Co., 115.96; J. J. Cassin, 75.00; Connon Nurseries, 21.71; R. L. Craig, 145.50; Dale Estate, Ltd., 154.60; De Laval Co., Ltd., 63.50; Doughty & McFarlane, 973.59; Dupuy & Ferguson, 41.20; Elliott & Moody, 48.00; Eureka Planter Co., Ltd., 13.69; Foster Pottery Co., 76.44; Dr. W. C. Galbraith, 432.90; General Steel Wares, Ltd., 19.23; Goodale Transport, 14.33; Carl Grobba, 160.00; J. H. Hagen, 1,397.55; Halton Cream & Butter Co., 35.47; Hayman & Mills, 165.33; Percy Hill, 104.50; Holstein-Friesian Association, 28.00; International Stock Foods & Consumers Co., Ltd., 30.00; Lang Tanning Co., Ltd., 34.65; Louden Machinery Co. of Canada, Ltd., 17.76; Maple Leaf Milling Co., Ltd., 855.62; B. J. McCabe, 191.18; Wm. McSkimming, 40.00; N. McTaggart, 500.00; Niagara Brand Spray Co., 42.81; Ontario Hardware Co., 18.50; Ontario Hospitals—Hamilton, 297.20; London, 75.70; Woodstock, 69.00; Ontario Reformatory Industries, 1,287.89; Ontario Veterinary College, 54.25; Parish & Heimbecker, Ltd., 1,538.41; D. T. Parker, 72.50; Penfold Hardware Co., 129.54; Pioneer Equipment Co., 292.02; Pratt Food Co. of Canada, Ltd., 759.40; Rae's Wagon & Truck Body Works, 19.80; Ralston Purina Co., Ltd., 718.25; Wm. Rennie's Seeds, Ltd., 18.15; C. Richardson & Co., Ltd., 49.20; Scottish Fertilizers, Ltd., 406.00; L. M. Smith, 10.46; Steele, Briggs Seed Co., Ltd., 86.30; F. W. Stull, 48.96; J. H. Sweeney, 105.90; Taylor-Forbes Co., Ltd., 126.45; A. J. Thomas, 52.10; Toronto-Guelph Express, Ltd., 17.30; Tremco Manufacturing Co., Ltd., 153.72; Vaughan Seed Store, 10.50; W. W. Walker & Sons, 16.00; Edward Webb & Sons, Ltd., 12.52; W. R. Welshman, 13.00; D. Young, 56.90; Young-Winfield, Ltd., 15.00; petty disbursements, 86.03............ 14,710 40

Contingencies, $14,305.71.

Bedford Motor Service, repairs, 88.61; Bogardus & Barton, decorations, etc., 226.65; F. Bogardus, developing and printing, 156.01; Bond Hardware Co., hardware, 18.14; Brunswick-Balke-Collender Co. of Canada, pool supplies, 37.14; F. E. Campbell, frames, 20.45; Canadian National Express, 27.31; Canadian National Railways, 68.25; Canadian Oil Companies, Ltd., gasolene, 4,215.33; Canadian Westinghouse Co., Ltd., electric supplies, 10.91; Chapple's, maps, 121.48; Church of Our Lady, religious services, 260.00; City Battery & Electric Service, repairs and supplies, 36.49; Cooke & Denison, repairs, 59.70; M. F. Cray, Ltd., charts, 13.00; J. H. Davenport, repairs, 25.93; Dept. of Highways, car repairs, 26.73; H. Evans, travelling expenses, 11.60; Expert Tire Repair, tires, 37.88; L. Godson, car insurance, 115.56; Goodyear Tire and Rubber Co. of Canada, Ltd., tires and tubes, 82.44; Guelph Cemetery Commission, burial fees, 23.00; Guelph Ministerial Association, religious services, 260.00; Guelph Paper Co., paper, 26.50; Guelph Tire Hospital & Battery Service, repairs, 23.65; Geo. M. Hendry Co., Ltd., supplies, 24.51; J. Hunter, travelling expenses, 12.90; Imperial Oil, Ltd., oil, 26.87; Imperial Tobacco Co. of Canada, Ltd., tobacco, 67.60; Instruments, Ltd., charts, 61.00; C. W. Kelly & Son, musical supplies, 33.45; Lehman's Taxi, transportation, 117.25; J. A. Livingstone, travelling expenses, 144.76; McColl-Frontenac Oil Co., Ltd., oil, 25.98; J. A. McDermott, burial fees, 161.40; A. McNiven, ambulance services, 60.00; R. J. Mitchell, tires, 157.84; National Grocers Co., Ltd.,

Public Institutions—Continued

Ontario Reformatory, Guelph—Continued

Expenses—Continued

Contingencies—Continued

paper bags, 24.95; J. D. O'Neil, legal costs, 200.00; Ontario Auto Spring & Supply Co., supplies, 38.05; Dr. Orton, medical services, 30.00; Province of Ontario Pictures, films, 13.00; Ratcliffe Paper Co., paper, 110.35; Robson Motor Corporation of Canada, repairs, 140.28; W. Rumball, travelling expenses, 10.00; Dr. L. M. Stewart, medical services, 15.00; Studebaker Sales & Service, repairs, etc., 44.95; F. W. Stull, transportation, 28.60; Sundry prisoners, gratuities, 6,462.15; Taylor & Munro, repairs, 11.25; J. Tocker, travelling expenses, 10.00; A. L. Torgis & Son, water heater, 25.09; A. Tovell, burial fees, 10.00; Victoria Paper & Twine Co., Ltd., twine, 10.28; H. A. Wilson & Co., Ltd., sporting goods, 36.94; petty disbursements, 198.50 .... 14,305 71

Repairs to Buildings ($16,675.22)

Maintenance and Repairs to all Buildings, Roads, Walks, Grounds and Fences, $5,671.25.

The Arco Co., Ltd., 54.97; Aulcraft Paints, Ltd., 28.17; Ault & Wiborg Co. of Canada, Ltd., 16.90; R. O. Barber, 41.17; The Bond Hardware Co., Ltd., 429.32; Brantford Roofing Co., Ltd., 309.67; The British American Oil Co., Ltd., 23.85; Canada Colors & Chemicals, Ltd., 11.50; Canada Paint Co., Ltd., 91.14; Canadian Gypsum Co., Ltd., 49.73; Canada Wire & Cable Co., Ltd., 73.95; Canadian National Railways, 33.64; Chapple's, 121.65; W. H. Cunningham & Hill, Ltd., 22.19; Department of Highways, 475.80; Galt Art Metal Co., Ltd., 474.91; Gowdy Bros., 297.16; Guelph Lumber Co., Ltd., 55.61; Knight-Whaley Co., 15.39; Marks Transport, 14.28; The Martin-Senour Co., Ltd., 337.27; J. H. Morin & Co., Ltd., 274.43; Ontario Hardware Co. of Guelph, 71.70; Ontario Reformatory Industries, 942.83; Pay lists, wages of men, 232.88; The Penfold Hardware Co., 203.85; H. W. Petrie, Ltd., 12.54; Pilkington Bros., Ltd., 246.96; Roofers Supply Co., Ltd., 347.83; G. F. Sterne & Sons, Ltd., 103.39; Robert Stewart, Ltd., 227.51; petty disbursements, 29.06 .... 5,671 25

Maintenance and Repairs of Plumbing, Steam and Electric Plants and Machinery, $5,016.24.

D. Anderson, 46.00; Baines & David, Ltd., 18.60; The Bowden Machine Co., Ltd., 16.00; Beardmore Leathers, Ltd., 22.78; Beldam's Asbestos Packing & General Mfg. Co., Ltd., 100.25; Board of Light and Heat Commissioners, Guelph, 20.08; Boiler Repair & Grate Bar Co., 404.30; Bond Hardware Co., Ltd., 59.22; Brooks Oil Co., 105.35; Canada Metal Co., Ltd., 48.40; Canadian Fairbanks-Morse Co., Ltd., 73.84; Canadian General Electric Co., Ltd., 242.70; Canadian Oil Companies, Ltd., 153.99; Canadian Westinghouse Co., Ltd., 84.46; W. H. Cunningham & Hill, Ltd., 35.36; Dawson's Iron Works, Ltd., 33.10; Direct Transport, 12.87; Dominion Rubber Co., Ltd., 720.15; Electric Boiler Compound Co., Ltd., 97.50; Ellis & Howard, Ltd., 26.75; Empire Brass Mfg. Co., Ltd., 114.90; English Electric Co. of Canada, Ltd., 139.50; Federal Wire & Cable Co., Ltd., 82.62; The Garlock Packing Co. of Canada, Ltd., 99.01; Greenfield Tap & Die Corp., 32.29; Gurney Foundry Co., Ltd., 26.81; Hoyt Metal Co. of Canada, Ltd., 23.45; Huston Oil Co., 70.38; Imperial Oil, Ltd., 70.28; La France Fire Engine & Foamite, Ltd., 83.09; Macdonald Electric Supply, Ltd., 135.13; The Masco Co., Ltd., 107.19; Mason Regulator Co. of Canada, Ltd., 33.35; J. A. McFarlane, 24.00; The Herbert Morris Crane & Hoist Co., Ltd., 26.31; The James Morrison Brass Mfg. Co., Ltd., 188.23; Nesbitt Electric Mfg. Co., Ltd., 34.30; Northern Electric Co., Ltd., 77.16; Otis-Fensom Elevator Co., Ltd., 20.70; Pendrith Machinery Co., 14.50; H. W. Petrie, Ltd., 27.77; Powerlite Devices, Ltd., 95.72; G. W. Sadler Belting Co., Ltd., 39.89; Smart-Turner Machine Co., Ltd., 41.75; Square D Co. of Canada, Ltd., 22.38; Sutherland Schultz Electric Co., Ltd., 73.00; Taylor-Forbes Co., Ltd., 447.02; Thompson Gordon, Ltd., 21.77; Van Camp, Ltd., 443.54; Wolverine, Ltd., 13.51; petty disbursements, 64.99 .... 5,016 24

Live Stock, Vehicles and Farm Implements, $5,987.73.

Geo. Brown, 250.00; Department of Agriculture, 3,300.00; Ontario Reformatory, Mimico, 133.00; Pioneer Equipment Co., 85.50; Rae's Wagon & Truck Body Works, 286.50; Robson Motor Corp. of Canada, 1,067.73; Treasury Department of Ontario, Sedan car, 800.00; David Young, 65.00 .... 5,987 73

Total		343,804 09	
Less Maintenance of Insane Patients	34,317 42		
Perquisites	11,528 31		
Sale of Produce	83,995 75		
		129,841 48	
Ontario Reformatory, Guelph		$213,962 61	

Public Institutions—Continued

Ontario Reformatory, Guelph—Continued

INDUSTRIAL OPERATIONS ($10,000.00)

Permanent Salaries ($12,500.00)

John Kirvan	Abattoir Manager	12 months	2,100 00
George E. Roberts	Clerk, Group 1	12 "	1,300 00
Herbert D. Doig	Head Tailor	12 "	1,600 00
Fred W. Couling	Foreman, Planing Mill	12 "	1,500 00
John Ditchfield	Assistant Foreman, Planing Mill	12 "	1,400 00
A. McDonald	Assistant Stationary Engineer	12 "	1,600 00
Edward Lamb	Blacksmith	12 "	1,600 00
Adam Hamill	Fireman	12 "	1,400 00

Temporary Salaries ($3,824.36)

M. S. McKay	Foreman, Woollen Mill	12 months	1,800 00	
		Less Leave of Absence	35 00	1,765 00
William E. Bahen	Clerk, Group 2	10⅓ months		842 29
Pay Lists, wages of men				1,217 17

Expenses ($405,395.38)

Alger Cartage, trucking, 41.60; A. A. Allan & Co., Ltd., caps, etc., 28.98; American Can Co., jam pails, cans, etc., 9,205.46; American Dyewood Co., logwood crystals, 268.87; J. W. Anderson, calves, 33.71; A. Andrews, blueberries, 500.00; Armstrong Cork & Insulation, cork covering, 339.85; John Armstrong, Ltd., cotton, etc., 719.64; W. J. Armstrong, Ltd., dry goods, 259.75; Associated Chemical Co. of Canada, Ltd., wax, 35.28; Aulcraft Paints, Ltd., paint, 150.16; Ault & Wiborg Co., of Canada, Ltd., paint, etc., 66.39; Baines & David, Ltd., iron, etc., 3,317.77; Chas W. Barber, cow, 48.00; T. Ross Barber, material for notice boards, 67.18; Beardmore Leathers, Ltd., belting, etc., 381.03; Beatty Bros., Ltd., galvanized tank, etc., 34.72; Beaver Laundry Machinery Co., Ltd., press rebuilt, 245.00; Belding-Corticelli, Ltd., silk thread, etc., 102.42; The Bell Telephone Co., rentals, 127.20; tolls, 119.64; Bell Thread Co., Ltd., thread, 1,094.53; Bond Engineering Works, Ltd., casters, 52.56; The Bond Hardware Co., Ltd., hardware, 1,907.05; H. Bottomley, wire, 39.90; A. Bradshaw & Son, Ltd., dry goods, etc., 2,009.63; British American Oil Co., Ltd., oil, gas, etc., 79.55; Brooks Oil Co., oil, etc., 58.80; Brown-Boggs Foundry & Machinery Co., Ltd., repairs, etc., 159.13; Brown's Transport, trucking, 52.68; P. Burns & Co., Ltd., coal, 1,234.61; Sandy Campbell Machinery Co., machinery parts, 481.91; Canada Barrels & Kegs, Ltd., barrels, etc., 236.61; Canada Colors & Chemicals, Ltd., soda ash, colouring, etc., 430.31; Canada & Dominion Sugar Co., Ltd., sugar, 12,074.34; Canada Glue Co., Ltd., glue, 117.04; Canada Label & Webbing Co., Ltd., labels, etc., 115.26; Canada Packers, Ltd., beef, pork, etc., 3,713.76; Canada Paint Co., Ltd., paint and enamel, 769.81; Canada Sand Papers, Ltd., sand paper, 93.10; Canada Starch Co., Ltd., glucose, 1,135.80; Canadian Colortype, Ltd., machinery, plant and supplies, 55,618.62; Canadian Co-operative Wool Growers, Ltd., wool, 3,206.70; Canadian Durex Abrasives, Ltd., durex paper, etc., 156.86; Canadian Fairbanks-Morse Co., Ltd., repairs, etc., 25.64; Canadian General Electric Co., Ltd., electrical supplies, 142.93; Canadian Hart Wheels Co., Ltd., wheels, 15.25; Canadian Ice Machine Co., Ltd., repairs and parts, 117.75; Canadian Industries, Ltd., leatherette, etc., 555.54; Canadian Liquid Air Co., Ltd., oxygen, 50.95; Canadian National Express, charges, 5,170.71; Canadian National Railways, freight, 1,981.96; Canadian Pacific Express, charges, 224.61; Canadian Pacific Railway Co., freight, 1,816.88; Canadian Wool Co., wool, 836.06; Casings, Ltd., curing salt, etc., 37.00; H. Chappell, hogs, calf, etc., 99.06; Conger Lehigh Coal Co., Ltd., coal, 2,771.86; Consolidated Dyestuff Corp., Ltd., acid, 24.50; Cooke & Denison, machinery repairs, etc., 106.55; Cotton Threads, Ltd., thread, 196.18; Cowan & Co. of Galt, Ltd., tools, etc., 69.14; M. F. Cray, Ltd., coal and wood, 65.00; Wm. Davies Co., Ltd., meat, etc., 1,829.76; Delaney & Pettit, Ltd., hair, etc., 211.50; Chas. W. Dempsey, patterns, etc., 28.00; Department of Highways, repairs to crusher, 251.26; Department of Trade and Commerce, inspection of scales, 42.25; Diamond Cleanser, Ltd., cleanser, 49.92; Doerr Transport, trucking, 17.75; Dominion Glass Co., Ltd., glass, 125.41; Dominion Oilcloth & Linoleum Co., Ltd., linoleum, cement, etc., 395.02; Dominion Reed Supplies, Ltd., reed, 69.75; Doon Twines, Ltd., rope, etc., 358.89; H. Dore & Fils, crusher parts, 37.00; Douglas-Pectin, Ltd., fruit pectin, 518.25; Edward A. Downey & C. H. Cummins, fruit, 9,453.49; John Duff & Sons, Ltd., hams,

Public Institutions—Continued

Ontario Reformatory, Guelph—Continued

Industrial Operations—Continued

141.14; Dumarts, Ltd., fat, 45.00; Dunham & Duggan, Ltd., linings, canvas, etc., 1,650.55; Dunlop Tire & Rubber Goods Co., Ltd., tires, 89.20; Dunn & Levack, Ltd., cattle, etc., 2,680.47; T. Eaton Co., Ltd., ticking, denim, etc., 8,660.11; Electric Boiler Compound Co., Ltd., soap flakes, etc., 165.75; Electric Delivery Co., trucking, 32.95; J. & R. Elliott, lard and oil, 239.00; Wm. Farrar & Co., Ltd., cutting and making suits, 732.35; F. W. Pearman Co., Ltd., meat, hams, etc., 1,047.96; The Forest Basket Co., Ltd., meat baskets, 327.99; Frank & Bryce, Ltd., twine, etc., 28.00; Galt Transport, trucking, 21.91; John Garde & Co., Ltd., sewing machines, etc., 1,684.03; General Steel Wares, Ltd., machine parts, 19.23; Georgetown Mfg. Co., needles, 22.50; Thos. Gilfillan, cattle, sheep, hogs, etc., 28,154.12; Gilfillan Coal Co., coal, 30.00; Goodale Transport, trucking, 60.03; W. Gordon Steel Works, Ltd., strainers, 27.00; Gowdy Bros., fire brick, etc., 87.20; Green & Moule, clothing, 685'00; Greenfield Tap & Die Corp., drills, dies, etc., 92.34; The Griffin Foundry Co., castings, etc., 10.25; Guelph Board of Light and Heat Commissioners, gas, 1,031.01; Guelph Creamery, butter, 12.75; Guelph Felt Co., Ltd., felt, 822.32; Guelph Lumber Co., Ltd., lumber, 4,102.38; Guelph Paper Co., paper, 196.76; The Guelph Soap Co., Ltd., soap, 442.25; Gunns, Ltd., meat, etc., 1,686.25; Hamilton Cotton Co., Ltd., cotton, 507.10; Hamilton & Johnston, cotton, etc., 993.39; A. Hanley, cattle, 3,241.22; Harley-Kay, Ltd., machine parts, 86.12; The Harris Abattoir Co., Ltd., beef, pork, wool, etc., 8,950.88; W. Harris & Co., Ltd., glue, 163.21; A. J. Hawkins, soap chips, etc., 465.86; Geo. H. Hees, Son & Co., Ltd., twine, reed, etc., 47.60; The Hicks-Groom Co., sugar peel, etc., 723.11; The Otto Homuth Sons, Ltd., cloth, 617.88; F. Hunisett, Jr., beef, pork, etc., 1,670.23; Hydro-Electric Power Commission, power, 4,548.12; Imperial Oil, Ltd., oil, gas, etc., 139.08; Industrial Farm, Burwash, cattle, wool, etc., 2,649.98; International Malleable Iron Co., Ltd., couplings, castings, etc., 1,043.97; G. Johnston, cattle, etc,, 89,742.07; R. Johnson, apples, 676.35; Julius Cohen & Joseph, wool, 1,830.12; Keenan Bros., Ltd., meat baskets, 262.00; Keenan Woodenware Mfg. Co., Ltd., lard tubs, 249.60; Albert Kerr Co., Ltd., wool, 910.26; J. J. Kirvan, travelling expenses, 64.15; Kitchener Buttons, Ltd., buttons, 253.96; Knight-Whaley Co., lumber, 6,233.74; Kraft Paper Products, Ltd., fibre cord, 327.35; The Laidlaw Bale Tie Co., Ltd., wire, 1,378.28; Lang Bros. Specialty Co., Ltd., frames, 16.55; S. F. Lawrason & Co., Ltd., lard, oil, etc., 827.55; Link-Belt, Ltd., machine parts, 44.24; J. A. Livingston, travelling expenses, 36.50; D. E. Macdonald & Bros., Ltd., cotton, silk, etc., 24.68; The Marshall Ventilated Mattress Co., Ltd., felt, springs, etc., 2,703.37; The Martin-Senour Co., Ltd., paints, etc., 638.78; Martin Transports, Ltd., trucking, 37.35; McArthur Beltings, Ltd., belting, 64.64; D. McArthur, apples, 375.00; D. McKenzie Machinery Co., machine parts, 316.84; J. C. McLaren Belting Co., Ltd., belting, 184.00; Meakins & Sons, Ltd., brushes, 133.64; Mercer Reformatory Industries, clothing, etc., 1,509.55; G. J. Merlihan Co., tapestry, 98.62; Monarch Belting Co., rubber aprons, 59.78; R. Moore, apples, 360.00; J. H. Morin & Co., Ltd., paint, 224.12; The Herbert Morris Crane & Hoist Co., Ltd., chain guard, etc., 20.32; John Morrow Screw & Nut Co., Ltd., drills, etc., 48.89; Mosser Transport, trucking, 15.16; Municipal Abattoir, Toronto, meat, pork, etc., 146.28; National Grocers Co., Ltd., salt, spices, etc., 435.96; National Mattress Felt & Batting Co., felt, 925.16; National Textiles, Ltd., flannel, 772.65; Northern Electric Co., Ltd., electrical supplies, 36.29; Office Specialty Mfg. Co., Ltd., furniture supplies, 443.90; Ontario Agricultural College (dept. of Horticulture) vegetables, 114.25; Ontario Reformatory, Mimico, cattle, hogs, etc., 590.07; Ontario Hardware Co., hardware, 157.40; Ontario Hospitals,—Brockville, wool rags, 36.64; Hamilton, cattle, hogs, etc., 3,703.01; London, cattle, hogs, etc., 8,627.87; Orillia, tweed, 326.50; Whitby, hogs, 2,829.42; Woodstock, hogs, 303.93; Ontario Reformatory, Guelph (Cannery), vegetables, 822.97; (Farm), cattle, hogs, etc., 1,528.23; Onward Mfg. Co., Ltd., supplies, 53.15; Page-Hersey Tubes, Ltd., pipe, 2,134.49; H. M. Pallett, fruit, 1,715.06; Pay list, wages of men, 911.80; Peckover's, Ltd., metal sheets, 830.97; Penfold Hardware Co., hardware, 249.43; H. W. Petrie, Ltd., machine parts, 82.00; Postmaster, postage, 600.00; Preston Woodworking Machinery Co., Ltd., machine parts, 10.64; Ratcliffe Paper Co., Ltd., paper, 532.49; P. L. Robertson Mfg. Co., Ltd., socket screws, etc., 171.42; W. Robinson & Son, Ltd., shirting, 2,948.41; Roofers' Supply Co., Ltd., galvanized iron, etc., 664.39; T. W. Ross, unloading stone, 45.92; G. W. Sadler Belting Co., Ltd., belting, 11.02; J. M. Schneider & Sons, Ltd., hams, bacon, etc., 7,176.00; Chas. Shaw, fruit, 22.75; Singer Sewing Machine Co., machine parts, 156.24; Chas. H. Smith, repairs, 61.95; I. Spegal, wool, 3,618.24; J. R. Spry, hogs and

Public Institutions—Continued

Ontario Reformatory, Guelph—Continued

Industrial Operations—Continued

cattle, 95.40; Standard Casing Co. of Canada, casings, 7,082.37; Standard Fuel Co., Ltd., coal, 3,538.37; Steel Co. of Canada, Ltd., spring wire, 191.54; Jas. Steele, Ltd., wire, etc., 227.03; Steep's Meat Market, poultry, 74.43; Robt. Stewart, Ltd., lumber, 1,564.63; H. W. Stillman, supplies, 14.15; Wm. Stone & Sons, Ltd., wool, 2,097.85; St. Lawrence Starch Co., glucose, 534.86; St. Lawrence Transport, Ltd., trucking, 17.34; F. W. Stull, trucking, 6,686.48; Sure-Way Products, sausage and meat flour, 41.46; Swift Canadian Co., Ltd., beef, pork, etc., 7,538.63; Talbot & Talbot, press cloths, 17.64; Taylor-Forbes Co., Ltd., floor flanges, etc., 114.80; Textan Co., Ltd., olive cream emulsion, 36.14; Textile Products Co., cotton, 1,116.15; Toronto Coppersmithing Co., kettles, 659.74; Toronto Guelph Express, Ltd., trucking, 14.57; J. J. Turner & Sons, Ltd., duck, 34.80; Union Special Machinery Co. of Canada, Ltd., machine parts, 12.91; United-Carr Fastener Co. of Canada, Ltd., cap fasteners, etc., 36.70; Universal Button Co., Ltd., loops, buttons, etc., 513.26; Victoria Paper & Twine Co., Ltd., twine, etc., 192.66; Wadsworth Coal Co., Ltd., coal, 281.45; Wagstaffe, Ltd., sugar peel, 27.60; Hugh Walker & Son, fruit, etc., 976.70; J. Walsh, cattle, 544.50; Wellington Metal & Waste, waste, 19.62; Wellington Packers, Ltd., beef, lard, etc., 3,755.04; Western Canada Flour Mills Co., Ltd., flour, 419.00; Wettlaufer Machinery Co., machine parts, 42.00; Whyte Packing Co., Ltd., pork, beef, etc., 174.26; W. Wight & Co., Ltd., pork, beef, etc., 1,622.28; Wilkinson-Kompass, Ltd., hardware, 636.50; Wilson Illumination Co., Ltd., brackets, 127.89; Woods Mfg. Co., Ltd., hessian, 351.00; Yocum-Faust, Ltd., lard oil, 269.00; Young, Winfield, Ltd., spices, etc., 597.03; petty disbursements, 130.66. .... 405,395 38

Total	421,719 74	
Less Sale of Products	411,719 74	
Industrial Operations, Guelph		10,000 00
Ontario Reformatory, Guelph	**$223,962.61**	

ONTARIO REFORMATORY, MIMICO

Permanent Salaries ($40,513.67)

J. R. Elliott	Superintendent	12 months	3,000 00
Edward Murray	Clerk, Group 1	8½ "	1,134 50
William K. Siddall	" " 1	3½ "	379 17
H. W. Eversfield	Stationary Engineer	12 "	1,400 00
Alfred Smith	Electrician (part time)		200 00
Guards			34,400 00

Temporary Salaries ($5,718.75)

W. J. Hall	Dentist (part time at $10.00 per day)	540 00
Guards		4,500 00
Pay Lists, wages of mechanics		678 75

Expenses ($53,698.95)

Medicines, $2,403.55.

Ash-Temple Co., Ltd., 37.70; Dominion Dental Co., Ltd., 79.39; Hargraft Bros., Ltd., 49.10; Imperial Tobacco Co., Ltd., 481.60; Ingram & Bell, Ltd., 133.66; W. C. Macdonald, Inc., 645.00; Parke, Davis & Co., Ltd., 60.65; Hugh M. Robertson, 49.00; W. E. Saunders Co., Ltd., 105.47; Scales & Roberts, Ltd., 392.02; E. B. Shuttleworth Chemical Co., Ltd., 66.76; Standard Tobacco Co. of Canada, 17.20; Switzer & Hanham Drugs, 239.05; Tuckett, Ltd., 20.40; petty disbursements, 26.55 .... 2,403 55

Groceries and Provisions, $16,764.29.

Barker's Bread, Ltd., 828.45; Booth Fisheries Canadian Co., 50.01; Bowes Co., Ltd., 138.60; Canadian National Railways, 26.23; Everist Bros., Ltd., 43.75; John J. Fee, 439.05; W. S. Fenwick & Sons, 12.60; K. C. Freeman, 271.33; Higgins & Burke, Ltd., 920.39; Hillside Dairy, 45.88; F. W. Humphreys Co., Ltd., 965.50; F. T. James Co., Ltd., 299.80; Loblaw Groceterias Co., Ltd., 625.51; Jas. Lumbers Co., Ltd., 33.76; D. McArthur, 150.00; Morland Coffee Co., 201.60; National Grocers Co., Ltd., 395.43; Donald Nicholson & Son, 424.80; Ontario Reformatory,

Public Institutions—Continued

Ontario Reformatory, Mimico—Continued

Expenses—Continued

Groceries and Provisions—Continued

Guelph, 12.56; Ontario Reformatory Industries, 8,093.16; Parkin's Bakery, 2,226.12; D. S. Perrin & Co., Ltd., 32.57; St. Lawrence Fish Market, 97.22; Swift Canadian Co., Ltd., 292.10; White Fish Co., Ltd., 97.16; petty disbursements, 40.71.... 16,764 29

Fuel, Light and Water, $6,313.66.

P. Burns Co., Ltd., 2,635.05; H. C. Burton & Co., 24.37; James Dunn, 913.20; Hydro-Electric Power Commission, 2,026.43; Public Utilities Commission, 714.61 6,313 66

Clothing, $9,410.31.

Adams Bros. Harness, Ltd., 78.08; A. A. Allen Co., Ltd., 77.50; Anglo-Canadian Leather Co., Ltd., 103.64; A. Bradshaw & Son, Ltd., 66.00; Carss Mackinaw Co., 276.75; Coghill Tailoring Co., 616.00; Dominion Rubber Co., Ltd., 133.27; Goodyear Tire & Rubber Co., Ltd., 10.12; Gutta Percha & Rubber, Ltd., 84.56; Hague & Hague, 159.00; Hamilton & Johnston, Ltd., 336.11; Jeffrey's & Taylor, 70.87; G. T. Lanning, 11.10; Mercer Reformatory Industries, 339.03; Morris Shoe & Slipper Co., 27.00; Northern Rubber Co., Ltd., 58.65; Ontario Reformatory Industries, Guelph, 3,981.24; Ontario Hospital, Orillia, Industries, 1,218.00; Palter Cap Co., Ltd., 45.00; C. Parsons & Sons, Ltd., 169.48; Quality Glove Co., 201.47; Schofield Woollen Co., Ltd., 600.00; Storey Glove Co., Ltd., 369.00; Western Shoe Co., 210.00; Wood Manufacturing Co., 96.00; petty disbursements, 72.44.... 9,410 31

Laundry and Cleaning, $5,784.72.

Aikenhead Hardware, Ltd., 19.77; Alpha Chemical Co., Ltd., 35.91; Associated Chemical Co., Ltd., 250.61; Boeckh Co., Ltd., 23.51; Canadian Germicide Co., Ltd., 36.77; Canadian National Institute for the Blind, 48.00; Colgate-Palmolive-Peet Co., 169.48; Diamond Cleansers, Ltd., 35.00; E. B. Eddy Co., Ltd., 97.50; Excelsior Brushes, Ltd., 285.84; T. G. Griffith, Ltd., 10.50; Guelph Soap Co., 21.00; Mercer Reformatory Industries, 3,849.55; J. H. Morin & Co., Ltd., 44.00; Ontario Reformatory Industries, 10.80; Procter & Gamble, Ltd., 26.02; Public Utilities Commission, 73.04; Rexo Chemical Cleaner Co., Ltd., 137.20; J. B. Sheppard, 54.70; Sunclo Products, 33.70; Swift Canadian Co., Ltd., 60.10; Switzer & Hanham Drugs, Ltd., 39.65; Victoria Paper & Twine Co., 29.13; West Disinfecting Co., 56.44; G. H. Wood & Co., Ltd., 227.38; petty disbursements, 109.12 5,784 72

Furniture and Furnishings, $2,225.11.

A. Bradshaw & Son, Ltd., 16.58; Canadian Speedo Co., 10.00; Cassidy's, Ltd., 78.97; J. H. Doughty, Ltd., 16.42; A. D. Gibson, 10.90; Gurney Foundry Co., Ltd., 47.62; Hospital & Kitchen Equipment Co., Ltd., 244.12; William Junor, Ltd., 188.65; Mercer Reformatory Industries, 326.17; Ontario Reformatory Industries, Guelph, 1,027.30; Robert Simpson Co., Ltd., 18.00; George Sparrow & Co., Ltd., 103.38; F. W. Stull Transport Co., 43.84; Toronto Feather & Down Co., Ltd., 18.80; W. Walker & Son, Ltd., 11.06; petty disbursements, 63.30...... 2,225 11

Office Expenses, $791.38.

Bell Telephone Co., rentals, 325.05; tolls, 54.89; Postmaster, stamps, 341.00; Thomas & Corney Typewriters, Ltd., 32.35; United Typewriter Co., Ltd., 18.73; petty disbursements, 19.36.... 791 38

Farm Expenses, $5,559.74.

Aikenhead Hardware, Ltd., 26.03; Alpha Chemical Co., Ltd., 62.75; Andrewes Mountain Seed Co., 40.00; Associated Chemical Co., Ltd., 526.67; H. A. Ball & Sons, 27.50; Fred Ball, 56.00; Belle Ewart Ice & Coal Co., Ltd., 102.05; Boys' Training School, Bowmanville, 189.05; Canadian Mineral Products, Ltd., 70.00; Canadian National Railways, 32.40; Canadian Pacific Railway Co., 63.80; J. T. Cassin, 60.00; S. J. Cherry & Son, Ltd., 468.75; Cockshutt Plow Co., 48.09; H. Cook, 158.52; Cosgrave's Brewery, 310.00; Everist Bros., Ltd., 10.00; Fairbanks Feed Co., 364.49; General Steel Wares, Ltd., 12.54; Ingram & Bell, Ltd., 22.25; Kelley Feed & Seed Co., 1,137.94; Lakeside Milling Co., Ltd., 233.00; George A. Lyons, 119.35; Massey-Harris Co., Ltd., 22.00; L. McKinnon, 19.25; O'Keefe Breweries, Ltd., 92.25; Ontario Fertilizers, Ltd., 171.00; W. A. Orr, 200.00; Reesors Marmill, Ltd., 18.63; Jas. A. Simmers, Ltd., 15.80; D. B. Snyder, 25.00; John Speers, 17.50; Steele, Briggs Seed Co., Ltd., 133.10; George Thomas, 15.00; Toronto Elevators Co., Ltd., 284.20; W. Vaughan & Sons, 117.90; Walker Wallace Co., Ltd., 16.84; W. Walker & Son, Ltd., 59.45; A. S. White, 114.78; petty disbursements, 95.86.... 5,559 74

Public Institutions—Continued

Ontario Reformatory, Mimico—Continued

Expenses—Continued

Contingencies, $4,446.19.

Aikenhead Hardware, Ltd., hardware, 13.99; British-American Oil Co., gas, 18.75; Confederation Petroleum Co., gas and oil, 280.45; Department of Highways, auto service, 214.73; Department of Public Works, repairs, 29.16; Eastman Kodak Stores, Ltd., supplies, 57.89; Lionel Godson, car insurance, 85.77; Harpham Bros., auto casing, 37.13; Gratuities, sundry prisoners, 2,542.50; R. M. Harden, travelling expenses, 19.73; Hargraft Bros., Ltd., pipes, etc., 10.00; F. W. Humphrey Co., Ltd., supplies, 186.58; McColl-Frontenac Oil Co., Ltd., gas and oil, 25.15; J. McGill, travelling expenses, 10.90; National Stationers, Ltd., art vellum, etc., 41.00; Ontario Reformatory Industries, supplies, 52.00; D. S. Perrin & Co., supplies, 16.05; Rogers Majestic Corporation, tubes, etc., 15.61; Solar Oil Co., gas and oil, 420.46; A. L. Torgis, repairs, 21.41; Victoria Paper & Twine Co., Ltd., supplies, 65.36; C. W. Wiegar, travelling expenses, 64.95; Wilkins Smallwares Co., Christmas decorations, 15.61; H. A. Wilson Co., Ltd., sporting goods, 15.69; petty disbursements, 185.32 ...... 4,446 19

Repairs to Buildings, etc. ($6,159.63)

Maintenance and Repairs to all Buildings, Roads, Walks, Grounds and Fences, $2,064.32.

Aikenhead Hardware, Ltd., 61.39; Aulcraft Paints, Ltd., 22.30; Brantford Roofing Co., Ltd., 170.30; Builders' Supplies, Ltd., 286.75; Canada Paint Co., Ltd., 123.42; J. H. Doughty, Ltd., 10.10; Graham Nail & Wire Products, Ltd., 26.26; Highway Hardware Stores, 10.21; Industrial Farm, Burwash, 108.96; La France Fire Engine & Foamite, Ltd., 13.20; R. Laidlaw Lumber Co., Ltd., 96.39; George B. Meadows, Ltd., 72.00; Mimico Planing Mills, 147.58; J. H. Morin & Co., Ltd., 112.45; Jas. Morrison Brass Manufacturing Co., Ltd., 536.49; Pay list, wages of men, 96.00; Pilkington Bros., Ltd., 20.60; Steel Co. of Canada, Ltd., 19.81; W. Walker & Son, Ltd., 59.74; petty disbursements, 70.37 ...... 2,064 32

Maintenance and Repairs of Plumbing, Steam and Electric Plants and Machinery, $2,105.75.

Aikenhead Hardware, Ltd., 14.67; Boiler Repair & Grate Bar Co., 84.08; Canadian Foundry Supply & Equipment, Ltd., 26.14; Canadian Industries, Ltd., 14.43; Canadian Rogers Sheet Metal Roofing, Ltd., 38.22; Dearborn Chemical Co., Ltd., 70.49; J. H. Doughty, Ltd., 53.50; C. A. Dunham Co., Ltd., 15.90; Empire Brass Manufacturing Co., Ltd., 275.04; Everlasting Valve Co., 30.68; Garlock Packing Co., Ltd., 25.01; Gurney Foundry Co., Ltd., 30.36; The Huston Oil Co., Ltd., 28.00; Linde-Canadian Refrigeration Co., Ltd., 58.63; The Masco Co., Ltd., 31.94; Mercer Reformatory, 35.00; James Morrison Brass Manufacturing Co., Ltd., 42.64; Pay list, wages of men, 1,135.70; Public Utilities Commission, 23.45; Steel Co. of Canada, Ltd., 10.52; F. W. Stull, 20.25; petty disbursements, 41.10 ...... 2,105 75

Live Stock, Vehicles and Farm Implements, $1,989.56.

A. B. Brubacker, 770.00; Canadian National Express, 7.56; Byron Jenvey, 300.00; Ontario Hospital, Hamilton, 42.00; Toronto Motor Car, Ltd., 700.00; W. C. Wood Co., Ltd., 170.00 ...... 1,989 56

Total		106,091 00	
Less Perquisites	4,836 50		
Sale of Produce	87,538 00		
		92,374 50	
Ontario Reformatory, Mimico		**$13,716.50**	

ONTARIO REFORMATORY, MIMICO INDUSTRIES

Salaries ($5,851.92)

Harry Loach	Machinist	12 months	1,800 00
S. Nicholl	Foreman	12 "	1,800 00
Pay Lists, wages of mechanics, fireman, etc.			2,251 92

Expenses ($39,801.91)

Aikenhead Hardware, Ltd., supplies, 176.49; Allanson Armature Exchange Co., repairs, 10.50; Barnett Lumber Co., lumber, 23.28; Baines & David, Ltd., iron and steel, 558.22; Bawden Machine Co., Ltd., repairs, 90.43; Berg Machinery Co., Ltd., patterns, 439.00; Beardmore Leather Co., Ltd., leather, 19.60; Boeckh Co., Ltd., brushes, 11.82; W. Bohne & Co., Ltd., supplies, 23.55; British-American

Public Institutions—Continued

Ontario Reformatory, Mimico, Industries—Continued

Expenses—Continned

Oil Co., Ltd., gas, 144.68; Builders Supplies, Ltd., lime, etc., 581.00; P. Burns & Co., Ltd., coal, 6,460.50; H. C. Burton & Co., Ltd., lamps, 73.17; Canada Customs, duty, 48.09; Canadian Foundry Supplies & Equipment, Ltd., fire clay, 11.43; Canadian General Electric Co., Ltd., electric supplies, 121.70; Canadian Industries, Ltd., explosives, 434.30; Canadian Laboratory Supplies, Ltd., supplies, 84.21; Canada Machinery & Supply Co., repairs, 10.00; Canada Metal Co., Ltd., lead, etc., 110.00; Canadian Metal Window & Steel Products, Ltd., sash, 23.00; Canadian National Express, charges, 29.33; Canadian National Railways, freight, etc., 406.63; Canadian Oil Companies, Ltd., oil, 51.73; Canadian Pacific Railway Co., freight, etc., 107.73; Canadian Rumely Co., Ltd., machinery supplies, 21.24; Canadian Westinghouse Co., Ltd., repairs, 69.50; Central Scientific Co. of Canada, Ltd., 57.32; Cling Surface Co., supplies, 59.41; Confederation Petroleum Co., Ltd., oil and gas, 249.87; Corman Engineering Co., repairs, 10.00; Crystal Gasoline Co., gas, 17.80; E. Davey, travelling expenses, 73.75; Dearborn Chemical Co., Ltd., supplies, 64.75; Henry Disston & Son, Ltd., saws, 14.31; Dominion Bridge Co., Ltd., steel work, 36.19; Dominion Wheel & Foundries, Ltd., castings, 701.95; J. H. Doughty, Ltd., plumbing supplies, 147.98; T. Dunn, coal, 8,961.96; Empire Brass Manufacturing Co., Ltd., fittings, 72.22; Federal Belting & Asbestos Co., Ltd., belting, etc., 276.18; A. Ganvin, moving and loading machinery, 200.00; Garlock Packing Co., 37.94; Gerrard Wire Tying Machine Co., repairs, etc., 61.68; A. Gibson, supplies, 11.75; W. J. Greey Co., Ltd., supplies, 244.70; B. Greening Wire Co., Ltd., steel rope, 63.58; G. Henshaw, cartage, 10.00; Huston Oil Co., Ltd., oil, etc., 396.14; Hydro-Electric Power Commission, power, 9,158.82; Imperial Oil, Ltd., oil and grease, 190.06; Industrial Farm, Burwash, lumber, 435.87; J. Johnson & Son, Ltd., castings, 394.80; M. Katz, fire brick, 403.12; King Refractories, Ltd., fire clay cement, 152.26; R. Laidlaw Lumber Co., Ltd., lumber, 205.57; Lake Shore Builders Supplies, Ltd., lime, etc., 32.96; Arthur S. Leitch Co., Ltd., valves, 17.60; The Masco Co., Ltd., electric supplies, 59.76; Thos. Meadows & Co., duty, etc., 63.32; W. H. Millman & Sons, cling surface, 59.41; Mimico Planing Mills, lumber, etc., 690.33; Mimico Reformatory, supplies, 11.98; Monarch Belting Co., belting, 94.20; J. H. Morin & Co., Ltd., paint, 31.90; James Morrison Brass Manufacturing Co., Ltd., supplies, 41.74; H. W. Petrie, Ltd., supplies, 31.12; Raliway & Power Engineering Corporation, supplies, 215.40; Regent Electric Supply Co., Ltd., supplies, 42.61; Roofers' Supply Co., Ltd., shingles, 21.08; Safety Supply Co., supplies, 10.19; W. G. S. Savage, lumber, 38.00; Shell Oil Co. of Canada, Ltd., gas, 12.41; Shultz Construction Co., freight, 92.16; Steel Co. of Canada, Ltd., bolts, 70.79; F. W. Stull, cartage, 20.00; Sundry persons, gratuities, 3,932.30; Thwing Instrument Co., supplies, 24.50; Toronto Asphalt Roofing Co., Ltd., repairs, 63.44; Toronto Brick Co., brick, 115.00; Victoria Paper & Twine Co., Ltd., bags, etc., 21.56; W. Walker & Son, Ltd., hardware, 145.68; W. A. Warwood, repairing kilns, 200.00; Wettlaufer Machinery Co., repair parts, 12.08; A. S. White, blacksmithing, 52.76; W. Williamson Lumber Co., Ltd., lumber, 437.84; York Belting Co., belting, 152.40; petty disbursements, 136.27 .... 39,801 91

Total	45,653 83	
Less Sale of Products	45,653 83	
Ontario Reformatory, Mimico		$13,716.50

MERCER REFORMATORY, TORONTO

Permanent Salaries ($30,784.63)

Letitia Scott	Superintendent	12 months	2,850 00
W. D. Watherston	Steward	12 "	1,900 00
Barbara C. Keith	Clerk Stenographer	12 "	1,200 00
Charles Macklin	Gardener	12 "	1,400 00
Thomas Thompson	Cleaner and Helper	12 "	1,400 00
A. Haughland	Stationary Engineer	12 "	2,000 00
Charlotte Hay	Teacher	12 "	1,200 00
Sybil E. Secord	Head Cook	12 "	1,300 00
Maria L. Ingram	Baker	12 "	1,200 00
Engineering Staff, Firemen			3,900 00
Chief Attendant and Attendants			12,434 63

Public Institutions—Continued

Mercer Reformatory, Toronto—Continued

Temporary Salaries ($11,578.77)

Edna M. Guest	Physician	12 months	2,400 00
Anna L. Dike	"	⅜ "	140 00
H. B. Black	Dentist (part time at $10.00 per day)		530 00
Lillian M. Gilbart	Clerk Stenographer, Group 2	12 "	825 00
Elmere Williams	" " " 2	⅜ "	48 12
Alfred Duck	Assistant Gardener	1 "	101 50
Thomas A. Courteney	Fireman, Group 3	12 "	1,050 00
Attendants			6,484 15

Expenses ($35,039.50)

Medicines, $532.45.

The Ash-Temple Co., Ltd., 29.98; J. F. Hartz Co., Ltd., 157.32; Ingram & Bell, Ltd., 150.08; F. E. Luke & Son, 57.00; Parke, Davis & Co., 36.37; The Stevens Companies, 94.70; petty disbursements, 7.00 .... 532 45

Groceries and Provisions, $12,396.52.

Belle Ewart Ice Co., 714.24; Booth Fisheries Canadian Co., 23.10; Bowes Co., Ltd., 399.75; City Dairy Co., Ltd., 40.00; Copeland Flour Mills, 114.10; Elder Flour Mills Co., Ltd., 731.18; Everist Bros., Ltd., 268.65; John J. Fee, 1,413.97; K. C. Freeman, 278.90; Higgins & Burke, Ltd., 279.77; F. W. Humphrey Co., Ltd., 725.67; F. T. James Co., Ltd., 171.14; Langley Harris & Co., 15.12; Jas. Lumbers Co., Ltd., 265.61; National Grocers Co., Ltd., 23.73; Donald Nicolson & Son, 547.80; Ontario Reformatory, Guelph, 914.48; Ontario Reformatory Industries, 4,452.86; Ontario Reformatory, Mimico, 174.48; H. M. Pallett, 90.00; D. S. Perrin & Co., Ltd., 39.23; P. J. Reynolds, 121.47; St. Lawrence Fish Market, 299.37; Silverwood's Milk Products, Ltd., 74.69; Standard Brands, Ltd., 68.38; Swift Canadian Co., Ltd., 27.39; White's Fish Co., Ltd., 93.02; petty disbursements, 28.42 .... 12,396 52

Fuel, Light and Water, $10,604.98.

H. C. Burton & Co., 124.12; Century Coal Co., Ltd., 2,400.35; The Consumers Gas Co. of Toronto, 117.91; Standard Fuel Co. of Toronto, Ltd., 4,644.79; Toronto Hydro-Electric System, 1,990.02; Toronto Water Works, 841.23; Wadsworth Coal Co., Ltd., 479.40; petty disbursements, 7.16 .... 10,604 98

Clothing, $1,928.51.

A. Bradshaw & Son, Ltd., 82.34; The Circle Bar Knitting Co., Ltd., 67.20; Corbett-Cowley Co., Ltd., 121.80; Hamilton & Johnston, 898.48; J. A. McLaren Co., Ltd., 284.30; Mercer Reformatory Industries, 168.56; Moodie's Underwear, Ltd., 158.40; I. Rovansky, 11.50; The T. Sisman Shoe Co., Ltd., 98.00; Textile Products Co., 28.20; petty disbursements. 9.73 .... 1,928 51

Laundry and Cleaning, $4,189.85.

The Alpha Chemical Co., Ltd., 12.85; Associated Chemical Co. of Canada, Ltd., 172.30; Bates Products, Ltd., 17.10; Beaver Laundry Machinery Co., Ltd., 101.23; Beldam's Asbestos Packing & General Manufacturing Co., Ltd., 35.69; Boeckh Co., Ltd., 18.00; Joseph Burns, 95.21; Canadian Germicide Co., Ltd., 51.86; Canadian National Institute for the Blind, 72.90; The Colgate-Palmolive-Peat Co., Ltd., 48.69; Diamond Cleanser, Ltd., 357.11; A. B. Drake Co., 25.88; Electric Boiler Compound Co., Ltd., 32.50; Ennis Wonder Polish Co., 10.50; Excelsior Brushes, Ltd., 97.56; Philip C. Garrett & Co., 242.00; General Steel Wares, Ltd., 12.85; R. S. Gillan, 21.16; Hamilton & Johnston, 88.91; G. A. Hardie & Co., 28.16; Higgins & Burke, 16.00; Hoar Transport, Ltd., 74.11; Howard Products Co., 12.25; Edward Howes & Co., Ltd., 10.80; F. W. Humphrey Co., Ltd., 24.51; Kennedy Manufacturing Co., 10.45; Lavoline Cleanser Co., Ltd., 47.78; Martin Transports, Ltd., 13.25; Mercer Reformatory Industries, 18.80; Midnite Express, 12.57; Anthony Mole, 32.65; Procter & Gamble, Co., of Canada, Ltd., 19.14; Ratcliffe Paper Co., Ltd., 53.55; Reckitts (Oversea), Ltd., 65.08; The Rexo Chemical Cleaner Co., Ltd., 1,611.97; St. Croix Soap Manufacturing Co., 15.10; K. Schiff, 75.56; Standard Wax Co., 25.28; Swift Canadian Co., Ltd., 228.74; C. V. Syrrett Paper Co., Ltd., 11.40; John Taylor & Co., Ltd., 41.33; Victoria Paper & Twine Co., Ltd., 94.88; West Disinfecting Co., 17.82; Wonder Products, 24.74; G. H. Wood & Co., Ltd., 67.13; petty disbursements, 22.50 .... 4,189 85

Public Institutions—Continued

Mercer Reformatory, Toronto—Continued

Expenses—Continued

Furniture and Furnishings, $1,951.46.

A. Bradshaw & Son, Ltd., 47.10; Canadian Speedo Co., 12.00; Cassidy's, Ltd., 80.76; Delaney & Pettit, Ltd., 29.85; Dominion Linens, Ltd., 33.76; Herbert Druiffe & Co., 64.35; T. Eaton Co., Ltd., 326.50; General Steel Wares, Ltd., 72.70; A. D. Gibson, 134.50; Grand & Toy, Ltd., 16.00; Gurney Foundry Co., Ltd., 17.36; Hamilton & Johnston, 70.09; Samuel Hobbs, 14.30; Industrial Farm, Fort William, 15.00; King's Printer, 155.00; The Masco Co., Ltd., 23.66; Mercer Reformatory Industries, 270.36; Anthony Mole, 28.67; Ontario Reformatory, Guelph, 136.70; Ontario Reformatory Industries, 205.00; Regent Electric Supply Co., Ltd., 14.00; The Robt. Simpson Co., Ltd., 126.75; Textile Products Co., Ltd., 37.50; petty disbursements, 19.55 .... 1,951 46

Office Expenses, $569.75.

Bell Telephone Co., rental, 256.80; tolls, 21.95; Postmaster, 238.00; United Typewriter Co., Ltd., 46.60; petty disbursements, 6.40 .... 569 75

Farm Expenses, $802.91.

Andrewes Mountain Seed Co., 177.75; J. Hall, 90.50; J. Lee, 34.10; Marchment Co., Ltd., 397.58; Anthony Mole, 44.75; Ontario Fertilizers, Ltd., 38.23; Ontario Reformatory, Guelph, 20.00 .... 802 91

Contingencies, $2,063.07.

Bates & Dodds, Ltd., funeral expenses, 40.00; Desmarais & Robitaille, Ltd., hymn books, 14.40; General Board of Religious Education, hymn books, 21.60; Gratton's Auto Livery, taxi service, 104.50; Hambleton Oil Co., gas and oil, 77.06; Hardinge Bros. of Canada, Ltd., time clock dials, 11.25; Might Directories, Ltd., directories, 18.00; Sundry prisoners, gratuities, 1,655.00; Toronto Transportation Commission, car tickets, 66.00; petty disbursements, 55.26 .... 2,063 07

Repairs to Buildings, etc. ($9,888.40)

Maintenance and Repairs of all Buildings, Grounds, Roads, Walks and Fences, $5,613.09.

Aulcraft Paints, Ltd., 91.14; Belleville Hardware & Lock Co., Ltd., 42.77; Builders Supplies, Ltd., 10.80; Canada Building Materials, Ltd., 36.87; Canada Paint Co., Ltd., 230.67; Samuel Hobbs, 21.75; LaFrance Fire Engine & Foamite, Ltd., 57.20; R. Laidlaw Lumber Co., Ltd., 328.63; Anthony Mole, 42.72; Pay list, wages of men, 4,170.15; Geo. Rathbone Lumber Co., Ltd., 203.07; Satin Finish Hardwood Flooring, Ltd., 168.28; Toronto Hydro-Electric System, 77.33; Tremco Manufacturing Co., Ltd., 36.31; Wilson & Cousins, Ltd., 45.00; petty disbursements, 50.40 .... 5,613 09

Maintenance and Repairs of Plumbing, Steam and Electric Plants, $4,275.31.

Beaver Laundry Machinery Co., Ltd., 25.79; Beldam's Asbestos Packing & General Manufacturing Co., Ltd., 200.13; Bond Engineering Works, Ltd., 13.68; Canadian Asbestos Co., 10.80; Crane Co., Ltd., 23.98; W. H. Cunningham & Hill, Ltd., 18.02; Dictograph Products Co., 54.40; C. A. Dunham Co., Ltd., 37.24; Ferranti Electric, Ltd., 403.80; General Steel Wares, Ltd., 89.47; The Huston Oil Co., 57.83; John Inglis Co., Ltd., 39.32; Lincoln Electric Co. of Canada, Ltd., 14.69; The Masco Co., Ltd., 28.10; National Refractories, Ltd., 350.00; Pay list, wages of men, 2,637.53; Price Chemical Co., 46.45; Regent Electric Supply Co., Ltd., 11.33; The Rexo Chemical Cleaner Co., Ltd., 16.63; Jas. Robertson Co., Ltd., 30.46; Rogers Electric Co., Ltd., 13.18; G. F. Sterne & Sons, Ltd., 57.33; Taylor-Forbes Co., Ltd., 26.56; R. Willett, 28.25; petty disbursements, 40.34 .... 4,275 31

Total		87,291 30
Less Perquisites	8,069 43	
Sale of Produce	19,647 92	
		27,717 35
Mercer Reformatory		$59,573 95

Public Institutions—Continued

MERCER REFORMATORY INDUSTRIES, TORONTO

Temporary Salary ($1,300.00)

Mary Miles	Forelady	12 months	1,300 00

Expenses ($108,089.33)

C. Adams, cases, 121.75; A. A. Allan & Co., monograms, 30.00; Bell Telephone Co., rentals, 92.95; tolls, 13.24; Bell Thread Co., Ltd., thread, 417.86; A. Bradshaw & Son, Ltd., shirting, etc., 615.94; Caldwell Linen Mills, Ltd., towelling, etc., 23,740.24; Canada Label & Webbing Co., Ltd., labels, 33.39; Canadian Industries, Ltd., hospital sheeting, 6,803.93; Canadian National Express, charges, 10.44; Canadian National Railways, freight, 105.00; Canadian Pacific Railway Co., freight, 36.08; Cluett Peabody & Co. of Canada, Ltd., shirting, etc., 1,338.66; Coghill Tailoring Co., nurses' capes, 2,143.00; Dominion Rubber Co., Ltd., rubber sheeting, 566.89; Dunham & Duggan, Ltd., worsted, etc., 5,827.14; Dupont Textiles, Ltd., uniform serge, 2,678.00; T. Eaton Co., Ltd., ticking, shirting, etc., 1,737.67; John Garde & Co., Ltd., machine parts, 112.26; A. D. Gibson, quilting, etc., 13,629.06; Hamilton Cotton Co., cotton, 110.13; Hamilton & Johnston, cotton, thread, etc., 10.452.47; Johnston, Crossley & McComb, Ltd., sateen, 544.90; John Leckie, Ltd., flannelette, etc., 1,614.66; K. B. McKellar & Co., hospital cloth, etc., 11,253.89; Anthony Mole, machine parts, 133.80; National Textiles, Ltd., serge, 2,726.75; Nisbet & Auld, Ltd., nurses' cloth, 1,739.73; Ontario Reformatory Industries, shirting, 135.13; Quality Button & Trimming Co., binding, etc., 406.42; W. Robinson & Son, Ltd., ticking, etc., 15,375.76; Sundry prisoners, gratuities, 389.00; C. V. Syrett Paper Co., Ltd., paper, 21.83; Textile Products Co., rubber sheeting, 2,893.91; Universal Button Fastener & Burton Co., buttons, etc., 88.40; Vail & Sheppard, cases, 90.00; Victoria Paper & Twine Co., Ltd., paper, etc., 23.10; petty disbursements, 35.95 .... 108,089 33

Total	109,389 33	
Less Sale of Products	109,389 33	
Mercer Reformatory		**$59,573.95**

INDUSTRIAL FARM, BURWASH

Permanent Salaries ($89,979.41)

Norman S. Oliver	Superintendent	12 months	3,000 00
Melvin R. Vincent	Storekeeper	12 "	1,600 00
W. Walker Cunningham	Clerk, Group 1	12 "	1,600 00
R. J. Shierson	" " 1	12 "	1,300 00
Herb Hollingshead	" " 1	12 "	1,200 00
Reginald Tomlinson	" " 1	12 "	1,200 00
Kenneth J. Lambie	" 1	12 "	1,050 00
Janet Reed	Nurse	8 "	868 00
Evelyn Loper	"	4	434 00
Fred H. Kennedy	Chef	12 "	1,300 00
Herbert J. Lawrence	Stationary Engineer	12 "	1,800 00
H. G. Boag	Farmer	12 "	1,600 00
L. Middleton	Carpenter	12 "	1,500 00
Herbert Stewart	Laundryman	12 "	1,325 00
Engineering Staff			4,225 00
Guards			65,977 41

Temporary Salaries ($39,603.15)

William Mosley	Physician	8 months	1,600 00
Donald R. Gunn	"	4 "	820 00
Thomas Dickie, Jr	Office Boy	6 "	262 50
Peter M. Scott	Principal	12 "	1,300 00
Edward D. Judd	Teacher	12 "	1,050 00
Harvey F. Crowder	Bush Foreman	12 "	1,500 00
Edwin W. Owen	Foreman, Planing Mill	10 "	1,250 00
Edward MacDonald	Blacksmith	12 "	1,200 00
G. Gibson	Gardener	12 "	1,125 00
Engineering Staff			2,017 50
Guards			27,478 15

Public Institutions—Continued
Industrial Farm, Burwash—Continued

Expenses ($166,637.96)

Medicines, $13,665.83.

Abbott Laboratories, Ltd., 91.00; Ash-Temple Co., Ltd., 57.97; Canadian National Express, 171.15; Carnahan's, Ltd., 30.70; Doctors Cook, Dales and Jones, professional services, 1928 to 1932, 2,000.00; J. F. Hartz Co., Ltd., 379.92; Imperial Optical Co., 15.84; Imperial Tobacco Co. of Canada, Ltd., 4,182.03; Ingram & Bell, Ltd., 187.06; Landau & Cormack, Ltd., 129.00; Liquor Control Board of Ontario, 31.90; W. C. MacDonald, Inc., 2,712.80; National Drug & Chemical Co. of Canada, Ltd., 209.74; Parke, Davis & Co., 76.05; Scales & Roberts, Ltd., 358.39; E. B. Shuttleworth Chemical Co., Ltd., 407.40; The Stevens Companies, 151.87; Dr. H. Stitt, 1,485.00; Tuckett, Ltd., 916.64; petty disbursements, 71.37 .... 13,665 83

Groceries and Provisions, $73,638.03.

Beaver Food Products, Ltd., 700.00; Booth Fisheries Canadian Co., Ltd., 23.55; Burns & Co., Ltd., 176.80; Cabot Macaroni Mfg. Co., 239.26; Canada & Dominion Sugar Co., 4,800.32; Canada Packers, Ltd., 862.49; Canadian Milk Products, Ltd., 1,160.78; Canadian National Express, 224.01; Canadian National Railways, 861.32; Christie, Brown & Co., Ltd., 46.48; Copeland Flour Mills, Ltd., 975.00; F. L. Dixon, 144.00; Edward A. Downey, 140.00; T. Eaton Co., Ltd., 179.74; K. C. Freeman, 276.00; Ga ble-Robinson Sudbury, Ltd., 155.45; The Edward Grain Co., 3,965.46; Harris Abattoir Co., Ltd., 2,828.73; T. G. Hemphill, 53.00; Higgins & Burke, Ltd., 3,792.19; F. T. James Co., Ltd., 1,498.70; Koffman Bros. & Fine, 25.00; K. W. Krouse & Sons, 43.20; Maguire Bros., 18.00; D. McArthur, 187.50; Moirs, Ltd., 72.17; National Grocers Co., Ltd., 4,952.01; Wm. Neilson, Ltd., 556.29; Donald Nicolson & Son, 1,136.43; Ontario Reformatory Industries, 30,670.05; Ontario Reformatory, Mimico, 320.00; Patterson's Chocolates, Ltd., 195.87; D. S. Perrin & Co., Ltd., 35.31; St. Lawrence Fish Market, 56.44; St. Lawrence Starch Co., Ltd., 1,390.69; Scales & Roberts, Ltd., 168.07; Standard Brands, Ltd., 443.26; J. B. Stringer & Co., 48.25; Swift Canadian Co., Ltd., 4,291.22; Tavistock Milling Co., Ltd., 930.00; United Farmers Co-operative Co., Ltd., 3,267.75; Geo. Weston, Ltd., 102.56; White's Fish Co., Ltd., 790.38; Young-Winfield, Ltd., 827.56; petty disbursements, 6.74 .. 73,638 03

Fuel, Light and Water, $4,983.35.

Higgins & Burke, Ltd., 97.67; Hydro-Electric Power Commission of Ontario, 3,789.57; Imperial Oil, Ltd., 664.63; Northern Electric Co., Ltd., 335.79; Scales & Roberts, Ltd., 74.03; petty disbursements, 21.66 .... 4,983 35

Clothing, $21,938.90.

A. A. Allan & Co., Ltd., 210.16; Beardmore Leathers, Ltd., 715.69; Beaver Laundry Machinery Co., Ltd., 20.83; Canadian National Express, 42.71; Canadian National Railways, 176.45; Canadian Pacific Railway Co., 14.74; Cochrane-Dunlop Hardware, Ltd., 23.60; The Coghill Tailoring Co., 1,758.48; Corbett-Cowley, Ltd., 19.06; Dominion Rubber Co., Ltd., 427.53; The Dotzert Glove Co., 695.87; The Fowler Hardware Co., Ltd., 32.25; Goodyear Tire & Rubber Co. of Canada, Ltd., 17.78; Gutta Percha & Rubber, Ltd., 283.71; Hamburg Felt Boot National Railways, 176.45; Canadian Pacific Railway, 14.74; Cochrane-Dunlop Hardware, Ltd., 23.60; The Coghill Tailoring Co., 1,758.48; Corbett-Cowley, 19.06; Dominion Rubber Co., Ltd., 427.53; The Datzert Glove Co., 695.87; The Fowler Hardware Co., Ltd., 32.25; Goodyear Tire & Rubber Co. of Canada, Ltd., 17.78; Gutta Percha & Rubber Co., Ltd., 283.71; Hamburg Felt Boot Co., Ltd., 434.70; Hamilton & Johnston, 776.01; McArthur Beltings, Ltd., 84.00; Mercer Reformatory Industries, 1,721.79; Northern Rubber Co., Ltd., 310.40; Ontario Hospital, Orillia, Industries, 2,989.00; Ontario Reformatory Industries, Guelph, 4,905.78; Quality Glove Co., Ltd., 562.94; Schofield Woollen Co., Ltd., 1,812.50; Scythes & Co., Ltd., 313.20; Sherry Leather Syndicate, 10.38; Singer Sewing Machine Co., Inc., 14.70; T. Sisman Shoe Co., Ltd., 386.40; Chas. R. Smith, 57.17; Storey Glove Co., Ltd., 250.95; Wm. Taylor, 156.52; United Shoe Machinery Co., of Canada, Ltd., 50.99; Waterloo Glove Mfg. Co., Ltd., 11.80; Woods Mfg. Co., Ltd., 2,625.15; T. C. Young, 10.45; petty disbursements, 15.21 .... 21,938 90

Laundry and Cleaning, $10,177.90.

Associated Chemical Co. of Canada, Ltd., 1,587.99; Canadian National Express, 23.43; Canadian National Institute for the Blind, 429.37; Canadian National Railways, 430.76; Canadian Pacific Railway Co., 19.84; Cochrane-Dunlop Hardware, Ltd., 254.19; Arthur Emond, 70.64; Excelsior Brushes, Ltd., 354.03; Fowler Hardware Co., Ltd., 246.01; Philip C. Garratt & Co., 168.00; Hamilton & Johnston, 108.79; Higgins & Burke, Ltd., 317.22; Imperial Oil, Ltd., 39.79; Interlake Tissue Mills, Ltd., 420.11; Andrew Jergens Co., Ltd., 156.61; Jones Bros. of Canada, Ltd., 47.00; S. F. Lawrason & Co., Ltd., 220.50; MacKinnon Sales, 45.00; National Drug & Chemical Co., of Canada, Ltd., 138.10; National

Public Institutions—Continued

Industrial Farm, Burwash—Continued

Expenses—Continued

Laundry and Cleaning—Continued

Grocers Co., Ltd., 359.38; Parke, Davis & Co., Ltd., 110.58; Rexo Chemical Cleaner Co., Ltd., 1,441.78; St. Croix Soap Mfg. Co., 365.73; Scales & Roberts, Ltd., 60.45; J. B. Sheppard, 1,124.54; Standard Brands, Ltd., 128.67; Swift Canadian Co., Ltd., 235.00; Victoria Paper & Twine Co., Ltd., 67.55; G. H. Wood & Co., Ltd., 1,203.02; petty disbursements, 3.82 .... 10,177 90

Furniture and Furnishings, $11,417.84.

Aluminum Goods, Ltd., 766.40; Associated Chemical Co. of Canada, Ltd., 78.39; Bannon Brothers, 321.21; A. Bradshaw & Son, Ltd., 37.12; Brantford Specialty Mfg. Co., Ltd., 10.17; Canadian Department Stores, Ltd., 36.41; Canadian National Express, 19.70; Canadian National Railways, 223.83; Canadian Scale Co., Ltd., 16.15; Cassidy's, Ltd., 559.82; Cochrane-Dunlop Hardware, Ltd., 155.10; The J. Coulter Co., Ltd., 163.00; Coulter Copper & Brass Co., Ltd., 114.00; T. Eaton Co., Ltd., 1,197.27; Fowler Hardware Co., Ltd., 346.94; General Steel Wares, Ltd., 43.44; A. D. Gibson, 106.92; Hamilton & Johnston, 528.14; Hospital & Kitchen Equipment Co., Ltd., 400.35; Ingram & Bell, Ltd., 228.00; Wm. Junor, Ltd., 54.32; John Leckie, Ltd., 37.92; Mercer Reformatory Industries, 1,511.62; Ontario Reformatory Industries, Guelph, 3,586.85; The Robt. Simpson Co., Ltd., 217.67; Smith & Nephew, Ltd., 121.27; Chas. R. Smith, 102.96; W. M. Smith, 76.10; Sully Aluminum, Ltd., 236.27; Toronto Butchers Supply Co., Ltd., 22.05; Toronto Feather & Down Co., Ltd., 47.00; Wrought Iron Range Co. of Canada, Ltd., 32.95; petty disbursements, 18.50 .... 11,417 84

Office Expenses, $1,540.23.

Bell Telephone Co., tolls, 127.86; Canadian National Express, 24.85; Canadian National Railways, 18.87; Canadian National Telegraphs, 26.95; Canadian Pacific Express, 10.12; Canadian Pacific Telegraph, 78.97; Grand & Toy, Ltd., 44.40; King's Printer, 164.67; Postmaster, 935.00; Royal Bank of Canada, 14.40; Sudbury Star, 80.50; United Typewriter Co., Ltd., 10.60; petty disbursements, 3.04 .... 1,540 23

Farm Expenses, $15,930.47.

B. F. Ackerman Son & Co., Ltd., 73.54; Adams Bros. Harness Manufacturing Co., Ltd., 534.01; Andrewes Mountain Seed Co., Ltd., 15.35; Beardmore Leathers, Ltd., 108.76; Beatty Bros., Ltd., 62.16; The Bond Engineering Works, Ltd., 32.49; Canadian Co-operative Wool Growers, Ltd., 65.35; Canadian National Express, 30.20; Canadian National Railways, 822.24; S. J. Cherry & Sons, Ltd., 481.26; Cochrane-Dunlop Hardware, Ltd., 1,275.35; Cockshutt Plow Co., Ltd., 185.07; Excelsior Brushes, Ltd., 29.11; The Edward Grain Co., 331.97; The Foster Pottery Co., 13.00; Fowler Hardware Co., Ltd., 430.38; Gunns, Ltd., 309.60; Stewart P. Hutton, 800.00; Imperial Oil, Ltd., 12.89; Massey-Harris Co., Ltd., 163.32; J. H. Morin & Co., Ltd., 29.51; National Drug & Chemical Co., Ltd., 81.48; National Grocers Co., Ltd., 105.55; Ontario Wind Engine & Pump Co., Ltd., 24.50; D. T. Parker, 370.00; Parrish & Heimbecker, Ltd., 3,708.81 Quaker Oats Co., 2,681.25; C. Richardson & Co., Ltd., 24.80; W. E. Saunders, Ltd., 69.04; Spramotor Co., 31.80; The Steel Co. of Canada, Ltd., 139.94; Steele, Briggs Seed Co., Ltd., 894.03; Terrell Fruit Co., Ltd., 24.40; Toronto Elevators, Ltd., 1,425.40; Tudhope-Anderson Co., Ltd., 26.79; Walker-Wallace, Ltd., 71.19; Geo. White & Sons Co., Ltd., 19.50; Wilkinson-Kompass, Ltd., 23.85; T. C. Young, 341.60; petty disbursements, 60.98 .... 15,930 47

Contingencies, $13,345.41.

Brunswick-Balke-Collender Co. of Canada, Ltd., repairs to billiard table, 24.84; Burke Electric & X-Ray Co., Ltd., x-ray supplies, 407.20; Canadian Canoe Co., Ltd., canoe, 75.20; Canadian National Carbon Co., Ltd., cells, etc., 87.87; Canadian National Express, charges, 183.51; Canadian National Railways, freight, 336.70; Canadian National Telegraphs, telegrams, 74.50; Canadian Oil Companies, Ltd., gas, etc., 959.51; Canadian Pacific Railway Co., freight, 28.85; Canadian Universal Film Co., Ltd., films, 222.00; F. Cheney, travelling expenses, 22.05; Cochrane-Dunlop Hardware, Ltd., hardware, 1,014.27; Davison's Garage, auto repairs, etc., 202.18; Wm. Dawson Subscription Service, Ltd., subscriptions, 12.00; Department of Highways, auto supplies, 60.58; Eastman Kodak Stores, Ltd., photo supplies, 144.17; Fowler Hardware Co., Ltd., hardware, 20.69; General Welding Co., batteries, 13.40; Lionel Godson, insurance on cars, 146.11; Imperial Oil, Ltd., gas, oil, etc., 2,269.01; International Nickel Co., Ltd., supplies, 25.00; Arthur A. Jackson, ambulance service, 103.50; Kilgour's, Ltd., bags, 11.64; Joseph A. Lobraico, auto tires, 286.53; A. C. Mason, travelling

Public Institutions—Continued

Industrial Farm, Burwash—Continued

Expenses—Continued

Contingencies—Continued

expenses, 54.95; McLeod Garage, auto repairs, etc., 512.62; Dr. Wm. Mosley, use of car, 14.00; Religious Services, 500.00; See & Duggan Motors, Ltd., auto parts, etc., 48.80; Sundry prisoners, gratuities, 4,292.70; A. L. Torgis & Son, cross chains, etc., 95.72; Victoria Paper & Twine Co., Ltd., paper, etc., 452.31; Dr. Walker, travelling expenses, 22.25; petty disbursements, 620.75........... 13,345 41

Repairs to Buildings ($32,417.56)

Maintenance and Repairs of all Buildings, Walks, Roads, Grounds and Fences, $8,312.16.

Aikenhead Hardware, Ltd., 152.60; Aulcraft Paints, Ltd., 108.82; Canada Machinery Corporation, Ltd., 25.55; Canada Paint Co., Ltd., 99.93; Canadian Johns-Manville Co., Ltd., 102.51; Canadian National Railways, 248.84; Cochrane-Dunlop Hardware, Ltd., 1,494.57; Department of Highways, 956.16; W. E. Dillon Co., Ltd., 17.00; The Evans Co., Ltd., 1,160.36; Excelsior Brushes, Ltd., 24.65; Fowler Hardware Co., Ltd., 417.01; General Welding Co., 22.25; Hill-Clark-Francis, Ltd., 36.62; J. H. Morin & Co., Ltd., 1,719.13; Ontario Reformatory, Mimico, 79.01; Ontario Reformatory Industries, Guelph, 905.00; Pay lists, wages of men, 301.80; The Pedlar People, Ltd., 34.62; H. W. Petrie, Ltd., 79.16; H. E. Smith, Ltd., 121.13; Toronto Lock Manufacturing Co., 14.17; W. Waterhouse, 19.25; Wilkinson-Kompass, Ltd., 81.67; A. R. Williams Machinery Co., Ltd., 40.23; petty disbursements, 50.12.................................. 8,312 16

Maintenance and Repairs to Plumbing, Steam and Electric Plants, $15,878.15.

Beldam's Asbestos Packing & General Manufacturing Co., Ltd., 95.04; Boiler Repair & Grate Bar Co., 68.33; Burke Electric & X-ray Co., Ltd., 1,674.35; H. C. Burton & Co., 28.80; Cactizona Products Co. of Canada, 58.75; Canadian Aluminate Co., Ltd., 73.33; Canadian Fairbanks-Morse Co., Ltd., 213.52; Canadian Foundry Supplies & Equipment, Ltd., 623.52; Canadian General Electric Co., Ltd., 195.40; Canadian Johns-Manville Co., Ltd., 30.43; Canadian National Express, 126.13; Canadian National Railways, 601.79; Canadian Pacific Express, 38.16; Canadian Pacific Railway Co., 15.35; Canadian Westinghouse Co., Ltd., 11.35; Cochrane-Dunlop Hardware, Ltd., 407.53; Crane, Ltd., 59.39; W. H. Cunningham & Hill, Ltd., 117.10; Dearborn Chemical Co., Ltd., 63.36; W. E. Dillon Co., Ltd., 30.00; Dominion Bridge Co., Ltd., 88.00; Dominion Wheel & Foundries, Ltd., 111.60; Downing & Co., 71.11; Drummond, McCall & Co., Ltd., 60.00; C. A. Dunham Co., Ltd., 206.19; Electrical Maintenance & Repairs Co., Ltd., 31.52; Empire Brass Manufacturing Co., Ltd., 1,207.20; The Evans Co., Ltd., 555.65; Everlasting Valve Co., Ltd., 15.67; Fowler Hardware Co., Ltd., 252.18; Garlock Packing Co., 20.25; General Welding Co., 20.80; The B. Greening Wire Co., Ltd., 66.15; Grinnell Co. of Canada, Ltd., 10.09; Gutta Percha & Rubber, Ltd., 168.68; Francis Hankin & Co., Ltd., 19.50; Hydro-Electric Power Commission of Ontario, 17.28; Imperial Oil, Ltd., 467.19; Insulation Manufacturing Co., 118.72; Kerr Engine Co., Ltd., 125.96; La France Fire Engine & Foamite, Ltd., 169.67; Arthur S. Leitch Co., Ltd., 366.56; The Masco Co., Ltd., 117.09; Mercer Reformatory, 30.47; J. H. Morin Co., Ltd., 80.50; Jas. Morrison Brass Manufacturing Co., Ltd., 499.95; National Drug & Chemical Co. of Canada, Ltd., 11.08; National Iron Corporation, Ltd., 312.48; Northern Electric Co., Ltd., 93.68; Ontario Reformatory Industries, 30.69; Ontario Wind Engine & Pump Co., Ltd., 10.85; Pay Lists, wages of men, 1,402.50; Pease Foundry Co., Ltd., 36.08; Peckover's, Ltd., 101.77; The Pedlar People, Ltd., 57.38; H. W. Petrie, Ltd., 52.91; Robt. T. Purves & Co., 29.70; Regent Electric Supply Co., Ltd., 54.58; Jas. Robertson Co., Ltd., 63.56; Rogers Electric Co., Ltd., 18.64; Sangamo Co., Ltd., 32.00; Geo. Sparrow & Co., Ltd., 449.00; Supplies & Insulation, Ltd., 52.02; Standard Sales Service, 16.50; G. F. Sterne & Sons, Ltd., 242.35; Storey Pump & Equipment Co., 390.19; Sudbury Construction & Machinery Co., Ltd., 344.74; Taylor-Forbes Co., Ltd., 1,191.54; Trane Co. of Canada, 206.54; Wallace & Tiernan, Ltd., 77.08; Waterloo Manufacturing Co., Ltd., 55.25; Watson Jack & Co., Ltd., 941.80; Wilkinson-Kompass, Ltd., 32.06; A. R. Williams Machinery Co., Ltd., 15.44; Wilson & Cousins, Ltd., 17.55; Wrought Iron Range Co., Ltd., 15.60; petty disbursements, 92.98............ 15,878 15

Live Stock, Vehicles and Farm Implements, $3,925.61.

Robt. Beatty, 89.94; Boys' Training School, Bowmanville, 30.00; Canadian National Express, 22.36; Canadian National Railways, 175.50; Cockshutt Plow Co., Ltd., 583.72; Estate of R. J. Fleming, 120.00; International Harvester Co. of Canada, Ltd., 171.00; Masssey-Harris Co., Ltd., 268.74; McLaughlin Motor

Public Institutions—Continued

Industrial Farm, Burwash—Continued

Repairs to Buildings, etc.—Continued

Live Stock, Vehicles and Farm Implements—Continued

Car Co., Ltd., 650.00; M. J. O'Brien, Ltd., 225.60; Ontario Hospital, Whitby, 25.00; Ontario Reformatory, Guelph, 1,530.00; Stevenson Farms, 25.00; petty disbursements, 8.75 ..... 3,925 61

Lumbering, $1,423.77.

Sandy Campbell Machinery Co., 426.30; Cochrane-Dunlop Hardware, Ltd., 447.71; Fowler Hardware Co., Ltd., 272.33; Pay Lists, wages of men, 275.40; petty disbursements, 2.03 ..... 1,423 77

Making Roads, $2,877.87.

Canadian Industries, Ltd., 383.40; Canadian National Railways, 30.75; Canadian Pacific Railway Co., 37.20; Cochrane-Dunlop Hardware, Ltd., 1,025.33; Fowler Hardware Co., Ltd., 816.66; W. Gordon Steel Works, Ltd., 352.80; The Pedlar People, Ltd., 115.54; Sawyer-Massey, Ltd., 114.79; petty disbursements, 1.40 ... 2,877 87

Total		328,638 08	
Less Miscellaneous Sales	22,562 84		
Perquisites	33,027 29		
		55,590 13	
Industrial Farm, Burwash		**$273,047.95**	

FORT WILLIAM INDUSTRIAL FARM

Permanent Salaries ($7,417.00)

Jas. Hosking	Senior Clerk Stenographer	12 months	1,400 00
Guards			6,017 00

Temporary Salaries ($13,467.57)

Hubert U. Western	Superintendent	12 months		2,400 00
R. McTavish	Physician	(1931) 12 "	1,000 00	
		(1932) 12 "	1,000 00	2,000 00
Robert Delmage	Chef	12 "		915 00
Guards				8,152 57

Expenses ($20,563.24)

Medicines, $1,031.73.

Imperial Tobacco Co. of Canada, Ltd., 511.32; Johnston & Boon Co., Ltd., 88.63; Dr. J. H. Langtry, 84.00; W. C. Macdonald, Inc., 90.00; Neville Drug Co., Ltd., 121.50; Spence Neville Drug Co., 10.90; Tuckett, Ltd., 124.10; petty disbursements, 1.28 ..... 1,031 73

Groceries and Provisions, $7,325.30.

Bole Elevator Co., Ltd. 36.77; Bole's Feed Store, 710.24; Burns & Co., Ltd., 120.00; Canadian National Railways, 61.38; Christie, Brown Co., Ltd., 22.48; Jas. Davidson & Co., Ltd., 24.00; Mrs. Denhardt, 17.50; T. H. Easterbrooke Co., Ltd., 30.00; Exclusive Fish Market, 105.51; Fitzsimmons Fruit Co., Ltd., 34.18; Harris Abattoir (Western), Ltd., 34.12; The Hub Grocery and Meat Market, 171.57; Lake Shore Wholesale & Packing Co., 2,210.19; Macdonald's Consolidated, Ltd., 832.40; H. L. McKinnon Co., Ltd., 569.55; Mount McKay Feed Co., Ltd., 128.25; Ogilvie Flour Mills, Co., Ltd., 19.75; Ontario Reformatory Industries, Guelph, 748.35; Palm Dairies, Ltd., 174.20; Standard Brands, Ltd., 43.05; Western Grocers, Ltd., 1,165.01; Young-Winfield, Ltd., 58.40; petty disbursements, 8.40 ..... 7,325 30

Fuel, Light and Water, $1,051.66.

Hydro-Electric Commission of Fort William, 953.17; Mahon Electric Co., Ltd., 21.60; Northern Electric Co., Ltd., 45.38; Western Grocers, Ltd., 14.04; petty disbursements, 17.47 ..... 1,051 66

Clothing, $3,843.12.

Bryans, Ltd., 18.35; Canadian National Express, 20.15; Canadian National Railways, 41.56; Carss Mackinaw Clothing Co., 108.00; Chapples', Ltd., 18.38; Coghill Tailoring Co., 110.00; Hamilton & Johnston, 136.62; Mercer Reformatory Industries, 138.61; Ontario Reformatory Industries, Guelph, 1,411.20; Ontario Hospital, Orillia, Industries, 547.40; C. Parson & Son, Ltd., 36.51; Schofield Woollen Co., Ltd., 362.50; Storey Glove Co., Ltd., 99.00; United Last Co., Ltd., 14.58; Woods Manufacturing Co., Ltd., 746.10; petty disbursements, 34.16 .... 3,843 12

Public Institutions—Continued

Fort William Industrial Farm—Continued

Expenses—Continued

Laundry and Cleaning, $639.24.

Associated Chemical Co. of Canada, Ltd., 27.64; Beaver Laundry Machinery Co., Ltd., 67.68; E. B. Eddy Co., Ltd., 78.64; Fife Hardware, Ltd., 47.85; Hub Grocery and Meat Market, 101.65; Johnston & Boon Co., Ltd., 33.80; Macdonalds Consolidated, Ltd., 107.94; Western Grocers, Ltd., 152.44; petty disbursements, 21.60........ 639 24

Furniture and Furnishings, $424.06.

Canadian National Railways, 21.09; Chapples', Ltd., 23.62; The Fife Hardware Ltd., 94.22; John Garde & Co., Ltd., 79.00; Mercer Reformatory Industries, 116.00; Ontario Reformatory Industries, Guelph, 35.00; Piper Hardware Co., 10.20; The Robert Simpson Co., Ltd., 32.39; petty disbursements, 12.54........ 424 06

Office Expenses, $444.91.

Canadian National Express, 18.20; Canadian National Telegraphs, 42.01; Canadian Pacific Express, 16.06; City of Fort William, 71.98; King's Printer, 165.00; postmaster, 116.00; petty disbursements, 15.66........ 444 91

Farm Expenses, $1,977.06.

Dr. B. C. Black, 31.00; Bole's Feed Store, 118.75; S. Campbell, 13.20; Canadian Pacific Railway Co., 36.49; Cordage Distributors, Ltd., 26.60; Coslett Machinery & Equipment Co., 30.50; The Coslett Hardware Co., 30.69; Jas. Davidson & Co., Ltd., 232.55; J. Edmond, 107.75; Fife Hardware, Ltd., 249.37; Dr. D. B. Fraser, 10.00; Johnston & Boon Co., Ltd., 10.54; C. Le Cocq, 30.65; A. MacDonald, 165.60; Massey-Harris Co., Ltd., 30.90; Mount McKay Feed Co., Ltd., 240.15; Hugh Parslow & Co., Ltd., 127.30; Piper Hardware Co., 17.48; Plumgrove Nurseries, 30.47; E. Prowse, 34.40; Edward Renwick, 298.50; Sid's Service Station, 21.75; Western Scrap Iron & Metal Co., 17.00; Woodside Bros., 15.00; petty disbursements, 50.42........ 1,977 06

Contingencies, $3,826.16.

J. Bucklow, travelling expenses, 32.05; Canadian Pacific Railway Co., freight, 38.20; Commissioner of Police for Ontario, escorting prisoners, 24.50; Delamater & Milligan, Ltd., gaskets, etc., 73.91; Department of Highways, repairs, 32.29; The Fife Hardware, Ltd., hardware, 41.54; Lionel Godson, insurance on cars, 57.78; Goodyear Tire & Rubber Co. of Canada, Ltd., tubes, etc., 87.29; Phillip Green, travelling expenses, 121.93; Gutta Percha & Rubber, Ltd., tubes, 57.81; Imperial Oil, Ltd., gas and oil, 88.53; Rice Lewis & Son, Ltd., hardware, 73.50; Mahon Electric Co., Ltd., supplies, 36.68; D. McIvor, religious services, 125.00; Monarch Oil Co., Ltd., gas and oil, 1,015.12; J. E. Rutledge, sporting goods, 12.00; Salvation Army, religious services, 104.00; Sid's Service Station, repairs, etc., 326.80; Sundry prisoners, gratuities, 1,127.50; A. L. Torgis & Son, auto parts, 23.62; Twinport Auto Sales, auto repairs and parts, 193.88; H. U. Western, travelling expenses, 85.00; petty disbursements, 47.23........ 3,826 16

Repairs to Buildings ($9,428.12)

Maintenance and Repairs of all Buildings, Walks, Roads, Grounds and Fences, $2,086.25.

Canada Paint Co., Ltd., 70.81; Fife Hardware, Ltd., 464.71; F. Gammond, 120.00; Matthews Sash & Door Co., Ltd., 807.11; Pay list, wages of men, 79.95; W. A. Pierce, 18.00; W. S. Piper, Ltd., 51.25; Piper Hardware Co., 373.40; F. J. Poulter, 20.57; Thunder Bay Lumber Co., Ltd., 40.40; Twisswire, Ltd., 25.80; petty disbursements, 14.85........ 2,086 85

Maintenance and Repairs of Plumbing, Steam and Electric Plants, $5,781.03.

Aikenhead Hardware, Ltd., 25.78; Beaver Laundry & Machinery Co., Ltd., 49.00; Canada Iron Foundries, Ltd., 464.87; Canadian Fairbanks-Morse Co., Ltd., 114.49; Canadian General Electric Co., Ltd., 59.37; Canadian Laundry Machinery Co., Ltd., 30.62; Canadian National Railways, 306.70; Canadian Transfer Co., 10.00; Crane, Ltd., 53.00; Dominion Wheel & Foundries, Ltd., 17.35; Empire Brass Mfg. Co., Ltd., 86.14; Fife Hardware, Ltd., 284.41; Gurney Foundry Co., Ltd., 49.79; Gutta Percha & Rubber, Ltd., 312.26; Hydro-Electric Power Commission of Ontario, 15.00; Kerr Engine Co., Ltd., 392.88; Mahon Electric Co., Ltd., 492.86; National Iron Corporation, Ltd., 278.23; J. R. McRae, 20.65; Northern Engineering & Supply Co., Ltd., 15.88; Ontario

Public Institutions—Continued

Fort William Industrial Farm—Continued

Repairs to Buildings, etc.—Continued

Maintenance and Repairs of Plumbing, etc.—Continued

Reformatory, Mimico, 266.52; Ontario Reformatory Industries, Guelph, 760.00; Ontario Wind Engine & Pump Co., Ltd., 1,387.00; Pay list, wages of men, 231.00; Western Engineering Service, Ltd., 14.77; petty disbursements, 42.46.. 5,781 03

Live Stock, Vehicles and Farm Implements, $3,466.16.

E. Anderson, 497.25; K. Baker, 325.00; Dr. D. C. Black, 30.00; D. Cameron, 600.00; Canadian National Express, 23.76; Canadian Pacific Railway Co., 181.55; G. S. Carver, 20.00; Cockshutt Plow Co., Ltd., 95.00; Coslett Machinery & Equipment Co., 201.10; G. Davidson, 15.00; L. Everett, 315.00; Fisher Dray Line, 13.00; Dr. D. B. Fraser, 10.00; R. Goodfellow, 40.60; F. A. Holmes, 340.00; Industrial Farm, Burwash, 25.00; Mrs. Ellen Moore, 90.00; J. T. Mulloy, 185.00; J. V. Sommers, 260.00; J. Swanson, 150.00; Taylor Forbes Co., Ltd., 18.00; Wm. Wild, 25.00; petty disbursements, 5.90.............................. 3,466 16

Making Roads, $251.51.

Canadian National Railways, 86.79; The Fife Hardware, Ltd., 164.72.......... 251 51

			11,585 55
Less sale of live stock			2,157 43
			9,428 12
Total		50,875 93	
Less Miscellaneous sales	1,128 40		
Perquisites	3,672 97		
		4,801 37	
Fort William Industrial Farm		**$46,074.56**	

STATUTORY

Minister's Salary (see page R6) 10,000 00

Statutory... **$10,000.00**

SPECIAL WARRANTS

Grant to Citizens' Service Association in Connection with the Re-establishment of Ex-prisoners ($3,500.00)

Citizens' Service Association.. 3,500 00

Payment to Dr. W. C. Morrison, Sudbury Gaol, for Special Services ($100.00)

Dr. W. C. Morrison.. 100 00

Special Warrants.................................. **$3,600.00**

Total	$835,260 05
Less Salary Assessment	10,771 57
Total Expenditure, Department of Provincial Secretary	**$824,488 48**

PART S

DEPARTMENT OF AGRICULTURE

FISCAL YEAR, 1931-32

TABLE OF CONTENTS

GENERAL INDEX AT BACK OF BOOK

PART S—DEPARTMENT OF AGRICULTURE

Statement of Expenditure Showing Amounts Expended, Unexpended and Overexpended for the Twelve Months Ended October 31st, 1932

Department of Agriculture	Page	Estimates	Expended			Un-expended	Over-expended	Treasury Board Minute
			Ordinary	Capital	Total Ordinary and Capital			
		$ c.	$ c.	$ c.	$ c.	$ c.	$ c.	$ c.
Main Office:								
Salaries	12	13,900 00	13,500 00	....	13,500 00	400 00	....	....
Contingencies	12	9,000 00	5,092 24	....	5,092 24	3,907 76	....	....
Main Office	..	22,900 00	18,592 24	....	18,592 24	4,307 76	....	....
Statistics and Publications:								
Salaries	12	12,725 00	7,600 00	....	7,600 00	5,125 00	....	....
Contingencies	12	4,000 00	3,035 47	....	3,035 47	964 53	....	....
Statistics and Publications Branch	..	16,725 00	10,635 47	....	10,635 47	6,089 53	....	....
Agricultural and Horticultural Societies Branch:								
Salaries	13	9,300 00	7,549 96	....	7,549 96	1,750 04	....	....
Contingencies	13	3,000 00	2,132 07	....	2,132 07	867 93	....	....
Grants,								
Pure Seed Fairs	..	500 00	....	....	....	500 00	....	....
Special grants under Section 25	13	5,000 00	5,000 00	....	5,000 00	....	....	....
Spring Stock Shows	13	3,500 00	640 27	....	640 27	2,859 73	....	....
Under Section 24, Subsection 1A to E	13	85,000 00	84,973 00	....	84,973 00	27 00	....	....
Agricultural Societies	15	1,000 00	990 00	....	990 00	10 00	....	....
Agricultural Societies in Districts, additional	..	5,000 00	....	....	....	5,000 00	....	....
Under Horticultural Societies Act	15	20,000 00	19,973 00	....	19,973 00	27 00	....	....
Ontario Horticultural Association	16	500 00	250 00	....	250 00	250 00	....	....
Vegetable Growers' Association	16	900 00	600 00	....	600 00	300 00	....	....
Ontario Plowmen's Association	16	500 00	400 00	....	400 00	100 00	....	....
Insurance against rainy weather, etc	16	10,000 00	9,653 00	....	9,653 00	347 00	....	....
Vegetable Specialist, salary	17	1,800 00	1,800 00	....	1,800 00	....	....	....
" " expenses	17	1,000 00	991 95	....	991 95	8 05	....	....
Field Crop Competition	17	25,000 00	9,534 65	....	9,534 65	15,465 35	....	....
" " Judges, services and expenses	18	10,000 00	268 50	....	268 50	9,731 50	....	....
Judges, services and expenses Fall Fairs	18	29,000 00	28,990 49	....	28,990 49	9 51	....	....

Short Courses for Field Crop Judges	18	3,600 00				3,600 00		
To encourage local plowing matches	18	6,000 00	5,995 67		5,995 67	4 33		
Special prizes, Provincial Plowing Match	18	500 00	500 00		500 00			
Services, travelling expenses, etc., of meetings	18	2,950 00	2,178 76		2,178 76	771 24		
Lecturer in Horticulture, salary	18	2,100 00	2,100 00		2,100 00			
" " expenses	18	1,000 00	939 34		939 34	60 66		
	..	227,150 00	185,460 66		185,460 66	41,689 34		
Less Judges' services, subventions, etc.	18		20,448 84		20,448 84	20,448 84		
Agricultural and Horticultural Societies Branch	..	227,150 00	165,011 82		165,011 82	62,138 18		
Live Stock Branch:								
Salaries	19	15,375 00	14,100 00		14,100 00	1,275 00		
Contingencies	19	6,000 00	5,260 10		5,260 10	739 90		
Grants,								
Ontario Provincial Winter Fair	19	14,500 00	14,500 00		14,500 00			
Ontario Provincial Winter Fair Building Account	19	1,000 00	1,000 00		1,000 00			
Royal Agricultural Winter Association	19	25,000 00	25,000 00		25,000 00			
Peninsula Winter Fair	..	5,000 00				5,000 00		
Ontario Horse Breeders' Association	19	1,000 00	1,000 00		1,000 00			
Ontario Cattle Breeders' Association	19	1,000 00	1,000 00		1,000 00			
Eastern Canada Live Stock Union	19	1,500 00	1,500 00		1,500 00			
Royal Winter Fair Association	19	35,000 00	35,000 00		35,000 00			
Ottawa Winter Fair	19	14,500 00	14,500 00		14,500 00			
Ottawa Winter Fair Building Account	19	9,750 00	9,750 00		9,750 00			
Western Fair, re Live Stock Arena	19	10,000 00	10,000 00		10,000 00			
Prince of Wales Prize	19	50 00	50 00		50 00			
Stallion Enrolment Act	19	15,000 00	10,286 47		10,286 47	4,713 53		
Field Man's salary	19	2,550 00	2,550 00		2,550 00			
Educational and Demonstration Work	19	75,900 00	59,989 33		59,989 33	15,910 67		
	..	233,125 00	205,485 90		205,485 90	27,639 10		
Less Sale of Stock, etc.	..		7,424 33		7,424 33	7,424 33		
Live Stock Branch	21	233,125 00	198,061 57		198,061 57	35,063 43		
Institutes Branch:								
Salaries	22	12,625 00	8,987 50		8,987 50	3,637 50		
Contingencies	22	3,000 00	2,995 14		2,995 14	4 86		
Grants, services and expenses, etc.	22	85,300 00	66,975 52		66,975 52	18,324 48		
Institutes Branch	..	100,925 00	78,958 16		78,958 16	21,966 84		

PART S—DEPARTMENT OF AGRICULTURE—Continued

Statement of Expenditure Showing Amounts Expended, Unexpended and Overexpended for the Twelve Months Ended October 31st, 1932

Department of Agriculture	Page	Estimates	Expended			Un-expended	Over-expended	Treasury Board Minute
			Ordinary	Capital	Total Ordinary and Capital			
		$ c.	$ c.	$ c.	$ c.	$ c.	$ c.	$ c.
Dairy Branch:								
Salaries	23	6,300 00	6,300 00		6,300 00			
Contingencies	23	3,000 00	2,854 33		2,854 33	145 67		
Grants,								
Dairymens' Association, Eastern Ontario	23	1,500 00	1,500 00		1,500 00			
" " Western Ontario	23	1,000 00	1,000 00		1,000 00			
Ontario Milk ard Cream Producers' Association	23	1,500 00	1,500 00		1,500 00			
Ontario Creamerymen's Association	..	200 00				200 00		
Central Ontario Cheesemakers' Association	23	200 00	150 00		150 00	50 00		
Eastern Ontario " "	23	350 00	200 00		200 00	150 00		
Western Ontario Cheesemakers' Association	23	150 00	100 00		100 00	50 00		
Instruction and inspection re Dairy Products	23	135,000 00	134,994 65		134,994 65	5 35		
Dairy products for grading purposes	24	40,000 00	14,316 16		14,316 16	25,683 84		
Eastern Dairy School	25	21,000 00	18,479 64		18,479 64	2,520 36		
Dairy exhibits, materials, etc.	25	2,000 00	26 40		26 40	1,973 60		
Chief Instructor, Western Ontario	26	3,000 00	3,000 00		3,000 00			
Experimental work in dairying	..	400 00				400 00		
	..	215,600 00	184,421 18		184,421 18	31,178 82		
Less Sale of Butter, Milk Testing Fees, etc.	26		38,785 43		38,785 43	38,785 43		
Dairy Branch	..	215,600 00	145,635 75		145,635 75	69,964 25		
Fruit Branch:								
Salaries	26	5,100 00	5,100 00		5,100 00			
Contingencies	26	2,800 00	1,908 81		1,908 81	891 19		
Grants,								
Fruit Growers' Association of Ontario	26	7,700 00	6,600 00		6,600 00	1,100 00		
Ontario Horticultural Exhibition Association	..	2,000 00				2,000 00		
Gardeners' and Florists' Association	26	150 00	150 00		150 00			

Niagara Fruit Growers' Association	..	150 00				150 00		
Ontario Beekeepers' Association	..	1,000 00				1,000 00		
Entomological Society of Ontario	26	1,000 00	500 00		500 00	500 00		
Toward erection of Co-operative Packing Houses	26	5,000 00	5,000 00		5,000 00			
Northumberland and Durham Fruit Growers	..	100 00				100 00		
Fruit Work, growing, handling, etc.	26	30,000 00	24,340 29		24,340 29	5,659 71		
Horticultural Experiment Station,								
Salaries	27	20,900 00	20,600 00		20,600 00	300 00		
Expenses	27	40,000 00	30,791 98		30,791 98	9,208 02		
Special experiments	28	4,500 00	1,600 75		1,600 75	2,899 25		
Cold storage experiments on fruit	..	1,500 00				1,500 00		
Expenses and maintenance of Fruit Stations	28	2,000 00	442 80		442 80	1,557 20		
Precooling station, Brighton, expenses	28	5,000 00	2,490 19		2,490 19	2,509 81		
Fruit Branch	..	128,900 00	99,524 82		99,524 82	29,375 18		
Agricultural Representatives Branch:								
Salaries	29	16,700 00	16,550 00		16,550 00	150 00		
Contingencies	29	8,000 00	6,054 92		6,054 92	1,945 08		
Agricultural Representative Work	29	375,000 00	327,034 98		327,034 98	47,965 02		
Demonstration Work on Farm, Sudbury District	..	1,000 00				1,000 00		
Household Science Demonstrator	30	2,000 00	881 40		881 40	1,118 60		
Free trip to Royal Winter Fair	30	15,000 00	11,953 25		11,953 25	3,046 75		
Short courses for winners in competition	30	2,000 00	1,459 83		1,459 83	540 17		
Agricultural Representatives Branch	..	419,700 00	363,934 38		363,934 38	55,765 62		
Markets and Co-operation Branch:								
Salaries	30	13,300 00	12,850 00		12,850 00	450 00		
Contingencies	31	6,550 00	3,200 35		3,200 35	3,349 65		
Loans: Co-operative Marketing	31	5,000 00		4,800 00	4,800 00	200 00		
Co-operative Marketing	31	7,500 00	5,786 80		5,786 80	1,713 20		
Grants to Community Halls, etc.	31	30,000 00	12,559 78		12,559 78	17,440 22		
Crop improvement, demonstrations, etc.	31	19,700 00	8,136 44		8,136 44	11,563 56		
Grants,								
Ontario Experimental Union	32	2,750 00	1,500 00		1,500 00	1,250 00		
Essex County Corn Improvement Association	32	300 00	200 00		200 00	100 00		
Ontario Corn Growers' Association	32	500 00	350 00		350 00	150 00		
Elgin Corn Growers' Association	..	350 00				350 00		
Lambton Corn Growers' Association	32	350 00	200 00		200 00	150 00		
Wentworth County Seed Association	32	150 00	100 00		100 00	50 00		
Brant County Seed Association	..	150 00				150 00		
Quinte Seed Society	32	250 00	200 00		200 00	50 00		

PART S—DEPARTMENT OF AGRICULTURE—Continued

Statement of Expenditure Showing Amounts Expended, Unexpended and Overexpended for the Twelve Months Ended October 31st, 1932

Department of Agriculture	Page	Estimates	Expended			Un-expended	Over expended	Treasury Board Minute
			Ordinary	Capital	Total Ordinary and Capital			
		$ c.	$ c.	$ c.	$ c.	$ c.	$ c.	$ c.
Markets and Co-operation Branch—Continued								
To promote Marketing Board	32	25,000 00	28,883 45	....	28,883 45	....	3,883 45	5,000 00
Subventions, seed cleaning plants	32	10,000 00	1,997 31	....	1,997 31	8,002 69	....	....
Subventions, freight on agricultural lime	33	10,000 00	1,105 36	....	1,105 36	8,894 64	....	....
Markets and Co-operation Branch	..	131,850 00	77,069 49	4,800 00	81,869 49	53,863 96	3,883 45	....
Agricultural Development Board:								
Salaries and expenses, etc	33	180,000 00	4,798 77	....	4,798 77	175,201 23	....	....
Colonization Branch:								
Salaries	35	9,575 00	5,181 25	....	5,181 25	4,393 75	....	....
Contingencies	35	2,000 00	150 97	....	150 97	1,849 03	....	....
General colonization purposes	36	20,000 00	5,268 01	....	5,268 01	14,731 99	....	....
Land guides	36	1,000 00	995 75	....	995 75	4 25	....	....
Grants,								
Canadian Women's Hostels, for maintenance	36	5,000 00	5,000 00	....	5,000 00	....	....	....
Salvation Army, to assist in procuring settlers	36	3,000 00	3,000 00	....	3,000 00	....	....	....
Work in Great Britain	36	60,000 00	55,412 24	....	55,412 24	4,587 76	....	....
Rental of Immigration Offices, etc	37	4,000 00	1,384 46	....	1,384 46	2,615 54	....	....
Wages and other expenses re Exhibits	..	2,000 00	....	....	....	2,000 00	....	....
Payments for after care of settlers	37	14,000 00	12,032 05	....	12,032 05	1,967 95	....	7,032 05
Salvation Army, placing boys	38	3,500 00	1,120 00	....	1,120 00	2,380 00	....	....
Expenses in after care of immigrants	..	2,000 00	....	....	....	2,000 00	....	....
Boy Land Settlement Administration	..	5,000 00	....	....	....	5,000 00	....	....
	..	131,075 00	89,544 73	....	89,544 73	41,530 27	....	....
Less Sale of Produce, Government Grants, etc	38	....	8,554 49	....	8,554 49	8,554 49	....	....
Colonization Branch	..	131,075 00	80,990 24	....	80,990 24	50,084 76	....	....

Kemptville Agricultural School:								
Salaries and expenses	38	80,000 00	58,270 87	....	58,270 87	21,729 13	....	....
Ontario Veterinary College:								
Salaries	40	12,750 00	12,750 00	....	12,750 00	....	....	....
Faculty and staff	40	23,050 00	24,775 00	....	24,775 00	....	1,725 00	1,725 00
Expenses	40	11,100 00	9,432 22	....	9,432 22	1,667 78	....	....
Scholarships	41	150 00	130 58	....	130 58	19 42	....	....
Research and investigations	41	5,000 00	4,135 61	....	4,135 61	864 39	....	....
	..	52,050 00	51,223 41	....	51,223 41	2,551 59	1,725 00	....
Less Tuition Fees, etc.	41	....	12,845 18	....	12,845 18	12,845 18	....	....
Ontario Veterinary College	..	52,050 00	38,378 23	....	38,378 23	15,396 77	1,725 00	....
Western Ontario Experimental Farm, Ridgetown:								
Maintenance, salaries, etc.	41	26,000 00	14,868 24	....	14,868 24	11,131 76	....	....
Stock and equipment	42	7,000 00	1,078 89	....	1,078 89	5,921 11	....	....
Western Ontario Experimental Farm, Ridgetown	..	33,000 00	15,947 13	....	15,947 13	17,052 87	....	....
Demonstration Farms:								
New Liskeard, construction of buildings, salaries, etc.	42	17,000 00	9,905 27	....	9,905 27	7,094 73	....	....
Hearst, maintenance, buildings, etc.	43	20,000 00	10,976 70	....	10,976 70	9,023 30	....	....
Demonstration Farms	..	37,000 00	20,881 97	....	20,881 97	16,118 03	....	....
[illegible] Agricultural College:								
Salaries, College Staff	43	356,941 00	346,119 61	....	346,119 61	10,821 39	....	....
" [illegible] and [illegible] assistants	43	6,400 00	6,302 37	....	6,302 37	97 63	....	....
" Herdsmen, [illegible]rs, etc.	43	13,770 00	13,770 00	....	13,770 00	....	....	....
" [illegible] foremen, farm hands, etc.	43	10,635 00	9,950 63	....	9,950 63	684 37	....	....
" [illegible]rs, etc.	43	13,450 00	13,149 44	....	13,149 44	300 56	....	....
" Temporary assistants, [illegible]	47	6,000 00	5,704 62	....	5,704 62	295 38	....	....
Contingencies	48	10,850 00	10,799 36	....	10,799 36	50 64	....	....
Travelling expenses	48	5,000 00	4,451 66	....	4,451 66	548 34	....	....
Library	48	4,500 00	3,933 23	....	3,933 23	566 77	....	....
Provisions, [illegible]	48	100,000 00	126,807 75	....	126,807 75	....	26,807 75	27,000 00
Furniture, repairs and equipment	49	20,050 00	14,982 12	....	14,982 12	5,067 88	....	....
Gymnasium	50	900 00	811 76	....	811 76	88 24	....	....
Student labour	50	4,500 00	4,463 46	....	4,463 46	36 54	....	....
Telephone service, rents, etc.	50	2,000 00	1,606 75	....	1,606 75	393 25	....	....
Scholarships	50	240 00	230 00	....	230 00	10 00	....	....
[illegible] Scholarships	50	2,000 00	1,999 92	....	1,999 92	08	....	....
Students judging teams	50	700 00	700 00	....	700 00	....	....	....

PART S—DEPARTMENT OF AGRICULTURE—Continued

Statement of Expenditure Showing Amounts Expended, Unexpended and Overexpended for the Twelve Months Ended October 31st, 1932

Department of Agriculture	Page	Estimates	Expended			Un-expended	Over-expended	Treasury Board Minute
			Ordinary	Capital	Total Ordinary and Capital			
		$ c.	$ c.	$ c.	$ c.	$ c.	$ c.	$ c.
[illegible]o Agricultural College—Continued								
Servants pay lists	51	17,100 00	16,735 31	....	16,735 31	364 69	....	1,000 00
Special Research Work	51	8,800 00	8,751 45	....	8,751 45	48 55	....	....
[illegible]se and [illegible]ce of autos, etc.	51	6,000 00	3,065 63	....	[illegible]5 63	2,93[illegible] 37	....	....
Bacteriology,								
Supplies, [illegible], etc.	51	3,100 00	2,273 81	....	2,273 81	826 19	....	....
Botany,								
Supplies, [illegible]es, etc.	51	4,000 00	2,674 52	....	[illegible]4 52	1,325 48	....	....
Chemistry,								
Soil survey, etc.	52	19,600 00	14,999 48	....	1[illegible]9 48	4,600 52	....	....
Trent [illegible]e,								
Services, [illegible]plies, etc.	52	3,475 00	2,446 18	....	2,446 18	1,028 82	....	....
Materials and labour of bakery	53	5, 00 00	4,986 69	....	4,986 69	13 31	....	....
Entomology,								
[illegible]s, [illegible]s, etc.	53	2,725 00	1,777 42	....	[illegible]7 42	947 58	....	....
[illegible]n borer investigations, etc.	53	3,500 00	1,674 94	....	[illegible]4 9[illegible]	1,825 06	....	....
English,								
Supplies, expenses, etc.	53	1,500 00	830 04	....	80 04	69 96	....	....
Agricultural Engineering,								
Services, [illegible]o equipment, etc.	54	11,600 00	4,854 11	....	4,854 11	6,745 89	....	....
[illegible]es, expenses, etc.	54	5,000 00	3,925 14	....	3,925 14	1,074 86	....	....
[illegible]l and [illegible]te broadcasting equipment	..	5,000 00	....	....	....	5,000 00	....	....
Farm [illegible]								
Farm surveys, [illegible]s, etc.	54	12, [illegible]0 00	6,171 14	....	6,171 14	5,928 86	....	....
Extension,								
Services, package li[illegible]y, etc.	55	10,000 00	8,492 34	....	8,492 34	1,507 66	....	....
[illegible]e and Hall:								
Home [illegible]s, [illegible]s, etc.	55	6,300 00	5,536 98	....	5,536 98	763 02	....	....
Animal [illegible]y Farm and Experimental Feeding Department,								
Permanent improvements	56	4,000 00	1,749 88	....	1,749 88	2,250 12	....	....
Wages, t[illegible]ry hel[illegible]	56	5,730 00	5,725 25	....	5,725 25	4 75	....	....

Purchase and maintenance of live stock	56	19,400 00	15,998 91		15,998 91	3,401 09		
Supplies, Equipment, etc.	56	6,850 00	4,998 86		4,998 86	1,851 14		
Field Experiments,								
Wages, temporary help	57	7,440 00	7,209 97		7,209 97	230 03		
Supplies, equipment, etc.	57	5,385 00	4,345 13		4,345 13	1,039 87		
Experimental Dairy and Dairy Schools,								
Wages, temporary help, etc.	57	2,900 00	2,364 90		2,364 90	535 10		
Purchase and hauling of milk	58	13,500 00	4,980 23		4,980 23	8,519 77		
Supplies, equipment, etc.	58	5,625 00	3,482 68		3,482 68	2,142 32		
Poultry Department,								
Wages, temporary help	58	7,625 00	7,541 00		7,541 00	84 00		
Experiments and feeds	58	15,400 00	12,657 44		12,657 44	2,742 56		
Extension work, autos, etc.	59	32,600 00	21,847 58		21,847 58	10,752 42		
Purchase and maintenance of horses, etc.	59	4,583 00	4,411 99		4,411 99	171 01		
Turkey Experimental Farm	60	7,300 00	2,566 20		2,566 20	4,733 80		
Empire Marketing Board Special Research	60	10,000 00	2,749 92		2,749 92	7,250 08		
Horticulture Department,								
Permanent improvements	60	3,700 00	3,699 42		3,699 42	58		
Wages, temporary help	60	11,365 00	11,362 85		11,362 85	2 15		
Trees, plants, seeds, etc.	60	10,950 00	9,942 67		9,942 67	1,007 33		
Extension work in Vegetable Growing	61	3,250 00	1,249 22		1,249 22	2,000 78		
Laying permanent roads, etc.	61	5,000 00	4,999 10		4,999 10	90		
Apiculture Department,								
Services, supplies, etc.	61	2,500 00	2,371 35		2,371 35	128 65		
Inspection of apiaries, etc.	61	13,875 00	8,992 35		8,992 35	4,882 65		
	..	881,714 00	800,224 76		800,224 76	108,296 99		
Less Board and Fees of Students, etc.	62		241,395 42		241,395 42	241,395 42		
Ontario Agricultural College	..	881,714 00	558,829 34		558,829 34	349,692 41	26,807 75	
Miscellaneous:								
Exhibits of grain, vegetables, etc.	63	10,000 00	6,219 08		6,219 08	3,780 92		
Removal expenses of officials	63	1,000 00	196 34		196 34	803 66		
Fees of officials	63	50 00	1 18		1 18	48 82		
Prize for most outstanding agricultural work	..	1,000 00				1,000 00		
Provincial Zoologist, services, expenses, etc.	63	15,000 00	9,069 10		9,069 10	5,930 90		
Administration of Corn Borer Act	63	10,250 00	9,834 14		9,834 14	415 86		
Incidentals	64	50,000 00	37,789 89		37,789 89	12,210 11		
Miscellaneous	..	87,300 00	63,109 73		63,109 73	24,190 27		
Supply Bill	..	2,979,014 00	1,998,629 98	4,800 00	2,003,429 98	1,008,000 22	32,416 20	

PART S—DEPARTMENT OF AGRICULTURE—Continued

Statement of Expenditure Showing Amounts Expended, Unexpended and Overexpended for the Twelve Months Ended October 31st, 1932

Department of Agriculture	Page	Estimates	Expended: Ordinary	Expended: Capital	Expended: Total Ordinary and Capital	Un-expended	Over-expended	Treasury Board Minute
		$ c.	$ c.	$ c.	$ c.	$ c.	$ c.	$ c.
Statutory:								
Minister's salary	65	....	10,000 00	....	10,000 00	....	....	....
Statutory	..	....	10,000 00	....	10,000 00	....	....	....
Special [illegible]:								
Co-[illegible] Marketing [illegible] Re Cold Storage [illegible], 22 [illegible] V, [illegible], Sec. 4, s.s. b,								
[illegible] Edward [illegible] [illegible] [illegible] Ltd.	65	....	....	30,000 00	30,000 00	....	....	....
[illegible] Cold Storage, Ltd.	65	....	....	50,000 00	50,000 00	....	....	....
[illegible] Bay [illegible] Growers, Ltd.	65	....	....	20,000 00	20,000 00	....	....	....
Mi[illegible] [illegible] Co-[illegible], Ltd.	65	....	....	26,000 00	26,000 00	....	....	....
[illegible] [illegible] Exhibition	65	....	1,200 00	....	1,200 00	....	....	....
[illegible] [illegible] on Boys' and Girls' Club	65	....	1,750 00	....	1,750 00	....	....	....
Investi[illegible] of the [illegible] of [illegible] milk, etc.	65	....	6,889 61	....	6,889 61	....	....	....
[illegible] [illegible] Export [illegible]	65	....	3,000 00	....	3,000 00	....	....	....
[illegible] to [illegible] Storage, Ltd.	65	....	5,000 00	....	5,000 00	....	....	....
[illegible] [illegible]tion re [illegible] [illegible]	65	....	11,148 25	....	11,148 25	....	....	....
Bank of [illegible] Scotia, re [illegible] [illegible]ative Creamery	65	....	3,327 82	....	3,327 82	....	....	....
[illegible] Board of Trade re Soya Bean [illegible]	65	....	1,500 00	....	1,500 00	....	....	....
Special Warrants	..	....	33,815 68	126,000 00	159,815 68	....	....	....
Total	..	....	2,042,445 66	130,800 00	2,173,245 66	....	....	....
Less Salary Assessment	..	....	24,827 16	....	24,827 16	....	....	....
Department of Agriculture	..	....	2,017,618 50	130,800 00	2,148,418 50	....	....	....

SUMMARY

Department of Agriculture	Page	Ordinary	Capital	Total
		$ c.	$ c.	$ c.
[illegible] [illegible]ffice	12	18,592 24	....	18,592 24
Statistics [illegible] Publi[illegible]ns Branch	12	10,635 47	....	10,635 47
[illegible] [illegible] [illegible] Societies Branch	13-18	165,011 82	....	165,011 82
Live Stock Branch	19-21	198,061 57	....	198,061 57
[illegible]s Branch	22	78,958 16	....	78,958 16
Dairy Branch	23-26	145,635 75	....	145,635 75
[illegible]t Branch	26-28	99,524 82	....	99,524 82
Agricultural [illegible]es Branch	29-30	363,934 38	....	363,934 38
Crops, Co-[illegible] and [illegible] [illegible]	30-33	77,069 49	4,800 00	81,869 [illegible]9
Agricultural [illegible]t Board	33-35	4,798 77	....	4,798 77
Colonization [illegible] Immigration Branch	35-38	80,990 24	....	80, 90 24
[illegible] [illegible] School	38-40	58,270 87	....	58 270 87
[illegible] Veterinary College	40-41	38,378 23	....	38,378 23
Western [illegible] Experimental [illegible]	41-42	15,947 13	....	15,[illegible]47 13
Demonstration Farm, [illegible] [illegible]	42	9,905 27	....	9,905 27
Demonstration [illegible], [illegible]t	43	10,976 70	....	10,976 70
[illegible] Agricul[illegible] College	43-62	558,829 34	....	558,829 34
[illegible]	63-65	63,109 73	....	63,[illegible]09 73
[illegible]	65	10,000 00	....	10,000 00
Special Warrants	65	33,815 68	126,000 00	159,815 68
		2,042,445 66	130,800 00	2,173,245 66
Deduct, Transferred to Loans and Special Funds (see Part U)			130,800 00	130,800 00
Total		2,042,445 66	....	2,042,445 66
Less Salary Assessment		24,827 16	....	24,827 16
Total, Department of Agriculture		2,017,618 50	....	2,017,618 50

DEPARTMENT OF AGRICULTURE

Hon. T. L. Kennedy..........Minister (Statutory).........10,000.00

MAIN OFFICE

Salaries ($13,500.00)

Jas. B. Fairbairn	Deputy Minister	12 months	5,200 00
B. McDonald	Secretary to Minister	12 "	2,000 00
Bessie Knowles	Senior Clerk Stenographer	12 "	1,400 00
Mary S. Martin	Accountant, Group 3	12 "	2,100 00
Florence M. Palmer	Senior Clerk Stenographer	6 "	650 02
Irene C. Jennings	Clerk, Group 1	6	649 98
J. C. McMillan	Senior Clerk Messenger	12 "	1,500 00

Contingencies ($5,092.24)

Temporary Services, $1,725.00.

L. A. Gibson	Clerk, Group 2	12 "	750 00
O. S. Wilson	Clerk Stenographer, Group 1	12	975 00

Travelling Expenses, $1,772.19.

H. Coleman, 26.90; J. B. Fairbairn, 725.49; Hon. T. L. Kennedy, 1,000.00; B. McDonald, 19.80 .... 1,772 19

Miscellaneous, $1,595.05.

R. J. L. Boyd, kodak, 15.00; Burroughs Adding Machine of Canada, Ltd., inspections, etc., 17.80; Canadian Poultry Review, advertising, 100.00; Dept. of Highways, auto service, 325.57; Dictaphone Sales Corporation, Ltd., inspections, etc., 22.00; L. Godson, Insurance Premium, 16.22; King's Printer, 676.80; Province of Ontario Pictures, films, etc., 90.45; Remington Typewriters, Ltd., inspections, etc., 12.00; United Typewriter Co., Ltd., inspections, etc., 48.00; Western Union Telegraph Code, renewal cable address, 25.00. Sundries—car tickets, 24.00; express, .95; newspapers and periodicals, 103.00; telegrams, 93.66; petty disbursements, 24.60 .... 1,595.05

Main Office..........$18,592.24

STATISTICS AND PUBLICATIONS BRANCH

Salaries ($7,600.00)

N. C. Engelter	Senior Clerk	12 months	2,000 00
S. Goodwins	Clerk, Group 1	12 "	1,600 00
C. J. Gale	" " 1	12 "	1,600 00
A. I. Benning	" " 2	12 "	1,200 00
M. E. Tuck	" " 2	12 "	1,200 00

Contingencies ($3,035.47)

Temporary Services, $1,411.28.

K. E. A. Redman..........Clerk Stenographer, Group 2..........11 .... 756 25

Clerks at 62.50 per month:—Wm. H. Godfrey, 84.13; Norman J. Kirvan, 98.55; W. E. McKinney, 84.13; E. F. Patterson, 96.15; John O. Whiting, 98.55; at 43.75 per month;—J. D. Florence, 58.90; Donald J. Jamieson, 65.63; David J. McFadden, 68.99 .... 655 03

Travelling Expenses, $28.00.

S. H. Symons 28 00

Miscellaneous, $1,596.19.

Burroughs Adding Machine of Canada, Ltd., inspections, etc., 27.75; J. V. Hennessey, compiling data, 80.00; A. S. Hustwitt, repairs, 67.60; King's Printer, stationery, etc., 1,322.06; United Typewriter Co., Ltd., rental, inspections, etc., 85.50. Sundries—freight, 2.60; telegrams, 10.68 .... 1,596 19

Statistics and Publications Branch..........$10,635.47

AGRICULTURAL AND HORTICULTURAL SOCIETIES BRANCH

Salaries ($7,549.96)

J. Lockie Wilson	Superintendent	(T) 12 months	1,749 96
O. Wickware	Clerk Stenographer, Group 1	12 "	1,200 00
V. Wagner	" " " 1	12 "	1,200 00
O. McArthur	Clerk " 1	12 "	1,600 00
D. H. Andrews	" " 1	12 "	1,200 00
A. F. Shields	Office Boy	12 "	600 00

Contingencies ($2,132.07)

Travelling Expenses, $464.86.

Olive McArthur, 74.90; J. L. Wilson, 389.96 .... 464 86

Miscellaneous, $1,667.21.

Dept. of Highways, auto service, 11.00; R. H. Fawcett, part cost Pontiac Sedan, 300.00; King's Printer, 1,165.75; Remington Typewriters, Ltd., inspections, 12.50; United Typewriter Co., Ltd., inspections, 60.14. Sundries—car tickets, 11.00; express, 29.85; newspapers and periodicals, 34.10; telegrams, 42.87 .... 1,667 21

Special Grants under Section 25, R.S.O. 1927, ($5,000.00)

Canadian National Exhibition, 2,500.00; Central Canada Exhibition, 1,225.00; Western Fair, London, 1,275.00 .... 5,000 00

Spring Stock Shows including Services, Travelling and Other Expenses of Judges ($640.27)

Grants, $341.00.

Arthur, 50.00; Erin, 50.00; Fenelon, 50.00; Forrest, 41.00; Millbrook, 50.00; Seaforth, 50.00; South Huron, 50.00 .... 341 00

Sundry Judges, $299.27.

Services, 125.00; Expenses, 174.27 .... 299 27

Agricultural Societies Act, R.S.O. 1927

Grants under Section 24, Subsection 1 (a) to (e) ($84,973.00)

Algoma.—Bruce Mines, 382.00; Central Algoma, 573.00; Desbarats, 197.00; Iron Bridge, 175.00; North Shore, 112.00; St. Joseph's Island, 127.00; Thessalon, 240.00 .... 1,806 00

Brant.—Paris, 467.00; South Brant, 521.00 .... 988 00

Bruce.—Arran and Tara, 378.00; Carrick, 305.00; Chesley, 233.00; Eastnor, 148.00; Hepworth, 165.00; Huron twp., 197.00; Kincardine, 137.00; Lucknow, 243.00; North Bruce and Saugeen, 256.00; Paisley, 215.00; Pinkerton, 85.00; Teeswater, 370.00; Tiverton, 159.00; Underwood, 113.00; Wiarton, 189.00 .... 3,193 00

Carleton.—Carleton County, 800.00; Carp, 652.00; Fitzroy, 183.00; Metcalfe, 666.00 .... 2,301 00

Cochrane.—Clute, 91.00; Cochrane, 308.00; Kapuskasing, 242.00; Porcupine, 252.00; Porquis Junction, 63.00; Val Gagne, 75.00 .... 1,031 00

Dufferin.—Dufferin, 390.00; Dufferin Central, 294.00; East Luther, 235.00 .... 919 00

Dundas.—Chesterville and District, 63.00; Mountain, 214.00 .... 277 00

Durham.—Cartwright, 178.00; Durham Central, 371.00; Millbrook, 308.00; Port Hope, 392.00 .... 1,249 00

Elgin.—Aldborough, 229.00; Aylmer and East Elgin, 371.00; South Dorchester, 156.00; Southwold and Dunwich, 143.00; West Elgin, 333.00; Yarmouth and Belmont, 137.00 .... 1,369 00

Essex.—Colchester North, 270.00; Colchester South, 202.00; Comber, 106.00; Cottam, 300.00; Essex County, 179.00; Mersea, Leamington and South Gosfield, 800.00; Oldcastle, 280.00; South Woodslee, 500.00 .... 2,637 00

Frontenac.—Kennebec, 50.00; Kingston Ind., 800.00; Parham, 98.00; Storrington, 76.00 .... 1,024 00

Glengarry.—Kenyon, 227.00; St. Lawrence, 171.00 .... 398 00

Grenville.—Kemptville, 354.00; Merrickville, 111.00; Spencerville, 157.00 .... 622 00

Grey.—Ayton, 109.00; Collingwood Township, 211.00; Desboro, 252.00; East Grey, 169.00; Egremont, 207.00; Hanover, Bentick and Brant, 265.00; Holland, 285.00; Keppel and Sarawak, 94.00; Kilsyth, 243.00; Markdale, 266.00; Meaford and St. Vincent, 339.00; Normanby, 110.00; Osprey, 133.00; Owen Sound, 531.00; Priceville, 93.00; Proton, 204.00; Rocklyn, 204.00; South Grey, 139.00; Sydenham, 107.00; Walter's Falls, 254.00 .... 4,215 00

Haldimand.—Caledonia, 611.00; Jarvis, 152.00 .... 763 00

Agricultural and Horticultural Societies Branch—Continued
Agricultural Societies Act, R.S.O. 1927—Continued
Grants under Section 24, Subsection 1 (a) to (e)—Continued

Haliburton.—Glamorgan, 90.00; Haliburton, 319.00; Minden, 245.00	654 00
Halton.—Acton, 284.00; Esquesing, 272.00; Halton, 451.00; Nelson and Burlington, 221.00	1,228 00
Hastings.—Bancroft, 155.00; Belleville, 800.00; Frankford, 91.00; Madoc, 376.00; Marmora, 210.00; Maynooth, 73.00; Shannonville, 127.00; Stirling, 268.00; Tweed, 350.00; Wollaston, 165.00	2,615 00
Huron.—Bayfield, 133.00; Blyth, 143.00; Dungannon, 119.00; East Huron, 246.00; Exeter, 207.00; Goderich, 238.00; Howick, 226.00; Kirkton, 235.00; Seaforth, 270.00; Turnberry, 243.00; Zurich, 134.00	2,194 00
Kenora.—Dryden, 391.00; Kenora, 575.00	966 00
Kent.—Camden, 272.00; East Kent, 193.00; Howard, 442.00; Orford, 224.00; Raleigh and Tillbury, 151.00; Romney and Wheatley, 111.00	1,393 00
Lambton.—Bosanquet, 147.00; Brooke and Alviston, 321.00; Florence, 211.00; Forest, 264.00; Moore, 347.00; Petrolia and Enniskillen, 199.00; Plymouth and Wyoming, 239.00; Sombra, 95.00; West Lambton, 384.00	2,207 00
Lanark.—Dalhousie, 114.00; Drummond, 60.00; Lanark Township, 161.00; Lanark Village and Bathurst, 143.00; Maberley, 56.00; North Lanark, 487.00; Pakenham, 180.00; South Lanark, 215.00	1,416 00
Leeds.—Delta, 222.00; Lansdowne, 237.00; Lombardy, 130.00	589 00
Lennox and Addington.—Addington, 233.00; Ernestown, 211.00; Lennox, 693.00	1,137 00
Lincoln.—Abingdon, 155.00; Clinton, 385.00; Monck, 107.00; Niagara Town and Township, 156.00; Peninsular Central, 96.00	899 00
Manitoulin Island.—Billings, 185.00; Gore Bay, 319.00; Howland, 270.00; Providence Bay, 169.00; Manitowaning, 227.00	1,170 00
Middlesex.—Caradoc, 169.00; Delaware, 172.00; Dorchester, 170.00; London Township, 246.00; Melbourne, 195.00; Mosa and Ekfrid, 152.00; North Middlesex, 115.00; Parkhill, 167.00; Strathroy, 393.00; Thorndale, 181.00; Westminster, 100.00	2,060 00
Muskoka.—Baysville, 149.00; Gravenhurst and Muskoka, 327.00; Medora and Wood, 350.00; Morrison, 170.00; North Muskoka, 419.00; South Muskoka, 800.00; Stephenson and Watt, 296.00; Stisted, 124.00	2,635 00
Nipissing.—Bonfield, 120.00; Sturgeon Falls, 485.00; Verner, 206.00	811 00
Norfolk.—Charlotteville, 131.00; Houghton, 84.00; Middleton, 100.00; Norfolk County, 756.00; North Walsingham, 65.00; Townsend, 81.00; Windham, 86.00	1,303 00
Northumberland.—Brighton, 264.00; Cramahe and Haldimand, 328.00; Percy Township, 650.00; Roseneath, 395.00; Seymour, 464.00; Wooler, 106.00	2,207 00
Ontario.—Brock, 195.00; North Ontario, 260.00; Port Perry, Reach and Scugog, 229.00; Rama, 72.00; Scott, 164.00; South Ontario, 667.00; Uxbridge, 264.00	1,851 00
Oxford.—Drumbo, 350.00; Ingersoll North and West Oxford, 243.00; North Norwich, 222.00; Tavistock, 265.00; Tilsonburg and Dereham, 242.00; West Zorra and Embro, 215.00; Woodstock, 800.00	2,337 00
Parry Sound.—Armour, Ryerson and Burk's Falls, 549.00; Christie, 244.00; Loring, 208.00; Machar, 294.00; Magnetawan, 324.00; McKellar, 414.00; McMurrich, 255.00; Perry, 296.00; Powassan, 395.00; Rosseau, 264.00; Strong, 473.00; Trout Creek, 171.00; United Townships, 317.00	4,204 00
Peel.—Albion and Bolton, 154.00; Caledon, 255.00; Cooksville, 424.00; Peel, 642.00; Toronto Core, 61.00; Toronto Township, 220.00	1,756 00
Perth.—Elma, 143.00; Fullarton, Logan and Hibbert, 323.00; Listowel, 211.00; Mornington, 212.00; South Perth, 308.00; Stratford, 791.00	1,988 00
Peterborough.—Apsley, 51.00; Drummer and Douro, 170.00; East Peterborough, 559.00; Galway and Somerville, 66.00; Lakefield, 214.00; Lakehurst, 190.00; Peterborough, 800.00	2,050 00
Prescott.—Alfred, 220.00; South Plantagenet, 171.00; Vankleek Hill, 579.00	970 00
Prince Edward.—Ameliasburg, 158.00; Prince Edward, 540.00; Sophiasburg, 99.00	797 00
Rainy River.—Rainy River Valley	755 00
Renfrew.—Arnprior, 399.00; Cobden, 285.00; North Renfrew, 425.00; Renfrew, 800.00	1,909 00
Russell.—Cassleman, 68.00; Clarence, 136.00; Osgoode, 155.00; Russell, 324.00	683 00
Simcoe.—Alliston, 235.00; Barrie, 550.00; Beeton, 148.00; Bradford and West Gwillimbury, 97.00; Cookstown, 241.00; East Simcoe, 218.00; Flos Township, 320.00; Matchedash, Coldwater, Medonte and Tay, 254.00; Notawassaga and Great Northern, 446.00; Oro, 244.00; Tiny and Tay, 264.00	3,017 00
Stormont.—Cornwall, 252.00; Roxborough, 271.00; Stormont, 253.00	776 00
Sudbury.—Martland and Cosby, 97.00; Massey, 244.00; Warren, 303.00	644 00
Temiskaming.—Charlton, 242.00; Earlton Junction, 47.00; Englehart, 432.00; New Liskeard, 452.00	1,173 00
Thunder Bay.—Canadian Lakehead, 800.00; Oliver, 538.00; Whitefish Valley, 141.00	1,479 00

Agricultural and Horticultural Societies Branch—Continued

Agricultural Societies Act, R.S.O. 1927—Continued

Grants under Section 24, Subsection 1 (a) to (e)—Continued

Victoria.—Emily, 170.00; Mariposa, 138.00; South Victoria, 800.00; Verulam, 318.00	1,426 CO
Waterloo.—Elmira and Woolwich, 278.00; South Waterloo, 800.00; Wellesley and North Easthope, 320.00; Wilmot, 420.00	1,818 00
Welland.—Bertie, 169.00; Fenwick, 168.00; Thorold Town and Township, 250.00; Welland, 700.00	1,287 00
Wellington.—Arthur, 238.00; Erin, 362.00; Mount Forest, 274.00; Palmerston, 154.00; Peel and Drayton, 196.00; Puslinch, 149.00; West Wellington, 186.00; Wellington, 316.00	1,875 00
Wentworth.—Ancaster, 527.00; Binbrook, 234.00; Rockton, 400.00	1,161 00
York.—Aurora, 230.00; Markham and East York, 705.00; Richmond Hill, 170.00; Scarborough, 254.00; Schomberg, 174.00; Sutton, 540.00; Woodbridge, 668.00	2,741 CO

Grants to Agricultural Societies Notwithstanding Provisions of Agricultural Societies Act ($990.00)

Amherst Island, 140.00; Cape Crocker, 50.00; Christian Island, 50.00; Garden River, 50.00; Georgian Island, 50.00; Hastings, 50.00; East Middlesex, 100.00; Manitoulin, 50.00; Moravian, 50.00; Oshweken, 100.00; Rama Ojibway, 50.00; Saugeen Indian, 50.00; Sarnia Reserve, 50.00; United Indian, 100.00; Walpole Island, 50.00	990 00

Grants under Horticultural Societies Act ($19,973.00)

Algoma.—Blind River, 53.00; Sault Ste. Marie, 76.00; Thessalon, 28.00; West Korah, 22.00	179 00
Brant.—Brantford, 179.00; Falkland, 22.00; Paris, 135.00; St. George, 69.00;	405 00
Bruce.—Albermarle, 18.00; Chesley, 53.00; Eastnor, 29.00; Huron, 130.00; Mildmay, 22.00; Paisley, 36.00; Port Elgin, 68.00; Southampton, 85.00; Tara, 31.00; Teeswater and Culross, 53.00; Walkerton, 79.00	604 00
Carleton.—Fitzroy, 18.00; Gloucester Township, 32.00; Goulbourn Township, 25.00; Huntley Township, 21.00; Kars, 27.00; Manotick, 35.00; North Gower, 34.00; Osgoode Township, 19.00; Ottawa, 232.00; Westboro, 145.00	588 00
Cochrane.—Cochrane, 42.00; Iroquois Falls, 72.00; Kapuskasing, 30.00; Smooth Rock Falls, 75.00; Timmins, 55.00	274 00
Dufferin.—Grand Valley, 46.00; Orangeville, 62.00; Shelburne, 71.00	179 00
Dundas.—Chesterville, 32.00; Iroquois, 65.00; Morrisburg, 27.00; Mountain Township, 23.00; Winchester, 44.00	191 00
Durham.—Bowmanville, 31.00; Hampton, 58.00; Newcastle, 37.00; Orono, 83.00; Port Hope, 81.00	290 CO
Elgin.—Aylmer, 84.00; Dutton and Dunwich, 23.00; Rodney, 50.00; St. Thomas, 97.00	254 00
Essex.—Amherstburg, 149.00; Comber, 75.00; East Windsor, 89.00; Essex, 29.00; Kingsville, 67.00; Leamington, 104.00; Sandwich, 98.00; Walkerville, 148.00; Windsor, 397.00	1,156 00
Frontenac.—Kingston	114 00
Glengarry.—Maxville	24 00
Grenville.—Maynard, 18.00; Merrickville, 31.00; North Augusta, 27.00; Prescott, 45.00; Spencerville, 47.00	168 00
Grey.—Chatsworth, 37.00; Dundalk, 23.00; Meaford, 28.00; Owen Sound, 160.00; Thornbury and Clarksburg, 15.00	263 00
Haldimand.—Caledonia, 48.00; Cayuga, 31.00; Dunnville, 78.00; Hagersville, 46.00; Oneida Township, 48.00; Rainham, 25.00	276 00
Haliburton.—Dysart Township	34 00
Halton.—Burlington, 134.00; Milton, 28.00; Nelson Township, 51.00; Oakville, 61.00	274 00
Hastings.—Belleville, 109.00; Stirling, 53.00; Trenton, 80.00; Tweed, 56.00	298 00
Huron.—Blyth, 106.00; Brucefield, 22.00; Brussels, 22.00; Carlaw, 22.00; Clinton, 41.00; Exeter, 45.00; Goderich, 155.00; Howick Township, 26.00; Kippen, 39.00; Kirkton, 63.00; Seaforth, 36.00; Walton, 14.00; Wingham, 78.00	669 00
Kent.—Blenheim and Harwich, 49.00; Bothwell, 43.00; Chatham, 422.00; Dresden, 76.00; Ridgetown, 52.00; Thamesville, 76.00; Tilbury, 54.00; Wallaceburg, 176.00; Wheatley, 133.00	1,081 00
Lambton.—Arkona, 29.00; Petrolia, 43.00; Sarnia, 373.00; Watford, 60.00; Wyoming, 37.00	542 00
Lanark.—Almonte, 55.00; Carleton Place, 71.00; Perth, 51.00; Smith's Falls, 26.00	203 00
Leeds.—Athens, 30.00; Brockville, 96.00; Delta, 31 00; Gananoque, 114.00	271 00
Lennox and Addington.—Napanee	18 00
Lincoln.—Beamsville, 36.00; Grimsby, 47.00; St. Catharines, 81.00; Smithville, 34.00.	198 00

Agricultural and Horticultural Societies Branch—Continued

Grants under Horticultural Societies Act—Continued

Manitoulin.—Billings, 9.00; Carnarvon, 16.00; Campbell Township, 11.00; Gordon Township, 40.00; Killarney Township, 19.00; Little Current, 42.00; Manitowaning, 8.00; Providence Bay, 13.00; Sheguiandah, 10.00; Silver Water, 17.00	185 00
Middlesex.—Ailsa Craig, 61.00; Lambeth, 27.00; London, 273.00; Lucan, 63.00; Parkhill, 48.00; Strathroy, 24.00	496 00
Muskoka.—Bracebridge, 75.00; Huntsville, 56.00; Stephenson, 43.00	174 00
Norfolk.—Atherton, 8.00; Boston, 19.00; Delhi, 46.00; Port Rowan and District, 40.00; Port Dover, 45.00; Simcoe, 73.00; South Walsingham, 26.00; Waterford and Townsend, 41.00	298 00
Northumberland.—Brighton, 35.00; Campbellford, 60.00; Colborne, 34.00; South Haldimand, 24.00; Wooler, 33.00	186 00
Ontario.—Beaverton, 94.00; Cannington, 28.00; Claremont, 17.00; Oshawa, 105.00; Port Perry, 20.00; Udney, 11.00; Uxbridge, 27.00	302 00
Oxford.—Dereham, 40.00; Drumbo, 86.00; East Zorra, 58.00; Ingersoll, 62.00; North Blenheim, 23.00; Norwich, 47.00; Princeton, 33.00; South Norwich, 19.00; Tavistock, 46.00; Thamesford, 20.00; Tilsonburg, 73.00; West Oxford, 9.00; West Zorra and Embro, 30.00; Woodstock, 52.00	598 00
Parry Sound.—Parry Sound, 19.00; Powassan, 10.00; Rosseau, 55.00	84 00
Peel.—Bolton, 22.00; Brampton, 75.00; Lorne Park, 18.00	115 00
Perth.—Cromarty, 17.00; Fullerton Township, 91.00; Listowel, 94.00; Mitchell, 38.00; St. Mary's, 65.00; Stratford, 500.00	805 00
Peterborough.—Havelock and Belmont, 75.00; Norwood, 30.00; Peterborough, 104.00	209 00
Prescott.—Plantagenet, 46.00; Vankleek Hill, 70.00	116 00
Prince Edward.—Picton	31 00
Rainy River.—Fort Francis	136 00
Renfrew.—Arnprior, 38.00; Pembroke, 109.00	147 00
Russell.—Billing's Bridge, 41.00; Cumberland, 43.00; Navan, 26.00; Russell, 32.00	142 00
Simcoe.—Angus, 29.00; Barrie, 133.00; Collingwood, 88.00; Creemore, 32.00; Elmvale-Flos, 38.00; Innisfil Township, 23.00; Midland, 107.00; Orillia, 222.00; Oro, 35.00; Washago, 31.00	738 00
Stormont.—Cornwall	111 00
Sudbury.—Sudbury	79 00
Temiskaming.—New Liskeard	46 00
Thunder Bay.—Port Arthur, 45.00; Slate River Valley, 31.00	76 00
Victoria.—Bobcaygeon, 57.00; Coboconk, 77.00; Fenelon Falls, 36.00; Lindsay, 84.00; Woodville, 75.00	329 00
Waterloo.—Ayr, 46.00; Elmira, 145.00; Galt, 192.00; Hespeler, 140.00; Kitchener, 471.00; Preston, 122.00; Waterloo, 251.00	1,367 00
Welland.—Bertie, 84.00; Fort Erie, 222.00; Niagara Falls, 226.00 Pelham, 38.00; Thorold, 81.00; Welland, 226.00	877 00
Wellington.—Arthur, 43.00; Clifford, 107.00; Elora and Salem, 77.00; Erin, 30.00; Fergus, 86.00; Guelph, 296.00; Guelph Township, 35.00; Hillsburg, 40.00; Maryboro, 25.00; Mount Forest, 73.00; Palmerston, 63.00; Puslinch Township, 19.00; Rockwood, 21.00	915 00
Wentworth.—Aldershot, 59.00; Ancaster, 16.00; Binbrooke, 33.00; Dundas, 55.00; Hamilton, 119.00; Lynden, 25.00; Mount Hamilton, 38.00; Mount Hope, 33.00; Stoney Creek, 27.00; Vinemount 29.00; Waterdown, 26.00; Winona, 24.00	484 00
York.—Aurora, 66.00; East York, 73.00; Eglinton District, 43.00; Etobicoke, 59.00; High Park, 120.00; King Township, 53.00; Lawrence Park, 178.00; Long Branch, 74.00; Maple, 46.00; Markham, 87.00; Mimico, 185.00; Mount Albert, 38.00; Newmarket, 46.00; New Toronto, 59.00; North Runnymede, 36.00; North York, 111.00; Richmond Hill, 65.00; Riverdale, 90.00; Roselands, 76.00; St. Clair and District, 102.00; Scarboro, 62.00; Stouffville, 47.00; Thornhill, 54.00; Toronto, 258.00; Unionville, 37.00; Weston, 161.00; Woodbridge, 148.00	2,374 00

Grants to Associations ($1,250.00)

Ontario Horticultural	250 00
Ontario Vegetable Growers	600 00
Ontario Plowmen's	400 00

Insurance to Indemnify Societies Suffering from Rainy Weather or Fire ($9,653.00)

Algoma.—Bruce Mines	141 00
Brant.—South Brant	500 00
Bruce.—Arran and Tara, 211.00; North Bruce, Saugeen, Lucknow, 159.00	370 00
Dufferin.—East Luther	115 00

Agricultural and Horticultural Societies Branch—Continued

Insurance to Indemnify Societies suffering from Rainy Weather or Fire —Continued

Elgin.—South Dorchester	132 00
Frontenac—Kingston Ind	492 00
Grey.—Desboro, 91.00; Markdale, 411.00; Rocklyn, 109.00; South Grey, 77.00	688 00
Hastings.—Belleville, 500.00; Madoc, 52.00	552 00
Huron.—Blyth, 61.00; Seaforth, 357.00	418 00
Kent.—Camden	500 00
Lambton.—Bosanquet, 169.00; Petrolia and Enniskillen, 453.00	622 00
Lanark.—Lanark Village and Bathurst	57 00
Manitoulin.—Howland	46 00
Middlesex.—Caradoc, 90.00; North Middlesex, 214.00	304 00
Norfolk.—Norfolk County	500 00
Northumberland.—Roseneath	500 00
Ontario.—South Ontario	500 00
Oxford.—Ingersoll North and West Oxford	395 00
Perth.—Mornington	347 00
Simcoe.—Nottawasaga and Great Northern, 500.00; Oro, 100.00	600 00
Waterloo.—South Waterloo	260 00
Welland.—Fenwick	500 00
Wellington.—Palmerston, 111.00; Puslinch, 92.00; Wellington, 50.00	253 00
Wentworth.—Rockton	361 00
York.—Schomberg	500 00

Vegetable Specialist ($2,791.95)

G. Rush	Vegetable Specialist	12 months	1,800 00

Expenses, $991.95.

G. Rush, travelling expenses, 419.64; Dept. of Highways, auto service, 56.09; R. H. Fawcett, part cost, Pontiac sedan, 500.00; L. Godson, insurance premium, 16.22 ..... 991 95

Field Crop Competitions, Prizes and Miscellaneous, Expenses of Exhibits at Exhibitions ($9,534.65)

Algoma.—North Shore	250 00
Brant.—Paris	250 00
Carleton.—Carleton Co., 236.36; Carp, 222.72; Fitzroy, 236.36	695 44
Cochrane.—Cochrane	250 00
Dufferin.—Dufferin Central	17 00
Essex.—Essex	250 00
Halton.—Acton, 250.00; Halton, 236.36	486 36
Hastings.—Belleville	222 72
Huron.—South Huron, 25.00; Twinberry, 204.55	229 55
Lanark.—Drummond, 236.36; Pakenham, 250.00	486 36
Lincoln.—Abbingdon	222 72
Lennox and Addington.—Addington	154 55
Nipissing.—Sturgeon Falls, 204.55; Verner, 250.00	454 55
Ontario.—Scott	204 55
Peel.—Peel County	236 36
Peterborough.—Peterborough Ind	236 36
Prescott.—Alfred	250 00
Renfrew.—Arnprior, 250.00; Renfrew, 181.82	431 82
Simcoe.—Alliston, 245.45; Barrie, 250.00; Norfolk, 50.00	545 45
Temiskaming.—Carleton, 245.45; New Liskeard, 250.00	495 45
Victoria.—Fenelon, 154.55; Verulam, 245.45	400 00
Waterloo.—South Waterloo	245 45
Welland.—Bertie, 181.82; Thorold, 204.55	386 37
Wellington.—Erin	222 72
Wentworth.—Binbrook, 245.45; Rockton, 204.55	450 00

Prizes.

Sundry persons, District No. 1	314 00
" " " " 2	268 00
" " Ottawa Valley Seed Fair	200 00

Miscellaneous, $678.87.

T. K. Aylmer, vegetables, 33.50; Canadian Bag Co., Ltd., bags, 19.00; F. A. Carter, services, 17.50; King's Printer, 66.77; E. W. Lucy, services, 20.00; G. R. Wilson, services, 157.00; expenses, 98.60. Sundries—cartage, 66.00; express, 174.55; petty disbursements, 25.95 ..... 678 87

Agricultural and Horticultural Societies Branch—Continued

Services, Travelling and Other Expenses of Judges in Field Crop Competitions ($268.50)

Sundry Judges, services, 82.50; expenses, 186.00	268 50

Judges' Services, Travelling and Other Expenses ($28,990.49)

Sundry Judges, services, 13,030.00; expenses, 15,960.49	28,990 49

To Encourage Local Plowing Matches ($5,995.67)

Grants.

Alderville, 25.00; Alfred, 50.00; Bowmanville Junior Farmers, 25.00; Brant County, 50.00; Caistor, 50.00; Cape Crocker, 25.00; Cavan and South Monaghan, 50.00; Christian Island, 34.00; Clarence Township, 100.00; Cochrane County, 89.50; Derby, 100.00; Dufferin County, 50.00; East York, 50.00; Egremont, 50.00; Elgin County Junior Farmers, 25.00; Frontenac, 50.00; Glengarry, 100.00; Grenville, 100.00; Haldimand County, 50.00; Haldimand County Junior Farmers, 25.00; Halton, 50.00; Halton Junior Farmers, 25.00; Huron, 50.00; Huron County Junior Farmers, 14.00; Kent, 50.00: King and Vaughan, 50.00; Kingston Junior Farmers, 15 00; Lambton, 50.00; Leeds County, 100.00; Leeds County Junior Farmers, 18.75; Lincoln County, 50.00; Logan, 100.00; Logan Junior Farmers, 15.00; London Kiwanis Club Junior Farmers, 22.25; Mackay's Corners, 40.00; Madoc Junior Farmers, 22.00; Middlesex, 50.00; Meaford Junior Farmers, 25.00; Mohawk, 50.00; Moraviantown, 43.00; Mount Pleasant, 50.00; Mount Pleasant Junior Farmers, 19.00; Norfolk, 50.00; North Bruce, 50.00; North Dumfries, 50.00; North Gower and Marlborough, 50.00; North Ontario, 50.00; North Wentworth, 30.00; North York, 50.00; Ontario, 50.00; Ontario County Junior Farmers, 24.00; Orillia, 50.00; Osgood Community Junior Farmers, 8.00; Parry Sound, 49.00; Peel, 50.00; Peel County Junior Farmers, 16.00; Perth County, 50.00; Peterborough County, 50.00; Peterborough County Junior Farmers, 16.00; Plantagenet, 100.00; Powassan, 50.00; Proton, 50.00; Puslinch County, 50.00; Russell, 50.00; Slate River, 40.50; Six Nation Indian, 50.00; South Bruce, 50.00; South Huron, 50.00; South Ontario, 50.00; Stormont West, 100.00; Sullivan Township, 100.00; Tilbury East, 50.00; Temiskaming Junior Farmers, 25.00; Thornloe Junior Farmers, 25.00; United Indian, 50.00; Victoria, 50.00; Victoria County Junior Farmers, 25.00; Walpole Island, 49.50; Waterloo, 37.50; Waterloo Junior Farmers, 25.00; Welland County, 50.00; Wellesley Township, 50.00; York Junior Farmers, 25.00	3,903 00
Sundry Judges and Demonstrators, services, 700.00; expenses, 971.14	1,671 14
King's Printer, 404.03; C. McKnight, livery, 15.00; Province of Ontario Pictures, prints, 1.00. Sundries—express, 1.50	421 53

Special Prizes, Provincial Plowing Match ($500.00)

Ontario Plowmen's Association	500 00

Horticultural, Agricultural and Vegetable Growers' Societies, Services, Travelling and Other Expenses of Meetings ($2,178.76)

Sundry Judges, services, 22.50; expenses, 1,845.06	1,867 56
E. M. Halter, reporting meetings, 217.85; King's Printer, 93.35	311 20

Lecturer in Horticulture ($3,039.34)

J. F. Clark	Lecturer	12 months	2,100 00

Expenses, $939.34.

J. F. Clark, travelling expenses, 692.94; Clarkson Garage & Service Station, Ltd., towing, etc., 13.50; Department of Highways, auto service, 140.44; L. Godson, insurance premium, 16.22; R. A. Malby & Co., slides, 17.19; United Church Publishing House, slides, 41.55; petty disbursements, 17.50	939 34

Total		185,460 66
Less Judges' Services	8,023 36	
Sale of Grain	110 98	
Dominion Government Subvention	12,314 50	
		20,448 84
Agricultural and Horticultural Societies Branch		$165,011 82

LIVE STOCK BRANCH

Salaries ($14,100.00)

R. W. Wade	Director		12 months	3,800 00
L. E. O'Neil	Assistant Director		12 "	3,000 00
C. Gardhouse	Clerk	Group 1	12 "	1,600 00
D. V. Bromley	"	" 2	12 "	1,200 00
F. B. Roberts	"	" 2	12 "	1,200 00
J. Hamlett	Clerk Stenographer,	" 1	12 "	1,200 00
E. Peacock	" "	" 1	12 "	1,125 00
B. N. Martin	Clerk Typist,	" 2	12 "	975 00

Contingencies ($5,260.10)

Temporary Services, $525.00.

G. S. Hutton	Office Boy	12 "	525 00

Travelling Expenses, $1,914.83.

L. E. O'Neil, 1,123.69; R. W. Wade, 791.14 .... 1,914 83

Miscellaneous, $2,820.27.

Burroughs Adding Machine of Canada, Ltd., maintenance, etc., 10.80; King's Printer, 2,579.97; McCann & Alexander, inspections, 12.00; United Typewriter Co., Ltd., inspections, 73.50. Sundries—car tickets, 24.00; express, 26.69; telegrams, 42.09; newspapers and periodicals, 49.72; petty disbursements, 1.50.. 2,820 27

Grants ($113,250.00)

Ontario Provincial Winter Fair (Guelph)	14,500 00
Ontario Provincial Winter Fair (Building Account)	1,000 00
Royal Agricultural Winter Fair	25,000 00
Ontario Horse Breeders' Association	1,000 00
Ontario Cattle Breeders' Association	1,000 00
Eastern Canada Live Stock Union	1,500 00
Royal Winter Fair Association, fifth annual payment (Building Account)	35,000 00
Ottawa Winter Fair	14,500 00
Ottawa Winter Fair (Building Account)	9,750 00
Western Fair	10,000 00

Prince of Wales Prize ($50.00)

J. K. Fetherston, 15.00; J. Lerch & Sons, 25.00; Oak Lodge Stock Farm, 10.00 .... 50 00

Stallion Enrolment Act ($10,286.47)

Inspectors, $1,536.47.

W. E. Baker, services, 280.00; expenses, 82.95; M. J. Duff, services, 253.00; expenses, 48.68; W. J. R. Fowler, services, 22.00; expenses, 35.77; F. J. Hassard, services, 247.50; expenses, 51.90; R. McEwen, services, 85.00; expenses, 29.12; W. L. Mossop, services, 313.50; expenses, 49.70; R. B. Smith, services, 10.00; expenses, 2.15; H. Spearman, services, 11.00; expenses, 1.20; J. White, services, 11.00; expenses, 2.00 .... 1,536 47

Premiums for Pure Bred Stallions, $8,750.00.

Sundry persons 8,750 00

Field Man ($2,550.00)

W. P. Watson	Field Man	12 months	2,550 00

Educational and Demonstration Work ($59,989.33)

Temporary Services, $1,800.00.

R. H. Graham	Field Man	12 months	1,800 00

Grants to Exhibitions, $1,323.33.

Canadian National Exhibition, 773.33; Royal Agricultural Winter Fair, 450.00; Wentworth Dairy Show, 100.00 .... 1,323 33

Live Stock Branch—Continued

Educational and Demonstration Work—Continued

Grants to Horse Shows, $2,658.00.

Canadian Hunter, Saddle and Light Horse Show Improvement Association, 1,000.00; Brantford Lions' Club Horse Show, 188.00; Drayton Spring Horse Show, 26.50; Elora Horse Show, 106.50; Linwood Spring Horse Show, 137.50; Ottawa Horse Parade and Show Association, 200.00; St. Clement's Spring Horse Show, 99.50; Toronto Horse Show, 600.00; Toronto Open Air Horse Parade, 300.00 .... 2,658 00

Bonuses to Live Stock Improvement Associations, $6,595.51.

Brant, 75.50; Bruce, 616.50; Carleton, 117.80; Dufferin, 211.90; Durham, 201.70; Elgin, 19.00; Essex, 110.50; Frontenac, 43.40; Greater Dundas, 238.00; Grey, 250.60; Hastings, 50.00· Huron, 671.10; Kent, 368.30; Lambton, 414.75; Leeds, 45.00; Lennox and Addington, 102.50; Middlesex, 430.30; Ontario, 303.20; Oxford, 133.00; Peel, 217.60; Perth, 209.60; Peterborough, 297.80; Prince Edward, 144.00; Renfrew, 191.86; Simcoe, 449.70; Victoria, 328.70; Wellington, 318.20; York, 35.00 .... 6,595 51

Bonuses re Purchase of Pure Bred Sires, $3,273.46.

W. R. Abbott, 25.50; H. Allen, 12.00; J. Alston, 30.00; J. J. Barnard, 30.50; J. Beattie, 15.00; C. Becker, 24.00; B. J. Becks, 13.80; F. Beaudry, 15.00; W. Beilhartz, 45.00; F. Belisle, 22.50; D. Bell, 19.50; J. Blackburn, 30.60; E. Bland, 22.50; F. Bradette, 27.97; R. Bradley, 12.90; J. Broad, 19.50; J. A. Bryant, 30.00; J. G. Boxwell, 21.00; G. Butler, 30.00; J. Campbell, 27.00; A. H. Carr, 21.00; N. D. Clark, 5.00; C. Coatois, 52.50; W. T. Colson, 29.50; W. E. Crawford, 5.00; G. Croft, 27.00; E. J. Cyr, 14.40; P. D. Dahl, 15.00; J. Dennis, 5.00; A. Dolson, 13.60; P. Donaldson, 22.50; N. Douglas, 17.50; J. A. Duguid, 13.50; H. T. Edmonds, 39.05; C. W. Egglesfield, 37.50; H. G. Enns, 24.00; S. I. Gallagher, 15.00; G. H. Gauthier, 112.50; E. Gignac, 59.95; E. George, 19.50; J. E. Greenfield, 22.50; J. Hall, 30.00; L. C. Hall, 25.70; Mrs. A. J. Hamilton, 100.00; F. Hicks, 15.00; J. E. Hill, 56.90; R. Hodge, 10.50; P. J. Honsinger, 45.20; C. Holland, 30.00; C. Hore, 30.00; R. Horricks, 21.00; A. Hunter, 13.60; G. Jaggard, 22.50; A. Jenkins, 22.50; W. Kebich, 39.00; H. T. Kenny, 50.10; D. H. Kirk, 24.00; L. Kent, 19.50; J. Klein & Sons, 35.50; A. J. Krohn, 18.00; W. J. Lamming, 21.00; P. Larabie, 21.00; L. Larochelle, 16.95; L. Lewis, 22.50; E. Lyons, 13.60; D. McDonald, 40.50; W. J. McDonald, 27.25; J. McKay, 18.00; T. H. McKillop, 173.60; J. McKinnon & Son, 40.50; D. McNaughton, 21.00; D. McRae, 75.83; A. McRoberts, 22.50; A. C. Mabbett, 18.30; M. Maki, 22.50; R. G. Marshall, 30.00; H. Martin, 22.50; N. Martin, 18.00; C. R. Maguire, 15.00; E. Melitzer, 15.00; A. E. Morphet, 27.00; W. H. Neville, 18.00; A. Odrowski, 22.50; J. E. Panmeer, 22.50; L. A. Peever, 25.50; A. B. Penny, 30.00; A. J. Phalen, 16.50; M. Proctor, 75.00; M. Proulx, 49.50; J. A. Purdon, 19.50; J. Purvis & Sons, 25.50; J. Ranta, 16.50; S. Richards, 18.00; W. D. Rodgers, 27.00; L. Roezel, 36.90; J. W. Rollins & Sons, 4.50; O. Ross, 30.00; E. E. Rostie, 24.00; R. Savoie, 30.00; W. Simon, 30.00; D. Sinclair, 30.00; W. Stewart, 15.00; W. L. Strigley, 5.00; A. Tessier, 60.00; G. M. Thompson, 33.00; V. Thompson, 12.00; U. Tousignant, 31.25; J. Trimble, 30.00; S. Vallee, 30.00; Wakegijig, 34.30; P. Williamson, 37.50; M. C. Willoughby, 22.50; H. Yelland, 56.21; T. Young, 18.00 .... 3,273 46

Bonuses on Graded Rams (Dominion Scheme), $4,001.00.

Sundry persons 4,001 00

Grants to Poultry Associations, $1,300.00.

Aurora, 50.00; Aylmer, 50.00; Beamsville, 50.00; Border Cities, 50.00; Brampton, 50.00; East York, 50.00; Galt, 50.00; Greater Toronto, 50.00; Guelph, 50.00; Hamilton and Wentworth, 50.00; Kimberley, 50.00; Kingston, 50.00; Kitchener, 50.00; Lake Shore, 50.00; Lennox and Addington, 50.00; Manitoulin, 50.00; Northern Ontario, 50.00; Oshawa, 50.00; Ottawa, 50.00; Owen Sound, 100.00; Peterborough, 50.00; Prince Edward County, 50.00; Sarnia, 50.00; Stratford, 50.00; Waterloo, 50.00 .... 1,300 00

Grants to Associations Holding Sales of Pure Bred Stock, $1,681.00.

Belleville Holstein-Friesian Breeders' Club, 153.00; Brant District Holstein Breeders' Club, 150.00; Caledonia Shorthorn Friesian Breeders' Club, 128.00; Canadian National Holstein Club, 124.00; Durham City Shorthorn Breeders' Association, 45.00; Guelph Fat Stock Club, 66.00; Halton-Peel Holstein Sale, 140.00; Inter-County Sales Association, 150.00; North Grey Shorthorn Breeders' Club, 52.00; South Simcoe Yorkshire Breeders' Club, 93.00; Strathroy Holstein

Live Stock Branch—Continued

Educational and Demonstration Work—Continued

Grants to Associations holding Sales of Pure Bred Stock—Continued

Breeders' Club, 75.00; Victoria County Shorthorn Association, 45.00; Waterloo and Wellington Holstein Breeders' Club, 150.00; Wentworth Holstein Club, 48.00; Western Ontario Consignment Sale Club, Ltd., 262.00.................. 1,681 00

Grants to Fairs, $900.00.

Aylmer Dairy Cattle Show, 100.00; Barrie Lamb Fair, 62.50; Brant County Dairy Cattle Show, 100.00; Brigden Bacon Hog Fair, 100.00; Douglas Lamb Fair, 47.00; Glencoe Bacon Hog Fair, 100.00; Kemptville Bacon Hog Fair, 100.00; Kenora District Lamb Fair, 48.50; Markdale Lamb Fair, 65.00; North Augusta Lamb Fair, 50.00; Rannock Lamb Fair, 25.00; St. Joseph's Island Lamb Fair, 52.00; Westport Lamb Fair, 50.00.. 900 00

Purchase of Stock, $4,937.07.

G. F. Aiken & Son, 68.00; P. Aikell & Sons, 30.00; J. Baxter, 65.00; Beatty Bros., 30.00; G. Bell, 350.00; C. Brethet, 87.50; J. G. Brethet, 140.00; F. T. Brignall, 30.00; R. F. Carscadden, 210.00; J. J. Clark, 84.00; A. Cochrane, 112.00; B. Cowan, 80.00; W. J. Culbert, 75.00; Dominion Experimental Farm, 60.00; W. R. Draper, 12.50; G. F. Dreman, 415.00; J. K. Featherstone, 75.00; E. Fleming, 15.00; W. Ford, 173.00; L. Forrest, 107.00; J. W. Freeborn, 75.00; H. W. Gibson 105.00; G. L. Graham, 15.00; G. N. Graham, 30.00; R. Heipel, 20.00; W. Henderson, 329.00; B. Houk, 47.00; F. G. Hutton, 100.00; W. Jones, 30.00; E. Kenny, 98.00; J. J. Lynch, 168.00; J. J. E. McCague, 237.50; W. J. McCorqudale, 60.00; A. B. MacDonald, 35.00; G. McDiarmid, 98.00; McLoughry Bros., 50.94; J. Metter, Jr., 26.00; L. E. Morgan, 60.00; Oak Lodge Stock Farms, 67.50; Ontario Agricultural College, 242.50; J. Payne, 49.00; C. W. Pollock, 12.50; W. G. Rennie, 15.00; L. Richardson, & Son 88.00; South Simcoe Yorkshire Breeders' Club, 15.00; Stevenson Farms, 15.00; D. W. Stewart, 28.00; R. Stonehouse, 30.00; B. Sutherland, 40.00; Telfer Bros., 30.00; E. Tolton, 75.00; J. L. Tolton, 75.00; H. Wharton, 90.00; F. Wiley, 5.63; G. Williams, 30.00; F. C. Willmott & Son, 75.00; A. S. Wilson, 45.00; W. Wittman, 60.00; A. E. Young, 45.50............ 4,937 07

Prizes.

Bacon Litter Competitions—Sundry persons................................	1,003 28
Swine Car Lot Competition—Sundry persons................................	276 00
Competition in the Improvements of Live Stock—Sundry persons.............	467 06

Judging, etc., $6,890.82.

Sundry persons, services, 2,375.00; expenses, 4,515.82........................ 6,890 82

Miscellaneous, $22,882.80.

Bain, Bicknell, White & Bristol, legal services, 51.40; Canadian National Live Stock Records, transfers, 24.25; Department of Highways, auto service, 68.05; Dominion Government Live Stock Department, proportionate cost of travelling expenses re tuberculosis tests, 16,206.07; C. Ferguson & Son, wire, 10.40; L. Godson, insurance premium, 32.44; A. D. Jackson, care of "Mainring," 75.00; Ketchum Manufacturing Co., Ltd., tags, 14.90; National Dairy Association, entry fees, 150.00; Ontario Cattle Breeders' Association, entry fees, 506.44; Province of Ontario Pictures, negatives, transparencies, etc., 166.15; W. K. Riddell, hardware, 10.20; Sundry boys, expenses, Colt Club Boys, R.W.F., 112.10; H. A. Strohmeyer, Jr., photos, 213.00; Union Stock Yards, feed, etc., 42.10; G. A. Walkey, ribbons, etc., 43.50. Sundries—cartage, 300.13; express, 356.29; freight, 4,475.78; petty disbursements, 44.93.............. 22,903 13

Less refund, 1931, T. Eaton Co., Ltd., discount..............		20 33	
			22,882 80
Total..		205,485 90	
Less Fees, Stallion Enrolment..............	2,450 12		
Fines, Breach of S.E. Act............	235 00		
Sale of Stock........................	4,453 91		
Miscellaneous.......................	285 30		
		7,424 33	
Live Stock Branch................................		$198,061 57	

INSTITUTES BRANCH

Salaries ($8,987.50)

G. A. Putnam	Superintendent	12 months		3,600 00
I. W. Brodie	Clerk Group 1	12 "		1,600 00
A. M. Hamilton	Clerk Stenographer, " 1	12 "		1,200 00
A. E. Smith	" " " 2	12 "		1,125 00
E. M. Little	" " " 2	12 "	975 00	
	Less Leave of Absence		487 50	487 50
S. T. Harvey	Junior Clerk Messenger	12 "		975 00

Contingencies ($2,995.14)

Temporary Services, $825.00.

Elsie McClure	Clerk Stenographer, Group 2	12 months	825 00

Travelling Expenses, $246.06.

W. Brodie, 17.05; E. M. Little, 13.10; G. A. Putnam, 211.61; A. E. Smith, 4.30 246 06

Miscellaneous, $1,924.08.

Addressograph-Multigraph of Canada, Ltd., supplies, etc., 50.41; Department of Highways, auto service, 213.46; L. Godson, insurance premium, on car 16.22; King's Printer, 1,342.09; National Stationers, Ltd., repairs, 16.10; H. E. Price, car repairs, 18.25; United Typwriter Co., Ltd., inspections, etc., 48.14; Remington Typewriters, Ltd., inspections, 13.75. Sundries—car tickets, 6.00; express, 95.05; freight, .88; newspapers and periodicals, 49.09; telegrams, 45.89; petty disbursements, 8.75 1,924 08

Grants, Services, Travelling and Other Expenses ($66,975.52)

Temporary Services, $9,850.00.

Pearl Church	Demonstrator and Lecturer	5½ months	550 00
Edith Collins	Field Assistant in Clothing	12 "	1,500 00
F. P. Eadie	" " Household Science	12 "	1,800 00
G. A. Gray	" " Nutrition	12 "	1,500 00
E. Hopkins	" " Junior Work	12 "	1,500 00
E. A. Slicter	" " Housing	12 "	1,500 00
M. V. Powell	General Assistant	12 "	1,500 00

Grants, $6,927.00.

Women's Institutes 6,927 00

Sundry Lecturers, $40,090.97.

Services, 23,096.90; expenses, 16,994.07 40,090 97

Miscellaneous, $10,107.55.

T. Allen, books, 35.52; Canadian National Railways, fares of farm girls to Royal Winter Fair, 911.80; Canadian Pacific Railway Co., fares re farm girls to Royal Winter Fair, 1,880.85; Clatworthy & Son, display rack, 106.00; G. Coles, Ltd., lunches, 167.40; Department of Highways, auto service, 33.78; J. M. Dent & Son, Ltd., books, 21.60; Dominion Glass Co., fruit jars, 10.12; T. Eaton Co., Ltd., lunches, dinners, etc., 306.09; Hotel Carls-Rite Co., Ltd., lunches, 462.15; T. S. Hubbard, reporting meeting, 12.00; Kemptville Agricultural School, meals, etc., re scholarship winners, 30.00; Ambrose Kent & Son, Ltd., medals and badges, 98.00; King's Printer, 1,917.49; Musson Book Co., books, 22.56; A. C. O'Connor, car repairs, 43.93; Ontario Agricultural College, Guelph, board, etc., re scholarships, 66.00; Peel County Agricultural Representatives Branch, Ford car, 300.00; Province of Ontario Pictures, photos, etc., 11.00; G. A. Putnam, meals, Institute officers, 20.60; Royal York Hotel, expenses re farm girls trip to Royal Winter Fair, 2,768.20; R. Simpson Co., Ltd., lunches, 91.50; Sundry Girls, travelling expenses re trip to Royal Winter Fair, 540.78; Treasurer, Women's Guild, Ottawa, service for overseas visitors, 60.00; Toronto Transportation Commission, special cars, 114.00; T. Wibby, badges, 55.68. Sundries—express, 3.90; petty disbursements, 16.60 10,107 55

Institutes Branch $78,958 16

DAIRY BRANCH

Salaries ($6,300.00)

G. H. Barr	Director	12 months	3,600 00
L. Nicholson	Senior Clerk Stenographer	12 "	1,500 00
H. Netterfield	Clerk, Group 2	12 "	1,200 00

Contingencies ($2,854.33)

Travelling Expenses.

G. H. Barr 845 05

Miscellaneou.

King's Printer, 1,907.29; United Typewriter Co., Ltd., inspections, 23.00; Sundries—express, 24.40; newspapers and periodicals, 15.40; telegrams, 25.75; petty disbursements, 13.44 .... 2,009 28

Grants ($4,450.00)

Dairymen's Association, Eastern Ontario	1,500 00
Dairymen's Association, Western Ontario	1,000 00
Ontario Milk and Cream Producers' Association	1,500 00
Central Ontario Cheesemakers' Association	150 00
Eastern " " "	200 00
Western " " "	100 00

Dairy Instruction and Inspection ($134,994.65)

Salaries, $26,400.08.

G. H. Barker	Chief Instructor	12 months	2,700 00
T. C. Adams	Creamery Instructor	12 "	1,700 00
J. L. Baker	" "	12 "	1,700 00
J. P. Bogaerts	" "	12 "	1,700 00
Geo. B. Brodie	" "	12 "	1,700 00
Jas. A. Hill	" "	12 "	1,700 00
C. A. Davies	" "	6 "	850 04
Roland Johnston	" "	12 "	1,700 00
C. E. Lackner	" "	12 "	1,700 00
D. McMillan	" "	12 "	1,700 00
W. S. McKenzie	" "	12 "	1,700 00
Arthur Legault	" "	12 "	1,700 00
Jno. Stubbs	" "	12 "	1,700 00
C. Chambers	Milk Test Inspector	12 "	1,700 00
A. P. Clark	" " "	6 "	850 04
J. C. Cumberland	" " "	12 "	1,600 00

Temporary Services, $61,523.64.

W. H. Bailey	Dairy Instructor and Inspector	9 months	1,555 54
T. F. Boyes	" " "	9 "	1,555 54
S. S. Cheetham	" " "	9 "	1,555 54
C. J. Brennan	" " "	9 "	1,555 54
D. Connell	" " "	9 "	1,555 54
H. W. Cunningham	" " "	9 "	1,555 54
Fred Dool	" " "	9 "	1,555 54
J. H. Eehlin	" " "	9 "	1,555 54
W. I. Hicks	" " "	9 "	1,555 54
Hugh Howey	" " "	9 "	1,555 54
C. F. Linn	" " "	9 "	1,555 54
Wm. C. Loughlin	" " "	9 "	1,555 54
Ed. McAllister	" " "	9 "	1,555 54
Jos. McAllister	" " "	9 "	1,555 54
E. McCormick	" " "	9 "	1,555 54
H. A. McKinley	" " "	9 "	1,555 54
G. A. McMillan	" " "	9 "	1,555 54
Jas. A. Mitchell	" " "	9 "	1,555 54
W. J. Moore	" " "	9 "	1,555 54
J. A. Murray	" " "	9 "	1,555 54
Peter Nolan	" " "	9 "	1,555 54
W. H. Olmstead	" " "	9 "	1,555 54
W. T. Oliver	" " "	9 "	1,555 54
G. Rancier	" " "	9 "	1,555 54
E. T. Rogers	" " "	9 "	1,555 54
H. B. Sandwith	" " "	9 "	1,555 54
R. A. Thompson	" " "	9 "	1,555 54

Dairy Branch—Continued

Dairy Instruction and Inspection—Continued

Temporary Services—Continued

M. O. Trickey	Dairy Instructor and Inspector	9 months	1,555 54
G. F. Wright	" " "	9 "	1,555 54
J. W. Bolton	" " "	9 "	1,544 46
H. Stinson	" " "	9 "	1,544 46
Fred Clark	" " "	9 "	1,533 31
W. J. Cobey	" " "	9 "	1,533 31
Geo. H. Alguire	" " "	5½ "	794 48
D. F. Brennan	Milk Test Inspector	12 "	1,599 96
E. D. Johnson	" " "	12 "	1,599 96
W. L. Misener	" " "	12 "	1,599 96
H. B. Welsh	" " "	12 "	1,500 00
F. G. Knowles	Assistant Creamery Inspector	4 "	437 50
S. G. Trevor	Assistant for Dairy Branch	3 "	273 08
Sundry Cheese Factory Instructors and Inspectors (broken periods)			2,452 50

Instructors and Inspectors, Travelling Expenses, $46,295.70.

T. C. Adams, 1,117.55; G. H. Alguire, 435.23; W. H. Bailey, 612.74; J. L. Baker, 1,782.13; G. H. Barker, 1,109.65; P. J. Bogarts, 1,539.33; J. W. Bolton, 690.74; T. F. Boys, 736.39; C. J. Brennan, 592.04; W. H. Brennan, 3.50; D. F. Brennan, 991.95; G. B. Brodie, 1,097.15; C. Chambers, 1,184.80; S. Cheetham, 646.89; A. P. Clark, 531.05; F. Clark, 696.64; W. J. Cobey, 691.69; D. Connell, 630.24; J. C. Cumberland, 1,320.75; H. W. Cunningham, 576.64; C. A. Davies, 1,029.95; F. Dool, 562.49; J. H. Echlin, 602.69; F. Herns, 490.69; T. Hicks, 7.20; W. I. Hicks, 593.89; J. A. Hill, 1,010.21; H. Howey, 555.94; E. D. Johnson, 993.50; R. Johnston, 1,392.20; F. G. Knowles, 262.75; C. E. Lackner, 939.71; A. Legault, 1,098.83; C. F. Linn, 603.44; W. C. Loughlin, 694.79; E. McAllister, 558.04; J. McAllister, 638.59; E. McCormick, 578.64; W. S. McKenzie, 1,345.41; H. A. McKinley, 590.19; D. McMillan, 715.70; G. A. McMillan, 596.79; W. L. Misener, 1,408.86; J. A. Mitchell, 617.69; W. J. Moore, 589.94; J. A. Murray, 613.67; P. Nolan, 621.14; W. T. Oliver, 667.39; W. H. Olmstead, 593.34; G. Rancier, 657.39; E. T. Rogers, 619.14; H. B. Sandwith, 573.29; J. H. Scott, 780.74; H. B. Strutt, 611.23; H. Stinson, 589.39; J. Stubbs, 1,292.18; R. A. Thompson, 648.74; H. G. Trevor, 42.70; M. O. Trickey, 635.19; H. B. Welsh, 1,307.10; G. F. Wright, 577.84 .... 46,295 70

Miscellaneous, $775.23.

J. V. Bourbonnais, rental of factory, 24.00; Canadian Laboratory Supplies, Ltd., heaters, 21.70; Cherry-Burrell Corporation, Ltd., bulbs, etc., 13.05; F. G. Evans, legal fees, 19.75; L. Godson, insurance premiums, 12.67; Hinde & Dauch Paper Co., Ltd., boxes, 14.09; King's Printer, 20.40; F. McKerkel, testing supplies, 35.10; Nichols' Chemical Co., Ltd., acid, 49.96; C. Richardson & Co., bottles, 42.45; A. Stewart, alcohol, 16.35; Sundry persons, washing bottles, 422.46; Toronto Municipal Abattoir, rental of milk test rooms, 45.00; petty disbursements, 38.25 .... 775 23

Ontario Butter Grading Station, Salaries, Travelling Expenses, Purchase of Dairy Products for Grading Purposes, etc. ($14,316.16)

Salaries, $6,299.92.

J. H. Scott	Butter Grader	12 months	3,000 00
A. P. Clark	Milk Test Checker	6 "	949 96
C. A. Davies	Creamery Inspector and Instructor	6 "	949 96
N. Nagle	Clerk Stenographer	12 "	1,400 00

Purchase of Dairy Products for Grading Purposes, $5,432.06.

Creameries—Arnprior, 42.12; Avonbank, 87.05; Belleville, 275.02; Bigham's, Ltd., 8.12; Bluevale, 10.61; Brampton, 36.55; Bridgen Cheese & Butter Co., 2.66; Caledon East, 2.45; Canada Milk Products, Ltd., 2.94; Canadian Packing Co., Ltd., 19.85; Central Smith, 1.40; Chesley, 80.30; Citizens, Belleville, 20.51; Citizens, Whitby, 16.80; Cobden, 51.57; Cobourg, 6.20; Corbett, 51.18; Elmira, 271.90; Elmvale, 17.22; Exeter, 73.78; Fenelon Falls, 10.92; Flavelle's, Ltd., 78.06; Forest, 192.45; Fullarton, 148.88; Galt, 2.73; German Union Cheese & Butter Co., Tavistock, 34.38; Grand River, 1.37; Grand Valley, 73.46; Hamilton Dairies, Ltd., Caledonia, 157.12; Hamilton Dairies, Ltd., Jarvis, 94.69; Harwood, 20.06; Hemlock Park, 47.12; J. A. Hughes Co., Shelburne, 123.10; Ingersoll, 4.10; J. B. Jackson, Ltd., 25.52; J. B. Kellar, Ltd., St. Jacobs, 7.63; Kerrwood, 41.84; Kingston Creameries, Ltd., Belleville, 154.76; Land O'Lanark, Perth, 149.33; Maitland, Wingham, 223.80; Malcolm's Condensing Co., 68.23; Maple, Woodstock, 93.81; Mutual, Brigden, 5.32; New Dundee, 443.59; New Hamburg,

Dairy Branch—Continued

Ontario Butter Grading Station, Salaries, etc.—Continued

Purchase of Dairy Products for Grading Purposes—Continued

67.46; Newmarket, 1.30; Norwood, 5.46; Paisley, 23.21; Peel, Brampton, 4.13; Renfrew, 63.04; St. Mary's, 19.43; St. Thomas, 1.47; Sarnia City Dairy, 1.40; Shamrock, Centralia, 19.95; Silverwood's—Cargill, 135.77; Cayuga, 107.88; Chatham, 69.56; Fergus, 131.38; Kitchener, 67.95; London, 264.24; Lucknow, 188.06; Niagara, 7.98; Peterborough, 86.09; St. Catharines, 46.75; Sarnia, 44.11; Stratford, 91.90; Stouffville, 1.40; Sutton, 79.61; Tamworth, 5.74; Teeswater, 27.27; Tilsonburg, 2.52; Trent Valley, Campbellford, 289.77; Trenton, 17.96; Wellington Produce Co., 21.28; Willow Grove, Mitchell, 231.30; Wiarton, 26.19. 5,432 06

Storage of Butter, $411.88.

Flavelle's, Ltd., 33.81; Fowlers Canadian Co., Ltd., 35.35; Graham Cold Storage, 3.15; Ontario Agricultural College, Dairy Dept., 9.80; Plaza Cold Storage, Ltd., 21.14; Silverwood's, Ltd., 171.64; Walkerton Egg & Dairy Co., Ltd., 87.57; Whyte Packing Co., Ltd., 49.42 .... 411 88

Miscellaneous, $2,172.30.

Bell Telephone Co., rentals, 33.80; tolls, 6.05; King's Printer, 67.36; Parisian Laundry, laundry, 17.89; J. H. Scott, travelling expenses, 117.90; Toronto Municipal Abattoir, rent and storage, 1,560.25. Sundries—cartage, 65.94; express, 220.28; postage, 63.00; petty disbursements, 19.83 .... 2,172 30

Eastern Dairy School ($18,479.64)

Salaries, $8,975.00.

Name	Position	Period		Amount
L. A. Zufelt	Superintendent	12	months	3,000 00
J. A. Craig	Buttermaker	12	"	2,000 00
J. F. Robinson	Cheesemaker	12	"	1,800 00
Ethel M. Lake	Clerk Stenographer, Group 1	12	"	1,200 00
Edgar Sheppard	Caretaker, " 2	12	"	975 00

Temporary Services, $3,680.00.

Name	Position	Period		Amount
C. F. Linn	Instructor, Separator Department	3	months	450 00
John H. Echlin	" Cheese "	3	"	450 00
H. B. Sandwith	" Milk Testing "	3	"	450 00
J. O. Cliff	Assistant, Butter "	12	"	1,010 00
S. E. Dennison	" Cheese "	3	"	195 00
J. W. Caverly	Fireman	12	"	900 00
Bruce Mitchell	Night Foreman	3	"	225 00

Miscellaneous, $5,824.64.

W. S. Anglin, cheese boxes, 230.36; Bell Telephone Co., rentals, 73.80; tolls, 3.32; Canadian Industries, Ltd., supplies, 47.28; Canadian Toledo Scale Co., Ltd., inspections, 26.25; Canadian Cheesemaker's Association, advertising, 10.00; Cherry-Burrell Corp. of Canada, Ltd., supplies, 22.60; City Steam Laundry, laundry, 52.35; J. Crawford & Sons, Ltd., cheese boxes, 45.15; W. B. Dalton & Sons, Ltd., supplies, 490.95; De Laval Co., Ltd., supplies, 15.00; J. R. C. Dobbs & Co., repairs, etc., 55.05; Douglas & McIlquham, repairs, 57.25; Dye & Chemical Co. of Canada, Ltd., butter colour, 17.33; Firstbrook Boxes, Ltd., boxes, 141.12; Hanson & Edgar, stationery, 68.35; Imperial Oil, Ltd., wax, 14.45; Jackson Press, stationery, 26.05; Jury & Peacock, bottles, etc., 18.05; Kingston Public Utilities Commission, light and power, 798.99; J. Laidlaw & Son, Ltd., supplies, 11.70; J. A. McFarlane & Son, salt, etc., 129.60; A. J. Mayo, machinery repairs, 21.10; Murdock Stationery, stationery, 19.85; Otis-Fensom Elevator Co., Ltd., inspection, 16.00; Pay list, wages of men, 214.00; C. Richardson Co., glassware, etc., 64.30; Robertson Grocery Co., groceries, 53.40; D. B. Shutt, travelling expenses, 175.70; Simmons Bros., Ltd., supplies and repairs, 686.50; J. Soward's Coal Co., coal, 1,768.98; Treasurer, City of Kingston, taxes, 70.92; S. G. Trevor, travelling expenses, 22.90; L. A. Zufelt, travelling expenses, 218.44. Sundries—cartage, 42.68; express, 4.15; freight, 1.08; newspapers and periodicals, 21.30; postage, 47.00; petty disbursements, 21.34 .... 5,824 64

Dairy Exhibitions, Purchase of Material and Incidentals, ($26.40)

Pudney Bros., expenses re Frigidaire equipment 26 40

Dairy Branch—Continued

Dairy Instructor ($3,000.00)

Frank Herns................Chief Instructor, Western Ontario......12 months 3,000 00

Total		181,421 18	
Less Milk Testing fees	11,010 15		
Cow Testing fees	98 25		
Sale of Butter	18,562 10		
Sale of Produce	27 00		
Fines D. P. Act	325 00		
Eastern D.S. Butter Making charges	8,762 93		
		38,785 43	
Dairy Branch		$145,635 75	

FRUIT BRANCH

Salaries ($5,100.00)

P. W. Hodgetts...............Director...........................12 months 3,600 00
G. Boehler...................Senior Clerk Stenographer, Group 1...12 " 1,500 00

Contingencies ($1,908.81)

Temporary Services, $74.52.

M. L. Gooderham........Clerk Typist, Group 2................1 1/5 months 74 52

Miscellaneous, $1,834.29.

Canadian Horticultural Council, membership fees, 200.00; L. Godson insurance premium, 66.18; P. W. Hodgetts, travelling expenses, 476.89; King's Printer, 264.47; C. R. Perry, strawberries, 13.00; Toronto Stamp & Stencil Works, Ltd., stamps and stencils, 17.90; United Typewriter Co., Ltd., inspections, 12.00; Sundries—car tickets, 5.00; express, 191.91; telegrams, 583.90; petty disbursements, 3.04........ 1,834 29

Grants ($7,250.00)

Fruit Growers' Association of Ontario........ 6,600 00
Gardeners' and Florists' Association........ 150 00
Entomological Society of Ontario........ 500 00

Grants Towards Erection of Co-Operative Packing Houses ($5,000.00)

Caradoc Fruit Growers' Association, 500.00; Meaford Co-operative Fruit Growers' Assciation, 1,500.00; Niagara Packers, Ltd., 1,500.00; Oxford Fruit Growers' Co-operative, Ltd., 1,500.00........ 5,000 00

Fruit Work including Expenditures under The Fruit Pests Act ($24,340.29)

Salaries, $3,800.00.

G. G. Dustan............Specialist in Fruit Pest Work...........12 months 2,000 00
A. Nelson...............Fruit Pest Inspector...................12 " 1,800 00

Municipalities' Half Cost of Inspection, $1,272.35

Beamsville, 23.20; Clinton, 215.30; Collingwood, 25.00; East Flamboro, 43.50; Fonthill, 30.00; Grantham, 25.00; Grimsby, 48.50; Hespeler, 50.00; Louth, 62.40; Niagara, 62.90; North Grimsby, 154.40; Saltfleet, 192.75; St. Catharines, 150.00; Stamford, 89.40; Walkerville, 100.00........ 1,272 35

Inspectors, $17,852.07.

H. V. Buckley, services, 418.00; expenses, 224.00; M. Blackburn, services, 1,084.50; expenses, 831.17; L. Caesar, expenses, 193.57; J. W. Casselman, services, 262.50; expenses, 262.50; N. H. Clement, services, 380.00; expenses, 152.00; K. Crews, expenses, 1,515.26; C. Copeland, services, 154.50; C. C. Duncan, services, 365.00; expenses, 146.00; G. G. Dustan, expenses, 234.28; J. A. Goldie, expenses, 459.42; W. L. Hamilton, services, 448.50; expenses, 240.04; W. Miles, services, 185.00; expenses, 55.14; J. Maxwell, services, 262.50; expenses, 262.50; C. A. Neil, services, 140.00; expenses, 68.95; A. Nelson, expenses, 837.86; E. J.

Fruit Branch—Continued

Fruit Work including Expenditures under Fruit Pests Act—Continued

Inspectors—Continued

Quail, services, 375.00; expenses, 326.53; I. E. Ronson, services, 346.50; expenses, 220.50; F. K. B. Stewart, services, 412.50; expenses, 263.50; G. E. Tregunno, services, 375.00; expenses, 150.00; E. Weese, services, 1,514.00; expenses, 783.61; C. A. Webster, services, 380.00; expenses, 208.99; H. M. Webster, services, 1,345.50; expenses, 1,023.23; H. N. Webster, services, 616.50; expenses, 327.52.. 17,852 07

Miscellaneous, $1,420.87.

Bell Telephone Co., rental, 7.55; tolls, 1.75; H. A. Berlette & Son, gasoline, etc., 16.85; Bowmanville Hydro-Electric Power Commission, power, 54.40; H. S. Britton, wiring, 69.25; J. Brown, apples, 14.00; Canadian Wirebound Boxes, Ltd., packing, 76.26; Department of Highways, auto service, 221.28; C. W. Dracup, apples, 30.00; Forbes Bros., gasoline, etc., 63.38; Goodyear Tire & Rubber Co., Ltd., tires, 23.84; Masco Co., Ltd., 11.15; Newcastle Hydro-Electric Power Commission, light, 16.43; Niagara Brand Spray Co., Ltd., wipers, etc., 595.43; Northumberland Packers, apples, 100.00. Sundries—express, 1.75; postage, 100.80; petty disbursements, 16.75 .... 1,420 87

Total	24,345 29	
Less Sale of Fruit	5 00	
		24,340 29

HORTICULTURAL EXPERIMENTAL STATION, VINELAND

Salaries ($20,600.00)

Name	Position		Period	Amount
E. F. Palmer	Director		12 months	3,600 00
W. H. Upshall	Research Specialist		12 "	3,000 00
O. J. Robb	Olericulturist		12 "	2,550 00
G. H. Dickson	Hybridist		12 "	2,400 00
W. J. Strong	"		12 "	2,400 00
D. L. Bailey	Pathologist	(T)	12 "	2,350 00
J. R. Van Haarlem	Hybridist		12 "	2,300 00
J. A. Goldie	Horticultural Representative, Group 2		12 "	2,000 00

Services and Expenses ($30,791.98)

Services, $24,103.28.

Name	Position	Period	Amount
S. Wylie	Foreman	12 months	1,600 00
E. A. H. Banks	Graduate Assistant	12 "	1,500 00
I. G. Burkholder	Clerk Stenographer, Group 1	12 "	1,200 00
I. Myers	Stationary Engineer, " 3	½ "	51 28
G. Marlow	Mechanic	12 "	1,300 00
J. Thornton	Fireman	12 "	1,200 00
A. Richardson	Gardener	12 "	1,400 00
S. Cass	"	12 "	1,300 00
W. H. Stephenson	Assistant Gardener	12 "	1,125 00
J. V. Ashwood	Farm Hand, Group 2	12 "	1,050 00
G. A. Ball	" " " 2	12 "	1,050 00
H. T. Eggleton	" " " 2	12 "	1,050 00
A. K. Meldrum	" " " 2	12 "	900 00
S. Peacock	" " " 2	12 "	1,050 00
G. Webb	Head Teamster	12 "	1,200 00
A. Barber	Teamster	12 "	1,050 00
J. Peacock	"	12 "	1,050 00
L. Webb	Maid	12 "	675 00
Pay list, wages of Farm Hands and Firemen			4,352 00

Travelling Expenses, $345.75.

G. H. Dickson, 5.55; J. A. Goldie, 31.78; E. F. Palmer, 185.91; O. J. Robb, 15.18; W. H. Upshall, 59.33; J. R. Van Haarlem, 48.00 .... 345 75

Miscellaneous, $15,663.79.

Battery & Electric Service, battery, 10.00; Beamsville Lumber & Supply Co., Ltd., lumber, 212.14; Bell Telephone Co., rental, 239.70; tolls, 94.41; E. E. Bossence, stationery, 49.00; Brooks Oil Co., oil, 128.11; Canadian Fairbanks-Morse Co., Ltd., machinery repairs, 13.68; Canadian Kodak, Ltd., films, 14.37; Canadian Oil Companies, Ltd., oil, 11.75; Carters, Ltd., tires, etc., 19.89; Central Scientific Co., Ltd., hydrometers, Instruments, etc., 211.03; C. Cigma, Ltd., stationery, 23.00; Cities Service Garage, tractor, 703.35; S. H. Clup, hay, 163.05;

Fruit Branch—Continued

Horticultural Experimental Station, Vineland—Continued

Services and Expenses—Continued

Miscellaneous—Continued

Coy Bros., hardware, 30.53; Crysler Machine Works, repairs, 159.00; Dale Estate, Ltd., boxes, etc., 17.80; Dupley & Ferguson, seed, etc., 24.50; T. Eaton Co., Ltd., heater, etc., 17.74; W. G. Fletcher, plumbing supplies, 25.67; C. Preitz, wreaths, 12.00; Garvin Hardware Co., Ltd., hardwaie, 31.84; General Casualty Insurance Co., premium, 11.92; L. Godson, insurance premium, 48.91; W. Holditch, hay, 230.25; Hydro-Electric Power Commission, light, 1,245.73; Imperial Oil, Ltd., gasoline, etc., 1,588.11; Instruments, Ltd., rain gauge, 111.00; International Garage, repairs, 175.20; International Harvester Co., Ltd., repair parts, 35.03; James Canadian Seeds, Ltd., seeds, 16.65; V. C. Juhlke, tires and tubes, 138.34; H. O. Keep, blacksmithing, 178.35; King's Printer, 252.44; Lee Hardware, Ltd., hardware, 22.39; Louth Township, taxes, 499.80; J. H. Mehlenbacher, team of horses, 350.00; S. Millen, veterinary services, 10.00; W. H. Moore, straw, 192.15; Moyer & Kennedy, anti-freeze, 18.25; National Drug & Chemical Co., Ltd., drugs and chemicals, 53.31; Niagara Packers, Ltd., hampers, etc., 754.28; Pay list, wages of men, 1,374.98; Queen City Coal Co., Ltd., coal, 1,258.20; Steele, Briggs Seed Co., Ltd., seeds, 22.66; Taylor-Forbes Co., Ltd., repairs, 13.88; Thompson-Gordon, Ltd., boiler repairs, 14.85; E. W. Townsend & Sons, strawberry plants, 21.40; Transport Oil, Ltd., oil and grease, 161.77; Tri-City Typewriter Service, repairs, 19.50; H. Tuffard, oats, 82.94; University of Pennsylvania, book, 15.00; Vic's Service, tires, etc., 22.24; Vineland General Store, Ltd., hardware, etc., 104.77; Vineland Growers' Co-operative, Ltd., cement, coal, oats, etc., 348.53; Wells Garage Co., Ltd., auto repairs and supplies, 193.16; R. O. Wilcox, harness supplies and repairs, 219.12; W. A. Wisemer, rent, 1,711.60. Sundries—cartage, 9.81; customs, 4.31; express, 41.07; freight, 1,476.48; newspapers and periodicals, 96.29; postage, 167.00; petty disbursements, 139.56..... 15,663 79

Total		40,112 82	
Less Dept. of Highways, gasoline tax	115 00		
Sale of Fruit	3,064 88		
Rent, Board, etc.	6,137 96		
Miscellaneous	3 00		
		9,320 84	
Horticultural Experimental Station, Vineland		$30,791 98	

Special Experiments ($1,600.75)

W. A. Crysler & Son, frames, etc., 23.69; Dominion Glass Co., jars, 28.07; Niagara Packers, Ltd., soda, acid, etc., 682.61; Pay list, wages of men, 655.49; Steele, Briggs Seed Co., Ltd., alfalfa, 49.25; Vineland Growers Co-operative, Ltd., posts, 37.51; Wellington & Davidson, nursery stock, 72.50; express, 7.70; petty disbursements, 43.93........ 1,600 75

Fruit Stations Expenses and Maintenance ($442.80)

H. M. Webster, services, 211.50; expenses, 231.30........ 442 80

Pre-Cooling Station, Brighton, Equipment, Services and Expenses ($2,490.19)

K. Crews........Manager and Horticulturist........12 months 1,800 00

Services and Expenses, $1,870.88.

K. Crews, expenses, 1,110.32; H. N. Webster, services, 567.00; expenses, 193.56 1,870 88

Miscellaneous, $1,293.20.

Acme Steel Co., Ltd., scales, etc., 25.00; Bell Telephone Co., rental, 12.50; tolls, 73.45; Brighton Hydro-Electric System, light and power, 697.57; Brighton Water Works, water, 150.00; J. Boes, labour, 124.00; Canadian Ice Machine Co., disc, 31.55; W. J. Gartshore, hardware, 21.55; C. Squire, labour, 141.50;. Sundries—express, 1.42; freight, 3.15; newspapers and periodicals, 7.10; telegrams, .61; petty disbursements, 3.80........ 1,293 20

Total	4,964 08	
Less refund, storage charges	2,473 89	
Pre-Cooling Station, Brighton	2,490 19	
Fruit Branch		$99,524 82

AGRICULTURAL REPRESENTATIVES BRANCH

Salaries ($16,550.00)

R. S. Duncan	Director	12 months	4,000 00
J. E. Whitelock	Assistant Director	12 "	3,300 00
M. C. McPhail	Second Assistant	12 "	3300 00
R. W. Froom	Clerk Stenographer, Group 1	12 "	1,200 00
N. Cooper	" " " 2	12 "	975 00
L. J. Neale	" " " 2	12 "	975 00
B. Ellis	Clerk 1	12 "	1,600 00
W. Wilson	" 2	12 "	1,200 00

Contingencies ($6,054.92)

Temporary Services, $750.00.

D. Mellor.............Clerk, Group 3...........................12 months 750 00

Travelling Expenses, $2,270.69.

N. J. Cooper, 10.90; R. S. Duncan, 649.47; B. Ellis, 10.90; R. W. Froom, 3.15; M. C. McPhail, 628.99; D. Mellor, 1.70; L. J. Neale, 10.90; J. E. Whitelock, 948.33; W. Wilson, 6.35........ 2,270 69

Miscellaneous, $3,034.23.

Cox & Andrew, chart, 20.00; Department of Highways, auto service, 314.51; King's Printer, 2,369.97; United Typewriter Co., Ltd., repairs and inspections, 120.03; T. Wibby, badges, etc., 19.60. Sundries—car tickets, 6.00; express, 28.47; freight, 3.16; newspapers and periocicals, 41.40; telegrams, 86.59; petty disbursements, 24.50........ 3,034 23

Agricultural Representatives Branch Services and Expenses ($327,034.98)

Permanent Salaries, $180,987.89.

Algoma, 3,975.00; Brant, 3,975.00; Bruce, 3,975.00; Carleton, 3,750.00; Cochrane, 2,200.00; Dufferin, 2,875.00; Dundas, 3,125.00; Durham, 2,700.00; Elgin, 4,550.00; Essex, 5,500.00; Frontenac, 3,375.00; Glengarry, 2,700.00; Grenville, 2,775.00; Grey, 5,350.00; Haldimand, 3,100.00; Halton, 2,700.00; Hastings, 3,075.00; Huron, 4,475.00; Kenora, 2,400.00; Kent, 3,600.00; Lambton, 3,975.00; Lanark, 2,975.00; Leeds, 2,000.00; Lennox and Addington, 2,900.00; Lincoln, 3,103.12; Manitoulin, 3,600.00; Middlesex, 5,125.00; Muskoka and Parry Sound, 3,825.00; Norfolk, 3,900.00; Northumberland, 3,825.00; Ontario, 3,975.00; Oxford, 3,975.00; Peel, 2,875.00; Perth, 2,875.00; Peterborough, 3,275.00; Prescott and Russell, 3,975.00; Prince Edward, 3,525.00; Rainy River, 2,975.00; Renfrew, 2,875.00; Simcoe North, 3,375.00; Simcoe South, 2,975.00; Sudbury, 2,859.77; Temiskaming, 3,375.00; Thunder Bay, Fort William, 3,275.00; Thunder Bay, Port Arthur, 3,675.00; Waterloo, 3,600.00; Welland, 3,525.00; Wellington, 5,575.00; Wentworth, 3,900.00; Victoria, 3,825.00; York, 5,300.00........ 180,987 89

Temporary Services, $8,146.18.

Algoma, 65.00; Bruce, 1,399.97; Cochrane, 731.25; Dundas, 93.75; Elgin, 825.00; Glengarry, 825.00; Kenora, 750.00; Leeds, 788.46; Lincoln, 756.25; Oxford, 1,661.50; Prescott and Russell, 250.00........ 8,146 18

Expenses, $116,806.44.

Algoma, 2,054.10; Brant, 1,556.02; Bruce, 2,457.65; Carleton, 2,288.39; Cochrane, 1,901.45; Dufferin, 1,477.79; Dundas, 1,914.59; Durham, 1,612.58; Elgin, 2,831.39; Essex, 2,376.49; Frontenac, 1,577.35; Glengarry, 1,921.74; Grenville, 768.21; Grey, 4,414.18; Haldimand, 1,676.50; Halton, 3,416.35; Hastings, 2,855.41; Huron, 1,820.38; Kenora, 2,159.07; Kent, 1,776.15; Lambton, 1,664.39; Lanark, 2,000.34; Leeds, 2,004.78; Lennox and Addington, 1,381.49; Lincoln, 4,187.45; Manitoulin, 2,149.47; Middlesex, 5,012.85; Muskoka and Parry Sound, 3,864.83; Norfolk, 1,989.46; Northumberland, 1,422.66; Ontario, 2,266.85; Oxford, 3,841.83; Peel, 2,008.18; Perth, 1,699.64; Peterborough, 2,027.68; Prescott and Russell, 1,758.17; Prince Edward, 1,425.72; Rainy River, 2,383.48; Renfrew, 2,524.36; Simcoe North, 2,229.63; Simcoe South, 1,700.86; Sudbury, 2,084.70; Temiskaming, 1,906.49; Thunder Bay, Fort William, 2,804.25; Thunder Bay, Port Arthur, 1,416.80; Waterloo, 3,072.03; Welland, 1,783.59; Wellington, 1,558.07; Wentworth, 5,678.48; Victoria, 1,448.95; York, 2,653.17........ 116,806 44

Short Courses, Lecturers' and Instructors' Services and Expenses, $3,895.03.

E. Armstrong, services, 12.80; J. Baker, services, 10.50; H. G. Bell, services, 6.20; J. Brethour, services, 7.00; expenses, 13.75; R. J. Bryden, expenses, 122.85; H. A. Bunt, services, 3.00; J. F. Clark, expenses, 30.94; G. L. Clute, services, 10.00; M. J. Duff, services, 10.00; expenses, 3.75; W. J. Gardhouse, services, 7.00;

Agricultural Representatives Branch—Continued

Services and Expenses—Continued

Short Courses, Lecturers and Instructors, Services and Expenses—Continued

expenses, 11.25; R. H. Harding, services, 10.00; expenses, 5.18; D. Hunter, services, 10.00; J. Y. Kellough, services, 7.50; J. S. Knapp, services, 133.00; expenses, 65.55; F. Larose, expenses, 22.25; F. H. Lee, services, 5.00; expenses, 7.61; J. Loughland, expenses, 163.56; J. J. E. McCague, services, 5.00; D. E. McEwen, services, 5.00; expenses, .98; C. H. McDougall, services, 32.00; N. D. McKenzie, services, 332.50; expenses, 167.54; R. M. McKenzie, services, 120.10; J. McLean, services, 84.00; expenses, 100.80; N. R. Martin, services, 168.00; expenses, 53.80; C. H. Mason, services, 20.00; expenses, 2.05; J. R. Ostler, expenses, 8.25; F. R. Page, services, 91.00; expenses, 101.20; H. E. Presaut, services, 252.00; expenses, 129.70; R. J. Rogers, services, 25.30; expenses, 9.45; H. J. Seymour, services, 5.50; J. H. Shaw, services, 518.00; expenses, 296.97; J. A. Sinclair, services, 252.00; expenses, 121.30; G. R. Snyder, expenses, 25.75; J. Spencer, services, 56.00; expenses, 53.85; H. Spearman, services, 35.00; expenses, 32.85; J. L. Stansell, services, 5.00; expenses, 8.50; F. K. B. Stewart, expenses, 60.90; N. J. Thomas, expenses, 12.90; J. Tisdale, services, 7.00; expenses, 4.55; G. Waldie, services, 10.00; expenses, 1.60 .... 3,895 03

Miscellaneous, $17,199.44.

Canadian Facts Publishing Co., copies, 16.50; Canadian Society of Technical Agriculturalists, subscriptions, 156.00; Darling's Garage, Ford Sedan, 441.00; W. Dawson Subscription Service, Ltd., subscriptions, 32.40; Dominion Motors, Chevrolet Coach, 456.63; L. Godson, insurance, 737.17; Imperial Oil, Ltd., oil, 21.90; A. Kent & Sons, Ltd., badges, etc., 1,125.55; King's Printer, 13,409.77; Ontario Agricultural College, Guelph, books, 22.50; Steele Briggs Seed Co., Ltd., seeds, 172.85; Tyne Motor Co., Ford Tudor, 395.31; T. Wibby, badges, 202.96. Sundries—petty disbursements, 8.90 .... 17,199 44

Household Science Demonstrator ($881.40)

Pearl E. Church .... Demonstrator .... 6½ months. 650 00

Bell Telephone Co., rentals, 23.60; Pearl E. Church, expenses, 37.95; W. A. Hamilton, gasoline, 69.91; Lee Sing laundry, .45; postage, 99.49 .... 231 40

Travelling and Living Expenses, Prizes for Essay Contests, Services and Supplies Necessary in Connection with Free Trips to Royal Winter Fair Offered to Winners in Competitions ($11,953.25)

Canadian National Railways, fares, 3,733.45; Canadian Pacific Railway Co., fares, 669.20; Geo. Coles, Ltd., catering, 850.80; Co-operative Supply Dept., O.A.C., books, 381.90; Cox & Andrew, banners, 2.50; L. B. Duff, services lecturing, 25.00; Kemptville Agricultural School, sundry boys' board, 36.00; A. Kent & Sons, Ltd., badges, 187.50; A. MacPherson, pipe band, services, 22.00; D. C. McArthur, drawings, 15.00; Royal York Hotel, accommodation, 4,871.60; Sundry Students' board, 75.77; Sundry Boys, travelling expenses, 832.53; Toronto Transportation Commission, hire of buses, 250.00 .... 11,953 25

Transportation and Living Expenses Attending Short Courses for Winners in Competitions under Agricultural Representatives ($1,459.83)

Canadian National Railways, fares, 301.15; Canadian Pacific Railway Co., fares, 265.65; Kemptville Agricultural School, meals, 102.00; Sundry Students, board, 618.93; Sundry Students, travelling expenses, 172.10 .... 1,459 83

Agricultural Representatives Branch $363,934 38

CROPS, MARRETS AND CO-OPERATION BRANCH

Salaries ($12,850.00)

Name	Position	Period		Amount
J. A. Carroll	Director	12 months		3,600 00
A. H. Martin	Assistant Director	12 "		2,700 00
G. R. Patterson	Fertilizer and Feed Specialist	12 months	2,700 00	
	Less leave of absence		225 00	2,475 00
S. H. H. Symons	Senior Clerk	12 months		1,600 00
I. E. Curtis	Clerk Stenographer, Group 2	12 "		900 00
D. J. Wiggins	Clerk Typist " 2	12 "		825 00
Doris E. Holder	" " " 2	12 "		750 00

Crops, Markets and Co-operation Branch—Continued

Contingencies ($3,200.35)

Temporary Services, $69.71.

Iris V. Logan..........Clerk Typist, Group 2.................... 1 month 69 71

Travelling Expenses, $1,319.98.

C. E. Broughton, 51.45; J. A. Carroll, 280.00; A. Goodwins, 7.77; A. H. Martin, 772.47; G. R. Patterson, 170.92; C. P. Walker, 37.37...................... 1,319 98

Miscellaneous, $1,810.66.

Department of Highways, auto service, 179.53; L. Godson, insurance premium, 32.44; King's Printer, 1,398.34; Remington Typewriters, Ltd., inspections, 14.00; United Typewriter Co., Ltd., inspections, etc., 24.75. Sundries—express, 28.86; newspapers and periodicals, 44.05; telegrams, 81.94; petty disbursements, 6.75... 1,810 66

Loans in accordance with The Co-operative Marketing Loan Act, 1920 ($4,800.00)

Harrow Fruit and Vegetable Co-operative, Ltd.................................. 1,200 00
Kingsville Fruit Growers Association, Ltd...................................... 1,200 00
Ruthven Growers Co-operative, Ltd.. 1,200 00
Seacliffe Growers Co-operative, Ltd.. 1,200 00

To Encourage Co-Operative Marketing ($5,786.80)

Services and Expenses, $5,207.24.

C. E. Broughton, services, 1,299.00; expenses, 678.30; J. T. Cassin, services, 1,527.00; expenses, 815.69; W. J. Price, services, 403.85; expenses, 483.40.... 5,207 24

Miscellaneous, $579.56.

Oxford Farmer's Co-operative Products Co., Ltd., freight on cheese, 520.21; Peel Seed Growers Co-operative, Ltd., alfalfa seed, 17.20; Robt. Redford Co., Ltd., strapping boxes for shipment, 23.40; Romeyn Co., Ltd., insurance on cheese, 13.75. Sundries—freight, 5.00.................................... 579 56

Grants under The Community Halls Act ($12,559.78)

Angus Community Park, 287.28; Craithie Community Hall, 144.37; Crossland Community Hall, 831.06; Elk Lake Community Park, 730.02; Finch Community Hall, 2,000.00; Janetsville Community Park, 455.68; Kemptville Community Park, 2,000.00; Myrtle Community Hall, 944.76; Rodney Community Hall, 2,000.00; Verner Community Park, 1,166.61; Wardsville Community Hall, 2,000.00.. 12,559 78

Crop Improvement Demonstrations, Purchase of Seed and Equipment, Services and Travelling Expenses, Printing, Advertising and Other Educational Work, Administration and Enforcement of The Weed Control Act ($8,136.44)

Services and Expenses, $5,868.44.

H. Cook, services, 300.00; expenses, 450.65; J. Laughland, expenses, 148.10; J. D. McLeod, services, 1,056.00; expenses, 860.50; A. R. G. Smith, services, 913.62; expenses, 593.57; A. S. Smith, services, 440.00; expenses, 1,080.80; E. H. Wallace, services, 7.50; expenses, 17.70............................. 5,868 44

Prizes.

International Grain and Hay Show, Chicago, sundry persons..................... 275 00
Boys' Grain and Potato Clubs, sundry persons.................................. 486 20

Miscellaneous, $3,486.49.

Department of Highways, auto service, 14.60; Goodyear Tire & Rubber Co., Ltd., tire, etc., 11.57; E. G. Hammer, Ltd., gas, 155.78; Harpham Bros., tires, 25.02; C. H. Jackson & Co., bags, 77.96; King's Printer, 483.32; C. O. Kruspe, garage rent, 12.00; Lake Shore Motors, Ford coupe, 394.00; Sundry persons, purchase of seed, 1,548.60; G. A. Walker, badges, 19.80. Sundries—express, 30.10; freight, 677.37; petty disbursements, 36.37......................... 3,486 49

Total..		10,116 13
Less refund F. R. Mallory, accountable warrant.....	50 00	
Sale of barley shipped to England............	1,929 69	
		1,979 69
		8,136 44

Crops, Markets and Co-operation Branch—Continued

Grants ($2,550.00)

Ontario Experimental Union	1,500 00
Essex County Corn Improvement Association	200 00
Ontario Corn Growers' Association	350 00
Lambton Corn Growers' Association	200 00
Wentworth County Seed Association	100 00
Quinte Seed Society	200 00

To Promote Marketing Board ($28,883.45)

Temporary Services, $4,624.96.

C. P. Walker	Director of Publicity	12 months	2,400 00
G. F. Perkin	Secretary	12 "	1,599 96
G. H. Duncan	Investigator	5 "	625 00

Travelling Expenses, $3,391.99.

J. A. Carroll, 285.87; G. H. Duncan, 747.35; B. Goodwins, 60.06; G. R. Patterson, 444.62; J. F. Perkin, 167.08; W. B. Somerset, 1,687.01 ..... 3,391 99

Miscellaneous, $4,866.54.

Associated Printers, Ltd., bulletins, etc., 61.75; C. E. Broughton, vegetables, 19.20; G. H. Carter, fruit, 11.14; A. Clark, erecting booth, 18.25; H. B. Clemes, honorarium, 300.00; Cooper Florist, flowers for booth, 12.00; Eastern Canada Fruit & Vegetable Jobbers Association, advertising, 60.00; King's Printer, 988.26; G. Kline, decorating booth, 12.00; C. T. LaSalle Sign Service, signs, 11.70; Province of Ontario Pictures, negatives, prints, etc., 18.15; Rapid Grip & Batten, Ltd., etchings, 29.50; Remington Typewriters, Ltd., inspections, etc., 19.85; Retail Merchants Association of Canada, circulars, etc., 85.00; Shepherd Printing Co., agreement forms, 30.00; W. B. Somerset, honorarium, 3,000.00; United Farmers Co-operative Co., Ltd., cheese, vegetables, etc., 19.19; Wolfe Photo Studio, photos, 24.00. Sundries—cartage, 14.28; express, 9.15; telegrams, 103.74; petty disbursements, 19.38 ..... 4,866 54

Expenses re Fruit and Vegetable Growers' Council, Hamilton

Services and Expenses, $10,974.41.

J. Baird, services, 100.90; C. W. Bauer, services, 2,765.92; expenses, 1,580.60; W. A. Broughton, expenses, 15.35; A. Campbell, services, 254.18; H. Carrothers, expenses, 22.50; K. B. Conger, services, 375.00; H. L. Craise, services, 175.00; expenses, 1,059.92; J. Cyr, expenses, 24.75; C. Dilworth, expenses, 11.80; A. H. Dixon, services, 154.59; expenses, 245.41; C. G. Kitney, expenses, 6.00; H. Leavens, expenses, 10.50; T. J. Mahoney, expenses, 33.70; J. O'Connor, expenses, 26.85; J. L. Smart, expenses, 10.00; B. Soper, services, 702.00; J. F. Thomas, services, 100.00; expenses, 17.50; H. E. Toms, services, 2,598.80; expenses, 570.07; F. J. Watson, expenses, 13.00; A. H. Wilford, services, 100.00 ..... 10,974 41

Miscellaneous, $5,025.55.

Bell Telephone Co., rental, 44.70; tolls, 189.79; E. E. Bossence, office supplies, 53.81; J. F. Bruce, rent, 280.00; J. A. Calvert, exhibit, 42.60; Canadian Horticultural Council, prize money, etc., 125.00; Cloke & Son, envelopes, 25.35; Eastern Canada Fruit & Vegetable Jobbers Association, advertisement, 60.00; D. Gestetner, Ltd., duplicating machine, supplies, etc., 341.44; Hughes & Wilkins, business cards, 37.28; McConnell & Ferguson, advertising, etc., 2,608.86; Ontario Growers Market Council, brokerage paid in error, 50.00; Reed Press, supplies, 291.71; V. Smith, board, 25.00; United Typewriter Co., Ltd., payment on machines, 75.00; United Farmers Co-operative, Ltd., addressograph charges, etc., 445.37; Vineland Growers Co-operative, machine, 15.00. Sundries—exchange, 1.10; postage, 120.00; telegrams, 154.84; petty disbursements, 38.70 ..... 5,025 55

Subventions Seed Cleaning Plants ($1,997.31)

Brownlee & Son, 141.65; J. H. Clement, 101.80; A. Coulter, 55.50; L. Currah, 51.72; Fennell & Wallace, 132.66; L. Hanlan, 133.75; C. L. Hartley, 129.90; W. A. MacEwen, 167.05; J. W. McRae, 183.20; J. W. Real, 71.48; St. Isidore Seed Growers' Association, 178.59; St. Pascal Seed Growers' Association, 233.75; Sangster & McQuaig, 197.28; L. Scissons, 11.63; A. J. Shantz, 130.28; Sturgeon Falls Agricultural Society, 206.22; Thunder Bay Co-operative Seed Growers, 135.00; Vankleek Hill Agricultural Society, 229.85; W. F. Weedmark & Son, 238.59 ..... 2,679 90

Less rebate Dominion Department of Agriculture, Ottawa 682 59

1,997 31

Crops, Markets and Co-operation Branch—Continued

Subventions—For Freight on Agricultural Lime ($1,105.36)

American Cyanamid Co., 804.70; Canada Crushed Stone Corporation, 721.23; Dominion Lime Co., 15.00; J. Schultz, 28.55; Standard Lime Co., 12.18; Wright Builders Supply, Ltd., 52.37 .... 1,634 03
Less refund Department of Agriculture, Ottawa .... 528 67 | 1,105 36

Crops, Markets and Co-operation Branch $81,869 49

AGRICULTURAL DEVELOPMENT BOARD

Ontario Farm Loans Act and Agricultural Development Act ($4,798.77)

Salaries, $75,140.62

Name	Position	Period		Amount
Executive Office,				
W. B. Roadhouse	Chairman	12 months		6,000 00
E. A. Western	Chief Inspector	12 "		2,850 00
C. C. McNeil	Inspector	12 "		2,200 00
H. W. Cruickshank	"	12 "		1,600 00
F. P. Johnston	Accountant	12 "		2,700 00
J. A. McBride	Principal Clerk	12 "		2,100 00
J. E. Hounsom	Senior Clerk	12 "		2,000 00
F. E. A. Trickey	" "	12 "		2,000 00
L. C. Axton	" "	12 "		1,700 00
G. Walliss	" "	12 "		1,700 00
W. E. Hunter	" "	12 "		1,700 00
E. A. Torrance	Clerk, Group 1	2 "		266 66
H. A. Roberts	" " 1	12 "		1,400 00
F. R. Dunlop	" " 1	12 "		1,600 00
E. M. Pearce	" " 2	12 "		1,125 00
G. Murphy	Senior Filing Clerk	12 "		1,400 00
M. I. Gray	Filing Clerk, Group 1	12 "		975 00
F. B. Selway	" " " 2	12 "		825 00
L. Taylor	" " " 2	12 "		825 00
E. Gott	Clerk Stenographer, " 1	12 "		1,125 00
M. V. Hillary	" " " 1	12 "		1,125 00
O. H. Bell	" " " 1	12 "		1,125 00
E. M. Crozier	" " " 1	11 "		1,031 25
F. M. Dunham	" " " 1	12 "		1,050 00
E. Sarginson	" " " 1	12 "		1,050 00
N. A. Allan	Clerk, " 2	12 "		1,050 00
A. L. Noble	Clerk Stenographer, " 2	12 "		975 00
M. E. Cooper	Junior Clerk Stenographer	12 "		975 00
M. Cardy	Clerk Stenographer, Group 2	12 "		975 00
E. O. Cope	" " " 2	12 "		975 00
E. E. James	" " " 2	12 "		900 00
E. Webb	" " " 2	12 "		900 00
Cora Hicks	" " " 2	12 months	975 00	
	Less leave of absence		765 62	209 38
Legal Department,				
H. W. Page	Solicitor	12 months		4,400 00
K. J. Crocker	Senior Assistant Solicitor	12 "		3,000 00
R. G. M. McDougall	" " "	12 "		2,400 00
V. H. Robinson	Assistant Solicitor	12 "		2,000 00
M. L. James	" "	12 "		1,800 00
M. E. Perney	Senior Filing Clerk	12 "		1,800 00
M. L. E. Burk	Clerk, Group 3	12 "		900 00
M. M. Soanes	" " 1	12 months	1,600 00	
	Less leave of absence		266 67	1,333 33
B. W. Smith	Filing Clerk, Group 1	12 months		1,200 00
H. V. Cullingworth	" " " 1	12 "		1,125 00
L. Livingstone	Senior Clerk Stenographer	12 "		1,400 00
F. Tuton	" " "	12 "		1,300 00
B. A. Shorey	Clerk Stenographer, Group 1	12 "		1,125 00
T. A. Gogo	" " " 1	12 "		1,125 00
E. E. Noble	" " " 2	12 "		900 00
B. Goodwins	" " " 2	12 "		900 00

Agricultural Development Board—Continued

Ontario Farm Loans Act and Agricultural Development Act—Continued

Temporary Services, $29,574.81.

Executive Office,

Name	Position	Group	Period	Amount
C. A. Hopkins	Clerk,	Group 1	12 months	1,200 00
R. L. Cooke	"	" 1	4 "	407 70
H. C. Henderson	"	" 2	12 "	975 00
H. Luscombe	"	" 3	12 "	750 00
M. T. Strathearn	Clerk Stenographer,	" 1	12 "	975 00
D. Brown	" "	" 2	12 "	825 00
K. Butler	" "	" 2	12 "	825 00
E. Langton	" "	" 2	12 "	825 00
M. B. Lee	" "	" 2	12 "	825 00
M. M. Quigley	" "	" 2	12 "	825 00
M. E. Fraser	" "	" 2	1 1/5 "	74 52
C. Rabbie	Filing Clerk,	" 2	12 "	750 00

Legal Department,

Name	Position	Group	Period	Amount
J. A. Gibson	Assistant Solicitor		12 months	1,599 96
B. Gordon	" "		12 "	1,599 96
H. Grossman	" "		12 "	1,599 96
D. F. Jackson	" "		12 "	1,599 96
L. Lees	" "		12 "	1,599 96
M. Henry	" "		7 1/3 "	923 08
G. J. McArthur	" "		6 "	900 00
M. S. Bennett	" "		12 "	1,500 00
J. McCormack	Clerk Stenographer,	Group 1	12 "	975 00
L. I. McLean	" "	" 1	12 "	975 00
M. Stuart	" "	" 1	12 "	975 00
F. Wright	" "	" 1	12 "	975 00
F. A. Stewart	" "	" 1	12 "	975 00
L. Denison	" "	" 2	12 "	825 00
G. M. Phasey	" "	" 2	12 "	825 00
M. Rawn	" "	" 2	12 "	825 00
M. E. Leggatt	" "	" 2	12 "	825 00
H. M. Newman	" "	" 2	1¼ "	69 71
M. Snider	Filing Clerk,	" 2	12 "	750 00

Inspectors—Services, $27,834.50; Expenses, $29,259.61.

R. Avery, services, 303.00; expenses, 420.35; C. O. Bowles, services, 1,257.00; expenses, 929.37; R. Bradey, services, 186.00; expenses, 141.22; D. Broderick, services, 300.00; expenses, 362.17; N. D. Buchan, services, 1,278.00; expenses, 1,075.38; H. W. Cruickshank, expenses, 195.92; S. N. Cleever, services, 510.00; expenses, 203.55; G. Duck, services, 1,224.00; expenses, 1,364.01; C. Fisher, services, 522.00; expenses, 474.35; W. Grice, services, 1,434.00; expenses, 1,752.42; R. J. S. Hill, services, 405.00; expenses, 493.10; J. E. Hounsom, expenses, 115.70; W. K. James, services, 366.00; expenses, 368.10; C. W. Ketcheson, services, 1,299.50; expenses, 1,501.70; C. H. Knight, services, 531.00; expenses, 351.09; J. A. McBride, expenses, 2.00; J. J. McCutcheon, services, 1,560.00; expenses, 1,322.89; D. McDonald, services, 335.30; R. G. M. McDougall, expenses, 15.85; D. A. McIntosh, services, 786.00; expenses, 775.03; L. T. McLaughlin, services, 1,713.00; expenses, 1,576.70; B. R. McMullin, services, 408.00; expenses, 527.10; C. C. McNeil, expenses, 939.24; A. B. McPhail, services, 903.00; expenses, 693.92; Neil McPhee, services, 447.00; expenses, 412.40; J. Mahoney, services, 264.00; expenses, 121.41; E. W. Morton, services, 1,860.00; expenses, 2,218.46; A. Mousseau, services, 330.00; expenses, 84.42; R. H. Murray, services, 781.00; expenses, 1,078.65; F. G. Pack, services, 1,407.00: expenses, 1,493.97; J. A. Riddell, services, 1,206.00; expenses, 1,492.32; W. B. Roadhouse, expenses, 551.89; E. Robson, services, 1,668.00; expenses, 1,569.46; J. W. Stewart, services, 882.00; expenses, 981.61; G. L. Van Patter, services, 871.20; expenses, 647.64; J. Vokes, services, 925.50; expenses, 672.06; F. J. Walker, services, 1,872.00; expenses, 2,207.96; E. A. Western, expenses, 126.20 .... 57,094 11

Miscellaneous, $28,683.71.

Burroughs Adding Machine of Canada, Ltd., inspections and repairs, 41.60; Burroughs & Co. (Eastern), Ltd., books, 13.00; Dept. of Highways, auto service, 314.43; Dictaphone Sales Corp., Ltd., inspections and repairs, 37.17; L. Godson, insurance premium, 27.50; Grant's Garage, auto repairs, 142.90; Hydro-Electric Power Commission, light, 42.91; King's Printer, 11,861.11; McCann & Alexander,

Agricultural Development Board—Continued

Ontario Farm Loans Act and Agricultural Development Act—Continued

Miscellaneous—Continued

inspections, 31.50; J. W. McKinley, auto supplies, 88.97; National Auto Sales, auto supplies, 118.50; Sundry legal disbursements, 12,508.89; Todd Sales Co., Ltd., repairs, 10.50; United Typewriter Co., Ltd., inspections and repairs, 504.82; Wawanesa Mutual Insurance Co., premiums, 2,127.56; Western Motor Sales, Dodge sedan, 465.47. Sundries—car tickets, 90.00; excise stamps, 34.00; express, 1.50; newspapers and periodicals, 106.00; telegrams, 110.58; petty disbursements, 4.80 .... 28,683 71

Expenses on Farms Foreclosed:

Arrears of Taxes, $49,879.17.

Augusta, 245.68; Arthur, 41.91; Binbrook, 102.91; Bromley, 262.01; Burford, 970.72; Caledon, 48.40; Caledonia, 304.36; Calvin, 49.59; Calvert, 481.61; Camden, 272.49; Carleton, 2,559.33; Casey, 28.60; Chapple, 758.91; Chatham, 114.53; Chinguacousy, 411.47; Chisholm, 250.20; Clarence, 70.40; Colchester North, 516.70; Colchester South, 103.23; Cornwall, 427.29; Dack, 269.27; Dorchester South, 324.22; Dymond, 229.99; Easthope North, 240.14; Eldon, 31.48; Elgin, 355.72; Ellice, 108.04; Emo, 685.41; Eramosa, 80.52; Essex, 3,158.12; Esquesing, 123.30; Euphrasia, 101.12; Finch, 85.47; Garafraxa, 179.16; Garafraxa West, 152.37; Gloucester, 351.44; Gosfield North, 200.91; Grey, 843.28; Grimsby North, 252.98; Grimbsy South, 161.67; Hallam, 57.20; Hanmer, 266.44; Herwood, 102.75; Hibbert, 91.72; Hillier, 376.37; Hislop, 48.26; Horton, 1,107.13; Howard, 136.60; Hudson, 39.60; Innisfil, 55.23; Kent, 4,662.02; Kenyon, 1,316.55; Kerns, 464.70; La Vallee, 604.35; Logan, 79.32; Luther West, 82.02; McKim, 274.63; Maidstone, 671.33; Mersea, 1,115.15; Morley, 505.79; Mulmer, 420.60; Nalden, 249.12; Nathers, 203.59; Nelson, 562.48; Nepean, 140.02; Niagara, 1,755.13; Nissouri West, 109.13; Norfolk, 203.34; Northumberland and Durham, 162.29; Orillia, 95.03; Oxford East, 67.70; Oxford-on-Rideau, 161.56; Paipoonge, 658.27; Pelee, 3,039.82; Pelham, 404.45; Prescott and Russell, 70.41; Rayside, 63.44; Renfrew, 1,032.44; Rochester, 1,072.14; Roxborough, 777.02; Russell, 1,014.46; Savard, 184.13; Shuniah, 1,197.87; Simcoe, 333.97; South River, 228.76; Stephenson, 89.18; Stormont, 129.43; Stormont, Dundas and Glengarry, 1,885.23; Tilbury North, 2,214.35; Tilbury West, 387.29; Trafalgar, 182.43; Tyendinaga, 89.10; Victoria, 102.60; Walford, 35.34; Walsingham South, 113.90; Waterloo, 1,086.37; Webbwood, 107.50; Wellington, 208.96; Wellesley, 426.34; Woolwich, 361.45; Yarmouth, 116.93; York, 123.49 .... 49,879 17

Miscllaneous, $1,749.88.

Allen's Hardware, hardware, 16.05; J. B. Arnett, cutting weeds, 16.20; Township of Burford, burning stubble, 11.44; W. N. Foster, seeding, 180.00; General Indemnity Corp., insurance premium, 15.00; R. Griffin, seed, 115.80; W. Habermehl, plowing, 49.50; W. D. Herbert, shingling, 19.00; R. Laidlaw Lumber Co., Ltd., shingles, 309.22; C. M. McCollum, fencing, 20.75; J. McGill, erection of bridge, 350.00; J. McGowan, tools, 21.50; A. J. McPhail, seed, 12.10; J. E. McQuaid, fertilizer, 52.42; J. W. Middleton, shingling, 25.00; M. Montgomery, shingling, 110.00; M. E. Mott, shingling, 12.15; W. E. Nairn, commission on sale, 40.00; Pedlar People, Ltd., nails, 50.10; Township of Rayside, cutting weeds, 35.00; L. R. Rillett, harvesting hay, 50.00; H. W. Rowden, roofing, 26.00; D. A. Stewart, services, valuator, 10.00; G. G. Thorne, seed, 67.50; H. L. Vauceleg, plowing, 27.70; W. Watson, plowing, 55.00; D. Williams, roofing material, 27.00; petty disbursements, 25.45 .... 1,749 88

Total	242,122 30	
Less refund of expenses	237,323 53	
Agricultural Development Board		4,798 77

COLONIZATION BRANCH

Salaries ($5,181.25)

G. A. Elliott	Director		12 months	3,300 00
R. Duggan	Clerk Typist,	Group 1	5 "	500 00
M. A. Wood	Clerk Stenographer,	" 2	1 "	81 25
C. Puttick	Clerk,	" 2	12 "	1,300 00

Contingencies ($150.97)

King's Printer, 82.57; United Typewriter Co., Ltd., inspections, etc., 20.00; Sundries.—express, 4.30; newspapers and periodicals, 25.50; telegrams, 18.60 .... 150 97

Colonization Branch—Continued

Pamphlets, Advertising, Maps and Other Expenses ($5,268.01)

Salaries, $2,974.97.

H. Tutt	Colonization Agent	12 months	2,000 00
J. R. Vaughan	Assistant	3 "	449 97
S. H. Wilson	Colonization Agent	9 "	450 00
L. G. Green	Colonization Agent (T)	3 "	75 00

Temporary Salaries, $1,708.00.

D. J. Matheson	Colonization Agent	12 months	1,500 00
J. R. Weir	Assistant	2 "	208 00

Travelling Expenses, $57.65.

J. R. Weir, 40.65; S. H. Wilson, 17.00 .... 57 65

Miscellaneous, $527.39.

British Welcome & Welfare League, maintenance, 100.25; Canadian Churchman, advertising, 42.00; Canadian National Railways, fares, 99.70; Canadian Pacific Railway Co., fares, 44.30; Dept. of Highways, auto service, 149.60; Farmer's Sun, advertising, 13.44; Wilson Publishing Co., advertising, 60.00; petty disbursements, 18.10 .... 527 39

Land Guides for Settlers and Veterans ($995.75)

Sundry persons, services as guides 995 75

Canadian Women's Hostel, Grant for Maintenance ($5,000.00)

Canadian Women's Hostel 5,000 00

Grant to Salvation Army to Assist in Procuring Farm Settlers, Farm Labourers and Domestic Servants ($3,000.00)

Salvation Army 3,000 00

Ontario House in Great Britain ($55,412.24)

Salaries ($40,275.00)

W. C. Noxon	Agent General	12 months	6,000 00
"	" " (living allowance)		9,000 00
"	" " (auto allowance)		2,500 00
S. E. Perceval	Assistant	12 months	3,600 00
H. Craig	Chief Clerk	12 "	3,000 00
J. P. Young	Publicity Agent	12 "	2,700 00
F. H. Stewart	Agent	12 "	3,400 00
E. Nicoll	Senior Clerk Stenographer	12 "	1,300 00
A. Abbott	" " "	12 "	1,350 00
F. M. Palmer	" " "	6 "	649 98
B. Dickinson	Clerk Stenographer, Group 1	8 "	650 00
Irene C. Jennings	Clerk, " 1	6 "	650 02
C. Campbell	" " 2	12 "	1,200 00
F. Thomas	" " 3	12 "	975 00
A. Hayhow	" " 3	12 "	825 00
M. P. Lewis	Senior Filing Clerk	12 "	1,300 00
P. Davis	Filing Clerk	2 "	125 00
K. Arnold	Caretaker, Group 3	12 "	1,050 00

Expenses Paid in London, England

(Converted into Canadian Currency, see page 37)

Travelling Expenses, £241:16:9.

K. Arnold	£ 1: 4: 5
H. Craig	13: 1: 3
A. Hayhow	12: 1: 5
W. C. Noxon	114: 8: 1
S. E. Perceval	53:18:10
F. H. Stewart	40: 1: 5
F. Thomas	7: 1: 4

Express, Freight and Cartage, £19:8:7.

Canadian Pacific Express Co.	£ 1:13: 2
F. A. Carey & Co.	2: 8: 3
Carter, Paterson & Co.	1: 7: 4
Great Western Railway	1: 0: 5
Kirkham & Co.	7: 6: 6
London, Midland and Scottish Railway	3: 6:10
Petty disbursements	2: 6: 1

Colonization Branch—Continued

Ontario House in Great Britain—Continued

Expenses Paid in London, England—Continued

Newspapers and Magazines...... £22: 2: 1

Postage, Telephone and Cables, £544:8:4.

Postmaster-General.

Postage stamps	£245: 0: 0
Telephone	93: 8: 2
Telegrams and cables	204: 0: 2
Telegraphic address	2: 0: 0

Rent, Taxes and Insurance, £1,036:15:8.

City of Westminster, taxes	£874:15: 4
Metropolitan Water Board, rates	90: 3: 9
C. W. Munn, rector's rate	2: 2: 6
National Health Insurance, office staff	12: 8: 3
Phoenix Assurance Co., Ltd., premiums	57: 5:10

Printing and Stationery, £741:2:5.

City Photo Engraving Co., Ltd., engraving photos	£46:16: 6
Eyre & Spottiswood, stationery supplies	11:14:11
Herring, Dewick & Cripps, Ltd., stationery supplies	15: 9: 0
Romney Press, Ltd., printing	613: 1: 5
H. G. Ryman, stationery supplies	1: 1: 2
Sellwood & Micklewright, Ltd., stationery supplies	36:14: 0
Waite & Cooke, printing	12:18: 0
Wesley, Ltd., stationery supplies	2:14: 3
Petty disbursements	0:13: 2

Heat and Light, £177:2:1.

Charing Cross Electricity Co. Ltd.	£79:11: 5
Gas, Light & Coke Co., Ltd.	41: 9: 0
General Electric Co., Ltd	8:13: 9
Shell Mex, Ltd.	47: 7:11

Advertising, £216:4:4.

British Passenger Agency	£ 6: 6: 0
Canadian Trade Publicity	6: 5: 0
Clougher Corporation	2:10: 0
Empire Mail	7:10: 0
G. Street & Co., Ltd.	193:13: 4

Miscellaneous, £564:3:5.

H. W. Alliott, auditor's fee	£16:11: 0
Baker's Typewriting Co., Ltd., repairs, etc.	7: 7: 9
Bank of Montreal, cheque books and interest	4:15: 1
Bedford, Lemere & Co., photos	7: 9: 6
Bovis, Ltd., painting flagpole	1: 2: 6
Canadian Chamber of Commerce, subscription	5: 5: 0
Eastman & Son, cleaning curtains	2:10: 3
Empire Forestry Association, subscription	2: 0: 0
Ericsen Telephones, Ltd., internal phones	2: 5: 0
W. G. Foye, book	1:10: 0
Hopwood Co., Ltd. photo	1:10: 0
F. C. Hornsey, lantern slides	1: 5: 0
Initial Towel Co., Ltd., towel supply	9:10: 9
Keith & Blackman, boiler repairs	1: 8: 0
Littlewood Bros., cleaning materials	2: 0: 6
London Provision Exchange, subscription	2: 2: 0
A. F. McKechnie, services re barley	10: 0: 0
New Century Co., Ltd., cleaning offices	321: 0: 0
North Finchley Garage, car and repairs	116:19: 0
Piggott Bros., flag	1:15: 0
Royal Agricultural Society, subscription	1: 1: 0
Royal Sanitary Institute, subscription	1:11: 6
Sheridan, Knowles & Co., frames	2:17: 0
Sport & General Press Agency, copyright	1: 1: 0
L. Stone & Co., repairs	1: 4: 6
Waygood Otis, Ltd., lift inspections, etc.	26:15: 1
Wootton & Son, glass	6: 7: 0
Petty disbursements	4:19: 6
	£3,563: 3: 8
Canadian Currency	$14,394 36

Expenses Paid in Ontario, $742.88.

H. Coleman, travelling expenses, 33.64; Dept. of Highways, gas, oil, etc., 96.84; W. C. Noxon, travelling expenses, 528.72. Sundries—newspapers and periodicals, 70.24; petty disbursements, 13.44 .... 742 88

Rental of Offices and Contingencies ($1,384.46)

Bell Telephone Co., rental, 70.20; tolls, 343.26; King's Printer, 30.50; G. A. MacGillivray, rental, London office, 840.00; H. Stainton, services as janitor, 55.00. Sundries—newspapers and periodicals, 30.50; petty disbursements, 15.00 .... 1,384 46

After-Care of Boy Settlers, etc. ($12,032.05)

Salaries ($949.98)

W. E. Sarel	Superintendent of Farm	3½ months	525 00
T. J. Lancaster	Inspector	3 "	424 98

Colonization Branch—Continued

After-care of Boy Settlers—Continued

Temporary Services, $733.31.

C. G. Johnson	Inspector	3 months	399 99
J. R. Weir	"	2 "	333 32

Travelling Expenses, $422.04.

C. G. Johnson, 192.36; T. J. Lancaster, 117.24; J. R. Vaughan, 112.44.......... 422 04

Miscellaneous, $9,941.72.

Bell Telephone Co., rental, 11.93; tolls, 14.65; Board of Home Missions, United Church, after-care of boys, 8,505.00; Bond Hardware, Ltd., supplies, 12.99; British Welcome & Welfare League, maintenance, 111.25; Brydges Coal Co., coal, 247.50; Canadian National Railways, fares, 44.50; Dept. of Highways, auto service, 34.17; Dept. of Immigration, Ottawa, railway fares, 20.57; Dr. J. A. Gandier, professional services, 50.00; Guelph General Hospital, maintenance, 196.00; Hydro-Electric Power Commission, light, 26.42; Imperial Oil, Ltd., gas and oil, 42.75; Dr. A. B. McCarter, professional services, 60.00; Ontario Agricultural College, butter, 12.50; Ontario Reformatory Industries, meat, 30.64; Dr. T. H. Orton, professional services, 250.00; Pearl Laundry Co., laundry, 27.32; Royal Alexandra Hospital, maintenance, 29.25; Dr. T. M. Savage, professional services, 152.50; J. G. Scott, fruit, 40.90; petty disbursements, 20.88.......... 9,941 72

Total			12,047 05	
Less repayment, Canadian Oil Companies			15 00	
			12,032 05	

Payment to Salvation Army for Special Work in Connection with the Placing of Boys ($1,120.00)

Salvation Army.......... 1,120 00

Total			85,544 73	
Less British Government Grant	362 56			
" Dominion Government Grant	2,614 83			
" Assisted Passages	2 40			
		2,979 79		
Less Vimy Ridge Farm:				
Rent, etc.	29 50			
Sale of Produce	5,545 20			
		5,574 70		
			8,554 49	
Total, Colonization Branch			**$80,990 24**	

KEMPTVILLE AGRICULTURAL SCHOOL

Salaries and Expenses ($58,270.87)

Salaries, $49,644.46.

W. J. Bell	Principal	12 months	4,200 00
A. J. Logsdail	Instructor	12 "	3,000 00
H. W. Graham	Instructor and Extension Specialist	12 "	2,700 00
J. F. Fraser	" " "	12 "	2,550 00
C. A. Warren	Instructor and Drainage Surveyor	12 "	2,400 00
V. C. Lowell	Instructor	12 "	2,400 00
W. B. George	"	12 "	2,200 00
Nellie Kidd	Instructress	12 "	2,100 00
H. Lacey	"	12 "	1,600 00
M. B. Perdue	"	12 "	1,500 00
G. A. Scott	Lecturer (T)	3 "	525 00
E. Bustard	Clerk Stenographer, Group 2	12 "	975 00
G. M. Dunfield	" " " 2 (T)	12 "	900 00
T. A. Smirle	Engineer	12 "	1,400 00
S. Clare	Farm Foreman	1 1/3 "	177 88
A. Johnston	Farmer	12 "	1,150 00
W. A. Crawford	Farm Hand, Group 2	12 "	975 00
S. Stevenson	Poultryman	12 "	1,300 00
J. J. Shanks	Assistant Poultryman	4 "	325 00

Kemptville Agricultural School—Continued

Salaries and Expenses—Continued

Salaries—Continued

T. Whates	Herdsman	12 months	1,300 00
E. Colborne	Assistant Herdsman	12 "	1,125 00
J. Levere	Teamster	12 "	1,050 00
J. Grier	"	1 "	87 50
F. Boals	"	12 "	975 00
Pay list, wages of men			12,729 08

Services, $972.00; Expenses, $1,703.58.

W. L. Bartley, services, 15.00; W. J. Bell, expenses, 909.70; L. R. Bryant, expenses, 27.25; J. F. Fraser, expenses, 128.22; W. B. George, expenses, 169.66; H. W. Graham, expenses, 229.57; F. Johnson, services, 96.00; N. Kidd, expenses, 7.00; A. J. Logsdail, expenses, 115.43; V. C. Lowell, expenses, 28.00; M. B. Perdue, expenses, 3.50; L. Reddick, services, 50.00; D. M. Robertson, services, 20.00; G. A. Scott, services, 525.00; expenses, 25.10; J. Spencer, services, 266.00; expenses, 47.60; C. A. Warren, expenses, 12.55 ..... 2,675 58

Equipment, $5,334.05.

Anderson & Langstaff Co., Ltd., 421.37; W. L. Bailey, 19.60; W. A. Barnes & Son, 404.23; H. Bustard, 41.50; Canadian Department Stores, Ltd., 50.00; W. J. Carson, Ltd., 10.67; Conn Bros., 90.46; Crane, Ltd., 16.05; B. F. Dangerfield, 150.00; J. A. Dobson, 854.08; T. Eaton Co., Ltd., 95.13; E. B. Eddy Co., Ltd., 65.00; Firstbrook Boxes, Ltd., 39.75; Frost & Wood Co., Ltd., 41.35; Ginn & Co., 12.66; Grand & Toy, Ltd., 117.30; Gurney Foundry Co., Ltd., 16.83; Gurney Massey Co., Ltd., 26.64; G. M. Hendry Co., Ltd., 55.35; Hotel and Hospital Supply Co., 327.50; Ingram & Bell, Ltd., 139.49; Instruments, Ltd., 14.96; Ketchum Mfg. Co., Ltd., 14.25; Keyes Supply Co., Ltd., 46.00; Kidd & Dickinson, 11.50; Langlier, Ltd., 11.84; McMaster Lumber Co., Ltd., 659.69; Ontario Agricultural College, Guelph, 32.10; Ontario Hughes-Owens Co., Ltd., 86.46; Pelton & Reynolds, 14.47; J. L. P. Sanders, 1,108.57; D. Seymour, 83.50; Spramotor Co., 29.20; W. B. Tuck, 35.00; University of Toronto, 18.50; Woods Mfg. Co., Ltd., 11.29; Yocum-Faust, Ltd., 34.80; petty disbursements, 126.96 ..... 5,334 05

Purchase and Maintenance of Stock, $5,805.19.

S. Anderson, 12.50; Anderson & Langstaffe Co., Ltd., 128.62; N. Brown, 15.75; Canadian National Live Stock Records, 161.50; F. C. Crowder & Son, 13.40; G. W. Davidson, 313.73; J. A. Dobson, 202.90; W. H. Dwyer Co., Ltd., 132.26; J. A. Eager, 1,526.03; J. A. B. Foster, 855.61; H. Higgins, 111.21; Holstein-Friesian Association, 19.00; L. Logan, 13.50; Magno-Davis Lumber Co., Ltd., 121.10; Maple Leaf Milling Co., Ltd., 734.26; T. McClenaghan, 75.00; A. McFarlane, 113.90; R. P. McGahey, 37.00; A. N. McLeod, 45.00; J. McLinton, 44.93; A. Moore, 138.40; G. Powell, 14.25; D. M. Robertson, 20.00; Stevenson's Farms, 300.00; Swift-Canadian Co., Ltd., 156.98; J. A. Tobin, 78.25; W. Waters, 388.70; G. H. Wood & Co., Ltd., 17.18; petty disbursements, 14.23 ..... 5,805 19

General Expenses, $16,537.77.

C. A. Adams, drugs, 309.45; T. E. Adams, syrup, 30.00; A. Ault, provisions, 669.08; J. M. Baker, seed, 38.10; Bell Telephone Co. of Canada, rentals, 90.70; tolls, 77.09; J. N. Berney, auto maintenance, 15.95; Blackie & Sons, Ltd., books, etc., 18.19; British Educational Society, books, etc., 46.25; J. B. Brown, ice, 33.00; Canadian Countryman Publishing Co., advertising, 92.40; Central Garage, auto maintenance, 317.75; Central Meat Market, provisions, 199.02; E. Colborne, alfalfa, 360.00; Dairy Dept. K.A.S., milk, 371.60; M. de Pencier, provisions, 210.89; E. M. Elliott, decorating, 11.00; Farm and Dairy, advertising, 75.60; Farmers' Advocate, advertising, 75.60; Farmer's Sun, advertising, 53.76; F. Fellows, provisions, 308.80; Frisby's Bakery, bread, 370.44; Frith's Flowers, flowers, 18.00; L. Godson, insurance premiums, 15.47; C. B. D. Graham, provisions, 661.50; Imperial Oil, Ltd., gas, 302.40; Kemptville Creameries, Ltd., butter, 940.23; Kemptville Hydro-Electric System, power, 2,154.35; Kemptville Printing Co., advertising, 84.06; Kemptville Public Library, fees, 10.00; King's Printer, 488.81; A. Langstaffe & Son, coal, 5,309.86; Lavoline Cleanser Co., Ltd., cleaning compound, 10.00; McClenaghan Bros., provisions, 962.08; K. McDonald & Sons, Ltd., supplies, 119.45; Macmillan Co. of Canada Ltd., books, 56.82; R. Moore & Sons, seed, 21.10; Ontario Milk Producers' Association, advertising, 12.50; Orme, Ltd., piano tuning, 18.00; Ottawa Farm Journal, advertising, 52.32; Ottawa Winter Fair, advertising, 25.00; Peel Seed Growers' Co-operative, Ltd., seed, 27.36; Plantagenet Seed Growers' Association, seed, 20.30; Poultry Dept.

Kemptville Agricultural School—Continued

Salaries and Expenses—Continued

General Expenses—Continued

K.A.S., eggs, 319.81; Scottish Fertilizers, Ltd., fertilizers, 38.00; Sheridan Nurseries, Ltd., shrubs, 18.45; Sport Shop, bulbs, 16.20; Mrs. G. Tuck, meals, 12.00; W. B. Tuck, ice cream, 59.00; E. Webb & Sons, Ltd., bulbs, 16.20; F. Whates, meals, 24.00; H. A. Wilson & Co., Ltd., sporting goods, 57.36; G. H. Wood & Co., Ltd., soap, etc., 150.00. Sundries—cartage, 51.25; express, 116.39; freight, 86.30; newspapers and periodicals, 45.63; postage, 338.75; telegrams, 19.76; petty disbursements, 84.39 .... 16,537 77

Total		79,997 05	
Less Sale of produce	4,383 42		
Rent, board, etc.	13,211 75		
Sale of stock and equipment	4,131 01		
		21,726 18	
Kemptville Agricultural School		58,270 87	

ONTARIO VETERINARY COLLEGE

Salaries ($37,525.00)

Staff:

Name	Position		Period	Amount
C. D. McGilvray	Principal		12 months	5,400 00
A. L. Shepherd	Senior Clerk		12 "	2,000 00
A. LeGrand	Clerk	Group 2	12 "	1,125 00
W. Graham	Caretaker	" 1	12 "	1,500 00
J. Newman	"	" 2	12 "	1,200 00
E. I. Twiss	"	" 2	12 "	1,050 00
C. B. Angell	Stationary Engineer	" 3	12 "	1,600 00
N. McColl	Fireman		12 "	1,300 00
J. Barnett	Veterinary Stableman		12 "	1,200 00

Faculty:

Name	Position	Period	Amount
R. A. McIntosh	Instructor	12 months	3,000 00
F. W. Schofield	"	12 "	3,000 00
H. E. Batt	"	12 "	3,000 00
A. A. Kingscote	"	12 "	2,550 00
J. S. Glover	"	12 "	2,550 00
W. J. R. Fowler	"	7 "	2,500 00
J. N. Pringle	"	7 "	2,100 00
H. D. Nelson	"	7 "	2,100 00
F. J. Cote	"	7 "	350 00

Expenses ($9,432.22)

Temporary Services, $1,600.00.

Name	Position	Period	Amount
B. Goulden	Fireman	7 months	560 00
T. Hubbard	"	6 "	480 00
A. Turner	Assistant Caretaker	7 "	560 00

Travelling Expenses, $298.35.

C. D. McGilvray, 263.40; R. A. McIntosh, 31.90; F. W. Schofield, 3.05 ...... 298 35

Miscellaneous, $7,533.87.

T. R. Barber, signs, glass, etc., 59.85; Bell Telephone Co., tolls, 45.83; rental, 123.60; Board of Light & Heat Commission, gas, light, etc., 110.02; Bond Hardware Co., Ltd., hardware, 301.18; H. W. Brown, examiner, 20.00; J. A. Campbell, lecturer, 13.05; Canadian General Electric Co., Ltd., lamps, 49.06; Commercial Oil Co., Ltd., polish, 26.00; Cook & Denison, valves, etc., 13.65; Crane, Ltd., plumbing supplies, 31.21; Cudahy Packing Co., cleanser, 19.11; Darling Bros., Ltd., plumbing, 33.40; J. Dietrich, hardware, 10.00; A. Dunbar, lecturer, 260.00; Edghill Tea Rooms, lunches, 29.50; Galt Brass Co., Ltd., valves, etc., 40.26; Garden City Paper Mill Co., towels, 84.80; Garlock Packing Co., packing, 14.67; J. J. Gibbons, Ltd., advertising, 648.48; J. Gould, boiler repairs, 24.00; F. C. Harrington & Son, coal, 127.18; L. Herringa, engraving diplomas, 11.25; Imperial Oil, Ltd., gasoline, 297.35; E. H. Kellog & Co., oil, 48.30; King's Printer, 571.51; S. F. Lawrason & Co., Ltd., soda ash, etc., 79.96; D. E. MacDonald, Ltd., dry goods, 74.32; Macmillan Co. of Canada, Ltd., books, 23.00; McArthur Engineering & Construction Co., Ltd., repairing drain, 12.00; Mrs. J. Newman, laundry, 101.58; Northern Coal Co., coal, 1,512.78; B. Oldfield, luncheons, 60.00; Ontario Reformatory Industries, chairs, 96.00; Perfection Brush Co., brooms, etc.,

Ontario Veterinary College—Continued

Expenses—Continued

Miscellaneous—Continued

15.80; E. E. Pettifer, plastering, 10.75; Royal City Laundry, laundry, 88.11; R. Stewart, lumber, 78.03; F. L. Stout, dry goods, 43.33; Solex Co., Ltd., lamps, 43.59; Sundry persons, anatomical subjects, 126.00; Taylor Forbes Co., Ltd., lawn mower, repairs, etc., 13.97; United Typewriter Co., Ltd., inspections, 12.00; Ward's Natural Science Est., Inc., laboratory supplies, 28.50; C. Yeates Co., Ltd., luncheons, 17.00. Sundries—car tickets, 10.00; cartage, 465.95; customs, 221.25; express, 11.77; freight, 989.58; newspapers and periodicals, 28.10; postage, 265.00; telegrams, 1.67; petty disbursements, 90.57.......... 7,533 87

Scholarships and Prizes ($130.58)

Cambridge Book Shop, Ltd., 17.60; A. Eger, 63.41; Macmillan Co. of Canada, Ltd., 43.07; W. L. Williams, 6.50.. 130 58

Research and Investigation ($4,135.61)

D. Anderson, straw, 41.50; Art Metropole, stationery, 11.15; A. F. Bain, services, 219.50; Bausch & Lomb Optical Co , microscope, 46.33; Bogardus & Barton, drugs, 64.65; Canadian Laboratory Supplies, Ltd., supplies, 158.61; Central Scientific Co., Ltd., laboratory supplies, 313.18; Doughty & McFarlane, feed, 335.00; J. Dunn, veterinary services, 94.00; J. S. Glover, travelling expenses, 20.50; J. H. Hagen, feed, 67.50; Haver-Glover Laboratories, instruments, 20.64; J. F. Hartz Co., Ltd., laboratory supplies, 27.42; Ingram & Bell, Ltd., laboratory supplies, 122.67; W. H. Johnston, fee, services, etc., 436.38; T. L. Jones, services, 17.00; G. H. Laird, hay, 201.20; P. Lariviere, hay, 78.75; W. E. LeGrange, services, 21.50; Liquor Control Board, alcohol, 143.13; Marshall's Drug Store, drugs, 263.11; R. A. McIntosh, travelling expenses, 148.99; Pay list, wages of men, 436.00; F. W. Schofield, travelling expenses, 190.00; Standard Chemical Co., Ltd., formaldehyde, etc., 57.00; A. Stewart, drugs, 29.57; Sundry persons, anatomical subjects, 180.10; University of Toronto, books, 36.50; Ward's Natural Science Establishment, crayfish, etc., 14.95; H. M. Warren, meat, 17.55; Wilson Scientific Co., Ltd., oil, 75.44; C. Yeates Co., Ltd., milk, 11.10. Sundries—cartage, 174.84; newspapers and periodicals, 31.20; petty disbursements, 28.65. 4,135 61

Total..		51,223 41
Less Tuition fees..............................	10,270 00	
Sale of feed, etc............................	150 60	
Rent, board, etc............................	444 00	
Miscellaneous..............................	1,980 58	
		12,845 18
Ontario Veterinary College............................		$38,378.23

WESTERN ONTARIO EXPERIMENTAL FARM, RIDGETOWN

Salaries and Expenses ($14,868.24)

Salaries, $13,720.00.

W. R. Reek	Director	12 months	3,600 00
E. Horsman	Junior Clerk Stenographer	12 "	825 00
George Mackay	Assistant Herdsman	12 "	1,125 00
Thomas White	Tobacco Specialist	12 "	1,500 00
Alvin Fraser	Farm Hand, Group 1	12 "	1,050 00
F. W. Ozanne	" " " 2	12 "	900 00
George Griffin	Teamster	12 "	1,125 00
Earl Barr	"	12 "	1,050 00
John Humble	"	12 "	975 00
J. M. Jones	"	12	900 00
J. Perrodou	Janitor	(T) 2 "	70 00
J. J. Neilson	Assistant (part time)		600 00

Travelling Expenses, $943.12.

J. J. Neilson, 56.96; W. R. Reek, 886.16.................................. 943 12

Miscellaneous, $6,265.58.

A. E. Baker, blacksmithing, 22.00; W. J. Bannister, veterinary services, 12.75; Bell Telephone Co., rentals, 58.20; tolls, 111.40; Bowden's Drug Store, drugs, 38.75; R. S. Brown & Son, dry goods, etc., 14.96; Canadian Fertilizer Co., Ltd., fertilizer, 40.37; Canadian National Live Stock Records, registrations, 38.50; Central Garage, gas, etc., 129.63; Clark & Son, provisions, 36.43; B. R. Cohoe, barley, 14.70; R. E. Cook, provisions, 73.74; Dale Estate, Ltd., labels, etc.,

Western Ontario Experimental Farm, Ridgetown—Continued

Salaries and Expenses—Continued

Miscellaneous—Continued

17.75; A. Delmege, implement parts, 31.51; C. F. Dickman, provisions, 68.72; Dominion Press, stationery, 15.30; H. English potatoes, 11.40; East End Garage, gas, etc., 106.42; E. Fish, gas and oil, 24.37; Gammage & Co., gas, etc., 853.73; C. Garton, coal, 627.50; L. Godson, insurance premium, 48.91; W. H. Goodhue, hardware, etc., 165.15; A. J. Green, repairs, etc., 10.80; Gunns, Ltd., manure, 25.10; Harrow Farmers' Co-operative Association, Ltd., oats, 769.33; D. A. Hitch, coal, 119.17; T. Hore, coal, 176.98; Irvin's Garage, gas and oil, 22.38; Kearney's Garage, gas, etc., 29.54; Ketchum Manufacturing Co., bands, 12.33; King's Printer, printing, etc., 72.03; J. H. Lampman & Son, seed, 64.00; J. G. Little, blinds, etc., 41.35; B. Lounsbury, shoeing, 30.75; Q. Lowing, cleaning, 22.50; J. MacGregor, harness repairs, 16.10; S. B. McCready, bulbs, 57.11; J. G. McIndoe, car repairs, 11.38; M. McLean, potatoes, 10.00; G. T. Mickle & Sons, feed, etc., 107.42; Pay list, wages of men, 247.85; Ridgetown Creamery, buttermilk, etc., 46.27; Ridgetown Public Utilities Commission, light, water, etc., 570.22; N. A. Roszell, provisions, 36.52; Shepherd Printing Co., printing, 10.00; A. J. Silcox, dustbane, etc., 86.12; Silverwood's Milk Products, Ltd., buttermilk, 161.85; Simpson Motor Sales, repairs, etc., 225.07; D. H. Stewart, oil, drugs, 46.30; Union Gas Co., Ltd., gas, 252.45; G. Wedge, feed, 94.65; Wilson Press, tags, etc., 11.50. Sundries—cartage, 12.75; custons, .43; express, 43.53; freight, 66.28; newspapers and periodicals, 32.65; postage, 73.00; telegrams, 6.65; petty disbursements, 119.43 .... 6,303 98

Less refund Dept. of Highways Gas Tax		38 40	6,265 58
Total		20,928 70	
Less Sale of Produce	2,359 88		
Rent	888 00		
Sale of stock and equipment	2,786 55		
Miscellaneous	26 03		
		6,060 46	
		14,868 24	

Purchase of Stock and Equipment ($1,078.89)

C. Brethet, sows, 42.00; G. F. Drennan, boar, 35.00; W. Knight & Son, steers, 907.89; Stevenson Farms, boar, 40.00; Sunny Crest Poultry Farm, cockerels, 54.00... 1,078 89

Western Ontario Experimental Farm, Ridgetown $15,947.13

DEMONSTRATION FARM, NEW LISREARD ($9,905.27)

Salaries, $5,550.00.

W. G. Nixon	Superintendent	12 months	3,600 00
J. McFarlane	Clerk Typist, Group 2	12 "	825 00
A. McGregor	Herdsman	12 "	1,125 00

Miscellaneous, $8,060.77.

P. H. Armstrong, auto supplies and repairs, 259.85; C. P. Ball, horse hair, 12.00; O. Blais, auto repairs, 12.40; Canadian Oil Companies, Ltd., gas and oil, 181.00; Canadian National Live Stock Records, registrations, 78.50; R. D. Chester, posts, 45.00; Conlin Bros., coal and wood, 150.75; Experimental Farm, Kapuskasing, cockerels, 14.00; L. Godson, insurance premium, 22.56; F. W. Hendry, seed, etc., 38.25; Holstein-Friesian Association, registrations, 42.00; Hovey & Evans, engine repairs, 21.71; Mrs. T. Hoyle, cleaning office, 31.00; Imperial Oil, Ltd., gasoline and oil, 211.45; King's Printer, 119.18; Liskeard Motors, auto supplies and repairs, 113.40; J. H. Long, feed, 119.15; McColl-Frontenac Oil Co., Ltd., gasandoil, 91.20; Town of New Liskeard, water, 174.00; W. G. Nixon, travelling expenses, 136.44; Northern Ontario Power Co., light, 483.83; Northern Telephone Co., rental, 94.48; tolls, 16.26; Pay list, wages of men, 5,007.97; P. J. Perry, blacksmithing, 21.10; T. J. Proud, wood, 36.88; H. W. Rowden, seed, hardware, etc., 96.21; Geo. Taylor Hardware, Ltd., hardware, 11.37; Temiskaming Motor League, road work, 42.00; S. E. Thicke, bags, 10.00; R. R. Wood, hardware, 35.60. Sundries—cartage, 1.55; express, 61.13; freight, 38.31; newspapers and periodicals, 12.00; postage, 94.00; telegrams, 14.10; petty disbursements, 110.14.. 8,060 77

Total		13,610 77
Less, Sale of Produce	1,488 10	
Sale of Stock and Equipment	1,962 25	
Rent	180 00	
Miscellaneous	75 15	
		3,705 50
Demonstration Farm, New Liskeard		9,905 27

DEMONSTRATION FARM, HEARST ($10,976.70)

Salaries, $2,000.00.

L. H. Hanlan..................Superintendent.................. 8 months 2,000 00

Miscellaneous, $11,476.71.

Beatty Bros., hardware, etc., 28.73; V. Brisson, coal, hardware, etc., 239.89; P. O. Brosseau, oats, 14.00; Canadian Fairbanks-Morse Co., Ltd., engine repairs, etc., 11.85; Canadian National Live Stock Records, registrations, 32.50; H. Carson Co., Ltd., harness, 27.11; Charcoal Supply Co., Ltd., charcoal, 10.00; Cherry-Burrell Corporation of Canada, Ltd., brushes, soda, etc., 21.25; Cockshutt Plow Co., Ltd., implement parts, 20.50; De Laval Co., Ltd., machinery parts, 12.38; Dominion Experimental Farm, cattle, 416.00; J. Doucet, machinery repairs, 64.00; T. Eaton Co., Ltd., blinds, etc., 26.10; Goodyear Tire & Rubber Co., Ltd., belting, 29.87; Graham Bros., seed, 48.00; Grieve & Powell, feed, 82.70; S. R. Griffin & Sons, oil, 14.95; Gunn's, Ltd., feed, 30.25; Halliday Co., Ltd., window sash, 10.86; L. H. Hanlan, travelling expenses, 873.00; Hearst Garage, repairs, 25.35; Imperial Oil, Ltd., gas and oil, 419.17; International Harvester Co., Ltd., implement repairs, 79.83; Kapuskasing Experimental Station, chicks, 75.00; Kemptville Agricultural School, sows, 166.50; Kenora District Co-operative Clover Seed Growers' Association, seed, 71.10; King's Printer, 73.70; Ketchum Mfg. Co., Ltd., tags, 10.39; J. Lepage, blacksmithing, 88.30; Lewis Bros., Ltd., hardware, 26.27; Lufken Rule Co. of Canada, Ltd., steel tapes, 14.88; A. G. H. Luxton, grease, 10.00; L. Martin, harness repairs, 15.20; Massey-Harris Co., Ltd., implement repairs, 27.06; Geo. McMeekin, wagon, etc., 175.00; Mercier & Shirley, feed, 595.86; Monarch Drug Store Co., Ltd., drugs, 29.05; R. Noble & Sons, sleighs, 116.00; Northern Garage, repairs, 42.25; Northern Telephone Co., Ltd., rental, 50.52; tolls, 33.43; Ogilvie Flour Mills Co., Ltd., feed, 76.94; Pay list, wages of men, 6,348.93; Peel Seed Growers Co-operative, Ltd., seed, 32.70; Pellow Lumber & Hardware Co., hardware, 245.81; Percival Plow & Stove Co., Ltd., stoves, 15.81; Plessisville Foundry, castings, 23.37; R. Senica, wood, 82.50; Spruce Falls Power & Paper Co., Ltd., posts, etc., 19.76; Telfer Paper Box Co , Ltd., egg cartons, 32.96; West & Co., auto supplies, 38.83; Western Canada Flour Mills Co., Ltd., feed, 27.05; Harry Yipp, laundry, 18.75. Sundries—cartage, 5.53; express, 58.09; freight, 136.19; newspapers and periodicals, 15.00; postage, 45.00; telegrams, 16.12; petty disbursements, 78.57............................. 11,476 71

Total..		13,476 71	
Less Sale of Produce....................	1,377 88		
Sale of Stock and Equipment.........	994 61		
Rent............................	112 00		
Miscellaneous......................	15 52		
		2,500 01	
Demonstration Farm, Hearst..........................		10,976 70	
Demonstration Farms..........................		$20,881.97	

ONTARIO AGRICULTURAL COLLEGE

Salaries ($389,292.05)

President's Office

G. I. Christie	President		12 months	8,000 00
J. B. Reynolds	President Emeritus	(T)	12 "	3,000 00
A. M. Porter	Registrar		12 "	2,000 00
W. M. Parke	Secretary to President	(T)	11 "	880 21
H. B. Grant	Clerk, Group 3		12 "	975 00
I. Eveleigh	Clerk Stenographer, " 2		12 "	900 00
D. R. Sands	Dean		12 "	500 00
E. T. Goring	Assistant Dean		12 "	312 00
F. G. Baldwin	Physical Director		12 "	2,400 00
W. Copp	Telephone Operator, Group 2		12 "	750 00
W. E. Sarel	Porter and Messenger		8½ "	850 00

Bursar's Office

T. H. Stuart	Bursar	12 months	2,850 00
R. D. Fowke	Senior Clerk	12 "	1,900 00
W. J. Precious	Clerk, Group 1	12 "	1,500 00
Lyle O'Neil	" " 1	12 "	1,300 00

Ontario Agricultural College—Continued

Salaries—Continued

Dining Hall, Dormitories, etc.

K. Beck	Dietitian	12 months	1,600 00
A. Ross	Matron	12 "	500 00
C. Moore	Baker	12 "	1,500 00
W. G. Moore	Chef	12 "	1,600 00
W. Colwell	Kitchen Porter	12 "	900 00
J. R. Jennings	" "	12 "	975 00
T. Buckley	Caretaker, Main Building	7 "	700 00
W. R. Walker	" Mills Hall	12 "	1,200 00
J. Taylor	" Dining Hall	12 "	1,200 00
J. C. Hersey	" Memorial Hall	12 "	1,050 00
W. Harper	" Gymnasium and Postmaster	12 "	1,050 00
C. Cockman	" Johnston Hall	12 "	975 00
William Macdonald	" Group 2 (T)	1 "	81 25

Engineer's Department

A. Green	Stationary Engineer	12 months	2,400 00
R. Yates	Assistant Stationary Engineer	12 "	1,600 00
T. Guthrie	Plumber	12 "	1,600 00
E. McGee	Fireman	12 "	1,500 00
F. Wakefield	Electrician	12 "	1,600 00
J. Quarrie	Fireman	12 "	1,300 00
J. Whittle	"	11 "	1,202 37
J. B. L. Good	"	12 "	1,300 00
O. McKay	"	12 "	1,200 00
G. Gibson		12 "	1,300 00

Mechanical Department

Roy S. Crawford	Foreman Carpenter	12 months	1,600 00
W. Swindell	Carpenter	12 "	1,300 00
T. Amos	"	12 "	1,600 00
J. Hayden	"	12 "	1,600 00
W. Holman	Foreman Painter	12 "	1,800 00
T. Vipond	Painter	12 "	1,500 00
A. Klein	Blacksmith	12 "	1,600 00

Library

L. Watt	Librarian	12 months	1,400 00
M. K. Macdonald	Assistant Librarian	12 "	1,125 00
M. I. Odroskie	" "	9 "	900 00
M. Healey	Janitress	12 "	625 00

Bacteriology Department

D. H. Jones	Professor	12 months	3,800 00
A. Davey	Associate Professor	12 "	3,000 00
D. B. Shutt	Lecturer, Group 1	12 "	2,400 00
E. H. Garrard	" " 1	12 "	2,200 00
N. Mills	Clerk Stenographer, " 1	12 "	1,125 00
T. J. Keenan	Caretaker, " 2	12 "	1,200 00

Botany Department

J. E. Howitt	Professor	12 months	3,800 00
R. E. Stone	Associate Professor	12 "	3,000 00
D. R. Sands	Assistant "	12 "	2,550 00
W. G. Evans	Lecturer, Group 1	12 "	2,200 00
M. Patrick	Clerk Stenographer, " 2	12 "	975 00
J. F. Mann	Caretaker, " 2	12 "	1,125 00

Chemistry Department

R. Harcourt	Professor	12 months	4,200 00
H. L. Fulmer	Associate Professor	12 "	3,000 00
A. L. Gibson	" "	12 "	3,000 00
H. G. Bell	" "	12 "	2,850 00
G. N. Ruhnke	Assistant Professor	12 "	2,700 00
L. R. Bryant	Lecturer, Group 1	12 "	2,400 00
W. W. Watson	" " 2	12 "	2,000 00

Ontario Agricultural College—Continued

Salaries—Continued

Chemistry Department—Continued

F. F. Merwick	Soil Specialist, Group 1	12 months	2,300 00
N. J. Thomas	" " " 1	12 "	2,200 00
D. MacKenzie	Fellow in Chemistry (T)	8 "	750 00
R. Bryant	Laboratory Assistant	12 "	1,600 00
Doris Johns	Clerk Stenographer, Group 2	12 "	975 00
A. Marshall	Clerk, " 3	12 "	900 00
D. Johns	Caretaker, " 2	12 "	1,200 00
R. Sunley	Janitress	3 "	161 42

Trent Institute

L. J. Bohn	Assistant Director	12 months	2,850 00
W. H. Croot	Instructor	12 "	2,550 00
R. P. Quance	Chemist and Instructor	12 "	2,000 00
W. Rushton	Baker	12 "	1,500 00
I. Wakefield	Clerk, Group 3	12 "	900 00

Entomology Department

L. Caesar	Professor	12 months	3,800 00
A. W. Baker	"	12 "	3,800 00
R. H. Ozburn	Lecturer, Group 1	12 "	2,300 00
W. E. Heming	" " 2	12 "	2,100 00
Robert Thompson	Assistant Entomologist	12 "	2,100 00
Rose King	Junior Laboratory Attendant	12 "	1,050 00
A. Comar	Clerk Stenographer, Group 2	12 "	900 00

English Department

O. J. Stevenson	Professor	12 months	3,800 00
E. C. McLean	Associate Professor	12 "	3,000 00
D. E. Calvert	Lecturer, Group 2	12 "	2,000 00

Agricultural Engineering

W. C. Blackwood	Professor	12 months	3,800 00
E. W. Kendall	Associate Professor	12 "	3,000 00
R. R. Graham	" "	12 "	3,000 00
F. L. Ferguson	Assistant Professor	12 "	2,700 00
R. C. Moffatt	" "	12 "	2,700 00
E. G. Webb	Demonstrator	12 "	1,900 00
W. P. Shorey	Drainage Supervisor, Group 1	12 "	2,100 00
M. A. Watt	" " " 2	12 "	1,800 00
C. Cox	" " " 2	12 "	1,900 00
A. King	Clerk Stenographer, " 2	12 "	975 00
J. M. Lillie	" " " 2	12 "	975 00
Wm. S. McDermid	Caretaker, " 2	12 "	975 00
Fred Lynch	" " 2	12 "	975 00

Farm Economics

F. C. Hart	Professor	12 months	3,650 00
C. W. Riley	Lecturer, Group 1	12 "	2,200 00
G. P. Collins	" " 2	12 "	2,000 00
W. S. Rowe	Enumerator	12 "	1,900 00
W. Fairweather	"	12 "	1,600 00

Extension Department

J. Buchanan	Director	12 months	3,800 00

Macdonald Institute and Hall

O. R. Cruikshank	Directress	12 months	3,450 00
J. M. Roddick	Instructress	12 "	2,000 00
M. C. Kay	Assistant Directress	12 "	2,200 00
G. B. Doughty	Instructress	12 "	2,100 00
G. G. Hassard	"	12 "	2,000 00
W. A. Schenck	"	12 "	2,000 00
A. Ross		12 "	2,000 00
E. Sommerfeld	"	12 "	1,700 00

Ontario Agricultural College—Continued

Salaries—Continued

Macdonald Institute and Hall—Continued

Name	Position	Term	Amount
A. D. Hicks	Instructress	12 months	1,700 00
E. Jean Miller	"	12 "	1,600 00
Mary M. Darby	"	12 "	1,600 00
Margaret C. Hall	"	(T) 8 "	1,066 64
Mary A. Clarke	"	(T) 2 "	266 66
M. A. McQueen	Physical Instructor	(T) 8 "	900 00
E. Sommerfeld	Superintendent, Watson Hall	12 "	312 00
E. Renouf	Clerk Stenographer, Group 1	12 "	1,050 00
M. Thompson	Clerk Typist " 2	12 "	900 00
P. Brown	Plumber and Steamfitter	12 "	1,400 00
Wm. S. Rumney	Fireman, Group 3	12 "	1,050 00
C. Stauffer	Caretaker " 2	12 "	1,200 00
E. Spiars	" " 2	12 "	1,200 00
T. Sheehy	Janitress	12 "	700 00
J. Abbott	"	(T) 11	572 88
A. Barber	Matron	(T) 12 "	1,125 00

Animal Husbandry, etc.

Name	Position	Term	Amount
J. C. Steckley	Professor	12 months	4,000 00
R. G. Knox	Associate Professor	12 "	3,000 00
G. E. Raithby	" "	12 "	3,000 00
E. C. Stillwell	Lecturer Group 1	12 "	2,550 00
M. W. Staples	" " 1	12 "	2,200 00
F. Mahoney	Clerk Stenographer " 1	12 "	1,125 00
J. Masson	Herdsman	12 "	1,320 00
A. Luscombe	"	12 "	1,300 00
J. Slinger	"	12 "	1,300 00
J. McLeod	"	12 "	1,300 00
J. Rae	"	12 "	1,125 00
H. Vassey	Assistant Herdsman	12 "	1,050 00
W. Harrison	Teamster	12 "	1,050 00
G. R. Rennie	"	12 "	1,050 00
H. Barbaree	"	12 "	1,050 00
A. Grant	Head Teamster	12 "	1,125 00
G. Head	Farm Hand	12 "	1,050 00
W. Hewitt	" "	12 "	1,050 00

Field Experiments

Name	Position	Term	Amount
W. J. Squirrell	Professor	12 months	4,200 00
J. W. McArthur	" (part time)	12 "	1,700 00
J. Laughland	Extension Specialist, Group 1	12 "	3,000 00
O. McConkey	Lecturer " 1	12 "	2,550 00
A. W. Mason	" " 1	12 "	2,550 00
R. Keegan	" 1	12 "	2,200 00
E. T. Goring	Lecturer	12 "	2,000 00
A. E. Whiteside	Plot Supervisor	12 "	1,800 00
E. E. Hood	Clerk Stenographer, Group 1	12 "	1,125 00
J. W. Crosbie	Clerk " 3	12 "	900 00
G. E. Westoby	" " 3	12 "	825 00
P. Daymond	Farm Hand	12 "	1,050 00
J. Barnet	" "	12 "	975 00
G. Binns	" "	12 "	1,050 00
Thos. Aiken	" "	12 "	975 00
William Burnett	" "	12 "	975 00
William McLeod	" "	12	975 00
J. Jennings	" "	12 "	1,050 00
William Hambley	" "	8½ "	800 63
J. F. McNally	Teamster	12 "	1,050 00
E. Emslie	"	12 "	1,050 00

Experimental Dairy and Dairy School

Name	Position	Term	Amount
H. E. Dean	Professor	10 months	3,166 60
W. H. Sproule	Assistant Professor	12 "	2,700 00
H. A. Smallfield	" "	12 "	2,400 00
F. W. Hamilton	Demonstrator	12 "	1,900 00
T. J. McKinney	"	12 "	1,900 00

Ontario Agricultural College—Continued

Salaries—Continued

Experimental Dairy and Dairy School—Continued

Name	Position	Group	Time		Amount
B. Millar	Demonstrator		12	months	1,800 00
M. Dougherty	Clerk Stenographer, Group	2	12	"	975 00
H. H. Matthews	Caretaker	" 2	12	"	1,125 00

Poultry Department

Name	Position	Group	Time		Amount
W. R. Graham	Professor		12	months	4,200 00
F. N. Marcellus	"		12	"	3,800 00
J. F. Francis	Extension Specialist, Group	1	12	"	2,700 00
E. S. Snyder	Assistant Professor		12	"	2,700 00
J. B. Smith	Research Specialist		12	"	2,200 00
J. E. Bergey	Extension Specialist, Group	2	12	"	2,100 00
H. M. Baron	" "	" 2	9	"	1,575 00
C. M. Huntsman	" "	" 2	12	"	1,800 00
E. H. Marston	" "	" 1	12 months 2,300 00		
		Less leave of absence	1,725 05		574 95
E. Parkinson	Clerk	" 2	12	months	1,125 00
E. I. Lewis	"	" 2	12	"	1,125 00
M. L. Cameron	"	" 3	12	"	750 00
L. LeGrande	Clerk Stenographer	" 2	12		975 00
G. Faull	Poultryman		12	"	1,500 00
W. Chapman	Assistant Poultryman		12	"	1,050 00
W. Lowe	Caretaker, Group 2		12	"	1,125 00

Horticulture Department

Name	Position	Group	Time		Amount
A. H. MacLennan	Professor		12	months	4,000 00
A. H. Tomlinson	Associate Professor		12	"	3,000 00
D. A. Kimball	Assistant Professor		12	"	2,550 00
P. B. Sanders	Lecturer	Group 1	12	"	2,200 00
T. H. Jones	"	" 1	12	"	2,300 00
W. H. Smith	"	" 1	12	"	2,400 00
E. Pears	Clerk Stenographer	" 2	12	"	975 00
G. Morris	Clerk	" 2	12	"	1,125 00
A. Gray	"	" 3	12	"	825 00
G. Winton	Floriculturist		11	"	1,659 89
G. I. Laidlaw	Orchardist		12	"	1,200 00
J. Renouf	Gardener		5	"	583 30
Simon Smith	"	(T)	7	"	656 25
W. Simmons	"		12	"	1,400 00
J. Slater	"		12	"	1,200 00
D. Clelland	Assistant Gardener		12	"	1,125 00
W. F. Johnston	" "		12	"	975 00
J. M. Markle	Teamster		12	"	1,050 00
S. Nisbet	"		12	"	1,050 00
N. Simmons	Truck Driver		12	"	1,125 00
J. Henry	Caretaker, Group 2		12	"	1,125 00

Apiculture Department

Name	Position	Group	Time		Amount
F. E. Millen	Professor		12	months	3,800 00
E. J. Dyce	Lecturer	Group 1	12	"	2,300 00
G. A. Hamilton	Clerk Stenographer	" 1	12	"	1,125 00
E. Smith	Clerk Typist	" 2	12	"	900 00
R. Sawyer	Caretaker	2	12	"	1,125 00

Expenses ($260,148.83)

Temporary Assistance ($5,704.62)

Mrs. A. Aldridge, 50.63; Mrs. L. E. Butchart, 52.08; Mrs. Brydon, 2.00; Mrs. D. Checkley, 25.69; I. Christie, 576.00; L. Currie, 90.00; R. A. Dempsey, 20.00; Mrs. G. Dickinson, 11.00; W. Dobbie, 160.00; A. Farquhar, 720.00; Mrs. N. Fitton, 11.25; W. Fitzgerald, 312.00; C. V. Fritz, 9.00; E. W. Hart, 702.00; C. Huck, 9.00; H. W. Jamieson, 81.00; J. Kendall, 2.50; Mrs. Lester, 17.81; N. Love, 11.20; Mrs. Macdonald, 9.50; E. Macmorine, 8.25; J. Massey, 7.50; C. McCarron, 9.00; A. McDermid, 786.00; Mrs. Nichols, 48.26; D. Nitingale, 10.50; F. G. Partridge, 30.00; J. Philpott, 540.00; A. Reed, 10.85; S. A. Simmons, 180.00; M. Simpson, 84.00; F. Steep, 509.60; Mrs. M. Thomas, 11.00; W. D. Tolton, 156.00; N. H. Wass, 312.00; G. W. West, 107.50; G. Wilson, 9.00; G. A. Wright, 7.50; J. Zavitz, 5.00 .... 5,704 62

Ontario Agricultural College—Continued

Expenses—Continued

Contingencies including Expenses of Short Courses ($10,799.36)

Autographic Register Systems, Ltd., registers, 213.40; Bell Telephone Co. of Canada, tolls, 203.81; M. Blackburn, expenses, 12.00; Bogardus & Barton, drug supplies, 33.84; Burnell Binding & Printing Co., binding, 19.25; Cafeteria, O.A.C., meals, 56.30; Canadian Passenger Association, certificates, 20.00; Canadian Universities Conference, fees, 10.00; Chapple's Ltd., stationery, 36.40; F. & E. Cheque Writer Sales, cheque writer, 101.30; Copp-Clark Co., Ltd., almanacs, 10.90; Dominion Bank, exchange, 447.78; Garden City Paper Mills Co., Ltd., toilet tissue, 300.00; Georgian Bay Fruit Growers, Ltd., apples, 24.00; Gray Coach Lines, Ltd., coach hire, 60.00; Guelph Tent & Awning Co., Ltd., marquee rental, 30.00; Gummer Press, Ltd., card covers, 18.25; M. L. Hancock, services, 10.00; expenses, 6.66; S. R. Hart & Co., Ltd., supplies, 24.30; Hydro-Electric Railway, repairs, 13.75; J. Kendall, lettering diplomas, 113.10; C. W. Kelly & Son, piano rental, 17.50; King's Printer, 4,438.59; Lavoline Cleanser Co., Ltd., crystals, 36.13; H. L. Lugsdin, toilet tissue, 63.00; Marshall's Drug Store, drugs, 108.49; Dr. A. B. McCarter, fees, 111.00; National Grocers Co., Ltd., towels, 23.25; F. Nunan, books, 19.50; L. O'Neil, expenses, 118.86; Sawyer-Massey, Ltd., bleacher seats, 650.00; C. C. Snowdon, oils, 25.50; G. Strome, hauling sludge, 12.00; O. A. Strome, hauling sludge, 10.63; Sundry persons, room rent, 2,139.24; United Typewriter Co., Ltd., inspections, ribbons, 67.50; Vernon Directories, Ltd., directories, 24.00; H. O. White, services, 45.00; G. H. Wood & Co., Ltd., blockettes, 45.00. Sundries—cartage, 11.68; express, 56.89; freight, 14.70; newspapers and periodicals, 23.51; postage, 843.50; telegrams, 42.36; petty disbursements, 86.49 .... 10,799 36

Travelling Expenses ($4,451.66)

A. W. Baker, 16.05; F. G. Baldwin, 61.85; K. Beck, 13.10; W. C. Blackwood, 11.00; A. N. L. Butler, 7.63; D. E. Calvert, 11.50; G. I. Christie, 552.65; G. Clarke, 3.55; T. A. Coleman, 75.00; O. R. Cruikshank, 15.75; A. Davey, 8.65; H. H. Dean, 8.00; G. B. Doughty, 11.25; V. E. Englebert, 8.85; W. J. Garnett, 2.50; E. H. Garrard, 35.25; A. L. Gibson, 14.30; M. P. Glover, 100.02; E. T. Goring, 9.61; R. Harcourt, 84.26; D. H. Jones, 4.48; T. H. Jones, 83.12; R. Keegan, 10.09; R. H. Keith, 2.00; D. A. Kimball, 174.08; A. L. Klein, 12.05; R. G. Knox, 408.13; H. R. Kraybill, 80.00; G. I. Laidlaw, 28.03; J. Laughland, 30.19; W. Macdonald, 25.00; A. H. MacLennan, 120.82; A. W. Mason, 73.12; E. Masson, 4.80; E. Matthews, 6.32; O. McConkey, 139.25; E. C. McLean, 16.80; G. McNeill, 1.70; L. O'Neil, 3.75; R. H. Ozburn, 4.20; E. Pettigrew, 5.20; A. M. Porter, 198.15; G. E. Raithby, 287.25; W. Renouf, 46.41; G. N. Ruhnke, 207.11; P. B. Saunders, 74.10; W. N. Simmons, 146.46; H. A. Smallfield, 50.76; W. H. Smith, 126.20; W. H. Sproule, 102.50; W. J. Squirrell, 172.08; M. W. Staples, 41.32; J. C. Steckley, 285.15; O. J. Stevenson, 21.25; E. C. Stillwell, 154.40; T. H. Stuart, 1.70; A. H. Tomlinson, 188.81; L. Watt, 5.00; A. Webster, 47.81; G. Winton, 11.30 .... 4,451 66

Library ($3,933.23)

E. G. Allen & Son, Ltd., 144.44; American Society for Horticultural Science, 12.60; Baker & Taylor Co., 170.03; Bond Hardware Co., Ltd., 12.91; E. E. Bossence, 42.65; C. Chivers, Ltd., 208.60; Co-operative Supply Dept., O.A.C., 24.50; Grolier Society, Ltd., 47.00; H. M. Stationery Office, 104.40; International Livestock Association, 10.00; James, Proctor & Redfern, 10.00; King's Printer, 149.12; Library of Congress, 59.91; Longmans, Green & Co., 30.95; Macmillan Co. of Canada, Ltd., 64.91; E. Masson, services as Asst. Librarian, 1,080.00; McGraw Hill Book Co., Inc., 14.68; Oxford University Press, 38.08; Peerless Windsow Cleaners, 24.00; Public Printing & Stationery, Ottawa, 25.00; Ryerson Press, 12.05; G. E. Steckhert & Co., 553.46; United Typewriter Co., Ltd., 10.50; Mrs. G. Webb, 226.50; Wheldon & Wesley, Ltd., 11.90; H. W. Wilson Co., 206.31. Sundries—customs, 3.57; express, 22.06; freight, 74.51; newspapers and periodicals, 430.74; postage, 29.74; petty disbursements, 78.11 .... 3,933 23

Provisions, Laundry, Engine Room Supplies and Fuel ($126,807.75)

Provisions, $64,200.32.

Associated Chemical Co. of Canada, Ltd., 37.50; Associated Quality Canners, Ltd., 401.80; Balfours, Ltd., 936.25; Black & Ferrie, 1,047.79; Canadian Canners, Ltd., 25.03; College Grocery, 35.50; Crosse & Blackwell, Ltd, 46.20; Dairy Dept., O.A.C, 847.11; W. H. Day & Son, 50.00; Doughty & McFarlane, 432.40; Downey & Cummins, 19.80; Elliott & Moody, 84.48; Farm Dept, O.A.C.,

Ontario Agricultural College—Continued

Expenses—Continued

Provisions, Laundry, etc.—Continued

Provisions—Continued

5,330.89; J. L. Fielding & Co., 329.93; A. B. Gordon Co., Ltd., 5,227.64; Guelph Creamery, 5,705.00; H. T. Heinz Co., 452.54; Hicks-Groom Co., 4,159.69; Horticultural Dept., O.A.C., 1,390.87; F. I. James Co., Ltd., 135.36; S. F. Lawrason & Co., Ltd., 155.77; E. H. Marston, 74.56; National Grocers Co., Ltd., 1,918.30; Norfolk Fruit Growers' Association, 223.50; Ontario Reformatory Industries, 13,978.67; Poultry Dept. O.A.C., 2,238.27; Pure Gold Manufacturing Co., Ltd., 351.59; Reinhart's Beverages, 27.95; Royal City Mineral Water Works, 10.10; Shephards, Ltd., 105.00; Silverwood's Guelph Dairy, Ltd., 80.27; Standard Brands, Ltd, 44.10; Steeps' Meat Market, 1,422.57; Swift Canadian Co., Ltd., 83.74; Trent Institute, O.A.C., 3,518.22; United Farmers Co-operative Co., Ltd., 174.00; H. Walker & Son, Ltd., 5,731.16; G. Williams, 16.60; C. Yeates Co., Ltd., 7,300.29. Sundries—cartage, 34.44; express, .60; freight, .80; petty disbursements, 14.04 .... 64,200 32

Laundry, $622.57.

Colgate-Palmolive-Peet Co., Ltd., 244.15; Dominion Linseed Oil Co., Ltd., 19.59; Electric Boiler Compound Co., Ltd., 112.13; Ellis & Howard, Ltd., 16.24; A. J. Hawkins, 58.14; S. F. Lawrason & Co., Ltd., 142.40; McCormack & Robinson, 12.00. Sundries—cartage, .50; petty disbursements, 17.42 .... 622 57

Engine Room Supplies, $1,860.20.

Bond Hardware Co., Ltd., 20.67; J. Brown, 53.00; Canadian Liquid Air Co., Ltd., 16.35; Combustion Engineerng Corporation, Ltd., 257.24; Crane, Ltd., 20.77; W. H. Cunningham & Hill, Ltd., 26.50; Darling Bros., Ltd., 11.00 Ellis & Howard, Ltd., 10.88; Engineer Co., 15.75; Hicks-Groom Co., 24.25; Imperial Oil, Ltd., 169.92; E. H. Kellogg & Co., 48.30; D. McKenzie Machinery Co., 16.89; National Meter Co. of Canada, Ltd., 73.75; Peacock Bros., Ltd., 21.42; Peerless Machine & Tool Co., Ltd., 168.31; Sheppard & Abbott, 48.51; R. Shorthill, 187.60; L. M. Smith, 334.85; W. W. Stuart, 25.56; Sutherland-Schultz Electric Co., Ltd., 155.25; Swedish General Electric, Ltd., 12.00; Taylor-Forbes Co., Ltd., 27.75; Thomson-Gordon, Ltd., 15.40; Yarnall-Waring Co., 15.10. Sundries—cartage, 21.43; customs, 5.07; express, 3.15; freight, 2.37; petty disbursements, 51.16 .... 1,860 20

Fuel, $60,124.66.

Board of Light & Heat Commission, 1,603.49; Canada Customs, 408.70; Canadian National Railways, 2,657.52; Canadian Pacific Railway Co., 24,911.87; Century Coal Co., Ltd., 86.88; Conger Lehigh Coal Co., Ltd., 741.61; F. C. Harrington & Son, 16.173.07; Hydro Electric Power Commission, 10,842.85; Kloepfer Coal Co., 333.25; Northern Coal Co., 726.74; Pay list, wages of men, 1,638.68.. 60,124 66

Furniture, Furnishings, Repairs and Equipment ($14,982.12)

Furniture and Furnishings, $8,352.38.

Acker Furniture Co., 172.50; Air Way Branch of Toronto, 12.00; Aluminum Goods, Ltd., 42.77; J. Armstrong, Ltd., 1,015.38; Associated Chemical Co., Ltd., 356.30; Beisser Key Machine Co., 59.75; Berkel Products Co., Ltd., 544 00; Boeckh Co., Ltd., 33.23; Bond Hardware Co., Ltd., 735.48; Canadian Office & School Furniture, Ltd., 25.44; Cassidy's, Ltd., 116.11; Crane, Ltd., 88.96; C. A. Dunham Co., Ltd., 12.85; Dustbane Products, Ltd., 114.60; T. Eaton Co., Ltd., 128.63; Guelph Tent & Awning Co., Ltd., 72.50; Guelph Paper Co., 147.63; Guelph Stove Co., Ltd., 58.40; E. Hawes & Co., Ltd., 115.00; Hicks-Groom Co., 197.56; Interlake Tissue Mills Co., Ltd., 214.07; C. W. Kelly & Son, 15.00; King's Printer, 10.00; Lavoline Cleanser Co., Ltd., 22.50; H. L. Lugsdin, 31.50; D. E. Macdonald & Bros., Ltd., 432.40; Mackenzie Manufacturing Co., Ltd., 81.00; Mackenzie Mop & Brush Co., 27.00; McGlashan, Clarke Co., Ltd., 545.30; M. G. Musselman, 18.00; National Grocers Co., Ltd., 10.65; National Stationers, Ltd., 100.00; Office Specialty Manufacturing Co., Ltd., 23.00; Ontario Hardware Co., 48.78; Ontario Reformatory Industries, 202.00; Ritchie Bros., 152.80; Schreiters, Ltd., 33.60; R. Simpson Co., Ltd., 288.62; R. E. Smith, 11.25; C. C. Snowdon, 53.00; Solex Co., Ltd., 40.32; Stevens, Hepner Co., Ltd., 42.32; W. W. Stuart, 969.92; Swift Canadian Co., Ltd., 54.00; L. Taylor, 463.42; R. G. Venn, 183.60; Wrought Iron Range Co. of Canada, Ltd., 95.75. Sundries—cartage, 30.86; customs, 32.55; express, 11.63; freight, 8.00; petty disbursements, 50.45 .... 8,352 38

Ontario Agricultural College—Continued

Expenses—Continued

Furniture, Furnishings, Repairs, etc.—Continued

Repairs, $6,629.74.

J. Anstice & Co., Inc., 21.75; Aulcraft Paints, Ltd., 62.50; T. R. Barber, 51.77; Beldam's Asbestos Packing & General Manufacturing Co., Ltd., 61.01; Berry Bros., 90.30; Board of Light & Heat Commission, 76.11; Bond Hardware Co., Ltd., 563.45; B. S. & M. Supply House, 118.75; Canadian Johns-Manville Co., Ltd., 39.15; Canadian Liquid Air Co., Ltd., 27.40; Canadian Paint Co., Ltd., 49.08; Commercial Oil Co., Ltd., 32.50; Cooke & Denison, 12.55; Crane, Ltd., 56.87; W. H. Cunningham & Hill, Ltd., 59.79; H. Disston & Sons, Ltd., 11.40; Dominion Cement Paint Co., 38.25; Dominion Linseed Oil Co., Ltd., 20.96; Downing & Co., 24.85; C. A. Dunham Co., Ltd., 45.50; Ellis & Howard, Ltd., 368 04; Federal Wire & Cable Co., Ltd., 102.25; T. J. Foster, 44.52; Good Specialties, Ltd., 24.92; Grand & Toy, Ltd., 23.80; Guelph Lumber Co., Ltd., 244.78; J. Hall, 571.50; G. A. Hardie & Co., 61.44; Hydro-Electric Power Commission, 12.19; C. W. Kelly & Son, 35.50; Knight, Whaley & Co., 45.92; M. Lasby, 11.75; Macdonald Electric Supply, Ltd., 87.29; P. Martin, 38.37; Masco Co., Ltd., 290.35; McCormack & Robinson, 160.65; J. A. McFarlane, 39.00; D. McKenzie Machinery Co., 36.23; J. H. Morin & Co., Ltd., 25.83; A. Muirhead Co., Ltd., 547.50; Northern Paint & Varnish Co., Ltd., 132.00; H. Occomore, 67.49; Ontario Hardware Co., 309.26; Ontario Reformatory Industries, 39.25; Ottawa Paint Works, Ltd., 180.00; R. Parker, 72.20; Pay list, wages of men, 122.10; Penfold Hardware Co., 69.71; Penfound Varnish Co., 12.90; R. T. Purves & Co., 12.00; Ritchie Bros., 32.25; Roelofson Elevator Works, 19.00; Scarfe & Co., Ltd., 33.75; J. A. Sexauer Manufacturing Co., Ltd., 51.58; R. Stewart, Ltd., 535.99; Sutherland-Schultz Electric Co., 66.80; Taylor Forbes Co., Ltd., 155.53; Thomson-Gordon, Ltd., 21.70; Thorp-Hambrock Co., Ltd., 125.00; Trelco, Ltd., 92.00; J. Watson Manufacturing Co., Ltd., 12.21; Wolverine, Ltd., 59.40. Sundries—cartage, 42.19; express, 10.50; freight, 6.07; petty disbursements, 113.09 .... 6,629 74

Maintenance of Gymnasium ($811.76)

Bond Hardware Co., Ltd., 37.91; Brown's Sports & Cycle Co., Ltd., 75.60; W. Fitzgerald, 663.00. Sundries—cartage, .90; express, 14.25; freight, 1.00; petty disbursements, 19.10 .... 811 76

Student Labour ($4,463.46)

Sundry Students 4,463 46

Telephone Service, Rent, etc. ($1,606.75)

Bell Telephone Co. of Canada, rental 1,606 75

Scholarships ($230.00)

T. Bell, 10.00; C. M. Brodie, 10.00; L. Butler, 10.00; H. D. L. Corby, 15.00 N. H. Denis, 10.00; T. A. Douglas, 10.00; J. D. Dryden, 15.00; R. E. Heal, 20.00; H. E. Markle, 10.00; J. C. Martin, 15.00; L. S. Matthews, 15.00; D. M. McMurchy, 10.00; J. G. McNiece, 15.00; W. L. Putman, 10.00; F. A. Stinson, 10.00; H. H. G. Strang, 15.00; G. F. H. Sumler, 15.00; R. Van Der Hoorn, 15.00. 230 00

Research Scholarships ($1,999.92)

W. M. Gammon, 999.96; W. R. Graham, Jr., 999.96 .... 1,999 92

Expenses Students' Teams Judging at Exhibitions ($700.00)

A. G. Douglas, 80.00; B. J. Dunsmore, 80.00; T. W. Gourlay, 80.00; D. J. McTaggart, 72.00; E. N. Needham, 80.00; J. W. Pawley, 72.00; H. J. Seymour, 84.00; M. D. Shearer, 80.00; J. Walker, 72.00 .... 700 00

Servants' Pay List ($16,735.31)

Sundry servants 16,735 31

Research Work O.A.C. Departments ($8,751.45)

Services, $7,251.75; Expenses, $196.33.

E. Bard, services, 720.00; J. W. Becker, services, 230.00; A. Beach, services, 50.00; R. Blythe, services, 10.00; A. N. L. Butler, services, 525.00; expenses, 58.05; W. Carr, services, 16.25; M. Darby, services, 200.00; E. J. Doyle, services, 302.00; W. Harris, services, 25.50; S. Henry, services, 300.00; D. M. Hewitt, services,

Ontario Agricultural College—Continued

Expenses—Continued

Research Work, O.A.C. Departments—Continued

Services and Expenses—Continued

90.00; A. B. Jackson, services, 750.00; B. Johnston, services, 5.00; T. H. Jones, expenses, 11.45; E. Mighton, services, 1,500.00; J. Millar, services, 200.00; E. R. Renouf, services, 1,500.00; expenses, 95.28; W. Renouf, services, 33.00; expenses, 31.55; R. C. Rosborough, services, 206.00; M. D. Shearer, services, 290.00; J. Whitehouse, services, 142.50; G. Willshire, services, 156.50 .... 7,448 08

Expenses, $1,303.37.

Brighton Garage, auto maintenance, 283.40; Canadian Canners Greenhouses, plants, 234.25; Canadian Industries, Ltd., fertilizer, 110.50; Cooper Bros., auto maintenance, 35.35; W. Davidson, beans, 24.00; G. G. Findlay, seeds, 202.01; K. Macklin, land rental, 50.00; C. Marshall, land rental, 50.00; Steele, Briggs Seed Co., Ltd., seeds, 159.23; R. Stewart, Ltd., prestwood, 14.20; Urbana Laboratories, corn stalk, 15.25; C. C. Wakefield & Co., Ltd., oils, 12.00. Sundries—cartage, 5.00; freight, 57.63; postage, 16.00; petty disbursements, 34.55 .... 1,303 37

Purchase and Maintenance of Automobiles, Trucks and Tractors ($3,065.63)

Brighton Garage, 62.91; Canadian Oil Companies, Ltd., 1,133.63; Daley's Tire Shop, 153.58; Dominion Linseed Oil Co., Ltd., 16.52; General Supply Co. of Canada, Ltd., 269.74; L. Godson, 466.26; Golf, Ltd., 10.00; Goodyear Tire & Rubber Co. of Canada, Ltd., 26.17; H. Little, 511.33; McCloskey's Service, 113.32; Reo Motor Sales Co. of Toronto, Ltd., 25.95; Robson Motor Corporation, 97.85; Tolton Bros., Ltd., 141.67; petty disbursements, 36.70 .... 3,065 63

BACTERIOLOGY

Supplies and Expenses ($2,273.81)

Supplies, $1,713.58.

Acker Furniture Co., 36.25; D. Appleton & Co., 12.00; Canadian Industries, Ltd., 17.51; Canadian Laboratory Supplies, Ltd., 27.92; Central Scientific Co. of Canada, Ltd., 354.76; Difco Laboratories, 69.15; Dominion Glass Co., Ltd., 45.44; Douglas, Gardner & Co., 40.00; Fisher Scientific Co., Ltd., 35.75; Guelph Paper Box Co., Ltd., 20.44; J. F. Hartz Co., Ltd., 23.22; Hinde & Dauch Paper Co. of Canada, Ltd., 12.84; King's Printer, 208.61; Palo Myers, Inc., 15.40; Stamped & Enamelled Ware, Ltd., 17.40; Torsion Balance Co., 76.00; Williams & Wilkins Co., 19.00; Wilson Scientific Co., Ltd., 570.95; petty disbursements, 110.94 1,713 58

Expenses, $560.23.

Bell Telephone Co. of Canada, rentals, 19.80; tolls, 8.66; Cooke & Denison, repairing sterilizers, 17.50; Mrs. L. Hammond, services, 12.00; McCormack & Robinson, repairs, 5.10; Suey Wah Laundry, laundry, 55.09; United Typewriter Co., Ltd., inspections, 19.00; G. Woods, services, 65.26; Sundries—cartage, 2.57; customs, 8.50; express, 21.83; freight, 9.79; newspapers and periodicals, 33.93; postage, 280.32; telegrams, .88 .... 560 23

BOTANY

Supplies and Expenses ($2,674.52)

Services, $398.30.

Pay lists, wages of men 398 30

Travelling Expenses, $732.92.

W. G. Evans, 7.15; J. E. Howitt, 237.13; E. Mighton, 178.52; D. R. Sands, 297.65; R. E. Stone, 12.47 .... 732 92

Supplies, $789.10.

C. Anderson & Co., 23.64; J. Armstrong, Ltd., 15.50; Bond Hardware Co., Ltd., 18.10; Central Scientific Co. of Canada, Ltd., 175.53; Commercial Oil Co., Ltd., 16.25; Co-operative Supply Dept., O.A.C., 16.64; T. Eaton Co., Ltd., 10.00; Guelph Lumber Co., Ltd., 20.37; Guelph Paper Box Co., Ltd., 14.28; Gummer Press, Ltd., 56.50; J. Hunter, 26.88; King's Printer, 222.93; Niagara Brand Spray Co., Ltd., 30.73; G. B. Ryan & Co., 11.34; R. Stewart, Ltd., 18.72; Taylor Forbes Co., Ltd., 10.44; petty disbursements, 101.25 .... 789 10

Expenses, $754.20.

Bell Telephone Co. of Canada, rentals, 34.20; tolls, 25.03; R. Blyth, rental, 25.00; W. R. Browne & Son, gas, 17.92; Canadian Canners Greenhouses, labour, 16.25; Cooper Bros., auto repairs, 161.67; H. Little, auto repairs, 169.99; Province of

Ontario Agricultural College—Continued

Botany—Continued

Supplies and Expenses—Continued

Expenses—Continued

Ontario Pictures, colouring, 110.70; United Typewriter Co., Ltd., inspections, 10.50. Sundries—cartage, 4.00; express, 13.67; freight, 9.33; postage, 145.00; petty disbursements, 10.94 .... 754 20

CHEMISTRY

Soil Survey and Demonstration Work ($14,999.48)

Services, $6,449.30.

L. A. Birk, 1,800.00; L. J. Chapman, 416.00; S. W. Fallis, 18.75; D. Mackenzie, 200.00; R. M. McKenzie, 150.00; F. Munro, 18.75; Pay list, wages of men, 439.80; W. H. Roberts, 80.00; H. M. Scollie, 1,542.00; G. R. Synder, 150.00; A. W. Taylor, 184.00; G. B. Whiteside, 1,450.00 .... 6,449 30

Travelling Expenses, $912.79.

H. G. Bell, 9.45; L. A. Birk, 11.35; R. J. Bryden, 17.60; G. Farley, 3.75; H. L. Fulmer, 16.50; R. Harcourt, 165.51; F. W. Lohse, 8.80; D. MacKenzie, 3.75; R. M. McKenzie, 13.37; F. F. Morwick, 97.21; J. E. Musgrave, 40.78; G. N. Ruhnke, 70.02; H. M. Scollie, 13.63; G. R. Snyder, 74.53; N. J. Thomas, 338.21; G. B. Whiteside, 28.33 .... 912 79

Maintenance of Automobiles, $974.04.

Daymond Bros., 152.04; Gram Bros., Ltd., 158.48; Guelph Tire Hospital, 588.68; Swanston's Garage, 53.50; petty disbursements, 21.34 .... 974 04

Supplies, $5,655.20.

Association of Official Agricultural Chemists, 31.00; J. T. Baker Chemical Co., 39.64; T. R. Barber, 25.48; F. H. Bell, 41.00; Bond Hardware Co., Ltd., 87.24; Canadian Bag Co., Ltd., 25.33; Canadian Industrial Alcohol Co., Ltd., 159.64; Canadian Fertilizer Co., Ltd., 13.39; Canadian Laboratory Supplies, Ltd., 66.70; Central Scientific Co. of Canada, Ltd., 2,493.88; College Grocery, 57.19; Co-operative Supply Dept., O.A.C., 27.30; Crane, Ltd., 27.86; J. H. Crow, 16.77; Dairy Dept., O.A.C., 13.90; Doughty & McFarlane, 21.55; Dustbane Products, Ltd., 10.50; Ellis & Howard, Ltd., 13.21; J. R. Garner, 171.75; Grand & Toy, Ltd., 12.10; Guelph Lumber Co., Ltd., 81.38; Guelph Paper Co., 11.81; Gunn's, Ltd., 72.39; Ingram & Bell, Ltd., 18.89; King's Printer, 620.38; Lambert Rogers Co., 21.29; D. E. Macdonald & Bros., Ltd., 42.50; Merck & Co., Ltd., 31.45; Modern Machine Co., Ltd., 38.50; National Fertilizers, Ltd., 36.30; National Grocers Co., Ltd., 34.11; L. J. Newcaster, 25.49; Nichols Chemical Co., Ltd., 206.68; H. Occomore, 66.14; Ontario Fertilizers, Ltd., 25.50; Scottish Fertilizers, Ltd., 45.65; R. Stewart, Ltd., 70.21; W. W. Stuart, 23.60; Taylor-Forbes Co., Ltd., 62.44; United Typewriter Co., Ltd., 18.00; Viozon Co. of Canada, 150.00; Wards Studio, 12.02; Wilson Scientific Co., Ltd., 384.10; Witts Fertilizer Works, 58.12; petty disbursements, 142.82 .... 5,655 20

Expenses, $1,008.15.

American Chemical Society, fees, 17.25; Bell Telephone Co., rental, 75.00 tolls, 123.41; H. Horton, rental of land, 232.80; Hydro-Electric Power Commission, power, 23.70; Mrs. D. Johns, washing, 29.40; United Typewriter Co., Ltd., inspections, 41.00. Sundries—cartage, 24.55; express, 76.61; freight, 86.82; postage, 211.00; newspapers and periodicals, 36.26; telegrams, 3.85; petty disbursements, 26.50 .... 1,008 15

TRENT INSTITUTE (SCHOOL OF BAKING) ($7,432.87)

Services, Supplies, Equipment and Contingencies ($2,446.18)

Services, $300.00.

C. J. Hanser 300 00

Travelling Expenses, $104.16.

L. J. Bohn, 75.01; W. H. Croat, 21.95; R. Harcourt, 7.20 .... 104 16

Supplies and Equipment, $1,596.27.

C. Anderson & Co., 10.10; Bond Hardware Co., Ltd., 47.97; Bowes Co., Ltd., 359.83; Central Scientific Co. of Canada, Ltd., 160.16; Crane, Ltd., 20.33; Despatch Oven Co., Ltd., 308.00; Fairfield Chemical Co., Ltd., 35.00; Fletcher Mfg. Co., Ltd., 379.50; Guelph Lumber Co., Ltd., 14.47; King's Printer, 95.76; Macdonald Electric Supply, Ltd., 32.62; Masco Co., Ltd., 51.86; Royal Paper & Supply Co., 19.07; W. S. Tierney, 11.60; petty disbursements, 50.00 .... 1,596 27

Ontario Agricultural College—Continued
Expenses—Continued
Trent Institute—Continued
Services, Supplies, Equipment, etc.—Continued

Contingencies, $445.75.

Bell Telephone Co., rental, 42.60; tolls, 8.27; Board of Light and Heat Commission, gas, 27.32; G. Fairley, repairs, 60.70; Fletcher Mfg. Co., Ltd., supplies, 56.56; H. W. Handbridge, weatherstripping, 66.90; Handbridge & Bohn, supplies, 11.00; H. Occomore, repairs, 23.81; Wong's O.K. Laundry, washing, 39.78. Sundries—cartage, 10.71; express, 13.48; postage, 51.32; newspapers and periodicals, 4.00; petty disbursements, 29.30 ..... 445 75

Materials for Bakery ($4,986.69)

Canadian Milk Products, Ltd., 91.78; S. J. Cherry & Sons, Ltd., 136.35; G. P. Coghill, 22.96; R. L. Craig, 31.95; J. Dawes, 996.00; Dininghall, O.A.C., 231.07; Doughty & McFarlane, 24.00; Drimilk Co., Ltd., 46.00; Elliott & Moody, 111.00; Fletcher Mfg. Co., Ltd., 15.15; Frigate Products Co., 13.40; Gowdy Bros., 130.00; Guelph Creamery, 150.50; Harris Abattoir Co., Ltd., 60.66; Hicks-Groom Co., 365.13; Lake of the Woods Milling Co., Ltd., 495.13; Lever Bros., Ltd., 15.25; Maple Leaf Milling Co., Ltd., 359.51; National Grocers Co., Ltd., 163.75; Ogilvie Flour Mills Co., Ltd., 112.00; People's Co-operative, 181.80; Procter & Gamble Co. of Canada, Ltd., 47.88; Quaker Oats Co., 105.30; Robin Hood Mills, Ltd., 128.75; Silverwood's Guelph Dairy, Ltd., 23.16; Silverwood's Milk Products, Ltd., 12.00; J. Stewart, 26.10; Standard Brands, Ltd., 368.49; F. L. Stout, 20.40; Swift-Canadian Co., Ltd., 127.30; Western Canada Flour Mills Co., Ltd., 304.90. Sundries—cartage, 9.00; express, 1.40; freight, 23.89; petty disbursements, 34.73 4,986 69

ENTOMOLOGY ($3,452.36)

Supplies, Expenses and Equipment ($1,777.42)

Services, $456.75.

J. M. Jackson, 45.00; C. A. Neil, 100.50; A. Wilkes, 311.25 ..... 456 75

Travelling Expenses, $31.00.

R. H. Ozburn 31 00

Supplies and Expenses, $1,289.67.

American Association of Economic Entomologists, 10.00; T. R. Barber, 10.70; Bell Telephone Co., rental, 19.80; tolls, 53 70; Biological Abstracts, 15.00; Bogardus & Barton, 20.14; Bond Hardware Co., Ltd., 10.26; E. E. Bossence, 30.15; Central Scientific Co. of Canada, Ltd., 145.28; Cole Bros. & Scott, 17.12; A. Gallenkamp & Co., Ltd., 16.50; B. Greening Wire Co., Ltd., 11.34; King's Printer, 269.73; Liquor Control Board, 45.27; Lockhart's Camera Exchange, 23.82; H. Occomore, 15.00; E. Paturel, 30.00; Penfold Hardware Co., 44.52; L. A. Philip & Co., 10.08; Rolls & Darlington, Ltd., 43.15; R. Stewart, Ltd., 59.51. Sundries—cartage, 5.15; express, 34.46; freight, 20.87; postage, 209.00; telegrams, 10.07; petty disbursements, 109.05 ..... 1,289 67

Cornborer Investigation ($1,674.94)

Services, $375.95.

W. C. Allan, 34.00; E. W. Kendall, Jr., 311.95; E. J. Quail, 30.00 ..... 375 95

Travelling Expenses, $862.50.

W. C. Allan, 40.33, L. Caesar, 451.72; E. W. Kendall, Jr., 50.70; E. J. Quail, 28.11; R. W. Thompson, 291.64 ..... 862 50

Expenses, $436.49.

Butler's One-Stop Service, auto maintenance, 11.15; Canadian Laboratory Supplies, Ltd., supplies, 18.88; Daley's Tire Shop, tires, 24.29; Fairfield Chemical Co., Ltd., supplies, 47.00; H. Little, auto maintenance, 119.52; Niagara Brand Spray Co., Ltd., supplies, 11.35; J. MacCallum & Son, auto repairs, 127.89; Rolls & Darlington, Ltd., supplies, 22.15; R. W. Thompson, garage rent, 18.00. Sundries—telegrams, 2.48; petty disbursements, 33.68 ..... 436 49

ENGLISH

Supplies and Expenses ($830.04)

Supplies, $694.81.

A. E. Byerly, 161.00; Eastman Kodak Stores, Ltd., 18.28; Mrs. T. Goldie, 15.00; D. Hood's Book Room, 74.50; King's Printer, 283.43; Mason & Risch, Ltd., 58.50; Ryerson Press, 44.52; petty disbursements, 39.58 ..... 694 81

Expenses, $135.23.

Bell Telephone Co., rental, 34.20; tolls, 16.21; Gill, Welch & Mulligan, Ltd., insurance, 42.04; H. J. D. Moss, services, 15.00; United Typewriter Co., Ltd., inspections, 3.50. Sundries—cartage, 4.26; express, 7.50; newspapers and periodicals, 11.01; telegrams, 1.51 ..... 135 23

Ontario Agricultural College—Continued

Expenses—Continued

AGRICULTURAL ENGINEERING ($8,779.25)

Expenses re Drainage Work ($4,854.11)

Services, $636.00.

J. Cullen, 28.00; T. Hands, 24.50; F. Jerome, 326.00; J. H. McLeod, 5.00; H. Parker, 217.50; R. Warren, 35.00 ..... 636 00

Travelling Expenses, $2,713.70.

C. Cox, 600.17; J. Cullen, 21.60; F. L. Ferguson, 137.11; W. P. Shorey, 749.64; C. A. Warren, 478.80; R. Warren, services, 35.00; M. A. Watt, 726.38 ..... 2,713 70

Equipment, $810.00.

Bond Hardware Co., Ltd., 15.44; M. N. Cummings, 13.00; Curtis Bros., 108.00; Hamilton Engineering Service, Ltd., 10.80; Instruments, Ltd., 272.05; Keuffel & Esser Co., 181.68; King's Printer, 67.17; W. Lamb, 20.00; Ontario Reformatory Industries, 75.00; R. Stewart, Ltd., 12.10; petty disbursements, 34.76 ..... 810 00

Expenses, $694.41.

W. O. Beattie, rental of machine, 70.90; Bell Telephone Co., rental, 19.80; tolls, 8.01; City Battery Service, battery, 10.92; Daley's Tire Shop, tires, 57.55; Grant & Thorpe, wiring, 12.00; H. Little, auto maintenance, 28.55; J. MacCallum & Son, auto maintenance, 123.91; W. J. Moore, repairs, 30.25; Muller Bros., repairs, 42 70; W. L. Sagar, testing pipes, 15.00; J. J. Turner & Sons, Ltd., 16.25. Sundries—cartage, .50; express, 25.60; freight, 140.27; newspapers and periodicals, 11.00; postage, 65.00; telegrams, 1.45; petty disbursements, 14.75 ..... 694 41

Engineering Supplies and Expenses ($3,925.14)

Services, $1,347.50.

J. Kendall, 733.50; E. Macdonald, 346.80; Pay list, wages of farm help, 131.20; R. Shortill, 126.00; E. G. Webb, 10.00 ..... 1,347 50

Travelling Expenses, $118.32.

W. C. Blackwood, 47.37; R. R. Graham, 11.05; R. C. Moffatt, 41.50; E. G. Webb, 18.40 ..... 118 32

Supplies, $1,974.33.

C. Anderson & Co., 13.35; T. R. Barber, 21.25; Beatty Bros., 48.93; Bogardus & Barton, 18.40; Bond Hardware Co., Ltd., 454.40; E. E. Bossence, 47.70; Canadian Industries, Ltd., 96.20; Canadian Liquid Air Co., Ltd., 56.79; Canadian Oil Companies, Ltd., 22 00; Central Scientific Co. of Canada, Ltd., 113.73; Co-operative Supply Dept. O.A.C., 98.95; Guelph Lumber Co., Ltd., 23.77; G. M. Hendry Co., Ltd., 37.75; Keuffel & Esser Co., 31.31; King's Printer, 250.27; Knight-Whaley Co., 115.85; Liquid Carbonic Canadian Corporation, Ltd., 12.50; D. E. Macdonald & Bros., Ltd., 13.48; D. McKenzie Machinery Co., 123.75; Ontario Hardware Co., 13.13; Penfold Hardware Co., 69.18; R. Stewart, Ltd., 120.44; J. L. Stout, 14.75; W. W. Stuart, 32.56; Taylor Instrument Co., 40.00; Wallace Printing Co., Ltd., 10.00; petty disbursements, 74.39 ..... 1,974 33

Expenses, $484.99.

Bell Telephone Co., rental, 39.60 ; tolls, 21.35 ; Board of Light and Heat Commission, meter, 10.00; Delco Appliance Corporation, repairs, 22.50; Guelph Tire Hospital, battery, 10.15; Imperial Oil, Ltd., oils, 15.50; J. A. Jeffery, repairs, 92.50; Kloepfer Coal Co., coal, 25.00; J. MacCallum & Son, gas, 27.15; McCormack & Robinson, repairs, 10.25; D. McKenzie Machinery Co., 16.30. Sundries—cartage, 48.25; express, 11.57; freight, 25.80; newspapers and periodicals, 18.75; postage, 60.00; telegrams, 1.50; petty disbursements, 28.82 ..... 484 99

FARM ECONOMICS

Expenses ($6,171.14)

Services, $3,663.50.

K. L. Butterfield, 75.00; W. Dobbie, 500.00; E. Martin, 840.00; J. R. Peet, 1,408.50; H. Reeves, 840.00 ..... 3,663 50

Travelling Expenses, $448.18.

G. P. Collins, 73.80; W. J. Fairweather, 117.05; F. C. Hart, 89.74; J. R. Peet, 4.00; C. W. Riley, 28.00; W. S. Rowe, 135.59 ..... 448 18

Equipment, $1,267.29.

American Institute of Co-operation, 12.00; B. H. Blackwell, Ltd., 25.73; Bond Hardware Co., Ltd., 14.66; E. E. Bossence, 51.20; Gowdy Bros., 12.25; Griffin Foundry Co., 122.50; Guelph Sand & Gravel, Ltd., 201.00; Instruments, Ltd., 26.00; King's Printer, 267.62; M. Lasby, 13.50; Penfold Hardware Co., 398.89; R. Stewart, Ltd., 68.56; petty disbursements, 53.38 ..... 1,267 29

Ontario Agricultural College—Continued
Expenses—Continued
Farm Economics, Expenses—Continued

Expenses, $792.17.

Bell Telephone Co., rental, 48.60; tolls, 7.82; Burroughs Adding Machine of Canada, Ltd., maintenance, 38.15; E. Lefler & Son, auto maintenance, 59.96; P. Martin, repairs, 13.13; Reinhart's Garage, auto maintenance, 492.90; United Typewriter Co., Ltd., inspection, 12.00. Sundries—cartage, 2.25; express, 3.74; newspapers and periodicals, 40.07; postage, 63.00; petty disbursements, 10.55. 792 17

EXTENSION

Expenses ($8,492.34)

Services, $2,671.00.

A. Aldridge, 720.00; F. H. Bell, 36.00; H. W. Cole, 42.00; Pay list, wages of men, 73.50; W. R. Peters, 40.00; Mrs. D. R. Sands, 37.50; W. D. Tolton, 1,722.00.... 2,671 00

Travelling Expenses, $777.49.

J. Buchanan, 147.30; R. Keegan, 5.21; J. Loughland, 243.02; W. D. Tolton, 381.96 777 49

Advertising, $1,445.80.

Acta Nostra, 15.00; The Beekeeper, 10.08; Canadian Countryman Publishing Co., Ltd., 165.00; Canadian Horticulturist, 41.05; Canadian Society of Technical Agriculturists, 200.00; Chatham Daily News, 37.80; H. B. Donovan, 34.50; J. Dougall & Son, 45.00; Farm & Dairy, 45.00; Farmers Advocate, 135.00; Farmers Sun, 96.00; Montreal Star Co., Ltd., 157.50; Ontario Farmer, 168.00; Ontario Milk Producers Association, 28.00; Ottawa Farm Journal, 72.00; Rural Publishing Co., Ltd., 45.00; Wilson Publishing Co. of Toronto, Ltd., 133.71; petty disbursements, 17.16... 1,445 80

Exhibits, $641.74.

T. R. Barber, 12.70; Davis Bulletin Co., Inc., 210.00; Guelph Cartage Co., 18.00; McKenzie Machinery Co., 85.57; Pringle & Booth, 22.98; Royal Agricultural Winter Fair, 32.87; Ruddy Manufacturing Co., Ltd., 16.71; J. B. Smith & Sons, Ltd., 26.88; R. Stewart, Ltd., 84.41; Swift Canadian Co., Ltd., 109.88; petty disbursements, 21.74.. 641 74

Supplies, $1,782.49.

Bogardus & Barton, 106.36; Bond Hardware Co., Ltd., 29.36; E. E. Bossence, 36.95; Chapple's, Ltd., 13.05; R. C. Christie Electric Co., Ltd., 22.00; C. W. Dempsey, 45.60; Eastman Kodak Stores, Ltd., 94.95; Guelph Lumber Co., Ltd., 92.28; King's Printer, 1,194.56; D. E. Macdonald & Bros., Ltd., 21.86; Mason & Risch, Ltd., 15.00; H. Occomore, 26.78; Walker Stores, Ltd., 17.46; petty disbursements, 66.28.. 1,782 49

Expenses, $1,173.82.

Battler & Freiburger, lining sink, 34.94; Bell Telephone Co., rental, 42.40; tolls, 26.65; Canadian Westinghouse Co., Ltd., repairs, 10.50; Tolton's Service Station, auto repairs, 13.47; Trans-Canada Broadcasting Co., Ltd., broadcast, 91.35; United Typewriter Co., Ltd., inspections, 12.00. Sundries—cartage, 211.83; express, 43.35; freight, 1.71; newspapers and periodicals, 396.44; postage, 270.25; telegrams, .80; petty disbursements, 18.13...................... 1,173 82

MACDONALD INSTITUTE AND HALL

Expenses ($5,536.98)

Services, $94.00.

J. Christie, 90.00; G. Kelso, 4.00.................................... 94 00

Travelling Expenses, $107.50.

O. R. Cruikshank, 15.20; G. B. Doughty, 14.55; A. D. Hicks, 18.20; M. C. Kay, 15.20; J. Miller, 10.50; M. A. McQueen, 19.35; W. A. Schenck, 14.50.......... 107 50

Supplies and Equipment, $4,881.73.

Aluminum Goods, Ltd., 33.24; C. Anderson & Co., 34.88; Appleford Paper Products, Ltd., 19.53; J. Armstrong, Ltd., 178.46; Bond Hardware Co., Ltd., 194.34; Cassidy's, Ltd., 46.20; College Grocery, 584.52; Copp, Clarke Co., Ltd., 23.15; Dairy Dept. O.A.C., 291.22; Dominion Linens, Ltd., 84.82; Fuller Brush Co., Ltd., 30.10; Guelph Paper Co., 60.15; Hales Meat Market, 338.18; Harris Abattoir Co., Ltd., 11.75; Horticulture Dept. O A.C., 89.06; Howard & Klinck, 12.00; King's Printer, 938.35; L. K. Liggett Co., Ltd., 72.56; D. E. Macdonald & Bros., Ltd., 13.25; Macmillan Co. of Canada, Ltd., 13.62; McAinsh & Co., Ltd., 21.75; G. J. Merlihan Co., 59.09; Meyer Bros., 14.38; National Grocers

Ontario Agricultural College—Continued

Expenses—Continued

Macdonald Institute and Hall—Continued

Supplies and Equipment—Continued

Co., Ltd., 317.27; Ontario Library Book Co., 18.00; Ontario Reformatory Industries, 14.40; Poultry Dept. O.A.C., 202.04; R. Simpson Co., Ltd., 31.20; L. Taylor, 781.55; Taylor Instrument Co., 30.55; Trent Institute O.A.C., 11.33; G. H. Wood & Co., Ltd., 26.00; C. Yeates Co., Ltd., 164.35; petty disbursements, 120.44 .... 4,881 73

Expenses, $453.75.

Aster Window Cleaning Co., 21.00; Bell Telephone Co., tolls, 61.19; Guelph Cartage Co., rental of chairs, 10.00; United Typewriter Co., Ltd., inspections, 12.00. Sundries—cartage, 6.25; express, 5.70; newspapers and periodicals, 70.75; postage, 250.00; telegrams, 13.51; petty disbursements, 3.35 .... 453 75

ANIMAL HUSBANDRY, FARM AND EXPERIMENTAL FEEDING DEPT.

Permanent Improvements ($1,749.88)

Bond Hardware Co., Ltd., 284.21; Ellis & Howard, Ltd., 38.13; Guelph Lumber Co., Ltd., 130.94; Kent Tile & Marble Co., Ltd., 125.00; M. Lasby, 68.25; Louden Machinery Co. of Canada, Ltd., 35.85; J. A. McAllister, 268.14; McArthur Engineering & Construction Co., Ltd., 256.00; Ontario Hardware Co., 11.34; Pay list, wages of men, 291.50; Pioneer Equipment Co., 41.20; J. Saunders, 78.40; R. Stewart, Ltd., 102.41; petty disbursements, 18.51 .... 1,749 88

Wages, Temporary Help ($5,725.25)

Sundry farm hands, labourers, etc. 5,725 25

Purchase and Maintenance of Live Stock ($15,998.91)

G. Auld, 170.27; W. W. Ballantyne & Sons, 75.00; T. Beal, 211.62; Bidwell Vegetable Oil Mills, Ltd., 135.00; N. Black, 45.40; R. Black & Sons, 90.00; Bogardus & Barton, 49.99; Bond Hardware Co., Ltd., 13.60; J. H. Borthwick, 10.00; J. Bovaird, 10.00; C. B. Boynton, 35.00; J. P. Brockel, 102.77; A. B. Brubacker, 310.00; B. H. Bull & Sons, 535.00; H. D. Cameron, 229.70; Canada & Dominion Sugar Co., Ltd., 180.00; Canada Packers, Ltd., 46.75; Canadian-American Lumber & Manufacturing Co., 194.17; Canadian National Live Stock Records, 358.25; Mrs. J. B. Carter, 200.00; A. Chatterton, 257.67; J. R. Curtis, 41.52; Dairy Dept. O.A.C., 399.86; H. D. Davison, 35.50; Dominion Linseed Oil Co., Ltd., 48.00; Doughty & McFarlane, 1,346.33; J. Douglas & Son, 500.00; R. G. Ford, 15.00; B. Gammie, 42.00; H. N. Gibson, 50.00; J. B. Gibson, 12.00; Guelph Casket Works, 27.00; Guelph Lumber Co., Ltd., 135.84; Haas Bros., 60.00; J. H. Hagen, 80.25; N. J. Halls, 21.97; W. E. Hamilton, 25.50; R. Harcourt, 68.67; Holstein-Friesian Association, 26.00; Imperial Oil, Ltd., 50.00; G. Johnson, 202.56; Mrs. C. Kay, 46.85; Kemptville Agricultural School, 75.00; J. S. Knapp, 160.00; R. G. Knox, 51.07; F. A. Lashley, 44.00; Lowe & Heibein, 275.00; A. Macdonald, 28.18; Maple Leaf Milling Co., Ltd., 1,111.17; E. Martin Estate, 522.35; J. J. McAnninch, 12.00; W. G. McCannell, 70.00; A. C. McDonald, 77.98; Michigan State College, 90.00; S. Mills, 150.00; T. H. Moore, 16.50; L. E. Morgan, 45.00; J. A. Ord, 50.40; G. A. Parkinson, 15.50; Quaker Oats Co., 538.75; Quinte Milk Products, Ltd., 33.00; M. T. Revell, 268.00; O. W. Rhynas & Son, Ltd., 454.60; G. Ross, 192.54; Seagram Stables, 25.00; Silverwood's Oxford Dairy, Ltd., 96.00; Mrs. J. Slinger, 19.00; J. L. Stansell, 160.00; M. W. Staples, 46.77; J. C. Steckley, 23.90; Stevenson's Farms, 120.00; A. Stewart, 22.70; E. C. Stillwell, 15.35; C. Stobbs, 120.00; G. Thompson, 36.00; Toronto Elevators, Ltd., 3,427.02; United Farmers Co-operative Co., Ltd., 86.20; N. Waggs, 186.00; J. Walsh, 101.33; F. W. Wood, 79.00; Mrs. W. Younge, 35.00. Sundries—customs, 4.40; express, 85.15; freight, 437.04; petty disbursements, 96.97 .... 15,998 91

Supplies, Equipment and Contingencies ($4,998.86)

Supplies and Equipment, $4,086.55.

Associated Chemical Co. of Canada, Ltd., 189.10; Beatty Bros., Ltd., 25.54; C. M. Blyth, 75.00; Bogardus & Barton, 13.95; Bond Hardware Co., Ltd., 327.66; E. E. Bossence, 99.00; Brantford Cordage Co., Ltd., 43.75; Canada Rex Spray Co., Ltd., 11.25; Canadian Co-operative Wool Growers, Ltd., 19.90; Canadian Oil Companies, Ltd., 39.63; Central Scientific Co. of Canada, Ltd., 24.12; Doughty & McFarlane, 231.85; Empire Milking Machine Co., Ltd.,

Ontario Agricultural College—Continued
Expenses—Continued
Animal Husbandry, etc.—Continued

Supplies and Equipment—Continued

25.26; W. J. Gardhouse, 118.60; General Supply Co. of Canada, Ltd., 31.59; Guelph Lumber Co., Ltd., 95.08; Gummer Press, Ltd., 83.53; J. H. Hogan, 56.40; Hygiene Products, Ltd., 17.50; Imperial Oil, Ltd., 1,058.27; International Harvester Co. of Canada, Ltd., 20.90; King's Printer, 425.28; London Cleansers Supply House, 12.50; Louden Machinery Co. of Canada, Ltd., 79.78; D. E. Macdonald & Bros., Ltd., 10.45; B. J. McCabe, 164.59; National Stationers, Ltd., 125.00; Ontario Hardware Co., 34.92; Pioneer Equipment Co., 76.38; Ritchie Bros., 28.45; R. Stewart, Ltd., 57.67; W. W. Stuart, 34.08; Sunelo Products, Ltd., 31.50; J. H. Sweeney, 15.40; Taylor-Forbes Co., Ltd., 11.68; Ward's Studio, 35.64; G. H. Wood & Co., Ltd., 97.50; D. Young, 95.52; petty disbursements, 142.33 .... 4,086 55

Contingencies, $912.31.

R. T. Amos, services, 35.00; Bell Telephone Co., rental, 123.60; tolls, 50.36; Canadian Countryman Publishing Co., Ltd., advertising, 50.00; Daley's Tire Shop, auto repairs, 29.60; Dept. of Trade & Commerce, inspecting scales, 20.45; Farmers' Advocate, advertising, 56.00; Harrison's Garage, auto maintenance, 116.24; A. R. Linn, services, 30.00; McCloskey's Service Station, auto maintenance, 11.88; Ontario Farmer, advertising, 25.00; Mrs. J. Slinger, washing, 56.25; W. G. Taylor, services, 15.00; United Typewriter Co., Ltd., inspections, 12.00. Sundries—cartage, 6.76; customs, 2.58; express, 63.10; freight, 13.05; postage, 120.00; newspapers and periodicals, 25.99; telegrams, 11.17; petty disbursements, 38.28 .... 912 31

FIELD EXPERIMENTS

Wages, Temporary Help ($7,209.97)

Sundry farm hands and labourers 7,209 97

Supplies, Equipment, etc. ($4,345.13)

Supplies, etc., $3,026.33.

J. Armstrong, Ltd., 29.68; J. Barclay, 110.90; Board of Light & Heat Commission, 11.43; Bogardus & Barton, 10.90; Bond Hardware Co., Ltd., 291.05; J. Carleton Co., 25.00; Central Scientific Co. of Canada, Ltd., 65.76; Daley's Tire Shop, 18.67; Doughty & McFarlane, 294.40; Ellis & Howard, Ltd., 21.51; Garden City Paper Mills Co., Ltd., 37.00; Golf, Ltd., 17.60; Guelph Lumber Co., Ltd., 176.13; Guelph Paper Co., 30.84; Gummer Press, Ltd., 18.70; Gunn's, Ltd., 55.78; G. A. Hardie & Co., Ltd., 125.00; Hart Emerson Co., Ltd., 44.80; Imperial Oil, Ltd., 48.11; King's Printer, 327.78; M. Lasby, 29.25; J. MacCallum & Son, 22.90; D. E. Macdonald & Bros., Ltd., 13.00; Mackey's Bakery, 24.50; Masco Co., Ltd., 20.02; McCormack & Robinson, 18.84; McGill & Smith, Ltd., 10.06; D. McKenzie Machinery Co., 22.05; National Grocers Co., Ltd., 10.60; Nichols Chemical Co., Ltd., 20.00; Ontario Hardware Co., 27.46; Ontario Paper Box Co., Ltd., 15.00; Ontario Provincial Winter Fair, 20.55; Penfold Hardware Co., 13.55; Pioneer Equipment Co., 62.70; Royal Dairy, Ltd., 41.50; Steele Briggs Seed Co., Ltd., 13.77; R. Stewart, Ltd., 461.45; Superior Clover Huller Co., 35.00; Sutton & Sons, Ltd., 17.97; J. H. Sweeney, 22.60; Taylor-Forbes Co., Ltd., 83.60; Walkerville Bag Manufacturing Co., 33.20; E. Webb & Sons, Ltd., 12.61; D. Young, 19.58; petty disbursements, 193.53 .... 3,026 33

Contingencies, $1,318.80.

T. R. Barber, spraying, 20.75; Bell Telephone Co., rental, 31.80; tolls, 25.65; Daley's Tire Shop, auto maintenance, 10.39; A. Ferguson, services, 75.00; J. Hastings, services, 75.00; H. Little, auto maintenance, 21.78; J. MacCallum & Son, auto maintenance, 32.83; McArthur Engineering & Construction Co., Ltd., paving, 656.00; McCormack & Robinson, 97.90; Trelco, Ltd., shellac, 11.50; United Typewriter Co., Ltd., 12.00; Waterworks Dept. City of Guelph, 14.49; D. Wright, services, 75.00. Sundries—cartage, 7.58; customs, 4.34; express, 59.24; freight, 38.88; newspapers and periodicals, 5.00; postage, 20.00; telegrams, 2.52; petty disbursements, 21.15 .... 1,318 80

EXPERIMENTAL DAIRY AND DAIRY SCHOOLS

Wages, Temporary Help ($2,364.90)

Sundry farm hands and labourers 2,364 90

Ontario Agricultural College—Continued

Expenses—Continued

Experimental Dairy and Dairy Schools—Continued

Purchasing, Hauling and Manufacturing Milk ($4,980.23)

J. Clair, 236.42; P. Crimless, 741.28; G. Deakin, 168.08; W. Deakin, 186.52; Farm Dept. O.A.C., 810.94; J. D. Gale, 662.96; M. Hanlon, 194.93; S. Headon, 621.14; Silverwood's Dairy, Ltd, 911.31; M. Walsh, 269.06; T. Walsh, 177.59........ 4,980 23

Supplies, Equipment, etc. ($3,482.68)

Supplies and Equipment, $947.22.

Appleford Paper Products, Ltd., 33.85; Bogardus & Barton, 12.83; Bond Hardware Co., Ltd., 49.62; Canada Colours & Chemicals, Ltd., 122.80; Canadian Milk Products, Ltd., 12.00; De Laval Co., Ltd., 139.00; Ellis & Howard, Ltd., 20.03; J. B. Ford Co., 26.42; C. Hansen's Canadian Laboratory, 21.10; King's Printer, 121.23; S. F. Lawrason & Co., Ltd., 67.20; Mackenzie Mop & Brush Co., 11.00; Masco Co., Ltd., 62.70; McArthur Engineering & Construction Co., Ltd., 33.00; National Grocers Co., Ltd., 15.43; Nichol's Chemical Co., Ltd., 39.61; C. Richardson & Co., Ltd., 63.05; petty disbursements, 96.35......... 947 22

Purchase of Machinery, $300.36.

Canadian Ice Machine Co., Ltd., 48.50; Cherry-Burrell Corporation of Canada, Ltd., 168.20; Ellis & Howard, Ltd., 21.88; J. B. Ford Co., 22.35; Purity Milk Cap, Ltd., 1.43; Sutherland Schultz Electric Co., Ltd., 38.00................ 300 36

Repairs and Contingencies, $2,235.10.

Bell Telephone Co., rental, 99.00; tolls, 8.67; Bond Hardware Co., Ltd., repair supplies, 29.93; Crane, Ltd., repair supplies, 90.72; Dairymen's Association of Western Ontario, advertising, 15.00; F. W. Hamilton, expenses, 216.85; C. E. Lackner, services, 225.00; E. L. Macdonald, services, 45.00; McCormack & Robinson, repairs, 53.40; T. J. McKinney, expenses, 191.49; D. McMillan, services, 225.00; A. Muirhead Co., Ltd., varnish, 38.70; H. Occomore, repairs, 92.96; Pay list, wages of men, 279.00; H. A. Smallfield, expenses, 101.76; W. H. Sproule, expenses, 26.12; Suey Wah Laundry, washing, 146.31; Taylor-Forbes Co., Ltd., repair supplies, 133.44. Sundries—cartage, 29.70; customs, 10.13; express, 20.92; freight, 4.48; newspapers and periodicals, 6.00; postage, 90.50; telegrams, 1.05; petty disbursements, 53.97................................ 2,235 10

POULTRY DEPARTMENT

Wages, Temporary Help ($7,541.00)

Sundry farm hands and labourers... 7,541 00

Experiments and Feeds ($12,657.44)

Services, $950.14.

G. B. Dale, 78.00; J. O'Connor, 144.00; Pay list, wages of men, 230.14; S. Scott, 108.00; J. Sykes, 312.00; N. B. Taylor, 78.00............................... 950 14

Travelling Expenses, $54.18.

H. Branion, 45.55; R. Daly, 8.63.. 54 18

Expenses, $11,653.12.

G. Amos, 127.35; G. Auld, 130.65; Ayearst, McKenna & Harrison, 156.60; J. T. Baker Chemical Co., 10.30; C. W. Barber, 104.66; Beaver Valley Alfalfa Meal Co., 125.00; Bowes Co., Ltd., 233.34; W. W. Buchanan, 140.28; Canada Packers, Ltd., 58.80; Central Scientific Co. of Canada, Ltd., 33.59; R. H. Chappell, 65.50; College Grocery, 22.21; Dairy Dept. O.A.C., 49.00; Doughty & McFarlane, 823.15; Eastern Dairies, Ltd., 100.00; Elliott & Moody, 121.50; Ellis & Howard, Ltd., 22.88; J. Gale, 29.30; J. B. Gibson, 268.00; Guelph Creamery, 165.00; Guelph Lumber Co., Ltd., 16.00; Gunn's, Ltd., 170.50; Harris Abattoir Co., Ltd., 92.40; Harrow Farmers Co-operative Association, Ltd., 540.00; N. C. Hayner Co., 17.50; Maple Leaf Milling Co., Ltd., 980.04; Mead, Johnson & Co. of Canada, Ltd., 201.75; National Grocers Co., Ltd., 102.38; Ontario Hardware Co., 22.35; J. A. Orde, 82.20; J. Paddcck, 12.40; Penfold Hardware Co., 14.44; Quaker Oats Co., 33.60; Quinte Milk Products, Ltd., 50.75; Reesors Marmill, Ltd., 393.02; Rideau Specialty Co., 37.25; St. Lawrence Starch Co., Ltd., 46.80; Silverwood's, Ltd., 66.88; A. Smith, 195.19; L. M. Smith, 1,542.40; Standard Brands, Ltd., 61.00; J. B. Stringer & Co., 69.00; J. E. Thomas, 128.20; Toronto Elevators, Ltd., 3,402.54; J. Walsh, 86.57; W. Whitelaw, 60.00; Wilson Scientific Co., Ltd., 35.85; Yocum-Faust, Ltd., 56.00. Sundries—cartage, 94.54; express, .80; freight, 224.58; petty disbursements, 29.08............. 11,653 12

Ontario Agricultural College—Continued

Expenses—Continued

Poultry Department—Continued

Poultry Extension Work ($21,847.58)

Services, $8,260.66.

M. S. Aplin, 187.00; N. C. Armstrong, 156.00; C. Castell, 76.00; J. R. Cavers, 460.00; C. Clelland, 187.00; C. C. Duncan, 532.00; H. C. Elliott, 234.00; N. Guthrie, 214.33; W. M. Hart, 516.00; J. Harvey, 25.00; B. Healey, 25.00; E. N. Healey, 234.00; G. Howell, 100.00; D. Jones, 145.00; M. J. Longstaff, 120.00; C. F. Luckham, 78.00; J. J. MacIlraith, 1,836.00; M. McArthur, 504.00; R. W. Morrison, 100.00; G. W. Mutrie, 569.50; E. Rivaz, 25.00; A. G. Robertson, 246.00; W. Strong, 515.50; P. D. Vahey, 432.00; H. B. Webster, 451.00; G. Woods, 292.33 .... 8,260 66

Travelling Expenses, $8,540.79.

H. M. Barron, 329.19; J. E. Bergey, 1,298.24; H. Branion, 103.97; J. R. Cavers, 252.78; G. B. Dale, 33.90; C. C. Duncan, 259.63; H. C. Elliott, 157.58; J. F. Francis, 750.70; W. R. Graham, Jr., 23.06; W. R. Graham, Sr., 194.52; W. M. Hart, 395.70; G. Howell, 63.40; C. M. Huntsman, 1,145.31; C. F. Luckham, 144.29; J. J. MacIlraith, 917.61; F. N. Marcellus, 381.80; E. H. Marston, 89.00; M. McArthur, 219.03; R. M. Morrison, 119.40; G. W. Mutrie, 487.21; A. W. Robertson, 227.41; J. B. Smith, 53.09; E. S. Snyder, 53.10; W. Strong, 206.49; W. D. Tolton, 41.50; P. D. Vahey, 300.22; H. N. Wass, 1.50; H. B. Webster, 291.16 .... 8,540 79

Purchase and Maintenance of Automobiles, $2,025.14.

Daley's Tire Shop, 86.40; H. Little, 270.42; Maguire Motors, Ltd., 750.00; Sutton Motors, Ltd., 904.00; petty disbursements, 14.32 .... 2,025 14

Supplies and Equipment, $3,020.99.

Bell Telephone Co. of Canada, tolls, 111.79; Canadian Poultry Journal, 18.00; Gummer Press, Ltd., 30.00; S. R. Hart & Co., Ltd., 66.83; J. F. Hartz Co., Ltd., 96.47; Holman Luggage, Ltd., 36.00; Ketchum Manufacturing Co., Ltd., 1,267.50; King's Printer, 721.71; H. Occomore, 30.20; Rideau Specialty Co., 44.15. Sundries—cartage, 1.25; express, 275.47; freight, 4.15; postage, 261.50; telegrams, 9.68; petty disbursements, 46.29 .... 3,020 99

Purchase and Maintenance of Horses, Supplies, Equipment and Contingencies ($4,411.99)

Supplies and Equipment, $3,509.58.

Acetol Products, Inc., 24.00; J. Armstrong, Ltd., 35.64; Associated Chemical Co. of Canada, Ltd., 32.50; G. Banta Publishing Co., 14.92; Bogardus & Barton, 13.10; Bond Hardware Co., Ltd., 222.58; Canadian Laboratory Supplies, Ltd., 131.63; S. C. Daniels Co., Ltd., 36.00; Doughty & McFarlane, 48.00; Garden City Paper Mills Co., Ltd., 30.00; General Steel Wares, Ltd., 51.62; Gowdy Bros., 27.10; Guelph Cartage Co., 20.00; Guelph Lumber Co., Ltd., 66.94; Hanovia Chemical & Manufacturing Co., 60.40; N. C. Hayner Co., 17.50; Imperial Oil, Ltd., 146.85; Ketchum Manufacturing Co., Ltd., 216.00; King's Printer, 191.06; Kloepfer Coal Co., 182.00; M. Lasby, 100.50; Marshall's Drug Store, 18.04; R. B. Millard, 77.00; National Grocers Co., Ltd., 81.41; Office Specialty Manufacturing Co., Ltd., 72.00; Ontario Hardware Co., 74.91; Penfold Hardware Co., 144.10; I. N. Petersine & Son, 31.50; Rideau Specialty Co., 59.57; Stevens Hepner Co., Ltd., 16.91; R. Stewart, Ltd., 797.88; W. W. Stuart, 55.38; Sutherland-Schultz Electric Co., 79.66; J. H. Sweeney, 25.20; Telfer Paper Box Co., Ltd., 150.00; R. D. White, 52.25; Wilson Scientific Co., Ltd., 16.69; petty disbursements, 88.74 .... 3,509 58

Contingencies, $902.41.

Bell Telephone Co., rental, 22.80; tolls, 18.76; McArthur Engineering & Construction Co., Ltd., paving, 352.64; McCormack & Robinson, repairs, 42.20; Ottawa Experimental Farm, entry fees re Egg Laying Contests, 30.00; Pay list, wages of men, 230.90; United Typewriter Co., Ltd., inspections, 13.50. Sundries—cargage, 18.06; customs, 9.45; express, 49.43; freight, 14.36; newspapers and periodicals, 18.50; postage, 50.00; telegrams, 5.25; petty disbursements, 26.56... 902 41

Ontario Agricultural College—Continued

Expenses—Continued

Poultry Department—Continued

Turkey Experimental Farm ($2,566.20)

Services, $499.70.

J. Aires, 11.70; A. Bullock, 75.00; E. Byers, 162.00; Mrs. E. Byers, 10.00; L. Carr, 3.00; Mrs. C. Rohrer, 6.00; S. Rohrer, 28.00; I. Wells, 10.00; C. Wolvin, 174.00; M. Wolvin, 20.00 .... 499 70

Travelling Expenses, $21.60.

E. H. Marston 21 60

Purchase and Maintenance of Stock, $1,818.36.

Farm Dept. O.A.C. 125.00; C. A. Fisher, 30.00; M. Howell, 60.00; E. H. Jackson Co. Ltd., 98.05; W. H. Jewell & Son, 168 22; F. E. Johnson & Co., 15.57; F. W. Kell, 14.45; A. T. Leedham, 1,036.63; McCall & Co., 183.93; Norfolk Co-operative Co., Ltd., 26.16; Tillsonburg Produce Co., 38.50; petty disbursements, 21.85 .... 1,818 36

Repairs and Contingencies, $226.54.

W. H. Abbey, repairs, 11.35; Bell Telephone Co., rental, 4.69; tolls, 17.46; Hydro-Electric Power Commission, power, 125.70; W. H. Jewell & Son, auto maintenance, 40.09. Sundries—express, 16.10; postage, 5.00; petty disbursements, 6.15 .... 226 54

Research Work under Arrangements with the Empire Marketing Board ($2,749.92)

Services, $2,749.92.

H. Branion, research expert, 1,999.92; G. Dale, research expert, 750.00 .... 2,749 92

HORTICULTURAL DEPARTMENT

Permanent Improvements ($3,699.42)

Bond Hardware Co., Ltd., 40.47; Gowdy Bros., 15.45; W. Grey, 33.00; Griffin Foundry Co., 49.50; Guelph Lumber Co., Ltd., 182.69; R. H. Keith, 90.00; King Construction Co., Ltd., 128.00; M. Lasby, 116.00; Lord & Burnham Co., Ltd., 31.40; D. E. Macdonald & Bros., Ltd., 51.34; McArthur Engineering & Construction Co., Ltd., 1,265.65; McCormack & Robinson, 108.80; Ontario Hardware Co., 155.99; Page-Hersey Tubes, Ltd., 10.60; Pay list, wages of men, 1,246.50; Roelofson Elevator Works, 17.00; R. Stewart, Ltd., 136.88; petty disbursements, 20.15 .... 3,699 42

Wages, Temporary Help ($11,362.85)

Sundry farm hands and labourers 11,362 85

Trees, Plants, Seeds, Fuel, Equipment, etc. ($9,942.67)

Trees, Plants and Seeds, $3,342.47.

J. B. Bridgman, 22.75; J. E. Carter, 26.00; Dale Estate, Ltd., 327.08; Dept. of Horticulture, South Dakota State College, 25.40; Douglas Seed Co., 809.95; Fisher Orchards, 18.00; J. Gammage & Sons, Ltd., 25.50; Graham's Nursery, 46.85; R. Grootendorst, 440.31; N. V. Konynenburg & Mark, 720.16; R. M. Lindley, 18.00; A. V. Main, 35.00; Norfolk Fruit Growers Association, 117.25; Northumberland Packers, 27.00; Ontario Reformatory Industries, 12.00; Papendrecht-Vandervoot, 309.30; Sheridan Nurseries, 106.80; Steele, Briggs Seed Co., Ltd., 114.55; Sutton & Sons, Ltd., 34.42; Toronto Produce, Ltd., 11.76; E. Webb & Sons, Ltd., 38.00; petty disbursements, 56.39 .... 3,342 47

Equipment, $5,220.74.

American Instrument Co., 75.00; C. Anderson & Co., 12.37; Apparatus & Specialty Co., 37.00; J. Armstrong, Ltd., 31.51; Art Metropole, 24.50; Associated Chemical Co. of Canada, Ltd., 89.95; Bailey, Grundy & Barrett, Ltd., 204.82; W. J. Bell Paper Co., Ltd., 15.36; Bogardus & Barton, 17.31; Bond Hardware Co., Ltd., 182.04; Canadian Ice Machine Co., Ltd., 37.91; Canadian Oil Companies, Ltd., 752.70; Canadian Wirebound Boxes, Ltd., 134.73; Central Scientific Co. of Canada, Ltd., 544.88; Co-operative Supply Dept. O.A.C., 11.75; Daley's Tire Shop, 39.25; Doughty & McFarlane, 470.50; Ellis & Howard, Ltd., 52.98; Foster Pottery Co., 134.25; Garden City Paper Mills Co., Ltd., 30.15; General Publishing Co., Ltd., 11.65; Goodyear Tire & Rubber Co. of Canada, Ltd., 71.71; Guelph Paper Co., 10.55; Instruments, Ltd., 577.47; Keuffel & Esser Co., 38.99; King's Printer, 389.37; Lavoline Cleanser Co., Ltd., 19.65; Liquor Control Board of Ontario, 18.99; D. E. Macdonald & Bros., Ltd., 15.25; Masco

Ontario Agricultural College—Continued

Expenses—Continued

Horticultural Department—Continued

Trees, Plants, Seeds, etc.—Continued

Equipment—Continued

Co., Ltd., 14.37; C. L. Muller, 42.60; Niagara Brand Spray Co., Ltd., 97.61; Norfolk Co-operative Co., Ltd., 52.50; F. Nunan, 74.50; Office Specialty Manufacturing Co., Ltd., 28.20; Ontario Hardware Co., 159.49; Pioneer Equipment Co., 19.35; E. Pullan Co., Ltd., 11.75; Rae's Wagon Works, 11.00; J. Richard, 485.60; Taylor-Forbes Co., Ltd., 11.10; J. Watson Manufacturing Co., Ltd., 68.46; petty disbursements, 91.62 .... 5,220 74

Fuel, Maintenance of Horses and Contingencies, $1,379.46.

W. J. Armstrong, Ltd., refinishing, 36.50; T. R. Barber, spraying, 71.26; Bell Telephone Co. of Canada, tolls, 126.73; Canadian Westinghouse Co., Ltd., repairs, 18.96; City Battery & Electrical Service, auto repairs, 18.23; H. Little, auto maintenance, 247.17; Province of Ontario Pictures, colouring, 21.40; Robson Motor Corporation, auto repairs, 19.05; Taylor-Forbes Co, Ltd., repairs, 48.70; United Typewriter Co., Ltd., inspections, 27.00. Sundries—cartage, 16.94; customs, 71.47; express, 106.93; freight, 259.72; newspapers and periodicals, 16.96; postage, 234.00; telegrams, 7.04; petty disbursements, 31.40 .... 1,379 46

Extension Work in Vegetable Growing ($1,249.22)

Services, $652.50.

Pay list, wages of farm help 652 50

Expenses, $596.72.

Art Metropole, cloth, 19.50; Bell Telephone Co. of Canada, tolls, 20.08; Dale Estate, Ltd., flowers, 37.85; Douglas Seed Co., seeds, 214.55; Golf, Ltd., nozzles, 11.50; R. Grootendorst, seeds, 18.10; King's Printer, printing, 34.44; R. Moore & Sons, seeds, 11.00; Ontario Hardware Co., hardware, 10.81; Steel Co. of Canada, Ltd., stakes, 30.15; Steele, Briggs Seed Co., Ltd., canes, 12.00; F. W. Thorold Co., Ltd., sprinkler, 17.00. Sundries—customs, .72; newspapers and periodicals, 1.78; postage, 85.32; telegrams, 1.85; petty disbursements, 70.07 .... 596 72

Laying Permanent Roads, College Grounds ($4,999.10)

The McArthur Engineering & Construction Co., Ltd 4,999 10

APICULTURE DEPARTMENT ($11,363.70)

Services, Supplies, Equipment and Contingencies ($2,371.35)

Services, $40.00.

J. D. Little, 10.00; M. Longstaff, 30.00 .... 40 00

Supplies and Equipment, $1,451.11.

Acme Steel Co., Ltd., 29.13; American Can Co., 64.98; Art Metropole, 133.25; Bond Hardware Co., Ltd., 33.10; E. E. Bossence, 42.00; J. Carleton Co., 12.50; Central Scientific Co. of Canada, Ltd., 81.23; Co-operative Supply Dept. O.A.C., 26.50; G. Dyce, 33.60; King's Printer, 434.61; Leeds & Northrup Co., 59.95; C. E. Lewis, 63.00; National Drug & Chemical Co. of Canada, Ltd., 60.85; H. Occomore, 36.00; Ontario Reformatory Industries, 24.00; Ruddy Manufacturing Co., Ltd., 52.08; Stephens Sales, Ltd., 13.50; United Typewriter Co., Ltd. 138.60; A. Zieman & Sons, 24.75; petty disbursements, 87.48 .... 1,451 11

Contingencies, $880.24.

T. R. Barber, lettering, 10.00; Bell Telephone Co., rental, 34.20; tolls, 50.95; H. Little, auto maintenance, 15.38; H. Occomore, repairs, 25.00; Robin-Hood Service Station, auto maintenance, 100.28; Taylor-Forbes Co., Ltd., repairs, 27.74; United Typewriter Co., Ltd., inspections, 12.00. Sundries—cartage, 7.03; express, 12.76; freight, 5.71; newspapers and periodicals, 30.58; postage, 511.36; telegrams, 5.99; petty disbursements, 31.26 .... 880 24

Inspection of Apiaries ($8,992.35)

Services, $6,153.25; Travelling Expenses, $2,839.10.

W. Abraham, services, 15.00; expenses, 12.00; R. E. Adamson, services, 85.00; expenses, 41.65; W. R. Agar, services, 10.00; H. C. Allen, services, 30.00; expenses, 25.55; C. F. Allyn, services, 15.00; expenses, 8.00; J. E. Bagnall, services, 32.50; expenses, 6.00; W. Barrett, services, 35.00; expenses, 24.00; J. Beattie, services, 50.00; expenses, 29.00; S. B. Bisbee, services, 22.50; expenses, 8.50; W. J. Boyce,

Ontario Agricultural College—Continued

Expenses—Continued

Apiculture Department—Continued

Inspection of Apiaries—Continued

Services and Expenses—Continued

services, 20.00; W. E. Boyes, services, 35.00; expenses, 28.00; A. Brown, services, 7.50; expenses, 2.00; A. T. Brown, services, 62.50; expenses, 43.55; H. Brown, services, 45.00; expenses, 20.81; H. W. Bryant, services, 1,457.50; expenses, 55.30; H. G. Burke, services, 10.00; expenses, 8.00; L. Butson, services, 27.50; F. S. Caldwell, services, 60.00; expenses, 48.00; C. W. Challand, services, 148.75; expenses, 121.76; C. F. Clarke, services, 35.00; expenses, 28.00; G. Collins, services, 20.00; expenses, 16.00; F. Congdon, services, 15.00; expenses, 4.00; G. Corneil, services, 20.00; expenses, 16.00; F. S. Craig, services, 45.50; expenses, 28.00; C. Davidson, services, 15.00; expenses, 4.00; J. M. Davies, services, 35.00; expenses, 28.00; R. Denham, services, 25.00; expenses, .20; R. R. Dixon, services, 22.50; expenses, 10.10; E. J. Dyce, expenses, 129.22; C. H. Dyment, services, 20.00; J. N. Dyment, services, 20.00; expenses, 16.00; E. A. Fiegehan, services, 60.00; expenses, 32.00; M. F. Fisher, services, 50.00; expenses, 35.00; R. H. Flagler, services, 22.50; expenses, 10.00; N. Foster, services, 37.50; expenses, 16.30; D. Galbraith, services, 22.50; R. V. Garbutt, services, 15.00; expenses, 8.00; B. M. Gilbert, services, 10.00; H. Giles, services, 21.25; expenses, 17.00; W. T. H. Gilroy, services, 85.00; expenses, 26.00; G. Gowan, services, 5.00; expenses, 4.00; T. Haberer, services, 15.00; expenses, 12.00; G. W. Hagerman, services, 37.50; expenses, 22.00; H. Haines, services, 17.50; expenses, 10.00; W. A. Hamilton, services, 15.00; expenses, 4.00; A. Hayslip, services, 17.50; expenses, 14.00; G. A. Howard, services, 36.00; expenses, 15.50; L. R. Hupfer, services, 15.00; H. Inch, services, 45.00; expenses, 20.98; M. Inch, services, 35.00; C. C. Jenkins, services, 57.50; expenses, 26.00; C. M. Johnson, services, 22.50; expenses, 2.00; C. G. Jones, services, 10.00; expenses, 8.00; G. S. Jones, services, 12.50; expenses, 4.00; G. J. Kinzie, services, 52.50; expenses, 22.00; O. G. A. Knoerck, services, 12.00; expenses, 6.00; F. W. Krouse, services, 40.00; expenses, 24.00; K. G. Lees, services, 15.00; expenses, 12.00; J. C. Legg, services, 20.00; expenses, 4.00; G. Leslie, services, 15.00; expenses, 4.00; J. D. Little, services, 12.50; expenses, 4.00; G. A. Locke, services, 90.00; expenses, 44.00; E. N. Lundy, services, 17.50; J. B. Macmath, services, 16.25; expenses, 8.75; A. E. Mallaby, services, 35.00; expenses, 20.00; R. Marsh, services, 40.00; expenses, 8.00; E. C. Martin, services, 642.50; expenses, 20.65; W. Martin, services, 19.00; expenses, 4.00; J. I. McArthur, services, 37.50; expenses, 30.00; G. McCarthy, services, 750.00; W. R. McGill, services, 27.50; expenses, 22.00; F. R. McGrogan, services, 17.50; expenses, 12.00; D. McKay, services, 80.00; expenses, 37.60; M. McTaggart, services, 10.00; F. E. Millen, expenses, 793.84; J. E. Morgan, services, 30.00; expenses, 16.00; W. A. Munro, services, 7.50; expenses, 6.00; A. E. Nash, services, 85.00; expenses, 71.65; G. Neil, services, 85.00; expenses, 71.00; J. Osborne, services, 20.00; expenses, 8.00; C. Perrin, services, 15.00; expenses, 15.00; B. J. Philp, services, 24.00; expenses, 19.00; G. Plant, services, 15.00; expenses, 10.00; W. H. Reed, services, 20.00; expenses, 12.00; S. S. Roth, services, 20.00; expenses, 4.00; R. G. Sawyer, expenses, 91.95; L. C. Schiedel, services, 15.00; expenses, 12.00; A. Schmidt, services, 17.50; expenses, 2.00; O. B. Shank, services, 12.50; expenses, 6.00; L. D. Shelly, services, 30.00; expenses, 12.00; B. H. Smith, services, 57.50; expenses, 46.00; W. C. Speers, services, 20.00; expenses, 13.50; C. H. Steen, services, 20.00; expenses, 12.25; J. A. Stephen, services, 245.00; expenses, 52.29; H. Stewart, services, 12.50; expenses, 10.00; R. Teeple, services, 10.00; expenses, 8.00; S. Trousdale, services, 10.00; expenses, 8,00; A. N. Ure, services, 12.50; expenses, 6.00; W. B. Vanderburg, services, 20.00; expenses, 5.00; A. C. Walker, services, 22.50; expenses, 16.35; E. C. Waller, services, 15.00; expenses, 5.00; E. N. Ward, services, 121.50; expenses, 93.20; H. O. White, services, 84.00; expenses, 65.65; R. L. Wilby, services, 10.00; expenses, 4.00; O. Williamson, services, 15.00; expenses, 12.00; S. Wright, services, 25.00 .... 8,992 35

Total		800,224 76	
Less Student fees	47,107 99		
Sale of produce	31,414 60		
Sale of stock and equipment	9,178 73		
Board of students, etc.	146,784 45		
Miscellaneous	3,606 52		
Empire Marketing Board	3,303 13		
		241,395 42	
Ontario Agricultural College		558,829 34	

GENERAL

Exhibit of Fruit, Grain, Vegetables, etc., at Exhibitions ($6,219.08)

Services, $419.50; Expenses, $484.57.

M. Blackburn, services, 135.00; expenses, 127.05; N. C. Engelter, expenses, 7.50; C. J. Gale, expenses, 7.75; W. L. Hamilton, services, 91.00; expenses, 72.80; G. R. Paterson, expenses, 126.24; A. P. Walker, expenses, 13.45; H. N. Webster, services, 193.50; expenses, 129.78 .... 904 07

Miscellaneous, $5,315.01.

Aikenhead Hardware, Ltd., painting, spraying unit, 120.00; C. E. Broughton, fruit and vegetables, 70.10; Canada Packers, Ltd., eggs, 16.90; Canadian Flood Lighting Co., Ltd., show case unit, 30.00; J. T. Cassin, vegetables, 44.93; G. DeGalantha, exhibits, 483.00; DeVita Studios, construction of exhibits at Royal Winter Fair, 2,189.00; Dick's Flowers, ferns, 16.50; T. Eaton Co., Ltd., rent of furniture, 255.42; Frigidaire Sales Corporation, rent of machines, 130.35; W. L. Hamilton, apples, 100.00; A. W. B. Hewitt, signs, 13.80; King's Printer, printing, 130.00; London Public Utilities, light, 30.19; Miller & Sons, rental of ferns, 50.00; Ontario Agricultural College, cheese, 17.22; Pringle & Booth, Ltd., photos, 15.00; Province of Ontario Pictures, photos, 100.00; Rapid-Grip & Batten, Ltd., enlargements, 24.70; H. C. Reed & Sons, rental of ferns, 31.00; Royal Agricultural Winter Fair, electric light and repairs of exhibit, 122.30; Ruddy Manufacturing Co., Ltd., rental of counter, etc., 67.31; Sheet Metal Service, supplies, 52.01; G. Sheppard Printing Co., cards, 27.91; Sheridan Nurseries, cedars, 37.50; Slichter's, Ltd., flowers, 14.00; W. W. Stillworthy, signs, 366.25; Swift-Canadian Co., Ltd., meat, etc., 23.46; Terry Bros., apples, 15.00; Thompson-Kline Studios, construction of booth at Canadian National Exhibition, etc., 524.00; Treasurer, Canadian National Exhibition, paint, etc., 30.16; United Farmers Co-operative Co., Ltd., vegetables, 13.45; Universal Refrigeration, Ltd., installing equipment, 50.00. Sundries—cartage, 53.50; express, 10.52; petty disbursements, 39.53.. 5,315 01

Removal Expenses of Officers of the Department ($196.34)

R. H. Clements, Arthur to Essex, 95.65; L. H. Hanlon, Kapuskasing to Hearst, 11.19; Hearst to Kapuskasing, 14.50; S. B. Stothers, Essex to Arthur, 75.00.... 196 34

Fees of Officers of the Department ($1.18)

Association of Marketing Officials, fee.. 1 18

Provincial Zoologist, Services, Equipment and Expenses ($9,069.10)

Lionel Stevenson............Provincial Zoologist...................12 months 3,800 00

Services, $1,835.20; Expenses, $1,218.60.

V. R. Brown, services, 1,800.00; expenses, 585.19; Lionel Stevenson, expenses, 633.41; W. D. Tolton, services, 35.20.................................... 3,053 80

Miscellaneous, $2,215.30.

T. R. Barber, signs, 154.10; Bogardus & Barton, drugs, films, etc., 87.24; Bond Hardware Co., Ltd., hardware, 133.74; G. L. Brown, storage, 25.00; Canadian Co-operative Wool Growers, Ltd., fly powder, 65.40; Canadian National Exhibition, wiring exhibit, 356.06; Central Scientific Co., Ltd., gears, etc., 40.03; Chapple's, Ltd., blinds, 26.23; H. D. Davidson, laboratory supplies, 62.55; Dick's Flowers, rental of palms, 11.00; Du-Art Film Laboratories, Inc., film, 25.88; O. F. Evans & Sons, houses, 76.95; Gibson Manufacturing Co., motor, etc., 20.00; L. Godson, insurance premium, 34.83; Guelph Tent & Awning Co., tents, 100.00; King's Printer, 235.39; H. Little, gas, etc., 18.83; Marshall's Drug Store, drugs, 28.01; J. H. Parker & Son, banners, etc., 39.00; Province of Ontario Pictures, lantern slides, etc., 209.15; Robson Motor Corporation, car repairs, 117.92; Royal Agricultural Winter Fair, electric work, 16.14; R. Stewart, Ltd., lumber, 158.83; W. W. Stillworthy, decorating exhibit, 75.00; J. J. Turner & Sons, Ltd., rental of tent, 25.00; Western Greenhouse, rental of palms, 16.00. Sundries—postage, 3.00; petty disbursements, 54.02.................................. 2,215 30

Administration and Enforcement of The Corn Borer Act
Half Cost of Inspections ($9,834.14)

Treasurer, City of

Guelph, 30.00; St. Catharines, 27.24...................................... 57 24

General—Continued

Administration and Enforcement of the Cornborer Act, etc.—Continued

Treasurer, County of

Brant, 316.50; Durham & Northumberland, 611.66; Elgin, 468.25; Essex, 1,259.37; Haldimand, 225.63; Halton, 188.82; Hastings, 478.84; Huron, 292.00; Kent, 978.52; Lambton, 548.88; Lennox and Addington, 63.00; Lincoln, 448.10; Middlesex, 418.50; Norfolk, 290.81; Ontario, 198.50; Oxford, 251.25; Peel, 79.50; Perth, 54.00; Prince Edward, 765.82; Waterloo, 168.62; Welland, 557.23; Wellington, 145.25; Wentworth, 460.38; York, 439.50...................... 9,708 93

Treasurer, Township of

Pelee Island.. 67 97

Incidentals ($37,789.89)

Salaries ($1,000.00)

L. H. Hanlan................Fieldman........................... 4 months 1,000 00

Temporary Services, $1,500.00.

J. F. B. Belford.........Extension Worker.....................12 months 1,500 00

Services, $4,811.18; Expenses, $4,907.51.

J. F. B. Belford, expenses, 282.06; H. Binkley, services, 99.00; expenses, 45.00; M. Blackburn, services, 135.00; expenses, 124.93; W. E. Breckon, services, 16.00; expenses, 25.80; J. W. Casselman, services, 66.50; expenses, 66.50; E. N. Clarke, expenses, 59.04; G. H. Dennis, services, 55.00; expenses, 119.83; J. B. Dingwall, services, 440.38; expenses, 608.60; G. Duck, services, 6.00; expenses, 18.55; G. H. Duncan, services, 72.00; expenses, 86.40; J. B. Fairburn, expenses, 8.65; J. P. Griffin, expenses, 114.11; L. H. Hanlan, expenses, 516.85; J. J. Jamieson, services, 16.00; expenses, 25.00; E. W. Kendall, services, 43.50; expenses, 91.88; F. W. Lee, expenses, 36.50; F. R. Mallory, services, 365.00; expenses, 363.64; J. Maxwell, services, 161.00; R. N. F. McFarlane, services, 50.00; V. S. Milburn, expenses, 42.83; C. A. Neil, services, 49.30; expenses, 83.28; W. G. Nixon, expenses, 167.04; J. K. Perritt, services, 2,089.50; expenses, 1,314.29; J. N. Pringle, services, 198.00; expenses, 95.22; R. J. Qua, services, 95.00; expenses, 138.88; E. J. Quail, services, 171.00; expenses, 63.43; J. B. Reynolds, expenses, 82.27; F. K. B. Stewart, services, 176.00; expenses, 112.00; C. B. Stock, expenses, 52.71; J. G. Waite, services, 121.00; expenses, 55.65; C. A. Webster, services, 246.00; expenses, 82.71; E. Weese, services, 140.00; expenses, 23.86.... 9,718 69

Miscellaneous, $25,571.20.

Associated Advertising Councillors, advertising service, 4,335.47; S. Ballantyne, rental of farm, 500.00; L. Burford, lettering titles re onion growing film, 13.50; Canadian Countryman Publishing Co., advertising, 50.00; Canadian Horticulturist, advertising, 50.00; Canadian Seed Growers Association, advertising, 30.00; Canadian Society of Technical Agriculturists, advertising and reprints, 339.70; Canadian Wirebound Boxes, Ltd., crates, 18.00; A. B. Clark, writing articles, 20.00; Clarkson, Gordon, Dilworth, Guilfoyle & Nash, services, financial report on First Co-operative Packers, Ltd., 814.65; Miss V. Engelbert, scholarship for research work, O.A.C., 1,200.00; Farm & Dairy, advertising, 50.40; Farmers' Advocate, advertising, 50.00; D. Gestetner, Ltd., stencils, etc., 24.75; Grey Coach Lines, hire of bus, 32.00; King's Printer, 11,708.86; E. Longstaffe, catering, 173.90; A. MacPherson, services of pipe band, C.N.E., 17.00; Mail and Empire, advertising, 128.80; Montreal Star Co., Ltd., advertising, 38.25; Municipal Intelligence Bureau, advertising, 50.00; National Council Women of Canada, advertising, 100.00; Ontario Agricultural Council, grant, 500.00; Ontario Farmer, advertising, 50.00; Ontario Milk Producers Association, advertising, 50.00; Ontario Veterinary College, horses, 200.00; B. M. Pearce, advertising, 897.00; Rapid-Grip & Batten, Ltd., zinc etching, 70.33; Rural Publishing Co., Ltd., advertising, 75.00; Smart & Biggar, services, re application for patent in Great Britain, 317.00; Strathcona Orchards, apples, 30.55; Sundry persons, prizes for women's and children's competitions, 659.20; The Secretary, Governor-General's Body Guard, band service, 70.00; The Secretary, 48th Highlanders' Band, band service, 70.00; Trans-Canada Broadcasting Co., broadcasting, 2,200.06. Sundries—express, 203.91; freight, 424.53; petty disbursements, 8.34.......................... 25,571 20

Miscellaneous.......................................$63,109 73

STATUTORY

Minister's Salary (see page S 12) 10,000 00

Statutory $10,000 00

SPECIAL WARRANTS

Co-operative Marketing Loans Re Cold Storage Plants. 22 Geo. V. Chapter 16, Section 4, S.S. (b)

Prince Edward County Fruit Growers, Ltd 30,000 00

Trenton Cold Storage, Ltd 50,000 00

Georgian Bay Fruit Growers, Ltd 20,000 00

Middlesex Growers' Co-operative, Ltd 26,000 00

Grant to Canadian Lakehead Exhibition for Special Expenses in Connection with Agricultural Short Courses for Young Men and Women in the District ($1,200.00)

Canadian Lakehead Exhibition 1,200 00

Grant to the Canadian Council on Boys and Girls Club Work ($1,750.00)

Canadian Council on Boys' and Girls' Club Work 1,750 00

Investigation of the Production and Marketing of Ontario Milk and Milk Products ($6,889.61)

G. Bain, travelling expenses, 11.20; W. E. Brennan, travelling expenses, 12.15; F. Perkins, travelling expenses, 49.41; W. B. Somerset, honorarium, 6,800.00; J. N. Truelove, travelling expenses, 16.85 .... 6,889 61

Ontario Honey Export Association to Defray Expenses of Representative on the British Market ($3,000.00)

Ontario Honey Export Association 3,000 00

To Pay Rent to Trenton Cold Storage, Ltd., Rent to October 1st, 1933 ($5,000.00)

Trenton Cold Storage, Ltd 5,000 00

To Pay Accounts Incurred by The Ontario Research Foundation re Investigation and Research with Regard to Bovine Infectious Abortion ($11,148.25)

Ontario Research Foundation, cost of investigation 11,148 25

To Pay The Bank of Nova Scotia re Indebtedness by Cochrane Co-operative Creamery ($3,327.82)

Bank of Nova Scotia 3,327 82

Grant to Chatham Board of Trade for Investigation in Connection with the Soya Bean Industry ($1,500.00)

Treasurer Chatham Board of Trade 1,500 00

Special Warrants $159,815 68

Total $2,173,245 66

Less Salary Assessment 24,827 16

Total Expenditure, Department of Agriculture $2,148,418 50

PART T

MISCELLANEOUS

FISCAL YEAR, 1931-32

TABLE OF CONTENTS

GENERAL INDEX AT BACK OF BOOK

PART T—GENERAL MISCELLANEOUS

Statement of Expenditure Showing Amounts Expended, Unexpended and Overexpended for the Twelve Months Ended October 31st, 1932

General Miscellaneous	Page	Estimates	Expended			Un-expended	Over-expended	Treasury Board Minute
			Ordinary	Capital	Total Ordinary and Capital			
		$ c.	$ c.	$ c.	$ c.	$ c.	$ c.	$ c.
Annuities and Bonuses to Indians	4	30,000 00	19,336 00	....	19,336 00	10,664 00	....	....
[illegible]	4	2,000 00	1,017 33	....	1,017 33	982 67	....	....
Unforeseen and Unprovided	4	10,000 00	6,421 91	....	6,421 91	3,578 09	....	....
Monument to Members C.E.F.	4	50,000 00	....	....	....	50,000 00	....	....
Compensation to Injured Workmen	4	125,000 00	57,428 41	45,114 50	102,542 81	22,457 19	....	23,387 89
Refunds Surplus Registry Office Fees	4	90,000 00	5,028 64	37,672 58	42,701 22	47,298 78	....	....
Wolf Bounty	4	75,345 00	69,046 24	....	69,046 24	6,298 76	....	....
Salary Increases	4	5,931 25	....	....	....	5,931 25	....	....
Fidelity Bonds	4	15,000 00	12,397 95	....	12,397 95	2,602 05	....	....
Grant to Canadian Institute for the Blind	5	60,000 00	60,000 00	....	60,000 00	....	....	....
" Ontario Safety League	5	10,000 00	10,000 00	....	10,000 00	....	....	....
Refunds	5	100,000 00	4,872 84	28,404 26	33,277 10	66,722 90	....	....
Supply Bill	..	573,276 25	245,549 22	111,191 34	356,740 56	216,535 69	....	....
Statutory:								
Administration of Workmen's Compensation Act	7	....	11,929 67	....	11,929 67	....	....	....
Special Warrants:								
Ontario Research Foundation, 19 Geo. V, Chap. 86, Sec. 4	7	....	301,120 00	....	301,120 00	....	....	....
Ontario Research Foundation, to cover cost of alterations and equipment of [illegible] and offices at 43, 47 Queen's Park	7	....	....	36,960 43	36,960 43	....	....	....
Grants:								
Labour Educational Association of Ontario	7	....	100 00	....	100 00	....	....	....
Technical Service Council	7	....	3,500 00	....	3,500 00	....	....	....
Navy League of Canada	7	....	1,000 00	....	1,000 00	....	....	....
Des Medicins de Langue Francaise, Ottawa	7	....	1,000 00	....	1,000 00	....	....	....
Civil Service Association re Red Cross	7	....	531 00	....	531 00	....	....	....
Canadian Red Cross Society, Ontario	7	....	22,180 00	....	22,180 00	....	....	....

Last Post Fund	7	....	2,000 00	....	2,000 00	....	....	....
Canadian Medical Association	7	....	500 00	....	500 00	....	....	....
Special Warrants	..	....	331,931 00	36,960 43	368,891 43	....	....	....
Total Miscellaneous	..	....	589,409 89	148,151 77	737,561 66	....	....	....

SUMMARY

General Miscellaneous	Page	Ordinary	Capital	Total
		$ c.	$ c.	$ c.
General Miscellaneous	4	245,549 22	111,191 34	356,740 56
Statutory	7	11,929 67	....	11,929 67
Special Warrants	7	331,931 00	36,960 43	368 891 43
	..	589,409 89	148,151 77	737,561 66
Deduct:				
Repayments on account of Special Funds (see part "U")	..	....	64,708 62	64,708 62
Total, General Miscellaneous	..	589,409 89	83,443 15	6[illegible]853 04

GENERAL MISCELLANEOUS

Annuities and Bonuses to Indians under Treaty No. 9 ($19,336.00)

Minister of Finance, Ottawa.. 19,336 00

Gratuities ($1,017.33)

Dr. W. M. English, retired Superintendent, Ontario Hospital, Brockville, 333.33; Estate of Mrs. Mabel M. Kell, former clerk in the Land Titles Office, Toronto, 534.00; Estate of A. R. Walker, former usher, Osgoode Hall, 150.00............ 1,017 33

Unforeseen and Unprovided ($6,421.91)

Expenses re Elevator Accident to Helen A. Boyd, Department of Education, $2,464.45.

Helen A. Boyd, allowance during convalescence, 240.00; W. R. Boyd, blood transfusion, 25.00; Dr. J. A. MacFarlane, professional services, 500.00; Laura L. Rowan, professional nursing services, 72.00; Dr. N. S. Shenstone, professional services, 75.00; Trustees, Toronto General Hospital, maintenance and services, 1,552.45.. 2,464 45

Miscellaneous, $3,957.46.

Arcade Florist, spray and flowers, 55.00; Bates & Dodds, Ltd., auto service re funeral of H. J. Tutt, Dept. of Labour, 10.00; John Brown, expenses re Arthur Bosquette and William Miller, Children's Aid, 68.70; Canadian Legion of British Empire Service League, poppy wreath, 15.00; Canadian Military Institute, grant, 600.00; Canadian National Railways, fares of indigents, 31.50; Canadian Westinghouse Co., Ltd., radio receiving set, Prime Minister's Offiee, 38.00; Clerk of the County Court, Essex, money paid H. Clay, deceased, not deposited in bank, 99.22; Dale Estate, Ltd., basket of flowers to Senator E. D. Smith, 11.05; Department of Provincial Highways, auto service for funeral, 5.38; Arthur E. Everest, funeral expenses re J. Merrifield and C. J. Mahoney, fire fighters accidently drowned in Onion Lake, District of Thunder Bay, 250.00; Gray Coach Lines, Canadian School of Missions, trip to Guelph, 112.00; R. V. V. Green, expenses re burial and shipping of bodies of officers killed in aircraft accident on Rainy Lake, 1,209.50; Samuel Hearst; hospital and doctor's bills for Betty Hearst, injured by Government truck, 264.25; A. Jackman, wreath, 5.00; C. Lecoca, wreath, 21.75; W. J. McLean, burial expenses, indigent, 30.00; F. J. Martyn & Son, ambulance service, 13.00; Miller & Sons, wreaths, 95.95; Misericordia Hospital, burial expenses, indigent, 30.00; S. Mustan, wreaths, 90.00; Ottawa General Hospital, railway fare home of indigent patient, 10.00; Parry Sound West, C. A. C., maintenance of Ellen Watts, 135.00; D. F. Quick, wreath, 15.00; Sundry disbursements, laying corner stone at Girls' Training School, Galt, 61.85; J. B. Tiefenbacher, burial expenses, indigents, 90.00; Toronto Orthopedic Hospital, railway fare home, indigent patient, 4.30; Veterans' Re-union Council, grant, Warrior's Day, C.N.E., 500.00; Mrs. C. G. Whitehurst, travelling expenses re Mrs. Hulton, 66.01; Estate of E. C. Wilkins, wreaths, 20.00................ 3,957 46

Compensation, Medical, Hospital and Other Accounts for Workmen Injured in Government Work, as Awarded by the Workmen's Compensation Board ($102,542.81)

Department of Agriculture, 466.25; Department of the Attorney-General, 2,119.72; Department of Education, 150.00; Department of Game and Fisheries, 961.93; Department of Lands and Forests, 1,406.50; Forestry Branch, 11,200.12; Department of Northern Development, 73,168.21; Colonization Roads Branch, 2,022.62; Department of Mines, 75.90; Department of the Provincial Secretary, 2,494.72; Department of Public Health, 378.86; Department of Public Works, 8,097.98... 102,542 81

Refunds of Surplus Registry Office and Land Titles Office Fees ($42,701.22)

City of St. Thomas, 146.80; City of Toronto, 16,696.68; County of Elgin, 808.11; County of Ontario, 100.40; County of York, 24,949.23........................ 42,701 22

Wolf Bounty ($69,046.24)

Sundry persons, 68,816.35; King's Printer, 165.06. Sundries—express, 64.83....... 69,046 24

Fidelity Bonds ($12,397.95)

Dominion of Canada General Insurance Co., 12,387.95; United States Fidelity and Guaranty Co., 10.00.. 12,397 95

General Miscellaneous—Continued

Grants ($70,000.00)

Canadian National Institute for the Blind		60,000 00
Ontario Safety League		10,000 00

Refunds ($33,277.10)

Prime Minister's Department:		
Sundry persons—Gazette advertising	39 70	
Contribution	10 75	
	50 45	
Deducted from Revenue	50 45	
Legislation:		
Sundry persons—Insurance Acts	1 00	
Overpaid for Statutes	22 20	
Private Bills, fees	1,558 25	
Publications	2 50	
	1,583 95	
Deducted from Revenue	1,583 95	
Attorney-General's Department:		
Sundry persons—Deductions for clothing	853 00	
Police Court fines	178 95	
Overpaid registrations	51 00	
Renewal fees	2,797 00	
Held in trust, re Insurance Investments, Ltd	25,000 00	
Overpayments, Legal Offices	309 21	
	29,189 16	
Deducted from Revenue	29,189 16	
Insurance Department:		
Sundry persons—License fees	1,568 00	
Deducted from Revenue	1,568 00	
Education Department:		
Sundry persons—Examination appeal fees	2,263 90	
Money sent in error	459 20	
Northern Academy fees,	30 00	
	2,753 10	
Deducted from Revenue	2,753 10	
Department of Lands and Forests:		
Sundry persons—Purchase of lots and rentals	3,650 78	
Timber dues and rights	5,182 44	
Land Improvement Fund	1,854 29	
Taxes, unpatented lands	115 75	
Sundries	128 00	
	10,931 26	
Deducted from Revenue	8,082 10	
		2,849 16
Department of Mines:		
Sundry persons—Mining claims and patents	720 00	
Miners' licenses	208 00	
Licenses to remove sand and gravel	100 00	
Recording fees	108 00	
Taxes and rentals	644 72	
Sundries	17 93	
	1,798 65	
Deducted from Revenue	1,798 65	

General Miscellaneous—Continued

Refunds—Continued

Game and Fisheries Department:		
Sundry persons—Licenses	6,184 98	
Fines	711 45	
Royalties	902 00	
Money sent in error	35 56	
Money not required	610 00	
Sale of mink pelt	10 80	
	8,454 79	
Deducted from Revenue	8,454 79	
Public Works Department:		
Sundry persons—Deposits re tenders	787 12	
Sundries	18 61	
	805 73	
Deducted from Revenue	805 73	
Department of Public Highways:		
Sundry persons—Gasoline Tax	921,576 20	
Licenses	2,181 50	
Fines	40 25	
Rental of cars and garage services	28,783 69	
	952,581 64	
Deducted from Revenue	952,581 64	
Health Department:		
Sundry persons—Nurses' registration fees	11 00	
Dental work	48 50	
Sundries	19 50	
	79 00	
Deducted from Revenue	79 00	
Labour Department:		
Sundry persons—Fees	279 00	
Fines	100 00	
	379 00	
Deducted from Revenue	379 00	
Public Welfare Department:		
Bursar, Boys' Training School, Bowmanville—Perquisites deducted from salary	31 75	
Deducted from Revenue	31 75	
Provincial Treasurer's Department.		
Sundry persons—Amusement Tax	9,687 83	
Stock Transfer Tax	335 91	
Law Stamps	76 10	
Corporations Tax	51,192 35	
Land Transfer Tax	160 45	
Luxury Tax	3,391 90	
Theatre and Show Licenses	669 39	
Operators' Licenses	50 00	
Censor Board, fees	250 50	
Sundries, Motion Picture Bureau	49 25	
Treasurer of Ontario—Reserve for farm loans	27,036 04	
United States exchange	93 82	
Overpayment on purchase of Bonds and Treasury Bills	1,084 97	
Department of Public Highways—Outstanding cheques	1,532 50	
Railway Tax—Distribution	110 95	
Sundries	606 80	
	96,328 76	
Deducted from Revenue	65,900 82	
		30,427 94

General Miscellaneous—Continued

Refunds—Continued

Provincial Secretary's Department:

Sundry persons—Company returns	2,852 00	
Brokers' registration	447 75	
Registrar-General, fees	2,612 25	
Marriage licenses	52 00	
Sundries	170 88	
Collector of Customs, Excise Tax	416 97	
	6,551 85	
Deducted from Revenue	6,551 85	

Agriculture Department:

Sundry persons—Stallion Enrolment fee	2 00	
Sundries	5 00	
Agricultural and Horticultural Societies Branch—subventions	1,211 26	
Department of Immigration and Colonization—Assisted passage	77 70	
Return passage	121 65	
Kemptville Agricultural School—Board	158 00	
Ontario Agricultural College—Board and Tuition Fees	927 92	
Interest, Students' deposits	461 30	
	2,964 83	
Deducted from Revenue	2,964 83	

General Miscellaneous $356,740.56

STATUTORY

Workmen's Compensation Act, Part I, Administration, R.S.O. 1927, Chap. 179, Sec. 77 ($11,929.67)

Workmen's Compensation Board, assistance in defraying expenses	11,929 67

Statutory $11,929.67

SPECIAL WARRANTS

Ontario Research Foundation, 19 Geo. V. Chap. 86, Sec. 4 ($301,120.00)

Ontario Research Foundation	301,120 00

Ontario Research Foundation, Repairs and Alterations to Laboratories and Offices at 43, 47 Queen's Park ($36,960.43)

Ontario Research Foundation	36,960 43

Grants ($30,811.00)

Labour Educational Association of Ontario	100 00
Technical Service Council	3,500 00
Navy League of Canada	1,000 00
Association des Medecins de Langue Francaise de l'Amerique du Nord	1,000 00
Civil Service Association re Red Cross Campaign	531 00
Canadian Red Cross Society	22,180 00
Last Post Fund	2,000 00
Canadian Medical Association, re expenses of Annual Meeting	500 00

Special Warrants $368,891.43

Total, General Miscellaneous $737,561.66

GOVERNMENT STATIONERY ACCOUNT

Contract Printing and Binding:

Noble Scott, Ltd.—Official Gazette, 4,342.00; Legislative printing, 14,914.83	19,256 83

Stock Paper:

Alliance Paper Mills, Ltd., 956.40; Buntin-Reid Co., Ltd., 1,062.31; F. W. Halls Paper Co., Ltd., 1,184.86; Howard Smith Paper Mills, Ltd., 9,001.18	12,204 75

Government Stationery Account—Continued

Stock and Printing Purchases:

Acton Publishing Co., Ltd., 8,630.13; Addressograph-Multigraph, Ltd., 2,586.13; Ailsa Craig Banner, 81.90; Alexander & Cable, 316.89; Alger Press, Ltd., 9.80; Alliance Paper Mills, Ltd., 1,009.74; Alliston Herald, 6.80; Almonte Gazette, 107.20; Angus Mack Co., 5.85; W. H. Apted, 195.95; Arcadian Press, 19.50; Arnprior Chronicle, 97.47; Arthurs Jones, Printers, 387.65; Artistic Stationery Co., Ltd., 1,327.19; Art Metropole, 1,972.90; Artists' Supply Co., 28.80; Associated Printers, Ltd., 6,004.14; Ault & Wiborg, Co. Ltd., 91.90; Autographic Register System, Ltd., 265.79; Aylmer Express, 755.42; J. and A. Aziz, 147.88; Bain & Cubitt, Ltd., 2,678.28; D. A. Balfour Co., 1,156.55; Banner Press, 48.65; Barber-Ellis, Ltd., 25,586.91; F. W. Barrett Co., Ltd., 456.25; Beares, Ltd., 1,901.33; J. W. Benson, 143.05; W. Bethune Co., .50; B. H. Press, 28.70; H. Birks & Son, 25.00; Blackhall & Co., 5,649.24; Blue Bird Ink Co., Ltd., 25.60; Bolander and Selby, 434.45; Bomac Electrotype Co., Ltd., 70.00; Booth Bros., 369.36; Bourne and Ironside, 290.40; R. Bourne, 91.25; Brantford Stationers, Ltd., 146.19; Brigden's, Ltd., 2,060.86; Broadview Press, 1,143.95; Brown Bros., Ltd., 9,760.31; B. H. & F. M. Brown, Ltd., 1,387.23; Brown Press, 40.00; Bryant Press, Ltd., 1,474.30; Buntin, Gillies Co., Ltd., 2,607.06; Buntin-Reid Co., Ltd., 20,512.70; Burnell Binding & Printing Co., 635.25; Burroughs Adding Machine Co., Ltd., 3,215.17; Bushnell Showcard Studios, 205.10; Burt Business Forms, Ltd., 177.07; Business Systems, Ltd., 975.18; Bernard Cairns, Ltd., 2,286.30; Calvert & Maynard Press, 50.60; Canadian Bonded Attorney and Legal Directory, Ltd., 15.00; Canadian Carbon & Ribbon Co., Ltd., 680.55; Canada Decalcomania Co., Ltd., 525.87; Canadian Engravers, Ltd., 22.86; Canadian Facts Publishing Co., 12.60; Canadian Gazeteer Publishing Co., 25.00; Canadian Law List Publishing Co., 259.00; Canadian Lithographing Co., 1,340.85; Canada Paper Wholesale, Ltd., 192.17; Canadian Parliamentary Guide, 469.75; Canadian Photo Copy Co., 9.55; Canadian Printing Co., Ltd., 145.39; Canadian Review Co., Ltd., 912.00; Canadian Statesman, 112.25; Canadian Supply Sales Co., 57.50; Carleton Place Canadian, 33.55; J. Carleton Co., 362.25; Hugh Carson Co., Ltd., 375.39; Carswell Co., Ltd., 3,134.41; Cassidy's, Ltd., 14.40; Carter-Thompson, Ltd., 8.00; Catholic Record, 54.98; John Catto Co., Ltd., 7.25; Central Scientific Co., Ltd., 37.81; Century Press, 781.05; C. Chapman Co., Ltd., 820.34; Charters Publishing Co., 1,601.05; Chatterson, Clifford, Ltd., 2,112.34; Circuit Guide Publishing Co., 54.50; F. F. Clarke & Co., 748.21; Cliffe Printing Co., 96.43; Cochrane Northland Post, Ltd., 183.19; Collett-Sproule, Ltd., 260.48; Comber Herald, 8.75; Commercial Press, 475.00; Commercial Printing Co., 85.61; Consolidated Sales Book Co., Ltd., 90.00; J. A. Cook & Son, Ltd., 1,701.56; W. A. Coon & Co., 139.68; Copeland-Chatterson Co., Ltd., 562.15; Co-operative Supply Department, Ontario Agricultural College, Guelph, 13.50; Copp, Clarke, Ltd., 3,743.42; Corrugated Paper Box Co., Ltd., 196.10; H. S. Crabtree Co., 694.90; Crain Printers, Ltd., 160.96; R. D. Croft, Ltd., 298.00; A. G. Cumming, Ltd., 6.00; Curran Bros., 285.60; Cutting, Ltd., 13.00; Davis & Henderson, 930.13; Day Sign Co., Ltd., 4.25; H. Degruchy Co., Ltd., 29.00; J. M. Dent & Sons, Ltd., 1.60; Dennison Manufacturing Co., Ltd., 49.26; Derrett, Ltd., 183.02; Deseronto Post, 85.75; W. Dickinson Co., 70.10; Dictaphone Sales Corporation, 95.20; Dominion Charts Publishing Co., 36.00; Dominion Envelope & Carton Co., Ltd., 1,367.08; Dominion Loose Leaf Co., 51.61; Dominion Paper Box Co., Ltd., 15.00; Dominion Printing Co., 1,088.90; Dominion Rubber Co., Ltd., 8.88; Donovan, Ltd., 65.45; Douglas Bros., 383.20; J. Doust, 563.03; T. Drinkwater & Co., 244.20; R. Duncan & Co., Ltd., 462.92; Durham Chronicle Printing House, 488.35; Dye & Durham, 18.75; Eastern Ontario Review, 15.62; Eastman Kodak Stores, Ltd., 57.23; T. Eaton Co., Ltd., 257.99; Ediphone Co., Ltd., 4.74; E. B. Eddy Co., Ltd., 89.34; J. E. Edwards & Sons, Ltd., 483.00; Elliott Adressing Machine Co., 6.35; Elliott Fisher Co., Ltd., 39.00; P. W. Ellis Co., Ltd., 28.50; Enterprise Printing Co., 175.05; Envelope Folders, Ltd., 944.30; Epworth Press, 193.88; Espie Printing Co., 1,979.55; G. Everall Co., Ltd., 152.67; Everatt & Malcolm, Ltd., 295.62; Excelsior Brushes, Ltd., 6.70; Express Herald, Newmarket, 117.03; Express Traffic Association of Canada, 2.00; Fairbanks-Morse Co., Ltd., 12.50; Fairbanks Printing Co., 429.68; Field, Love & House, 99.27; Forest Standard Printing & Publishing Co., Ltd., 27.00; J. H. French & Co., 410.47; Frontier Printing Co., 45.59; W. J. Gage Co., Ltd., 3,556.20; Galt Press, 25.36; Gardner Press, 96.75; Georgetown Herald, 15.55; D. Gestetner Co., Ltd., 7,519.45; Gibbard Furniture Shops, Ltd., 6.00; Goldie & McCulloch Co., Ltd., 336.00; Good Printing Co., 446.65; Gordon Mackay Co., Ltd., 91.12; Grand & Toy, Ltd., 11,104.78; Griffin & Richmond Co., Ltd., 145.05; Gummer Press, Ltd., 2,479.12; F. W. Halls Paper Co., Ltd., 36,601.09; Hambly Bros., Ltd., 13,221.08; Hanson & Edgar, Ltd., 90.95; Harcourt & Son, Ltd., 56.00; W. J. Hargrave, 39.15; Wm. Harper, Ltd., 2.25; S. R. Hart & Co., Ltd., 5,021.52; J. F. Hartz Co., Ltd., 294.52; Heaton Publishing Co., 5.00; Henderson Bros., Ltd., 14,185.34;

Government Stationery Account—Continued

Stock and Printing Purchases—Continued

G. M. Hendry Co., Ltd., 1,654.89; Hollin's Press, 24.70; Holman Leather Goods Co., 180.05; Holman Luggage, Ltd., 5.75; Hood, Rankin, Ltd., 195.30; Hunter Printing Co., 45.42; Hunter Rose Co., Ltd., 140.25; Huntsville Forester, 47.60; Hurley Printing Co., Ltd., 355.15; A. S. Hustwitt, 158.15; Imperial Engraving Co., 5.76; Imperial Trunk & Leather Goods Co., 319.90; Ingram & Bell, Ltd., 1.80; Inland Printing House, Ltd., 206.75; Instruments, Ltd., 1,071.10; Interlake Tissue Mills, Ltd., 40.00; International Business Machines Co., 30.00; Jackson Press, 446.55; Jarrett Printing Co., 183.40; W. S. Johnston Co., Ltd., 1,190.25; Julian Sale Leather Goods Co., Ltd., 332.62; Kelso Printing Co., 121.50; Kilgours, Ltd., 667.48; J. J. Knight Co., 3.75; Lawson & Jones, Ltd., 12.87; Lawson & Wilson, Ltd., 164.30; Leader Publishing Co., Ltd., 123.42; Legge Bros., 1,136.60; Litho Print, Ltd., 13,888.05; C. E. Locke, Ltd., 1,275.71; London Luggage Shop, 418.34; R. J. Lovell Co., Ltd., 11.70; Lowe-Martin Co., Ltd., 5,735.59; Lumley & Hewitt, 356.30; Lytle & Lytle, 2,411.79; Machan Sealing Wax Co., 220.00; Macoomb Press, 8,248.15; Mackinnon Sales, 11.00; L. McBrine Co., Ltd., 1,068.09; McCallum Press, Ltd., 1,063.75; McCann & Alexander, 412.94; J. M. McCrae & Son, 2.85; R. G. McLean, Ltd., 674.00; Menzies Co., Ltd., 1,547.00; Mercantile Press, 177.50; Merchants Press, 23.25; Merchants Printing Co., 4.50; The Mercury-Sun, 9.50; Meredith & Simmons Co., Ltd., 1.30; Midland Argus, 45.05; Might Directories, Ltd., 1,012.11; Miln-Bingham Printing Co., 477.71; Miner Publishing Co., 87.45; Mitchell & McGill, 3,160.71; Monetary Times Printing Co., 1,029.82; J. L. Morrison Co., 4.50; Moyer Printing Co., 352.25; Multigraph Sales Agency, 78.98; Munson Supply Co., 44.00; Murdoch Stationery Co., 742.02; Muskoka Publishing Co., 20.15; Musson Book Co., Ltd., 242.82; National Cash Register Co., Ltd., 47.26; National Stationers, Ltd., 19,156.28; National Drug & Chemical Co., Ltd., 79.97; Newsome & Gilbert, 103.55; North Bay Nugget, 196.47; Northern Miner Press, Ltd., 1,325.94; Norwich Gazette, 11.50; F. Nunan Bookbinder, 125.50; Oakwood Printing House, 486.05; Office Specialty Manufacturing Co., Ltd., 5,040.88; Office Sales Co., 41.50; Office Supplies, Ltd., 16.00; Ontario Citator, 17.00; Ontario Intelligencer, Belleville, 298.00; Ontario Press, Ltd., 453.30; Ontario Engraving Co., Ltd., 154.98; Ontario Safety League, 185.00; Parkdale Press, 82.45; Pembroke Standard Observer, 835.71; Perth Expositor, 154.00; Peterborough Review Co., 111.80; L. A. Philips & Co., 30.00; W. E. Phillips Co., Ltd., 3.14; Phoenic Sales Co., 6.00; Photo Engavers, Ltd., 885.74; Picton Gazette Publishing Co., Ltd., 607.27; Sir Isaac Pitman & Sons, Ltd., 28.66; Planet, Chatham, 63.83; T. Pocklington Co., 909.55; J. E. Poole, 30.69; Porcupine Advance, 119.08; Port Arthur News Chronicle, 299.00; Preston Progress Printing Co., 450.48; The Print Shop, 19.50; Public Printing & Stationery, Ottawa, 79.00; Publishers, Ltd., 3,012.92; E. Pullan, Ltd., 17.80; B. J. Rae & Son, 232.84; Rapid-Grip & Batten, Ltd., 4,909.46; Ratcliffe & Ovey, 538.91; Ratcliffe Paper Co., Ltd., 384.34; J. F. Raw Co., Ltd., 2,150.19; Robert Raw Co., 137.75; Recorder, Gore Bay, 26.14; A. P. Reed, 30.60; Reed-Canadian Engravers, Ltd., 228.44; Reeves Ink Co., 66.25; Regent Press, 2,406.49; Reid Press, Ltd., 87.00; Reliance Engravers, Ltd., 248.48; Remington Typewriters, Ltd., 1,339.89; Ribbons, Ltd., 65.40; Rice Lewis & Son, Ltd., 772.37; Ritchie Supply Co., 6.65; Robb Press, 109.01; Chas. Roddy Printing, 27.00; Rogers Electric Co., Ltd., 86.18; G. F. Rogers, 2.25; Rolph-Clarke-Stone, Ltd., 1,004.54; Roneo Co. of Canada, Ltd., 1,180.55; Royal City Press, 158.95; Runge Press, Ltd., 134.10; Ryan Printing Co., Ltd., 200.95; Ryerson Press, 1,005.23; A. Saywell, 16.00; Noble Scott, Ltd., 52,556.69; Saturday Night Press, 265.00; Scythes & Co., Ltd., 147.74; Service Press, 491.58; Shaw Schools, Ltd., 3.60; Geo. Shepard Printing Co., 12,003.89; Shepherd Printing Co., 507.95; Simcoe Reformer, 544.83; Robt. Simpson Co., Ltd., 72.50; L. C. Smith & Corona Typewriters, Ltd., 2.00; Southam Press, Ltd., 157.35; Sovereign Press, Ltd., 204.15; H. H. Sparks, 756.30; Stainton & Evis, 2,623.59; Standard Embossing Co., Ltd., 1,363.36; Star Office Specialty Co., Ltd., 178.20; Stephens Sales, Ltd., 3,594.85; Sterling Press, 41.30; W. N. Stock, Ltd., 34.00; Student's Book Department, U. of T., 4.25; Sudbury Star, 325.76; Superior Manufacturing Co., Ltd., 356.20; C. V. Syrett Paper Co., Ltd., 131.89; C. Tarling Map Mounting Co., 1,325.35; Taylor Instrument Co., Ltd., 10.88; Telford & Craddock, 269.90; Templeton & Son, 74.80; E. G. Thomas & Son, 4,608.86; F. S. Thomas & Co., 1,686.60; Thomas & Corney Typewriters, Ltd., 480.27; Thompson Bros., 841.75; Todd Sales Co., 116.14; Toronto Envelope Co., Ltd., 1.89; Torontonian Society Blue Book, 15.00; W. J. Travis, 22.75; Samuel Trees & Co., Ltd., 50.03; Trevelyan Manufacturing Co., 54.15; C. L. Turnbull Co., Ltd., 8,687.78; Tweed News, 159.45; United Paper Mills, Ltd., 7,974.27; United Typewriter Co., Ltd., 10,734.33; University of Toronto Press, 6.95; Uxbridge Times Journal, 8.20; A. VanKoughnet & Co., 1,029.97; Victoria Paper & Twine Co., Ltd., 350.95; Wade & Butcher, Canada,

Government Stationery Account—Continued

Stock and Printing Purchases—Continued

Ltd., 33.15; Walkerville Printing Co., 39.25; Wallace Printing Co., 296.65; Warwick Bros. & Rutter, 895.54; Watchman-Warder, Lindsay, 1,197.30; Waterloo Chronicle, 779.58; Weekly Times, 27.00; Welch & Quest, 1,025.91; Welland Printing Co., 26.40; Wellinger & Dunn, Ltd., 33.00; West Toronto Printing House, Ltd., 282.86; Whyte-Hooke Paper Co., Ltd., 5,429.76; Wilkes Press, 72.00; Wilson-Munroe, Ltd., 8,469.21; Wilson Press, Ltd., 3,093.02; Wilson Publishing Co., 116.50; Wilson Stationery & Printing Co., Ltd., 1,906.27; Winchester Press, 304.25; C. J. B. Wood, Ltd., 190.52; G. H. Wood & Co., Ltd., 19.00; York Publishing Co., Ltd., 955.72 .... 487,911 80

Total			519,373 38
Purchased		519,373 38	
Distributed	511,037 70		
Cash sales	26,153 62		
		537,191 32	
Excess of Distribution over Purchases			17,817 94

PART U

PUBLIC DEBT, LOANS ADVANCED, SPECIAL FUND REPAYMENTS, ETC. FISCAL YEAR 1931-1932

	Page	Amount	Total
PUBLIC DEBT:			
Loans matured and paid (Statutory)	P4	....	$135,675,950 34
LOANS ADVANCED, ETC.:			
Hydro-Electric Power Commission	B5	4,860,320 00	
" " Rural Loans	B5	65,000 00	
Settlers Loan Commission (Statutory)	H3	106,595 00	
Drainage Debentures—Municipal (Statutory)	P3	8,055 50	
" " Tile (Statutory)	P3	99,096 40	
Debenture Guarantee Act (Statutory)	P3	42,168 56	
" " "	F15	2,313 92	
Agricultural Development Finance Act (Statutory)	P4	8,500,000 00	
Farm Loans Act (Statutory)	P4	33,790 00	
Mothers' Allowances—Municipalities	O4	121,165 00	
Old Age Pensions—Dominion Government, Municipalities, and Interprovincial	O4	687,403 17	
Co-operative Marketing Loans	S5-10	130,800 00	14,656,707 55
SPECIAL FUNDS:			
Public Service Superannuation Fund:			
Allowances and Refunds (Statutory)	B5	502,993 28	
Back to Land Movement	G3	2,933 93	
Accountable Warrants—Administration of Justice in Districts	D7	6,209 84	
Reserve for Farm Loans	T2	27,036 04	
Assurance Fund—Land Titles Act (Statutory)	P3	765 15	
Municipal Sinking Funds:			
Deposits repaid (Statutory)	P3	100,462 23	
Surplus Registry Office Fees:			
Refunds	T2	37,672 58	678,073 05
			$151,010,730 94

INDEX

B

H

I

N

O

P

S

U

Supplementary Estimates

of the

Province of Ontario

for the

Fiscal Year

Ending October 31st, 1933

PRINTED BY ORDER OF
THE LEGISLATIVE ASSEMBLY OF ONTARIO
SESSIONAL PAPER No. 2, 1933

TORONTO
Printed and Published by Herbert H. Ball, Printer to the King's Most Excellent Majesty
1933

SUMMARY OF AMOUNTS TO BE VOTED

Vote No.	Departments	Deduction	Addition
1	Lieutenant-Governor	$1,150 00	$1,900 00
2	Legislation	31,200 00	7,080 00
3	Prime Minister	11,608 00	215,711 00
4	Hydro-Electric Power Commission	....	1,225,000 00
5	Attorney-General	215,425 65	3,000 00
6	Insurance	720 00	825 00
7–31	Education	468,874 22	1,883,230 00
32	Lands and Forests	875,210 00	82,650 00
33	Northern Development	395,425 00	....
34	Mines	56,957 73	31,990 50
35	Game and Fisheries	164,200 00	4,375 00
36	Public Works	324,973 74	732,916 36
37	Highways	60,866 52	....
38–39	Health	390,300 00	483,655 00
40	Labour	32,470 00	34,925 00
41	Welfare	66,782 00	36,624 25
42	Provincial Treasurer	52,958 58	32,125 00
43	Provincial Auditor	2,391 00	7,625 00
44–45	Provincial Secretary	205,630 00	15,500 00
46–62	Agriculture	276,316 03	22,055 89
63	Miscellaneous	81,675 00	....
	Total	$3,715,133 47	$4,821,188 00

Supplementary Estimates

For the Fiscal Year ending October 31st, 1933

No. of Vote	No. of Item	Service	Main Estimates Old Vote	Main Estimates Old Item	Reduction	Addition
1		**OFFICE OF THE LIEUTENANT-GOVERNOR**				
	1	Salaries	1	1-5	1,150 00	
	2	Contingencies	1	6		1,900 00
					1,150 00	1,900 00
2		**DEPARTMENT OF LEGISLATION**				
		Office of the Speaker				
	1	Clerks of Committees		7	600 00	
	2	Sessional Writers		8	15,000 00	
	3	Indemnity to Members, including mileage		9	200 00	
	4	Stationery, including printing, etc	8	10		5,000 00
		Office of Law Clerks				
	5	Salaries	8	14-17	6,000 00	2,080 00
		Office of Clerk of the Crown-in-Chancery				
	6	Contingencies	8	20	200 00	
					22,000 00	7,080 00
		Legislative Library				
	7	Salaries	8	21-23	1,750 00	
	8	Purchase of books, subscriptions, fees and dues; binding, rebinding, stationery, printing and contingencies	8	24	7,400 00	
	9	Purchase of legal publications	8	25	50 00	
					9,200 00	
3		**DEPARTMENT OF PRIME MINISTER**				
		Main Office				
	1	Salaries	2	1-5	3,110 00	
	2	Contingencies	2	8		6,146 00
	3	Entertainment	2	6	4,500 00	
	4	General Advertising	New	New		2,500 00
		Grants:				
	5	Last Post Fund	New	New		2,000 00
	6	Navy League of Canada	New	New		800 00
	7	Ontario Research Foundation	New	New		155,000 00
	8	Technical Service Council	New	New		3,000 00
	9	Canadian Red Cross (Ontario Division)	New	New		26,115 00
	10	Canadian Medical Association	New	New		400 00
	11	Veterans' Reunion Council	New	New		500 00
	12	Canadian Military Institute	New	New		500 00
	13	Ontario Safety League	New	New		8,000 00
		Tourist and Publicity Bureau				
	14	To provide for printing and distributing booklets, etc	4	3		10,000 00

No. of Vote	No. of Item	Service	Main Estimates Old Vote	Main Estimates Old Item	Reduction	Addition
3		**DEPARTMENT OF PRIME MINISTER —Continued**				
		Office of Civil Service Commissioner				
	15	Contingencies..........................	5	8	898 00	
		Office of King's Printer				
	16	Salaries..............................	6	1–10		750 00
	17	Contingencies..........................	6	11	2,126 00	
	18	Cartage..............................	6	12	212 00	
	19	Gazette..............................	6	13	762 00	
					11,608 00	215,711 00
4		**HYDRO-ELECTRIC POWER COMMISSION**			Additions,	
	1	*Niagara System*........................	7	1		
		(1) Developments:				
		(a) Chats Falls:				
		Generation and transformation			230,000 00	
		(2) Transformer Stations:				
		(b) 110 K.V. Stations..............			150,000 00	
		(3) Transmission Lines:				
		(a) 220 K.V. Lines................			100,000 00	
		(4) Miscellaneous:				
		(a) Special equipment and services for power sales..................			350,000 00	
						830,000 00
	2	*Georgian Bay System*....................	7	2		
		(3) (b) Rural distribution............			55,000 00	
						55,000 00
	3	*Eastern Ontario System*..................	7	3		
		(3) (b) Rural distribution............			55,000 00	
						55,000 00
	4	*Thunder Bay System*....................	7	4		
		(3) (b) Rural distribution............			20,000 00	
		(4) Special equipment and services for power sales....................			150,000 00	
						170,000 00
	5	*Northern System*........................	7	5		
		(1) Developments....................			100,000 00	
		Rural distribution..................			15,000 00	115,000 00
						1,225,000 00
5		**DEPARTMENT OF ATTORNEY-GENERAL**			Reduction	Addition
		Main Office				
	1	Salaries, permanent....................	9	1–8		3,000 00
	2	Law Library..........................	9	10	100 00	
	3	Contingencies..........................	9	11	1,000 00	
	4	Crown Counsel prosecutions............	9	15	10,000 00	
	5	General litigation......................	9	16	2,000 00	
	6	Grants to conferences, etc...............	9	19	400 00	
	7	County law libraries....................	9	20	2,000 00	
	8	Compassionate allowances...............	9	21	1,600 00	
					17,100 00	3,000 00

No. of Vote	No. of Item	Service	Main Estimates Old Vote	Main Estimates Old Item	Reduction	Addition
5		**DEPARTMENT OF ATTORNEY-GENERAL —Continued**				
		Supreme Court				
	9	Grants to Judges' Library for upkeep......	10	2	400 00	
	10	Grant to Judges' Library (Chancery) S.C.O.	10	3	400 00	
	11	Allowance to Treasurer of Judges' petty expense fund for petty expenses of Judges	10	4	1,000 00	
		Office of Master				
	12	Salaries..............................	10	8-10	3,100 00	
		Office of Registrar				
	13	Salaries..............................	10	11-21	2,120 00	
					7,020 00	
		Law Enforcement Branch				
	14	Law Enforcement Fund.................	11	1	11,045 65	
		Toronto and York Crown Attorney's Office				
	15	Contingencies..........................	12	6	200 00	
		Audit of Criminal Justice Accounts Branch				
	16	Administration of Justice in counties......	13	7	100,000 00	
		Administration of Justice in Districts—Fuel, light and water for Gaols, Court House and Registry Office, etc., including maintenance of prisoners, including clothing. Districts of—				
	17	Algoma............................	13	16	2,600 00	
	18	Cochrane...........................	13	20	1,500 00	
	19	Kenora.............................	13	25	1,000 00	
	20	Muskoka............................	13	39	500 00	
	21	Thunder Bay.......................	13	74	2,050 00	
					107,650 00	
		Inspector of Legal Offices				
	22	Fidelity Bonds.........................	14	9	1,000 00	
	23	Contingencies..........................	14	10	2,000 00	
	24	Typewriters, office equipment, etc., for judicial officers, etc....................	14	11	500 00	
					3,500 00	
		Land Titles Office				
	25	Contingencies..........................	15	6	2,470 00	
		Local Masters of Titles				
	26	Salaries, etc...........................	16	1-4	3,200 00	
	27	Forms, copying, etc....................	16	5	1,000 00	
	28	Registration of patents..................	16	6	1,000 00	
					5,200 00	
		Ontario Municipal Board				
	29	Transferred to Statutory................	17	1-11	44,750 00	
		Office of Drainage Trials				
	30	Contingencies..........................	18	3	350 00	

No. of Vote	No. of Item	Service	Main Estimates Old Vote	Main Estimates Old Item	Reduction	Addition
5		**DEPARTMENT OF ATTORNEY-GENERAL —Continued**				
		Fire Marshal's Branch				
		General Office:				
	31	Salaries	20	1–4	2,000 00	
		Fire Investigation Division:				
	32	Salaries	20	5–8	150 00	
	33	Contingencies, etc.	20	9	4,000 00	
		Fire Prevention Division:				
	34	Contingencies, etc.	20	12	2,000 00	
		Lightning Rod Division:				
	35	Contingencies, etc.	20	15	1,400 00	
					9,550 00	
		Ontario Securities Commission				
	36	Salaries	21	1–12	6,375 00	
	37	Contingencies	21	13	215 00	
					6,590 00	
					215,425 65	3,000 00
6		**DEPARTMENT OF INSURANCE**				
	1	Salaries	22	1–15	150 00	825 00
	2	Printing Reports, etc.	22	16	500 00	
	3	Contingencies	22	17	70 00	
					720 00	825 00
		DEPARTMENT OF EDUCATION				
		SUMMARY				
	7	Main Office			20,290 00	2,475 00
	8	Public and Separate School Education, grants and contingencies			76,184 22	320,815 00
	9	Inspection of Schools			35,000 00	825 00
	10	Departmental Examinations			34,600 00	
	11	Text Books			17,500 00	
	12	Training Schools, General			14,650 00	17,300 00
	13	Toronto Normal and Model Schools			11,675 00	3,350 00
	14	Ottawa Normal and Model Schools			11,265 00	
	15	London Normal School			4,200 00	
	16	Hamilton Normal School			3,210 00	
	17	Peterborough Normal School			5,590 00	
	18	Stratford Normal School			2,725 00	300 00
	19	North Bay Normal School			45,285 00	
	20	University of Ottawa Normal School				28,980 00
	21	Sturgeon Falls Model School			17,350 00	
	22	Sandwich Model School			3,350 00	
	23	Embrun Model School			13,600 00	700 00
	24	High Schools and Collegiate Institutes			52,850 00	
	25	Departmental Museum			5,500 00	
	26	Public Libraries			14,900 00	500 00
	27	Vocational Education			3,200 00	219,150 00
	28	Ontario Training College for Technical Teachers			6,800 00	1,000 00

No. of Vote	No. of Item	Service	Main Estimates Old Vote	Old Item	Reduction	Addition
		DEPARTMENT OF EDUCATION—Continued				
		SUMMARY—*Continued*				
	29	Superannuated Teachers			6,650 00	1,800 00
	30	Provincial and other universities			62,500 00	1,275,000 00
	31	Belleville School for the Deaf				11,035 00
					468,874 22	1,883,230 00
		Main Office				
7	1	Salaries	23	1-16	7,515 00	2,475 00
	2	Contingencies	23	17	5,000 00	
	3	Extra services as may be directed by the Lieutenant-Governor in Council	23	18	3,000 00	
	4	Proportion of cost of Minister's Report	23	19	1,250 00	
	5	Cost of litigation	23	20	850 00	
	6	Consolidation and revision of the Acts of the Department of Education, including services, travelling expenses, printing and supplying Acts to Trustees and contingencies	23	21	2,400 00	
	7	Fees of various officials, Department of Education to archaeological and other associations	23	23	275 00	
					20,290 00	2,475 00
8		PUBLIC AND SEPARATE SCHOOL EDUCATION				
		Grants and Contingencies				
	1	Public and Separate Schools, grants and contingencies	24	1		143,000 00
	2	Assisted Public and Separate Schools, grants and contingencies	24	2		40,000 00
	3	Special grant to Tarentorus Township School Board in aid of education of children at Children's Shelter	24	4	175 00	
	4	Redemption of debentures issued by Boards of Public or Separate School Trustees which are guaranteed by the Province of Ontario to be paid as they become due when the Boards of Trustees through unforeseen circumstances cannot meet their obligations punctually	24	5	1,869 22	
	5	Rural School Libraries, grants and contingencies	24	6	5,000 00	
	6	Public, Separate and Continuation Schools, Cadet Corps, grants and contingencies	24	7	3,350 00	
	7	Kindergarten Schools, grants and contingencies	24	8	1,300 00	
	8	Night Schools, grants and contingencies	24	9		1,015 00
	9	Consolidated Schools, including grants, organizations, services, travelling expenses and contingencies	24	10	30,540 00	
	10	Agricultural and Horticultural Grants to School Boards, teachers and inspectors, for Public and Separate Schools and contingencies	24	11		60,000 00
	11	Industrial Arts, Manual Training and Household Science, grants to Boards and teachers, and contingencies	24	12		33,500 00

No. of Vote	No. of Item	Service	Main Estimates Old Vote	Main Estimates Old Item	Reduction	Addition
8		**DEPARTMENT OF EDUCATION—Continued** *Grants and Contingencies—Continued*				
	12	Correspondence courses and courses by itinerant teachers for pupils in isolated districts, including services, equipment, supplies and contingencies	24	13	3,000 00	
	13	Auxiliary Classes, grants, services, travelling expenses and contingencies	24	14		22,500 00
	14	Continuation Schools, grants and contingencies	24	15	1,500 00	
	15	Fifth Classes, grants and contingencies	24	16		1,500 00
	16	Spring and Summer Schools, including services, board and travelling expenses of instructors and students and transportation expenses of children and contingencies	24	17		15,000 00
	17	Expenses in connection with the League of the Empire	24	18	400 00	
	18	Grants to Art Departments and teachers in Art in Public, Separate and Continuation Schools and contingencies	24	19		300 00
	19	Grants to School Boards, Supervisors and Teachers to encourage Courses of Music in Public, Separate and Continuation Schools and to provide for inspection, travelling expenses and contingencies	24	20	8,000 00	
	20	Medical and Dental Inspection, including grants, services, travelling expenses and contingencies	24	21	3,000 00	
	21	Visual instruction in the schools, including grants, services, expenses and contingencies	24	22	1,000 00	
	22	Purchase of text-books by schools, grants and contingencies	24	23	1,000 00	
	23	Public and Separate School Registers, printing and contingencies	24	24	3,000 00	
	24	School Journey Association (Ontario Branch), services, travelling expenses and contingencies	24	25	500 00	
	25	Teachers' Association, including grants, services, travelling expenses and contingencies	24	26	2,200 00	
	26	Grant to Ontario Educational Association	24	27	1,000 00	
	27	Grant to Trustees' Section, Ontario Educational Association	24	28	2,000 00	
	28	Grant to Urban Trustees Association	24	29	250 00	
	29	Grant to Canadian Educational Association	24	30	200 00	
	30	Grant to National Council of Education for secretarial work	24	31	1,400 00	
	31	Grant to Ontario Federation of Home and School Association	24	32	1,000 00	
	32	Grant to Frontier College to be paid as may be directed by the Lieutenant-Governor in Council	24	33	2,500 00	
	33	Grant to Penny Bank of Ontario	24	34		4,000 00
	34	Grant to Soldiers' Aid Hostel, Bon Air (to be transferred to Public Welfare Department)	24	35	1,500 00	
	35	Grant to Canadian Bureau for the advancement of music	24	36	500 00	
					76,184 22	320,815 00
9		*Inspection of Schools*				
	1	Salaries	24	37–53	4,000 00	
	2	Salaries	24	55–56		825 00

No. of Vote	No. of Item	Service	Main Estimates Old Vote	Main Estimates Old Item	Reduction	Addition
		DEPARTMENT OF EDUCATION—Continued				
9		*Inspection of Schools—Continued*				
	3	Inspection of Public Schools............	24	54	10,000 00	
	4	Travelling and moving expenses of inspectors and other officials and for clerical assistance, office rent, office furniture and contingencies........................	24	57	20,000 00	
	5	Inspection of Indian Schools, including services, travelling expenses and contingencies............................	24	58	1,000 00	
					35,000 00	825 00
10		*Departmental Examinations*				
	1	Departmental Examinations, including services and travelling expenses..........	24	69	22,000 00	
	2	Paper, postage, printing, typewriters, adding machines, multigraphs and other office equipment and contingencies for Departmental Examinations..........	24	70	1,500 00	
	3	Assistants in connection with Departmental Examinations.......................	24	71	10,000 00	
	4	Extra services in connection with Departmental Examinations as may be directed by order of the Lieutenant-Governor in Council...........................	24	72	1,000 00	
	5	Extra services of professional Supervising Board of Examiners as may be directed by the Lieutenant-Governor in Council, Departmental Examinations..........	24	73	100 00	
					34,600 00	
11		*Text-Books*				
	1	Preparation of text-books, including plates, services, etc., services, travelling expenses and contingencies.....................	24	76	2,500 00	
	2	Subventions to publisher as supplementing retail prices of text-books.............	24	77	15,000 00	
					17,500 00	
		TRAINING SCHOOLS				
12		*General*				
	1	Travelling and moving expenses and contingencies...........................	25	3	600 00	
	2	Grants to teachers engaged in Model School Training in connection with Normal and other Training Schools................	25	4		14,000 00
	3	Services and expenses for lecturers in connection with the course for training first-class teachers.......................	25	6	800 00	
	4	Temporary teachers, Normal and Model Schools, in case of illness or on leave....	25	7	3,000 00	
	5	Travelling and moving expenses of Normal and Model School teachers transferred..	25	8	1,700 00	
	6	Grants to Public, Separate, High and Continuation School Boards for use of schools for observation purposes and contingencies............................	25	9		500 00

No. of Vote	No. of Item	Service	Main Estimates Old Vote	Main Estimates Old Item	Reduction	Addition
		DEPARTMENT OF EDUCATION—Continued				
12		TRAINING SCHOOLS—*Continued*				
	7	Grants to teachers in Public, Separate, High and Continuation Schools used for observation purposes	25	10		2,500 00
	8	Travelling expenses of Normal School students to Rural Public and Separate Schools and for Nature Study	25	11		300 00
	9	Grants to Public and Separate School Inspectors for services in connection with visits to Public and Separate Schools of Normal School students and Masters	25	12	600 00	
	10	Travelling expenses of Normal School Masters and Inspectors in visiting Rural Schools with Public and Separate School Inspectors	25	13	500 00	
	11	Classes in Manual Training and Household Science for Rural School teachers, including services, per diem allowances, to assist in paying travelling and other expenses of students and contingencies	25	14	1,500 00	
	12	Payment of fees of returned soldiers attending academic and professional courses to qualify as teachers	25	15	1,000 00	
	13	Payment of per diem allowances to and travelling expenses incurred by returned soldiers attending academic and professional courses to qualify as teachers	25	16	4,950 00	
					14,650 00	17,300 00
13		TORONTO NORMAL AND MODEL SCHOOLS				
	1	Salaries	26	1–18	1,400 00	3,150 00
	2	Extra services and additional teachers	26	19	500 00	
	3	Reference Books, periodicals, stationary, text and blank books, services and contingencies	26	20	1,400 00	
	4	Apparatus, chemicals, musical instruments, Domestic Science and Manual Training supplies	26	21	100 00	
	5	Supplies for Kindergarten	26	22	500 00	
	6	Annual grant in aid of Boys' and Girls' Model School games	26	24	100 00	
	7	Annual grant for rink	26	25	25 00	
	8	Payment to the Toronto Board of Education	26	26		200 00
		Maintenance of Toronto Normal and Model Schools and Departmental Museum				
	9	Fuel, light and power	26	27	1,500 00	
	10	Water	26	28	450 00	
	11	Furniture and furnishings	26	29	800 00	
	12	Expenses of grounds, trees, supplies, etc.	26	30	750 00	
	13	Wages of porters and extra firemen and labourers on grounds	26	31	2,650 00	
	14	Scrubbing, cleaning and supplies	26	32	500 00	
	15	Repairs, including services, materials and incidentals	26	33	1,000 00	
					11,675 00	3,350 00

No. of Vote	No. of Item	Service	Main Estimates Old Vote	Main Estimates Old Item	Reduction	Addition
		DEPARTMENT OF EDUCATION—Continued				
14		OTTAWA NORMAL AND MODEL SCHOOLS				
	1	Salaries	27	1–17	4,950 00	
	2	Extra services and additional teachers	27	18	500 00	
	3	Reference books, periodicals, stationery, text and blank books	27	19	2,000 00	
	4	Apparatus, chemicals, musical instruments, Domestic Science and Manual Training supplies	27	20	500 00	
	5	Physical training, including apparatus and athletic supplies	27	21	50 00	
	6	Supplies for Kindergarten	27	22	200 00	
	7	Annual grant in aid of Boys' and Girls' Model School games	27	23	100 00	
		Maintenance				
	8	Fuel, light and power	27	26	500 00	
	9	Water	27	27	140 00	
	10	Furniture, repairs and incidentals	27	28	400 00	
	11	Expenses of grounds	27	29	650 00	
	12	Scrubbing, cleaning, etc.	27	30	500 00	
	13	Snow cleaning, cartage, etc.	27	31	775 00	
					11,265 00	
15		LONDON NORMAL SCHOOL				
	1	Salaries	28	1–9	1,000 00	
	2	Extra services and additional teachers	28	10	500 00	
	3	Reference books, periodicals, stationery, services and contingencies	28	11	300 00	
	4	Apparatus, chemicals, musical instruments, Domestic Science and Manual Training supplies	28	12	200 00	
	5	Physical Training, including apparatus and athletic supplies	28	13	50 00	
	6	Payment to the London Board of Education	28	14	300 00	
		Maintenance				
	7	Fuel, light and power	28	15	50 00	
	8	Water	28	16	200 00	
	9	Furniture, repairs and incidentals	28	17	500 00	
	10	Expenses of grounds, trees, etc.	28	18	600 00	
	11	Scrubbing, cleaning, cartage, etc.	28	19	500 00	
					4,200 00	
16		HAMILTON NORMAL SCHOOL				
	1	Salaries	29	1–9	600 00	
	2	Extra services and additional teachers	29	10	500 00	
	3	Apparatus, chemicals, musical instruments, Domestic Science and Manual Training supplies	29	12	200 00	
	4	Physical Training, including apparatus and athletic supplies	29	13	100 00	
	5	Payment to the Hamilton Board of Education	29	14	100 00	

No. of Vote	No. of Item	Service	Main Estimates Old Vote	Main Estimates Old Item	Reduction	Addition
		DEPARTMENT OF EDUCATION—Continued				
16		HAMILTON NORMAL SCHOOL—*Continued*				
		Maintenance				
	6	Fuel, light and power	29	15	500 00	
	7	Water	29	16	60 00	
	8	Furniture, repairs and incidentals	29	17	500 00	
	9	Expenses of grounds, trees, etc	29	18	250 00	
	10	Scrubbing, cleaning, cartage, etc	29	19	400 00	
					3,210 00	
17		PETERBOROUGH NORMAL SCHOOL				
	1	Salaries	30	1–9	3,600 00	
	2	Extra services and additional teachers	30	10	500 00	
	3	Physical Training, including apparatus and athletic supplies	30	13	75 00	
		Maintenance				
	4	Fuel, light and power	30	15	300 00	
	5	Water	30	16	140 00	
	6	Furniture, repairs and incidentals	30	17	375 00	
	7	Expenses of grounds, trees, etc	30	18	400 00	
	8	Scrubbing, cleaning, cartage, etc	30	19	200 00	
					5,590 00	
18		STRATFORD NORMAL SCHOOL				
	1	Extra services and additional teachers	31	9	500 00	
	2	Apparatus, chemicals, musical instruments, Domestic Science and Manual Training supplies	31	11	400 00	
	3	Physical Training, including apparatus and athletic supplies	31	12	50 00	
	4	Payment to Stratford Board of Education	31	14		300 00
		Maintenance				
	5	Fuel, light and power	31	15	600 00	
	6	Water	31	16	175 00	
	7	Furniture, repairs and incidentals	31	17	300 00	
	8	Expenses of grounds, trees, etc	31	18	500 00	
	9	Scrubbing, cleaning, cartage, etc	31	19	200 00	
					2,725 00	300 00
19		NORTH BAY NORMAL SCHOOL				
	1	Salaries	32	1–6	1,400 00	
	2	Extra services and additional teachers	32	7	500 00	
	3	Reference books, periodicals, stationery, services and contingencies	32	8	100 00	
	4	Apparatus, chemicals, musical instruments, Domestic Science and Manual Training supplies	32	9	200 00	
	5	Physical Training, including apparatus and athletic supplies	32	10	50 00	
	6	Students' Board and travelling expenses	32	11	41,000 00	

No. of Vote	No. of Item	Service	Main Estimates Old Vote	Main Estimates Old Item	Reduction	Addition
		DEPARTMENT OF EDUCATION—Continued				
19		NORTH BAY NORMAL SCHOOL—*Continued*				
		Maintenance				
	7	Fuel, light and power..................	32	12	200 00	
	8	Water................................	32	13	135 00	
	9	Furniture, repairs and incidentals.........	32	14	800 00	
	10	Expenses of grounds, trees, etc...........	32	15	700 00	
	11	Scrubbing, cleaning, cartage, etc..........	32	16	200 00	
					45,285 00	
20		UNIVERSITY OF OTTAWA NORMAL SCHOOL				
	1	Salaries..............................	33	1-3		3,600 00
	2	Payment to Roman Catholic Separate School Board, Ottawa, for use of schools for training of teachers................	33	6		380 00
	3	Board and travelling expenses of students attending the University of Ottawa Normal School and of students preparing for admission to this school............	33	7		25,000 00
						28,980 00
21		STURGEON FALLS NORMAL SCHOOL				
	1	Reference books, periodicals, stationery, equipment, musical instruments, services and contingencies.....................	34	6	500 00	
	2	Physical Training, including apparatus and athletic supplies......................	34	7	100 00	
	3	Payment to the Roman Catholic Separate School Board, Sturgeon Falls, for use of schools for training of teachers.........	34	8	200 00	
	4	Students' Board and travelling expenses...	34	9	15,000 00	
		Maintenance				
	5	Fuel, light and power..................	34	10	500 00	
	6	Water................................	34	11	25 00	
	7	Furniture, repairs and incidentals.........	34	12	575 00	
	8	Expenses of grounds....................	34	13	300 00	
	9	Scrubbing, cleaning and supplies..........	34	14	150 00	
					17,350 00	
22		SANDWICH MODEL SCHOOL				
	1	Reference books, periodicals, stationery, equipment, musical instruments, services and contingencies.....................	34	18	100 00	
	2	Physical Training, including apparatus and athletic supplies......................	34	19	100 00	
	3	Payment to the Roman Catholic Separate School Board, Sandwich, for use of schools for training of teachers..........	34	20	600 00	
	4	Students' Board and travelling expenses...	34	21	1,500 00	

No. of Vote	No. of Item	Service	Main Estimates Old Vote	Main Estimates Old Item	Reduction	Addition
		DEPARTMENT OF EDUCATION—Continued				
22		SANDWICH MODEL SCHOOL—*Continued*				
		Maintenance				
	5	Fuel, light and power	34	22	475 00	
	6	Water	34	23	75 00	
	7	Furniture, repairs and incidentals	34	24	350 00	
	8	Expenses of grounds	34	25	100 00	
	9	Scrubbing, cleaning and supplies	34	26	50 00	
					3,350 00	
23		EMBRUN MODEL SCHOOL				
	1	Reference books, periodicals, stationery, equipment, musical instruments, services and contingencies	34	30		700 00
	2	Physical Training, including apparatus and athletic supplies	34	31	50 00	
	3	Annual grant for rink	34	32	25 00	
	4	Students Board and travelling expenses	34	34	12,000 00	
		Maintenance				
	5	Fuel, light and power	34	35	600 00	
	6	Water	34	36	150 00	
	7	Furniture, repairs and incidentals	34	37	475 00	
	8	Expenses of grounds	34	38	200 00	
	9	Scrubbing, cleaning, supplies, etc	34	39	100 00	
					13,600 00	700 00
24		HIGH SCHOOLS AND COLLEGIATE INSTITUTES				
	1	High Schools and Collegiate Institutes, including Districts, grants	35	1	42,000 00	
	2	Night High Schools, grants	35	2	2,300 00	
	3	High School Cadet Corps, grants	35	3	750 00	
	4	Grants to School Boards, Supervisors and Teachers to encourage courses of music in High Schools and Collegiate Institutes	35	4	100 00	
	5	Grants to High Schools and Collegiate Institutes to offset losses occasioned by unassessed Crown property (to be paid as may be directed by the Lieutenant-Governor in Council) (to be transferred to the Health Department)	35	5	1,200 00	
	6	Salaries	35	6–8	2,000 00	
	7	Travelling expenses of Ontario teachers to France, to be paid as may be directed by the Lieutenant-Governor in Council	35	10	1,000 00	
	8	Grant to Students' Hostel, Paris	35	11	1,000 00	
	9	High School Registers, printing and contingencies	35	12	500 00	
	10	Stationery, postage, printing, services and contingencies	35	13	2,000 00	
					52,850 00	

No. of Vote	No. of Item	Service	Main Estimates Old Vote	Main Estimates Old Item	Reduction	Addition
		DEPARTMENT OF EDUCATION—Continued				
25		DEPARTMENTAL MUSEUM				
	1	Salaries	36	1-3	1,050 00	
	2	Contingencies, including services, postage, stationery, typewriters and office equipment, printing, labels, etc.	36	4	2,800 00	
	3	Expenses of archaeological researches, purchase of collections, pictures, busts, cases, paintings, services, manuscripts, furnishings, travelling expenses	36	5	1,200 00	
	4	Natural History, collections and supplies, incidentals and inspection	36	6	450 00	
					5,500 00	
26		PUBLIC LIBRARIES				
	1	Salaries	37	1-5	600 00	
	2	Public Libraries, grants, organizations, services, cost of books, expenses and contingencies	37	6	10,000 00	
	3	Travelling expenses	37	7		500 00
	4	Travelling Libraries, cost of books, services and contingencies	37		1,900 00	
	5	Services and expenses in connection with Historical Research Work in Ontario	37		2,000 00	
	6	Grant to Royal Astronomical Society of Canada	37	1	100 00	
	7	Grant to Institute Canadian Francais, Ottawa	37	18	300 00	
					14,900 00	500 00
27		VOCATIONAL EDUCATION				
	1	Salary of Inspector Group 1, Vocational Education (transferring from Inspection of Schools, Vote 24, Item 42)	38	1-6		3,800 00
	2	Manual Training and Household Science Departments, including grants, Scholarships, services, equipments, books, stationery, printing and contingencies	38	7		5,350 00
	3	Grant to Haileybury High School for Mining Department. The payment of the whole or part of this sum to be made on the recommendation of the Director or Assistant Director of Vocational Education, approved by the Lieutenant-Governor in Council	38	9	1,000 00	
	4	Agricultural Training in High Schools and Collegiate Institutes, Continuation Schools and Fifth Classes, grants to Boards and teachers and contingencies	38	10	2,200 00	
	5	Vocational Education, Day and Evening Classes, including grants, services and contingencies	38	11		210,000 00
					3,200 00	219,150 00

No. of Vote	No. of Item	Service	Main Estimates Old Vote	Main Estimates Old Item	Reduction	Addition
		DEPARTMENT OF EDUCATION—Continued				
28		ONTARIO TRAINING COLLEGE FOR TECHNICAL TEACHERS				
	1	Salaries	38	13–16	2,000 00	
	2	Reference books, periodicals, stationery, furniture, services and contingencies	38	18	700 00	
	3	Apparatus, chemical and shop supplies	38	19	1,200 00	
	4	Payment to Hamilton Board of Education	38	20		1,000 00
		Maintenance				
	5	Heat, light and power	38	21	500 00	
	6	Water	38	22	50 00	
	7	Expenses of grounds, trees and flowers, etc.	38	23	550 00	
	8	Repairs and incidentals	38	24	425 00	
	9	Scrubbing, cleaning, cartage, etc	38	25	1,375 00	
					6,800 00	1,000 00
29		SUPERANNUATED TEACHERS				
	1	Annual retiring allowance to Teachers' and Inspectors'	39	1	6,500 00	
	2	Compassionate allowance for ex-teachers to to be paid as may be directed by the Lieutenant-Governor in Council	39	2		1,800 00
	3	Medical examination, fees, printing, paper, and contingencies	39	3	150 00	
					6,650 00	1,800 00
30		PROVINCIAL AND OTHER UNIVERSITIES				
	1	Grant to University of Toronto to provide in the Ontario College of Education for the training of High School Assistants and for graduate courses of instruction in education, and for such other courses for certificates of the Department of Education as the Minister of Education may direct	40	1	25,000 00	
	2	Grant to University of Western Ontario (to be paid as may be directed by the Lieutenant-Governor in Council)	40	2	25,000 00	
	3	Grant to Royal Ontario Museum (to be paid as may be directed by the Lieutenant-Governor in Council	40	3	10,000 00	
	4	Grant to Royal Ontario Museum for cataloguing	40	4	2,500 00	
	5	Special grant to University of Toronto	New	New		1,000,000 00
	6	Grant to Queen's University (to be paid as may be directed by the Lieutenant-Governor in Council)	New	New		275,000 00
					62,500 00	1,275,000 00
31		BELLEVILLE SCHOOL FOR THE DEAF				
		Expenses				
	1	Medicine and medical comforts; groceries and provisions; bedding, clothing and shoes, soap and cleaning; furniture and furnishings; farm expenses; repairs and alterations, including supplies, tools, etc.;				

No. of Vote	No. of Item	Service	Main Estimates Old Vote	Main Estimates Old Item	Reduction	Addition
		DEPARTMENT OF EDUCATION—Continued				
31		BELLEVILLE SCHOOL FOR THE DEAF—*Continued*				
		school supplies and equipment, including books, apparatus and appliances; sewage works, chemicals, etc.; purchase and maintenance of motor conveyances, contingencies	41	28		10,000 00
	2	To provide for refunds to teachers-in-training	New	New		1,035 00
						11,035 00
32		**DEPARTMENT OF LANDS AND FORESTS**				
		Main Office				
	1	Salaries	44	1-7	75 00	
	2	Contingencies	44	40	5,000 00	
	3	Advertising	44	41	1,500 00	
	4	Back to the Land Movement	New	New		75,000 00
	5	Payment to Canadian Lumbermen's Association as Ontario's contribution towards expenses of Representative to England in connection with working out Article 21 of Trade Agreement between Canada and United Kingdom	New	New		1,500 00
	6	Settlement of claim of Hudsons Bay Company covering La Cloche Reserve	New	New		1,500 00
		Branches				
		Salaries:				
	7	Lands	44	8-17	6,010 00	2,775 00
	8	Woods and Forests	44	18-24	5,100 00	900 00
	9	Files Branch	44	32-34	8,900 00	975 00
		General				
	10	Legal Fees and Expenses	44	42	800 00	
	11	Insurance	44	43	500 00	
	12	Display, Toronto Exhibition	44	44	1,000 00	
	13	Moving expenses of officials	44	45	50 00	
	14	Agents' salaries, etc.	44	47	10,000 00	
	15	Forest Ranging, etc.	44	48	70,000 00	
		Parks				
	16	Algonquin Provincial Park	45	2	15,000 00	
	17	Algonquin Provincial Park, clearing right-of-way, etc.	45	3	500 00	
	18	Rondeau Provincial Park	46	4	5,000 00	
	19	Quetico Provincial Park	46	5	5,000 00	
	20	Creation and extension of parks, etc.	46	6	450 00	
					134,885 00	82,650 00
		Forestry Branch				
	21	Contingencies	46	12	3,725 00	
	22	Forest Reserves	44	49	300 00	
	23	Forestry Act	45	1	10,000 00	

No. of Vote	No. of Item	Service	Main Estimates Old Vote	Main Estimates Old Item	Reduction	Addition
32		**DEPARTMENT OF LANDS AND FORESTS —Continued**				
		Forestry Branch—Continued				
	24	Reforestation	46	13	100,000 00	
	25	Fire Ranging	46	14	500,000 00	
	26	Clearing Townsites	46	15	6,500 00	
	27	Forest Research	46	17	3,500 00	
	28	Insect Control	46	22	2,000 00	
	29	Display at Exhibitions and Fall Fairs	46	23	500 00	
					626,525 00	
		Surveys Branch				
	30	Salaries	47	1-15	7,000 00	
	31	Surveys	47	16	57,000 00	
	32	Lac Seul Storage Dam, maintenance, etc.	47	19	49,400 00	
	33	Salaries, expenses, etc., re inspection of dams, etc.	47	20	400 00	
					113,800 00	
					875,210 00	82,650 00
33		**DEPARTMENT OF NORTHERN DEVELOPMENT**				
		COLONIZATION ROADS BRANCH				
	1	Salaries	48	1-6	6,550 00	
	2	Contingencies	48	7	1,200 00	
	3	By-laws	48	8	100,000 00	
	4	Construction and maintenance	48	9	275,000 00	
	5	Inspections	48	10	10,000 00	
	6	Storage and insurance	48	11	375 00	
	7	Engineering and surveying	48	12	1,500 00	
	8	Salaries, travelling and other expenses, not otherwise provided for	48	13	800 00	
					395,425 00	
34		**DEPARTMENT OF MINES**				
		Main Office				
	1	Salaries	49	1-13	5,757 73	2,000 00
	2	Contingencies	49	42	6,000 00	
		BRANCHES				
		Salaries:				
	3	Geological	49	14-17	1,500 00	
	4	Inspection	49	24-27		1,300 00
	5	Mining Court	49	35-39	3,000 00	
		General				
	6	Salaries, etc., gas and oil wells	49	43	3,500 00	
	7	Temiskaming Testing Laboratories	49	46	5,000 00	
	8	Mining Recorders	49	47		5,000 00
	9	Draughtsman, North Bay	49	49	2,000 00	
	10	Legal Assistance re Mining Act	49	50	500 00	
	11	Salaries, etc., Temporary Field Assistants	49	51		4,000 00

No. of Vote	No. of Item	Service	Main Estimates Old Vote	Main Estimates Old Item	Reduction	Addition
34		**DEPARTMENT OF MINES—Continued**				
		General—Continued				
	12	Surveys Mining Areas	49	52	1,000 00	
	13	Trails, clearing streams, etc.	49	53	1,000 00	
	14	Mineral collections	49	54	1,500 00	
	15	Insurance	49	55	200 00	
	16	Research Work	49	57	10,000 00	
	17	Purchase of gold and silver ores	49	59	500 00	
	18	Services, etc., unprovided for	49	60	500 00	
	19	Diamond drilling re lignite	49	61	15,000 00	
	20	Erection of New Milling Building at University of Toronto	New	New		19,690 50
					56,957 73	31,990 50
35		**DEPARTMENT OF GAME AND FISHERIES**				
		Main Office				
	1	Salaries	50	1–13	....	3,675 00
	2	Contingencies	50	14	4,000 00	
		Biological and Fish Culture Branch				
	3	Contingencies	50	19	1,500 00	
	4	Services and Expenses of Hatcheries	50	20	50,000 00	
		General				
	5	Erecting Ponds, Buildings	50	21	55,000 00	
	6	Enforcement of Act	50	22	50,000 00	
	7	Moving Expenses	50	23	1,500 00	
	8	Wild Rice Seed	50	28	500 00	
	9	Exhibits	50	29	600 00	
	10	Adjustment of Claims	50	30	500 00	
	11	Annual Membership Fees	50	31	100 00	
	12	Unforeseen and unprovided	50	32	500 00	
	13	Grants	New	New		700 00
					164,200 00	4,375 00
36		**DEPARTMENT OF PUBLIC WORKS**				
		Main Office				
	1	Salaries	51	1–21	11,200 00	
	2	Contingencies	51	22	3,700 00	
	3	Travelling expenses	51	23	500 00	
	4	Local improvement taxes	51	25	15,500 00	
		General Superintendent				
	5	Salaries	52	1–7	3,400 00	
	6	Services—Travelling and other expenses	52	8	1,000 00	
		Government House				
	7	Salaries	53	1–8	1,850 00	
	8	Pay List—For other help; repairs to grounds, flowers, shrubs, etc.	53	9	1,300 00	
	9	Water, fuel, light and power	53	10	3,000 00	
	10	Repairs, contingencies, etc.	53	11		1,700 00
	11	Furniture and furnishings	53	12		1,000 00
	12	Telephone service	53	14		350 00

No. of Vote	No. of Item	Service	Main Estimates Old Vote	Main Estimates Old Item	Reduction	Addition
36		**DEPARTMENT OF PUBLIC WORKS—Continued**				
		Parliament Buildings				
	13	Salaries	54	1–21 & 27	17,848 74	
	14	Electric power and light, current and gas	54	23		4,000 00
	15	Supplies, tools, etc., for engine room, and general repairs	54	24	500 00	
	16	Caretakers of grounds and maintenance of grounds, drives and walks	54	25	1,000 00	
	17	Repairs and cleaning of buildings, etc	54	26	10,000 00	
	18	Shelving for library	54	28	100 00	
	19	Vault fittings and shelving	54	29		1,000 00
	10	Interior alterations	54	31		1,000 00
	21	Flowers, shrubs, plants, etc	54	32	2,000 00	
	22	Uniforms for messengers, attendants, etc	54	33	100 00	
	23	Painting outside and inside work	54	34	10,000 00	
	24	Fire protection	54	36	700 00	300 00
	25	Rental of property and office space	54	37		
	26	Motion picture sound equipment	New	New		4,500 00
	27	Motion Picture Studio, Trenton, repairs and incidentals	54	38	80 00	
	28	Typewriter inspection and repairs	New	New		2,500 00
	29	Sewage Experimental Station, Toronto, repairs	54	39	50 00	
	30	110 University Avenue, Toronto, repairs, alterations, painting and incidentals	54	40		18,000 00
		Osgoode Hall				
	31	Salaries	55	1–8 & 13	6,650 00	
	32	Water, fuel, light, and power	55	9	2,000 00	
	33	Furniture and incidentals	55	10	1,000 00	
	34	Telephone service	55	11	500 00	
	35	Fire protection	55	14	50 00	
	36	Electric wiring and fixtures	55	16	100 00	
	37	Painting interior and exterior	55	17	1,000 00	
	38	Alterations to provide additional fire protection	New	New		1,500 00
		EDUCATIONAL BUILDINGS				
		Toronto Normal School				
	39	Repairs and incidentals	56	1	2,500 00	
		Ottawa Normal School				
	40	Repairs and incidentals	56	2	1,000 00	
		London Normal School				
	41	Repairs and incidentals	56	3	300 00	
		Hamilton Normal School				
	42	Repairs and incidentals	56	4	300 00	

No. of Vote	No. of Item	Service	Main Estimates Old Vote	Main Estimates Old Item	Reduction	Addition
36		**DEPARTMENT OF PUBLIC WORKS—Continued**				
		EDUCATIONAL BUILDINGS—*Continued*				
		Peterborough Normal School				
	43	Repairs and incidentals	56	5	300 00	
	44	Repairs to existing fence	New	New		220 00
		Stratford Normal School				
	45	Repairs and incidentals	56	6	300 00	
	46	To renew and reconstruct roof	New	New		500 00
		North Bay Normal School				
	47	Repairs and incidentals	56	7		100 00
		Belleville School for Deaf				
	48	Reconstruction of fireman's cottage detroyed by fire (to complete)	New	New		78 55
	49	Remodelling bathroom and other plumbing	New	New		1,550 00
	50	Furniture and furnishings	New	New		850 00
	51	Linotype machine and installation	New	New		1,600 00
	52	Auricular appliances	New	New		1,000 00
		Brantford School for Blind				
	53	Repairs and incidentals	56	9	1,000 00	
		Sandwich Training School				
	54	Repairs and incidentals	56	10	200 00	
		Sturgeon Falls Training School				
	55	Repairs and incidentals	56	11	300 00	
		Northern Academy, Monteith				
	56	Repairs and incidentals	56	12		300 00
		Embrun Training School				
	57	Repairs and incidentals	56	13	200 00	
		Ontario Training School for Technical Teachers, Hamilton				
	58	Repairs and incidentals	New	New		1,000 00
	59	Painting	New	New		500 00
		General				
	60	Repairs and incidentals to boilers and heating plants in Educational Buildings	New	New		1,500 00
	61	To provide for fire protection and equipment in Educational Buildings	New	New		250 00

No. of Vote	No. of Item	Service	Main Estimates Old Vote	Main Estimates Old Item	Reduction	Addition
36		**DEPARTMENT OF PUBLIC WORKS—Continued**				
		AGRICULTURAL BUILDINGS				
		Ontario Agricultural College, Guelph				
	62	Repairs and incidentals	57	1		1,000 00
	63	Dismantling boilers and remodelling boiler room	New	New		1,000 00
	64	Furniture and furnishings	New	New		1,000 00
	65	Surfacing driveway in front of College	New	New		250 00
		Horticultural Experimental Station, Vineland				
	66	Repairs and incidentals	57	3	1,000 00	
		Western Ontario Experimental Farm, Ridgetown				
	67	Repairs and incidentals	57	4	500 00	
		Agricultural School, Ridgetown				
	68	Repairs and incidentals	57	5	200 00	
		Eastern Dairy School, Kingston				
	69	Repairs and incidentals	57	6	900 00	
		Agricultural School, Kemptville				
	70	Repairs and incidentals	57	7		350 00
	71	Kitchen equipment	New	New		300 00
		Hearst Demonstration Farm				
	72	Repairs and incidentals	57	8	300 00	
		WELFARE BUILDINGS				
		Boys' Training School, Bowmanville				
	73	Repairs and incidentals, including drives and walks	58	1		400 00
		DISTRICT BUILDINGS				
		Algoma District				
	74	Repairs and alterations to Court House, Gaol, Registry Office, Land Titles Office, and Lock-ups, including improvements to grounds	59	1	200 00	
	75	Furniture and furnishings	59	2	200 00	

No. of Vote	No. of Item	Service	Main Estimates Old Vote	Main Estimates Old Item	Reduction	Addition
36		**DEPARTMENT OF PUBLIC WORKS—Continued**				
		DISTRICT BUILDINGS—*Continued*				
		Cochrane District				
	66	Repairs and alterations to all buildings, including Court House, Gaols and Lock-ups, and Mining Recorder's offices, including improvements and upkeep of grounds	59	3	200 00	
	67	Furniture and furnishings	59	4	200 00	
	68	Repairs and incidentals to Lock-up at Matheson	New	New		250 00
		Kenora District				
	69	Repairs and alterations to Court House, Gaol, Registry Office, Land Titles Office, and Lock-ups, including improvements to grounds	59	5	200 00	
	70	Furniture and furnishings	59	6		70 00
		Manitoulin Island				
	71	Repairs to Court House, Gaol, Registry Office and Lock-ups, including improvements to grounds	59	7	200 00	
	72	Furniture and furnishings	59	8		40 00
		Nipissing District				
	73	Repairs and alterations to Court House, Gaol, Registry Office, Land Titles Office, and Lock-ups, including improvements to grounds	59	11	250 00	
	74	Furniture and furnishings	59	12	55 00	
	75	Salary of caretaker, North Bay	59	13	650 00	
		Parry Sound District				
	76	Repairs and alterations to Court House, Gaol, Registry Office, Land Titles Office, and Lock-ups, including improvements to grounds	59	14		200 00
	77	Furniture and furnishings	59	15	100 00	
	78	Repairs and incidentals for Lock-up, Burk's Falls	New	New		200 00
		Rainy River District				
	79	Repairs and alterations to Court House, Gaol, Registry Office, Land Titles Office, and Lock-ups, including improvements to grounds	59	16	400 00	
	80	Furniture and furnishings	59	17	140 00	
	81	Painting Court House	New	New		1,000 00
		Sudbury District				
	82	Repairs and alterations to Court House, Gaol, Registry Office and Lock-ups, including improvements to grounds	59	18	200 00	
	83	Furniture and furnishings	59	19		35 00

No. of Vote	No. of Item	Service	Main Estimates Old Vote	Main Estimates Old Item	Reduction	Addition
36		**DEPARTMENT OF PUBLIC WORKS—Continued**				
		DISTRICT BUILDINGS—*Continued*				
		Thunder Bay District				
	84	Repairs and alterations to Court House, Gaol, Registry Office, Land Titles Office, Lock-ups, and Government buildings, including improvements to grounds.....	59	23		525 00
		General				
	85	To provide for repairs, installation of boilers and heating plants in Districts.........	New	New		1,500 00
		GENERAL BUILDINGS				
		Ontario Government Building, Exhibition Park, Toronto				
	86	Preparing and installing exhibits and electric energy......................	60	1	2,000 00	
		PUBLIC WORKS AND BRIDGES				
	87	Lockmasters, bridge-tenders, caretakers, etc.	61	1	700 00	
	88	Maintenance, locks, dams, bridges, dredging, etc............................	61	2	15,000 00	
	89	Surveys and inspections.................	61	3	4,000 00	
	90	Equipment, instruments, machinery, scows, rubber boots, motor trucks and cars....	61	4	5,100 00	
	91	Wages and expenses of Supervising Foremen	61	5	1,000 00	
		CAPITAL				
		Public Works Construction				
	92	Storage dams..........................	61	6	6,500 00	
	93	Cutting and purchase of timber and construction materials....................	61	7	3,750 00	
	94	Municipal bridges......................	New	New		40,000 00
	95	Municipal drainage.....................	New	New		10,000 00
	96	To continue works in progress............	61	8	50,000 00	
	97	Grant to Dominion Government for Hawkesbury-Grenville bridge..........	New	New		4,397 81
	98	Grant to Culross-Kinloss for Black Creek drain and extension (not to exceed).....	New	New		3,500 00
		PUBLIC BUILDINGS				
		Parliament and Departmental Buildings				
	99	To provide additional accommodation.....	62	1		110,000 00
	100	Painting East Block....................	New	New		2,500 00
		PUBLIC INSTITUTIONS BUILDINGS				
		Ontario Hospitals and Public Institutions				
	101	Additions, alterations and equipment, including laundry machinery............	62	2	20,000 00	

No. of Vote	No. of Item	Service	Main Estimates Old Vote	Main Estimates Old Item	Reduction	Addition
36		**DEPARTMENT OF PUBLIC WORKS—Continued**				
		PUBLIC INSTITUTIONS BUILDINGS—*Continued*				
		Ontario Reformatory, Guelph				
	102	Additions, alterations, etc.	62	3	5,000 00	
		Brockville Hospital				
	103	To complete additional home for nurses, furniture and furnishings, grading and sidewalks, and expenses in connection therewith	New	New		12,000 00
		Hamilton Hospital				
	104	To complete New Assembly Hall, furniture and furnishings, and equipment and expenses in connection therewith	New	New		10,800 00
		Orillia Hospital				
	105	New barns destroyed by fire	New	New		17,500 00
	106	New buildings for patients, furniture, furnishings and expenses in connection therewith	New	New		10,000 00
	107	Water service and expenses in connection therewith, including pumps, engines and electrical apparatus	New	New		14,500 00
		Penetanguishene Hospital				
	108	To complete building for criminally insane prisoners, furniture, furnishing, including roads and grading, screens, lighting of grounds and expenses in connection therewith	New	New		36,500 00
	109	Laundry machinery	New	New		2,000 00
	110	New boiler, stack and stoker, including alterations to boiler house and expenses in connection therewith	New	New		20,000 00
		Woodstock Hospital				
	111	To complete new buildings, walks and grading and expenses in connection therewith	New	New		12,950 00
	112	To complete new laundry building, machinery and equipment, weigh scale, walks and grading, and expenses in connection therewith	New	New		10,500 00
		Industrial Farm, Burwash				
	113	New reformatory building for men, furniture and furnishings, deep well, chlorinators, pipes, pumps and equipment for water supply and expenses in connection therewith	New	New		100,000 00

No. of Vote	No. of Item	Service	Main Estimates Old Vote	Main Estimates Old Item	Reduction	Addition
36		**DEPARTMENT OF PUBLIC WORKS—Continued**				
		PUBLIC INSTITUTIONS BUILDINGS—*Continued*				
		Fort William Industrial Farm				
	114	Pipes, pump and chlorinator equipment for water supply	New	New		1,750 00
	115	Boiler and heating equipment	New	New		6,000 00
		WELFARE BUILDINGS				
		Girls' Training School, Galt				
	116	To complete construction of works and buildings, furniture and furnishings, laying out of grounds and expenses in connection therewith	New	New		113,700 00
	117	Building for poultry raising	New	New		600 00
	118	Gardeners' tool shed and equipment	New	New		200 00
		EDUCATIONAL BUILDINGS				
		Peterborough Normal School				
	119	New fence enclosing property	New	New		600 00
		Belleville School for Deaf				
	120	New dormitory building, furniture and furnishings and expenses in connection therewith	New	New		50,000 00
		Brantford School for Blind				
	121	Fire alarm system	New	New		350 00
		AGRICULTURAL BUILDINGS				
		Ontario Agricultural College, Guelph				
	122	To complete Administration Building and students' residence buildings, including section 3, electric substation service tunnels, heating mains, electric service, furniture and furnishings and expenses in connection therewith	New	New		12,000 00
	123	Steam distributing mains	New	New		15,000 00
	124	To complete girls' residence	New	New		25 00
	125	Extension of electric cables	New	New		7,000 00
	126	Taking down old laundry, levelling and grading court and forming back roadway	New	New		200 00
		DISTRICTS				
		Cochrane District				
	127	District gaol, Cochrane, installation of steel cells in Court House	New	New		5,000 00

No. of Vote	No. of Item	Service	Main Estimates Old Vote	Main Estimates Old Item	Reduction	Addition
36		**DEPARTMENT OF PUBLIC WORKS—Continued**				
		DISTRICTS—*Continued*				
		Kenora District				
	128	Porch and steps to gaoler's residence......	New	New		250 00
	129	Mining Recorder's Office and Lock-up, Sioux Lookout (to complete)...........	New	New		4,200 00
		Nipissing District				
	130	Wall around gaol, North Bay............	New	New		200 00
		Rainy River District				
	131	District gaol, Fort Frances, fencing of property for gaol yard................	New	New		100 00
		Miscellaneous				
	132	Purchase of property....................	62	6	4,500 00	
	133	Special Relief Work......................	New	New		35,000 00
	134	To continue buildings in progress at close of fiscal year 1931-32, including fittings and furnishings (to be paid as directed by the Lieutenant-Governor in Council).	62	4	100,000 00	
	135	To continue buildings in progress at close of fiscal year 1932-31, including fittings and furnishings (to be paid as directed by the Lieutenant-Governor in Council) Amount unallotted..................	New	New		10,175 00
					324,973 74	732,916 36
37		**DEPARTMENT OF HIGHWAYS**				
		Main Office				
	1	Salaries..............................	63	1–31	1,075 00	
	2	Contingencies..........................	63	32	13,879 08	
	3	Taxes................................	63	35	216 40	
		Grants:				
	4	Ontario Good Roads..................	63	37	100 00	
	5	Canadian Good Roads................	63	38	500 00	
					15,770 48	
		Motor Vehicles Branch				
	6	Salaries..............................	63	42–54 & 58	9,600 00	
	7	Contingencies..........................	63	55	171 04	
	8	Testing headlights......................	63	56	325 00	
	9	Markers...............................	63	57	25,000 00	
	10	Advertising............................	63	59	10,000 00	
					45,096 04	
					60,866 52	

No. of Vote	No. of Item	Service	Main Estimates Old Vote	Old Item	Reduction	Addition
38		**DEPARTMENT OF HEALTH**				
		Main Office				
	1	Salaries	64	1–13		2,475 00
	2	Contingencies	64	14	500 00	
	3	Library and Fees	64	15	300 00	
		Cancer Work:				
	4	Purchase of Radium	New	New		61,000 00
	5	Operation of Emanation Plant	New	New		2,000 00
		Grants:				
	6	Ontario Institute of Radio-Therapy, Toronto	New	New		45,000 00
	7	Ontario Institute of Radio-Therapy, Kingston	New	New		9,000 00
		District Officers of Health Branch				
	8	Services, Equipment Expenses	64	20	1,800 00	
		Maternal and Child Hygiene and Public Health Nursing Branch				
	9	Salaries	64	22–27		3,000 00
	10	Services, Equipment Expenses and for the Employment of District Nurses. The payment of such Grants as may be certied by the Department of Health	64	28	2,000 00	
		Dental Services Branch				
	11	Services, expenses, supplies and equipment and for payment of such grants to municipalities for the organization and maintenance of school and community dental services as may be certified by the Department of Health	64	31	50 00	
		Inspection of Training School for Nurses Branch				
	12	Services and expenses in connection with the administration and enforcement of The Registration of Nurses Act, 1922	64	35	300 00	1,000 00
		Preventable Diseases Branch				
	13	Salaries	64	36–41	250 00	
	14	Outbreaks of diseases, sanitary investigations and free distribution of biological products for the prevention and cure of disease, services and expenses	64	42	40,000 00	
	15	Services and expenses—for payments of the treatment of patients in hospitals and clinics and legally qualified medical practitioners for equipment of and grants to clinics as may be certified by the Department of Health and generally for the enforcement of the law and regulations	64	43	8,200. 00	
	16	Services and expenses, X-ray equipment and travelling clinical services	64	44	1,700 00	
	17	Grant, Social Hygiene Council	64	45	4,500 00	

No. of Vote	No. of Item	Service	Main Estimates Old Vote	Main Estimates Old Item	Reduction	Addition
38		**DEPARTMENT OF HEALTH—Continued**				
		Industrial Hygiene Branch				
	18	Services and Expenses	64	54	100 00	
		Sanitary Engineering Branch				
	19	Services and Expenses	64	64	1,000 00	
		Main Laboratory				
	20	Salaries	64	65–79		10,675 00
	21	Services and Expenses	64	80	1,500 00	
		Branch Laboratories				
	22	Salaries	64	82–91		3,825 00
	23	Services and Expenses	64	92	1,000 00	
		Public Health Education Branch				
	24	Contingencies, including Public Health Exhibits	64	102	1,050 00	
					64,250 00	137,975 00
39		**Hospitals Branch**				
		Main Office				
	1	Salaries	65	1–23		12,510 00
	2	Contingencies	65	24	1,350 00	
		Hospitals and Charities				
	3	Salaries	66	1–4	10,350 00	
	4	General Hospitals	66	5	103,000 00	
	5	Homes for Incurables	66	6		5,500 00
	6	Maintenance of patients in Municipal Sanatoria for Consumptives	66	7		114,000 00
	7	Grant to Victorian Order of Nurses	66	9	500 00	
	8	Grant to The Haven, Toronto, for feeble-minded women	New	New		500 00
	9	Contingencies	66	12	4,950 00	
	10	To provide special grants to municipalities	New	New		12,000 00
		Hospitals, General Expense				
	11	Removal of patients	67	3		3,000 00
	12	Travelling expenses of social service workers at Ontario Hospitals	67	6	500 00	
	13	Minor comforts for indigent patients in Ontario Hospitals, on certified statements from Superintendents	67	7	1,000 00	
	14	Provision for expenses in connection with conventions held at various institutions	67	8	2,900 00	
	15	Removal expenses (other than patients) in connection with the Public Institutions	67	9		500 00

No. of Vote	No. of Item	Service	Main Estimates Old Vote	Main Estimates Old Item	Reduction	Addition
39		**DEPARTMENT OF HEALTH—Continued** **Hospitals Branch—Continued**				
		Hospitals, General Expense—Continued				
	16	Printing and stationery for Public Institutions	67	10	7,000 00	
	17	Treatment of patients and inmates of Public Institutions in Hospitals and Sanatoria	67	12	800 00	
	18	Legal costs and expenses covering sundry investigations	67	13	500 00	
	19	Expenses in connection with exhibit of the the Department of Health, Hospitals Division, at the Canadian National and other Exhibitions	67	15	500 00	
	20	Maintenance of criminal insane at the Ontario Reformatory, Guelph, from October 14th, 1932, to date of transfer to the Ontario Hospital, Penetanguishene	New	New		10,000 00
	21	Grant to Municipality of Town of Portsmouth re maintenance of that part of King Street approaching the Ontario Hospital, Kingston	New	New		200 00
	22	Grants to schools for education of children of Ontario Hospitals Staff	New	New		4,000 00
		Brockville				
	23	Salaries	68	1–7	8,300 00	
	24	Maintenance	68	8		10,000 00
		Cobourg				
	25	Salaries	69	1–7	3,000 00	
	26	Maintenance	69	8		8,000 00
		Hamilton				
	27	Salaries	70	1–7		2,300 00
	28	Maintenance	70	8	25,000 00	
	29	Repairs to buildings, etc	70	9	5,000 00	
		Kingston				
	30	Salaries	71	1–7	1,000 00	
	31	Maintenance	71	8		20,000 00
	32	Repairs to buildings, etc	71	9		10,000 00
		London				
	33	Salaries	72	1–7	14,900 00	
	34	Repairs to buildings, etc	72	9	25,000 00	
		Mimico				
	35	Salaries	73	1–7		8,600 00
	36	Maintenance	73	8		30,000 00
	37	Repairs to buildings, etc	73	9	75,000 00	
		Orillia				
		Industries				
	38	Salaries, operating expenses, etc	74	11	15,000 00	

No. of Vote	No. of Item	Service	Main Estimates Old Vote	Old Item	Reduction	Addition
39		**DEPARTMENT OF HEALTH—Continued**				
		Hospitals Branch—Continued				
		Penetanguishene				
	39	Salaries	75	1-7		23,850 00
	40	Maintenance	75	8		30,000 00
		Toronto				
	41	Salaries	76	1-7		6,500 00
		Whitby				
	42	Salaries	77	1-7	9,500 00	
	43	Repairs to buildings, etc.	77	9	10,000 00	
		Woodstock				
	44	Salaries	78	1-7		24,100 00
	45	Repairs to buildings, etc.	78	9		3,000 00
		Toronto Psychiatric				
	46	Salaries	79	1-5		2,120 00
	47	Maintenance	79	6		5,000 00
	48	Repairs to buildings, etc.	79	7	1,000 00	
					326,050 00	345,680 00
					390,300 00	483,655 00
40		**DEPARTMENT OF LABOUR**				
		Main Office				
	1	Salaries	80	1-9	2,575 00	750 00
	2	Contingencies	80	10	5,500 00	
	3	Purchase of supplies, General Stores	New	New		4,000 00
	4	Labour Exhibit	80	11	200 00	
	5	Investigations, Library, etc.	80	12	750 00	
	6	General—Educational work, advertising, etc.	80	14	1,000 00	
	7	Litigation of constitutional and other questions	80	15	195 00	
	8	Grant to School for Girls, LeFoyer	New	New		600 00
	9	*Building Trades Protection Act*	80	39	900 00	
		Apprenticeship Branch				
	10	Salaries	80	16-23	4,900 00	
	11	Contingencies	80	24	1,500 00	
		Boiler Inspection Branch				
	12	Salaries	80	25-29	100 00	
	13	Contingencies	80	30	5,300 00	

No. of Vote	No. of Item	Service	Main Estimates Old Vote	Old Item	Reduction	Addition
40		**DEPARTMENT OF LABOUR—Continued**				
		Factory Inspection Branch				
	14	Salaries	80	31–37	1,875 00	
		Board of Examiners, Operating Engineers				
	15	Salaries	80	40–46	825 00	
	16	Contingencies	80	47	1,500 00	
		Ontario Government Employment Offices				
	17	Salaries	80	48–58	3,250 00	4,575 00
	18	Contingencies	80	59		25,000 00
	19	Travelling expenses and per diem allowances to members of Provincial Employment Service Council	80	60	750 00	
	20	Administration of Provincial Employment Service Council	80	61	750 00	
		Minimum Wage Board				
	21	Administration of Act	80	64	600 00	
					32,470 00	34,925 00
41		**DEPARTMENT OF PUBLIC WELFARE**				
		Main Office				
	1	Contingencies	81	5		350 00
	2	Expense of exhibits at C.N.E., etc	81	6	200 00	
	3	Maintenance of indigents	81	7		1,000 00
	4	Memorial wreaths	New	New		1,850 00
	5	Standard Relief Forms for the Municipalities of the Province of Ontario	New	New		6,000 00
					200 00	9,200 00
		Grants:				
	6	Salvation Army	82	4	1,500 00	
	7	Ontario Society for prevention of cruelty to animals	82	5	750 00	
	8	Royal Humane Society	82	6	250 00	
	9	Girl Guides' Association	82	7	1,000 00	
	10	Boys Scouts' Association	82	8	1,000 00	
	11	Soldiers' Aid Commission	82	9	12,500 00	
	12	Ex-service Men	82	10	500 00	
	13	Ontario Society for Crippled Children	New	New		5,000 00
	14	Community Welfare Council	New	New		1,000 00
	15	Canadian Council, Child and Family Welfare	New	New		800 00
	16	Soldiers' Aid Hostel, Bon Air	New	New		1,500 00
					17,500 00	8,300 00
		Children's Aid Branch				
	17	Salaries	83	1–10	975 00	
	18	C. P. Act and C. U. P. Act	83	11	16,000 00	
	19	Grant to Children's Aid Society	83	12	500 00	
	20	Contingencies	83	13	2,357 00	
					19,832 00	

No. of Vote	No. of Item	Service	Main Estimates Old Vote	Main Estimates Old Item	Reduction	Addition
41		**DEPARTMENT OF PUBLIC WELFARE—Continued**				
		Boys' Training School, Bowmanville				
	21	Salaries	84	1-2 & 7	2,100 00	2,150 00
	22	Medicine and medical comforts, groceries and provisions, fuel, light, water, clothing, laundry and cleaning, furniture and furnishings, office expense, farm expense, recreation equipment and contingencies, including boys' travelling expenses and maintenance of boys in foster homes. (This wording in lieu of wording Main Estimates, vote 84, item 8-1932-33)	84	8	6,000 00	
	23	Maintenance and repairs	84	9	4,500 00	
	24	Toronto Club	84	10	1,650 00	
	25	Gratuities to boys	84	11	1,000 00	
					15,250 00	2,150 00
		Mothers' Allowances Commission				
	26	Salaries	85	1-8		2,025 00
	27	Contingencies	85	9	14,000 00	
					14,000 00	2,025 00
		Old Age Pensions Commission				
	28	Salaries	86	1-7		3,975 00
	29	Contingencies	86	9		4,825 00
						8,800 00
		Girls Training School, Galt				
	30	Salaries and operating expenses (2 months)	New	New		6,149 25
					66,782 00	36,624 25
42		**DEPARTMENT OF PROVINCIAL TREASURER**				
		Main Office				
	1	Salaries	87	1-14	5,779 16	5,950 00
	2	Contingencies	87	15	783 00	
					6,562 16	5,950 00
		Office of Budget Committee				
	3	Salaries	New	New		4,000 00
	4	Contingencies	New	New		5,500 00
						9,500 00
		Office of Controller of Revenue				
	5	Salaries	88	1-26	4,000 00	9,175 00
	6	Contingencies	88	28	776 00	
	7	Stock transfer stamps, printing, etc.	88	29	2,000 00	
	8	Law stamps, printing, commissions, etc.	88	30	1,000 00	
	9	Membership and annual fees in associations	88	31	50 00	
	10	Legal expenses, valuations, arbitrations and commissions	88	32		2,000 00
					7,826 00	11,175 00

No. of Vote	No. of Item	Service	Main Estimates Old Vote	Main Estimates Old Item	Reduction	Addition
42		**DEPARTMENT OF PROVINCIAL TREASURER —Continued**				
		Board of Censors				
	11	Salaries	89	1–5		2,750 00
	12	Contingencies	89	6	2,324 42	
					2,324 42	2,750 00
		Motion Picture Bureau				
		Administration and Distribution				
	13	Salaries	90	1–9	737 50	125 00
	14	Contingencies	90	10	2,350 00	
	15	Express and Customs charges (circulation of film)	90	11	4,000 00	
		Laboratory				
	16	Salaries	90	12–17 19–22	568 75	
	17	Purchase and maintenance of equipment, machines and film, film laboratory, still pictures and lantern slides	90	18	19,118 75	
					26,775 00	125 00
		Public Records and Archives				
	18	Salaries	91	1–7	2,900 00	1,125 00
	19	Purchase of documents, pamphlets, books, relics, etc.	91	8	2,330 00	
	20	Contingencies	91	9		1,500 00
					5,230 00	2,625 00
		House Post Office				
	21	Postage and cost of House Post Office	92	4	4,241 00	
					52,958 58	32,12[illegible] 00
43		**PROVINCIAL AUDITOR'S OFFICE**				
	1	Salaries	93	1–13	2,391 00	5,300 00
	2	Contingencies	93	14		2,325 00
					2,391 00	7,625 00

No. of Vote	No. of Item	Service	Main Estimates Old Vote	Main Estimates Old Item	Reduction	Addition
44		**DEPARTMENT OF PROVINCIAL SECRETARY**				
		Main Office				
	1	Salaries	94	1–14	3,650 00	3,825 00
	2	Contingencies	94	16	2,200 00	
	3	Travelling and other expenses, Real Estate Brokers Act	94	15	8,500 00	
					14,350 00	3,825 00
		Registrar-General's Branch				
	4	Salaries	95	1–8	1,050 00	2,625 00
	5	Contingencies	95	10	5,580 00	
	6	Fees, District Registrar	95	9	200 00	
					6,830 00	2,625 00
					21,180 00	6,450 00
5		PUBLIC INSTITUTIONS BRANCH				
		Main Office				
	1	Contingencies	97	13	850 00	
		General				
	2	Travelling expenses of bailiff and prisoners	97	14	5,000 00	
	3	Railway fares and clothing of discharged prisoners	97	15		300 00
	4	Printing and stationery for Public Institutions	97	17	1,500 00	
	5	Medical attendance, funeral, transportation and burial expenses of officials and employees of the Public Institutions where death or illness arises from nature of employment	97	18	300 00	
	6	Treatments of patients and inmates of Public Institutions in Hospitals and Sanatoria	97	19	200 00	
	7	Expenses re Exhibit of the Provincial Secretary's Department at the C.N.E. and other Exhibitions	97	20	1,000 00	
	8	Compassionate allowance	97	21	1,700 00	
	9	Citizens' Service Association	New	New		5,000 00
	10	Grant for Public School No. 1, Guelph Township	New	New		325 00
	11	Sundries	New	New		500 00
	12	Unforeseen and unprovided	97	23	400 00	
		Board of Parole				
	13	Allowance and expenses for Parole Board	98	7		600 00
	14	Prisoners' Assistance Fund	98	8	400 00	
	15	Expenses of returning to prison parole and permit violators	98	9	100 00	

No. of Vote	No. of Item	Service	Main Estimates Old Vote	Main Estimates Old Item	Reduction	Addition
45		**DEPARTMENT OF PROVINCIAL SECRETARY —Continued**				
		REFORMATORIES				
		Ontario Reformatory, Guelph				
	16	Expenses	99	9	30,000 00	
	17	Repairs to buildings	99	10	7,000 00	
	18	Ontario Reformatory—Guelph Industries	100	1	25,000 00	
		Ontario Reformatory, Mimico				
	19	Expenses	101	2	10,000 00	
	20	Repairs to buildings, etc.	101	3	4,000 00	
	21	Purchase of materials, machinery, repairs, expenses, etc.	102	1	30,000 00	
		Mercer Reformatory, Toronto				
	22	Salaries	103	1–15		825 00
	23	Expenses	103	16	6,500 00	
	24	Repairs to buildings, etc.	103	17	7,000 00	
	25	Purchase of materials, machinery, repairs, expenses, etc.	104	1	10,000 00	
		INDUSTRIAL FARMS				
		Industrial Farm, Burwash				
	26	Salaries	105	1–20	1,500 00	1,500 00
	27	Expenses	105	21	35,000 00	
		Industrial Farm, Fort William				
	28	Expenses	106	6	4,000 00	
	29	Repairs to buildings, etc.	106	7	3,000 00	
					184,450 00	9,050 00
					205,630 00	15,500 00
		DEPARTMENT OF AGRICULTURE				
		Summary				
	46	Main Office			Net	Net 18,130 89
		Branches:				
	47	Statistics and Publications			2,925 00	
	48	Agricultural and Horticultural Societies			69,100 00	
	49	Live Stock			2,250 00	
	50	Institutes			16,306 25	
	51	Dairy				1,425 00
	52	Fruit			17,750 00	
	53	Agricultural Representatives			32,231 78	
	54	Crops, Co-operation and Markets			26,950 00	
	55	Agricultural Development Board				2,500 00
	56	Colonization and Immigration			18,000 00	
	57	Kemptville Agricultural School			7,000 00	
	58	Ontario Veterinary College			1,275 00	

No. of Vote	No. of Item	Service	Main Estimates Old Vote	Main Estimates Old Item	Reduction	Addition
		DEPARTMENT OF AGRICULTURE —Continued				
		Summary—Continued				
	59	Western Experimental Farm...........			7,000 00	
	60	Demonstration Farm, New Liskeard....			5,000 00	
	61	Demonstration Farm, Hearst..........			7,000 00	
	62	Ontario Agricultural College...........			63,528 00	
			•		276,316 03	22,055 89
46		*Main Office*				
	1	Salaries...............................	107	1-6	200 00	3,606 25
	2	Contingencies..........................	107	7	2,000 00	
		General				
	3	Fieldman, Northern Ontario, salary and expenses............................	New	New		5,000 00
	4	Provincial Zoologist, services, equipment and expenses.........................	107	11	3,000 00	
	5	Publicity work in Great Britain; promotion and sale of Ontario farm products; services, travelling and other expenses of Ontario House. (This wording to be used in lieu of wording Vote 117, Item 9 of Main Estimates, 1932-33)............	117	9	10,000 00	
	6	Services and expenses in connection with agricultural work; preparation, printing and distributing reports, bulletins and circulars; special investigations into agricultural conditions or the production of crops; advertising and publicity, including special educational campaigns; agricultural instruction, agricultural education, including Scholarships, bursaries, prizes or awards; expenses in connection with outbreaks of diseases; services and expenses in connection with exhibits, including prizes, trophies, etc.; travelling expenses, equipment, supplies and contingencies not otherwise provided for....	107	12	15,000 00	
	7	Administration and enforcement of *The Corn Borer Act*......................	113	18		551 32
	8	Expenses of exhibit of grain, fruit, vegetables and other products at Exhibitions	107	8	2,500 00	
	9	Inspection of apiaries, automobiles, services and other expenses...............	123	232		3,125 00
	10	Removal expenses of officials in the Public Service............................	107	9	500 00	
	11	Fees of officers of Department...........	107	10	50 00	
		Grants occasioned by unassessable Crown lands:				
	12	Union School No. 1, Clinton and Louth..	New	New		350 00
	13	Macdonald Consolidated School, Guelph	New	New		817 46
	14	Kemptville Public School..............	New	New		69 94
	15	S.S. No. 10, Oxford Township..........	New	New		15 69
		Grants:				
	16	City of Toronto re horse stables in Exhibition Park........................	New	New		26,407 50
	17	Ontario Agricultural Council...........	New	New		750 00
	18	Ontario Research Foundation..........	New	New		8,213 73
	19	Matheson Co-operative Dairy..........	New	New		2,375 00
					33,250 00	51,380 89

No. of Vote	No. of Item	Service	Main Estimates Old Vote	Main Estimates Old Item	Reduction	Addition
		DEPARTMENT OF AGRICULTURE—Continued				
47		*Statistics and Publications Branch*				
	1	Salaries	108	1–6	1,925 00	
	2	Contingencies	108	7	1,000 00	
					2,925 00	
48		*Agricultural and Horticultural Societies Branch*				
	1	Salaries	109	1–2 & 22	1,200 00	2,200 00
	2	Contingencies	109	6		1,200 00
		Grants:				
	3	Grants under Section 22, subsection 1(*a*) to (*e*), inclusive	109	12	25,000 00	
	4	Grants under Horticultural Societies Act	109	18	10,000 00	
		Grants:				
	5	To encourage local plowing matches, to be paid in grants or otherwise, as may be approved by the Lieutenant-Governor in Council	109	19	1,000 00	
		Grants under Agricultural Societies Act:				
	6	Spring Stock Shows (including services, travelling and other expenses of Judges)	109	10	700 00	
	7	Special grants under Section 23	109	11	1,000 00	
	8	Agricultural Societies notwithstanding provisions of Agricultural Societies Act	109	13	200 00	
	9	Ontario Plowmen's Association	109	9	100 00	
	10	Ontario Vegetable Growers' Association	109	8	150 00	
	11	Ontario Horticultural Association	109	7	50 00	
	12	Judges, services, travelling and other expenses	109	17	19,000 00	
	13	Services, travelling and other expenses of Judges in Field Crop Competitions	109	16	5,000 00	
	14	Horticultural, Agricultural and Vegetable Growers' Societies, services, travelling and other expenses of meetings at the direction of the Department, investigations and unforeseen expenditure	109	21		1,000 00
	15	Field Crop Competitions, prizes and miscellaneous expenses, including transportation and other expenses of exhibits at Exhibitions	109	15	9,000 00	
	16	Special prizes, Provincial Plowing Match	109	20	100 00	
	17	Vegetable Specialist, expenses	109	23	1,000 00	
					73,500 00	4,400 00
49		*Live Stock Branch*				
	1	Salaries	110	1–6 & 15		1,250 00
	2	Contingencies	110	7	1,500 00	
		Grants:				
	3	Educational and Demonstration Work in any Branch of Live Stock, Judges, Lecturers, Valuators and other Assistants, salaries, expenses and equipment, live stock exhibits and transportation charges; travelling expenses, fieldmen; purchase, maintenance and distribution of live stock; to pay such grants for the encouragement of live stock as may be fixed by the Lieutenant Governor in Council	110	16	15,000 00	

No. of Vote	No. of Item	Service	Main Estimates		Reduction	Addition
			Old Vote	Old Item		
		DEPARTMENT OF AGRICULTURE—Continued				
49		*Live Stock Branch—Continued*				
	4	Expenses in connection with T.B. testing work	New	New		15,000 00
	5	Services, travelling and other expenses in connection with the administration of *The Stallion Enrolment Act*, and payment of premiums for pure-bred stallions	110	17	2,000 00	
					18,500 00	16,250 00
50		*Institutes Branch*				
	1	Salaries	111	1-7	2,806 25	
	2	Contingencies	111	8	500 00	
		Grants:				
	3	Services, travelling, equipment, supplies and other expenses in connection with Women's Institutes, Junior Institutes, demonstration lecture courses, one-month and three-months courses, Household Science, judging, instruction and competitions, exhibits, conferences, conventions, and Women's Institute and agricultural meetings	111	9	13,000 00	
					16,306 25	
51		*Dairy Branch*				
	1	Salaries	112	1-3 & 13		3,000 00
	2	Contingencies	112	4	1,000 00	
		Grants:				
	3	Dairymen's Association, Eastern Ontario	112	5	500 00	
	4	Dairymen's Association, Western Ontario	112	6	500 00	
	5	Ontario Whole Milk Producers' Association. (This wording in lieu of wording of Vote 112, Item 7, Main Estimates, 1932-33)	112	7		700 00
	6	Central Ontario Cheesemakers' Association	112	9	50 00	
	7	Western Ontario Cheesemakers' Association	112	8	25 00	
	8	Experimental work	112	12	200 00	
					2,275 00	3,700 00
52		*Fruit Branch*				
	1	Salaries	113	1-2		3,800 00
	2	Contingencies	113	3	300 00	
	3	For the carrying on of work in the growing, handling, exhibiting, and advertising of fruit, including expenditure under *The Fruit Pests' Act*, leasing of orchards, travelling and other expenses	113	6	12,800 00	
		Grants:				
	4	Entomological Society of Ontario	113	4	150 00	
	5	Towards erection of packing houses	113	17	4,000 00	
	6	Special experiments	113	15	1,500 00	
	7	Apple Maggot Survey and expenses therewith in accordance with agreement with Dominion Department of Agriculture	New	New		2,500 00

No. of Vote	No. of Item	Service	Main Estimates Old Vote	Main Estimates Old Item	Reduction	Addition
		DEPARTMENT OF AGRICULTURE—Continued				
52		*Fruit Branch—Continued*				
		Horticultural Experiment Station:				
	8	Salaries	113	7–13	300 00	18,200 00
	9	Services, travelling and other expenses in connection with maintenance of Horticultural Experiment Station, rent of additional land, purchase and maintenance of automobiles, trucks, tractors, and farm machinery	113	14	23,200 00	
					42,250 00	24,500 00
53		*Agricultural Representatives Branch*				
	1	Salaries	114	4	150 00	750 00
	2	Contingencies	114	7	2,000 00	
	3	Agricultural Representative work, services, expenses and equipment	114	8	35,000 00	
	4	Transportation and living expenses attending Short Courses for winners in competitions under Agricultural Representives	114	10	800 00	
	5	Household Science Demonstrator, services and expenses	114	9	2,000 00	
	6	Canadian Council on Boys' and Girls' Club Work	New	New		1,750 00
	7	Royal Winter Fair Party	New	New		5,218 22
					39,950 00	7,718 22
54		*Crops, Co-operation and Markets Branch*				
	1	Salaries	115	1	8,125 00	
	2	Contingencies	115	7	2,550 00	
	3	Loans in accordance with *The Co-operative Marketing Loan Act, 1920*	115	8	2,500 00	
	4	To encourage co-operative marketing	115	9	5,000 00	
	5	Crop improvement, demonstrations, purchase of seed and equipment, services and travelling expenses, printing, advertising and other educational work, prizes, trophies and awards, etc., administration and enforcement of *The Weed Control Act*	115	11	5,000 00	
		Grants:				
	6	Ontario Experimental Union	115	12	500 00	
	7	Essex County Corn Improvement Association	115	13	50 00	
	8	Ontario Corn Growers' Association	115	14	100 00	
	9	Lambton Corn Growers' Association	115	15	50 00	
	10	Wentworth County Seed Association	115	16	25 00	
	11	Quinte Seed Society	115	17	50 00	
		Subventions:				
	12	Seed cleaning plants	115	19	1,000 00	
	13	For freight on agricultural lime	115	20	2,000 00	
					26,950 00	

No. of Vote	No. of Item	Service	Main Estimates Old Vote	Main Estimates Old Item	Reduction	Addition
		DEPARTMENT OF AGRICULTURE—Continued				
55		*Agricultural Development Board*				
	1	Salaries and expenses in connection with operation of Ontario Farm Loans Act and Agricultural Development Act, including prepayment of insurance premiums	116	1		2,500 00
56		*Colonization and Immigration Branch*				
	1	Salaries	117	1	1,050 00	
	2	Contingencies	117	4	700 00	
		Grants:				
	3	Canadian Women's Hostels	117	5	4,000 00	
	4	Salvation Army	117	6	3,000 00	
	5	Printing pamphlets for publicity purposes; expenses incurred in distributing settlers; photographs, maps, advertising, services, travelling and other expenses in connection with colonization. (This wording to be used in lieu of wording Vote 117, Item 7, Main Estimates, 1932-33)	117	7	3,000 00	
	6	Land Guides for settlers and veterans	117	8	500 00	
	7	Rental of offices, including equipment, heating, lighting, furnishing and contingencies	117	10	2,000 00	
	8	Payments for after-care of boy settlers as per agreement with the Overseas Settlement Board; payments in accordance with the agreement entered into with the Board of Home Missions of the United Church	117	11	1,000 00	
	9	Salvation Army special work in connection with placing of boys in the Province of Ontario, to be paid in accordance with terms approved by the Lieutenant-Governor in Council	117	12	1,750 00	
	10	Expenses in after-care of immigrants	117	13	1,000 00	
					18,000 00	
57		*Kemptville Agricultural School*				
	1	Wages, travelling expenses, equipment, purchase and maintenance of stock, general expenses	118	1	7,000 00	
58		*Ontario Veterinary College*				
	1	Faculty and staff not otherwise provided for to be paid out as directed by Order of the Lieutenant-Governor in Council	119	6		3,325 00
	2	Fuel, light, water, telephone service, books, apparatus, appliances, library supplies and equipment, furnishings, repairs, temporary lecturers or other assistance, printing, advertising and contingencies	119	7	2,100 00	
	3	Research and investigation	119	9	2,500 00	
					4,600 00	3,325 00

No. of Vote	No. of Item	Service	Main Estimates Old Vote	Main Estimates Old Item	Reduction	Addition
		DEPARTMENT OF AGRICULTURE—Continued				
59		*Western Experimental Farm*				
	1	Purchase of stock and equipment, wages, seed, feed, fertilizer, fuel, light, supplies; travelling expenses, education work, contingencies	120	1	7,000 00	
					7,000 00	
60		*Demonstration Farm, New Liskeard*				
	1	Expenses of clearing, construction of buildings, salaries and wages, provisions, purchases and shipping of live stock, equipment, travelling and miscellaneous expenses, including expenses incurred in connection with entertaining visitors to the Farm	121	1	5,000 00	
					5,000 00	
61		*Demonstration Farm, Hearst*				
	1	Expenses of clearing, construction of buildings, salaries and wages, provisions, purchase of land, buildings, live stock and equipment, travelling and miscellaneous expenses, including expenses incurred in connection with entertaining visitors to the Farm	122	1	7,000 00	
					7,000 00	
62		ONTARIO AGRICULTURAL COLLEGE				
		Administration and Maintenance				
	1	Salaries	123	39	1,500 00	
		Administrative Expenses				
	2	Temporary assistance, including extra lectures	123	46	1,000 00	
	3	Contingencies, including expenses of Short Courses	123	47	850 00	
	4	Travelling expenses	123	48	500 00	
	5	Library	123	49	500 00	
	6	Provisions, laundry, engine-room supplies and fuel	123	50		10,000 00
	7	Furniture, furnishings, repairs and equipment	123	51	1,000 00	
	8	Student labour	123	53		2,000 00
	9	Servants' pay list	123	58	2,100 00	
	10	Special research work in different Departments under the direction of the President	123	59	1,800 00	
	11	Purchase and maintenance of automobiles, trucks and tractors	123	60	1,000 00	
					10,250 00	12,000 00

No. of Vote	No. of Item	Service	Main Estimates Old Vote	Main Estimates Old Item	Reduction	Addition
		DEPARTMENT OF AGRICULTURE—Continued				
62		ONTARIO AGRICULTURAL COLLEGE—*Con.*				
		Bacteriology Division				
		Expenses:				
	12	Supplies, expenses and equipment......	123	67	350 00	
					350 00	
		Botany Division				
		Expenses:				
	13	Supplies, expenses and equipment......	123	74	1,000 00	
					1,000 00	
		Chemistry Division				
	14	Salaries..............................	123	89	625 00	
		Expenses:				
	15	Soil survey and field work, automobiles, supplies, expenses and equipment.....	123	90	3,000 00	
					3,625 00	
		Trent Institute Division				
	16	Salaries..............................	123	95	1,700 00	
		Expenses:				
	17	Services, supplies, equipment, maintenance and contingencies..............	123	97	475 00	
	18	Materials and labour for bakery........	123	98	1,000 00	
					3,175 00	
		Entomology Division				
		Expenses:				
	19	Supplies, expenses and equipment......	123	106	725 00	
	20	Cornborer investigations, including automobiles..........................	123	107	1,000 00	
					1,725 00	
		Agricultural Engineering Division				
		Expenses:				
	21	Services, automobiles, equipment and expenses re drainage work...........	123	123	3,600 00	
	22	Supplies, expenses and equipment......	123	124	1,000 00	
					4,600 00	
		Farm Economics Division				
		Expenses:				
	23	Farm surveys, automobiles, services, equipment and other expenses........	123	130	2,000 00	
					2,000 00	

No. of Vote	No. of Item	Service	Main Estimates Old Vote	Main Estimates Old Item	Reduction	Addition
		DEPARTMENT OF AGRICULTURE—Continued				
62		ONTARIO AGRICULTURAL COLLEGE—*Con.*				
		Animal Husbandry Division				
		Expenses:				
	24	Wages, temporary help	123	163	730 00	
	25	Purchase and maintenance of live stock	123	164	3,000 00	
					3,730 00	
		Field Experiments Division				
		Expenses:				
	26	Wages, temporary help	123	177	940 00	
	27	Supplies, equipment, purchase and maintenance of horses, and contingencies	123	178	885 00	
					1,825 00	
		Experimental Dairy and Dairy School Division				
	28	Salaries	123	179	3,800 00	
		Expenses:				
	29	Wages, temporary help, and instructors in Dairy Schools	123	187	1,400 00	
	30	Purchase, hauling and manufacturing milk	123	188	5,000 00	
					10,200 00	
		Poultry Division				
	31	Salaries	123	196–198	4,300 00	
		Expenses:				
	32	Wages, temporary help	123	204	1,625 00	
	33	Experiments and feeds	123	205	3,400 00	
	34	Poultry extension work, automobiles, services, supplies and equipment	123	206	9,000 00	
	35	Purchase and maintenance of horses, supplies, equipment and contingencies	123	207	1,583 00	
	36	Turkey Experimental Farm, services, maintenance and purchase of stock, repairs and contingencies	123	208	1,300 00	
	37	Empire Marketing Board, special research, services, expenses and equipment	123	209	3,000 00	
					24,208 00	
		Horticulture Division				
	38	Salaries	123	219	2,075 00	
		Expenses:				
	39	Wages, temporary help	123	221	365 00	
	40	Trees, plants, seeds, equipment, fuel, purchase and maintenance of horses, forestry contingencies	123	222	1,500 00	
	41	Laying permanent roads, College grounds	123	224	3,000 00	
					6,940 00	

No. of Vote	No. of Item	Service	Main Estimates Old Vote	Old Item	Reduction	Addition
		DEPARTMENT OF AGRICULTURE—Continued				
62		ONTARIO AGRICULTURAL COLLEGE—*Con.*				
		Apiculture Division				
	42	Salaries..............................	123	227	1,900 00	
					75,528 00	12,000 00
63		**GENERAL MISCELLANEOUS**				
	1	Annuities and bonus to Indians...........	124	1	10,000 00	
	2	Gratuities.............................	124	2	1,900 00	
	3	Unforeseen and unprovided..............	124	3	5,775 00	
	4	Grant to Canadian National Institute for the Blind...........................	124	5	10,000 00	
	5	Compensation, medical and hospital accounts, etc., for workmen injured while engaged on Government work, etc., as awarded by Workmen's Compensation Board..............................	124	6	25,000 00	
	6	Refunds of surplus, Registry fees.........	124	7	12,000 00	
	7	Wolf Bounty—and for payment for portion of skins already submitted that do not comply with the requirements of *The Wolf Bounty Act.* (This wording in addition to wording of Vote 124, Item 8, Main Estimates, 1932-33.).............	124	8	15,000 00	
	8	Fidelity Bonds.........................	124	10	2,000 00	
					81,675 00	

No. of Vote	No. of Item	Service	Main Estimates	Old Item	Reduction	Additi
		DEPARTMENT OF AGRICULTURE **Continued**				
62		ONTARIO AGRICULTURAL COLLEGE—*Con*				
		Animal Husbandry Division				
		Expenses:				
	24	Wages, temporary help	123	163	730 00	
	25	Purchase and maintenance of live stock	123	164	3,000 00	
					3,730 00	
		Field Experiments Division				
		Expenses:				
	26	Wages, temporary help	123	177	940 00	
	27	Supplies, equipment, purchase and ma tenance of horses, and contingencies	123	178	885 00	
					1,825 00	
		Experimental Dairy and Dairy School Division				
	28	Salaries	23	179	3,800 0	
		Expenses:				
	29	Wages, temporary help, and instruct in Dairy Schools	123	187	1,400	
	30	Purchase, hauling and manufactur milk	12	188	5,000	
					10,200	
		Poultry Division				
	31	Salaries	123	196-198	4,3	
		Expenses:				
	32	Wages, temporary help	123	204	1,	
	33	Experiments and feeds	123	205	3,	
	34	Poultry extension work, automobi services, supplies and equipment	123	206		
	35	Purchase and maintenance of hor supplies, equipment and contingen	123	207		
	36	Turkey Experimental Farm, servi maintenance and purchase of st , repairs and contingencies	123	208		
	37	Empire Marketing Board, special search, services, expenses and eq ment	123	209		
		Horticulture Division				
	38	Salaries	123	219		
		Expenses:				
	39	Wages, temporary help	123	221		
	40	Trees, plants, seeds, equipment, fl, purchase and maintenance of hors, forestry contingencies	123	222		
	41	Laying permanent roads, College grouds	123	224		

ESTIMATES

of

Ordinary and Capital Expenditure

of the

Province of Ontario

for the

Fiscal Year

Ending October 31st, 1934

PRINTED BY ORDER OF
THE LEGISLATIVE ASSEMBLY OF ONTARIO

SESSIONAL PAPER No. 2, 1933

TORONTO
Printed and Published by Herbert H. Ball, Printer to the King's Most Excellent Majesty
1933

ESTIMATES

OF

Ordinary and Capital Expenditure

OF THE

PROVINCE OF ONTARIO

For the Fiscal Year Ending

OCTOBER 31st, 1934

SUMMARY

No. of Dept.	Departments	Vote No.	Page No.	To be Voted	Statutory
I	Lieutenant-Governor	1	5	$ 7,200 00	
II	Legislation	2-4	6	314,305 00	
III	Prime Minister	5-10	7	1,471,837 00	1,304,000 00
IV	Attorney-General	11-26	10	2,352,730 00	243,882 00
V	Insurance	27	16	66,300 00	
VI	Education	28-55	17	9,708,209 00	1,337,638 43
VII	Lands and Forests	56-61	33	1,513,625 00	10,000 00
VIII	Northern Development	62	37	471,025 00	3,768,325 00
IX	Mines	63-69	38	311,925 00	10,000 00
X	Game and Fisheries	70-71	41	590,400 00	
XI	Public Works	72-83	44	871,111 00	35,000 00
XII	Highways	84-85	50	532,675 00	6,777,000 00
XIII	Health	86-109	52	7,249,470 00	64,000 00
XIV	Labour	110-116	58	417,596 50	
XV	Public Welfare	117-122	61	5,225,618 00	10,000 00
XVI	Provincial Treasurer	123-129	64	596,215 00	18,798,794 48
XVII	Provincial Auditor	130	68	104,925 00	6,500 00
XVIII	Provincial Secretary	131-139	69	1,109,335 00	10,000 00
XIX	Agriculture	140-153	73	2,043,849 50	192,500 00
XX	Miscellaneous	154	84	200,000 00	
				35,158,351 00	32,567,639 91

I.—OFFICE OF LIEUTENANT-GOVERNOR

No. of Vote	No. of Item	Service	Fiscal Year 1934	
			To be Voted	Statutory
1		**Office of Lieutenant-Governor**		
		Salaries:		
	1	Permanent	3,600 00	
		Expenses:		
	2	Allowance for contingencies	3,600 00	
			7,200 00	

II.—DEPARTMENT OF LEGISLATION

No. of Vote	No. of Item	Service		Fiscal Year 1934 To be Voted	Fiscal Year 1934 Statutory
2		**Office of the Speaker**			
		Salaries:			
	1	The Speaker		2,500 00	
	2	Permanent		11,425 00	
	3	Temporary—Secretary to Speaker, clerks of committees, Sessional writers, messengers, elevator men, charwomen and pages		12,000 00	
	4	Indemnities—Members, including mileage		230,300 00	
	5	Stationery, including printing, paper, printing bills, distribution of the Statutes, printing and binding		35,000 00	
	6	Contingencies		5,000 00	
		Details:			
		Travelling expenses	$ 300 00		
		Advertising	800 00		
		Papers (subscriptions)	200 00		
		Express, cartage	125 00		
		Maintenance of equipment	50 00		
		Telegraph	75 00		
		Late suppers for Members	300 00		
		Rental, machines for Session	350 00		
		Committee Fees	400 00		
		Miscellaneous	2,400 00		
	7	Allowance to Mr. Speaker in lieu of contingencies		1,000 00	
	8	Legislative Committee for Art Purposes		1,500 00	
				298,725 00	
3		**Office of Law Clerk**			
		Salaries:			
	1	Permanent		12,080 00	
4		**Office of Clerk of the Crown-in-Chancery**			
		Salaries:			
	1	Permanent		3,200 00	
	2	Contingencies		300 00	
		Details:			
		Papers (subscriptions)	$ 12 00		
		Maintenance of equipment	25 00		
		Printing and stationery	75 00		
		Miscellaneous	188 00		
				3,500 00	
				314,305 00	

III.—DEPARTMENT OF PRIME MINISTER

No. of Vote	No. of Item	Service	Fiscal Year 1934 To be Voted	Fiscal Year 1934 Statutory
		Summary		
5		Main Office	29,685 00	1,304,000 00
		Branches:		
6		Office of Executive Council	10,525 00	
7		Tourist and Publicity Bureau	43,800 00	
8		Office of Civil Service Commissioner	15,602 00	
9		" " King's Printer	37,225 00	
			136,837 00	1,304,000 00
10		Hydro-Electric Power Commission of Ontario	1,335,000 00	
			1,471,837 00	1,304,000 00
5		**Main Office**		
		Salaries:		
	S	Prime Minister		14,000 00
	1	Permanent	11,540 00	
	2	Contingencies	10,145 00	
		Details:		
		Salaries—Temporary $8,350 00		
		Travelling expenses 200 00		
		Books, magazines, papers 200 00		
		Maintenance of equipment 100 00		
		Stationery, printing, etc. 750 00		
		Telegraph, telephone 500 00		
		Miscellaneous 45 00		
	3	Entertainment of distinguished visitors	500 00	
	4	Sundry investigations	5,000 00	
	5	General advertising	2,500 00	
	S	Ontario Public Service Superannuation Fund—Payments to Superannuates and Refunds		600,000 00
	S	Rural Transmission Lines—Bonus		650,000 00
	S	Rural Power Distribution Act—Loans		40,000 00
			29,685 00	1,304,000 00
6		**Office of Executive Council**		
		Salaries:		
	1	Permanent	10,525 00	
7		**Tourist and Publicity Bureau**		
		Salaries:		
	1	Permanent	3,800 00	
	2	Printing and distributing booklets, advertising tourist attractions, and the expenses of the Tourist and Publicity Bureau	40,000 00	
			43,800 00	
8		**Office of Civil Service Commissioner**		
		Salaries:		
	1	Permanent	15,000 00	
	2	Contingencies	602 00	
		Details:		
		Travelling expenses $ 200 00		
		Stationery, etc. 350 00		
		Maintenance of equipment 50 00		
		Telegraphs, telephone 2 00		
			15,602 00	

III.—DEPARTMENT OF PRIME MINISTER—Continued

No. of Vote	No. of Item	Service	Fiscal Year 1934	
			To be Voted	Statutory
9		**Office of King's Printer**		
		Salaries:		
	1	Permanent	29,925 00	
	2	Contingencies	1,374 00	
		Details:		
		Stationery and printing $1,250 00		
		Maintenance of equipment 50 00		
		Freight and express 62 00		
		Miscellaneous 12 00		
	3	Cartage	188 00	
	4	Official Gazette	5,738 00	
			37,225 00	
			136,837 00	1,304,000 00
10		**Hydro-Electric Power Commission of Ontario**		
	1	**Niagara System**		
		1 Developments:		
		(a) Chats Falls Generation and Transformation: Land purchases and miscellaneous betterments	75,000 00	
		(b) Niagara River: Miscellaneous betterments	50,000 00	
		(c) St. Lawrence and Ottawa River: Preliminary engineering and co-operation	50,000 00	
		2 Transformer and distributing stations	200,000 00	
		3 Transmission:		
		(a) Lines of all voltages	100,000 00	
		(b) Rural systems (ex bonus)	250,000 00	
			725,000 00	
	2	**Georgian Bay System**		
		1 Developments	30,000 00	
		2 Distributing stations	50,000 00	
		3 Transmission:		
		(a) Lines	25,000 00	
		(b) Rural systems (ex bonus)	75,000 00	
			180,000 00	
	3	**Eastern Ontario System**		
		1 Developments	25,000 00	
		2 Transformer and distributing stations	50,000 00	
		3 Transmission:		
		(a) Lines of all voltages	25,000 00	
		(b) Rural systems (ex bonus)	100,000 00	
			200,000 00	

III.—DEPARTMENT OF PRIME MINISTER—Continued

No. of Vote	No. of Item	Service	Fiscal Year 1934	
			To be Voted	Statutory
10	4	**Thunder Bay System**		
		1 Developments	10,000 00	
		2 Transformer stations	5,000 00	
		3 Transmission:		
		(a) Lines of all voltages	5,000 00	
		(b) Rural systems (ex bonus)	10,000 00	
			30,000 00	
	5	**Northern System**		
		1 Developments:		
		Wahnapitae dam reconstruction and general betterments	50,000 00	
		2 Transformer stations	10,000 00	
		3 Transmission:		
		(a) Lines of all voltages	30,000 00	
		(b) Rural systems (ex bonus)	10,000 00	
			100,000 00	
	6	**Miscellaneous**		
		(a) Administration and service buildings	100,000 00	
			1,335,000 00	

IV.—DEPARTMENT OF ATTORNEY-GENERAL

No. of Vote	No. of Item	Service		Fiscal Year 1934 To be Voted	Fiscal Year 1934 Statutory
		Summary			
11		Main Office		95,250 00	20,000 00
12		Supreme Court of Ontario		107,580 00	
13		Judges of Surrogate		1,600 00	
S		" in Counties			71,532 00
14		Deputy Clerks of the Crown and Local Registrars		25,050 00	
15		Shorthand Reporters		31,000 00	
16		Office of Toronto and York Crown Attorney		27,525 00	
17		" Land Titles		32,630 00	
18		" Local Masters of Titles		30,300 00	
19		" Drainage Trials		4,550 00	
20		Audit of Crinimal Justice Accounts Branch		803,230 00	82,375 00
S		Ontario Municipal Board			48,375 00
21		Office of Public Trustee		57,800 00	
22		" Fire Marshal		75,300 00	
23		" Inspector of Legal Offices		31,500 00	10,100 00
24		Law Enforcement Branch (Provincial Police)		888,955 00	
25		Ontario Securities Commission		40,460 00	1,500 00
				2,252,730 00	233,882 00
26		Workmen's Compensation Board		100,000 00	10,000 00
				2,352,730 00	243,882 00
11		**Main Office**			
		Salaries:			
	S	Minister			10,000 00
	1	Permanent		48,050 00	
	2	Contingencies		4,000 00	
		Details:			
		Salaries—Temporary	$ 525 00		
		Travelling expenses	900 00		
		Books, magazines, papers	45 00		
		Freight, express, cartage	5 00		
		Stationery, printing	1,525 00		
		Telegraph, telephone	500 00		
		Miscellaneous	500 00		
	S	Special investigations			10,000 00
	3	Crown Counsel prosecutions		25,000 00	
	4	General litigation		8,000 00	
	5	Commissions and sundry investigations		5,000 00	
	6	Services not otherwise provided for, to be paid as directed by the Lieutenant-Governor in Council		1,000 00	
		Grants:			
	7	Conferences on improving laws		400 00	
	8	County Law Libraries		2,000 00	
	9	Compassionate allowances for incapacitated officers not entitled to superannuation allowances, to be paid as may be directed by order of the Lieutenant-Governor in Council		1,400 00	
		LAW LIBRARY			
	10	Books, reports, etc		400 00	
				95,250 00	20,000 00

IV.—DEPARTMENT OF ATTORNEY-GENERAL—Continued

No. of Vote	No. of Item	Service		Fiscal Year 1934 To be Voted	Fiscal Year 1934 Statutory
12		**Supreme Court of Ontario**			
	1	Allowances to Judges under R.S.O., Cap. 89		19,000 00	
	2	Grants to Judges' Libraries		500 00	
	3	Salaries		7,925 00	
				27,425 00	
		MASTER'S OFFICE			
	4	Salaries		17,950 00	
		REGISTRAR'S OFFICE			
		Salaries:			
	5	Permanent		50,805 00	
	6	Contingencies		6,000 00	
		Details:			
		Reporting expenses	$600 00		
		Books, magazines, papers	80 00		
		Freight, express, cartage	20 00		
		Postage	300 00		
		Stationery, printing	4,000 00		
		Telegraph, telephone	200 00		
		Miscellaneous	800 00		
		TAXING OFFICE			
	7	Salaries		5,400 00	
				107,580 00	
13		**Judges of Surrogate**			
	1	Commutation of fees		1,600 00	
S		**Judges in Counties**			
	S	Allowances			71,532 00
14		**Deputy Clerks of the Crown and Local Registrars**			
	1	Salaries		25,050 00	
15		**Shorthand Reporters**			
	1	Salaries including allowance in lieu of stationery		24,000 00	
	2	Contingencies—Services, reporting, and travelling expenses		7,000 00	
				31,000 00	

IV.—**DEPARTMENT OF** ATTORNEY-GENERAL—Continued

No. of Vote	No. of Item	Service		Fiscal Year 1934	
				To be Voted	Statutory
16		Office of Toronto **and** York **Crown** Attorney			
		Salaries:			
	1	Permanent		22,725 00	
	2	Contingencies		4,800 00	
		Details:			
		Salaries—Temporary	$4,500 00		
		Books, magazines, papers	135 00		
		Telegraph and telephone	65 00		
		Miscellaneous	100 00		
				27,525 00	
17		**Land Titles Office**			
	1	Salaries		32,100 00	
	2	Contingencies		530 00	
		Details:			
		Stationery, printing	$ 400 00		
		Maintenance of equipment	100 00		
		Miscellaneous	30 00		
				32,630 00	
18		**Office** of Local **Masters of** Titles			
	1	Salaries and office expenses		24,300 00	
	2	Forms, copying and contingencies		2,000 00	
	3	Registration of Patents under R.S.O., Cap. 158, S. 158, including allowance for postage and for ordinary stationery		4,000 00	
				30,300 00	
19		**Office of Drainage** Trials			
		Salaries:			
	1	Permanent		4,000 00	
	2	Contingencies		550 00	
				4,550 00	
20		**Audit** of **Criminal Justice** Accounts **Branch**			
		Salaries:			
	1	Permanent		10,875 00	
	2	Contingencies		1,000 00	
		Details:			
		Travelling expenses	$ 300 00		
		Freight, express, cartage	50 00		
		Maintenance of equipment	50 00		
		Stationery, printing	500 00		
		Telegraph, telephone	50 00		
		Miscellaneous	50 00		
	S	Administration of Justice Expense Act: Special expenses			50,000 00
	3	Annual revision of Municipal Voter's Lists: Services and expenses of County and District Court Judges		2,500 00	
				14,375 00	50,000 00

IV.—**DEPARTMENT OF ATTORNEY-GENERAL**—Continued

No. of Vote	No. of Item	Service	Fiscal Year 1934 To be Voted	Fiscal Year 1934 Statutory
20		**Audit of Criminal Justice Accounts Branch—Continued**		
		COUNTIES AND CITIES		
	4	Administration of Justice: Reimbursement for maintenance and accounts under The Administration of Justice Expenses Act; also direct payments under other Acts.....	375,000 00	
	5	DISTRICTS		
		Salaries: Permanent and temporary..................	92,840 00	
	6	General Administration of Justice including Fuel, light, water, rent, maintenance and clothing of prisoners, and contingencies	200,815 00	
			293,655 00	
		POLICE MAGISTRATES		
	7	Salaries, travelling expenses and contingencies......	120,000 00	
		REGISTRAR OF DEEDS, HALIBURTON		
	8	Allowance.......................................	200 00	
		PROBATION OFFICES		
	S	Salaries..		30,000 00
	S	Contingencies..................................		2,375 00
		Details:		
		Travelling expenses............... $1,375 00		
		Stationery, printing............... 500 00		
		Miscellaneous.................... 500 00		
				32,375 00
			803,230 00	82,375 00
S		**Ontario Municipal Board**		
		Salaries:		
	S	Permanent..................................		40,275 00
	S	Contingencies................................		8,100 00
		Details:		
		Salaries—Temporary.............. $1,600 00		
		Travelling expenses............... 3,000 00		
		Stationery, printing............... 2,300 00		
		Periodicals, membership fees, etc..... 175 00		
		Court Reporter, engineer.......... 750 00		
		Miscellaneous.................... 275 00		
				48,375 00

IV.—DEPARTMENT OF ATTORNEY-GENERAL—Continued

No. of Vote	No. of Item	Service		Fiscal Year 1934 To be Voted	Fiscal Year 1934 Statutory
21		**Office of Public Trustee**			
		Salaries:			
	1	Permanent		45,300 00	
	2	Remuneration of Advisory Committee		4,500 00	
	3	Auditor's fees		3,000 00	
	3	Contingencies		5,000 00	
				57,800 00	
22		**Office of Fire Marshal**			
		Salaries:			
	1	Permanent		44,050 00	
	2	Contingencies		31,250 00	
		Details:			
		Salaries—Temporary	$1,275 00		
		Travelling expenses	16,000 00		
		Advertising	500 00		
		Books, magazines, papers	175 00		
		Freight, express, cartage	50 00		
		Maintenance of equipment	1,500 00		
		Purchase of equipment	250 00		
		Stationery, printing	5,000 00		
		Telegraph, telephone	750 00		
		Rent	3,000 00		
		Miscellaneous	2,750 00		
				75,300 00	
23		**Office of Inspector of Legal Offices**			
		Salaries:			
	1	Permanent		22,000 00	
	2	Fidelity bonds		2,000 00	
	3	Contingencies		6,000 00	
		Details:			
		Travelling expenses	$4,000 00		
		Stationery, printing	1,400 00		
		Telegraph, telephone	25 00		
		Freight, express, cartage	25 00		
		Maintenance of equipment	60 00		
		Postage	425 00		
		Books, magazines, papers	18 00		
		Miscellaneous	47 00		
				30,000 00	
	4	Typewriters, office equipment and contingencies for Judicial Officers, Registrars, and Local Masters of Titles		1,500 00	
	S	Sheriffs—To make up incomes to $1,800.00			1,300 00
	S	Registrars of Deeds—To make up incomes to $1,800.00			8,800 00
				31,500 00	10,100 00

IV.—DEPARTMENT OF ATTORNEY-GENERAL—Continued

No. of Vote	No. of Item	Service		Fiscal Year 1934 To be Voted	Fiscal Year 1934 Statutory
24		**Law Enforcement Branch**			
		(Ontario Provincial Police)			
	1	Law Enforcement Fund		888,955 00	
		Salaries—Permanent	$670,000 00		
		Temporary	15,000 00		
		Miscellaneous	203,955 00		
25		**Ontario Securities Commission**			
	1	Salaries		25,675 00	
	2	Contingencies		14,785 00	
		Details:			
		Salaries—Temporary	$4,650 00		
		Travelling expenses	550 00		
		Books, magazines, papers	100 00		
		Freight, express, cartage	25 00		
		Maintenance of equipment	200 00		
		Purchase of equipment	1,160 00		
		Stationery, printing	2,000 00		
		Telegraph, telephone	100 00		
		Services	6,000 00		
	S	Accounting services			1,500 00
				40,460 00	1,500 00
				2,252,730 00	233,882 00
26		**Workmen's Compensation Board**			
	S	Assistance in defraying expenses			10,000 00
		General to all Departments:			
	1	Compensation, medical, hospital and other accounts for workmen injured in Government work as awarded by Board		100,000 00	
				100,000 00	10,000 00
				2,352,730 00	243,882 00

V.—DEPARTMENT OF INSURANCE

No. of Vote	No. of Item	Service	Fiscal Year 1934 To be Voted	Fiscal Year 1934 Statutory
27		**Main Office**		
		Salaries:		
	1	Permanent	48,200 00	
	2	Contingencies	12,000 00	
		Details:		
		Salaries—Temporary $3,800		
		Travelling expenses 4,800		
		Books, magazines, papers 300		
		Maintenance of equipment 200		
		Stationery, printing 1,300		
		Telephone, telegraph 300		
		Miscellaneous 1,300		
	3	Printing annual reports, and financial statements of insurance, loan and trust corporations, licenses, forms, etc	6,000 00	
	4	Grant to Association of Superintendents of Insurance of the provinces of Canada, toward expense of annual conference	100 00	
			66,300 00	

VI.—DEPARTMENT OF EDUCATION

No. of Vote	No. of Item	Service	Fiscal Year 1934	
			To be Voted	Statutory
		Summary		
28		Main Office	90,275 00	
		Branches:		
29		Legislative Library	18,575 00	
30		Public and Separate School Education	3,784,305 00	
31		Inspection of schools	564,300 00	
32		Departmental examinations	296,075 00	
33		Text-books	58,900 00	
34		Training Schools	119,600 00	
35		Toronto Normal and Model Schools	125,475 00	
36		Ottawa Normal and Model Schools	81,360 00	
37		London Normal School	40,800 00	
38		Hamilton Normal School	38,515 00	
39		Peterborough Normal School	38,260 00	
40		Stratford Normal School	42,200 00	
41		North Bay Normal School	38,815 00	
42		University of Ottawa Normal School	112,475 00	
43		Sturgeon Falls Model School	41,500 00	
44		Sandwich Model School	13,575 00	
45		Embrun Model School	37,175 00	
46		High Schools and Collegiate Institutes	425,425 00	11,000 00
47		Departmental Museum	4,400 00	
48		Public Libraries	94,900 00	
49		Vocational Education	1,517,325 00	
50		Ontario Training College of Technical Teachers	20,050 00	
51		Superannuated Teachers	20,300 00	700,000 00
52		Provincial and other universities	1,800,500 00	626,638 43
53		Belleville School for the Deaf	152,750 00	
54		Brantford School for the Blind	85,724 00	
55		Monteith Northern Academy	44,655 00	
			9,708,209 00	1,337,638 43
		Main Office		
28		Salaries:		
	1	Permanent	76,275 00	
	2	Contingencies	7,000 00	
		Details:		
		Salaries—Temporary $2,200 00		
		Travelling expenses 500 00		
		Advertising 50 00		
		Books, magazines, papers 400 00		
		Freight, express, cartage 100 00		
		Maintenance of equipment 400 00		
		Purchase of equipment 400 00		
		Stationery, printing 2,200 00		
		Telegraph, telephone 250 00		
		Miscellaneous 500 00		
		Proportion of cost of Minister's Report	1,250 00	
		Cost of litigation	150 00	
	3	Consolidation and revision of the Acts of the Department of Education and contingencies	600 00	
		Details:		
		Printing $ 550 00		
		Miscellaneous 50 00		
	6	Advertising in Educational and other papers and magazines	5,000 00	
			90,275 00	

VI.—DEPARTMENT OF EDUCATION—Continued

No. of Vote	No. of Item	Service		Fiscal Year 1934 To be Voted	Fiscal Year 1934 Statutory
29		**Legislative Library**			
		Salaries:			
	1	Permanent		14,475 00	
	2	Purchase of books, subscriptions, fees and dues, binding, rebinding stationery, printing and contingencies		3,600 00	
		Details:			
		Salaries—Temporary	$ 500 00		
		Purchase of books	1,500 00		
		Subscriptions	500 00		
		Stationery, printing and binding	1,000 00		
		Miscellaneous	100 00		
	3	Purchase of legal publications		500 00	
				18,575 00	
30		**Public and Separate School Education**			
	1	Public and Separate Schools' grants and contingencies		2,900,000 00	
		Details:			
		Grants	$2,898,000 00		
		Contingencies	2,000 00		
	2	Assisted Public and Separate Schools, grants and contingencies		150,000 00	
		Details:			
		Grants	$149,800 00		
		Contingencies	200 00		
	3	Special grant to school at Whitefish Falls, District of Algoma		500 00	
	4	Special grant to Tarentorus Township School Board in aid of education of children at Children's Shelter		325 00	
	5	Redemption of debentures issued by Boards of Public or Separate School Trustees which are guaranteed by the Province of Ontario to be paid as they become due when the Boards of Trustees through unforeseen circumstances cannot meet their obligations punctually		200 00	
	6	Public, Separate and Continuation Schools, Cadet Corps, grants and contingencies		7,320 00	
		Details:			
		Grants	$7,300 00		
		Contingencies	20 00		
	7	Kindergarten Schools, grants and contingencies		11,700 00	
		Details:			
		Grants	$11,650 00		
		Contingencies	50 00		
	8	Night Schools, grants and contingencies		5,200 00	
		Details:			
		Grants	$5,150 00		
		Contingencies	50 00		
	9	Consolidated Schools including grants, organizations, services, travelling expenses and contingencies		34,460 00	
		Details:			
		Grants	$34,400 00		
		Contingencies	60 00		

VI.—DEPARTMENT OF EDUCATION—Continued

No. of Vote	No. of Item	Service	Fiscal Year 1934 To be Voted	Fiscal Year 1934 Statutory
30		**Public and Separate School Education—Continued**		
	10	Agricultural and Horticultural grants to School Boards, teachers and inspectors for Public and Separate Schools and contingencies.............	170,000 00	
		Details:		
		Grants....................... $169,800 00		
		Contingencies................ 200 00		
	11	Industrial Arts, Manual Training and Household Science, grants to Boards and teachers and contingencies..................................	78,500 00	
		Details:		
		Grants........................ $78,450 00		
		Contingencies.................. 50 00		
	12	Correspondence Courses and courses by itinerant teachers for pupils in isolated districts, including services, equipment, supplies and contingencies...	22,000 00	
		Details:		
		Salaries—Permanent............ $13,400 00		
		Temporary........... 3,500 00		
		School cars.................... 3,500 00		
		Books, stationery, printing...... 1,500 00		
		Miscellaneous.................. 100 00		
	13	Auxiliary classes, grants, services, travelling expenses and contingencies............................	43,500 00	
		Details:		
		Grants........................ $43,000 00		
		Contingencies.................. 500 00		
	14	Continuation Schools, grants and contingencies.....	190,500 00	
		Details:		
		Grants........................ $190,300 00		
		Contingencies.................. 200 00		
	15	Fifth Classes, grants and contingencies............	51,500 00	
		Details:		
		Grants......................... $51,400 00		
		Contingencies................... 100 00		
	16	Spring and Summer Schools, including services, board and travelling expenses of Instructors and students and transportation expenses of children and contingencies............................	70,000 00	
		Details:		
		Services....................... $68,000 00		
		Travelling expenses............ 500 00		
		Books, supplies................ 600 00		
		Stationery, printing............ 300 00		
		Miscellaneous.................. 600 00		
	17	Grants to Art Departments and teachers in art in Public, Separate and Continuation Schools and contingencies...............................	7,600 00	
		Details:		
		Grants........................ $7,550 00		
		Contingencies.................. 50 00		

VI.—DEPARTMENT OF EDUCATION—Continued

No. of Vote	No. of Item	SERVICE		Fiscal Year 1934 To be Voted	Fiscal Year 1934 Statutory
30		**Public and Separate School Education—Continued**			
	18	Grants to School Boards, supervisors and teachers to encourage courses of music in Public, Separate and Continuation Schools, and contingencies.........		12,000 00	
		Details:			
		Grants........................	$11,950 00		
		Contingencies..................	50 00		
	19	Medical and Dental Inspection including grants, services, travelling expenses and contingencies....		12,000 00	
		Details:			
		Grants........................	$11,950 00		
		Contingencies..................	50 00		
		Grants:			
	20	Ontario Educational Association................		2,500 00	
	21	Trustees' Section, Ontario Educational Association		2,000 00	
	22	National Council of Education for Secretarial work....................................		1,000 00	
	23	Ontario Federation of Home and School Association.....................................		1,000 00	
	24	Frontier College to be paid as may be directed by the Lieutenant-Governor in Council..........		5,000 00	
	25	Penny Bank of Ontario......................		5,000 00	
	26	Canadian Bureau for the advancement of music..		500 00	
				3,784,305 00	
31		**Inspection of Schools Branch**			
		Salaries:			
	1	Permanent................................		196,800 00	
	2	Inspection of Public Schools, Counties............		285,000 00	
		Details:			
		Salaries.......................	$259,850 00		
		Grants.......................	25,150 00		
	3	Travelling and moving expenses of Inspectors and other officials and for clerical assistance, office rent, office furniture and contingencies..............		80,000 00	
		Details:			
		Salaries—Temporary............	$ 500 00		
		Travelling expenses.............	51,600 00		
		Office expenses of County Inspectors........................	15,000 00		
		Books, magazines, papers........	100 00		
		Freight, express, cartage.........	25 00		
		Maintenance of equipment......	500 00		
		Purchase of equipment..........	150 00		
		Stationery, printing.............	12,000 00		
		Telegraph, telephone............	50 00		
		Miscellaneous..................	75 00		
	4	Inspection of Indian Schools, including services, travelling expenses and contingencies...........		2,500 00	
		Details:			
		Services.......................	$1,700 00		
		Travelling expenses.............	800 00		
				564,300 00	

VI.—DEPARTMENT OF EDUCATION—Continued

No. of Vote	No. of Item	Service	Fiscal Year 1934	
			To be Voted	Statutory
32		**Departmental Examinations Branch**		
		Salaries:		
	1	Permanent	41,425 00	
	2	Departmental Examinations including services and travelling expenses	200,000 00	
		Details:		
		Services $180,000 00		
		Travelling expenses 20,000 00		
	3	Contingencies	17,000 00	
		Details:		
		Travelling expenses $ 100 00		
		Books, magazines, papers 50 00		
		Freight, express, cartage 150 00		
		Maintenance of equipment 500 00		
		Purchase of equipment 500 00		
		Stationery, printing 14,000 00		
		Telegraph, telephone 100 00		
		Miscellaneous 1,600 00		
	4	Assistants in connection with Departmental Examinations	30,000 00	
	5	Extra services of Professional Supervising Board of Examiners as may be directed by the Lieutenant-Governor in Council, Departmental Examinations	7,650 00	
			296,075 00	
33		**Text-Books Branch**		
		Salaries:		
	1	Permanent	6,400 00	
	2	Preparation of text-books, including plates, etc., services, travelling expenses and contingencies	12,500 00	
		Details:		
		Services $9,000 00		
		Travelling expenses 500 00		
		Advertising 75 00		
		Books, magazines, papers, plates 1,000 00		
		Freight, express, cartage 100 00		
		Stationery, printing 1,700 00		
		Miscellaneous 125 00		
	3	Subventions to publishers as supplementing retail prices of text-books	40,000 00	
			58,900 00	
34		**Training Schools**		
		Salaries:		
	1	Permanent	6,200 00	
	2	Travelling and moving expenses and contingencies	400 00	
		Details:		
		Travelling expenses $ 300 00		
		Contingencies 100 00		
	3	Grants to teachers engaged in Model School Training in connection with Normal and other Training Schools	74,000 00	
	4	Grants to caretakers for services in Model Schools used for training teachers in connection with Normal and other Training Schools	1,700 00	

VI.—**DEPARTMENT OF EDUCATION**—Continued

No. of Vote	No. of Item	Service		Fiscal Year 1934 To be Voted	Fiscal Year 1934 Statutory
34		**Training Schools**—Continued			
	5	Temporary teachers, Normal and Model Schools in case of illness or on leave		4,000 00	
	6	Travelling and moving expenses of Normal and Model School Teachers transferred		300 00	
	7	Grants to Public, Separate, High and Continuation School Boards for use of schools for observation purposes		5,500 00	
	8	Grants to teachers in Public, Separate, High and Continuation Schools used for observation purposes		15,500 00	
	9	Travelling expenses of Normal School students to Rural Public and Separate Schools and for Nature Study		7,000 00	
	10	Classes in Manual Training and Household Science for teachers including services, per diem allowances to assist in paying travelling and other expenses of students and contingencies		5,000 00	
		Details:			
		Services	$4,500 00		
		Contingencies	500 00		
				119,600 00	
35		Toronto Normal and Model Schools			
		Salaries:			
	1	Permanent		102,350 00	
	2	Contingencies		4,000 00	
		Details:			
		Advertising	$ 25 00		
		Books, magazines, papers	500 00		
		Maintenance of equipment	50 00		
		Purchase of equipment	100 00		
		Stationery, printing	3,000 00		
		Telegraph, telephone	150 00		
		Miscellaneous	175 00		
	3	Apparatus, chemicals, musical instruments, domestic science and manual training supplies		1,000 00	
	4	Supplies for Kindergarten		500 00	
	5	Physical Training including apparatus and athletic supplies		375 00	
	6	Payment to the Toronto Board of Education		2,200 00	
	7	Maintenance		15,050 00	
		Fuel, light and power	$4,500 00		
		Water	1,000 00		
		Furniture and furnishings	200 00		
		Expenses of grounds, trees, supplies, etc	500 00		
		Wages of porters and extra fireman and labourers on grounds	3,350 00		
		Scrubbing, cleaning and supplies	5,000 00		
		Details:			
		Charwomen $4,500 00			
		Supplies 500 00			
		Repairs, including services, materials and incidentals	500 00		
				125,475 00	

VI.—DEPARTMENT OF EDUCATION—Continued

No. of Vote	No. of Item	Service		Fiscal Year 1934 To be Voted	Fiscal Year 1934 Statutory
36		**Ottawa Normal and Model Schools**			
		Salaries:			
	1	Permanent		69,575 00	
	2	Contingencies		2,500 00	
		Details:			
		Advertising	$ 25 00		
		Books, magazines, papers	600 00		
		Freight, express, cartage	50 00		
		Maintenance of equipment	50 00		
		Purchase of equipment	100 00		
		Stationery, printing	1,200 00		
		Telegraph, telephone	150 00		
		Miscellaneous	325 00		
	3	Apparatus, chemicals, musical instruments, domestic science and manual training supplies		500 00	
	4	Physical training including apparatus and athletic supplies		50 00	
	5	Supplies for Kindergarten		600 00	
	6	Payment to the Ottawa Public School Board		1,000 00	
	7	Maintenance		7,135 00	
		Fuel, light and power	$3,500 00		
		Water	660 00		
		Furniture, repairs, incidentals	600 00		
		Expenses of grounds	250 00		
		Scrubbing, cleaning, etc	2,000 00		
		Details:			
		Charwomen $1,800 00			
		Supplies 200 00			
		Snow-cleaning, cartage, etc	125 00		
				81,360 00	
37		**London Normal School**			
		Salaries:			
	1	Permanent		33,100 00	
	2	Contingencies		1,200 00	
		Details:			
		Travelling expenses	$ 50 00		
		Books, magazines, papers	400 00		
		Maintenance of equipment	100 00		
		Stationery, printing	500 00		
		Telegraph, telephone	100 00		
		Miscellaneous	50 00		
	3	Apparatus, chemicals, musical instruments, domestic science and manual training supplies		400 00	
	4	Physical training including apparatus and athletic supplies		50 00	
	5	Payment to the London Board of Education		1,600 00	
	6	Maintenance		4,450 00	
		Fuel, light and power	$1,450 00		
		Water	100 00		
		Furniture, repairs and incidentals	500 00		
		Expenses of grounds, trees, etc	900 00		

VI.—DEPARTMENT OF EDUCATION—Continued

No. of Vote	No. of Item	Service		Fiscal Year 1934 To be Voted	Fiscal Year 1934 Statutory
37		**London Normal School—Continued**			
		Scrubbing, cleaning, cartage, etc......	1,500 00		
		Details:			
		Charwomen.......... $1,400 00			
		Supplies............ 100 00			
				40,800 00	
38		**Hamilton Normal School**			
		Salaries:			
	1	Permanent..................................		32,125 00	
	2	Contingencies..................................		1,000 00	
		Details:			
		Travelling expenses...............	$ 50 00		
		Books, magazines, papers..........	500 00		
		Maintenance of equipment........	100 00		
		Stationery, printing...............	250 00		
		Telegraph, telephone..............	50 00		
		Miscellaneous....................	50 00		
	3	Apparatus, chemicals, musical instruments, domestic science and manual training supplies............		500 00	
	4	Physical training including apparatus and athletic supplies..................................		100 00	
	5	Payment to the Hamilton Board of Education.....		1,800 00	
	6	Maintenance..................................		2,990 00	
		Fuel, light and power...............	$1,000 00		
		Water............................	140 00		
		Furniture, repairs and incidentals.....	500 00		
		Expenses of grounds, trees, etc.......	250 00		
		Scrubbing, cleaning, cartage, etc......	1,100 00		
		Details:			
		Charwomen.......... $1,000 00			
		Supplies............ 100 00			
				38,515 00	
39		**Peterborough Normal School**			
		Salaries:			
	1	Permanent..................................		32,900 00	
	2	Contingencies..................................		1,000 00	
		Details:			
		Travelling expenses...............	$ 50 00		
		Books, magazines, papers..........	400 00		
		Maintenance of equipment........	50 00		
		Stationery, printing...............	400 00		
		Telegraph, telephone..............	50 00		
		Miscellaneous....................	50 00		
	3	Apparatus, chemicals, musical instruments, domestic science and manual training supplies............		500 00	
	4	Physical training including apparatus and athletic supplies..................................		25 00	
	5	Payment to Peterborough Board of Education.....		1,100 00	

VI.—DEPARTMENT OF EDUCATION—Continued

No. of Vote	No. of Item	Service		Fiscal Year 1934 To be Voted	Fiscal Year 1934 Statutory
39		**Peterborough Normal School—Continued**			
	6	Maintenance		2,735 00	
		Fuel, light and power	$1,200 00		
		Water	210 00		
		Furniture, repairs and incidentals	125 00		
		Expenses of grounds, trees, etc	200 00		
		Scrubbing, cleaning, cartage, etc	1,000 00		
		Details:			
		Charwomen $ 900 00			
		Supplies 100 00			
				38,260 00	
40		**Stratford Normal School**			
		Salaries:			
	1	Permanent		36,050 00	
	2	Contingencies		1,000 00	
		Details:			
		Travelling expenses	$ 200 00		
		Books, magazines, papers	400 00		
		Maintenance of equipment	50 00		
		Stationery, printing	250 00		
		Telegraph, telephone	50 00		
		Miscellaneous	50 00		
	3	Apparatus, chemicals, musical instruments, domestic science and manual training supplies		500 00	
	4	Physical training including apparatus and athletic supplies		325 00	
	5	Payment to the Stratford Board of Education		1,500 00	
	6	Maintenance		2,825 00	
		Fuel, light and power	$ 900 00		
		Water	125 00		
		Furniture, repairs and incidentals	500 00		
		Expenses of grounds, trees, etc	300 00		
		Scrubbing, cleaning, cartage, etc	1,000 00		
		Details:			
		Charwomen $ 900 00			
		Supplies 100 00			
				42,200 00	
41		**North Bay Normal School**			
		Salaries:			
	1	Permanent		30,700 00	
	2	Contingencies		900 00	
		Details:			
		Travelling expenses	$ 50 00		
		Books, magazines, papers	400 00		
		Maintenance of equipment	50 00		
		Stationery, printing	300 00		
		Telegraph, telephone	50 00		
		Miscellaneous	50 00		
	3	Apparatus, chemicals, musical instruments, domestic science and manual training supplies		300 00	

VI.—DEPARTMENT OF EDUCATION—Continued

No. of Vote	No. of Item	Service		Fiscal Year 1934 To be Voted	Fiscal Year 1934 Statutory
41		North Bay Normal School—Continued			
	4	Physical training including apparatus and athletic supplies		50 00	
	5	Students' board and travelling expenses		4,000 00	
	6	Maintenance		2,865 00	
		Fuel, light and power	$1,300 00		
		Water	165 00		
		Furniture, repairs and incidentals	200 00		
		Expenses of grounds, trees, etc	200 00		
		Scrubbing, cleaning, cartage, etc	1,000 00		
		Details:			
		Charwomen $ 900 00			
		Supplies 100 00			
				38,815 00	
42		University of Ottawa Normal School			
		Salaries:			
	1	Permanent		19,475 00	
	2	Contingencies		3,000 00	
		Details:			
		Salaries—Temporary	$2,000 00		
		Travelling expenses	50 00		
		Books, magazines, papers	400 00		
		Maintenance of equipment	50 00		
		Purchase of equipment	200 00		
		Stationery, printing	200 00		
		Telegraph, telephone	50 00		
		Miscellaneous	50 00		
	3	Payment to the University of Ottawa for use of building, equipment and accommodation		14,000 00	
	4	Payment to R.C. Separate School Board, Ottawa, for use of schools for training of teachers		1,000 00	
	5	Board and travelling expenses of students attending the University of Ottawa Normal School and of students preparing for admission to this school		75,000 00	
				112,475 00	
43		Sturgeon Falls Model School			
		Salaries:			
	1	Permanent		11,900 00	
	2	Contingencies		500 00	
		Details:			
		Travelling expenses	$ 50 00		
		Books, magazines, papers	100 00		
		Maintenance of equipment	50 00		
		Purchase of equipment	100 00		
		Stationery, printing	100 00		
		Telegraph, telephone	50 00		
		Miscellaneous	50 00		
	3	Payment to the R.C. Separate School Board, Sturgeon Falls, for use of schools for the training of teachers		400 00	
	4	Students' board and travelling expenses		28,000 00	

VI.—DEPARTMENT OF EDUCATION—Continued

No. of Vote	No. of Item	Service		Fiscal Year 1934 To be Voted	Fiscal Year 1934 Statutory
43		**Sturgeon Falls Model School—Continued**			
	5	Maintenance		700 00	
		Fuel, light and power	$ 500 00		
		Water	125 00		
		Furniture, repairs and incidentals	25 00		
		Scrubbing, cleaning and supplies	50 00		
				41,500 00	
44		**Sandwich Model School**			
		Salaries:			
	1	Permanent		6,475 00	
	2	Contingencies		250 00	
		Details:			
		Books, magazines, papers	$ 50 00		
		Maintenance of equipment	25 00		
		Purchase of equipment	50 00		
		Stationery, printing	50 00		
		Telegraph, telephone	50 00		
		Miscellaneous	25 00		
	3	Students' board and travelling expenses		6,500 00	
	4	Maintenance		350 00	
		Fuel, light and power	$ 225 00		
		Water	25 00		
		Furniture, repairs and incidentals	50 00		
		Scrubbing, cleaning and supplies	50 00		
				13,575 00	
45		**Embrun Model School**			
		Salaries:			
	1	Permanent		10,050 00	
	2	Contingencies		1,200 00	
		Details:			
		Travelling expenses	$ 50 00		
		Books, magazines, papers	300 00		
		Maintenance of equipment	50 00		
		Purchase of equipment	100 00		
		Rent	500 00		
		Stationery, printing	100 00		
		Telegraph, telephone	50 00		
		Miscellaneous	50 00		
	3	Physical training including apparatus and athletic supplies		50 00	
	4	Payment to R.C. Separate School Board, Embrun, for use of schools for training of teachers		300 00	
	5	Students' board and travelling expenses		25,000 00	
	6	Maintenance		575 00	
		Fuel, light and power	$ 400 00		
		Water	50 00		
		Furniture, repairs and incidentals	25 00		
		Scrubbing, cleaning, supplies, etc	100 00		
				37,175 00	

VI.—DEPARTMENT OF EDUCATION—Continued

No. of Vote	No. of Item	Service	Details	Fiscal Year 1934 To be Voted	Fiscal Year 1934 Statutory
46		**High Schools and Collegiate Institutes Branch**			
		Salaries:			
	1	Permanent		23,450 00	
		Grants:			
	2	High Schools and Collegiate Institutes including Districts		378,000 00	
	3	Night High Schools		11,700 00	
	4	High School Cadet Corps		3,375 00	
	5	School Boards, Supervisors and teachers to encourage courses of music in High Schools and Collegiate Institutes		900 00	
	6	Travelling and moving expenses		5,000 00	
	7	Contingencies		3,000 00	
		Details:			
		Books, magazines, papers	$ 200 00		
		Maintenance of equipment	50 00		
		Stationery, printing	2,500 00		
		Miscellaneous	250 00		
	S	French Scholarships (10 Geo. V, Chapter 103, Section 2)			6,000 00
	S	Carter Scholarships (R.S.O. 1927, Chapter 22, Section 6)			5,000 00
				425,425 00	11,000 00
47		**Departmental Museum**			
		Salaries:			
	1	Permanent		3,850 00	
	2	Contingencies		200 00	
		Details:			
		Travelling expenses	$ 50 00		
		Books, magazines, papers	50 00		
		Maintenance of equipment	25 00		
		Stationery, printing	25 00		
		Miscellaneous	50 00		
	3	Expenses of archaeological researches, purchase of collections, pictures, busts, cases, paintings, services, manuscripts, furnishings, travelling expenses		300 00	
	4	Natural History collections and supplies, incidentals and inspection		50 00	
				4,400 00	
48		**Public Libraries Branch**			
		Salaries:			
	1	Permanent		10,400 00	
	2	Public Libraries, grants, organizations, services, cost of books, expenses and contingencies		50,000 00	
		Details:			
		Grants	$42,500 00		
		Salaries—Temporary	200 00		
		Books, magazines, papers	500 00		
		Freight, express, cartage	100 00		
		Maintenance of equipment	100 00		
		Purchase of equipment	100 00		
		Stationery, printing	6,000 00		
		Miscellaneous	500 00		

VI.—DEPARTMENT OF EDUCATION—Continued

No. of Vote	No. of Item	Service	Fiscal Year 1934	
			To be Voted	Statutory
48		Public Libraries Branch—Continued		
	3	Travelling expenses	1,500 00	
	4	Travelling Libraries, cost of books, services and contingencies	2,500 00	
		Details:		
		Books, magazines, papers........ $2,000 00		
		Freight, express, cartage......... 200 00		
		Maintenance of equipment...... 50 00		
		Purchase of equipment.......... 100 00		
		Stationery, printing............. 100 00		
		Miscellaneous.................. 50 00		
	5	Services and expenses in connection with Historical Research Work in Ontario	1,000 00	
		Grants:		
	6	Ottawa Association for the Blind	1,000 00	
	7	Ontario College of Art and other Art Societies	25,500 00	
	8	Grant to Royal Canadian Institute, Toronto	2,500 00	
	9	Royal Astronomical Society of Canada	500 00	
			94,900 00	
49		Vocational Education Branch		
		Salaries:		
	1	Permanent	29,175 00	
	2	Manual Training and Household Science Departments, including grants and contingencies	69,350 00	
		Details:		
		Grants......................... $69,000 00		
		Contingencies.................. 350 00		
		Grants:		
	3	Sudbury High School for Mining Education. The payment of the whole or part of this sum to be made on recommendation of the Director of Vocational Education approved by the Lieutenant-Governor in Council	7,000 00	
	4	Haileybury High School for Mining Department. The payment of the whole or part of this sum to be made on the recommendation of the Director of Vocational Education approved by the Lieutenant-Governor in Council	9,000 00	
	5	Agricultural Training in High Schools and Collegiate Institutes, Continuation Schools and Fifth Classes, grants to Boards and teachers and contingencies	37,800 00	
		Details:		
		Grants......................... $37,500 00		
		Contingencies.................. 300 00		
	6	Vocational Education, Day and Evening Classes, including grants, services and contingencies	1,310,000 00	
		Details:		
		Grants......................$1,308,500 00		
		Books, magazines, papers...... 100 00		
		Maintenance of equipment.... 100 00		
		Stationery, printing........... 800 00		
		Miscellaneous................ 500 00		
	7	Travelling expenses	5,000 00	

VI.—DEPARTMENT OF EDUCATION—Continued

No. of Vote	No. of Item	Service		Fiscal Year 1934 To be Voted	Fiscal Year 1934 Statutory
49		Vocational Education Branch—Continued			
	8	Grant to Canadian National Institute for the Blind to assist in maintaining and developing its activities on behalf of the adult blind of the Province to be paid as may be directed by the Lieutenant-Governor in Council		50,000 00	
				1,517,325 00	
50		Ontario Training College for Technical Teachers			
		Salaries:			
	1	Permanent		11,700 00	
	2	Critic teachers and other additional teachers		3,700 00	
	3	Contingencies		800 00	
		Details:			
		Travelling expenses	$ 100 00		
		Books, magazines, papers	250 00		
		Stationery, printing	300 00		
		Telegraph, telephone	100 00		
		Miscellaneous	50 00		
	4	Apparatus, chemicals and shop supplies		300 00	
	5	Payment to Hamilton Board of Education		1,550 00	
	6	Maintenance		2,000 00	
		Heat, light and power	$1,500 00		
		Water	50 00		
		Expenses of grounds, trees and flowers, etc	250 00		
		Repairs and incidentals	75 00		
		Scrubbing, cleaning, cartage, etc	125 00		
				20,050 00	
51		Superannuated Teachers			
	1	Annual retiring allowance to Teachers and Inspectors		13,500 00	
	2	Compassionate allowance for ex-teachers to be paid as may be directed by the Lieutenant-Governor in Council		6,800 00	
	S	Teachers' and Inspectors' Superannuation Fund (R.S.O., Chapter 331, Section 4)			700,000 00
				20,300 00	700,000 00
52		Provincial and Other Universities			
		Grants:			
	1	University of Toronto to provide in the Ontario College of Education for the training of High School Assistants and for graduate courses of instruction in education, and for such other courses for certificates of the Department of Education as the Minister of Education may direct		208,000 00	
	2	Special grant to University of Toronto		1,000,000 00	
	S	University of Toronto (R.S.O. 1927, Chapter 337, Section 129)			500,000 00

VI.—DEPARTMENT OF EDUCATION—Continued

No. of Vote	No. of Item	Service		Fiscal Year 1934 To be Voted	Fiscal Year 1934 Statutory
52		**Provincial and Other Universities—Continued**			
	S	University of Toronto (R.S.O. 1927, Chapter 337, Section 9, Subsection 3)			7,000 00
	S	University of Toronto (16 Geo. V, Chapter 69, Section 2)			13,480 75
	S	University of Toronto (18 Geo. V, Chapter 55, Section 3)			52,157 68
	3	Royal Ontario Museum (to be paid as may be directed by the Lieutenant-Governor in Council)		40,000 00	
	4	Royal Ontario Museum for cataloguing		2,500 00	
	S	Royal Ontario Museum for maintenance (R.S.O. 1927, Chapter 343, Section 16)			54,000 00
	5	University of Western Ontario (to be paid as may be directed by the Lieutenant-Governor in Council)		275,000 00	
	6	Queen's University (to be paid as may be directed by the Lieutenant-Governor in Council)		275,000 00	
				1,800,500 00	626,638 43
53		**Belleville School for the Deaf**			
		Salaries:			
	1	Permanent		77,275 00	
	2	Temporary		15,475 00	
		Details:			
		Supervisors	$3,250 00		
		Domestic help	5,500 00		
		Engineering staff, fireman	2,500 00		
		Farm hands	1,025 00		
		Temporary assistance	3,200 00		
	3	Expenses		60,000 00	
		Details:			
		Medicine and medical comforts	$ 700 00		
		Groceries and provisions	18,600 00		
		Bedding, clothing and shoes	3,700 00		
		Fuel, light and power	15,000 00		
		Laundry, soap and cleaning	2,000 00		
		Furniture and furnishings	2,600 00		
		Farm expenses	2,500 00		
		Repairs and alterations	4,000 00		
		School supplies and equipment	6,300 00		
		Purchase and maintenance of motor conveyances	1,300 00		
		Travelling expenses	1,000 00		
		Contingencies	2,300 00		
				152,750 00	
54		**Brantford School for the Blind**			
		Salaries:			
	1	Permanent		44,524 00	
	2	Temporary		11,200 00	
		Details:			
		Domestic help	$6,900 00		
		Engineering staff, fireman, night watchman, etc	1,000 00		
		Farm hands, etc	1,000 00		
		Temporary assistance	2,300 00		

VI.—DEPARTMENT OF EDUCATION—Continued

No. of Vote	No. of Item	Service		Fiscal Year 1934 To be Voted	Fiscal Year 1934 Statutory
54		**Brantford School for the Blind—Continued**			
	3	Expenses		30,000 00	
		Details:			
		Medicine and medical comforts	$ 400 00		
		Groceries and provisions	11,000 00		
		Bedding, clothing and shoes	200 00		
		Fuel, light, power and water	9,600 00		
		Laundry, soap and cleaning	600 00		
		Furniture and furnishings	400 00		
		Farm and garden	1,500 00		
		Repairs and alterations	900 00		
		School supplies and equipment	1,600 00		
		Inspection of literature and musical classes	300 00		
		Dental and oculist services	400 00		
		Purchase and maintenance of motor conveyances	800 00		
		Travelling expenses	100 00		
		Contingencies	2,200 00		
				85,724 00	
55		**Monteith Northern Academy**			
		Salaries:			
	1	Permanent		21,175 00	
	2	Temporary		9,980 00	
		Details:			
		Domestic help	$2,500 00		
		Engineering staff, fireman and night watchman, etc	3,000 00		
		Farm hands, etc	4,000 00		
		Temporary assistance	480 00		
	3	Expenses		13,500 00	
		Details:			
		Medicine and medical comforts	$ 100 00		
		Groceries and provisions	6,000 00		
		Bedding, clothing and shoes	200 00		
		Fuel, light, power and water	2,900 00		
		Furniture and furnishings	200 00		
		Laundry, soap and cleaning	400 00		
		Grounds and garden	600 00		
		Repairs and alterations	400 00		
		Books, apparatus, chemicals, etc	800 00		
		Physical culture supplies	50 00		
		Travelling expenses	250 00		
		Contingencies	600 00		
		Farm and power plant	1,000 00		
				44,655 00	
				9,708,209 00	1,337,638 43

VII.—DEPARTMENT OF LANDS AND FORESTS

No. of Vote	No. of Item	Service	Fiscal Year 1934	
			To be Voted	Statutory
		Summary		
56		Main Office and Branches	142,825 00	10,000 00
		General	103,000 00	
		Branches:		
57		Agents	90,000 00	
58		Foresters and Scalers	130,000 00	
59		Provincial Parks	65,050 00	
			530,875 00	10,000 00
60		Forestry	896,325 00	
61		Surveys	86,425 00	
			1,513,625 00	10,000 00
56		**Main Office**		
		Salaries:		
	S	Minister		10,000 00
	1	Permanent	18,300 00	
		Lands Branch		
	2	Permanent	34,250 00	
		Woods and Forests Branch		
	3	Permanent	27,175 00	
		Accounts Branch		
	4	Permanent	20,600 00	
		Files Branch		
	5	Permanent	10,375 00	
		Provincial Lands Tax Branch		
	6	Permanent	11,625 00	
	7	Contingencies	20,500 00	
		Details:		
		Salaries—Temporary ... $4,200 00		
		Travelling expenses ... 2,000 00		
		Advertising ... 500 00		
		Subscriptions ... 180 00		
		Freight, cartage, etc ... 200 00		
		Purchase of equipment ... 300 00		
		Maintenance of equipment ... 300 00		
		Stationery, printing ... 11,600 00		
		Telegraph and telephone ... 1,000 00		
		Miscellaneous ... 220 00		
			142,825 00	10,000 00

VII.—DEPARTMENT OF LANDS AND FORESTS—Continued

No. of Vote	No. of Item	SERVICE		Fiscal Year 1934 To be Voted	Fiscal Year 1934 Statutory
56		General:			
	8	Legal fees and expenses		200 00	
	9	Insurance		7,000 00	
	10	Exhibits—Canadian National Exhibition, etc.		500 00	
	11	Moving expenses of officials		200 00	
	12	Commutation, Veterans' land grants		100 00	
	13	Annuities and bonuses to Indians under Treaty No. 9		20,000 00	
	14	Back to the Land Movement		75,000 00	
				103,000 00	
57		**Agents**			
	1	Salaries, disbursements, rent, etc.		90,000 00	
		Details:			
		Salaries—Permanent	$61,350 00		
		Temporary	4,500 00		
		Miscellaneous	24,150 00		
				90,000 00	
58		**Foresters and Scalers**			
	1	Forest ranging and measurement of timber		130,000 00	
		Details:			
		Salaries—Permanent	$45,250 00		
		Temporary	70,000 00		
		Miscellaneous	14,750 00		
				130,000 00	
59		**Provincial Parks**			
		Algonquin			
	1	Operating expenses		35,000 00	
		Details:			
		Salaries—Permanent	$25,950 00		
		Temporary	7,000 00		
		Miscellaneous	2,050 00		
		Rondeau			
	2	Operating expenses		15,000 00	
		Details:			
		Salaries—Permanent	$5,925 00		
		Temporary	8,000 00		
		Miscellaneous	1,075 00		

VII.—DEPARTMENT OF LANDS AND FORESTS—Continued

No. of Vote	No. of Item	Service		Fiscal Year 1934 To be Voted	Fiscal Year 1934 Statutory
59		Provincial Parks—Continued			
		Quetico			
	3	Operating expenses		15,000 00	
		Details:			
		Salaries—Permanent	$4,525 00		
		Temporary	10,000 00		
		Miscellaneous	475 00		
		General:			
	4	Creation and extension of parks		50 00	
				65,050 00	
				530,875 00	10,000 00
60		Forestry Branch			
		Main Office			
		Salaries:			
	1	Permanent		44,650 00	
	2	Contingencies		6,275 00	
		Details:			
		Salaries—Temporary	$ 825 00		
		Travelling expenses	300 00		
		Advertising	325 00		
		Subscriptions	13 00		
		Freight, cartage, etc	12 00		
		Purchase of equipment	100 00		
		Maintenance of equipment	200 00		
		Stationery and printing	3,300 00		
		Telegraphs, telephone	900 00		
		Miscellaneous	300 00		
	3	Forest Reserves		7,700 00	
		Salaries—Permanent	3,150 00		
		Temporary	3,000 00		
		Miscellaneous	1,550 00		
	4	Forestry Act		15,000 00	
		Salaries—Permanent	3,000 00		
		Temporary	7,000 00		
		Miscellaneous	5,000 00		
	5	Reforestation		150,000 00	
		Salaries—Permanent	51,525 00		
		Temporary	68,475 00		
		Miscellaneous	30,000 00		
	6	Fire Ranging		650,000 00	
		Salaries—Permanent	105,450 00		
		Temporary	250,000 00		
		Miscellaneous	294,550 00		
	7	Clearing Townsites etc		18,500 00	
	8	Forest Research		1,500 00	
		Salaries—Temporary	1,200 00		
		Miscellaneous	300 00		

VII.—DEPARTMENT OF LANDS AND FORESTS—Continued

No. of Vote	No. of Item	Service		Fiscal Year 1934 To be Voted	Statutory
60		**Forestry Branch—Continued**			
		Main Office—Continued			
	9	Insect Control		1,000 00	
		Allowance to Township School Sections—			
	10	In South Walsingham		150 00	
	11	In Vespra		250 00	
	12	In Charlotteville, Norfolk County		150 00	
	13	In Clarke, Durham County		150 00	
	14	Grant to Canadian Forestry Association		1,000 00	
				$896,325 00	
61		**Surveys Branch**			
		Main Office			
		Salaries:			
	1	Permanent		32,525 00	
	2	Contingencies		10,000 00	
		Details:			
		Salaries—Temporary	$2,850 00		
		Travelling expenses	930 00		
		Advertising	30 00		
		Subscriptions	15 00		
		Freight, cartage, etc	160 00		
		Maintenance of equipment	60 00		
		Stationery and printing	3,000 00		
		Telegraph and telephone	40 00		
		Miscellaneous	2,915 00		
		General:			
	3	Surveys		43,000 00	
	4	Lac Seul Storage Dam: Maintenance, operation and damage accruing from flooding or other causes by reason of dam		600 00	
	5	Salaries, expenses and equipment in connection with inspection of dams and other engineering works and valuations		100 00	
		Grants:			
	6	Boatd of Surveyors		200 00	
				86,425 00	

VIII.—DEPARTMENT OF NORTHERN DEVELOPMENT

No. of Vote	No. of Item	Service		Fiscal Year 1934 To be Voted	Fiscal Year 1934 Statutory
		Summary			
S		Main Office			3,658,075 00
		Branches:			
S		Settlers' Loan			110,250 00
62		Colonization Roads		471,025 00	
				471,025 00	3,768,325 00
S		**Main Office**			
	S	Salaries			118,575 00
		Permanent	$102,250 00		
		Temporary	16,325 00		
	S	Contingencies			24,000 00
		Details:			
		Travelling expenses	$4,000 00		
		Stationery, printing, etc	20,000 00		
	S	Roads and Bridges:			
		Construction and maintenance			3,500,000 00
		Seed grain			10,000 00
		Creameries			500 00
	S	Cattle purchase			5,000 00
					3,658,075 00
S		**Settlers' Loan Commission**			
	S	Salaries			7,750 00
		Permanent	$4,750 00		
		Temporary	3,000 00		
	S	Contingencies			2,500 00
		Details:			
		Stationery, printing, etc	$2,500 00		
	S	Settlers' loans			100,000 00
					110,250 00
62		**Colonization Roads Branch**			
		Salaries:			
	1	Permanent		8,800 00	
	2	Contingencies		800 00	
		Details:			
		Stationery, printing, etc	$800 00		
	3	By-laws		200,000 00	
	4	Construction and maintenance		250,000 00	
	5	Inspections		10,000 00	
	6	Storage and insurance		225 00	
	7	Engineering and surveying		1,000 00	
	8	Miscellaneous not otherwise provided		200 00	
				471,025 00	
				471,025 00	3,768,325 00

IX.—DEPARTMENT OF MINES

No. of Vote	No. of Item	Service	Fiscal Year 1934 To be Voted	Fiscal Year 1934 Statutory
		Summary		
63		Main Office and Branches	175,425 00	10,000 00
		General	55,500 00	
		Branches:		
64		Gas and Well Inspectors	8,500 00	
65		Office of Fuel Controller	500 00	
66		Sulphur Fumes Arbitrator	5,000 00	
67		Temiskaming Testing Laboratories	17,000 00	
68		Offices of Mining Recorders	43,500 00	
69		" " Draughtsman, North Bay	6,500 00	
			311,925 00	10,000 00
63		**Main Office**		
		Salaries:		
	S	Minister		10,000 00
	1	Permanent	35,750 00	
		Geological Branch		
	2	Permanent	17,550 00	
		Publications and Statistics Branch		
	3	Permanent	20,775 00	
		Mine Inspection Branch		
	4	Permanent	22,300 00	
		Mine Assessment Branch		
	5	Permanent	6,800 00	
		Chemical and Assay Branch		
	6	Permanent	10,400 00	
		Natural Gas Commissioner's Branch		
	7	Permanent	5,525 00	
		Mining Court of Ontario		
	8	Permanent	9,950 00	
		Files Branch		
	9	Permanent	2,375 00	
	10	Contingencies	44,000 00	
		Details:		
		Salaries—Temporary $8,200 00		
		Travelling expenses 7,100 00		
		Advertising 8,400 00		
		Subscriptions 525 00		
		Freight, express, cartage, etc 125 00		
		Maintenance of equipment 275 00		
		Printing, stationery 10,250 00		
		Telegraph and telephone 375 00		
		Miscellaneous 8,750 00		
			175,425 00	10,000 00

IX.—DEPARTMENT OF MINES—Continued

No. of Vote	No. of Item	Service	Fiscal Year 1934 To be Voted	Fiscal Year 1934 Statutory
63		General:		
	11	Salaries, equipment and expenses of temporary field and other assistants, including educational work	34,000 00	
	12	Trails, clearing streams, opening routes and roads	2,000 00	
	13	Mineral collections, including cases, and displays at exhibitions, also services and expenses	2,500 00	
	14	Insurance	800 00	
	15	Moving expenses of officials	100 00	
	16	Research work, salaries, equipment and expenses	10,000 00	
	17	Maintenance and operation of cable-testing machine	600 00	
	18	Purchase and treatment of gold and silver ores	500 00	
	19	Expenses of development, mining operations and experimentation re lignite and other deposits, Northern Ontario	5,000 00	
			55,500 00	
64		**Gas and Oil Well Inspectors**		
	1	Salaries, equipment and expenes of Gas and Oil Well Inspectors, also office expenses, temporary assistance and expenses enforcing The Natural Gas Conservation Act and The Well Drillers Act	8,500 00	
		Salaries—Permanent $5,700 00		
		Miscellaneous 2,800 00		
65		**Office of Fuel Controller**		
	1	Expenses of administering The Fuel Supply Act, 1918, including salaries, expenses and assistance	500 00	
66		**Sulphur Fumes Arbitrator**		
	1	Salary, travelling and other expenses, Sulphur Fumes Arbitrator, 14 Geo. V, Cap. 76 (to be refunded by smelting companies)	5,000 00	
		Salary—Permanent $3,000 00		
		Miscellaneous 2,000 00		
67		**Temiskaming Testing Laboratories**		
	1	Maintenance and operation of plant	17,000 00	
		Salaries—Permanent $5,400 00		
		Temporary 5,600 00		
		Miscellaneons 6,000 00		
68		**Offices of Mining Recorders**		
	1	Salaries and expenses, and for buildings, land and repairs	40,000 00	
		Salaries—Permanent $25,550 00		
		Temporary 3,150 00		
		Miscellaneous 11,300 00		

IX.—MINES DEPARTMENT—Continued

No. of Vote	No. of Item	Service		Fiscal Year 1934 To be Voted	Fiscal Year 1934 Statutory
68		**Inspector of Mining Recorders' Office**			
	2	Salary, travelling and other expenses		3,500 00	
		Salaries—Permanent	$2,000 00		
		Miscellaneous	1,500 00		
				43,500 00	
69		**Draughtsman, North Bay**			
	1	Salary, expenses and apparatus		6,500 00	
		Salaries—Permanent	$ 975 00		
		Temporary	4,950 00		
		Miscellaneous	575 00		
				311,925 00	10,000 00

X.—DEPARTMENT OF GAME AND FISHERIES

No. of Vote	No. of Item	Service		Fiscal Year 1934 To be Voted	Fiscal Year 1934 Statutory
		Summary			
70		Main Office		52,250 00	
		General		318,400 00	
		Branches:			
		Biological and Fish Culture Branch and Hatcheries		139,450 00	
		Experimental Fur Farm		15,000 00	
		MacDiarmid Station		5,300 00	
71		Wolf Bounty		60,000 00	
				590,400 00	
70		**Main Office**			
		Salaries:			
	1	Permanent		46,250 00	
	2	Contingencies		6,000 00	
		Details:			
		Salaries—Temporary	$2,625 00		
		Advertising	284 00		
		Stationery and printing	2,325 00		
		Telegraph	240 00		
		Travelling expenses	300 00		
		Sundries	226 00		
				52,250 00	
		Biological and Fish Culture Branch			
		Salaries:			
	3	Permanent		9,450 00	
	4	Contingencies		5,000 00	
		Details:			
		Salaries—Temporary	$2,575 00		
		Garage rent	60 00		
		Laboratory supplies	50 00		
		Stationery and printing	700 00		
		Telegraph	200 00		
		Travelling expenses	1,300 00		
		Sundries	115 00		
		Hatcheries			
	5	Services, maintenance and operation		125,000 00	
		Details:			
		Salaries—Permanent	$49,000 00		
		Temporary	20,715 00		
		Expenses	47,085 00		
		Salaries and expenses (truck drivers)	7,000 00		
		Stationery and printing	450 00		
		Miscellaneous	750 00		
				139,450 00	

X.—DEPARTMENT OF GAME AND FISHERIES—Continued

No. of Vote	No. of Item	Service		Fiscal Year 1934 To be Voted	Fiscal Year 1934 Statutory
70		General:			
	6	Erecting ponds and buildings, for propagation of fish, game animals and birds and equipment of same, and purchase of land		35,000 00	
		Details:			
		Salary—Permanent	$2,700 00		
		Expenses	32,300 00		
	7	Services and expenses in connection with the enforcement of The Ontario Game and Fisheries Act		250,000 00	
		Details:			
		Salaries—Permanent	$124,525 00		
		Temporary	21,425 00		
		Expenses	60,950 00		
		Issuers of Special Export Permits (services)	500 00		
		Advertising	100 00		
		Express, freight and cartage	700 00		
		Insurance (on cars)	450 00		
		Stationery and printing	10,000 00		
		Miscellaneous	1,350 00		
		Patrol boats	30,000 00		
	8	Moving expenses of officers of the Department		500 00	
	9	Purchase or building of and repairs to boats, boathouses, machinery and vehicles		15,000 00	
		Details:			
		Salary—Permanent	$1,800 00		
		Expenses	13,200 00		
	10	Services and expenses in connection with the purchase, importation, rearing and distribution of game animals, and birds and equipment of same		15,000 00	
		Details:			
		Salaries—Permanent	$3,300 00		
		Temporary	4,350 00		
		Expenses	7,350 00		
	11	Exhibits—Services and expenses including prizes and trophies, etc		2,400 00	
	12	Unforeseen and unprovided		500 00	
				318,400 00	
		Experimental Fur Farm			
	13	Services and expenses		15,000 00	
		Details:			
		Salaries—Permanent	$7,150 00		
		Temporary	1,650 00		
		Expenses	6,200 00		

X.—DEPARTMENT OF GAME AND FISHERIES—Continued

No. of Vote	No. of Item	Service		Fiscal Year 1934	
				To be Voted	Statutory
70		**MacDiarmid Station**			
	14	Services, expenses, repairs, maintenance and equipment..		5,300 00	
		Details:			
		Salaries—Temporary............	$1,800 00		
		Expenses......................	3,500 00		
				530,400 00	
71	1	Wolf Bounty: services and expenses in connection with same, including any equipment, expenses or services for the destruction of wolves and the tanning of pelts............................		60,000 00	
				590,400 00	

XI.—DEPARTMENT OF PUBLIC WORKS

No. of Vote	No. of Item	Service		Fiscal Year 1934 To be Voted	Fiscal Year 1934 Statutory
		Summary			
72		Main Office		89,750 00	10,000 00
73-81		Public Buildings—Maintenance and repairs		520,811 00	
82		Public works and bridges—Maintenance and construction		70,050 00	25,000 00
83		Public Buildings—Construction		190,500 00	
				871,111 00	35,000 00
		Main Office			
72		Salaries:			
	S	Minister			10,000 00
	1	Permanent		66,150 00	
	2	Contingencies		6,300 00	
		Details:			
		Salaries—Temporary	$1,200 00		
		Advertising	500 00		
		Books, magazines, papers	100 00		
		Freight, express, cartage	100 00		
		Maintenance of equipment	1,500 00		
		Purchase of equipment	300 00		
		Stationery, printing	2,000 00		
		Telegraph, telephone	200 00		
		Miscellaneous	400 00		
	3	Travelling expenses		3,000 00	
				75,450 00	
		General:			
	4	Insurance, including installation of lightning rods		9,000 00	
	5	Local Improvement taxes		4,500 00	
	6	Gratuities		100 00	
	7	Unforeseen and unprovided		200 00	
	8	Compensation, medical, hospital and other accounts for workmen injured while engaged on Government work, as awarded by the Workmen's Compensation Board		500 00	
				89,750 00	10,000 00
73		**General Superintendence**			
	1	Salaries		24,350 00	
	2	Services, travelling and other expenses		7,000 00	
	3	Contingencies		100 00	
				31,450 00	
74		**Government House**			
	1	Salaries		15,100 00	
	2	Pay List—Gardeners, firemen, repairs to grounds		2,500 00	
	3	Water, fuel, light and power		7,000 00	
	4	Repairs, contingencies		5,000 00	
	5	Furniture and furnishings		3,000 00	
	6	Uniforms for messengers, gardeners and other help		200 00	
	7	Telephone service		700 00	
				33,500 00	

XL—DEPARTMENT OF PUBLIC WORKS—Continued

No. of Vote	No. of Item	Service	Fiscal Year 1934	
			To be Voted	Statutory
75		**Parliament and Departmental Buildings**		
	1	Salaries	155,926 00	
	2	Water and fuel	30,000 00	
	3	Electric power and light current and gas	18,500 00	
	4	Supplies, tools, etc., for engine room and general repairs	3,000 00	
	5	Caretakers of grounds and maintenance of grounds, drives and walks	4,000 00	
	6	Repairs and cleaning of buildings, etc	90,000 00	
	7	Furniture and furnishings and equipment for buildings	15,000 00	
	8	Interior alterations	6,000 00	
	9	Flowers, shrubs, plants, etc	500 00	
	10	Uniforms for messengers, attendants, etc	100 00	
	11	Painting outside and inside work	5,000 00	
	12	Telephone service	46,000 00	
	13	Fire protection	500 00	
	14	Rental of property and office space	1,300 00	
	15	Motion Picture Studio, Trenton, repairs and incidentals	400 00	
	16	Typewriter inspection and repairs	5,000 00	
	17	Sewage Experimental Station, Toronto, repairs, etc	100 00	
	18	110 University Avenue, Toronto, repairs, alterations, painting and incidentals	1,000 00	
			382,326 00	
76		**Osgoode Hall**		
	1	Salaries	17,315 00	
	2	Fuel, light, water and power	5,500 00	
	3	Furniture, furnishings and equipment	2,000 00	
	4	Telephone service	3,500 00	
	5	Cleaning of building and incidentals	5,000 00	
	6	Fire protection	50 00	
	7	General repairs and alterations	5,000 00	
	8	Painting interior and exterior	1,000 00	
			39,365 00	
77		**Educational Buildings**		
		Toronto Normal and Model Schools		
	1	Repairs and incidentals	2,500 00	
		Ottawa Normal and Model Schools		
	2	Repairs and incidentals	1,000 00	
		London Normal School		
	3	Repairs and incidentals	300 00	
		Hamilton Normal School		
	4	Repairs and incidentals	300 00	
		Peterborough Normal School		
	5	Repairs and incidentals	300 00	

XI.—DEPARTMENT OF PUBLIC WORKS—Continued

No. of Vote	No. of Item	Service	Fiscal Year 1934 To be Voted	Fiscal Year 1934 Statutory
77		**Educational Buildings—Continued**		
		Stratford Normal School		
	6	Repairs and incidentals........................	300 00	
		North Bay Normal School		
	7	Repairs and incidentals........................	300 00	
		Belleville School for the Deaf		
	8	Repairs and incidentals........................	2,000 00	
		Brantford School for the Blind		
	9	Repairs and incidentals........................	1,000 00	
		Sandwich Model School		
	10	Repairs and incidentals........................	200 00	
		Sturgeon Falls Model School		
	11	Repairs and incidentals........................	200 00	
		Monteith Northern Academy		
	12	Repairs and incidentals........................	500 00	
		Embrun Model School		
	13	Repairs and incidentals........................	200 00	
		Ontario Training School for Technical Teachers, Hamilton		
	14	Repairs and incidentals........................	400 00	
		General		
	15	Repairs and incidentals to boilers and heating plants in Educational Buildings and fire protection.....	1,750 00	
			11,250 00	
78		**Agricultural Buildings**		
		Ontario Agricultural College, Guelph		
	1	Repairs and incidentals........................	3,500 00	
		Ontario Veterinary College, Guelph		
	2	Repairs and incidentals........................	500 00	
		Horticultural Experiment Station, Vineland		
	3	Repairs and incidentals........................	1,000 00	

XI.—DEPARTMENT OF PUBLIC WORKS—Continued

No. of Vote	No. of Item	Service	Fiscal Year 1934 To be Voted	Fiscal Year 1934 Statutory
78		**Agricultural Buildings—Continued**		
		Western Ontario Experimental Farm, Ridgetown		
	4	Repairs and incidentals	500 00	
		Agricultural School, Ridgetown		
	5	Repairs and incidentals	100 00	
		Eastern Dairy School, Kingston		
	6	Repairs and incidentals	100 00	
		Kemptville, Agricultural School		
	7	Repairs and incidentals	750 00	
		Demonstration Farm, New Liskeard		
	8	Repairs and incidentals	200 00	
			6,650 00	
79		Welfare Buildings		
		Ontario Training School for Boys, Bowmanville		
	1	Repairs and incidentals	750 00	
		Ontario Training School for Girls, Galt		
	2	Repairs and incidentals	200 00	
			950 00	
80		District Buildings		
		Algoma		
	1	Repairs and alterations, furniture and furnishings and improvements to grounds to all District Buildings	900 00	
		Cochrane		
	2	Repairs and alterations, furniture and furnishings and improvements to grounds to all District Buildings	900 00	
		Kenora		
	3	Repairs and alterations, furniture and furnishings and improvements to grounds to all District Buildings	900 00	

XI.—DEPARTMENT OF PUBLIC WORKS—Continued

No. of Vote	No. of Item	SERVICE	Fiscal Year 1934	
			To be Voted	Statutory
80		**District Buildings—Continued**		
		Manitoulin		
	4	Repairs and alterations, furniture and furnishings and improvements to grounds to all District Buildings	500 00	
		Muskoka		
	5	Repairs and alterations, furniture and furnishings and improvements to grounds to all District Buildings	500 00	
		Nipissing		
	6	Repairs and alterations, furniture and furnishings and improvements to grounds to all District Buildings	900 00	
		Parry Sound		
	7	Repairs and alterations, furniture and furnishings and improvements to grounds to all District Buildings	900 00	
		Rainy River		
	8	Repairs and alterations, furniture and furnishings and improvements to grounds to all District Buildings	900 00	
		Sudbury		
	9	Repairs and alterations, furniture and furnishings and improvements to grounds to all District Buildings	900 00	
		Temiskaming		
	10	Repairs and alterations, furniture and furnishings and improvements to grounds to all District Buildings	900 00	
	11	Salary of caretaker, New Liskeard	720 00	
		Thunder Bay		
	12	Repairs and alterations, furniture and furnishings and improvements to grounds to all District Buildings	900 00	
		General		
	13	To provide for repairs, installation of boilers and heating plants in Districts and fire protection	1,500 00	
			11,320 00	

XI.—DEPARTMENT OF PUBLIC WORKS—Continued

No. of Vote	No. of Item	Service	Fiscal Year 1934 To be Voted	Fiscal Year 1934 Statutory
81		**General Buildings**		
	1	Ontario Government Building, C.N. Exhibition Park, Toronto: Preparing and installing exhibits and electric energy	4,000 00	
			531,411 00	
82		**Public Works and Bridges**		
		Ordinary:		
	1	Equipment, instruments, machinery, scows, boats, rubber boots, motor trucks and cars	900 00	
	2	Lockmasters, bridgetenders, caretakers, etc	4,800 00	
	3	Maintenance of locks, dams, bridges, dredging, etc.	10,000 00	
	4	Surveys and inspections	1,000 00	
	5	Wages and expenses of Supervising Foremen	2,000 00	
			18,700 00	
		Capital:		
	S	Drainage aid grants		25,000 00
	6	Cutting and purchase of timber and construction materials	1,250 00	
	7	Storage dams	100 00	
	8	To continue works in progress at end of fiscal year 1932-33, including expenditures in excess of appropriations (to be paid as directed by the Lieutenant-Governor in Council)	50,000 00	
			51,350 00	25,000 00
			70,050 00	25,000 00
83		**Public Buildings**		
		Parliament and Departmental Buildings		
		Capital:		
	1	To provide additional accommodation	25,000 00	
		Ontario Hospitals and Reformatories		
		Capital:		
	2	Additions, alterations and equipment	15,000 00	
		Miscellaneous		
		Capital:		
	3	To continue buildings in progress at close of fiscal year 1932-33, including fittings and furnishings (to be paid as directed by the Lieutenant-Governor in Council)	100,000 00	
	4	Ontario Government Building, Exhibition Park, Toronto: Grant to City of Toronto	50,000 00	
	5	Purchase of property	500 00	
			150,500 00	
			190,500 00	
			871,111 00	35,000 00

XII.—DEPARTMENT OF HIGHWAYS

No. of Vote	No. of Item	Service	Fiscal Year 1934 To be Voted	Fiscal Year 1934 Statutory
		Summary		
84		Main Office	319,975 00	6,777,000 00
85		Motor Vchicles Branch	212,700 00	
			532,675 00	6,777,000 00
84		**Main Office**		
		Salaries:		
	S	Minister		10,000 00
	1	Permanent	177,575 00	
	2	Contingencies	66,900 00	
		Details:		
		Salaries—Temporary $19,500 00		
		Travelling expenses 25,250 00		
		Stationery, printing, etc. 21,000 00		
		Telephone and telegraph 150 00		
		Advertising 1,000 00		
	3	Exhibits—Highways	5,000 00	
	4	Unforeseen and unprovided	1,000 00	
	5	Taxes—Due or accruing on properties, gravel pits, stone quarries, sidings, properties for storage purposes, etc., notwithstanding any general clause in The Municipal Act, or in any other Act to the contrary	300 00	
	6	Fees, etc.—Educational work, membership, conferences	3,000 00	
		Grants:		
	7	Ontario Good Roads Association	300 00	
	8	Canadian Good Roads Association	1,500 00	
	9	Road surveys, inspection, traffic census, and reports, surveyors' equipment, etc	29,000 00	
		Roads:		
	S	King's Highways		4,000,000 00
	S	County roads		1,750,000 00
	S	Township roads		1,000,000 00
	S	Indian reserves		10,000 00
	S	Connecting links		7,000 00
	10	Salaries—Chauffeurs	17,400 00	
	11	Automobiles—Purchases, repairs, maintenance, equipment, etc	18,000 00	
			319,975 00	6,777,000 00
85		**Motor Vehicles Branch**		
		Salaries:		
	1	Permanent	92,775 00	
	2	Contingencies	44,850 00	
		Details:		
		Salaries—Temporary $18,750 00		
		Travelling expenses 7,000 00		
		Stationery, printing, etc. 17,500 00		
		Telegraph and telephone 100 00		
		Freight 1,500 00		

XII.—DEPARTMENT OF HIGHWAYS—Continued

No. of Vote	No. of Item	Service	Fiscal Year 1934	
			To be Voted	Statutory
85		Motor Vehicles Branch—Continued		
	3	Safety Committee, to pay ccst of advertising, etc...	25,000 00	
	4	Testing automobile headlights....................	75 00	
	5	Automobile markers and supplies.................	40,000 00	
	6	Services and expenses—In connection with and enforcement of The Highway Traffic Act, Public Vehicles Act and Public Commercial Vehicle Act.	10,000 00	
			212,700 00	
			532,675 00	6,777,000 00

XIII.—DEPARTMENT OF HEALTH

No. of Vote	No. of Item	Service	Details	Fiscal Year 1934 To be Voted	Fiscal Year 1934 Statutory
		Summary			
86		Main Office		128,700 00	64,000 00
		Branches:			
87		District Officers of Health		43,200 00	
88		Maternal and Child Hygiene and Public Health Nursing		86,425 00	
89		Dental Service		24,100 00	
90		Inspection of Training Schools for Nurses		12,275 00	
91		Preventable Diseases		295,250 00	
92		Industrial Hygiene		53,300 00	
93		Sanitary Engineering		47,125 00	
94		Laboratory		111,250 00	
95		Laboratory Divisions		50,900 00	
96		Public Health Education		28,625 00	
				881,150 00	64,000 00
97–109		Hospitals		6,368,320 00	
				7,249,470 00	64,000 00
86		**Main Office**			
		Salaries:			
	S	Minister			10,000 00
	1	Permanent		34,700 00	
	2	Contingencies		9,000 00	
		Details:			
		Salaries—Temporary	$ 1,575 00		
		Travelling expenses	1,800 00		
		Maintenance of equipment	400 00		
		Purchase of equipment	500 00		
		Stationery, printing	3,500 00		
		Telegraph—Telephone	325 00		
		Miscellaneous	900 00		
	3	Fees, books, magazines, papers		2,000 00	
		Grants:			
	4	Connaught Laboratories		18,000 00	
	5	St. Johns Ambulance Association		2,000 00	
		Cancer Control:			
	6	Services and expenses and for the operation of Radium Emanation Plant and for the purchase of radium		63,000 00	
		Grants:			
		The Ontario Institutes of Radio Therapy:			
	S	Toronto General Hospital			45,000 00
	S	Kingston General Hospital			9,000 00
				128,700 00	64,000 00
87		**District Officers of Health Branches**			
		Salaries:			
	1	Permanent		32,975 00	
		Services, equipment and expenses		9,925 00	
	3	Annual conference of Health Officers		300 00	
				43,200 00	

XIII.—DEPARTMENT OF HEALTH—Continued

No. of Vote	No. of Item	Service	Fiscal Year 1934	
			To be Voted	Statutory
88		**Maternal and Child Hygiene and Public Health Nursing Branch**		
		Salaries:		
	1	Permanent	36,425 00	
	2	Services, equipment, expenses and for the employment of District Nurses	25,000 00	
		Grants:		
	3	To municipalities operating a system of school medical inspection and employing Public Health Nurses in school service	25,000 00	
			86,425 00	
89		**Dental Service Branch**		
		Salaries:		
	1	Permanent	6,100 00	
	2	Services, expenses, supplies and equipment and for Dental Services in unorganized Districts in Northern Ontario	8,000 00	
		Grants:		
	3	To municipalities for organization and maintenance of School and Community Dental Services	10,000 00	
			24,100 00	
90		**Inspection of Training Schools for Nurses Branch**		
		Salaries:		
	1	Permanent	7,575 00	
	2	Services and expenses in connection with administration and enforcement of The Registration of Nurses Act, 1922	4,700 00	
			12,275 00	
91		**Preventable Diseases Branch**		
		Salaries:		
	1	Permanent	24,500 00	
	2	Outbreaks of diseases, sanitary investigations and free distribution of biological products for the prevention and cure of disease, services and expenses	152,000 00	
	3	Services and expenses for payment of the treatment of patients in hospitals and clinics and by legally qualified medical practitioners and generally for the enforcement of the law and regulations relating to venereal disease and communicable diseases	75,000 00	
	4	Services and expenses X-ray equipment and travelling clinical services	20,000 00	
		Grants:		
	5	For the operation of venereal disease clinics	20,750 00	
	6	Canadian Social Hygiene Council	3,000 00	
			295,250 00	
92		**Industrial Hygiene Branch**		
		Salaries:		
	1	Permanent	35,300 00	
	2	Services and expenses	18,000 00	
			53,300 00	

XIII.—DEPARTMENT OF HEALTH—Continued

No. of Vote	No. of Item	Service	Fiscal Year 1934	
			To be Voted	Statutory
93		**Sanitary Engineering Branch**		
		Salaries:		
	1	Permanent	28,125 00	
	2	Services and expenses	19,000 00	
			47,125 00	
94		**Laboratory Branch**		
		Salaries:		
	1	Permanent	66,250 00	
		Services and expenses	30,000 00	
	3	For the establishment, equipment, maintenance, salaries and expenses connected with Clinical Laboratory Centres	15,000 00	
			111,250 00	
95		**Laboratory Divisions**		
		Salaries:		
	1	Permanent	25,100 00	
	2	Services and expenses	14,000 00	
		Grants:		
	3	Public Health Laboratory, Queen's University, Kingston	3,300 00	
	4	Public Health Laboratory, Peterborough	2,000 00	
	5	Public Health Laboratory, Peterborough, for equipment, maintenance and supplies	500 00	
	6	Public Health Laboratory, Institute of Public Health, Western University, London, Ontario	6,000 00	
			50,900 00	
96		**Public Health Education Branch**		
		Salaries:		
	1	Permanent	8,625 00	
	2	Contingencies	20,000 00	
		Details:		
		Exhibits $2,000 00		
		Advertising 1,000 00		
		Stationery, printing, etc. 17,000 00		
			28,625 00	
			881,150 00	64,000 00
		Hospitals Branch		
		Summary		
97		Main Office	139,850 00	
		Grants, etc—General Hospitals and Charities	1,886,400 00	
98–109		Ontario Hospitals	4,342,070 00	
			6,368,320 00	

XIII.—DEPARTMENT OF HEALTH—Continued

No. of Vote	No. of Item	Service		Fiscal Year 1934 To be Voted	Fiscal Year 1934 Statutory
97		**Main Office**			
		Salaries:			
	1	Permanent		104,850 00	
	2	Contingencies		35,000 00	
		Details:			
		Salaries—Temporary	$10,000 00		
		Travelling expenses	7,200 00		
		Maintenance of motor vehicles	1,800 00		
		Maintenance of office equipment	350 00		
		Analyses of purchases	150 00		
		Advertising	100 00		
		Stationery and printing	14,000 00		
		Newspapers and periodicals	150 00		
		Postage and telegrams	250 00		
		Miscellaneous	1,000 00		
				139,850 00	
		Grants, etc.—General Hospitals and Charities:			
	3	General Hospitals		990,000 00	
	4	Homes for Incurables		159,000 00	
	5	Maintenance of patients in Municipal Sanatoria for Consumptives		704,000 00	
	6	Travelling and incidental expenses for the removal and escort of indigent patients of unorganized territory, to and from Public Hospitals, Hospitals for Incurables, and Sanatoria for Consumptives; and for the expenses of burial, not exceeding $30.00 in each case, of such indigent patients when their death occurs in such institutions		1,000 00	
	7	Victorian Order of Nurses		2,000 00	
	8	Hospital for Sick Children, Toronto, to pay expenses incurred during the year ending September 30, 1933, in connection with the Out-Patients Branch as may be directed by the Lieutenant-Governor in Council		7,000 00	
	9	Hospital for Sick Children to erect a 100-bed Country Hospital		10,900 00	
	10	The Haven, Toronto, for Feeble-Minded Women		500 00	
	11	Special grants to municipalities in a territorial district, other than a city, under The Public Hospitals Act, 1931, Sec. 18, Subsection 2, and The Sanatoria for Consumptives Act, 1931, Section 38, Subsection 2		12,000 00	
				1,886,400 00	
	12	General Expense—Ontario Hospitals: Printing examination papers, stationery, badges and prizes for annual examinations in Training School for Nurses		500 00	
	13	Board of Examiners, Training School for Nurses, Ontario Hospitals, $100 each and travelling and other expenses		600 00	
	14	Removal of patients		13,000 00	
	15	Clothing for Bailiffs removing patients		500 00	
	16	Grants to recovered indigent patients from Ontario Hospitals, and removal expenses to their legal domicile		600 00	
	17	Travelling expenses of Social Service Workers at Ontario Hospitals		500 00	

XIII.—DEPARTMENT OF HEALTH—Continued

No. of Vote	No. of Item	Service	Fiscal Year 1934	
			To be Voted	Statutory
97		**Main Office—Continued**		
	18	Minor comforts for indigent patients in Ontario Hospitals, on certified statements from Superintendents	500 00	
	19	Provision for expenses in connection with conventions held at various institutions	100 00	
	20	Removal expenses (other than patients) in connection with the Public Institutions	1,500 00	
	21	Printing and stationery for Public Institutions	15,000 00	
	22	Medical attendance, funeral transportation and burial expenses of officials and employees of the Public Institutions, where death or illness arises from nature of employment	650 00	
	23	Treatment of patients and inmates of Public Institutions in Hospitals and Sanatoria	500 00	
	24	Legal costs and expenses covering sundry investigations	500 00	
	25	Unforeseen and unprovided	1,500 00	
	26	Exhibits of the Department of Health, Hospitals Branch, at the Canadian National and other exhibitions	1,500 00	
	27	Ontario Research Foundation in connection with contagious abortion in farm herds	3,000 00	
			40,450 00	
		Ontario Hospitals		
98		**Brockville**		
	1	Salaries	205,700 00	
		Maintenance	160,000 00	
	3	Repairs to buildings, etc	25,000 00	
			390,700 00	
99		**Cobourg**		
	1	Salaries	59,700 00	
		Maintenance	68,000 00	
	3	Repairs to buildings, etc	15,000 00	
			142,700 00	
100		**Hamilton**		
	1	Salaries	248,875 00	
	2	Maintenance	190,000 00	
	3	Repairs to buildings, etc	35,000 00	
			473,875 00	
101		**Kingston**		
	1	Salaries	205,375 00	
	2	Maintenance	155,000 00	
	3	Repairs to buildings, etc	35,000 00	
			395,375 00	

XIII.—DEPARTMENT OF HEALTH—Continued

No. of Vote	No. of Item	Service	Fiscal Year 1934	
			To be Voted	Statutory
		Ontario Hospitals—Continued		
102		**London**		
	1	Salaries	273,700 00	
	2	Maintenance	180,000 00	
	3	Repairs to buildings, etc	50,000 00	
			503,700 00	
103		**Mimico**		
	1	Salaries	201,400 00	
	2	Maintenance	165,000 00	
	3	Repairs to buildings, etc	25,000 00	
			391,400 00	
104		**Orillia**		
	1	Salaries	258,550 00	
	2	Maintenance	240,000 00	
	3	Repairs to buildings	35,000 00	
	4	Industries	10,000 00	
			543,550 00	
105		**Penetanguishene**		
	1	Salaries	101,400 00	
		Maintenance	80,000 00	
	3	Repairs to buildings, etc	30,000 00	
			211,400 00	
106		**Toronto**		
	1	Salaries	174,725 00	
	2	Maintenance	140,000 00	
	3	Repairs to buildings, etc	25,000 00	
			339,725 00	
107		**Whitby**		
	1	Salaries	297,350 00	
	2	Maintenance	255,000 00	
	3	Repairs to buildings, etc	15,000 00	
			567,350 00	
108		**Woodstock**		
	1	Salaries	121,000 00	
	2	Maintenance	76,000 00	
	3	Repairs to buildings, etc	10,000 00	
			207,000 00	
109		**Toronto Psychiatric**		
	1	Salaries	97,845 00	
	2	Maintenance	35,000 00	
	3	Repairs to buildings, etc	2,000 00	
			134,845 00	
			4,342,070 00	

XIV.—DEPARTMENT OF LABOUR

No. of Vote	No. of Item	Service	Fiscal Year 1934		
				To be Voted	Statutory
		Summary			
110		Main Office		38,096 50	
		Branches:			
111		Apprenticeship Board		26,575 00	
112		Boiler Inspection		25,550 00	
113		Factory Inspection		72,900 00	
114		Board of Examiners of Operating Engineers		27,275 00	
115		Employment Offices		212,000 00	
116		Minimum Wage Board		15,200 00	
				417,596 50	
110		**Main Office**			
		Salaries:			
	1	Permanent		21,275 00	
	2	Contingencies		4,500 00	
		Details:			
		Salaries—Temporary	$3,000 00		
		Travelling expenses	600 00		
		Freight, express, cartage	5 00		
		Maintenance of equipment	50 00		
		Purchase of equipment	200 00		
		Stationery, printing	600 00		
		Telegraph, telephone	10 00		
		Miscellaneous	35 00		
	3	General Stores		4,000 00	
		Details:			
		Purchase of stationery, printing and supplies for all Branches	$4,000 00		
	4	Exhibits—Services and expenses		1,800 00	
	5	Investigations, Library publications, journals, subscriptions, dues, etc		250 00	
	6	Insurance premium of Caisson Inspector against injury, death or permanent disability, etc		266 50	
	7	Advertising, educational work, conferences, speakers, membership fees, publicity, administration of justice, witnesses and interpreters in the Department of Labour, including Apprenticeship Board, Factory Inspection Branch, Boiler Inspection Branch, Board of Examiners of Operating Engineers, and the administration of the Employment Agencies Act		6,000 00	
	8	Litigation of constitutional and other questions		5 00	
				38,096 50	
111		**Apprenticeship Board**			
		Salaries:			
	1	Permanent		20,575 00	
	2	Contingencies		6,000 00	
		Details:			
		Allowances (per diem)	$1,440 00		
		Travelling expenses	2,400 00		
		Freight, express, cartage	4 00		
		Maintenance of equipment	50 00		
		Purchase of equipment	160 00		
		Stationery, printing	600 00		
		Telegraph, telephones	314 00		
		Rent	792 00		

XIV.—DEPARTMENT OF LABOUR —Continued

No. of Vote	No. of Item	Service		Fiscal Year 1934 To be Voted	Fiscal Year 1934 Statutory
111		**Apprenticeship Board—Continued**			
		Postage	40 00		
		Miscellaneous	200 00		
				26,575 00	
112		**Boiler Inspection Branch**			
		Salaries:			
	1	Permanent		20,850 00	
	2	Contingencies		4,700 00	
		Details:			
		Travelling expenses	$3,600 00		
		Freight, express, cartage	5 00		
		Maintenance of equipment	50 00		
		Purchase of equipment	50 00		
		Stationery, printing, etc	800 00		
		Telegraph, telephone	25 00		
		Miscellaneous	170 00		
				25,550 00	
113		**Factory Inspection Branch**			
		Salaries:			
	1	Permanent		57,800 00	
	2	Contingencies		15,000 00	
		Details:			
		Travelling expenses	$14,000 00		
		Freight, express, cartage	10 00		
		Maintenance of equipment	25 00		
		Purchases of equipment	50 00		
		Stationery, printing	800 00		
		Telegraph, telephone	5 00		
		Miscellaneous	110 00		
	3	Building Trades Protection Act Contingencies, salaries, other services, travelling expenses, etc., incidental to the enforcement of the Act.		100 00	
				72,900 00	
114		**Board of Examiners of Operating Engineers**			
		Salaries:			
	1	Permanent		20,275 00	
	2	Contingencies		7,000 00	
		Details:			
		Salaries—Temporary	$ 825 00		
		Travelling expenses	3,000 00		
		Freight, express, cartage	5 00		
		Maintenance of equipment	50 00		
		Purchase of equipment	200 00		
		Stationery, printing	2,800 00		
		Telegraph, telephones	20 00		
		Miscellaneous	100 00		
				27,275 00	

XIV.—DEPARTMENT OF LABOUR—Continued

No. of Vote	No. of Item	Service		Fiscal Year 1934	
				To be Voted	Statutory
115		**Ontario Government Employment Offices**			
		Salaries:			
	1	Permanent		136,500 00	
	2	Contingencies		75,000 00	
		Details:			
		Salaries—Temporary	$22,200 00		
		Travelling expenses	3,600 00		
		Advertising	80 00		
		Books, magazines, papers and subscriptions	100 00		
		Freight, express, cartage	170 00		
		Maintenance of equipment	200 00		
		Purchase of equipment	200 00		
		Stationery, printing supplies	2,100 00		
		Telegraph, telephone	6,500 00		
		Postage	950 00		
		Rent	33,000 00		
		Janitor service and cleaning, etc	2,600 00		
		Light, heat, water	1,800 00		
		Repairs and alterations	500 00		
		Miscellaneous	1,000 00		
	3	Provincial Employment Service Council		500 00	
		Details:			
		Administration	$ 250 00		
		Expenses	250 00		
				212,000 00	
116		**Minimum Wage Board**			
		Salaries:			
	1	Permanent		3,800 00	
	2	Contingencies		11,400 00	
		Details:			
		Allowances (per diem)	$9,800 00		
		Travelling expenses	1,000 00		
		Advertising	30 00		
		Books, magazines and papers	15 00		
		Freight, express, cartage	5 00		
		Maintenance of Equipment	50 00		
		Purchase of equipment	50 00		
		Stationery, printing	300 00		
		Telegraph, telephone	15 00		
		Legal and witness fees	100 00		
		Miscellaneous	35 00		
				15,200 00	
				417,596 50	

XV.—DEPARTMENT OF PUBLIC WELFARE

No. of Vote	No. of Item	Service	Fiscal Year 1934 To be Voted	Fiscal Year 1934 Statutory
		Summary		
117		Main Office	27,550 00	10,000 00
		Grants—Refuges, Orphanages and Charities	303,750 00	
		Branches:		
118		Children's Aid Branch	130,018 00	
119		Ontario Training School for Boys	94,275 00	
120		" " " " Girls	26,850 00	
121		Mothers' Allowances Commission	1,825,575 00	
122		Old Age Pensions Commission	2,817,600 00	
			5,225,618 00	10,000 00
117		**Main Office**		
		Salaries:		
	S	Minister		10,000 00
	1	Permanent	12,400 00	
	2	Contingencies	12,350 00	
		Details:		
		Temporary salaries $8,025 00		
		Travelling expenses 1,500 00		
		Purchase of equipment 125 00		
		Stationery, printing 2,000 00		
		Telegraph, telephone 200 00		
		Miscellaneous 500 00		
	3	Exhibits—Canadian National and other exhibitions	800 00	
	4	Maintenance of indigents from unorganized territory	2,000 00	
			27,550 00	10,000 00
		Grants:		
	5	Refuges	83,000 00	
	6	Orphanages	60,000 00	
	7	Industrial Schools	110,000 00	
	8	Salvation Army for Prison Gate Work	2,500 00	
	9	Society for Prevention of Cruelty to Animals	750 00	
	10	Canadian Girl Guides' Association, to be paid as may be directed by the Lieutenant-Governor in Council	1,000 00	
	11	Boy Scouts' Association	1,500 00	
	12	Soldiers' Aid Commission for payment of Travelling, office and other expenses of the Commission, and for such other purposes as provided by the Soldiers' Aid Commission Act	45,000 00	
			303,750 00	
118		**Children's Aid Branch**		
		Salaries:		
	1	Permanent	47,875 00	
	2	Services and expenses in connection with the administration of The Children's Protection Act of Ontario and The Children of Unmarried Parents' Act, 1921, including travelling expenses	75,000 00	
		Details:		
		Salaries—Temporary $38,200 00		
		Travelling expenses 6,000 00		
		Maintenance 29,300 00		
		Legal 1,500 00		
	3	Grant—Association of Children's Aid Societies	500 00	
	4	Contingencies	6,643 00	

XV.—DEPARTMENT OF PUBLIC WELFARE—Continued

No. of Vote	No. of Item	Service		Fiscal Year 1934	
				To be Voted	Statutory
118		**Children's Aid Branch—Continued**			
		Details:			
		Salaries—Temporary..............	$2,850 00		
		Travelling expenses...............	1,400 00		
		Maintenance of equipment........	300 00		
		Stationery, printing...............	1,200 00		
		Miscellaneous....................	893 00		
				130,018 00	
119		**Ontario Training School for Boys (Bowmanville)**			
		Salaries:			
	1	Permanent and Temporary....................		42,575 00	
		Operating Expenses:			
	2	Medicine and medical comforts, groceries and provisions, fuel, light and water, clothing, laundry and cleaning, furniture and furnishings, office expenses, farm expenses, recreation, equipment and contingencies including boys' travelling expenses and maintenance of boys in foster homes....................................		44,000 00	
	3	Maintenance and repairs of all buildings, roads, walks, grounds and fences; purchase, maintenance and repair of plumbing, steam and electric plants, and machinery attached thereto; live stock, vehicles and farm implements..........		7,500 00	
	4	Car allowance to Superintendent.		200 00	
				94,275 00	
120		**Ontario Training School for Girls (Galt)**			
		Salaries:			
	1	Permanent and Temporary....................		11,850 00	
		Operating Expenses:			
	2	Medicine and medical comforts, groceries and provisions, fuel, light and water, etc.; clothing, laundry and cleaning, furniture and furnishings, office expenses, garden expenses, recreation, equipment and contingencies................		15,000 00	
				26,850 00	
121		**Mothers' Allowances Commission**			
		Salaries:			
	1	Permanent..................................		49,575 00	
	2	Contingencies..................................		26,000 00	
		Details:			
		Salaries—Temporary..............	$4,050 00		
		Travelling expenses...............	16,000 00		
		Local Board expense..............	2,000 00		
		Stationery, printing...............	2,000 00		
		Miscellaneous....................	1,950 00		
	3	Allowances in accordance with The Mothers' Allowances Act...............................		1,750,000 00	
				1,825,575 00	

XVI.—**DEPARTMENT OF PUBLIC WELFARE**—Continued

No. of Vote	No. of Item	Service		Fiscal Year 1934	
				To be Voted	Statutory
122		**Old Age Pensions Commission**			
		Salaries:			
	1	Permanent		22,775 00	
	2	Contingencies		44,825 00	
		Details:			
		Salaries—Temporary	$22,925 00		
		Travelling expenses	12,000 00		
		Local Board expense	2,400 00		
		Maintenance of equipment	300 00		
		Purchase of equipment	200 00		
		Stationery, printing	7,000 00		
	3	Pensions in accordance with The Old Age Pensions Act		2,750,000 00	
				2,817,600 00	
				5,225,618 00	10,000 00

XVI.—DEPARTMENT OF PROVINCIAL TREASURER

No. of Vote	No. of Item	Service	Fiscal Year 1934	
			To be Voted	Statutory
		Summary		
123		Main Office	130,800 00	841,394 48
	S	Public Debt		17,750,000 00
		Branches:		
124		Office of Budget Committee	5,800 00	
125		Office of Controller of Revenue	218,550 00	
S		Savings Office		207,400 00
126		Board of Censors	24,215 00	
127		Motion Picture Bureau	75,000 00	
128		Public Records and Archives	20,950 00	
129		Post Office	120,900 00	
			596,215 00	18,798,794 48
123		**Main Office**		
		Salaries:		
	S	Minister		10,000 00
	1	Permanent	63,300 00	
	2	Contingencies	16,500 00	
		Details:		
		Salaries—Temporary $2,250 00		
		Travelling expenses 1,850 00		
		Advertising in financial papers, etc. 1,800 00		
		Books, magazines, papers 175 00		
		Maintenance of equipment 500 00		
		Purchase of equipment 1,500 00		
		Stationery, printing, office supplies 8,275 00		
		Telephone and telegraph 80 00		
		Miscellaneous 70 00		
	3	Fidelity bonds	13,000 00	
		Registry and Land Titles Office:		
	4	Refund of surplus fees deposited	38,000 00	
		Municipalities:		
	S	Railway tax distribution		41,000 00
	S	Sinking Fund—Repayment of deposits (Capital)		65,000 00
	S	" Accumulated Interest		45,000 00
	S	Tile Drainage Debentures (Capital)		75,000 00
	S	Municipal Drainage Debentures(Capital)		8,000 00
	S	Debentures guaranteed by Province (Capital)		140,000 00
		Grants:		
	S	Banting-Best Medical Research		10,000 00
	S	Banting Research Aid		10,000 00
	S	Northern Ontario Fire Relief		3,894 48
		Dominion Government:		
	S	Common School Fund re sale of school lands		2,500 00
	S	Farm Loan Associations (Capital)		30,000 00
		Public Service:		
	S	Superannuation Fund—Government contribution		400,000 00
		Bequests and Scholarships:		
	S	Interest		1,000 00
			130,800 00	841,394 48
	S	Public Debt—Interest and expenses—Less repayments		17,750,000 00

XVI.—DEPARTMENT OF PROVINCIAL TREASURER—Continued

No. of Vote	No. of Item	SERVICE		Fiscal Year 1934 To be Voted	Statutory
124		**Office of Budget Committee**			
		Salaries:			
	1	Permanent		4,800 00	
	2	Contingencies		1,000 00	
		Details:			
		Travelling expenses	$ 500 00		
		Books, magazines, papers	25 00		
		Maintenance of equipment	100 00		
		Stationery, printing	300 00		
		Miscellaneous	75 00		
				5,800 00	
125		**Office of Controller of Revenue**			
		Salaries:			
	1	Permanent		134,700 00	
	2	Contingencies		62,500 00	
		Details:			
		Salaries—Temporary	$34,075 00		
		Travelling expenses	16,200 00		
		Books, magazines, papers	500 00		
		Freight, express, cartage	50 00		
		Maintenance of equipment	525 00		
		Stationery, printing	11,000 00		
		Telegraph, telephone	150 00		
	3	Fees and Commissions		21,050 00	
		Details:			
		Law stamps	$14,000 00		
		Membership	50 00		
		Legal	7,000 00		
	4	Miscellaneous		300 00	
		Details:			
		Unforeseen	$100 00		
		Insurance premiums	200 00		
				218,550 00	
		Savings Office			
S		**Head Office and Branches**			
		Salaries:			
	S	Permanent			124,000 00
	S	Contingencies			83,400 00
		Details:			
		Salaries—Temporary	$10,000 00		
		Travelling expenses	750 00		
		Advertising	20,000 00		
		Purchase of equipment	3,000 00		
		Stationery, printing	10,000 00		
		Telegraph, telephone	150 00		
		Miscellaneous	2,500 00		
		Rent	36,000 00		
		Postage	1,000 00		
					207,400 00

DEPARTMENT OF PROVINCIAL TREASURER—Continued

No. of Vote	No. of Item	Service		Fiscal Year 1934	
				To be Voted	Statutory
126		**Board of Censors**			
		Salaries:			
	1	Permanent		20,575 00	
	2	Contingencies		3,640 00	
		Details:			
		Salaries—Temporary	$2,325 00		
		Travelling expenses	300 00		
		Books, magazines	125 00		
		Stationery, printing	700 00		
		Telegraph, telephone	15 00		
		Miscellaneous	175 00		
				24,215 00	
127		**Motion Picture Bureau**			
		General Office			
		Salaries:			
	1	Permanent		15,525 00	
	2	Contingencies		5,450 00	
		Details:			
		Salaries—Temporary	$2,100 00		
		Services	300 00		
		Travelling expenses	300 00		
		Auto mileage	200 00		
		Auto maintenance and repairs	600 00		
		Stationery and printing	1,000 00		
		Telephone and telegraph	75 00		
		Books, magazines and papers	50 00		
		Membership fees	20 00		
		Laundry	30 00		
		Exhibition and miscellaneous	775 00		
	3	Express and Customs Charges		3,150 00	
		Details:			
		Express	$2,500 00		
		Freight and cartage	250 00		
		Customs and brokerage	400 00		
		Laboratory, Still Pictures, Lantern Slide Divisions and Trenton Studio			
		Salaries:			
	4	Permanent		24,125 00	
	5	Purchase and maintenance of equipment and film operations		26,750 00	
		Details:			
		Salaries—Temporary	$10,375 00		
		Services	1,200 00		
		Travelling expenses	1,500 00		
		Rental of equipment	100 00		
		Royalties and reproducing rights	100 00		
		Raw film, chemicals and paper	10,000 00		
		Negatives and prints	145 00		
		Equipment (machine and tools)	1,500 00		
		Miscellaneous	400 00		
		Maintenance and repairs	200 00		
		Telephone and telegraphs	100 00		
		Laundry	50 00		
		Postage	30 00		

DEPARTMENT OF PROVINCIAL TREASURER—Continued

No. of Vote	No. of Item	Service		Fiscal Year 1934 To be Voted	Fiscal Year 1934 Statutory
127		Motion Picture Bureau—Continued			
		Electricity, gas and water.........	450 00		
		Fuel...........................	600 00		
				75,000 00	
128		**Department of Public Records and Archives**			
		Salaries:			
	1	Permanent..................................		14,550 00	
	2	Purchase of documents..........................		200 00	
	3	Contingencies..................................		6,200 00	
		Details:			
		Salaries—Temporary..............	$5,000 00		
		Stationery, printing...............	500 00		
		Maintenance of equipment........	235 00		
		Travelling expenses...............	450 00		
		Freight, express, cartage..........	15 00		
				20,950 00	
129		House Post Office			
		Salaries:			
	1	Permanent..................................		10,125 00	
	2	Postage and postal machines.....................		110,525 00	
		Details:			
		Postage........................	$110,000 00		
		Meter rental and supplies........	500 00		
		Cash register....................	10 00		
		Cartage........................	15 00		
	3	Contingencies.................................		250 00	
		Details:			
		Stationery......................	$225 00		
		Miscellaneous...................	25 00		
				120,900 00	
				596,215 00	18,798,794 48

XVII.—OFFICE OF PROVINCIAL AUDITOR

No. of Vote	No. of Item	Service		Fiscal Year 1934	
				To be Voted	Statutory
130		Salaries:			
	S	Provincial Auditor			6,500 00
	1	Permanent		87,425 00	
	2	Contingencies		17,500 00	
		Details:			
		Salaries—Temporary	$13,650 00		
		Travelling expenses	2,000 00		
		Blank books, stationery and printing	1,500 00		
		Maintenance of equipment	100 00		
		Miscellaneous	250 00		
				104,925 00	6,500 00

XVIII.—DEPARTMENT OF PROVINCIAL SECRETARY

No. of Vote	No. of Item	Service		Fiscal Year 1934 To be Voted	Fiscal Year 1934 Statutory
		Summary			
131		Main Office		64,805 00	10,000 00
		Branches:			
132		Registrar-General		57,975 00	
				122,780 00	10,000 00
133-139		Reformatories and Prisons		986,555 00	
				1,109,335 00	10,000 00
131		**Main Office**			
		Salaries:			
	S	Minister			10,000 00
	1	Permanent		52,025 00	
	2	Contingencies		12,780 00	
		Details:			
		Salaries—Temporary	$2,700 00		
		Travelling expenses	600 00		
		Car rentals	30 00		
		Advertising	100 00		
		Books, magazines, papers	200 00		
		Stationery, printing	9,000 00		
		Telegraph, telephone	100 00		
		Miscellaneous	50 00		
				64,805 00	10,000 00
132		**Registrar-General's Branch**			
		Salaries:			
	1	Permanent		51,575 00	
	2	Contingencies		6,400 00	
		Details:			
		District Registrars' fees	$ 325 00		
		Supreme Court Registrars' fees	400 00		
		Freight, express, cartage	35 00		
		Stationery, printing	5,000 00		
		Binding	500 00		
		Money order charges	110 00		
		Telegraph, telephone	30 00		
				57,975 00	
				122,780 00	10,000 00
		Reformatories and Prisons Branch			
		Summary			
133		Main Office		79,750 00	
134		Board of Parole		22,975 00	
135		Ontario Reformatory, Guelph		323,005 00	
136		Mimico Reformatory, Mimico		103,025 00	
137		Mercer Reformatory, Toronto		94,125 00	
138		Industrial Farm, Burwash		322,325 00	
139		Industrial Farm, Fort William		41,350 00	
				986,555 00	

XVIII.—**DEPARTMENT OF** PROVINCIAL SECRETARY—**Continued**

No. of Vote	No. of Item	Service		Fiscal Year 1934	
				To be Voted	Statutory
		Reformatories and Prisons Branch—Continued			
133		**Main Office**			
		Salaries:			
	1	Permanent		33,275 00	
	2	Contingencies		6,150 00	
		Details:			
		Salaries—Temporary	$1,650 00		
		Travelling expenses	2,323 00		
		Freight, express, cartage	10 00		
		Books, magazines, papers	25 00		
		Maintenance of equipment	210 00		
		Stationery, printing, etc	1,900 00		
		Insurance on cars	32 00		
		General:			
	3	Travelling and other expenses of bailiff and prisoners		15,000 00	
	4	Railway fares and clothing of discharged prisoners		12,000 00	
	5	Removal expenses (other than patients) in connection with the Reformatories		350 00	
	6	Printing and stationery		4,500 00	
	7	Medical attendance, funeral transportation and burial expenses of officials and employees where death or illness arises from nature of employment		50 00	
	8	Treatment of patients and inmates in hospitals and sanatoria		500 00	
	9	Expenses in connection with the exhibit of the Provincial Secretary's Department at the Canadian National and other exhibitions		2,000 00	
	10	Legal costs and expenses covering sundry investigations		500 00	
	11	Unforeseen and unprovided		100 00	
		Grants:			
	12	Citizens' Service Association		5,000 00	
	13	Public School No. 1, Guelph Township		325 00	
				79,750 00	
134		**Board of Parole**			
		Salaries:			
	1	Permanent		11,775 00	
	2	Allowance and expenses for Parole Board		4,200 00	
	3	Prisoners' Assistance Fund		100 00	
	4	Expenses of returning to prison parole violators and permit violators		900 00	
	5	Contingencies		6,000 00	
		Details:			
		Salaries—Temporary	$1,950 00		
		Travelling expenses	3,200 00		
		Freight, express, cartage	2 00		
		Books, magazines, papers	20 00		
		Maintenance of equipment	50 00		
		Stationery, printing, etc	718 00		
		Telegrams	60 00		
				22,975 00	

XVIII.—DEPARTMENT OF PROVINCIAL SECRETARY—Continued

No. of Vote	No. of Item	SERVICE.	Fiscal Year 1934	
			To be Voted	Statutory
		Reformatories and Prisons Branch—Continued		
		Ontario Reformatories		
135		**Guelph**		
	1	Salaries	145,005 00	
	2	Medicines and medical comforts including tobacco; groceries and provisions; fuel, light and water; clothing; laundry and cleaning; furniture and furnishings; office expenses; farm expenses; recreation, equipment and contingencies; gratuities to inmates	150,000 00	
	3	Maintenance and repairs of all buildings, roads, walks, grounds and fences; purchase, maintenance and repair of plumbing, steam and electric plants, and machinery attached thereto; live stock, vehicles and farm implements	18,000 00	
		INDUSTRIES		
	4	Purchase of materials, machinery, repairs, expenses and services in connection with industrial operations	10,000 00	
			323,005 00	
136		**Mimico**		
	1	Salaries	47,025 00	
	2	Medicines and medical comforts, including tobacco; groceries and provisions, fuel, light and water; clothing; laundry and cleaning; furniture and furnishings; office expenses; farm expenses; recreation, equipment and contingencies; gratuities to inmates	40,000 00	
	3	Maintenance and repairs of all buildings, roads, walks, grounds and fences; purchase, maintenance and repair of plumbing, steam and electric plants, and machinery attached thereto; live stock, vehicles and farm implements	6,000 00	
		INDUSTRIES		
	4	Purchase of materials, machinery, repairs, expenses and services in connection with industrial operations	10,000 00	
			103,025 00	
137		**Mercer—Toronto**		
	1	Salaries	47,625 00	
	2	Medicines and medical comforts; groceries and provisions; fuel, light and water; clothing; laundry and cleaning; furniture and furnishings; office expenses; farm expenses; recreation, equipment and contingencies	28,500 00	
	3	Maintenance and repairs of all buildings, roads, walks, grounds and fences; purchase, maintenance and repair of plumbing, steam and electric plants, and machinery attached thereto; live stock, vehicles and farm implements	8,000 00	

XVIII.—DEPARTMENT OF PROVINCIAL SECRETARY—Continued

No. of Vote	No. of Item	Service	Fiscal Year 1934	
			To be Voted	Statutory
		Mercer—Toronto—Continued		
137		INDUSTRIES		
	4	Purchase of materials, machinery, repairs, expenses and services in connection with industrial operations	10,000 00	
			94,125 00	
		Industrial Farms		
138		**Burwash**		
	1	Salaries	152,325 00	
	2	Medicines and medical comforts, including tobacco; groceries and provisions; fuel, light and water; clothing; laundry and cleaning; furniture and furnishings; office expenses; farm expenses; recreation, equipment and contingencies; gratuities to inmates	145,000 00	
	3	Maintenance and repairs of all buildings, walks, grounds and fences, purchase, maintenance and repair of plumbing, steam and electric plants, and machinery attached thereto; live stock, vehicles and farm implements; making roads, clearing lands and fencing; lumbering and saw-mill operations	25,000 00	
			322,325 00	
139		**Fort William**		
	1	Salaries	18,350 00	
	2	Medicines and medical comforts, including tobacco; groceries and provisions; fuel, light and water, clothing; laundry and cleaning; furniture and furnishings; office expenses; farm expenses; recreation, equipment and contingencies; gratuities	16,000 00	
	3	Maintenance and repairs of all buildings, roads, walks, grounds and fences; purchase, maintenance and repair of plumbing, steam and electric plants, and machinery attached thereto; live stock, vehicles and farm implements	7,000 00	
			41,350 00	
			986,555 00	

XIX.—DEPARTMENT OF AGRICULTURE

No. of Vote	No. of Item	Service	Fiscal Year 1934 To be Voted	Fiscal Year 1934 Statutory
		Summary		
140		Main Office	273,532 50	10,000 00
		Branches:—		
141		Statistics and Publications	13,800 00	
142		Agricultural and Horticultural Societies	110,750 00	
143		Live Stock	96,725 00	
144		Institutes	68,975 00	
145		Dairy $ 152,175 00		
		Eastern Dairy School, Kingston 18,000 00	170,175 00	
146		Fruit $ 29,050 00		
		Pre-Cooling Station, Brighton 3,200 00		
		Horticultural Experiment Station, Vineland 55,700 00	87,950 00	
147		Agricultural Representatives	316,250 00	
148		Crops, Co-operation and Markets	36,950 00	
S		Agricultural Development Board		182,500 00
149		Colonization and Immigration	5,900 00	
150		Kemptville Agricultural School	63,000 00	
151		Ontario Veterinary College, Guelph	50,820 00	
152		Western Ontario Experimental Farm, Ridgetown	18,050 00	
153		Ontario Agricultural College, Guelph	730,972 00	
			2,043,849 50	192,500 00
140		**Main Office**		
		Salaries:		
	S	Minister		10,000 00
	1	Permanent	17,450 00	
	2	Contingencies	5,000 00	
		Details:		
		Salaries—Temporary $ 750 00		
		Travelling expenses 2,000 00		
		Books, magazines, papers 100 00		
		Freight, express, cartage 10 00		
		Purchase of equipment 400 00		
		Maintenance of equipment 275 00		
		Stationery, printing 1,000 00		
		Telegraph, telephone 125 00		
		Miscellaneous 340 00		
			22,450 00	10,000 00
		General:		
	3	Field man, Northern Ontario, services and expenses	5,000 00	
	4	Provincial Zoologist, services, equipment and expenses	9,000 00	
	5	Publicity work in Great Britain; promotion and sale of Ontario farm products; services, travelling and other expenses of officials; rentals and expenses of offices; advertising; alterations to premises and equipment, repairs and miscellaneous expenses in connection with administration of Ontario House	35,000 00	
	6	Services and expenses in connection with agricultural work; preparation, printing and distributing reports, bulletins and circulars, special investigations into agricultural conditions o[illegible]		

XIX.—DEPARTMENT OF AGRICULTURE—Continued

No. of Vote	No. of Item	Service	Fiscal Year 1934	
			To be Voted	Statutory
140		**Main Office—Continued**		
		the production of crops; advertising and publicity, including special educational campaigns; agricultural instruction, agricultural education, including scholarships, bursaries, prizes or awards; expenses in connection with outbreaks of diseases; services and expenses in connection with exhibits, including prizes, trophies, etc.; travelling expenses, equipment, supplies and contingencies not otherwise provided for.......	35,000 00	
	7	To promote Marketing Board..................	25,000 00	
	8	Administration and enforcement of The Corn Borer Act................................	8,500 00	
	9	Expenses of exhibits of grain, fruit, vegetables and other products at exhibitions.............	5,000 00	
	10	Inspection of apiaries; automobiles, services and other expenses............................	3,875 00	
	11	Removal expenses of officials in the Public Service	500 00	
		Grants:		
	12	Royal Agricultural Winter Fair Association....	25,000 00	
	13	Ontario Provincial Winter Fair...............	8,000 00	
	14	Ottawa Winter Fair........................	8,000 00	
		Grants occasioned by unassessable Crown lands:		
	15	Union School No. 1, Clinton and Louth.....	350 00	
	16	Macdonald Consolidated School, Guelph....	850 00	
	17	S.S. No. 10, Oxford Township.............	20 00	
	18	Kemptville Public School..................	75 00	
	29	Ontario Agricultural Council.................	750 00	
	20	City of Toronto re Horse Stables in Exhibition Park (1933-1952)........................	26,412 50	
	21	Royal Winter Fair Association—in accordance with, and approving Order-in-Council dated August 14th, 1925 (1927-1943)............	35,000 00	
	22	Ottawa Winter Fair, building account as per agreement (1927-1936)....................	9,750 00	
	23	Western Fair, grant in accordance with agreement in connection with Live Stock Arena, (1929-1938)..............................	10,000 00	
			273,532 50	10,000 00
141		**Statistics and Publications Branch**		
		Salaries:		
	1	Permanent..................................	10,800 00	
	2	Contingencies..................................	3,000 00	
		Details:		
		Salaries—Temporary.............. $ 800 00		
		Travelling expenses............... 50 00		
		Freight, express, cartage........... 10 00		
		Purchase of equipment............ 1,000 00		
		Maintenance of equipment........ 125 00		
		Stationery, printing............... 700 00		
		Telegraph, telephone.............. 15 00		
		Miscellaneous.................... 300 00		
			13,800 00	

XIX.—DEPARTMENT OF AGRICULTURE—Continued

No. of Vote	No. of Item	Service		Fiscal Year 1934 To be Voted	Fiscal Year 1934 Statutory
142		**Agricultural and Horticultural Societies Branch**			
		Salaries:			
	1	Permanent		12,100 00	
	2	Contingencies		4,000 00	
		Details:			
		Travelling expenses	2,300 00		
		Books, magazines, papers	35 00		
		Freight, express, cartage	30 00		
		Maintenance of equipment	75 00		
		Stationery, printing	1,200 00		
		Telegraph, telephone	45 00		
		Miscellaneous	315 00		
	3	Judges' services, travelling and other expenses		2,500 00	
	4	Horticultural, Agricultural and Vegetable Growers' Societies, services, travelling and other expenses of meetings at the direction of the Department, investigations and unforeseen expenditures		2,500 00	
	5	Field Crop Competitions, prizes and miscellanoues expenses, including transportation and other expenses of exhibits at exhibitions		1,000 00	
	6	Special Prizes, Provincial Plowing Match		400 00	
		Grants:			
	7	Grants under Section 22, subsection 1 (a) to (e) inclusive		60,000 00	
	8	Insurance to indemnify societies suffering from rainy weather or fire, to be paid in accordance with R.S.O. 1927, Cap. 71, Section 22, subsections 2 and 3		5,000 00	
	9	To encourage local plowing matches, to be paid in grants or otherwise, as may be approved by the Lieutenant-Governor in Council		5,000 00	
	10	Grants under Horticultural Societies' Act		12,000 00	
		Grants under Agricultural Societies' Act:			
	11	Spring Stock Shows (including services, travelling and other expenses of judges)		500 00	
	12	Special grants under Section 23		4,000 00	
	13	Grants to Agricultural Societies notwithstanding provisions of Agricultural Societies' Act		800 0C	
	14	Ontario Plowmen's Association		300 00	
	15	Ontario Vegetable Growers' Association		450 00	
	16	Ontario Horticultural Association		200 00	
				110,750 00	
143		**Live Stock Branch**			
		Salaries:			
	1	Permanent		19,175 00	
	2	Contingencies		4,500 00	
		Details:			
		Travelling expenses	2,800 00		
		Books, magazines, papers	50 00		
		Freight, express, cartage	25 00		
		Maintenance of equipment	100 00		
		Stationery, printing	1,200 00		
		Telegraph, telephone	45 00		
		Miscellaneous	280 00		
	3	Educational and demonstration work in any branch of live stock, judges, lecturers, valuators and other assistants, salaries, expenses and equipment, live			

XIX.—DEPARTMENT OF AGRICULTURE—Continued

No. of Vote	No. of Item	Service		Fiscal Year 1934 To be Voted	Fiscal Year 1934 Statutory
143		**Live Stock Branch—Continued**			
		stock exhibits, and transportation charges, travelling expenses, fieldmen; purchase, maintenance and distribution of live stock; to pay such grants for the encouragement of live stock as may be fixed by the Lieutenant-Governor in Council.....		30,000 00	
	4	Expenses in connection with T.B. testing work.....		15,000 00	
	5	Services, travelling and other expenses in connection with the administration of The Stallion Enrolment Act and payment of premiums for Pure Bred Stallions....		10,000 00	
	6	To encourage and promote Federal-Provincial Bull Policy....		15,000 00	
		Grants:			
	7	Canadian Hunter, Saddle and Light Horse Improvement Society....		750 00	
	8	Ontario Horsebreeders' Association....		750 00	
	9	Ontario Cattlebreeders' Association....		750 00	
	10	Eastern Canada Live Stock Union....		750 00	
	11	Prince of Wales prize....		50 00	
				96,725 00	
144		**Institutes Branch**			
		Salaries:			
	1	Permanent....		9,475 00	
	2	Contingencies....		2,500 00	
		Details:			
		Travelling expenses....	600 00		
		Books, magazines, papers....	50 00		
		Freight, express, cartage....	100 00		
		Maintenance of equipment....	300 00		
		Stationery, printing....	1,000 00		
		Telegraph, telephone....	45 00		
		Miscellaneous....	405 00		
	3	Services, travelling, equipment, grants, supplies and other expenses in connection with Women's Institutes, Junior Institutes, Demonstration Lecture Courses, One-month and Three-months, Courses, Household Science Judging Instruction and Competitions, Exhibits, Conferences, Conventions and Women's Institutes and Agricultural meetings....		57,000 00	
				68,975 00	
145		**Dairy Branch**			
		Salaries:			
	1	Permanent....		12,300 00	
	2	Contingencies....		2,000 00	
		Details:			
		Travelling expenses....	850 00		
		Books, magazines, papers....	15 00		
		Freight, express, cartage....	25 00		
		Maintenance of equipment....	25 00		
		Stationery, printing....	1,035 00		
		Telegraph, telephone....	25 00		
		Miscellaneous....	25 00		

XIX.—DEPARTMENT OF AGRICULTURE—Continued

No. of Vote	No. of Item	Service	Fiscal Year 1934 To be Voted	Fiscal Year 1934 Statutory
145		**Dairy Branch—Continued**		
	3	Dairy Instruction and Inspection; Instructors' and Inspectors' salaries and expenses; purchase and and maintentance of automobiles, dairy equipment, stationery and supplies; to pay such expenses for the encouragement of the industry as may be fixed by the Lieutenant-Governor in Council	135,000 00	
	4	Grants:		
	5	Dairymen's Association, Eastern Ontario	1,000 00	
		Dairymen's Association, Western Ontario	500 00	
	6	Ontario Whole Milk Producers' Association	1,000 00	
	7	Eastern Ontario Cheesemakers' Association	200 00	
	8	Central Ontario Cheesemakers' Association	100 00	
	9	Western Ontario Cheesemakers' Association	75 00	
			152,175 00	
		EASTERN DAIRY SCHOOL		
	10	Salaries:		
	11	Permanent	8,975 00	
	12	Equipment, services and expenses	9,025 00	
			18,000 00	
			170,175 00	
146		**Fruit Branch**		
		Salaries:		
	1	Permanent	10,700 00	
	2	Contingencies	2,500 00	
		Details:		
		Salaries—Temporary $ 750 00		
		Travelling expenses 475 00		
		Freight, express, cartage 200 00		
		Maintenance of equipment 50 00		
		Stationery, printing 275 00		
		Telegraph, telephone 600 00		
		Miscellaneous 150 00		
	3	For the carrying on of work in the growing, handling, exhibiting, and advertising of fruit, including expenditure under The Fruit Pests Act, leasing of orchards, travelling and other expenses	11,200 00	
		Grants:		
	4	Fruit Growers' Association of Ontario	800 00	
	5	Entomological Society of Ontario	350 00	
	6	Grants towards the erection of Co-operative packing houses	1,000 00	
	7	Apple Maggot Survey and expenses therwith in accordance with agreement with Dominion Department of Agriculture	2,500 00	
			29,050 00	
		PRE-COOLING STATION, BRIGHTON		
	8	Equipment, services and expenses	3,200 00	

XIX.—DEPARTMENT OF AGRICULTURE—Continued

No. of Vote	No. of Item	Service	Fiscal Year 1934 To be Voted	Fiscal Year 1934 Statutory
146		**Fruit Branch—Continued**		
		HORTICULTURAL EXPERIMENT STATION, VINELAND		
		Salaries:		
	9	Permanent	38,900 00	
	10	Services, travelling and other expenses in connection with maintenance of Horticultural Experiment Station, rent of additional land, purchase and maintenance of automobiles, trucks, tractors and farm machinery	16,800 00	
			55,700 00	
			87,950 00	
147		**Agricultural Representatives Branch**		
		Salaries:		
	1	Permanent	17,300 00	
	2	Contingencies	6,000 00	
		Details:		
		Travelling expenses $ 2,300 00		
		Books, magazines, papers 40 00		
		Freight, express, cartage 30 00		
		Maintenance of equipment 425 00		
		Stationery, printing 2,400 00		
		Telegraph, telephone 85 00		
		Miscellaneous 720 00		
	3	Agricultural Representative work, services, expenses and equipment	290,000 00	
	4	Transportation and living expenses attending Short Courses for winners in competitions under Agricultural Representatives	1,200 00	
	5	Grant to Canadian Council on Boys' and Girls' Club work	1,750 00	
			316,250 00	
148		**Crops, Co-operation and Markets Branch**		
		Salaries:		
	1	Permanent	5,175 00	
	2	Contingencies	4,000 00	
		Details:		
		Salaries—Temporary $ 750 00		
		Travelling expenses 1,000 00		
		Books, magazines, papers 40 00		
		Freight, express, cartage 30 00		
		Maintenance of equipment 225 00		
		Stationery, printing 1,400 00		
		Telegraph, telephone 80 0C		
		Miscellaneous 475 00		
	3	Loans in accordance with The Co-operative Marketing Loan Act, 1932	2,500 00	
	4	To encourage co-operative marketing	2,500 00	

XIX.—DEPARTMENT OF AGRICULTURE—Continued

No. of Vote	No. of Item	Service		Fiscal Year 1934 To be Voted	Fiscal Year 1934 Statutory
148		**Crops, Co-operation and Markets Branch—Continued**			
	5	Crop improvement, demonstrations, purchase of seed and equipment, services and travelling expenses, printing, advertising, and other educational work, prizes, trophies, and awards, etc., administration and enforcement of The Weed Control Act......		8,000 00	
		Subventions:			
	6	Seed cleaning plants..........................		2,000 00	
	7	Freight on agricultural lime....................		1,000 00	
		Grants:			
	8	Grants under The Community Halls Act........		10,000 00	
	9	Ontario Experimental Union..................		1,000 00	
	10	Essex County Corn Improvement Association....		150 00	
	11	Ontario Corn Growers' Association............		250 00	
	12	Lambton Corn Growers' Association...........		150 00	
	13	Wentworth County Seed Association...........		75 00	
	14	Quinte Seed Society..........................		150 00	
				36,950 00	
S		**Agricultural Development Board**			
	S	Salaries and expenses in connection with operation of Ontario Farm Loans Act and Agricultural Development Act, including prepayment of insurance premiums................................			182,500 00
					182,500 00
149		**Colonization and Immigration Branch**			
		Salaries:			
	1	Permanent................................		4,600 00	
	2	Contingencies................................		300 00	
		Details:			
		Travelling expenses...............	$ 75 00		
		Books, magazines, papers..........	20 00		
		Freight, express, cartage...........	5 00		
		Maintenance of equipment........	20 00		
		Stationery, printing...............	75 00		
		Telegraph, telephone..............	15 00		
		Miscellaneous....................	90 00		
	3	Printing pamphlets for publicity purposes; expenses incurred in distributing settlers; photographs, maps, advertising, services, travelling and other expenses in connection with colonization.........		500 00	
	4	Payments for aftercare of boy settlers as per agreement with the Overseas Settlement Board; payments in accordance with the agreement entered into with the Board of Home Missions of the United Church............................		500 00	
				5,900 00	
150		**Kemptville Agricultural School**			
		Salaries:			
	1	Permanent................................		34,950 00	
	2	Wages, travelling expenses, equipment, purchase and maintenance of stock, general expenses..........		28,050 00	
				63,000 00	

XIX.—DEPARTMENT OF AGRICULTURE—Continued

No. of Vote	No. of Item	Service	Fiscal Year 1934	
			To be Voted	Statutory
151		**Ontario Veterinary College, Guelph**		
		Salaries:		
	1	Permanent	30,475 00	
	2	Temporary	8,695 00	
	3	Fuel, light, water, telephone service, books, apparatus, appliances, library supplies and equipment, furnishings, repairs, temporary lecturers or other assistance, printing, advertising and contingencies	9,000 00	
	4	Scholarships and prizes	150 00	
	5	Research and investigation	2,500 00	
			50,820 00	
152		**Western Ontario Experimental Farm, Ridgetown**		
		Salaries:		
	1	Permanent	13,050 00	
	2	Purchase of stock and equipment, wages, seed, feed, fertilizer, fuel, light, supplies, travelling expenses, educational work, contingencies	5,000 00	
			18,050 00	
153		**Ontario Agricultural College, Guelph**		
		General Offices		
		Salaries:		
	1	Permanent	72,062 00	
		Administrative expenses:		
	2	Temporary assistance, including extra lectures	5,000 00	
	3	Contingencies, including expenses of Short Courses	10,000 00	
	4	Travelling expenses	4,000 00	
	5	Library	3,500 00	
	6	Provisions, laundry, engine-room, supplies and fuel	110,000 00	
	7	Furniture, furnishings, repairs and equipment	14,000 00	
	8	Gymnasium	900 00	
	9	Student labour	6,500 00	
	10	Telephone service, rents, etc	2,000 00	
	11	Scholarships	240 00	
	12	Research scholarships, to be awarded as directed by the Lieutenant-Governor in Council	2,000 00	
	13	Students' teams, judging at exhibitions	700 00	
	14	Servants' pay list	15,000 00	
	15	Special research work in different divisions under the direction of the President	7,000 00	
	16	Purchase and maintenance of automobiles, trucks and tractors	3,000 00	
			255,902 00	
		Bacteriology Division		
		Salaries:		
	17	Permanent	13,725 00	
		Expenses:		
	18	Supplies, expenses and equipment	2,000 00	
			15,725 00	

XIX.—DEPARTMENT OF AGRICULTURE—Continued

No. of Vote	No. of Item	SERVICE	Fiscal Year 1934 To be Voted	Fiscal Year 1934 Statutory
153		**Ontario Agricultural College—Continued**		
		BOTANY DIVISION		
		Salaries:		
	19	Permanent	13,650 00	
		Expenses:		
	20	Supplies, expenses and equipment	2,000 00	
			15,650 00	
		CHEMISTRY DIVISION		
		Salaries:		
	21	Permanent	30,075 00	
		Expenses:		
	22	Purchase and maintenance of laboratory equipment and supplies; contingencies	7,000 00	
	23	Soil survey and field work, automobiles, supplies, expenses and equipment	5,000 00	
			42,075 00	
		TRENT INSTITUTE DIVISION		
		Salaries:		
	24	Permanent	9,800 00	
		Expenses:		
	25	Supplies, expenses and equipment	2,000 00	
	26	Materials and labour for bakery	4,000 00	
			15,800 00	
		ENTOMOLOGY DIVISION		
		Salaries:		
	27	Permanent	16,050 00	
		Expenses:		
	28	Supplies, expenses and equipment	1,500 00	
	29	Cornborer investigations, including automobiles	1,500 00	
			19,050 00	
		ENGLISH DIVISION		
		Salaries:		
	30	Permanent	8,800 00	
		Expenses:		
	31	Supplies, expenses and equipment	1,000 00	
			9,800 00	
		AGRICULTURAL ENGINEERING DIVISION		
		Salaries:		
	32	Permanent	26,800 00	
		Expenses:		
	33	Services, automobiles, equipment, expenses re drainage work	3,000 00	
	34	Supplies, expenses and equipment	3,000 00	
			32,800 00	
		FARM ECONOMICS DIVISION		
		Salaries:		
	35	Permanent	11,350 00	
		Expenses:		
	36	Farm surveys, automobiles, services, equipment and other expenses	6,000 00	
			17,350 00	

XIX.—DEPARTMENT OF AGRICULTURE—Continued

No. of Vote	No. of Item	Service	Fiscal Year 1934	
			To be Voted	Statutory
153		**Ontario Agricultural College—Continued**		
		Extension Division		
		Salaries:		
	37	Permanent	3,800 00	
		Expenses:		
	38	Services, package library, exhibits, equipment, supplies and contingencies	8,500 00	
			12,300 00	
		Macdonald Institute and Hall		
		Salaries:		
	39	Permanent	35,925 00	
		Expenses:		
	40	Home Economics, services, supplies, expenses and equipment	6,300 00	
			42,225 00	
		Animal Husbandry Division		
		Salaries:		
	41	Permanent	29,645 00	
		Expenses:		
	42	Permanent improvements	2,000 00	
	43	Wages, temporary help	5,000 00	
	44	Purchase and maintenance of live stock	13,000 00	
	45	Supplies, equipment and contingencies	5,000 00	
			54,645 00	
		Field Experiments Division		
		Salaries:		
	46	Permanent	33,125 00	
		Expenses:		
	47	Wages, temporary help	6,500 00	
	48	Supplies, equipment, purchase and maintenance of horses, and contingencies	3,500 00	
			43,125 00	
		Experimental Dairy and Dairy School Division		
		Salaries:		
	49	Permanent	12,800 00	
		Expenses:		
	50	Wages, temporary help, and Instructors in Dairy School	1,500 00	
	51	Purchase, hauling and manufacturing milk	4,500 00	
	52	Supplies, equipment, machinery, repairs and contingencies	3,625 00	
			22,425 00	
		Poultry Division		
		Salaries:		
	53	Permanent	27,150 00	
		Expenses:		
	54	Wages, temporary help	6,000 00	
	55	Experiments and feed	10,000 00	
	56	Poultry extension work, automobiles, services supplies and equipment	18,000 00	

XIX.—DEPARTMENT OF AGRICULTURE—Continued

No. of Vote	No. of Item	Service	Fiscal Year 1934	
			To be Voted	Statutory
153		**Ontario Agricultural College—Continued**		
		Poultry Division—Continued		
	57	Purchase and maintenance of horses, supplies, equipment and contingencies	3,000 00	
	58	Empire Marketing Board, special research, services expenses and equipment	2,000 00	
			66,150 00	
		Horticulture Division		
		Salaries:		
	59	Permanent	30,750 00	
		Expenses:		
	60	Permanent improvements	2,700 00	
	61	Wages, temporary help	11,000 00	
	62	Trees, plants, seeds, equipment, fuel, purchase and maintenance of horses, forestry, contingencies	8,500 00	
	63	Extension work in vegetable growing, services and expenses	1,250 00	
			54,200 00	
		Apiculture Division		
		Salaries:		
	64	Permanent	9,250 00	
		Expenses:		
	65	Services, supplies, equipment and contingencies	2,500 00	
			11,750 00	
			730,972 00	
			2,043,849 50	192,500 00

XX.—MISCELLANEOUS

No. of Vote	No. of Item	Service	Fiscal Year 1934	
			To be Voted	Statutory
154		**Miscellaneous**		
	1	Monument to the members of the Canadian Expeditionary Forces from the Province of Ontario who lost their lives in the Great War, and for carrying out recommendations of War Memorial Committee in accordance with report adopted by the Legislature, 1921, or for such other War Memorials as the Lieutenant-Governor in Council may direct (revote)	50,000 00	
	2	Increases in salaries during current and previous year to employees of any Department or Branch of the Public Service, to be paid as directed by the Lieutenant-Governor in Council, during the fiscal year 1933-34. Every such increase to form part of the salary of the officer or servant and to be the same in all respects as if such increase had been specifically voted in the Estimates and appropriated by the Legislature for that purpose	50,000 00	
	3	Miscellaneous refunds	100,000 00	
			200,000 00	

Lightning Source UK Ltd.
Milton Keynes UK
UKHW022201140219
337291UK00006B/617/P